Contemporary
Literary Criticism

Guide to Gale Literary Criticism Series

When you need to review criticism of literary works, these are the Gale series to use:

If the author's death date is: **You should turn to:**

After Dec. 31, 1959
(or author is still living)

CONTEMPORARY LITERARY CRITICISM

for example: Jorge Luis Borges, Anthony Burgess,
William Faulkner, Mary Gordon,
Ernest Hemingway, Iris Murdoch

1900 through 1959

TWENTIETH-CENTURY LITERARY CRITICISM

for example: Willa Cather, F. Scott Fitzgerald,
Henry James, Mark Twain, Virginia Woolf

1800 through 1899

NINETEENTH-CENTURY LITERATURE CRITICISM

for example: Emily Dickinson, Fedor Dostoevski,
Gerard Manley Hopkins, George Sand

1400 through 1799

LITERATURE CRITICISM FROM 1400 TO 1800
(excluding Shakespeare)

for example: Anne Bradstreet, Pierre Corneille,
Daniel Defoe, Alexander Pope,
Jonathan Swift, Phillis Wheatley

SHAKESPEAREAN CRITICISM

Shakespeare's plays and poetry

Antiquity through 1399

CLASSICAL AND MEDIEVAL LITERATURE CRITICISM

for example: Dante, Plato, Homer, Sophocles, Vergil,
the Beowulf poet

(Volume 1 forthcoming)

Gale also publishes related criticism series:

CHILDREN'S LITERATURE REVIEW

This ongoing series covers authors of all eras. Presents criticism on
authors and author/illustrators who write for the preschool
through high school audience.

CONTEMPORARY ISSUES CRITICISM

This two volume set presents criticism on contemporary authors
writing on current issues. Topics covered include the social sciences,
philosophy, economics, natural science, law, and related areas.

ISSN 0091-3421

Volume 40

Contemporary Literary Criticism

Excerpts from Criticism of the
Works of Today's Novelists, Poets,
Playwrights, Short Story Writers, Scriptwriters,
and Other Creative Writers

Daniel G. Marowski
EDITOR

Roger Matuz
Jane E. Neidhardt
Robyn V. Young
ASSOCIATE EDITORS

Gale Research Company
Book Tower
Detroit, Michigan 48226

STAFF

Daniel G. Marowski, *Editor*

Roger Matuz, Jane E. Neidhardt, Robyn V. Young, *Associate Editors*

Molly L. Norris, Sean R. Pollock, Jane C. Thacker, Debra A. Wells, *Senior Assistant Editors*

Kelly King Howes, Thomas J. Votteler, Bruce Walker, *Assistant Editors*

Sharon R. Gunton, Jean C. Stine, *Contributing Editors*

Lizbeth A. Purdy, *Production Supervisor*
Denise Michlewicz Broderick, *Production Coordinator*
Eric Berger, *Assistant Production Coordinator*
Kathleen M. Cook, Maureen Duffy, Sheila J. Nasea, *Editorial Assistants*

Linda M. Pugliese, *Manuscript Coordinator*
Donna Craft, *Assistant Manuscript Coordinator*
Maureen A. Puhl, Rosetta Irene Simms, *Manuscript Assistants*

Victoria B. Cariappa, *Research Coordinator*
Maureen R. Richards, *Assistant Research Coordinator*
Daniel Kurt Gilbert, Kent Graham, Michele R. O'Connell,
Keith E. Schooley, Filomena Sgambati, Vincenza G. Tranchida,
Mary D. Wise, *Research Assistants*

Jeanne A. Gough, *Permissions Supervisor*
Janice M. Mach, *Permissions Coordinator, Text*
Patricia A. Seefelt, *Permissions Coordinator, Illustrations*
Susan D. Battista, *Assistant Permissions Coordinator*
Margaret A. Chamberlain, Sandra C. Davis, Kathy Grell, Josephine M. Keene,
Mary M. Matuz, *Senior Permissions Assistants*
H. Diane Cooper, Colleen M. Crane,
Mabel E. Schoening, *Permissions Assistants*
Margaret A. Carson, Helen Hernandez,
Anita Williams, *Permissions Clerks*

Frederick G. Ruffner, *Publisher*
Dedria Bryfonski, *Editorial Director*
Ellen T. Crowley, *Associate Editorial Director*
Christine Nasso, *Director, Literature Division*
Laurie Lanzen Harris, *Senior Editor, Literary Criticism Series*
Dennis Poupard, *Managing Editor, Literary Criticism Series*

Computerized photocomposition by
Typographics, Incorporated
Kansas City, Missouri

Printed in the United States

Contents

Preface

Literary criticism is, by definition, "the art of evaluating or analyzing with knowledge and propriety works of literature." The complexity and variety of the themes and forms of contemporary literature make the function of the critic especially important to today's reader. It is the critic who assists the reader in identifying significant new writers, recognizing trends in critical methods, mastering new terminology, and monitoring scholarly and popular sources of critical opinion.

Until the publication of the first volume of *Contemporary Literary Criticism (CLC)* in 1973, there existed no ongoing digest of current literary opinion. *CLC,* therefore, has fulfilled an essential need.

Scope of the Work

CLC presents significant passages from published criticism of works by today's creative writers. Each volume of *CLC* includes excerpted criticism on about 50 authors who are now living or who died after December 31, 1959. Since the series began publication, almost 1,800 authors have been included. The majority of authors covered by *CLC* are living writers who continue to publish; therefore, an author frequently appears in more than one volume. There is, of course, no duplication of reprinted criticism.

Authors are selected for inclusion for a variety of reasons, among them the publication of a critically acclaimed new work, the reception of a major literary award, or the dramatization of a literary work as a movie or television screenplay. For example, the present volume includes Marguerite Duras, who was awarded the 1984 Prix Goncourt for her novel *The Lover*; Fred Chappell, recipient of the 1986 Bollingen Prize in poetry; and Peter Carey, whose novel *Bliss* was adapted into a critically acclaimed film. Perhaps most importantly, authors who appear frequently on the syllabuses of high school and college literature classes are heavily represented in *CLC;* Jean Anouilh and Kurt Vonnegut, Jr. are examples of writers of this stature in the present volume. Attention is also given to several other groups of writers—authors of considerable public interest—about whose work criticism is often difficult to locate. These are the contributors to the well-loved but nonscholarly genres of mystery and science fiction, as well as literary and social critics whose insights are considered valuable and informative. Foreign writers and authors who represent particular ethnic groups in the United States are also featured in each volume.

Format of the Book

Altogether there are about 700 individual excerpts in each volume—with an average of about 14 excerpts per author—taken from hundreds of literary reviews, general magazines, scholarly journals, and monographs. Contemporary criticism is loosely defined as that which is relevant to the evaluation of the author under discussion; this includes criticism written at the beginning of an author's career as well as current commentary. Emphasis has been placed on expanding the sources for criticism by including an increasing number of scholarly and specialized periodicals. Students, teachers, librarians, and researchers frequently find that the generous excerpts and supplementary material provided by the editors supply them with all the information needed to write a term paper, analyze a poem, or lead a book discussion group. However, complete bibliographical citations facilitate the location of the original source as well as provide all of the information necessary for a term paper footnote or bibliography.

A *CLC* author entry consists of the following elements:

• The **author heading** cites the author's full name, followed by birth date, and death date when applicable. The portion of the name outside the parentheses denotes the form under which the author has most commonly published. If an author has written consistently under a pseudonym, the pseudonym will be listed in the author heading and the real name given on the first line of the biographical and critical introduction. Also located at the beginning of the introduction to the author entry are any important name variations under which an author has written. Uncertainty as to a birth or death date is indicated by question marks.

- A **portrait** of the author is included when available.

- A brief **biographical and critical introduction** to the author and his or her work precedes the excerpted criticism. However, *CLC* is not intended to be a definitive biographical source. Therefore, *cross-references* have been included to direct the reader to other useful sources published by the Gale Research Company: *Contemporary Authors* now includes detailed biographical and bibliographical sketches on nearly 86,000 authors; *Children's Literature Review* presents excerpted criticism on the works of authors of children's books; *Something about the Author* contains heavily illustrated biographical sketches on writers and illustrators who create books for children and young adults; *Contemporary Issues Criticism* presents excerpted commentary on the nonfiction works of authors who influence contemporary thought; *Dictionary of Literary Biography* provides original evaluations of authors important to literary history; *Contemporary Authors Autobiography Series* offers autobiographical essays by prominent writers; and the new *Something about the Author Autobiography Series* presents autobiographical essays by authors of interest to young readers. Previous volumes of *CLC* in which the author has been featured are also listed in the introduction.

- The **excerpted criticism** represents various kinds of critical writing—a particular essay may be normative, descriptive, interpretive, textual, appreciative, comparative, or generic. It may range in form from the brief review to the scholarly monograph. Essays are selected by the editors to reflect the spectrum of opinion about a specific work or about an author's literary career in general. The excerpts are presented chronologically, adding a useful perspective to the entry. All titles by the author featured in the entry are printed in boldface type, which enables the reader to easily identify the works being discussed.

- A complete **bibliographical citation** designed to help the user find the original essay or book follows each excerpt. An asterisk (*) at the end of a citation indicates that the essay is on more than one author.

Other Features

- A list of **Authors Forthcoming in** *CLC* previews the authors to be researched for future volumes.

- An **Appendix** lists the sources from which material in the volume has been reprinted. Many other sources have also been consulted during the preparation of the volume.

- A **Cumulative Author Index** lists all the authors who have appeared in *Contemporary Literary Criticism, Twentieth-Century Literary Criticism, Nineteenth-Century Literature Criticism,* and *Literature Criticism from 1400 to 1800,* along with cross-references to other Gale series: *Children's Literature Review, Authors in the News, Contemporary Authors, Contemporary Authors Autobiography Series, Dictionary of Literary Biography, Something about the Author, Something about the Author Autobiography Series,* and *Yesterday's Authors of Books for Children.* Users will welcome this cumulated author index as a useful tool for locating an author within the various series. The index, which lists birth and death dates when available, will be particularly valuable for those authors who are identified with a certain period but whose death date causes them to be placed in another, or for those authors whose careers span two periods. For example, F. Scott Fitzgerald is found in *Twentieth-Century Literary Criticism,* yet a writer often associated with him, Ernest Hemingway, is found in *Contemporary Literary Criticism.*

- A **Cumulative Title Index** lists titles reviewed in *CLC* (novels, novellas, short stories, poems, dramas, essays, films, songs) in alphabetical order. Titles are followed by the corresponding volume and page numbers where they may be located; all titles reviewed in *CLC* from Volume 1 through the current volume are cited. In cases where the same title is used by different authors, the author's surname is given in parentheses after the title, e.g., *Collected Poems* (Berryman), *Collected Poems* (Eliot). For foreign titles, a cross-reference is given to the translated English title. Titles of novels, novellas, dramas, films, record albums, and poetry, short story, and essay collections are printed in italics, while all individual poems, short stories, essays, and songs are printed in roman type within quotation marks; when published separately (e.g., T.S. Eliot's poem *The Waste Land*), the title will also be printed in italics.

Acknowledgments

The editors wish to thank the copyright holders of the excerpted articles included in this volume for permission to use the material and the photographers and other individuals who provided photographs for us. We are grateful to the staffs of the following libraries for making their resources available to us: Detroit Public Library and the libraries of Wayne State University, the University of Michigan, and the University of Detroit. We also wish to thank Anthony Bogucki for his assistance with copyright research.

Suggestions Are Welcome

The editors welcome the comments and suggestions of readers to expand the coverage and enhance the usefulness of the series.

Authors Forthcoming in *CLC*

To Be Included in Volume 41

Reinaldo Arenas (Cuban novelist and poet)—Censored by the Cuban government for his controversial fiction and poetry and for his homosexuality, Arenas now lives in the United States. His recent acclaimed novel, *Farewell to the Sea,* recounts the psychic struggles of a disillusioned writer and his wife.

John Ashbery (American poet and critic)—A widely respected contemporary poet, Ashbery is regarded as a talented stylist whose work often remains elusive to interpretation. His recent works include *A Wave,* which won the Lenore Marshall/Nation Poetry Prize, and *Selected Poems,* which features many of his most important works.

Morley Callaghan (Canadian novelist, short story writer, essayist, and dramatist)—Described by Edmund Wilson as "perhaps the most unjustly neglected novelist in the English-speaking world," Callaghan has been active in literature for over sixty years. His latest novel, *Our Lady of the Snows,* like much of his work, is characterized by its journalistic prose style, ironic tone, and moralistic themes.

T.S. Eliot (American-born English poet, critic, dramatist, and essayist)—One of the most important literary figures of the twentieth century, Eliot is recognized as a major contributor to the modern age in poetry and criticism. The twentieth anniversary of Eliot's death has sparked renewed evaluation of his achievements.

Carlos Fuentes (Mexican novelist, dramatist, short story writer, essayist, and critic)—In his internationally acclaimed works, Fuentes draws upon Mexican history and legend to explore and define the identity of his homeland. His recent novels include *The Old Gringo* and *Distant Relations.*

Ernest Hemingway (American short story writer, novelist, and nonfiction writer)—Regarded as one of the greatest writers of the twentieth century, Hemingway has received renewed critical attention for the posthumous publication of such works as *The Dangerous Summer* and *The Garden of Eden.* Criticism on these books, as well as recent scholarly essays, will be featured in Hemingway's entry.

Eugène Ionesco (Rumanian-born French dramatist, essayist, scriptwriter, and novelist)—One of the most renowned exponents of the Theater of the Absurd, Ionesco employs exaggeration and black humor to explore the alienation of individuals searching for meaning in an irrational and meaningless world.

Peter Levi (English poet, novelist, travel writer, and editor)—A former Jesuit priest whose poetry often employs such Elizabethan and classical forms as the sonnet and the elegy, Levi has also written two adventure novels, *Head in the Soup* and *Grave Witness.*

Janet Lewis (American novelist, poet, short story writer, dramatist, and author of children's books)—The author of *The Wife of Martin Guerre* and other acclaimed historical novels, Lewis has also gained considerable respect for her poetry about the Ojibway and Navajo tribes of North America.

Ross Macdonald (American novelist, short story writer, essayist, and autobiographer)—A prolific and popular author of detective fiction, Macdonald is best known as the creator of sleuth Lew Archer. In his recent volume of essays, *Self-Portrait: Ceaselessly Into the Past,* Macdonald examines his long career and the geneses of his novels.

Anne Rice (American novelist and critic)—The author of the popular novel *Interview with the Vampire,* Rice has recently published *The Vampire Lestat,* the second installment of *The Vampire Chronicles.*

Nayantara Sahgal (Indian novelist, short story writer, autobiographer, and nonfiction writer)—Sahgal's writings are noted for their insightful portraits of life in contemporary India. Her recent novels, *Rich like Us* and *Plans for Departure,* are considered important additions to her canon.

James Baldwin (American novelist, essayist, and critic)—A prolific and popular author of such novels as *Go Tell It on the Mountain* and *Giovanni's Room*, Baldwin examines the state of black people in the United States in *The Price of the Ticket*, which features essays from his entire career.

Julian Barnes (English novelist, editor, and critic)—Barnes's novel *Flaubert's Parrot*, an insightful and humorous combination of fiction and criticism, has garnered considerable praise and has inspired renewed interest in his earlier novels, *Metroland* and *Before She Met Me*.

William S. Burroughs (American novelist and short story writer)—In his recent novels, *The Place of Dead Roads* and *Cities of the Red Night*, Burroughs continues to employ the experimental techniques that won him fame for such works as *Naked Lunch*.

Robertson Davies (Canadian novelist, dramatist, short story writer, and nonfiction writer)—An outstanding figure in Canadian letters, Davies has recently published *What's Bred in the Bone*, a novel that has furthered his reputation as an important contemporary author.

Harlan Ellison (American short story writer, novelist, scriptwriter, and nonfiction writer)—*An Edge in My Voice*, a collection of essays on nonfiction topics, displays the controversial moralistic approach that distinguishes Ellison's award-winning science fiction works.

Dick Francis (Welsh-born English novelist)—Francis is a popular and respected mystery author whose experiences as a jockey have influenced his novels centered in the world of horse racing. His recent novel, *Proof*, is a tale of murder and intrigue involving the wine and liquor industries.

Zbigniew Herbert (Polish poet, dramatist, and essayist)—One of Poland's most important contemporary poets, Herbert often explores historical and political themes and centers on the conflict between ideals and reality. His recently translated works include *Report from the Besieged City*, a collection of verse, and *Barbarian in the Garden*, a volume of essays.

Larry Kramer (American dramatist, novelist, and scriptwriter)—In his acclaimed play *The Normal Heart*, Kramer seeks to broaden public awareness of the physical and psychological effects of AIDS.

Harry Mulisch (Dutch novelist, short story writer, dramatist, poet, and essayist)—One of Holland's most acclaimed and popular authors, Mulisch has gained attention in the United States for his novel *The Assault*. This work examines four years in the life of a man whose family was unjustly executed by Nazi forces during World War II.

Dave Smith (American poet, novelist, and nonfiction writer)—Regarded as one of the most important poets to have emerged in the United States during the 1970s, Smith explores a wide range of themes in his verse. His recent collection, *The Roundhouse Voices: Selected and New Poems*, has received significant critical attention.

Mario Vargas Llosa (Peruvian novelist, short story writer, and nonfiction writer)—Criticism on this leading contemporary Latin American writer will focus on *The War of the End of the World* and *The Real Life of Alejandro Mayta*, his latest novels.

Derek Walcott (West Indian poet and dramatist)—In his poetry Walcott explores themes related to his mixed heritage while evoking his life in the Caribbean islands. The publication of *Collected Poems, 1948-1984* has secured Walcott's position as an important and versatile poet.

Brian W(ilson) Aldiss

1925-

(Has also written under pseudonyms of Peter Pica and C. C. Shackleton) English novelist, short story writer, critic, historian, editor, autobiographer, nonfiction writer, travel writer, and poet.

An author who has experimented with a variety of literary forms and styles throughout his career, Aldiss is best known as a prolific and popular author and critic of contemporary science fiction. His major contribution to the science fiction field has been to develop a more thoughtful and humane literature which challenges the standard assumptions and beliefs of its audience. In his fiction Aldiss usually focuses on ambiguities, dualities, and paradoxes not generally attempted by other science fiction authors. Although some critics consider Aldiss's dialogue to be overly pedantic and his characters unconvincing, he is frequently praised for his confident, energetic style and the depth and scope of his ideas.

Aldiss's experiences as a soldier in the Far East during World War II have had a strong impact on his fiction. Jungle settings and the sense of exile he felt upon returning to postwar England are reflected in much of his work. Aldiss began his career writing what he termed "ordinary fiction," but he soon became interested in a variety of genres, including moralistic comedy, poetry, occult literature, detective fiction, and science fiction. His first mainstream book, *The Brightfount Diaries* (1955), written under the pseudonym of Peter Pica, is a collection of interrelated short stories about the domestic life of a bookshop assistant. Aldiss's first novel, *Non-Stop* (1958), anticipates his later themes of exile and solitude in the story of a crew of space explorers orbiting the earth who have lost all communication with the planet.

Much of Aldiss's early science fiction originally appeared as short stories in various magazines. Aldiss received a Hugo Award for most promising new author for the collection *The Canopy of Time* (1959; published in the United States as *Galaxies like Grains of Sand*). This book contains his most popular and widely anthologized short story, "Who Can Replace a Man?," which chronicles the end of humanity and the ascendance of machines. Aldiss received the Hugo Award for best short fiction for the short stories he later revised as the novel *Hothouse* (1962). This work is set in a jungle of giant plants and insects and relates the adventures of dwarfish humans attempting to survive in a hostile environment. Aldiss won the Nebula Award for best novella for *The Saliva Tree*, the title story of *The Saliva Tree and Other Strange Growths* (1966). In this tribute to H. G. Wells, a space machine arrives on an English farm in order to fatten animals and humans for alien consumption. *The Moment of Eclipse* (1972), another of Aldiss's well-regarded collections of short stories, is a diverse blend of science fiction, comedy, horror, and mainstream literature.

Aldiss's interest in taboo social issues, particularly sex, has at various times prompted him to write moralistic comedies in which he challenges conventional notions of sexual restraint. In *The Male Response* (1961), Aldiss centers on a group of Britishers forced to confront the casual sexuality of a tribe of

© Jerry Bauer

Africans, and in *The Primal Urge* (1961), his characters are outraged by the most controversial aspects of Freudian theory. Both novels received scathing reviews but achieved best-seller status in England. Aldiss's series of novels about Horatio Stubbs, a sexually obsessed Englishman, met with the resistance of critics and publishers alike. In *The Hand-Reared Boy* (1970), a book about adolescent masturbation, Aldiss strives to avoid lewdness in favor of blunt, honest comedy. In *A Soldier Erect* (1971) and *A Rude Awakening* (1978), the protagonist's sexual experiences as a soldier in Burma and Sumatra are developed as a metaphor for survival amidst the brutal realities of war. Most critics faulted Aldiss for indulging in tasteless, nonliterary subject matter, but the novels were popular successes.

Together with such acclaimed authors as Thomas M. Disch and John Sladek, Aldiss became a major force in the "new wave" movement in science fiction, which originated in England during the mid-1960s. Proponents of the movement, determined to break with the overworked conventions of traditional science fiction, argued that the genre should not be thought of as a single mode of literature but as a varied, developing hybrid of many literary forms. Several of Aldiss's novels from this period were originally published as short stories. His experimental novel *The Dark Light Years* (1964) centers on humanity's inability to relate to an intellectual alien race who profess a liking for their own excrement. *Barefoot in the Head: A European Fantasia* (1967) is the story of a displaced Yugoslavian's journeys through a futuristic Europe inundated by hallucinogenic gas. Timothy White characterized the novel's blend of surreal and literary language as a narrative "written as though Timothy Leary had collaborated with James Joyce." In *Report on Probability A* (1968), Aldiss, influenced by the French antinovelists Michel Butor and Alain Robbe-Grillet, develops a quasi-documentary style through which details are observed but meanings remain obscure. Throughout the book's length, nothing is developed or resolved. These novels received largely negative reviews but established Aldiss's reputation as an author who prefers innovation over reliable literary formulas.

Aldiss's best-received fiction of the 1970s is diverse both in theme and subject matter. In *Frankenstein Unbound* (1973), a fantasy novel written as a philosophic treatise on the moral responsibilities of art and science, a futuristic narrator travels back in time, where he converses with nineteenth-century literary figures and with the fictitious Dr. Frankenstein. *The Malacia Tapestry* (1976) is a utopian novel in which Aldiss returns to a subject he often explored in his early fiction—that of absolute stasis, or the concept of entropy. In this book, citizens of a wealthy city-state believe they are descended from dinosaurs and prohibit art, technology, or any stimulus which could conceivably cause change. Aldiss reverses this situation in *Enemies of the System: A Tale of Homo Uniformis* (1978). In this dystopian novel, a futuristic military elite is faced with an impending need for evolutionary adaptation and must decide whether or not to defy the fixed beliefs of their totalitarian system.

Aldiss's Helliconia trilogy has been hailed as his major return to popular science fiction. In these novels Aldiss integrates such scientific concerns as ecology, biology, physics, geology, and chemistry to explore the effects of severe change on a planet circling two stars. Because Helliconia's orbit around its larger, hotter sun lasts 2592 earth years and its orbit around its smaller, colder sun lasts only 480 earth days, the planet's inhabitants are continuously forced to adapt to extremes in weather and temperature. In *Helliconia Spring* (1981), for which Aldiss received the John W. Campbell Award for best science fiction novel, viruses and a rival race known as phagors play a part in natural selection, with phagors becoming dominant in the winter when the humanoid population decreases and the humanoids becoming dominant in summer. In *Helliconia Summer* (1983), a novel of more personal concerns, Aldiss examines the moral implications of politics and the massacre of the phagors. *Helliconia Winter* (1984) centers on the attempts of the humanoids to survive the encroaching ice age and on the efforts of phagors and humanoids to come to terms with their mutual hatred.

Aldiss is also respected as an observant critic of the science fiction genre. He has published numerous essays, reviews, and columns both under his own name and under the pseudonym of C. C. Shackleton. *Billion Year Spree: The History of Science Fiction* (1973) is regarded as a definitive study of the genre, serving as both an introduction to the field and as a reference volume for enthusiasts.

(See also *CLC*, Vols. 5, 14; *Contemporary Authors*, Vols. 5-8, rev. ed.; *Contemporary Authors New Revision Series,* Vol. 5; *Contemporary Authors Autobiography Series,* Vol. 2; *Something about the Author,* Vol. 34; and *Dictionary of Literary Biography,* Vol. 14.)

NEIL HEPBURN

[In *The Malacia Tapestry,* Mr Aldiss] suggests that the past enslaves the present. Malacia itself is a rich city-state, with the texture of renaissance Venice, but a mien bellicosely fixed against change of any sort. The ruling council imposes a belief in man's descent from 'ancestral beasts'—biped dinosaurs—performs a ferocious positive vetting on any development of technology or art that might lead to change, and quietly murders those whom it judges to be progressives.

Perian de Chirolo is an actor scratching for parts in this strange place, which seems to be in the real world but not of it; and, to advance himself to a social position in which he can be a serious suitor to the rich and beautiful Armida, agrees to perform in a series of tableaux for the inventor of a kind of colour-photography. . . . But it all collapses as the Galileo-figure is denounced and made away with.

Somewhere in this entertaining farrago, with its science-fiction intrusions which Mr Aldiss seems unable to resist, there is a serious novel crying to be understood. But the questions—about class, authority, wealth, the effect of all of them on the capacity to feel, the weight of the past, the problem of change—are asked in a trite way, and never answered. It is best, perhaps, just to enjoy the continuous pleasure of reading Mr Aldiss's prose . . . and being struck by his felicitous invention of fantastications which never jar with the milieu he is describing. (p. 95)

> Neil Hepburn, "A Quick Tweak," in The Listener,
> Vol. 96, No. 2467, July 22, 1976, pp. 94-5.*

HARRIET WAUGH

[In *The Malacia Tapestry,* Aldiss] has attempted an exceptionally difficult form of fiction, and one in which there is a wide chasm between the first-rate and the rest. While a novel does not necessarily have to be very good in order to be enjoyable, this form of fiction does require a very high order of imaginative and intellectual power for it to work successfully; by these criteria, *The Malacia Tapestry* fails.

Mr Aldiss takes the reader into an imagined country on the borders of Byzantium. The people of the country evolved from prehistoric monsters, who still exist and are hunted at certain times of the year. Because of this killing, the religion of the country insists that man is basically evil. According to one version, if the people try hard enough they might achieve goodness, but in the other version there is so little chance of such grace that they must appease instead the gods of evil. . . .

The plot itself is a simple tale of romantic infidelity and betrayal, concerning a hero who is a handsome, empty-headed and essentially uninteresting actor who skids through life looking for a jolly time, not too concerned with the state of the nation. . . . The hero sums up the predicament of the novel rather well when he complains that the plot of the tableau in which he acts for a revolutionary photographic inventor, and which turns out to mirror his own story, is banal. It is a sad case of the emperor having no clothes.

> Harriet Waugh, "The Front Line," in The Spectator,
> Vol. 237, No. 7727, July 31, 1976, p. 23.*

TOM PAULIN

Brian Aldiss knows how to be witty about the wilder reaches of subjectivity. The stories in *Last Orders* are hilarious fantasies which turn Wittgenstein's *Tractatus* into space-age musicals and Neffpanimate Holman Hunt's "The Awakening Conscience". This act of cinematic ingenuity shows 'Turner's little steam train cross a viaduct in a storm and its passengers alight at Maidenhead'. A similar ingenuity effortlessly imagines blank-faced clone-serfs, obsolescing futures, 'ashes in the air, and traces of older destinations'. And what's so appealing about Aldiss's surreal universe is his way of introducing both quirky comedy and an obstinate humanity. In one story he quotes Auden's "Musée des Beaux Arts" and then shows how suffering happens in its ordinary way while galaxies explode and expensive, delicate space-ships plunge into infinity. (p. 745)

> Tom Paulin, "Mortem Virumque Cano," in *New Statesman, Vol. 94, No. 2436, November 25, 1977, pp. 744-45.**

ALEX DE JONGE

[*Last Orders*] is vintage stuff. Some of the pieces are fairly conventional, others dazzling little narratives set on Aldiss's favourite territory—those glistening and frequently wild zodiacal planets. More ambitious compositions are musical in conception, reminiscent of symbolist prose poetry in their use of names and images to explore dreamscapes and work variations on their basic themes. Like symbolist writing, only less pretentious, they are beautiful but enigmatic. Mr Aldiss succeeds in leaving rational understanding behind without lapsing into gratuity. The writing conveys a sense of necessity and pleases greatly although I sometimes lacked any clear idea of what was going on—my fault I suppose. The writing is poetic in a good sense, a million miles from pseud's corner, authentically imagined probings into the deepest areas of inner space. . . . Real writing this. (p. 21)

> Alex de Jonge, "January SF," in *The Spectator, Vol. 240, No. 7802, January 14, 1978, pp. 20-1.**

A. N. WILSON

Told in the first person, [*A Rude Awakening*] chronicles the discreditable doings of Harry Stubbs, a name aptly suggesting unpleasantness of character and perpetual chain-smoking. The main flaw in this often clever book is that, while presenting the drunken antics of Stubbs (now a sergeant in Sumatra) in a realistic enough way to show that he is a mindless reprobate, it has no other voice but his in which to comment on things in general. Why should we accept his (of all people's) banal reflections on the political situation in the Far East in 1946?

And the obsession with whoring seems excessive. . . . Doubtless true, *A Rude Awakening* shows why the experience is distinctive, but not why it is one that a man could conceivably wish to have had. Aldiss is too fond of these dull tarts to think that some of his readers might find them boring.

> A. N. Wilson, "No Offence," in *New Statesman, Vol. 95, No. 2455, April 7, 1978, p. 471.**

PAUL ABLEMAN

Life In The West is primarily a novel of ideas, and a pretty good one. It shares with the kind (and it is the best kind) of SF that Aldiss writes the property of using character and situation to explore ideas rather than ideas to reveal character. The 300-odd pages of the book are divided into 14 sections.

Half of these are set in Ermalpa, Sicily where one Thomas Squire is participating, as guest of honour, in the 'First International Congress of Intergraphic Criticism' and much of these sections is taken up with a detailed account, complete with long extracts from delegates' speeches, of the proceedings. What is 'Intergraphic Criticism'? It seems to be the treatment of popular art forms, and even diversions, as serious cultural manifestations. One delegate reads a paper on pin-ball machines and another, perhaps not surprisingly, on science fiction which, again perhaps not surprisingly, he manages to elevate to the status of literature. . . . [Squire] is the dynastic master of Pippet Hall, a country seat in Norfolk, and also a businessman and spare-time publicist who really knows where culture's at. It fleetingly occurred to me, while reading these sections, that perhaps Aldiss had originally aimed at a television spectacular and, unable to launch it, had settled for this prose version. But then there is the other half of the book to consider.

This consists of a series of flashbacks which jumps about rather confusingly and, I felt, gratuitously in time in order to reveal Squire's past. This turns out to contain a number of lurid elements. For example, his father was killed and partially eaten by his own mastiffs and, as a Freudian result, Squire, also feeling deprived at having been too young for the second World war, gets himself recruited into a Special Ops unit and sent to Yugoslavia to shoot Russians. He then returns to England, college, the family seat, the city and marriage. The blurb talks of his 'many affairs with women' but I counted only four. This is hardly Casanova stuff but suffices to alienate his wife who takes the kids and leaves the hall. . . . While recognizing that real people often do display contradictory qualities, I was never convinced that the disparate elements in Squire's character really fitted together. He remained for me essentially a talking head. Indeed, all the characters are chiefly talking heads but many of them generate more sense of being autonomous people than the hero does. Amongst the notable creations is the reluctant Russian Vasily Rugorsky.

But somehow, the places in the book seem much more real than the people. Singapore, Sicily, Serbia and Norfolk are all crisply evoked as is a cave in the jungle decorated with thousands of images of hands which are alleged to be the oldest works of art in the world. . . .

But most real of all are the ideas. Mr Aldiss is first-rate at unpicking the blurred fabric of thought in which we all live and showing its constituent threads. . . . [He] is acute and even profound on the nature of the great ideological conflicts of the contemporary world, on the rise of cities, on race and on many other things.

Selina Ajdini, whom Squire fancies, reads the congress a paper on Aldous Huxley, maintaining that 'Huxley's life typified the end of one great strand of English and European bougeois Romantic thought' and also that the type of elite that Huxley represented 'typified a repressive class structuralism cloaked by a veneer of scientific and humanistic enlightenment'. Squire pencils 'higher foolishness' on his note-pad. Squire reveres Huxley, whose ghost hovers over these pages, and almost certainly Brian Aldiss does too.

It is a pity, then, that Aldiss did not emulate his master and limit his aspiration to a slender novel of ideas in which the characters make little pretence of being other than points of view. It would probably have resulted in a stronger work than this lopsided one which strives to incorporate flesh and blood but thereby only succeeds in obscuring the thought. The sense of strain can be felt in the pretentious title. What we really have here is not 'Life in the West' but 'Certain Currents of Thought in the West.' Still, while they are flowing, the reader enjoys an exhilerating dip.

Paul Ableman, "Ideas Man," in The Spectator, *Vol. 244, No. 7913, March 8, 1980, p. 21.*

MICHAEL BISHOP

[The] least popular of Wells' early scientific romances was *The Island of Doctor Moreau,* undoubtedly because it smudges the conventional distinctions between the bestial and the human. Also, in the person of Moreau, it confronts the reader with an unsavory parodic God, an almost archetypal "mad scientist" whose obsession is (. . . according to [Frank] McConnell) "to recapitulate and improve upon the process whereby men evolve from beasts." Although Wells called this novel "an exercise in youthful blasphemy," its themes still disturb us, and much of *Doctor Moreau*'s power derives from our continuing, perhaps innate interest in these questions. . . .

[Aldiss] attempts to tap the sources of this power by casting his newest novel as a modern sequel to Wells' evolutionary nightmare. *An Island Called Moreau* . . . takes place in 1996, exactly a century after the publication of its famous predecessor, during a global war. Particularly Wellsian is Aldiss' adoption of a prophetic, cautionary voice. In a brief, italicized coda he writes, *"The question was whether humanity's instinct for survival would impel it to find a way to permanent peace. Otherwise, all would be lost."* (p. 10)

U.S. Undersecretary of State Calvert Madle Roberts ends up on a mysterious Pacific island. He soon learns that Wells' late Victorian allegory was triggered by his acquaintance with a "real" person, one Angus McMoreau (like Wells, a student of Thomas Huxley), and that the descendants of the Scottish doctor's grotesque beast-men are undergoing further experiments at the hands of a British thalidomide victim and genetic specialist by the name of Mortimer Dart.

To synopsize too much more of the story would be to explode a few of its crucial "surprises"—but it is significant that Dart's work, which depends not on the knife but on gene-manipulating drugs, has acquired a kind of legitimacy from the *institutionalized* conviction that the suicide of our species is inevitable as well as imminent. By dramatizing this concept, Aldiss' fable effectively argues against such a chilling surrender. And in an age when talk of "limited nuclear war" provokes casual ho-hums rather than outright horror, we can scarcely fault Aldiss for going to the Wells too often.

But I do quarrel with certain aspects of the *presentation* of this message. First, the American narrator occasionally stumbles into phrasing that betrays the author's nationality, and outdated Americanisms like "Why not cool it, Mr. Dart?" do not offset the elegant fishiness of these lapses. Further, when Roberts repeats his mother's tale of how Americans escaped the thalidomide disaster of the early 1960s . . . , Aldiss' dramaturgical string-pulling becomes embarrassingly clanky and conspicuous.

The novel's most damaging flaw, however, is the introduction of a female character, Heather, whom Aldiss wants to behave both as a silly exhibitionist and an ideologically committed government agent—without this latter role's in any credible way dictating her assumption of the former. . . . Beyond in-

jecting S-E-X into the narrative, it depicts Heather as a stupidly tractable wench and Roberts, in his response, as a paragon of priggish nobility. Although later events rescue Roberts from this assessment, Heather remains an ill-defined and therefore unbelievable creation. (pp. 10, 14)

Michael Bishop, "Marvels and Monsters from the Wells Spring," in Book World—The Washington Post, *March 22, 1981, pp. 10, 14.**

ROBERT E. COLBERT

While Brian Aldiss is the least programmatic of critics—in striking contrast to such earlier, highly influential spokesmen for the [science fiction] genre as John W. Campbell—there does, nevertheless, emerge from the body of his critical work (and even to some extent from the designedly popular historical survey *Billion Year Spree*) a set of inter-related critical principles; it is to these principles that his discussions and evaluations of individual works and writers can be seen to have reference. Paramount among these principles is the high value placed on authorial autonomy. It is this central concern which governs a cluster of related concerns and the value judgments that ensue. It is, for example, Aldiss' concern for authorial autonomy that causes him to cast a skeptical glance at a great number of genre (i.e., magazine) science fiction's sacred cows. One of the distinctive features of his criticism is his advocacy of the necessity for thematic originality. Aldiss finds modern science fiction all too prone to ancestor worship, a major consequence of which is the resort to thematic and formal clichés. (pp. 333-34)

Aldiss rightly detects a paradoxical conservatism in a genre that professes to be concerned with change and diversity; instead, he discovers time and again in modern science fiction a strikingly unimaginative adherence to old stock formulas of theme, plot, and characterization, many of which derive from the technology-worshipping, gadget-oriented fiction printed in Gernsback's *Amazing Stories.* The "orthodoxies" initiated by Gernsback and his followers are seen to have inhibited severely the development of modern science fiction in two paramount ways, either one of which would seem to doom the form to inconsequence. The conservatism introduced by the magazines "shows itself in two ways in science fiction: in the way that posited (future societies) . . . are still but thinly veiled versions of today's capitalist West. The other ways [this] conservatism shows is in an almost frantic fight to retain old forms of fiction and even the old subjects—forms and subjects not exactly fresh when [genre] science fiction began in 1926! So the ostensibly forward-looking is often the backward-looking."

The price that writers pay for their all-too-frequent reliance on old, outdated formulas is that, lacking any genuine originality, their works rapidly date, become essentially unreadable. . . . (p. 334)

[Integrity] does not come easily; a great many forces within the field exert pressure on the writer to compromise with his craft and his conscience. From the time of Gernsback, for example, the weight of genre magazine editors and editorial policies has played a major role in turning writers into mere "producers," men lacking in any genuine creativity due to their subservient role to editors, fans, and financial pressures. . . . [Aldiss] only really came into his own as an artist once he made the decision to place his stories and novels in other markets where editors were more accepting of independent work. Such editors were often younger men who were not wedded to the old tried-and-true formulas of the so-called "Golden Age" of science fiction. (p. 335)

It should be noted that Aldiss is by no means bereft of social and moral concerns of his own; numerous comments found throughout his work make it clear that he is no supporter of a rigorous and exclusive art-for-art's-sake position. While he is keenly aware of the need for authorial autonomy and individual artistic vision, he is at the same time concerned that writers in the medium make a concerted effort to stay faithful to "a real world of . . . sensitive, sinful, defeated" human beings. The relationship here with Aldiss' concern for the dearth of ordinary human feeling in so much genre science fiction, its lack of warmth and compassion, is clear. And the specifically literary benefits of the reintroduction of such concerns are also clear: an art which renders situations, depicts characters, closer to the more immediate human concerns can only benefit artistically.

Aldiss' championship of J. G. Ballard, as of Philip K. Dick, is due in large part to his appreciation of both writers' unwavering concern for "real, fallible human beings." Aldiss rightly comments that the themes and protagonists of his fellow Britishers constitute "a conscious reaction against conservative s[cience] f[iction]. His central characters . . . defeated, wry, are poles away from Heinlein's swaggering heroes, Asimov's world savers. . . ." Aldiss' very considerable admiration for Philip Dick and for the later novels of Ursula Le Guin stems from much the same reason: both writers have succeeded in wedding significant science fiction themes—often social and/or psychological rather than the more conventional "hard science," technological themes favored by Heinlein and Asimov—to stories about recognizable human beings in recognizable social and moral situations (i.e., no swaggerers need apply).

The gain for science fiction as a viable art form is enormous. But no less considerable is the gain for the medium as a valid mode of social criticism. Significantly [in **"The Year of the Big Spring Clean"**], Aldiss points to the presence of "conservative science fiction's infallible heroes [as] useless as protagonists *in novels of social criticism.* For them, one needs fallible people who are only marginally better than the society in which they exist; that was the H. G. Wells tradition." (pp. 337-38)

One of the satisfactions of reading [Aldiss'] . . . criticism is that of discovering that Aldiss rarely loses his sense of the necessary *balance* to be maintained between narrative and aesthetic values on the one hand, and matters of content and commentary on the other. Thus, he is sincere when he insists that "the vital history of sf in the 60's lies precisely in its taking itself more seriously: not as prediction: not as *Practical Mechanics* . . . not even as satire: but as science fiction. As one of the . . . arts." This is all well and good, a commendable position; that is, it is so in the abstract. But Aldiss is nothing if not a reader and critic of the concrete text; and it is a consequence of his fidelity to the work itself, and his relative freedom from any particular overriding dogma, that his actual response to a given work or writer cannot readily be predicted. (p. 340)

In another context, striving yet again to loosen the editorial constrictions on writers, Aldiss very shrewdly (and wittily) arrives at the conclusion that, in fact, science fiction does not exist; it is only "a paper empire," one which has been invented for the convenience of editors and publishers. "'Science Fic-

tion' has to be a vague term in order to cover everything; and so it applies to nothing. . . . By the time you have a definition broad enough to cover all the components, you are left with no viable definition. There is no such thing as science fiction. . . .' " . . . [For] the newer writers of Aldiss' generation and later, this formulation is the necessary prerequisite to artistic freedom; without some such freeing proposition, it is difficult to see how writers could ever have successfully extricated themselves from the much-loved but increasingly stultifying formulas of conservative editors and readers. The conclusion Aldiss draws from his "proof" of the genre's non-existence is that, as a consequence, novelists and short story writers "can write their own thing, can attempt to satisfy themselves instead of bowing to some vague set of external standards, can be free of all the trappings of the medium that have become so stale—clichés that no longer work." . . . These clichés are those of magazine science fiction: "spaceships that travel faster than light, and robots that can't be distinguished from humans, and telepathy." (pp. 335-36)

While Aldiss clearly regrets the disproportionate influence of a few editors in the field, he is aware also that writers as well bear no little responsibility for their plight. . . . In the context of an earlier essay [**"Knights of the Paper Spaceship"**], Aldiss scathingly comments on the fact that during the early fifties "many SF writers . . . became more or less propagandists for the space race. . . . Science fiction was . . . being prostituted to the space race . . . it was not merely espousing a cause but sucking up to a source of power, just like the storytellers of *Analog* who affect at various times to believe in (Campbell's) editorial notions from Dianetics onward."

The potential danger to a body of work that is produced on demand for reasons extrinsic to art and the writer's personal vision is extremely clear; the work that results will in all likelihood be uninspired in style, derivative in content. . . .

Didacticism poses a similar threat [to the integrity of the artist]—and temptation—to the science fiction writer and to the achievement of genuinely literary values. Thus, even in those cases where the editor and his writers are focused on intrinsic issues of purely intellectual and scientific interest—in contrast to extrinsic causes, as, for example, the space race—there still remains the problem of achieving a satisfying *balance* of science *and* fiction. Here, too, Aldiss finds a startlingly high proportion of the stories and novels published in the "Golden Age" of Campbell's *Astounding* bereft of any durable artistic significance and, thereby, a negative influence on the growth and development of the genre. (p. 336)

[Aldiss' strictures] and his candid expression of boredom in the face of the ponderous and the pretentious, are consistent with the insights and asides found elsewhere in his work. He welcomes art, but he is suspicious of artifice—certainly of cold and ponderous artifice. He looks always for evidence of the humane. And he relishes stylistic grace, the equipoise of art. Thus, a striking feature of his criticism is the sensitivity it exhibits to wit and humor. There is his delight, for example, in the balletic lightness of touch of Robert Sheckley. . . . And it is this same pleasure, taken in the play of intellectual wit, that contributes to his appreciation of J. G. Ballard and Philip K. Dick. . . . [He] knows full well that they draw their material from their own experience of life, from personal joy and suffering, and that they transmute this individually perceived material into stories and novels in significant part by means of intellectual "play" and verbal wit. The very feel, look, tone, smell, texture of their prose testify to the originality, the authenticity, of their style and vision. . . . Such writers are significant artists because they are free men. (p. 341)

Robert E. Colbert, "Unbinding Frankenstein: The Science Fiction Criticism of Brian Aldiss," in Extrapolation, *Vol. 23, No. 4, Winter, 1982, pp. 333-44.*

MICHAEL BISHOP

[In *Helliconia Spring*], the first volume of a projected trilogy, [Aldiss] has written a novel of wide-screen panorama, imaginative incident, and suspenseful foreshadowing of events yet to come. . . . Liner notes attribute to Aldiss the heady ambition of creating "one of the half-dozen truly wonderful novels of scientific romance," . . . just the sort of self-important puffery that invites a deflating pin prick. And I, after snowshoeing through this fat book's first 50 pages, grimacing at such ugly obligatory coinages as *Yuli, yelk, phagor, Batalix, gunnadu,* and others, desperately wanted to administer that pin prick.

What stayed my hand? Among other virtues, Aldiss' unflagging narrative energy, his gift for drawing character (including female characters, an area in which he has not always excelled), and the many overt or subtle hints of larger, more portentous mysteries underlying the Viking-saga surface of his story. Since the publication of *The Long Afternoon of Earth* [published in Great Britain as *Hothouse*] 20 years ago, Aldiss has obviously seen, read, and absorbed much.

The planet Helliconia has two suns. Its Great Year—the period in which it and its nearer sun revolve about the larger and more distant star—lasts 2592 terrestrial years; and as this novel unfolds, Helliconia is moving inexorably toward the promise and peril of spring, a season that none of its winter-born inhabitants has ever before imagined much less experienced. Moreover, the coming of spring has metaphorical correspondences with the blossoming of new cultural patterns among the planet's people, particularly those in the crossroads settlement of Oldorando.

Aldiss is working on a vast, almost Stapledonian scale, not neglecting the complex ecology of a world where a single season endures nearly 6½ centuries, where great galumphing animals and tiny tick-transmitted viruses play equally important roles in planetary history. Against his human characters Aldiss stands a species of intelligent beast, phagors, who unfortunately resemble the befurred and bicorned villains on Saturday-morning cartoons, but who eventually acquire a touching credibility as both the foes and victims of their human counterparts. . . .

Do the scrupulous scientific underpinnings of *Helliconia Spring* add anything completely indispensable to either its enjoyment or its message? Distance? A new perspective? A rationale for the marshaling of unearthly wonders? Well, maybe. I am not really sure. This is *War and Peace* as distilled through the mind of a troubled futurologist, *Shogun* as penned by a professional visionary; and whatever the second and third volumes contribute to this saga, as either pure story or fictional exegesis of our own historical predicament, I am anxious to read them.

Michael Bishop, in a review of "Helliconia Spring," in Book World—The Washington Post, *February 28, 1982, p. 8.*

GEORGE MORTIMER

[*Helliconia Spring*] deals with weather on a large scale, and the effect this has on the life systems within [Aldiss's] imag-

inary planet. . . . *Homo sapiens* on Helliconia seem to cope less well with the changes of temperature from sub-zero ice age to tropical profusion than the flora and fauna and other beasties of the planet. As on our own earth, presumably, man is a relative newcomer.

Throughout the book—and it is a long one—Aldiss wrestles with language, rescuing archaic words, successfully playing with the forms of others (*cf* fossie) and creating new ones where necessary. . . . [It] becomes clearer and clearer that the humane mantle of H. G. Wells is falling into place more and more comfortably on the shoulders of Aldiss.

Helliconia Spring begins at the very end of one of the planet's recurring ice ages. The book's title suggests a neat blend of Dante and the Muses. Its contents definitely begin in Purgatorio, yet with an optimistic hint of human aspiration reaching beyond the brutal and savage hardships which its inhabitants must endure. (pp. 82-3)

The book begins with an expedition, Yuli hunting with his father. Yuli is to be the protagonist. We are told that he has arrived at a full grown man's estate at the tender age of *nine*. However, this proves to be not entirely to do with precociousness but to a vagary of differing calendars. Helliconia revolves around Balatix, its neighbouring planet, once every 480 days. My pocket calculator reveals his 'true' age to be nearly twelve and a half.

During the initial hunting scene he has the misfortune to see his father, paralyzed with fear, captured by two beast-like Phagors and led away into captivity as a slave. It is impossible here to encapsulate Yuli's further adventures, but they can be compressed to two periods. The first occurs during his life in a fascist community which dwells inside a hollowed out mountainous hill. Like a true hero, he escapes from his perils in this underground community, enlisting other rebels en route. Together they enter into a farming/hunting community called Embruddock. Yuli has grown up to be a natural leader, and takes over, secures and maintains Embruddock, widening its boundaries in the process.

Following his death, interest shifts to the growing prosperity of the community and the internecine struggles for power that take place. If much of this reminds us of the wild west of America this may both be intentional and far from implausible, given Embruddock's burgeoning history. In view of the primitive nature of the settlement, and its initial natural poverty, it comes as a surprise to find the introduction of a remarkable lady, Shay Tal, who founds an academy for women. . . . She believes that the ruins of a past civilization lying not far away may give some clue to the past of the planet, and that in turn may help its inhabitants in the future.

At this point volume one ends. If I have not conveyed the sheer excitement of the book, it is not for lack of admiration for the skill that involves one with the carefully humanised characters, and for the very real fear created by the hostile environment, in which animals and plants are more menacing than useful to the 'human' inhabitants. (pp. 83-4)

George Mortimer, "Weather Forecast," in London Magazine, *n.s. Vol. 21, No. 12, March, 1982, pp. 82-4.**

WILLIS E. McNELLY

What place does *Helliconia Spring* have in the Aldiss canon? The question admits of no simple answer. . . . [It's] not oversimplification to say that [Aldiss's] major concern in most of his major fiction has been the problem of change and its consequences. Aldiss himself prefers to call it the problem of entropy. Yet however designated, change and/or stasis has been the artistic center about which most of his major work revolves.

At one end of the stasis-change spectrum is his neglected minor masterpiece, *Report on Probability A* (1968). He once told me that in this short novel he executed his original plan more closely than in any other of his books. He wanted to show, as he once put it to me, "actionless stasis" in a virtual freeze frame world. Strongly influenced by the French anti-novel of Alain Robbe-Grillet and the provocative Alain Resnais motion picture, *Last Year at Marienbad, Report* gives the reader nothing but phenomena. Three characters, known only as G, S, and C, live in separate hovels, each invisible to the others. . . . Nothing happens . . . for 200 pages. They remain virtually motionless in their static world, *per omnia secula seculorum*. Both brilliant and annoying, *Report* shows the degradation of matter/phenomena to inert uniformity.

Aldiss's 1980 mainstream novel *Life in the West*, occupied the author prior to his embarking on the Helliconia epic. Here too the subject is change and its effects. . . . Its themes are delightfully familiar to scholarly SF buffs. It's so good I urge Aldiss fans to acquire the British edition.

Helliconia Spring is at the opposite end of the spectrum. The world of Helliconia is drenched with action; character after character and incident after incident cascade from Aldiss's fertile imagination. The book is thus more than a mere change in the weather; it details the results of severe climatic changes on a metamorphic, psychological, even theological level. If all things change, what remains unchanged? he seems to ask, aside from the process of change itself.

Coupled with this most inventive situation is the presence of an observer ship from Earth, the *Avernus*. . . . In a profound sense, Earth is dependent upon Helliconia for its artistic, intellectual, theological, even teleological sustenance. Yet in some kind of absolute reality, Helliconia is only a phantasm, the show place of events 1000 light years away and of people long since dead.

Thus Aldiss wishes us to consider still one more aspect of our own life: how much of its vitality is dependent upon artistic constructs? He has assured me that he intends to develop this theme in the next two books in the series. Art. Life, Reality, Change. Essence. Existence. Stasis. Entropy. These are the themes that make Aldiss's writing and *Helliconia Spring* so important. (pp. 18-19)

Willis E. McNelly, "A Second Opinion," in Science Fiction & Fantasy Book Review, *No. 5, June, 1982, pp. 18-19.*

PHILIP SMITH

The stories in *Foreign Bodies* and Aldiss's decision to have them published in Singapore show his continued fascination with the fantasy and the reality of S.E. Asia. All but one of the six stories are set in the region; four of the six were written especially for this book. Three stories are fables, three are non-SF, realistic stories.

The collection is unified by a concern for finding the emotional truth in a part of the world where everything seems to be a deception. In the title story a displaced European who has returned to Sumatra 30 years after his wartime experiences there tells an exiled Indonesian about his frustrating attempts to find a dead lover's house in Medan. He has discovered instead the depth of his own feelings about the past. In "**Frontiers**" a British doctor on assignment from the U.N. must try to discern the truth of the refugee problem in a fictional country much like Cambodia. He views the facts of suffering through the lenses of his own skepticism, his hosts' Communist ideology, and the reports of a young Dutch girl he meets and rescues. "**Boat Animals**" makes into a beast fable the problems and politics of refugee Vietnamese boat people in Singapore. "**A Romance of the Equator**" and "**Back from Java**" are concerned with love and the tropics—the first story is a fable of a man who cannot choose between two magical lovers, one dark, one fair; the second is about the dream vision of an academic who has returned from Java to England and to his dying grandmother, absent wife, and a punk teenage temptress. The closing fable, "**The Skeleton**," captures in one and a half pages the wish of a Westerner to be one with the people of the East, even if he must affirm his likeness by stripping away flesh and skin.

These are minor stories from a major writer, but they are worth reading as visions of an important part of Aldiss's, and our, world.

Philip Smith, in a review of "Foreign Bodies: Stories," in Science Fiction & Fantasy Book Review, *No. 7, September, 1982, p. 16.*

GERALD JONAS

In a sense, the hero of the first two volumes in [Aldiss's] projected trilogy that truly deserves the label "epic" is Charles Darwin. . . . [In *Helliconia Summer*] Aldiss writes science fiction on the grandest possible scale. He writes of the evolution of cultures, of entire species, of the ever-changing physical environment that shapes and is itself shaped by the forces of life. Yet he does not forget—what true Darwinian could?—that the key unit of evolutionary change is the individual, struggling, sometimes blindly and sometimes with hard-earned foresight, to survive and multiply.

Helliconia is a planet that resembles Earth in many ways. It has mountains, plains, deserts, oceans and rivers and a variety of Earthlike flora and fauna, including a species of intelligent bipeds virtually indistinguishable from human beings. But these Helliconians share their world with a second sentient species, horned, hairy creatures called phagors, who might pass for intelligent mountain goats on Earth. Humans and phagors vie for dominance, but both species are subjected to periodic extremes in climates that test the limits that living creatures can endure. . . .

The adaptation of the two sentient species of Helliconia to their environment—and to each other—is the theme that holds the trilogy together. But Mr. Aldiss's focus is always on the individual. He writes of young Yuli, who accidently discovers the underground city of Pannoval, where men live out the long winter and maintain the old writings that tell of the day when "the sky of ice" will become "a sky of fire." The story of spring becomes the story of a small community, founded by Yuli, that grows into a major trading center and eventually a city. Strong men contend for political mastery, but they are barely able to keep pace with the changes prompted by the long thaw. . . .

As it happens, the evolutionary epic unfolding on Helliconia is being monitored by humans from Earth who have set up an orbiting observation station called Avernus. Although the inhabitants of Avernus try to maintain a scientific detachment, they cannot resist sending one of their number down to the planet from time to time to mingle with the Helliconians. For the emissary, this assignment is a death sentence, since an Earth-bred immune system is powerless against Helliconian microbes. But life in the unchanging environment of Avernus is so deadly to the spirit that the observers compete for the chance to die an interesting death on Helliconia, and to provide all Avernus with vicarious thrills. Meanwhile, a running record of *everything* that happens on Helliconia is beamed back to Earth, where the words and deeds of the Helliconians are treated as entertainment—an edifying kind of soap opera.

One might ask why Mr. Aldiss has gone to the trouble to invent an entire planetary ecology as a setting for his Darwinian drama, when he could have found sufficient material to dramatize in our own prehistory, as Jean M. Auel has done in *The Clan of the Cave Bear* and *The Valley of Horses*. Miss Auel's novels represent a considerable achievement, but there is a built-in limit to her work that Mr. Aldiss soars beyond. A scientifically plausible recreation of the human past must reflect the conventional wisdom of paleontology, archaeology and anthropology. No matter how cleverly Miss Auel weaves her story around these givens, the reader cannot help keeping an eye out for the bits of science sustaining the plot.

Mr. Aldiss is free of such constraints. So long as he remains within the broad scope of modern evolutionary theory, he can illuminate the complex interactions between individual and environment without having to pick his way around the detritus of documentation and controversy. The ingenious and diverse methods employed by the flora and fauna of Helliconia to adapt to profound climatic change gave me a clearer picture of Darwinian mechanisms than most traditional explanations.

But Mr. Aldiss's strategy has an even more important advantage. In the second book of his trilogy, the onset of summer allows the humans on Helliconia to organize ever-larger social entities, with all the benefits and drawbacks that go with a "higher" civilization, including experimental science and war. In describing these developments, Mr. Aldiss teases the reader with narratives that hint at parallels to terrestrial history yet veer off at crucial moments on purely Helliconian tangents. JandolAnganol, King of Bortien, a religious fanatic burdened by his own lusty nature and beset by powerful political rivals, might be a figure out of some medieval chronicle. But it is his curious relationship with his personal guard of phagors that determines his fate and that of his kingdom.

Mr. Aldiss is attempting nothing less than an evolutionary gloss on the rise—and possibly fall—of a civilization, in which complex personalities like JandolAnganol take their place along with more "primitive" types like Yuli and Laintal Ay as links in a chain that runs from the products of stellar fusion to the products of the imagination. Final judgment on the trilogy must, of course, await publication of the third book, which will presumably carry the story of Helliconia through the rest of its enormously eventful "year." Given the brilliant success of the first two books, I would say that Mr. Aldiss is now in competition with no one but himself.

*Gerald Jonas, in a review of "Helliconia Summer,"
in* The New York Times Book Review, *February
26, 1984, p. 31.*

PHILIP E. SMITH II

In contrast to the centuries-long time span of *Helliconia Spring*, [*Helliconia Summer*] narrates the events of only six months. Beginning *in medias res*, the first chapters present a densely figured tapestry full of characters, incidents, and background. The blindly ambitious King and beautiful, sorrowful Queen of Borlien, a minor country, are about to be divorced. The cause and consequences of this event, together with revelations about Helliconia's surprising history, inhabitants, languages, flora, fauna, and ecology, are woven together in the rest of the book. The reader's early confusions in trying to assimilate so much seemingly unrelated information are appropriately analogous to the interpretive incomprehensions experienced when first viewing a finely detailed picture. Delving deeper into the novel, though, the reader is gradually returned to the causes of events and is rewarded with successively more inclusive perceptions about the complex structure of plot, character, idea, and image.

Aldiss's design, fully revealed only in the conclusion, surprises, delights, and challenges the reader; it also prepares suspensefully for the third volume. Finally, it provides a cosmic stage for Aldiss to dramatize his fascination with the aesthetic relationships amongst creator, observer, and observed, amongst author, audience, and artifact. This theme, apparent in his work as early as *Starship* (1959), permeates other fictions like *Report on Probability A* (1969) and the stories in *Last Orders* (1977). . . .

Aldiss has said that he thinks of this three-part novel as "scientific romance." If so, its imaginative extrapolations, scope, and perspective of cosmic irony suggest Aldiss's regard for and debt to H. G. Wells and Olaf Stapledon. Ironies aside, though, Aldiss's plot also contains much of the swash and buckle of melodramatic historical romance, and there are several scenes where narrative and dialogue do not rise above the grandiloquent cliches of novels by Walter Scott, R. L. Stevenson, H. R. Haggard, and their twentieth-century followers. Since Aldiss's plot and setting have many analogues in Renaissance and early modern European history, such echoes of historical fiction may be unavoidable, or even intentional and affectionate stylistic recollections, but I find them the one truly distracting feature of this volume.

If a small part of *Helliconia Summer* seems dissonant, the whole is nonetheless remarkable; the book belongs in any serious library of science fiction. I await the third volume with confidence that it will complete and fulfill the great pattern and promise of this tapestry of the Helliconian seasons.

*Philip E. Smith II, "Swash, Buckle and Hints of
Greatness," in* Fantasy Review, *Vol. 7, No. 2, March,
1984, p. 24.*

TOM EASTON

For a change of pace, how about Brian Aldiss's *Helliconia Summer*? Aldiss's world is a magnificent creation, broad and intricate, with echoes of relevance and influence, a gold-mine for future literary scholars. Even present-day critics are raving, and the series is selling well.

But it's dreadful. Aldiss tries for Morgenstern's elegance but achieves only pretentiousness. *Helliconia Spring* had verve and originality, and I called it stodgy. *Helliconia Summer* has only the stodginess. It's slow-moving, long, windy, and occasionally ludicrous, as when Aldiss has a king assemble "his wife behind him to make an attractive composition." . . .

The story is fairly simple: Helliconia's complex orbit gives it a 2600-year "year," with an excessively frigid winter and a thoroughly hellish summer. In this book, the planet is approaching the peak of summer, when its forests will burst into flames. The people are aware of this, and they are maneuvering to maximize their chances of survival till fall. King JandolAnganol of Borlien is divorcing his Queen of queens, MyrdemInggala, to marry a wanton nymphet and cement a queasy alliance. There are plots and counterplots, strange names and personalities galore, treason and friendship, and revelations of evolution.... And the reader never gives a damn.

Aldiss here reminds me of Jack Vance at his worst and least empathic. For all the richness of imagination that shows in names, scenes, incidents, and history, there is no involvement for the reader. There is too much of manner and preciosity, and not enough of humanity. Perhaps there is simply too much authorial cleverness. (pp. 166-67)

> *Tom Easton, in a review of "Helliconia Summer,"*
> *in* Analog Science Fiction/Science Fact, *Vol. CIV,*
> *No. 7, July, 1984, pp. 166-67.*

CAROLE MANSUR

[Aldiss's] latest collection [of short stories, *Seasons in Flight*,] should be circulated to schools or, better still, read aloud over a camp fire, where it would mesmerise any huddle of listeners into forgetting the draught at their backs. Not that Aldiss draws attention to himself; on the contrary, he wastes no words in getting straight down to business, with an opening sentence that both introduces his subject and by its rhythm precipitates the reader into the next.... The language is simple, as are the several communities where the tales unfold, as is the narrative development, which often follows a symmetrical or repetitive pattern typical of fables....

Strangely, the absence of complexity enhances the narrator's tone of authority so that he almost resembles a sage or sooth-sayer, whose conclusions leave a question mark in the air. Even when the final act is annihilation, as in **"The Plain, the Endless Plain"**, there remains the feeling that everything sits in a cosmic perspective: what is the "dazzling brilliance such as they had never known"? Similarly, at the end of the **"The Blue Background"**, the snapshot of the Crucifix fails to capture the "delicate sky tint" behind—"the glimpses of infinity, that Lajah had once loved, before life closed in."

> *Carole Mansur, in a review of "Seasons in Flight,"*
> *in* Punch, *Vol. 287, No. 7512, November 21, 1984,*
> *p. 74.*

PAUL KINCAID

This slim collection of ten stories [*Seasons in Flight*] reveals Aldiss at his most spare and, apparently, most simple. Yet they are mostly fables and allegories charged with carrying a great weight upon their slim shoulders. In the main they manage to do just this, often surprisingly well. The theme is generally one of tolerance for human differences and the virtues of communication, a message sometimes handicapped by the strangely distancing technique Aldiss has chosen, describing the geography then the society and only then, like a camera slowly zooming in on its subject, depicting his characters. The result is that the message tends to come across on an intellectual rather than on an emotional level. The best stories are the ones that avoid this pitfall, such as **"The Gods in Flight"** in which

an island just off Sumatra, vaguely aware that the rest of the world has destroyed itself in a nuclear holocaust, uneasily awaits the arrival of a planeload of high-ranking American refugees, or **"The Girl Who Sang"**, set in the world of his Helliconia trilogy, though it could as easily and perhaps more effectively belong in the vaguely Balkan realm inhabited by most of the other stories. In this story a young man finds himself sacrificing the girl he loves, but doesn't understand, in vague hope of gain. Nevertheless, the other stories, particularly **"The Other Side of the Lake"**—[and **"Consolations of Age"**] ... reveal the author's familiar dark humour and real compassion. Only one tale, **"The O in Jose"**, doesn't quite fit in with the rest; it was first published in 1966 and mostly serves to demonstrate how Aldiss has refined his talent over the intervening years.

> *Paul Kincaid, in a review of "Seasons in Flight,"*
> *in* British Book News, *February, 1985, p. 108.*

MICHAEL R. COLLINGS

Rarely have I waited for a book with as much anticipation as for the third and final volume of Aldiss's Helliconia series; and even more rarely has the wait been rewarded so fully. *Helliconia Winter* is a fitting culmination, not only for the trilogy which began with *Helliconia Spring* (1982) and *Helliconia Summer* (1983) but for Aldiss's career to date. Implicit within *Winter* are concerns that reach back as far as his first novel, *Starship* (1958) [published in Great Britain as *Non-Stop*] and recur throughout intervening novels and short stories, here clearly focused upon and in many instances finally resolved. In addition, the magnitude of his attempt, the sheer sweep of the novel is ambitious enough to merit particular attention; only an author such as Aldiss, who has immersed himself in questions of stasis and change, entropy, ecological balance, and definitions of what it is to be human—and has explored their possibilities for almost three decades—could have completed such a vision.

As one expects in an Aldiss novel, he does so without resorting to easy, dramatic, space-opera endings. Building on *Spring* and *Summer*, the overwhelming imagery of *Winter*—encroaching ice and cold and darkness—creates a sense that to have survived change is itself heroic. Aldiss simultaneously makes even closer connections between Earth and Helliconia in this final volume, shifting his vision from one to another as he suggests a balance between the two, an empathic tie that reveals how deeply his Helliconians reflect ourselves and our social and cultural preoccupations. *Winter* combines the best of the Helliconia volumes—the breadth, scope, and historical sweep of *Spring* with the finely crafted details and narrow focus of *Summer*, as it translates what Aldiss attempted in his main-stream *Life in the West* into science fictional form and carries the reader stages beyond the change-in-stasis of *The Malacia Tapestry*.

Aldiss wisely concludes the series without trying to tie up all of the details; he occasionally leaves me wanting more. I would like to see more closely how the human/phagor conduct is resolved, for instance, but such a resolution lies outside the purposes of the novel—change is what is essential, and adaptation to that change....

Helliconia Winter successfully completes the series; it simultaneously stands on its own as a coherent novel. I highly recommend it to all readers interested in that kind of science fiction that requires thought and care, repaying the reader with a broader and deeper understanding of human potential. It is not an easy novel, but it is certainly an important statement by a master in the genre.

Michael R. Collings, "A Fitting Culmination by a Master," in Fantasy Review, *Vol. 8, No. 4, April, 1985, p. 14.*

GERALD JONAS

[*Helliconia Winter*] is the concluding volume in Brian W. Aldiss's masterful trilogy whose theme is nothing less than the interrelationship of all living (and nonliving) things. This time Mr. Aldiss has narrowed his focus a bit. Unlike *Helliconia Spring* and *Helliconia Summer,* which told of the rise and fall of entire cultures, the new novel has a single protagonist, Luterin Shokerandit, a princeling on Helliconia's northernmost continent, where efforts are being made to preserve law and order during the long freeze.

As in the previous books, the impact of climate on behavior is dramatized in a way that does full justice to the maddening unpredictability of individuals who remain free to resist the environmental imperatives they cannot escape. In a novel filled with memorable scenes, two marvelous set pieces stand out: a dog sled ride through a frozen land that loses nothing in comparison with the classic snow-and-ice-scapes in Ursula K. Le Guin's *Left Hand of Darkness;* and Shokerandit's incarceration in the Great Wheel of Kharnabhar—prison, religious shrine and bitter symbol of hope for the Helliconians. . . .

The links between Helliconia and Earth form a subplot that Mr. Aldiss was careful to leave somewhat vague in the trilogy's first two books. In this novel, we learn more about events on Earth, where the human species nearly destroys itself before the survivors learn to appreciate their role in the superorganism that constitutes all life on the planet. Here, I think, Mr. Aldiss has made a mistake. His insights into evolution and ecology come across far more powerfully in the Helliconian setting than in the breathless summaries of terrestrial "future history" that read like synopses of *another* trilogy. But this is a forgivable flaw in a splendid work of imagination that weds grandeur of concept to a mastery of detail and a sense of style unmatched in modern science fiction.

Gerald Jonas, in a review of "Helliconia Winter," in The New York Times Book Review, *April 28, 1985, p. 20.*

PATRICK PARRINDER

Helliconia is a remarkable instance of what is nowadays called world-building, a specialist activity. . . . Nowadays a team of expert consultants is recommended, including a biologist, a geologist, an anthropologist, an astronomer, and preferably Professor Tom Shippey of Leeds University to advise on the philology. A novel written under such conditions needs as much planning as a mountaineering expedition; and Brian Aldiss has performed the Science Fictional equivalent of scaling the Matterhorn.

The production of new matter demands neologisms. To signify an alien planet we require unfamiliar names. Philological expertise or sensitivity to language are crucial adjuncts to space travel, at least of the fictional sort (the lesson we all learned from C. S. Lewis's *Out of the Silent Planet*). Aldiss's habits of word coinage perhaps owe something to Lewis's. *Helliconia*

Spring, the first volume in the trilogy, began with a barrage of outlandish names, the purpose of the naming being to emphasise those parts of the alien world which in our case we had not got. The new names have become steadily naturalised as the trilogy progressed. . . . With *Helliconia Winter* the strange world has become a relatively familiar world whose deeps have been plumbed and charted. The map of the planet which Aldiss's new novel (unlike its predecessors) carries on its endpapers thus conveys the same pleasures as a map of Houyhnhnmland or of Treasure Island. In *Helliconia Winter* it is the developments on Earth during the next half-dozen millennia, which Aldiss reports in summary form, which strike us as truly disorienting. . . .

Helliconia is evidently a fictive metaphor for certain aspects of terrestrial life, and this metaphorical dimension is reinforced in the latest volume by explicit references to the concept of the nuclear winter. In addition, events on Helliconia are watched, down to their smallest detail, by scientists on an observation satellite beaming television pictures back to Earth. The Helliconia transmissions—Earth's last art- or 'Eductainment'-form—are screened to crowds of people in huge communal auditoria. The transmissions run parallel to Aldiss's narrative.

Seen as 'Eductainment', the *Helliconia Trilogy* is an embodiment of Science Fiction's claim to be the Bible of the future, an estranged and parabolical structure conveying knowledge of man's place on Earth and in the universe. Human life on Helliconia survives within a delicate ecosystem, which its more ruthless and rational members are unwittingly trying to destroy. The individual episodes of Aldiss's planetary history are chosen to illustrate the dilemmas of knowledge and power, and the prickly and acrimonious [relationships between fathers and sons]. . . .

Naming is crucial here at several levels: naming as metaphor, naming as melodramatic revelation, naming as the key to human survival. Aldiss's dense specification of Helliconia as metaphor produces a species-rich world of kaidaws, arang, hoxneys, nondads, brassimips and many others, not to mention the phagors with their cowbirds. . . . As the year draws on, the hoxneys lose their stripes, the phagors begin to roll back the frontiers of human civilisation, and other species prepare for hibernation. Luterin, the hero of *Helliconia Winter,* spends ten years' imprisonment in the caves of the Great Wheel to escape the consequences of exposing his father as the Oligarch. His eventual re-emergence seems to symbolise the possibility of human beings surviving the forthcoming Ice Age. On the fateful day of Myrkwyr, the autumn solstice, the ruling classes carouse away their fears while the common people cry out to Freyr 'as if by naming the star they could have power over it'. It is a fittingly epic moment, a moving conclusion to Aldiss's boldly-conceived and sturdily-executed history. Where *Helliconia* differs from the admonitory visions of earlier Science Fiction writers such as Wells, Orwell and Stapledon is in its refusal to pretend that it is anything other than a fantasy-construct devised for metaphorical ends. Aldiss's warning of the perils facing mankind is reared on purely nominalist foundations. To this extent *Helliconia* belongs to the category of the self-conscious novel, not to the fiction of attempted prophecy. (p. 22)

Patrick Parrinder, "Naming of Parts," in London Review of Books, *Vol. 7, No. 10, June 6, 1985, pp. 22-3.**

Jorge Amado

1912-

Brazilian novelist, short story writer, and nonfiction writer.

Amado is a major figure in Brazilian literature and an internationally acclaimed author whose novels have been translated into over forty languages. The majority of his works are set in the Bahia region of northeastern Brazil, where Amado has lived most of his life, and draw upon the physical, social, and cultural milieu of the region. Amado's works reveal his fascination with the rich mixture of heritages among Bahia's inhabitants, who are of European, African, and native Indian ancestry. While describing the local color of Bahia, Amado centers on political and social themes. In his early works, written in the mode of social realism, Amado focused on the settling of the region for the cultivation of cacao and on characters involved in class conflicts. These works depict a violent, squalid society which the protagonists strive to improve through actions based on communist ideals. Amado's later works, which have made him an international best-selling author, are more expansive and less politically didactic, as he tempers his social criticism with satire, ironic humor, and raucous comedy.

Amado's first three novels, *O pais do carnaval* (1931), *Cacáu* (1933), and *Suór* (1934), are generally faulted for being excessively pedantic in expressing communist solutions to social problems. While the artistic merits of these works were debated, they drew significant attention in Brazil and in the Soviet Union for their political implications. A member of the Brazilian Communist Party during this period, Amado was briefly imprisoned for his political beliefs in 1935—the first of a succession of controversial events that resulted in the banning of his books by the Brazilian government in 1937 and in his exile on two occasions. *Jubiabá* (1935) is generally considered his first success at blending political themes and art. In this work, Amado details a young black man's struggles against social injustice while infusing into the story elements of Brazilian and African folk traditions. *Terras do sem fim* (1942; *The Violent Land*), Amado's most significant early work, focuses on the cultivation of cacao and its potential for bringing economic prosperity to the Bahia region. In this novel, rival planters become involved in a violent struggle to gain control of a tract of forest land that will be cleared to produce huge cacao groves. Critics praised Amado's development of a large cast of characters and his deft use of irony; the economic prosperity of the region comes at the expense of moral values and human blood. Carlos Fuentes viewed *The Violent Land* as "the novel of a master craftsman, richly endowed with the narrative art and the humor, distance, beauty and perceptiveness that distinguishes a classic work."

Following *The Violent Land*, Amado wrote several more novels of social realism, as well as a number of nonfiction works and political treatises. His literary career took a major shift with the publication of *Gabriela, cravo e canela* (1958; *Gabriela, Clove and Cinnamon*), a best-selling novel in several countries, including the United States. This work initiates a significant change in Amado's style, as he began to create comic situations while continuing to examine social, cultural, and political themes. *Gabriela, Clove and Cinnamon* is set in the town of Ilheus, in Bahia, after the region has prospered from the cultivation

of cacao. Gabriela, a lovely migrant worker, and Mundinho Falçao, a wealthy young man, arrive in Ilheus and play major roles in overturning restrictive social values and in freeing the town from domination by wealthy landowners. This novel also exemplifies Amado's increasing interest in the themes of love, sexuality, and friendship. *A morte e a morte de Quincas Berra Dágua* (1961; *The Two Deaths of Quincas Wateryell*) is a tall tale concerning a man who rejects the stability of his family life and becomes a vagabond; he finds love, truth, and happiness as a tramp as opposed to the materialistic values and shallowness he experienced as a respectable citizen. Gregory Rabassa called this work "Amado's masterpiece." *Os velhos marinheros* (1961; *Home Is the Sailor*) is written in the form of a biography of an old man who came to a small town and charmed the local residents by relating his adventures as a sea captain. Amado purposefully obscures this work, leaving the reader to ponder whether the man was actually a heroic sailor or simply a great storyteller. *Dona Flor e seus dois maridos: Historia moral e de amor* (1966; *Dona Flor and Her Two Husbands: A Moral and Amorous Tale*), another of Amado's novels that became a best-seller in several countries, centers on a vivacious and virtuous woman whose roguish husband died in drunken revelry. Soon after Dona Flor marries a proper and meticulous pharmacist, her first husband returns as a ghost capable of enjoying physical pleasures. Amado examines character in this work, focusing on the dilemma of Dona Flor; she is still deeply in love with her passionate first husband, of whom society disapproved, yet she respects the well-ordered life of her socially reputable second husband. The novel is rich in sensual descriptions of fragrances, gourmet dining, and sexual activity. This work and Amado's preceding comic novels helped secure his reputation and led to the republication in many languages of such earlier works as *The Violent Land* and *Jubiabá. Dona Flor and Her Two Husbands* and *Gabriela, Clove and Cinnamon* have been adapted for film.

During the 1970s, Amado continued to examine social themes within the context of comedy. *Tereza Batista, consada de guerra* (1975; *Tereza Batista, Home from the Wars*) and *Tieta do agreste* (1979; *Tieta*) center on strong female protagonists who overcome degrading circumstances to affect profound changes in their societies. *Tenda dos milagres* (1971; *Tent of Miracles*) evidences Amado's interest in African influences on Brazilian culture. This work centers on a town's anniversary celebration for a black man who was persecuted for promoting interracial harmony during his lifetime. *Farda fardao, camisola de dormir* (1979; *Pen, Sword, Camisole: A Fable to Kindle a Hope*) centers on the struggle between two military men who attempt to gain a seat in the Brazilian Academy of Letters despite objections by other writers. These later works have helped affirm Amado's importance in Brazilian and Portugese-language literature.

(See also *CLC*, Vol. 13 and *Contemporary Authors*, Vols. 77-80.)

BERTRAM D. WOLFE

The Violent Land is a novel of the Brazilian frontier. It tells the story of the opening up of the forest region of southern Bahia to the planting of cacao, earlier in the century when cacao was king, and of a war to the death between two powerful, upstart planter families for the possession of the last unclaimed virgin forest lying between their rival estates. The stakes are high, for whoever wins the forest will be lord of the region. The means employed are chicanery, subornation and intimidation, arson, murder from ambush, pitched battle between rival armies of gunmen. Literally all the inhabitants of the region are drawn into the struggle to one degree or another. . . .

The leading contestants send out men to kill as they would to prune a grove, to kill in ambush and in open battle, to kill each other's laborers and armed retainers, the owners of the lesser groves that stand in their way, and finally each other. . . . Besides being destroyers and coveters, the lords of this land are clearers and builders; the cacao tree is the incarnation of wealth and power, the true object of worship, the fetish which, once it has been created by the labor of men, assumes a mysterious mastery over their actions, their fates, their very souls.

This is the second novel by Jorge Amado on the theme of cacao. The first, a "short and violent tale," [*Cacao*, was] written when he was only nineteen. . . . The present one, written ten years later, after his talents have ripened through the writing of seven other novels, two biographies and many poems, and after his experience has been enriched by political struggle, imprisonment and exile, shows how the theme obsesses him,

with a hatred (relieved by involuntary admiration and lyrical pity) that is almost akin to love—and almost as effective. He was a boy in this very land when the last great struggle was being fought to a conclusion, the forest was turning into groves and the squalid huts and mud tracks into towns and cities. His childish imagination was nourished on tales of violent deeds. His social sensibilities were nourished by his own experiences as a worker on a cacao plantation, where he learned to know the humble and pitiful lot of those sacrificed to the god of greed, materialized in the cacao tree. . . .

[In *The Violent Land* Amado] has achieved mastery of the theme that obsessed him. Despite the vast panorama comprehended, the plot is more tightly constructed than is usual in Latin-American novels. The whole region has been caught in its pages with all its social types, yet not a personage great or small is introduced carelessly or left at loose ends, not an act or gesture is wasted.

To the raw violence and action of one of our gold-rush, claim-jumping, frontier tales, this novel adds an exuberant, tropical lyricism. Only study of one or more characters in depth is lacking to complete the full humanity of the work—largely because its true concern is not the individual human being but a society, a region and an industry. It is one of the most important novels to have come North in some time, and, because of its frontier character and crowded action, one of the most accessible to the American reader.

> *Bertram D. Wolfe, "Panorama of a Tropic Frontier," in* New York Herald Tribune Weekly Book Review, *June 17, 1945, p. 4.*

FRED P. ELLISON

The European as well as the Brazilian vogue of Amado has often been the result of political rather than literary qualities. He reacted violently to his times, and some of his books have been marred by extreme partisanship to the left. Nevertheless, he is a novelist, and an important one. Brazilian literature would be deprived of several impressive works should critics decide to rule out his writings as political. (p. 83)

Amado was sent by his father to Rio de Janeiro to study law. There, at the age of eighteen, he began his first novel, *Carnival Land (O País do Carnaval),* which was published in 1932. Although devoid of literary merit, the book is worth noticing, first, for its reflection of the confusion and excitement before and after the revolution of 1930, with its boiling ideological currents, and second, for the evidence it bears of Jorge's own search as a young Brazilian for something in which to believe.

Amado's subsequent evolution in political thinking seems to have paralleled that of José Lopes, the Communist figure of *Carnival Land.* Although he did not identify himself with the Communist party until many years later, his entire career as a man of letters was intimately connected with radical political movements in Brazil during the 'thirties and thereafter. (pp. 84-5)

With the exception of *Carnival Land,* the least typical of his works, everything that Jorge Amado has written has a sociological foundation. Brazilians themselves do not deny the fundamental truth of the situations and institutions studied by Amado. They do not tax him with misrepresentation. He is merely one of many Brazilian novelists of the 'thirties who had cause to interpret the terrible social drama of his times. Amado draws critical fire only when, unlike Lins do Rego, Graciliano Ramos, or Rachel de Queiroz, he combines the objectivity of the *document* with the impassioned subjectivity of the *protest*. Sociologists may confirm the factual portions of his writing, but must make reservations in regard to the novelist's analysis of the facts.

The question of the rightness or wrongness of Amado's sociopolitical views, or of his humanitarian philosophy, is not at issue here. From the strictly literary standpoint, however, it must be observed that such a philosophy, when projected in the novels, has grave consequences for art. Their frankly political aim requires some justification in literary works. (p. 85)

Carnival Land is the story of Paulo Rigger, the European-educated son of a Brazilian cacao grower, and of his search for a philosophy of life. Morally adrift, Rigger seeks happiness first in the cultivation of his instincts, particularly the sexual. Later he has a love affair with a girl of the lower classes, abandoning her when his social prejudices assert themselves. He becomes a journalist and a follower of an old intellectual of Bahia, Pedro Ticiano, who gathers about him a small band of younger men dissatisfied with their generation and anxious for new solutions to their problems. Religion, politics, love, marriage, and philosophy are discussed, usually in a bar, with the noisy vehemence of youth turning over new ideas. (pp. 86-7)

The rather primitive work is full of the impulsiveness and impatience to be expected of a youth of eighteen. (p. 88)

Amado has written three novels about cacao. Their scene is southern Bahia, which since the middle of the nineteenth century has been the center of Brazil's richest area of production of the so-called "chocolate bean." *Cacao (Cacáu)*, his first attempt at portraying the region, was a rather crude sketch of life on a plantation near Ilhéus. From all parts of the Northeast, migrant workers come each year to harvest the multicolored pods, which, hanging from trunks and branches, have been compared to Chinese lanterns casting a beautiful but unreal glow on the jungle. Amado describes the culture of a modern "forbidden fruit"—because of its economic value, denied to the undernourished workers by the growers—and he details the appallingly low standard of living among the *alugados,* mostly Negroes, mulattoes, and poor whites, who "rent themselves" to the contractors for the harvest and are often slaves to their unpaid bills at the planter's commissary.

The prostitutes in the cacao region, old at twenty, are victims of the harsh Brazilian sexual code about which the novel's slender plot revolves. When the planter's son seduces the sweetheart of a workman, Colodino, the latter stabs him, and is aided in his escape by the Negro jagunço hired to kill him—an example of "class consciousness"—and becomes a leftist organizer. One of the motives for social protest is the fact that the seducer is not even censured, while his victim is forced into prostitution. Sociologists acknowledge the existence of this Brazilian practice. As literature, however, this immature novel founders because of its ideological bias.

The *Sergipano* (man from Sergipe) is the real hero of *Cacao*. Though a worker, he has the opportunity to marry the planter's daughter, but chooses instead to better his class. (pp. 88-9)

In strong contrast is the next novel of the cacao cycle, which appeared ten years later. Of all his works, *The Violent Land (Terras do Sem Fim)* remains Amado's masterpiece, a story of almost epic grandeur. This description of the struggle between

rival planters for possession of the cacao groves is the only novel by Amado that contains no propaganda. (p. 89)

Fighting for the golden fruit were the Badarós—Juca, his brother Sinhô, and the latter's daughter Don'Ana—and Colonel Horácio Silveira. Although the Badarós are aristocratic and Colonel Horácio is plebeian, they are alike in their passion for the land, their veneration of brute force, and their quest for power. Cacao has leveled them. Individual differences, however, sharpen the characterizations. Sinhô Badaró hates killing but kills nonetheless, especially when he can find a passage from the family Bible to justify him. Horació's great weaknesses are cacao and his young wife Ester. . . . Ester, however, repays his crude veneration by an affair with the Colonel's lawyer Virgílio. After Ester's death and Horació's discovery of her letters to Virgílio, his decision to put the lawyer "out of the way" comes as naturally as his next breath. (p. 90)

Artistically the best of his novels, *The Violent Land* shows what Amado can achieve when art is not encumbered with the millstone of political argument. The hostility and proletarian purpose which in *Cacao* made of the fazendeiro a fat, mean-eyed ogre exploiting his workers are absent from the characterizations of Juca and Sinhô Badaró and Colonel Horácio Silveira, who are among the novelist's most acute psychological studies.

Both the Colonel and Don'Ana, as well as the latter's husband, João Magalhães, reappear in *St. George of Ilhéus (São Jorge dos Ilhéus)*, which describes the cacao economy in terms of the present day. The central action is the seizure of the land from the fazendeiros by a group of exporters who employ a different means of conquest. (p. 91)

Fortunately for the novel as literature, [Amado] has infused life and movement into his study of Ilhéus, "Queen of the Southland," in successive periods of "boom and bust." The complicated plot, involving exporters, planters, workers, labor agitators, Communists, Integralistas, and, for added spice, assorted cabaret entertainers, is skillfully handled. Amado repeats from the preceding work a number of effective scenes dealing with cacao cultivation, political intrigue, and the technique of the notorious *caxixe,* or "ouster," by means of which owners are dispossessed of their property, as through the recording of forged documents in the legal registers. (pp. 91-2)

In his novels dealing with the historic city of São Salvador da Bahia de Todos os Santos, or Bahia, Amado exhibits many of the qualities found in the cacao cycle. There are moments of supreme artistry but, probably more often, moments when art is absent. The early work *Sweat* is on a par with the proletarian *Cacao;* likewise a bit sketchy and vindictive, it is also crudely realistic. *Jubiabá* reveals the hand of one who could create *The Violent Land;* sometimes argued to be Amado's best, *Jubiabá* at least deserves to rank alongside that book. Two other novels of the cycle display the good and bad characteristics of Amado, the excessive attachment to the proletarian theme set over against a first-rate storytelling talent that makes his work readable.

In almost all these novels Amado has been able to capture the mystery that he says flows like oil upon the city. He has caught the spirit of "the mother of all Brazilian cities." Historically the first Brazilian metropolis, Bahia is also called "black Rome," because, even though it is a place of imposing Catholic churches and basilicas, one may also hear African drums booming from the Negro districts, where the fetish cults, or *candomblés,* are still very much in existence. In no Brazilian city is the influence of Africa more evident. It is truly "a medieval city surrounded by African villages."

Bahia may also be viewed in terms of the rich and the poor rather than in terms of black and white. Indeed, although the juxtaposition of Negro and European is a valid one, there are to be found in Bahia, as in all Brazil, whites, blacks, mulattoes, and other mix bloods in all the economic categories. Social distances are measured in degrees of economic class rather than in terms of race or caste, as, for example, in the United States. (pp. 92-3)

Amado is the novelist of this class struggle in the lowest social echelon. *Sweat (Suor)* describes one of the proletarian quarters of Bahia. Like Michael Gold's *Jews without Money,* which is widely known in Latin America and has influenced Amado, *Sweat* is rather a propagandist's notebook than a novel in the usual sense. It is a sheaf of sketches of types observed at 68 Whipping Post Hill, a vast tenement where Amado lived in 1928.... (p. 93)

Since there are no central characters, unity is supplied by the tenement itself; the account is given a political orientation when its inhabitants join in a mass protest against the arrest of strikers and are fired upon by police. Bitter in tone, the novel's depressing view of life is almost unrelieved. Despite the author's ability to record incident vividly and to capture the essence of lower-class speech, *Sweat,* more than any of the novelist's other books, deserves to be called reporting. No one, however, could deny the truthfulness and power of the book as a record of man's brutality to man.

Jubiabá, Amado's fourth book, and second in the series on Bahia, marks an important advance in his conception of the novel. Hitherto he had been feeling his way, first with *Carnival Land,* then with the two short novels *Cacao* and *Sweat,* both strongly in the proletarian vein and purposely (it would seem) without literary adornment. Originally Amado may have felt it a political obligation to keep his novels as lean and unprepossessing as the people he described.... He then wrote *Jubiabá,* which is surely a minor masterpiece of the literature of the 'thirties. The proletarian theme remains, but thereafter he stated it more artistically, often symbolically. (p. 94)

It should be considered a product of the campaign during the 'thirties in Brazil to vindicate the Negro, who, always wearing the badge of slavery, ascends more slowly in the social scale than any other part of the population. Everywhere Amado champions the black man, and nowhere more effectively than in his Negro hero António Balduíno.

Born in a quarter of Bahia in which the African footprint is still visible, Balduíno is a moleque of the streets who "was pure as an animal and knew only the law of the instincts." The lad is consumed with hatred for his oppressors. After a boyhood spent between the Negro district and the fine home of a Portuguese who momentarily befriends him, the lad becomes the leader of a band of homeless waifs, and, eventually, a *malandro,* or good-for-nothing, who strums his guitar, composes sambas, drinks rum, learns the art of *capoeira* fighting, and pays passionate court to the *mulatas* of the city.

Balduíno's unrequited love for Lindinalva, the white daughter of his benefactor, may be regarded as a symbol of the Negro's unconscious quest for purity. Lindinalva did not even know of Balduíno's lifelong devotion. When she dies a prostitute, he maintains that she was chaste and that only he had been her husband. (pp. 94-5)

After successes and one great failure as a boxing champion, and various adventures while wandering through the outlying agricultural districts, Balduíno, still the malandro, returns to Bahia. There, for the first time in his life, he becomes a working man, then a labor agitator, and in this pursuit finds a new purpose and usefulness in life. His sudden conversion from aimless malandro to a man of social awareness belongs in the realm of the miraculous, but because he is a myth it is easier to accept this social miracle. (p. 95)

As a Negro of the present, Balduíno stands in striking contrast to the Negro Jubiabá, from whom the novel takes its name and around whom the African cultural survivals in Bahia are studied.... The hundred-year-old man is a *pai de santo,* or leader of a fetish cult, at whose *terreiro,* or temple, the religious ceremonies called candomblé, or *macumba,* are observed. Amado was himself an *ogan,* or male initiate, of a Bahian fetish cult, and his undisputed knowledge of Negro life is based on personal experience.

A high point of the novel is the author's description of a candomblé, in which the female ceremonial dancers (*filhas de santo*) whirl about Jubiabá and his retinue of ogans until "made" (*feitas*), or possessed, by the spirit of one of the African deities (*orixás*). (p. 96)

Jubiabá symbolizes the African past, which, as assimilation progresses, is fast disappearing. In a final scene, illustrating the new symbolism in Amado's novels of political outcry, Jubiabá bows to the Negro Balduíno after the latter has participated in a successful general strike against the city....

The novelist of the Negro, Amado may also be called the Brazilian novelist of the sea, which is an indispensable part of the Brazilian scene. With him, the sea becomes another personage of the novel. In *Sea of the Dead (Mar Morto)* Amado describes the maritime life of the city, and especially of the men who sail the small, sturdy sailing vessels, known as *saveiros,* that ply between Bahia and the little ports of the Recôncavo or along the Paraguassu River. One of Amado's most lyrical novels, *Sea of the Dead* is a web of adventure and of superstition. The chief characters are Guma, a mulatto sailor, and his sweetheart Lívia, who fears the sea goddess Yemanjá....

Yemanjá is another of the African deities frequently met in the Bahian novels of Amado. (p. 97)

With the folklore elements Amado has artistically integrated his message of social protest: after Guma drowns during a heroic rescue at sea, his wife, though a landlubber, goes to sea in her husband's saveiro, thus "fighting back," as Amado calls it, against her destiny, against the grinding poverty that condemns the seamen to a bare subsistence. (pp. 97-8)

Amado's sentimental conception of the primatively "pure" lower classes may be carried too far, as in his final novel of Bahia, *The Beach Waifs (Capitães da Areia).* A band of homeless urchins, "dressed in tatters, filthy, half starved, aggressive, hurling obscenities and smoking cigarette butts, were, in truth, the lords of the city: they knew it completely, they loved it completely, they were its poets." Some forty of them live in an abandoned warehouse near the beach, boys with nicknames like "Peter Bullet," "Big John," "Professor," "Limpy," "Skinny," "The Cat"—each a symbol of a racial or social type. The group has innumerable adventures, brawls, beatings, thefts, imprisonments, escapes, and sex experiences. "Lords of the city" these children may have been to Amado—

they were nonetheless a social menace, which the novelist shrugs off with sentimental pleadings. (p. 98)

When the gang breaks up, the boys drift into various pursuits, several to become criminals, one a friar, another a "bum," and one a famous painter. . . .

The novel is replete with pathetic scenes demanding an emotional response: Pirulito's theft of a statue of the Christ-child, Pedro Bala's punishments in a reformatory, Boa Vida's self-sacrifice in quarantining himself in a compound from which few return alive, and the death scene of Dora, who was "mother, sister, and sweetheart" to the gang of urchins. The critic is never sure whether Amado's sentimentality is not merely an immoderate expression of the author's compassion for the unhappy humanity he describes. One thing, however, is certain: lack of restraint is a defect in his novels. (p. 99)

The Beach Waifs was a product of its times. Some episodes are effectively described, and possess literary value. In general, however, the book's angry spirit and obvious propaganda for a political party negate most of its worth. In 1937, the year of its appearance, it was, along with the earlier and equally contentious *Cacao,* banned in Brazil. All the novelist's works have been banned in Portugal.

Jorge Amado's most recent novel, *Red Harvest (Seara Vermelha),* has as its setting the same forbidding Bahian backlands described by Euclydes da Cunha [in *Rebellion in the Backlands*]. . . . Amado concerns himself with fanaticism and banditry, but his penchant for social problems as texts for political preachment causes him to study a further problem associated with the sertão: the migration of sertanejo families, uprooted by the loss of their lands or by drought, who journey more than a thousand miles, by way of the São Francisco River, to the "promised land" of São Paulo.

Amado blames the latifundiary system of landholding for the plight of the old mulatto farmer Jerónimo, who, after being forced off the land he had worked for years as a sharecropper, sets out with a little band of children, grandchildren, and others—thirteen in number, including a goat and a cat—to seek work in the south. In a journey which would make that of the Joads of *The Grapes of Wrath* appear a pleasure outing in comparison, Jerónimo's group disintegrates, either through starvation in the *caatinga,* disease aboard an overcrowded river vessel, or other misfortunes—such as the daughter's resorting to prostitution in order to get a bill of health for her tuberculous old father, who straightway ostracizes her. (pp. 100-01)

The merits of *Red Harvest,* which are to be found in vivid scenes and action-filled episodes, are virtually nullified by a final chapter (comprising one-fifth of the novel) dealing with the Communist-abetted revolution of 1935 by the National Liberation Alliance. The link with the preceding portions of the novel is the character Juvêncio (or Nenén), another of Jerónimo's sons, who runs away from home and becomes a Communist conspirator. The final episode is jarringly inappropriate, suggesting that in this latest work, if not in the majority of the earlier novels, Amado has used his talents to disseminate a political message.

In plot construction, characterization, and other phases of novelistic technique, the author's *parti pris* leads him to commit errors. In his effort to prove the thesis that the masses are unjustly exploited and should unite against their oppressors, Amado gives to his novels a broad sameness that permits the reader to predict with accuracy the final outcome of nearly any plot situation. Aside from *Carnival Land* and *The Violent Land,* both of which are unrepresentative (one because of its weakness, the other because of its strength), the story pattern of the novels is generally that of *Cacao,* in which the workers, after long enduring their economic servitude, are driven to collective action in a strike or some act of violence.

Sweat, Jubiabá, Sea of the Dead, and *The Beach Waifs* follow the same plot formula as *Cacao,* although after *Sweat* the stories contain more complication and are more subtle. The exhortation to arise and fight against oppression may be given a more artistic and symbolic form, as in *Sea of the Dead,* in which the urge to class struggle is made part of a folklore motif. Of the later novels, written in the 'forties, both *St. George of Ilhéus* and *Red Harvest* run true to type, except that, curiously, in the former it is not so much the lower classes as the fazendeiros themselves who are exploited and dispossessed by "capitalists." One cacao planter actually joins a leftist movement; some capitulate to their new masters; others, notably the Sergipano António Víctor and his wife Raimunda, workers who had become landowners, die defending their roças. (pp. 101-02)

Amado employs the vernacular in all his writing. He goes out of his way to avoid anything that might be called "literature," in the pejorative meaning the word sometimes had among writers of his generation. His sentences have little or no stylistic grace and appear to be set down, often in haste, in a monotonous fashion. However, although he is no architect of the sentence, Amado can impart to his language "a savor as of flesh, and a rhythm almost like music," as Olívio Montenegro has observed. (p. 107)

Amado's stories have something strangely in common with the epic poems of the Middle Ages, in their disregard for proportion, their admiration for the hero, the preference for action over character, and, finally, a wonderful mingling of the fancied and the real. He has always depended on episodes, not always well integrated, to give movement to the novel. In reviewing his total work, we think not of precisely constructed plots but rather of a succession of episodes, some of which, taken individually, are nothing short of masterpieces.

In the works of this most controversial of modern Brazilian writers, unevenness is the salient characteristic. Amado seems to write solely by instinct. Of conscious art intellectually arrived at, the result of reflection and high craftsmanship, there is relatively little. Yet his novels have a mysterious power to sweep the reader along. Serious defects in artistry are overcome by the novelist's ability to weave a story, to construct vivid scenes, and to create fascinating characters. "An incomplete and mutilated novelist," as Álvaro Lins has well characterized him, he offers the "spectacle of a great talent for creating fiction in contrast with enormous deficiencies as a writer and as an intellectual." Though his literary career now covers more than twenty years, Jorge Amado is barely forty years old. No writer holds out a greater promise, and his future works will be eagerly read by those who expect the promise, made manifest in *The Violent Land,* some day to be fulfilled. (pp. 107-08)

Fred P. Ellison, "Jorge Amado," in his Brazil's New Novel, Four Northeastern Masters: José Lins do Rego, Jorge Amado, Graciliano Ramos, Rachel de Queiroz, *University of California Press, 1954, pp. 83-108.*

HARRIET DE ONIS

In his first novel—published in 1931, when he was twenty-one years old—Jorge Amado gave clear evidence of the gifts that make him one of today's major novelists. He has the narrative art to a superlative degree, the ability to create three-dimensional characters, a deep awareness of the problems of his country and his epoch, a style as flexible and colorful as it is lyrical. Much of his early work belongs to the literature of protest, for the major problem of Brazil, a land so prodigiously endowed, is the inequity and the iniquity in the distribution of its wealth, the exploitation of the many by the few. *Seára Vermelha,* one of Amado's best novels, is a Brazilian counterpart of *The Grapes of Wrath.*

But it is in *Gabriela, Clove and Cinnamon* that he really finds himself. One hardly knows what to admire most: the dexterity with which Amado can keep half a dozen plots spinning; the gossamer texture of the writing; or his humor, tenderness, and humanity. . . .

The novel gets off to a fast start, and its pace never slackens. (p. 36)

The time is 1925, the setting Ilhéus, a small port city in the rich cacao-growing region of Bahia. Mundino Falcão, a member of a prominent and politically powerful São Paulo family and a newcomer to Ilhéus, is largely responsible for the city's sudden rash of progress. It is his contention that if the harbor of Ilhéus were dredged, the cacao could be loaded directly, without need for transshipment to Bahia. But this is opposed by Colonel Bastos, a hidebound reactionary and the political boss of Ilhéus. How Mundino Falcão achieves his ends and brings the old colonel down with ruthlessness, deviousness, and exquisitely Brazilian politeness is a study in political shenanigans from which even Boston could take pointers.

And the inauguration of a bus line between Ilhéus and Bahia—also opposed by Colonel Bastos—changes the life of Nacib the Arab (Syrian, to be exact, but 100-percent Brazilian, as all immigrants to that fabulous land quickly become). How, without a cook, is he to handle the banquet scheduled for the next day in his Vesuvius Bar to celebrate this giant step forward? After scouring the city, he goes in desperation to the camp of migrant workers from the drought-stricken backlands of the Northeast. There in the "slave market" he finds a woman who says she can cook; and, though Nacib does not believe it, he hires her.

She is in rags, and so covered with dirt from the long trek that he can not make out her features or guess her age. The first thing he tells her to do when they get home is to take a bath and put on clean clothes. When she next appears the effect is that of Venus arising from the sea. This is Gabriela. Not only is she young, beautiful, merry, sweet, but such a cook and, very soon, such a bedfellow as Nacib has never encountered. Word of her presence quickly spreads, and business at the Vesuvius booms.

But, alas, Nacib falls head over heels in love with her, and nothing will do but he must marry her, against the advice of his friends and of Gabriela, who sees no need to change their completely satisfactory relationship. Subsequent events more than justify her misgivings. Nacib has become a man of substance, and his wife has to be a lady. No longer can she serve in the bar and revel in the compliments to her cooking and her beauty. She has to wear shoes that pinch her feet, go to lectures instead of the circus, and to the Christmas Eve dance at the Progress Club instead of joining the street revelers. Amado's solution to this and the many other problems the new order in Ilhéus gives rise to is wise, witty, and profoundly Brazilian. (pp. 36-7)

Harriet de Onis, "Nacib's Fair Lady," in Saturday Review, *Vol. XLV, No. 37, September 15, 1962, pp. 36-7.*

JUAN DE ONIS

Gabriela, Clove and Cinnamon is an exciting and enjoyable romp of a book, rich in literary delights, and was a record-smashing runaway when it first appeared in Portuguese four years ago. . . .

Gabriela, Clove and Cinnamon is a "chronicle of a city in the interior." The city is Ilhéus, in Eastern Brazil, center of the Bahia cacao boom of the nineteen-twenties. But Ilhéus is also Brazil, a microcosm of that immense and turbulent land of divers races, cultures and traditions which is still evolving from a patriarchial plantation society into a modern, integrated, urban nation. Peasant revolt, creole communism, racial fusion, political intrigue, mongrel religion, tropical sexuality, lawless violence—these are all in the immediate present of the people of Ilhéus. The tensions of Brazil's dynamism and contradictory psyche are the flesh and sinew of Amado's tale, but its theme is the ultimate triumph of accommodation, of social tolerance over violence, of life over death.

The story takes place in 1925-26 when the cacao boom is transforming Ilhéus under everyone's very eyes, including those of the old provincial city's patron, Saint George. Money flows, ships arrive, there are new streets, automobiles, mansions, clubs, even newspapers. Almost overnight, bourgeois, mercantile society has arisen and is challenging the traditional dominance of the landowners—the "colonels"—masters of peasants and trustees of political power and social customs.

Gabriela opens on an act of vengeance under the "unwritten law," the code of conduct of the cacao "colonels" which requires that the besmirched honor of a cuckolded husband can be cleansed only by the blood of his deceivers. The conflict between this antiquated code and rapidly changing social attitudes in the boom city is one of two main threads running through the chronicle. The other is the struggle for political power, the decline of the "colonels" and the rise of the forces of "progress."

Senhor Amado builds his story around two superbly alive characters, Gabriela and Mundinho Falcao, both of whom are in a sense "outsiders" in Ilhéus. Gabriela is the mulatto girl with the cinnamon thighs and a perfume of clove in her hair—innocent yet knowing, unquenchable and enticing—who arrives in Ilhéus as a refugee migrant worker from the drought-seared backlands, and becomes the mistress of the kitchen and heart of Nacib, a Syrian-born "Brazilian of the Arabies," the fat, comical proprietor of the Vesuvius bar. But before Gabriela is done, she has enchanted half the town, and forced the repeal forever of the "unwritten law."

A parallel thread is followed in the person of Mundinho Falcao, youngest son of a wealthy, politically powerful São Paulo family, who comes to Ilhéus to prove to himself and to his family that he can conquer wealth and power on his own merits. As an enterprising cacao exporter, he takes it upon himself to persuade the government in Rio to remove a sandbar holding back development of the port of Ilhéus—and thus fires the political struggle that divides Ilhéus into two warring factions.

In his earlier novels on the cacao region, on the drought-ridden backlands, on the slums of Salvador, or on the industrial center of São Paulo, Senhor Amado tended to paint caricatures rather than characters: the girl from the backlands was either a prostitute or a Communist militant: a young man of wealth was either a deflowerer of working girls or an effete representative of a decadent oligarchy. In striking contrast to these flat symbols, the characters in *Gabriela* are created in-the-round; they live, breathe and feel as genuine individuals—and none more so than Gabriela herself.

A contrast is also apparent in the tone of the earlier works as compared to that of the present book. The only Amado novel previously published in America, *The Violent Land* (1945)—also set in Ilhéus, and concerned with a blood feud between two land-owning families—is spun out with grim, humorless indignation. In *Gabriela*, however, irony, satire and plain high spirits illumine every page, and even section headings. . . .

Explanation for these contrasts in character and tone between the earlier novels and *Gabriela* can be found in the author's own political history, for Amado, who is now 50, was, for the greater part of his writing career, one of Brazil's active and influential Communists. (p. 1)

Gabriela represents undoubtedly the artistic liberation of Senhor Amado from a long period of ideological commitment to Communist orthodoxy. He has not had to make a public profession of his present views to show that his artistic integrity has prevailed over the intellectual "Party line." He was shocked by the Hungarian bloodbath and publicly criticized the Soviet handling of the Pasternak case, and in these reactions he is very close to European intellectuals, such as Jean-Paul Sartre, with whom he is personally friendly. (pp. 1, 22)

In a retrospective look at the first ten years of his career as a writer, Senhor Amado wrote in 1942: "I find with immense happiness that one line of unity, never broken, binds together not only the work I have accomplished in these ten years but also the life which I lived: a line of hope—more than hope, of certainty—that tomorrow will be better and more beautiful." *Gabriela*, in its exultation of the basic gift for tolerance in the Brazilian personality, is testimony to this belief. (p. 22)

> *Juan de Onis, "The Town's Story Is the Land's,"
> in* The New York Times Book Review, *September
> 16, 1962, pp. 1, 22.*

VIRGILIA PETERSON

[It is] hard to find a writer in English today—at least since the death of James Thurber—with as gay an imagination and as fond a sense of the absurd as the Brazilian, Jorge Amado. No one who read his recent novel, *Gabriela, Clove and Cinnamon* will have forgotten its spice and charm. His new book, *Home Is the Sailor,* is both funnier on the surface and more serious underneath, but no less spicy and charming.

Home Is the Sailor purports to be written by a young man aspiring to a prize for a work of historical research who undertakes in 1961 the biography of a certain Capt. Vasco Moscoso de Aragão, dead for some 10 years before the narrator begins his investigations. The choice of the captain for subject is fitting and logical, since the narrator himself lives in the little backwater village of Periperi—a suburb of the port of Salvador da Bahia—to which the captain had come upon retirement and where, long years later, he had died. . . .

The captain's life was the subject of two diametrically conflicting versions, his own and that of his archenemy. According to the captain himself (and who should know better?) he had

spent his life on the high seas as a Master Mariner in the merchant marine. According to Chico Pacheco, the lawyer whose pre-eminence the captain had stolen the very day he disembarked at the Periperi railroad station, he had grown up in his grandfather's warehouse amid beef and codfish, had stayed on in Bahia to squander his inheritance in gambling and whoring, and had never so much as set foot, so to speak, on the sea. Which of these stories is the truth? In *Home Is the Sailor,* the young historian tells them both and leaves the reader to decide whether dream or reality is the truer.

Like another, now legendary, character, Walter Mitty, Captain Vasco lived his life in his head. But the captain had also made his appearance fit his dream. . . .

Inside his decorated bosom, under the braid and the vainglory, the captain's heart was quick with life, and, however fierce life's challenge, he saw himself meeting them head on. When at last the challenge came in that most unforseeable way challenges always come, he was game enough, but his imagination had not sufficiently prepared him. If Providence had not intervened, the captain's legend would have died at the very moment of verifying it, and his biographer would have been left with only a burst bubble.

Thanks to Providence, however, and to the inventive powers lavishly bestowed on Jorge Amado . . . , *Home Is the Sailor* makes a wondrously amusing and thought-provoking tale.

> *Virgilia Peterson, "The Captain and the Sea," in*
> The New York Times Book Review, *March 22, 1964,
> p. 4.*

WILLIAM L. GROSSMAN

One of the happiest developments in world literature during the past few years has been the mellowing of the Brazilian novelist Jorge Amado. . . . Always a gifted storyteller, with an appeal so universal that he has been published in thirty-one languages, Amado nevertheless used to suffer under the self-imposed handicap of a preoccupation with violence and with the misery resulting from economic and social "conditions." An avowed communist, he sometimes sacrificed literary values to ideology. Then, in 1958, came *Gabriela, Clove and Cinnamon,* which achieved critical and popular success in both Brazil and the United States, followed in 1961 by *Home Is the Sailor.* These novels give us a radically new and improved Amado, humorous, gently ironic, broadly human.

Vasco, the hero of *Home Is the Sailor,* is an undistinguished, somewhat ineffectual man of inherited wealth. At the age of sixty he moves to a suburb of Salvador, the capital of Bahia, and lets it be known that he is a retired sea captain. . . . With his Mitty-like fantasies about a captain's life and his heroic but benevolent manner, he becomes the idol of the community—until a jealous skeptic discovers his landlubber past. . . .

To make matters worse, "Captain" Vasco is pressed into service to command a coastal passenger ship in the emergency caused by its master's death. . . . The story here becomes a bit contrived; but this is not a book of stark realism, and the contrivance is all part of the fun.

The narrative is related long after the event by an amateur historian, who interrupts it from time to time to philosophize on the nature of truth or to tell us about his affair with the playfully amorous mulatto mistress of a retired judge. This device contributes to the ironic detachment that seems to be

an essential element in the new Amado and which, in paradoxical combination with his affection for his characters, gives
his work a special charm—that of an indulgent, tropical, heart-
warming smile at the human comedy.

*William L. Grossman, "The Captain Was All at Sea,"
in* Saturday Review, *Vol. XLVII, No. 13, March 28,
1964, p. 43.*

THE TIMES LITERARY SUPPLEMENT

Jorge Amado's long-standing popularity in Brazil is due to his
remarkably adroit and faithful interpretation of the way of life
of the country stretching from Bahia northward to the Amazon.
In the 1930s he was the most popular, even if not the most
talented from a strictly literary point of view, of the *Nordeste*
school of authors who fought the social ills of the time. Today
he is one of the few writers in Brazil still uninfluenced by
outside literary trends. He is consequently greatly cherished
by a public swamped with translations of north American,
British and French authors. He is Brazilian through and through
and they love him for it. . . .

Amado seems most at ease when culling from his memory of
what must for him have been the most impressionable period
of his life. He does not look back in anger but there are occasional blows against social injustice and false social values.
These protests are not voiced as violently as in his earlier novels
and in fact in *Home is the Sailor* they seldom rise above the
level of sly digs. Jorge Amado sets out more to please than to
preach and so this is a humorous book. . . .

The story is excellent; Vasco Moscoso de Aragão was an orphan brought up by his thrifty grandfather who was assiduously
dedicated to grocery. On the threshold of middle age, and
financially well provided for, he becomes acutely aware of the
need to acquire a professional qualification if he is to feel at
home in Bahia's smart society. . . . It does not take him long
to divest himself of the restraints of reality, to assume the rank
of captain, and to become every inch an old sea dog. In due
course, after his friends have left Bahia to marry or to take
other appointments, and feeling his facade grow thin, he moves
to a nearby town complete with uniforms, a telescope, a sex-
tant, and a great deal of miscellaneous nautical paraphernalia.
He is soon accepted as the most entertaining and sought-after
member of the new community, anxious to please and to regale
all and sundry with spectacular accounts of shipwrecks, romances and acts of daring on voyages across the seven seas.

Attempts are made to unmask him, and the camp becomes
divided; but the "Captain's" ingenuity keeps him securely in
pleasurable prominence. The situation, however, takes a turn
for the worse when a ship calls in Bahia, with its captain in a
coffin. As he is registered as being qualified "to be in command
of any type of vessel and under any circumstances", Vasco is
put in command for the remainder of its journey north to Belem.
A very funny series of events ensues, leading to a touching
love affair, and to a climax which it would be inconsiderate
to reveal.

These are the bones of the story, but there is also flesh, much
of it of a bed and brothel kind. Some of this is in keeping with
the need to convey the atmosphere of the place and the period,
but there are a few incidents which add nothing to the twin
themes of self-fulfilment by living out dreams, and the elusive
quality of truth in human affairs. It would have been preferable,
for instance, to have omitted the private adventures of the

person telling the story, and to have trimmed the work down
to the size of a novella. . . .

All told, *Home is the Sailor* provides a humorous and original
diversion. Had it told less, it might have become a minor classic
of its kind.

"In Bahia's Bay," in The Times Literary Supplement, *No. 3274, November 26, 1964, p. 1053.*

ELIOT FREMONT-SMITH

No one could explain how Quincas [the title character of *The
Two Deaths of Quincas Wateryell*] had come into being. He
was once just Joaquin Soares da Cunha, respectable functionary
of the Bahia State Rent Board. . . .

How, the family wondered, could this model of middle-class
propriety suddenly, at 50, and without warning, "leave his
home, his family, his life-long habits, and his old acquaintances
to wander the streets, drink in cheap bars, visit whorehouses,
go around dirty and unshaved, live in a filthy hole in the worst
part of town, and sleep on an old cot that was falling to pieces?"

But that was what Joaquin had done. It was shocking. And
embarrassing. But even more shocking and embarrassing were
the newspaper stories in which he was called "Vagabond king
of Bahia," "Champion rum-drinker of Salvador," "Tattered
philosopher of the marketplace," "Senator of the honky-tonks"
and "Patriarch of the prostitutes." Well, the family couldn't
really be sorry that he was now dead and almost buried. If
only that "scruffy riff-raff" hanging around outside the funeral
parlor would go away.

Of course, the riff-raff, Quincas's waterfront pals, knew Quincas better than did his bereft family. They knew, for one thing,
that Quincas claimed to be an "old sea dog," by blood-line
at least—and like an old sea dog he had vowed that he was
"too tough and ornery for any kind of grave but one: the sea
washed in moonlight, the endless ocean."

Now, the vows of old sea dogs, not to mention champion rum-
swillers, are not to be sneered at. They should be respected,
indeed, (if possible) celebrated. Furthermore, none of his pals
could be sure that Quincas was really dead; he was a great one
for practical jokes.

And so it happened that Quincas (or Quincas's corpse) disappeared from the funeral parlor and went on a wild tour of
his old underworld haunts, guzzling rum (anyway taking it
between his lips) and making indecent proposals and filthy
observations (it was hard to tell, for all the noise), until it was
time for a second try at departure—the details of which the
reader will have to discover for himself.

The Two Deaths of Quincas Wateryell is what is known as a
tall tale, and a delight—a sort of *Old Man and the Sea* as it
might have been told by W. C. Fields. In fact, Quincas and
Fields share a good many characteristics, including a celebrated
dislike of drinking water. . . .

As usual in the tall tale false and hypocritical morality is the
target, but Amado surmounts the genre and makes an ancient
heroic type newly winning in a rollicking story that does not
seem twice-told.

*Eliot Fremont-Smith, "What a Way for a Corpse to
Act!" in* The New York Times, *November 19, 1965,
p. 37.*

DUDLEY FITTS

The Two Deaths of Quincas Wateryell is a raucous, impudent little book. Hardly more than a long short story, its dimensions, like its scope, are admirably calculated. The demonstration may be rowdy, but the form is as strict and composed as a theorem in Euclid—whence much of the ironic charm of the narrative. On the surface it would appear to be a tall tale in the familiar American manner—the outrageous exaggerations, the tough talk, monstrous felicities of booze and bumming: an urban proletarian pastoral.

Its hero, too, is familiar enough: the "successful" middleclass citizen, respectable and predictable, who reverts to nature, goes wild. Here, however, Nature is not a matter of Thoreau-like communion with chipmunks and toadstools, but the low bars and devoted-drunken stevedores and fishermen of the water-front, where our Prodigal Father lives in the odor of scandal. Lives, and dies; for the story hardly gets under way before his wake, when his methylated pals circumvent the decorous family mourners and kidnap the corpse. They have the confused impression that the dead man has revived; and such is the strength of the swaying, swaggering prose—even in translation!—that the reader half falls under the same spell. . . .

The immediate effect is that of the tall tale, the frontier tale, as I have said. On this level, the story is convincingly irresponsible, a fine specimen of its kind. Perhaps inevitably, but none the less unhappily, much of the apparatus is deployed in such a way as to enforce a recognition of symbols. The tall tale is also a social parable. What is unhappy about it is not the parable impulse itself, the diving below the surface. Rather it is the fact that the symbols themselves so often turn out to be worn counters, the clichés of thought. The drunken paterfamilias, the outraged prim wife, the scandalized relatives; the whore, a battered but loving mistress, with the heart of gold; the ragged, redolent, credulous, faithful companions of the bottle, likewise hearts of gold; the middle class shown bankrupt, the proletariat triumphant—all well and good; but how tired, how done to death, these types, these portents!

Anyone who remembers the between-the-wars proletarian novel will feel uncomfortably back home again in these pages, back home and haunted. Perhaps it was inevitable from the start; certainly the allegorical intention was central. Nevertheless, symbols conceived less crudely and handled less expectably would have allowed the tragic and hilarious male space to move in, more room for play. The Social Muse—her name is Mopsia—crashed Wateryell's wake. She should've stood in bed.

> Dudley Fitts, "The Delightful Odor of Scandal," in The New York Times Book Review, *November 28, 1965, p. 5.*

ROBERT ANTHONY PARKER

The heroes of Jorge Amado's new work [*Shepherds of the Night*] are once again the poor and raffish citizens of northeastern Brazil, people whose lives and loves match the exuberance, the grace and the earthiness of his prose. It is a world that Amado, after his early works of bitter indignation, evokes with a gay, romantic heart.

Romanticism has been the key to Amado's work since he wrote the popular *Gabriela, Clove, and Cinnamon.* . . . [In *Shepherds of the Night* he] assembles a trio of long stories with one cast of characters and tells about a marriage, a baptism and the siege of a shanty town. (pp. 470-71)

"Cat Wood" shows us the author's strengths and weaknesses. His rakes and ruffians build a shanty town on private property, then find their position turned into a cause by self-seeking "friends"—a publisher, a legislator, a governor, a reporter. A story of political finagling that Amado has also told, and better, in *Gabriela*, it features two love stories that, even at the climax, frustratingly remain separate from the main theme.

The question arises, is there a contradiction between Amado's romanticism and his political and social message? Why do the conflicts between his characters—as in the story of Corporal Martim—rarely rise to the surface? Why do his heroes on the underside of poverty lead only gay lives? Is Amado using the absurdity of his romanticism to interest us in a society whose emptiness we would prefer to ignore?

If so, the result is closer to legend than to reality. And if this is what Amado seeks—to turn these tales into folk legends—he achieves it at the expense of drama and characterization, although not at the expense of being entertaining. (p. 471)

> Robert Anthony Parker, in a review of "Shepherds of the Night," in America, *Vol. 116, No. 12, March 25, 1967, pp. 470-71.*

JOHN WAIN

[*Shepherds of the Night* can] be described tersely but not unfairly as a contribution to the debate on Brazilian self-definition, rendered ineffective by being cast in the form of pastoral. Amado's theme is the life of the Bahian poor: not the whole of their lives, for we seldom glimpse them at the back-breaking work that must occupy some of their waking hours, but their leisure life. His scene is laid in cheap brothels, alleys, shanties on the beaches, and in those hidden shrines on the mountainsides where the priests and priestesses of Ogun or Oxalá enact their rites. His characters bear colorful, Runyonesque names: Corporal Martim, Wing-Foot, Jesuino Crazy Cock, Negro Massu, Bullfinch, Carnation-in-his-Buttonhole. No one, except the personnel of the brothel, has a fixed address. Life flows in a natural tide, governed by no routine, given structure only by the religious festivals which everyone observes with uninhibited rejoicing, be they *candomblé* or Catholic.

As in all pastoral, everything that makes middle-class life irksome is screened out, and the actual sufferings of the poor, the price they pay for this immunity, are—at most—sketched in lightly. Corporal Martim, the handsome card-sharper, makes an unfortunate marriage to a selfish beauty; but there's no harm done—as soon as his eyes are opened to her faults, he takes off and goes back to his old life, which centers on Madame Tibéria's brothel. This, of course, is a happy place: the girls worship Tibéria, who treats them as daughters and the younger clients as sons, herself secure in the calm of a perfect marriage to a husband who makes clerical vestments. Begone, dull care. There may, even in Bahia, be bawds who are greedy and cruel, there may be prostitutes who chafe against the fate that has put them where they are, there may be brothels that are like disease-ridden prisons, there may be card-sharpers whose lives are anxious and miserable, but naturally we are not going to read about them in this kind of book, whose object is mainly to suggest that the poor people of Bahia are the salt of the earth and that to be one of them is, on the whole, great fun.

But there is another side to *Shepherds of the Night* as well as its pastoral side. Amado has obviously made a deep and sympathetic study of Afro-Brazilian religious cults. One of the three main episodes, which tells of the christening of Negro Massu's bastard child, concerns itself entirely with the bifurcated religious life that so easily reconciles saint with voodoo, Ogun with Christ. Not that this reconciliation goes very deep. It appears to be mainly on a social level. As a true religious belief—i.e., one that provides motives and modifies conduct—the *candomblé* has it every time over the Church. (pp. 35-6)

Still the baby must have a Church christening, with regular godparents, and finally Ogun, god of iron and of war, accepts the role of *compadre*. The whole episode is told in the manner of a lyrically extravagant folk-tale, which is exactly right, because it assimilates important anthropological and sociological questions into the pastoral mode, so that they don't have to be answered. The reader who starts out with no knowledge of Afro-Brazilian cults will find that by reading attentively and making use of the glossary, he will end up with a clear sense of these cults.

Shepherds of the Night is a strange, rich, unsatisfactory book. Naturally intended mainly for home consumption—to read a translation is always to eavesdrop a little—it must have had a curiously self-cancelling effect. On the one hand the author takes pride in his characters and carefully avoids showing them as mere victims of poverty and social inertia. Brazil, he seems to be saying, is not a transplanted European country; it is at once more colorful, more exotic, more extreme, and basically happier. On the other hand, since he implies strongly that these people are superior to their masters (when politicians, journalists, and high-ups appear in the concluding episode, they are seen as uniformly contemptible), the effect is of a vote cast in favor of non-interference, and therefore for the *status quo* which keeps the European oligarchy on top. Novels aren't, of course, any the worse for having no "social message"; but it's strange to find one which handles so much social material without taking it somewhere, only moving it from place to place. (p. 36)

> John Wain, "Versions of Pastoral," *in* The New York Review of Books, *Vol. VIII, No. 8, May 4, 1967, pp. 35-6.**

LEO L. BARROW

Jorge Amado must have enjoyed writing this novel about Dona Flor and her two husbands [*Dona Flor e seus dois maridos*], the first a lovable lover, gambler and general all around good-for-nothing, the second a strong, honest, hard working druggist who had a well ordered routine for everything including sex. The events and scenes of this long and some-what diffuse novel are centered around and are intimately linked to the poor real life in the magic city of Bahia. The frankness and candor with which he treats the problems of this poor real life are laudable. He doesn't avoid, over-romanticize or use them for their shock value. Everyday problems like sex, money, and getting along with neighbors and mothers-in-law are treated with honesty, insight, and understanding.

The novel is like *Gabriela cravo e canela, Os velhos marineros,* and *Os pastores da noite* in that each character tends to create his own personal truth which may seem absurd when tested by reality but which enables him to live in a reality which might otherwise be difficult and harsh. Jorge Amado smiles at all these little self-created truths, at the absurd prejudices and ambitions with compassionate amusement. Then he takes these same liberties, goes beyond the pale of reality, and gives the work a novel twist which enriches its humor and lends pro-

fundity to its social, moral, and philosophical implications. This bold step, at least in part, is justified by the African witchcraft and superstition, still very much a living tradition in Bahia.

Basically, the characters in this novel are revealed rather than developed. This revelation is unhurried and easy going. (pp. 371-72)

Our knowledge, understanding, and acceptance of these characters is greatly enhanced by Jorge Amado's new philosophy of live and let live which is evident throughout the work. We see human examples of almost all the social segments of Bahia, from the great and fine gentlemen and ladies who frequent the Palace Hotel to the most insignificant humans caught up in life's many vices. Jorge Amado gives them all their place in the world and a compassionate slap on the back. Even Flor's bitter, absurdly ambitious, and sharp-tongued mother is viewed with more benign amusement than with scorn.

This same philosophy becomes an integral part of most of the characters. They tend to give their fellow *baianos* their place in the world, even though their ideas, ideals, and self-created truths may seem absurd or be diametrically opposed to their own. (p. 372)

> Leo L. Barrow, in a review of "Dona Flor e seus dois maridos," in Hispania, *Vol. LI, No. 2, May, 1968, pp. 371-72.*

TIME

As proprietress of the Cooking School of Savor and Art, pretty, plump Dona Flor [in *Dona Flor and Her Two Husbands*] is a well-loved member of the community. She is also pitied because of her impulsive marriage to Vadinho, one of the great gamblers and womanizers in all Brazil. The novel begins at carnival time with Vadinho's sudden death while dancing the samba in drag, "with that exemplary enthusiasm he brought to everything he did except work." (p. 88)

Her second husband is Dr. Teodoro, a hard-working druggist and part-time bassoonist. A man moderate in everything, he makes love to his wife on Wednesdays and Saturdays—with an optional encore on Wednesday. She thinks she is content, until she enters her bedroom and finds Vadinho stretched out naked. The next morning he parades unclad about her cooking class—invisible except to Dona Flor but capable of exerting physical pressure on the breasts of an astonished student. Mostly he can be found in her bed, stating with humorous logic his legitimate posthumous rights as a husband.

Of course, Vadinho could not make his way back from the blue except in a land as saturated with voodoo and ghostly *candomblé* rituals as Bahia. "God is fat," he confides to Dona Flor. He came back, he adds, because, despite her love for Dr. Teodoro, she called him. She cannot deny it, nor can she bring herself to send him packing back to his corpulent deity.

Dona Flor is rich and leisurely, as much verbal aphrodisiac as novel. Flor is a close cousin to Amado's most celebrated heroine, Gabriela (in *Gabriela, Clove and Cinnamon*), another lady capable of cooking up a storm in the kitchen or in bed. In lavishing details of color, touch and taste, Amado so ignores the canons of construction that at times he seems embarked on little more than an engaging shaggy-dog story.

One reason for his expansive mood is that he is really writing a love letter to Bahia. . . . [Amado] romanticizes his Bahians into virile lovers, darkly sensual *morenas*, whores and neighbors, all larger than life. According to rumor, Dona Flor's friends are not the Bahian poor, but Amado's own circle of artists and intellectuals, whom he has costumed as peasants for a literary romp *à clé*. To that degree, **Dona Flor** is a long, savory inside joke. It is not, however, malicious. Amado too plainly believes that he lives in God's country. He may even be trying to provide some benevolent fat deity with a narrative blueprint for his own future return. (pp. 88-9)

> *"Sugar and Spice," in* Time, *Vol. 94, No. 10, September 5, 1969, pp. 88-9.*

JOHN WAIN

Amado's books contain a good deal of froth; at least, I understand that his early novels of social consciousness are deadly serious, but since the international success of **Gabriela, Clove and Cinnamon** in 1962 he has, justifiably, given his extravagant comic sense full play, and this alone would put out of court the claim made for him as the "Brazilian Balzac." He gives us a Balzacian torrent of detail and a colossal *dramatis personae* (the sheer number of people mentioned by name in an Amado novel does indeed take one back to the nineteenth century), but the structure itself is constantly enveloped in a spume of fanciful and slightly sentimental humor, so that one cannot take it as a serious Balzacian analysis of a society. Amado's view of the *demi-monde*, for instance, is consistently flavored with saccharine; or, at least, if Bahia really is a paradise where all the whorehouses and gambling dives are owned and operated by such wise, tolerant, and harmless people, and frequented by loveable and amusing scamps with hearts of gold, then I am ready for a one-way ticket there.

On the other hand, underneath all the fol-de-rols, Amado has a consistent view of life and makes it credible, which is perhaps the most we have a right to ask of any writer, anything else he gives us being lagniappe. He is well inside the Latin tradition of taking pleasure, and particularly sensual pleasure, with intense seriousness and building the rest of life around it; he loves rogues for the usual reason that rogues are loved, i.e., that they are honest and frank about their pleasures, and, having cast off hypocrisy, are likely to be more honest in their relationships than people who keep up appearances. The unashamed lyricism of Amado's descriptions of physical pleasure reflects his engaging inverse Puritanism, his sense that hedonism is what makes life worth living, so that it is important enough to be preached about.

Certainly **Dona Flor and Her Two Husbands** is a powerful frontal attack on the theme of human completeness. Dona Flor, a pretty young teacher of cookery from the respectable middle class, is swept into marriage by a loveable picaro of the type Amado so much admires, who causes her great suffering but also great joy (in bed); he then dies, and after an uncomfortable period of widowhood she marries a steady, reliable man who brings all the joys of regularity and security, while being if anything a little too regular (in bed). Dona Flor does not exactly solve her problem, but she manages, like most human beings, to find a way of soldiering on, and, as she sensibly observes in a note to the author which he uses as a preface, "that which is crooked cannot be made straight." Amado is a good-natured writer, and, the way things are going, that is a lot to be grateful for. (pp. 37-8)

> *John Wain, "The Very Thing," in* The New York Review of Books, *Vol. XIV, No. 4, February 26, 1970, pp. 35-8.**

L. J. DAVIS

[**Tent of Miracles**] is far too sentimental and haphazard to qualify as a good novel, but it is certainly a very rich and exotic one, and I confess that I loved every minute of it. Its plotting is fortuitous, its bad guys are straw men, its good guys are angels, its message is superficial, its victories are cheaply won, its mayhem is jolly, its irony is facile, its Africanisms are frequently unintelligible, and its sorrows verge on bathos. Yet Amado's enthusiasm for his subject, his proficiency in its lore, his humanism, and his considerable powers of description result in a warmth and richness that are impossible to resist. . . .

The novel's faults shrink to insignificance when set in the context of Amado's joyous, exuberant, almost magical descriptions of festivals, puppet shows, African rituals, local legends, fascinating customs, strange and wonderful characters—this is the heart of the book, the reason one continues to read on despite the Mickey Mouse machinations of the plot and the homiletic simplicities of Amado's theories of race.

One doesn't read a novel like this because it is good but because it is fun. A very special kind of suspension of disbelief is involved, and against Amado's rich backdrop one is soon unabashedly cheering on Archanjo and his friends, booing the villains, and misting over in the love scenes. Perhaps the reason is that we want to believe so badly in Amado's world that we are willing to believe in everything that happens in it, especially because the author is so good-hearted and sincere.

> *L. J. Davis, "Brazilian Magic," in* Book World— The Washington Post, *September 12, 1971, p. 2.*

GREGORY RABASSA

Tent of Miracles is the tale of an alert Bahian mulatto who serves as a messenger at the Medical School at the turn of the century but also dabbles in folkloric writing and is an adept of the Afro-Brazilian rites of *candomblé*. This Pedro Archanjo has also delved into the ancestry of old Bahian families and found a goodly admixture of African blood. He discovers that his archenemy, the racist Prof. Nilo Argolo, is actually his distant cousin through a common black ancestor. Yet these revelations are never published, for the police raid the Tent of Miracles, a shop run by Pedro's best friend, and destroy its printing press and haul Pedro off to jail.

This story is told in the present, 100 years after Pedro's birth, by one Fausto Pena, a caricature of the Brazilian type called a *cabide de emprêgos* (literally a "coatrack of jobs," or jack-of-all-trades). He is narrating it, we learn, at the insistence of one Prof. James D. Levenson, Columbia University anthropologist and Nobel Prize winner. . . . The central irony of the book is that Pedro has retroactively become an honored son of Bahia. Since Levenson, a foreign notable, has "discovered" him and hailed him as a great "protoanthropologist," the city is celebrating the centenary of his birth. Though he had been persecuted when alive, he is celebrated now that African ceremonies are tolerated and even extolled from lofty places that are themselves, of course, free of "contamination." There is a feeling in all this that Jorge Amado may be hinting at new persecutions of a somewhat different color.

Despite the attraction of Amado's picaresque satire and the inclusion of a most useful glossary at the end, I fear that neophytes in things Bahian (and that would include many native Brazilians) will find themselves frequently at sea and unable to follow the tale. At these points the book becomes something of a textbook and vocabulary exercise. It is too bad that Amado has let this happen, for his theme here is his strongest since his first phase of heavy-handed protest. What is missing in this book is the tightness of his masterpiece, the novella *The Two Deaths of Quincas Wateryell*.

The race question in Brazil has mostly been evaded by her writers. The dreary official line has always been geared to public relations, while Rio's famous carnival too often reminds one of those excursions in the twenties up to Harlem's Cotton Club, where blacks were not admitted except on stage. *Tent of Miracles* does give the American reader a look into Afro-Brazilian life, and Amado's forthright espousal of racial mixture is most refreshing in these Neanderthal times of ever-reductive tribalism. His book also shows that ethnic identification among African descendants in Brazil is comparable to that of European descendants in the United States. . . .

Tent of Miracles is a most enjoyable romp, puckish and bawdy a good deal of the time, but a more stringent picture of the race issue requires the anger of an Eldridge Cleaver, and the colonels in charge have artfully divided and dispersed anger to the four winds.

> *Gregory Rabassa, "In Bahia, It's Living Theater," in* The New York Times Book Review, *October 24, 1971, p. 52.*

GREGORY McNAB

For one who is acquainted with Amado's work, the reading of the first few pages of *Tereza Batista* appeared to hold nothing substantially new. He had already immortalized two heroines. First, in 1958, there was the celebrated Gabriela of *Gabriela, Clove and Cinnamon*. . . . Then in 1966, the second of Amado's charmingly amorous heroines, Dona Flor of *Dona Flor and Her Two Husbands*, appeared. She, too, was joyfully welcomed by the international reading public. This reviewer's suspicion was that Tereza Batista would be another in the same lineage with little to differentiate her from her two literary ancestors.

But first impressions are notoriously unreliable, and the initial view of *Tereza Batista, Home from the Wars* was no exception. Her adventures are different and more varied than the others'. Sold into slavery, she suffers the most humiliating degradations at the hands of the sadistic Justiniano Duarte da Rosa. Then almost single-handedly she defeats a small-pox epidemic, emerging unscathed herself. From that she goes to a gloriously satisfying affair with the older, patrician Emiliano Guedes. Next she leads a prostitutes' strike against a forced eviction. And finally, as if as a reward for her dedication to the people and her sincerity, she is reunited with her one true love, Januário Gereba, to live happily ever-after.

Amado has surpassed all his previous efforts because of the uniqueness of Tereza, but also because of the varied quality of the narrative itself. There seems to be no end to the diversity in the tone of the narrative, and the author seems to have drawn from every conceivable story-telling convention and situation to maintain his readers' interest.

To begin with, we have the distinct impression that the novel has been informed by the *ABC*, the popular rimed account of

disaster and deeds of derringdo which is sung and read in the market places of northeastern Brazil. In the case of *Tereza Batista,* we have a series of five major episodes of which the third one is divided into chapters, not by numbers, but by the letters of the alphabet.

This is not the first time Amado has used the *ABC* in his works. He did it in his 1935 novel, *Jubiabá,* and in his imaginative rendition of the life of the nineteenth century Brazilian poet Castro Alves in the *ABC de Castro Alves*. By giving literary dignity to a popular form, Amado pays homage to the people, but he also finds much in popular culture to fit his needs. Only the robust, ribald, bigger-than-life tall-tale of the Bahian people could contain his subject matter.

Indeed, the happenings of the novel's world seem beyond the reach of our conventional reality. The spirits of *candomblé* appear to watch over events and Tereza Batista as she passes through adventure after adventure.

To understand this world, we must return to the traditions from which the *ABC* derives and to the stock motifs of literature which Amado uses so freely. Tereza's story of toils and long separation from her true love, Januário Gereba, are akin to the journey and final reconciliation of Greek romance. The prostitutes' strike, one of the key episodes in the novel, is descended from the strike in Aristophanes' *Lysistra*. The cultivation of Tereza by Emiliano Guedes is the Pygmalion story retold. The whorehouse master, Vavá, is straight out of Fellini's *Satyricon*. Tereza's battle against the small-pox is a duel between St. George and the Dragon. And Januário's return to Tereza at the end, after presumed dead, recalls Ulysses' return to Penelope.

All of this is held together by a narrator who makes us only too willing to suspend our disbelief. He is a story-teller who can first present the reader with the most incredibly violent scenes and then confront him with vividly erotic ones which are sometimes narrated with the ingenuousness of Fanny Hill and other times presented with the brutal frankness of D. H. Lawrence. There is no skimping on the taboo words with him, but he is also a narrator capable of great tenderness without being maudlin. Tereza's poignant good-bye to Emiliano is a case in point. (pp. 107-08)

What remains after the novel is over is a bigger than life impression of Tereza, who combines vigor and energy with helplessness and compassion. With her unflagging stamina in the face of frequently overwhelming odds, she is the complete picture of the indestructable female, a Bahian mother-earth. (p. 108)

> *Gregory McNab, in a review of "Tereza Batista, Home from the Wars," in* Latin American Literary Review, *Vol. IV, No. 8, Spring-Summer, 1976, pp. 106-08.*

MALCOLM SILVERMAN

In *Tieta do Agreste,* as in all his post-1958 works, [Amado] continues with his brand of humorous satire, lambasting bourgeois shortcomings in an atmosphere of picaresque adventures and contagious optimism. (p. 573)

Tieta returns victorious to Agreste, the pastoral Bahian town from where, as an adolescent, she was forced to flee because of sexual indiscretions. As it turns out, during the intervening years, Tieta has led a very successful life of prostitution, allowing her to shower money and gifts on far-off family and friends. They, of course, are ignorant of any sordid details, believing instead that Tieta was married to a recently deceased São Paulo industrialist. Her arrival triggers a series of social confrontations on the personal level and also coincides with potential upheaval on the collective level: the acquisition of hydroelectric power (progress) and the threat of a chemical installation (pollution). In both cases, Tieta's clout saves the day, although the disparity between her unabashed openmindedness and Agreste's hypocritic conservatism proves too great a gap to breech—at least for one visit. In the end, she leaves a dazzled populace amid a confusing hail of praise and vituperation.

Amado presents his tragicomic story through the eyes of an obtrusive narrator whose humorous interjections serve to enhance further the light-hearted tone evident throughout the narrative.... Amid almost continuous action, tongue in cheek suspense and profuse dialogue, Tieta and Agreste's colorful personae get to know each other on several fronts. Subplots center around the usual gamut of small town sexual mores, which Amado realistically portrays with appropriate (and often comical) language. While colloquialisms abound, however, the infusion of cosmopolitan Paulista ways into Agreste's provincialism clearly makes for a story of national appeal—and universal undercurrents.

Jorge Amado has always been at his novelistic best in recreating Bahian life with its mixture of poetry, mystery and telluric regionalism. (pp. 573-74)

> *Malcolm Silverman, in a review of "Tieta do Agreste,"* in Hispania, *Vol. 61, No. 3, September, 1978, pp. 573-74.*

JOHN STURROCK

In Jorge Amado's picturesquely rundown stretch of Brazil [as depicted in *Tieta*] it is the local goats that set the tone. The ostentatious venery of these lusty ruminants is set before us as something we might all profitably learn from. The more sympathetic inhabitants of ruttish Sant'Ana do Agreste have grown up doing as the goats do and coupling to their loins' content, while the pathetic minority, whom we can but scorn, turns a blind eye to nature and stays chaste, prisoner of its absurd repressions. Mr. Amado is Brazil's most illustrious and venerable novelist, and a veteran rhapsodist of its native assets. He has also taken a radical line politically, and spoken up emotively for the poor and disfavored. In *Tieta* he has gone soft, celebrating the goodness and vitality of his home province of Bahia, more from memory than conviction, and at crushing length. This is a slow, explicit, sentimental novel with a theme that might have made a short, sharp fable.

The heroine of the piece, Tieta—"spirited, sexy, adorable," the blurb thoughtfully warns us—is encountered in a symbolical preface, spiritedly, sexily and adorably surrendering her maidenhead on the sand dunes to a randy peddler. The one-time goat-girl has begun as she means to go on, and quickly fornicates her way to the heights. She becomes the cherished mistress of a summarily rich, generally accomplished tycoon in São Paolo, and the madam of that city's ritziest bordello, where sooner or later most of the nation's truly significant political and economic decisions seem likely to be taken.

Tieta does not, however, in her innate generosity, forget the folks back home, and to her sisters in Sant'Ana, prim Perpétua and envious Elisa, she regularly mails her surplus cash and her Christian Dior castoffs. Then, in her mid-40's, with her superb lover dead and a manageress looking after the business, Tieta comes boisterously back to her hometown in the still-ripe flesh, her bags stuffed with cruzeiros whose source she keeps decently secret from the curious Sant'Anans. Her descent on Sant'Ana is the cue for much strenuous comedy, as she stirs the neighborhood up sexually, economically and politically. Her city ways spread havoc in the sticks....

Her goings-on would be more entertaining if they didn't go on so. Mr. Amado spells everything out and tells us again and again what sort of people his very simple characters are, as if there were some danger of our forgetting. In short chapters of commentary he interrupts the story to make ironical or dismissive remarks about it, calling it "a threepenny novel" and a "soap opera," and complaining about its length. Well, *Tieta* is too long, and it does have a lot of the blandness and cheap contrasts in character of the soap opera. It is as if Mr. Amado had one eye on the film or television rights and another on his more sophisticated readers, who need to be reassured that he knows just what sort of book he is writing. (p. 11)

Corruption and industrialization are presumably urgent matters in Brazil, but they are less than urgent matters in *Tieta*. Mr. Amado's businessmen are absurd, inadequate even as caricatures, graduates from the fantasies of Harold Robbins, never the Harvard Business School, and more likely to titillate (with their immoralities) than to appall. Indeed, the satire as a whole, when it comes, is stale and discounted by the oppressive benignity of the rest of the novel. The people whom Mr. Amado would protect, in Sant'Ana do Agreste, may seem worth protecting to their creator, but few of them will seem so to his readers. His Rousseauesque trust in the survival and benevolence of human instinct strikes one as horribly insufficient to cope with the genuine moral and economic dilemmas raised here in fun. (p. 25)

> *John Sturrock, "Brazilian Soap Opera," in* The New York Times Book Review, *July 1, 1979, pp. 11, 25.*

STEPHEN BROOK

Readers of Amado's previous novels (such as *Gabriela, Dona Flor* and *Tieta*) will not be surprised to learn that the heroine [of *Tereza Batista, Home from the Wars*] is, among other things, a prostitute, and that she is blessed with a heart of gold. Though many men pass through her bed, that heart is reserved for a big brawny hulk of a sailor. Amado chronicles Tereza's deeds and misdeeds, her sufferings and her heroism. It's all depicted on a vast canvas with a huge supporting cast (all, maddeningly, named) and the result is like a box of marshmallows. Amado has vigour, panache, raciness, exoticism, but not a grain of discernible literary intelligence. Everything lies on the glittering and over-generous surface....

Amado has a reputation as a master storyteller, but his skills are constantly undermined by his garrulity. The Emiliano section opens with his death, and the main narrative follows the reactions of the bereft Tereza, the petty-minded servants, the scandalized relatives; this is interwoven with flashbacks portraying different stages of the relationship while Emiliano was alive. There are tender, even moving, passages, and moments of ironic comedy, but everything is repeated over and over. Amado simply doesn't know when to stop, and his lyricism is excessive and cloying....

Tereza Batista also has some equally verbose though far more dramatic and vivid passages describing Tereza's endless violations and beatings at the hands of the thug who enslaves her; and there's some delightful comedy in the final section, when the forces of law and order use all possible means to persuade the whores to reopen the brothels, which play a vital part in the corrupt local economy. Fine too is the way Amado personifies the epidemic: "The smallpox was hopping mad by the time it got to Buquim. It had an old grudge against the place and the people in it, and it went there on purpose to kill." Sadly, these good moments of the novel are drowned by the tidal wave of words. Amado is too sentimental, too self-indulgent, too lush, too sprawling; but, like his heroine's, his heart is in the right place.

> *Stephen Brook, "All Heart," in* The Times Literary Supplement, *No. 4154, November 12, 1982, p. 1254.*

IRWIN STERN

Jubiabá and *Sea of Death,* first published during the turbulent 1930's, enhance the English-language reader's acquaintance with Amado, the political activist and promoter of his country's popular culture.

Referring to a Latin American novelist of the 30's in those terms may surprise fans of contemporary Latin American fiction. Critics of this fiction have so stressed the political persuasions of writers of the last two decades that one might be left with the impression that sociopolitical consciousness and the defense of national culture in Latin America date only from the appearance of Che Guevara and Fidel Castro. . . .

Mr. Amado participated in the Brazilian Communist Party's programs during the 1930's in response to the authoritarian policies of President Getúlio Vargas. For Mr. Amado, the novel became a means of awakening *o povo*, the Brazilian poor, to the class struggle and to their rich cultural heritage.

Jubiabá (1935) is a "people's" biography of Antônio Balduíno, a fictional Brazilian *pícaro*, or rogue, in the author's native city of Bahia. Through his experiences as a street urchin, boxer, tobacco picker and strike organizer, Balduíno discovers that the "fetters of slavery" still entrap the Brazilian poor—be they blacks, whites or of mixed race. Mr. Amado deftly avoids a doctrinaire socialist plot by melding the mythical/magical elements of Bahian life into the action: the *cordel*, or popular literature, the city's cooking aromas, the people's sexual allure and, most important, the pervasive Afro-Brazilian traditions. . . .

In *Sea of Death* (1936), the Bahian fishermen's drinking, whoring and brawling with the well-to-do from the upper city are highlighted by the chanteys and *cordel* of the docks. Livia and her lover, Guma, are the rather drab protagonists of a superficial ideological tract—poverty leads men to crime and women to prostitution. Love, death, happiness and guilt: everything in Bahia comes under the dominion of Iemanjá, the Afro-Brazilian goddess of the sea. The code of honor she tacitly imposes upon all justifies both brutality and heroic achievement in daily life. . . .

In 1947, when the Brazilian Communist Party was declared illegal, Mr. Amado went into exile, first in Europe and later in the Soviet Union and China. Upon his return to Brazil in 1952, he turned from the overt socio-political novel to his "Bahian comedy." No longer are his protagonists the machos of the city, the seas or the interior, but rather, voluptuous, sensuous and, oftentimes, calculating women like Gabriela and Dona Flor. He abandons the epic novel for a mock epic of brash humor, wild exaggeration and colorful sexual exploits. But to this day he has never deserted the Bahian poor as the source of his characters and themes, most of which are sketched in these early novels.

Ironically, Mr. Amado's more recent fiction has come under attack from widely different Brazilian political and literary circles for what has been called his "patronizing glorification" of poverty and exploitation of female characters. But no matter. No other Latin American writer is more genuinely admired by his peers, nor has any other exerted so great a creative influence on the course of Latin American fiction. Mr. Amado's is truly a golden anniversary.

> *Irwin Stern, "Magic Socialism," in* The New York Times Book Review, *October 28, 1984, p. 16.*

KRISTIANA GREGORY

The beauty of the sea and those who live and die by its power are gracefully portrayed by Brazilian novelist Jorge Amado in *Sea of Death.* . . . In a lyrical, almost mystical style, he tells about Guma, the penniless sailor who lives on his sloop in Bahia with his devoted Livia. Set in the 1930s, their story is one of struggle, of love and of their ever-present terror that he will perish in a storm and she will be widowed. . . .

Also by Amado and equally vivid is *Jubiaba* . . . , a powerful tale about the street urchin Antonio Balduino. He roams alleys and docks of Bahia, king of tramps, balladeer and heroic lover. As he matures into his 20s, abandoning a career as circus boxer, his life suddenly holds purpose, he learns the meaning of freedom and love. Among the many strange, wonderful characters in this odyssey is Jubiaba, the medicine man he's known since childhood. Oppression and slavery of the masses, depressing themes, are drawn so brightly, so adroitly, that there is a triumph in their telling.

> *Kristiana Gregory, in a review of "Sea of Death" and "Jubiaba," in* Los Angeles Times Book Review, *December 9, 1984, p. 14.*

PUBLISHERS WEEKLY

In his charming new novel [*Pen, Sword, Camisole: A Fable to Kindle a Hope*] Amado displays all the humor, sensuality and joie de vivre readers have come to expect from this most accessible and populist of the great Latin American writers. His tale of the 1940 struggle to keep two military men—one an outright fascist, the other an obnoxious authoritarian—from gaining a seat in the Brazilian Academy of Letters is an impassioned cry for freedom, but that word is never defined in narrowly sectarian terms. . . . Each of his characters is a complete person, rambunctious with individuality and vibrant with life. His ringing avowal that "oppression, violence, death would never succeed in destroying freedom, life, man" is inspiring, and *Pen, Sword, Camisole* radiates a profound joy it's impossible not to share.

> *A review of "Pen, Sword, Camisole: A Fable to Kindle a Hope," in* Publishers Weekly, *Vol. 227, No. 11, March 15, 1985, p. 102.*

NANCY RAMSEY

[The] Brazilian poet António Bruno has just died in Paris [in the beginning of *Pen, Sword, Camisole*], after hearing a radio bulletin announcing the fall of the city to the Nazis. In his home country, where martial law has been imposed, the search to fill his seat in the Brazilian Academy of Letters begins. Two candidates emerge, neither of whom shares Bruno's freedom-loving, bohemian spirit: the calculating, brutal Col. Agnaldo Sampaio Pereira, a Nazi sympathizer, and Gen. Waldomiro Moreira, author of polemical tracts, ''a windbag and a braggart'' who plays both sides of the political fence. Four months of political infighting and plotting—including a hemlock poisoning—ensue, the subject of *Pen, Sword, Camisole*. . . . Mr. Amado shows—largely through two leftist octogenarians—that hope can be maintained even in bleak, repressive times. Some likeable characters weave their way among the military bureaucrats. . . . But Mr. Amado has stripped away details and nuances of character. And while there are some surprising turns of events, for the most part political maneuverings are presented in such labored detail that even life-and-death matters seem like brokering at a convention. . . . Mr. Amado's didactic style is unfortunate, because his intent is an honorable one.

> *Nancy Ramsey, in a review of "Pen, Sword, Camisole: A Fable to Kindle a Hope," in* The New York Times Book Review, *May 19, 1985, p. 22.*

Kingsley (William) Amis

1922-

(Has also written under pseudonyms of Robert Markham and William Tanner) English novelist, poet, short story writer, editor, nonfiction writer, biographer, scriptwriter, and journalist.

An eclectic, prolific, and controversial author, Amis is best known for his popular and acclaimed novel, *Lucky Jim* (1954). Although he began his career as a poet and has since explored a number of styles and genres, Amis's most frequently praised works are predominantly satirical. He generally writes in a witty, irreverent style, challenging his readers' beliefs and attitudes by focusing in his fiction upon cynical male protagonists who hold controversial or illiberal views on such topics as sex, feminism, culture, and related moral concerns. Amis has been characterized at various times in his career as a comic writer with serious overtones, a moral satirist similar to Evelyn Waugh, and a realist in the manner of Henry Fielding. Whatever his inclination, Amis has established a reputation as an author who values innovation over easy categorization.

Amis defines modern satire as "fiction that attacks vice and folly as manifested in the individual." His heroes are typically cynical, condemnatory individuals who combine intelligence and wit with curiously lowbrow or middle-class values. Jim Dixon, the sardonic and engaging protagonist of Amis's first novel, *Lucky Jim,* is a junior lecturer at a provincial university who flouts the pseudointellectual demands of academia as a way of rejecting its affectation and hypocrisy. Although some reviewers considered the book to be a savage polemic on British culture, Amis received much critical attention and was highly praised for his apt characterizations, deft use of understatement, and biting, sarcastic humor. The cynical tone of this and later novels led critics to associate Amis with the "Angry Young Men," a group of British writers who bitterly condemned their country's social and political values during the 1950s and 1960s. The characters of Amis's subsequent novels are similar to Jim Dixon in temperament but grow increasingly mean-spirited and repellent in their attitudes. The hero of *That Uncertain Feeling* (1955), a young Welsh librarian obsessed with the sexual opportunities of university life, is alternately kind, lecherous, and cruel. In *Take a Girl like You* (1960), an attractive but insincere grammar school instructor seduces, then all but sexually assaults, a newly-arrived preschool teacher. The title character of *One Fat Englishman* (1963), a bigoted Oxford snob, is left with no redeeming human values at the novel's end as he fails to realize the fundamental contradictions in his own nature.

Amis disavowed the use of polemic and experimented with a variety of forms and styles in his fiction of the mid-1960s and 1970s. *The Anti-Death League* (1966) is a dark, humorless novel in which he combines elements of the spy thriller, love story, and ideological novel. *Colonel Sun* (1968), a novel written under the pseudonym of Robert Markham, features as its protagonist Ian Fleming's hero, James Bond. In this novel, Amis attempts to humanize the flamboyant secret agent and ground his adventures in contemporary reality. *The Green Man* (1969) is a comic ghost story in which a malevolent spirit awakens in a rundown pub, believing it has found an ally in the establishment's drunken and lecherous but essentially de-

© Jerry Bauer

cent proprietor. Amis received the John W. Campbell Award for *The Alteration* (1976), an example of the "alternate worlds" subgenre of science fiction. In this work, Amis postulates that the Protestant Reformation never took place in Europe and that, as a result, England is overwhelmingly Catholic. The novel centers on the complex moral and psychological issues raised by a Papal decision to castrate, or "alter," a young boy to preserve his voice for the choir. *Russian Hide-and-Seek* (1980), another example of the "alternate worlds" novel, centers on a future England overrun by the Soviets, who abandoned Marxism in favor of the ancient system of czarist rule.

In his recent mainstream novels, Amis expands on the concerns of his early work, focusing on characteristic heroes in modern situations. These books elicited sharply divided critical opinions due to their controversial or challenging conclusions. The central character of *Jake's Thing* (1978), a middle-aged man who was once sexually active, seeks psychiatric help in restoring his failing libido but concludes that indifference is preferable to commitment. The bigoted protagonist of *Stanley and the Women* (1984) is unable to understand the women in his life—his wife, his ex-wife, and his son's feminist psychiatrist. While Susan Fromberg Schaeffer called the book "a *misanthropic* work in which Mr. Amis attacks everything in sight," Marilyn Butler contended: "The messages conveyed by the packaging, that the book is stupid, old-fashioned, illiberal and likely to displease women, are nonsense, the very reverse of the novel's actual messages.''

Amis began writing poetry while a student at Oxford University, where he came into contact with such poets as Philip Larkin and John Wain. The poems in his first collection, *Bright November* (1947), are colloquial, traditional in structure, and reflect the influence of W. H. Auden. In "Release," Amis contemplates the demobilization of the armed forces after World War II; in other poems, he attempts to define his new roles as poet, teacher, father, and husband. Amis disavows Romanticism and its influence in *A Frame of Mind* (1953), contrasting humorous observations with serious, often surprising conclusions about human nature. Much of this poetry, along with works from other Oxford writers of the era, was anthologized in Robert Conquest's *New Lines* in 1956. The writers included in this volume, who came to be known as members of "The Movement," favored clear, rational writing over the highly symbolic works of W. B. Yeats, the experimental prose of James Joyce, and the obscurity of such modernists as Ezra Pound and T. S. Eliot. Many of Amis's poems were collected with earlier verse in *A Case of Samples: Poems 1946-1956* (1956). *The Evans Country* (1962) centers on a sly, lecherous character, reminiscent of Amis's fictional heroes, who lives eternally in the present and learns nothing from experience. Verse from this volume is reprinted with uncollected poetry in *A Look round the Estate: Poems 1957-1967* (1967). Many critics detect in the recent verse in Amis's *Collected Poems 1944-1979* (1979) a greater maturity and heightened awareness of the external world.

Amis has been involved throughout his career with other literary ventures. In addition to coediting the *Spectrum* series of science fiction anthologies, among other works, Amis is the author of *New Maps of Hell: A Survey of Science Fiction* (1960), which is considered the first detailed overview of the genre. Among Amis's well-regarded collections of essays on political topics are *Socialism and the Intellectuals* (1957) and *Lucky Jim's Politics* (1968). In the biography *Rudyard Kipling and His World* (1975), Amis deals with the issue of Kipling's racism and imperialism. Amis has also written several television scripts, and some of his novels have been adapted for film, including *Lucky Jim, That Uncertain Feeling* (under the title *Only Two Can Play*), and *Take a Girl like You*.

(See also *CLC*, Vols. 1, 2, 3, 5, 8, 13; *Contemporary Authors*, Vols. 9-12, rev. ed.; *Contemporary Authors New Revision Series*, Vol. 8; and *Dictionary of Literary Biography*, Vols. 15, 27.)

CLIVE JAMES

Kingsley Amis has had to go on and on proving that he is as interesting a poet as he is a novelist. It was inevitable. He is a very interesting novelist. That he should be equally good at the other thing seems unjust. But this volume [*Collected Poems 1944-79*], which collects all of his verse that he wishes to preserve, should finally be proof positive. Accomplished, literate and entertaining, it is a richly various expression of a moral personality coming to terms with the world.

Since the arrangement of poems is chronological, the personality can be heard discovering its own voice in the opening

pages. To become himself, Amis had first of all to absorb the bewitching influence of Auden, whose tones pervade his early poems just as thoroughly as the tones of Yeats pervade the early poems of Philip Larkin. . . .

Amis has done us a double service by not suppressing these early poems. In the first place, they give us an object lesson in what a gifted young poet finds fascinating about an older master: clearly it was the way Auden made the *prosaic* sound poetic that Amis wanted to steal the secret of. In the second place, they are substantial poems in their own right. He wasn't just scrambling a few borrowed effects together in order to conjure up an air of meaning. He actually had clear themes, even when the themes were callow.

When he discovered what he really wanted to say, he quickly began sounding like himself. This process is usually known as 'finding your own voice'. There is nothing automatic about it. Most poets never find their own voice. Instead they employ quirks to give their anonymity identity. To speak naturally and still be immediately recognisable is a rare thing. . . .

[Early in his career, Amis began to develop] the ability to discipline a principal strength. It would have been easy for him to indulge his capacity for comic invention. But he used it sparingly from the start. Comedy was always subordinated to argument. Amis's tone has never been less than densely serious, so it was no surprise that Dr Leavis found him frivolous.

> Half-shut, our eye dawdles down the page
> Seeing the word love, the word death, the
>   word life,
> Rhyme-words of poets in a silver age:
> Silver of the bauble, not of the knife.

Knives, not baubles, are what poems should be like: a very rigorous aesthetic, which Amis had begun holding to long before he got round to formulating it. Poets find their guiding principles by assessing the implications of what they have done already. Similarly, they increase their range of vision by gazing within. By comically dramatising his own introspection, Amis found a way of taking the conceit out of self-regard. In **"A Dream of Fair Women"**, the 'squadron of draped nudes' who mob him in his sexual fantasy are banal enough to be flying around in ours too. . . .

The poet goes on to admit the sad triteness of that imaginary harem; to contend that if it were real then only 'the best' would settle for anything else; and to regret the fact that everyone else would come along with him to seek 'the halls of theoretical delight'. It is notable that he does not include himself among 'the best', even though the mere ability to analyse the problem would give him some justification to place himself above it. But Amis's insistence on his own propensity for all moral failings is based on deep conviction, quite apart from its being a useful creative device. In Amis's view, we all have similar impulses. What we do about them is a matter of choice. The callous and the stupid have *chosen* to be that way.

Not to be swept up by feelings but to control them—both ethically and aesthetically it is an anti-romantic standpoint. In **"Against Romanticism"** he made the connection explicit. Admitting that it does not seem quite enough to be a 'traveller who walks a temperate zone', nevertheless he distrusts the irrepressible hunger for 'a grand meaning' that

> . . . sets the brain raging with prophecy,
> Raging to discard real time and place . . .

It is true that there must be visions, but they should be visions that do not leave the real world out. . . .

Those of us who are always re-reading Amis's novels have grown used to finding his later themes presaged in early works. The same applies to his poetry, where his later set-piece struggles with Eros and Thanatos are merely the culmination of a string of skirmishes that go back to the very beginning. (p. 521)

Only the fabled travelling salesman of **"A Song of Experience"** ('And so he knew, where we can only fumble') can unthinkingly do the right thing about sex. Amis's own conclusion—that at the moment of being overwhelmed by our strongest instinct we are obliged to turn our brains on instead of off—is once again an anti-romantic one. The best we can hope for is to go through life with our eyes open. Those who take short cuts have nothing to tell us: a stricture from which Jesus Christ is not excluded. (pp. 521-22)

Dai Evans [of *The Evans Country*] is the final development of the travelling salesman. The Evans Country is the land of heart's desire—a version of Wales less stridently fabulous than Llaregubb, yet still mythical, because in it life acts itself out without an inward look. Evans firmly quells all intimations of morality. Staging a bonfire of his second-rate pornography, he still keeps the first-rate stuff upstairs. . . .

Amis does not withhold his admiration from this most indefatigable of all stick-men. Yet it is made clear that the void which awaits Evans already has its counterpart in his head: by not noticing he has solved nothing. Facing reality has its own value. That is the sole, but strong, affirmation underlying Amis's later poems. Some of these are merrily contemptuous of what modern life has become. . . .

Others tragically accept the brute facts about what life has always been. **"A Reunion"**, for example, . . . is really an extended and painful encounter with the truth about how we grow apart from and forget each other. Two things lie between such a poem and despair. The first is the perfection of the poet's craft, which in Amis as in any other true artist is essentially a moral property. The second is the unspoken corollary of Socrates' insistence that the unexamined life is not worth living. The examined life *is* worth living. Only the fact that he is so marvellously readable can now stop Kingsley Amis from being placed in the front rank of contemporary poets. He has attained his grand meaning after all. (p. 522)

Clive James, "The Examined Life," in New Statesman, *Vol. 97, No. 2508, April 13, 1979, pp. 521-22.*

WILLIAM H. PRITCHARD

Kingsley Amis's poems have always made critics a trifle nervous, partly because he is such a re-readable novelist that it seems hardly fair he should perform so well in verse. Then there is the presence of Larkin over his shoulder, a writer whose poems take on depths of gloomy richness that Amis, wisely I think, doesn't attempt to match. Transatlantically speaking, it's my impression that news of Amis the poet has barely reached these shores. . . . As someone who for years has been sending people copies of **"Lovely"** ('Look thy last on all things lovely / Every hour, an old shag said'), I should like to suggest here why his poetry is one of civilization's resources, the sort of thing you want to read aloud to another person.

What the *Collected Poems* reveals is Amis's development into one of the two best writers of light verse extant (the book is dedicated to John Betjeman, the other one). Reviewers of his poems in the past have sometimes disagreed over whether they qualified for that label or were of a higher (or heavier) nature. But we can now draw on his introduction to the *New Oxford Book of English Light Verse* for a useful criticism of his own work:

> I described *vers de société* earlier as in some degree a continuation of satire. This move can be seen as already in progress by the time of Swift, who was certainly not writing satire in the normal sense of the term, as his avoidance of the heroic couplet would be enough to suggest. . . . We are dealing with a kind of realistic verse that is close to some of the interests of the novel: men and women among their fellows, seen as members of a group or class in a way that emphasizes manners, social forms, amusements, fashion (from millinery to philosophy), topicality, even gossip, all these treated in a bright, perspicuous style.

These perspicuous sentences about one kind of light verse are so partly because they have roots in Amis's own poetry and suggest the way in which, like Swift, he was not writing 'satire in the normal sense'.

Yet in the earliest poems from the collection . . . there is little of the flexibility needed for writing *vers de société*. The portentous style is more contrived than 'bright', and contrived in the manner of Auden. . . . [There are] Audenesque 'fumbling gestures', and resolutions to 'speak straight' and 'walk without a strut'. John Bayley has said of Larkin's first book of poems, *The North Ship,* that 'there is a high degree of competence and of effective Yeatsian usage, but no Larkin at all'. A similar judgment might be passed on the presence of Auden in Amis's early poems.

Audenesque was not a plausible style for Amis because there is little suggestion of an unexpressed or inexpressible content, a 'secret' behind the words. (pp. 58-9)

The flare of a more personal voice is there though in **"A Dream of Fair Women"**, which like Amis's other poems has a principled point to make, but on the way to making it provides us with something other than a dispassionate presentation—as when, in the dream, a bevy of females exercises its varied charms on the narrator. . . . Here the 'bright, perspicuous style' emerges, as it does in **"A Bookshop Idyll"**, when after the narrator (may we call him Amis?) finds that gents and ladies tend to title their volumes of poetry in discernibly different ways, he finds also that 'a moral beckons'. . . . (p. 60)

By not reading [Amis's] poems or novels very carefully, one could assume that he is simply a professional squasher of the human heart, that he merely delights in letting the hot air out of pumped-up dreams and visions. It is useful then to consider **"Romance"**, the concluding poem in *A Case of Samples,* to suggest how disturbed and moved he has been by this whole matter of romantic inflation. . . . This lovely and delicate poem does something interesting with the Yeatsian motto 'In dreams begins responsibility', by rewriting it more ruefully and disillusionedly: in dreams begins disappointment or weakness—the heart turned out and away, unable for more than a moment to scale the 'forest-fence', to capture or to live in that 'high romantic citadel' where you must be as glamorous and undaunted as the others. It is Amis's Fitzgerald poem, as written by a Nick Carraway who had read Empson. (pp. 61-2)

Amis has always held on hard to the images and truths of youthful—one could say boyish—perception (his imagining of the youth, Peter, in *The Riverside Villas Murder* is finely done), which is perhaps why in his poems from the last fifteen or so years, the oldster speaking them is scornful and sad. **"A Chromatic Passing-Note"**, from *A Look Round the Estate* (1967) begins with an oldster talking this way:

> 'That slimy tune' I said, and got a laugh,
> In the middle of old Franck's D minor thing:
> The dotted-rhythm clarinet motif.

Amis invariably does something fresh with his musical references, classical or jazz. Here it would be a mistake to remember 'filthy Mozart' and presume that a Lucky Jim is up again to his old debunking tricks. The poem goes on to point out, quite didactically, that the tune wasn't 'slimy' when the speaker was fifteen, but showed rather 'that real love was found / At the far end of the right country lane'. Now, having learned different, '"Slimy" was a snarl of disappointment'. What saves the **"A Chromatic Passing-Note"** from abstractedness and mere lesson-teaching is that there *is* such a clarinet motif in the second movement of the Franck symphony; that one loves it when young and (in my experience) eventually turns on it or away from it as too plangent, too much of a dream. (pp. 62-3)

From here it is but a step, and with hindsight a predictable one, to **"The Evans Country"**. 'Adulthood's high romantic citadel' has been too pricey a dream, the human heart too weak to engage it for long. So Amis imagines, with fierce satisfaction, the unromantic architecture against which Evans's courting takes place:

> By the new Boots, a tool-chest with flagpoles
> Glued on, and flanges, and a dirty great
> Baronial doorway, and things like portholes,
> Evan met Mrs Rhys on their first date.

Here we have moved completely and successfully into the 'manners, social forms, amusements, fashion (from millinery to philosophy)' which distinguish *vers de Société*, Amis's brand of light verse. The 'bright, perspicuous style' continues to engage us as further items of 'romance' are catalogued 'the time they slunk / Back from that lousy week-end in Porthcawl;' then the poem reaches conclusion in a strongly assured and compelling rhythm. . . . In *The Waste Land* Eliot is also supposed to have squashed flat the human heart; but if one feels, as I do, that the encounter between the typist and her young man carbuncular ('Flushed and decided he assaults at once') has been bicycle-pumped by language into a great caricature that is beautiful (Eliot's language about Ben Jonson), then one can also be truly moved by this moment in the Amis poem:

> But how disparage what so well reflects
> Permanent tendencies of heart and mind?

The question can be asked only when the poet moves beyond the complacencies of more ordinary 'satire' ('poking fun', as the undergraduates say) and acts instead as a true witness to love, even Evans's love, by measuring, thus celebrating it in verse.

By the time we reach the end of the final poem in **"The Evans Country"** (**"Aberdarcy: The Chaucer Road"**) the poet-as-commentator has disappeared. On his way to a quick one with 'Mrs No-holds-barred', Evans reflects on 'How much in life he's never going to know: / All it must mean to really love a woman'. Yet, the poem suggests, there are compensations, as after the event Evans returns home for a quiet evening:

> 'Hallo now, Megan.
> No worse than usual, love. You been all right?
> Well, this looks good. And there's a lot on later;
> Don't think I'll bother with the club tonight.'

> Nice bit of haddock with poached egg, Dundee cake,
> Buckets of tea, then a light ale or two,
> And 'Gunsmoke', 'Danger Man', the Late Night
>   Movie—
> Who's doing better, then? What about you?

It is a marvellous stroke to take us, by the flash and movement of the catalogue of anticipated delights, inside Evans country to the extent that the final question totally disarms us. And the tendencies of Evans's heart and mind have been permanently etched.

One might say the same about Amis, after reading through the eighteen poems, some of them very short, which follow **"The Evans Country"** and make up his published output of verse for the last twelve years. Often they are recited (Amis has recently edited *The Faber Popular Reciter*—'poems that sound well and go well when spoken in a declamatory style') by the radical-reactionary controversialist we've become familiar with from various letters and columns in newspapers and weeklies since the later sixties. Aging and rigidifying, he salutes himself on his fiftieth birthday for having at least lived through *those* fifty years rather than the fifty to come: 'After a whole generation / Of phasing out education, / Throwing the past away, / Letting the language decay, / And expanding the general mind / Till it bursts'. At least he was born with a 'chance of happiness. / Before unchangeable crappiness / Spreads over all the land'. (pp. 63-5)

Robert Frost used to say that rather than entertaining ideas he liked to try them out to see whether they entertained him. Amis's poems, especially the recent ones, work this way by invoking contemporary crappiness so magnificently and expertly that—like the poet, and perhaps the man himself—we are positively exhilarated by the awful spectacle. The next-to-last poem in the book, **"Farewell Blues"** uses Hardy's "Friends Beyond" (the Mellstock Churchyard poem) to eulogize dead jazz musicians, much of whose music moulders in the vaults of dead 1930's record companies. . . . In the immortal language of another recent poem, the contemporary improvisor is 'A nitwit not fit to shift shit'. But the final stanza of **"Farewell Blues"** brings together much of what makes up Amis's version of things: contempt and disgust for the crappy present; nostalgia for a time when things were different, just possibly better; commitment to rhyme and exactly measured lines (fifteen syllables in the first three lines, twenty-four in the fourth one); respect helplessly paid to the 'dream' which was once entertained and which, because it was so good, helped ruin the present. The stanza is about jazz but about more than just jazz. . . . (pp. 66-7)

Light verse no longer feels very light, has gone 'high' instead into a version of pastoral that is affecting and moving. But I speak for myself here, as one for whom since the day I first read *Lucky Jim* back then, Amis has been the most entertaining, the most exhilarating of contemporary writers. Who's doing better then? What about you? (p. 67)

William H. Pritchard, "Entertaining Amis," in Essays in Criticism, *Vol. XXX, No. 1, January, 1980, pp. 58-67.*

D.A.N. JONES

[*Russian Hide-and-Seek*] is the second of Kingsley Amis's 'might-have-been' novels. In *The Alteration,* he imagined a 20th-century world in which the Reformation had never taken place, and Britain was dominated by an authoritarian Papacy. In *Russian Hide-and-Seek,* he imagines a 21st-century world in which Britain has lost a war (in the 1980s, I think) and is occupied by Soviet troops. (p. 659)

This novel is more serious, more grave, than *The Alteration.* It is as serious as *The Anti-Death League,* which it somewhat resembles. 'Kingsley Amis's story of sinister military plans, spies, double agents and triple bluffs is set against a background of indolent officers' fun and games with women and with each other. . . .' That [publisher's] blurb for *The Anti-Death League* would serve for *Russian Hide-and-Seek.*

While reading the first chapter, about a rather attractive Russian cavalryman riding through our countryside, we may look back at the emblem on the cover, wondering in fascinated indignation how that bear got hold of our possessions. Where is the Resistance? Where is the King? The story grips by offering clues, by referring to Britain as 'what used to be the Kingdom', by making a character say 'when the King of England gets to sit on his throne'—as a proverbial phrase, meaning 'never'. The only person now alive who is mentioned in the book is the Queen: she appears in a powerful paragraph in the final chapter, when a hateful Russian security man is at last telling the long-concealed truth about the Soviet conquest of Britain, half a century before. (pp. 659-60)

[Amis] is, in this book about a possible future, writing partly about things that are happening now, about the sorts of behaviour and opinions that might lead to a successful foreign invasion, to treachery and collaboration.

It is delicately done. We see among the Russian soldiers and officials the faults and weaknesses that lead to disaster, the flaws that brought Britain down. There are two feeble, 'wet-liberal', permissive fathers in the book, bringing disaster upon their respective houses with all the incompetence of old Montagu and old Capulet. One is a Russian administrator, the other an English doctor.

Kingsley Amis has long been interested in incompetent fathers. . . . Vandervane, in *Girl, 20,* could see girls only as ages, in sexy advertisements; he ruined his family, particularly his daughter, through adherence to a social theory about youth, freedom and permissiveness.

The Vandervane figure in *Russian Hide-and-Seek* is called Petrovsky. He is told by another Russian officer: 'You're the all-round liberal, unreservedly tolerant, not least of what others condemn, in favour of equal treatment for unequals, exercising no authority over his children, the master who's patient but firm, but more patient than firm . . . [Your] greatest fear is to be caught disapproving of something . . .' Old Petrovsky's son, Alexander, is the Romeo of this story: because of his upbringing he is devoid of loyalty, prepared to kill his army comrades and even his own father for the sake of an idealistic cause which he has taken up in wantonness.

The Juliet of the story is called Kitty. Her father, Dr Wright, is a feeble opponent of the Soviet occupying forces, resentfully entertaining the young officers in his house and whining to his daughter: 'I wish you wouldn't call that fellow *golubchik* in front of me. I mean, he *is* helping to hold us all down by force . . . It might have been his grandfather who killed my

parents . . .' It is characteristic of the hopeless Wright that he has given his daughter no idea of her heritage. In the course of the story, Alexander and Kitty go to a rotten production of *Romeo and Juliet:* the actors cannot speak the verse and the audience cannot understand. But something gets through to Kitty. In the last chapter, after the death of Alexander, Kitty is almost mourning her lover, it is almost a tragedy—as far as possible in this dehumanised, non-tragic society—and she is trying to remember a line of Juliet's: 'Take him and cut him out in little stars.' But she can't quite get it. This is very moving. The characters in this novel are not lay-figures—as they might well be in such a schematic book, such an unreal world. One can feel for them.

This is a story about losing. Losing a war, first of all—and losing too (as cause and effect) faith, loyalty, history, language and the loving feeling in sex. Alexander is a cold-hearted lover, fortified by chilly, Frenchified epigrams. . . . [He] has not the wit to analyse the nature of his disease, to recognise that the times are out of joint, that he lives in a non-ethical state. Robert Conquest has suggested, recently, that the next generation in the Russian ruling class may be worse than their predecessors, because they have no faith. Alexander seems to be an example of this possibility. . . .

[As in *The Anti-Death League*], there is a sermon, there is prayer, and things look hopeful—and then there is a disaster, as if to prove the truth of Sod's Law. The last chapter of *The Anti-Death League* destroyed hope, was anti-life. Similarly here, the result of the old parson's fine sermon is this: 'That was the day Wright finally despaired.' It looks as if Kingsley Amis will be able to bring a serious novel to a happy conclusion only if he comes to believe in God.

What the novel needs, perhaps, is a bit more 'optimism of the will' to balance 'the pessimism of the intellect', to use Gramsci's terms. (p. 660)

D.A.N. Jones, "After Conquest," in The Listener, *Vol. 103, No. 2662, May 22, 1980, pp. 659-60.*

PAUL BINDING

The title of Kingsley Amis's new novel [*Russian Hide & Seek*] refers to a [Russian-roulette-like] game played during its course by army officers. . . . For Amis this game is a cultural epitome of the society to which its players belong—one motiveless, bored, callous, self-indulgent, yet infatuated with violent death. It is that of Imperialist Russia—its period 50 years hence, when the Soviet Union has overrun England, and abandoned Marxism to revert to the style of the Ancien Régime. The protagonists of *Russian Hide & Seek* are members of the Russian ruling-class of England; its plot concerns the attempt by some of these to stage a revolution which will restore England to the English, an attempt doomed from the first both through the naivety of the revolutionaries and through the strength and efficiency of an eternally paranoid Central Government.

Amis has long been fascinated by the challenge of genre fiction—thus in *The Green Man* he produced a ghost-story, in *The Riverside Villas Murder* a Thirties-style whodunnit. This new novel, subtitled a 'Melodrama', is at once a pastiche of certain aspects of 19th-century Russian fiction and an exercise in cloak-and-dagger adventure. The two genres unite to form a work far more ambitious than those earlier *jeux*—a fictional expression of the author's obsessive conviction that, whatever its avatar, Russian culture is beastly, thriving on conscious exploitation, enamoured of brutality. . . .

In order to succeed as an indictment of Russian culture, the novel must of course provide a plausible picture of it. Inevitably its characters derive from literature rather than life, but from literature wilfully read with only one eye. Amis has eliminated from the subjects of Turgenev and Tolstoy their moral preoccupations and questionings, their religious sense, their awareness of both the desirability and the inevitability of the transformation of their society. For the most part he has accorded his 21st-century Russians only the outward rituals and attitudes—and indeed attitudinisings—of their ancestors. These, it hardly need be said, are totally inadequate if we are to be convinced by the characters as logical heirs to a culture. But of course the very existence of the novels to which Amis has turned for source-material, and of which, as we read, we are constantly aware, constitutes a major refutation of his thesis; no society which produced them can be thus dismissed. And this is to say nothing (as indeed the author himself virtually does) of the ideologies and social structure of the Soviet Union. If Amis believes that these now contain the germinating seeds of reversion, then—even in a fictional parable—evidence should be given. . . .

Amis naturally feels obliged to pay tributes to the mores of the defeated English; their capacity for luck is emphasised, and this was never better exhibited—according to his fantasy-history—than in their demonstrations when they learned of the death of the Queen! The attempted revolution is carried out under the guise of a Festival of English Culture, something resurrected with difficulty: a muddled Anglican service is held, Shakespeare is bizarrely produced. These scenes are among the most imaginative in the book, since they are animated by Amis's characteristic verbal inventiveness, yet they leave one with curiously little sense of any belief on the author's part in the cultural realities behind the garbled versions presented. . . .

What is it then that draws Amis so compulsively to the subject of the destruction of his country when both here and elsewhere he exhibits such lukewarm enthusiasm for many of its most characteristic attainments? It is hard not to detect in his insistent harping on the theme something of that very death-wish, that bored hunger for violent defeat that distinguish the players of 'hide-and-seek'. But I imagine Amis knows this only too well himself.

> Paul Binding, *"Snow on Their Boots," in* New Statesman, *Vol. 99, No. 2566, May 23, 1980, p. 784.*

JAMES FENTON

[Kingsley Amis's *Collected Short Stories*] collects nearly all the author's short stories (but what a pity that **"The Sacred Rhino of Uganda"**, 1932, was omitted as uncharacteristic). There are two parts. The second part includes science fiction of a straightforward kind (**"Something Strange"** describes a group who have been living through an experiment in which, unknown to them, the element of fear has been entirely removed) and three stories by way of a humorous futurological spoof (**"The 2003 Claret"**, **"The Friends of Plonk"** and **"Too Much Trouble"**). The best of the sci-fi is a short item . . . entitled **"Hemingway In Space"**, in which machismo of epic proportions is pitched in mortal struggle against a xeeb. Hunting xeebs is a man's job—and there is an invigoratingly committed misogyny in this five-page story. The remainder of Part

Two includes a mystery solved by Doctor Watson, an expert vampirological dossier, a dream study and Mr Amis's radio piece from the early Seventies, in which the listener was intended to be temporarily hoaxed into the belief that Elizabeth Jane Howard had been tampered with by God. (Instead, everyone either believed the story or—worse—believed that Mr Amis believed it.)

Part Two, then, is entertainment. Part One includes three stories from military life—**"My Enemy's Enemy"**, **"Court of Inquiry"** and **"I Spy Strangers"** which together form a miniature novel, a study of personal vindictiveness and enmity between ranks at the end of the Second World War. These are by far the best thing in the book. Of the other serious stories, **"Moral Fibre"** is an attack on the interfering behaviour of social workers, **"All the Blood Within Me"** describes an aged man at the funeral of the woman he loved, while **"Dear Illusion"** . . . calls into being a sad protagonist in order to play a cruel joke at his expense. It is a story which makes a critic think hard before praising a man's work—before praising this book, for instance. But it is a fine collection, worth reading and, for that matter, worth *buying*.

> James Fenton, *" 'He Is Obliged to Find a Few Plausible Reasons for Anger'," in* The Listener, *Vol. 104, No. 2684, October 23, 1980, p. 543.*

JOHN LUCAS

Among the stories brought together in [Amis's *Collected Short Stories*] is one called **"The Darkwater Hall Mystery"**. It's a pastiche of the Sherlock Holmes stories. . . . [The villain] is Black Ralph, would-be murderer of Sir Harry Fairfax, identified by Watson as 'one of the finest types of English country gentlemen'. Amis does a pretty good imitation of Conan Doyle's style, and of Watson's prejudices, which isn't surprising since he's a first-rate mimic. Proof of that is contained in the story **"Hemingway in Space"**, which exactly echoes the tight-lipped fake-stoical manner of *The Old Man and the Sea*. But that isn't to say very much, especially since Hemingway has often enough been parodied, not least by himself. On the other hand, **"Hemingway in Space"** nails some of Papa's most tiresome clichés, whereas **"The Darkwater Hall Mystery"** supplies its own, and ones for which Amis, rather than Watson, is responsible.

It may be Watson who remarks that Black Ralph is a figure of 'indescribable menace' but it's Amis who has the plot reveal that he's obviously a villain because he's obviously a villain. . . . The objection to this has to be that it cuts out any interest in the character himself, so that all we have is a tale of indulged prejudices, in which we know how matters are going to turn out: the surprise of there being no surprise simply doesn't work. And this is only partly due to the fact that Amis is short on skill when it comes to handling the detective story, a criticism which extends not only to the clumsy *Riverside Villas Murder*, but also to the one story in this collection which hasn't previously seen the light of day. **"To See the Sun"** is a very awkwardly told story of vampirism. In fact, all the later stories seem awkward, badly told and for the most part badly written. The one exception is **"Who or What Was It"**, and although this brilliant fancy about Amis finding himself in a 'real-life situation' which repeats much of *The Green Man* has its rough moments that's probably because it was written to be heard rather than read.

'This collection is really one of chips from a novelist's bench', Amis says in his introduction. No doubt, but the wood from which the more recent stories come is inferior stuff. In Amis's case, later means worse. Earlier is a different matter, and that's particularly true of the clutch of stories dealing with army life at the end of the second world war. These allow for the springing of reversal and surprise which by the time of **"Dear Illusion"**—about a non-poet's recognition of his utter absence of talent—has hardened into a gimmick. . . .

But in the early stories the surprise works. It's pretty good in **"My Enemy's Enemy"**, where the unregarded 'regular' officer is given a speech that stingingly rebukes the liberal conscience of the central character, Thurston, who hasn't done all that he might have done to help another officer he knows is the object of the Adjutant's dislike. . . . Amis effectively makes the point that from where others stand we are not what we are but what we do—and that those others can surprise us by their capacity for acting in ways that we hadn't expected but which make sense. . . .

Amis's ability to spring surprises about his characters, which upset the complacent certainties that he adopts in **"The Darkwater Hall Mystery"**, is at its best in **"I Spy Strangers"**. This story is surely a masterpiece? It brilliantly catches the feel of those days in 1945 leading up to the overwhelming victory of the Attlee government, and the puzzled inability of conservative-minded people to understand what was happening. It also manages to be just to and interesting about all the characters, from the right-wing Major Raleigh, through the trim fascist, Sergeant Doll, the quintessential liberal Archer, to Hargreaves, the socialist intellectual whom Doll hates almost as much as he hates the Major. Doll seems to be a parody. In fact, however, we are made to take him seriously. He may be unlovely, but he's understandable; and he's no fool. The writer who imagined Doll had a wit and intelligence that aren't much in evidence in the latter part of *Collected Short Stories*.

> John Lucas, *"Early Is Best,"* in New Statesman, *Vol. 100, No. 2594, December 5, 1980, p. 30.*

DANA GIOIA

Collected Poems, 1944-1979 finally makes all of Amis' ingratiating poetry available for American readers. Looking over the volume, it is interesting to trace the author's development over those 35 years and compare him to his close friend and contemporary, Philip Larkin. In the mid-fifties Amis and Larkin must have seemed very much alike as writers. Both of them were novelists who had also written a small, carefully-crafted body of poetry. Yet by the mid-sixties it was clear that Amis had chosen the role of a minor poet while Larkin had become one of the best poets writing in English. It was not that Amis' work had declined in quality. For Amis proved Auden's *dictum* that minor poetry is as well-written as major poetry. Nor was it solely that Amis poured his genius into his novels and his talent into his verse. Instead, his development seems primarily temperamental. Amis chose the role of anti-romantic in his poetry, and he has lived with that decision and its consequences. . . . Amis never gives in to what used to be called "the oceanic feeling." Amis never loses a sense of distance from his subject, even when it is himself. In **"A Dream of Fair Women,"** one of his finest poems, he explores his own sexual fantasies in a formal set piece about an imaginary bordello that makes its revelations indirectly through wit and diction rather than bald confession. . . . (p. 615)

Amis may limit himself by dwelling within the "temperate zone" of experience, but within these latitudes he writes with memorable precision and zest. He demonstrates a lesson it is too easy to forget—that to write well about ordinary events takes extraordinary skill. And so in its peculiar way, Amis' *Collected Poems* is a necessary book, especially for those American readers who do not share his anti-romantic assumption that intelligence, wit, form, and verbal ingenuity are the essentials of poetry. Readers who find Rimbaud, Whitman, Ginsberg, and Snyder especially sympathetic, can be assured that in this sense at least Amis' work will prove a mind-expanding experience. (p. 616)

> *Dana Gioia, in a review of "Collected Poems, 1944-1979," in* The Hudson Review, *Vol. XXXIII, No. 4, Winter, 1980-81, pp. 615-16.*

PETER BLAND

Amis's poems [in *Collected Poems 1944-1979*] draw a good deal of their strength from their sense of period but, even so, the best of them (a good dozen or so) lightly outlive their most fruitful decade (middle 50's to early 60's). Amis is both a raconteur and a moralist and it's the tensions between such opposites in his *own* nature that gives his poems their edge. Reason and passion, idea and action, the social man and the outsider, all vie with each other in poems that are often deceptively off-hand. Sex is the great catalyst and in the more recent poems where Thanatos rather than Eros presides, there's no doubting the author's sense of loss. (p. 66)

Reading these poems chronologically one can follow the younger Amis improbably trying to fit his early 'social' lyrics to Empson's enticing but austere tunes—**"Lessons," "Masters,"** etc—and, equally improbably, getting away with it! Then he throws in his lot with the ideas of the movement—**"Wrong Words," "Against Romanticism,"**—although his own language, even at this time, is straining to be more honestly colloquial than most of his academic contemporaries. It's in such poems as **"A Bookshop Idyll," "They Only Move," "A Note on Wyatt,"** and **"A Song of Experience,"** that his talent, for me, finds its maturity. The success of these poems perhaps ties in with his development as a novelist. One can sense that the pressure is suddenly off him to be 'a poet'. The inverted 'humility' and intellectual exclusiveness of some of the movement poets often resulted in its own form of hubris. But with Amis one always warms to the personality. His 'morality' is genuine. He wants to understand things for *himself*. He isn't preaching. Well, perhaps a little in a poem such as **"Masters,"** but the moral proverbs with which he peppers the page have a charm of their own. . . . It's with his elbow on the bar and his lips to one's ear that Amis comes into his own. Paradoxically, his growing use of the lighter mode allows his personality to express itself with greater depth. In **"A Song of Experience,"** for example, all the best elements of an Amis poem come together. It's a fine poem and worth some discussion. The social scene is aptly set: 'A quiet start: the tavern, our small party', and the central figure of 'the stranger' who joins them, has all the mystery of a Flying Dutchman, Ancient Mariner, or Wandering Jew, without any of these mythological figures being mentioned. In fact, 'the stranger' turns out to be a commercial traveller with tales of his sexual conquests. (pp. 66-7)

The poem suddenly sharpens when we learn that the stranger seeks his sexual 'grail' with all the passion of a religious fanatic. He really 'loves' and is prepared to pay the price for his obsession, ie, sacrificing safety, domesticity, conventional morality etc. Even the suffering he causes others is not done out of deliberate cruelty but blind commitment. It's the Robert Burns syndrome. Amis is always fascinated by the moral issues that underline such sexual tug-of-wars.

Later poems—**"Their Oxford,"** **"A Reunion"**—use extended narrative to look back at a world beyond recall. The present is always seen through a personalized past. The poems are still witty and vastly entertaining but the 'now' is increasingly co-cooned in personal nostalgias. . . . [This collection] must be currently one of the best reads around. (pp. 67-8)

> *Peter Bland, "Elbow on the Bar," in* London Magazine, *n.s. Vol. 20, No. 10, January, 1981, pp. 66-8.*

IAN STEWART

In the introduction to his *Collected Short Stories* Kingsley Amis describes the pieces as "chips from a novelist's work-bench", even as "telescoped novels". . . . Whatever his prejudices or preconceptions the reader will, I think, find some of these "chips", the science fiction and time-travel pieces among them, insubstantial and ineffective. A previously unpublished story, **"To See the Sun"**, is an accomplished pastiche of the Dracula legend, but those that give most satisfaction and most scope to the distinctive Amis qualities are **"My Enemy's Enemy"**, **"Court of Inquiry"**, **"I Spy Strangers"** and **"Moral Fibre"**. The first three of these are telling studies of class antagonism and vindictiveness among officers of a Signals regiment in Belgium and Germany towards the end of the last war, **"Court of Inquiry"** displaying the author's sure touch in putting farce at the service of his derisive intentions. The complacency, pretensions and insensitivity of social workers get a characteristically rude but entertaining knock in **"Moral Fibre"**.

> *Ian Stewart, in a review of "Collected Short Stories," in* The Illustrated London News, *Vol. 269, No. 6992, March, 1981, p. 58.*

ALAN BROWNJOHN

Kingsley Amis's *Collected Short Stories* brings together the services stories from *My Enemy's Enemy,* three other "straightforward" stories, including the entertaining **"Dear Illusion"**, with the fairly frequent Kingsley Amis motif of a false impression gained and later corrected; several sci-fi pieces; and one or two diverting pastiches. The collection doesn't have to have a unity, or a development, and it hasn't got either. Read all at once, which is the wrong way to do it, the stories leave a hit-and-miss impression. The hits are **"All the Blood Within Me"**, [**"Too Much Trouble"**], and **"The Darkwater Hall Mystery"**]. . . . They make it seem sad that Amis's stories have not visited him more regularly, more chips fallen "from the novelist's work-bench." Strangely, though, many of them do not have the narrative inevitability and pace of the novels, even within the shorter compass; as if he had always found the marathon easier to cope with than the one hundred yards. (p. 91)

> *Alan Brownjohn, "Breaking the Rules," in* Encounter, *Vol. LVI, No. 5, May, 1981, pp. 86-91.**

RUSSELL DAVIES

It's been apparent for some time (say, about 30 years) that Kingsley Amis goes through life in the expectation of disgust. His greatest pleasure is to come across something which, or

someone who, for even the briefest time, defeats that expectation by being, you know, tolerable. . . .

So perhaps we should not be too shocked to find that the list of things from which nothing but woe can be expected—modernists, foreigners, teetotallers, book reviewers and the like—has now been joined by women. Not only joined, but topped. Women go straight to Number One. They are, after all, inescapable and, according to *Stanley and the Women,* they are all mad. . . .

[Stanley Duke] is a Fleet Street advertising manager, married for the second time. First wife: an actress, Nowell ('somebody had been plain bleeding ignorant' is Stanley's explanation of the spelling). Second wife: Susan, a writer. One son, by Nowell, name of Steve: a mad person, or so it proves as the novel gets under way. A loud crash, as of a heavy glass ashtray breaking and entering a television screen, signals that Steve is not merely sulking. Something Is Up.

It would have been a different story, or no story at all, if the psychiatrist assigned to Steve at St Kevin's (*sic*) had been a man. No such, speaking from Stanley's viewpoint, luck. Dr Trish Collings is not only a woman, but apparently determined to prove it to Stanley's dissatisfaction. She is an exponent of fashionable psycho-speak; a keen jumper to the conclusion that it's probably all Daddy's fault; and, disconcertingly, a physical presence not utterly out of the question where a spot of unprofessional conduct might be concerned. At least, there are flickers of a fancy for Stanley on her side. Stan's position is roughly summed up by the phrase 'Still, they were breasts', a summary which slips out of him in a moment of generosity. (p. 23)

[The] complexities of the book cluster around the wives. It is no secret that Amis himself has undergone some of the same domestic turbulences that beset Stanley, and the authorial voice is touchingly close to the narrative surface, I imagine, in Stanley's plaintive observation: 'Stopping being married to someone is an incredibly violent thing to happen to you, not easy to take in completely, ever.' But in Nowell's case, and perhaps to Stanley's surprise, a small upward revaluation takes place. 'I miss you,' he finally finds himself saying, 'Every day.' The feeling comes over strongly that this kind of thing takes a lot of saying.

With Susan I am less happy. Her character is not only misleading, which, in Stanley's estimation, would be no more than par for the course; it is warped to fit the story. That we should not take Susan at face value is an idea cunningly planted by Amis right at the start, where an objective account of one of her dinner parties has us believing that the whole novel is going to be a third-person narrative. Two pages later, in an unusual technical coup, she is revealed as the narrator's wife.

This successfully suggests that Susan may be more formidable than she looks, an effect backed up by *(a)* a glimpse of her dreadful titled mother, and *(b)* by the opinion of Lindsey, Stanley's Fleet Street confidante, that 'according to me she's slightly mad, you know.' But the evidence for this comes too late. Susan, for the most part, is astoundingly agreeable, not only backing Stan up against Dr Collings's accusations but doing it on Stanley's own terms: 'You know what women are like.' (Have women *ever* been known to say these words—let alone in 1984, and to *Stanley*?) So, when we are asked to believe that at the height of Steve's paranoid mania Susan would, or could, go so far as to do physical injury to herself in order to reassume the limelight, it feels too much. Even her walking out on Stanley takes more accepting than he has prepared us for—it's as though either he, or Amis, were punishing Susan for being comparatively unimplicated in the origins of Steve's decline.

But the tenor of Stan's saloon-bar existentialism remains constant, and it carries us through. Closing the book (thankful as ever for so many laughs, by the way) we are left with a need to pronounce sentence, or at least a diagnosis, on our hero. Much of what he says is excused by a pain which the incidental hilarities of his intolerant career do not disguise. He feels people *need* to be married, but look what happens when they are. Stan excuses himself, though, much too easily. To explain his racism, or his exaggerated awe of doctors, he pleads conditioning . . . but seems unprepared to allow that he is a large, perhaps the largest, component in the conditioning of the luckless Steve. . . . He shifts the blame to women in ways he scarcely notices ('. . . she had boarded him out with friends more than she should have', and so on—what about Stan's *own* responsibility for this policy?); and it ought perhaps to worry him more that Lindsey, his only solace (apart from drink), is so plainly an honorary chap.

In fact, one disagrees with a good deal of what Stanley says, does and stands for. Yet he is, well, strikingly unrepulsive. And I do have my wife's permission to say so. (pp. 23-4)

Russell Davies, "'Amis Has Undergone Some of the Same Domestic Turbulences as His Hero'," in The Listener, *Vol. 111, No. 2859, May 24, 1984, pp. 23-4.*

MARILYN BUTLER

[In *Stanley and the Women,* Amis] has created a world in which only men appear to communicate with one another, and their favourite topic is their dislike of women. . . .

The title proclaims another skirmish in the sex war, and an unprepossessing jacket reinforces this theme: an unnaturally small, weakly-looking male, the hero, Stanley Duke, is threatened by a half-circle of four towering women. The blurb beckons to women to read, in order to be outraged: 'it is not a book that is likely to win many prizes for fairness or fashionable social attitudes.' It is certainly not a book that is likely to win many prizes for accurate representation of itself. After the coat-trailing comes a sensitive, thoughtful and open-minded novel. What can be discerned of social philosophy seems humane, nondoctrinaire, neither radical nor Thatcherite, but clearly preferring state intervention to the-devil-take-the-hindmost. On this showing, the worst that can be said of Amis's disposition towards his women readers is that he mischievously hopes to make fools of them, by showing them in advance how to read him superficially.

It would have to be a superficial reading that perceived this novel as an anti-feminist tract. A good feminist book, according to one current dictum, is a book that inverts the feminine stereotype: instead of depicting women as passive and subordinate, as in current society and in literature they generally are, a feminist book depicts them as authoritative, so that it presents women with wholesome models to follow, and men with objects of chastening respect, or terror. Stanley, whose surname Duke recalls notions of status and of a male hierarchy, spends the novel lamenting his lot as the perennial victim of women who are self-centred, bossy, exploitative and vengeful. Amis's subject is not man's objective hold on power in our

times, but his morale; tougher-minded women readers are going to feel gratified rather than insulted by Stanley's witness, because he is delightfully demoralised. A somewhat less polemic definition of a feminist book is one that exposes the formative influence of the arbitrary concept of gender on our thinking. Relevantly again, Stanley spends the novel contrasting the characteristics of women with those of men—who to him represent the human norm—for the purpose of getting women declared constitutionally, generically mad. This must be one of the most persuasive accounts in fiction of a mind imprisoned in received categories, a condition so impenetrable to evidence and common sense that it might itself be labelled delusory, except that much of the population shares it. . . .

At first sight, *Stanley and the Women* seems to be, despite the title, less about gender than about madness. The story begins when Steve, Stanley's 19-year-old son by a previous marriage, arrives at his father's new marital home in a state which a layman like Stanley simply describes as mad. On one level the plot unfolds as a tightly written and acutely observed study of Steve's advancing disorder and of its effect upon Stanley, his first wife Nowell, his current wife Susan, their relationships and their relations. As well as domestic drama, the topic gives scope for a satire of that classic kind which anatomises some current intellectual folly—in this case, competing theories about madness. . . .

Amis stirs things up by making Stanley, the narrator, a bigot of the most unabashed kind. He announces early in the book that women are mad, using his first wife Nowell as an instance. . . . He is given to random asides against the rich Jew-boys down the road. Though he feels for Steve, and feels guilty about him, he despises his son's friends, his clothes, his language, his pursuits and his mental equipment. 'Poor old Steve of course belonged to one of the generations which had never been taught anything about anything.' What Stanley does like includes drink, casual encounters with women, the police, and above all his powerful car, an Apfelsine FK3, with which he has a relationship passing the love of women. At the beginning you can imagine that Amis likes Stanley, but it soon becomes hard to believe that he could ever be caught confessing the 'secret admiration' Mailer has owned to feeling for his sadistic Sergeant Croft in *The Naked and the Dead.* In fact, Amis maintains his distance from the petty chauvinist Stanley more unmistakably than he did from the sexual separatist Jake, so that what Stanley says and what the book says must be two very different things. (p. 7)

In practice, Amis upholds a vein of criticism primarily associated with feminists, of the male and 'orthodox' habit of so structuring the world that male comes out superior to female, sane to mad, and who gets into which category is left to the gerrymandering of men themselves. The messages conveyed by the packaging, that the book is stupid, old-fashioned, illiberal and likely to displease women, are nonsense, the very reverse of the novel's actual messages—unless the 'fashionable social attitudes' which it is alleged not to have are some of the current conservative ones. It may be silly to wonder why Amis or his publisher chose to present the book this way, if it was only in order to sell more copies off station bookstalls. But there could be another reason, if the 'labelling' and 'fashionable attitudes' that rile Amis are really literary. Could he be tilting in advance at some of his critics?

Some academics are going to call the novel old-fashioned, not because of its subject-matter or its attitudes, but because of its format. Amis belongs to what is perhaps the dominant school of ambitious novels in England since about 1930, the school of Waugh, a type of intellectual comedy with a naturalistic veneer and a more or less covert philosophic dimension. The world represented in such novels has to correspond to an observable real-life community, inhabited by articulate and generally professional people. . . . The more recent campus novels have allowed more serious, 'shop' conversations into their dialogues than ever *Lucky Jim* did, but then *Stanley and the Women* does too: it's not the university setting but a general taste for intellectual controversy that seems to be raising the comic tone. . . .

It must be quite hard for an intellectual novelist like Amis to shrug off those literary academics who deny him the status appropriate to his talents because he is writing for the wrong market. Academics have numbers, organisation, a captive audience, and considerable money and influence at their command. But they are not gods, and their judgments, like everyone else's, can be interested. In one respect at least, Amis's type of novel, or a first-class example like *Stanley and the Women,* has the advantage over the self-referential and new campus novels in its capacity to criticise the intellectual community, the collusive large family in which readers as well as characters and author are included. In *Stanley and the Women,* it isn't only the male who is closely and sometimes humiliatingly scrutinised: medical professionalism, institutionalised intellectuality, proves as mad and riven as the common-or-garden North London household. . . .

As the judgment of good new novels passes more and more to professionals in universities, the criteria become technically more refined, while the intellectual and ethical range looked for may actually be more confined. If Amis's pose of anti-intellectualism is a protest against that creeping progress, that move to standardise what we call serious, it's worth attending to. (p. 8)

> Marilyn Butler, "Women and the Novel," in London Review of Books, *Vol. 6, No. 10, June 7 to June 20, 1984, pp. 7-8.*

JAMES LASDUN

Stanley and the Women is alarmingly enjoyable. It's like a perfect crime: you know something reprehensible has been done, you know who the villain is, but he has an answer or alibi for every piece of evidence you offer. You find yourself admiring him for his sheer professionalism. The reprehensible something is the book's more or less unqualified conclusion that the behaviour of women is worse than that of the clinically insane. Amis arrives there by way of an extremely good, at times harrowing, novel about the effect of a son's crack-up on his father, mother, and stepmother.

Stanley, the father, is a down-to earth Fleet Street advertising manager currently married to Susan, a deputy literary editor whom he appears to love dearly. He narrates the novel in a genial, saloon-bar idiom that positively drips with common sense, unpretentiousness, and a sincere willingness to be proved wrong in any reservations its speaker might have about women, Jews, artists, homosexuals, etc. It is a measure of Amis's great skill in handling this idiom that he is able to use it, without ever lapsing into anything more refined, to express a range of moods and subjects that include discussions about madness in literature, knockabout comedy of drunkenness, media-world satire, schizophrenic behaviour, and the subtlest of nuances in a domestic conversation. A comparable achievement would be rewriting a philosophical tract in Pidgin English. (pp. 49-50)

So it goes for 216 pages; quite a feat of self-suppression on Amis's part. But on page 217 he snaps; or rather, he snaps Susan, turning her from a model of sanity into a monster; she stabs herself in the arm, claims that the deranged son did it, then, thinking Stanley suspects her ruse, abuses him grotesquely and walks out on him—all this because she is jealous of the attention the son is getting. A history of such outbursts is duly provided in the remaining thirty pages, but it does not succeed in making Susan's violent volte-face remotely plausible (which isn't to say that it fails to be dramatically engaging—it most certainly is).

The effect is retroactive: no longer counterpointed by Susan, the selfishness and stupidity of Nowell and Trish Collings, so vividly conveyed in the previous pages, expands into a characteristic of Womankind, coercing the reader into a particularly distasteful sympathy with the male chorus of unbridled misogyny that concludes the book.

It's a trick, albeit a very clever one, and while it provides Amis with a context in which he can air some deeply unpleasant views with apparent impunity, it does so at the cost of the book's integrity. I was left feeling that Amis wanted a good deal more provocation than his story would have generated naturally. To that end he distorted the character of Susan; it says something for the inherent judiciousness of the novel form that this distortion is so glaringly visible. Among those unpleasant views is that of Stanley's pal Cliff, who ends up as an apologist for wife-battering: "'Just goes to show what an easy lot English husbands are, only one in four of them bashing his wife.'" (p. 50)

> James Lasdun, "The Fictions of Experience," in Encounter, *Vol. LXIII, No. 3, September-October, 1984, pp. 47-51.**

SUSAN FROMBERG SCHAEFFER

[In *Stanley and the Women,* Stanley] wants to know *why* women are so terrible. Women, according to Stanley, are extremely dangerous creatures dedicated to screwing men up and "attention getting." In fact, they may all be collectively insane. Whether they are or not is the question that animates Mr. Amis's book. . . . It is not so much that his narrator is uncontrollably angry at women. He is in a rage against all creation and its creator, that idiot who made the mistake of creating only two sexes, each utterly dependent on and absolutely incompatible with the other.

Because the entire natural order seems to be the target of Stanley's rage, I would not call *Stanley and the Women* a fundamentally misogynist work. It is a *misanthropic* work in which Mr. Amis attacks almost everything in sight: the young (their ways are, according to him, as incomprehensible as the world of "medieval Patagonia"), psychoanalysts of all types (whenever he mentions an analyst, the word quack is never more than three syntactical units away), liberals who believe the police ought to maintain law and order, actresses, editors of newspapers, modern education (the lack of) and mental hospitals (the buildings are dubbed "Rorschach House" or "Ebbinghaus House"). This is only a partial listing. . . .

Stanley and the Women is an ingeniously contrived book. It is divided into four sections: "Onset," "Progress," "Relapse" and "Prognosis," all terms that ostensibly refer to the stages in son Steve's acute paranoid schizophrenia, but which also refer to the progress of Susan's mental disorder, as well as the progress of Stanley's disillusionment with women, especially Susan. Steve is, however, a schizophrenic who might have been ordered from a waxworks, nothing but a catalyst. He ought to be able to command our sympathy, but as a cartoon cannot. He is present to show how people react to him. He is present to show that, crazy as he is, women are even crazier. (p. 9)

Mr. Amis has often been castigated for his anti-feminist views. How fair is it to identify the author with his protagonist? No more fair than it would be to identify Vladimir Nabokov with Humbert Humbert, the child molester of *Lolita*. Moreover, there are hints throughout this work that Stanley's reactions are meant to be viewed as extreme. At various points, he is referred to as "Mr. Joke." Mr. Amis is, therefore, either playing devil's advocate or has come to his conclusions (as he says of the mad child, Steve), "at the sacrifice of all the common sense and humour in the world." The reader should begin to suspect that there is something not entirely reliable about a man who cannot poke out his nose without a madwoman biting it off. Stanley's former wife, a monster of egotism, and his second wife, another monster of the same breed, are as nothing compared to the demented psychiatrist who treats Steve in the hospital, tracks Stanley down in his office, pretends she is someone else, then interviews him in a pub and finally threatens to release Steve simply because the boy's father has not found her sexually attractive.

Men do most of the talking in this book, unhappy men, and naturally they sympathize with and agree with one another. But are they meant to be sane? One of them mimics a constant state of drunkenness to avoid fighting with his wife. Another refuses to consort with women more than is absolutely necessary because he cannot bear to part with money. There is enough material here for a volume entitled *Susan and the Men*.

But overwhelming textual evidence does support certain conclusions about the author himself. From *Lucky Jim* to *Stanley and the Women*, most of Mr. Amis's protagonists have shown an alarming fear of other humans, whom they seem to regard as bombs that, if not defused, are likely to blow them up at any minute. . . . Their view of the world is mildly—and often not so mildly—paranoid. Stanley walks into a room, catches a glimpse of his mother-in-law, and thinks how much she looks like Ingrid Bergman "interrupted in a bit of spying." . . . *Stanley* suffers, as the abominable female psychiatrist says his son suffers, from "an appalling fear of being hurt." And in *Stanley and the Women,* as in his other books, Mr. Amis's protagonist is afflicted with a fear of what women will do to him. . . . It is this fear that in turn generates a paranoia (comically described) the protagonist and the author seem to share.

Those who are unhappy to see women attacked in print *ever*— and I am not one of those people . . .—will get their revenge by reading *Stanley and the Women* very carefully. Although everywhere and always Mr. Amis expresses his contempt for analysts, those "quacks," what do Stanley and his cohorts decide (albeit drunkenly) motivates all women? A desire to be desired. A thirst for revenge against men who refuse to desire them. An irrational insistence that they are superior because their characters are "based on a gigantic sense of insecurity." But what has he, after so much digging, come up with this time? Nothing but Freud's theory of penis envy—the castration complex. To go to so much trouble only to provide further evidence for the theories of one's bête noire is revenge enough. Apparently, there is a wild, Amislike justice in the world.

Finally, a book must be judged by what it sets out to do. *Stanley and the Women* sets out to be a comic *and* serious exploration of the trouble between men and women. In the end it is neither comic nor truly serious. It suffers from long stretches of tedium, an almost neurotic repetitiveness and a certain straining for effect. It is not, for the most part, interesting. We find vitriol where we would like to find intelligence or truth. Many of its characters—most noticeably Steve—never become more than caricatures. The intricate scheme of the book, Mr. Amis's commendable willingness to say whatever he thinks, *ought* to have made this a better book than it is. *Stanley and the Women* is finally a courageous but failed attempt, a book that shows that Mr. Amis has perhaps treated his theme once too often, or prematurely, before having time to expand upon what he has already said so well. This is, however, a book with a vision, and it is an extremely sad one. Theoreticians of comedy claim sadness is at the heart of all humor. It is the very heart and soul of this seriously flawed and disappointing book. (pp. 9, 11)

Susan Fromberg Schaeffer, "Only Two Sexes, Both Crazy," in The New York Times Book Review, *September 22, 1985, pp. 9, 11.*

Jean (Marie Lucien Pierre) Anouilh

1910-

French dramatist, editor, translator, short story writer, and scriptwriter.

One of France's foremost modern dramatists, Anouilh has written over forty plays in a wide variety of modes. Central to his work is a skeptical, often bitter view of the human condition. According to Joseph Chiari, Anouilh's pessimism results from "the revolt of a sensitive being appalled and wounded by the cruelty of life and expressing man's despair at never being able to know his true self." Discovering and remaining true to one's self is the theme that consistently resurfaces in Anouilh's work. His protagonists typically strive to maintain their integrity in a world of compromise and corruption; however, to be successful often necessitates existing in a fantasy world or dying for one's convictions. Anouilh's work reflects the classical theater of Molière in its comic portrayal of human folly and misery and the experimental theater of Luigi Pirandello in its overt use of theatrical devices to explore the nature of reality and illusion. Anouilh writes in such varied dramatic forms as tragedy, farce, and romance. He has rejected these classifications, however, and instead categorizes his plays as follows: *pièces noires* (black plays), *nouvelles pièces noires* (new black plays), *pièces roses* (rosy plays), *pièces brillantes* (brilliant plays), *pièces grinçantes* (grating plays), *pièces costumees* (costume plays), and *pièces baroques* (baroque plays).

Anouilh's early plays reflect the influence of Jean Giraudoux, whose stylized drama dominated the post-World War I French theater. Like Giraudoux, Anouilh approaches drama as a means of expressing a particular philosophy rather than as an exploration of character. Anouilh's earliest plays were produced during the 1930s and generally fall under the categories of *pièces noires* and *pièces roses*. As their titles suggest, the former plays are dark in tone and explore evil and deception, while the latter include fantastical elements and convey a lighthearted mood. Among the major conflicts Anouilh addresses in both groups are those between wealth and poverty and the burden of the past as it relates to the present. In two of the *pièces noires*, for example, the protagonists attempt to deny their pasts. In *Le voyageur sans bagage* (1937; *Traveler without Luggage*), an amnesia victim escapes his previous identity as a cruel, wealthy man by claiming a young orphan as his kin, while in *La sauvage* (1938; *Restless Heart*), a young heroine realizes that she cannot be free of her base, poverty-stricken background and runs away as she is about to be married to her upper-class suitor. In *La bal des voleurs* (1938; *Thieves' Carnival*), one of Anouilh's *pièces roses,* a band of thieves misrepresent themselves as noblemen to an aristocratic woman, who allows the deception to continue for her amusement. Anouilh furthers the illusion and explores the theme of appearance versus reality by setting later scenes at a masked ball. As the play concludes, the thieves must assume their true identities when the woman finds that her pearls are missing and calls a halt to the charade.

Beginning in the 1940s, Anouilh wrote a number of plays that adapt Greek myth to modern settings and are classified as *pièces noires*. These works include *Eurydice* (1941; *Legend of Lovers*), *Antigone* (1944), and *Médée* (1953; *Medea*). *Antigone*

was the most popular of the three and remains one of Anouilh's most respected works. Based on Sophocles's classical tragedy, the play concerns Antigone's burial of her dead brother in direct defiance of an edict issued by her uncle Creon, a statesman. By thus placing sacred law above civil law, Antigone faces a sentence of death. This play was first produced during World War II in Nazi-occupied France; many critics interpreted the conflict between Antigone and Creon as representing the conflict between the French Resistance and occupying forces. Because Anouilh created convincing arguments for both characters, some viewed Antigone's refusal to compromise as an affirmation of Resistance efforts, while others found in the rational, pragmatic speeches of Creon an indication that Anouilh favored the Nazi collaborators. Many now regard *Antigone* as an illustration of his belief that one must refuse compromise at all costs, even in the face of death. In all of Anouilh's plays based on myth, the protagonists favor death over the capitulation of their ideals.

Following World War II, Anouilh's dramas became dominated by *pièces grinçantes* and *pièces brillantes*. The *pièces grinçantes* are marked by black humor, while the *pièces brillantes* convey a less bitter tone and employ witty dialogue. In these plays, the conflict between good and evil is not as sharply defined as in Anouilh's early work. Some critics have noted that as Anouilh ages, so too do his protagonists, and their outlook on life is tempered by an acceptance of human faults. The plot of *La valse des toréadors* (1952; *The Waltz of the Toreadors*), one of Anouilh's most acclaimed works, centers on General Leon Saint-Pé and his infatuation with a woman he had danced with eighteen years earlier. The couple's love had remained unconsummated because of the general's commitment to his marriage; when the two meet again, the woman falls in love with a younger man. As is characteristic of the *pièces grinçantes,* this play has sardonic overtones, as Anouilh explores the disillusionment and pettiness that occur in the aftermath of lost love. Anouilh also uses coincidence as a dramatic device to highlight the artificiality of theatrical conventions.

Among Anouilh's later plays are *pièces costumees,* which are based on historical personages, and *pièces baroques.* When using history as a background for his drama, Anouilh draws upon figures of heroic dimension. For example, *L'alouette* (1953; *The Lark*) dramatizes the life of Joan of Arc, and *Becket, ou l'honneur de dieu* (1959; *Becket, or the Honor of God*) concerns Thomas à Becket. Both plays use spare sets and are reminiscent of *Antigone* in their focus on protagonists who remain true to their sense of honor even when confronted with death. The theatrical elements of Anouilh's work come to the forefront in his *pièces baroques.* In *Cher Antoine, ou l'amour rate* (1969; *Dear Antoine, or The Love that Failed*), the central character is a prominent playwright and the story unfolds as a play within a play, and in *Ne reveillez pas Madame* (1970), the protagonist is an actor. By stressing the artificiality of the theater, Anouilh probes the relationship between reality and illusion and works to create a dramatization of ideas rather than a representation of reality.

While Anouilh is among the most successful "boulevard" playwrights, having enjoyed many well-attended productions of his works in the Paris theater district, critics have debated his importance in contemporary drama. Some have faulted Anouilh for repetition of theme, lack of intellectualism, and for his reliance on theatricality. However, others note that Anouilh's strength as a dramatist lies in his mastery of stagecraft, which makes his work entertaining while he investigates serious themes. Lewis W. Falb comments: "Although not as intellectual as some other twentieth-century French dramatists, Anouilh is unquestionably a master playmaker, one of the most accomplished craftsmen in modern French theater—indeed, in world theater. We respond deeply to the humanity of Anouilh's writing as we are dazzled by the brilliance of its form, for his work is both a synthesis of and a contribution to the most creative elements in modern drama." Several of Anouilh's works have been adapted for film and television.

(See also *CLC,* Vols. 1, 3, 8, 13 and *Contemporary Authors,* Vols. 17-20, rev. ed.)

ANTHONY CURTIS

[In the work of Anouilh one finds] an almost complete freedom from didacticism together with a conscious delight in aesthetic and technical problems, problems not of philosophy but of art and the theatre. It is M. Anouilh who has created an appropriate modern idiom in which to write formal tragedy based on the Racinian model and using the characters of Greek mythology; it is in his work that one discovers a perception of the dramatic

significance of a clash between the worlds of fantasy and reality, and a mastery of such dramatic devices as the use of the omniscient character, who is not an integral part of the story of the play, who, like Monsieur Henri in *Eurydice,* is almost the dramatist himself, and provides both a means of manipulating events without destroying credulity and also at crucial moments a view of existence antithetical to that of the hero. One finds, too, in his plays such traditional devices as the letter, the messenger, the twins, all used with unquestionable ease and certainty.

His characters, in contrast to his range of effects, are limited to a number of types. They consist chiefly of the young rebellious hero or heroine, uncorruptible, uncompromising, poor, 'exigeant' (a favourite word); the sensual price-minded bourgeois, who has little self-respect and who is often ignoble; the embittered cynic; the man of power, who has submitted to the demands upon personal integrity, which power makes of its human instruments; and the woman, sometimes comic, sometimes tragic, who, no longer young, is still the tormented slave of passion.

To those who know M. Anouilh's work well, what is exciting and original in each new play as it appears is not the characters, for these same types are constantly recurring, nor is it even his message, for ever being shown as having more universal implications, but rather the form which the new drama takes, its conception. Throughout the *pièces roses* (those of his plays which end happily), M. Anouilh has emphasised a contrast between the purity, enchantment and transience of the ideal, imagined world with the unsatisfying permanence of present reality. In the series of *pièces noires* the isolation of the rebel from society, of the exception from the universal, of the hero from the community, has been the basic theme. . . . (pp. 32-4)

In each play hand in hand with the restatement and development of these ideas have appeared new discoveries of dramatic technique, new ways of presenting the different aspects of the conflict, of communicating more accurately, and more forcefully the truth of this division.

It was, as early as 1934, in *La Sauvage,* that M. Anouilh achieved his first real success in the theatre. In the relationship between the heroine Thérèse and her fiancé, the rich, talented Hartman, he shows how Thérèse's poverty and the squalid involuntary promiscuity of her past life create an inexorable breach between the two lovers. It forces her, in spite of herself and her deep love for Hartman, to rebel against the security, the comfort, the happiness which he offers her. . . . (pp. 34-5)

It is instructive to compare *La Sauvage* with *Eurydice* (1941). Once again the play has as its theme the story of two young lovers who become isolated from each other through the impingement upon their lives of the irredeemable events of the past. This time, however, the separation is not caused by the poverty of one and the affluence of the other. Orpheus and Eurydice belong to the same class, they are both surrounded and humiliated by the same type of parent; what isolates them is the impossibility, for Eurydice, who has let herself be violated by the blackmailer Dulac, of existing under the intolerable compulsion of trying to *be* the image which Orpheus, her lover, has in his mind. It is this, and not her real self, with which, as she tries to explain to him, she believes he is in love. . . . A shift of emphasis in the later play from what was primarily a social distinction to a moral one is paralleled in *Eurydice* by daring experiments of construction; of these both the reappearance of Eurydice after her death and the symbolical significance of some of the secondary characters are obvious; less obvious, however, is the way the final act is used as a counterpoint to the tragedy, to show what might have happened if Orpheus and Eurydice had belonged to the race of those who choose to shrug the shoulders and accept.

In *Le Rendez-vous de Senlis* (1937), one of the *pièces roses,* this concept of the purity of the imagined world and of the image of the beloved is contrasted with the sordid actuality of the real. A young man who has as his mistress the wife of his best friend suddenly falls deeply in love with a young girl of unspoiled innocence called Isabelle. The play opens in a large house at Senlis which the young man has just rented, and to which he has invited two provincial actors to be for the evening his mother and father, in addition a hired servant is to masquerade as an old family retainer. These three are to people the dream world of domestic peace and happiness which his love for Isabelle has inspired him to desire, and which he had been deluding her to believe was his environment. As soon as she arrives, however, the deception is discovered. His former mistress Barbara and her husband appear with frantic messages from his wife. Barbara and Isabelle meet and when they discuss the hero it is almost as if they are talking about two different people. Finally, he appears himself, and at the climax of the play has to choose between the world of Barbara and the purity of Isabelle. He chooses the latter.... [This decision demonstrates] one of the central ideas of M. Anouilh's theatre, the attempt of one individual to regain innocence through a self-denying devotion to the purity of another. (pp. 35-8)

In *Léocadia* (1939), a play in the same romantic genre as *Le Rendez-vous,* it is again a contrast of the real and the ideal which is portrayed. Here, however, the ideal is seen as part of the past and not of the future; it has become a tyrannical nostalgia from which in order to achieve happiness, 'le Prince', the hero, must now liberate himself.

In order to arrive at a complete comprehension of M. Anouilh's vision, the possibility of escaping to happiness through a rediscovered purity, a regained innocence and an acceptance of reality, which such plays as *Léocadia* and *Le Rendez-vous* embody, must be set beside his conception of that other race of people for whom acceptance is not possible, the passionate rebels against the compromises and deceptions of existence to whom in *Antigone* [1942] and *Medea* [1946], throughout one act of concentrated intensity, he returns to create tragedy. In the former, the play, staged in modern dress, begins at the point where Creon, representing power and authority, has commanded that the corpse of Polynices, Antigone's brother, the leader of an unsuccessful rebellion against the state, shall be left to rot without due funeral rites. Antigone defies him and, leaving the palace in the early morning, using only a child's spade, she covers over the body. Most of the play is exhausted by the long argument between Creon and Antigone. Creon tries to persuade her to abandon 'ce geste absurde'. He is prepared to give her another chance. He even confides to her that the law refusing due funeral rites to the corpse of Polynices is merely a political expedient; and he then proceeds to whittle away every possible rational motive that Antigone can have for defending her brother's honour. He is revealed to her as having been a vicious bully, who on one occasion in a fit of temper struck his father. However, despite its absurdity, she persists in her revolt, and is sentenced to death. (pp. 38-9)

Medea is something of a companion piece to *Antigone.* The conflict between passion and reason is seen in the second play with the interest centering more on personal rather than political

relations. It is, I feel, mistaken to interpret these later plays as having a direct allegorical meaning. Obviously Antigone, in one sense, symbolises resistance, and Jason the cool, rational administrator who sets to work to restore order after the calamity is over, but on a deeper level they represent that state of mind, in the one case rebellion, in the other humility, at which an individual, perceiving the imperative necessity of sacrifice, may at any time arrive.

Among modern dramatists no one has made more subtle use of the dramatic force of a passion which is seen to embrace in a conflicting relationship members of the same family than M. Anouilh. His play *Jézabel* (1932) is the most terrifying evidence of this: in Marc's relationship with his mother, his sense of sharing her guilt, which prevents him from devoting himself to Isabel, the drama is of a Strindbergian intensity. *Jézabel* is, I feel, the blackest of the *pièces noires.* (pp. 39-40)

More recently in *Roméo and Jeannette* (1945) and *Invitation au Château* (1948), M. Anouilh has shown in a conflicting relationship two sisters both of whom, in the former play, are in love with the same man; and, in the latter, two brothers who are twins and who, as they are played by the same actor, never appear on the stage at the same time. The skill with which this highly comic situation is handled, the large number of important characters, the complexity of the plot and the artistic audacity with which what purports to be a tragic ending is in a few minutes made a comic one are indications that the play is the work of a dramatist at the height of his power. Such scenes as that between Isabelle and Messerschmann, reminiscent of the scene between Creon and Antigone, where the man of power finds himself defeated by integrity, and ends by tearing up his fortune in the attempt to regain the one moment of enchantment of his life, leads one to suspect that this is one of those comedies where the happiness achieved by the characters at the end of the play is a convention, not a reality. (pp. 40-1)

> *Anthony Curtis, in his* New Developments in the French Theatre: A Critical Introduction to the Plays of Jean-Paul Sartre, Simone de Beauvoir, Albert Camus and Jean Anouilh, *The Curtain Press, 1948, 42 p.**

ROBERT CHAMPIGNY

The modern French theatre offers significant examples of a reflexive theatre, of a theatre which, more or less consciously, calls its own existence into question. The theatre thrives on possession, on the eagerness with which a "real" person transforms a *persona* into a person and expects the *persona* to justify and verify his existence. How can the theatre avoid this exploitation without destroying itself? In several plays Anouilh raises the question in an anxious, helpless manner.

Anouilh often takes pains to remind the spectator that the characters in the play are *personae,* not persons. In *Antigone,* the Prologue presents the play as a play. The characters will have to "play their part." Anouilh shows a preference for social situations in which the part has absorbed the reality: idle bourgeois, actors, strolling players. The device of the play within the play is presented in such a way that the boundary with the play itself is effaced: thus the whole fabric of the play is infected. (p. 58)

In *L'Invitation au château* and in *Léocadia,* the plot is contrived within the play. After playing Léocadia, the heroine is allowed "to be herself," but this only means playing the part written by Anouilh. The most elegant presentation of the device may be found in *Eurydice.* Vincent says to Eurydice's mother: "There is on the earth one holy, sublime thing, the union of these two beings so imperfect and so horrible"; and a few lines below: "It is I who have lived, not a contrived character created by my pride and ennui." This eulogy of love and this opposition between dream and reality are generally used by the theatre to hide its own unreality. The spectator is supposed to be taken in: how can someone who speaks about Love with a capital letter, who is able to distinguish between dream and reality, not be real? But this time, the spectator will be brutally awakened: Eurydice's mother recognizes quotations from Musset. The remarks about dream and reality occurred within a dream. When the second generation, Eurydice and Orpheus, improvise their own love duet, the spectator has been warned: what they are reciting may not be Musset, but it is most certainly Anouilh.

And this, in the last analysis, under the usual talk about love, life and death, is the plight of Anouilh's characters: whether they play "child" or "adult," "wild" or "tame," they cannot leap beyond the limits of the play, of the dream which is the stuff they are made of; whatever they do, they remain the characters of Anouilh.

Time and space are our reality: past, future and the actuality of things. It is in relation to other people that we may have to play a role, to assume the unreality of stage characters. The actuality of things is denied to the *persona.* The theatre is an "absolute place," in which things are but props. The character exists only in relation to other characters. When we read a poem or even a novel, we feel the existence of things behind the descriptions and images, behind this symbolical appropriation of reality. Not so when we watch a play.

The past gives us reality: in so far as we are, we are what we have been. The *dramatis personae* have a past only in so far as it is told, as it is projected into the other *personae.* Their past as well as their present is alienated. Thus, in *La Sauvage:* Thérèse wants to be faithful to her past, but she has to see it in the character of her father. When she wants to oppose her "reality" to that of her fiancé, she opposes her father to her fiancé's mother, she makes her father play and overplay her past. The impossibility of disposing of one's past is also exemplified by Eurydice. She succumbs to the meaning which the other characters give her past. Hence the role played by the family, in particular the parents, in Anouilh's plays. Superficially, the parents are a burden because they are always presented by Anouilh as "bad." But, beneath this conventional "badness," the parents are fundamentally bad because they are the alienated past of the *persona.* They maintain the *persona* in a possessed condition even beyond the time limits of the play.

The subject is perhaps best treated in *Le Voyageur sans bagage.* The hero is suffering from amnesia. The members of the family are eager to recognize him as a son who has disappeared. He knows that they are not mistaken, yet he refuses to recognize himself in the portrait that they have composed for him. The superficial reason, the reason within the play, is that he has changed. The fundamental reason, which calls the theatre into question, is that he cannot coincide with the *persona* into which the others have transformed his past. He refuses it. The character has refused to be himself, but the theatre was the stuff of which this "self" was made. The character has chosen inauthenticity with regard to the other characters, to the spectator. What he has chosen to escape is the nightmare of the theatre, an escape which cannot be achieved until he ceases to

be a character, until the play ends. The *malaise* which the *dénouement* has produced in certain critics is due to the unwillingness of the spectator to awake from the theatrical dream. The character escapes the grasp not only of the other characters, but also of the spectator. (pp. 58-60)

In Anouilh's *Antigone,* an uneasy romantic irony is applied to the classic myth. The Prologue tells the spectator what is going to happen. The Chorus presents the tragedy as a clean, well-oiled machine. Now the spectator cannot take the Chorus seriously as an oracle of the gods, of the *moira.* The theatrical metaphors which the Chorus uses to outline the destiny of the *personae* are more than metaphors. The god who dictates the destiny of the characters is the dramatist and the Chorus stands for Anouilh. Anouilh undermines the theatrical illusion, the sacred drug of the myth, by putting himself on the stage.

The play reveals a conflict between dramatist and *persona.* In the words of the Chorus, the dramatist tries to find a certain artistic purity in the tragic *genre.* It will be purity of inhuman necessity: "tragedy is clean." The *personae* are despoiled of their pretension to represent the spontaneity of life; they are nailed to a part, they are cogs in a machine: "Her name is Antigone and she will have to play her role to the end."

Let us turn from Anouilh to Antigone. Before the play, when she had not yet been reduced to a *persona,* her "purity" was the poetic purity of the child, that of a cosmic rather than a human being. Her first pilgrimage was neither a religious rite nor a theatrical "act"; it was a poetic game. Antigone was real and she was pure because she was dealing with things, not men. But now she has entered the unreality of the play, the anti-world of interhuman relations. As she speaks first with the nurse, then with her sister, then with the fiancé, she becomes a *persona.* She said she loved life; but the theatre has taken hold of her; in order to live as *persona,* she must die to real life.

Symbolic of this death is her second pilgrimage. This time, she does not have her toy shovel. This time, her action is not a poetic game, but a theatrical "act." She has chosen the alienation of the actress. Sophocles' Antigone was supposed to have chosen religious possession. Anouilh's Antigone apes Sophocles' Antigone, thus breaking the unwholesome spell of the sacred. (pp. 60-1)

The Chorus rejoices over Antigone's theatrical repetition of her action. She can no longer escape: "Now, she will be able to be herself," that is, since we are within the theatrical dream herself as *persona.* The Chorus has presented his view of theatrical purity: the *persona* is a cog in a machine. As for Antigone herself, her vision of theatrical purity can be but that of the "pure heroine." The play ruins these two hopes of finding purity within the theatre.

The development of the play bears no resemblance to the silent, precise working of a machine. Whether the Chorus likes it or not, a tragedy is words, words, words, rhetoric piled on rhetoric. And, at any moment, we are made to feel that Antigone could very easily escape her fate.

We are thus rejected toward the point of view of the *persona.* The fate of Antigone depends upon herself. Yet, as a tragic character, she tries to deny this responsibility. Her purity as a heroine depends on alienation. Thus, at the beginning of her discussion with Creon, she recites her Sophoclean lesson. Unfortunately, one of the guards has already likened her to an exhibitionist. And Creon correctly diagnoses a case of tragic hybris. Antigone longed to play the brilliant role of the daughter of Oedipus: "You wanted a *tête-à-tête* with destiny and death"; "Polynices was but a pretext."

Thus exposed as a *persona*, Antigone tries to return from the theatre to reality. She asserts that her action was meant for no one but for herself. She denies possession. But it is too late. The theatrical repetition has effaced what could be poetically authentic in her action. After a moment of hesitation, Antigone steps back into the role of the heroine, for fear Creon should steal the show: "I am a queen." She did not want "to be touched," but as a *persona*, she was at the mercy of the other *personae*.

"I no longer know why I die." The reasons within the play, the "noble" reasons, have been dismissed. Antigone dies because she chose to be the heroine of a tragedy. The *dénouement* is but the recognition of an already accomplished fact: to live as a *persona* is to die to "real" life. In the case of Antigone, however, extenuating circumstances could be pleaded. She played her role so badly that it became a cathartic caricature. But the Chorus had prepared his final speech. He was not to be denied; and he was probably glad to put an end to a show which had ridiculed his concept of tragedy.

The theatre of Anouilh is said to be dominated by a pessimistic outlook on life. This common judgment is valid only if the *persona* is assumed to be an adequate image of the person. It is not valid insofar as the theatre, the *persona* call themselves into question. Whatever the personal philosophy of Anouilh, if any, may be, the pessimistic color of his plays bears on the theatre, not on life, at least not on "real" life (since life can take the theatre as a model and thus become unreal, possessed).

The case is not clear-cut. Anouilh has somehow to maintain the theatrical illusion. In some of his plays, generally *pièces roses* or *brillantes,* no rupture is indicated between theatre and "real" life. The hero leaves the stage alive, which tends to confirm the illusion that the *persona* is a person. In *Le Voyageur sans bagage,* the hero rejects the theatrical past which the other characters have tried to impose on him and is supposed to find a life of innocence in the company of a little boy. The *persona* is seen as a person since the play, thanks to the little boy, suddenly appears as a nightmare from which the hero awakens. In other plays, however, Anouilh does not let his *persona* off so easily. Outside the play, the *persona* can but be dead. There is no little boy conveniently set beyond the reach of the theatrical myth.

Antigone presents these two relations of the theatre to life. There is no rupture, at the beginning of the play, between Antigone's action and the theatrical repetition. There is a break at the end: Antigone chooses to remain a *persona* and thus chooses death.

The gratuitousness of the theatrical *dénouement,* its fundamental inauthenticity are bravely presented in *L'Alouette.* The dreaming spectator was ready for a gripping *dénouement.* But the scene of St. Joan at the stake at Rouen is suddenly whisked away and the scene of the coronation at Rheims is substituted for it. This is not a passage from the theatrical dream to real life: historically, the stake at Rouen is the "true" *dénouement.* The master stroke consists in substituting as a "real" ending the dream within the dream for the dream itself. The play could give to the spectator the illusion of reality by putting an end to the play within the play. But it is the play within the play which meaningfully supplants the play.

This *dénouement* may be interpreted as an obliteration of the theatrical dream in another way. It may be interpreted as an obliteration not only of the play but of the play within the play too, as a return to the poetic game of the child Jeanne, to her vision of the coronation: the other characters are only props, the obedient creatures of the game of the child. The spectator is thus robbed of his own dream, as certain uneasy comments on the play would seem to indicate.

Anouilh is not the only dramatist who has used the theatre to expose what may be unreal and inauthentic in life. The characters of Sartre, of example, also try to escape the possession which is their lot. Sartre's intention is even clearer than Anouilh's. Yet his criticism of theatrical bad faith is not so far-reaching as Anouilh's, even though it is more deliberate. For the authenticity which Sartre sets up as an ideal is not the poetic "purity" of Anouilh. Sartre's morals are ethical, not poetic. They concern interhuman relations, in which a certain amount of theatricality is unavoidable. Sartre's morals can but aim at a compromise between the for-self and the for-others.

The romantic purity to which Anouilh alludes is more exacting. It can perhaps be found in man's relation to the world, not in man's relation to man. It is the purity of the physicist, of the craftsman, of the artist (but not of the dramatist). It requires the elimination of the other as such. In Anouilh's theatre, the theatre aspires to commit suicide.

The dramatic critic may confine himself to a technical analysis; most of the time, however, he will try to find a human meaning and he will launch into psychological and moral considerations. These questions necessarily involve a discussion of the status of the theatre with regard to life; yet the dramatic critic frequently seems to be talking in his sleep, under the spell of the theatrical dream. The concept of the catharsis has been forgotten. The alienation, the possession, the irresponsibility of the *persona* are accepted as moral values. The mask becomes a model.

A moral theatre can but be negative, critical, pessimistic, caricatural. For the theatre can successfully represent life only in so far as life is theatrical: unreal and possessed. (pp. 61-4)

*Robert Champigny, "Theatre in a Mirror: Anouilh,"
in* Yale French Studies, *No. 14, Winter, 1954-55,
pp. 57-64.*

J. CHIARI

[Anouilh] has a dramatic skill unequalled on the contemporary stage. His blend of comedy and seriousness, whimsicality and wry pathos is typically his own, and his remarkably fluent style is a perfect medium for the swift changing moods which it is meant to convey. He moves from naturalism to fantasy with grace and ease, and only O'Casey can so stab comedy with poignancy. With Anouilh, as with Giraudoux and Tennessee Williams, time always degrades and soils. Growing old is a degenerating process, children soon pass from innocence to corruption and pure love cannot live. Happiness is not of this world, and Orpheus, whether born from Cocteau, Anouilh or Tennessee Williams, can only find bliss in death. This is anything but an original attitude; it is nothing else but romantic necrophilia, and Anouilh, who handles this theme with greater success than the other two, has criss-crossed the romantic longing for death with a bitter, social satire and cynicism completely alien to the seriousness of the devotees of Werther and René, although not so remote from Byron's Don Juan.

All Anouilh's heroes are obsessed with purity and with the uncompromising attitude which it entails. Thérèse, Antigone, Joan of Arc, Becket, search for purity and say no to life and to what they call in different ways, *le sale bonheur.* Becket who leads his King to despair through jealousy and unrequited love says no to the King's pleas for reasonableness in the same way as Antigone says *no* to Creon and Joan of Arc to her judges. It is obvious that in each case, these heroes and heroines of negation have been defeated by rational arguments and in fact, say no to reason and logic. "Be logical", says the King to Becket, who replies, "No, it's not necessary, one has only to do absurdly what one has been entrusted with doing to the very end." Absurdly, obviously means without reflection and without reasoning. But the problem is that life not being a series of gratuitous acts, it is rather difficult to set about doing anything absurdly to the very end; although, of course, one may adopt an absurd attitude, which is the case with Anouilh's heroes. In that case the word absurd has a very clear meaning which has no connotations whatever with metaphysical absurdity. It simply means that life degrades and corrupts; therefore, if one wants to remain pure one can only do so by rejecting life. This rejection is absurd in the sense that it cannot be rationally justified; it is a defiance to reason, apparently based on the notion that, reason having failed, life is not worth living. In fact, such an attitude rests upon immaturity and the childish notion that since life cannot be understood, the only way to deal with it is to reject it. Becket does not quite say no because he has failed to understand life; he has not even tried, he is not interested. He was a libertine and a detached hedonist without any principles except that of doing well whatever he did, and when the King appoints him Archbishop, he decides to be the paragon of the function with which he has been entrusted; and so, forsaking the spirit for the letter, he equates the honour of man as well as the honour of God with an absolute no to any aspect of life. He becomes possessed by the game and the game is all. He is what he appears to be. He is a perfect phenomenalist and an example of Pascal's truth contained in the words: "Begin by kneeling down and praying, and faith will perhaps come." Doing whatever one does to the best of one's abilities is an act of faith which can carry with it a sense of truth which may redeem all appearances and inform all actions with true reality. Acting in such conditions ceases being a game and is the real thing, or rather is a means of reaching truth through one's own consciousness and dedication. This means that life itself is only a game or a set of appearances which can only be given reality by what one puts into them. Dramatic action reveals the place where hidden truths lie, and sometimes a character can only reveal his truth by identifying himself with a dramatis persona. Anouilh's plays abound in plays within the play and in masks, impersonations and acting. Playing the game with earnestness is a way of reaching truth and of keeping boredom at bay. The shades of Pirandello are at times hovering very close to Anouilh's theatre. (pp. 51-3)

> J. Chiari, "Drama in France," in his *Landmarks of Contemporary Drama, Herbert Jenkins, 1965, pp. 49-80.* *

B. A. LENSKI

In the *Pièces roses, Pièces brillantes* and two of the *Pièces grinçantes* (*Ardèle* and *La Valse des toréadors*), the settings, with very few exceptions, have one thing in common: they represent places far removed from the turmoil of reality. A castle is the setting for *Léocadia, L'Invitation au château* and

La Répétition; a theatre, for *Colombe;* a general's provincial home, for *Ardèle* and *La Valse des toréadors.* In *Le Bal des voleurs,* we see an old-fashioned drawing room in the villa of an extravagant old lady; in *Le Rendez-vous de Senlis,* a rococo drawing room in a house several miles outside Paris, rented to serve as a secluded spot for a lovers' meeting.

Anouilh puts his lovers in these closed-in worlds where—from *Le Bal des voleurs* to *La Valse des toréadors*—we witness their quest for happiness through love, conducted, as a rule, by the male protagonists whose female counterparts in the *Pièces roses* and *Pièces brillantes* are, without exception, young working-class girls invited into a milieu very different from their own. Isabelle in *Le Rendez-vous de Senlis,* Amanda in *Léocadia,* Isabelle in *L'Invitation au château,* Colombe in *Colombe* and Lucile in *La Répétition* all could be called *invitées au château.*

These twenty-year-old *invitées* possess unusual powers. They can relieve their partners' sorrows and longings, provide them with safe islands of escape and inspire in them hopes for a happy future. (pp. 17-18)

In the *Pièces roses,* Anouilh confronts us with more young lovers. Gustave and Juliette in *Le Bal des voleurs* are in harmony with the world and for them alone the comedy turns into success, because they have played it with all the zest of youth "and only because they were playing their youth, a thing which always succeeds. They were not even aware of the comedy". . . . By the end of the play, they leave the stage hand in hand, with a promising future lying ahead of them. In *Le Rendez-vous de Senlis,* we have an identical situation; by the end of the play, Isabelle proves strong enough to lead Georges over all the environmental hurdles toward a future full of hope.

The third hero in the *Pièces roses* who is saved by a young girl is the Prince in *Léocadia* who earlier in his life experienced three unforgettable days with Léocadia, an extravagant woman who strangled herself with a scarf, involuntarily it seems. Since then he has refused to acknowledge time's victory over those three days and lives surrounded by people who in one way or another witnessed his short-lived happiness. When street urchins run after him, jeering at his folly, the Prince finds an easy refuge in the castle garden behind the walls encircling his aunt's property. There, among those who have been hired to foster his dreams, he can forget the *others,* a luxury not granted the heroes of the *Pièces noires.* The Prince finally is saved by Amanda, the young *invitée* who is stronger than nostalgia because she is hope. She makes him forget Léocadia by becoming a new Léocadia for him, and—most likely—a source of future regrets.

Love is triumphant in the *Pièces roses,* and the pervading optimistic point of view suggests that a person can be saved by another person. Anouilh was between nineteen and twenty-nine years old when he wrote his *Pièces roses,* and if there is hope in these early plays, it is because he focuses on young lovers, whereas the aging characters, who incarnate the *noir,* are given roles of secondary importance.

When Anouilh wrote his *Pièces brillantes,* he was older, between thirty-seven and forty years old, like Héro and Tigre in *La Répétition ou L'Amour puni. L'Amour puni* could serve as an epigraph for the whole collection of *Pièces brillantes.* To be sure, the young girls "bright and clean in their little cotton dresses" reappear, but they are no longer so strong and firm as in the *Pièces roses.* Their partners have aged too and are burdened with the fatigue of life. (pp. 18-19)

In contrast to the *Pièces roses,* in which nostalgia is overcome by hope, in the *Pièces brillantes* hope is crushed and ground into nostalgia, a process that reaches its climax in the *Pièces grinçantes.*

A power stronger than love makes itself felt in the *Pièces brillantes,* one against which love is helpless: time. (pp. 19-20)

At curtain fall, the young *invitées* have been hurt, and the love seekers, having pursued a dream in vain, must content themselves with a sigh of regret or take refuge in the cult of a single moment of beauty already buried in the past. The question at the end of *Le Rendez-vous de Senlis*—How long will they be happy?—becomes at the end of *La Répétition:* How long will they be able to play the game?

In two of the *Pièces grinçantes, Ardèle* and *La Valse des toréadors,* Anouilh's love seekers have progressed further on the curve of time along which they are traveling. Anouilh now centers his plays on aging couples; the young are relegated to secondary roles. After seventeen years of marriage, General Saint-Pé is still dreaming of his "Léocadia," Mademoiselle de Sainte-Euverte, with whom he danced an unforgettable waltz seventeen years earlier at a military ball at Saumur. In all the years he has spent at the side of his hated and hateful wife, *la générale,* Saint-Pé has never stopped thinking about the young girl from the Saumur dance floor. Miraculously, after seventeen years, Mademoiselle de Sainte-Euverte arrives at the General's home, only to throw herself into the arms of Saint-Pé's young secretary Gaston. The General's dream of lasting love, confronted with its embodiment seventeen years later, crumbles to pieces, and Saint-Pé is left with the sole consolation of pinching the new maid, Pamela. As he approaches the end of his life, his dream has shrunk to the size of this gesture, and time is so precious that he cannot afford to lose a single minute on hope or regret. Time is definitely the enemy of love. The greater the intensity of love, the greater the final solitude; the more desperate the nostalgia, the heavier the fall from hope. In the end all that remains of Léocadia is a scarf; of love, in the final analysis, probably no more than pinching Pamela. "Don't think about me, ever. Don't ever think about love".... These two sentences from *Ardèle* seem to express Anouilh's final verdict at the end of his trial of love. (pp. 20-1)

In the *Pièces roses, Pièces brillantes* and two of the *Pièces grinçantes,* the value of love is weighed against the universal background of time. In the *Pièces noires* and *Nouvelles Pièces noires,* written during the same period, the value of love is examined within the much narrower perspective of an immediate environment, not as a plea for permanence, but rather as a plea for understanding. (p. 24)

In the *Pièces noires,* in contrast to the *Pièces roses* and *Pièces brillantes,* Anouilh's characters function in the midst of life's turmoil. More often than not, we are introduced into milieus where poverty is prevalent. This is true of the setting in the first act of *La Sauvage* where a bandstand occupies the better part of the stage, arranged to represent the interior of a seaside resort café. In the first act of *Eurydice,* we see a refreshment room in a provincial railway station. In the second and fourth acts of *Eurydice,* the characters are in a big, somber, dirty room in a provincial hotel; in the three acts of *Jézabel,* in the room of an impoverished young man. Even in the bourgeois home of the father of Julia, Jeannette and Lucien in *Roméo et Jeannette,* the accent is on shabbiness; the action in Acts I, II and IV of *Roméo et Jeannette* takes place in a large, badly furnished room in a sprawling, dilapidated house.

This is the type of setting in which Anouilh places his young lovers: Florent and Thérèse in *La Sauvage,* Frantz and Monime in *L'Hermine,* Marc and Jacqueline in *Jézabel,* Frédéric and Jeannette in *Roméo et Jeannette* and Orpheus and Eurydice in *Eurydice.* With the exception of Orpheus and Eurydice, who are both poor, the lovers in the *Pièces noires* belong to different social classes. One partner is rich, the other poor, and it is always the poor one who is seeking perfection in love, dreaming of finding an absolute in love, hoping to be completely understood by his partner.

The twenty-year-old working-class girl in her cheap cotton dress reappears in the *Pièces noires,* but here, from the very outset, she lacks the innocence of her counterpart in the *Pièces roses* and *Pièces brillantes.* Thérèse, Jeannette and Eurydice, all are deeply marked by their environments. At the time of their meetings with their ideal partners, these girls have already acquired burdensome pasts, filled with events which they would rather forget. But struggle as they may, with themselves and against others, Thérèse, Jeannette and Eurydice are unable to forget their memories of the past: it weighs upon the present and intensifies their search for a different way of life. Each in his own way, Marc, Frantz, Thérèse, Eurydice and Jeannette finds himself engulfed in the squalor of an environment inhabited by three distinct categories of people who constitute Anouilh's stage humanity: the mediocre race, the compromisers and the heroes. (pp. 25-6)

The most distinctive representatives of the mediocre race in the *Pièces noires,* are the parents whom Anouilh depicts as having been reduced by life to the last dregs of humanity, to one-dimensionality; mechanisms reacting to stimuli in an almost animal-like manner. Seemingly unaware of the freedom of choice, they accept without questioning whatever comes their way. They are machines for eating, drinking, belching, penny-squeezing and fornicating. An occasional infidelity and from time to time chicken Italian-style with Armagnac is all the father in *La Sauvage* asks of life. His language abounds with clichés and vulgarisms. At the table he hiccups and scratches himself, shedding dandruff into his food. His subjection to money is pathological. While a taxicab waits outside he can hardly speak: he seems umbilically tied to the taximeter; a spasm of pain runs through him whenever he senses that the fatal money machine outside is registering a new unit. (p. 27)

The mothers and fathers in the *Pièces noires* are *ugly parents.* The mother in *Jézabel* goes from one infidelity to the next, drinks heavily and begs her husband for money to prevent her latest and possibly last lover from leaving her. The fathers in *Eurydice* and *Roméo et Jeannette* cannot grasp anything going on outside their little worlds. Confronted by tragedies unfolding in spheres totally alien to them, all they can do is sit back in wonderment, puffing on cigars, uttering platitudes.

The compromisers in the *Pièces noires* are a different category of stage characters. They are clearsighted and sensitive enough to perceive the two sides of the game being played. They are an in-between species, neither mediocre nor heroic. They understand both the sordid condition of the mediocre race and the plight of the heroes. They might have been heroes themselves had they been cut out for a big role. However, they never had the courage to take the first step. So they have become the eternal arguers, philosopher-friends, advisers, intelligent wits, ironical toward themselves, often cynical and resigned. They see clearly but do not know how to, or do not dare or simply refuse to live in the light of this clarity. Such is Frantz's friend Philippe in *L'Hermine,* Florent's friend Hartman in *La Sauvage,* Jeannette's brother Lucien in *Roméo et Jeannette* and M. Henri in *Eurydice.* (p. 28)

Anouilh judges reality from the height of the ideal and inevitably, seen from high up, the world seems a very sad place to live. At the same time, in showing reality in black coloring, Anouilh places the ideal into proper perspective. (p. 29)

If the decor and angle of observation in the *Pièces noires* differs from those in the *Pièces roses, Pièces brillantes* and two of the *Pièces grinçantes,* the basic idea inherent in the plays in both these groups is the same: He who commits all his hopes and desires to Love must sooner or later dearly pay for such poor judgment. In the *Pièces roses, Pièces brillantes* and two of the *Pièces grinçantes,* Anouilh insists more on what time does to love. In the *Pièces noires* he shows to what extent love itself appears to be love's worst enemy. His heroes in these plays place love too high, as if, compelled by some masochistic urge, they want its failure. (p. 31)

The heroes in the *Pièces noires* are deaf to arguments in favor of a humble sort of happiness. They want all or nothing at all, and the lower they stand, the greater their claims on the Ideal, the louder their plea for help from the companion meant to share it. As Thérèse, Orpheus and Jeannette rebel against their environments with growing impatience, they become more demanding of their partners. To conform with their idea of the perfect couple, their partners ultimately would have to become simple extensions of the hero himself. Because Florent, Eurydice and Frédéric are *other,* products of their own pasts, fashioned by their own environments, they can never fully respond to the yearnings of Thérèse, Orpheus and Jeannette, unable to save them from their thirst for the absolute. (p. 32)

In *Antigone* and *L'Alouette,* Anouilh takes his twenty-year-old girls from mythology and history. Attracted to the exceptional, he found in Antigone and in Joan of Arc two of the clearest and most touching figures of mankind that have braved authority in the name of personal conviction. In making these two voices echo his own innermost voice, Anouilh wrote his two clearest and most touching plays. (p. 34)

In *Antigone* and *L'Alouette* a new philosophical dimension makes itself felt in Anouilh's theatre. Parallel with the deepening of philosophical content, we find a change in the plays' settings to suggest an expansion from the local to the universal. The scene shifts from the stifling bourgeois interiors, maids' rooms, cheap hotel rooms, castle drawing rooms, refreshment counters in provincial stations and parks at health resorts. Anouilh's characters have exchanged these shut-in private family worlds for the broader and more neutral settings of *Antigone* and *L'Alouette* and the historical backgrounds of the royal palaces of *Becket* and *La Foire d'Empoigne.* At the same time, Anouilh adds characters to each of his three fundamental groups: the mediocre race, the compromisers and the heroes.

In *Antigone,* mediocrity is incarnated in the guards Jonas, Boudousse, and Durand. Having delivered Antigone to Creon, the guards expect double pay and discuss rapturously the way they will spend it without their wives' knowledge. No tragedy can affect the Boudousses of this world who are here to do their work and draw their salaries. They serve the powers that be, and should the devil himself seize power one day, they will serve him faithfully. Boudousse may indeed be "immortal." Two millenia elapse between Antigone's rebellion in mythological Greece and the rebellion of Joan of Arc in medieval France, but Boudousse ironically reappears in *L'Alouette.*

In *Antigone, L'Alouette* and *Pauvre Bitos,* Anouilh applies the term *mediocre* to a much broader segment of humanity than, for example, in *La Sauvage.* Although the *ugly parents* are present in *L'Alouette,* they are not isolated units like the families in *La Sauvage* but archipelagos in the vast sea of mediocrity referred to in *Antigone* as *the crowd,* a conglomerate of everyday people, an indeterminate clay-like mass of human flesh. The characteristics of the crowd are extreme opportunism, short memory and an acute need to turn in the direction in which the wind is blowing. (pp. 35-6)

Without exception, all the compromisers in Anouilh's theatre regard ideals as children's diseases which must be overcome early in life, like measles or smallpox. Life's veterans in Anouilh's plays watch the awkward heroes with amusement, tenderness and chagrin, referring to them as *mon pĕtit* or *mon enfant.* From the heights of their experience they repeat that life is not what the heroes playing with knives, pistols, shovels or banners think it is. Creon urges Antigone to get plump, marry and have children. With babies crying in the house, according to the Inquisitor in *L'Alouette,* there will be no danger of Joan's hearing other voices, particularly those likely to cause disturbance to the state and church. (p. 37)

In *Antigone,* Anouilh glorifies the childhood years, contrasting their purity and innocence with the compromises of age. Ideally, Antigone would like for childhood to go on indefinitely. Beyond childhood, she finds the certitude she demands of life only in total identification with the cause she has chosen to defend: the burial of her brother's uncovered body. In her rebellion, Antigone prolongs her childhood; in death, she crowns it with an aura of eternity.

A child's weapon stands out in the play as a touching symbol of the heroine's rebellion; to cover her brother's body with earth, Antigone uses the same shovel which she used when she was a little girl building sand castles on the beach. Another object that is suggestive of a child's universe is the paper flower Polynices once gave to her. She has kept it like a sacred relic, and on the morning of her fatal decision she sought in its sight the necessary courage to leave her room and go bury the uninterred body.

In *L'Alouette,* Anouilh likewise exalts childhood and early youth. Joan, the "Christian Antigone," wants the story of her life to begin with a scene in her father's house, when she was still a little girl, at the time she was tending sheep in the fields, when the Voices addressed her for the first time.

Both Joan and Antigone have sudden revelations concerning duties to be performed. Antigone must bury the uninterred body of Polynices which lies exposed to vultures; Joan must save the Kingdom of France from the exposure to the abuse of the English soldiers. Their heroic acts having been accomplished, both are being judged as enemies of the established order. They express identical views on courage, have the same horror of old age and, at about the same stage in the development of the two plays, experience a moment of doubt. Antigone agrees to repudiate her cause after Creon has shown her that Polynices was far from the ideal brother she thought he was. Joan signs the act of renunciation when she realizes that all her friends have deserted her. Ultimately, both heroines withdraw their renunciations and reaffirm their rebellions. They refuse to accept the trite everyday happiness described by Creon and Warwick as the only possible way of life.

The endings of both *Antigone* and *L'Alouette* are ironical as in both cases the stage is occupied by representatives of the mediocre race. In *Antigone* the last image seen by the spectator is that of the guards playing cards. The last words in *L'Alouette* are spoken by Joan's father, who used to break sticks on his daughter's back to teach her to be reasonable and who appears just before curtain fall to claim a share of Joan's posthumous glory for himself.

Antigone and Joan remain Anouilh's purest and most cherished heroines, in whom he glorifies intuition at the expense of reason and scientific investigation. (pp. 41-2)

After *Antigone* and *L'Alouette*, *Becket* provided Anouilh with a new opportunity to exalt a person chosen for the fulfillment of a mission. In four acts and twenty-seven tableaux, Anouilh carries us through sixteen years of Becket's life, from the time that Becket became Henry's Chancellor at the age of thirty-six to the day of his murder in the cathedral at the age of fifty-two.

From the moment the curtain rises, Becket behaves like a man who is familiar with the extent of nature's and man's indifference toward man. For him, trees, flowers and blades of grass have long since lost the luster they have for Antigone and Joan at the outset of their rebellions. Becket is a person who has already experienced the moment of truth which, as Camus points out in *Le Mythe de Sisyphe*, is likely to steal into life at about the age of thirty, bringing with it the revelation of the absurd.

To counteract the absurd, Becket identifies with his role. He is willing to play whatever part he is given and to play it as best he can. . . . As the king's companion in pleasure, he applies himself to his task so well that he succeeds in outwenching the king himself, who is fifteen years his junior. As Chancellor of England, he serves the state with utmost zeal. . . . And when the king finally makes him Archbishop of Canterbury he once again proves himself a most faithful servant, not the king's, however, but God's.

Anouilh traces Becket's evolution through his various roles. All the time—while brilliantly playing the role of Henry's companion and counselor, while saying the right words and making the proper gestures to conform to the political expedients of the moment—deep within himself, he preserves a firm sense of honor. In the absence of a noble cause with which to identify, Becket is obliged to improvise his honor for many years. And he would have never discovered it had not the role of archbishop suddenly been entrusted to him. Made into God's servant, Becket's honor becomes identical with the honor of God.

Becket is a more complex character than Antigone and Joan who play their roles with youthful fervor, feeling intuitively that somewhere, somehow they are right in doing what they do. More logical, Becket controls his feelings and does not permit himself the moments of weakness which make Joan and Antigone temporarily waver in their causes. Antigone and Joan, who die young, are spared the debasing effects of life. . . . To Antigone, the bitter truth about Polynices comes as a revelation, just as Joan is stunned to learn that her best friends have forsaken her. Having lived longer, Becket knows about the Polyniceses of this world. In him, Antigone's determination to fight for an ideal is combined with Creon's rich experience of life.

Like the ending of *L'Alouette*, the ending of *Becket* barely conceals bitter irony. The king, who has had Becket murdered, entrusts the inquiry into his murder to none other than one of Becket's assassins, and, moreover, forced to act in just that way for reasons of political expediency, he hastens to acknowledge publicly his total solidarity with his dead friend's views, vying before the Saxon crowd for a share in Becket's posthumous glory.

Becket, a "rebel at forty," represents Anouilh's last attempt to depict metaphysical rebellion in all its vainglorious splendor. (pp. 43-5)

Anouilh's dramatic opus reflects an imposing scope of vision and diversity of tone. Anouilh has the comical verve of Molière and the elegance of Marivaux, the skill and light touch of a boulevard entertainer and the intellectual power of a popular philosopher. Critics have compared him to Sardou, Guitry, Labiche, Salacrou, Giraudoux and Shakespeare. . . . Through his modern versions of ancient myths in *Antigone*, *Eurydice*, *Médée* and *Tu étais si gentil quand tu étais petit*, Anouilh is an heir to Aeschylus, Euripides and Sophocles. For both his intellectual content and his expression, Anouilh is an heir to the moralist tradition in French literature, an heir to Montaigne, Pascal, La Rochefoucauld, La Bruyère, Vauvenargues and Chamfort.

Antigone, L'Alouette, Becket, Pauvre Bitos, L'Hurluberlu, La Foire d'Empoigne and *Les Poissons rouges* best represent a moral, political and, to a certain extent, philosophical theatre in Anouilh's opus. However, the concern with morality, politics and philosophy in these plays is always subdued to the primary concern of theatricality. By allying the sublime and the grotesque, Anouilh skillfully avoids the solemnity and the boredom usually associated with the theatre of ideas. In *Le Songe du critique*, he voices his dislike for Berthold Brecht and all the so-called committed theatre, considering it, on the whole, very boring, reminding those who solemnly preach commitment of the lesson they could learn from Molière and, implicitly, from Anouilh himself: that despite everything, man can always rise above his wretched condition through laughter and defiance. From *Humulus le muet* to *Le Directeur de l'Opéra*, mixing laughter and tears, Anouilh creates an entire theatrical universe based upon this essential belief.

What are the chances that this universe will survive in the years to come? (pp. 73-4)

By the end of the fifties Anouilh was well aware that Beckett and Ionesco were capable of crystallizing and conveying the poetry of the stage more effectively than Giraudoux twenty or thirty years earlier. Like Giraudoux's theatre, the theatre of Anouilh is predominantly auditive and cerebral, its poetry generated almost exclusively through language, which in turn serves certain attitudes and myths dear to his heart. In comparison with the stage of Beckett in *En Attendant Godot* and Ionesco in *Les Chaises*, Anouilh's stage falls short when it comes to language incorporated in objects and gestures. But it would be out of place to hold against Anouilh the fact that he belongs to one literary tradition and not to another one, to reproach him for not writing the kind of plays that with all that made up his childhood, youth and mature years he could never have written. . . . Still, the avant-garde compelled Anouilh to assert with added conviction his role of provider of entertainment— light as in *Le Bal des voleurs* or more serious as when in plays like *Antigone* and *L'Alouette* he ventures into boulevard metaphysics. Often Anouilh exaggerates when claiming to be no more than a skillful manufacturer of solid theatrical merchandise geared to appeal to the market, but it is true that within these limits he can withstand any criticism whatsoever from whatever side it may come.

For thirty years, year after year, Anouilh has been peopling the stage with one René after another, each in his own way craving for or lamenting the loss of his Amélie and each reprimanded for his excessive romantic ambitions by an argumentative Father Souel. For thirty years, through bedroom as well as metaphysical farces, Anouilh has been providing us with his orchestration of the eternal debate between the body and the soul. The question of whether the philosopher is going to outlive the entertainer or the entertainer the philosopher does not seem very relevant in determining Anouilh's place in the history of modern theatre. One may at the very best express the wish that it be the philosopher, the historian and the moralizer of **Antigone** and **Pauvre Bitos**, the author so close to Camus, so fond of rebellion in the face of man's and nature's indifference to man. One may hope that the one who will endure the longer will be the chronicler, the journalist and the witness of hard times during and after World War Two, whose voice rises in indignation before certain historical crimes and yet always remains stylized, elegant and perfectly allied to the action on stage.

Contrary to the "new dramatists" who cultivate distantiation from their works, Anouilh is the type of playwright who pours all his life into his plays, crying, laughing, vituperating, battling, confessing, telling in transposition the story of his childhood, youth, old age, his loves, his disappointments, expressing thoughts about his own theatre. It may very well be, as Anouilh's Playwrights admit, that such theatre often exhibits cheap sentimentality, is talkative, abounds in locker-room jokes, relies on vaudeville gimmicks—yet in so doing it is only true to life. Anouilh works in the twilight zone between light and darkness, laughter and tears, coarse humor and elevated thoughts, part Feydeau, part Pascal. He belongs to a very old tradition, the one that gave Shakespeare and Molière. The theatrical historian will be likely to say that the thirties in which Anouilh began his career as playwright were most prominently marked by Giraudoux and Cocteau, the forties by Sartre and Camus, the fifties by Ionesco, Beckett and Genet. Yet Anouilh is the only outstanding French playwright who in his own sphere exercised a steady influence during all three of these decades. The true reason for his withdrawal during most of the sixties, the decade of "new criticism" rather than "new theatre," remains open to conjecture. It seems unlikely that for six years he would have offered no new play because of an alleged disagreement with De Gaulle. (pp. 76-8)

Early in 1972, in the midst of much mediocre theatre, two outstanding plays were performed—Ionesco's *Macbett* and Anouilh's modern version of the Orestes story **Tu étais si gentil quand tu étais petit**. It is probably the play whose completion and performance filled Anouilh with the greatest satisfaction since for over twenty years he had been unable to go beyond a fragment of **Oreste** published in 1945. Anouilh, embarking on his fifth decade of playwriting, thereby added still another masterpiece to those of his plays that contain a commentary on our times and man's fate in general. Ionesco and Anouilh, much closer to one another than it seemed in the fifties and sixties, appear in the early seventies as two unsurpassable masters of the metaphysical boulevard. Anouilh's **Becket** and Ionesco's *La Soif et la faim* have entered the repertory of the Comédie-Française. In the light of these facts, if today one were to play prophet it would seem justified to say that for many years the chances of reviving Anouilh, Beckett and Io-

nesco are likely to be equal. For traditions that remain young and avant-gardes that age fast both live together for a long time as classic repertory. (pp. 79-80)

B. A. Lenski, in his Jean Anouilh: Stages in Rebellion, *Humanities Press, 1975, 104 p.*

LEWIS W. FALB

The themes of the *nouvelles pièces grinçantes* are familiar. As in the earlier *pièces grinçantes,* Anouilh concentrates on those grating and irritating elements that express so well his bitter and cynical viewpoint. But the style of the *nouvelles pièces grinçantes* reveals a confidence, a virtuosity, and an occasional daring unequaled in Anouilh's theater. These works—**L'hurluberlu; ou Le réactionnaire amoureux, La grotte, L'orchestre, Le boulanger, la boulangère et le petit mitron,** and **Les poissons rouges; ou Mon père, ce héros**—are the creations of a resourceful and inventive genius, surely one of the supreme technicians in contemporary theater.

By the time these plays were written, Anouilh's audiences had come to expect from him a great deal of sophisticated experimentation with theatrical form. And these remarkable works of Anouilh's maturity fully satisfy these expectations. It should be kept in mind, however, that Anouilh was far from alone in making French audiences accept dramatic innovation. The *nouvelles pièces grinçantes* were first performed from 1959 to 1970, a period in which the structural and technical experiments of the theater of the absurd were particularly important and influential. Therefore, Anouilh's audiences had their theatrical education broadened by the more radical departures of Beckett, Ionesco, Genet, and others. Accordingly, when they came to the fashionable Comédie des Champs Élysées to see an Anouilh play, their experiences in other theaters enabled them to take delight in his unconventional structure. Although not strictly an absurdist dramatist, Anouilh in the *nouvelles pièces grinçantes* engages in experiments as bold as many of the absurdists.

L'hurluberlu (1959), the earliest of the *nouvelles pièces grinçantes,* displays an interest in contemporary political and social issues unusual in Anouilh's theater. The scatter-brained title character is a retired general engaged in a quixotic conspiracy to rid France of all that deprives it of glory. His efforts are doomed to failure because the world belongs to the scions of plastics manufacturers, and only the foolish try to struggle against "reason" and "progress." In **L'hurluberlu** Anouilh combines political commentary with the compassionate portrayal of a foolish idealist, but the combination does not entirely work. What seems especially lacking here is that characteristic touch of unreality which leads Anouilh's best plays to greater truthfulness and persuasiveness.

La grotte (1961) is one of Anouilh's bleakest works. Because the plot is so sordid and unpleasant, Anouilh had to find some way to make this material acceptable and believable. He borrowed the Pirandellian device of an "author" trying to deal on stage with a group of difficult characters. But this clever form cannot successfully overcome the crudeness of the story— a saga of rape, incest, and murder. Indeed, in the second act, when the characters insist on performing their roles without the author's interference, melodrama completely dominates the play. The device of the author-as-character, which offers Anouilh the means to express highly personal and illuminating views about the art of theater and of artistic creation, is sacrificed to an unpleasant and ultimately unconvincing plot.

L'orchestre (1962) is considerably more successful than *La grotte* in transforming sordid and melodramatic material through exciting theatrical technique. For the framework of this short play Anouilh returns to the world of a third-rate café orchestra, which he had used in earlier plays, but this time his musicians are seen in performance, and their individual tales of love, frustration, cruelty, and even madness are underscored by the banal and cloying music they play. The central story of the unhappy and doomed love affair between two musicians has great sentimental potential. And when other members of the orchestra contribute their anecdotes about cruelty to children and aged parents, the work seems close to approaching the mood of Anouilh's earliest plays, the *pièces noires*. But by giving his story the framework of a performance within a performance, Anouilh undercuts the melodrama and achieves a more powerful play. The orchestra becomes a disturbing and particularly unsparing image of human activity. That these characters live desperate and unhappy lives in a world of bad music, bored audiences, and indifferent companions, a world that seems to mock their private sufferings, turns a play that could have been merely maudlin into a disturbing and provocative work.

In *Le boulanger, la boulangère et le petit mitron* (1968) Anouilh experiments, as he had in *La valse des toréadors,* with the use of farce as a means of commenting seriously on the human condition. One of the characters in the play even says that Feydeau was the only writer to have spoken truly about the life of man. Low comedy—*vaudeville*—he goes on to say, portrays man as he really is, a superbly ridiculous creature in top hat and nightgown, "one hand on his heart, the other on the maid's rear end."

The play deals with a favorite Anouilh theme—the incompatibility of a married couple. Their individual needs are so strong, so selfish, that harmony is impossible. This situation, repeatedly encountered in Anouilh's theater, is presented as a turn-of-the-century farce. But to heighten the irony, the comedy, and the seriousness, Anouilh presents the fantasies of his characters, allowing dream and reality to exist side by side. The effect is almost surrealistic. Anouilh's purpose here is to show us a reality beyond the every day, deeper and truer.

Each of the characters escapes from his discontent in the present by dreaming of another, better, and, above all, more tranquil life. But only in the dreams of the young son do we get any of the compassion that is so important a part of Anouilh's best work. Anouilh seems to have misgauged his effects here. The ferocity, cruelty, and painful lucidity of the battling couple make laughter difficult, if not impossible. We are no longer in the world of comedy, not even of grating comedy.

Les poissons rouges (1970) is the play of this group in which Anouilh best maintains the balance between the serious and comic vision, and offers a humanity and density the other *nouvelles pièces grinçantes* lack. Like the others, the structure of *Les poissons rouges* is remarkably flexible. Its nonlinear development allows Anouilh to present a series of brief glimpses into the protagonist's life, free from any time sequence. Past and present can exist simultaneously, the one calling forth the other. It is reminiscent of the stream-of-consciousness technique in the novel.

Antoine de Saint-Flour, the protagonist, is a very successful playwright. His private life, however, is a shambles, and the play dramatizes a series of conflicts in which Antoine wages battles against wife, mistress, children, and friends in a desperate struggle to retain his freedom and individuality. (pp. 114-18)

[*Les poissons rouges*] is concerned with the nature of responsibility to oneself and to others; it deals with solitude, frustration, and, in a somewhat mocking but nonetheless moving way, heroism. Victory here, as elsewhere in Anouilh's theater, is personal—it is the maintaining of self-identity against all the pressures of family, friends, and society. The play reveals the terrible, unchanging nature of this struggle, the loneliness of the well-intentioned individual constantly forced to repeat his mistakes. But it is also an optimistic play, ultimately displaying a faith in man's ability to withstand these terrible attacks and finally to sustain honor and dignity. (pp. 126-27)

Anouilh's *pièces baroques—Cher Antoine; ou, L'amour raté, Ne réveillez pas madame, Le directeur de l'Opéra*—extend his metaphor of the theatrical performance as an image of the real world. In fact, all these plays involve actors, actresses, performers, and playwrights. (pp. 129-30)

The protagonist of *Ne réveillez pas Madame* (1970), Julien Paluche, is a successful actor-director who is quite miserably unsuccessful in his private life, a typical combination for an Anouilh hero. A loving but ineffectual and neglectful father, a demanding but perhaps selfish husband, and a well-intentioned but puritanical pain-in-the-neck to his friends and co-workers, Julien is something of a misfit, unable to accept the many compromises others seem to make with such ease. Like his namesake in *Colombe,* this Julien, too, ends up totally alone on a bare stage.

In *Ne réveillez pas Madame* Anouilh seems determined to strip his writing of all trappings—of plot, of situation, and of setting. The play is presented on the bare stage the director Jacques Copeau had demanded in his attempt to purify and revivify the French theater. Sets or parts of a setting are flown in on occasion, but each time the process discourages the suspension of disbelief that conventional scenery encourages. Anouilh, reducing theater to its essential elements, demands the kind of intellectual awareness and response from his audience that comes from watching the very act of theatrical creation.

Of the various works that the actors in Julien's troupe rehearse during the play, the most important is the final one, in which Julien attempts to realize his long-standing ambition to direct *Hamlet.* What we watch is a rehearsal of the closet scene, and indeed, the confrontation between Gertrude and Hamlet is brilliantly used by Anouilh. Their quarrel mirrors that between Julien and his own mother, a vain, flirtatious actress who had neglected her son for her career. The antagonism between mother and son has been a key subject throughout Anouilh's career, but here, with Shakespeare's help, it is stated with a depth of understanding and compassion rather new in his treatment of this material. The adult Julien realizes that the roles of woman and mother were not compatible in the case of his own mother. This understanding, however, does not alleviate his pain. Julien's "weakness," found in many other Anouilh heroes, is that he understands too much.

In the next *pièce baroque* Anouilh seems to repeat material he has treated better elsewhere. *Le directeur de l'Opéra* (1972) takes place in an opera house in Italy. Antonio di San-Floura seeks in the theater something of the stability and ideal order absent in the world outside. To elude the excessive demands of his family, he now lives backstage in his office at the theater. His attempt to escape is unsuccessful, for during the course of the play he must deal with the unhappy love affairs and attempted suicide of his daughter, the financial demands of his estranged wife, and the misdeeds of his spoiled, ne'er-do-well son, Toto. Apart from a moving scene between Antonio and Toto, and another between Antonio and his accountant, much of the material is familiar, perhaps overly familiar. Compared with his French namesakes—the two Antoines in *Les poissons rouges* and *Cher Antoine*—or even with Julien Paluche in *Ne réveillez pas madame,* Antonio lacks complexity and depth.

Written and staged before *Les poissons rouges, Cher Antoine* (1969) is, in fact, the first of Anouilh's plays to use a playwright as central character and one of Anouilh's most successful "theatrical" plays. (pp. 130-31)

In *Cher Antoine* Anouilh continues to explore the intellectual and theatrical possibilities of presenting an image of what is conventionally called "real life" through a milieu in which everything is artificial, distorted, and exaggerated. Moreover, the allusions that occur throughout *Cher Antoine* to the theatrical nature of the events are particularly appropriate to this story. Furthermore, these references and devices remind us not only that we are dealing with the story of people who work in the theater but also that we ourselves are sitting in a theater. Anouilh calls attention to his theatrical devices so that we are completely aware of their artificiality. An example of this is his blatant duplication of the ending of *The Cherry Orchard.* Anouilh makes Chekhov's closing scene appropriate for his play and at the same time makes sure that we know he copied it. Anouilh achieves both an emotional response from his audience and a more complicated intellectual one.

The multiplicity of responses results in still another kind of counterpoint in the play, one that is consistently comic. Anouilh repeatedly encourages and discourages an identification between the writer of the play and the writer in the play. This allows him the opportunity of answering some of the most frequent charges leveled at his art. At the same time it provides the spectator with the pleasure of watching a play, *Cher Antoine,* about a playwright who writes a play, *Cher Antoine,* about a playwright.

Anouilh employs such devices to lighten material that could be, in other hands, profoundly depressing. Characteristically, Anouilh presents an unrelievedly dark view of man; and, typically, although the message is unhappy, the vehicle is witty. (pp. 141-42)

Anouilh may choose to present his observations in the guise of amusing fables, but one must not be deceived by their often pleasing surfaces; the vision underlying them is brutal and unpleasant. . . . But in his theater, even at his most misanthropic, Anouilh offers a glimpse of an ideal, which, although faint or parodied, is not forgotten. In addition, Anouilh's belief in the possibility of man's survival in an inhospitable environment provides a note of optimism that lightens much of his writing. Anouilh the cynic cannot entirely suppress the frustrated idealist.

Anouilh's strength as a playwright, the reason for his eminence as a contemporary dramatist, comes from his ability to present in a large body of work and to an extremely wide audience a rich statement of a personal vision, a lucid yet entertaining exploration of themes that involve the anxieties and preoccupations of contemporary audiences. Although not as intellectual as some other twentieth-century French dramatists, Anouilh is unquestionably a master playmaker, one of the most accomplished craftsmen in modern French theater—indeed, in world theater. We respond deeply to the humanity of Anouilh's writ-ing as we are dazzled by the brilliance of its form, for his work is both a synthesis of and a contribution to the most creative elements in modern drama. (pp. 149-50)

> *Lewis W. Falb, in his* Jean Anouilh, *Frederick Ungar Publishing Co., 1977, 169 p.*

H.G. McINTYRE

It is hardly an exaggeration to say that there is only one central theme running through the whole of Anouilh's work—the eternal and universal conflict between idealism and reality. All his other themes are related to this, either as expressions of the idealistic rejection of life or as explorations of the various obstacles to idealism and self-realization in an imperfect world. In the plays of the thirties and forties we find a direct conflict between the intense, idealistic expectations of Anouilh's "heroic race" and the pedestrian *bonheur* and inevitable compromises of life. In the fifties it is still the same theme which is debated in terms of *rigueur* and *facilité.* Anouilh's earlier idealism is caricatured in the *rigueur* of Julien in *Colombe* or of Ludovic in *L'Hurluberlu,* but there is also an undercurrent of poignant nostalgia for earlier times. Those characters, especially the dramatist-heroes of the fifties and sixties who play at life with deliberate *facilité,* do so because they are at heart disillusioned idealists. As his heroes age, marital love and family life naturally loom larger in the plays, but still we have not forsaken the central theme. True love in Anouilh is a glimpse of an ideal state which by definition cannot endure. His couples' mutual recriminations over dead love and fading desire are one more instance of the degradation of all ideals in an imperfect world.

This is not to say, however, that Anouilh's preoccupations, while remaining constant, have not matured. On the contrary, Anouilh's attitudes and sympathies have altered significantly over the years. (p. 130)

In fact, there is no better illustration of both his consistency and maturation than the childhood theme. In the plays of his first period childhood is, implicitly or explicitly, a time of sheltered innocence into which one may escape from the realities of adult life, as in *Le Voyageur sans bagage,* or by which one may measure the deceptions of growing up, as in *Antigone.* After *L'Invitation au château* the view of childhood innocence changes radically. In *Ardèle* and *La Valse des Toréadors,* the later *L'Hurluberlu* and, most recently, in *Chers Zoiseaux,* Anouilh's youngsters are sexually precocious and adept at imitating their elders' more unpleasant habits. In the works of the sixties and seventies as a whole, childhood, far from being a haven of innocence, security and happiness, is a traumatic time and the source of all adult discontent and hence many of society's ills. There was a childish or childlike quality about the stubborn intransigence of Anouilh's former heroes and heroines, which set them apart. Now the whole of adult society stands accused of immaturity and infantilism. Childhood has, then, remained one of that nucleus of characteristic themes throughout the plays, becoming, if anything, even more central to Anouilh's view of his fellow man. The perspective has, however, changed substantially. (p. 131)

[Anouilh's] fondness for a traditional, outmoded style of theatre is . . . a symptom or an expression of Anouilh's instinctively theatrical view of life. . . . Just as some people are sensitive to light, noise or pollens in the air, so others are sensitive to the theatrical side of human behaviour. This is probably more of an affliction than an advantage. It seems to become progressively more pervasive to the point where nothing appears real or where what may be genuine also has a simultaneously theatrical side. . . .

In the first plays we can see a distinction between real and theatrical living. [Anouilh's earliest characters] are presented as 'real' people, surrounded by lesser theatrical characters. When Anouilh embraces theatricalism in 1936 all his characters are henceforth presented as conscious or unconscious role-players and his plays give up any pretence at realism to concentrate on demonstrating and underlining their own artificiality. It is an integral part of his theatricalist approach that he toys with the conventions of his medium and plundering the repertoire of theatrical effects also contributes to the creation of an unreal, fantasy world into which he invites us to escape from everyday reality. (p. 132)

As Anouilh continues to explore the intricacies of role-playing in life his defence of his practice goes deeper. Even after his adoption of theatricalism it is still possible on occasion to see some distinction between theatre and some kind of reality. Antigone, for example, who begins by seeing herself playing the role of a heroine in a Greek tragedy, is disillusioned as the action progresses and brought to face the reality of her situation. The old gods are dead and she is alone in an absurd world with no absolute values. The cause in which she claims to be acting is inauthentic and her real motives are personal. Her initial vision of herself as an *héroïne de théâtre* is shattered, even if it is replaced by an equally theatrical reality—a vision of herself condemned to act out a role in which destiny has arbitrarily cast her in an absurd world. By the time we come to *L'Alouette* and *Becket,* even this theatrical reality has receded and it is now the characters' theatrical vision of themselves which is allowed to triumph. Whereas Antigone was made to see the inauthenticity of her cause, Joan and Becket do not suspect the ironies and ambiguities which undermine their claims to be acting in the name of a greater authority than themselves. They are dominated by their roles and, as in the case of Bitos, the roles in which they see themselves have supplanted true self-awareness.

This view of the human mind at work is the core of Anouilh's justification for his use of conventionalized forms in the theatre. If that image we have of our innermost selves is only an inauthentic, theatrical image of a real self which we do not know, then the possibility of discovering any ultimate truth about existence seems remote. In fact, Anouilh goes further by suggesting that we can only conceive of any such ultimate reality in conventionalized terms. In this lies both a defence of and a function for his own brand of *théâtre artificiel.* (p. 133)

[The] play can only ever be a kind of façade . . . for the real play, the *pièce secrète* of life, which the dramatist cannot write. On the other hand, if what we think of as real life is only a theatrical image of an ultimately unknowable reality, then the dramatist can at least, by producing an even more artificial and conventionalized image of life in his plays, begin to suggest what lies beyond.

This apparently resigned and defeatist attitude should not be equated with a lack of artistic or social commitment. On the contrary, the history of Anouilh's development as an artist is . . . one of sustained self-scrutiny and criticism. He has always been anxious to define a function for his theatre and to reappraise his approach in keeping with that function and his maturing vision of life. If this self-renewal has led him, not to the more obviously experimental types of modern theatre, but

back to a seemingly outmoded style of drama, that is because he has realized the limits and the futility of the Avant-garde. This is a vague designation which covers a multitude, but it is clear from the parody of avant-garde drama in *L'Hurluberlu* what Anouilh has in mind and why he takes issue with it. This kind of theatre only captures the surface banalities of life and cannot, therefore, reveal or suggest either life's theatricality or the *vraie vie* which lies beneath. . . . (pp. 133-34)

Moreover, as Antoine realized in *Cher Antoine,* all new approaches quickly degenerate into recognizable 'styles' with their own conventions and the Avant-garde is no exception. . . .

When the first shock of novelty has passed, we are no nearer glimpsing *la vraie vie* than we were before. Even so, Anouilh's attitude to innovation is ambiguous. Despite his ultimate pessimism, he has not given up the struggle to improve his own work. But innovation, in his view, is relative and draws its real vitality from tradition. . . . (p. 134)

Those whom he admires as the greatest innovators in the modern theatre since Pirandello, for example Vitrac, Beckett, Ionesco and Genet, he sees as having transcended the Avant-garde and grafted their preoccupations on to an older tradition. . . . (pp. 134-35)

Although he has not himself produced as new a style as Beckett or Ionesco, Anouilh is none the less proud to be 'modern' in the broadest sense. By virtue of his rejection of realism and the well-made play, his theatricalism and his unflagging interest in the conventions of his medium, he includes himself in that broad movement in twentieth-century theatre which is descended from Pirandello. . . .

Where he is unrepentantly less modern is in his refusal to commit himself to any political ideology, espouse any social cause or even discuss, as Camus and Sartre do for example, the philosophical principles behind political action. . . . (p. 135)

[Anouilh's view] is that all other restrictions on men, social, political or economic, pale into insignificance beside the greatest oppression of all—the inevitability of death in an absurd world. Helping to remedy this 'injustice', which afflicts all men equally, is, in Anouilh's view, the proper concern and function of the writer. In fact, Anouilh would probably shrink from such generalizations but this is the background to his own proud assertion that he is a humble craftsman of the theatre, providing employment for actors and an opportunity for the public to escape from themselves and their worries for the space of an evening. This view of the theatre's function in turn elevates Anouilh's incorrigible lack of *sérieux* in the theatre to something more deliberate and purposeful. The dramatic form he has evolved has its roots in an age-old comic tradition which, as he indicates, goes back at least as far as the Atellan farces of ancient Rome. This comic tradition is not trivial and escapist. On the contrary, it is positive in Anouilh's eyes because mankind has used it from time immemorial as a means of facing the harsh realities of existence and defending itself against them by transposing them into comic terms and laughing at them. . . . (p. 137)

Anouilh's debt to this comic tradition places his anti-intellectualism on a more reasonable basis. Two things have become associated in his mind. One is the growing democratization of modern society and the other the contemporary tendency to despair and to take a tragic view of life. They are related because democracy and, especially, the spread of education have increased both the number and the influence of intellectuals in present-day society.... Anouilh, by dipping into an ancient and unintellectual tradition of comic theatre, is inviting us ... not to despair at our misery but to laugh at our absurdity.

The comic dramatist is, in Anouilh's estimation, an aristocrat in an increasingly egalitarian age because he has inherited at birth this gift of being able to laugh at himself and of not taking life seriously which cannot be acquired by any amount of study, personal merit or intellectual prowess.... (pp. 137-38)

Anouilh's anti-intellectualism does not contradict his view of the theatre as a *jeu de l'esprit*. The safest translation of this phrase might be 'game of the imagination' and not of the 'mind' or 'intellect'....

[The] comic theatre has no need of intellectual or rational analysis in order to get its message across. In his preface to a volume of Labiche's plays Anouilh explains how the comic theatre works....

This preface is also interesting for Anouilh's view of Labiche's place in the nineteenth-century theatre. One comes away with the distinct impression that Anouilh is comparing it to his own in the twentieth. Labiche was a "petit bourgeois tranquille" who excelled in the minor genre of light comedy. He produced no grand theories on his art but applied himself competently and methodically to making audiences laugh and earning as much money as possible in the process. The audiences of the 1850s and 60s no doubt felt that the great and enduring drama of the age was being written by Augier and Alexandre Dumas *fils*. Yet Labiche's gift for making people laugh at themselves ensures that he is still enjoyed today when Augier and Dumas are gathering dust on library shelves. Anouilh is nothing if not a modest man. [He has stated: "I am aiming neither at posterity nor the respect of my contemporaries."] ... (p. 138)

Whether or not his modesty is justified only time will tell; but the chances are high that audiences will still be laughing at Anouilh when the Augiers and the Dumas of our own century have been forgotten. (p. 139)

     H. G. McIntyre, in his The Theatre of Jean Anouilh, *Barnes & Noble Books, 1981, 165 p.*

Ann Beattie

1947-

American short story writer and novelist.

In her fiction Beattie records the disillusionment of the "Woodstock generation" as her protagonists approach middle age. Echoing the views of many critics, Pico Iyer calls Beattie "perhaps the first and finest laureate of that generation of Americans born to a society built on quicksand and doomed to life in the long, ambiguous shadow of the 'sixties." Her characters are typically well-educated, affluent people who experience a sense of loss as they attempt to reconcile the idealistic convictions of their youth with their present lifestyles. They drift from one relationship to another, and their inability to make commitments results in an aimless and ultimately empty existence. Maintaining a narrative distance, Beattie rarely explores the inner motivations or emotional complexities of her characters. She instead focuses on their external environment, and through her detailed references to brand-name goods and popular songs Beattie establishes a distinct mood and setting.

Beattie began her career writing short stories, many of which were published in *The New Yorker*. By depicting the quiet despair of New England's chic upper middle class, Beattie's early short fiction elicited comparison with celebrated *New Yorker* contributors John Cheever and John Updike. Beattie has published three short story collections: *Distortions* (1976), *Secrets and Surprises* (1978), and *The Burning House* (1982). Most of the stories in these volumes concern characters whose lack of permanent ties and consequent sense of aimlessness is reflected in the story titles, which include "Gravity," "Afloat," and "Learning to Fall" in *The Burning House*. Beattie employs a prose style which parallels the listlessness of the characters through flat, declarative sentences and detached observations; she maintains an even tone whether describing a dinner party or a miscarriage. While critics praise the crystalline quality of Beattie's prose, her dispassionate style is often considered unsettling.

Beattie's novels concern the same milieu as her short stories, with the settings changing slightly as the members of her generation grow older. In *Chilly Scenes of Winter* (1976), the 1960s are again a dominant presence as the protagonist seeks emotional solace by romanticizing his past. In *Falling in Place* (1980), the range of Beattie's characters expands as she reveals a concern for the various members of a suburban family. With *Love Always* (1985), Beattie's references to the 1960s become less frequent as her characters surround themselves with upscale and trendy consumer items while engaging in tangled relationships. Some critics consider these novels to be less polished than her previous work and contend that Beattie's episodic style is best suited to the short story. *Chilly Scenes of Winter* was adapted for film.

(See also *CLC*, Vols. 8, 13, 18; *Contemporary Authors*, Vols. 81-84; and *Dictionary of Literary Biography Yearbook: 1982*.)

© 1986 Thomas Victor

ANATOLE BROYARD

When I was a child, I got lost at Coney Island one day and ended up in a pound—like a dog pound—for lost children. What was curious about the place, as I remember it, was the fact that most of the children were not crying, but sitting and staring into space, waiting to be rescued.

This is how the people in Ann Beattie's first two volumes of stories [*Distortions* and *Secrets and Surprises*] struck me. They were lost in a Coney Island world, waiting for something to happen. But in *The Burning House*, her third collection, Miss Beattie seems to be changing—in my opinion, for the better. Most of her characters now have recognizable desires, color in their cheeks, energy in their movements. Sometimes they even cry.

In one piece, a young woman actually asks her husband, in italics, mind you, "*You don't love me?*" Another story ends with the sentence: "I am really at some out-of-the-way beach house, with a man I am not married to and people I do not love, in labor." In her earlier stories, the first two clauses of that last sentence would almost have gone without saying....

[In another piece] a man says to a weeping woman, "Just tell me what you've done." Not what's been done to you, but what you've done, as if to suggest that she is at least partly responsible for her own unhappiness. A husband urges his wife to say "I have a nice life."

After she's divorced, one of these women of Ann Beattie's goes to the house of another unhappy divorced woman and they take turns holding and kicking a tambourine, as if it's the only thing left in this world for them to do. There's pathos in these stories, in the characters themselves, rather than in the sadness of what's missing in their makeup.

There's one long story, **"Winter: 1978,"** that strikes me as a regression. The actions of the characters are determinedly, even implacably gratuitous, and to obscure them even further they are buried in the paraphernalia of verisimilitude. At times, I wondered whether there might not be a wild laugh echoing through this story, but this is just a guess, probably a wrong one, for writers are never so serious as when they are bad.

Miss Beattie used to have a reticence about language that seemed to be the trauma of her generation, but she now allows herself an occasional pretty or rhythmical sentence. She doesn't take refuge any longer in a deadpan style. In the whole book, I noticed only three bad sentences....

Still, Miss Beattie has come so close to the normal in this book that when I found six people cheering a sponge as it expanded in the water of a bathtub, I wasn't sure whether she was cheering with them or mocking them. I wish she had not made two other people drive through the night to Brattleboro, Vt., just because a friend called and said he was besieged by wasps—but no reader can have it all his own way.

There's a lovely scene of a baby sitter named Inez reading a bedtime story in Spanish to a contented child who doesn't understand a word. And another moment in which a young mother imagines her son and his dubious father ascending in a glass elevator somewhere in California. Perhaps my favorite image is the one in which a divorced woman goes to a dance class and "learns to fall."

I think Miss Beattie is learning to fall, too. She may even be falling for us—her all-too-human readers. While it may be a risky thing to do, it's more fun than kicking a tambourine.

> Anatole Broyard, *"Kicking and Falling," in* The New York Times, *September 25, 1982, p. 16.*

MARGARET ATWOOD

A new Beattie is almost like a fresh bulletin from the front: We snatch it up, eager to know what's happening out there on the edge of that shifting and dubious no man's land known as interpersonal relations. How goes the fray, at least in the area roughly defined as New York, with Vermont on the upper perimeter and Virginia on the lower one? ... How are life, liberty and the pursuit of happiness getting along these days?

Not too well, going by the evidence of [the stories collected in **The Burning House**].... Happiness is still being pursued, sort of; at least, the characters in these stories can remember what it was like when they were pursuing it. By now, many have flagged and are substituting Valium. (pp. 1, 34)

What ails them? ... Life is too easy an answer. It seems to be more a matter, strangely enough, of liberty. There are no longer any ties that bind, not securely, not definitively: jobs, marriages, the commitments of love, even the status of parent and child—all are in a state of flux. Thus everything is pro-

visional, to be re-invented tomorrow, and no one can depend on anyone else....

Freedom, that catchword of sixties America, has translated into free fall, or a condition of weightlessness, and the most repeated motifs in the book are variants of this. **"Learning to Fall," "Gravity," "Afloat"** and **"Running Dreams"** are titles of stories. "Space cadet" is a phrase used by one character of another, but in some ways all the protagonists, both men and women, are defined by their relationship to this label. Zipped in, petrified, like the little boy in a beekeeper's suit in **"Sunshine and Shadow,"** they peer out through Plexiglas at the dangerous collisions around them, at the fatal stars.... These are stories not of suspense but of suspension.

Freedom is the freedom to take off, but when you're being taken off from, as happens to most of the people in these stories, it doesn't feel quite the same. What many of these characters want is to be grounded. Like spies on the run, they're searching for a safe house, and houses and their furnishings loom large. But the houses tend to be booby-trapped: Home is no longer a comfy fortress, as the book title more than hints. Even the most domestic of activities—cooking dinner, fun with the dog—are fraught with a jittery sense of wrongness. Sometimes the characters, nostalgic for Christmas trees the way they used to be, return to their own pasts, but the lovely Pennsylvania farmhouse of **"Sunshine and Shadow,"** which lulls us into security with its patchwork quilts and golden oldie records, is indicative of what is likely to happen to anyone who gets sucked in by the décor: "When he moved his head nose-close to the window he could see the cement driveway ... where his mother had run a hose into the car and killed herself with carbon monoxide."

This is also a good example of Ann Beattie's method. The detail is casually dropped on the reader's head in passing, not treated with special rhetoric, just *there*, like a vase or a clock; and it is the evenness of tone used to describe both horrific event and trivial observation alike that accounts perhaps for the eerie, shell-shocked effect of Miss Beattie's prose. By now this is a technique she wields with absolute control. Compared to the earlier stories, these are less grotesque, more narrowly and intensely focused, more accomplished; they are also less outrageous and less outraged and more sympathetic to their characters. The mood is not bloody-minded; rather it is sorrowful....

No one is better at the plangent detail, at evoking the floating, unreal ambiance of grief. I would say Ann Beattie is at her best here, except that I think she can do even better. One admires, while becoming nonetheless slightly impatient at the sheer passivity of these remarkably sensitive instruments. When that formidable technique is used on a subject large enough for it, the results will be extraordinary indeed. Still, that's like caviling because Wayne Gretzky misses one shot. If Miss Beattie were a ballerina you could sell tickets to the warm-ups. (p. 34)

> Margaret Atwood, *"Stories from the American Front," in* The New York Times Book Review, *September 26, 1982, pp. 1, 34.*

PICO IYER

The *New Yorker* has long seemed to be written for, by and about those who lead lives of quiet desperation. In its discreet, fearfully subdued stories the usual milieu is peripheral suburbia, the usual mood penumbral regret. Indeed, many of the magazine's most celebrated contributors—Salinger, Cheever and Updike among them—have distinguished themselves by coolly chronicling the sad eccentricities, plaintive longings and quiet frustrations of their generation. The newest inheritor of this tradition, speaking for a new and peculiarly displaced generation, is Ann Beattie. . . .

[In *The Burning House* the] surface details of Ann Beattie's stories so strikingly resemble Cheever's that one can almost read them as a sequel. For although her characters swallow pills instead of booze; although they flee to California instead of Europe; although their hassles are those of cohabitation instead of marriage—they might well be the offspring of Cheever's well-heeled lonelyhearts, raised on expectations they frequently let down. Like their literary forefathers, Beattie's well-educated vagrants often reside in Connecticut and pursue moderately successful careers. In truth, they could almost be mistaken for the charmed, witty bright young things who inhabit beer ads on TV, but their urbanity ensures that their lives, like their words, sidestep all the obvious clichés. Most of them are haunted by a cool sorrow and a listless despair.

For Ann Beattie is perhaps the first and finest laureate of that generation of Americans born to a society built on quicksand and doomed to a life in the long, ambiguous shadow of the 'sixties. (p. 87)

[Her characters] are, in every sense, between engagements, forever commuting between one another's homes and lives, both of which they enter and leave with casual frequency. As one nameless figure remarks, 'Everybody who doesn't take hold of something has something take hold of them'. And Ann Beattie evokes this atmosphere of dangling conversations between people deaf to one another's griefs with characteristic compression: her characters are constantly calling each other up, being answered by machines and left to whisper their secrets and endearments into thin air. (p. 88)

Numbness pervades the parched, exhausted mood of her stories. Utterly toneless, she reads them herself into a plain, flat voice that suggests deadened feelings or, on occasion, a determined attempt to fight back tears. Her wan sentences and neutral cadences follow one upon another with sharp, chill clarity. Wandering like their protagonists' days, her stories have no resolution—in part because their people cannot make sense of life, in part because nothing ends in any case. As if to invert the eventful frenzy and clamourous manic swings of the world according to television, a Beattie story is naked of explosions or alarums. It has no strain, and no looseness; no lyricism or radiance or rhythm or hope. Reading it is like driving for mile after mile down a straight road through a snow-covered desert.

One of Beattie's deftest narrative tricks is to catch the blur of personal relations in today's America by plunging her reader without any introduction or reference into a chaos of first names (uninterested in the public world, she rarely mentions surnames). Upon beginning one of her stories, it always takes a while to determine the relations between the floating soap-bubbles: a child can easily be mistaken for a boy friend, a gay lover for a brother, or a son. For the family structure of middle-class America has imploded, and domestic structures have been grotesquely distorted and distended. People seem to change spouses, disguises, even sexual preferences at random: thus children do not know their uncles, girls are older than their step-mothers and many need calculators to count their siblings

or parents. Everybody cares about 'relating' to everybody else in part, perhaps, because relatives are unknown. Nothing is quite as it seems or as it should be: in one Beattie story, a woman shares roller-coaster rides, confidences and a joint with her husband's gay brother; in another, the narrator must try to win over her lover's teenage daughter; and in a third, a woman commiserates with her husband's live-in male lover as all three try to cope with separation.

Elsewhere, again and again we see men boyishly wooing their children. For it is the dark and perverse paradox of modern America's broken families that adults and children have effectively exchanged places. . . . While all too many adults lust after adolescence, all too many kids are thrust into a precocious maturity. Forced to fend for themselves, to confront both the sins of their fathers and the vices of their peers, more and more children are hustled by privilege and negligence into a hard wisdom they must reluctantly assume. . . . In Beattie's stories, children are knowing before they are discriminating: a six-year-old refuses stories with morals, dismissing them as 'kid's stuff'; parents read their children R. D. Laing instead of fairy tales; one nine-year-old carries around Samuel Beckett. Even as these children are turning into tough little realists, their parents are tumbling into stolen romances and irresponsible rites, belatedly courting an innocence they had earlier squandered. We see them dressing up as bears, playing with frisbees, devising quirky surprises for their lovers and running with dogs. And we come to see that their prankish charm is part of their affliction, a refuge and a mask. . . . It is sad that the children of Beattie's world are afraid, confused, disenchanted; it may be sadder that their elders are no wiser and no better off.

It cannot be denied that Ann Beattie's stories are perfect mirror-images of the protagonists and predicaments they describe. But because her theme so rarely varies or evolves (save for one gay and giddy interlude called **"Happy"**, an exception to prove the rule), her tales seem almost mass-produced. All the off-beat tunes she plays are in the same (minor) key; after reading a few, one feels that one could write a few. Collect some characters, and name them Jason, say, or Barrett or Hilary. Give them trendy occupations and some engaging idiosyncrasies. Place their homes in the woods, and supply them with shaggy dogs, coffee and conversation around the kitchen table. Make it a grey day in winter. Let there be a phone call to a former lover, a child from a sometime marriage. Ensure that someone takes Valium and someone refers to a gynecological operation. Write in a withered present tense and end before the conclusion (it was once noted that a *New Yorker* story is a regular story with the final paragraph lopped off to give the impression of restrained subtlety and truthful complexity).

This is not entirely to disparage Ann Beattie's commanding talents. Her spare, soft-spoken prose is singularly observant: she can conjure up a dog without a single physical detail, so keen is her sense of gesture. She clearly knows the very pulse and heartbeat of her dreamless drifters—indeed, with her long fair hair, air of seraphic funkiness, and apparently itinerant, make-shift life-style she seems to belong in their midst. She performs many tasks with unrivalled skill: conveying the weary braveness of children and their secret wish to be children again, or the poignancy of the grown men who try to entertain them, equally eager and equally desperate; pinning down voguish tastes, brand-name allusions and aimless dialogue; sketching pale, lead-coloured skies. The harsh transparency of her unblinking, unstinting realism seems almost photographic.

And ultimately these stories may be best regarded as a collection of photos in an album: each records a situation, revives a memory and redeems nothing. Reading them is like consulting a doctor's X-ray of contemporary America. But just as a doctor is vulnerable to the very disease he treats, the closeness of Beattie's manner to her matter can be suffocating. Privy to anomie, her stories become party to it; faithful to the details of the world, they seem treacherous to the energy and heroic idealism that are America's saving grace. (pp. 89-91)

Pico Iyer, "Shadows of the 'Sixties," in London Magazine, *n.s. Vol. 22, No. 12, March, 1983, pp. 87-91.*

DEAN FLOWER

Ann Beattie's stories exert a continuing, almost morbid fascination. What seemed funny and satiric in her first collection, *Distortions,* has disappeared on longer acquaintance: she wasn't kidding. The distortions are us, Beattie tells her readers, over and over again. Lest that meaning be evaded by the affluent and educated audience she appeals to, Beattie has made her characters all pretty much the same sort that Updike and Cheever used to chronicle, bringing them up to date. Now, with [*The Burning House*] . . . Beattie seems unable to break the mold. Her titles hint at this: *Secrets and Surprises,* her second collection, suggested an effort to charm and entice, and so in her present collection do stories labeled **"Sunshine and Shadow,"** **"Desire,"** **"Afloat"** and **"Happy"**; but other titles tell us the truth. These are stories of loss and emotional dearth, *Chilly Scenes of Winter,* about people so stuck in failing relationships that they're *Falling in Place.* The dust jacket assures us that Beattie's stories "'aim for grace,' and invariably achieve it," but when we turn to the story from which the phrase was hopefully plucked (**"Learning to Fall"**), we learn that each character is locked in disappointments and failures, that fall they must, and that the only choice is whether to do so gracefully or to take another bruising. Reasonably, the narrator opts for the former.

The word *grace* has no religious reverberations, in Beattie's realm, nor is that what she seems to be after stylistically; deliberate gracelessness might be a better description, or scrupulous undernourishment. She remains a severe stylist, allowing few metaphors, lulling rhythms, or rich sense appeals, and no verbal play. Beckett's prose has been thought an influence; I am more often reminded of Harold Pinter. The following passage from the first page of **"Winter: 1978"** may be an unconscious Pinter-parody or a self-parody, but it's typical of the almost perverse way Beattie launches her stories:

> Benton and Olivia had just arrived in L.A. Nick had gone to the airport to meet them. Olivia said she wasn't feeling well and insisted on getting a cab to the hotel, even though Nick offered to drive her and meet Benton at Allen Tompkins's house later.

Four characters have been mentioned so far, but note the refusal to focus anything with a perceiver's emotions or a narrator's explanations. The passage continues:

> The man who had also come to the airport to meet Benton was Tompkins's driver. Nick could never remember the man's name. Benton was in L.A. to show his paintings to Tompkins. Tompkins would buy everything he had brought.

> Benton was wary of Tompkins, and of his driver, so he had asked Nick to meet him at the airport and to go with him.

One hardly knows whether to laugh or draw a diagram. It reads like a story problem in Algebra 1, a puzzle with a catch to it (How many were going to Tompkins's house?), nearly a farce. Yet such enigmatic openings are fundamental to Beattie's storytelling. . . . Stories that begin in bizarre tangles of ambiguous relationships end not with explanations or solutions but usually with clarified enigmas. **"Cinderella Waltz,"** for example, turns out to be almost precise. It is not about the wife's shocked discovery that her husband (Milo) left her for a man (Bradley) or that Milo is now dumping Bradley and his nine-year-old daughter for a new life on the West Coast. It proves rather to be about the peculiar relationship that now exists between the wife and Bradley, less sympathy than identification. (pp. 359-60)

Despite all the oddity and particularity, Beattie's stories suffer from sameness. Sixteen in a row is too much. What the poor sensitive gentleman was to Henry James, the angst-ridden catatonic woman is to Ann Beattie. Ruth in **"Learning to Fall"** goes on other people's errands in spasms of impure self-abnegation; Amy in **"The Burning House"** hovers in her kitchen like a mere eavesdropper to all the voices addressing her. The remarried wife in **"Afloat"** finds her gestures so fruitless she wishes "simply to get off the earth." The woman in **"Waiting,"** whose friends cannot console her while her husband is away, imagines the dog has died. Looked at one way, these women—and most of the men too—are all powerless to change. Looked at another, their stasis is not so bad. If marriage and the family have cracked apart and the metaphoric house is in flames, why isn't all changed utterly? An early Beattie story says why: "Nothing ever came entirely apart." For all the lamentation over failing relationships and disintegrating families, Beattie keeps showing where the rifts stop. Memories which so often torment still connect us, sometimes savingly, with the past. Children who seem the victims of broken marriages have a way of insisting on the irrevocability of the old roles, no matter what the new arrangements are. A touching, nearly comic instance of this is in **"Desire,"** where a man named B. B. cares for his ten-year-old Bryce during spring vacation. . . . Whatever the sorrow and confusion, some things—like being a parent—do not change. Things fall apart, Beattie shows us, but only so much. (p. 361)

Dean Flower, in a review of "The Burning House," in The Hudson Review, *Vol. XXXVI, No. 2, Summer, 1983, pp. 359-62.*

CHRISTOPHER LEHMANN-HAUPT

It is easy enough for a reader to keep his distance from the story and the people of Ann Beattie's *Love Always*. . . .

After all, the plot of *Love Always* is often almost cruelly satirical, involving as it does the visit of a 14-year-old soap-opera star named Nicole Nelson with an aunt in Vermont who writes a parody lonely-hearts column under the byline Cindi Coeur for a counterculture magazine called Country Daze.

After all, some of the novel's best moments are funny at the expense of its characters: for instance, the scene in which Nicole's agent, P. G. (Piggy) Proctor, discovers that her soap opera's title, "Passionate Intensity," comes from the line in Yeats's "The Second Coming" that reads, "The best lack all conviction and the worst are full of passionate intensity." . . .

After all, Miss Beattie's narrative technique is essentially Keystone comedy, with sudden jump-cuts from one character's point of view to another and outrageous collisions among the various subplots of the comedy. For instance, in a typical scene, two local Dogberrys nearly crash their squad car into a limousine inside which Nicole, the child star, is busy taking pornographic photographs of a man who wants to make his girlfriend jealous.

Indeed, film and videotape are used everywhere in the story, and this too invites us to keep our distance, to view the novel's events in the scale of a television screen, and above all not, for heaven's sake, to make things more complicated than they are or take them as if they were real. We come to feel like Nicole's aunt Lucy Spenser, who sees even the rural New England scenery as a kind of stage set. . . .

Yet underneath all the clowning, Miss Beattie's message is ambiguous. Her theme is a somber one, the failure of love between parents and children, between husbands and wives, between couples of every sexual persuasion—people's inclination to treat the message "Love Always" as a variation of "Yours truly." At the climax of the novel, when Nicole's mother is killed in an automobile accident, we are asked to believe that beneath the plastic veneer that Miss Beattie has worked so skillfully to polish, Nicole is really just a vulnerable child. People were never just one thing, Miss Beattie reminds us in another significant scene, and "if people weren't any one thing, then of course situations weren't." The world "could change in a second."

These apparent pleas for a deeper reading of *Love Always* would seem ludicrous if Miss Beattie lacked a talent to turn our emotions on a dime and send them speeding off in a direction altogether different from satirical comedy. But she has this ability in abundance. In the midst of the jokes, there are remarkable passages of introspection that plunge us off the edge of satire into depths where we even feel empathy for her people.

And then there is Miss Beattie's amazing eye for detail, which, whether she is describing a landscape, a roomful of objects, a gathering of people or a collection of character traits, serves to remove what she observes from any familiar category, most of all from a satirically comic one.

Unfortunately, this astonishing versatility works against the success of *Love Always*. Miss Beattie's talent simply goes off too far in too many conflicting directions for her to pull everything together at the end. It happens to be one of those books that contains a number of comments that can mischievously be turned against itself, as if the author was half-consciously pre-empting possible criticism. . . .

[A grieving mother's comment, for example]: "I believe that in Oriental rugs, there is often an irregularity in the pattern—a key, it is called—woven that way deliberately, to allow the spirit to escape." It isn't altogether clear what meaning this is supposed to have in context, but Miss Beattie's deliberate misweaving of her novel's pattern has allowed too much of its spirit to escape. In *Love Always*, she continues to grow as a novelist, but her talent is still somewhat ahead of her command of it.

       Christopher Lehmann-Haupt, "Key for Escaping Spirit," in The New York Times, *May 27, 1985, p. 14.*

FRANK RICH

Whatever else Ann Beattie may or may not tell us in her fiction, no one need ever fear that she'll fail to record her characters' background music. In the opening sentence of her third novel, *Love Always,* we learn that Barbra Streisand is singing "Happy Days Are Here Again"—and, from there, it's onward, if not necessarily upward, to the Eurythmics, Duran Duran, Procol Harum, Madonna, Carly Simon, James Taylor, and most persistently, Cyndi Lauper. The sound track forms an ironic counterpoint to the fictional doings, of course. Girls don't just want to have fun in *Love Always,* and happy days are never going to be here again. Beattie's shell-shocked survivors of the 1960s are lucky if they can snort, let alone slouch, towards Bethlehem. (p. 42)

[Beattie's characters are] colorlessly anomic—which is to say that they are often interchangeable with one another, as well as with the personnel of other Beattie fictions. (The otherwise undifferentiated male staffers of *Country Daze* come in two generic flavors, straight and gay.) Everyone is as bored and self-indulgent as the Buchanans—Fitzgerald is also on the hit parade of golden oldies in *Love Always*—but no one is in sharp focus. "Set the camera on infinity, and you're bound to get the long view," says *Country Daze*'s ace photographer. Beattie, who opens her novel with a party being videotaped for posterity, seems to swing her own camera around as if it were dangling idly from a cord around her neck. Only when brand names are in view (Dalmane, the Horchow collection, Perrier, Nike, Dom Pérignon, Gold American Express Card, Datsun 280ZX, Sportsac) does she move in for the tight close-up. It's not until violence strikes in the book's final section that she gives some of her characters (Lucy's family) a past—a tiresome feat accomplished with a somber, journalistic voice that seems intended to emulate the belated chronicling of Gatz's history in *Gatsby*.

Up until then, the tone of *Love Always* is relentlessly jokey, without being funny. The tone is set by the scattered excerpts from Lucy's Cindi Coeur columns. When a fictive young girl writes that she and her brother have suffered parental punishment for playing an innocent hide-and-seek game they call "Deep Throat," the terribly knowing Cindi advises that the game be renamed "Woodward and Bernstein." Such shtick is not only flat, it also adds little to our understanding of the book's principal characters. Beattie would rather have a few contemptuous laughs at the expense of the downtrodden bit players. Hildon's much-betrayed wife, Maureen, is presented strictly as a running gag. She gets back at her husband by signing up with a $50-an-hour, crypto-feminist guru who teaches a "holistic approach to man-hating" that is "part psychotherapy, part whole body reconditioning, and part assertiveness training." The author also shares Hildon's condescending attitude toward the redneck townies. The cops, delivery men, and other local yokels who cross the paths of the well-heeled *Country Daze* crew stand accused of eating regularly at McDonald's, shopping at K-Mart, and writing illiterate letters. And if Lucy is a latter-day Miss Lonelyhearts, so her niece's New England fans are mindless latter-day locusts, erecting pathetic little shrines to their favorite star.

If anything, show biz is Beattie's favorite satirical target in *Love Always*. It's hard to understand why, given the novel's prefab contributions to this well-rehearsed genre. . . . The familiar Hollywood types in *Love Always* include Nicole's vulgar agent (known as "Piggy," no less) and a young hack writer, Andrew Steinborn, who's preparing a novelization of "Passionate Intensity.'' Steinborn's other literary projects, we're told in another representative display of Beattie's wit, include a real novel titled *Buzz* (''about people at a fashionable resort in Southampton, as seen from the perspective of a mosquito'') and *I Will Always Love You,* the unauthorized biography of Dolly Parton. This young man, however, commits the cardinal sin of *Love Always*—he takes his work seriously. Steinborn's girlfriend is always chastising him for refusing to admit that ''Passionate Intensity'' was only a soap opera: ''Why did he insist that it was something more—that there were subtleties and hidden complexities in the characters, and that to the intelligent viewer the show was more than entertainment.''

This, one assumes, is Beattie's aesthetic rationalization for her own novel. We are to take the book's flaccidly assembled jumble of melodramatic plot bombshells, buzzwords, and helter-skelter wisecracks as its own entertaining reward, subtleties and complexities be damned. Call this collage a cool slice of Magic Realism, if you will—life among the Yuppies as documented on a single videocassette, unedited. Yet skeptics may feel that *Love Always* is simply a freeze-dried *Big Chill,* still awaiting its infusion of hot water (or blood). (p. 44)

As a spokesperson for a generation, Ann Beattie is beginning to sound like a broken record. And the needle is stuck in a narrow groove that emits only the muffled sounds of the wealthy, Waspy, childless, and most narcissistic baby boomers. If there are any insights here, they pertain mainly to the collapse of the Hart campaign. The blank idlers who traipse through these chilly scenes of summer are the kind of rarefied preppies who throw wine-and-cheese fund-raisers by night, only to find themselves too tranqued-out to pile into their Datsuns on election day. *Love Always* is no novel, but it can, at least, be read as a persuasive chapter in *The Making of the President 1984.* (pp. 44-5)

Frank Rich, ''Chilly Scenes of Summer,'' in The New Republic, Vol. 193, Nos. 3 & 4, July 15 & 22, 1985, pp. 42, 44-5.

JOSH RUBINS

[In *Love Always*] Beattie has taken on more than she can handle. She still adopts a variety of authorial voices, remaining loose and noncommittal, mixing *Angst* with grace-note amusement. But here, while clinging to remnants of her graver, more delicate and life-sized tragicomedy, Beattie sets out to be a satirist-*farceur* as well—even if that aim results in unpleasant clashes of mood and tone, more crazy quilt than pointillism.

Take, for example, the novel's brief opening chapter—set on June 30, 1984, the day of the third annual party for the city-bred, Vermont-based staff of *Country Daze,* a chic humor magazine founded by handsome entrepreneur Hildon (apparently so *macho* and hip that he has no first name). The hostess is Hildon's wife, Maureen, whom Beattie immediately sets up as a cartoonlike simp: we're invited to laugh at Maureen's complacent pleasure in the giving of ''perfect'' parties (with inane motifs), at her discomfiture in the presence of *Country Daze* writer Lucy Spenser (Hildon's longtime, off-and-on lover), at her limited erudition. (Silently fuming at Lucy's blithe-spirit manner, Maureen thinks: ''She acted a little like that woman, whatever her name was, whom the Great Gatsby had been in love with.'') Some readers will resist the faint smugness of the caricature, of course. But those who cheerfully go along with Beattie as a disdainful satirist will be jolted by an abrupt shift in the chapter's final lines—as Maureen recalls herself at last

year's *Country Daze* fete: ''She had worn a toga. She had served pita bread and hummus. It had rained on the Fourth of July. Two days later she had been on the phone, ordering a set of glasses from the Horchow collection, when she suddenly felt blood soaking her pants, and miscarried, without having known she was pregnant.''

What is Beattie after here? Are we meant to giggle scornfully at Maureen, then to gag on the laughter when Beattie suddenly switches gears? Apparently so—because most of the characters in *Love Always* receive much the same having-it-both-ways treatment: an ill-prepared lurch from giddy sendup to maudlin, undeveloped psychological revelation. . . .

Pathos as punch line: that, unfortunately, is Beattie's favored strategem in this centerless, disjointed novel—which is uncharacteristically heavy-handed in both its comic and poignant extremes. . . . True, the jump-cuts from mockery to insight to sentiment may be intended as a demonstration of Beattie's belief in human nature's many-sidedness. ''Nobody is really a hero or a heroine; they're all confused and pulled in different directions.'' So says Lucy of Nicole's soap-opera script. So says Beattie, it seems, about her company of *pagliacci,* clowns and jokers and poseurs who are almost always revealed to be crying on the inside. (p. 40)

But with nearly a dozen principal players wandering through a hectic yet static plot, Beattie's skittish narration never settles down long enough to bring any of them into rounded focus; the attempt to invest them with emotional heft registers only as a mawkish gimmick. . . . Meanwhile, the comic potential in these wayward personalities remains diffused, largely unexploited: as if to cancel out her few bold squiggles of burlesque, Beattie is constantly hedging and justifying, distancing and blurring, declining to give her characters coherent identities—or to adopt one of her own.

Such ambivalence may not be enough to alienate those readers who come to *Love Always* with a preexisting faith in Beattie-as-soulmate, as trend spotter and generational guide. Others, however, will find themselves distrusting Beattie-as-narrator, especially since the uncoordinated attempts at social satire fare only slightly better than the manipulations of character. (pp. 40-1)

Throughout, in fact, Beattie seems uneasy as a cartoonist, while her proven talents—as a fine-tuner of casual dialogue, an observer of post-Sixties mores, and a collector of late-twentieth-century artifacts—are subverted by the distracting clamor all around, by the erosion of the reader's confidence in an over-extended, capricious narrator. Few readers, certainly, will be inclined to look for—or be much affected by—the starker, quieter motifs that Beattie (in yet another mode) has rather elegantly laced through this inelegant novel. On its busy surface *Love Always* would appear to be most seriously concerned with the ironic dynamics of loveless love and hollow ambitions. But there's also, barely discernible amid the narrative chaos, a potentially powerful, largely squandered counter-theme: Maureen's remembered miscarriage is the first in a series of references, throughout the book, to childless women (including characters on Nicole's soap) and orphaned children (including Elvis Presley's daughter)—perhaps suggesting that the only love with an ''always'' guarantee is the link between parent and child. . . .

Finally, then, this hard-working jumble of comic/portentous gestures becomes—like most of the anecdotes Lucy Spenser knows—just ''another story that made things tenuous and a bit ironic," enervating and thin. Beattie's technical limitations as a novelist (her inert, summarizing style has never transferred well to full-length fiction) are partly to blame, exacerbated by the sheer busyness of her Vermont/Hollywood variations on *La Ronde*. Above all, however, *Love Always* fails because Beattie recoils from the liberating embrace that gives any heightened comedy its energy and conviction. Villain or fool, Tartuffe or Falstaff, Roth's Mrs. Portnoy, John Kennedy Toole's Ignatius Reilly, or (on a more modest level) the eccentric Tula Springs denizens of the young novelist James Wilcox (*Modern Baptists, North Gladiola*)—comic characters must on some level be surrendered to, even celebrated, not just scrutinized and explained. In *Love Always* only Nicole's carnage-loving dog, St. Francis, "a monster, pure and simple," is allowed that kind of zestful autonomy. With her two-legged characters Beattie never lets go, never gives in; she's alternately intrusive and standoffish, Having It All by way of authorial distance and safety but missing nearly every opportunity for persuasive, exhilarating human comedy. (p. 41)

> Josh Rubins, "Having It All," in The New York Review of Books, *Vol. XXXII, No. 12, July 18, 1985, pp. 40-1.*

JOHN UPDIKE

Ann Beattie, though there has always been a kind of fond humor in her deadpan, delicate stories of languishing young lives and her willingness to transcribe the grotesquer details of American popular culture, has not hitherto been satirical. Satire must stand outside a world and its values; it implies a better way of doing things, a certain credal position, whether it be Waugh's Catholicism, Orwell's anti-Communism, Twain's roughneck skepticism, or Beerbohm's hermetic dandyism. There must be some energy of indignation, of rejection. Miss Beattie's power and influence, on the contrary, arise from her seemingly resistless immersion in the stoic bewilderment of a generation without a cause, a generation for whom love as well as politics is a consumer item too long on the shelves and whose deflationary mood is but dimly brightened by the background chirping of nostalgia-inducing pop tunes and the faithful attendance of personable pet dogs; in the now swollen chorus of minimalist fiction, it was she who first found the tone for the post-Vietnam, post-engagé mood, much as Hemingway found the tone for his own generation's disenchantment with all brands of officially promoted importance. Both authors remade reality out of short, concrete sentences and certifiable, if small, sensations; in the absence of any greater good, the chronic appearance of food on the table becomes an event worth celebrating. . . .

[In *Love Always*], Miss Beattie seems to be on the attack, though her targets dissolve so quickly that she keeps popping new characters into the gallery. (p. 80)

The novel holds a dazing wealth of anecdote and attributed eccentricity: Noonan, a homosexual writer for the magazine, likes to steal things; Peter, his lover and a specialist in *in utero* surgery, drives a refurbished Checker cab with leopardskin jump seats and a black bear rug; Piggy Proctor, Nicole's agent, communicates with her by taping antic TDK cassettes; Hildon likes to make love while viewing videotapes from other moments of his life and further enhances his existence by disguising himself, in a "Born to Lose T-shirt, torn jeans, pointed-toe boots with spurs," as a "shit kicker"—that is, a normal, local person. These locals, however, seem as prone to personality tics and infestation by media-think as the Manhattan émigrés, and the Forest of Arden called Vermont offers little contrast to the pageant of imported dissatisfaction that serves, in *Love Always,* for comedy.

The author's view of the world is not comedic: no conceivable social order could be drawn firm, in Shakespearean style, when her romantic hurly-burly exhausts itself. Marriage, the traditional end of comedy and of Jane Austen novels (Austen and Scott Fitzgerald haunt this book along with Yeats), ranks here as a disaster area: Lucy and Jane's father deserted them, Jane's husbands are wildly loserish, Lucy helps to break up Hildon's marriage without a flinch of compunction, and she, momentarily considered as wife material by a longtime suitor, is rejected for the fey reason that "she was wonderful, but she wasn't right." The changing nature of heterosexual relations and, particularly, the ineluctable unsatisfactoriness of men prompt Lucy's most earnest meditations. . . . There is, in short, no pleasing men, on any kind of substantial basis; indeed, they have no substance, they are all pose and fantasy. Lucy accuses Les Whitehall, a previous beau: "When I tried to deal with you as a real person instead of idolizing you, you left." She reflects that, for all Les's charm, "in reality he did not approve of himself or of anyone else. Anyone who had less than he had wasn't worth his time, and anyone who had more was a threat." Hildon ends by perceiving that "nobody was his type." Les has written Lucy claiming of Hildon that he is in Vermont "in hiding from being a serious person." Hildon hates Les. These two rivals, the two romantic leads of Lucy's inner videotape, are yet so interchangeable that Les finally slips into Hildon's job, while Hildon sinks into an ending as bitter and smoky as that of a Don DeLillo novel.

Unreality, insubstantiality, interchangeability: these make up the novel's agenda, and are built disturbingly into its texture. Many of the characters seem superfluous, but then perhaps they all, and we all, are superfluous. Several introduced early with a promising flourish, like Nigel the photographer and Cameron Petrus the Bostonian and Matt Smith the new publisher of *Country Daze*, fade away as if forgotten by their creator; others, such as Myra DeVane the investigative reporter, have a continuing presence in the novel but no defined personality. (p. 81)

The characters are oddly transparent—jellyfish through which one keeps seeing the same salt water. Myra DeVane has a tryst at the Plaza, while Andrew Steinborn defends it as still a fashionable place. Nicole tries to read *Pride and Prejudice*, the same book Lucy's mother read to her as a girl. Are these connections, or symptoms of a blithe carelessness? The events do not feel consecutive, scenes that we want to witness are left out, scenes developed at length come to little, and the plot meanders as if in mimicry of "Passionate Intensity"'s episodes.

"The best lack all conviction," Yeats wrote, "while the worst Are full of passionate intensity." These best and brightest lack conviction and, with it, the coherence that makes fictional characters in the old-fashioned sense; they are not so much round or flat, in E. M. Forster's geometrical terminology, as on or off. Images on a cathode-ray tube are produced by a bombardment of electrons; a pointillist bombardment from the culture at large seems to conjure up Lucy and her friends, who wink out in their own minds as readily as in our own. Too much self-consciousness evaporates the self. All pursuits end up trivialized. Take away the brand names, the slogans, the nicely worked-out costumes and postures, and you have blank tape. Lucy intermittently looks around her, at what she imagines is Vermont:

> From where Lucy sat, she couldn't see the trickle of muddy river below. The farmhouse with the blue roof she had always loved was visible on the hillside, and people hardly larger than dots were moving around it—people and cows—more of those mysterious people who thought something and felt some way Lucy couldn't fathom. People who lived in a house in the valley.

Yet the reader has no reason to suppose that the house in the valley holds anything different; it is just a blue blip and some jiggling dots on Lucy's screen. This novel is sadder than satire, for it is about the emptiness not of these lives but of our lives. (pp. 81-2)

> *John Updike, "Beattieniks," in* The New Yorker, *Vol. LXI, No. 24, August 5, 1985, pp. 80-2.*

S(amuel) N(athaniel) Behrman

1893-1973

American dramatist, memoirist, essayist, biographer, short story writer, scriptwriter, translator, and novelist.

An important exponent of the American comedy of manners, Behrman combined social, political, and philosophical commentary with sophisticated humor to expose the incongruities of human behavior. In his plays, Behrman underscored the distinctive qualities of his characters through contrast; his protagonists are usually upper-class sophisticates whose impassive social and philosophical attitudes are challenged by the intolerant views of their adversaries. Among the major themes in Behrman's work are success and the acquisition of wealth and power, morality, Jewishness, and the conflict between political activism and tolerance. Behrman is often praised for his use of witty and urbane dialogue, his incisive characterizations, and for the intelligence of his comic vision. Like the works of many of his contemporaries, including Noël Coward and Philip Barry, Behrman's dramatic comedies are products of their time and have not enjoyed continued success in the decades since their original productions. His prose memoirs, however, are considered important for their depiction of the coming of age of a talented young playwright and their portraits of various personalities of the World War I era.

Behrman's first play, *The Second Man* (1927), a subtly humorous story about a dilettante writer who forsakes romantic love for the comforts of wealth, established Behrman's reputation as an insightful writer of high comedy. Several of his succeeding plays, including *Serena Blandish; or the Difficulty of Getting Married* (1929), based on a novel by Enid Bagnold, *Brief Moment* (1931), and *Biography* (1932), resemble *The Second Man* in their emphasis on the love interests of complex, upper-class characters. These plays, as is true of most comedies of manners, are clearly removed from reality; as Joseph Wood Krutch noted, "Mr. Behrman's plays are obviously 'artificial'—both in the sense that they deal with an artificial and privileged section of society and in the sense that the characters themselves are less real persons than idealized embodiments of intelligence and wit." Behrman's plays of this period were well received both by critics and the public. By the 1930s, however, the disturbing economic and political climate in the United States and the volatile state of world affairs deemed Behrman's light comedies inappropriate, and he began to consider more serious themes.

In *Rain from Heaven* (1934), *End of Summer* (1936), and *Wine of Choice* (1938), Behrman introduced some of the important political issues of the time, notably the assault on individual freedom from both the radical right and left, into the reserved social commentary of traditional drawing-room comedy. These plays were less successful with playgoers than his earlier comedies and were faulted by many critics for being overly didactic and lacking focus. *No Time for Comedy* (1939), Behrman's semiautobiographical account of a successful playwright's efforts to reconcile his desire to continue writing comedy with society's demand for serious drama, is generally regarded as marking the end of the most creative phase of his career. Most of Behrman's plays after *No Time for Comedy* are adaptations from the works of other authors or collaborations with other

playwrights. Despite a mixed critical response, some of these works, including *I Know My Love* (1948), adapted from a work by Marcel Achard, and *Fanny* (1954), written in collaboration with Joshua Logan and adapted from the work of Marcel Pagnol, were popular successes and enjoyed long runs on Broadway.

During the 1950s, Behrman turned his attention to producing prose works, many of which were originally published as essays in *The New Yorker* and later collected in book form. *Duveen* (1952) is an anecdotal biography of the infamous art dealer Joseph Duveen. *The Worcester Account* (1954) reveals Behrman's early years in the Jewish enclave of Worcester, Massachusetts, and is the basis for one of his later plays, *The Cold Wind and the Warm* (1958). Behrman's only novel, *The Burning Glass* (1968), details the experiences of a successful young Jewish playwright from Ohio amid the cosmopolitan worlds of Salzburg and Hollywood in the late 1930s. Behrman's final work, *People in a Diary: A Memoir* (1972), begins where *The Worcester Account* ended, retracing his career in the theater through portraits of the people he knew and with whom he worked. Behrman also wrote or collaborated on the scripts of many films throughout his long career.

Critics generally agree that the quality of Behrman's drama declined after the 1930s and that by the 1950s both the material and the manner of high comedy had become dated. Although Behrman's plays are rarely revived, Cyrus Hoy observed that they "deserve to be remembered for both the individual excellencies of single plays and their collective testimony to a humane and intelligent playwright's attempt to mirror the complexities and the anxieties of modern society in one of the most traditional of dramatic forms."

(See also *Contemporary Authors*, Vols. 15-16, Vols. 45-48 [obituary]; *Contemporary Authors Permanent Series*, Vol. 1; and *Dictionary of Literary Biography*, Vols. 7, 44.)

J. BROOKS ATKINSON

[In *The Second Man*] Mr. Behrman is uncommonly facile with his dialogue, and perhaps wiser about his own generation than the violent course of his comedy indicates. Nor has he been slovenly with his four principal characters; they are ably described as individuals representing distinct points of view. After a cyclone season of blurting melodramas it is good to welcome such true characters back on the stage. But the story of *The Second Man* is beaten too thin for an evening of compact entertainment. Mr. Behrman's theatrical devices for bringing it swiftly to life again wrench his comedy out of its natural course among four people of forthright, unequivocal character.

It is a comedy of two groups of young people muddled by love in the timeless manner of stage and poetry. Clark Storey, a complacently humorous and cynical novelist, wants to marry Mrs. Kendall Frayne because she is wealthy and tolerant. "Outside of the fact that I love comfort—and that you are rich—I like you very much," he confesses without superfluous passion. Mrs. Frayne is not actively displeased. The second couple consists of a talented scientist, Austin Lowe, who is passionately devoted to Monica Grey. As Clark cleverly remarks of her, "Her talk is not small. It is infinitesimal. Your microscopic training should help you." If Monica had seen the worldly light as clearly as her elders and if she had gone obediently to the man who loved her, Mr. Behrman might have had no play at all. But for some childish whim she persists in loving Storey. How she is disillusioned, how the glamour surrounding Storey suddenly fades, and how she tenderly goes to her suitor involves three acts and one or two factitious theatrical devices.

In the expression of this engagingly simple fable Mr. Behrman rather vexes his play with innumerable exits and entrances, and when the story begins to grow tame in the second and third acts he administers the shocks of one scandalous revelation and of one pistol shot. Candidly, they shock more than Mr. Behrman intended; they very nearly shock his study of character off the stage.

Inasmuch as he has been so adroit in his anatomizing of human motives and so delightful in his dialogue, these purely esthetic faults are all the more disappointing. For between the rippling lines of his patter one feels that Mr. Behrman has looked searchingly into the hearts of his four modern people. If you care to be stern about them, they are indeed alarming. They are selfish to the point of cruelty; they mock the finer things of life; they are flaccid; they risk nothing for an ideal; they never let go.

Only Monica retains the impulses of youth; and as every one takes pains to remind her, she merely lacks understanding. But if you care to regard them sympathetically, they are not bad young people at all; on the contrary, they are ingratiating, wise, self-reliant, with a hard code of honor that is really good sportsmanship. Their gayety may be overshadowed with worldly sadness, but it is not false. If it has any fault it is too militantly honest. All these subtle qualities Mr. Behrman has managed to express deftly in his first produced play.

> *J. Brooks Atkinson, in a review of "The Second Man,"*
> *in* The New York Times, *April 12, 1927, p. 24.*

JOSEPH WOOD KRUTCH

It would be easy, and perhaps not entirely unjust, to dismiss S. N. Behrman's tenuous little comedy *The Second Man* . . . as no more than a bit of inconsequential fluff kept pretty constantly amusing by . . . expert direction . . . and by the suave acting of an excellent company. . . . The plot, concerning itself with the successful effort of an honest and amiable but indolent short-story writer to disentangle himself from the determined embraces of an infatuated flapper in order that he may marry an old friend with an income, is developed with liveliness rather than with any remarkable inevitability; and so, I say, one might dismiss the piece with no more than what has already been said. Yet it would, I think, be more profitable to consider it rather in connection with the thing which it and many other similar plays are striving to be and which it in a measure succeeds in being; for it is,. in effect, sentimental comedy on the point of becoming that much higher thing, pure comedy.

Mr. Behrman, it is to be noted first of all, has chosen as his milieu the American equivalent of the smart bohemia so extensively and so cheaply exploited by that nine days' wonder, Noel Coward. Occupied exclusively by well-decorated studios, inhabited by a race of near-artists and their semi-fashionable hangers-on, and dedicated less to the practice of the seven arts than to fastidious experimentation with both the Ten Commandments of Moses and the ten thousand of the social code, it is a semi-mythical region not unanalogous to that which constitutes the scene of the plays of Congreve, but it has a sort of ideal existence. Its denizens, all well enough off to be pleasantly irresponsible, represent rather the ideal aspired to than the actuality achieved by the class of real people from which they are imitated, and their artistic function is to strive to create a comedy of manners in the old sense, a comedy, that is to say, which takes its rise from the fact that its characters order their lives by their minds rather than by their emotions and frankly acknowledge prudence rather than sentiment as their guide. . . .

Mr. Coward's comedy was, as comedy, completely destroyed both by the extent to which he introduced sentiment and by a half-hypocritical, half-muddle-headed tendency to conventional moralizing which gave his plays a tone quite as much suggestive of nurse-maid literature as of high comedy; but from this Mr. Behrman has entirely escaped. He has, to be sure, satisfied the sentimental half of his audience by disposing of the little flapper safely in the arms of the romanticist who really loves her, but he preserves the comic spirit of his hero intact and he shows no moralistic incapacity to accept that hero, for he leaves him, not as Mr. Coward would have done, desolately aware of the charming romance he has thrown away, but contentedly talking over the telephone to the amiable lady with the amiable income who will serve to make him comically content. Moreover, to say that Mr. Behrman's lines are bright is not enough. We must revive the distinction which seventeenth-century critics made between wit and humor, a distinction which may be translated into the modern vocabulary as the difference between that kind of comic writing which consists in giving to the personages lines which are funny because they are in character and that kind which consists in allowing everybody without distinction to indulge in some current form of wise-cracking. Most of Mr. Behrman's characters are fairly conventional types, but his hero is individually conceived and his lines amusing because they serve constantly to define his point of view. "It is terrible," he remarks, "to take money from a woman. But then for the life of me I can't see why it is any worse than taking it from anybody else."

Very few writers, and those few are among the greatest that the world has produced, have ever succeeded in completely accepting and completely expressing the comic attitude. It requires a sophistication, a disillusion if you like, far deeper than that which can be acquired by a little free thinking and a little loose talking, for it is a difficult philosophy of life and one very easy to corrupt by ever so little concessive toying with romantic sentiment. No one (not Goldsmith, not Sheridan, and not Wilde) has written pure comedy since Congreve, and certainly Mr. Behrman does not do it; but he is just a little bit better than most of the Americans and Englishmen who are struggling toward it and that little bit is important.

Joseph Wood Krutch, "Comedy of Manners," in The Nation, *Vol. CXXIV, No. 3225, April 27, 1927, p. 484.**

JOHN MASON BROWN

The Second Man, by S. N. Behrman, is a comedy that aims at being very *haut-monde* but that somehow does not admit its characters beyond the vestibule of authentic sophistication. Starting with a crisp first act that glitters with the wit of disillusionment, and maintaining a certain pleasurable effervescence to the end, it is far more enjoyable than most of the comedies that trail into New York and has its spurts of genuine high comedy. But it runs thin too soon and falls back rather helplessly upon farce to gain a last minute consistency. . . . Mr. Behrman's people . . . [seem] blasé in a counterfeit way. In part, the fault lies with the talkiness and the unavoidable monotony of a play that enlists only four characters for three long acts. But a more important flaw is the insistency with which Mr. Behrman drives home his very simple underlying idea. Certainly a contemporary audience does not have to be informed more than once that a man may have two selves which are in constant conflict. But Mr. Behrman seems to think differently. First of all he quotes a letter of Lord Leighton's in his programme that says, "for, together with, and as it were behind, so much pleasurable emotion, there is always that other strange second man in me, calm, critical, observant, unmoved, blasé, odious," which more than sums up the play. Then he has his novelist, whose natural self has been suppressed by just such a second man and who is consequently engaged to a wealthy widow, though he is really in love with a young girl, state the theorem all over again . . . and again . . . and state it baldly and explicitly, when the action itself has been doing just that very thing since the rise of the first curtain. (p. 404)

John Mason Brown, "The Merry Month of May," in Theatre Arts Monthly, *Vol. XI, No. 6, June, 1927, pp. 401-13.**

JOSEPH WOOD KRUTCH

[In *Meteor*] Mr. S. N. Behrman has drawn a dramatic portrait of extraordinary richness and originality. Even the casual observer cannot fail to be intrigued by the vivid personality of his central character, but I doubt if such a casual observer is very likely to realize what a difficult feat the author has achieved. It is easy to say that your hero is a genius and it is not especially difficult to make the other dramatis personae act as though he were, but it is a very different matter to convince your audience and that is exactly what Mr. Behrman does.

The story which he has chosen to tell is not, in itself, very novel or very important. Indeed there is something artificial about this tale of his hero's rise to financial eminence—something factitious which suggests that it was invented without great enthusiasm and for no other reason than that a story of some sort was necessary. But this relative conventionality of plot is thrown into sharp relief by the vivid reality of its protagonist. From the very moment when this consummate and yet ingratiating egotist appears upon the scene he seizes upon the imagination of the spectator and holds it by virtue of that very fascination which is supposed to reduce his companions to impotent wonder. We are not asked to understand him and we never do. For us as for those who share the play with him he remains an all but incredible mixture of vanity and power—a man to be laughed at and to be labeled with all the names which psychologists have invented to chastise the pride of those who think abnormally well of themselves. But his reality is as indubitable as his secret is dear, and though the last curtain leaves us still wondering how much of his success is due to genius and how much to a delusion so powerful that it hypnotizes others as completely as it does its victim, the one thing we never doubt is the existence of the man whose portrait Mr. Behrman has so skilfully drawn. His vigor, his confidence, and his maniacal self-absorption are all there. So, too, are the touches of weakness and folly which make him human. Sometimes we suspect, as his companions sometimes do, that he is merely naive, but our doubts are never so strong as his faith and that, perhaps, is the secret of his power. (pp. 78-9)

[Mr. Behrman] has, I think, succeeded because of the extent to which he has been willing (and able!) to let his hero speak for himself. Whenever Mr. Behrman succumbs to the temptation to explain or analyze he is relatively weak. Even the touch of mysticism seems to me a blemish and so do all the other efforts to get inside the character or to explain him in terms of normal human nature. We can know such a man only from the outside. He takes our breath away with the directness of his vanity; he dazzles us with his success in realizing his own conception of his powers; and it is in the representation of these things that Mr. Behrman excels. In one sense his character is too much for him just as he is too much for his companions, but the record of his words and deeds is too vivid to be forgotten. If *Meteor* be considered as a whole it is doubtless far from perfect, but I cannot, at least offhand, think of any character in American drama who is likely to remain longer in the imagination of the spectator. (p. 79)

Joseph Wood Krutch, "Portrait of an Egotist," in The Nation, *Vol. CXXX, No. 3367, January 15, 1930, pp. 78-9.*

JANE DRANSFIELD

With his first two plays, *The Second Man* and *Serena Blandish,* Mr. S. N. Behrman established himself as an American playwright capable of excellent work in high comedy. In this, his third play, *Meteor,* he enhances his own reputation for skill in character drawing and absorbing dialogue. While neither profound nor richly imaginative in his work, Mr. Behrman is a keen observer, with a tendency, however, toward the unusual and particular rather than to the universal. This new play, for instance, is a study of a supreme egotist, but the "I am God" complex of Raphael Lord is far different from the bourgeois self confidence of George Kelly's *The Show Off.* There is a certain spiritual quality about Lord, his belief in himself being founded upon his possession of clairvoyant powers. As drawn in the early parts of the play he is a fascinating, romantic figure, and his final downfall, with his lapse into ruthless and blatant personal egotism, comes almost as a shock. The character, moreover, is not mere invention on the part of the author. The superiority complex, while not exactly common, exists among us today to an astonishing degree, a product, perhaps, of our popular superman metaphysics. To justify his theme, therefore, Mr. Behrman needs no Napoleonic quotation (as on the title page). We first see Lord, "febrile, restless, his mind an incessant gyroscope," as an impatient student in a middle western college, older than most of the students, his past shrouded in mystery. Next we see him, five years later, as a master of finance, a metropolitan multimillionaire. Success has been easy. He has simply followed his clairvoyant leadings. In the reliance upon these powers lie his tragedy and his downfall. When these fail him, however, his egotism comes to his rescue: "This sets me free. Now, for the first time, I'm ready for my destiny." The play is satire in its essence, but not pure satire in development, and consequently is unsatisfactory as a whole in its final reaction. There is a flaw in the psychology.... Nevertheless, *Meteor* is unique and arresting.

> Jane Dransfield, in a review of "Meteor," in The Saturday Review of Literature, Vol. VI, No. 42, May 10, 1930, p. 1024.

J. BROOKS ATKINSON

[In *Brief Moment* Mr. Behrman] is among his contemporaries again, analyzing them with rare understanding and writing a light dialogue that is a joy to hear. It is the story, suggested by a recent episode in New York life, of a wealthy banker's son who marries a night club singer. To Mr. Behrman this is no occasion for random theatricals. He is interested in his characters, and he is willing to let them discover their own salvation. As a play *Brief Moment* is limp and for half its length apparently aimless. If you are looking for rapid-fire patter you will be disappointed. What distinguishes it is the flavor of the dialogue and the thoroughness of its characterizations....

Brief Moment is tepid and discursive as a play. As a study of modern characters, it has the sort of fineness Mr. Behrman can impart to his work.... Like newspaper work, *Brief Moment* introduces you to interesting people.

> J. Brooks Atkinson, "Woollcott and Contemporaries," in The New York Times, November 10, 1931, p. 28.

STARK YOUNG

[*Brief Moment*] does not always progress steadily, perhaps, as a continuous dramatic line, though the line in comedy is rather loose and obliging. But it tries to extract from the characters and from the situation an assemblage of thoughts and reactions such as intelligent people might recognize as lying in their own region. This sounds a simple matter, but is far from it. We do not, with the most wretched settings or with the rawest coincidences of fate in the plot and stage hokum in the acting, accept more than we do in the stage realm of thoughts, reactions and conversation. Very little of the poorest scenery is poorer than the ideas in most plays, though the presence of living vehicles for these ideas, human beings and human voices, gives them some degree of interest and enlists our patience and humanity for stuff that we all know is miles beneath our most ordinary level of intelligence.

The mere mental responses and emotional states of Mr. Behrman's play are a contribution to our stage. What he tries for we are better accustomed to in books than in the theatre, where cerebral activity and civilized analysis have not seemed very plausible. Broadway is therefore heavily in his debt. The subtleties of our general drama are mostly only expedite and obvious; and work like much of that in *Brief Moment* is more of an innovation on Broadway than writing the play backward, or foiling time and space with revolving stages. To have carried his thoughts and shadings into theatricality and entertainment is something for Mr. Behrman to crow about. (p. 70)

> Stark Young, "Three More Plays," in The New Republic, Vol. LXIX, No. 887, December 2, 1931, pp. 69-71.*

STARK YOUNG

Mr. Behrman in *Biography* ... remains one of the few playwrights that we have ever had in America who does not cause embarrassment to dramatist, actors and audience when he indulges in brains or sophisticated statement. The underlying basis of *Biography* proceeds from a mind that is mature, that suggests a degree of association with literature and that, once it has found out that people do say from time to time intelligent things and that there is nothing to be nervous about when the characters and motivations are not Broadway or primitive or traditional or idiotic, is not afraid. He is one of those rare authors in the theatre who do not mistrust civilized society and do not think that Times Square must understand or no tickets will be sold....

In his new comedy there appears a certain roundness or sweetness, more in solution than expressed, that marks a definite advance for him. The play tells the story of Marion Froude, a sort of big laissez-faire girl, as she says of herself, who is not vicious but very casual, who has painted portraits of diverse celebrities at home and abroad, even in Russia, and who at the opening of the play is confronted with a young journalist, Richard Kurt, the child of disillusion, in whom rage the storms of revolt, candors and strenuosity. He has come to arrange with her for the story of her life, which is to appear in the magazine he works for. At the same time, her first lover from her own Tennessee appears. He is about to become a Senator by marriage with the daughter of the leading editor in his state. As a matter of fact, he has never forgotten Marion and the renewal of her presence disturbs him profoundly, leads to the order for a portrait, and so on. The complications around her biography—to cut the matter short—become finally the exhibition point of all characters in the play; the editor, the Tennessee Senator suitor, the young revolter, the editor's daughter and Melchior Feydak, a Viennese composer, brother of a famous dead musician who was the lover, still deeply remembered, of Marion.... The play, as it draws towards its conclusion, therefore, shows everyone in character and leaves Marion in character also, for, at the very last, she understands that what she would do to her young man is to destroy in him the very thing she loves. He, on his part, explodes himself out of the scene, heart-broken and more distorted than ever.

This is, of course, an absurd account of a play not without intricacy of character and motivation. *Biography* has a great deal of subtle and beautiful insight, and the characters, certainly so at the highest point of their dramatic expression in the play, are revealed in a matrix very much superior to the ordinary run of plays.

In the first scene the effect is the least happy in all the play. There is, as a matter of fact, something very close to common, next to vulgar, in the way its people crack at each other. It is the influence, perhaps, of the vulgarity in our social drama generally, where bad manners are confused with wit. What Mr. Behrman needs in this passage of the play is to put over it something a little more subtle in taste. The best thing to be said, perhaps, for this side of *Biography*, is that more grace of mind and an impression of a more distinguished breeding in the dramatist would drown all we see and hear in a bath of humor, leave it less blunt and half-crude in its impact, and leave it more carefully wrought as to the dramatist's own comment on the characters and scene. The play, also, in spots—for example, in the last act—appears to be a little pieced up, not wholly fluent in its progress. On the other hand, it exhibits no scenes of mere vulgar adequacy, good as far as it goes, which is not very far. It refreshes rhythm, in the dialogue especially. The fact remains us by being civilized as well as blessed with a good theatre however, that much of the dialogue needs reworking at various spots, some of which as they stand now are only job lots that get nowhere at all. The whole play needs to be slightly stressed in the crucial emphases of the dramatic situation. But in the scenes themselves there is a plenitude of insight and self-respecting mentality that makes Mr. Behrman one of the interesting playwrights in English and *Biography* one of the interesting things of the season, a play before which you can sit not alone with the lethargy of being there already and in seats that are comfortable, but also with self-respect. (p. 188)

> Stark Young, "Without Embarrassment," *in* The New Republic, *Vol. LXXIII, No. 943, December 28, 1932, pp. 188-89.*

BROOKS ATKINSON

If S. N. Behrman wrote with more fever and crackle, his comedies of manners would no doubt arouse more excitement in the theatre. For pace and hilarity his first comedy, *The Second Man,* is still his most successful. But in the last six years Mr. Behrman has been steadily refining his gifts for writing and observation, and his current play, *Biography,* is in every respect his best. No one who is writing for the theatre today can match him for limpidity of character portrayal. . . .

You have only to read the script of *Biography* . . . to realize that Mr. Behrman has here become the master of his art. He has given his characters free rein to govern the tone and direction of his play. If *Biography* seems a little tenuous as drama, it is because his chief character is instinctively too complaisant and tolerant for pyrotechnics. Mr. Behrman is a scrupulous dramatist. Although he writes with a subdued hum of wit, he never once sacrifices a character or a situation to a brilliant remark. Story and dialogue proceed naturally out of the thoughts and impulses of these seven or eight modern people. But let us not commit the fallacy of assuming that any work of art lives independent of its author. Whether it is a drama, a novel or a painting, every figure in it is in the image of its creator. And if *Biography* seems remarkable for its neatness and dexterity and its quietly amused understanding of life, it is because those are the qualities of Mr. Behrman's mind. He writes with the tranquillity of an observant and reflective artist. . . .

It is the weakness of comedy of manners that nothing of tremendous importance is at stake. As a play in the theatre *Biography* does not altogether escape that pallor of theme. Marion Froude is attractive, wise, generous and straightforward . . . ; but she is incorrigibly tolerant, which is only a modest virtue. . . . Overwrought and demoniac as the editor may be, he puts his finger on the essential weakness of that submissive scheme of life: "I see now why everything is this way," he says, "why the injustice and the cruelty go on, year after year, century after century, without change, because, as they grow older, people become tolerant! Things amuse them. I hate you and I hate your tolerance. I always did." Of all the characters in *Biography* the editor is the only one whom Mr. Behrman has overdrawn. Amusing and startling as he is on the stage, his excesses, especially in the company of strangers, put you on your critical guard. But something is at stake in this editor's passionate scheme of existence. He is the stuff of which exciting plays are made.

But when you are one of Mr. Behrman's guests prepare yourself not for jeremiads or fulminations, but for skill, understanding, neatly phrased humors and for the integrity of a fine artist. . . . In *The Second Man* Mr. Behrman proved that he knew how to manipulate a comic story shrewdly. In *Brief Moment* he moved among the moderns he knew with mature assurance. And now in *Biography* he resolves character, story and dialogue into a finely textured comedy of manners. It is a modest play, for that is Mr. Behrman's nature, and it comes lightly and beguilingly out of the scrambled lives we moderns are living.

> Brooks Atkinson, "Maker of Modern Comedy," *in* The New York Times, *Section 9, January 22, 1933, p. 1.*

MORTON EUSTIS

Biography, despite an excellent initial idea and many flashes of expert high comedy dialogue, never measures up in the sum total to the expectations in store for it. After a good first act, and a less good second act, it seems to be continually on the verge of coming to grips with its main theme only to skate blithely away from it in the field of farce. In his characterization, too, Mr. Behrman, except in the subtle delineation of his leading character, has only sketched types, which are all the more obviously types in contrast to the central figure. As *Biography* does afford considerable amusement, it may seem unnecessarily perverse to dwell at length on its failings. If *Biography* were the work of a less gifted playwright this might be true. We should be thankful for what we had received and hope for more next time. But Mr. Behrman, by right of being one of our most brilliant writers of high comedy—a field in which American dramatists are notable chiefly because of their rarity—must be judged by standards considerably more severe. (pp. 103-04)

In brief outline *Biography* seems to bear the elements of a splendid comedy and in brief outline it does. The trouble is that Mr. Behrman was not content to let his story tell itself in the terms of the characters but must needs introduce many extraneous scenes which detract from his main plot—notably the farcical one in the third act wherein the first lover, his fiancée, and prospective father-in-law all argue it out in the woman's studio. Some of these interludes are comic in themselves, but high comedy should spring primarily from the characterization, and even brilliant dialogue cannot disguise this fact. (p. 104)

Morton Eustis, "Wonderland," in Theatre Arts Monthly, Vol. XVII, No. 2, February, 1933, pp. 101-15.*

JOSEPH WOOD KRUTCH

[The essay from which this excerpt is taken was originally published in The Nation, July 19, 1933.]

When the Theatre Guild produced *The Second Man* in the fall of 1928 S. N. Behrman was totally unknown. Since then he has written only two other plays which achieved an outstanding success, but there is no American dramatist who has more clearly defined or more convincingly defended an individual and specific talent. (p. 272)

The public was given no opportunity to discover Mr. Behrman until he had completely discovered himself, and *The Second Man* was not only a mature play—quite as good as anything he has written since—but actually a comedy about Comedy and therefore, by implication, the announcement of a program. All its accidental qualities were, of course, those common to nearly every work which even approaches the type of which it represents the fully developed form. The locale was luxurious, the people privileged enough to spend most of their time adjusting amorous or other complications, and the conversation sparkling with wit. But the theme was the Comic Spirit itself and the hero a man forced to make that decision between the heroic and the merely intelligent which must be made before comedy really begins.

Like Mr. Behrman himself, his hero belongs to a society which still pretends rather unsuccessfully to affirm its faith in moral ideals. Romantic love, for example, is still theoretically so tremendous a thing that no man or woman worthy of the name would hesitate to give up everything else in its favor. Life, below even the frivolous surface of fashionable existence, is supposed to be real and supposed to be earnest. But our hero—a second-rate story writer—has brains enough to know, not only that his stories are second rate, but also that he does not really believe what he is supposed to believe. He can strike the heroic attitude, but the steam is not really there. A "second man" inside himself whispers the counsel of prudence and common sense, tells him that he does not really prefer love to comfort, or exaltation to pleasure. The only integrity he has is the only one which is necessary to a comic hero—the one which makes it impossible for him either to be a conscious hypocrite on the one hand or, on the other, so to befuddle himself with sentiment as to conceal from even his own mind the fact that he is making one choice while pretending to make the other.

In terms of action the result is that he sends packing the determined flapper who wants to marry him and returns to the wealthy mistress who can support him in the luxury to which he has been accustomed. . . . Incidentally, and in the course of this action, the result is also to develop with bold clarity the whole philosophy of a hero who has surrendered the effort to be heroic and is ready to explain without equivocation why such as he must take themselves and the world as they find them without either trying to pretend that they are different or trying to make them so. The originality of the whole—so far as our particular stage is concerned—consists just in the fact that the play neither shirks the logic of its own conclusions nor presents itself as a simple "shocker" but remains essentially "serious" in the sense that it accepts and defends the premises of all pure comedy. "Life is a tragedy to those who feel and a comedy to those who think." Follow the emotions and you may reach ecstasy; but if you cannot do that, then listen to the dictates of common sense and there is a very good chance that you will be comfortable—even, God willing, witty besides. (pp. 273-74)

Since his first play [Mr. Behrman] has spent a good deal of time in Hollywood and he ought, it would seem, to share the weaknesses as well as the strengths of the typical Broadway group into which he seems so obviously to fit. But by now it is evident that *The Second Man* was no accident. He shows no tendency to become submerged in the commmon tradition, to write merely in the current manner. Instead, each of his succeeding plays has been quite obviously the product of the same talent and the same integral attitude.

It is true that once—in the comedy-drama *Meteor*—he fumbled the intended effect for the very reason that he had, apparently, not thought the situation through to the point where it could be stated in purely intellectual terms. This history of a rebellious and disorganized genius seen through the eyes of a bewildered but admiring acquaintance is not pure comedy because it is suffused with a sense of wonder, because its subject is a mystery, whereas comedy, almost by definition, admits no mysteries and adopts *nil admirari* as its motto. But since that time Mr. Behrman has not faltered. He made a delightful play out of the delightful English *conte Serena Blandish* and then, in *Brief Moment* and *Biography*, he extended his demonstration of the comic solution to the problem of civilized living. (p. 275)

Brief Moment is concerned with a very rich, intelligent, and disillusioned young man who marries a cabaret singer because he fancies her somehow "elemental," and then discovers that she is all too capable of becoming a very convincing imitation of the women of his own class—not only by adopting all their manners, but by developing a genuine enthusiasm for all the manifestations of fashionable pseudo-culture. One of its points, therefore, is that those "simple souls" which sometimes fascinate the too complicated are really less "beyond" than simply not yet "up to" the follies from which they seem so refreshingly free; but the real theme of the play is larger. Its hero is an inhabitant of that Wasteland described in so many contemporary poems and novels. He is the heir of all our culture, the end product of education and privilege, eclectically familiar with so many enthusiasms and faiths that there is none to which he can give a real allegiance. But instead of gesturing magniloquently in the void, instead of trying, like most of his prototypes in contemporary literature, to turn his predicament into tragedy despite the obvious absence of the necessary tragic exaltation, he is content, first to analyze the situation intellectually and then to compensate for the absence of ecstasy by the cultivation of that grace and wit which no one can be too sophisticated to achieve.

Biography is again the vehicle for a comment made by the Comic Spirit upon one of the predicaments of contemporary life. Its heroine is a mediocre portrait painter with a genius for comely living. Her dilemma arises out of the apparent necessity of choosing between two men—the one a likable but abandoned opportunist in public life, the other a financial revolutionary idealist. Her solution is ultimately to choose neither, and the play is essentially her defense of her right to be a spectator and to cultivate the spectator's virtue—a detached tolerance. The revolutionist says everything which can be said against her attitude. He denounces it as, at bottom, only a compound of indolence and cowardice which parades as a superiority when it is really responsible for the continuance of all the injustices of the world which the intelligent profess themselves too "wise" to correct. But the heroine sticks to her contention that a contemplative, understanding neutrality is "right" for her. She may be wholly ineffectual. The world's work may be done by persons less reasonable and less amiable than she. But wit and tolerance are forms of beauty and, as such, their own excuse for being.

Mr. Behrman's plays are obviously "artificial"—both in the sense that they deal with an artificial and privileged section of society and in the sense that the characters themselves are less real persons than idealized embodiments of intelligence and wit. No person was ever so triple plated with the armor of comic intelligence as his hero; no society ever existed in which all problems were solved—as in his plays they are—when good sense had analyzed them. Just as the tragic writer endows all his characters with his own gift of poetry, so Mr. Behrman endows all his with his own gift for the phrase which lays bare to the mind a meaning which emotion has been unable to disentangle. No drawing room ever existed in which people talked so well or acted so sensibly at last, but this idealization is the final business of comedy. It first deflates man's aspirations and pretensions, accepting the inevitable failure of his attempt to live by his passions or up to his enthusiasms. But when it has done this, it demonstrates what is still left to him—his intelligence, his wit, his tolerance, and his grace—and then, finally, it imagines with what charm he could live if he were freed, not merely from the stern necessities of the struggle for physical existence, but also from the perverse and unexpected quixoticisms of his heart. (pp. 276-77)

> *Joseph Wood Krutch, "The Comic Wisdom of S. N. Behrman," in* The American Theatre as Seen by Its Critics: 1752-1934, *edited by Montrose J. Moses and John Mason Brown, W. W. Norton & Company, Inc., 1934, pp. 272-77.*

GRENVILLE VERNON

Mr. S. N. Behrman is at his best a most accomplished writer of dialogue and an exceedingly subtle etcher of sophisticated human beings. In his latest play [*Rain from Heaven*] both of these qualities are present. His drawing of the charming Lady Violet Wyngate; of the German music critic, Hugo Willens; of the Russian refugee, Nikolai Jurin, are masterly both in conception and execution. Indeed I can recall no American play of recent years which contains three more sensitively drawn, civilized men and women. When these three talk, and they talk rather than do, the evening proves one of unalloyed pleasure. Nothing happens except the expression of ideas, but ideas so subtly evolved, so poignantly expressed, that we forget all else. If these three characters had continued only to talk I, for one, would have been enchanted at the end of the evening, but Mr. Behrman found it necessary after a while to inject a play, and the play was utterly unimportant, and often false to the characters themselves. And for the purposes of the play he had to create other characters, notably a preposterous American fi-

nancier and his equally preposterous wife. These characters might have done in a farce, but they are certainly out of place in a comedy of manners. The story, if it can be dignified by that name, concerns a house-party at Lady Violet's, and Lady Violet's realization that the young aviator she is engaged to is not the man for her. She realizes this when she meets the German music critic, and though the critic at the end goes back to Germany to face the hate of the Nazis, we feel that probably he will some day return to Lady Violet. But the story is trivial, false in its working out, and does not count. But much of the dialogue does. Some day Mr. Behrman will find a theme and a story worthy of his literary gifts.

> *Grenville Vernon, in a review of "Rain from Heaven," in* Commonweal, *Vol. XXI, No. 11, January 11, 1935, p. 318.*

STARK YOUNG

One of Mr. Behrman's attributes as a dramatist is that he surprises people with things on the stage that they take for granted off it, or at least those do who ever heard a conversation or read a book. This is to say that Mr. Behrman's intention and direction are toward the civilized and literate. . . . However it may drag at times and however entertain, *Rain from Heaven* at least moves among words and thoughts and cerebral values. It is also as gentle as Shakespeare could ever have wanted justice to be. I am not sure that the play is not too gentle, in that it softens and glozes the tragic point so often, and falls into a mild analysis that merely brings up another line of Shakespeare's: 'twere to consider too curiously to consider so.

Mr. Behrman's play more or less talks its way through to the dénouement, which is one way of doing it. The talk varies, sometimes quick, subtle and good, sometimes rather lost between the epigrammatic or comic intention and a more direct realism. In Lady Wyngate's house a number of people are met: a rich American and the brother he has made famous by paying for expeditions to the South Pole—Hobart Eldridge and Rand Eldridge—plus, for the ladies, Phoebe Eldridge and Joan Eldridge, the latter in love with a Jewish musician whom we are to believe a fine artist but a sorry piece of humanity. Meanwhile there is Nikolai Jurin, the Russian exile, supposed, doubtless, to afford us the lubrications of a sort of objective and detached subjectivity. And meanwhile there is, also, Hugo Willens, the Wandering Jew of the mind, so to speak, composed of an ancient unrest, wailing wall, personal charm, deliberately self-accepted powers of suffering, and a certain contempt for such emotions and simple ructions that mean nothing to him either racially or profitably. He does not wish contentment, he devotes his self-consciousness to the luxury of the tortured and timeless. Meanwhile, too, there is Lady Wyngate—Lady Violet—who endows a liberal weekly, but is not a Communist or pattern for Hobart Eldridge's conservative fears and dreads. She represents, in a way, a certain British adjustability or unlogical muddling through, comfortable living along with unconcern about worldly assets, simplicity based on complete assurance of position. We must add to that the poignancy of feeling in Lady Violet and the liberation of impulse and commitment that makes her start a love affair with the Jew, Hugo Willens. You can scarcely blame her for the choice, since the dramatist has chosen to present an Anglo-Saxon South Polar hero whose nature and processes are as simple as a motto, though not so well written. . . .

Rain from Heaven needs a more distinct marking of its inner rhythm. That is to say, there will be passages where the action of the story is to be forwarded, passages where the emotional intensity gathers, or where the talk should score for its own sake and the sake of the dramatic aftermath. We may add, moreover, that so far as the delivery end of it goes, such dialogue as Mr. Behrman's might even do well to annotate the lines as a musician might his score, to slow up here, hasten there, to rest, to staccato the expression, et cetera.

The trouble, what's more, would not be wasted if Mr. Behrman went through his dialogue to find where it is weakened by a certain explicitness. For example, there is a place where Lady Violet says something about being given enough time and she will pick herself up. It is not necessary to add, "I am irrepressible." . . . In a great many places the dialogue lines go on to make more articulate things that are already inherent and clear—which means that we have sections of dead organism piled on what is alive.

As racial discussion Mr. Behrman's play is, we may say, somewhat oblique and a little vulgar.

Stark Young, "It Droppeth As," in The New Republic, *Vol. LXXXI, No. 1051, January 23, 1935, p. 308.*

BRIAN DOHERTY

There is little wrong with S. N. Behrman's latest play *Rain from Heaven.* . . . Behrman is in a class by himself when it comes to writing brilliant and intelligent dialogue; and it's really intelligent, not just a series of clever wise-cracks such as those indulged in by Mr. Coward, which depend on their sophistication to hide their emptiness. It is one of those plays in which practically nothing happens and yet you're sitting on the edge of your seat with your ears pricked up the whole time. This phenomenon results partly from the playwright's uncanny gift for writing absorbing dialogue and partly from . . . Lady Wyngate, a charming and understanding English lady if ever there was one. She and her guests talk about Germany, the Nazis, capitalism and other topics arising out of the changing social and economic order, and it's all very much like listening to a group of interesting people conversing for several hours, except that it's much more interesting. (pp. 194-95)

Brian Doherty, in a review of "Rain from Heaven," in The Canadian Forum, *Vol. XV, No. 173, February, 1935, pp. 194-95.*

JAMES P. CUNNINGHAM

When Mr. S. N. Behrman hits on an interesting story or even on a single vitalizing and unifying idea he ought to write the first great American comedy. He has the equipment for it possessed by no other dramatist. He has a mind at once thoughtful and subtle; he has that virtue rare among important modern playwrights, urbanity of spirit; he sees character in the round and as it is rather than as a projection of his own prejudices and desires; he understands the subtleties of character and is able to portray them subtly and incisively; he welcomes ideas, no matter how divergent, and delights to play with them; he has a keen sense of character contrast; he writes dialog which in pith and wit is surpassed by no living dramatist and equaled by no American one. Yet with all these splendid virtues he has not yet written the play worthy of them. What is the reason? I, for one, do not believe, as it has been suggested by one

critic, that it is lack of innate feeling. Mr. Behrman is certainly an intellectual, but his ability to get within the skin of utterly divergent characters and make them act and speak as they would themselves is not the mark of a man without emotional sensibility. Moreover in the clash of these characters there is feeling and even heat. It is true that Mr. Behrman does not take sides, that he does not project his own beliefs at the expense of his characters' integrity, or that he is unfair to the characters themselves; but this certainly is not necessarily due to a lack of personal feeling. The real weakness of Mr. Behrman is that he does not tie together the actions of his characters in a definite, firm enough pattern; in short, his plays lack form.

End of Summer is an example in point. It deals with a millionaire family and the differences of its three generations. The grandmother is four-square, a product of the pioneer age, her daughter is a pleasure-loving and rather loose-living woman of social charm, and her granddaughter has liberal ideas and is in love with a young radical. The daughter, Leonie, has been in love with a Russian and is falling in love with Dr. Rice, a cynical psychoanalyst with an eye to the main chance, and with an eye also both for Leonie and her daughter Paula. In the end Paula shows up the doctor, by whom she has been tempted, and the play ends with her going off to recapture her young radical through being necessary to him, while Leonie is apparently about to become interested in another young liberal, an Irish-American Catholic, who wants her to finance his magazine. Thus we end about where we began. Nothing very much happens, but we undergo some very brilliant and at times really profound presentations of the points of view of the various characters. . . . To seek for any moral or any meaning in *End of Summer* would be to seek in vain, but as a projection of modern moral confusion it has its use. And it is magnificently written.

James P. Cunningham, in a review of "End of Summer," in Commonweal, *Vol. XXIII, No. 18, February 28, 1936, p. 497.*

JOHN MASON BROWN

[*The essay from which this excerpt is taken was originally published in the* New York Evening Post, *March 6, 1936.*]

Although Mr. Behrman is a stylist whose choice of words belongs to a vanished period of candlelight and polished marquetry, his mind is not closed to the grim dilemmas presented by Marx. As a comic dramatist he cares almost as little for plot as Congreve did when he came to write *The Way of the World.* From the time he wrote *The Second Man* and dramatized *Serena Blandish,* through such of his scripts as *Meteor, Brief Moment* and *Rain From Heaven,* right up until *End of Summer,* his major concern has been how his characters are affected by the world rather than how the world is affected by them. In this sense his plays have been as passive as they are reflective. Occasionally they have suffered from being so, just as *Rain From Heaven* did by withdrawing too far from the specific instance which, by its author's own confession in his preface, provided him with his subject matter.

Interested as Mr. Behrman is in ideas, he is no rabid propagandist. He is too rational, too intelligent, too wise to limit his vision to what his eyes would be permitted to see if he covered them with the blinders of any single social panacea. He is aware (as who is not?) that mighty forces are at work today which are destined to make the world of tomorrow different from the world of yesterday. His *End of Summer* finds him recording some of the first impacts of those changes in the kind of special world of privilege which has always been the realm of high comedy. His very title shows he is keen-witted and warm-hearted enough to know that all changes, however beneficent they may prove, do not come without their toll in suffering, and hence have their elements of pathos.

It is this sense of change, with all it implies, which really provides *End of Summer* with what little action it contains. Mr. Behrman's central figure is Leonie, a kindly, flighty but irresistible woman of great wealth who has been brought up in a protected social order to judge people solely by such pleasant standards as their niceness or their charm. She is the summer flowering of a family oil has made far richer than it needs to be or than it can survive being. Not only Leonie but also her social-minded and far more adult daughter are the victims of their great wealth. Leonie, in particular, has been separated by it from reality and lived a radiant, if a futile, life in a playroom of her fortune's creation. Little by little the stern present intrudes upon her standards and her world in terms of the talk and action of her very different house guests. And little by little Leonie becomes aware of the changing values of the present, and more and more of a delightful, if poignant, anchronism. Even her charities doom her, for she is finally reduced to backing a radical magazine which, if it succeeds, will work to outlaw her and her kind.

Some people have been bothered because Mr. Behrman takes no final stand in *End of Summer.* Others have objected to the play's lack of plot. But to my way of thinking Mr. Behrman's Sir Roger de Coverley attitude is alive with dramatic strength, and his dialogue is so brilliant and perceptive that it far more than compensates for the comedy's defiant dearth of action. His symposium is scintillant in his best manner. Yes, and more than that. It is as thoughtful as it is witty, and its very irresolution is part of its validity as well as of its charm. (pp. 143-45)

> John Mason Brown, "S. N. Behrman as a Comic
> Dramatist," in his Two on the Aisle: Ten Years of
> the American Theatre in Performance, W. W. Norton
> & Company, Inc. Publishers, 1938, pp. 142-45.

JOSEPH WOOD KRUTCH

S. N. Behrman's new comedy [*Wine of Choice*] . . . certainly exhibits no new facets of the author's talent. The scene is again a sumptuous drawing-room through which his characters move with their accustomed ease, and the subject under discussion is not unrelated to subjects which similar characters have taken in hand on previous occasions. That is no doubt the reason why not all the reviewers seem to have found as much delight in the performance as I myself found, but I do not think I shall be inclined to enter any complaints so long as Mr. Behrman can discourse with the wit and incisiveness he again displays in *Wine of Choice.*

His method, like every other method, has of course its limitations. Certain dramatic aspects of the conflict between the philosophy of those who have and the philosophy of those who have not obviously cannot be observed in a drawing-room. If the real significance of that conflict does not emerge except on the battlefield where concrete things are being fought for, then it is plain enough that only plays which move through the factory and the field can communicate that significance. But a fundamental assumption of intellectual comedy is that one kind of understanding of any conflict is possible only on the

sidelines, or at some other place where, for the moment at least, the battle is not raging. And Mr. Behrman's drawing-rooms are merely realistic substitutes for a spot of enchanted ground upon which deadly enemies can meet, fragments of neutral territory over which flies the flag of social convention guaranteeing against any breaches of the peace other than those which come within the definition of the "scene" as opposed to the brawl. Here the contented sybarite can exchange thrusts with the reformer, but here also the revolutionist can, not too improbably, come to express his exclusive contempt for all the rules of a game which is not to him worth playing.

Mr. Behrman's clarity and wit being what they are, the result is an exhilarating exploration of minds and temperaments which can be as clear and stimulating as it is only because he has adopted still another convention—that by virtue of which each character is permitted to speak as wittily as the author can make him. For this same reason the battle is, moreover, almost necessarily a draw. That does not mean that Mr. Behrman conceals the direction in which his own sympathies lie. He is, as clearly here as in the other plays, among those who hold that the sensibilities and loyalties of his liberals—"inhibited by scruple and emasculated by charm," as one character puts it—are indispensable to any possible good life, however insufficient they alone may be to guarantee it. But this revelation of his own conviction does not involve any failure to give the revolutionist an opportunity to make the best possible statement of his case, and there is no reason whatever why many spectators should not conclude that he actually has the best of the argument. (pp. 280-81)

> Joseph Wood Krutch, "Drawing-Rooms and Battle-
> fields," in The Nation, Vol. 146, No. 10, March 5,
> 1938, pp. 280-81.*

GRENVILLE VERNON

Wine of Choice seems almost a parody of Mr. Behrman's two last plays, *Rain from Heaven* and *End of Summer.* It contains the same sophisticated people, Liberals, Communists, hedonists, staying in the same sort of charming house; it contains even less action and more chatter; it gets nowhere. This of course is not the parody, but only the likeness; the parody consists in its exaggeration of these things. The people, with the exception of the senator and the Communist, are no longer living beings, but ticketed attitudes; the house is even more charming than its predecessors, but who owns it and just why everybody is there is so vague that it might vanish with its inhabitants into thin air and nobody would be much surprised; as for the action, it is so indeterminate that often we don't know what it means, and the chatter is so sophisticated that it floats through the air with the greatest of ease, but with little regard for that one touch of nature without which phrases become pretentious. It is a hard thing to say, that Mr. Behrman's dialogue has become pretentious, for up to now he has been the wittiest, most truly sophisticated of American dramatists. The trouble seems to be that in his latest play he hasn't known just what he is writing about, and in the confusion his characters utter not ideas, but words to conceal the lack of any clear idea. It would be useless to attempt to tell the story except to say that it concerns a Communist and a Liberal who are in love with the same girl. The Communist wins her and then refuses to marry her because it would hurt his Communism, whereupon the Liberal denounces him and his Communism. It is not until this last moment that the play begins to live, and Mr. Behrman has written for the Liberal an eloquent and passionate speech in defense of democracy. If only that passion, and eloquence, and incisive meaning had informed the rest of the play! Then we would have had a drama worthy of Mr. Behrman and interesting to the rest of us.

Grenville Vernon, in a review of "Wine of Choice," in Commonweal, *Vol. XXVII, No. 20, March 11, 1938, p. 554.*

JOSEPH WOOD KRUTCH

Certain virtues can almost be taken for granted in any play by S. N. Behrman, but *No Time for Comedy* . . . seems to me distinctly less successful than any other of his recent works and at least relatively superficial as well as relatively unfunny.

As the title suggests, the problem is specifically that with which Mr. Behrman himself has been repeatedly faced—the problem of a comic writer living in an age which forces upon his attention conflicts which the comic spirit seems incapable of resolving. He is faced therefore with an unhappy choice: either he must abandon the form and spirit of pure comedy, or he must confine himself to subjects which are bound to seem remote for the simple reason that they are bound to avoid reference to the topics most persistently under discussion. In the past Mr. Behrman has got around the difficulty in more than one way. In *Biography,* for instance, he eluded it by making the two proponents of conflicting political philosophies so plainly mere talkers that they could be satisfactorily disposed of by the talk of the brilliant woman who embodied the comic philosophy. In *Rain from Heaven* he sent the German exile back to his native land to fight the battle which he could no longer honorably avoid, while he left his heroine to continue life in her own land, where, for the time being at least, the comic virtues of tolerance and common sense still have their place. Both of these plays were successful, but *No Time for Comedy* ceases almost to be comedy at all while failing to become very much more than a rather tepid problem play.

The central situation seems decidedly promising. It concerns the dilemma of a brilliant young writer who, just as he is beginning to be tired of writing smart comedies for his actress wife, falls into the hands of a sort of up-to-date Dulcy, a rich woman who goes in for serious problems and is accustomed to use as a technique of seduction the discovery that successive men are wasting their talents by not realizing the depths of their souls. Inevitably our hero writes a play about death, asks his Dulcy to marry him, and plans to go off to Spain to fight for democracy. But when he realizes that the play is wretched stuff, it is almost equally inevitable that he should return to his wife and, presumably, forget about Spain. Perhaps the fundamental trouble with the play is that it has really two themes, here related but not identical, which are never clearly distinguished and which get in each other's way. One theme, specifically stated, is concerned with a conflict over a man between two types of women—the shrewd, intelligent critic and the yearning flatterer or, as the former puts it, the tearer-downer and the builder-upper. The other theme, and the one to which the title of the play refers, is concerned with the question whether or not the comic virtues have any place in a world where, as a character in one of the author's previous plays remarked, "while you are trying to understand your enemy he will kill you." This second theme Mr. Behrman takes seriously and seems by no means willing to dispose of out of hand. Yet he has begged the question and made the conclusion inevitable by making the protagonist of the graver view a pre-

tentious imbecile while letting the hero's choice of an attitude nevertheless depend largely upon his choice between the two women. Perhaps because the two themes are confused, neither of the issues is ever directly faced, and at no time does either conflict really come to a head. The play is brought to a close by an ingenious theatrical trick, but brought to a close while one is still waiting for the decisive confrontation of the problem with which it ostensibly proposes to deal. The big scene has simply not been written, and even the hero's conclusions concerning the place of comedy in his world are left almost sentimentally vague.

Only occasionally does the dialogue exhibit the crisp and witty precision one has come to expect from Mr. Behrman, and it may be that the central confusion is also responsible both for that and for the fact that the characters seem to lack the charm which even his rattle-brains have managed so often in the past to suggest. Under the transforming touch of pure comedy even bores become entertaining, though we still recognize the fact that they would be intolerable in any drawing-room except the enchanted one which the comic writer has conjured up, and in the same magic realm even fools make themselves welcome. But in *No Time for Comedy* Mr. Behrman's characters are seen without enchantment. . . . Probably Mr. Behrman was not very happy in writing this play, and he does not make the spectator very happy either. (pp. 509-10)

Joseph Wood Krutch, "Mr. Behrman Goes Astray," in The Nation, *Vol. 148, No. 18, April 29, 1939, pp. 509-10.*

JOSEPH WOOD KRUTCH

It would be too much to say that *The Talley Method* . . . reveals any new aspects of the talent of S. N. Behrman. In fact, the play is very precisely in the manner of such of his later pieces as *Rain from Heaven* and *End of Summer*. But so far at least as I am concerned, it is enough that he should have found again that true way which he seemed momentarily to have lost in *No Time for Comedy,* and that *The Talley Method* should again exhibit so delightfully the special kind of charm and special kind of wit which are his.

There is no contemporary writer whose gift is more exclusively or more purely comic. I have no doubt that he could, if he chose, write polite comedies of a more conventional sort, dealing with drawing-rooms, from which had been carefully excluded everything capable either of disturbing the pleasant tenor of events or of challenging, by implication, the adequacy of the comic approach to life. . . . But it had been evident for a long time that Mr. Behrman's conscience has made it impossible for him to disregard the dilemma created for the comic writer by the terrible urgency of these times. He has not lost faith in the value of those virtues which a genuinely comic wisdom almost inevitably generates, but he is fully aware of the fact that ours is not a world in which all existing problems can be solved by wit, tolerance, and good will. He is willing neither to pretend that they can nor to choose themes which exclude from the field of awareness those facts which pure comedy cannot digest. He must create a kind of comedy which, in less skilful hands, would rapidly become no comedy at all because it must continually keep at the periphery an awareness of situations by no stretch of the imagination comic. All his recent plays have been, in one aspect, attempts to define the limits up to which comic wisdom is relevant. Sentimentality could easily obscure the issue; cynicism could attempt to cross the line. But Mr. Behrman is neither sentimental nor cynical. He is extraordinarily clear-sighted.

In the present instance the play revolves around the contrasting characters of a humanely intelligent woman and a great surgeon. She has fallen in love with him because, as a patient, she had observed in him a scientific competence which seemed to implement humane impulses like her own. But it presently becomes evident from his relations with his two rebellious children that both his skill and his apparent good will are strictly limited to his profession. He can and he will save a life with what looks from the outside like benevolence—but only if that life is threatened by way of the duodenum, the twelve-finger-broad segment of man to which alone the Talley method is applicable. In human relations he is clumsy; in his attitude toward men as men rather than as creatures in need of surgery he is unimaginative and brutal. Nothing in the world except the duodenum is likely to be the better for his existence.

The play is a comedy in the sense that it makes the audience laugh, and also in a more philosophical sense, and it need not, perhaps, mean any more than is here suggested. But without being in any formal way symbolic it almost inevitably (and no doubt intentionally) suggests a larger thesis which Mr. Behrman has suggested before. "Scientific" and revolutionary social philosophers are right when they proclaim that sympathy and benevolence and humanitarianism are as incapable as wit and fairmindedness of creating by themselves a better world. But it is also true, as "scientific" social philosophers so generally seem to forget, that a good world cannot be created without them. They are not sufficient, but they are indispensable. They are indispensable because a world in which they did not exist would not *be* a good world, but also because without them no Talley method and no aggregation of Talley methods can bring a good world about. Mr. Behrman first preached that thesis at a time when most intellectuals were extremely unsympathetic to it. Since then, the most famous of all Talley methods has come to be less widely acclaimed as the beginning and end of wisdom.

> *Joseph Wood Krutch, in a review of "The Talley Method," in* The Nation, *Vol. 152, No. 10, March 8, 1941, p. 277.*

GRAHAM GREENE

[Mr. Behrman] is bold enough to believe that audiences are interested in the professional problems of playwrights. True, he tries to ease it all down with a little adultery or near-adultery, and such smart thirtyish lines as "Sleep with him if you must, but don't ruin his style"; but the interest of [*No Time for Comedy*]—and very interesting it is—really lies in the professional fate of a playwright like Mr. Behrman at a time when nations are breaking. The doom of Europe broods over the American cocktail-bar, and the Martini cherries are bitter with cordite. What, in such a world, is the writer of brilliant brittle comedies about nothing at all to do? "I wish I had first principles," moans Gaylord Easterbrook. But go on writing comedies, the playwright's wife—an actress, argues. Trivial comedies are better than shallow tragedies. Millions of people already have learnt how to die: they don't need any more lessons. To be gay is also a duty.

But the playwright's dilemma is another woman's opportunity. Amanda Smith is young and blonde and intense and a rather dull man's wife—"a Lorelei," Mr. Smith calls her, "with an intellectual patter." She persuades Easterbrook that he ought to write a "serious" play, and in a delicious scene, which hung fire with an audience who were quite prepared to take the serious play seriously, she runs over the plot to him—all about survival after death, spiritualism, enormous moral problems. The play, of course, is a flop as soon as it's on paper—the author can see that as well as anyone, and while Amanda waits for her lover in the cocktail-bar, his wife has already won the battle and suggested the plot of his next comedy—their own story. And the comedy's curtain-line? He has to supply it himself over the telephone to Amanda, impatient to know what detains him from her arms and the European war, and speechless, baffled, he cannot find it, as *our* curtain falls on a play lively, intelligent, admirably acted.

> *Graham Greene, in a review of "No Time for Comedy," in* The Spectator, *Vol. 166, No. 5885, April 11, 1941, p. 395.*

CHARLES KAPLAN

In the gallery of contemporary American playwrights, Behrman occupies a rather special niche, which, upon examination, turns out to be more a corner into which he has backed himself.

The period of Behrman's productivity (which is not yet at an end) covers the end of the hectic boom times, the depression, the rise of totalitarianism, the war, and today's confused and uneasy peace. It is against this troubled background that he has written his comedies: it is relevant to note at the start that they are more than merely comical, witty pastiches set in Never-Never Land, that they reflect the times in which we live. Behrman's sense of society's maladjustments is strong; his feelings about the relationship between man and the state are equally powerful; and his sympathy is all for the individual caught up in the complexities of his age. But the satirical note is lacking. Instead of exposing the shortcomings and follies of the world about him by illustrating them in action, he uses the technique of the discussion. Behrman is frequently praised for his witty and polished dialogue and his highly urbane patter. It is a mistake to assume, however, that this dazzling rhetoric is merely an ornamental virtue; on the contrary, it is the very heart and substance of his dramatic method, in which his characters talk about their problems, frequently without much relationship to what is going on in the action. In certain instances he embodies his problems in characterizations and lets the resulting action resolve the difficulty; but his more common practice (and failing) is that of turning his conversationalists loose and letting them air their opinions in brittle and sophisticated prose. Behrman's comic spirit is not a mocking one, satirical in nature, but is rather a highly refined and glittering one, civilized to a high degree, and articulate to the point of oververbalization.

What are the results of this union between the powerful social consciousness and the nonsatiric comic instinct? It must be admitted that, though always entertaining, the results are somewhat unsatisfactory and, as might be expected, sometimes confused. In this confusion he merely reflects the larger confusions of our day. In one significant instance, the way in which Behrman's comedies mirror his times might be cited: at a time when security, certitude, and calm were (and are) almost entirely lacking, one of his principal themes is that of incompatibility. No less than six plays make prominent use of this symbol of the loss of love, of frustration, of the failure to achieve harmony.

The smartness and sophistication that are the trademarks of a Behrman play are both apparent in *The Second Man,* which introduced him to playgoers in 1927. What might be called the play's "intellectual content" is the position in society of the detached, amused observer, viewing with a keen but tolerant eye the world in which he happens to live. The connection between this intellectual content and the plot, which is basically only a very deft refinement of the "boy meets girl" story, is extremely tenuous: they touch at one or two points, but there is no organic relationship between them. The archetypal sophisticate who is the leading figure, Clark Storey, makes what is perhaps the only social comment in the play. "Real emotions and real feelings," he says, "are destructive. I've learned to do without them. That's civilization." In the kind of world we live in, only the deliberately superficial and flippant is of any validity, as being most in harmony with the age. This is as much of a social comment as may safely be inferred from this play, a kind of generalized, implied criticism of modern social incongruities.

The anti-idealism that Storey utters throughout becomes a more important theme in later plays, with the important difference that this and similar attitudes are put into the mouths of the "villains." The social criticism becomes more explicit, sometimes didactically so. And what is perhaps the most obvious social theme in Behrman's plays—that of the Strong Man, the individual with dictatorial ambition—becomes more evident.

Meteor (1929) is an analysis of such a superhuman egotist and his rise to success and power. It is the closest to pure melodrama of any of Behrman's plays and the one with the loosest plot construction. . . . (pp. 317-18)

In *Meteor*, Behrman is highly critical of "oil imperialism" and of the benevolent dictator who can make trains run on time. It shows very clearly his concern over specific social problems, but as a play it suffers from lack of clarity. Lord is the supreme egotist, but Behrman treats him heroically. He is certainly the only strong figure in the play; at the final curtain, just after his wife has left him without a word of regret on his part (he has been shouting threats over the telephone to his rival), he "hangs up the receiver and stands silent, his body taut, keyed for the impending combat"—bloody but unbowed.

The figure of the Strong Man takes on a subtler form in a more polished play, *Biography* [1932], which combines a good deal of direct and indirect social criticism with a comic situation, some penetrating characterizations, and a high degree of integration between what is going on in the action and what is being discussed in the dialogue. . . .

In *Biography* Behrman embodies two conflicting outlooks in his principal figures rather than merely having people talk about the questions raised. In Marion we see the adapter to circumstance, the one who "gets around" people. She is warmhearted, impulsive, kind, and independent; she is tolerant to a degree that only irritates Kurt. He, on the other hand, is the uncompromising rebel. He is rude, fanatical, and arrogant. To him life is not only serious but tragic; Marion agrees but adds that one may as well be relaxed about it. (p. 319)

Behrman skilfully maintains his balance between the love story of two people with immutable temperamental differences and the political implications of the existence of such unbridgeable differences. Finally, however, with the recognition by both of their essential incompatibility, they leave each other, despite their love.

In the curtain line of *Rain from Heaven* (1934), the leading character says: "We're all shut in behind our little fences."

The title, too, would seem to indicate Behrman's belief that more mercy and understanding, which would humanize people and make civilized living possible, are necessary in these complex times. But, whereas in *Biography* Behrman kept his artistic balance, this play sees him totter.

An involved love story interweaves with an anti-Fascist statement. Behrman's sensitivity to the dangers to the human spirit implicit in fascism makes him sound a loud warning, but it is, unfortunately, a trifle discordant amid all the fashionable philanderings; the two strains are reconciled only rhetorically and not organically in the plot. (pp. 319-20)

The propagandistic element, which is not thoroughly assimilated into the bloodstream of the play, is the problem that Behrman most often stumbles over. In *Rain from Heaven* the results of that failure to integrate are clearly evident.

The two actions of *End of Summer* (1936) are almost entirely disparate, their only connection being that the major characters of one plot are the minor figures in the other. The chief problem is how the disinherited, unemployed generation fits into the hard world of 1936; the other concerns the designs made upon warmhearted and uncritical Leonie Frothingham by Dr. Kenneth Rice, a psychoanalyst and the Strong Man in a new guise. In the "young generation" plot, Will Dexter, the poor young liberal, is in love with Leonie's daughter, Paula; the "poor boy—rich girl" situation is embarrassingly familiar, and so is the familiar ending, which, incidentally, evades the issue that has been raised throughout. (p. 320)

With its melodramatic villain and a plot condition that is almost fatal, *End of Summer* falls far short of being high comedy. For other reasons the same verdict may be passed on *Wine of Choice* (1938). The plot elements are related in a thematic way more closely than they are in *End of Summer:* the philosophy of the Communist zealot who denies the existence of "free choice" is played off against the story of Wilda Doran, who epitomizes the romantic "instinct rampant" in choosing by heart rather than coolly by head. But Behrman's earnestness and sincere convictions, which are put into the mouth of Senator Ryder Gerrard, a liberal senator who gives Chris, the Communist, a tongue-lashing in the third-act climax, represents a failure to stick to the plane of intellectual comedy. (pp. 320-21)

A significant, if incidental, speech in *Wine of Choice* reveals Behrman's attitude toward the "proletarian" writers, who were dealing more frontally and "realistically" with social issues than he was. His democratic ideas and humanitarian feelings were probably as strong as those of the proletarians, but his invincibly sophisticated point of view prevented him from approving of their approach. Rumination over the implications of his attitude might very easily have led to the formulation of his theory of the function of comedy, expressed in *No Time for Comedy* (1939). As though trying to justify the continual production of comedies of high society, set in fashionable surroundings, and peopled with witty and glamorous individuals, at a time when fascism had already struck in Ethiopia and Spain, Behrman pictures a playwright (appropriately named Gay) torn between his social consciousness and his comic spirit. . . .

The theory of comedy expressed by Behrman's *raisonneur* is apparently the one on which he thinks that he has been operating and through which he announces his intention to continue in the same vein. But the gap between theory and practice is often a large one. Far from writing "escape" comedies, Behrman has been unable to keep the outside world from intruding. The theory makes no mention of the place of the propagandistic element in comedy; but it is precisely this intrusive and unassimilated element that weakens his plays. In trying to effect a compromise between preaching a social message and creating a light comedy, the usual result is a verbally entertaining, but intellectually and artistically unhappy, combination.

Both *The Talley Method* (1941) and *Dunnigan's Daughter* (1945) give further evidence of Behrman's quandary. Neither shows any indication that the verbalization of the theory in *No Time for Comedy* has had any effect on the practice. (p. 321)

Dunnigan's Daughter is the most specifically propagandistic of Behrman's later plays: It is based on an actual political situation and incident, it condemns the specific practice of "mine imperialism," and it is designed to illustrate the maxim: "Power corrupts. Absolute power corrupts absolutely."

This theme is combined with a melodramatic romance and an analysis of Clay Rainier, the symbol of the quest for power, who operates on the principle that evil is the mainspring of human nature. (p. 322)

The theme of incompatibility which runs through Behrman's comedies reflects, as I have suggested, the stresses and strains of the outside world. The reason for this failure to agree is suggested by a line in *The Talley Method*. When Axton learns of Enid's resolution not to marry him, he exclaims: "My God, you're not going to let a difference in point of view separate us!" To which she replies: "But that's all that ever does separate people." Differences in point of view—differences which on a greater scale lead to troubles that rack the world—are inescapable in the nature of human beings. Behrman would be the last person to insist on conformity. But his humanism does imply a recognition of these differences and at least a civilized attempt to try to reconcile them by intelligent discussion.

Where Behrman's peculiar problem has led him in recent years is apparent. Instead of adhering to his own comic theory, he has been tempted, under the overpowering and well-nigh irresistible pressure of social incongruities, to forsake the sock for the soapbox. It may be asking too much of a writer to produce serious comedy in an era which is far from being amusing. Others, at other times, have done it by hewing to the line of satire. But Behrman, as we have seen, is no satirist; and his comic spirit wrestles with serious problems to the detriment of ultimate artistic success.

It is significant that in the most recent phase of his career, Behrman has been more and more exercising his talent in translations and adaptations of the works of other playwrights. . . . In the sense that these plays had long runs, made good theater, and in three cases provided brilliant starring opportunities for Behrman's favorite acting team, he may be said to have achieved a high degree of success as a playwright. In another sense, however, this retreat from originality, which may be either an inability or a reluctance to come to grips with one's self, looks more like an evasion, and not a solution, of his problems as a comic playwright. (pp. 322-23)

> *Charles Kaplan, "S. N. Behrman: The Quandary of the Comic Spirit," in* College English, *Vol. 11, No. 4, January, 1950, pp. 317-23.*

LLOYD MORRIS

Like the best of Mr. Behrman's plays, *Duveen* reflects its author's subtle intelligence, urbane wit, and flair for irony.

Like them also, it has a sparking surface and serious implications. In it, Mr. Behrman portrays a small segment of American society during an opulent, festive era—and the finished portrait is a little masterpiece of social satire.

Duveen tells the story of "the most spectacular art dealer of all time," whose amazing career was founded on the simple observation that, while Europe had plenty of art, America had plenty of money. The adroitness with which Joseph Duveen persuaded America's wealthiest tycoons to part with millions for paintings enabled him to become a monopolist and an autocrat. It also enabled him, over the years, to give away ten million dollars in public benefactions, chiefly in England, so that he was successively elevated to knighthood, baronetage, and peerage, dying as Lord Duveen of Millbank with—as Mr. Behrman puts it—"fifteen million dollars in the bank, an inventory worth ten million, and his self-confidence intact." (p. 14)

Duveen resembled some of his clients, in the earlier phases of their careers. Intent upon creating and maintaining a monopoly, he was obsessed by business and ruthless to all competitors. His object, as Mr. Behrman notes, was "to teach millionaire American collectors what the great works of art were, and to teach them that they could get these works of art only through him." The tactics he employed in this educational mission yield Mr. Behrman a treasury of astonishing anecdotes that makes *Duveen* the most diverting book of this season. . . .

Mr. Behrman suggests that it was [a] . . . sense of devastating failure, notwithstanding their grandiose material success, that impelled American multimillionaires to devote their last years to the acquisition of art under Duveen's tutelage. In their consuming avidity there was "a hint of desperation, of loneliness, of futility, even of fear." These magnates, with their incalculable wealth, "felt the need, as they grew older, to ally themselves with reputations that were solid and unassailable and, as far as the mind could project, eternal." Some of them even craved an immortality which might result from this alliance. They obtained vicarious survival through the great public institutions which Duveen helped them to create: Huntington with the superb gallery at San Marino; Frick with the beautiful museum on Fifth Avenue; Mellon with the National Gallery at Washington. The odd, snobbish, devious-minded little tradesman in beauty managed, in the end, to make it possible "for the American people to see a large share of the world's most beautiful art without having to go abroad." Mr. Behrman's book provides a fascinating account of how he did it. (p. 15)

> *Lloyd Morris, "Tradesman in Beauty," in* The Saturday Review, *New York, Vol. XXXV, No. 12, March 22, 1952, pp. 14-15.*

FRANCIS HENRY TAYLOR

A successful playwright is not necessarily a good biographer. Nor does it follow that he can qualify as a social historian; even less as an art critic. On all counts Mr. Behrman with *Duveen* has hit the jackpot in reverse. Seldom has there been a book so misleading or so false. Because of its hilarious humor and its infectious quality of letting the reader in on "the real low-down of the art world," it will be widely read and immensely popular. . . .

Purporting to depict "the most spectacular art dealer of all time," the author has instead presented a series of *tableaux vivants*. Each episode is a theatrical entrance building up to a moment of farce when the asbestos curtain is rung down on a poor, benighted, red-faced millionaire who has just received the stigmata from Sir Joseph da Vinci. It would make a good musical with Bert Lahr or Jimmy Durante in the title role. Maybe that is what Mr. Behrman has in mind. (p. 5)

The sins of omission in this biographical sketch are so glaring that one hesitates to call attention to those of fact which already have been committed. The author seems to be gripped by a tractarian obsession with the folly of the man of wealth. He cannot forgive the rich for being rich. "The bigger they come, the harder they fall" and "You can't take it with you" are the antiphonal jeremiads that greet the reader on every page. Nowhere is there any attempt to put the multimillionaire, who, Mr. Behrman says, "was all dressed up with no place to go," into the context of his time. The growth of corporations, the changing attitude toward money and, most of all, the incredible story of American philanthropy, seem to have passed the author by. It is indeed strange that the museums and art galleries of this country were built up in the first quarter of this century by the very men whom Mr. Behrman has included in the sucker chorus of his Duveen Comedy. They were, moreover, assisted in their purpose by a score of connoisseurs and merchants who were anything but clowns and who will make the memory of Fifty-seventh Street sing in the pages of American social history.

The artistic chronicles of this epoch must yet be written by someone with a sense of the accomplishment of the art trade as a whole. The present book is at best a curtain raiser, a rather ineffective spotlight on a career which glowed for so many reasons never here disclosed. Joe Duveen was a phenomenon placed against the background of the most prodigal age the world has ever seen. His was a career which would never suffer by comparison. It seems therefore hardly worth the effort to denigrate the colleagues and the clients who set him off with such perfection. (p. 28)

> *Francis Henry Taylor, "'The Last Sunburst'," in The New York Times Book Review, March 23, 1952, pp. 5, 28.*

NATHANIEL BENCHLEY

Ten out of eleven pieces in S. N. Behrman's *The Worcester Account* have appeared in *The New Yorker,* but any one who thinks that by reading them he has thereby read the book is sadly mistaken. Unified as they are, and altered imperceptibly for the sake of continuity, they result in a profoundly moving and sometimes hilarious picture of Behrman's early years in Worcester, Mass., of his family, his relatives, and his friends, and of the darkly brooding religious atmosphere that hung like a storm cloud over the tenements of Providence Street. Individuals who, in the separate pieces, are of minor or secondary importance, come to full life in the collection as a whole, and Behrman treats them with an insight and a compassion that make most of them likable and all of them understandable. There isn't a false or a shallow character in the lot.

> *Nathaniel Benchley, "Compassion, Insight, Wit," in New York Herald Tribune Book Review, October 24, 1954, p. 7.*

SAUL BELLOW

S. N. Behrman's *The Worcester Account* is an engaging collection of reminiscences of the author's early years in a small,

devout Jewish community in New England at the turn of the century. It is a book of warmth and nostalgia and it is sometimes very touching. . . .

To one who comes, as I do, from a similar place, the half-ghetto of an American city, these people are immediately familiar. I recognize them in Mr. Behrman's skillful reproduction and wonder why they often appear shortened, flattened, and lacking in vigor and primitive idiosyncrasy. They have been written of with charm and in the process have emerged somewhat tamed and weakened. Somehow the charm does not seem to belong to them; it is not their native charm but one which the writer has lent them, returning to them after long separation. The air of nostalgia which pervades the book is often appealing but many times emphasizes the quaintness of Providence Street rather than its difficulty and poverty. Even tragedy moves a little too smoothly and lives often come to an end with too round a period.

> *Saul Bellow, "Old World in the New," in The Saturday Review, New York, Vol. XXXVII, No. 47, November 20, 1954, p. 41.*

RICHARD WATTS, JR.

Out of the memories of his youthful years in New England, S. N. Behrman wrote a graceful, charming, humorous and rueful book of reminiscences called *The Worcester Account*. In *The Cold Wind and the Warm*, . . . he has made a play based on some of its stories and characters, and it retains many of the glowing qualities of heart and mind that gave the volume such an endearing spirit, even though its transference to the stage has resulted in a dramatic structure harmful to its emotional effectiveness.

The framework of the play is one of the basic themes of the contemporary American theater. It is the tale of the sensitive young man with artistic aspirations, who has plans to go to New York, learns something about life from the people at home, and experiences tragedy when he watches the sadness and death of a friend who had been his philosopher and guide. It is a good story, but it inevitably calls up recollections of such a powerful drama as *Look Homeward, Angel,* and the comparison is not helpful to its mildness of manner.

Although the inescapable parallel is there, *The Cold Wind and the Warm* is far from a pallid copy. Its special quality is the characterization of the relatives and neighbors of the young man, and they form a closely-knit Jewish community of warm and engaging people. Even a wealthy and self-satisfied suitor and a shallowly flirtatious girl are disarmingly likable, and the matchmaking widow, the rabbinical father, the attractive and love-lorn girl from out of town, and the boy, himself, are genuinely lovable. This is the play at its finest.

> *Richard Watts, Jr., "A Drama by S. N. Behrman On Memories of Youth," in New York Post, December 9, 1958. Reprinted in New York Theatre Critics' Reviews, Vol. XIX, No. 25, Year ending December 31, 1958, p. 175.*

KENNETH TYNAN

[*The essay from which this excerpt is taken was originally published in* The New Yorker, *December 20, 1958.*]

[*The Cold Wind and the Warm* is founded on episodes from Mr. Behrman's] book *The Worcester Account,* a collection of reminiscent *contes* whose quality I cannot judge, since I have not read them. There is always, however, a sizeable gap between the printed page and viable drama, and it does not seem to me that Mr. Behrman has succeeded in bridging it. Prose in stiff covers (or soft, for that matter) is addressed to only one reader at a time; drama, by contrast, is aimed at a thousand spectators simultaneously assembled. Where a bored reader would skip, a bored audience walks out. To prevent this, the playwright must concentrate his action, narrow his focus, and resolutely shun those digressive details that are at once the novelist's province and his pride. . . . The dangers of getting too particular are multiplied when drama verges on autobiography. Fondly ransacking the attics of his mind, the author grows more and more reluctant to throw anything away, and frequently ends up by convincing himself that nothing could be more fascinating to an audience than a lengthy procession of the most unforgettable characters he has ever met, including, of course, himself. The result, almost invariably, is something that might have achieved a modest sale as a volume of memoirs but has about as much to do with drama as a police line-up. The awkward art of writing a good memory play demands far more in the way of self-discipline and condensation. The two great examples of the genre are *The Glass Menagerie* and *Long Day's Journey into Night*, and it is significant that neither of them was adapted from a book. In each case the author, looking back on his life, singled out a turning point—a crucial, indelible event that somehow determined the course of his maturity. Mr. Behrman is inspired by a similar conception; where he falters is in the matter of execution. Both Williams and O'Neill confined their *dramatis personae* to people who were actively involved in the crisis—in Williams' play, his mother, his sister, and the latter's "gentleman caller"; in O'Neill's, his parents and his elder brother, plus a harmless necessary maid. And both of them were careful to select incidents in which they themselves figured not merely as observers but as participants, not just recording but contributing. Mr. Behrman slips up on both counts. Not only is his plotting vagrant and diffuse; he has imposed on it a character who does nothing but impede it—to wit, himself as a child. This is a camera-type (or perhaps I should say daguerreotype) play that has been thrown off balance by the photographer's insistence on being in the picture. (pp. 290-91)

> *Kenneth Tynan, "The American Theatre: 'The Cold Wind and the Warm',"* in his *Curtains: Selections from the Drama Criticism and Related Writings, Atheneum, 1961, pp. 290-95.*

JOHN McCARTEN

[*Lord Pengo*] is a witty, affectionate, and perceptive account of the life and times of a highflying art dealer of the thirties who had an uncanny knack for convincing plutocratic merchants and industrialists that they could immortalize their names by investing in Old Masters. . . . Perhaps Mr. Behrman hasn't managed to introduce much suspense or conflict into this comedy, but as it goes along he does succeed in interesting us in Pengo's unsuccessful efforts to make his son a worthy heir to the business, his meddling in the private lives of his clients, his determination to convince his clients that the masterpieces he has sold them should be assembled in a National Gallery in Washington, and his struggle to establish the fact that "The Adoration of the Shepherds" is a Giorgione, even though the eminent Bernard Berenson has pronounced it an early Titian. *Lord Pengo* is a loquacious comedy, but the talk, for the most

part, is worth listening to, and if the crises in the career of the hero aren't exactly spellbinding, the author has seen to it that the hero himself is always an attractive sort, even when his delight in salesmanship makes him neglect a loving wife or take advantage of the innocents he deals with. (p. 118)

> *John McCarten, "Sweet Personality, Full of Rascality," in* The New Yorker, *Vol. XXXVIII, No. 41, December 1, 1962, pp. 118, 120.**

THEOPHILUS LEWIS

The word on the theatrical grapevine is that [*Lord Pengo*] is based on the career of an English lord who became a distinguished art dealer in America. Since the title character is a recognizable international personality, it is not surprising that *Lord Pengo* can be compared with a palimpsest. On the surface, it is an affectionately drawn portrait of a man who ferreted out hidden works of art and made them available for contemporary buyers as a benevolence. He did not neglect to pocket a profit, of course; but he cherished the dream that the most precious items he sold would eventually be willed to public galleries. Under the surface, however, there are traces of a darker pattern, and we detect a man hag-ridden by the incubus of power. . . .

Behrman's portraiture shows his subject in a favorable light, with warts and wrinkles obscured by shadows. In high light, Pengo is an affable man who has a lot of fun making a lot of money. Even when one discovers his inner urge, the enjoyment of power, which enables him to deal with hard-bargaining giants of dollar royalty on equal footing, he remains an engaging fellow, and one becomes emotionally involved in his success. One's involvement, of course, is the result of the author's trick that keeps Pengo confronted with less attractive characters.

The confrontations, while not highly dramatic, are interesting episodes in the life of a colorful personality. For theatregoers who have not forgotten how to enjoy urbane drama . . . , *Lord Pengo* is a nostalgic delight.

> *Theophilus Lewis, in a review of "Lord Pengo," in* America, *Vol. 108, No. 2, January 12, 1963, p. 52.*

GRANVILLE HICKS

In his middle seventies, after a lifetime of writing successful plays, as well as such biographical sketches as *Duveen* and *Portrait of Max*, S. N. Behrman has published his first novel, *The Burning Glass*. . . . Not surprisingly, it is a novel about the world of the theater, laid in Salzburg, Hollywood, and New York, in the years from 1937 to 1940. It is also a novel about the love affairs of a young dramatist on the way up, Stanley Grant. Finally, it is a novel about the effect that the triumph of Nazism has on Grant and on his world.

Since a major fact of contemporary history is at the center of the book, it is to some extent a historical novel. I was therefore surprised to find this note: "I have not striven, in this book, for strict chronological accuracy of world events. I have tried rather to convey the atmosphere of the time." Certainly chronological accuracy has not been achieved; there are many slips that are troubling to a reader who likes facts to be facts.

The serious question, however, is whether Behrman has succeeded in conveying "the atmosphere of the time." The novel opens on the *Normandie*, which is carrying several of the principal characters on their way to the Salzburg Festival. . . . "It was the summer of 1937," Behrman notes, "and the Jewish question had been given acrid stimulus by the goings-on in Germany." I don't know exactly what Behrman means by "acrid," but surely "goings-on" is a mild way of describing what had happened after Hitler took power in 1933. . . .

In Salzburg, it is true, the young dramatist, who has changed his name to Stanley Grant in order to minimize his Jewishness, becomes more conscious of organized anti-Semitism, and he views with alarm the lights of Berchtesgaden, where Hitler is plotting the subjugation of Austria. But he is almost as much disturbed by the description of the Jewish owner in T. S. Eliot's "Gerontion" as he is by the painting of a swastika on the lawn of his hostess. Indeed, it is the casual, thoughtless anti-Semitism of the "upper classes," American and European, that Behrman renders most successfully. . . .

Grant has many things on his mind, especially his career and his women. He has had one Broadway success, which is what enables him to mingle with the cultural élite at Salzburg, and he is determined to have another. Meanwhile there are Sally and Eileen and Stephanie, and there will be Naomi and Doris and Emmeline. Stanley's love affairs never prosper because he has a habit of falling in love with women who are indifferent to him if not hostile, whereas the girls who fall in love with him leave him cold.

Although the reader assumes at the outset that this is Stanley's story, his older friend and benefactor, Alexander Löwe, nicknamed Kaetchen, comes to occupy more and more of Behrman's attention; and, because he is a much pleasanter person than his protégé, the reader welcomes this change of emphasis. (p. 21)

A third male character is of some importance, a psychiatrist named Kenneth Ogden, who attracts the women Grant doesn't attract and ruthlessly exploits them. His predatory activities become the theme of Grant's second play, but in fact he and Grant get on well together, for he appeals to the opportunism in Grant's personality as Löwe appeals to his more generous inclinations.

Dramatist that he is, Behrman makes considerable use of dialogue, and his lines are often amusing. (He even gives a scene or two from Grant's new play.) Grant and various other characters move from Salzburg to Hollywood, and in the midst of a variety of subplots history almost completely drops out of sight. After an indefinite period of time, we hear about the Soviet-Nazi Pact and realize that we have arrived at August 1939. The novel ends soon after New Year's Day, 1940.

Grant is complex enough to interest the reader. . . . I wish Behrman had concentrated on him instead of devoting so much space to other characters and introducing so many episodes that have no bearing on his life. As a result of this diffuseness, Behrman treats Grant's ultimate reversion to Jewishness in so summary a fashion that it is not convincing, though we have known from the beginning that it was bound to happen.

Behrman felt, I suppose, that his experiences had been rich enough to make an interesting novel, and to that extent he was right. But what he did was to throw together a lot of these experiences, without much imaginative processing. He would not, I am sure, have knocked together a play in this offhand way. . . . [He] has not conveyed "the atmosphere of a time," nor has he gone to the heart of Stanley Grant. (pp. 21-2)

Granville Hicks, "The Odd One," in Saturday Review, *Vol. LI, No. 29, July 20, 1968, pp. 21-2.*

SAUL MALOFF

S. N. Behrman compels us to see [*The Burning Glass*] as an infinitely extended version by other means of a Behrman play. . . .

Since these are Behrman characters, they are—typically—rich, fashionable, glamorous, the sort who dine late, speak burnished phrases, frequently address one another as "darling," and attend the Festival at Salzburg, where in fact much of the action takes place, roundabout 1937. . . .

While the little lives unfold beneath, the lights of Berchtesgaden burn the night through; while the characters pursue their vain and idle course, the Mustache—as [Hitler] is not infrequently called—has other plans for them. This is intended, of course, to give weight and gravity to the novel's frivolities. It fails to do so: history is an accident of the novel's time; the characters and actions are in no important way affected; the pathos is superimposed, does not solemnize the events even retrospectively. These men and women, themselves jaded, are the collectors of jade; and though they, too, live in the shadow of the holocaust about to engulf the world, they are phantoms, wraiths. When the war finally descends, it is hardly alluded to. . . .

The novel is not without its pleasant moments. Behrman is Behrman: he can and does write elegantly. He is a composer of deft, and sometimes witty, dialogue; but the lines, which fade from the memory a moment after they are uttered, are disembodied mots spoken by spectres. The purling, ingratiating tone flattens everything to the same level. If Behrman had written the Book of Job, the central character would have been a charming, cultivated man no longer young, world-weary beyond his years, perhaps a gentleman farmer, a kind of Near Eastern Montaigne, Jewish but cosmopolitan, a collector of rare scrolls, who had suffered some minor business reverses and—as if he didn't have enough trouble—was further afflicted by an embarrassing skin condition.

Saul Maloff, "Of Sin and Acne," in The New York Times Book Review, *July 21, 1968, p. 31.*

HAROLD CLURMAN

At the age of 77, S. N. Behrman, author of five books and 20 plays, has extracted [*People in a Diary: A Memoir*] from the 60 volumes of a diary he has kept since 1915. It is, to begin with, a delightful and endearing collection of anecdotes involving such people as George and Ira Gershwin, Ina Claire, Garbo, Ernst Lubitsch, the Lunts and many eminent literary figures. . . .

A largesse of such stories, however, is not the main interest of a book like *People in a Diary*. What is crucial in a memoir is the narrator. In the present instance, the author, at first glance, appears invisible. The reason for this apparent "absence" offers a clue to his nature. (p. 7)

Behrman is fascinated, he says "by the idea of pluralism in personality, in duality." The dominant trait of his own character is a peculiar timorousness in expressing all he thinks and feels due to worry that utter frankness may cause him as much pain as it would others. Because he finds reality appalling he retreats to laughter and to an almost constant affability. "Comedy is the saving grace," he says, "which makes life bearable." Behrman, a man of genuine sensibility, knows life and fears its hurt.

We come to perceive the melancholy face of the memorialist through the veil of his jests. Born in poverty of immigrant Jewish parents, the man grows up with a hankering for comfort and luxury. But he is the scion of ''the people of the Book''; they revere learning and intellect. Within the limits of his means, Sam Behrman's father had both. The son aspires to exceed these limits. He goes to Harvard; he moves toward a polished style in life and literature, to breeding and gentility. He harbors ''a nostalgia for England,'' the England which in his mind exemplifies these attributes. He is impressed by high position, is attracted to wealth, gracious manners, to everything which smooths the rough edges of existence.

But he is no snob. He sees in Max Beerbohm a model of serene self-acceptance within a modest creative scope marked by gentle irony and elegance of expression. In Somerset Maugham (the chapter devoted to him is the best in the book) Behrman recognizes bitterness and suffering turned to the ends of hard work and literary skill. (pp. 7, 18)

Despite the twinkle of skepticism, Behrman remains a constant hero-worshiper. He always seems amazed and gratified that he has won entry into the magic circle of the extremely gifted, the splendidly glamorous, the seers, the world-beaters. He never once suggests that he is equally pleased with his own achievements. For he is deficient, he confesses, ''in courage and self-belief.''

What is most sympathetic in Behrman, what gives his book a special enchantment, apart from the transparent silkiness of his prose, is his awareness that the structure of his personality, which makes him avoid overt self-revelation, also impels him to a recognition of its pathos. Writing of the vertiginous twenties, he says, ''I found myself in a millstream of gregariousness in New York and London: incessant contact with great theatre stars, with rich people and social people, at posh hotels, at parties, and on yachts. But through it all I never shook off the plaintive counterpoint of my parents, their religion and their poverty.''

This explains both the mask and the face underneath: the two comprising the total person. . . . He may entertain severe critical judgments but he is very rarely forthright or rude in voicing them. He is conscious of cruel truths, but he sidesteps too complete a confrontation with them; fleetingly he simply indicates their presence. He wishes to preserve a precarious balance lest life become too shattering. . . . With *People in a Diary* he provides an ingratiating glimpse into his ''secret'' through the decorative trellis of scintillating reminiscences, where possible candid, and always self-effacing. (p. 18)

> Harold Clurman, ''A Playwright's Biography, a Playwright's Memoir,'' in The New York Times Book Review, *June 25, 1972, pp. 7, 18.**

ELIOT FREMONT-SMITH

In *People in a Diary,* S. N. Behrman deliberately eschews any autobiographical intent. ''An odd quirk of destiny has put a great many people in my way,'' he writes. ''I want, in this book, to return to them.'' He notes the eerie effect of rereading what he wrote in his diary about friends and colleagues:

> Characters keep appearing whose very existence I had forgotten, and yet they keep reappearing, vivid ghosts, taut in their momentary preoccupations, clamped, as I myself was, in the imperatives of NOW. Reading through these pages, I can foresee their destinies; their futures are laid out, all the criss-crossed lines where my life intersected theirs. It is somewhat terrible to become possessed, suddenly, of all that foresight, a pointillism of time. They seem blindfolded, as I myself was.

It is a lovely beginning, both graceful and honest, and it leads to many exquisite miniature portraits. (p. 53)

The chapters on Berenson, Maugham, the Gershwins are perfect small portraits, and throughout there are a hundred tiny, swift, almost offhand observations, recordings of facial expression or something said, that thrust these people into sharp and shimmering focus and momentarily make the whole book come alive and glow. But there are also long stretches of dimness, where the reader feels he has been given the wrong end of the telescope to look through. We see the suffering Sassoon often in this book but always at a great distance; his suffering is not doubted, but neither is it understood, and it and he grow tiresome. Behrman himself we see hardly at all.

As noted, Behrman's absence is deliberate. ''By this time,'' he writes, ''—seventy-five plus—I have had just about all I can take of myself.'' But his presence is nonetheless very keenly missed. It is not so much a matter of the facts of his life and career . . . or of his personality—these can be discerned in the book—but a matter of his *presence*. For what we want to experience is not simply vignettes of these people in his diary, but their relationship to him, and his to them—and thereby our relationship to both. We are with, in this book, a nearly invisible guide, and it is disconcerting. Only at the end, when he talks about feeling old and bequeaths an unfinished play to any young playwright who will take it over, does Behrman begin to come into focus himself. He seems a wonderful man, civilized and civilizing, which is, of course, why one is so conscious of missing him. (p. 54)

> Eliot Fremont-Smith, ''Broadway, Hollywood, and the Years that Were,'' in Saturday Review, *Vol. LV, No. 30, July 22, 1972, pp. 52-4.**

KENNETH T. REED

S. N. Behrman differs in certain important respects from most American writers of his generation. His literary upbringing was initially an academic one, and the works he was destined to write tend to reflect the subtle influences of having had a fairly structured exposure to literature in the classrooms of Clark, Harvard, and Columbia in the second decade of the twentieth century. (p. 131)

As early as 1939, Joseph Wood Krutch recognized that Behrman had secured for himself ''as sure a position in the contemporary American theater as any writer can claim''; and in 1952 John Gassner, writing appreciatively of Behrman, called him ''the only remaining writer of high comedy . . . [and] perhaps the only consistently brilliant stylist in our drama.'' . . . His relationship with other playwrights aside, Behrman shares a number of characteristics in common with another New Englander, Nathaniel Hawthorne. Like Hawthorne, he has a gnawing preoccupation with moral problems, as is quite apparent in such plays as *Meteor, Jane* and *Lord Pengo* where he raises ethical questions about money and matrimony. He also shares with Hawthorne a markedly suspicious attitude toward modern science, as is evidenced in *The Second Man* and in *The Talley Method.* Skepticism toward social reformers (*End of Summer*) and Oedipal conflicts between parents and children (*Lord Pengo, But for Whom Charlie*) are themes also found in Hawthorne's works.

In common with the arch-cosmopolitan Henry James, Behrman possesses an almost instinctive repugnance toward American vulgarity and narrow provincialism, both of which he treats in *Duveen;* but, in spite of this attitude, he maintained a certain mannered, polished, subtly humorous, and yet humanistic vision of the world and its people. . . . Like James, Behrman is a limited social realist with a special awareness of, and appreciation for, the psychological implications of human behavior. It is with a certain wry detachment that Behrman, along with James, treats life in the upper economic (if not social) classes that are closely identified with modern urban life along the eastern seaboard and in Europe. Consistent with Hawthorne and James, Behrman has but little feeling for nature in her primal state. Obviously no Agrarian, Behrman's world is the world of streets and buildings, restaurants and living rooms. (pp. 131-32)

As a young writer of short fiction particularly in the pages of *The Smart Set,* Behrman obviously patterned himself after the American realists such as Howells, Norris, and Dreiser, who harbored serious reservations about the American Dream; and Behrman's early fiction embraced the familiar tendencies associated with turn of the century realism: deprived characters, leftist politics, and a threateningly competitive economic system. In his later, more established drama and prose essays, it is possible to see Behrman in the context of American Jewish writers, especially after he gradually devoted more attention to the dilemmas of Jewish life posed by the rise of fascism in the 1930s. (pp. 132-33)

Like [Abraham] Cahan and the whole tradition of Jewish writers in America, Behrman writes primarily of the city. His enlightened liberal political views, his penchant for analyzing the moral consequences of everyday acts and gestures, and his occasional reference to Jewish social and religious rituals are not so different in character from the writing of such younger American Jews as Bernard Malamud and Saul Bellow. (p. 133)

[The] flavor of Behrman's theatrical comedy is closest to playwrights like Shaw, Coward, and Maugham, although in America his closest resemblence is to Philip Barry. Unlike most playwrights, however, Behrman designed plays that he believed would bring out the best in his favorite players: the Lunts, Alexander Woollcott, Ina Claire, Laurence Olivier, and others. These were performers who, in one sense or another, were best able to infuse life into a Behrman script. It is therefore understandable that Behrman wrote plays around living actors, inasmuch as two of his chief concerns were with people and with theatrical success.

As an essayist, Behrman owes much to those other magnificent essayists of his time who, like himself, contributed to *The New Yorker:* James Thurber, E. B. White, and S. J. Perelman. It was the combined influence of such persons that created and nurtured *The New Yorker* prose style, a style characterized in part by its urbane, intelligent, and subtle appeal to a sophisticated audience. Indeed, Behrman's own prose style is at times scarcely distinguishable from that of his peers.

As for an assessment of Behrman in his own right, considered apart from those literary influences that were brought to bear on him, there is the inescapable conclusion that some of his plays and published books were a critical success; some were not. Only his prose essays remained at a high level of achievement and survive today as the best of his work. His one attempt at writing a novel . . . was, by common consensus and by his own estimation, a failure. In truth, the often commended brilliance of his stage dialogues has been overstressed through the years by friendly critics such as Joseph Wood Krutch. It required, after all, such theatrical talent as that of the Lunts, Katherine Cornell, and Ina Claire to bring Behrman his stage successes. (pp. 133-34)

Probably the most astute assessment of Behrman is that of John Gassner who wrote that "Behrman's art of comedy, including his so-called comic detachment consists of an ambivalence of attitudes that has as its sources the simultaneous possession of a nimble mind and a mellow temperament." For Behrman is at the same time critical and forgiving of human weakness. The "nimble mind" of which Gassner speaks allowed Behrman to form moral judgments in a great many plays, among them *Meteor, Amphitryon 38,* and *Jane;* but the mellow temperament prevented him from possessing an outright vindictiveness, even in a play like *Jacobowsky and the Colonel* where, with a certain comic detachment, he chose at the conclusion to look toward the dawning of a better era in human history than to treat the horrors of fascism with all of the vindictiveness he might have. (p. 134)

Throughout his career Behrman appealed to his public through the intellect and the heart, never through the glands. He believed quite realistically and without naiveté in the proposition that life can be savored and refined and that the human race can, if it wishes, be perfected and improved upon beyond anything commonly considered possible. He preferred to think of man as a fragment of God, as he wrote in *Rain from Heaven,* rather than as a highly developed animal. Most of all, he illustrated in his own life and writing that it is not only preferable but reasonable that human beings can laugh and yet come to terms with the stark reality of life. (pp. 135-36)

Kenneth T. Reed, in his S. N. Behrman, *Twayne Publishers, 1975, 151 p.*

Chaim Bermant

1929-

Polish-born English novelist, nonfiction writer, journalist, editor, author of books for children, memoirist, and scriptwriter.

Bermant is an author of humorous novels about Anglo-Jewish culture. These works, which typically center on family situations and the often improbable misfortunes of Bermant's characters, usually conclude on an upbeat note. Bermant employs a straightforward, spare prose style as he examines different aspects of the Jewish experience. His first novel, *Jericho Sleep Alone* (1964), concerns the misadventures of a Jewish youth living in Glasgow; *Now Dowager* (1971) involves a wealthy woman whose attempts to convert a young gentile girl to Judaism end with the girl observing the faith more rigidly than the woman; *The Last Supper* (1973) begins with a mother's death and chronicles the reminiscences of her eccentric family during *shiva,* the Jewish ritual of mourning; and *The Patriarch* (1981), which is described by Annie Gottlieb as "a Jewish comedy of affairs," concerns the adventures of a Russian Jew who flees persecution by relocating to Glasgow. Bermant occasionally departs from this milieu, as in *Diary of an Old Man* (1966), a well-received work about a month in the life of a man who must come to terms with the reality of death. Bermant is also a respected nonfiction writer, having published such works as *Troubled Eden: An Anatomy of British Jewry* (1969) and *The Cousinhood: The Anglo-Jewish Gentry* (1971).

(See also *Contemporary Authors,* Vols. 57-60 and *Contemporary Authors New Revision Series,* Vol. 6.)

Photograph by Mark Gerson

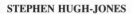

STEPHEN HUGH-JONES

No doubt which book takes this week's medal, and not a tin one either: *Jericho Sleep Alone.* Which is odd, because the Jewish family and particularly Jewish growing-up is getting to be one of the most overworked themes of fiction, and Jewish humour by now has all the novelty of that one about the Scotsman and saxpence. In short, a book like Mr Bermant's has to work rather harder to make an impression than most. It succeeds.

Jericho Broch lives in Glasgow. His friends or cousins of the same age are good with words or money or girls. Jericho is ham-handed with all of them. His father, his mother, his uncles and aunts have ambitions for him; he has really no ambitions except to make out (and what does he mean by that? Does Jericho Broch know?) with Ninna, the attractive but inconstant daughter of another comprehensive Jewish family.

The story, though, is not a great deal; what is, is the sense of place, of age, the particularities of word and feeling. I cannot swear personally for the Jewish background, though I suspect that it is one of those caricatures that achieve truth precisely by exaggeration. But the windiness and cold, and at the same time dignity, of Glasgow are exact enough. Very exact indeed are the hopes and indecisions of Jericho Broch's adolescence, his uncertainty at any given moment just what he feels about

Ninna, his certainty that it matters desperately—or 10 minutes later not at all—what she feels about him, his development from the imagined pleasures of sexual fantasy to the young man's take-it-or-leave-it reality (not with Ninna, one should add—she remains a kind of earthbound, unromantic *princesse lointaine*).

All this is told with (and in no way diminished by) a very lively and unsubtly funny wit. There are few set-pieces but anyone who keeps a straight face for more than half a dozen pages of this perfectly serious novel deserves sympathy. Unless the world's got it in for Mr Bermant as hard as for Jericho Broch, his publishers should be laughing too.

> Stephen Hugh-Jones, "Jericho's Colony," in New Statesman, Vol. LXVII, No. 1725, April 3, 1964, p. 533.*

THE TIMES LITERARY SUPPLEMENT

A good *raconteur* does not necessarily make a good novelist; it is easier to get away with the flat parts of a joke or even a whole flat joke if one has an expressive voice or a mobile face to help. Mr. Bermant is clearly a good *raconteur,* and at first sight his novel [*Berl Make Tea*] appears to be an excuse for stringing together a series of stories of the "Then I said to him

..." variety, leading up to epigrams which may or may not misfire. "Please, Brisker, don't make epigrams out of my grief", the hero's employer, Mr. Urbane-Urban, asks him; both Berl Brisker and Mr. Bermant have a *penchant* for making epigrams out of grief. . . .

The first part of the novel is concerned with Berl's fear that his wife may return after running away with the gardener, the second with his indecision over whether to marry the Home's ex-cook, Mrs. Kamenetz-Podolsk, who loves him but cooks atrociously. Berl has an urge to live rootlessly and irresponsibly; he is a man who invites—and provokes—the world to deal hardly with him. His career is a typical mixture of "outrageous comedy" and "underlying sadness". It is when the two coincide that *Berl Make Tea* becomes upsetting. Mr. Bermant is too fond of the grotesquely comic aspects of sudden death and his need to cram every page with jokes interferes with his development of the pleasantly knotty tug-of-war between Berl and Mrs. K.-P. This is an uncertain, maddening book; but, in spite of pages of an unamusing broad humour, and the sketchiness of the characters, the overall impression is appealing.

> *"Sad and Merry," in* The Times Literary Supplement, *No. 3289, March 11, 1965, p. 201.*

BRIGID BROPHY

Much as I prefer the Jewish to the Irish, Scottish or Welsh joke, I cannot find its inconsequence enough to sustain a whole novel. [In *Berl Make Tea*] Mr Bermant's indefatigably little hero undergoes a series of indefatigably pointless indefatigably misadventures, kicking off from his being kicked out as warden of a Jewish old people's home. The dialogue or, rather, crosstalk plays in music hall fashion on such misunderstandings as between 'substitute' and 'prostitute'. This sort of comedy, like sentimental postcards, is better aged than merely faded. I prefer that older but still definitive collection of what one rabbi said to another outside the public baths, Freud's *Wit and its Relation to the Unconscious*.

> *Brigid Brophy, "Formal Modes," in* New Statesman, *Vol. LXIX, No. 1774, March 12, 1965, p. 409.**

THE TIMES LITERARY SUPPLEMENT

[*Ben Preserve Us*] is amusing and slightly saddening. Ben tells his own story, accurately recording [his] whimsical, awkward or hilarious encounters [as a Rabbi in Scotland] . . . , but at the same time revealing little by little his own temperamental differences from those he meets. As he tells a prostitute who has happily fabricated some sociological sophistry to justify her life, glibness is a form of corruption. And he views with gentle scepticism the glib and unspiritual ways of his parishioners and his voluble mother. He finds the Jewish obsession with family particularly trying.

There is a fair selection of the obvious Jewish jokes . . . ; but it is also genuinely funny with an absorbing collection of characters, such as the Catholic priest who thinks the Israelites had a lot of Irish in them or the beadle, so confident of disaster that he rejoices he cannot believe in the Messiah's coming, because if he did, it would never happen. Such figures provide the amusement as well as the context in which Rabbi Bindle has to adjust his ideas and conduct to fit a world of Mammonism and uncongenial obsessions.

> *"Braes-Bound Rabbi," in* The Times Literary Supplement, *No. 3317, September 23, 1965, p. 820.*

RICHARD MAYNE

[In *Ben Preserve Us*] Bermant goes for laughter: 'Your poor father, if he was alive now he would be turning in his grave.' This is a Jewish mother, all Yiddisher tags and speech-rhythms, berating her son for going to be a Rabbi in Scotland. He rockets off, pursued by reproaches: 'I should live to see the day.' If you enjoy this kind of vaudeville act, all right already; even if you think the fashion for being Jewish gets a bit cloying, I suspect you'll come to like the repartee and the in-group digs at weaknesses that goys daren't deride. The Rabbi turns out to have a heart of steel, in some respects, which is refreshing: faced with his synagogue's Board of Management, he needs it. Like a hole in the head, they'd no doubt answer; but he finds his feet quite firmly, although the path is strewn with misers, eccentrics, lascivious girls, and Oedipus-schmoedipus mommas. A nice light *hors-d'oeuvre*. So you want it should be fattening? (p. 488)

> *Richard Mayne, "Make 'em Wait," in* New Statesman, *Vol. LXX, No. 1803, October 1, 1965, pp. 488-89.**

MARTIN LEVIN

Another novel about middle-class Jewish life? Before you say "All right already!"—read *Jericho Sleep Alone* . . . and discover for yourself a fresh landscape in which some familiar figures are animated with a wit often subtle and oblique. Mr. Bermant writes of Glasgow Jews, in particular of Jericho Broch, a perennial loser who sleeps alone and hates it. Jericho pursues a beautiful, fickle medical student, wins an honors degree at the University of Glasgow, gets a scholarship to Jerusalem, and amounts to absolutely nothing. But Jericho's failures in love and work are Mr. Bermant's triumphs; his style is epigrammatic . . . and pithy. . . . And it makes one curious about the author's next novel—which is easily satisfied since *Berl Make Tea* is on the flip side of the book, like a record.

This novella amplifies the bulk of the book without adding to its quality. It is in the vein of Jewish low comedy, and concerns a ne'er-do-well named Berl Brisker, who first appears in the novel as a caretaker in a home for the aged, and thereafter slides downhill. Berl becomes, among many other things, bodyguard to a dowager's cat, and engages in some bizarre encounters that reveal the author's penchant for ethnic humor but do not reflect the controlled style so visible in the first book.

> *Martin Levin, in a review of "Jericho Sleep Alone" and "Berl Make Tea," in* The New York Times Book Review, *June 12, 1966, p. 32.*

ROBERT TAUBMAN

First-person teenage narrators are frequent enough, but it's a shock to find the practice extending to the very old. From absolute beginners to the absolute end: yet Chaim Bermant's old man has the same colloquial style, scepticism and liveliness as the 60-years-younger lot—and less sentimentality. In the month covered in *Diary of an Old Man* the narrator sees his last two friends into the grave—besides his landlady, who has been murdered—and it's a relief to read a novel so much about death that doesn't do it for black jokes. Yet one could say it's a quiet month: other things—like his stove and wireless—are more immediate to Cyril, and assert themselves in the midst of death. The book has solid charm. It only seems to me precarious on the difficult question of impersonation: one can't altogether shelve the objection that it's only half true, because the old man couldn't have written it this way. Mr Bermant, incidentally, plays Cyril's relation with the Pakistani upstairs dangerously close to *Huckleberry Finn*, from which he lifts a famous line.

　　　　　Robert Taubman, "Last Straws," in New Statesman,
　　　　　Vol. 71, No. 1841, June 24, 1966, p. 934.*

NICHOLAS SAMSTAG

"The more time we have, / The less time we have, / And the less time we have, / The more . . . ." That quatrain might well have been the epigraph of [*Diary of an Old Man*]. It also seems to be a bafflingly true statement once we get the two sets of time straightened out. The young (or, rather, the non-old), with much of their lives ahead of them, race around at their work or play as if their time is very little and getting less; while the old, with so little time left, have an astonishing patience and try to prolong everything not actually unpleasant as if they are drawing on a private supply of infinity. The fact that the patience of the old is a benign condition and imminently curable makes it both a comfort and a terror to contemplate.

Their problem, of course, is to make the time pass as easily as possible until they die—which, expressed perhaps too bluntly, is the problem of us all at any age. That this is their chief preoccupation is made clear, without sentimentality but with great skill and a wry precision, by Chaim Bermant in *The Diary of an Old Man,* which covers an ordinary month in an average London winter. . . .

Because they are both on relief and must pay for the fuel they burn in their rented rooms in their freezing, cold-water flats, Cyril and his friend, George, spend all the time possible at the public library, reading newspapers, trade papers, directories, anything they haven't read before that is not too elevated for their very moderate educations. At home they doze most of their hours away listening to the wireless . . . , and on Sundays, when the air is all mucked up with sermons and such, the men do their darning or straighten their rooms or cook something special on their gas-rings. . . .

There is also the interminable problem and ineffable solace of the w.c., which is always occupied while someone's bladder is bursting outside because someone inside is using the place as a retreat. . . .

The diary opens: "They buried old Harry this morning." It closes with "The rain came down heavily and rapped on the roof like machine-gun fire," after having created a sandwich of cold funeral meats that may not be to every reader's taste. Old Harry was a friend of the two cronies, one of whom, George, drops dead of sheer joy and overexertion on the first balmy day when they can return to their beloved park. Meanwhile a young East Indian boarder at Cyril's house is almost burned to death in a fire started by Cyril's paraffin stove, and the aging but still randy landlady (a dedicated Commie) has her head smashed by a fancy man who makes her think he pants for her favors when all he wants is her rent receipts. After that, things get no more cheerful. . . .

Why, then, is this a little masterpiece?

Because Mr. Bermant has written here a superb fantasy disguised as a realistic novel. Into his dreary tapestry he has managed to work threads of gold, crimson, and lettuce green, expressing gallantry, gusto, gaiety, and a human goodness that I wish I believed in. For a little while, experiencing that suspension of disbelief which only the most artful of fantasists can create, I was convinced that all those heartening things really could accompany extreme old age. I expect you'll believe it briefly, too—unless you're too old.

　　　　　*Nicholas Samstag, "On the Dole without Dol-
　　　　　drums," in* Saturday Review, *Vol. L, No. 19, May
　　　　　13, 1967, p. 42.*

AILEEN PIPPETT

[In *Diary of an Old Man* the protagonist's] name is Cyril, which has a Tennysonian tang. Otherwise the diarist is a most bedraggled hero. He is not only old, he is poor and, in all probability, dirty. It is winter when his story opens. He has trudged through slush from a funeral to his one room. His oil heater won't work, so he puts on a sweater over his pajamas and goes to bed, because "a man's best friend is his bed, as long as he can get in and out as he wants." It is this wanting, this determination, to cling to life to the last moment that keeps the heart beating in the half-starved, bronchitic body of an octogenarian.

With equal tenacity he grips your attention, laying his skinny hand on your arm like a latter-day Ancient Mariner. It is no use pretending that his tale has the moral lesson or wild imagery of Coleridge's poem. His philosophy is summed up in that remark about bed; his religion is limited to listening to Choral Evensong on the radio, because hymns are nice at tea time. As for art, he likes a bit of music. . . .

The special quality of Chaim Bermant's most unusual novel can only be conveyed in the expressions—trite, foolish, coarse or ironic as they are—used by Cyril and his friends, all as opinionated and garrulous as he is. The author reproduces them with exactitude, never striking a false note, giving unforgettable glimpses into the tragicomic life of lonely old age in Britain's welfare state today.

Each character is firmly realized. There is George, who has his moods, knows everything, including what day of the week it is ("a sort of gift"), loves his rubber plant and waits eagerly for the fine weather when he and Cyril can go to the park and see the crocuses. Or Mrs. M., Cyril's landlady, who loses her school-crossing attendant job because, says George, of her foul mouth and loose morals. . . .

Or Sayed, the Pakistani student in Mrs. M.'s top room, whom Cyril drives to distraction by his chatter. They are irritating, absurd, unlovely and immensely touching. To meet them is a rewarding experience.

The portrait of Cyril is masterly. As impudent as a cock sparrow, snatching at every crumb of amusement and friendship thrown his way, he somehow manages to bring to mind the Scriptural assurance that to the All Seeing the fall of no sparrow to the ground shall pass unnoticed.

　　　　　Aileen Pippett, "Courage to the End," in The New
　　　　　York Times Book Review, *May 21, 1967, p. 40.*

KENITH TRODD

[*Swinging in the Rain*] is just right for sun-dozing; indeed it could hardly be right for a more waking state because full faculties resist such an impudently strung-out load of ancient gags, titillations and competing themes. But Bermant writes engagingly and just about gets away with it. (p. 262)

Kenith Trodd, "Hell for Mum," in New Statesman, Vol. 74, No. 1903, September 1, 1967, pp. 261-62.*

THE TIMES LITERARY SUPPLEMENT

Swinging in the Rain makes its appearance rather belatedly. It should be strictly summer holiday reading or—so slight is it—bank-holiday weekend reading. The book is the reverse of compulsive reading. Yet the author claims in an "Historical Warning" which takes the place of a preface, that its purpose remains at least semi-serious, "a protest against the pace of change and against instant everything, including instant—indeed, constant—sex. In essence, it is a sigh for mellowness."

Unfortunately Mr. Bermant's targets are only too obvious. His central character is a Conservative chocolate manufacturer, with a fading, querulous and vaguely dissatisfied wife, a daughter who is "a pseudo-problem", particularly with respect to her chastity, and a son whom he regards with some reason as "an imbecile". The chocolate maker's main ambition is to standardize the shape, flavour and wrapping of chocolates throughout the nations of the world; hence the founding of "Inter-Choc", a tiny and indeed liquefying basis which nevertheless allows the author to tilt at the United Nations, the Foreign Office, the Common Market, television interviews, parties for gossip-column "personalities", the *New Statesman* (by the foundation of a rival called the *Old Statesman* with a leader headed "Outdated Virtues"), the law, and a private school which is but the dimmest dim shade of Llanabba.

Most of the jokes are on the level of "I'm all for sex, if, perhaps, in an old-fashioned way. I like it to be conducted through the usual channels" or (when the manufacturer explains how he feels after being shot through the stomach) "My colon has been reduced to a semi-colon". Sweetness and light and mellowness? If so it is the sweetness of the soft-centre, the lightness of the Light Programme and the mellowness, after all, of the autumnal.

"Mellow," in The Times Literary Supplement, *No. 3421, September 21, 1967, p. 844.*

STUART HOOD

[The hero of *Here Endeth the Lesson*], David Garbett, is a teacher in a secondary modern coeducational school, where corporal punishment is forbidden but some of his colleagues (himself for that matter) are not beyond using a fist or a boot if necessary. This is familiar country inhabited by cynical, impoverished, socially depressed schoolmasters, randy adolescents and ravenous Lolitas. Garbett is suffering from a kind of *couvade,* a long pre-natal depression brought on by the interminable length of his wife's gestation. One result of his ailment is heightened sexual activity. He is seduced by Moira, his teenage pupil whom he tutors at home; seduces—or is seduced by—Miss Sutton, a half-caste supply teacher with expensive tastes, and the gym-mistress, Miss Butterworth (in the showers after tennis). Retribution comes as he mucks up his teaching career and is finally sacked for befriending a boy

from his class whom he finds on the prowl in Soho and sends home saved from sex but a victim to alcohol. The final scene takes place in the waiting room of a maternity hospital, where life, hope and reconciliation appear to Garbett and his cronies in the person of a nine-and-a-half-pound boy. It is a sentimental end to a book which is often brutal, always sharply observant and nearly always funny. (p. 120)

Stuart Hood, "Incestuous Brood," in The Listener, *Vol. LXXXII, No. 2104, July 24, 1969, pp. 119-20.*

THE TIMES LITERARY SUPPLEMENT

It is often said that, punch-drunk from the assaults of reformist zealots-in-a-hurry, our schools are edging steadily towards the snake-pit. [In *Here Endeth the Lesson*] Chaim Bermant's Crumleigh High School has already tumbled in. Masters fraternize with boys in Soho strip-clubs. A girl pupil (Crumleigh is coed) seduces one of the male staff and then blackmails him for £25 in order to procure a mythical abortion. A nymphomaniac supply teacher neglects her netball in order to glut the appetite of the head-boy. Pickering, the English master, goes immediately out of his mind when he sees a colleague tearing a page out of one of his exercise books. Miss Pearson marks steadily on through riot and rape. Dr. Harris does no sinful action, speaks appropriately angry words, but remains to the end a non-headmaster. David Garbett, central character and narrator, a Cambridge man (who irritatingly persists in describing himself as belonging to Kings' when he means King's) has considerable trouble with his rampant libido while Tilly his wife, pregnant for what seems to him an elephantine time, tolerates him and his inadequate Burnham Scale more patiently than he deserves.

In the past Mr. Bermant has shown that he has a light touch, an exact ear for speech rhythms, and enough boldness of line in his character-drawing to ensure what puppeteers call animation. One thinks of an earlier book of his, *Diary of an Old Man,* with particular pleasure. But in *Here Endeth the Lesson* nothing goes right for him. The note he seems to be aiming at—funny-fantastic with an accompaniment of (perfectly valid) social commentary—is never held confidently or for long. Too soon he is back with just a tired Cambridge light-blue farce on his hands.

"If . . . ," in The Times Literary Supplement, *No. 3522, August 28, 1969, p. 945.*

D.A.N. JONES

[*Now Dowager* is] a light comedy flawed by lapses into unsuccessful farce. A new addition to Chaim Bermant's gallery of amusing British Jews, Mrs Fentzter is a wealthy septuagenarian widow with certain of the characteristics he has gently mocked in his earlier novels: a great regard for the rules of her faith so long as she is not expected to know them all, and for the nation of Israel so long as she doesn't have to live there. She has a gentile au pair, a wild young woman whom she converts to Judaism and who becomes embarrassingly orthodox about washing up, carrying umbrellas on Saturday, and whether Cohens can marry divorcées. The old lady would have been touchingly plausible, had not the author plunged her into contrived children's-comic situations (costumed as Long John Silver at a fancy-dress party, she collars a burglar with his swag) which even a Wodehouse could hardly bring off.

D.A.N. Jones, ''God Sent a Family of Gazelles,'' in The Listener, *Vol. 85, No. 2200, May 27, 1971, p. 688.**

F. J. BROWN

Yiddisher Mommery written in the first person by the Yiddisher Momma herself, is the theme of *Now Dowager.* There is a note of desperation sounding through the surface gaiety that lifts this novel out of the ordinary. Lotte Fentzter was seized by the idea that her Gentile maid, Mary, should embrace the Jewish faith as a convert. After great difficulties, Mary became an Orthodox Jew. Then the difficulties really began. For one thing, Lotte had reckoned without the burning zeal of the convert. She felt less than grateful to Mary for sitting in her kitchen pointing out her trifling sins!

That the narrator, Lotte, can be witty is shown by her comment on her doctor: 'He was treating me like a National Health patient, the anti-semite.' There are problems solved and unsolved at the end, but the most important thing is Mary's discovery that at the heart of Judaism, as at the heart of most religions, is the practice of caring for others.

Mr Bermant has written about what he knows, and has done so in such a way that the reader knows too; learning even while he laughs.

F. J. Brown, in a review of ''Now Dowager,'' in Books and Bookmen, *Vol. 16, No. 10, July, 1971, p. 42.*

JIM HUNTER

Chaim Bermant's wry Jewish story [*Roses are blooming in Picardy*] is about as substantial in outline as one of Singer's, but is blown up unconvincingly to the length of a short novel. Sam Zucker's orchestra used to play for *Music While you Work;* now he is over seventy and living on his past and his one recording, 'Roses are blooming in Picardy'. He chats winsomely to us in the first person, but we gradually come to see that he is an old boor. The main wriggle of the book is our slow revaluation of his wife Sybil and his bandsmen friends as we learn to distrust Sam's account of them. The novel attempts to be funny and touching, without success.

Jim Hunter, ''Wriggles,'' in The Listener, *Vol. 87, No. 2241, March 9, 1972, p. 317.**

THE TIMES LITERARY SUPPLEMENT

Is it inherently funny to be Jewish? Or Welsh, Neapolitan, Texan, Irish, or Panamanian? In the hands of the right writer, it is a gift. . . . [More] mileage has been got out of the Jewish joke than any of the others based on the endearing ridiculousness of a people: Chaim Bermant's aging musician Sam Zucker [the protagonist of *Roses Are Blooming in Picardy*] would need to be more crisply drawn, more skilfully plotted in, if he were just any old elderly Gentile trying to keep a whole book revolving around him.

As it is, Mr Bermant burbles along relying rather too much on his own *chutzpah* to keep us entertained, as Sam grows old, loses his monumental wife, and is whisked off to spend his last days in the sunny land of his ancestors, pining for the soot and rain of exiled Hackney. Sad, like so many funny stories. Through the burbling the bell can be heard tolling on three

specifically Jewish themes: family—Sam's love-hate for large, stupid Mrs Zucker; inspiration—his longing to be a real musician, known for his Bach and not his ''Roses of Picardy''; and exile, which follows you wherever you go. ''By the waters of Jordan he sat, yea, he cried when he remembered Hackney.''

It is a bit too slick, a bit too slight: the ingredients have been cooked up too often before. Without the sweet-sour taste it would be nowhere. It takes a bit of sadness to keep a funny book together.

''Any Old Zion?'' in The Times Literary Supplement, *No. 3657, March 31, 1972, p. 352.*

AUBERON WAUGH

[*The Last Supper* is] about a young Jewish author writing a saga about his own family and discovering various skeletons in the cupboard one by one. It is also a psychological study of a man who has cut his own roots by renouncing his Judaism yet nevertheless passionately needs a hero figure for at least one of his antecedents. Well, there you are. But although the idea for the novel is a fairly boring one, and although Mr Bermant's occasional attempts at Jewish jokes are quite catastrophic, there is a simple skill in the unfolding of the narrative which rescues it and makes it readable, as well as a wealth of intriguing detail about the Jewish customs of *shiva* and *seder* which makes it nearly compulsory reading for those like the reviewer who take pleasure in second-hand social voyeurism.

It is written in a very leisurely fashion. Mr Bermant takes 153 pages before his hero decides to write his saga and have any very solid idea of what the novel is going to be about. The hero's mother has died, and the first part describes the gathering of the family for the week-long *shiva*, where brothers, sisters, sons and daughters of the departed sit around to receive the condolences of friends. Mrs Coggan was of aristocratic—though recently so—Russian Jewish origin; her marriage to a rich but wayward cinema tycoon called Koch was generally thought a misalliance. Our hero, James Coggan-Koch, decides to find out why his father is regarded as such a black sheep. Above all, he must discover which of his parents is the heroic figure he requires for his own, slightly obscure, self-respect. After talking with various business associates, mistresses and friends of his father he decides that his father was the victim of his mother. On learning that his father died in a brothel, he mysteriously reverses this judgement and takes to drink. On discovering that his father was the victim of financial manipulation by his rich uncle and on being reconciled with his estranged wife, he reaches a middle judgement. Never mind. Although there are some absurd moments which seem to invite parody, there is certainly enough original material and enough skill in the presenting of it to make a worthwhile read. Nor does Mr Bermant expect his gentile readers to cringe with Hitler-guilt on every twentieth page, and this is a development in the Jewish novel for which we should be grateful. (pp. 427-28)

Auberon Waugh, ''Variations on Familiar Themes,'' in The Spectator, *Vol. 230, No. 7554, April 7, 1973, pp. 427-28.**

THE NEW YORKER

[*The Last Supper* is a] slow-moving, irritatingly self-conscious novel. . . . This book would have been fine entertainment if the author had been able to restrain himself from allowing his characters to constantly point out how fabulous and unusual they all are. They *are* an interesting lot: wall-to-wall eccentricities and a fascinating *haut-bourgeois* Russian past mingle nicely in their late-night reminiscence. But the self-admiring note is so piercing (and so frequent) that it is hard to keep one's mind on what is happening—especially after the author coyly (and erroneously) suggests that readers will probably consider him a cross between Chekhov and Ivy Compton-Burnett. (pp. 118-19)

A review of "The Last Supper," in The New Yorker, *Vol. XCIX, No. 52, February 18, 1974, pp. 118-19.*

NICK TOTTON

What can one say of a novelist who fills his first eight pages with exquisite thumbnail sketches of a terraceful of characters, most of whom promptly move out, hardly to reappear? This kind of delighted generosity of invention is typical of *The Second Mrs Whitberg*. But the wide mouth of the cornucopia rests on a narrow base: wealthy Glaswegian Jewish family life.

Mr Bermant has decked out as domestic comedy the classic contours of a mystery novel; except that the question is not, whodunnit? but who'll do it?—become, that is, the second wife of Josh Whitberg, respectable widower, pillar of the synagogue, and narrator of the story. And even having correctly guessed the eventual wife by page twenty-three, it was still possible to admire the stately unrolling of marital manoeuvres, intertwined with the alternating joys and sorrows of Jewish parenthood. . . .

It would be worrying to think that Mr Bermant endorsed the attitudes—chiefly, this generalisation of the ego to the family—which he portrays. But one does not suspect the anthropologist of cannibalism; and like any self-respecting anthropologist, Mr Bermant's formal role is not to judge but to describe. However, as with the most interesting anthropology, scientific objectivity is tempered with enough pure affection to leave the reader gently wondering if civilisation is worth so much after all. The characters of *The Second Mrs Whitberg* are anything but 'uncivilised'; but they lack completely one civilised characteristic, which Mr Bermant does not provide—a sense of intercultural comparison, a knowledge that the habits and rituals of one's own tribe are ultimately convenient agreements, social cement.

Arguably, it may be demanded of the novel form that it provides this relativist context to the particular culture portrayed. But in this case the culture is an attractive and entertaining one—from a good distance; and Josh Whitberg, its quintessence, is a likeable and (within his cultural norms) a good man. The version of middle-class Jewish culture may be presumed accurate—at least, it is consistent with the worlds of other Jewish novelists. Information, wit, invention, style, conviction—what more can one ask from an anthropological whodunnit?

Nick Totton, "Lost Tribes," in The Spectator, *Vol. 237, No. 7731, August 28, 1976, p. 16.**

MARTIN LEVIN

If you haven't run into Chaim Bermant before, you are in for a treat. His field of specialization [in *The Second Mrs. Whitberg*] concerns middle-class Orthodox Jews, habitat Glasgow. But you don't have to be Jewish to enjoy his wry humor, any more than you have to be a Mississippian to appreciate Faulk-

ner. Mr. Bermant excels at creating a social climate rich in ethnic commonalities and personal differences. Both are instantly recognizable.

The second Mrs. Whitberg doesn't come into this episodic ramble until the first Mrs. Whitberg has been gone for 16 years. During this time, Joshua Whitberg lives at 22 Tulloch Terrace, where he has spent most of his adult life. . . . [Nothing] remains constant on Tulloch Terrace except the mellow ambiance with which the author invests it.

Martin Levin, in a review of "The Second Mrs. Whitberg," in The New York Times Book Review, *October 3, 1976, p. 38.*

VICTORIA GLENDINNING

At the age of seventy Henry Hoch emigrates with his wife Celeste from Isleworth to a small town in Israel. What happens next is the subject of Chaim Bermant's very readable new novel *The Squire of Bor Shachor*. It is all told in letters from Henry, who is a gentlemanly, Jewish Mr Pooter, mild, ineffective and optimistic. The reader realizes long before he does that his wife is a terror: described in an early letter as "one of those frail English ladies who are sustained by periodic bursts of fury", she blossoms in Bor Shachor into the scourge of garage-men, builders, developers and orthodoxy. . . .

The insights into Israeli society, and into the troubles of the very British Hochs in adapting to it, are both entertaining and salutary. But Henry's letters are equally preoccupied with what is going on back in England. Hoch *père*, founder of the family firm, is about to celebrate his hundredth birthday at Fetlock Hall, where he lives with his eldest son Berthold, approaching eighty, and his spinster daughter Gwendolen. Another aging brother has made his fortune in America; yet another, Matthew, gets romantically entangled with Henry's (married) neighbour on a visit to Bor Shachor and runs away with her. . . .

Mr Bermant is at his best and sharpest on the petulant malice of the old and on familial obsession.

Victoria Glendinning, "Middle-Class Families," in The Times Literary Supplement, *No. 3929, July 1, 1977, p. 812.*

ANNIE GOTTLIEB

Perhaps [*The Patriarch*'s] title is ironic; at any rate, it is misleading. The word "patriarch," for me, evokes a domineering Old Testament figure, who awes and intimidates his children and haunts their imaginations long after they flee his iron love. The "patriarch" of this book, Nahum Raeburn (né Rabinovitz), on the contrary, jokes plaintively that his ever more rambunctious and far-flung clan dominates *him*. Nahum is gentle, stalwart, decent and ambivalent—hardly a weak man, but he lacks the patriarch's authoritarian certainty. And yet he is definitely the *genius familias*, the generative source from which "the Jewish family Raeburn" has sprung, who sustains it against the disintegrative forces of world wars, adventure, morality and scandal. The family is the triumphant fruit of Nahum's confused yearnings, his dubious exuberance for life, his inarticulate, almost maternal, love.

Nahum Rabinovitz arrives in Glasgow, Scotland, from Volkovysk, Russia, in 1892, the 16-year-old emissary of his father's hopes and fears. In Volkovysk the family is well-off but uneasy; pogroms are sweeping the South and business is declining as the great Jewish exodus begins. Nahum has a head start, and eventually, reluctantly, he profits from it, first as a go-between for Yiddish-speaking Jews seeking passage to America and then as an overland transporter of their household goods. He acquires an English-speaking business partner, Goodkind; a Scottish clerk, Colquhoun (with whom there will be decades of inter-ethnic repartee); and a lawyer who advises him to change his name: "You'll be asked to spell it every time you say it." And so the firm of Goodkind-Raeburn is born.

Unbeknownst to Nahum, some of the foundations of the future family Raeburn are also being laid. But at this point he feels doomed to eternal virgin bachelorhood. The object of his first shy crush, a chicken merchant's daughter, has married a pious fraud who, imported from Volkovysk as a sort of mail-order rabbi, quickly turns secular and libertine and changes his name from Yerucham to James. (The spirited adaptability of the Jews, forever converting exile into enterprise, is a trait Chaim Bermant details with fond comic energy.) (p. 14).

What we have here so far is a Jewish comedy of affairs, owing at least as much to Thackeray as to Sholom Aleichem. It's a refreshing new flavor of Jewish humor, civilized, expansive, ironic, quite unlike the claustrophobic New York brand, with its edge of imminent hysteria, its sense of mingled specialness and shame. Chaim Bermant, who was himself born in Russia and educated in Glasgow and London, writes about Jews with a curious blend of intimacy and objectivity, like an affectionate anthropologist; he captures the specialness without the shame.

What's special about the Jews, of course, is their homelessness, their ambiguous relationship of love and fear to any homeland, including Palestine. In *The Patriarch,* Nahum Raeburn and his compatriots are permanently nostalgic for Russia, which they have fled; they do have their moments of thrilled British patriotism, but these are shattered when the press labels them "alien scum." After World War II they turn toward Zion, only to find the ground under their feet shaken by shells once again. It is perhaps the need for a home that impels Nahum to create and hold together his large, eccentric family. Most of *The Patriarch* chronicles that beleaguered act of creation. (pp. 14-15)

People die, new people are born, grow up, fall in love, get in trouble, vanish, reappear years later out of the blue. With each death, disappearance, betrayal, Nahum sinks a little toward death; with each birth, marriage, reappearance, he is reborn, revives, forgives. The family Raeburn—which embodies Nahum's affections—proves able to absorb goyim and gunrunners, to stretch from Mexico to Palestine, to regenerate itself, giving newborns the names and faces of the dead—and finally even to laugh at death. The family is a living organism, precarious yet tenacious, woven of the conflict between persistence and change. In *The Patriarch,* Chaim Bermant has written its ebullient, wistful chronicle. (p. 15)

Annie Gottlieb, "Joy and Tzores," in The New York Times Book Review, *August 2, 1981, pp. 14-15.*

MARGARET GORMAN

[With *The House of Women*] Chaim Bermant has once again produced an engaging portrait of Jewish family life. Courlander is not a practising Jew, and largely ignores the family business in order to play the English country gentleman. The family, despite its social aspirations, is rather déclassé, and its fluctuating fortunes are wryly observed by Ducks, the least attractive of Courlander's four daughters. Ducks may not share her sisters' looks but she more than compensates with a strong personality, a fine mind and a searing wit. . . .

At the core of the novel is Ducks herself: pert child, then promiscuous young woman with something of a father complex, touchingly trying to make sense of her relationships with men and putting a good face on her failures. For Ducks' ability to be independent is undermined by a strong pull towards marriage, and her growing feeling of panic and isolation. Her fear that, like Aunt Stevie before her, she will be left on the shelf while her sisters are all married, is one of the most affecting aspects of this light, lively and accomplished novel.

Margaret Gorman, in a review of "The House of Women," in Books and Bookmen, *No. 332, May, 1983, p. 34.*

KATE FULLBROOK

The generational novel has been a favourite form for Middle and East European authors for more than a century. Tolstoy, Thomas Mann and Isaac Bashevis Singer set an exceedingly high standard for this tradition, and Chaim Bermant is perhaps not to be blamed for falling far short of success in this field in [*The House of Women*]. . . . The dynastic undertones of the title are present throughout the novel, as the central character, Henrietta 'Ducks' Courlander, relates the story of her family's life in contemporary England. (pp. 514-15)

Bermant struggles not to allow his novel to degenerate into Zionist propaganda but this is, nevertheless, the most striking impression left by the book. He has trouble, too, in controlling his narrator who is supposed to be a woman and a highly successful economic scholar, and who sounds like neither. Further, Ducks seems to have no significant inner life so it is difficult to see what is gained by allowing her to narrate the story. This lack of self is a mark of the other characters as well. They just 'do' things, with little coherence or development evident in their portrayal. *The House of Women,* then, has all the marks of a pot-boiler—a lot of action, juicy adventures of the rich, and a spoonful of gung-ho Zionism for the seasoning. (p. 515)

Kate Fullbrook, in a review of "The House of Women," in British Book News, *August, 1983, pp. 514-15.*

Eavan (Aisling) Boland

1944-

Irish poet and critic.

Boland is one of Ireland's most significant female poets. Focusing her work on both political and private concerns, Boland writes of the condition of woman as poet and social outcast. Female sensuality, domestic details, and the spiritual torment of the oppressed intertwine in many of her poems; she also addresses the state of her craft and the social turmoil and violence of present-day Ireland. Most critics agree that Boland's poetry provides a valuable counterpoint to the male-dominated tradition of Irish poetry.

Boland's first collection to appear outside of Ireland, *Introducing Eavan Boland* (1981), reprints in whole *The War Horse* (1975) and *In Her Own Image* (1980), the two collections following her first full-length publication, *New Territory* (1967). The poems in *The War Horse,* directed primarily at such external issues as Ireland's political unrest and the confinement of conventional suburbia, are traditionally metered, often rhymed, and characterized by their formal control and keen imaginative power. *In Her Own Image* evidences a shift in both style and focus. Often linked to the work of Sylvia Plath, the poems in this collection are terser than Boland's earlier verse; the lines are shorter, the diction more striking, and the syntax more abrupt. Intensely focused on humanist and feminist concerns, the poems "blaze on the page," according to Jay Parini, challenging traditional notions of femininity and raging against the forces that imprison people in their lives. In *Night Feed* (1982), Boland continues her exploration of political, domestic, and artistic concerns. While some critics have detected a degree of literary affectation in Boland's work, most agree that the eloquence, grace, and intensity of her strongest poems mark her as a vital contributor to contemporary Irish poetry.

(See also *Dictionary of Literary Biography,* Vol. 40.)

MARTIN DODSWORTH

[In *The War Horse*] Eavan Boland uses rhyme and conventional form, with a clear cool diction. At its best the result is a kind of modern metaphysical, but the book is rather patchy. There is a tendency to lapse into the obvious, and the fact that she does so with an air of innocent grace doesn't really compensate the reader adequately. . . .

> Martin Dodsworth, "Under Duress," *in* The Guardian Weekly, *Vol. 112, No. 25, June 21, 1975, p. 23.*

DESMOND GRAHAM

Eavan Boland's second collection [*The War Horse*] possesses . . . unity and consistency of concern. . . . Between the title poem which opens the book, **"The War Horse,"** and the concluding poem, **"The Hanging Judge,"** Boland seeks a perspective which will encompass the domestic and the atavistic, the tender and the brutal, the Irish present and the Irish past.

> Our unease
> Vanishes with one smile
> As each suburban, modern detail
>
> Distances us from old lives
> Old deaths, but nightly on our screen
> New ones are lost, wounds open,
> And I despair of what perspective
> On this sudden Irish fury
> Will solve it to a folk memory.
>
> **("Naoise at Four")**

Here, the focus of the poem, is a child inheriting death and an Irish myth with his name. Elsewhere we have **"A Soldier's Son,"** **"The Famine Road"** and **"The Family Tree"** where 'On the right my cousins, lace at the wrists . . . Will wage their sterile fight' like laburnums, 'Pleasuring to poison enemy cattle.' Images of battle, murder, weaponry and bloodshed recur, even when Boland takes earlier writers for her source.

But too often the urgent violence of real suffering has been appropriated to sustain a metaphor; and however acute the pain of the poem's subject, Boland's failure to discriminate between the bleeding of a wounded past and of a wounded man amounts to more than a lack of taste.

On the face of it *The War Horse* combines skill in traditional metrics and versification with themes of immediate importance: a quest for the order which compassion might bring. In fact we have the accessible solutions of art imposed on the tangles of suffering.

> Come to the country where justice is seen to be done,
> Done daily. Come to the country where
> Sentence is passed by word of mouth and raw
> Boys split like infinitives. Look, here
> We hanged our son, our only son
> And hang him still and still we call it law.

The rhythms and repititions make the anger literary: the conceit in the middle makes death a verbal challenge. And as we come to the end of the collection we feel it is not our false sense of security which muffles the impact of violence but the taming capacity of artifice. (p. 78)

> *Desmond Graham, in a review of "The War Horse,"*
> *in* Stand, *Vol. 17, No. 3 (1976), p. 78.*

ANNE STEVENSON

What shall we say of women poets? Is there such a category? Is it not absurd to divide the ranks of the world's writers by sex? I myself am visited by puzzled resentment every time I suspect I have been injected into a poetry reading simply because I am female. On the other hand, there is a tendency, even today, for academic gentlemen to assume that literary history is, as it always was, safely in masculine hands. . . . In 1938, which seems a long time ago, John Crowe Ransom published an uneasy essay on Edna St. Vincent Millay.

> She is also a woman. No poet ever registered herself more deliberately in that light. She therefore fascinates the male reviewer but at the same time horrifies him a little too. He will probably swing between attachment and antipathy, which may be the very attitudes provoked in him by generic women in the flesh, as well as by the literary remains of Emily Dickinson, Elizabeth Barrett, Christina Rossetti and doubtless, if we only had enough of her, Sappho.

Significant about this passage is Ransom's honesty, and also his covert defence. He admits to horror and fascination, but he implies too, that there have been so *few* women poets, and those few so disconcerting (he fears their hysteria as King Pentheus feared the Maenads) that the 'male reviewer' had better not come too close. 'Our age,' Ransom continues stiffly, 'is the age which, among other things, has recovered the admirable John Donne; it is hardly the age of which it may be said Miss Millay is the voice.' (pp. 57-8)

Ransom was right; Millay's style was weak and over-emotional. . . . But what Ransom could not have seen in 1938 was that women have access to enormous areas of experience about which men, in their poetry, have had little to say. Without denying the importance to 'the age' of Eliot, Pound, Stevens, Williams, Auden, etc. (all of whom can be credited for having recovered not only the admirable John Donne but the entire tradition of English poetry as we are now taught it)—without denying the importance of this tradition, I think it is possible that the poets of the future will look back on the second half of the Twentieth Century as an age when, for the first time in civilized Western history, women found multiple and original tongues of their own.

If we have to give *a* voice to the age, let it be that of Sylvia Plath. Let us hope that Sylvia Plath, Anne Sexton and the other women for whom poetry has been literally a matter of life and death in our time will be remembered as *Kamikaze* heroines, as martyrs to the cause of an experiential language for women which no poet would have dreamed of exploring before.

It is a tribute to Plath and Sexton, too, that so few books by good women poets in 1980 take up artificial postures of martyrdom. Of the six books by women which are on my desk as I write, one only—Eavan Boland's *In Her Own Image*—could be described as destructively feminist. A note of anger spoils a real talent here. A great deal of self-pity masks as passion. I could wish for a broader, more generous view of a woman's life, than that which centres on a frenzied preoccupation with her body.

For there is much power in Ms Boland's work:

> I've caught you out. You slut. You fat trout.
> So here you are fumed in candle-stink . . .
> Anyone would think you were a whore—
> An ageing out-of-work kind-hearted tart.
> I know you for the ruthless bitch you are:
> Our criminal, our tricoteuse, our Muse—
> Our Muse of Mimic Art.

The criminal here, apparently, is femininity, womanhood, the lie about women Mr. Ransom would have liked to perpetuate. Ms Boland would have thrown her mirror at him:

> I will wake you from your sluttish sleep.
> I will show you true reflections, terrors.
> You are the Muse of all our mirrors.
> Look in them and weep.

All this is very well, but it isn't the whole story, and Eavan Boland knows it. Sex, childbirth, menstruation, nappies, fury—yes, vital, frightening, and after all, eternal. Mr. Ransom shouldn't have looked the other way, but neither should Eavan Boland steep herself in 'hips and breasts / and lips and heat / and sweat and fat and greed'. Not if she wants to represent more than a little human experience. (pp. 58-9)

> *Anne Stevenson, "Houses of Choice," in* Poetry Review, *Vol. 70, No. 3, 1980, pp. 57-65.**

DAVE SMITH

Eavan Boland's poetry is, I would judge, pretty much unknown to American readers but the Ontario Review Press . . . has set out to change that with *Introducing Eavan Boland*. . . .

As contemporary poets go, Boland is an eccentric becoming more ordinary. That is, she has been intensely and traditionally formal in the poems from *The War Horse* (1975), with a consistent adherence to rhymes, metrics, puns, wit, and conceit, and has moved in *In Her Own Image* (1980) to shorter, more colloquial lines that have at least the look and feel of Robert Creeley, though they possess greater dramatic substance. Not surprisingly the early poems concern, at the oblique and at the direct, that Irish violence which leaves dead children, maimed spirits, a world for "whose anguish no reprieve / exists unless new citizens, / And, as we found, laws of love—." Yet her poetry is no more partisan than Seamus Heaney's and might be about almost any human violation. She is less a poet of cultural and social issues than a lyric voice lamenting our blindness to and our abuse of love. Indeed she imagines us all prisoners of love as of other forces and imprisonment is the metaphor which underwrites her work. (p. 42)

Yet if love imprisons us she regards that emotion as entrapped itself, caged, tamed, dispossessed of its ancestral and shaggy power. Eavan Boland yearns for ferocity to burst through the tidy discretion of her poetry. She is caught like so many others in a life which seems a mockery of what life ought to be, that suburban angst which is the stock in trade of television soaps. Part II of **"Suburban Woman"** is a familiar, if slightly skewed, portrait:

> Morning: mistress of talcums, spun
> and second cottons, run tights
> she is, courtesan to the lethal
> rapine of routine. The room invites.
> She reaches to fluoresce the dawn.
> The kitchen lights like a brothel.

One imagines she must mean the kitchen appears hideously alien, perhaps ugly, disheveled. If not, what? Still this suburban woman wakes to a context different from many, that continuing Irish bloodletting which is "the romperings, the rape on either side, / the smiling killing" within which she discovers she "is the sole survivor." As survivor, she becomes a mother: "Waking, her cheeks dried, to a brighter / dawn she sensed in her as in April earth / a seed, a life ransoming her death." Soon enough this joy fades as Boland finds herself in her dusky garden where she "stares / at her life falling with her flowers . . . (like) the tears of shell-shocked men. . . ." This report of wars leads us to think we are going to have the full impression of life in the combat zone, and of that old shaggy passion which endures and breaks our heart. But section V disabuses us of that notion for "veterans of a defeat / no truce will heal, no formula prevent" turn out to be the combatants of suburban woman and the poem. Boland turns out to be imprisoned in "my compromise, my craft" and we are left less with shaggy passion than its ghost.

Perhaps it is pointless to complain about a book published six years ago but there is such graceful promise in *The War Horse* that I resent its tameness as much as Boland herself evidently did. She has a talent for sharp imagery, for consistency of metaphor, for knifing lines, and knows how to make verse speak with power. Yet she allows herself an excess of bruises in the keeper apples. She is coy to no purpose. **"Song"** is neatly turned but is little more than an adolescent joke about sex. A woman chases a man over a stream, the Irish image of the liberated lady I guess, and the poem concludes "He late that night / Followed the leaping tide." Subtlety? Yet in such poems as **"The War Horse," "The Soldier's Son,"** and **"Anon"** there is that dependably Irish muse as tragic as it is rough and ragged, the one known to Lady Gregory and Synge and Yeats.

The poems of *In Her Own Image* are conversions to Black Mountain rhetoric, feminism, and polemics of all sorts. I do not know if Boland has found shaggy atavistic love but she has made a raw poetry. Smooth iambics are chucked out, though some rhymes—like man's little toe—remain, and there are stanzas which evoke the ghost of good Dr. Williams. The spirit of patient passion, Yeats, is replaced by a cellular thumping: "my aesthetic: / a hip first, / a breast / a slow / shadow strip / out of clothes / that bushelled me / asleep." Boland has also found a use for figures of disease and, like Louise Gluck,

submits her suburban woman to anorexia's war of spirit and flesh. (pp. 42-3)

In the largest sense contemporary poetry has been an experiment in how to use what the Modernist improvisers concocted. If they were revolutionaries, so must we be. If they were extreme formalists, technicians, so must we be. How easy it is to understand Boland's feeling of entrapment in the old language, those pleasant turns which take the edge off things until the poem is not only expressive of our problem but is our problem. But how much of your life must you change, how much shall be made new before you find yourself pointlessly howling? Boland's poems feel the violent and vulgar powerfully enough. They hear Sylvia Plath in **"Menses"** when Boland writes "I am sick of it, / filled with it, / dulled by it, / thick with it." But in every case it is art, poetry, that Eavan Boland is writing about. Everywhere she is struggling to rid poetry of its worldly uselessness, its glibness, to make it visceral, strong stuff that thuds and bumps with whatever life now is. This is admirable, of course, but shaggy assertion is not necessarily any more than what Yeats calls "an old bellows full of angry wind." God knows it must be incumbent on an Irish poet to escape *his* shadow but I cannot help thinking Eavan Boland's view of things has taken her to write too much of writing poetry about writing poetry. I think, too, she has abandoned her generally effective verse, effective for poems only she can write, in preference for a form which will not afford her a sufficient scope or flexibility. Nevertheless *Introducing Eavan Boland* is a book worth more than a little attention from American readers. . . . (p. 43)

> Dave Smith, *"Some Recent American Poetry: Come All Ye Fair and Tender Ladies,"* in The American Poetry Review, *Vol. II, No. 1, January-February, 1982, pp. 36-46.**

VERNON YOUNG

From the quarterlies I have received the impression that in Ireland all poets face the east every dawn and pray, "Please, Mary Mother of God, let me not write like W. B. Yeats!" I expect it's an exaggeration. Eavan Boland (the only female Irish poet I've heard of since Oscar Wilde's grandmother), is in no danger. If there's a principal Irishman among her influences, it would be James Joyce; but I could be in error, persuaded by her very latest poems [collected in *Introducing Eavan Boland*] in which she sounds like Molly Bloom whipped into fury by seeing herself, in a crucial flash, as woman and fatally beset. Whoever may be the fount of her vindictive eloquence (the root is of course the daily speech in a country where language has not been emasculated by the radical separation of thought from culture), hers is the most startling arrival since Seamus Heaney's. The contents of *Introducing Eavan Boland* represent two slim volumes five years apart, 1975 and 1980; what happened to her poetry in those interim years is what happened to her, better defined as a mutation than as a development; even better, as an eruption. Clues to the subsequent poems are latent in the motifs of imprisonment that surface in such earlier works as **"Prisoners."** . . . The motif is sustained in two measured diatribes on that rational fungus of our age, Suburbia ("the claustrophobia / Of your back gardens varicose / With shrubs") and reaches a climax with the archetype Eavan Boland finds in a man named Lynch, magistrate and First Citizen of Galway in 1493, who hanged his son in the interests of justice. ("We hanged our son, our only son / And hang him still and still we call it law.")

From the first lines of her first poem in the most recent group, **"In Her Own Image,"** all forensic subjects are exiled. Increasingly self-concentrated and impeccably scornful, she wants revenge. . . . Her stanzas thereafter are shortened into trimeters that rush down the page, partita-like, as if she were only restraining with her eye the angered fluency of her hand and ear. The result is not ingratiating but it is stunning. From **"Anorexic"**: "Flesh is heretic. / My body is a witch. / I am burning it. / Yes, I am torching / her curves and paps and wiles. / They scorch in my self-denials / How she meshed my head / in the half-truths / of her fevers / till I renounced / milk and honey / and the taste of lunch. / I vomited / her hungers. / Now the bitch is burning . . ." From **"Witching"**: My gifts are nightly, / shifty, bookish. / By my craft / I bald the grass, / abort the birth / of calves / and warts / I study dark." We have been here before, have we not? but American feminist resentment has little of Miss Boland's art: the spare, polished invective, the speed and punctiliousness of vowels and alliterations clashing or consorting, the almost contemptuous economy of statement in a single poem. Whether or not the tigers of wrath are *wiser* than the horses of instruction, when leashed they are formidably more sensuous. Eavan Boland's language shortens the distance between the condition and the image: in its own ferocious way confirming Seamus Heaney's peerless definition, "that moment when the bird sings very close / To the music of what happens." (pp. 146-47)

Vernon Young, "The Experts," in The Hudson Review, Vol. XXXV, No. 1, Spring, 1982, pp. 139-50.*

JAY PARINI

[Eavan Boland is] a young woman whose poems blaze on the page. Her range is as considerable as her talents, and she can be hushed or strident by turns. **"Child of Our Time"** [from *Introducing Eavan Boland*] is an elegy for her dead infant, and its restraint makes it all the more powerful:

We who should have known how to instruct
With rhymes for your waking, rhythms for your sleep,
Names for the animals you took to bed,
Tales to distract, legends to protect,
Later an idiom for you to keep
And living, learn, must learn from you, dead.

The poem ends with this injunction to the child: "Sleep in a world your final sleep has woken." Beside such magisterial poise, we have Boland's rage against suburbia, the "back gardens varicose / With shrubs," as well as against the "rituals and flatteries of war, / Chants and pipes and witless empty rites / And war-like men." A well-tempered ferocity characterizes her latest work, such as **"Witching"**: "By my craft / I bald the grass, / abort the birth / of calves / and warts." This same craft informs her poetry as she studies the darker sides of nature and transmogrifies inarticulate yearnings into hard clear verse. Eavan Boland may well become the first important Irish *woman* poet since God-knows-when. (p. 633)

Jay Parini, "The Celtic Center," in The Sewanee Review, Vol. XC, No. 4, Fall, 1982, pp. 623-33.*

MAURICE HARMON

Eavan Boland occupies a unique position in Irish poetry. Her energies reflect a personal, domestic, feminist world; the poems [in *Night Feed*] register the everyday and glance at its possible mythic connections, but with ironic reservation. The obser-

vations of contingency are touched with a wry humour: "I shall be here forever / putting out the tea". In that "forever" we are invited to hear both the lost opportunity and the accepted-acceptable reality—"there's a way of life / that is its own witness". In this area of acceptance she creates her "fictions of evasion"—again the ambiguity is potent. The language enables us to face the implications: the ironies and the parallels, the beauty of the ordinary, the courage of the living, the artistry that creates this complex response. The persona is both present and detached, at times accepting, at times enacting a drama of escape and metamorphosis. The consciousness is intelligent, civilised and literary in the best sense. **"The New Pastoral"**, for example, is a sophisticated redefinition of old conventions. Eavan Boland has a reflective manner; she is quiet within the spaces in which a modern woman exists, seeing the objects, activities and duties, but seeing also potential around them. Like certain paintings the poems articulate these spaces and the life they sustain. (pp. 114-15)

Maurice Harmon, in a review of "Night Feed," in Irish University Review: A Journal of Irish Studies, Vol. 13, No. 1, Spring, 1983, pp. 114-15.

VERNON YOUNG

God help an Englishman who tries to establish hierarchy among Irish poets, who pits the North against Eire or vice versa. I am prepared to live dangerously by asserting that there are few poets writing English anywhere whose verses so purely exhibit the fusion of passion with euphony as those [in *Night Feed*] by Eavan Boland of Dublin. Her poems ring like bells across the snow. . . . The most formidable poems in her previous volume were leveled at the torments of fruitless womanhood; some, in the present collection, sing (vehemently!) the burden of time and the ineluctable demotion of the flesh (**"The Woman Changes Her Skin"**; **"The Woman Turns Herself into a Fish"**; **"The Woman as Mummy's Head"**). Many others, half of the total, I'd say, celebrate the wonders of motherhood and the lactic poetry of the everyday, the domain of bottles, of washers and driers, of feeding and tucking-in. I hope I am pardoned if I remark that these recitals are not calculated to convert *my* sounds of woe into hey nonny nonny! But this woman is a witch of poetry; she can make you believe in anything—even the marriage of heaven and hell.

I would guess that the tenacity with which she circumscribes and exalts a chosen subject depends closely on her emotional fortunes in life. She transcends solipsism by the perfection with which she models a *poem* from its subjective source. Nothing is left to chance: the click of consonants, the echo of vowels, internal rhyme, syllabic counterpoint. Her art often consists in the impression she gives of having rushed to the page, her eye in a fine frenzy rolling, but we know it couldn't have happened that way; it's safe to assume that she has consigned thousands of imprecisions to the waste basket. It will be interesting to see for just how long she will be able to sustain her almost unremitting exclusion of the inhabited poem that introduced her eight years ago. A handful of poems in the current volume, neither denunciatory nor domestic, may predict a future shift from her self-intensive phase. The following quotations are, respectively, a sestet and an octet from two sonnets. From **"Woman Posing,"** after the painting, "Mrs. Badham," by Ingres:

She smirks uneasily at what she's shirking
Sitting on this chair in silly clothes
Posing in a truancy of frills.

There's no repose in her broad knees.
The shawl she shoulders just upholsters her.
She hands the open book like pantry keys.

From **"On Renoir's *The Grape-Pickers*"**:

They seem to be what they are harvesting:
Rumps, elbows, hips clustering
Plumply in the sun, a fuss of shines
Wining from the ovals of their elbows.
The brush plucks them from a tied vine.
Such roundness, such a sound vintage
Of circles, such a work of pure spheres!
Flesh and shadow mesh inside each other.

Flesh and shadow mesh inside each other! If these stanzas were not so intrinsically musical, one would be tempted to call them sculptural. Compact yet plastic, they fashion before one's eyes the living shape and ambience of a personality. W. H. Auden once proclaimed: "Whatever else it may be, I want every poem I write to be a hymn in praise of the English language." Few of his stoutest admirers (I am one) would agree that this fervent hope accurately describes the substance of his achievement. For my purpose, it comes near to explaining the resonance of Eavan Boland's achievement. (pp. 408-10)

Vernon Young, "Some Others and the Irish," in The Hudson Review, *Vol. XXXVI, No. 2, Summer, 1983, pp. 399-410.**

JAMES McELROY

[Modern] critics tend to overlook the normative silence of women, this being especially true in contemporary Ireland where it is simply assumed that Yeat's poetic heir will be male. And given that Ireland's women poets are consistently ignored as serious challengers to the Yeats name, this remains a strong possibility. . . .

Any suggestion that this inequity has more to do with the intrinsic weaknesses of Ireland's female verse than the conscious or unconscious biases of male editors somehow misses the point that it is men who define quality—quality of theme; quality of tone; quality of language; also perhaps the quality of rhythm? Even the more recent critics mesmerized by the male pulse of Montague, Kinsella, Heaney, Mahon, et al. have failed to bring women poets to mind and have left them all but unthought. Consequently, women's marginal presence in the major anthologies has been taken for granted and the hidden but powerful assumption that Irish women poets, especially 'quality' Irish women poets, do not exist, remains unexposed.

One woman who dispels this kind of unspoken opinion is Eavan Boland. Not only does she have four full-sized collections in print, *New Territory* (1967), *The War Horse* (1975), *In Her Own Image* (1980), and *Night Feed* (1982), but she has also proven herself to be a sophisticated mediator of technique. So much so, in fact, that her treatment of less popular and sequestered themes like child-rearing, domestic chores and "the quiet barbarities of the suburbs" are kept from going slack or becoming commonplace. Despite Boland's occasional fall into romanticism (notably in poems like **"Migration,"** **"Lullaby"** and **"Song"**) she successfully manipulates the romantic form so it projects subtle but defiant attitudes into marriage and maternalism and the sentimentality so often associated with these heteronomous institutions.

One almost random example of this tear between the uncomplaining and the disillusioned housewife comes in the recent poem **"Dedication"**:

The woman is as round
as the new ring
ambering her finger.
The mirror weds her.
She has long since been bedded.

There is
about it all
a quiet search for attention,
like the unexpected shine
of a despised utensil.

Here, the sting in the tail comes with "She has long since been bedded" and the dismissive cynicism of "despised utensil." Neither stanza is quite as demure or archaic as it appears and both press the lines of a malcontent; someone who wants to register mature regrets against domestic ordinance. But Boland is more than just a poet of pots and pans who goes public with her private exasperations; she is also an exposer of suburban episodes and how they connect with (create) circumstantial selves. (p. 32)

[Boland extends] frustrations and disappointments and builds them into an explicit critique of the female social self through the utterly strident **"Witching"** where the images and archetypes of women are repeatedly attacked in order to annihilate not women, but the emotive ideas that transfix women. So, in addition to its internal power, this poem should also be read as a disciplined bid to poeticize a specifically female experience, and not, as the masculinist critic might suggest, as some kind of unnecessary self-pity or indulgence. In fact, the poem's ready obligation to feminism continues in negativity only as a means of berating the mysogynist. . . . With even more vituperation, Boland castigates the shackled body and mind of contemporary women in **"Anorexic"** with its stark: "Flesh is heretic / My body is a witch": and **"Mastectomy,"** where she indicts the masculine other. . . . Directed at the body as some thing to be treated impersonally ("It has gone"), **"Mastectomy"** enables Boland to identify the complex authors—the masculine "they"—who have calibrated the lives of women. Taking this conviction one step futher, Boland dramatizes the generic man role through her allegorical **"In His Own Image."** . . . Boland orchestrates a further series of poems that rally a radical womanist stand: **"It's a Woman's World," "The Woman Changes her Skin," "The Woman Turns Herself into a Fish," "The Woman as a Mummy's Head"** and the polemical **"Daphne with her Thighs in Bark."** . . . (pp. 32-3)

Alongside these feminist-inspired lines Boland has written a number of verses that have their first inspiration in painting. For example, the poem **"From the Painting 'Back from the Market'"** (on the work by Chardin), is a Boland reflection that bears down on the rural figure, and in the process, demonstrates her capacity to handle concise episodes and mount a kind of recovery; a recouping of biographical, historical, even perhaps religious meaning where there was assumed to be none. That Boland's gaze penetrates beneath the (painting's) surface of things and problematizes that forgotten character known as woman only reassures us of both the conceptual and literary value of her poetry. . . . [The phrase from this poem] *Woman's secret history* is, in one expression or another, the premise of Boland's literature. It is not inappropriate then that she chose a work of Chardin, himself a painter of domestic things—of "despised utensils"—to advance her sensual ideology. After all, Chardin's element was also the mundane and forgotten objects that contained (for him at least) some fleeting epiphany. And it was also through those objects and the world they represented that a subject arrived at self-identity. . . . (pp. 33-4)

In part explained by the fact that her mother, Frances Kelly, was an artist with the Post-Expressionists in Paris in the 1930s, Boland's intimate relationship with painting is very visible in the 1982 collection *Night Feed*. Here we find references to Van Eyck and a set of poems which reflect a deep interest and profound appreciation of the painted image. In **"Fruit on a Straight-sided Tray,"** society's aesthetic is said to be shaped "When the painter takes the straight-sided tray / and arranges late melons with grapes and lemons" *forgetting* that "the true subject is the space between them." For Boland, this interstice is usually the female figure. **"Woman Posing"** (after the painting "Mrs. Badham" by Ingres) and **"On Renoir's 'The Grape-Pickers,'"** along with the very cleverly narrated poem **"Degas's Laundresses,"** are powerful and secure verses that bring women into the foreground as subjects in their own rights. . . . (p. 34)

Boland's mild literary affectation . . . should not, however, blind us to the general and valuable truth that . . . [she provides] an alternative voice and [deals] with a very un-Irish theme: the self. Ironically, this theme, instead of being encouraged or allowed to blossom, has been sniped at as ego-centric indulgence. Thus, Vernon Young, in his recent article "Poetry Chronicle: Some Others and the Irish" [see excerpt above], while lavishly praising Boland, also falls into an old masculinist trap with his speculative conclusion:

> It will be interesting to see for just how long she will be able to sustain her almost unremitting exclusion of the inhabited poem that introduced her eight years ago. A handful of poems in the current volume, neither denunciatory nor domestic, may predict a future shift from her self-intensive phase.

This discussion of the *Night Feed* volume and the critic's desire for a return to the "inhabited poem" and a turn away from some "self-intensive phase" only reminds us that a woman's range of themes are less valued than the masculine concerns of land, labor, and animal—the provinces of men. It also fails to remind us of the fact that male Irish poets have traditionally neglected precisely the questions of intimacy, self and sexuality in all but a cursory way. . . . (p. 36)

James McElroy, "'Night Feed': An Overview of Ireland's Women Poets," in The American Poetry Review, *Vol. 14, No. 1, January-February, 1985, pp. 32-9.*

Christine Brooke-Rose

1926-

English novelist, critic, translator, short story writer, and poet.

In her novels Brooke-Rose experiments with such elements as time, structure, and language. Her fiction demonstrates the influence of James Joyce and such practitioners of the *nouveau roman* as Alain Robbe-Grillet and Nathalie Sarraute in its de-emphasis of plot, characterization, and linear narrative. Brooke-Rose explores themes related to language, often using free association and stream-of-consciousness narrative together with unconventional, often technical phraseology. Although many critics find her work obscure, Brooke-Rose is generally praised for her wit and verbal wordplay.

Brooke-Rose's early novels are more conventionally structured than her later fiction. Her first two novels, *The Languages of Love* (1957) and *The Sycamore Tree* (1958), combine love stories with satiric portrayals of English intellectuals. These novels have been compared to the works of Iris Murdoch for their examination of English society. In her most ambitious novel of this period, *The Dear Deceit* (1960), Brooke-Rose recounts the life of her protagonist backward from his death to his birth. This novel is considered Brooke-Rose's first attempt to move away from traditional, realistic fiction.

In 1962, Brooke-Rose became gravely ill, and her approach to writing underwent drastic changes. She renounced her earlier novels and developed a fascination for scientific language. Brooke-Rose stated: "Such phrases, of precise significance to the scientist, fired my imagination as poetic metaphors for what happens between people." *Out* (1964), written during her illness, reflects Brooke-Rose's new interests and is her first overtly experimental novel. Classified by some critics as a science fiction novel, *Out* is set in a future world recently devastated by nuclear war in which white people are victims of racial prejudice. The language of *Out* is highly technical, containing many references to scientific concepts, and the story is related through the protagonist's randomly connected thoughts and observations. These elements recur in Brooke-Rose's succeeding novels, in which she continues her examination of language and the lack of meaningful communication between individuals. *Such* (1966), a cowinner of the James Tait Black Memorial Prize, centers on an astronomer who dies and comes back to life; the narrative, which takes place during the astronomer's three minutes of death, relates his past through scientific and technical language that reflects his knowledge of astronomy. *Between* (1968) explores language-related themes and associative wordplay in its story about a professional translator. *Thru* (1975) is perhaps Brooke-Rose's most difficult novel because of its alternating narrative focus and detailed exploration of the nature of fiction and its relation to reality. *Amalgamemnon* (1984) further demonstrates Brooke-Rose's linguistic dexterity through her use of puns, allusions, and narrative shifts.

Brooke-Rose is also respected as a literary critic, having published three volumes of structural analysis: *A Grammar of Metaphor* (1958), *A ZBC of Ezra Pound* (1971), and *A Rhetoric of the Unreal: Studies in Narrative and Structure, Especially of the Fantastic* (1982). In addition, she has published a long

poem, *Gold* (1955), and a collection of short stories, *Go When You See the Green Man Walking* (1970).

(See also *Contemporary Authors,* Vols. 13-16, rev. ed. and *Dictionary of Literary Biography,* Vol. 14.)

WALTER ALLEN

The Sycamore Tree, according to the blurb, 'will be enjoyed and treasured by readers of both Wolfenden and Wittgenstein'. Oh dear! Miss Brooke-Rose is a learned writer and, as her admirable first novel *The Languages of Love* showed, she can wear her learning lightly. She doesn't in *The Sycamore Tree,* which sinks under a mass of elaboration. Synopsised, her novel would sound, I am afraid, like a farrago of nonsense. It isn't that, but it is much too crammed with disparate material tenuously linked together, and nothing quite convinces; not the Oxford-don novelist who can get into telepathic *rapport* with his wife, nor his beautiful wife who has blackouts in which she solicits in the streets as a tart (Wolfenden), nor the nasty book-reviewer whose mistress she becomes after he has sued her husband for libel, nor the Hungarian refugee poet who identifies himself in his persecution with a dead poet of a century ago, nor the great central theme, the nature of reality (Wittgenstein). It's a great pity that she has tried to do too much here, because one day Miss Brooke-Rose may very well write a very good novel.

> *Walter Allen, in a review of "The Sycamore Tree,"*
> *in* New Statesman, *Vol. LVI, No. 1439, October 11,*
> *1958, p. 500.*

WIRT WILLIAMS

[*The Sycamore Tree*] is at once a brilliant contemporary love story and philosophical fiction of a high order. It is as good a novel as I have read by any of the new British writers, and should establish poet-critic Christine Brooke-Rose as one of the best.

Like so much serious contemporary writing, it is thematically concerned with the quest for those much-sought Siamese twins, identity and reality. But it is also dazzling entertainment, rendering the world of literary and fashionable London with poised irony and wit, and dramatizing some interlocked love affairs with insight and unabashed physical vitality.

These love stories make a five-pointed (though far from perfectly pentagonal) design. Gael Jackson, a novelist and an Oxford tutor, loves his wife, Nina. She loves him too, but is seduced by critic Howard Cutting—who is fond enough of his own wife, Elizabeth. She in turn loves a Hungarian refugee poet who is also her student—*he* loves *her*, but unsuccessfully. The poet, Zoltan Corday, completes the figure with his friendship for Jackson.

At the outset of the action Cutting suppresses Jackson's book, *The Sycamore Tree,* with a libel suit. Simultaneously he develops a tremendous yen for Jackson's wife. She loathes him at first—then is inescapably attracted by his vulgar vigor. Once seduced, she becomes, almost, two separate personalities.

Meanwhile Zoltan turns out to be the supposedly liquidated countryman about whom he is writing a critical study. More and more he finds himself, like Nina, bewildered and threatened by this sharp division of soul. From the fatal division tragedy flows. So does the author's theme: all parts of a personality, both good and evil, must be contained and kept in balance, or destruction follows. (p. 4)

The sycamore tree of the title is reality. And, says Christine Brooke-Rose, it is fixed and permanent, no matter from what angle viewed. . . .

But the novel, like an artfully contrived hall of mirrors, refracts many other angles. It offers strong evidence that British fiction—which has lagged far behind American in the intensity and variety of its techniques through most of the last fifteen years—has about caught up. (p. 33)

> *Wirt Williams, "Good and Evil Got Out of Balance,"*
> *in* The New York Times Book Review, *January 11,*
> *1959, pp. 4, 33.*

JEREMY WARBURG

[*A Grammar of Metaphor*] is not 'just another book on metaphor'. That would imply that it had nothing, or very little but its mass, to add to what has already accumulated since the days of Aristotle. But remarkably little of that material has been concerned—as *A Grammar of Metaphor* is concerned—with the variety of grammatical and syntactical ways, and with the significance of the ways, in which metaphors have been expressed; and what little there is, is qualitatively as well as quantitatively inadequate. Of course, 'a purely grammatical analysis of metaphor has', as Miss Brooke-Rose points out, 'many limitations', but, for all its limitations, it is not only an original but an important, a salutary analysis to make, and Miss Brooke-Rose's is, it seems to me, an admirable one. She examines 'the syntactic groups on which metaphor must, willy-nilly, be based', and provides us with a helpful and more than usually objective typology of metaphor. She describes the different linguistic forms of metaphor, and, often felicitously, the general intention and effects of each . . . as well as observing the tendencies which the use of one or other has revealed, or at the least illuminated, in the texts she has chosen from the work of fifteen English poets from Chaucer to Dylan Thomas. . . . She also points out, undogmatically and in passing, some of the advantages which may be conferred, and some of the limitations which may be imposed, by the structure of the particular language in which the poetry is written. And she does, I think, clear up, as she had hoped, 'certain confusions which are so constantly found in works on figurative language'—the muddling of metaphor with comparison and simile . . . , the abuse of the term 'imagery', and the confusion between metaphor and symbol.

But *A Grammar of Metaphor* demonstrates something more than the value of a grammatical approach to metaphor; it also provides a scholarly and stimulating demonstration of the value of a linguistic approach to literature, one which should add considerably to the understanding and appreciation which a purely 'literary' approach to literature can give. Some may complain that a linguistic approach cannot take them very far: others may agree, but might justifiably point out that the places it will lead them to undoubtedly exist, have far too seldom been visited, and are well worth the rigours of the trip. (pp. 97-8)

> *Jeremy Warburg, in a review of "A Grammar of*
> *Metaphor," in* The Modern Language Review, *Vol.*
> *LV, No. 1, January, 1960, pp. 97-8.*

KEITH WATERHOUSE

I have read many novels that appeared to have been written backwards, but only one that was intentionally so, and that is *The Dear Deceit*. Miss Brooke-Rose starts with the funeral of Alfred Northbrook Hayley, liar, thief, pornographer, prude, hypocrite, snob, fanatic, and she finishes up with his childhood. It isn't flashback; the reader is simply taken back and back and further back through the years as though he were a psycho-analyst delving deeper and deeper into the character of this horrible yet pathetic and engaging man. Now one hesitates to use the word 'gimmick' when dealing with so scholarly a writer as Miss Brooke-Rose, but the question must be asked: would Alfred Northbrook Hayley be such a fascinating character if his story were told the right way round, if, so to speak, one were to *read* it backwards? And the answer is yes: he is an original. But the way Miss Brooke-Rose has dealt with him, letting the outer husk fall away and then stripping off layer after layer of character formation until we see the shivering village boy at the beginning of it all, is enlightening and technically superb.

> *Keith Waterhouse, in a review of "The Dear Deceit," in* New Statesman, *Vol. LX, No. 1544, October 15, 1960, p. 580.*

MARY ROSE

The Dear Deceit etches a caustic and often witty portrait of a thoroughgoing bounder whose slippery course in love and business met with only one real fall. Its chief suspense is that one does not know until nearly the end in just what way the agile Alfred came a cropper. The novel is distinguished in characterization and in the particulars of contemporary settings in England and America during the last quarter of the nineteenth century and the first part of the twentieth.

During a spell when Hayley was a partner in a dull publishing business in New York, a budding author sent him a manuscript comparing Herman Melville to an onion from which layer after layer of meaning can be peeled. In somewhat the same way, each of the chapters of this novel except the first and last peels back time to progressively earlier years of Alfred's life until one sees him as a rather horrid little boy in a middle-class family with pretensions to gentility, already beginning to ape and impose upon his betters.

Even though the technical tour de force of the plotting does not quite come off—as in my opinion it does not—readers of *The Dear Deceit* are not likely to forget Alfred. Conceivably they may remember him the better because they have stumbled a little in following him to progressively more youthful, but also outrageous, misdoings.

Mary Rose, "A Bounder Comes a Cropper," in Books, *September 10, 1961, p. 11.*

KAY DICK

[*Out*] is a very unusual book indeed, particularly when related to this novelist's past work and to the circumstances of how it was written.

Out presents a landscape of sickness in worldwide terms, through a futuristic view of the human race, following a disaster classified as 'the displacement,' which has upset the whole chemistry of man and nature. The main feature is the rising supremacy of the coloured races as distinct from the decaying whites whose philosophy, sciences and humanities were not strong enough to prevent their self-destruction. The picture, one of terrifying proportions, visual and psychological, is made absolutely acceptable to the reader simply because Miss Brooke-Rose herself has experienced an illness which, temporarily, cut her off from the greater part of daily realities. Such an experience enabled Miss Brooke-Rose to extend her perception and, what is more important, to free herself from social and personal trivia and apply her writer's imagination, intelligence and understanding to basic truths. (pp. 613-14)

On the whole this author's previous fiction presents witty and satirical views of contemporary, mostly metropolitan, social life, with the exception of *The Dear Deceit* which explored an autobiographical theme. *Out* is a complete breakaway, and shows remarkable courage. It is not an easy book and demands intense concentration because it makes no concessions. This does not imply incomprehensibility. On the contrary, it strikes vivid images in terms recognisable to all of us. The weak and the strong, the sick and the healthy, epitomised by the colourless (that is the whites) and the Afro-Eurasian groups, cope with a distorted natural world where famine, poverty and radiation are daily realities. Danger is constant, survival is the main issue, and the experience of both are illustrated through the dimmed perception and enfeebled mind of a colourless male, whose intelligence and memory are in a state of shock.

He is, psychologically, a mutated individual, who was once a professor, a humanist, in status reduced to the ranks of the unskilled, the almost incapacitated. In this man, crippled though he is as an individual, there is still love, intellectual passion and hope, although physiological deficiency controls the quality and action of such positive virtues which are almost fossilised. To have attempted such a book is a triumph in itself: that Miss Brooke-Rose has achieved her purpose with such unfaltering dedication and creative integrity is an exciting fact. *Out* must be read. (p. 614)

Kay Dick, "The Magic Mountain," in The Spectator, *Vol. 213, No. 7115, November 6, 1964, pp. 613-14.*

FRANCIS HOPE

[In *Out* Christine Brooke-Rose's story] presupposes a nuclear disaster referred to as 'the displacement', as a result of which the map is a different shape and the present racial hierarchy upside down. The sickly, displaced, demoralised whites have become a shanty-town subspecies, scratching for jobs on the fringes of established black or brown society. The whole book unrolls through the consciousness of one of these 'Colourless' pariahs, struggling to get a bare conceptual hold on life and a job at the local big house. It would therefore be unreasonable to expect a level-headed narrative; but it does seem a pity that Miss Brooke-Rose has trotted out the whole Left Bank box of *trues*—meaningless confusions, solipsistic riddles, obsessive galaxies of 'objective' scientific terms. Vague incantations like 'diagnosis merely prognosticates aetiology' are passed around like fake currency; intimations of epistemology peep out from each repetitive paragraph. . . .

An anti-novel should perhaps be judged for anti-standards. This one, then, has the virtues of moral nullity and crucifying dullness: it is resplendently unreadable. But it remains possible that the anti-author (perhaps anti-reader is nearer the truth) really is trying to say something more interesting than that uncertainty is a state in which one is uncertain. Those healthy blacks and dwindling whites suggest (as does the blurb) some warning about neglected dark forces in the mind, about the mental breakdown of an intelligence with shallowly rationalistic roots—the sort of intelligence which produces anti-novels, in fact. Commendably old stuff, of course, but Miss Brooke-Rose's persistent intelligence once or twice threatens to make something of it. The possibility that we have to deal with an anti-anti-novel can't quite be ruled out. (p. 742)

Francis Hope, "I, Julian," in New Statesman, *Vol. LXVIII, No. 1757, November 13, 1964, pp. 741-42.*

WILLIAM COOPER

The jacket tells us that *Such,* Christine Brooke-Rose's new post-James Joycean novel, is about 'a physicist turned psychiatrist for a university radio-astronomy unit'. Certainly it's useful to know before one starts reading the book, because it's difficult to tell after. Through the stream of scientific 'hithering thithering of', one glimpses Miss Brooke-Rose grappling with the theory that our individual natures are particulate—a theory arrived at by inference, I imagine, from the theory (which underlies Joycean writing) that our experience of living is particulate. As the latter theory is not borne out by experiment, it's understandable that she gets into difficulties with the former. However, it's possible that we're supposed to take it that 'all is in the writing'—not in the content. On this level her stream of scientific terms used with an engagingly learned air in metaphor that doesn't figure, and simile that can't relate is fun, a sort of nonsense poetry. What seems to me the danger Miss Brooke-Rose may not have foreseen is that it asks to be taken as 110 percent serious by people who fancy their chance as highbrows. It would be a sad and inappropriate fate for her, a clever and gifted artist, to find herself acclaimed their queen.

William Cooper, in a review of "Such," in The Listener, *Vol. LXXVI, No. 1960, October 20, 1966, p. 583.*

MARTIN SEYMOUR-SMITH

[*Such*] is very sophisticated SF. Larry, a physicist, has died and then come back to life. The structure is highly complex and ingenious: during death he has encountered Something, a girl who carries five planets on her arms, each of which—after his resurrection—comes back representing some aspect of his real past, and of the people under whose influence he has come. The cleverness of all this is dazzling, and so are its intellectual implications. The difficulty is that the reader needs to work too hard, intellectually, all the way; the fabric is not well enough informed with feeling or psychological depth; the whole is too much a stark ideological structure. One wants to work hard on books only when one has enjoyed them, responded to them . . . : I admired this novel, but I could not enjoy it. (p. 593)

Martin Seymour-Smith, "Heroic Qualities," in The Spectator, *Vol. 217, No. 7219, November 4, 1966, pp. 592-93.**

DAVID WILLIAMS

Between is a multilingual reverie, a seven-terraced Tower of Babel broadcasting a swirling, recurring pattern of words— English, French, German, with an exotic peppering of the less familiar. The words are those remembered by one woman— no name is given her—jet-borne around the world on her way from conference to congress where she acts as simultaneous interpreter.

We are to imagine this woman dozing and dreaming, mixing her languages up, never bothering about time because the jets make time jump forward or backward too often to make a watch worthwhile. Bits of poetry—"Kubla Khan," "Erlkönig," *King Lear*—mingle with the sleepy, tangential, autobiographical flow; clusters of phrases, images . . . keep returning; a platitude from the conference-room rises to the surface of consciousness like a hippo surfacing in a swamp. You watch a verbal roundabout trundling, and gradually the pattern of her life-till-now emerges: her divorce from the Englishman, her comic, half-hearted attitude to possible successors, her confused loyalties—to a French mother or to Tante Frieda, the Nurnberg Nazi to whom she was handed over at fifteen before the war—or to places, the Paris flat, the Wiltshire cottage, loved fixed points in a world where landing and take-off are diurnal.

The book is a continuously exciting, often funny, Pentecostal experiment which I enjoyed greatly. It owes much to Joyce, but all the same Christine Brooke-Rose speaks with her own voice, and speaks with authority.

David Williams, in a review of "Between," in Punch, *Vol. CCLV, No. 6687, November 6, 1968, p. 672.*

MALCOLM BRADBURY

Christine Brooke-Rose is one of the few novelists we have who are seriously experimenting still in neo-modernist techniques, and for that reason alone she's important. At the same time her own tackling of form and language has an intelligent distinctiveness. *Between* is a novel centred in the consciousness of a cosmopolitan girl of French and German background, a "simultaneous interpreter" who lives between hotel rooms, airplane flights, cultures, languages, and lovers. The working frame of the action is a plane-flight which intersects with all the many other such flights she takes, with its symbolic significance; and with a body of cosmopolitan recollections that ultimately draw our attention to the problem of language itself; how does it descend into matter and culture and experience?

Miss Brooke-Rose runs, it seems to me, into some of the slippery traps of this kind of experimental novel: on the one hand we are concerned with the free associative system of the central consciousness, that process of penetration of time by space, and space by time, which gives images and symbols; while on the other we are concerned with a system of *verbal* associations, the jokes of "simultaneous interpretation" which produces punning and wit, the way themselves words fraternise and fornicate with syntax. But Miss Brooke-Rose produces as neat a reconciliation as this kind of novel can, by making her central character an interpreter, attempting to bridge the gap between Saussure and love. And so her sense of emotional suspension and transition, her state between marriage and divorce, guilt and innocence, can be given a real relationship with the linguistic world of the modern Tower of Babel in which she lives.

Malcolm Bradbury, "As the Rot Sets In," in The Guardian Weekly, *Vol. 99, No. 19, November 7, 1968, p. 15.**

WALLACE HILDICK

In art an unorthodox technique can be employed for various purposes. . . . On the credit side, unorthodox technique may be necessary if an artist is to explore new ground or genuinely to experiment. Since genuine experiments are, by definition, as likely to have negative as positive results, the risks here are great and the artists taking them worthy of our deepest respect if not highest praise.

Miss Christine Brooke-Rose's *Between* comes into this category of genuine high-risk experiment. Basically an account of a number of air journeys undertaken by a professional interpreter in the course of her work, it is narrated as a stream of consciousness which, logically faithful to the heroine's life and habits of thought, flows along in several languages—chiefly English, French and German. After a very few pages—long before the heroine had echoed the belief that languages behave as if they 'loved each other behind their own facades . . . as if words fraternised silently beneath the syntax, finding each other funny and delicious in a Misch-Masch of tender fornication'—I was finding it comparatively easy to follow. Partly this was because of the author's care to juxtapose, paraphrase and generally act as procuress for the fornication she was to speak of later; and partly it was because of the fascination engendered by the nature of the expedition. For this is a truly exploratory book; as the title suggests, a journey into transition itself, into the territories between sleeping and waking, take-off and landing, the utterance and its apprehension, language and language, medium and message, the gadget and its uses, between everything and everything else, as it were, from aerosol to breakfast-time. The risks are appalling, but Miss Brooke-Rose is so completely in charge of her material that the result is most satisfying: an elegant, witty, deeply moving hymn to St. Christopher, whose medallion dangles between the breasts of the between-age heroine as she flies between meals and affairs from one conference to another.

Wallace Hildick, "Divided Loyalties," in The Listener, Vol. LXXX, No. 2068, November 14, 1968, p. 649.*

SUSAN HILL

["**Queenie Fat and Thin**" is the] only half-way memorable story in Miss Brooke-Rose's schematic collection [*Go When You See the Green Man Walking*]. . . . Otherwise, this is a sterile and rather dated assortment, heavily influenced, as are Miss Brooke-Rose's novels, by the Robbe-Grillet school. Some highbrow ghost stories here sent me straight back to Muriel Spark, who does this kind of thing so much better.

Susan Hill, "Signs of the Times," in New Statesman, Vol. 80, No. 2070, November 20, 1970, p. 687.*

TOM MacINTYRE

Christine Brooke-Rose, though a novelist of repute, is not altogether at ease in the shorter form. She has, however, the right kind of vulnerability and tremendous fluency, and she does come up with at least two excellent stories in her first collection [*Go When You See the Green Man Walking*]. To take the less exciting pieces first: her ventures into fantasy, as in "**George and the Seraph**", lack the confidently light touch that is necessary—one has the sense of a writer straining to beat the material and the effect is calamitous. Leaving that zone, she at once moves more freely—two Italians discussing the good old days when girl-tourists were theirs for the picking in "**They all go to the mountains now**" or a young woman locked in religious obsession in "**The Religious Button**". These pieces are obviously competent if not altogether successful—the Italians escape really telling exposure, and one's concern for the young woman is mitigated by a diffuse quality in the account of her dilemma. Perhaps the most interesting thing about the latter story is that it points to the area where Miss Brooke-Rose is at her best—that area where the sexual and the obsessive commingle. The book's finest achievements—the title story and "**Medium Loser and Small Winner**"—are placed there. In both these stories the writing, fluent and flexible as ever, is abruptly urgent, with its theme clearly in sight, and one has the delight of encountering form and material perfectly fused. (pp. 755-56)

Tom MacIntyre, "Small Winners," in The Listener, Vol. 84, No. 2174, November 26, 1970, pp. 755-56.*

JONATHAN RABAN

[In *A ZBC of Ezra Pound*] Miss Brooke-Rose addresses her students, whom she calls, as grown-ups will, 'the younger generation', and puts on a special voice for the purpose. 'Goodness me!' she exclaims in the middle of a sentence about the appropriateness of epic form; 'you don't have to go and look it up,' she reassures us, when she announces that she's written an article on the spiral structure of the *Cantos* and *Piers Plowman;* she calls an early poem 'Pre-Raphish', and a few pages later says that an Arthur Rackham painting is 'very Pre-Raphish'. She borrows some of the finger-wagging manner of Pound's own *Guide to Kulchur,* and spices it with the giggling raffishness of a chain-smoking lady don, in an attempt to jolly us along over the rocky terrain of her extremely detailed and thickly documented argument. Her book reads like a pile of hectically compiled lecture notes, complete with coffee-stains and knots in mental handkerchiefs as evidence of the human touch.

Her obvious embarrassment is understandable, but it is to be regretted nevertheless. For it is her coyness that gets her out of every tight critical spot. She approaches Pound with love, insight, and a store of hard knowledge unrivalled by any other commentator. She knows about ideograms . . . , is tireless in her pursuit of allusion, and communicates her own excitement in reading Pound . . . with an infectiousness I've found entirely lacking in Dekker, and even in Kenner and Davie. But one reads the book with a growing conviction that the whole enterprise is founded upon a massive tautology. Its effect is merely to reduplicate the problems of the *Cantos* themselves, as if Pound had decided to 'explain' the poem by just telling us more about all the personages and literary works mentioned in it.

This isn't, of course, her intention. Indeed most of the book is occupied in producing elaborate arguments to justify Pound's method. But they all reduce to a single strategy. Where I see a haphazard collision, a private and unarticulated association, she discerns a 'juxtaposition', a 'tension', a 'fusion', a 'telescoping', a 'metamorphosis', all terms which assert, but in no way demonstrate, the formal coherence which she claims for the poem. She, like Pound, showers us with a fine confetti of historical and literary snippets, then announces that she has proved the richness and 'complexity' of the poem. As long ago as 1934, R. P. Blackmur . . . said that the verse of the *Cantos* was 'complicated' but not 'complex', and that 'the difficulties of the *Cantos* are superficial and their valuable qualities are all qualities or virtues of a well-managed verbal surface'. It's a distinction and an argument that any critic of Pound must begin by taking seriously, even if only to counter it. It's also, sadly, true that discussions of the *Cantos* which go straight for their 'complexity' tend to lose the verbal surface altogether. But Miss Brooke-Rose has no time for such elementary matters. Among all the other things which, in her frantic plunge, she engagingly forgets to tell us about—including the fact that Pound himself, by the 1960s, was saying that the *Cantos* were 'botched'—is, goodness me, why she's jumped in in the first place.

I suppose the proof of the pudding is meant to lie in the exegesis, which may be true of life but makes a bad standard for the judgment of art. The *Cantos,* like the world, are endlessly amenable to observation and theories; their physics, history, biology and gossip are clearly potentially absorbing, but you could say the same about a random copy of the *Daily Telegraph.* And Poundians, unfortunately, are the last people we should consult about their real merits, which are still profoundly in question. Lovers, however morally admirable may be their ardour, make poor referees; and Pound, now more than ever . . . , needs some solid references before he gets the job for which Miss Brooke-Rose is promoting him. (pp. 928-29)

Jonathan Raban, "Goodness Me!" in New Statesman, Vol. 82, No. 2128, December 31, 1971, pp. 928-29.

PETER ACKROYD

Thru is too little, and it is also too late. It tries to do for the English language what Denis Roche and a host of experimentalists did to the French, but *Thru* is neither here nor there. It also tries to be very modern: there is no linear narrative, no 'characterisation,' and no plot, and it employs all sizes and shapes of prose. It is very brave of Miss Brooke-Rose to apply certain European strategies to the indigenous product, but like a great many Europeanisms they have a faded date-stamp upon them. The English have missed that particular development of modernism but it is too late to imitate it: we must go beyond it.

The first impression of the book is of some harmless and quite funny game-playing: there are anagrams, acrostics, and even some light-hearted references to things known as "trace" and "text." Miss Brooke-Rose has clearly been reading what are known, with the breathless successiveness of French orthodoxies, "the second-generation structuralists" like Jaques Lacan and Jaques Derrida . . . , but all she does is apply their terminology flatly to the surface of her writing. If *Thru* had assimilated them in the normal manner, there would have been no point to the passages of Roland Barthes, for example, which are dropped quite gaily into the narrative. Barthes is an easy academic lay, being the most flashy, the most predictable and the least rigorous of the French 'masters.'

But *Thru* does not stop at that point. Allusions to other and earlier literatures are folded into its writing, in much the same spirit but with rather less success than James Joyce; this sort of inventiveness can be witty and even astonishing, but it is only the first stage in the creation of a viable language: Miss Brooke-Rose displays it as an achievement in itself. There is also some magpie scholarship in her tedious discussions about the nature of narrative linear, but this is evidence only of good intentions. In fact, it says something about the pallid nature of most Anglo-Saxon experimentalism that critical theory should become not only its method but also its substance: *Thru* becomes as much a victim of content as those poor nineteenth century, three-volume novels which are the *Bêtes noires* of all good Frenchmen.

I don't mind the book being self-conscious, since only self-conscious emotions can be effectively conveyed, I don't mind its eclecticism, . . . but I do mind its clumsiness and its obviousness. And when Frank Kermode is said to describe the book as "funny," I can only suspect that this nice, old-fashioned academic is willing to find *some* merit in something which he does not understand. The book is not funny ha-ha, and, despite Miss Brooke-Rose's efforts, it is not even funny peculiar.

Peter Ackroyd, "Modernist?" in The Spectator, *Vol. 235, No. 7672, July 12, 1975, p. 52.**

C. J. DRIVER

On the back cover of *Thru* Professor Kermode tells us that

> If we are ever to experience in English the serious practice of narrative as the French have developed it over the last few years, we shall have to attend to Christine Brooke-Rose. There has been writing in English about the subject, and even a small amount of timid pastiche, but Christine Brooke-Rose is the sole practitioner of the real thing. Incidentally, the word 'seri-

ous' doesn't rule out the word 'funny.' *Thru* is both.

Because one has learned to trust Kermode in other things, one wishes to believe him here and certainly two of the three grounds he advances for attending *Thru* seem valid. It is good to have an English example of French narrative practice, especially if one is ignorant of French writing; and *Thru* is often very funny, especially if one has a taste for allusion, parody and pun.

Its seriousness is, I think, essentially linguistic, based on a notion that (in the words of the blurb)

> *Thru* could be described as a mirror of modern consciousness, viewed, necessarily, as a series of texts: society is a text, the human body is a text. *Thru* is also about the production of texts, this text, and language itself, without which there would be no politics, no marriage and families, no psycho-analysis, no universities, no revolution, no human relationships.

Oh yeah? Suppose one substituted "sexual act" for "text," and "sex" for "language": one is happily back in the days of early Freudianism. Everything was explained then: understand sexuality, understand all. Now, understand language, understand all.

I for one am not buying the package. Literary creation and criticism are to do with value, and the critical study of enacted language, though it may not encompass our values, is not value-free. Linguistics has added some useful tools to the writer's and critic's baggage, but they haven't replaced the others.

And so with this novel: the surface glitters, all right; it is witty and funny; it contains some hilarious dialogue; it raises some interesting questions about the conventions of the written language (that we read from left to right, for instance) and of the novel; the professorial comments interspersed variously make the reader writhe with embarrassment at his own internal comments; and the author is obviously a very clever person indeed and I guess would be pleasant and entertaining to know. "In this text everyone has a voice." If at the end I was left wanting more of a single voice, desiring discourse rather than false and fresh starts and snippets, it is perhaps because I want the wrong things from a novel—the text in the context of time and value. One of the characters (only they're not really characters, you see—they're texts . . .) in fact makes much the same point.

C. J. Driver, "Text and Context," in The Guardian, *Vol. 113, No. 3, July 19, 1975, p. 20.**

ERIC PARTRIDGE

The blurb suggests that '*Thru* could be described as a mirror of modern consciousness': but isn't every sincere work, whether in literature or in art or, come to that, in music, a mirror, even if a necessarily somewhat defective mirror and sometimes a distorting mirror, of modern consciousness, usually of the here-and-now? The blurb continues, 'viewed, necessarily, as a series of texts': but why *necessarily* texts? I should have thought that consciousness was concerned with something rather more vivid and real and compulsive than a series of texts. To assert that 'society is a text' is to narrow and depreciate it; to call the human body a text is to desiccate it; to regard the mind and the spirit as a conjoint text would be to try to contain 'the water of life' in a very leaky sieve and virtually to deny its very existence. The blurb (which presumably meets with the author's approval and was conceivably written by her) proceeds to mention 'language itself, without which there would be no politics, no marriage and families, no psycho-analysis, no universities, no revolution, no human relationships', a statement clearly needing violent modification, for whereas there would be perhaps no revolution or politics and certainly no psychoanalysis, or universities, the absence of *verbal* language would not preclude marriage (except in a restrictively legal sense)—families—other human relationships. To overstate a case is to weaken it. Nevertheless, it would be grossly unfair to the author to omit this demurrer: she is far from being so intransigent, so doctrinaire, as all that.

Perhaps yet graver issues are involved in the interlinked admissions that 'the author . . . seems implicity to pose the question: why come to terms with the author?' and that 'the text destroys itself as it goes along'. No text *destroys* itself as it goes along; it doesn't even—except, of course, unintentionally—contradict itself, unless the author is deliberately setting up the skittles merely to knock 'em down, or raising difficulties in order to have the pleasure of showing they either don't exist or are really trivial or rudimentary. . . .

I should have liked to examine in detail, both destructively and constructively, some self-contained passage (and there are more, often many more, than one on virtually every page) of this teasing, mocking, challenging, delightful, immensely worthwhile book. Although you mightn't at first think so, it is remarkably readable, providing you accept the principle that a book does not have to be *easy* reading in order to be good. Christine Brooke-Rose manifestly owes a vast amount to James Joyce; perhaps a little to Swift-being-diabolically-ingenious; maybe something to 'the daddy of 'em all' in the minor as well as in the major aspects and activities of wordplay 'raised to the *n*th', I mean Rabelais.

I do, however, propose to her those potentialities for the mutual good of the writer and her public alike which are inherent in a relationship of greater tolerance, profounder sympathy, a far-reaching empathy: she has in her growing public aroused curiosity, interest, willingness to be persuaded: she does (I feel, think, believe) fail, just occasionally, to realise that there exist thousands of people capable of enjoying her verbal acrobatics, her dazzling pyrotechnics, her delicate and subtle virtuosity, and that they would respond to an attitude devoid of unflaunted linguistic ambivalence.

Eric Partridge, "Verbal Pyrotechnics," in Books and Bookmen, *Vol. 20, No. 12, September, 1975, p. 47.*

EMMA KAFALENOS

Composed without chapter divisions, [*Thru*] contains few pages that even resemble traditional fiction in appearance. "Painstakingly typeset," as the credit reads with good reason, the novel's 164 pages contain charts, lists, diagrams, concrete poems, linguistic formulae, letters, graded student papers accompanied by the teacher's handwritten comments, an academic vita, and occasional Chinese characters.

The novel is not plotless. Instead there are a number of plots, each of which is cut off (almost as soon as it begins) by the introduction of another plot, only to recur later, often in a quite altered form. Originally titled *Texttermination*, the novel's central concern is the fictionality of fiction—both this particular fiction and the fiction we share with the author as a common

background. In a prodigious display of intertextuality, the novel refers to the *Odyssey, Tristram Shandy, I promessi sposi, La Princesse de Clèves, Clarissa, Pamela, Les Liaisons dangereuses, Gulliver's Travels, The Marble Faun, The Portrait of Dorian Grey, The Wings of the Dove.* There are also discussions about Beckett, Isherwood, Pound's *Cantos,* Dicken's "deathoflittlenell," and quotations, among others, of Lewis Carroll's "brillig" and "tove," Eliot's "young man carbuncular" as well as his "hollow man," the "nailparings" of Joyce's God, and, several times, a "blue guitar," reminding us of Wallace Stevens's:

> They said, "You have a blue guitar,
> You do not play things as they are."

> The man replied, "Things as they are
> Are changed upon the blue guitar."
> ("The Man with the Blue Guitar")

Like Stevens, Brooke-Rose is well aware of the fictionality of fiction, and uses quotations from previous works of fiction to demonstrate her point. Within the novel we read about the "text in its moment . . . of dialogue with all preceding texts as death and birth in a dialectic to the death with one another" . . . , and also of "the text within the text that generates another text." . . . Both the text of the novel itself and the texts quoted within it function in the same two ways. The first of these, to use her term, is to bring "death" to the immediately preceding fiction, by cutting it off in the midst of its development, or by altering it so radically that it is no longer the same fiction. The second way is to give "birth" to the ensuing fiction by generating it out of a previous text. Two forms of generation are customarily distinguished in discussions of contemporary French fiction; Brooke-Rose uses both. One is verbal generation, in which a word reminds an author of another word that is similar either in sound (perhaps a rhyme) or appearance (often a rearrangement of the same letters). A semantic relationship between the two words is both unnecessary and rare. In *Thru,* for example, the word "eye" is often used interchangeably with its homonym, the first-person pronoun "I." Or Wallace Stevens's "The Emperor of Ice-Cream" becomes "the naked emperor of I-scream." . . . Or "wrought iron" becomes "wrought irony" which becomes "ire on eye." . . . "Textasy" . . . combines the similar sounds in "text" and "ecstasy." As these examples suggest, many forms of verbal generation are impossible to translate into another language. This is not a problem for the other form of generation, thematic generation, which (as its name implies) is the development of a text from the semantic meanings of a word, phrase, or image. The opening image of *Thru* is a thematic generator for large sections of the novel and for the structure of the whole novel.

The novel begins with the word which is its title: "Through the driving-mirror four eyes stare back two of them in their proper place [two of them] nearer the hairline further up the brow but dimmed as in a glass tarnished by the close-cropped mat of hair they peer through." . . . The image is the rearview mirror of a car; Brooke-Rose uses the French term "rétroviseur" and thereafter anglicizes it to retrovizor. As Brooke-Rose has said in an interview, it conveys the "idea of looking forward but actually looking back," which as we have seen is a way of describing the relationships among the texts that compose the novel. The rearview mirror, or retrovizor, is necessarily one of the modern ones equipped with an anti-glare device, which has two particular characteristics. If one looks at oneself in one of these mirrors, one can see a second reflection of oneself, higher up than the clearer one, with the eyes (which seem to be the most prominent feature of the second reflection) juxtaposed on the primary reflection approximately at the hairline. This is the literal image which the novel's opening words describe: "Through the driving-mirror four eyes stare back." The other characteristic of rearview mirrors equipped with anti-glare devices is that at night they sometimes double the pair of headlights of the car behind, producing what Brooke-Rose describes as "dancing hoops." ... From this image she develops the "black recumbent street" (still seen through the mirror) as "very short and fat for a magician" juggling the hoops, until (changing the setting but not the scene) the magician walks off "leaving me alone on stage to cope somehow in the glare of lights that hits the mirror." ... The fat magician recurs in the dreams of a girl whom the male narrator tells the female narrator that he really does not want.... The four eyes in the rearview mirror generate the two main narrators of the novel, a man and a woman, Armel Santores and Larissa Toren. As another character in the novel discovers, "the names are anagrams. Except for ME in hers and I in his." ... That is, the two names have eleven letters in common. These eleven letters plus the two letters in the word "me" form the name Armel Santores; the same eleven letters plus the letter "I" form Larissa Toren.

The problem of narration in *Thru,* however, is a very complex one. The "floating I" in fiction—a first-person narration in which the "I" that narrates sometimes refers to one character and sometimes another—has been a recognized possibility since the publication of Alain Robbe-Grillet's *La Maison de rendez-vous* in 1965. Much of *Thru* is told in the first person, and often the "I" is either Larissa or Armel. Both characterizations are extremely fluid. Larissa and Armel are both listed as instructors of university-level courses in literature. The first time the reader is sure that an "I" refers to Armel, he is writing a letter to Larissa while attending a faculty meeting. Later we come across a letter from Larissa to Armel in which she is a graduate student writing a dissertation on his poetry and hoping to meet him. On another occasion Armel, now darkened into an Arab through the properties of the retrovizor, interrupts Larissa while she is writing a novel, wanting to discuss her previously published novels with her. Early in the novel Larissa seems to be with a Marco or a Stavro rather than Armel. Later a possible explanation is given: "As to the first name, well of course she could have changed whatever original name she gave to the man she was inventing, maybe it was Marco or Stavro." ... But near the end of the novel Larissa arranges for Armel, from whom she is separated but to whom she has been married for fifteen years, to meet Stavro and give her his opinion of him. There seems to be no doubt that one invents the other: "... if Larissa invents Armel inventing Larissa, Armel also invents Larissa inventing Armel." ... Occasionally the master of Diderot's *Jacques le Fataliste* takes over the narration, sometimes in his own right and sometimes as Armel. Midway through the novel he decides that "it looks mightily as if [Larissa] were producing this [novel] and not, as previously appeared, Armel," ... which, as he tells Jacques, transforms their relationship, since Jacques's master is being changed into a mistress.... In addition, it often appears as if the novel were being written by a creative-writing class, perhaps taught by Armel, perhaps by Larissa.

The confusion is Brooke-Rose's method of illustrating the untrustworthy nature of the role of the narrator in contemporary fiction, the "absently unreliable or unreliably absent narrator." ... (pp. 43-5)

Yet Larissa and Armel both are clearly aspects of the author. Brooke-Rose has spoken of talking to herself in French, of addressing herself either as "je" or "tu" ("I" or "you"); in similar fashion Armel refers to Larissa as his "second person singular." ... The two characters complement each other. We are told, reversing the stereotype, that Larissa's "mental diagrams seem to be also a good deal more complex than [Armel's] though his emotional ones seem more complex than hers." ... Elsewhere Larissa tells Stavro (who may be Armel), "you have your list of women, children and languages, I have my list of publications." ... Just as the two pairs of eyes in the opening image are the reflection of one person, Larissa and Armel together (the one intellectual, the other emotional) seem to form one complete human being, perhaps in many respects Brooke-Rose herself.

Writing is a creative endeavor, and Brooke-Rose is not the first to describe it in sexual terms. She does, however, stress it throughout the text, in addition to providing both a male and a female narrator for the novel. The "winedark sea of infratextuality" ... recurs some fifteen pages later as the "wine dark sea of infrasexuality." ... Plagiarism is described as a form of false "paternity." ... Linguistics is defined in terms of sexual relationships, "the double standard" for male and female adultery, she tells us, "is useful even in semiotics." ... There are several references to "heterotextuality," ... a term that seems perfectly coined to describe the fictional creation of this piece of fiction. *Thru* is a generative textasy. (pp. 45-6)

Emma Kafalenos, "Textasy: Christine Brooke-Rose's 'Thru'," in The International Fiction Review, *Vol. 7, No. 1, Winter, 1980, pp. 43-6.*

BERNARD BERGONZI

Christine Brooke-Rose's *A Rhetoric of the Unreal* is ... a work by a dazzlingly brainy writer who conveys unfamiliar ideas and attitudes in a familiar, apprehensible manner. She is an English novelist, critic and academic of francophone upbringing who has taught in France for several years, and though she once read English at Oxford her intellectual world is now largely formed by Russian formalists and French structuralists, whom she takes for granted and discusses in a matter-of-fact way, without fuss or special advocacy. Their effect is balanced or offset by her surviving English empiricism, common sense, and directness of style.

For a critic to be immensely well-read is perhaps no more than one expects of a true professional; but with Brooke-Rose the range is unusually wide and available, all the way from medieval romance to the latest forms of French or American postmodernist fiction. She is a highly competent critical technician, who can do all jobs herself, from the most fiddling up to the largest; she has a stimulating capacity to switch within a page or two from the intensive reading of a small unit of narrative to a wide historical sweep. Even her frequent recourse to charts, diagrams and tables, which usually get up the nose of the English reader, is done with style and dash. Parts of her book are tough reading, but well worth persisting with, and it considerably increased my understanding of the nature and implications of fantasy as a genre.

Her most extended single discussion is a hundred-page close examination of *The Turn of the Screw,* which employs the methods of Chomskyan linguistics and is less arid than one might expect, though some way before the end weariness sets in. Brooke-Rose on James's novella has some affinities with Barthes on Balzac's *Sarrasine* in *S/Z*, though she is more responsive to the historical author. She reveals the extraordinary capacity of the creative literary intelligence to generate micro-patterns of parallel, contrast, repetition, and so forth, on the lexical, phonological and syntactical levels. Something similar emerged from Jakobson's exhaustive analyses of poems by Shakespeare and Baudelaire.... Brooke-Rose on James may attract the same objections that Jakobson did; of providing too much information, which is redundant and irrelevant to any possible interpretation of the text, though to say this both opens up and begs the question of what literary interpretation is, and what we expect from it.

She is an extraordinarily acute and suggestive reader, though. My final response to her book, which is a product of the contemporary French intellectual milieu, is: what are the conditions of academic practice that permit or encourage such rigorous minuteness of examination? (pp. 64-5)

Bernard Bergonzi, "A Strange Disturbing World," in Encounter, *Vol. LVIII & LIX, Nos. 6 & 1, June & July, 1982, pp. 58, 60-7.**

GEORGE CRAIG

A distinction used to be (perhaps still is) made between a compound, where diverse elements fused, and a mixture, in which they were merely added together. [*Amalgamemnon*] is unquestionably a mixture, and rather an odd one, for it lays high verbal sophistication (an almost uninterrupted display of it) alongside a persistent concern with humiliation, loss and man's inhumanity to woman.

The "I" of the novel, a woman no longer young, deprived by "cuts" of her job as teacher of literature/philosophy/history, speaks her response to this and to the world in which she must now move: the world of economic realism, power politics and the computer.... The "suave and portly man at the National Education Computer" will explain her profound redundancy, hint at new possibilities but make clear that the price is a share of her bed. His approaches are presented with fastidious and allusive distaste and capped with "If he were someone in a nineteenth-century novel I might ironically detach him".

But this confident handling is verbal only. Her capacity to mock merely sharpens her awareness of how ineffective it is within her world: there will always be suave and portly men (and "portly" carries more than a hint of euphemism), and they will always get their way. Nor is there rescue in fantasy. In one recurrent sequence she is drawn to Orion; but he will put or let her down no less surely than the latest Willy or Wally. The sequences multiply and expand, set off by things remembered, read or heard; but in almost all, the playful-casual and the prodigiously inventive alike, a clever and sensitive woman will be exploited and undervalued. Ideologically and personally she is a loser.

The contrast between linguistic vitality and existential defeat could easily become the matter of rancorous demonstration ... or élitist demolition.... The blurb-writer, dutifully focusing on Christine Brooke-Rose's word-play, simply dismisses the contrast: the "verve and gaiety of her experimentation", her "infectious joy in language" ensure that "the narrator's personal crisis disappears". It is the narrator herself who makes sure that nothing of the kind happens; that we are given an immediate awareness both of the central preoccupation and of

tone. There are indeed moments of anger and contempt, there is an abundance of experimentation, but they never hide the continually reiterated sense of loss, fear and bewilderment: now rueful, now bitter, now resigned. The verbal inventiveness, the easy familiarity with European literary culture are a defence against hopelessness, pain and the intrusive other. Even the best of the sequences ... do no more than bring a moment's ease; hardly different in this from the radio to which she turns for solace in the small hours. Both will soon let back in the reminders of her plight.

But the plight is not just what a hostile or indifferent world has imposed: more destructive still are the narrator's malleability and failure of nerve. If she can mimic her overbearers, she can also mimic her own capitulation, the ease and speed with which she colludes with them. After one put-down she exclaims: "I would seem to be unpopular with these characters. How long shall I continue to rush into over-friendliness obscurely to make up for the overfreeness of my solitude?" This sort of talk is not cancelled out by some such answer as "Let sex equal why." What *is* clear is the difficulty of reconciling, in a single fiction, smart word-play with the equivalent of the old theatrical aside. What we have in the end is a plangent tale of vulnerability and timid hope decked out with puns and portmanteaux, names and knowingness. In a word, a mixture.

George Craig, "The Pain and the Portmanteaux," in The Times Literary Supplement, *No. 4254, October 12, 1984, p. 1168.*

LORNA SAGE

[*Amalgamemnon*] is an elegant, rueful and witty word-game about what it feels like to be a word-addict—worse, a writing-addict—in the brave new world of communications technology. In a word, says the heroine Cassandra, we're redundant. She's about to lose her job as a teacher of 'dead languages' ('like literature, philosophy, history') and in the interval before the National Education Computer pronounces sentence (or whatever it does) she speculates on her thankless role. Who needs an old-fashioned oracle when history is instant?

'Amalgamemnon' is the name of the composite monster that's stealing the future—the mind-set that turns vision into information, and churns out predictions like weather-forecasts.... Cassandra could, she muses, live off the literary heritage ... or even find some nourishment in gaudy, subliterary fantasies.... But no, the romance is tarnished by present anxieties. Cassandra listens riveted to the radio (sport, pop, the World News, phone-ins) and what she hears shapes her imaginings into the prison-camp plot, the terrorist plot, the kidnapping plot.... And not least the plot in which she has an absurd love-affair with 'the suave and portly man' from the National Education Computer who's called Willy at the beginning and is solidly smug, but seems to have become Wallace by the end, when he's redundant too.

'You shall see what you shall see and may the beast man wane' says Cassandra oracularly. However, ring the changes as she may ('and may the boast man whine'?) she's breathing the atmosphere of the 'black cloud of news enveloping the earth', and what she imagines comes out always in the future or conditional tenses ('we'll all go on as if') that belong to the enemy. It would, of course, be all right—as one hard-nosed character points out—if you could *just* play games with words, give up entirely on meanings, and on any claim to the real, but Cassandra can't:

All words should be played with and names most of all he'll answer but she'll say for fun yes, not all the time though, or you'd undermine the fragile fabric of communication.

This is very much Christine Brooke-Rose's feeling—that if the violent gaps she's disclosing between humanities and technology, the first world and the third, women and men (not to get the order too tidy), *are* becoming uncrossable, then it's an occasion for passionate concern, not indifference.

Lorna Sage, "Word Addict," in The Observer, *November 18, 1984, p. 29.*

IHAB HASSAN

Christine Brooke-Rose's earliest books were always deft and alert fictions about love, loss, death, faith, about people and a continent of troubles. The manner was traditional, realistic. Then, with *Out* (1964), followed by *Such* (1965), *Between* (1968) and *Thru* (1975), the manner changed, becoming satiric, antic, fantastic. This author, however, is laconic only in her titles. She has also written several works of criticism, notably *A ZBC of Ezra Pound* (1971) and *A Rhetoric of the Unreal* (1981), well regarded among academics. Yet she remains obscure in her distinction. Why?

I can address the question only in a certain slant of language. I say language because Miss Brooke-Rose is a confessed graphomaniac, and her later fiction, like so much of postmodern literature, takes a self-delighting, linguistic turn. That is, fiction, which has always attended to language, now makes it the center of its reflexive concern, and explodes in ludic, parodic, ironic forms. It is carnival time for the Logos, with all the anarchic exuberance that the 20th-century Russian critic Mikhail Bakhtin has invested in the term "carnivalesque." But now, alas, the lights have begun to dim on such frolics.

Let us admit it: the language (or postmodern) novel never had many readers, though it could boast an honorable, if mildly daft, pedigree. Postmodern fiction may revert to Sterne's *Tristram Shandy*, certainly to Joyce's *Finnegans Wake*. It can claim such high masters of verbal jinks as Raymond Roussel, Raymond Queneau, Vladimir Nabokov, Witold Gombrowicz, Jorge Luis Borges, and even the dour, incomparable Samuel Beckett. In this tradition, which flourished till recently in France and the United States . . . , Miss Brooke-Rose has made a place of her own.

But writers share with us all what Auden called the "error bred in the bone"—they want "to be loved alone." Miss Brooke-Rose certainly asks for, and deserves, our precise, wakeful attention, unencumbered by the generalities of literary history. What, then, is *Amalgamemnon* about? Consider the title: King Agamemnon Amalgamated or Incorporated (and finally by his mate mated), warlord, sacker of cities, Cassandra's master, the immanent male whose mastery precludes heeding the voice of true prophecy. In this fiction, Cassandra speaks up against him, often in her guise as a professor of humanities, wavering between a "portly lover" who offers marriage and a terminal academic career. And when she speaks, her voice persuades us, almost, to heed her.

There are actually many voices in this novel, echoes and whispers. Mostly they continue the eternal conversation between man and woman. He could be Willy or Wally or Hans; she Cassandra, Sandra Enkeltei, Miss Inkytie, or Miss Inkytea. Her voice is more insistent, clairvoyant, dire as befits Cassandra. She wants her worth and independence, as a woman teaching the obsolete art of letters; she wants a saner world. Everything is here: history, myth, astronomy, technology, ecology, capitalism, terrorism, feminism, the humanities, the third world, all the gods that failed.

And it's done with puns, parodies, allusions, self-ironies ("Cassandra Castratrix"), genealogical tables, shifts in narrative, rifts. The puns can be very good. . . . No plot is needed for this travesty of intermittent verbal revelations, though Miss Brooke-Rose can "mimirender" Mozartean dialogue worthy of Ivy Compton-Burnett or Barbara Pym, as if to say: "Look, I can do this, too, if I want."

Yet underneath all its acute frolics, *Amalgamemnon* is an aggrieved book, at once brave and drear. Its central persona feels that she is "for ever channeled into the mysterious voices of the night, gathering up solitude as a needed strength that will nevertheless be resented by one and all especially one." She derives strength from language, and gratefully returns it there; she calls on imagination, the great As If, and says:

> What will you be when you grow up? A maniac. Ego pyro sexo mytho clepto mono? No none of these but a graphomaniac—oh come that will include them all—to be imprisoned for graffitism as poor Cassandra will be enslaved by all Amalgamemnons and die with them not out of love but of amalgamation to silence her for ever.

> But my words will carve through dungeon walls and I shall crawl priestlike through the hole into a neighbouring cell, carrying a secret about buried treasure, then montecristoid plummet as a faked corpse into the black sea of oblivion and swim ashore.

This is an impeccable sentiment for a female character in a novel written by a woman in our Age of Language. But it does not do complex justice to the vision of Christine Brooke-Rose herself, who knows that enlightened paranoia is not enough, and that the great As If can also lie behind every accommodation, deceit, illusion, in our lives. Reflexive, perhaps even autobiographical in parts, this book surrenders little to the cant of the day, especially the cant of one's own ranting heart. In the end, its fault may be generic. Like much post-modern or linguistic fiction, it substitutes intelligence, verbal virtuosity, for whatever brings us to literature: that pathos of being by which many of us recognize ourselves as intensely alive. *Amalgamemnon* can move us, but only with music on a narrower band.

Ihab Hassan, "Revillusionary Punorama," in The New York Times Book Review, *September 8, 1985, p. 20.*

(John) Anthony Burgess (Wilson)

1917-

(Has also written as John Burgess Wilson and under pseudonym of Joseph Kell) English novelist, essayist, critic, dramatist, translator, editor, scriptwriter, short story writer, author of books for children, poet, and composer.

A prolific writer who examines a vast range of topics, Burgess is regarded as one of the most important novelists in contemporary literature. Burgess frequently applies his knowledge of music and linguistics to his fiction; his fascination with languages is particularly evident in his best-known novel, *A Clockwork Orange* (1962). Describing himself as a "renegade Catholic," Burgess often explores the dilemma of free will versus determinism in his works. Although his fictional worlds are sometimes disordered and Burgess remains pessimistic about the state of modern society, his use of humor and inventive wordplay serve to lighten his cynical vision. Burgess's canon, consisting of more than forty volumes, is considered by many critics to be uneven. Nevertheless, his contribution to contemporary literature is widely acknowledged, and Michael Dirda stated that Burgess "may be the most consummate professional writer now alive."

Burgess enrolled at the University of Manchester in 1936 to study musical composition, but he soon began to study English literature and languages. After graduating in 1940, Burgess enlisted in the British Army. His assignments included a tour as a musician with a mobile entertainment unit and surveillance work in Gibraltar. Following his discharge in 1946, Burgess worked at a variety of jobs, among them playing piano in a jazz band in London and teaching various subjects, including English literature, in a grammar school. In 1954, Burgess accepted a teaching position in Malaya as an education officer for the British Colonial Service. His experiences there supplied material for his early novels, *Time for a Tiger* (1956), *The Enemy in the Blanket* (1958), and *Beds in the East* (1959). Following the adventures of Victor Crabbe, a young British teacher living in Malaya, the novels examine the demise of British rule and present a detailed portrait of the conflicts between the British colonists and the diverse indigenous populations. Robert K. Morris stated that the novels are "a continuing drama of change; how one man encounters and experiences it, founders upon and succumbs to it." These novels, collectively known as the *Malayan Trilogy,* were published in the United States as *The Long Day Wanes: A Malayan Trilogy* in 1965. Burgess returned to England in 1959 when he was diagnosed as having a brain tumor. He was given less than a year to live, yet Burgess produced five novels during that year, including *The Doctor Is Sick* (1960), which relates his experiences while undergoing medical treatment.

A Clockwork Orange, Burgess's most popular and widely discussed work, was reportedly influenced by an assault on his pregnant wife and by his trip to the Soviet Union in 1961. The novel takes place in a near-future city dominated by lawless juvenile gangs. Burgess's proficiency in linguistics is evident by his invention of *Nadsat,* a crude combination of Russian and Cockney slang spoken by Alex, the protagonist, and his peers, which underscores the cultural fusion of East and West in the novel. Alex is a maladjusted youth who, after committing

© *Jerry Bauer*

a series of violent crimes, becomes the subject of a government-sponsored behavioral experiment. He is given drugs which induce severe physical pain and nausea whenever he has sexual or violent thoughts. After the treatment is completed, Alex is released from prison and is subjected to attacks of revenge by his past victims. Several critics have suggested that in his depiction of Alex's experiences Burgess is protesting similar experiments performed by behavioral scientists during the 1960s. *A Clockwork Orange* was adapted for film in 1971 by Stanley Kubrick, and many critics regard the popular film as the catalyst for Burgess's subsequent rise to literary prominence.

Burgess has also written a series of humorous novels centering on the exploits of F. X. Enderby, a moderately successful lyric poet who some critics suggest is Burgess's alter ego. *Inside Mr. Enderby* (1963), written under the pseudonym of Joseph Kell, introduces Enderby and places him in several ridiculous situations. The middle-aged Enderby is portrayed as a latent adolescent who can create poetry only in the privacy of his bathroom. His adventures continue in *Enderby Outside* (1968) and *The Clockwork Testament; Or Enderby's End* (1974), in which the hero dies of a heart attack. *Enderby's Dark Lady; Or No End to Enderby* (1984) marks the return of Enderby. Critics noted similarities between Enderby's resurrection and Sir Arthur Conan Doyle's restoration of Sherlock Holmes. The recent Enderby novel, structured as a story within a story, presents the hero engaged in writing the libretto for a musical based on the life of William Shakespeare. Although entertaining, the Enderby novels include serious examinations on the role of the artist in contemporary society.

In *Earthly Powers* (1980), a novel dense with philosophical and theological themes, Burgess further examines the nature of good and evil and the necessity for free will. The novel, which took Burgess ten years to write, follows the intertwining lives of a homosexual British novelist and a charismatic Italian cleric through world events of the past fifty years. As participants and observers of human cruelty and degradation, both characters conclude that God has created evil to allow humanity the freedom of choice. *Earthly Powers* was well received by critics and is regarded as Burgess's most ambitious recent work. With *The End of the World News* (1983), Burgess returned to light fiction. Described by the author as "an entertainment," the novel consists of three separate narratives that are, according to Burgess, "all about the end of history as man has known it." The first story is a fictional biography of Sigmund Freud; the second section is a musical based on Leon Trotsky's visit to New York in 1917; and the third story is a fantasy about a cosmic disaster in the year 2000. Although not as highly acclaimed as *Earthly Powers,* Thomas Mallon called *The End of the World News* a "satisfying verbal comedy." *The Kingdom of the Wicked* (1985), a historical novel about the early years of Christianity, likewise drew a cool reception, but critics acknowledged Burgess's thorough research of the writings of the Twelve Apostles and the works of ancient Roman historians. *The Kingdom of the Wicked* was the basis for Burgess's script for the television mini-series "A.D."

Burgess is highly regarded for several scholarly works of criticism, including *Here Comes Everybody: An Introduction to James Joyce for the Ordinary Reader* (1965; published in the United States as *Re Joyce*), and he has also published several textbooks on English literature. In addition, he is renowned as a translator, particularly for his 1972 adaptation of Sophocles's drama *Oedipus Rex*. Among Burgess's recent critical volumes are *Flame into Being: The Life and Works of D. H. Lawrence* (1985) and *But Do Blondes Prefer Gentlemen? Homage to Qwert Yuiop and Other Writings* (1986), a collection of reviews and critical essays.

(See also *CLC*, Vols. 1, 2, 4, 5, 8, 10, 13, 15, 22; *Contemporary Authors*, Vols. 1-4, rev. ed.; *Contemporary Authors New Revision Series*, Vol. 2; and *Dictionary of Literary Biography*, Vol. 14.)

GEOFFREY AGGELER

Many of Burgess's novels have a recurrent motif related to his dualistic concept of ultimate reality: his work thus portrays cultures that embody, either literally or metaphorically, some forms of "darkness" and cultures that lack this darkness. The protagonists of these novels tend to be derived from the latter and drawn to the former. For example, in *A Vision of Battlements,* Richard Ennis is caught between the cultural values represented by his fair Protestant English wife and the love he finds with a Spanish Catholic girl in Gibraltar. Other aspects of a darker culture, including the Rock's Moorish heritage, which he seeks to capture in music and his own residual Catholicism, draw him to this Mediterranean darkness and in-

crease his sense of alienation from the culture he has left. In *The Long Day Wanes,* the darkness of Malaya draws Victor Crabbe into itself and reveals the mystery of a dark girl he had loved and killed. An obsessive desire to be reunited with this girl causes him to give himself wholly to the country. In *Devil of a State,* on the other hand, darkness is a negative thing for Lydgate, a means of escape from responsibility and guilt. In fleeing his past, he seeks shelter in various dark corners of Asia and Africa before he is finally caught in a dark little state called "Dunia." Unlike the protagonists in those novels, Christopher Howarth in *The Worm and the Ring* is not actually shown within a darker civilization. But his residual Catholicism deprives him of any sense of community in fair Protestant England, and he finally decides to leave it for a darker Catholic Mediterranean community. (p. 30)

There is much more to *A Vision of Battlements* than the mere dreariness of soldiering on the Rock. Much of it is riotously entertaining, and Burgess's gift for comic description is evident throughout. The book also contains partial treatments of philosophical and religious themes that become central preoccupations in his later work. Also, in some respects, it anticipates later developments in the novel generally. Its form, for instance, is that of a mock epic quest structured around the misfortunes of an antihero of the type introduced by Kingsley Amis and others during the fifties. Although it is by no means one of Burgess's finest achievements in the novel, it is a very respectable apprentice piece; moreover, it deserves recognition as one of the more successful attempts to capture satirically an aspect of a war that inspired surprisingly little in the way of significant fiction. (p. 31)

When a writer such as Burgess, living in another empire, chooses to burlesque such an epic [as Vergil's *Aeneid*] by reducing Aeneas to a bumbling sergeant and his Mediterranean wanderings to the Rock, we can see that his diminishing irony extends beyond characters and events to the tradition-hallowed, imperial self-images and ideals that inspire the creation of national epics. The passing of the empire is not itself one of Burgess's main focuses in this novel, as it is in the *Malayan Trilogy* and *Devil of a State,* but it is an important part of the backdrop against which we watch the antiheroic exploits of Sergeant Richard Ennis. For this empire, which had so drained itself in the fight against fascism that its ability and will to preserve itself against other foes had gone, Ennis is an appropriate Aeneas. In short, it is not merely the antiheroism of an individual we are seeing, but the antiheroism of Britain herself at the end of the war. Vergil could overlook debauchery at court and other blemishes and still celebrate Roman greatness, but few writers who had experienced World War II could overlook its dehumanizing effects and still sing in traditional heroic terms of arms and men. (p. 32)

[*A Vision of Battlements*] is a kind of potpourri of subjects—the plight of the artist oppressed by a philistine Establishment, the attractions of Manichaeism, the inescapable hold of Catholicism, the Pelagian heresy in the twentieth century—that he treats fully and brilliantly in his later novels but that are not intimately related here except in the mind of Ennis and his chance conversations with others. Although, to an extent, this can be justified in terms of the comic epic form, inclusion of too much intrusive, loosely related material has a vitiating effect on a book that seeks to present an author's vision of what World War II meant to one nonheroic participant and, by implication, what it meant to the weary victors generally. This is not to say that the subjects are not in any way relevant to each other or to his main focus. They can in fact be related closely, as Burgess himself shows in *Tremor of Intent, Enderby,* and other later novels. It seems, however, that Burgess had not fully thought through the connections when he was writing *A Vision of Battlements*. Still, he introduces his material in an intriguing fashion, and while he is entertaining us with respectable comedy, he whets our appetites for later, fuller treatments of the same material. (pp. 36-7)

Devil of a State is . . . both farce and parable. Like the satire of Swift, it is pointed in an overwhelming variety of directions. For certain types of subjects, including life in a fantastic colonial setting, such satire is eminently suitable. The reader is detached and moved primarily to mocking laughter, and the only way in which a writer can fail in this vein is by inconsistency, by failing to sustain his irony throughout. But Burgess does not fail in this way; he is consistently, brilliantly ironic in his presentation of the farce of life in Dunia and the horribly funny practical jokes that life plays on men like Lydgate. . . . Burgess's description of Waugh's *The Loved One* as "a satire . . . told heartlessly but brilliantly" would fit *Devil of a State* very well, and a less sentimental reader might find it more satisfying than *The Long Day Wanes*. (p. 58)

The Worm and the Ring is a kind of mock epic. More exactly, it is a mock opera, a burlesque of Wagner's *Der Ring des Nibelungen*. Wagner's allegorical struggle for power between Nibelung dwarfs, giants, and gods is translated into a struggle for the control of a grammar school in a little English borough. (p. 59)

The Worm and the Ring is one of Burgess's better novels, not merely because it is such a memorable record of conditions that should have generated national shame in the year of the Festival; it also reveals Burgess's extraordinary capacity to make absorbing dramatic entertainment out of the most unlikely material. The hidden comedy and pathos of life in the dreary little grammar school are revealed with sensitivity, sympathy, and irresistible wit. In addition to the main characters—Howarth, Woolton, Gardner—there are some splendidly drawn minor portraits. One of them is Mr. Lodge, whose humdrum existence as an uninspired purveyor of elementary scientific truths would seem to be most unpromising material for hilarity or pathos; yet Burgess manages to evoke both. (pp. 64-5)

Nothing Like the Sun is Burgess's finest achievement so far in the novel. His rendering of Elizabethan idiom is faultless; yet the book is lucid enough to be enjoyed fully by the average reader. The only difficulty it may present is in the shifting personae and the novelist's identification with [William Shakespeare]. If the reader, like some of the critics, ignores the opening announcement that the book is "Mr. Burgess's farewell lecture to his *special* students," he may not be fully aware of what is happening. . . .

Another source of distress to some readers will be the portrait of WS and its utter humanity. Again, like some of the critics, they may have entertained an image of Shakespeare as some sort of ethereal being who, through a mysterious process, was granted unparalleled understanding of the human condition without being a part thereof. Or they may have thought of him as a good, solid burgher cranking out money-making dramas about the power of evil he had never felt merely because that was as they liked it and what they willed. . . . Burgess understands WS as few academic scholars do, and I am convinced of the comparative worth of his contribution to our understanding of Shakespeare. One cannot document the poet's syphilis

with reference to parish records any more than one can "document" Joyce's provocative theories about him in *Ulysses*. But there is a ring of truth in the "unscholarly" disquisitions of both Dedalus and Burgess's drunken persona. The portrait of the man himself may not be entirely accurate. He may not have had syphilis (cancer perhaps?). But the man we are given in these novels is the kind of man who could have created the Shakespeare canon. He loves, suffers, and beholds the face of evil as surely as Shakespeare must actually have done.

This is not to suggest that Burgess simply used his imagination in lieu of doing his homework. His knowledge of the period and its well-documented events is considerable, and by his deft use of allusion and descriptive detail, he has given us an extremely convincing picture of the vigor, violence, filth, and color of Elizabethan town and country life. We see how amply WS could have been provided with material within the limited world he knew. (p. 79)

[In] the *Enderby* novels, Burgess is primarily concerned with the condition of poetry and the poet in the latter half of the twentieth century. He intended *Inside Mr. Enderby* [published in the United States with *Enderby Outside* as *Enderby*] to be "a kind of trumpet blast on behalf of the besieged poet of today—the man who tries to be independent, tries to write his poetry not on the campus, but in the smallest room in the house," where he can have some privacy. Again and again, he emphasizes that the poet must be independent. (p. 84)

As a "trumpet blast," *Inside Mr. Enderby* may not shake the walls of conventional thinking surrounding the practice of poetry, but it is, as one critic has said, "a little masterpiece." The uncontrollable laughter it arouses somehow increases our sympathy for Enderby and artists like him. He presents a ludicrous figure as he scribbles away under the watchful gaze of the mice inhabiting his bathtub or wards off an intruder with his faithful toilet seat. But the great world, which is in many ways more ludicrous than he is, cannot see the humor. It can only bend a stern, stepmotherly gaze on him and coerce him into a more "serious" way of life. Before this is accomplished, he is an extremely lovable character, even though there is very little love in his life, and his forced conversion to useful citizenship is quite as painful as the conversion of Alex in *A Clockwork Orange*. Although we cannot help laughing at Enderby, we also cannot help but share Burgess's intense anger at the enemies who surround him. In a sense, he is doing for the besieged artist what Somerset Maugham did in *The Moon and Sixpence,* but Burgess's trumpet blast is the more powerful because it shows just how vulnerable the artist really is. (pp. 85-6)

What began [in *Inside Mr. Enderby*] as a trumpet blast on behalf of artists besieged by the great world has become [in *Enderby Outside*] an overall assessment of the condition of modern poetry—a pessimistic assessment, to be sure. But just as there is at least implied optimism within Swift's generally pessimistic assessment of humanity, *Gulliver's Travels,* so there is some basis for hope in *Enderby Outside*. Though neither Enderby nor any of the other would-be poets have what it takes to make love to the muse, at least she is available—downing champagne in cafés, swimming naked in the surf, throwing four-letter words at cab drivers, walking the dirty streets. Poetry is there for the making in all these places and things. If and when a poet arrives, the goddess will have her orgasm and poetry will be made.

Burgess's first two *Enderby* novels comprise his most complete positive statement concerning the role of the artist. The duties of that role are to maintain one's responsibilities to one's art, which means essentially committing oneself to the fullest extent of one's talent and energy and resisting social and other pressures from the great world that would "impinge" and interfere with this commitment. In *MF* Burgess defines the role in another way, by opposition. The "incestuous" works of "Sib Legeru" represent everything that art is not, and the attitudes of the admiring narrator/protagonist in search of "Sib Legeru" reveal the irresponsibility of the antiartist who cultivates chaos. (pp. 93-4)

In the third *Enderby* novel, *The Clockwork Testament or Enderby's End,* he again uses an American setting and places within it his besieged true artist, the poet Enderby. In this novel, it is not the artist that is besieged so much as art itself. (p. 94)

The Clockwork Testament is by no means one of Burgess's major achievements in the novel, and one suspects it was never intended to be. His treatments of the same themes in other novels are richer, more complex, and comparison with these other longer novels can only make this one appear rather slight.... Those who are ready for a fuller, subtler satiric treatment of American culture should read *MF*. Of course, the role of the artist receives its fullest definition in the two novels that appeared in the United States as one *Enderby* novel. This is not to say that *The Clockwork Testament* is not worth reading. It is a superb little satire, animated throughout by a fine rage and an unwearying wit. It occupies a place in the Burgess canon very much analogous to that of *The Loved One* in Evelyn Waugh's canon—slight when compared with the major novels but a brilliant minor work.... Burgess's impulse to write *The Clockwork Testament* came presumably from the experience of being "demoted" as an artist by the filming of *A Clockwork Orange.* It is his answer to those who would so demote him and the art of fiction itself. Like the rapier thrusts of Enderby on the subway, the thrusts of its multipronged satire are shrewdly placed. (pp. 108-09)

In a group of novels written between 1960 and 1964 Burgess presented assessments, from various points of view, of the quality of life in midtwentieth-century England. One of them, *The Worm and the Ring,* ... seems to be primarily concerned with the ways in which an Englishman can be drawn away from his native country into a darker, foreign culture. The others include *The Right to an Answer, The Doctor Is Sick, One Hand Clapping, Honey for the Bears,* and *The Eve of St. Venus.* Not all of these novels are set in England, but the one that is not, *Honey for the Bears,* is in fact largely concerned with English attitudes and values and the question of love. (p. 110)

The Right to an Answer is ... a well-filled package. Burgess can incorporate and develop more of the matter of serious fiction in fifty pages than most writers can in five hundred. *The Right to an Answer* is so loaded with fascinating insights and characterization that one has a sense of reading the distillation, the quintessential best, of a much larger work. This is not because anything seems to be missing but because Burgess has presented so much with such faultless economy and wit. The range of subjects treated—from culture clashes to love and moral responsibility—is considerable; yet the relevance of each subject to the others is clearly evident. (p. 118)

In addition to being Burgess's meatiest treatment of love and decay in the West, *The Right to an Answer* is also his funniest. Some of Denham's descriptions of what he sees make one ache with laughter. Even a dreary event such as a Sunday dinner at the house of his sister becomes thoroughly hilarious, and his description of a voyage back to the Orient aboard a Dutch liner is a marvelous piece of comedy worthy of any anthology. We may not share Denham's feelings about what he sees, but we cannot resist being entertained by his descriptions and commentaries. His detached outsider's testimony is a tempting invitation to view England through the eyes of other Burgess protagonists, protagonists who are less witty but more involved with life, love, and decay in the West. (p. 119)

For Mr. Tomlin, the long-suffering United Nations adviser in *Devil of a State,* the problems of gaining or maintaining a grasp on "reality" weigh heavily. Faced with impossible tasks, frustrated by irrational human obstacles, looking forward to a retirement even more dismal and meaningless than his last term, he wonders whether he or anyone around him is genuinely aware of what is or is not real. His doubts can be related largely to his "fantasticated" tropical surroundings and the various strange or hostile human types with whom he must associate. However, as another Burgess novel, *The Doctor Is Sick,* suggests, such doubts are by no means peculiar to Englishmen in the tropics. The protagonist of *The Doctor Is Sick,* Dr. Edwin Spindrift, has been in the tropics, in Burma, but when he, like Burgess, collapses on a lecture-room floor, he is flown immediately to England and hospitalized. The action begins in the depressing atmosphere of his hospital ward, a place where all that has previously sustained and protected him in the great world suddenly becomes quite irrelevant and meaningless. (p. 119)

[The] analysis of interacting theological, mythological, artistic, and philosophical motifs in *The Doctor Is Sick* should not suggest that a reader must bring to the novel a bookish, Spindriftian sensibility in order to enjoy it. If one *wants* to play the professional game of critical exegesis, to hunt for symbols, motifs, and so forth, there is plenty to keep one occupied just digging into aspects of the novel not even touched here. But the book is very nearly as funny as *The Right to an Answer,* and anyone with a feeling for life and language will find it hard to lay aside.... The way in which Burgess effortlessly wrings the full comic possibilities out of thoroughly dreary material is continually amazing. (p. 130)

Like *The Doctor Is Sick, Honey for the Bears* chronicles a Ulyssean quest for understanding and self-awareness. Set in Leningrad during the Khrushchev regime, it is based in part on Burgess's own experiences there in 1961....

To an extent, what Paul Hussey, the protagonist of *Honey for the Bears,* learns about Russia is what Burgess himself learned, and many of his more improbable adventures are based on experiences that Burgess himself had. But this is the fullest extent to which *Honey for the Bears* could be termed autobiographical. Between Hussey and Burgess, there is no appreciable resemblance. Hussey is a rather colorless, apparently asexual antique dealer who goes to Leningrad solely for the purpose of smuggling in twenty-dozen drilon dresses to be sold on the black market at a substantial profit. His motives for engaging in this risky trade are far more complex than simple greed. Mainly it is a matter of doing a favor for a deceased friend named Robert who had planned before his sudden death to sell the dresses himself. Robert's widow, Sandra, needs the money and Paul feels bound to help her. Along with her need, however, is a stronger, related motive. Robert's memory is a constant fond presence and carrying out the venture is a ritual of devotion to it. The real nature of the relationship he had had with Robert is suggested subtly early in the novel but not fully revealed either to Paul himself or the reader until later, when he is about to lose his voluptuous American wife, Belinda, to Russia. (p. 131)

[*Honey for the Bears*] is an irresistibly entertaining experience throughout, and one is apt to enjoy it more than, say, *MF* or *One Hand Clapping* because even its satire and criticism are informed by an obvious faith in the regenerative power of love. This is probably due largely to Burgess's feelings for Russia, as opposed to his feelings for the settings of these other novels. It would appear that Russia gave him some hope for the West, while Malta ("Castita" in *MF*) and the America that could breed Miles Faber and export so much of the vulgarity and cheapness that gratify Janet Shirley in *One Hand Clapping* made him wonder whether the West could be saved from the various forms of "incest" mirrored in its racial attitudes and cultural values. Burgess's faith in the regenerative power of love appears again strongly reaffirmed in *The Eve of St. Venus,* but it may be significant that love's triumph in a decadent Western setting requires the miraculous intervention of the goddess herself. (p. 144)

One Hand Clapping first appeared in England in 1960 under the pseudonym Joseph Kell and, largely because of this, failed to attract the attention it deserved. Although it is not one of Burgess's best novels—it is not on the same level with the *Enderby* books and *The Right to an Answer*—it is nonetheless a very competently written, provocative, and entertaining work. Like *The Right to an Answer,* it is a first-person commentary on life in present-day England. What makes it less dazzling and witty than that commentary is not careless craftsmanship but simply the narrator/protagonist Burgess has chosen to use. Instead of somone like the urbane, worldly wise Denham, a highly literate, clever man capable of articulating brilliant insights, we have a very limited narrator/protagonist—an ill-educated young Englishwoman named Janet Shirley who possesses no more than an average share of native cleverness. Burgess thus limits himself from the start both in the ideas he can express and the language he can use to express them. But what he gains is an authentic testimony from a contented product of a decaying philistine culture. (p. 145)

The limitations of *One Hand Clapping* are not due to any artistic deficiency. To give us an authentic picture of England through a young Englishwoman's mind, Burgess has deliberately handicapped himself considerably, but what he has produced in the process is no mean achievement. There are few male writers in any age who can draw women convincingly.... Although Janet Shirley is by no means the most interesting female in Burgess's fiction—she is less interesting than the women in *Nothing Like the Sun* and *Enderby*—she is a very convincing portrait of a type of woman that American as well as British readers should recognize readily. Her ways of reasoning, her values, her fears, and her reactions ring true and are not contrived to fit in with themes, as so often happens when a male writer seeks to present a female character as a commentary on a society. A reader may be a bit startled by the callousness and ruthlessness she exhibits near the end of the novel, but this seems to be one of Burgess's purposes. As a product of her society, Janet is so lacking in stable, meaningful values that the transition from loving wife to calculating murderess is quite easy. (p. 149)

The temptation to label [Burgess "liberal" or "conservative"] is ... strong because so many of the conflicts in his novels are between *Pelagian liberals* and *Augustinian conservatives.* By his use of these *terms,* Burgess intends to remind us of the ultimate origins of much of the so-called liberalism and conservatism in Western thinking. In Burgess's view, the liberal's optimism, his belief in the fundamental goodness and perfectability of man, derives from an ancient heresy—the Pelagian denial of original sin. Not surprisingly, he believes the doctrinal bases of much of the pessimism pervading Western conservative thinking can be traced to Augustine's well-known refutations of Pelagian doctrine. (p. 158)

The Wanting Seed is Burgess's fullest and most explicit treatment of the Augustinian/Pelagian conflict. In this Orwellian/Malthusian proleptic nightmare, he presents a cyclical theory of history—as essentially a perpetual oscillation or "waltz" between two philosophical "phases"—a Pelagian phase and an Augustinian. As the novel opens, we behold a world in which our undernourished descendants have little more than standing room. England, as suffocatingly crowded as the rest of the world, is under the benevolent guidance of a "Pelagian" government. Official attitudes and policies are, however, more distinctively Rousseauvian than Pelagian. Indeed, the shocking vision of the Malthusian nightmare itself may remind one of Jean-Jacques's pronouncement that "the government under which, without external aids, without naturalization of colonies, the citizens increase and multiply most is beyond question the best." Just as the folly of this assumption is revealed, the incredible naïveté of the Pelagian government's Rousseauvian political philosophy is also revealed.... Burgess's sardine-can civilization comes into being largely because the government has been unshakable in its trust in *la volonté générale.* Despite massive proof to the contrary, it maintains an optimistic belief that "the great liberal dream seems capable of fulfillment." (pp. 162-63)

The Wanting Seed is, in [Thomas] Mann's sense, a "grotesque" drama, and, like Shakespeare's sonnets, it is a relatively late but fresh and enduring contribution to a subgenre that seemed to have been worked to death. It antagonized some influential critics but is greatly admired by more youthful intellectuals, especially in America, who see in it a book that passes the test of "relevance," not merely because it depicts some possible consequences of the population explosion we all fear, but also because it gives a horribly convincing picture of the alternatives modern man may face at some time in the near future in his endless quest for social stability: If he isn't, in one sense or another, "eaten" by a military/industrial complex, he will be persuaded to castrate himself, in one way or another, for the sake of social stability. (p. 169)

Like *The Wanting Seed,* [*A Clockwork Orange*] is a proleptic nightmare with dystopian implications. Although it can be read as an answer to and a rejection of the main ideas of B. F. Skinner, the author of such works as *Walden Two* and *Beyond Freedom and Dignity,* Burgess seems to have been directly influenced less by Skinner's ideas in particular than by accounts he had read of behaviorist methods of reforming criminals that were being tried in American prisons with the avowed purpose of limiting the subjects' freedom of choice to what society called "goodness." This struck Burgess as "most sinful," and his novel is, among other things, an attempt to clarify the issues involved in the use of such methods. (pp. 169-70)

[*A Clockwork Orange* is] one of the most devastating pieces of multipronged social satire in recent fiction, and, like *The Wanting Seed,* it passes the test of "relevance." Although most people have been made aware of the assumptions of behavioral psychology through the recent uproar caused by Skinner's polemical restatement of his ideas in *Beyond Freedom and Dig-*

nity, it is perhaps less generally realized that Skinner's schemes for imposing goodness on the human "mechanism" are among the less radical of those being proposed by behavioral technologists. As of this writing, a sociologist, Professor Gerald Smith of the University of Utah, is engaged in promoting the development of a device that can be implanted within the person of a paroled convict. The device, which measures adrenalin, is designed to send signals to a receiver in the home or office of his parole officer if the convict becomes excited by committing a crime. How this gadget would separate criminal stimuli from activities such as love making that might signal "false positives" has not been revealed. What is certain, at least in the mind of the sociologist, is that the beneficial effects of such devices would completely justify their use. A convict would lose nothing, since, as a prisoner, he is already without freedom, and the benefits to society would be incalculable.

It is this line of thinking that Burgess challenges in *A Clockwork Orange.* (pp. 172-73)

Whether or not we choose to agree with [*A Clockwork Orange*] as "a sermon on the power of choice," we have been forced to view clearly the implications of limiting that power. It is providential that the Kubrick film should come out in the same year as the publication of *Beyond Freedom and Dignity*. For those who were disturbed by Skinner's book but unable to articulate a refutation, Burgess and Kubrick have provided an eloquent answer. (p. 182)

In 1966 Burgess, having already experimented successfully with a wide variety of subgenres of the novel—mock epic, historical romance, picaresque, proleptic satire—turned his hand to a type that seems to be, by its very nature and purpose, fatally constricting to a writer with Burgess's philosophical and artistic concerns. *Tremor of Intent* is a spy thriller. If one reckons literary success purely in terms of sales, unquestionably Ian Fleming has been the most successful creator of spy thrillers. . . . But one wonders about just how many generations of readers will be thrilled by the exploits of James Bond. (p. 185)

Burgess is by no means the only novelist to perceive that Fleming and his imitators had not exhausted the possibilities of the spy thriller. . . . There has been, however, nothing to compare with Burgess's *Tremor of Intent.* Upon the well-worn framework of the Bond formula, he has fleshed out and molded a tale of intrigue that must fire the senses of even the most Bond-weary aficionado of the spy thriller. The typical Bond feats of appetite are duplicated and surpassed, sometimes to a ridiculous extent. The protagonist, Denis Hillier, has bedroom adventures that make Bond's conquests seem as crude and unfulfilling as an acneed adolescent's evening affair with an issue of *Playboy*. His gastronomic awareness is such that Bond is by comparison an epicurean tyro. In addition, Hillier possesses a mind that is good for something besides devising booby traps and playing games with supervillains. Unlike Bond, he has a moral awareness that extends beyond ideology. In his view, the specter of nuclear holocaust that causes East and West to tremble before each other, ponder genocide, and play their murderous little pranks is illusory. . . . (p. 186)

Burgess has accomplished something rather amazing in *Tremor of Intent.* He presents violence and a variety of sensual experience with an evocative linguistic verve that must dazzle even the most jaded sensibility. At the same time, he makes some very provocative eschatological statements and conjectures. This in itself is amazing because the spy thriller by its very nature tends to avoid eschatology. If a reader is compelled to think about what may occur long after the Pentagon and the Kremlin are reduced to rock dust, he may find it difficult to worry about whether James Bond or Matt Helm can win another round for the Free World. Indeed, in the hands of a less competent novelist, any involved religious or philosophical questions would be a fatally distracting burden, but *Tremor of Intent* is such a brilliantly integrated package that somehow we pass quite easily from an irresistible, corrupting vicarious involvement in gastronomy, fornication, and bloodshed to involved questions of ethics and eschatology and back again. (pp. 193-94)

In a number of his novels, notably *The Wanting Seed, The Eve of St. Venus, The Worm and the Ring,* and *Enderby,* Burgess builds deliberately upon mythic frames and, like his master Joyce, even reveals some mythopoeic tendencies. Many of Burgess's characters are ironically modified archetypes who undergo archetypal experiences or ironic parodies of such experience. In addition, we find literal goddesses as well as goddess figures intervening in human affairs in order to revive and regenerate. However, none of these novels fits wholly within a mythic frame, presumably because Burgess found such archetypes too confining for his purposes. In *MF* he seems to have found a framework large enough to accommodate his total artistic design. He has fused incest myths—Algonquin Indian and Greek—and given them new meaning as a devastating satiric indictment of contemporary Western cultural values that goes well beyond the criticisms levelled in the *Enderby* novels. (p. 195)

The focus of *MF* is broader than art—much broader. The whole pattern of Western culture, as Burgess sees it, is incestuous. Race consciousness in particular, which has in no way diminished in recent years, is symptomatic of an incestuous pull. In Burgess's view, "the time has come for the big miscegnation." All of the races must overcome their morbid preoccupation with color identity and face the merger that is inevitable in any event. As *The Wanting Seed* suggests, population pressures will make any notion of racial compartmentalization utterly absurd in the not-too-distant future. But aside from this, Burgess sees race consciousness itself as fundamentally absurd, and he has illuminated the absurdity in a number of books. . . . Throughout the *Malayan Trilogy* race consciousness is shown to be the major factor that will inhibit cultural progress in the new Malaysia. In *MF* Burgess focuses on what he regards as the absurd and incestuous black preoccupation with race. . . . In *MF* itself, he attempts to jolt his readers out of their race consciousness by allowing them to finish the entire novel before he reveals a racial factor that most writers would feel compelled to clarify on their first page. (p. 204)

MF can also, as suggested, be seen as a continuation of those novels in which Burgess focuses on Western man's myopic view of his own nature. In his dystopian books *A Clockwork Orange* and *The Wanting Seed* especially, he focuses on Western man's insane compulsion to generalize about the nature of "man" at the expense of any true understanding of human problems. As social order is sought on the basis of preconceived "Pelagian" or "Augustinian" notions about the nature of man, society is propelled toward moral chaos. Similarly, in *MF* we see that the yearning for freedom through chaos is actually a yearning for slavery. Another "alembicated moral" Faber offers his readers is that "a mania for total liberty is really a mania for prison, and you'll get there by way of incest." . . . Taking the application of this at its broadest, one realizes that Western man's failure to understand himself causes him to develop a spurious concept of freedom and to seek ruinous avenues to that freedom. Narrowing the focus to America (and *MF* invites this focus), one can see a strong tendency to preserve "freedom" through incestuous avenues. . . . World federalism, the concept of world government, is viewed as un-American and dangerously subversive. This incestuous tendency of America, this feeling that it can be saved only if it turns in upon itself and either excludes or converts the corrupting influences from the great world outside, is not an avenue to freedom. It imprisons America. (p. 205)

[In *Napoleon Symphony*] Burgess is concerned and worried, perhaps unduly, that his artistic purposes will not manifest themselves clearly enough to be understood by his audience. He is worried that some critics may compare his portrait of Napoleon with Tolstoy's in *War and Peace*. Such comparisons diminish unfairly Hardy's achievement in *The Dynasts,* and he seems to fear the same fate for *Napoleon Symphony*. Such a comparison would of course be pointless because it would be apple and orange, both in terms of subject and subgenre. Burgess's subject is ostensibly Napoleon, but his real, "implied," subject is Beethoven, the creative will of Beethoven manifesting itself in an achievement that utterly dwarfs that of its ostensible subject. Burgess asks that the novel be judged as a "comic novel," but he does not wish to have it assessed in terms of hilarity generated by contrivances. In short, Burgess is asking his critics to have a *sense de mesure* and a *sense de métier*. (p. 230)

Thematically, *Napoleon Symphony* does not represent any "new directions" in Burgess's fiction. As in *MF* and *Enderby Outside,* he is mainly preoccupied with summarizing and clarifying his views concerning the role of the artist in the modern world. *Enderby* defines the artist in terms of his concerns and identifies the forces that threaten him. *MF* is a satirical polemic against antiart and pseudoartists that also attempts to define the role of the artist: *Napoleon Symphony* carries the definitions of these novels somewhat further by exalting the true artist's creative will and imagination, which could have created perhaps a better modern world without Napoleon. It is a much subtler handling of the theme than either *MF* or *Enderby,* but in some ways it is more successful than both. Although all three novels emphasize the theme of the artist's role with didactic dialogues near their conclusions, we are perhaps more likely to be convinced by *Napoleon Symphony,* in which the didacticism is not overheavy. . . . Burgess . . . [makes] his point regarding the awesome powers and concomitant responsibilities of the artist far more effectively than he has in the other two novels by such devices as having a muse figure quote Shelley on the role of the poet as unacknowledged legislator of the world or having a protagonist discourse directly to the reader on the irresponsibility of antiart. (pp. 231-32)

It can be argued that Burgess deals with essentially the same themes in nearly all his novels. What *Napoleon Symphony* reveals is that the themes are inexhaustible when subjected to the will and creative genius of a true artist. (p. 232)

> *Geoffrey Aggeler, in his* Anthony Burgess: The Artist
> as Novelist, *The University of Alabama Press, 1979,*
> *245 p.*

SAMUEL COALE

Burgess has often spoken about life's being a game:

> God had no necessity to create the world . . .
> He must have created it to amuse himself, not

out of necessity, because the ludic element has nothing to do with necessity. It's just an extra. This I accept. The important things in life are games, are ludic . . . I mean, nature gets on with her own or of sustaining us, but as for the rest of the things we do, it must be ludic.

(p. 195)

Burgess's sense of the game pervades his fiction. To play games, exploit myths, structure realistic novels around all kinds of war games, musical patterns, fables, and legends, is to create one's own independence, experience one's delight in his imagination. Language itself becomes a game, emanating as it does mysteriously from the unconscious shape of the imagination and mind: to grapple with it, stretch and explore it, is to grapple with the mind's ability to create. The choice of a particular structure, a form, assists the writer in coming to grips with his themes. The function of playing the game is to see how far it will carry you into some genuine revelation of insight.

Both game and myth partake of ritual and ceremony, forms of experience that lay very close to Burgess's lapsed-Catholic, modernistic heart. Thus the sense of the writer as mythmaker and game player—the artist as conscious conjuror—pervades his vision. (pp. 195-96)

Guilt, loneliness, isolation, and corruption stalk the landscapes of Burgess's novels. History embodies them all: politics, sex, and human betrayal reveal these qualities over and over again. The comic form of these novels, however, is quite another thing. (p. 196)

He views the modern world as a chaotic, ambiguous place, fallen away—like himself?—from the solid, moral virtues and values of the past, and yet the sheer exuberance and delight, both in his style and in his crazy-guilt plots, comes through. . . . Burgess's plots have a tendency to twitch and gyrate, absurd episodes tumbling one upon the other. They're roller-coaster rides, filled with coincidence, mistaken identities, and labyrinthine journeys. These coincidences, parallel situations, and outrageous circumstances become cyclical, repetitive, and are often suddenly transformed, suggesting the possibility that all is not lost, that situations and even guilt itself can be redeemed or at least partially transcended. In a few pages a new circumstance, another coincidence, a shift in perspective will occur, and the realm of guilt and isolation may be miraculously overcome. Comedy, however bleak, relies on such cycles and transformations.

At the center of these outrageous, almost ramshackle tales lies one harried soul, struggling for some way out, trying to seek some accommodation with ultimate meaning and personal belief. . . . In Burgess's case the rollicking plot often overshadows the personality of the man at the center. The main character registers dissatisfaction, but only in rare instances—such as Enderby, Alex, and Toomey, and to a lesser degree Burgess's Napoleon and Shakespeare—does he reveal any deep human complexities. His character is often sacrificed to the comic coincidences and gerrymandered structure of the plot. Certainly such a theme can be treated tragically, but all of Burgess's authorial inventions—his style, his plots, his structures—provide the necessary distance to treat them, and his characters, comically.

Burgess's comedy raises some difficult questions. Often there seems to be a separation in his work between his intellectual grasp of a theme or idea and his emotional response to that theme or idea. Perhaps Burgess's sixteen years as a teacher may account for this, the sacrificing of character and honest emotion to theme and a specific thesis. Many of the novels delight and instruct, but they often fail to capture the heart of the matter. One recognizes the lines and shapes of his elaborate designs and structures, but they often seem superficial and thin as if he'd drawn the lines of his vision but failed to color it in. This is not necessarily true of comedy in general, but it does seem to be true of Burgess's comedies in particular.

Burgess may have used these mythic and comic devices as an attempt to overcome his own deep-seated feelings of guilt. To avoid what seems to be his most obsessive subject, to surround it with artifice and game, may account for the split between his verbal wit, his "throw-away" plots, his whirl of coincidence and design, and the very real Manichean concern about the nature of reality and moral choice. It's as if Burgess chose these particular forms for his novels to take the sting of guilt out of their content, to defuse the forces of guilt and isolation which seem to consume his characters. Their actions, then, become gestures in a game, self-conscious postures in a comic whirligig of modern angst and alienation.

The price, however, in such an approach is that such other emotions as love, joy, and terror are also defused. The landscape flattens, and truth becomes not a passionate conviction dredged up from the soul of full-bodied characters, but a windy lecture in a world where nobody else is listening. Perhaps the force of guilt has crushed the fragile bloom of love in Burgess's view. And in order to assuage such ferocious and dark feelings, ritual has replaced real emotion. The urge to cleanse oneself in an act of contrition and deliverance has surpassed the need to create the emotional and passionate fullness of love, grief, and other human feelings.

When the artist, the mythmaker, the poet, and the word-player become the focus of a novel—when love and language become inseparable—Burgess's art triumphs. His best characters are men like himself—Enderby, the poet, and even Alex, the droog, who in a brutal futuristic world, still likes to "shine artistic." And Napoleon and Shakespeare come alive with their vast visions of humanity and expert enjoyment of language, gamesmanship, sexual appetite, and irrepressible spirits. Even some of the lesser characters, such as Denis Hillier and J. W. Denham and Kenneth Toomey, share his delight in language and concern about moral values in the contemporary world. When the single dogged consciousness of the artist occupies Burgess's energies in a novel, the vision of restorative, redemptive powers of art and language blossom fully, no matter how brutal the world which surrounds it continues to be.

In the portrayal of each of these characters, Burgess does not by-pass human frailty, disease, and guilt; in each, he confronts these fully, suggesting the very real possibility of redemption and fulfillment—especially in art and in his own Manichean "faith"—that may grow out of the very human soil in which they are planted. This is his triumph. In playing serious but comic games, in devising new myths or replaying old ones, in constantly celebrating the continuous display of man's imagination and creativity through word and deed, Burgess views the artist as a man capable of constructing his own salvation. It doesn't always work. In his best novels, however, he convinces us it can. (pp. 196-99)

> *Samuel Coale, in his* Anthony Burgess, *Frederick Ungar Publishing Co., 1981, 223 p.*

MICHAEL DIRDA

Anthony Burgess may be the most consummate professional writer now alive. His knowledge of literary, linguistic and musical arcana rivals that of any Oxford don; he writes with a lyrical verve; and he seems willing to turn his hand to anything whatever. In between ambitious novels (*Earthly Powers,* being the most recent), he has constructed languages for the movie *Quest for Fire,* reviewed regularly for British newspapers, and composed operas. This new book, *On Going to Bed,* is clearly an example of his Grub Street work: a slight but engaging essay, supplemented by pretty pictures, yet an altogether pleasant scrapbook to fall asleep over.

The bed, Burgess suggests, is among the most universal of human inventions, preceding fire and the wheel, and coming soon after the discovery of sex. In bed we are conceived, given birth, and laid to rest; beds provide the one pleasure we never tire of—sleep—and they are where we go when we feel depressed, put upon, or sick. As children we fight with pillows or jump on mattresses like trampoline acrobats. . . . And for many, reading just the right book while propped against pillows and warm beneath a blanket remains the cheapest of all luxuries. . . .

The real delight [of this essay] comes when Burgess remembers his childhood fears of the dark and cold or reveals that he himself has given up on the bed per se, preferring a mattress on the floor with his books, papers, and phonographic equipment spread around him. Of course, none of this is in the least important, but it all reads wonderfully well—especially with a big cup of tea during a stormy night, snug between the sheets.

> *Michael Dirda, in a review of "On Going to Bed,"* in Book World—The Washington Post, *June 13, 1982, p. 4.*

PETER PORTER

If, like me, you've thought that any parallel to Anthony Burgess's copious production must be sought outside literature altogether, in the works of composers whose legacies so often become the life's work of a Köchel or a Hoboken, then the master's new book [*This Man and Music*] holds a surprise for you. Anthony Burgess, man of letters, is also John Wilson, seasoned composer. . . .

The only music of Burgess/Wilson I have encountered is the Joyce operetta and a short virtuoso piano accompaniment he wrote in the Sixties as melodrama to a poem by Martin Bell. **"The Blooms of Dublin"** affected me differently from the way it struck Hans Keller. It was eclectic, but that didn't matter. It just didn't have enough music in it. At all times words dominated; not dramatic shapes but words at their wordiest. In the chapter 'Under the Bam' in his new book, Burgess offers a brilliant analysis of the relationship of music to words in popular songs and musical comedy—Lorenz Hart is properly canonised and T. S. Eliot gently admonished for not trusting sufficiently his own ear and instincts. . . .

Burgess writes: 'It was, I suppose, a doubt about the capacity of music to provide me with a language that drove me to the craft of the novel, where there are solidities of character and *récit* and corresponding semantic and syntactical solidities.' This comes at the end of a discussion of the decay of music's power in our age, but surely he would have felt the same doubts even before Schoenberg. There have been composers, some of conservative bent and others more progressive, who have found a workable musical language in our time. Might it not be that the sensible and economical spirit of creation in Burgess directed him away from music, so much an art of 'given' genius, towards literature, a field of speculation, reference and memory?

Everything he writes about the relations of the two arts is full of wisdom and challenges the glib parallels which too many well-wishers impose on them. Since he became a literary man, Burgess has produced some of the richest semi-fictional writing of the age. Perhaps only Nabokov has done as much. The novelist and the composer were twinned in him at birth, but the first has gone on to become a major artist. Until we hear some more of those listed compositions we shan't know how talented the composer is. Unfortunately, music's closed shop operates against even so famous a figure as Burgess, which is why the furore which greeted **"The Blooms of Dublin"** is so depressing.

Meanwhile, we have Burgess opinionated, Burgess autobiographical, Burgess expository, and it is all very readable. Poets could benefit from his discussion of Hopkinsian 'sprung rhythm,' which he persuaded me for the first time is more than a literary con for those with cloth ears. He is excellent again on Joyce, and on Eliot, especially the Wagnerian themes in *Finnegans Wake* and *The Waste Land*. His description of his pioneering structuralist novel *MF* is more eye-goggling than the work itself.

Best of all, Burgess loves to play. Good literary man that he is, he writes variations on a theme of Shakespeare as finale to his Third Symphony. Shakespeare's tune is the bit where Holofernes gets the gamut wrong in *Love's Labour's Lost*. It is not much of a theme even if it can readily be inverted, reversed, etc. Perhaps Shakespeare wanted to be a composer too. And it surprises me that Burgess, the great connector, forbears to point out that the early opera credited to Thomas Mann's invented composer, Adrian Leverkühn, in *Doctor Faustus,* is *Love's Labour's Lost*.

> Peter Porter, "Novelist as Composer," in The Observer, September 12, 1982, p. 33.

MICHAEL POOLE

It takes a special kind of nerve to write a novel about the end of the world and then gloss it as an 'entertainment'. But then everything about [*The End of the World News*] is audacious—from the bitchiness of the foreword, penned by one wholly fictitious James B. Wilson, BA, which uses the occasion to settle old literary scores, to the wilful casting of Trotsky in a 1917 Broadway musical, and the fact that the dustjacket blurb has been written by none other than the author himself, 'acting as his own puffer'....

The End of the World News takes its cue from two diametrically opposed broadcast mediums—old-style radio as practised by the BBC World Service, and the brash panache of the American television networks. Burgess was struck by an unintentional irony in the sonorous way Bush House concludes its actuality bulletins with the phrase, 'That is the end of the World News'. Hence the title and theme: news about how the world might indeed 'end'. The form, though—a triptych-like structure containing three separate narratives—grew out of an image from the 1980 American Presidential Campaign: Jimmy and Rosalynn Carter sitting in the White House eating hamburgers and watching three television screens simultaneously. This faintly absurd vignette of the hopelessly fractured quality of modern living provides the novel with a rationale—of sorts. In order to understand Burgess's apocalyptic scenario, we have constantly to keep in play the story of two conceptual *bouleversements*—the advent of Freudianism and the development of Marxism—both of which in their time signalled the frailty of established world views and thus, metaphorically at least, can be seen to have anticipated the Big Bang.

The Freud strand, the opening thread in the weave, offers a potted history of the psychoanalytical movement from the initial discovery of infantile sexuality through to the various personality clashes and theoretical rows that were to split it long before its founding father's death in 1939. Convincingly researched and written with real verve, this is far and away the best part of the book and one gulps it down whole. Burgess pulls out all the stops to humanise Freud—off-setting the towering intellectual stature of the man against his all too petty failings as a husband and a father; hinting at the impetuousness that led him to extrapolate recklessly from the particular to the general; and, most tellingly, teasing out the contradictions in his own sexuality, which were precisely those of the repressed Viennese bourgeoisie who formed his clientele. But it's all done with warmth and a great deal of wit.... (p. 27)

The writing, however, takes a discernible dive whenever Trotsky enters the proceedings as the unlikeliest song-and-dance man in history. Indeed, apart from making a song and dance *about* history, it is never really clear what he is doing in the novel. Cursorily dumped in a New York that fails to come into any kind of focus and all too predictably bloated on his own rhetoric, he rarely emerges as anything more than a caricature, a figure of fun—there, it would seem, simply to allow Burgess to indulge himself as a librettist and to secure a further peg on which to hang the Reds-under-the-beds paranoia of *1985*.

New York also features prominently in the planetary end-game Burgess confects for the novel's key futuristic strand. The city Trotsky failed to woo for socialism is first in the firing-line when the planet Lynx enters on a collision course with the earth. A combination of massive tides and landslips have decimated the whole eastern seaboard of what is now the Commonwealth of the Democratic Americas. Plans to gather together the cream of this super-technological civilisation, and blast them out into the safety of space, include a hack SF writer who is to 'chronicle' their sojourn in the void. One last earthly binge, however, almost sees him missing the boat, and much of the narrative is taken up with his desperate attempt to reach the launch-pad in time—and the various philosophical reasons for going down with the rest of mankind he encounters on the way, and rejects. There's an elaborate literary irony at work here. The world, it seems, will end in an imaginative whimper, with Literature in the new space order being delivered up into the hands of an alcoholic pulp writer. And yet, as the epilogue—set in outer space several generations on—informs us, the hack will excel himself. His 'chronicle', now imbibed like Holy Writ, has, willy-nilly, turned the old civilisation—Freud, Trotsky *et al*—into Myth as effectively as might his *semblable*, the author described in the foreword as 'serving truth through a lying medium'—Burgess himself.

The End of the World News is a frustratingly uneven read. One looks hard for connections between the shifting storylines, but apart from a sort of metaphorical apocalypticism, one looks in vain.... [The] triptych structure is pretty redundant, a bogus set of mirrors that reflect very little off one another. For once, Burgess's energy seems to have got the better of him. Still, he could never yarn a yawn and there's an infectious vigour about this book even when it's at its most tenuous. Perhaps he was simply Freudened by Trotting out the End? (pp. 27-8)

Michael Poole, "End-Games," in The Listener, *Vol. 108, No. 2788, November 25, 1982, pp. 27-8.*

MICHAEL WOOD

Mr. Burgess, borrowing a term from his Riviera neighbor and literary sparring partner, Graham Greene, calls [*The End of the World News*] "an entertainment." He doesn't seem to mean that it's lightweight—its 389 pages sit a bit too bulkily in the hand for that. He means to parody the forms of writing that might survive the death of literature: the libretto, the novel ripe for a television series and science fiction. In fact, we get one of each here, spliced together by what Mr. Burgess, masquerading as his own editor, calls sub-literary devices: A character goes to the window in one story; a character is found at the window in another; the whole mixture is offered as a chronicle told to children in the far future. We don't have to take the splicing seriously. Mr. Burgess simply alludes to the problem of structure and then ignores it.

The three stories are a life of Freud ("novelised, or very nearly televisualised," Mr. Burgess says), a musical about Trotsky in New York in 1917 and a tale about a hefty planet crashing into the earth and thus ending our world around the year 2,000. The stories "are all the same story: they are all about the end of history as man has known it." This declaration is not entirely to be trusted, since it appears in the cheerfully overblown blurb Mr. Burgess has written for himself—"the author . . . who is past all shame, is acting as his own puffer"—but it is not to be dismissed either. The stories are not all the same, and they are not exactly about the end of history. But they are all about dreams of ending, about old worlds that go off with a bang, not a whimper, leaving us with less history than we thought we had but maybe more than we can manage. (p. 3)

The world won't end tonight, and Anthony Burgess doesn't think it will. His is not the scorching apocalypse of Lawrence or Yeats but a love song to what would be lost if the world went away: all its colors and tastes and smells and finally forgivable mistakes. It is an old song but a good one, made attractive not by its newness but by its steady virtue and the liveliness of Mr. Burgess's arrangement of it. "This is the end of the world," a character in the book says. "I presume anybody can join in." Sure. And we can also, in the words of Sam Goldwyn, include ourselves out. (p. 25)

Michael Wood, "A Love Song to What Would Be Lost," in The New York Times Book Review, *March 6, 1983, pp. 3, 25.*

REID BUCKLEY

Burgess, one would swear, has it all. He is fecund and prolific (dear God, *is* he!) and a master of language. There seems to be almost nothing that he cannot *say,* and so say it that it sticks to the tastebuds deliciously long after. (p. 38)

Mr. Burgess's wit is wicked, he is hilarious, and his characters, when he bothers, are *observed,* by which I mean that they are so incarnated by the imagination that he seems to be writing biography. His personae are often zany; they can be delightful; yet, somehow, there's the wanting love that he dramatizes so eloquently in *The Wanting Seed,* one's emotions are rarely engaged, one is rarely brought to feel about the characters or truly care for them, so that their predicaments (and their lot) scarcely ever entail more than our amused attention. Like Mr. Burgess himself, the reader remains at a remove.

The End of the World News is a mish-mash with fewer of Mr. Burgess's virtues hitting than his faults missing. Like many prodigiously talented folk, he can be too clever by half. The title is precious—a terrible pun. The publisher's puff, which he composes himself, and where he assures us of the seriousness of the novel, is both precious and sententious. The ho-ho-ho introduction, which is a take-off on an Edwardian adventure novel's conceit, is a bore. And then follows his three-ring circus, the yoking of unrelated stories in a single work of fiction. . . . (pp. 38-9)

The apocalyptic third storyline is fun. Despite lengthy (and repeated) interruptions by the other two narratives, Burgess builds tingling suspense, and two characters in this sequence, Courtland Willett, the out of work actor, and Val Brodie, a writer of science fiction, gain our affection. As we follow their debauches through the floods and earthquakes that attend the first swipe of the onrushing planet, we hope they survive, but like all the other characters in this miscegenated novel, each in his way, they are finally a stereotype. Willett is the Bohemian who Breaks Molds. Brodie is the Nice Guy, the Liberal Humanist, the Error-prone, Sinning, Everyman (but *lovable*). Brodie's wife is the Blonde Intellectual Iceberg (that is, she freezes Brodie's libido). Hubert Frame, her Man of Science father, is wooden, predictable, and entirely dialectical. Others in the cast are mini-series television, such as the neo-Nazi Bartlett who takes command of the escape spaceship project, and one, the President of the new meganation called The Commonwealth of the Democratic Americas, is little more than a snapshot that Burgess, in a bad fall from grace, uses to milk unearned tears out of the reader. This is *bad* stuff, and *bad* writing, and it is the more inexcusable because it is served up by a pro whose craft never entirely deserts him. (p. 39)

Reid Buckley, in a review of "The End of the World News," in The American Spectator, *Vol. 16, No. 8, August, 1983, pp. 38-40.*

THOMAS MALLON

The worst bit of news about the future is that they're going to name an airport after John Lindsay. The second worst is that the world is going to end after a rogue planet named Lynx plays havoc with the earth's tides and then, after a sneaky retreat around the sun, comes back for a direct apocalyptic hit. *The End of the World News,* Anthony Burgess's 26th or so novel (counts may vary), does not, however, find this a big enough subject by itself. Alternating with this Lynx story is a biography of Sigmund Freud (intended as background for a TV docu-drama) and the script for a musical about Trotsky's visit to New York in 1917. . . .

I defy you to take any three novels from your bookshelves and fail to fashion among them any spurious thematic links you wish. So let's get any pretense that there's a point to this trinity disposed of right away.

But, that being done, stay a minute. Anthony Burgess is too nimble a writer to give up on so quickly. He may know how to write a bad book, but he finds it very hard to write a bad page. *The End of the World News,* a whole that is decidedly less than the sum of its parts, remains full of silly incidental pleasures and satisfying verbal comedy. (p. 1349)

In his criticism Burgess has written often and well about Shakespeare and Joyce. And sure enough, Courtland Willett and Valentine Brodie, an actor and a writer escaping from flooded

New York to Kansas (the spaceship will take off from there), have more than a little of Falstaff and Prince Hal—as well as Leopold Bloom and Stephen Dedalus—in them. In further homage to his literary gods, Burgess fills this book with puns and neologisms and freshly baked acronyms. Plenty of the jokes are groan-makingly witless—when Freud and colleagues eat garnished sausages, they munch "with relish and with relish"—but that's part of the fun. Supposedly, anyway; and often enough in fact. Burgess also occasionally throws in some lovely bits of lyricism. When the Canadian president of the Commonwealth of the Democratic Americas flies one last time over New York, we are told: "He was coming to the region where it all began—the seaboard where men had kissed the earth and cursed the sea and shaken fists at a Europe that had condemned them to poverty or the tyranny of fools and bigots. They had come seeking a living, peace, tolerance, slow in finding any of the three." These are beautiful sentences, not so far in feeling from the last ones in *Gatsby*. But in a few pages we're back to verbal end-runs and pratfalls.

Burgess's trouble is that he is too exuberantly gifted to be contained by even that great 18-wheeler of genres, the novel. He is bursting with doggerel and dactyls and data, and he can't bear not to get everything down, even if it means stitching three stories together with spaghetti instead of wire. He proffers this novel, precisely, as "an entertainment." It is a very likable, very inconsequential book. As Falstaffian Courtland Willett says to his writing sidekick, Val: "'Fine words, sound. They don't have to mean much, of course.'" (p. 1350)

> *Thomas Mallon, "Holey Trinity," in* National Review, *Vol. XXXV, No. 21, October 28, 1983, pp. 1349-50.*

ROGER LEWIS

Enderby has a talent for disaster. His comic escapades palliate for Burgess his own unhappy ventures. Being a receptacle for incidents in his creator's life, when Burgess had a malady of the brain, Enderby followed suit by going completely mad. He lost his memory and appropriated the name Piggy Hogg. This was *Inside Mr. Enderby* (1963). Perhaps we were intended to make a connection with *The Private Memoirs and Confessions of a Justified Sinner*, published by James Hogg in 1824. This is a tale about the relationship between two brothers. The vagaries of the fraternal bond are what link Enderby and Burgess. It is as though the novelist did not father a character but produced a somewhat older sibling for himself. In Hogg's novel, George, the eldest, is killed by his younger brother, Wringhim. In *The Clockwork Testament* (1974), a book dedicated to Burt Lancaster, Enderby is killed off by Burgess in a New York bedroom after coronaries induced by seeing his screenplay of Hopkins's *The Wreck of the Deutschland* altered by moguls into a pornographic movie about Nazis and raped nuns.

Now, a decade later, Enderby stirs again [in *Enderby's Dark Lady Or, No End to Enderby*]. He has been resurrected as Holmes had to be by Doyle. . . . Invent a ruse, and a reprise can occur. The novelist can pretend, for instance, that new details have come to light. Watson used regularly to find new bundles of manuscript about old cases—and to hell with the Reichenbach Falls. Burgess's conceit with *Enderby's Dark Lady* is that his character once published a short-story about Shakespeare in a Canadian magazine and has been invited, on the strength of it (the hippy dialect suggests the very early Sev-

enties), to Indiana to work on a musical about the life of Stratford's upstart crow. . . .

The book begins with Enderby's fantasy about Shakespeare. Even though it covers much the same ground as Burgess's *Nothing Like the Sun* (1964) it is still very amusing. The playwright is discovered, 46 years of age, living in London and occasionally working as an artistic adviser on those Jacobean plays with a composite authorship. Though Burgess doesn't press the parallel, there is an ironic connection to be made here between the pooling of talent when creating such dramas and the writers who congregated in Hollywood to contribute lines of dialogue to a sprawling epic. The heterodox talent conflated into a movie is similar to having Dekker, Middleton and Rowley meet and come up with *The Witch of Edmonton*. In Burgess's novel, when Shakespeare is kept waiting by the Earl of Salisbury, he "took to sketching of a drinking song he had been asked for by Beaumont." When Ben Jonson appears at his friend's lodgings, he has just been released from prison. He had been incarcerated for submitting a line mocking the Scots to Marston and Chapman's *Eastward Ho!* The early years of King James's reign seem replete with communal projects. . . .

In *Earthly Powers* new causes were ascribed to the effects known as history. Now Burgess has tinkled with seventeenth century activities in a similar, puckish way. His cold Elizabethan prose is commendable, too. It is a trick he learned from Joyce. In *Here Comes Everybody* (1965) he singled out sentences from *Ulysses* which were constructed with tight economy. Joyce, like Shakespeare, "presses every drop of water out of his cooked cabbage".

When Enderby enters, the Elizabethan energy gives way to a style more appropriate to a weary progress through American theatreland. The text submitted for the musical will not do ("You got too many long words . . . You got to consider the public") and Enderby once more finds his artistic standards being stormed by the vulgarisms of the market. Will he have to make compromises to earn his fee? There are a number of comic scenes which involve mad widows, theosophists and monstrous impresarios. Enderby falls in love with April Elgar, the alluring negress who plays the Dark Lady of the Sonnets. On the opening night, of course, the leading actor is indisposed and it is Enderby who is put into doublet and hose and pushed onto the stage to play the part of Will.

Enderby becomes Shakespeare. Hence he is called either Enderspeare or Shakeserby. If Burgess and Enderby are virtually interchangeable, this identification with Shakespeare is both blasphemously hyperbolic and comically hubristic. Burgess is aware of this. The musical had been called *Leave Will Alone*.

> *Roger Lewis, "No End to Enderby," in* Punch, *Vol. 286, No. 7478, March 28, 1984, p. 59.*

D.A.N. JONES

Shakespeare, Beethoven, Napoleon, Freud, Trotsky . . . These are but a few of the great and/or famous men who have been presented as fictional characters in Anthony Burgess's witty, learned and musical novels. . . . *Enderby's Dark Lady* offers two more of Burgess's fantasies about what Shakespeare might have been like. Between this pair of agreeable yarns is sandwiched a story about a character whom Burgess made up all by himself—and who has found favour with the reading public. This is the poet Enderby, a 20th-century man, a closet Falstaff.

Best known from *Inside Mr Enderby,* he was revived in *Enderby Outside* and killed off, like Sherlock Holmes, in *The Clockwork Testament Or, Enderby's End.* Enderby has now been resuscitated by his creator and brought into contact with the spirit of Shakespeare, towards whom Enderby sometimes displays a decent humility. . . .

The first chapter is an admirable 'historical' story about Shakespeare and Ben Jonson in 1606 and 1610, offering a theory or fantasy about their connection with the Gunpowder Plot and the King James Bible. In the second chapter we are told that this story is the work of the 20th-century poet Enderby and that it has won him an invitation to the United States where he has been commissioned to write the book and lyrics for a musical about Shakespeare's life. Enderby is taken by the theory that the Dark Lady of Shakespeare's sonnet was an African girl in London, called Lucy Negro: this theory becomes real to him when he meets the leading actress in the show, a beautiful black American called April Elgar. . . . April Elgar puts Enderby through several hoops—not unlike the hoops through which Enderby had put Shakespeare in the first chapter—and Enderby fails, partly through his superstitious fear of the curse engraved on Shakespeare's tomb at Stratford:

> . . . Blest be the man who spares these stones
> But curst be he who moves my bones.

Another of the American showbiz people introduces Enderby to science fiction—and we are invited to suppose that the 12th and final chapter of the book, an agreeably horrid time-travel story, is a new literary effort by the poet Enderby, imagining what would happen to a man of the 23rd century who managed to get back to Elizabethan London, looking for the real-life Shakespeare.

Anthony Burgess offered a not dissimilar three-part story in 1982, with *The End of the World News* . . . , but Burgess melded them, according to some musical pattern, perhaps a three-part fugue. *Enderby's Dark Lady* is easier reading, since the stories are kept separate, like a three-piece suite, and we may relax with each one of them while admiring the matching design of the upholstery. (p. 24)

The trouble with Anthony Burgess is that he bewilders his readers both with his ancient scholarship and his modern 'streetwise' knowingness. In this he resembles Ben Jonson more than any other of the famous men he plays with in his fiction. But, like Ben Jonson, when he stops dazzling or befogging us with word-play he can create real characters and tell a good tale. Enderby is a great help. He may be a corruption of 'entropy' (a word with many meanings) or he may be just a rhyme for 'Neither a borrower nor a lender be'. But he comes over as real, with all his erections and eructations, and he anchors us to middle earth. (p. 25)

> *D.A.N. Jones, "Rattle Dem Bones," in* The Listener, *Vol. 111, No. 2852, April 5, 1984, pp. 24-5.*

PATRICK SKENE CATLING

What [*Enderby's Dark Lady*] needs most of all is a bit of serious relief. . . . It is set partly in Elizabethan London, where the language of the taverns was almost as fruity—as over-ripely fruity—as Burgess's own can be, and partly in Indiana, where our hero, our seedy scholar, our stumblebum buffoon, our flatulent wordsmith, has been hired to write the book of a Shakespearean musical.

As in previous instalments of the saga (*Inside Mr. Enderby,* which seemed the best, mainly because it was the first, *Enderby Outside* and *The Clockwork Testament*), the poet's bowels disturb him, and he suffers from the inconvenience of untimely onsets of tumescence. Although I attended an orthodox English school, I am bound to admit that I am a bit squeamish about traditional lavatorial and masturbatory humour. My fault, perhaps. . . .

Enderby's respectful lust for the gorgeous black singer who plays the Dark Lady in the musical provides some funny dialogue and accurate black American dialect. But throughout the novel, the Joycean excesses often are really no more than exhibitions of Burgess's remarkable linguistic knowledge. They impede communication. The novel's subtitle is 'No End to Enderby', but there *must* be. (p. 29)

> *Patrick Skene Catling, "Revelations," in* The Spectator, *Vol. 252, No. 8126, April 7, 1984, pp. 28-9.**

WALTER KERR

What is interesting about Mr. Burgess's willingness to restore his man to life [in *Enderby's Dark Lady*] is that he does not bother to do it in the old Universal Pictures way: He doesn't have the monster fall through the floor of the flaming mill into a saving pool of water, or anything ridiculous like that. No. He simply supposes that two opposites can concur at one and the same time, and why not? Of course, no existentialist philosopher would let him do that. Your average existentialist would point out that the choice of Enderby dead in New York eliminates the choice of Enderby alive in Indiana, and that it is precisely all those eliminated choices that fill modern man with *Angst,* with a sense of living among rejections, above a void.

But Enderby, you see, does not really suffer from *Angst,* nor does Mr. Burgess. Enderby suffers from cholesterol buildup and bad cigars, Mr. Burgess suffers from a fondness for adverbs like "queenlily" and a growing reliance on irrelevant set-pieces. But we must grant the two writers their double-jointed universe, partly because they have so often provided us with savage fun, and partly because we're all headed for science-fiction anyway.

In point of fact, the final chapter of *Enderby's Dark Lady* is sci-fi, and, though it does not feature Enderby because Enderby is its author, it is quite shiveringly written, especially when a space-time visitor to Elizabethan England is struggling to keep the rooms he is passing through from dissolving before he has passed through them.

Considerably less felicitous, I am sorry to say, is an opening stretch in *Jacobean* England that purports to be a short narrative, also imagined by Enderby, detailing Ben Jonson's role in the Gunpowder Plot (spy for the Court) and Shakespeare's contribution to the King James Bible (worked his name into the 46th Psalm). While this particular set-piece does serve to secure Enderby an invitation to a university theater in Indiana (where he will be expected to concoct a musical based on Shakespeare's life, times and dark lady), it is otherwise quite unnecessary. Also, it's not really much better than the standard semischolarly, faintly impertinent stabs at evoking the period that college students have been turning out, and turning in as term papers, for years.

There are other curious collapses of tone. An improvised sermon delivered by an uncomfortable Enderby before a black congregation in North Carolina is simply bewildering, neither amusing nor to any discernible point. And when Enderby, just arrived in Indiana, is attempting to deal with a supercilious stage director (Toplady) and an arrogant if untutored composer (Silversmith) at the Peter Brook Theater, Mr. Burgess seems suddenly uncertain of his targets. . . .

But shortly Enderby is supposing that Toplady "seemed to know what he wanted" and is obligingly doing foolish rewrites (on what was presumably a foolish script to begin with). But the arrows aren't flying either way—the mild flings at parody seem to cancel each other out. Mr. Burgess appears to have lost real enthusiasm for the cultural battle as he has waged it before.

Until, that is to say, the dark lady herself puts in a delayed appearance. She is a black pop singing star doing a guest stint on campus, she has been on campuses before and can give you noumenon and/or phenomenon at the least whiff of Kant, and, when Kant is not wanted, she can always slip into her "Topsy act." As she says, bestowing her blessing on Enderby, "Baby, you may be an uptight ofay milktoast limey bastard, but you ain't no fag." She is good for the poet's self-esteem, and he seriously falls in love with her, as many of Mr. Burgess's readers are apt to do, starting here, starting now.

When I say that Enderby "seriously" falls in love with her, I mean that this aging, rhyme-drunk near-misogynist who was frightened by sex at an early age . . . is forced to define both his ardor and his sexual reluctance ruthlessly. His open declaration of love is filled with an entirely plausible rage. His bitter analysis of the interdependence of love and lust is masterly. We understand him better by the time he's exhausted his fury, still preposterous and sad and honest and hopeless, still undecided as to whether he's more nearly Falstaff or Silenus.

He's neither. He's an original, this out-of-sync singer of earnestly obscure melodies, who prefers to write his verse while seated on a toilet and has "always found it difficult to be insincere." And, in this fourth book of Mr. Burgess's Enderbean Apocalypse, it is the dark lady and the dark lady alone who brings him to pitch. . . .

The novel, as novel, is more nearly patchwork than clockwork. And pretty brazen about it, too. But, now that April's here, it can safely be welcomed by all those Burgess fans who simply cannot conceive of a world without Enderby.

Walter Kerr, "The Poet and the Pop Star," in The New York Times Book Review, April 22, 1984, p. 10.

LYNTON LESSERDAY

One opens [*The Kingdom of the Wicked*] at random and there one comes upon a character hearing "an octopudium of hoofs" and seeing "a nimbus of dust". Turning and opening again at random we come across a chap who is "untrue to his cognomen". Why, one wonders, does Anthony do this sort of thing. It is most annoying and it does not make him sound like his great hero James Joyce but more like that irritating fellow who uses all those long words introducing the acts on *The Good Old Days* on BBC1. . . . *The Kingdom of the Wicked* is probably the worst novel Anthony Burgess has ever produced. One reviews it only to give warning to the unwary, to those many fans of Mr Burgess's Mr Enderby or of such good, old fashioned "reads" as *Earthly Powers*. They are warned. Shy away from this absolute nonsense about St Paul and the early years of Christianity and the corruption of the Roman Empire.

This is a half-baked mixture of that dreadful film *Caligula* and one of those TV documentary-dramas which tries to retell the New Testament in contemporary language.

Lynton Lesserday, in a review of "The Kingdom of the Wicked," in Punch, Vol. 288, No. 7535, May 15, 1985, p. 63.

GERALD PRIESTLAND

What we have [in *The Kingdom of the Wicked*] is a historical novel about the birth of the Early Church out of the Empty Tomb. According to Mr Burgess—or rather, his narrator—it was empty, right enough, for the simple reason that Jesus did not die on the Cross but revived and let Himself out. Contrary to the tradition of Clement, Origen and Tertullian that Jesus was physically ill-favoured and frail, Burgess's narrator asserts that "He was, by all accounts, a man of immense stature and strength with huge lungs. . . . It was no great act of strength for such a colossus to shove aside the stone that served as a door to his tomb." (pp. 28-9)

Behind the muscular, macho prose there is a basic cynicism about *The Kingdom of the Wicked*. One feels that the author was contracted to write it, so he wrote it, well-researched but without any conviction that the Early Church was either a fraud or a miracle. In a brave but rather humdrum way it took over where Stoicism left off, though from the evidence in the book it is hard to see how it managed to survive the years between Caligula and Constantine. If this is all there was, it does not make sense; and that, I think, is not just the reaction of a believer but will be echoed by many readers who are uncommitted.

Yet of course, being by Burgess, it still makes a good read—especially for anyone addicted to the world of *I, Claudius* and *Quo Vadis*. . . . (p. 29)

Gerald Priestland, "Out of an Empty Tomb," in Books and Bookmen, No. 356, June, 1985, pp. 28-9.

FRANK KERMODE

Most people would call Mr. Burgess a prodigiously fluent writer, but he would demur, pointing out that a professional should be capable of a thousand words a day, which is 365,000 a year, or five moderate-sized books, with plenty of time left over to deal with the input of information required for at least some of the output. It's obvious that his powers of assimilation are, by the standards of normal or normally lazy writers, exceptional. Nor does he squander the knowledge thus acquired: it goes into a TV series *and* a novel or a critical biography. One's admiration for all this prudent industry may sometimes by tempered by a feeling that the product, efficient as it is, lacks aura, lacks the zest we associate with this writer in his more exuberant, less mechanical novels. His last novel-of-the-TV-series, *The Kingdom of the Wicked,* combines Acts and other early Christian evidence with a rehandling of the *I, Claudius* historical material into a large, well-conceived and doggedly executed novel, inventive but also well-researched, and authenticated by a scattering or smattering of Greek, Latin and Aramaic words from his polyglot store. For all its informative energy, the book somehow seems a bit dull.

[*Flame Into Being*, Burgess's] biography of Lawrence is also related to something for television. One may see it as continuing Burgess's survey of his favourite writers (Shakespeare,

Keats, Joyce, Enderby). It required him once again to process a lot of information, the extent of which is suggested by his subtitle [*The Life and Works of D. H. Lawrence*], and by his insistence that you have to take on the whole of Lawrence, all the life and all the works, if you are properly to grasp his importance. Here, though, there is small danger of his simply or routinely rehandling the facts, and this book, for all its oddness, is much better Burgess than its predecessor, partly because Burgess himself comes into it a lot, having a much livelier relationship with Lawrence than with St Paul. . . .

What gives this small but quite ambitious book its quality is simply the freedom of comment and the independence of opinion that a good craftsman may enjoy as he contemplates, without envy, a great one. Lawrence could be silly, and Burgess will say so, though without ceasing to admire him; he will offer rational explanations for irrational conduct and give some account of themes and doctrines he doesn't much like. He will sometimes say that in respect of one thing or another—Lawrence's paintings, for instance—he lacks competence to speak. He even rather oddly excuses himself from sympathy with his subject's Oedipal relation to his mother by saying that his own mother died very early, leaving him free of that supposedly universal plight. But all through the book, however outrageous Lawrence's beliefs and behaviour, however careless and rushed his writing, Burgess is celebrating a stubborn intransigence he greatly admires, and a prophetic nerve that Blake, though very few of his countrymen then or since, would have applauded. And he catches very well the quality of Lawrence's fiction that corresponds to this prophetic power. . . .

For the most part, Burgess treats everything, even the pieces that fall far short of the best, with professional respect. He speaks well of *The White Peacock*, applauding its restraint, and pointing out that it lacks the usual characteristics of a first novel, which Lawrence held back until his third, *Sons and Lovers*. On the second, *The Trespasser*, he is jolly and censorious, disliking its refinement and its merely smouldering sex, but he hasn't the space or inclination to explain how, at that particular moment, the young Lawrence would want to write such a book. On the new, fuller version of *Mr Noon*, which must have become available just as he was at work on the book, Burgess rightly notes that its value lies partly in the testimony it provides that Lawrence in going off with Frieda was moving out of the world of respectability and of conventional cultural aspirations. He was obviously a bit surprised, even shocked, to realise that there was in his partner a guiltless aristocratic libertinism extremely remote from the sexuality of Jessie Chambers or indeed Helen Corke. . . .

On the 'nightmare' war years the book has little to add except a note of sympathy. . . . Of the major works of the war period, *The Rainbow* is called something of a failure, though the work of a great novelist; the *Studies in Classic American Literature* are commended for their amazing novelty, but their merits cannot be properly exhibited in so brief an allusion. Burgess keeps his space, and his enthusiasm, for the other great war novel, *Women in Love*. . . . What he rightly admires *Women in Love* for is the way in which Lawrence desocialises fiction, creating 'naked primitives' who are also civilised, social beings. Though this achievement must owe something to Hardy, it is for Burgess Lawrence's great contribution to the modern: the introduction of the poetry of nakedness into the heavily socialised genre. . . .

His most serious censure is reserved for *Lady Chatterley's Lover*, which he sees as occupying in the Lawrence canon the disgraced position of *A Clockwork Orange* in his own. That Lawrence's most notorious book should also be so generally misread is, according to Burgess, the novelist's own fault, since he made it difficult for people to read it as an exaltation of fidelity and chastity (among other things) by including the forbidden words, and especially 'fuck'. (p. 7)

Burgess says the book is longer than he at first meant it to be, and yet it is possible to say that it is too short. He often quotes a passage he thinks especially fine or characteristic, but rarely says enough about why it is so. Some of the more dubious beliefs he is content to adumbrate rather than discuss with the energy he gives to the sexual questions touched on above. Yet his book, though very personal and, where it chooses, opinionated, seems truly lacking in self-interest, a genuine tribute, sent, with deep respect, from one thousand-word-a-day man, living in exile out of disgust for his beloved country, to another who did the same, more restlessly, more absurdly even, yet not less patriotically. And the homage is properly formulated: Burgess's book never ceases to remind one that Lawrence was a great writer, and that argument about him should always begin from a shared assumption of that greatness. (p. 8)

Frank Kermode, "Lawrence and Burgess," in London Review of Books, *Vol. 7, No. 16, September 19, 1985, pp. 7-8.*

JOHN CROWLEY

Simone Weil once noted an intractable literary problem: in literature goodness tends to appear banal, dull and colorless, and evil seems thrilling, fulfilling and rich—while in life it's just the reverse. This problem must necessarily be hardest to solve when the author sets, as Anthony Burgess does in [*The Kingdom of the Wicked*], an enterprise of absolute, even divine, goodness against one of history's great examples of wickedness.

The Kingdom of the Wicked takes up where Mr. Burgess's *Man of Nazareth* left off, with the apostles of Jesus in a state of dismay and wild hope after the Crucifixion. It is narrated by the son of the skeptical Jew who narrated the earlier novel, and follows very closely the events related in The Acts of the Apostles in the Bible: how the tiny Nazarene sect was persecuted by orthodox Judaism and the Roman Empire, how it became a religion chiefly of gentiles, and how Peter and the original leadership were eclipsed by the vigorous evangelizing of Paul.

That's the good. The evil is taken out of those horrific (and tendentious) Roman histories of Tacitus and Suetonius that tell of the lurid misdeeds and endless bloodlust of the last Claudian emperors and their wives, Caligula, Nero, Messalina and the rest. Mr. Burgess—or his narrator, rather—retells these scandals with straightforward credulity, just as he retells the miracles and blessings that accompanied the disciples' missions. He takes exception to very little, and since the style of the book is no careful counterfeit of classical writings, as Marguerite Yourcenar's *Memoirs of Hadrian* was, but is written in a very modern and Burgess-like voice, it seems that it is Mr. Burgess who takes no exception to the extraordinary story he has to tell.

But if the moral oppositions and the pious anecdotes are not different from those of a dozen old novels—*The Robe, The Silver Chalice, Quo Vadis?*—the tone is utterly lacking in the solemnity that once seemed mandatory. The supper at Emmaus, the Pentecost, the healings and visitations and exorcisms are completely matter-of-fact, and some miraculous events—the raising of Dorcas from the dead is one—approach slapstick. As one solution to the Weil problem, this method holds the attention, but the fire of mystic apprehension, the sense of living in the last days before the world's destruction and renewal, is missing almost entirely from these Christians. And this earthbound quality paradoxically makes the story seem even more extraordinary: sometimes, indeed, downright unlikely. . . .

The Kingdom of the Wicked is not Mr. Burgess at the top of his bent. It is not schlock. It is too individual, too original for that; but unlike one or two of his other historical pieces (*Nothing Like the Sun, Napoleon Symphony*), it can't be immediately classed as literature. You might call it "glitterature." But Mr. Burgess does expend much wealth of language, wit and energy, and marshals masses of intriguing and funny historical detail, and in the end his two-dimensional cartoons pile up to make an almost three-dimensional world.

> John Crowley, "St. Paul Meets Nero," in The New York Times Book Review, *September 22, 1985, p. 20.*

CECELIA HOLLAND

The noble scale and huge moral theme of such a project [as *The Kingdom of the Wicked*] demands a writer of considerable skill, and Burgess writes wonderfully well. The surface of his book, as in all his novels, flashes with intelligence, with wry wit, with presence, with style. Unfortunately the substance is amazingly trivial.

For one thing, in writing about the Caesars, Burgess invites, foolishly, comparison with Robert Graves, whose *I, Claudius* deals with the same material.

The great dynasty that Julius Caesar founded reached the seat of ultimate power and its members immediately set about destroying one another; the decline and fall of this extraordinary family marks the beginning of the terrible collapse of ancient civilization. Graves, through his profound knowledge of and

empathy for the ancient world, penetrated the monstrous deeds of individual people to expose an underlying crisis, the fundamental disjointing of society.

Without some such resonance of meaning, the careers of such as Tiberius and Caligula are grotesque and crazy, a black comedy. Burgess has always had a taste for black comedy, and yielding to it here he lets it drown his story. . . .

If Burgess had developed some idea here of what was going wrong with Rome, of how the traditional ways were failing these people, he could have shown why the doctrines of Christ and Saint Paul had such a widespread appeal.

The first Christians lived in daily expectation of the Second Coming and the end of the world, yet none of this apocalyptic intensity comes through in this novel.

Burgess has chosen to place a narrator between his readers and his plot, a narrator of ironic detachment and very little commitment, whose physical and intellectual distance from events makes even miracles seem humdrum. The Apostles are mouthpieces, actors, who've read the script and know what happens next.

Kingdom of the Wicked is a television show in disguise, **"A.D."** in hardcovers. Exactly what is missing here are the complexity, the depth, the difficulty of real fiction. . . .

Rome was "the kingdom of the wicked," as the Jews called it: a vacuum, a negative, the world made blind and stupid by sin, the absence of Christian love. Yet, to save the people of this same kingdom, the saints of the early Church subverted the Jewish bedrock of their faith and borrowed rituals like baptism and concepts like the Holy Spirit from the very same pagan religions they abhorred.

There's a great story here, but Anthony Burgess has not written it. *Kingdom of the Wicked* leaves Christianity as it began: a mystery religion.

> Cecelia Holland, "Anthony Burgess and the Fall of the House of Caesar," in Book World—The Washington Post, *October 6, 1985, p. 9.*

Peter Carey

1943-

Australian novelist and short story writer.

Carey has earned critical respect for his first three works: *The Fat Man in History* (1974), a collection of short stories, and the novels *Bliss* (1981) and *Illywhacker* (1985). He is praised for his inventive mixture of the fantastic and the ordinary, which he renders in an exuberant yet controlled prose style. Carey commonly creates detailed, realistic settings into which he introduces surreal and fabulous events. He often satirizes contemporary social values and explores through comedic devices the illusory nature of reality. In addition, Carey self-consciously examines the art of fiction in much of his work.

Most of the stories in *The Fat Man in History* depict individuals who experience sudden anxieties when they encounter surreal events in commonplace situations. In other stories, Carey satirizes the effects of technology and foreign influences on Australian culture and society. In *Bliss,* Carey centers on a man who dies for nine minutes and has an out-of-body experience through which he observes family members and friends involved in unseemly activities. Carey uses black humor and satire to examine hypocrisy and moral poverty in contemporary society. While much of this work is related in straightforward, realistic detail, the allegorical plot transports Carey's protagonist from the "hell" of contemporary suburban life through a mental hospital and eventually to a blissful life in a rain forest.

Illywhacker, Carey's most ambitious work, is an expansive comic novel that relates the adventures of Herbert Badgery, a man who claims to be 139 years old. The novel's title is an Australian slang expression variously defined as "taleteller," "trickster," "con man," and "liar," all of which describe Badgery's main talents. A central focus of this novel involves the art of lying; Badgery lies constantly in order to survive and improve his life, and Carey employs lying as a metaphor for writing fiction. The picaresque adventures of Badgery are related to Australian historical themes: Badgery was born near the time of Australia's independence from Great Britain, and the book's epigraph is a quote by Mark Twain: "Australian history does not read like history, but like the most beautiful lies. . . ." While introducing many characters and events and developing an intricate series of symbolic references involving animals, Carey explores such themes as colonization, technology, and human relationships. Most critics praised *Illywhacker* as a major work of Australian fiction. D. J. Taylor called the novel "a masterpiece of comic invention, a ragbag of unfocused events given connection and design by symbolic coat-pegs negligently distributed through the text."

© 1986 Thomas Victor

CARL HARRISON-FORD

The Fat Man in History was the *succes d'estime* of 1974. The twelve stories in the collection are in fact fairly uneven and their range could even suggest the work of more than one author or a confused one. But at all times there is an assurance and a precision in the prose that is stunning in itself and for its sustained pace.

Apart from Carey's exemplary prose, the factors going for him are his effortlessly diverse imagination and the skill with which he incorporates and controls it. In **"Withdrawal"**, the story of a necrophile antique dealer who deals in corpses, severed limbs and the paraphernalia of death, the chance comes to sell the complete tableau—House with Undiscovered Corpse. But the gruesome trail of events gets complicated and then resolved by a series of even more extraordinary events—including the presence of a junkie pig, addicted after eating junkie shit—that have seemed disparate but which dovetail.

At the more mundane level of passing images, the stories are equally well constructed. The shadow images in **"Report on the Shadow Industry"** lead effortlessly to the broader implications about writing. The crewcut like worn carpet on the American soldier going rationally insane as he patrols a base in central Australia takes on a suggestive presence without becoming too much a key image or a talisman. The truck mentioned early in **"American Dreams"**, and seemingly of no real importance, suddenly becomes a rational means of transport when the action speeds up and transport is needed. Time and again, the raw materials for the action are incorporated with enough ease to suggest sleight of hand.

"**American Dreams**" is an extraordinarily good story. It tells, briefly, of a retired man in a small town who builds a scale model of it which the inhabitants find only after his death. Once embarrassing exhibits have been removed it becomes important for the American tourist trade, but the tourists' expectations of the originals are restricting and stultifying. However, characteristically for Carey, the implications are enormously diverse as a sense of lazy nostalgia, dreams of America, revelation, invasion combine to give the thirteen pages a novelistic complexity.

Carey's success, generally again in the longer stories, swamps the lesser stories and makes *The Fat Man in History* one of the key books in recent Australian fiction. (pp. 43-4)

> Carl Harrison-Ford, "New Australian Fiction," in Stand, Vol. 16, No. 3 (1975), pp. 40-4.*

BRUCE BENNETT

Peter Carey's first collection of stories, *The Fat Man in History* (1974) stamps him as the major talent among . . . new writers. Literary parallels can be discerned, in particular Barthelme, Vonnegut, and Evelyn Waugh, but the shaping imagination is Carey's own. He is a true fabulator according to Scholes's criteria, one whose inventive, witty fictions both delight and instruct. By leading his readers out of the "real" world Carey enables them to look back on its everyday concerns with new eyes. In "**Conversations with Unicorns**" for instance, the first person narrator recounts his several meetings with these mythical beasts. The matter-of-factness of tone, attention to detail, and consistency of logic compel our belief in the fiction and its consequences. Man's destructive tendencies and his naive unawareness of the consequences of his actions are skilfully revealed, as is the possibility of his madness. (p. 363)

These stories set up anti-utopian situations: they satirise an increasingly technologised and Americanised society. In "**American Dreams**" an apparently conventional shire clerk in a country town "goes mad" in his retirement and builds a high wall around his house on top of a hill overlooking the town. When he dies the townspeople discover behind the wall a perfect replica of their town, which reveals hidden truths about each of them. They are doubly repaid for their "American dreams" of wealth and fame by an influx of American tourists who expect the inhabitants to remain frozen in the postures that have made their town famous. Carey's fertile imagination and narrative skill do away with the need for the verbal or structural gimmickry that has sometimes marred modern experiments in short fiction. He is a true fabulator. (pp. 363-64)

> Bruce Bennett, "Australian Experiments in Short Fiction," in World Literature Written in English, Vol. 15, No. 2, November, 1976, pp. 359-66.*

DAVID GILBEY

Beneath the matter-of-fact tonal surface of Peter Carey's prose in *The Fat Man in History* is a control sometimes deadly (if not horribly) serious and at other times crazily fantastical. The writing reads simply. It is idiomatic and colloquial (not the archetypal Australian bush vernacular of Lawson and Rudd, or the more contemporary suburban clichés of Buzo and Williamson, but)—a kind of international argot which is commonplace and not particularly articulate. It is almost wearily bored, pedestrian. . . . And yet the stories are carefully composed, like a painting. (p. 467)

[In "**Peeling**," the] persona tries to peel back the layers of his relationship with a mysterious woman named Nile (goddess, slut, nurse, murderess) to discover what is "real" and to try to discover her "true self". Carey is preoccupied with a metaphysical and logical problem as much as trying to unravel threads of metaphor. Like a predecessor in Kafka's *Metamorphosis*, the more the persona tries to unravel the threads, the further embroiled he is in the web of a surreal nightmare. (p. 468)

During one particular conversation, Nile makes a couple of remarks the "thread" of which the narrator is reluctant to pick up for fear of "unravelling the whole sweater". In an attempt to soothe Nile, the narrator, out of a sense of tenderness and ritual adoration begins slowly to undress her—and finds himself rushing it. Peculiarly, there are lots of clothes to remove—a shawl, a coat, a football jumper, a blue cardigan, three blouses, two skirts, a petticoat, stockings and girdle. Then, as he pulls off her earring, it seems to be a zip and Nile's face, then her breasts are peeled away. A young male handling his penis stands before the narrator who sees a second earring, pulls it and peels away the male layer, revealing a slimmer tauter Nile than before. As he unrolls the stockings she now has, so her legs unroll. At a touch her hair, hands, limbs fall away. The trunk falls to the floor and shatters. Among the fragments the persona notices "a small doll, hairless, eyeless and white from head to toe".

The story is tightly written and unashamedly rich in ambiguous meanings. What is the real Nile? Who is she? Does the undressing (or something like it) really happen or does the persona's imagination take over completely? In one sense Carey has performed a spectacular *reductio ad absurdum* by peeling back layers of meaning (cf. clothes) only to find, not the "real" person but several possible realities the final one of which (the broken doll) parodies the very attempt. That is, the story is a trick played on a reading public which cautiously suspends disbelief to try to enter the brittle fantasy world of fiction.

It is a tribute to the success of "**Peeling**" that we believe in it sufficiently to follow it through in such a short space. The colourless evenness of the prose is consistent with the continual emphasis on white (persona's hair; Nile's dolls, neck, association with milk, etc.) which creates both a static and a fruitful environment. Its deadpan tones also create a sense of the lonely, self-critical world of an old man on the fringe of society, but not an unbelievable eccentric. Hence we accept its reality from this social base although its full impact is an imaginative one.

"**Peeling**" suggests the nature of the fictional world of the stories in this book and to some degree the techniques Carey has employed in writing them. . . . The stories invite belief and imply empirical development and extenuation. Most of them dramatize layers of a persona's mind or situation. Carey does this by unfolding the perceptions of a persona through whom either directly in the first person or indirectly through a kind of oblique consciousness, each "story" is perceived. It is in the course of this imaginative awareness that the reader gets caught up in an ambiguous and often frightening solipsism. Thus, for example, in "**Withdrawal**" we are drawn into a guarded sympathy for Eddie Rayner "a pornographer of death" who exhibits shocking and obscene photographs and *objets trouvés* in a notorious backroom. Gradually we begin to distrust Eddie's credibility (he exaggerates his enemies' faults) but are drawn ineluctably into the freaky, coprophiliac hallucinations. When his companions desert him we are abandoned too, and left floundering in Eddie's nightmares which we have accepted as plausible but now see as insane.

Most of Carey's personae are introspective failures like the old man of **"Peeling"** or the weak, down-and-out traveller of **"Room No. 5"** or at least victims of an institution or a society (e.g. the soldier posted at an unidentified border in the middle of the Australian desert, **"A Windmill in the West"**). Often they are anonymous or given names which while appropriate, do not reveal the person or invite intimacy. Most are fighting against a "them" of some kind (e.g. small town prejudice and suspicion in **"American Dreams"**; the "Shadow Industry"; the "Committee" ruling the world of the fat men) and have little control over their own destinies and environment. The macrocosm is viewed from within a microcosm and the outside world appears darkly absurd. The perspectives adopted are those of the outsider, the minority, the freak . . . the fat man. (pp. 468-70)

The Fat Man in History has already established its reputation in literary circles and Peter Carey's talents have been recognized by other writers such as Frank Moorhouse and Barry Oakley. The book *is* impressive; it dramatizes some of the dark myths beneath uncertainty and anxiety in contemporary life and does so with deadly, though not humourless, seriousness. His work is intricately and surreally resonant and stands out markedly amongst contemporary Australian writing. (p. 471)

> *David Gilbey, "Experiments in Narrative," in Southerly, Vol. 37, No. 4, December, 1977, pp. 461-74.**

NEIL PHILIP

[Carey's stories in *The Fat Man in History*] prove him capable of a sustained, controlled intensity of a very special order. His writing is disturbing but not depressing, for it is shot through with a dry, unnerving wit. Carey writes with a taut deliberation which shades at times into poetry. **"The Last Days of a Famous Mime"**, for instance, is compressed almost to the point of dispensing with character and plot; yet both actor and story are brilliantly implied. The stories take a wide variety of subjects, but they are linked by the way in which they distort our known world into something unknown yet still frighteningly applicable, and by the way in which they hint at unhappy truths: that we are all manipulated, all foolish, all alone. The fat men in the title story think they are survivors, scavenging off a society in which to be fat has suddenly become a crime; really they, and by implication the reader too, are just the subjects of a monstrous controlled experiment in psychology. . . .

All the stories in *The Fat Man in History* could loosely be termed science fiction, and their use of the genre's conventions to probe ideas and relationships is incisive and ironic. . . . Certainly these grim, funny, disciplined, inventive stories reveal a talent to watch.

> *Neil Philip, in a review of "The Fat Man in History," in British Book News, February, 1981, p. 117.*

JUDY COOKE

'Harry Joy was 39 years old and believed what he read in the papers.' Peter Carey's hero [in *Bliss*] is a happy innocent; he remembers his childhood as a Vision Splendid, indulges his wife and children, and is universally regarded as a Good Bloke. Then he dies—only for nine minutes, it's a heart attack—and wakes up in Hell. His wife is unfaithful, his partner's a rat, his son pushes drugs, his daughter sells herself, his advertising company promotes products that cause cancer; Aldo, head waiter at Milano's, actually laughs when an elephant sits on Harry's car. Yes, an elephant. Carey's short stories explored a talent for the fantastic and the surreal; his first novel is even better than might have been expected, a sustained and sardonic fable on the folly of being wise.

Hell turns out to be an Australian provincial town 'on the outposts of the American Empire'. Harry cautiously observes it and classifies it; certain that his only chance of survival lies in Being Good, he fires his largest client, Krappe Products, and is promptly committed to Alice Watson's mental hospital, an institution run on the principle that 'mental illness is a business, just like any other'.

Against these torments (which are narrated in faultless, elegant prose) Carey provides a saviour: hippy Honey Barbara, 'pantheist, healer, whore'. . . . Honey is to Harry as Isis to Osiris, as Diana to Charles; together they conquer Hell and retire to the forest, where their children inherit the legend of paradise regained. Perhaps it takes an Australian to revive English romanticism? We have novelists of Carey's calibre who are like him in being both sceptical and inventive; they can turn a pretty moral and often cut sharp and deep. What they lack is the sense of profusion and celebration that comes spilling out of *Bliss*.

> *Judy Cooke, "Paradise," in New Statesman, Vol. 102, No. 2644, November 20, 1981, p. 22.**

FRANCIS KING

Mephistophilis's stonily despairing 'Why this is hell, nor am I out of it', in Marlowe's *Dr Faustus*, might stand as a suitable epigraph for this remarkable first novel [*Bliss*].

The protagonist, Harry Joy, is a successful advertising executive (Mr Carey himself works, part-time, in advertising) in some subtropical country near to the United States both spatially and spiritually and yet not of it. . . . Then, felled by a coronary at the age of 39, he 'dies' for nine minutes, during which his spirit, floating free of his body spreadeagled on the lawn of his suburban home, has a vision of Heaven and Hell—in neither of which he has ever believed before.

While subsequently submitting to open-heart surgery, he 'dies' again on the operating-table and, when he comes round, 'ripped with huge wounds, a vast punishment down his chest', it is in the conviction that he is now in Hell. . . .

His eyes opened at last, he sees what previously had been concealed from him. . . . All the people around him are hypocritical, venal, dishonest, brutal or vengeful, with the exception of a tough, beautiful country girl, Honey Barbara, who each year leaves her home in a primitive community in a rainforest in order to descend into the Hell of the city, to sell both her body and pot.

There follows a section, both comic and horrifying, in which, disquieted and angered by this man, now a stranger, who seems always to be passing moral judgments on them, Joy's family have him certified and confined in a lunatic-asylum, the director of which is a tough, unhappy woman, convinced that mental illness is merely a growth industry from which money can be minted with the right mixture of ruthlessness and cunning. In this circle of hell, Joy becomes filthy from neglect, lethargic from drugs, and fearful from the constant threat of

ECT. After many vicissitudes, he buys himself and Honey Barbara, now similarly incarcerated, out of the bin and returns home with her, to a hell more comfortable but no less terrible.... [Barbara] escapes back to her wild, primitive life with her beekeeping father in the rain-forest.

There, after adventures even more ghastly than those that he has suffered already, Joy arrives to join her; and it is in this other Eden, where he works as a woodman and lives with his Eve, fathering children on her, that Hell slowly becomes Heaven for him through a succession of 'days, nights, meals, storms, fires, trees, bees, many things that were tedious, repetitive, as expected as peas uncurling through the red soil.' This final vision of prelapsarian bliss has about it a sentimentality from which the rest of the novel, so remorseless in its exposure of human cruelty, corruption and guile, is mercifully free; and as the author softens, so too, interestingly, does his style, acquiring the texture and taste of a sleepy pear.

Mr Carey is no more a realistic writer than Kafka was; but, like Kafka, he is scrupulous in maintaining both the inexorable logic of every happening and the detailed accuracy of every description. The suburban house, once tidy and elegant and then slowly deliquescing as the lives of its inhabitants deliquesce; the mad-house, with its smells of rotting bodies, floor polish, stale orange peel, urine, chlorine and methylated spirits; the rain-forest, 'the air festooned with creeper like some deserted vegetable exchange': all are evoked with an eerie precision.

In both the breadth of his vision of human life, in all its misery and happiness, and in the profundity of his insight into moral dilemmas, Mr Carey makes the work of most of our 'promising' young and not so young novelists seem tinselly and trivial. Not since Patrick White's *The Aunt's Story* has a novel so much convinced me of the emergence of a potentially major talent.

Francis King, "Suburban Inferno," in The Spectator, *Vol. 247, No. 8005, December 12, 1981, p. 21.*

NEIL PHILIP

A novel called *Bliss,* centred on a character called Joy, concerned with the reality of Heaven and Hell: it sounds dire. But this is no heavy-handed allegory or whimsical trifle: Peter Carey's first novel is as sure-footed and exciting as his recent volume of short stories, *The Fat Man in History....* Harry Joy 'dies' twice for short periods. When he recovers, he is convinced he is in Hell. There are three categories of inhabitants in Hell: 'Captives, like us. Actors. And Those in Charge.' The trick is to work out which is which. This simple conceit allows Carey to maintain three levels of narrative: simple reporting; a symbolic drama of sin, punishment and redemption; and a wickedly funny black comedy.... The ending, in which Joy finds peace with his lover Honey Barbara in a rural, tribal Paradise, is simplistic. Carey is more at home in Hell—especially the mendacious, seductive world of advertising—than Heaven. The Oscar Wilde-like fables Joy tells throughout the book, and understands only at the end, are never convincing as a potent counter-agent to the carcinogens which represent for Carey the moral and spiritual pollution of the technological age. Nevertheless, this is a rich, rewarding novel: crisply written, daringly conceived, brilliantly achieved.

Neil Philip, in a review of "Bliss," in British Book News, *May, 1982, p. 320.*

JUDITH CHETTLE

Most of us, if we think about it, have more precise ideas about what Hell is like than the other place.... Heaven is paradoxically the place of negatives—no disease, no pain, no naughtiness—while Hell tends to be the vivid, highly-colored place, well-illuminated by the eternal fires, populated with interesting people, that captures the imagination. In *Bliss,* his second book, the Australian novelist Peter Carey describes both places, and Hell is again the more memorable....

Harry Joy's Hell is more than the cruel and greedy behavior of people. It is also where they exist: cities full of population, impersonal, air-conditioned hotels, sapping humid weather and unhealthy wet seasons that produce food too water-logged to have any flavor, derelict cars on front lawns, cancer in epidemic proportions and houses whose "timbers are saturated with the ultrasonic hiss of television." A bleak contemporary landscape more universal than Australian and tellingly described by Carey.

Carey is a writer of power and imagination. Harry Joy's descent into Hell and his trip back is a masterful amalgam of black humor, satire, perceptive observation and empathy for Harry, his damned family and his friends. But Carey has also written a book that in its evocation of Heaven and Hell relies on rather trendy answers to the fundamental questions of good and evil. Having so vividly described Harry Joy's anguish on returning from the dead, Carey disappoints us, in this book of serious intent, by portraying Heaven once more as a place of negatives—a pallid, goody-goody place of less than universal appeal whose inhabitants do not like cities, conventional religion nor meat on the dinner table. The people of Honey Barbara's commune while away their time in tasks of repetitive simplicity like digging holes, planting trees and telling stories around the fire.

If Heaven seems rather dull, Hell is surely more than the product of unconscionable collusion between businessmen, ad agencies and Americans. Regrettably, the Hell that most of us know first-hand festers within us, generated by our own impulses and disappointments, and following us the length of our days from culture to counterculture. Carey's *Bliss* has all the virtues of a modern fable and all its vices, but he is nevertheless a writer of impressive promise.

Judith Chettle, "Paradise Lost and Found," in Book World—The Washington Post, *May 2, 1982, p. 8.*

NICHOLAS SPICE

With the publication of his latest novel, *Illywhacker,* the author of *The Fat Man in History* has secured himself a prominent place in the history of the fat book. If you're not normally a fat book reader, you mustn't be outfaced by the fatness of *Illywhacker....*

While some fat books take up the space of several thin ones, spreading themselves over more than their fair share of the available mental furniture, threatening breakages, *Illywhacker* contrives to seem slim. Not that its content is thin, but that its stories are so splendidly tall, making the fatness proportionate and proving again that longueurs have less to do with length than with pace, which Peter Carey controls like a master, thwacking his prose along with all the exuberant free energy of a boy thwacking a hoop with a stick.

To Herbert Badgery—funny man, raconteur and compère extraordinary of *Illywhacker*—the notion that a book might seem slimmer than it is, would be commonplace, that his own book should practise such a trick, inevitable. Sleight of being, or the ability to appear other than one is, is Herbert's natural gift, although the specific techniques of looking bigger and smaller, as well as how to give an impression of great wealth by shining your shoes, and how to modify accents and modulate walks, were taught him back in 1896, when he was ten, by Goon Tse Ying, the Melbourne Chinaman.... *Illywhacker* is Herbert Badgery's account of how he applied these and other arts of seeming to the tricky business of life, managing by their lights to survive to 139 and become the chief attraction of the 'Best Pet Shop in the World', a giant menagerie of Australiana, situated in Sydney, run by his grandson, but owned by the Mitsubishi Company of Japan.

If Herbert really is 139, then he is speaking to us from the year 2025. This contributes to our sense of him as partly a mythical being, but otherwise, except at the end of *Illywhacker,* where the idea of a vague and worrying future helps to lift the story into the symbolic, the exorbitance of Herbert's age plays little part in the book....

Funny men, like books, come in two sizes: fat and thin. *Illywhacker* is a fat book, but Herbert Badgery is a thin funny man: agile, alert, beady-eyed and shifty, dry but slippery—a snake.... Sharp character and charmer, ruffian and trickster, scoundrel and con man, lounge lizard, quandong, ripperty man, shark—in the course of the book, Herbert has many names. To himself he is a liar. To Leah Goldstein he is an illywhacker. And what *is* an illywhacker? It is, she explains, a 'Spieler ... Eelerspee. It's like pig Latin. Spieler is ieler-spe and iely-whacker. Illywhacker. See?'

Of the two definitions, Leah's is the more accurate, because it incorporates the element of play. Herbert's insistence on bundling the total effects of his personality into the one capacious conceptual hold-all, 'lie', is typical of his animus against himself, but it is misleading. For lies are mean and diminishing things, and Herbert is generous and an augmenter. Balancing his compulsive dishonesty is an equally compulsive creativity. Herbert the bullshitter, the salesman of T Model Fords, is also Herbert the builder who can make houses out of the wooden crates they are shipped in. The same genius animates both personae, a genius for invention, the genius of a hessian bag:

> It is my belief that there are few things in this world more useful than a hessian bag, and no matter what part of my story I wish to reflect on I find that a hessian bag, or the lack of one, assumes some importance. They soften the edge of a hard bench, can be split open to line a wall, can provide a blanket for a cold night, a safe container for a snake, a rabbit or a duck. They are useful when beheading hens or to place under car tyres in sandy soil....

Making the most of scarce resources, exploiting the potential of every encounter, turning the least promising situation to good account—such is the principle of the hessian bag, and for Herbert and Leah telling lies is just a way of applying the principle, a strategy for survival, and a source of sustenance and comfort when conditions are poor and the going is not good. Thus, when Herbert is in gaol and Leah is caged by a dismal existence looking after the Kaletskys—Izzie maimed and bitter, Rosa dying of cancer ('suffering that filthy rot that left her all eaten out inside, as light and fragile as a pine long infested with white ant')—Leah saves her sanity through her

imagination, filling volumes of letters to Herbert with a vision of things as they might have been.... Lying to subsist, mind you, has nothing whatever to do with 'subsistence lying', which is simply saying anything that comes into your head rather than admit the truth. What Leah does to get through hard times has a nobility about it, and when Herbert outfaces the railway police by pretending to be tough, his lie is principled and heroic. By contrast, the subsistence lie, being a lie without heed to use and regardless of plausibility or potential, is altogether a low thing and 'has no lasting value no matter how you look at it'. Herbert's idiom when talking about lies, his favourite theme, reveals him as a dedicated professional, a purist and an aesthete—a moralist, no less, of mendacity. In Herbert's view, if a lie is well constructed it deserves the respect of a great building, and a badly-built building is no better than a subsistence lie. Likewise, while a lie can have the beauty of a poem, poetry itself works with the resourcefulness of lies: 'a poem can take any form, can be a sleight of hand, a magician's trick, be built from string and paper, fish or animals, bricks and wire.' Thrift, magic and cunning are, appropriately, the creative forces that govern Herbert Badgery's own great poem, *Illywhacker,* in which the principle of the hessian bag and the energies for life of the lie are definitively exemplified and embodied.

The lie is a wonderful narrative instrument and a powerful generator of funny stories. It makes the distinction between art and reality unnecessary. Whether in a book or in life, a lie is a master key to adventure, unlocking doors to the right and the left of the straight, the schematic and the narrow. Telling a lie is the surest way to turn your life into a story. But, as the Germans are too fond of saying, *'Lügen haben kurze Beine'*— lies have short legs, and this is what makes them such good generators of comic material. When a master liar like Herbert Badgery lets loose a lie, he is able to sustain its running time far beyond its natural capabilities. Once Herbert has told Phoebe that the deadly king brown snake he has just picked up is his pet, he is committed to a ludicrous sequence of risks and responsibilities. The working out of these consequences, interwoven with the consequences of the parallel lie that he is involved in developing the prototype of the Australian aeroplane, generates much of the first book of *Illywhacker.* The process is enthralling because it appears to take place on the page, as though the book were being invented as it went along. It is impossible to convey in a review the cumulative brilliance and accelerating hilarity of Herbert Badgery's prose. He plays the language like Hardy's rustic virtuoso, 'bowing it higher and higher', or like a great jazz improviser, always just ahead of the pulse and galvanising boredom with astonishing syncopations.

If I have given the impression that *Illywhacker* is a rollicking, affirmative sort of book, then it is time I corrected the mistake. Energy, play, life, extravagance, invention are all aspects of Peter Carey's art, and they make *Illywhacker,* in one sense, a refreshing and invigorating entertainment. But the positive forces of the book are expended in the elaboration of a dark, disturbing and unhappy vision. *Illywhacker* is a distasteful book. It gets under the skin. The further one is drawn into it, the more one longs to shake free. The origins of this malaise sit deep in Herbert Badgery. Herbert tells lies to cheer people up, but he is himself far from a cheerful person. Like all good funny men, he lacks a sense of humour. He finds little in life to recommend, and even less in life as it is lived in Australia. Wherever he looks he sees lies, and Australia is the biggest lie of all: the people pretending to be English or American, the buildings pretending to be European, and a history based upon the lie 'that the continent, at the time of the first settlement, was said to be occupied but not cultivated'—justifying the eviction of the aborigines.

Herbert's acute sensitivity to the shams and delusions of what he calls 'this lonely rotten world' is one of the chief spurs to his own dishonesty. He lies to harmonise with creation, to defeat lies with lies, to replace an ugly sham with a less ugly sham. His iconoclasm is radical, his refusal to compromise ascetic. At heart, he is a fanatic truth-teller. This expresses itself in open scorn for the pretensions he finds around him, but it is everywhere implicit in his idiom, in his unflagging insistence on naming every aspect of things as they are. Where most of us flinch from sticking our noses or soiling our hands, Herbert is at home. His imagination reaches out and embraces the insides of filthy pockets, the undersides of carpets, the contents of bathroom pedal bins, the basket of dirty underwear. No indignity is allowed to be suppressed: unwashed sheets and unmade beds, ties stained with luncheon gravy, fingernail-bitten hands, urine and vomit, tummy rumbles and globs of spittle, liquid shit and giant unflushable turds, bile and warts, farts and scaly skin. Herbert's similes are invariably bathetic, keeping the general style low. . . . (p. 20)

Against all the nastiness, cruelty, strangeness and pain, *Illywhacker* invokes one supremely healing value: kindness. 'If kindness is not the point, what point is there?' Jack McGrath's plea is reformulated over and over again throughout the book. The tragedy for Herbert Badgery is that, never having had kindness as a child, he does not know how to attract kindness as an adult. . . . The pattern of abandonment in his life is cruel. Each time it is repeated, it provokes a terrible anger. . . . Herbert contends that no one allows him to be himself, that his lies and performances are forced upon him. But the real motivation of his lies is emotional deprivation, his lack of a mother, his lack of mothering. Herbert tells lies to hide his true feelings. They are his revenge upon a world that refuses to meet his needs, his instrument of power to control it. As strategies of omnipotence, Herbert's lies grant him temporary satisfactions, but at the cost of a deep loneliness and a fear that he may in fact be an evil, unkind man.

The roots of Herbert Badgery's personality are damaged, and it is this which ultimately limits the scope of *Illywhacker*. Herbert dominates the book. Even Charles Badgery is really a way of defining Herbert—a necessary antithesis. Wherever the narrative strays from these two characters to fill in the background, the spark in the writing fades, the energy flags. Peter Carey writes most truly in the voice of Herbert. But the very qualities that make Herbert such a strong and distinctive character also preclude his being taken as representative, whether of humanity in general or Australians in particular. There are other ways of looking at life and other ways of looking at Australia. In an extraordinary interpolation, *Illywhacker* acknowledges this limitation. While Herbert is in hospital suffering the after-effects of a stroke, Leah Goldstein finds the notebooks in which he has been writing the book. What distresses her about what she reads is not that Herbert has plagiarised her own writings, but that he has distorted what he has stolen, turning all the sweet things sour, or simply leaving them out. 'And why have you been so unfair to us, to yourself most of all? . . . You have treated us all badly, as if we were your creatures.' It is as though Peter Carey were talking to himself.

In time (probably in a week or two), *Illywhacker* will be seized upon by the academic establishment in 'English' literature and subjected to intensely competitive manipulations. Like *Tristram Shandy*, it will become a Venus fly-trap for the buzzing PhDs. They will write of it as moral philosophy (invoking Sissela Bok), as a discourse upon Book Ten of the *Republic*, as a commentary on *Le Neveu de Rameau* and the *Paradoxe sur le Comédien*, as a brilliant experiment in textuality, as an instantly self-deconstructing text. 'Am I a prisoner in the midst of a sign or am I a spider at its centre?' asks Herbert innocently, pondering the position of his bedroom window in the middle of the neon lights that announce the best pet shop in the world. He won't have to stay long for an answer.

Meanwhile the large numbers of people outside academia who will buy and enjoy *Illywhacker* will do so because Herbert Badgery is a great fictional character, but mainly, I think, because of his irresistible and addictive style. This in the end is where the quality of the book lies. (pp. 20-1)

Nicholas Spice, "Phattbookia Stupenda," in London Review of Books, *Vol. 7, No. 7, April 18, 1985, pp. 20-1.*

ANDREW HISLOP

Peter Carey's first published novel, *Bliss*, began with a death, that of Harry Joy, a benign, complacent advertising executive who has inherited some of the talents, or at least some of the tales, of his story-telling father. . . .

Carey's massive, ambitious new novel, *Illywhacker*, a comic mixture of myth and history, tall stories of small town life and telling moralities of city society, starts with a painfully and implausibly extended life: "My name is Herbert Badgery. I am a hundred and thirty-nine years old. . . . It is hard to believe that you can feel so bad and still not die." Badgery also tells tales—whoppers. He is a true illywhacker: conman, trickster, liar ("illywhacker" derives, according to *A Dictionary of Australian Colloquialisms*, from "spieler", teller of tales, swindler)—and our narrator.

We are in untrustworthy hands. Tricks are played on us. Badgery slips in and out of the first person narrative. "You have invented yourself Mr Badgery. . . . You can be anything you want", says one of his admirers. Not only Badgery; every character is subject to his whims, even when he is off-stage. They may intrude on the narrative, like another of his lovers, to complain in a letter that he has got things wrong, but their dissent is by his special permission. Death forces upon Joy a reassessment of his subjective view of the world; Badgery's extended life reduces the world to his subjectivity.

For the most part, we are only too glad to have him along as guide. The pity is that the humorous zest of his exploits as youthful but balding trickster are not sustained and he is allowed, if not to die, at least to age into enervation and physical decay. The other characters, not having his narrative authority, can never quite replace him on the stage.

The attenuation of Badgery as a dramatic presence (though not as spieler) coincides with the gradual change in the background of *Illywhacker* from a broad, rollicking historical canvas to a cramped, futuristic vision whose menacing symbolic luggage is lightened only by black comedy. . . .

Illywhacker ends in familiar Carey territory, so successfully delineated in his short stories which economically summon up other worlds far from, yet very near to our own. What is unusual, however, is that it takes 600 pages to get there, and that those pages are preoccupied with a place, only too well known to Carey, which he has hitherto almost completely ignored in his writing: his native Australia.

The locations of Carey's earlier work are mostly nameless or imaginary, often defined only by their relation to another country—usually the Mecca of his modern materialist nightmares, America. This perspective is "colonial" in that its authority depends on the values, accepted or rejected, of an outside power. *Bliss* is situated in "the outposts of the American Empire". The stories **"American Dreams"** and **"A Windmill in the West",** about an American guard on a foreign US base, are also parables of a "colonized" culture. Australia makes an appearance in **"The Puzzling Nature of Blue",** but only as itself the colonizer of a group of islands.

Not surprisingly, themes of colonization abound in *Illywhacker;* colonization is a kind of confidence trick, a game of false identities. Australia is explored in relation to other economically dominant powers—first the British, then the Americans and, predicatively, the Japanese. The country itself, we are reminded, was founded on a lie: that Australia was unoccupied, or at least uncultivated, by its aborigines.... *Illywhacker,* however, does not settle down with the black residents but follows the tourists. There are a host of them....

[They form a] cast of hundreds in a book dizzy with movement. Our picaresque narrator apart, what holds this erupting conglomeration together and promotes its themes is the persistent symbolic juxtaposition and curious symbiosis of two essentials of our lives, whose relationship Carey has already explored in such stories as **"Exotic Pleasures":** animals and machines.

The links between machinery and colonization in *Illywhacker* are direct and obvious. Badgery, aviator and reluctant salesman for Henry Ford, ditches his plane near the picnicing family of Jack McGrath whom he involves in a fanciful plan to build an Australian aeroplane. The project fails because of lack of support from Anglophile backers. A mechanical genius of a farmer also fails to get finance for his new plough. General Motors is given Australian money to build an Australian car but takes the profits out of the country.

This "politics" of machinery is, however, from the first bound up with the symbolism of the animal kingdom. Badgery on landing bags a snake "as silky as 50 SAE motor oil". (As this literary ark fills up, the snake becomes a symbol of the untamed, uncolonized, as opposed to domesticated, mastered animals such as "chooks".) Badgery throws it at the crypto-English would-be plane financiers whom he regards as "rabbits" that the country should be rid of. He tells Jake, who later dies from a snake-bite, of a serpent that makes itself into a wheel before attack, and us of a plane, succulent with castor oil, eaten by cows....

With the failure, however, of Badgery's mechanical indigenes to get off the ground, the animal ones, in particular a host of parrots, rosellas and cockatoos, are increasingly the focus of national identity. Man and beast become, with the help of magic *and* economics, more and more symbolically entwined.

A cryptic schema such as this does injustice, though, to the dazzling heterogeneity of Carey's work. *Illywhacker* has many brilliant moments but in the end it overreaches itself. The performance cannot be sustained, and there is something unsatisfactory about the reduction of the broad canvas. It seems

almost a form of fictional "colonialism", as though Carey's imagination had occupied his homeland, and made hilarious use of whatever it offered, only to deprive it of its vibrant identity by imposing his symbolic interpretation on it. But then there are snakes such as Ouroboros who belie the masterful independence of their species by biting their own tails.

Andrew Hislop, "Whoppers and Warnings," in The Times Literary Supplement, *No. 4283, May 3, 1985,* p. 492.

CURT SUPLEE

The comic novel these days is no laughing matter. As the world seems ever more menacing and less comprehensible, fiction's central characters shrivel accordingly. Too often they are bland, feckless, both or worse ... ; and the "comedy" derives from watching those sensitive but spunkless entities get squashed like bugs on the windshield of life. And too often the humor is fueled by mere hostility ..., the tone shrill, the aftertaste sour.

The grander comic vision, from Rabelais to Dickens, *Huckleberry Finn* to *Garp,* is ultimately compassionate, its protagonists worth our sympathy, its purport auspicious. It gives our vanities and failings a wholesome thrashing, but in the end refreshes our sense of human possibility. Such books are rare and valuable, particularly in this lugubrious era. And such a book is *Illywhacker,* Peter Carey's huge and hugely rewarding second novel.

The title is Australian slang for "confidence man." The man is Herbert Badgery, hero, narrator and madcap patriarch. The con is exquisite: For sheer melodious deceit, Badgery makes W. C. Fields look like Beaver Cleaver. "Lying is my subject, my speciality, my skill"—and his perennial means of survival as ill fate or public outrage drive him from place to place in this exotic picaresque that sprawls across 60 years and three generations of Badgery's eccentric and cunning tribe. He is 139 years old as he begins his life story, and is in no hurry. It will take a quarter of a million words to contain two wives and a mattress-load of consorts; scams aplenty and stints as a carnival performer, aviator, snakehandler, salesman of Model Ts (which he loves for their efficiency and loathes for their foreign origin); surreal vignettes and digressions by the dozen; 10 years in prison for stealing from the mysterious Chinaman who teaches him to become invisible; scores of cameoed characters from florid to doughty to dumb. (pp. 1, 14)

Carey rarely lets a minor character remain minor. Thus the McGrath clan and its history are limned in lavish particular, from mother Molly (daughter and granddaughter of suicides, she is kept sane only by wearing a battery-operated "electric invigorator belt") to her maniacally enthusiastic father Jack, made rich by decades as a bullock-driver, whose jerry-rigged "improvements" to his vintage Victorian house are a neighborhood scandal. Ditto for the decorous Goldsteins, the squabbling Kaletskys, etc. All are portrayed with such affection for their foibles and fantasies and such rich descriptive detail that the novel's world achieves the kind of depth and texture found in Garcia Marquez's *One Hundred Years of Solitude.*

This scope is a function of Badgery's itinerant proclivities. An obsessive nest-builder who wants nothing more than "a place in this rotten lonely world," he is forever erecting dwellings, only to vacate them on the lam. "I was an expert, however, at getting 'put up' "—which he accomplishes with an adjustable amalgam of charm, sexual allure, formidable wile and plain utility.

The last is essential. Traditionally, the con man in literature, from Tartuffe to Melville's deaf-mute to Twain's mysterious stranger, serves to darken our view of human nature. But Badgery is an ethical impostor ("I delivered value in whatever way was required") who regards himself as evil and keeps trying to make amends, however ineffectual. After persuading a farmer to buy a Ford, he is stricken by conscience and refuses to sell it, urging the gent to buy an Australian model instead: "You'd be better off with a worse car if the money stayed here." Whereupon the offended rustic tries to kill him with a poker. . . .

Badgery's elegant deceptions—like the ephemeral jingoisms and pop moral nostrums by which we live, the author suggests—have a magical tonic effect on their audience. Carey's vision is relentlessly ironic, and it is his genius to acknowledge that the same lies which distort our lives also enrich them, fueling our dreams, stoking our resolve and getting the world's work done even if for deranged reasons.

At one point, forced by suspicious burghers to explain his presence in a town, Badgery cobbles together the hasty excuse that he is planning a factory to build the first Australian airplane. To his amazement, the idea ignites the townsmen's ardor. And his, as well. . . . The novel provides a broad catalogue of such inflammatory delusions, from hilarious to pathetic. And it suggests that nations are subject to the same syndrome. "Australian history," says the epigraph from Twain, "does not read like history, but like the most beautiful lies . . . but they are all true, they all happened." . . .

[*Illywhacker*] has an ample metaphorical heft. Themes of appearance and reality are accentuated by images of skin; aspirations and delusions alike find counterparts in persistent references to birds. Moreover, the elder Badgery's history serves as a sort of synecdoche for Australia's evolution. He dates his spiritual birth from a ferocious beating administered by his father, whom he fled in 1895 to become a Melbourne street urchin. (Australia's constitution was drafted in 1897-98; it became a commonwealth in 1900.) Similarly, his financial condition—like Australia's, Carey implies—is invariably determined by some foreign power: first by the British (his father, who masqueraded as an Englishman, worked for a British cannon company), then Americans (Ford Motors, as well as the Yankee hustler who becomes Charles' partner in the pet-export business). And finally by Japanese at the story's appalling surprise conclusion, in which Herbert's original dream of a native-owned enterprise free of colonial exploitation is realized with particularly vicious irony.

Those who make it to the climax will have had to excuse the author's occasional lapses. Carey is a vivid depictor (a magpie's cry sounds like "an angel gargling in a crystal vase"; Izzie speaks in quiet confidence "with a rhythm like soft erratic rain") whose style is never far from overkill, and he is capable of protracted redundancies and sloppy repetitions of unusual words like "verdigris" and "singlet." And though his control of plot is usually masterful, the structure starts to wobble toward the end. Major figures such as Izzie's mother disappear in a single sentence after chapters of attention; yet new characters (notably a superfluous Chinese named Mr. Lo) are introduced to no visible purpose. But given the awesome breadth, ambition and downright narrative joy of this book, these are quibbles. *Illywhacker* is a triumph. (p. 14)

Curt Suplee, "Con Man of the Outback," in Book World—The Washington Post, *August 18, 1985, pp. 1, 14.*

D. J. TAYLOR

The fabulist at the centre of Peter Carey's *Illywhacker* is 139-year-old Herbert Badgery, found reminiscing about a specious and eventful life. "Illywhacker" is demotic for confidence-man, a role Badgery gaily entertains from the moment in 1919 when his Morris Farman lands at Balliary East and introduces him to the entrancing Phoebe McGrath. A brief married idyll ends upon her elopement with Horace, the travelling poet. The novel then fast-forwards to 1931 when Badgery, seven years on the road with his precocious offspring, encounters Leah Goldstein, a dancer of obstinate virtue attempting to support her maimed husband. These are the tornado years. As Badgery and Goldstein Theatricals they traverse the 1930s "like flies on the face of a great painting" until Leah returns to her husband, while Badgery, his world falling apart, revisits his childhood mentor, the scrutable Goon Tse Ying, and abstracts his magical *Book of the Dragon*.

With Herbert sentenced to ten years in Rankin Downs gaol, the novel's focus switches to 17-year-old Charles, "Snake Boy Badgery", and his role in the Great Victoria Mouse Plague. Deaf, cretinous, but likeable, he marries Emma, a teacher rescued from the saurian clutches of a Gould's Monitor. Charles and Emma establish a pet-shop in Sydney and everything prospers until the dreadful afternoon when Emma imagines that Charles has enlisted for war, and the lizard, blithely stepping to freedom from its cage, has a leg excised by an excited fox-terrier. It is a symbolic incident. Emma retreats into the cage and resists extraction, and in a period coincident with Herbert's return the fortunes of the Badgery family, *quondam* owners of the world's greatest pet emporium, go into irreversible decline.

This is only the most restrained summary of a vast, diffuse plot chock-full of luminous characters and incident, in whose arbitrary nature it is possible to detect unflinching ulterior motive. "Illywhacker" is Carey's metaphor for fiction, "a trickster, a ripperty man, a conman"—on one level the book can be interpreted as a debate about truth and the novel. Badgery contends that lies enliven. "You call it a lie. I call it a gift."

True or not (an irrelevant distinction, possibly), *Illywhacker* is a masterpiece of comic invention, a ragbag of unfocused events given connection and design by symbolic coat-pegs negligently distributed through the text. . . . This is a comic novel, and something more. Rereading establishes the fact that Carey has constructed his narrative with beguiling artfulness, confronting the reader on the one hand with a sensation of stories falling off trees on either side of the path, each demanding investigation and comment, on the other a sneaky, manipulative continuity, a panoramic awareness of past and future contingency.

Carey's language is as enterprising as that of the stories contained in *The Fat Man in History*. An umbrella attack on Badgery's Morris Farman does no more damage than "a knife in water"; an old man's skin hangs from his arm "like a roast chicken wing." Form and content, dextrously interwoven, contrive to illumine an entire country. Watching Badgery's dealings with his canny, assured countrymen, noting his complaint that "the country is full of bloody salesmen", we can also speculate that "Illywhacker" is a metaphor for the Australian past. Traditionalists might deplore the obvious contrivance but *Illywhacker* is a dazzling and hilarious book. (p. 52)

D. J. Taylor, "Down Under with Waltzing Jane: Australia in Fiction," in Encounter, *Vol. LXV, No. 3, September-October, 1985, pp. 51-4.**

HOWARD JACOBSON

[With *Illywhacker*] Carey shows he can spin a yarn with the best of them. It's a big, garrulous, funny novel, touching, farcical and passionately bad-tempered. It begins arbitrarily in 1919 as Annette Davidson, who trained in Reading, England, to be a teacher, finds herself earning her living at the Hermitage Church of England Girls' Grammar School in Geelong, Australia. In between she stopped off in Paris, where she had an affair with an obscure Impressionist, Jacques Dussoir. In 1946 she will publish a book about her few months in Paris and say nothing about the 28 years in her reluctantly adopted country.

But Annette Davidson's story is just the first to be told by the narrator, Herbert Badgery, an illywhacker—that is, a trickster or con man—aged 139, give or take the odd half-century. By the time he has told his tale and brought us to the present, Francophilia has given way to whatever the word is for being dependent on the Japanese, and the dreamy reminiscence of Paris nights, 13,000 miles away, has become Robert Hawke-speak, the language of supersalesmanship and the current Australian Prime Minister.

I feared initially that Mr. Carey might have ditched distemper rather too unreservedly in favor of teeming life, miraculous incident, marvels, dragons, myths and an incorrigibly untrustworthy narrator whose fabulosity mirrors that of the Artist himself. He uses all the paraphernalia of that creaking movement known as magic realism, the literature of wonder, which writers who aren't South American (and even some who are) manage very badly. There is a strong whiff of this, a laboriousness of invention sometimes, an overfertility of metaphor, one dragon and one traveling Australian illusionist too many.

Yet reading *Illywhacker* is not unlike spending a week in the company of the best kind of Australian. The stories keep coming, told with deceptive guilelessness and innocence. The talk is bawdy, the jokes are throwaway and rank, the sex is avid but democratic. Withal there is that haunting nostalgia and desolation that seems to be the immutable condition of the country. If you haven't been to Australia, read *Illywhacker.* It will give you the feel of it like nothing else I know.

Howard Jacobson, "Dirty Very Old Man," in The New York Times Book Review, *November 17, 1985, p. 15.*

Fred Chappell

1936-

American novelist, poet, and short story writer.

Chappell is praised for his imaginative use of language and for the philosophical depth of both his poetry and fiction. He is considered a talented stylist whose extensive use of image and symbol contribute to the subtle complexity of his writing. In much of his work, Chappell draws upon the North Carolina mountain region where he has lived most of his life. He describes the lush natural environment and depicts characters who are involved in intense emotional situations. Several critics contend that Chappell's novels belong to the ''Southern Gothic'' tradition, citing their dark, brooding atmosphere and their violent and grotesque elements. Chappell's poetry, like his fiction, is rooted in rural North Carolina; critics note that the power and impact of his verse derives from the deep affection he obviously feels for the area and from the richly varied poetic diction he uses to describe it.

James Christopher, the protagonist of Chappell's first novel, *It Is Time, Lord* (1963), is a disillusioned man whose life lacks meaning and purpose. Considered experimental in its free flow between past and present, this novel juxtaposes images from Christopher's childhood with present-day scenes of idleness, drinking, and infidelity. Although faulted for weak character development, *It Is Time, Lord* won praise for its convincing depiction of a rural North Carolina boyhood. *The Inkling* (1965) concerns a sensitive boy confronted with the pressures of growing up in a disturbed family situation. While noting that the novel contains ''pretensions and verbal lapses,'' Orville Prescott claimed that Chappell ''writes with power and passion and with flashes of humor.'' *Dagon* (1968) centers on a minister who, after moving to a small town with his wife, becomes obsessed with and transformed by a strange, sadistic daughter of a tenant farmer. The book is infused with elements of fantasy, mythology, psychic horror, and violence.

Chappell's next two novels are notably lighter in tone. *The Gaudy Place* (1973), while again located in North Carolina, takes place in an urban rather than a rural milieu. Centered on the residents of Gimlet Street—a seedy district populated by hustlers, prostitutes, and thieves—this novel explores, among other themes, the randomness of life and the ways in which intentions go awry. *I Am One of You Forever* (1985) is an affectionate coming-of-age tale about a young boy in the mountainous region of western North Carolina. In the short stories collected in *Moments of Light* (1980), Chappell explores such themes as justice, the loss of innocence, and moral conflicts, suggesting that art can serve as a means for attaining order and harmony in life. In a laudatory foreword, Annie Dillard characterizes the stories in *Moments of Light* as representing ''man as a whole [as] a fallen innocent and sojourner newly-bewildered in a life of unfathomable moral complexity, a life which engenders in every generation a thousand new forms of injustice.'' Dillard also praises Chappell's powerful depiction of humankind's yearning for order and transcendence.

Although Chappell first attracted critical attention as a novelist, he considers himself primarily a poet. His first volume of poems, *The World between the Eyes* (1971), anticipates his

Photograph by Bob Cavin. Courtesy of Fred Chappell

later work in its inclusion of long, descriptive verse built around his impressions of life in a North Carolina mountain town. *Midquest* (1981), his most highly acclaimed work, comprises four previously published volumes: *River* (1975), *Bloodfire* (1978), *Wind Mountain* (1979), and *Earthsleep* (1980). The four sections are metaphorically structured around the four essential elements—water, fire, air, and earth—and each is ''spoken'' on the poet's thirty-fifth birthday, which he identifies as the midpoint of his life. The poems incorporate a variety of poetic forms and voices, blending past and present, narration, meditation, and dialogue. Kelly Cherry noted: ''[The] narrative thread that binds these four books into one is that of the journey, the voyage, the long wandering among events that edify and reveal.''

Castle Tzingal (1984) represents a departure from Chappell's characteristic poetic technique. A narrative written in the form of a revenge tragedy, this volume combines an eerie medieval setting and an elaborately suspenseful plot with modern language and humor. Reviewers lauded Chappell for his skillful storytelling and the imaginative, compelling language he employs in *Castle Tzingal*. Chappell's recent collection, *Source* (1985), also differs from his previous poetry. The poems in this volume show Chappell working in a more varied, exploratory mode. Chappell shared the Bollingen Prize in Poetry with John Ashbery in 1986.

(See also *Contemporary Authors*, Vols. 5-8, rev. ed.; *Contemporary Authors New Revision Series*, Vol. 8; and *Dictionary of Literary Biography*, Vol. 6.)

GRANVILLE HICKS

[The narrator of *It Is Time, Lord*], James Christopher, begins with reminiscences of his childhood. These are not arranged in chronological order but according to some pattern of association, so that the boy may be three or ten or thirteen. Dreams and made-up stories mingle with memories, and quite different versions are given of the same incident. The uncertainty of memory is one of Chappell's major themes.

Despite a certain deliberate vagueness, the hill-country farm is real enough, and so are its people. James lives with his mother and father, who are schoolteachers, with his grandfather and grandmother, and with a younger sister. The grandparents play a larger part in his life than do his parents. His grandmother is enormously energetic and hard-working, taking most of the responsibility for the management of the farm. The grandfather, a builder, talks to the boy intimately, plays chess and other games with him, and tells him stories.

As James's memories unfold, there are many touches of great vividness. (p. 17)

Abruptly the manuscript shifts to the present, with James in his thirtieth year. He tells the reader something about himself, but this is to some extent an imagined self—he says, for instance, that he is a Methodist minister, which is not true. What we do know about James is that he is in a desperate situation. He has given up his job, drinks too much, is unfaithful to his wife.... All and all, he is in a bad way.

The novel now moves freely between past and present. We are given more episodes from James's past, including the death and burial of his grandfather, and new light is thrown on other incidents. As for James at present, his life seems singularly unpleasant. We see his dull drinking companions and the stupid woman with whom he sleeps. He is as disgusted with his life as we are, but he does not know how to change it.

Yet he wants to change, and he is searching his past in order to find some guidepost for his future, but the search is difficult.... (pp. 17-18)

I must admit that not all of Chappell's philosophizing about the relationship between past and present is clear to me. Furthermore, I am not sure how James got into the mess that he is in. Nor do I understand the ending: has James found a solution of his problems, and, if so, how? Chappell has tried hard to be both profound and subtle, but I am afraid that some of the time he is merely obscure.

Nevertheless, in spite of these reservations, I like the novel very much.... [The] writing is fresh and vigorous. Chappell has a sharp eye for telling details, and his imagery is powerful. Although I feel confident that he will write better novels than *It Is Time, Lord,* this is by no means a bad book. If the self-searching hero sometimes loses himself and us in morasses of speculation, he is at other times perfectly clear and wholly alive. Chappell has many gifts, and it will be interesting to watch him bring them to maturity. (p. 18)

Granville Hicks, *"Thirty Years with a Stranger,"* in Saturday Review, *Vol. XLVI, No. 31, August 10, 1963, pp. 17-18.*

DENIS DONOGHUE

I think of style as 'heavenly labials in a world of gutturals', Wallace Stevens's phrase driven beyond his contract only a little outrageously. Or, from the same context, 'veracious page on page, exact'. This is to say that Fred Chappell has style. *It is Time, Lord* is beautifully written, page on page; written, composed, balanced from word to word. This is to say that Mr Chappell is an artist, a stylist, that his way with words gives the same kind of delight as the different ways of John Crowe Ransom or Janet Lewis or, on his good days, Saul Bellow. Mr Chappell's story began as a sketch called 'January', about a boy, James, his young sister, Sandra, and a group of displaced men in North Carolina. In the novel the girl is Julia, James has grown up to read Nietzsche, Blake, Tolstoy and Eliot, the displaced men turn out to be escaped convicts, and North Carolina has gone the way of Texas in *Hud*. James has given up his job for no official reason; he drinks too much, reads pulp and tries to write. In the novel he declares himself and his themes: the stain of the past upon the present page, the counterfeiting of memory, the hope of understanding what has happened. Finally, released from the ghosts, he buries his dead.

It is a remarkable first novel.... *It is Time, Lord* is not faultless. For one thing, James's wife Sylvia is poorly imagined, holy, fair and wise to an incredible degree. Most of the other characters emerge with remarkable vitality, especially James's mother and his grandfather. (p. 811)

Denis Donoghue, *"Style,"* in New Statesman, *Vol. LXIX, No. 1784, May 21, 1965, pp. 811-12.**

ORVILLE PRESCOTT

The Inkling is a work of genuine talent and a good one of its kind. The question is: Is its kind rewarding reading? ...

[*The Inkling*] is further proof of Mr. Chappell's ear for dialogue, his skill in suggesting an atmosphere of emotional tension and impending disaster, his love of words. But *The Inkling* is in some ways a curiously unsatisfactory performance.

Instead of a story about people one can understand and care about it is a story about people as doomed by fate as Oedipus or Electra. One never feels that these are human beings doing their poor best to cope with their troubles. They are victims of the cruelty of life sternly manipulated and maneuvered by Mr. Chappell. And in superfluous addition, Mr. Chappell has opened and closed his novel with scenes that twist time out of order and confuse with unexpected fantasy. The trickery is ingenious, but labored and artificial.

This is the story of the Anderson family that lived in a six-room house on the outskirts of a town in Western North Carolina. The father had been killed at Pearl Harbor. Jenny Anderson, always called "the mother," was gentle, patient, loving, exhausted, helpless and passive. She worked as a secretary in the paper mill. Her worthless brother, Uncle Hake, also worked at the mill. A glum, stupid, malevolent alcoholic, Uncle Hake "lived in the languorous luxury of blind ignorance." Timmie, the daughter, was abnormally timid, dependent on her brother for comfort and protection. Jan, a silent, fierce, imaginative boy, did his watchful best to care for his sister, but could do nothing to prevent her descent into madness.

Although Mr. Chappell never allows his readers to see very deeply into the minds of any of his characters, he deftly portrays them in speech and action. Uncle Hake is contemptible. "The mother" is pitiful. Jan is enigmatic, capable of drastic and melodramatic action. Timmie is pathetic when little, alarming when demented. Mr. Chappell's excursions into the dreams and hallucinations of the mad Timmie are dark and confusing. But through the murky gloom clues appear which pave the way for future events.

The Inkling is flawed by laborious figures of speech and spotted with recondite words: xanthic, intemerate. It does not command unquestioning belief. But it casts a spell of its own. Mr. Chappell writes with power and passion and with flashes of humor. His book holds one's attention and inspires respect.

Any writer who can produce a book as good as this can surely produce a better one. Stripped of its pretensions and verbal lapses, *The Inkling* would be a chilling melodrama. Endowed with more human warmth and depth of individual character, it would be moving. As it is, *The Inkling* is brilliant, but unsatisfying.

> *Orville Prescott, "Brilliant, but Unsatisfying," in* The New York Times, *August 11, 1965, p. 33.*

CARMEN P. COLLIER

[*The Inkling* is a] short complex novel with a fine sense of dramatic assurance, disarming simplicity, and disquieting perception. With the opening words, the aura of fatality is recognized and is subtly built up to a climax of fear, frustration, hopelessness, and violence.

With superb dialogue and striking detail, Mr. Chappell brings together five unlovely characters in a small house in North Carolina in the early Forties. . . .

It is a wondrous piece of fresh and vigorous writing. Mr. Chappell moves smoothly from passions and cruelties to the beautiful imagery of dreams and the musings of a deluded mind. Certainly, this is not a book to be read for entertainment, but for those readers who like good writing, in spite of the subject or the incidents, this is a small masterpiece.

> *Carmen P. Collier, in a review of "The Inkling," in* Best Sellers, *Vol. 25, No. 10, August 15, 1965, p. 204.*

KENNETH LAMOTT

Fred Chappell writes like a whiz, but I finished *The Inkling* with the distressing feeling that I had been there several times before. I don't mean that Mr. Chappell lacks imagination or ingenuity, but only that I cannot promise to keep the peace if I am exposed to another bright young Southern writer who is hooked on incest, barnyard sadism, imbecility and domestic bloodletting.

The characters include a blond young boy who is doomed by the circumstances of his life: his older sister, a mental incompetent who becomes sexually active; their mother, who dies; their uncle, who owns a pistol and a book of pornographic photos; and a red-haired hill girl with cheerful breasts and

buttocks, who comes to do the housework and stays to marry the uncle and seduce the boy.

There is nothing, in principle, that I object to here, for surely people such as these are as proper subjects for the novelist as any others. Furthermore, it has been amply demonstrated that their lives can be transmuted into fiction that is moving in its revelations of the true condition of the human animal. Yet, it has been done before, again and again, and I can't resist the suspicion that Mr. Chappell, like others of the current generation of Southern novelists, took on this project much as he would a thesis for an M. A., as a demonstration that he, too, can find universal meanings in such a traditional theme as the drab and violent circumstances of country life in the South.

> *Kenneth Lamott, "Deja Vu, Y'all," in* Book Week— San Francisco Examiner, *August 15, 1965, p. 10.*

PETER BUITENHUIS

Dagon is another horse from the dilapidated stable of the Southern gothic novel. It is decked in the time-honored trappings of the breed: the rotting house set in the steaming countryside, the puritanical hero tempted tragically by the flesh, the po' white trash, the beatings, the blood and the death. The question about *Dagon* is whether Fred Chappell fleshes out a winner or merely futilely whips a dead horse.

He has a clergyman for a hero, and this is almost the oldest trick of American gothic romance, but he at least does not preach at his unsuspecting congregation. Peter Leland is on leave from his parish, writing a book to be called *Remnant Pagan Forces in American Puritanism.* Somehow he can't seem to settle down to work in the old house that he has recently inherited from his grandparents. The reason for this is mainly Mina, the sluttish daughter of a moonshine-making squatter on Peter's land. Mina, a witch of the first water, takes a liking to Peter, and it's not long before he murders his pretty blonde wife and shacks up with Mina in the rancid hole where she and her family live. . . .

The style of the novel is of a very high order. Its precise, dry elegance contrasts piquantly with its sleazy material, just as the shy, scholarly Peter himself contrasts strangely with the brutal illiterates who surround him. These contrasts belong, however, merely to the surface of the book. At the fundamental level, they are contradictory. Mr. Chappell does not show adequately why Peter suddenly nosedives from melancholy to mayhem and from scholarship to sadomasochism. . . .

Mr. Chappell has tried to lend depth to his character and story by recourse to literary symbolism. A key figure in Peter's researches into pagan Puritanism is Dagon, the god whom Milton characterized in *Paradise Lost* as "Sea Monster, upward Man! And downward Fish"—a figure who also appears in American Puritan literature. The debased Peter comes to resemble this monster, whom he had once cursed in sermons and studied in books. Again, this contrast seems contradictory. Peter is a cold fish at best, and not a bit like the vigorous pagan fertility god that mythology painted Dagon to be.

Peter's weakness is in fact the central flaw of the book. He has none of the agonized moral fervor of Hawthorne's clergyman, Dimmesdale, nor the rhetorical flamboyance of Hightower, Faulkner's parson. Peter is simply bored and often boring. Though this may reflect a torpor common to our time, it simply won't do as a trait in the hero of a gothic romance, which must either have passion and panache, or founder under the weight of its conventions. In the hands of Mr. Chappell . . . , Southern gothic seems to have provided an opportunity for an academic exercise rather than for a searching analysis of individual conscience and social decay, which is its special province.

Peter Buitenhuis, *"Desire under the Magnolias," in* The New York Times Book Review, *September 29, 1968, p. 58.*

THE VIRGINIA QUARTERLY REVIEW

Witchcraft and murder are but two of the expedients used by the abundantly endowed Mr. Chappell in [*Dagon*], a tale of terror almost Gothic in its atmosphere of absolute dread, decay, and desolation. . . . Symbolism is scattered throughout with almost too heavy a hand, and credulity is sometimes lost for the reader as a result of the author's failure to elaborate upon the weaknesses inherent in the minister's character and to develop even further than he has the element of doom represented by the long-untenanted ancestral home. Whatever defects the story may possess in a technical sense are far outweighed by the brilliance and sureness of the writing. In so tenebrous a yarn Mr. Chappell needs greater length by half and much more diligence in character development to assure conviction and to separate his participants from the status of mere automatons.

A review of *"Dagon," in* The Virginia Quarterly Review, *Vol. 45, No. 1 (Winter, 1969), p. viii.*

EDWARD M. MOORE

[*Dagon*] is an interesting book, if the writing is occasionally careless, but I do not think it finally comes off. If one wants to categorize it, it belongs to the gothic or fantasy tradition of Southern writing, though just plain weird seems a better term (and this is the weirdest of Chappell's three books). His image is Dagon, a fertility god mentioned in First Samuel, a merman in later tradition, broken and left with "only the stump". The protagonist, a Puritan minister named Peter Leland, falls under his power through the agency of a monster, Mina, a figure of the fertility-death symbol: he first sees her after being interrupted as he is about to have sexual relations with his wife. Her house smells "fishlike", it gives the "impression of dark vegetation of immense luxuriance blooming up and momentarily rotting away" and has "the smell of rank incredibly rich semen" (the symbolic associations are rather overdone), and Mina herself looks like a fish. She leads him to the final consummation of the flesh, death. Leland, subconsciously under the power of the image, dreams of murdering his wife as if he were making love to her, a dream of impotence and fertility. He does soon murder her. With this symbolic background as it were, Leland falls complete victim to Dagon and is systematically destroyed through the flesh—by physical torture, having been left mindless long before. (pp. 376-77)

It is an interesting book and an interesting image, but besides some carelessness and awkwardness, the vision as rendered (if I have understood it) seems to me weak. The action becomes too fantastic and is not sustained. The first half of the book is rendered naturalistically. It is only after the episode with the torture instruments (a brilliant scene) that we move into fantasy or gothic, and the natural does not sustain the exploration; at the same time we are not deep enough into Leland's mind to accept the fantasy without the natural. Comparison with Welty (who I should think is a major influence on Chappell) or O'Con-

nor is perhaps instructive: in both of these writers, in their different ways, the fantastic or grotesque is sustained and made believable and meaningful by a consistent blend with the natural setting. The fantastic, or allegorical, or symbolical truth is embodied in the visible world. Another way, frequent in Welty, is to have the action almost entirely in the imaginative world of a character. Here neither is done—in effect we leave one world for another. I don't think this was the author's intention—the action proper is related naturalistically throughout but becomes unbelievable and hence the vision unacceptable. . . . The point of view is central intelligence, but we are only on the surface of Leland's mind. For example, the scene in which Leland murders his wife: the murder is appropriately melodramatic and senseless; there is no other motivation than what we understand Leland has become; Leland is under Dagon's power and this is Dagon's universe. But there is no drama for the reader. If we were deeper in Leland's mind there could be drama there, but the natural details alone do not sustain it. As the novel moves further into the incredible and weird we do not move deeper into his mind where the incredible could be carried. But Chappell is an interesting writer; if I understand him correctly he is trying to take off from Eudora Welty's way of using the world of the imagination but not trying to redo what she has done so superbly. He may bring it off yet. (pp. 377-78)

Edward M. Moore, *"Some Recent Southern Things," in* The Sewanee Review, *Vol. LXXVIII, No. 2, Spring, 1970, pp. 366-78.**

R. H. W. DILLARD

The reasons for [Fred Chappell's] audience in this country's not being larger are not hard to find. In the first place, he is a Southerner, and his novels are set in the mountains of North Carolina. The phrase "Southern Gothic" has all too easily been attached to his work, and that phrase has automatically excluded him from much of the audience he deserves, those readers who savor the wonders and complexities of a Barth or Coover or Hawkes. . . .

And not only is he Southern, but he is Gothic. The landscape of his fiction is most often frighteningly ugly, and it is peopled with grotesques, with grotesques and with ordinary people awash in the flesh, drowning in its pains, suffocating in an absence of spirit. It is a world which, at least at first acquaintance, is as barren and deadly as Lovecraft's Arkham or Kafka's castled K-land. Or, if it is not barren, even its very fecundity can be as deadly. (p. 2)

But, of course, his being Southern and Gothic are not the whole answer. Styron and Price and Dickey, not to mention O'Connor and McCullers and Capote, have made the Southern grotesque quite acceptable and even profitable. The difference between the work of these familiar Southern Gothic writers and that of Fred Chappell is that, despite the clarity and ease of his prose, Chappell is a difficult writer—a consciously, uncompromisingly and originally difficult writer. He is what used to be known as an "experimental" writer, a writer deeply and intensely involved with the complexity of his vision who writes a fiction which demands of its reader an imaginative commitment of an equivalent depth and intensity. Like Alain Robbe-Grillet or John Hawkes or Borges or Nabokov, Chappell demands of his reader that he "read the page, every page, as hard as if it were a letter from a distant, and reticent, lover. Which is, in a way, exactly what a page from a novel is."

The difficulty of Chappell's fiction is further compounded by the nature of his perception. The sources of his understanding are not psychological or social like those of a Thomas Wolfe or a Styron. They are, rather, philosophical. In the early 1920's, Wolfe complained to his notebook that North Carolina seemed incapable of producing any genuine thought.... And so Wolfe, logically enough, set out to devour the whole of the vast world of impenetrable fact that his upbringing seemed to deny him. Fred Chappell's is a new generation, however, one raised on science fiction, to whom the galaxy seems and feels as real and immediate as the stonecutter's lot down the street or the whores at the foot of the hill. They are a generation ready for and at ease with ideas and no longer able to write a fiction which is unaware of the vast curve of space or the lawless variety of sub-atomic matter even though it may be focussed on the conversation in the room or the mysterious events next door. (p. 3)

Edgar Allan Poe, who was also Southern and Gothic and difficult and philosophical, ... felt the need in the preface to the 1840 edition of *Tales of the Grotesque and Arabesque* to assure his readers that his work was not of the school of German "pseudo-horror" which was popular at the time, but rather that "If in many of my productions terror has been the thesis, I maintain that terror is not of Germany, but of the soul,—that I have deduced this terror only from its legitimate sources, and urged it only to its legitimate results." Like Poe, Fred Chappell has deduced his terrors from their legitimate sources; they are not of the South but of the soul, the mind and the heart. If his pages are, as he says, letters from a distant, and reticent, lover, then I should like this essay to be read as a hesitant, uncertain, but very enthusiastic and excited reply. (p. 4)

[It] is in Fred Chappell's new novel, *The Gaudy Place* (1973), that we find the fullest rendering of society, of the social and economic levels of a small town from bottom to top, from A(rkie) to Z(ebulon Johns Mackie). The novel is a tracing of the events leading up to an act of violence, an act comic and trivial in itself but which reveals with a startling clarity the terrible patterns of human striving and knowing.

The novel is comic; its tone is far lighter than anything Chappell has written before, the prose lively and witty. Its characters are the familiar victims of vice and folly that we have come to know from centuries of comic art—Arkie, the fourteen-year-old boy who ranges tawdry Gimlet Street and his fourteen block world looking for a good con; Clemmie, the nineteen-year-old whore tied to her life because the rest of the world seems to her "as flossy and unbelievable as a Technicolor movie"; ... Andrew Harper, ... [the historian] whose "muddied perceptions and not particularly admirable life" have led him to believe in a "humanity helpless because choice is absent"; and Zebulon Johns Mackie, Andrew's uncle by marriage, a corrupt small town political boss and businessman, an expert at urban charading, a gangster who looks like our sentimentalized image of Benjamin Franklin. Assorted characters mixed ready to begin the morning right, and their lives do mix and mingle, all of them ready, for one reason or another, to turn their backs "on this feverish gaudy place for good," all of them knowing that Gimlet Street "could take you anywhere in the world, it was joined to all the other streets there were," but none of them able to leave that gaudy place behind.

Chappell's first three novels, dark in texture, filled with physical and spiritual suffering, all have at center a faith in life, in something inexpressibly larger than the bare self in the barren world. But *The Gaudy Place,* the brightest and lightest of them

all, has at its heart the deepest darkness of them all, for at the center of this exercise in cause and effect is an absence of meaning, of first cause. It is as if, in these lives, design does not govern at all. (pp. 12-13)

The characters in *The Gaudy Place* all feel themselves to be at a turning place, but when the turn comes it is unexpected, and the road leads into a new and strange country quite different from anything they might have dreamed. "I don't know whether a novelist believes finally and philosophically in cause and effect," Fred Chappell admitted to John Graham. "I don't frankly philosophically believe in it.... But, in human terms, I think there is a cause and effect. In sub-atomic physics, I'm sure there isn't." In *The Gaudy Place,* this purgatory without apparent exit, the chaos of the sub-atomic world seems to be the metaphorical figure at the moral center of the novel.

"Anything can happen," Clemmie says when discussing a science fiction book with a barfly named Teacher, "but I don't believe in it." But anything can and does happen, believe it or not. Arkie gets up his courage and tells his dream to Clemmie. When it begins to come true, partly because he told it, she invents a lie to tell back to Arkie. Arkie, who has come to love Clemmie, acts upon her lie, leading Clemmie to believe that she is "on the verge of a strange and important revelation. She was going to know things that she had never known before ... Something big was going to take place and she was going to have a piece of it." And it does, but with consequences neither of them could imagine. Dreams feed fact; new fact gives rise to new dreams which feed new fact; the whole process careening along, a giddy nightmare of cause and effect, unpredictable and formless, the mad world of "anything can happen." (pp. 13-14)

But there is more to the gaudy place than this random mix of blind cause and effect. We do live "upon this lonely blue planet Earth, burning like a sunny atom of dust on the farthest rim of its galaxy," and "The universe is, after all, a gaudy place in which to live." Andrew Harper, speaking of the shooting at the end of the novel, does manage to find a way of coming to terms with events:

> What happened next was at first almost incomprehensible to me—and, in fact, I do not yet understand it. That is, I cannot know the causes and mechanics of the event. But it does take a shape in my mind, it does make itself at least credible. Even at the time it occurred it must have appealed to me as a pattern, for by the time it was over I was laughing uncontrollably.

Laughing out of control, but laughing; unaware of causes and mechanics, but taking pleasure in the shape of things. Andrew Harper's laughter rings with Jan's [of *The Inkling*] and Peter Leland's [of *Dagon*]. Oh, we learn the hard way, the hardest ways, but we learn. And we forgive. And we love. We care for these poor fools in Gimlet Street, and by that caring, we love life itself a bit more....

"The act of literature is a moral act," Fred Chappell told John Carr and John Sopko in an interview in 1969, and certainly the care and caring at the heart of *The Gaudy Place* make it a moral act. "What's right and wrong?" That we cannot ever know, because the right and the wrong are as fluid as the chaotic moment itself. But we can know the good. "I think the human spirit can surmount its materialism," Fred Chappell continued. "After all, materialism is really just an invention of the spirit. Anything we can invent we can get over. I hope." And that hope is at the source of *The Gaudy Place* as well as the earlier novels. The universe is, after all, such a grand and gaudy place in which to live. (p. 15)

R. H. W. Dillard, "Letters from a Distant Lover: The Novels of Fred Chappell," in The Hollins Critic, Vol. X, No. 2, April, 1973, pp. 1-15.

JONATHAN YARDLEY

Fred Chappell's fourth novel [*The Gaudy Place*] departs rather dramatically from the dense, dark mood of the first three. *The Gaudy Place* is light, almost airy, and it is as different in setting as in mood. He has moved from the Southern countryside into the new Southern city, from the settings and themes of the past into a fiction that reflects the South of the present. This "new" South is a greatly changed place, and it is appropriate that Chappell should explore it in a novel so unlike its predecessors.

"The Gaudy Place" is a seedy section of Braceboro, N.C., centered on Gimlet Street. Its occupants are small-time hustlers, prostitutes, bail bondsmen—shifty folk trying to find an angle. One of the shiftiest is Arkie, a precocious 14-year-old who is looking for "a real fine con, not a big one, but a good solid one that it didn't take a lot of capital to get off the ground with." Before his various maneuverings in that direction have ended, he has entangled a good many more people in his web than he had originally intended.

It is an improbable chain of circumstances, but that is what Chappell has in mind.... Chance, circumstance, coincidence—these are the determining factors in the world of *The Gaudy Place*. People do things, make plans, largely out of greed, but they cannot control the consequences. Life boils along on Gimlet Street, and eventually it spills over into the rest of the city.

If there is a serious problem to *The Gaudy Place*, it is structural: it is told from five points of view, and in shifting from one to another Chappell does not maintain a consistent flow. But Chappell is a serious and uncommonly skillful writer, and the novel has considerable strengths: sharp, precise prose; several fine comic scenes; good dialogue; and, most important, an accurate feel for the new urban South, "rotten at the heart, but bright and shiny on the outside, jacketed with golf links and shopping centers." That, alas, is the way it is, and Chappell has depicted it honestly and vividly.

Jonathan Yardley, in a review of "The Gaudy Place," in The New York Times Book Review, May 13, 1973, p. 36.

ANNIE DILLARD

[In *Moments of Light*] we find pleasure for the heart and the mind, and further evidence of Chappell's broad intellectual passion and deep artistic gift.

Like the stories in the Bible, the stories in *Moments of Light* appear in moral chronological order. Together they narrate the history of man.

The book opens with **"The Three Boxes,"** a hieratic parable the action of which occurs at the beginning of things, at the time of the creation of man and the origin of human culture. The story introduces in broad terms the notions of justice and destiny. The idea of justice, at this point, is large and plain.

Then follows a complementary tale, **"Judas."** Already man has fallen, and Christ is betrayed. Judas's zealot's hope for a secular moral order, a powerful kingdom on earth, meets a new thing: Christ's idea of transcendence. Christ is characterized by his indifference to secular values and at the same time by his insistence on man's absolute responsibility to the transcendent order in which the material order is fully grounded. You can't abandon the place. From here on the hope of justice is in man's hands; and he will botch it every time.

These two stories sound many of the book's major themes: man's hope of a just moral order and his responsibility to things as they are; man's longing for transcendence and the obdurate difficulty of the temporal destiny he faces instead; and man's art (the music of **"The Three Boxes"**) which reconciles, if anything can, man's hope of harmony with his experience of chaos.

Now three stories appear which take place in the 18th Century. The tone of these stories, steeped in Enlightenment thought, is airy, spacious, and reasonable. Man is still in most ways innocent. He still hopes for a just secular order based on human reasonableness—if not in the old world, then in the new. And he still hopes that his science will verify his religion by discerning a universal moral order.

In **"Mrs. Franklin Ascends,"** Chappell introduces these themes. Sweet Mrs. Franklin is, I'm afraid, as simple and material as a bolt of cloth. And Benjamin Franklin leaves her bed for a higher level, for the attic where he plays his "armonica"—a musical device which imitates the music of the spheres. The music of the spheres is the central notion of the book, and one to which I shall return.

"Thatch Retaliates" follows the career of Enlightenment hopes for the new society in the new world. It takes place in the wilderness (or garden) of North Carolina in the 18th Century. There, plain as day, an enlightened European who hopes to help establish the new order meets Blackbeard, who kills him at whim. Blackbeard in fact holds the region in terror, and the governor is in league with him: the secular order is already as essentially corrupt as the incorrigibly chaotic heart of man. The light of reason dies, overcome by "the relentless American nighttime."

The title story, **"Moments of Light,"** completes both the 18th Century section and the first half of man's moral history. It chronicles both the end of man's intellectual innocence and the beginning of a new kind of hope. In this story, Franz Joseph Haydn looks through a telescope at the heavens.

Throughout most of this story, Haydn, a man of reason and the old order, is afraid to look. He dreads seeing what he knows he must see: chaos, the senseless universe whose guiding principles reason cannot discover because there are none. At last he looks, and is lost, but not as he had feared. Instead of seeing the flung wreck of materials, he sees beauty bare. He has a vision. The human hope of order is not just a veneer: it is ontologically grounded in what-is. What-is is beauty. Out there at the very fringes of human perception, a transcendent spiritual order sockets into materials. We do not find this incarnation in our days; we cannot found perfect societies upon it; but it is there.

Reason can neither discern nor describe this miracle at the heart of being. Reason invents the telescope which in turn informs reason that the jig is up. But the new science also informs the old order that the jig is up. Haydn is a composer. Now, in the modern world, in the fallen world, in the world in which neither the old order nor the new science has any answers, human vision must take over as the sole epistemological tool. In these new realms, only art can speak. Spiritually, this is the New Genesis; temporally, historically, it is the beginning of the Romantic Movement. Now in his old age Haydn writes his great oratorio, *The Creation*. He hails Beethoven as a genius. The heavenly spheres are disorderly and glorious, and their music is our music: not a given harmony handed down by decree, but some wild and hopeful creation offered up.

The first part of **Moments of Light** establishes a theoretical and historical framework for the second part, which takes place in the world we know. The characters in the second group of stories struggle as we do. Gone is the parabolic plainness of the first group of stories. Here instead is a world thick with materials, emotions, and a thousand ambiguities. These latter stories, narrative in both content and method, carefully loving in tone, are as emotionally engaging as they are artistically profound. Moral complexity characterizes their world. And in every one of them, in narrative structure and in vivid detail, over and over, innocence is lost.

In **"The Thousand Ways"**—one of the very finest of stories—a wise and innocent man grieves for the heartbreak of the world, for the thousand ways lives are lost through human carelessness, human moral and intellectual innocence, and human irresponsibility. This is a major theme of this section and of the book (first introduced in **"Judas"**): this world is the big time. We alone are accountable for the world and for our lives in the world. The moral complexity of the world is urgent and irreducible. And we are called to wake up and take notice.

In **"January,"** Chappell again explores the moral complexity of things. I will describe this story in some detail because it is so small, so subtle, so winning, and so telling of Chappell's various gifts for telling a story well, for thinking well, and for loving well.

A little boy's three-year-old sister follows him up a road to the barn. It is January, freezing, and she is wearing only a thin little dress. The men in the barn tell him he'd better strike out for home; it is cold, and his little sister will freeze to death. "I told her not to come," he says.

He starts home, urging his sister on. Now she is too cold to budge; she is in fact freezing to death; she sits on a log by the roadside. The boy is terrified; he pulls at her, pleading. Just then their father appears: "What are you doing to her? Why don't you leave her alone?" and, "What makes you hurt her? What gets into you?" The father gathers up the little girl and carries her home without speaking. The boy follows. The father will tell the mother; the boy cannot speak in his own defence.

For what could his defence be? Is he unjustly accused or not? He has all our sympathy; we feel at first that he has just learned the injustice of the world. Or has he? It is more accurate to say that he has just learned the moral ambiguity at the heart of things, and the moral imperative. (pp. ix-xiii)

The boy is alone now, his childhood over. He stands inside at the cold window, his breath obscuring "the total moon." This beautiful little story reiterates, as do all the stories in this second section, the fall of man: his loss of innocence and his moral coming of age.

In **"The Weather,"** it happens again. The child is now an adolescent. And innocence lies spread in its true color: a kind of dreaming passivity. The languors of innocence are not only

behind us; they are best left behind us. For their sweet passivity is a shirking of the real burden of things, the injunction to love in a responsible and even an engendering way.

"Broken Blossoms," which is about as pleasing a story as you will ever read, treats these themes fully. I don't want to ruin it, especially because much of it is so funny. I will merely indicate that it fits into the moral chronology in this wise, that a dreaming, unconscious boy discovers that he *must* wake up. (pp. xiii-xiv)

In **"Children of Strikers,"** Chappell makes manifest, vividly and subtly, the real and grave nature of human suffering. This is a brilliant story whose narrative gradually uncovers its own locus. We wake, as the children wake, to the import of what they have found by the roadside; but we know, as they do not, what it means about the world. The many layers of this story separate the reader from pain while forcing him, unaware, to seek it out at the center of the narrative riddle, and forcing him to find it, accidentally as it were, at the center of human experience.

The final, capping story in this collection is **"Blue Dive."** It is a great, complex, and enduring work of fiction. It completes the moral chronology to date. Here we are again, still alone, and experienced now in the world's evil and in our complicity in that evil. We meet good people and bad, try to make our way with our eyes open, and have only our old-timey music—the soul's transcendent longing—between us and ruin.

"Blue Dive" chronicles our eternal blue dive into sin and knowledge and our eternal blue dive towards heaven, leaping as high as we can. And in this story, Christ is betrayed once again. We all have power over other lives. One man of such power rejects, like Judas, another man, and in so doing rejects all hope of transcendence in favor of a material kingdom. And art, old art, disenfranchised as usual, takes it on the road.

Do not mistake these abstractions for Chappell's stories. These are living, vivid narratives whose rich actions lodge in the imagination. . . . These stories are as real as days; the moral calendar I have outlined merely orders them without giving any sense of their texture, solidity, warmth, and color.

Very briefly, what do these stories suggest of Chappell's vision? What can be said of the world, and of the people who inhabit it?

The world itself is, I believe, morally neutral, like the many stars. But in the light of human experience and ideals, the world's moral neutrality amounts to profound moral disarray. That of the world which we experience most forcibly is its passive resistance. "Matter retains its smirking hardness," Chappell writes in the poem **Bloodfire**. The universe passively resists our heartbreaking efforts to live well within it, to avoid pain to ourselves and others, to know it, and to reconcile it with any order beyond it.

The material world requires and inspires our active resistance. It is a January hard frost, a river current which bears us away from our goals, or a dread Carolina forest wilderness. Human nature and culture struggle against these things. But there is another material level which is a step removed from human knowledge and culture: the troubled earth spins in a setpiece of stars. And the multitudes of moving spheres have nothing to do with us, nor we with them. We need not act. The spheres' passive resistance and their obduracy occur at the other side of human pain. And, paradoxically, their very material unfathomableness meets and answers our most spiritual longings.

Our wishing always to escape or redeem the material world leads at last and always to the very heart of matter: its mystery. And there, in the thick of the mystery where spirit and matter meet, there is the faintly-perceived harmony, the world's great grounding in beauty: the music of the spheres.

And what of man? Chappell's characters, excepting the two Judas figures, are all beloved, known, and forgiven. Man as a whole is a fallen innocent and a sojourner newly-bewildered in a life of unfathomable moral complexity, a life which engenders in every generation a thousand new forms of injustice. (pp. xiv-xvi)

At his very worst, man betrays the human longing for a kingdom not of this world. Like Judas, and like Locklear Hawkins who owns the Blue Dive, he shuts his eyes to all he knows and gives himself over to idolatry, seeking the merciless secular power of a material kingdom. And at his moral best—like George Palinopolous, like B. J. and Darlene, Mark Vance, and Mr. Cody—man is his brother's keeper, a sojourner among sojourners, awake enough to help.

And at his metaphysical best, man never abandons his furious longing for order. He casts that spiritual longing into the very teeth of matter—and comes up with art. In *Moments of Light* that art is music. . . . It's all we've got, and so it is enough. "Daddy," the little boy says of Stovebolt Johnson and his blues guitar; "Daddy," the little boy says, "he can play the *blue pee* out of that thing!"

And so can Chappell. He can play it, and the rest of the stricken world can dance. (pp. xvi-xvii)

> *Annie Dillard, in a foreword to* Moments of Light
> *by Fred Chappell, The New South Company, 1980,*
> *pp. ix-xvii.*

CHOICE

[The pieces in *Moments of Light* are] mainly stories of moral initiation or insight, of characters who discover the discrepancy between the moral order and justice they dream of and the hardness and injustice that surround them in the real world, or of young people who learn that they must take responsibility for their moral choices. Some of Chappell's characters, though, do envision a moral order in the universe and use their musical art to express it. Chappell's stories are consistently thought-provoking and well written. And while they reflect complex moral and aesthetic themes, these themes are grounded in the concrete elaboration of character, setting, and incident.

> *A review of "Moments of Light," in* Choice, *Vol.*
> *18, No. 7, March, 1981, p. 946.*

ELLEN TUCKER

With *Earthsleep*, Fred Chappell completed last year his tetralogy *Midquest*. A poetic autobiography, it provides—in four versions—a view of the poet's life as seen from a day in midcourse. The second poem of *River*, **"Birthday 35: Diary Entry,"** serves as critical preface to the text that follows, explaining first of all the need for reflection: "Multiplying my age by two in my head, / I'm a Grandfather. Or dead." The poet reviews the time he has spent and is disappointed, yet not really bemused, to find no accumulations of understanding. What he has garnered through one half of a life is an amicable relationship with the cranky questioner, shifty declaimer, in-

temperate lover that he is. . . . Despite moral and spiritual doubt, Chappell retains a sense of his own constant identity. (p. 85)

One might expect so protracted an inquiry to lead not to a summary of the self but to possibly endless revisions of it. Yet Chappell seems unimpressed by the argument that the mind which begins a poem is not the mind which finishes it. It is after all not in certainties that he hopes to fix himself, but in the gregarious projection of his voice through the possibilities. (pp. 85-6)

Or perhaps it is more accurate to say that Chappell's autobiography presents not evolving self-consciousness but a series of masks. Chappell's is a highly flexible, theatrical voice. His mind is intensely engaged with what he calls "moral ideas," but these he tests less through their logical or analogical development than through the assumption of the posture appropriate to each. He relishes the music in language, and a fine ear enables him to invent meters suitable to each pose. These range from the comically inept heroic couplets of the **"Diary Entry"** to a long, lyrical line, used in his dream poems, which searches the left and right margins of the page. . . . Occasionally his theatricality appears in the shameless ease with which he dons the rhythms and diction of other poets. (p. 86)

His real gift emerges when he brings to us voices out of Appalachia, seldom recorded in our poetry. Chappell confronts in *Midquest* life's daily crises; to find out how commitments arise, he does not merely reexamine his own (largely literary) experience; he recalls the voices of family elders. Each has not so much opinions as stories to tell.

Explanations for crucial choices are shaped through narrative, and narrative is shaped through the unique qualities of the voice which tells the story. . . . These voices are defined and authenticated by their address to a specific audience. Most often the audience is the poet—not the thirty-five-year-old poet whose birthday is the occasion for reflection and remembrance, but the poet's former self, a child or adolescent who has just begun to wonder about his parents' pasts, about the decisions that made them who they are. Questioned by youth, age shapes a tale of inevitability, proclaiming more assurance than perhaps it knew it felt. The elders speak not to instruct the young person so much as to justify themselves in front of the young person, for Chappell reminds us that adults, becoming parents, are jolted into responsibility not only for their children but for their own lives. They seek a tale that will do justice to their own sense of reality, often announcing at the outset that *this* time age will speak to youth without white-washing the past. Yet they design the tale not to pursue complexities, forestalling judgment, but to clarify harsher certainties. Chappell does not deny the slippery tendencies of belief. For example, in **"My Mother's Hard Row to Hoe,"** he records the difficulty, despite the determined machinery of rhyme and refrain, of keeping a single harsh perspective in focus. Still, he is convinced of the fatefulness of decision; and he sees narrative as a form of explanation which satisfies the self's desire for coherence by accounting for life's crucial choices.

Speaking for himself, Chappell's voice remains flexible, largely because it almost always retains a specific sense of audience. (pp. 87-8)

Chappell addresses to his wife Susan the lyrical, visionary poems which begin and end each volume. Although tentative, the voice is prophetic, striving for insight that it might guide the woman's entrance into a foreign world, at the same time as it appeals to her for companionship and looks to her beauty for revelation. The opening poems of each volume of *Midquest* register the waking poet's dismay at his exile from the world of dream. And the address of these poems—loving, slightly condescending, supportive—reveals Chappell's sense of entrance into the waking day as analogous to Adam and Eve's entrance into the world after being barred from Eden. Before waking the woman enacts a kind of fall that the man warns her of and yet will share in. . . . Chappell subscribes not to that part of the myth which assigns first error to the woman (whenever Susan speaks she is a witty innocent) but to that part which testifies that loss of the woman would have been the price of paradise. In Chappell's poetic universe love precedes and conditions choice, and love is inextricably connected with mortality. If Chappell spoke *about* this love it would become, perhaps, a thing to be questioned, a force which threatened. Instead, he enacts his love, by inviting the woman into the poem and speaking to her.

There are private meditations among the poems, usually resulting when the poet seeks an unlikely auditor. The voice of **"Firewood"** harangues the material world, yet admits that the unsolicited performance is unheeded and unappreciated. In **"The Autumn Bleat of the Weathervane Trombone"** and **"The Peaceable Kingdom of Emerald Windows"** the talkative mind addresses a sluggish body, which grows bored, and cries for real food. Here Chappell displays a need to talk which persists even when no one is listening. Yet in the absence of audience his talk is different. For the sake of friends or family Chappell will pursue meanings and fashion explanations. But in private meditations he affronts the reader with a blatant lack of responsible concern for the audience at large. For here he does not commit himself to any single inquiry. Stream-of-consciousness perorations test Chappell's ability to sustain a mood, whether facetious or philosophical (usually both); they do not test knowledge or belief. The strategy here, as Chappell points out in the **"Diary Entry,"** is to "veer and slide and wobble / Immorally eavesdropping my own babble." He stages the performance for his own use, on the off chance that understanding will surface during it.

I think monologues like these Chappell's least impressive poems. Yet they demonstrate perhaps better than his other work the extent of his singularity among contemporary poets. To insist that such experimental flights of fancy are the necessary recreation of the mind, to implicitly class us with Caliban for growing bored and impatient, is to challenge our desire for a poetry that takes us inside a poet's head and there shapes for us clarities. Chappell makes fun of our fascination with the private. He invites us inside his mind, yet he will gratify neither a voyeur's appetite for confession nor an earnest romantic's hope for a glimpse of the center of consciousness. For he knows quite well that to journey into inward experience, looking there for meaning, is to surrender consciousness to the determinations of time: each successive insight will alter what has gone before, and will stimulate a new search, which will alter all again. That is why his solitary meditations concern outward objects and perennial ideas. Nevertheless, although they examine a range of possibilities, these poems remain essentially static—or rather, they continually orbit some stubborn skepticism, some unresigned will, which persists to give Chappell his constant sense of self. The forward impulse of his gab, like the momentum of a moving satellite, keeps him from crashing into his center; but the gravitational pull of the self restrains him from a hurtle through outer space. (pp. 89-91)

> *Ellen Tucker, "His Life in Mid-course," in* Chicago
> Review, *Vol. 33, No. 1, Summer, 1981, pp. 85-91.*

ROBERT MORGAN

[The] art of prose is as difficult as any poetry. But in our culture it does not carry the same aura of pretension and expectation. Poetry is something to be worshipped from afar, not read, while it is to prose we turn for entertainment, information, authority. We should value all the more, therefore, a writer such as Fred Chappell who can combine the two arts. He is both poet and novelist, and also a short story writer. But he is at his best in what can only be called narrative poetry. By this designation I do not mean prose broken into lines, and I will distinguish what Chappell does best by calling it a lyric narrative, implying that the local texture of the lines is as interesting and concise as lyric poetry, while the overall movement of each piece is essentially narrative. . . .

There is a wholeness about the work of Chappell. Everything he does seems a piece of the same cloth, whether story, poem, novel or essay, and whatever he does fits with all the rest. It is the voice that dominates and is recognizable, no matter where you start any of his works, speaking with great richness of mind and language, deeply learned, acid at times, but always improvising, engaging whatever is at hand with all its attention, true overall to a wonderful good will and wit. Whether the subject be his parents or Linnaeus, he demonstrates the same gift for luminous phrase and detail. All his work has the tone of the gifted rememberer and tale teller delighting in his powers and flights of merrymaking memory. The voice is often self-deprecating and parodic, and the range of reference from the learned and reverent to the grotesque and mock-heroic. But there is an enormous amount of affection here for these people and their brief triumphs and losing battles with the sad facts of their lives. . . .

Each volume [of *Midquest*] is a separate poem, and all are spoken on the same day, May 28, 1971, the Dantean thirty-fifth birthday of the poet. Each poem, *River, Bloodfire, Wind Mountain,* and now *Earthsleep,* symbolizes one of the four classical elements. The centering of these poems in all of experience, midway in a lifetime, is important in more ways than the merely chronological. While touching extremes of usage and allusion at times, the work clearly derives its elan from the middle range of experience, stressing no angle of vision over another, and rendering with utmost care and humor the lives of grandmother, parents, aging mountain Falstaffs and storekeepers. With his fluent "prose" style Chappell has achieved a kind of middle poetry, centered in the actual, familiar as conversation, but often as wry and learnedly comic as the poetry of, say, John Crowe Ransom. He uses elaborate traditional forms for the most humble subjects, often making stilnovist terza rima a vehicle for Appalachian whoppering.

This very middleness about *Midquest* is one of its most daring features, for it enables Chappell to avoid the safe and accepted manners of so much contemporary poetry and navigate far beyond the surrealist, confessional, formalist and agrarian limits so many contemporaries have imposed on themselves. Chappell has found a "synthetic" style that enables him to assimilate all he knows into his work. Steering a middle course, he has avoided the siren call of the safely ambiguous on the one side, and the heady maelstrom of manner on the other. Starting from the harbor of a northern port he has crossed the Equator and been baptized in new tropical waters and, like the true yarn-teller he is, has incorporated the new figures seamlessly into his old tales.

But having said all this I must point out that the very difference of Chappell's work puts it exactly in the tradition of American poetry. Only by turning away from the accepted poetic norms into its own eccentricities and obsessions can the American gift seem to work. It is the veering away that brings one toward the middle. Chappell follows the pattern almost exactly, turning away from the high serious and meticulously chiseled understatement of verse to an explosion of free verse, hyperbole, flamboyant experimentation with French forms and autobiography. In the rejection of poetry for the playfulness and wrinkles of self he finds his true Poetry. In the contrasts of form and freedom, idea and facts, sad failure and guilt against rebellious joy, we find an authentic gift.

There are formal complexities in *Midquest* which will, and should, go unnoticed until a second or third reading. The whole is interwoven and subtly counterpointed with motifs and repetitions. Characters appear and later reappear in the poems. The variety of form and tone is used as a narrative as well as a poetic pacing device. Each volume is complete in itself, yet completes the whole structure, beginning with the surfacing from the unity of sleep at dawn, beside Susan the wife-muse, and moving through a long day of remembering and story telling, shaggydogging and drinksinging, and outright powerful poetry, to night and the return to unity and sleep with Susan, the earth-death muse and mother.

Part of Chappell's power is his willingness to put all of himself into this work. He gives to his poetry a great reservoir of learning, lyric hymning, alternating with science fiction and fantasy, country music (''I went walking up Chunky Gal / To watch the blackbird whup the owl''). That he is willing to invest so many facets of himself is our gain. For we come to feel the wholeness of a human being. There is the recognition that this is truly a man, in the gaudy landscape of our times, yes, and seen from more angles than we normally see, and with greater focus and knowledge, but nevertheless a man in touch at times with the absurd and corny, at times with the sublime.

Midquest is about curvature and rondure, the return of that which goes out in the morning from its bed, and the turning of the earth and seasons, the sweep from the marriage of all in sleep (death) out through the almost overwhelming detail and near-chaos of experience back to the unity of love and dream. The theme is also the recurrence of everything from the least *deja-vu* to the grandest rhyme of history, and the night of stars beyond human history. The central thread is perhaps the deja-vuness of being, and each volume recapitulates the others and repeats the whole. Thus the hill in **''Stillpoint Hill at Midnight''** in *River* returns near the end of *Earthsleep* in **''Stillpoint Hill that Other Shore,''** and the Virgil Campbell of **''Dead Soldiers''** in the first volume returns again and again, most notably in **''Firewater''** of *Bloodfire* and **''Three Sheets in the Wind''** in *Wind Mountain* and finally in **''At the Grave of Virgil Campbell''** in *Earthsleep*. (p. 45)

It is in *Bloodfire* that the central metaphor, the middle of life, becomes clear, for there we see that the thirty-fifth birthday, the being born again to the second half of one's life, means to be born to death. The implication is not just that as one passes the mid-point of his life he becomes increasingly aware of approaching death. Rather, it is the perception that one's life has become the process of death. Every breath is an act in the long dying back into the earth. And the recognition is that life is exactly the same as death, though to be alive is the opposite of being dead. (pp. 45-6)

Chappell has integrated into his epic story the details and names of his region as no one else has. ''Chunky Gal,'' ''Greasy Creek,'' ''Standing Indian'' do not just give a sense of local usage; they become part of the thick texture of the style, giving at once intimacy and distance to the poetry. It is as though the speaker is of two minds at once, the mountain boy telling of the places and people of which he is derived, and the learned and wise poet who knows Latin, Italian, French, neoplatonism and quantum mechanics. The complexity of tone is rendered most clearly in the sections about the poet's parents, in their constant harping of the hardness of the old days on their hard-scrabble farms from the comfort of their prosperous suburban lives. There is a parodic overtone in their monologues, a teasing, as though the poet knows that while they do miss the sweat and poverty of their childhoods, they are exaggerating all around. Even if they could travel back they would not, yet probably it was not as hard as they make it sound. This essential paradox is what Chappell communicates so affectionately, and it partly explains his enormous popularity in the South. No one has rendered so accurately the sense of displacement amid so much prosperity, and the jealous holding on to the phrases and accents of the old as both an amused conning of the self and an irreplaceable touchstone.

Typical of this half-serious teasing are the stories about fundamentalist religion. The little white churches in these poems cast cold shadows over the coves, and their preachers and doctrine are never absent long from the mind of the speaker. Whether in the mock-heroics of the terza-rima **''My Grandfather Gets Doused''** or the mock-epic alliterative line of **''My Grandfather's Church Goes Up,''** or the Dantean **''In Parte Ove Non E Che''** which, part translation, part original, tours hell with the Master and finds James Dickey in the Inferno for lechery; or finally in the drinking hymns of **''At the Grave of Virgil Campbell,''** we see a mind coming to terms with one of the terrors of its world through the jujitsu of humor. Since the church and its work-ethic and hellfire can't be ignored, it must be defused a little with parody, while the more humble, everyday things are treated reverently. . . .

There is a spirit in this work I find remarkable, and rare in contemporary poetry. Much of what we read these days is often at best hardbitten and stingy, sometimes downright nasty to the reader. Though Chappell is often outrageous about himself, his family and neighbors, there is an assumption of community in all his work, a sense of belonging not just to a family and place, and to a place in terms of geography, but to the terrain of history. It is a community *in time* that is implied and evoked, a world of parents and ancestors both literal and literary, as real as the expressways and gaudy vernacular of the present.

Interestingly enough, this sureness of who he is, in a community both poetic and familial, gives Chappell a truer rapport with contemporary culture. His imagination lives not only among the things that were, but also the things that are. That is, to paraphrase Wallace Stevens, his gift is equal to the pressure of reality. This partly explains his popularity as a poet and as a reader of his poetry. He speaks to people as they are and as he is. The authenticity is instantly perceivable, on the page and in his voice. There is no precious regionalism here, no easy agrarian indignation, no sentimental celebrations. (p. 46)

Robert Morgan, '' 'Midquest','' in The American Poetry Review, *Vol. 11, No. 4, July-August, 1982, pp. 45-7.*

MICHAEL J. BUGEJA

The revenge play—so popular in Shakespeare's day that theater owners had to trot out *The Spanish Tragedy* when a new production flopped—has been revived, at least in spirit, by Fred Chappell. Although his latest poetry collection, *Castle Tzingal,* may be somewhat overshadowed by the acclaimed *Midquest* tetralogy that established him as a major voice in contemporary poetry, this slim volume is, nevertheless, timelessly appealing and suspenseful. It would have served nicely in the Tudor era when London playhouses were closed because of plague, and royalty had to resort to poetry for entertainment.

The book is offbeat. First of all, it is dramatic poetry, the genre we tend to omit in our overemphasis of the narrative and lyric. The poems, each a scene of a play, are arranged to tell a story about the disappearance of the harpist-poet Marco, whose songs echo through the sinister castle. Thus, the collection embodies the three genres of poetry, thereby reminding us of Shakespeare's sonnet sequence about love. Love is at the heart of the typical revenge, and Chappell makes the most of it in his book. Frynna, the forlorn queen of "an iron and fruitless man," King Tzingal, has fallen for the song of Marco, even though she fears he has been attacked by robbers or has abandoned her for a new mistress. The setting . . . is described by Frynna in her introductory poem, **"The Queen":**

> Here no man walks;
> But sneaks or stamps or stalks.
> And no one tells a tale but the telltale.
> And no one thrives here but the mad
> Or guilty.

To make matters worse, the queen's love for Marco causes problems for the kingdom because he is the nephew of the rival King Reynal, half-brother to Tzingal. Via such family ties, Chappell endows his revenge with overplot, again in the Tudor tradition: the security of the state may be at stake. If Reynal discovers Tzingal has harmed Marco, he may take the advice of his envoy Petrus and go to war. The reader knows that Marco has been "harmed"—beheaded by the jealous king and metamorphosed into a disembodied poetic voice—but suspense and plot revolve around the envoy's trying to learn the facts, and we question whether he will succeed in the ominous castle. . . . In Chappell's book, we experience theater along with the poetry. We weigh the evidence the envoy gathers for Reynal in a series of secret reports; we watch, among others, a deviant homunculus, a seductive page, and a manipulative astrologer as they weave the intrigue that transpires at court.

Although plot is important for suspense in this book, it is subservient—in the mode of good drama—to characterization. Chappell, in a grand display of his poetic gift, varies the voices and styles of each player. We are drawn to the grotesquerie of the homunculus, marvel at the equivocation of the page, feel for the captive queen, admire the shrewdness of the envoy, and so on, until Chappell—through his characters—triggers a range of emotions in his reader that the typical narrative or lyric poet simply cannot evoke. (pp. 896-97)

[*Castle Tzingal* succeeds through] brilliant exposition, the most difficult device of dramatic poetry. Too often, the lesser poet makes flat statements so the reader can understand plot or situation. Chappell not only communicates such information in his exposition but also colors the character through it and furthers the action.

While exposition and characterization, so skillfully wrought, enhance the dramatic and narrative elements of *Castle Tzingal,* Chappell's songs for the harpist-poet add the lyric element that is the soul of this collection. (p. 898)

Chappell's book captures the music and flame of a revenge that also sheds light on realities that exist today. The promotional copy on the back cover states that *Castle Tzingal* "is a political fairy tale that speaks with the vivid, sometimes harsh truth and knowledge of our own most fevered nightmares," but other metaphors are also afoot. The homunculus may be grotesquely cast as an eighteen-inch beast, but practitioners of his deception have such stature in real life. Opportunists like the page exist on all social levels, and even serious-minded envoys like Petrus resort to bribe when intellect fails. Moreover, Marco, who represents poetry, cannot be silenced by king or government; his song becomes more powerful in death. Those who hear it—a hapless queen yearning for affection, or a reader who understands the theme of this ambitious book— come to understand that love, like art, is eternal. (p. 899)

> *Michael J. Bugeja, in a review of "Castle Tzingal,"*
> *in* The Georgia Review, *Vol. XXXIX, No. 4, Winter,*
> *1985, pp. 896-99.*

GEORGE CORE

Both [*I Am One of You Forever,* by Fred Chappell, and *Raney,* by Clyde Edgerton] are Southern; both are written in the first-person vernacular mode that harks back to Mark Twain; and both should be read in a rush—a sitting or two. The comedy in both ranges from the quick thigh-slapping humor of the guffaw to the slow and indirect response of the faint smile. There is a wider range of experience embodied in *I Am One of You Forever,* a novel in which the author often uses tall tale and other forms of hyperbole to show life's possibilities, and the fell hand of death on one occasion darkens the otherwise sunny action, tinging it with pathos and privation. . . .

I Am One of You Forever involves growing up on a mountain farm in western North Carolina. The action unwinds through the consciousness of a man looking back on his youth, but seldom are you aware that events aren't occurring in the present. We are carried quickly and surely from one situation to the next, and the scene changes when each new character— usually an uncle from the mother's side of the family—appears to pay a visit. The first of these is Uncle Luden, the prodigal son. "Any fatted calf, his days are numbered," says the boy's father, who goes on: "When Uncle Luden walks the street, strong men tremble and women squeal." Uncle Luden is followed by a series of uncles still more preposterous and finally by Aunt Samantha Barefoot, a country singer who is the most colorful of all this scattered tribe.

I Am One of You Forever is a series of farfetched and winning stories, one following hard on the heels of the other. It is a novel to read and reread for its tales, its lovely cast of characters, and its poetry. It is also a novel to put on the shelf with Mark Twain, William Faulkner, and Eudora Welty.

> *George Core, "Tall Tales, Guffaws, and Sly South-*
> *ern Humor," in* Book World—The Washington Post,
> *June 30, 1985, p. 11.* *

DAVID GUY

[*I Am One of You Forever* is not] a conventional novel. Though it is told from the point of view of a single character, a boy named Jess, and though the entire book concerns him and his family—father, mother and grandmother—in the North Carolina mountains in the 1940's, it is actually a series of vignettes about people who visit the family and does not tell a continuous narrative. One character, an orphan named Johnson Gibbs, comes to work on the farm and figures in a number of the stories.

The psychic structure of this family seems typical of the back-woods South. Jess's father is 30 and Johnson Gibbs nearing 20, but the day after they meet they become fast friends by fighting "like tomcats." From then on their lives revolve around dodging work, telling tall tales and staging elaborate practical jokes. "We three males might have been the same age," the 10-year-old Jess says, and he is dead right; the women are essentially mothers to the three of them, trying to keep them out of trouble, scolding them when they go wrong.

I can easily grow tired of reading about the Southern boy-man and his idea of a wild time, but just as I was gritting my teeth at yet another stupid prank, Mr. Chappell woke me up with a superb piece of writing. He is a fine technician of narrative prose who writes with marvelous economy, gives his characters letter-perfect dialogue and describes them with wonderful vividness. . . .

There are whole sections in the middle of this book that succeed beautifully—a surrealistic passage in which an uncle's 40-year-old beard expands to fill the entire house, an allegory about a telegram that perfectly portrays the human need to mourn, a section that speculates hauntingly on the nature of storytelling talent. Mr. Chappell also saves his best vignettes for last: a simple story about Jess fishing with his father and their encounter with a broken-down alcoholic and the story of Aunt Samantha Barefoot, a 60-ish country singer who "knows how to live with her feelings." Mr. Chappell in all his writing is a poet, who can touch us suddenly and deeply with a single phrase. Though some early sections of this book are tiresome, I would have waded through all the dumb practical jokes in the world to experience its best moments.

> David Guy, "Coming of Age in Carolina," in The New York Times Book Review, September 15, 1985, p. 21.*

R. T. SMITH

Castle Tzingal is a composition in a decided minor key, a cat's fugue after Fred Chappell's important *Midquest*, and I admit to being at once fascinated by and disappointed in this work. . . .

What fascinates me is the liquid weaving of voices and motives from monologue to monologue. The triumph there lies in the songs of "Disembodied Voice," which haunt the palace to report the crime in dream, a dream that takes various forms for the several denizens of Tzingal and serves as keystone for guilts and needs and wishes. The lyricism of these songs rings of the troubadours' "music that silvers the wind with shadow"—appropriate, since the victim is a poet. In counterpoint, Chappell gives us the thorny words and self-devouring intrigues of the king, the spy, the homunculus, and the astrologer's ambitious page.

There is, mind you, meaning in this self-described king of frogs' inadequacies and schemes, but Chappell does not aim accusation at any particular politician through any code that I've deciphered, though with this writer I always suspect more richness buried beyond the casual reader's eye, am always

aware that I may be duped if I judge prematurely. The necrophagia of the king's spite strikes me as particularly contemporary, as the king continues to torture a half-buried half corpse, and the cave-in of this malignant court, like Poe's *House of Usher,* augurs ill for the isolated and self-blinded regent whose own self-destructive imp dooms him.

The facets I dislike most in this elegant masque are: the quickness with which the reader is told the fate of the missing poet . . . and the weakness of the monologues of the fay admiral. I might also wish the pest king more cannily mad, the queen less wispy, the assassination plot more mystifying. The performances I have no quarrel with are: the manipulation of rhyme and line and cold-sobering tone . . . that dominates and the urgent confrontation of evil in its mesmeric courtly forms, however briskly masked as lore and bottle manuscript. Though I wish for the sense of necessity and practical beauty of the more American, colloquial, and familiar subjects of *River* and *Bloodfire,* I find myself returning to re-read many passages of *Castle Tzingal* with appreciation for a skillful maestro at his craft and an enigma spinning against his native drift, and I feel fortunate for one more glimpse of this angel of the odd at his Lovecraftish work. (p. 391)

> R. T. Smith, in a review of "Castle Tzingal, a Poem," in The Southern Humanities Review, Vol. XIX, No. 4, Fall, 1985, pp. 390-91.

PUBLISHERS WEEKLY

In this new collection of lyrics, [*Source*], Chappell is freed of the exigencies of framework, and his powers seem to have responded with ever-greater enthusiasm. A serious end-of-the-world nightmare poem, **"The Evening of the Second Day,"** contrasts with the comic celebration of **"Recovery of Sexual Desire After a Bad Cold."** The peculiarly rich Chappell diction, combining strictly poetic language with country dialect, is more effective than ever. Even with a masterpiece [*Midquest*] behind him, Chappell has not exhausted his gifts, as these virtuoso songs, prayers, elegies and fables prove.

> A review of "Source," in Publishers Weekly, Vol. 228, No. 18, November 1, 1985, p. 63.

BETH COOLEY

As he tells the thirteen stories that make up [*I Am One of You Forever*], Fred Chappell seems to reside in a poetical penumbra reminiscent of Hawthorne's "neutral ground," a contiguous sphere that not only touches reality but flows over into it with natural fluidity and grace. With the first brief story, "The Overspill" (one of the three italicized vignettes at the beginning, middle, and end of the novel), one realizes that this is a novel of extremes. Yet the literal and fantastic, the physical and metaphysical never collide; instead they blend to create a world that quite comfortably, even courteously, includes both. (p. 87)

[The] novel begins with straightforward traditional realism. Jess and his father, Joe Robert, work on the banks of a mountain creek attempting to transform "a half-acre of fallow ground considered unsalable because of its marshiness and the impenetrable clot of blackberry vines in the south corner" into a garden complete with ornamental bridge for Jess' mother. The clear description, the honest ring of the dialogue, even the homey details of Joe Robert's attempt to tie a red silk bow onto the bridge ("He growled in a low tone like a bear trying to dislodge a groundhog from its hole"), do nothing to prepare us for the final paragraph of the vignette. With the simultaneous opening of floodgates upstream, the collapse of the bridge, and the arrival of Jess' mother, the down-home realism of the vignette is flooded with the translucence of poetry. Not only does the style become poetic, but the event itself becomes fantastically figurative. The young husband's disappointment, the wife's keen sympathetic understanding and the son's indefinable emotion are transformed into metaphor. The very real tear that glistens on Jess' mother's cheek, "silver in the cheerful light of midafternoon," detaches itself from her face, and becomes "a shiny globe widening outward like an inflating balloon . . . as it expanded it took my mother and father into itself." Here the "metaphysicality" of the event becomes quite specific and also quite literary. As in the tear poems of Herbert, Marvell, and especially Donne, the tear becomes the metaphorical little world excluding the mundane catastrophes of physical reality. And yet in *I Am One of You Forever* the metaphysical often *is* the physical. "The tear enlarged until at last it took me in too. It was warm and salt. As soon as I got used to the strange light inside the tear, I began to swim clumsily toward my parents." Jess' experience is real, not just poetic; he swims clumsily, as any ten year old would.

While the symbolically fantastic is most pervasive in the three short vignettes, in Jess' other recollections of childhood we find the realistic and fantastic mixed in varying proportions. Uncle Luden, the prodigal son who spends much of his time "sniffing the breeze and chewing his ole mustache and patrolling the female gender" (much to the amusement and chagrin of members of Jess' family), is eccentric, but there is nothing outside the possible, if not the probable, in his story. Similarly, Aunt Samantha Barefoot, the aging country music star, is unusual but believable enough. Uncle Gurton, however, presents another matter; his tale is the most fantastic in the novel. As if his disconcerting tendency to appear and disappear, his warm, friendly, but mysterious smile ("as informative as a spoon"), and his single utterance were not enough, there is the amazing beard. Here, Chappell becomes positively surrealistic. Time and space alter completely as Jess and his father watch everything from life size mermaids to Moby Dick swim through the billowing waves of immaculate white fleece.

The tendency to permit worlds to seep into each other is as apparent in Chappell's style as in his plot. At times this can be annoying, as when Jess describes a picnic, "We ate hunkered or standing up, turning slow pirouettes around the fire," or explains the care he takes not to "squash the innards" out of the grub that will attract "black filigreed" fish. However, with the poet's keen sense of language, Chappell usually succeeds in taking liberties with style that parallel the sometimes outrageous poetic license of his tales. (pp. 87-8)

After the initial but pleasant surprise at Chappell's refusal to remain in either one world or the other, the reader simply listens to his stories and ponders them. Like Uncle Zeno, Chappell is not interested in answering questions, at least not questions pertaining to facts. If *I Am One of You Forever* answers any questions, and I believe it does, these are questions about imagination, art, and the role of the storyteller in creating and ordering reality. There are many would-be storytellers in the novel. Johnson Gibbs, for instance, who "ain't no hand at ghostally tales," goes for hunting, fishing, and baseball stories,

"he-man stuff" instead. The problem with Johnson is that he leaves out important details such as how the hero can cross the ravine without a bridge and how the alligator can climb up 500 feet of sheer rock wall. Joe Robert also tells tales; in fact he tells Jess the *Iliad* in ten minutes flat. He begins by propping a picture of Betty Grable (Helen of Troy) on the mantle piece and ends by lugging a sofa cushion (Hector) around the living room. Despite the special effects, Joe Robert fails simply because he is too "entranced with mischief and effect" and "unable to keep his hands off things." Uncle Zeno is the only true storyteller in the bunch. "He told stories," Jess recalls, "endless stories, and these stories worked upon the fabric of our daily lives in such manner that we began to doubt our own outlines." In the sixth chapter, "The Storytellers," the outlines between the believable and unbelievable again blur, but the hazy realm just outside the pale of both reality and fantasy is the realm of art.

For Jess and his father, Uncle Zeno is an Appalachian Homer, a "necessary part of nature" through which divinely inspired fiction manifests itself. Yet the "real world" has a part in the telling too. Jess explains, "Homer and Uncle Zeno did not merely describe the world, they used it up. My father said that one reason Homer was reckoned such a top-notch poet was that you couldn't tell where the world left off and the *Iliad* began." Of course inflexible rationality tells us where the real world, or at least the believable world, ends in Chappell's art. Yet, Chappell is himself, if not a Homer, an Uncle Zeno. And that is no shallow compliment. (pp. 88-9)

Beth Cooley, in a review of "I Am One of You Forever," in Carolina Quarterly, *Vol. 38, No. 2, Winter, 1986, pp. 87-9.*

CHRISTOPHER BENFEY

You might call Fred Chappell an ornery poet, especially if, as my dictionary says, "ornery" is a variant of "ordinary." This poet is irritable, oblique, shape-changing, antic. . . . Chappell is most ornery when he is protecting the rhythms and rituals of ordinary life—"love and fresh coffee." His name is familiar here and there, especially in North Carolina, where he has lived for most of his life. But his healthy spells should have more sway, more readers.

Chappell was given the Bollingen Prize for poetry earlier this year, along with John Ashbery. The completion of his tetralogy *Midquest* was one reason for this unexpected honor. *Midquest* is partly Chappell's *Prelude,* looking back to his childhood in the mountains of North Carolina, his extended family, and his poetic apprenticeship. . . .

Chappell uses a variety of meters, forms, and genres in *Midquest*; there are verse letters, dramatic monologues, conversation poems, elemental odes. . . . "My model," he remarks, "was that elder American art form, the sampler, each form standing for a different fancy stitch." . . .

One of Chappell's distinctions is the way he introduces humor into his work. He often plays off two sides of himself: the "Haywood County hillbilly," born and raised in the Carolina mountains, and the Duke-educated poet, schooled in French symbolist poetry. . . .

Chappell's recent poetry is haunted less by French Symbolism than by German Romanticism. In his medieval fable **Castle Tzingal** (1984) and in the short lyrics of **Source** (1985) Chappell shows a fascination with Märchen, fairy tales, opera—there's even a Lieder cycle in **Source**. And many of these poems, such as the beautiful **"Humility,"** reveal a Hölderlin-like reverence for the earth. Chappell is claiming a larger cultural territory for himself in his recent work, but he retains his love for the ordinary, "the country we return to when / For a moment we forget ourselves."

Christopher Benfey, "A Poet's Sampler: Fred Chappell," in Boston Review, *Vol. XI, No. 1, February, 1986, p. 11.*

John (Anthony) Ciardi

1916-1986

American poet, editor, critic, author of books for children, nonfiction writer, and translator.

Highly respected as a translator, critic, educator, and editor of poetry, Ciardi initiated his prolific literary career as a poet in the late 1930s. Based primarily upon personal experience and narrated in a personal voice, Ciardi's poetry reflects his life as the son of Italian immigrants. In much of his verse he writes realistically of the myth of the American dream, detailing social and domestic aspects of a country preoccupied with material gain. Ciardi's poetry written after World War II expresses his concern with materialism and inhumanity while also focusing on his family and home life.

Ciardi's first volume of verse, *Homeward to America* (1940), presents a United States not yet recovered from the Depression and fully aware of the imminence of war. The realization of war is recounted in his next volume, *Other Skies* (1947), which contains poems chronicling Ciardi's military service during World War II. *Live Another Day: Poems* (1949) and *From Time to Time* (1951) place increasing emphasis on daily concerns and include love poems to his wife. The love poems, reprinted in the ''To Judith'' section of *As If: Poems New and Selected* (1955) and in *I Marry You: A Sheaf of Love Poems* (1958), are distinctive in that the social realism of much of Ciardi's other poems is tempered by a more romantic vision and lyrical sensibility. *Live Another Day* also contains ''Foreword to the Reader of (Some) General Culture,'' an acclaimed essay in which Ciardi addresses the nature of poetry. Although Ciardi's own poetry has sometimes been faulted for obscurity, this essay reveals his belief that poetry should be accessible to a general audience.

In the Stoneworks (1961), *In Fact* (1962), and *Person to Person* (1964) detail Ciardi's efforts to remain loyal to his values and retain artistic vitality while becoming increasingly popular and financially successful. Commenting on this struggle, Ernest Sandeen noted: ''The irony is his fortunate discovery that he can enjoy the best of both worlds and so defy the quaint tradition that associates primitive nature with plain living and high thinking.'' *This Strangest Everything* (1966) and *An Alphabestiary: Twenty-Six Poems* (1966) continue Ciardi's observations of contemporary society and reflect his increased acceptance of modern conditions. In *The Little That Is All* (1974) and *For Instance* (1979), Ciardi parodies himself and his suburban lifestyle in poems dealing with such domestic details as family matters, neighborhood disputes, and power lawn mowers. Critical reception to Ciardi's later poetry has been less uniformly favorable than that of his early work. Steven Ratiner found the verse of *For Instance* ''more an example of the malaise of American culture than an examination of its problems,'' and although David Wojahn noted of *Selected Poems* (1984) that ''there's some fine detail about growing up in an Italian immigrant family,'' he also asserted that ''Ciardi's smug tone can weaken his effect.'' Nevertheless, as Dana Gioia noted, Ciardi at his best has created poems ''that are strong, memorable, and unmistakably personal.''

Ciardi's reputation as a prominent literary figure is founded on a wide range of accomplishments in addition to his verse.

As poetry editor of *Saturday Review* for more than fifteen years, Ciardi's discriminating tastes and strict demands on poetry generated much controversy. Many of the pieces he wrote for this magazine are collected in *Manner of Speaking* (1972). His prominence as a teacher and critic of poetry is evidenced by *How Does a Poem Mean?* (1960), a highly regarded introduction to the rudiments of poetry. Ciardi's translation of Dante's *Divine Comedy* is also widely respected. *The Browser's Dictionary and Native's Guide to the Unknown American Language* (1980) and *A Second Browser's Dictionary and Native's Guide to the Unknown American Language* (1983) display Ciardi's fascination with the English language, as do his numerous books for children, which are noted for their humor and wordplay.

(See also *CLC,* Vol. 10; *Contemporary Authors,* Vols. 5-8, rev. ed., Vol. 118 [obituary]; *Contemporary Authors New Revision Series,* Vol. 5; *Contemporary Authors Autobiography Series,* Vol. 2; *Something about the Author,* Vol. 1; and *Dictionary of Literary Biography,* Vol. 5.)

EDA LOU WALTON

[In *Homeward to America*, Ciardi] proves that for the young American poet as for the English, the personal themes of love, friendship and family relationships cannot be divorced from the social theme. His title is ironical, for although he advocates the poetic exploration of what America means, it means to him quite clearly that in this country too youth may "lose beauty in terror, terror in inquisition."

John Ciardi is not a propagandist, nor a satirist, but he states that the young poets are "reporting merely," and that what they report is their own feeling that Spain, Europe, the world of horrors, enters into every conscious moment. Even in his love poems, he notes that the playful moment of wooing is slanted across by the idea that the night in which lovers walk would be fine for snipers, that the landscape would lend itself to defense.

The romantic mood in poetry is gone. . . .

In place of the romantic mood, this poet interprets youth's awareness of coming danger within America itself. Traveling west, he notes the unemployed and the desolated farms. His poetry, which is a clear and condensed exposition of youth's sensibility to the modern scene, rises now and then to an image which projects the emotion more violently than can the terse statement. I venture to guess that this poet will move more and more away from exposition toward the dramatic method of combining interpretive action with observation. He can write (as in **"Valediction"**) the symbolic lyric—and beautifully. But for his purposes—the precise representation of the American scene without utopian thinking, and of the growing psychology of general apprehension—his poetry of statement rather more than that of song or of violent image is successful. He is haunted by the sense of a possibly dangerous future for himself and his generation.

Eda Lou Walton, "Poems in a Time of Conflict," in The New York Times Book Review, February 25, 1940, p. 5.

RUTH LECHLITNER

[The poems in Ciardi's *Homeward to America*] are by way of discovery, of learning about America. Mr. Ciardi has looked about him, and made a good many well-observed notes. He is aware that most poetry today, brought down from the thinness of upper air, becomes "time's journalism"—a way of reporting. And Mr. Ciardi is a good reporter, as all good poets must be. If anything stands in his way it is not journalism, but the class-room. Evident in his work are book-gathered symbols and references not yet wholly assimilated by or subordinated to his own experiences. Sometimes a formal, academic manner influences his expression and (fortunately to a lesser degree) encroaches upon his viewpoint. The use of coldly colorless words not common to American speech—calibrating, ectoplasm, euphemism, catharsis—chill the hard, earthy impact of his writing, often stiffen up the vigorous free rhythms, the natural music of his lines. Obviously it is second-hand literary-derived observation that goes into such phrases as

> Grasses and galaxies merge in one
> Mysticism
> Freudian, the moon smiles.

Mr. Ciardi gets away from this in his better poems. He turns from the myth at the continent's edge and faces west. **"To**

Westward" is a strong poem, gritty and plain-seeing. It follows neither the Paul Engle variety of windy patriotism nor the soap-box brand of social oratory. A young man travels across the great plains, the names of the makers of America rich in his mind: Clarke, Custer, Pike, Johnny Appleseed. He sees miles of parched earth, rusted iron in barnyards, towns rotting; not historic place names but other names: Eureka Dishpan, Inc., Hi-Jinx Novelty Company. . . .

There are other good poems; one on the innocent pretenses and imaginings of boys growing up together that pointedly concludes: "Are we ready yet? Is the Pretense ended? May we advance now?" **"Letter to My Sisters at Home"** presents through acidly sharp images the psychological differences between two world cultures, and why allegiance to the new makes it necessary to deny even blood-ties in rejecting the decay and death of the old.

He writes of cities: not so much in terms of skyline and factory as in terms of human history: the weight of generations of migrations from times past bearing upon the present. He is less sure when he attempts a transposition of figures from legend—Elaine and Lancelot, Hamlet and the "dark lady of a single sonnet"—to such modern city types as counter-girl and clerk. And he is least successful when he tries to analyze personal conflict in metaphysical terms. But in **"Spring Song"** he writes delightfully of the careless happiness of boy and girl walking out, playing at love; but the boy's mind planning also how a sniper might clean this hilltop, or a machine-gun bottle this pass. . . .

The tragedy in Spain enters two of the poems—a tragedy that has done something to an American boy's ideas of honor, that forces him either to leave his world of books and dreams and face the "enemy known," or cling to innocence and "leave his world undone." There are no false heroics in Mr. Ciardi's deeply felt contemplation upon the events of his time, no passionate rebellions that are more romantic than the "romancing" he decries. He looks at disaster calmly and squarely. His ability to get beneath the surface, to find purpose and meaning under "the scattering fact of incident," his efforts to fit these into ordered patterns of evaluation, are rare in the work of a young poet.

Ruth Lechlitner, "First Generation U.S.A.," in New York Herald Tribune Books, May 26, 1940, p. 13.

FRAJAM TAYLOR

"The Foolish Wing," writes John Ciardi in *Homeward to America,*

> Is done now with bright thinness of upper air. Weight
> Of body sinks earthward: good capture. Probing of
>   wing's
> Torn muscle under the raised and eager feathers
> Points obvious and necessary truth. Time grows too late
> For the torn ligament to attempt heaven. There is
> Nothing either in rememberings.

And it is just this spirit of practical realism and undaunted recognition of "obvious and necessary truth" that dominates this first volume in which all the fiery eagerness of youth colors and quickens the sober reflections of maturity. While only four out of the thirty-four poems have America for their immediate theme, the titular emphasis is well founded; for though Ciardi experiments occasionally with more intimate themes—as in **"The Visit"** and **"Valediction"**—he is at his best when inspired by the problems pertinent or auxiliary to the furtherance of his avowed purpose. Furthermore, having made it clear in the excellent **"Letter to Mother"** that the "dynastic example" of her coming to America may be emulated only in a traveling "across the sprung longitudes of the mind—And the blood's latitudes" he not merely indicates the nature of his turning "inland," but brings to the projected adventure all the earnestness and sturdy vigor—the hope in, and courage to meet, the future—which the early American pioneers brought to theirs.

Like his mother, who encountered "the rankness of steerage, the landing in fog . . . the tenements, the reek and the shouting in the streets," and those earlier arrivals whose dreams of a heavenly Arcadia struck against the awakening reality of a hard and savage earth, he, too, has had his disappointments; and in the fine poem **"To Westward"** he writes tersely but feelingly of the disillusionment attendant upon a trip west, where he had expected to find reminders of all that marked the age and achievement of such national heroes as Clarke, Custer, Pike and Johnny Appleseed, but found instead only parched earth, soot, smelteries and slums where gray-muscled men loitered and drifted in unrhythmical routine—with nothing to say, and nothing to do—just waiting. . . . He accepts the unromantic truth rather as a challenge than as a deterrent; and by this convincing attestation of his own ability to find adventure "natively" adds weight and beauty to his hope and faith in America.

But Ciardi brings something more than the sober realism and earnest maturity of his apprehensions to his task and to his poetry. And if he is wise enough, and honest enough, to say that

> The romance is dead,
> Childhood gone under. Time is the offense:
> What work we do against the shriveling head
> Of years is done in self-defense

and reasonable enough to ask:

> What are we sure of but the stated purpose,
> The hope to make it real and the long fear
> That time may stamp it VOID, and close
> A canceled journal for our meaning here?

he is also passionate enough to be filled with pity and indignation that there should be so little time for love; while at the same time bitterly resenting the indifference to disaster of some, and growing ever more hotly impatient over the fear and timid vacillation of others—who, in a time of great danger to the integrity of their country and their ideals, feed "steel-caged hearts" on hesitations and allow all "necessary murder" to rise high in the mind only: "Falling limp and undone from the hand's grasp." (pp. 337-39)

> *Frajam Taylor, "A New Adventure," in* Poetry, *Vol. LVI, No. 6, September, 1940, pp. 337-40.*

PEARL STRACHAN

The scientific and machine age is blessed with a considerable number of poets of ability. Some of the best poets writing today in the English tongue served in the armed forces of the second world war. And one of the best of these is John Ciardi. . . .

[*Other Skies*] is the work of one who knows how to make poetry and loves it enough to work at it; of one who has taken hold on his own scientific machine age, an age of violence and atomic warfare, an age of winged men and sky traveling, and from it has extracted all he can get of truth and beauty.

The diction is fresh and inspired. Kansas fields, from cloud height, become "a plaid abstraction." Morning, to the air-corps sergeant, is the "brass jazz of bugles hurled like sudden weathers on the field of mind." Embarkation for the Pacific theater of war gives the poet a view of planes "arranged on fields of concrete flowered with lights."

While the personal experiences which accompanied the making of the poems occurred, for the most part, during the recent world war, the poet does not offer the collection as "war poetry." Poetry, in his opinion, doesn't amount to much unless it has a far more universal value than mere war records.

The satire is mellow. In the first section of the book, which reflects a young man's memory of the world he knew before the outbreak of war, he sketches in the crowded beaches of America, the school graduation exercises and so forth, and prepares the stage for part number two, where: "The stars fade down the angles of their rank." . . .

A graphic piece in this collection is **"Death of a Bomber,"** describing the landing of a bombing plane which had caught fire. . . .

Mr. Ciardi's poetry is not the sort to lull the reader into dreams. It stabs him wide awake.

> *Pearl Strachan, "A Poet of Today," in* The Christian Science Monitor, *December 20, 1947, p. 11.*

WINFIELD TOWNLEY SCOTT

The stresses of [Ciardi's] new book, *Live Another Day,* indicate marked development of an intellectual poet. These accumulate in the three poems with which the book closes: the **"Letter to Virginia Johnson,"** the **"Letter to Dante,"** and (really another letter-poem) **"A Guide to Poetry."** They are not the best poems in the book. But that, with a young poet, is not necessarily the basic question. New poems which are not so good as other poems are often transitional poems. In them the poet is working toward something neither more nor less mysterious than himself. And since all of Ciardi's poetry is woven out of the belly of "personal record" these are a consistent development.

They exhibit qualities found throughout Ciardi's poetry. They bring to a head the tendency toward wit, an off-the-top-of-the-mind yet serious playing with concepts of contemporary experience. Although not thoroughly remarked, this is a dominant tendency in recent poetry; from Auden to Viereck. The verse is, I suppose, more in the tradition of the 18th century than any other. (pp. 119-20)

Ciardi's three poems respectively discuss man and his universe, man within a special System, and, most lightly of all, the realistic politics of esoteric poets. . . . In general these poems thrive on the language of science and materialism which Ciardi has long since used with ease. They flourish with his agility of mind, his meaningful playfulness. They expose what seems to me his danger: too much ease, too loose and wordy a way of writing.

Let me extenuate, in terms of Ciardi's language. He is extraordinarily adept in employing the imagery of our times; all those things, whether of laboratory or airport or city street, which mark the ways in which our mid-twentieth century America looks, sounds and acts. And his vocabulary is contiguous.

Again and again his language, as he uses it, seems a set of fine tools. He can employ it with concentration, or he can employ it casually. It is the latter glibness which, I should guess, he must most guard against. . . .

Already I have suggested consistency of organic growth in John Ciardi's work. In *Homeward to America* certain dispositions of the later books are readily discoverable; and I should like to tick off some of them, for they are interesting.

The very young Ciardi was a shade rhetoric-happy in those days. He was learning tricks from MacLeish (who, to be sure, had learnt his here and there beforehand); and yet, though of course sometimes imitatively, Ciardi was working not slavishly but cleanly. (p. 120)

There is the attraction of the contemporary scene, names and places and gadgetry, and political atmospherics (depression and pre-war). . . .

The memoir-poem, which he is fascinated by, appears in **"Letter for Those Who Grew Up Together."** A few pages farther on, the tragedy of war is first sounded, with reference to the civil war in Spain. Immediately following, political injustice is slated in a Yeatsian piece more relevant now than when it was new—**"To One 'Investigated' By the Last Senate Committee, or the Next."**

All these reflect a specific era recorded by a sensitized young man. From the first Ciardi has had that basic instinct of the lyric poet, to personalize the extraneous. To let it come through himself. . . . These first are the poems of a youth of "foreign extraction"; poor; lonely and lost enough to suit the American literary tradition; charging toward his own identity, as toward his real birthright, through a greed for books and learning. . . .

Some of the poems are slight. Many are made of mood-music. The forms are generally irregular—but the ear is generally good.

There is some anti-romance going on. At least, the mind tends to have the last word on *l'amour*. Baleful prophecy thunders over both love and its season in **"Spring Song."** And if planes appear as "silver hawks" it is now, in retrospect, only to remind us that such imagery is to be turned upside down in the maturer poems of *Other Skies*. . . . (p. 121)

Other Skies is Ciardi's testament of war: going off to it, living through it, coming home from it. I have swiped the phrase "personal record" not from Conrad but from the jacket of that second book: it is perfectly accurate. It applies, as I have said, to all his poetry: through himself. War experience was of course bound to be a tremendous chapter. . . .

Without question, *Other Skies* is a part of the important poetic record of the war. Only Karl Shapiro's and Randall Jarrell's verse ranks with it. The work of each is already selecting itself out, so to speak; but moments in the best of it stay in the mind. (p. 122)

The suppression of emotionalism in poetry of "personal record" genre is a threat to its potency. Where Ciardi yields to it, in war poems and others, I suspect he is also exploring the methods of his art. Through a series of **"Birthday"** poems, but in many more not obviously connected, he has pursued the development of his own thought out of his own experience. As an artist he has properly sought to objectify the expression and thus raise its significance. So far, so good. He accomplishes his objective an enviable number of times. Only when typicality drains the color of his own voice do the sleek tools

of his language take over; simplicity murmurs into stylelessness, and poems slide together slippery and journalistic. His difficult course runs between personality and impersonality. (p. 123)

[Ciardi] is at his best . . . when he performs in just the way his sardonic final line of *Other Skies* puts it:

> The camera photographs the camera
> man.

Succinct finality again, one of many in *Other Skies*. The forms have tightened to a favored iambic pentameter and a penchant for a five-line or six-line stanza, often rhymed. But rhymed or unrhymed, a stanza which usually avoids ruminant monotony by tight-packed, nervous statement. The style achieves authority in the massively-dense poem **"To Judith Asleep"** which opens *Live Another Day*.

This is a very beautiful poem, a superb example of Ciardi's work at highly concentrated efficiency. Though he remarks in his new book that metaphysics "must end in boredom or neurosis," elsewhere he resolves "to keep the symbol but to shoot the bird;" and in **"To Judith Asleep"** there is passionate blending of the real and the idea. Only its fourth stanza trembles a little in enumerative detail, yet it contains the loveliest image in a poem assertive with valid rhetoric.

Why is the rhetoric valid? Because it is tense with sexuality. The authentic emotions of the man contemplating the naked, sleeping body of his wife against the frightening concept of death, is unquestionable in terms of experienced love and unquestionable as a specific for the generality of art. (pp. 123-24)

I should also mention, in [*Live Another Day*], such typical interweavings, knittings-together, as **"Sunday Afternoon Near the Naval Air Base."** Here we link back to the war poems of *Other Skies* and even come full circle to a phrase or two in *Homeward to America;* for now civilian-Ciardi watches the new aviator as

> . . . awed as children are
> At his pure motion, but I cannot
> guess
> What tokens will be on his battle
> dress
> When all his Sunday practice goes
> to war.

This, and such pregnant phrasing as the "huge forgetting" of the Easter Island stone faces, reminds us that here is the poet of the first book; sadder, wiser, more intellectual and more substantial. It has been a real, indigenous growing, and it would seem to avoid definition as yet. (p. 124)

Winfield Townley Scott, "Three Books by John Ciardi," in The University of Kansas City Review, *Vol. XVI, No. 2, Winter, 1949, pp. 119-25.*

MILTON CRANE

In his fourth volume of poetry, *From Time to Time,* John Ciardi displays his striking and original talent exercised upon a diversity of themes. Although many of his poems are quite explicit studies of a limited number of recurring subjects—death, the father, birth—one is always aware of the particularity and immediacy of the experiences that inspired these poems. The sense of excitement that is communicated stems from the naturalness and effortlessness with which Mr. Ciardi's imagination moves from these experiences to large and complex artistic statements.

The figure of the father broods large over many of the poems, particularly in **"My Father's Watch,"** in which the poet is locked in a watch which is at once the Ptolemaic universe and the symbol of a lost orthodoxy. And the elegiac tone is predominant in such pieces as **"Anatomy Lab," "Three Songs for a Cadaver,"** and **"Elegy for Sam."**

Along with the richness and strangeness of conception that characterize the best poems in *From Time to Time* goes a curious and sometimes distressing unevenness of diction and tone. . . . And one cannot avoid the suspicion that some of the more fantastic images in such a poem as **"High Tension Lines Across a Landscape"** are dictated by a desire to dazzle the reader rather than by the needs of the poem itself.

> Milton Crane, *"Elegies, Rich and Strange," in* The New York Times Book Review, *May 25, 1952, p. 27.*

F. CUDWORTH FLINT

To poems selected from three previous books, *Other Skies, Live Another Day,* and *From Time to Time,* Mr. Ciardi has added a number of hitherto uncollected poems to make up *As If,* a book which, of those I have seen by this poet, best performs for him the role he assigns to poetry when, as quoted on the dust-jacket, he says: "Poetry is AS IF's reality. . . ."

It is in poems of family reminiscence that Mr. Ciardi is least an excogitator of symbols—and how many poets, after Rimbaud, have dared refrain?—and most a *person,* affectionately detached ("having survived a theology and a war"), and warmly, appreciatively amused. **"The Evil Eye,"** recounting the efforts of worried female relatives to avert from him at his birth the curse indicated by the title, renders delightfully a scene of primitive flurry. In such poems, Mr. Ciardi does not try for dialect, or artificially limit his own point of view; he does not forget what he has learned as student of poetry. But his style is at its simplest. Any reader will find these poems immediately accessible.

The eight poems grouped under the rubric **"War Poems"** occasionally show a side of Mr. Ciardi presumably fostered by his years as a B-29 gunner in the Pacific—the now tight-lipped, now sardonic, and determinedly tough warrior who will not allow any situation or feeling to carry him overboard. . . .

[In other pieces] Mr. Ciardi's considerable gift of satire finds expression, as in **"Childe Horvald to the Dark Tower Came,"** in which he spoofs, deflatingly rather than crushingly, the chivalric-romantic-impetuous stance. . . .

Critics in quarterlies and other places where they pontificate may be inclined to rate Mr. Ciardi by his poems in the more difficult modern manner—a hop-skip-and-jump from one fragment of imagery to another, across bottomless gulfs of implication; by such poems as **"Two Egrets"** in the section labelled **"Prayers,"** with its three fine concluding lines and its six distracting lines just preceding; or **"The Size of a Universe"** in the section **"Poems Looking In,"** where the gyrations of relativistic galaxies, super-added to the saltations of a symbolist presentation, left one reader both macrocosmically and microcosmically astray. Similarly confusing was some of the imagery in the sequence of poems **"To Judith"** with which the book opens, though here, on a second and third reading, some of

the phrases presenting the body of the beloved lying beneath a wavering moonlight attained a precarious rightness. To my taste, Mr. Ciardi is most successful in this manner when the scheme of a particular poem allows him to reiterate his images. The chiming, heard and unheard, in **"Home Revisited: Midnight and Thursday"** is effective. Where the theme of a poem is embodied in ever new images, the reader comes to feel too much like a man hunting for a dozen different objects in a large and crowded Woolworth's with which he is imperfectly acquainted.

> F. Cudworth Flint, *"Ciardi's New Poems," in* The Nation, *Vol. 181, No. 21, November 19, 1955, p. 444.*

MAURICE IRVINE

"As If," says John Ciardi in explanation of his title, "strikes me as the enduring mode of poetry. IS is the mode of prose. Poetry is AS IF's reality." And if that statement isn't clear enough, read the poems, because it becomes increasingly clear that with [*As If*], his fifth volume, John Ciardi is one of our most rewarding and one of our most active poets. . . .

To describe what Mr. Ciardi does in these poems is not easy. There are words like "wit," "perception," "humanity," "vitality," but the labels don't seem very satisfactory, although they are certainly descriptive of the qualities one finds in the poems. . . .

This collection has been justly described as a generous one, for Mr. Ciardi has a wide range of interest. There are love lyrics, war poems, family poems, prayers, observations, occasional, introspective, and flights-of-witty-fancy poems. In fact, everything but the expositional and the exhortatory. It is true that a few of the poems are to be understood only through strenuous effort, but the proper (perhaps ideal) reader will share his thought and feeling as a sort of privilege.

Mr. Ciardi has truly all kinds of technical skill. What is more impressive is a keenly intelligent and witty humanity, easy to assume, most difficult to possess. When you have read the book, you have been for a while in remarkably good company.

> Maurice Irvine, *"No Labels Available," in* The New York Times Book Review, *November 20, 1955, p. 16.*

RANDALL JARRELL

The most notable thing about John Ciardi's *As If* is a kind of crude power. The hesitations, reticences, and inabilities of the poetic nature—for to be able to say what it does say is to be unable to say everything else—are unknown to natures of such ready force, natures more akin to those of born executives, men ripe for running things. This writer uses Stevens', or Shapiro's, or half a dozen other poets' tricks and techniques as easily, and with as much justification, as a salesman would use a competitor's sales-talk—it works, doesn't it? But he doesn't use the styles as delicately and helplessly as these poets used them—after all, he *can* help himself, has helped himself. He resembles, as a poet, what Helene Deutsch calls "persons of the 'as if' type, because in every new object-relation they live *as if* they were really living their own life and expressing their own feelings, opinions, and views." He is much at his best as a translator, where his native force can put on a more sensitive and individual mask—his translation of the *Inferno* has more narrative power, strength of action, than any other I know. (p. 479)

Randall Jarrell, "Graves and the White Goddess—Part II," in The Yale Review, *Vol. XLV, No. 3, Spring, 1956, pp. 467-80.**

JAMES WRIGHT

Mr. Ciardi's book [*I Marry You*] is called "a sheaf of love-poems", and one is at once struck by that special combination of tenderness and roughness which characterizes this poet when he is in form. These are fine qualities in combination—they are Hardyesque—and, if they were always recorded in perfect balance, we should have a fantastically good book. As it is, *I Marry You* is easily the best single book of Mr. Ciardi's that I have ever read; and that, in spite of his numerous other activities as teacher and editor, he should continue the essentially personal experimentation of his poetry is the best possible sign. In short, it seems to me that he is still searching for the proper balance between tenderness and roughness, between the lyrical delicacy and the world it must sing about, between the human and the "modern". When he finds his own balance, we shall have a remarkable love-poet indeed. Even in this book, he comes close to what I imagine to be his own true harmony. In the title-poem, for example, there are lines in which the clarity of the music and the depth of the emotion are splendidly fused: "I marry you from time and a great door / is shut and stays shut against wind, sea, stone. . . ." What a relief it would be if Mr. Ciardi would only let the two magnificent lines alone! But no. Wind, sea, stone are not enough for him; he has to add "sunburst and heavenfall" to his list. I think these two Hopkinsisms (an ugly word for an ugly effect) ruin Mr. Ciardi's lines just as those lines have begun to find their characteristic beauty—their simplicity, humanity, strength. The quality of a fine excess can be one of the glories of lyric poetry; but at what point does fine excess become mere "modernism"? I ask this question in the hope that it may be useful. Certainly Mr. Ciardi's book as a whole is a document of considerable human importance. The distinguishing feature of his love-poetry is its ability to include the concrete physical realities in his poetic vision, as indeed love includes them. Once again, a poet is returning to Nature; that is, he searches behind the conventions of love-poetry in order to rediscover their true sources, and so to restore himself. In so far as he is successful in his search, he strengthens all of us, and he restores poetry too. Most of the poems, taken singly, are marred by "modernisms" like the "sunburst and heavenfall" I have mentioned. Yet, as a whole, the book is beautiful and alive. If my remarks are quibbles, then I justify them by expressing my belief that Mr. Ciardi is a good poet—good enough to be nagged. (pp. 46-7)

James Wright, "Four New Volumes," in Poetry, *Vol. XCIII, No. 1, October, 1958, pp. 46-50.**

JANET FISCALINI

John Ciardi's new book is likely to be taken up by those who admire frankly emotional poetry, likely to be given up by those who resent rhetorical exaggeration. But in fact, I think, the *39 Poems* are rather unequal. Ciardi has divided the book into three subtitled sections: **"In the ego with us all"**; **"In the year of the longest Cadillac"**; and **"Certainties."** The poems in the second group have political or public subjects, those in the third group are concerned with poets, artists, and poetry, those in the first group—well, those in the first group are the ones which are *not* concerned with art nor with public conditions. One finds various developments of familiar lyric themes.

The second and longest section is by far the best. There is clean observation and detail, and clear passion; many of the poems are moving and strongly made. I would rather not think how many poets have written "Letters from Rome," but Ciardi's **"Letter"** hasn't a baroque fountain in it. It has Romans in it, instead, and Mussolini, and several unpleasant, significant scenes. **"Captain Nicholas Strong"** may not hold together as a complete poem, but the central scene, in which prisoner-corpses break from a liberated concentration camp, is frighteningly successful. Some of the quieter things are excellent; one might mention **"Gift," "Massive Retaliation,"** and **"Letter from Paris."** (pp. 503-04)

Unfortunately, Ciardi's "violent style" tends toward a familiar kind of bombast. He crowds his lines, but the things he crowds into them simply aren't good enough: "Small / they were, yes, a boy-race, but men, too, / the deaths they played with being god-grabbed old / as their blood's night fit. . . ."

The bombast is worst in the third section, **"Certainties."** Most of these poems are celebrations, praises of "good poets in a bad age." The theme is vague and popular—popular among poets, at least—and liable to thick oratory. It would take more discrimination, more thought, than Ciardi shows here, to define it.

The first section, **"In the ego with us all,"** has some very good things: the title poem; **"Shark Hunter"**; parts of **"Abundance."** But again, there is a tendency to fall into facile solutions or facile writing. . . .

And one is irritated by sleepily rhythmed repetitions, by dully pretentious "sentences." Ciardi can be graceful enough, at other times. But it is the clear, unspecialized eye that one remembers, and the spare narrative rendering. (p. 504)

Janet Fiscalini, "Unequal Value," in Commonweal, *Vol. LXXI, No. 18, January 29, 1960, pp. 503-04.*

JOSEPHINE JACOBSEN

"There is no feast but energy," says John Ciardi. Mr. Ciardi's never-disputed energy, as passionate as ever, is more sharply disciplined than in the past. *39 Poems* is his best book by a handsome margin. His personal poetic dangers dog him and make an occasional successful foray, but their total elimination would eliminate too the quintessence of his flavor. He is still sometimes harried by zeal bursting its poetic bounds, oversimplification, and the conviction that the smell of sweat is the opposite of the smell of ink—a not wholly unwelcome tenet. Sometimes instead of the simplification in which singleness of viewpoint is understood to be the choice, there is the implication that no choice is necessary or indeed possible. Infamy strikes Mr. Ciardi with such admirable immediacy that he is apt to give it a single face. The passionate sincerity which produced **"After the Street Fighting"** has the sense of ignoring the ramifications of infamy and its antiquity as our bedfellow. We are indeed paid for by deaths—but at what point was this not true? Mr. Ciardi is well aware of this, but ignoring it as a poetic device is dangerous. (Yet it is noticeable how often in this book Mr. Ciardi does relate the object of his anger to its roots—as in the poem on Giordano Bruno:

man's tongue, confused to meat, and still
bursting from carrion like a gull surprised—
the sprung word's wing-spread, taking all the air.)

It is possible also to carp at the lavishness of hyphens, scattered for pace and roughness, but effective in inverse proportion to their use. There are fourteen of these in a five verse poem; the first verse alone has camp-sung; roar-boys; god-sent; runt-running; deep-seized; goat-scented. But these marginal defects are nearly obliterated by the tide of the poetry. Mr. Ciardi is a poet whose tempo often obscures the fact that his best accent yields itself slowly, through the mass of his poems. There are lines whose single beauty is heavily reinforced by their kinship with other lines in other poems. (pp. 235-36)

This work is nourished by three outstanding qualities: a marriage of passion and intelligence; a brilliantly assimilated technique, and a refusal to play safe. By the last is not meant Mr. Ciardi's legendary willingness to stand up and be counted, but—far more important—his refusal to devitalize his verse by limiting his demands upon it. . . . Like that of Joyce, Mr. Ciardi's work is the heir of a fruitful tension. It is subtly and consistently enriched by the symbols and ambience of a religion to which he cannot accede. Increasingly this has been true of his work; in this book seven out of thirty-nine poems contain no hieratic reference. These echoes, and this preoccupation with "the thing behind the name of the thing", the white elk, unseen but sensed in the thicket, preclude the powdery finish which so many poems make in the mind. (p. 236)

The curiously ominous meter of **"Dialogue in the Stoneworks,"** which, in the first four lines, falls like a shadow over the reader, is an example of Mr. Ciardi's ability to use meter as a tuning-fork to mood; which stands him in good stead in one of his fortes—the narrative poem. Two of the book's best poems, **"Ulysses,"** and **"Captain Nicholas Strong,"** are narratives. In each case neither the pace nor drama of the poem deflects it from its core of significance—a sufficiently rare accomplishment. The book has, also and notably, **"A Dream"**; **"In Ego with Us All"**; **"Bridal Photo, 1906"**; **"Of History Fiction"**; **"Language"**; and **"Homage to Lorca."** And, for a stunner, a poem on Dylan Thomas which one does not wish omitted. Like his saint, Mr. Ciardi "comes and throws rocks through the window". A little shattered glass seems a small price to pay for this book. (p. 237)

> *Josephine Jacobsen, "Whittemore, Engle, Scott, Ciardi," in* Poetry, *Vol. XCVI, No. 4, July, 1960, pp. 230-37.**

JAMES G. SOUTHWORTH

Some poetry is easy to write about; some is not. That of John Ciardi is not. The difficulty is not that of interpretation of any single poem because, for the most part, a few readings are enough to clear up any one poem's obscurity. The difficulty is of a different sort—that of a synthesized evaluation. In other words it is the problem of evaluating a poet rather than a poem. The careful reader senses unresolved inner conflicts in Ciardi's work. There is, for example, the conflict between the romantic and the realist; between the man needing solitude and the man requiring an audience; between the man proud of his immigrant family and the compulsive drive of the man struggling against a sense of inferiority because of that family; between the man of feeling and the man of thought; between the poet's theory and his practice.

Ciardi's first volume of poetry—*Homeward to America*—is not only an outstanding achievement from the point of view of youthful quality, but in it Ciardi touches upon most of the subjects treated in his later poetry; as well as his contradictory

attitudes toward some of those subjects: anti-materialism, his immigrant background, imagination, intellectual courage, love, nature, patriotism, political convictions, and realism. All these are important in shaping his humanistic approach. The essential difference between this and the later volumes is the greater degree to which Ciardi permits his feelings to control his expression, his greater surface lyricism. Later the rhythms become more taut, a little drier, the feeling more restrained, the emotion more mature. Whereas none of the early poems is obscure, several readings of a few in the later volumes fail to communicate the poet's purpose. Some of his later love poems are more tightly metaphoric and therefore more difficult.

Ciardi has enunciated as axioms for poetry three statements about its subject matter that immediately concern us: "Poetry should be about the lives of people," "Poetry should be specific," and "There is no subject not fit for poetry and no word not fit for poetry." (p. 583)

Although reminiscences of childhood, youth, and early manhood occur in many poems of the early volumes, it is not until in *As If,* in a somewhat lengthy section called **"Tribal Poems,"** that he discards his romantic attitude toward his family and writes out much of his insecurity stemming from his origins. His honesty in these poems helps free him from a compensatory overassertive ego. He recreates many incidents of childhood, of peasant superstitions, of his pride in the earthliness of his father and mother, or of some sudden act (like the flight of starlings) that made him aware of himself and of other miscellaneous incidents. Of these poems, many have a therapeutic value for the poet, but small survival value except as sociological or biographical documents; little as poetry *per se.* Those to his father and mother have a depth not readily apparent. . . .

The knowledge of the poet derived from the **"Tribal Poems"** makes more understandable Ciardi's poems on love. Particularly in *I Marry You,* he strives for a frankness somewhat akin to that of Benton's *This Is My Beloved,* an attitude that contrasts strongly with the New England reticence of the proper Bostonians. In the early poems about love, **"Valediction," "Action and Epilogue,"** and **"Anniversary,"** from *Homeward to America,* the emotion is more direct and less cerebral than that of the later ones among which are **"To Judith Asleep"** (first published in *Live Another Day* and again . . . published in *I Marry You*). Judith is more than his wife; she is a symbol of all desired women. Probably because it is less sensuously passionate than others of the love poems but possesses a quiet inward depth **"Most Like an Arch This Marriage"** carries greater conviction and is the best of his love poems. . . .

"The Stone without Edges" is an expansion of Ciardi's statement about marriage: that no marriage is perpetually smooth, but that from the annoyances springs a deeper love. **"That Summer Shore"** further communicates his feeling for his wife. Closely bound up with his love is the fear that death will terminate the relationship, a fear that haunts many of the poems. In several instances, Ciardi reveals a predilection for the macabre and likes, metaphorically at least, "shelves of mouse turds, dusts, and dirty damps." Does this predilection arise from a compulsive desire to show that he is strong, realistic, and not bound by the genteel tradition? (p. 584)

Ciardi's realistic attitude possibly arises from his realization of the danger of excessive idealism. He not only tells a young American that "the world is not the world you dream," but that to cling to his bright innocence is to leave his "world to be undone'' (**"To a Young American the Day after the Fall of Barcelona"**). (pp. 584-85)

Ciardi puts this ability to view life critically to excellent use as a positive force by buttressing his realism with an intense intellectual courage. **"The Night Lies," "Letter to J.R.R., the Last Transcendentalist,"** and **"To One 'Investigated' By the Last Senate Committee, or the Next,"** all from *Homeward to America,* comprise an early statement of his clear and courageous attitude. His intense interest in the world as it is and its meaning in the light of our new scientific knowledge prevents discouragement.... To him no one period is better than another and a man of character (a poet?) will be the same regardless of his time or environment (**"A Sermon Beginning with the Portrait of a Man"**)....

His courage is visible, in both his patriotic and political poems. Just as a convert to religion is often more intense in his faith than a person whose entire life has been spent in the church (and Ciardi touches on this in **"The Convert"**), so often does an immigrant or the son of an immigrant evince a more active patriotism than one whose family has lived in America for generations. Ciardi's patriotism is not chauvinistic; it springs from a sincere realization of what America has to offer. (p. 585)

Every volume of Ciardi's poetry contains attacks against the too-prevalent materialism of America's culture, and these attacks take many forms: sometimes head on, sometimes oblique, sometimes with all the force of a reformer, sometimes satirical. Since this materialism is not endemic to any one stratum of society, his attack may be general and implied (**"The Coming"**); against the average man in the street (**"Biography," "On the Year of Many Conversions etc."**); may have a political cast (**"On Flying to a Political Convention"**); or be a self-examination (**"Poem for My Thirty-Second Birthday"**); the celebration of the Christmas season (**"A Christmas Carol," "Christmas Eve"**); symbolic (**"The Hawk," "Child Horvald to the Dark Tower Came"**); religious (**"Sunday Morning"**); or as a warning to future ages (**"Letters for the Next Time"**).

Were the reader, however, to confine himself to the poems falling under the foregoing categories, even were he to include many of the poet's war poems, he would have an inaccurate picture of Ciardi. As a poet, he is often at his best in those poems where his love and accurate observation of nature enhance the communicative power of his experience. I have already mentioned **"The Hawk"**; but it may be a gull (**"Gulls from a Fantail"**), a snowy heron (**"Snowy Heron"**), spring in its many moods (**"Spring Song," "Flowering Quince," "March Morning," "Morning in the Park"**), even a cow (**"The Cow"**).

Obviously Ciardi is not a poet of a few recurring ideas. He is gregarious and his poems reveal this characteristic. He may long for solitude and enjoy it when it comes, but he soon tires of it (**"Letter from a Metaphysical Countryside"**). (pp. 585-86)

But what has Ciardi contributed to poetry as poetry and not as source material for the biographer, the psychologist, and/or the social historian? Can the reader focus his critical eye on the individual poem and admire it as an entity in which the subject matter is the mere skeleton? Or does he commend the poet rather than the poem? Granted that the poet's subject matter must not be trivial, and Ciardi's is not, the survival value as poetry nevertheless lies in the poem's craftsmanship, the molding of idea into form.

Although Ciardi makes occasional use of a rhymed stanza, his predilection is strongly against the use of rhyme in favor of rhythms that more obviously capture those of speech. The rhythms in *Homeward to America,* more traditional than those in his later volumes, communicate a stronger sense of "heart," and accomplish this effect, I think, through their more deliberate pace. With **"A Drive Through Spring"** in *Live Another Day* he introduces a different rhythm which is crisper, drier, more cerebral, and more matter-of-fact. (p. 586)

Although it is possible that Ciardi's line is somewhat controlled by his subconscious memory of the five-beat line [traditionally dominating English metrics], his achievement is an extension of the freer line of contemporary poetry.... Ciardi's verse is essentially a rhythmical verse varying from ten to seventeen syllables with five or six stresses as a basis. In order to achieve a satirical effect as in **"Elegy Just in Case,"** he uses a four-stress a-b-a-b stanza reminiscent of Eliot's Sweeney poems. This dry, tight trochaic movement is admirably suited to such a purpose. In fact, Ciardi's best satirical verse (**"New Year's Eve," "A Guide to Poetry," "On a Photo of Sgt. Ciardi a Year Later"**) depends heavily for its effectiveness on his use of rhyme and the lack of a fluid inward rhythm. In striving for the rhythms of contemporary speech he often takes the easy way out, and by so doing keeps any poem from the ranks of the truly great. The effect is sometimes one of superficiality (**"Prologue for a Play"**). In place of poetry one finds rhetoric, and far too often. This is, of course, a subjective matter that each reader must decide for himself. More careful revision on the poet's part would have resolved much of the doubt.

In general the tone of the poems is right, but one poem, obviously a favorite of Ciardi's, is not. This is **"Chorus."** The children returning to their homes in the school bus are singing "Old MacDonald." At a precipitous turn in the road the defective brakes give way and the bus hurtles over the side of the road sending the occupants to their deaths. The incident is horrible and the poet fails to inject a sense of the tragic into it. The rhythms are incongruous with the subject and communicate a sense of joviality and triviality. Properly handled the theme is capable of high tragedy. It resembles superficially the theme of Auden's "Musée des Beaux Arts" except that Auden by interpreting the story of Icarus from classic mythology as represented by Breughel achieves a communication in which mere horror has no place. In Auden's poem the perfect fusion of the elements that make up a complete work of art communicates an experience of tragedy that far transcends the merely shock-effect of **"Chorus."** (p. 587)

One cannot call Ciardi a myth-maker; one can scarcely call him an image-maker although some of his images are excellent. As he drives along Boston's north shore he speaks of "the mandarin festival of shore lights" which is evocative. In speaking of his love for his wife he speaks of himself as standing, "a spinning coin of wish and dread."

In order to make a fair appraisal of Ciardi's images, however, as well as of his stature as a poet, it is important that we look closely at a few of his more successful poems. Let us select the four in which I think he most nearly effects a perfect fusion of thought and form. In two of them he comes close (**"The Deaths about You When You Stir in Sleep," "To Judith Asleep"**); in two he succeeds (**"Most Like an Arch This Marriage," "Snowy Heron"**). Ciardi's practice of republishing in each successive volume those poems of the previous volume for which he obviously has the highest regard provides the critic with the external evidence for Ciardi's self-criticism.

"**The Deaths About You**" . . . communicates the unparaphrasable experience of the lover so deeply in love that the thought that death can end this love is an ever-present fear. . . . I think the important significance of the poem is the feeling of a deeply passionate man whose alert and observing mind never permits him wholly to surrender himself to his love. . . . The poem fails to the extent that the reader is never quite certain that he has grasped the poet's intention.

"**To Judith Asleep**" is universal. Written in unrhymed eight-line stanzas, no recurring sound ties stanza to stanza, and yet the connection is tighter than in "**The Deaths About You**" . . . The first stanza with its richly vivid images describes the moonlight on the sleeping woman. When she silently and suddenly turns in her sleep, her movement deeply stirs her husband watching her. The second stanza and the first six lines of the third speak of her as the symbol of woman who "drowns male centuries in [her] chiaroscuro tide / of breast and breath." The last two lines of stanza 3 and stanza 4 describe the ferment in the husband's mind. . . . In stanza 5, seized by the fear that death might rob him of her, he would have her stir to reassure him that she lives. He regains his poise and confidence, convinced that "Time still must tick *this is, I am,* we are." This is a crude paraphrase and is a desecration of the poem's full meaning. The imagery, texture of the verse, and the poem's structure reveal what Ciardi is capable of doing when he devotes himself to his task. (pp. 587-88)

What Ciardi can do best reveals itself in another love poem, "**Most Like an Arch This Marriage**." In addition to bolstering the feeling of the poem by the use of a four-line stanza a⁵ - b⁵ - b⁵ - a⁵, the dominant image of the arch closely integrates the four stanzas. It is only by a happy marriage that man completes himself, experiences "half-heaven," feels security. From each facet of the arch the poet creates an image that builds up the unique power of a happy marriage by which man can fulfill himself. A full explication of this poem is not here possible, but unerringly the poet builds up a powerful communication of all the things that make the ideal marriage. . . . There is less exuberance than in "**To Judith Asleep**," but the poem gains by the greater discipline. In no other poem does Ciardi employ the objective correlative with such force and economy.

Ciardi's most perfect poem is probably "**Snowy Heron**," consisting of only two five-stress stanzas, rhyming a - a - b - a - c - c. Again the concentration of images, in verse with a texture suitable to the subject, aided by the poet's sharp observation and intellectual courage combine to show what the poet is capable of when he concentrates his effort, has a firm grasp of his idea, and takes the time and trouble to give us his best. His use of cesurae is excellent. (pp. 588-89)

Ciardi is, I believe, now at the crossroads of his career. Were he to give himself the time he could make a valuable contribution to American poetry. Except for a very few poems, he has not yet produced enough work of expert craftsmanship to insure the longevity of the worth of what he has to say. "**Snowy Heron**" reveals that he has the ability. So, too, does "**Fragments from Italy**" with its deep pathos. . . . He should be in less of a hurry to publish. He should, too, remember Auden's statement that "Time . . . worships language." Interesting as his ideas often are—and he is rich in subject matter and not too narrowly egocentric—he has not heretofore been careful enough to supply the necessary craftsmanship for those ideas. And in no case has he been wholly successful in a poem of more than four stanzas. This should give him pause. He has been one of our most passionate voices against the materialism

of the present age. Has he, however, unwittingly placed himself in the ranks of those content to fight only the materialism of the present day and not to be an ally of that minority that must fight it in the future? Were he to subject himself to severe self examination, he could possibly do both. . . .

His latest volume, *39 Poems,* largely satirical, often deeply perceptive, and inherent with the stuff of poetry, contains no poem that will withstand a sharp critical analysis, no poem in which the various elements of a poem are fused into really significant form. If his is a conscious choice of the immediate plaudits of the uncritical I have no quarrel with him; but if he is not to descend into obscurity as a poet and ultimately be forgotten except for a possible three or four poems which will find their way into various anthologies, it is time that he subject himself to a severe questioning of his motives, purposes, and goals. (p. 589)

James G. Southworth, "The Poetry of John Ciardi,"
in English Journal, *Vol. L, No. 9, December, 1961,
pp. 583-89.*

M. L. ROSENTHAL

[*In the Stoneworks* shows that John Ciardi] has not God's loveliest gift to poets, the gift of breathing in impressions and letting them gather in silence into a perfect richness. He is a controversialist, a banger-together of arguments, an anecdotalist of sorts, full of memories of his childhood in an Italian immigrant family. He likes to make loud noises, sometimes to impress a political point, sometimes in wryly comic deference to the family life he remembers, sometimes out of sheer exuberance and a purely technical interest in being noisy like Ezra Pound's when he was writing "Sestina: Altaforte." Ciardi's "**Launcelot in Hell**" is another such poem. No comparable clatter has been heard since Pound gave us Bertrans de Born, that black-hearted warrior-troubadour whom "Dante put in Hell for that he was a stirrer-up of strife," shouting "Damn it all! all this our South stinks peace" and "Hell grant soon we hear again the swords clash!" (p. 50)

If this were all there is to Mr. Ciardi, we could simply set him down as a splendid Master of Fireworks to be trotted out without shame for popular reading tours, television programs about poetry, and other enterprises in which he does, indeed, perform splendidly. We would certainly recommend him as a model for schoolboy poets were he not, in this poem and elsewhere, so "wholesomely frank" about sex: or at least he would provide wonderful texts for the endless discussions about just what degree of realism the young are ready for. And yet [a] quieter sensitivity . . . is never altogether absent. . . . It is precisely this felt sensitivity, present but neglected in so many poems that leap about and shout and run as fast as their impatient metric can carry them, that is irritating in his poetry. . . . [Too] often the realizing inwardness is blocked off from its sufficient expression. We feel its presence, wait for it to emerge, and are frustrated. (pp. 50-1)

[The ultimate feeling of Mr. Ciardi's *In the Stoneworks* is expressed in] the culminating poem of the section of his book entitled "**Back Home in Pompeii**." A preoccupation with the death of civilizations and with the fact that the heart—that is, the sphere of consciousness which involves emotional conviction—must learn to recognize what that death means has produced the most incisive poetry. . . . [Mr. Ciardi also asserts] the sweetness of our world as we know it, its hidden beauties that blaze into view unexpectedly, and its worth despite the harsh and tragic discipline it imposes on most of us on occasion. . . .

Of course, the rather bitter "set" of Mr. Ciardi's most serious work is not the whole picture of this ebullient poet, who can write with . . . much joy and wit. . . . (p. 51)

M. L. Rosenthal, "An Unfair Question," in The Reporter, *Vol. 26, No. 4, February 15, 1962, pp. 48, 50-1.**

JOSEPH LANGLAND

John Ciardi is one of America's best-known figures in poetry. He has been a lively editor of it and an energetic public defender of its meaning and nature.

[*Person to Person*] has the wit and sharp images and tough language we have come to expect, the observant talk about contemporary civilization. Ciardi here is not a maker of new ways in language and feeling. But he is an expert user of the ways we have. There is a strong effort here to be quiet in a noisy life, to be more "with" the birds, animals, vegetation, seasons and elements.

Ciardi begins with a Frostian poem on **"The Size of Song,"** wondering "What happens as they [birds] move along / to power and size?" This is one of the central concerns of this book: how to maintain song and quality in a heavy, pervasive civilization ready to make the most tempting superficial rewards. . . .

In some poems Ciardi, one of the world's talkers, simply cannot resist talking too far beyond his suggestion, depriving his reader of the discovery he has prepared for him. He takes on his role of guide with full seriousness, despite such passages as:

> Because words find me, I go
> to find
> words, the food of my kind.
> I walk
> by nowheres to the luck of a
> word, its found wild
> honey.

Though many of these poems do not achieve this singing ideal, laboring with a raised voice at wit and metaphor, some of them do. And this book is lively and warm with affection for our sometimes desperate lives. It is a pleasure to think and feel along with it.

Joseph Langland, "Quiet Songs about Life," in The New York Times Book Review, *October 4, 1964, p. 22.*

WILLIAM DICKEY

The quality that I find most notable in [Mr. Ciardi's *Person to Person*] is that of observation; he sees things with an intensity and an accuracy that no conventional language can wholly contain. The effect of a convention is to smooth out the differences between things; it expects, having established a form of language, that all objects will be equally amenable to its ministrations. But Mr. Ciardi's objects break these bounds; his sight is defined by the object itself, and he accepts and uses the object's own recalcitrance toward language that will soften it. "Hunchback bees in pirate pants" is a phrase wholly determined by what its object looks like, rather than by a kind of language which is felt to be appropriate to the discussion

of objects in general. Mr. Ciardi is often sententious or sentimental in his attitudes toward the things he discusses, but those attitudes never prevent him from seeing what is before him. This ability to see is neither easy nor usual, and it represents one of the most important ways in which the floating world of poetic language can be given a persistent human relevance, a persistent reference back to the solidities of existence. (p. 591)

William Dickey, "Poetic Language," in The Hudson Review, *Vol. XVII, No. 4, Winter, 1964-65, pp. 587-96.**

ERNEST SANDEEN

Person to Person is a book of middle age in which the poet takes stock of his situation and finds the important commitments and repudiations already settled. Foremost is his commitment to his own astonishing success with its rewards of popularity, status, and, not least, money. In the second, middle section which gives its title to the book the poet who is "trying / as simple and as marvelous a thing as honesty" deals in explicit, loving detail with the old, ever new American success story which has happened to him. (pp. 231-32)

In **"Sequence"** the poet travels through the rugged scenery of the far west and is found at day's end lounging on an inflated raft at the edge of a heated swimming pool with a waitress leaning down to hand him a bourbon, "tinkling like money". The contrast is ironic but is not drawn at the poet's expense. Rather, the irony is his fortunate discovery that he can enjoy the best of both worlds and so defy the quaint tradition that associates primitive nature with plain living and high thinking.

Whether it is the effect of his success or not, this book shows Ciardi writing from a vantage point of self-assurance which gives him greater control and disciplined detachment than his earlier books displayed. It also brings him clearly into the orbit of the Frost tradition. Although he lacks Frost's sly, countryman's reticence, he shares the same cheerful scepticism, the same easy, offhand way with the reader, the same delight in words and fancies that sometimes slide off momentarily into the merely clever, and the same robust but often delicate clarity of image. Perhaps he is most of all like Frost in his suspicion of merely verbal subtleties, having learned by dint of frequent temptations, he tells us, to resist such plausible trumperies as the hypothetical line, "Nothing is really hard but to be real."

Not only solemn shams but important realities have been excluded or at least attenuated in order to accommodate this happy consolidation of poetic personality. For example, although death appears several times as a finality of dust that comes upon father, friends, a favorite uncle, an obscure filing clerk, it demands of the poet no immediate, decisive confrontation. ("Not even my hair is thinning.") Other dark and ugly unalterables are honestly met (**"To No End Ever," "Coq au Vin"**), but they look like isolated occurrences that do not affect basic attitudes.

In the last section, **"Wholly Numbers, or the Meditations of St. Stitch,** the poet moves from autobiography to larger concerns involving the race. The pun on "Holy Verses" announces a non-religious intention, and "St. Stitch" which may be a word-play on "stich" (a line of verse) suggests "poet". At any rate these are in fact the meditations of a secular poet and are centered upon the history of man's image of himself from the early time when men "had the idea / of being man confused wth the idea of being God'' to the present age of Doubt. The master figure is that of a colossus slowly sinking into quicksand. As it is disappearing below the surface, the poet sees in the eyes of the colossus the image of itself "still standing higher than the sky''. But man's best hope is of the earth and is evolutionary: "Think, given time enough, / what languages [man] might yet learn to speak / . . . when the last ape has grunted from his throat.'' Meanwhile, what about the individual? The epitaph which the poet requests for himself—to be carved at the proper time—is *"Thank you / for the experience which I, lovingly, did not / understand.''* (pp. 232-33)

Ernest Sandeen, "'A More Comic Spirit'," *in* Poetry, *Vol. CVI, No. 3, June, 1965, pp. 231-33.*

CHARLES PHILBRICK

[John Ciardi's *This Strangest Everything*] must be somewhere around his fifteenth book of verse. Nor is it surprising that his latest poems are done with quiet but expert craft, and that what he has to say is, as always, interesting to hear, for he says it so arrestingly and yet with such apparently easy clarity. A poem called **"Boy"** begins with "He is in his room sulked shut,'' and ends with "May sons forgive the fathers they obey.'' Perhaps one has to be middle-aged to appreciate fully such a poem as this, as well as several others in which he reflects—in a mellow mood, but in crisp language—on his parents, whose world was so far away in time and style, or on himself in his successful present and on all the selves he's been. **"Talking myself to sleep at one more Hilton"** is a wry and regretful acceptance of the rootlessness of contemporary American life.

Here and elsewhere, with perception and amusement, Mr. Ciardi has come to terms with himself in mid-career, and with his relationships to others. His poem on Roethke, for example, rollicks with admiration; wonderfully, it is more a celebration of Roethke's life than an expression of Ciardi's feelings about his death. Throughout the book runs concern (even satire requires concern) for Man and for men; and, without abandoning concern, Mr. Ciardi sees to it that wit and gusto triumph over regret and despair—always in active language. (p. 33)

Charles Philbrick, "Debuts and Encores," *in* Saturday Review, *Vol. L, No. 22, June 3, 1967, pp. 32-4.**

WILLIAM STAFFORD

[In *This Strangest Everything*] John Ciardi delivers the quick, sharp image: he stands for the ready man caught up but not overwhelmed by his time. . . . More than most, Ciardi establishes his ideas in definite meters and forms. He is wild and reckless in fancy, but guarded about any hint of being constantly serious or off balance in his commitments: "Not that it matters, or not much. . . .'' But the personality back of the poems is definite, with an engaging, generous intelligence. (p. 187)

He is so adept with the surface of the language that some readers feel a lack of engagement with its depths, and with the depths of the writer's own feelings; but Ciardi disarmingly identifies that frivolity in himself, saying of one of his teachers who at first withheld approval:

> Well, I learned what to say.
> I grabbed the whole hot crockful with both hands
> and slopped it to her till I got my A. . . .

It is this headlong communication about slant moral issues that most distinguishes the poems in this book; the force is a moral force though the language is offhand. (pp. 187-88)

William Stafford, "A Five-Book Shelf," *in* Poetry, *Vol. CXI, No. 3, December, 1967, pp. 184-88.**

MILLER WILLIAMS

[Ciardi] is haunted by John Ciardi. As we see Ciardi moving from loss to discovery, to a ringing celebration of the self that is conscious of that celebration and therefore real, through all the lines of all the poems of affirmation, through all the voices in which Ciardi says, "This is, I am, we are,'' there is the inescapable feeling that he is not always as sure as he seems to be that even the self, love, and logic are what they appear to be, that they will work to carry us through. There is a reasoning, a rationalism, in his poems that is clear and consoling, and a mercy that tempers them well. Indeed, these qualities make the name of John Ciardi possible and understandable. Everything shapes up, but on the shoulder of the self, affirmed in the celebrated world, is a shapeless incubus, whispering confusions that are almost audible in the poems.

The introspective search is not so much a part of Ciardi's earlier work, where the most distinctive characteristic is rather an iconoclasm set forth with the matter-of-factness that has persisted and grown stronger in Ciardi's voice at its best. This iconoclasm comes to us as a quiet sort of "knock it off'' attitude, a poetic expression of anger, the voice of the social critic. It is seen first, as we would expect, in the war poetry. (pp. 10-11)

The poems of Ciardi that are not intensely introspective—and even some that are—fall loosely under the heading of social criticism: disapproving, often angry comment on the world man has made. They are pointedly—and increasingly—directed at the gods and demigods we have constructed. (pp. 11-12)

Idol-breaking is an intrinsic part of the angry humanism in Ciardi's poetry. It comes with the rejection of metaphysics and the refusal to relegate anything that matters to another, later world. This is the humanism that forms when a man gives his whole attention to the moment he is living—whether he does it by nature, or because he senses that no other moment exists, or because he believes that that is the only way to make the next moment be anything but another sentence to be served while waiting for the next one. Whatever the reason, the affirmation of the eternal present demands an honest eye for things as they are, a refusal to settle for pretense, for mere superficiality. It demands that the face behind the face be seen. And Ciardi's social criticism stems, I think, from this honesty.

His refusal to accept the pomp of the world as reality, which strikes us somehow as an angry and violent refusal, and his great rage, which seems to tear like an underground river just beneath the words of the poem, are probably caused to a great extent by an inner turmoil that has nothing to do with society as such. I suspect that a hundred angers—against all that was lost for having been lost, against the absence, the past which is no past—that have nowhere else to go fire the furnaces of the poet's impatience with society.

It is possible for the poems of Ciardi to bring Alexander Pope to mind, not only—or primarily—because both men have channeled the energies of inner turmoil into social criticism but also because of the tone and the directness of their criticism, and of the rational terms in which it is usually couched. It is as if in Ciardi, as in Pope, the raging furnaces are banked by an objectivity that is all but classical.

When Ciardi goes wrong in a poem, it is more often than not the result of a tendency grown—paradoxically—out of this rationalism: he will make things clear that were clear already. (Even more paradoxically, he does not do this in the poems of social criticism, where we would expect this rationalism to be a greater peril.) It happens at the ends of poems, and sometimes, especially in his earlier work, he has injured a good piece by telling us what he was about. Even as late as *In Fact* (1962), he would let some poems go pat, with an all-to-clear resolution, a sense, not of inevitable surprise, but of the obvious, the just-right truth. Thus, in **"In My Father's House There Are a Few Mansions, More Hovels, and Probably Even More Ranch Houses,"** he tells us at the end that we should

> Given a picture-window . . .
> make sure it looks out onto some-
> thing. Which is also to say, out from
> something, preferably, I suggest, a Self.

The last five words show that he has decided not to trust us, that he fears we might not understand without the explication. In fact, it is the poem he has not trusted. (pp. 12-14)

[A] part of Ciardi's growth as a poet [is] his increasing willingness to trust his instincts and our willingness—our need—to go with him without too many signposts. The development has been impressive. (p. 14)

Probably the poem that best tells of the man, important and nothing, a little higher than the animals and yet also dust, at the center and yet seen from the center, is one of Ciardi's most read and best remembered, **"On a Photo of Sgt. Ciardi a Year Later."** Here is the man who in every sense is both subject and object. Here the humanism, the humility, the social criticism, the quiet anger, and all the plain agony of introspection come together. (p. 17)

There are two things beyond his humility which save Ciardi's poems from intellectual pride, and so set them apart from many that look with a hard eye at society. One is his relative willingness, his wish, to accept, even to love the world. Few write with more open and unembarrassed compassion than does Ciardi. He cares for the world . . . and celebrates it.

Now this is easy to do if by world we mean cows and freight trains, but Ciardi is larger than that. He cares for everything that honestly is. . . .

The other redeeming grace is his sense of the comic, which with love is the only antidote to madness for the humanist who is a critic of a world he is committed to. We think of Pope . . . , and of Swift. There is almost nothing in which Ciardi does not see the ridiculous, almost no pose—especially his own—in which he does not see the fool. (p. 18)

All of this, the honesty, the insistence on fact, the impatience with hypocrisy, is of course part of the poet's search for himself. A man whose concern is with his own identity, with recognizing who he is, is likely to be concerned with masks, or, more simply, with the face behind the face. This is Ciardi's total concern, what he looks for and writes toward. It is what he is after when he turns to his father and where the man stood; to his family and the country they came from; to himself.

He wants to relate those things—all things of this world—to himself, and to understand that relationship. Without an ab-

solute, without a Father, he wants confirmation of the family of things or, as we more conventionally put it, the *relativity* of things. This is the heart of Ciardi's work. (p. 19)

> *Miller Williams, "Introduction: John Ciardi, 'Nothing Is Really Hard but to Be Real',"* in The Achievement of John Ciardi: A Comprehensive Selection of His Poems with a Critical Introduction *by John Ciardi, edited by Miller Williams, Scott, Foresman and Company, 1969, pp. 1-19.*

JOSEPH PARISI

John Ciardi's poems indicate a generous soul, a wide-ranging intelligence, and a sharp eye for spotting the unexpected in the commonplace. *The Little That Is All* is a virtuoso performance, in which the poet focuses his attention on, among other things, the Muse, 2:00 a.m., a hole in his front yard, Leonardo, Francis of Assisi, feet, the System, East Sixty-Seventh St., and the so-called Generation Gap. With his pleasantly skewed perception, he makes this eclectic group of subjects new, or at least novel, and he is very often amusing and always enlightening. (p. 220)

Family matters form a large interest in this collection. In **"A Fool Too Fast,"** the motorist kills his daughter Kate's dog, and "she feels / what we only know . . . can't learn to ask nor father nor school / answer . . ." **"Addio"** is a touching farewell to his mother, obedient to her "old-country" father even on her deathbed. Memories of friend and former student Frank O'Hara's bizarre death mingle with thoughts of his own son Jamie: "His mother, a Jewish princess . . . taught him to expect". The son feels we are all worthless, while the father concludes: "we are what we are and some of it hurts." Ciardi heads the second section of his book **"Generation Gap,"** but the poems therein belie the title. **"A Prayer to the Mountain"** is a father's doleful lay, uttered after twelve-hour days filled with a son's electric guitar. Those visits to the assistant principal ("always at 9:00 impossible o'clock A.M.") are recalled in **"Poem for Benn's Graduation from High School"**; while **"Memo: Preliminary Draft of a Prayer to God the Father"** shows an indulgent if road-weary father listing the bills, for lawyers (son's pot bust), wrecked cars, daughter's piano lessons (and piano), wife's elderly parents, in the "only slightly embalmed" motel room. His real and exaggerated exasperation is, however, only equalled by his good humor. The remarkable **"Letter from a Pander"** begins by mocking our limited vision and transitory nature in the light of countless stars, eons, the vast universe ("no scale speaks another", "We are newer than newts here"), and concludes in human terms with a surprising message to his daughter. . . . (p. 221)

If the universe *in toto* is beyond comprehension, immediate surroundings are not, and the poet attempts to take their measure. In **"Notes,"** Ciardi asks: "Is it purposeful, I wonder, to endure this / stumped straddle of observation posts . . . the banality of recorded impressions?" But, of course, "there will be experiences and they should be noted." . . . However unpredictable his subjects or points-of-view, Ciardi's poems convey a sense of order, interconnectedness, reinforced by long, smooth lines and associative development. In **"Driving Across the American Desert and Thinking of the Sahara,"** he notes: "I breathe some million molecules of argon / breathed by Christ once. Part of His pronunciation." From the variety he discovers and delights in, Ciardi fashions his personal Great Chain of Being. (pp. 221-22)

Joseph Parisi, "Personae, Personalities," in Poetry, *Vol. CXXVI, No. 4, July, 1975, pp. 219-42.**

STEVEN RATINER

John Ciardi is an elder statesman of American poetry. In 40 years he has given us volumes of poems, criticism, children's verse, and an extremely fine translation of Dante's *Divine Comedy*. But his recent work has become more an example of the malaise of American culture than an examination of its problems.

For Instance is Ciardi's 14th book of poetry. In it we are given a glimpse of the poet's struggles with semiretirement, Key West, suburbia, youth culture, alcohol, insomnia, and a growing sense of futility.

In the course of 40 poems, Ciardi turns a cold eye on the world's difficulties.

There are examples of biting humor throughout the text ("**Suburbia**," "**Censorship**," "**The Abstract Calorie**"), but barely enough to relieve the acid taste. The few shining moments occur when the poems aim a clear eye at the human place in a still-mysterious world. . . .

Although Ciardi possesses all the style and nuance, charged syntax and verbal authority that poetry requires, what is missing too often here is the image, the focus, the passion that drive mere "talk" to poetic climax, convert thinking to envisioning. We already *know* the world of these poems—we want to know it better.

A poet who writes as well as Ciardi makes more than just books. He creates a human architecture, a city of the mind— a place a reader can visit in his everyday life, not just during literary excursions. If there is to be construction constantly going on, we need that poet to build the care-crafted houses and personal temples where we can retreat to consider life and devotion.

Steven Ratiner, "Poetry from Two Grand Masters of Nuance: John Ciardi Struggles with Futility," in The Christian Science Monitor, *January 2, 1980, p. 17.*

DANA GIOIA

It may be fashionable to consider John Ciardi a poet long past his prime, and anyone who would venture to defend his recent work in print risks being labelled hopelessly out-of-touch. Ciardi has certainly made it difficult for any would-be defender; for years he has published no new volume in which the bad poems do not greatly outnumber the good. Yet the good, at least in art, do sometimes prevail against the bad, whatever the odds, and a few times in each book Ciardi has struck exactly the right notes, creating poems that are strong, memorable, and unmistakably personal.

The problem is in finding them, and many a braver soul than I would give up in Ciardi's latest collection, *For Instance*. Here one must push through dozens of weak, occasional poems before suddenly, nearly at the end of the book, coming upon two excellent poems literally face to face—"**Roman Diary: 1951**" and "**Firsts.**" These pieces represent the unique tone of Ciardi's best work—not the private lyric voice he so often exercises and definitely not his brand of heavy-handed satire but the civilized, level voice of a man talking to his equals.

"**Roman Diary: 1951**" is an anecdotal poem. In twenty-four lines it tells a complete story with economy and precision, recounting an argument Ciardi had thirty years ago with another expatriate over giving money to a street beggar. . . . Ciardi develops this incident into a revealing story that captures all too accurately a certain mean-spiritedness one sees more often than one would like. While it is refreshing to see a simple narrative handled so well in verse, Ciardi's real achievement here is that he deals so credibly with the complex social and psychological dimensions of the story. He evokes just the right details to make the incident stick in the reader's mind like a troubling personal memory.

"**Firsts**" is a more complex poem which counterpoints four episodes, three of them personal and one drawn from James Baldwin's life. Each episode is an example of the world (in this case specifically a linguistic world) one loses in breaking way from one's childhood roots. . . . "**Firsts**" is both a personal elegy for Ciardi's own lost childhood and a public one for the dying languages of American immigrants. Ciardi writes about a dialect of Italian, but it could as easily be Yiddish, or pre-Soviet Russian, any of those languages which adapted to America and briefly became a living *patois* before vanishing forever. One hopes that poems like "**Firsts**" or the more modest "**Scene Twelve: Take Seven**" show Ciardi on the verge of an important new phase. Till that proves true, however, I recommend a highly selective reading of *For Instance*. (pp. 112-14)

Dana Gioia, "Eight Poets," in Poetry, *Vol. CXL, No. 2, May, 1982, pp. 102-14.**

JOSEPH PARISI

[John Ciardi] has endeared with a warm, personal voice speaking directly to the heart from a broadly human understanding. From almost a score of books, he has chosen some of his most telling and touching poems [for *Selected Poems*], arranged topically upon his central concerns: family history, love and marriage, friendship, World War II, the way we live now. Here are poignant verses on his influential mother, the father he imagines but could not know, his wife, and assorted quirky relatives and acquaintances. His portraits from an interesting marriage and from life in the suburbs are sharply, shrewdly drawn, with plenty of aperçus, mixed emotions, and sardonic humor to fill in the outlines. The war poems are equally memorable, while the satiric sketches of contemporary follies, now somewhat faded, still make valid points. Throughout this generous selection, the poet proves a most personable companion: bright, unpredictable, entertaining.

Joseph Parisi, in a review of "Selected Poems," in Booklist, *Vol. 81, No. 8, December 15, 1984, p. 554.*

DAVID WOJAHN

Writing of [the 1955 collection *As If*, Randall] Jarrell made a typically snide remark that still applies to Ciardi's new volume [*Selected Poems*]: "This writer uses Stevens's, or Shapiro's, or half a dozen other poets' tricks as easily, and with as much justification, as a salesman would use a competitor's sales talk—it works, doesn't it?" [see excerpt above]. When Ciardi did find a voice, in the late Fifties, it was in poems of trivial social satire. While Shapiro employed the sarcasm of outrage to rail against bigotry and oppression, Ciardi opted for odes to his power mower and descriptions of quarrels in suburbia regarding the origin of a dog turd beside a neighbor's rosebush. In the case of the latter poem, the gallant Mr. Ciardi admits defeat in the argument, and scoops the offending object up. What's remarkable about this poem is not its silly scatological humor, but the fact that a speaker so consistently smug and self-important would even care to own a dog. Shapiro is an iconoclast, but Ciardi is mostly just a crank. Poems like his dog dropping opus are meant, one supposes, to be light verse, but there's so much of a nasty streak in all of Ciardi's work that he can't achieve the playfulness that characterizes good light verse.

Ciardi is a personal poet, but he is not a personable one. Some of his better poems, included in the book's first section . . . , concern his parents and relatives, and he has some interesting stories to tell about them. There's some fine detail about growing up in an Italian immigrant family, and there are some affectionate portraits of Ciardi's father, who died when the poet was still an infant. But even in these poems, and in the recollections of his days as a bomber gunner during World War II, Ciardi's smug tone can weaken his effect. He invariably lets his irony turn into ridicule of his subjects or into preposterousness. . . . There are times in the volume when Ciardi abandons his curmudgeonly pose, but when he does so, he is apt to become saccharine. The book includes a section of love poems, most of them taken from Ciardi's 1959 volume, *I Marry You,* and these come close to being greeting card verse. Perhaps, in trying to strip his approach of nastiness, Ciardi overcompensates.

The most notable poems in the book are the more recent autobiographical narratives included in the closing section, **"Lives of X."** They're long and rangy pieces, mostly about Ciardi's youth. Perhaps because they're the work of an older man looking back, they have a charm and generosity of spirit not found in Ciardi's other efforts. It's unfortunate that he did not discover this style at an earlier point in his career. (pp. 169-70)

David Wojahn, in a review of "Selected Poems," in
Poetry, *Vol. CXLVI, No. 3, June, 1985, pp. 169-70.*

Douglas (Eaglesham) Dunn

1942-

Scottish poet, scriptwriter, short story writer, editor, and critic.

Dunn's poetry is marked by richly descriptive language, flashes of wit, and attention to both social and personal concerns. Although several reviewers have detected a cynical tone in some of Dunn's work—particularly those poems in which he addresses social issues—he is often praised for his observations and for the emotional depth of his verse. Michael O'Neill provided a succinct description of Dunn's accomplishment: "Landscapes in his work are ticketed with social and cultural meanings, there to be emblematized. This cast of mind can make him contentiously wordy. But it is yoked, more often, to an enriching humanism." Born in Scotland, Dunn lived most of his adult life in England before returning to his native country in 1984.

In his first volume of poetry, *Terry Street* (1969), Dunn created a vivid portrait of the English working-class neighborhood where he lived while working as a librarian at the University of Hull. He was lauded for portraying ordinary situations and characters with color and conviction and for his poignant observations of cultural malaise. Evident in *Terry Street* is a deep awareness of social inequality, a theme which recurs in several of Dunn's later works. Reviewers noted that in his next major collection, *The Happier Life* (1972), Dunn employs rhyme and meter more frequently and is concerned with a broader spectrum of topics. These developments continue in the poems collected in *Love or Nothing* (1974), which include elements of fantasy and allegory as well as Dunn's characteristic social realism. Several critics viewed *Barbarians* (1979), with its emphasis on social injustice and its tone of resentment toward those whom Dunn considers elitist, as directly expressing Marxist ideologies. However, in an interview, Dunn denied any overtly polemical intent, stressing that "I don't really put much store upon the political meanings of my poems in terms of political reality."

Dunn's interest in community concerns blends with a greater attention to his Scottish heritage in *St. Kilda's Parliament* (1981). The title poem of this volume relates an imaginary town meeting in a small Scottish village; Dunn describes people, objects, and issues that are representative of Scotland. *Europa's Lover* (1983), his next work, is a long poem that explores and celebrates European culture. In *Elegies* (1985), perhaps his most acclaimed volume of poetry, Dunn mourns his wife, who died of cancer at age thirty-seven. The poems chronicle their relationship, particularly the pain and love shared during their final months together, and Dunn's grief after her death. Dunn was praised for effectively evoking strong emotions without allowing self-pity and sentimentality to overwhelm the poetry. Peter Porter observed that the poems in *Elegies* "have their bitternesses, but their extraordinary, naked naturalness owes much to there being no admixture of guilt in [Dunn's] recreation of the life he and his wife lived." Dunn has also published a collection of short stories, *Secret Villages* (1985), and he has edited a number of poetry anthologies.

(See also *CLC*, Vol. 6; *Contemporary Authors*, Vols. 45-48; *Contemporary Authors New Revision Series*, Vol. 2; and *Dictionary of Literary Biography*, Vol. 40.)

RONALD HAYMAN

In *Terry Street,* Douglas Dunn displays an admirable sureness of touch, particularly in the first part of the book, which consists of eighteen poems dealing with life in the slums of Hull. Without using any dialogue, he vividly recreates the life of the streets, commenting on it at the same time. When it occurs, the question of his own involvement in it, whether as an insider or outsider, is perfectly focused, as in the final poem, about his decision to leave Terry Street.

At first much of the statement appears to be about the surfaces of appearance and behaviour but examine it more closely and you see that particular details are very judiciously fused into generalisations which are then built into a montage that takes us, partly by implication, over a wide range of experience. . . . [Dunn organises] his fragments of fact to create a truthful emotional atmosphere. Taken together, the eighteen poems give off an unusually strong—and not at all unattractive—smell of life as it is actually lived.

The poems in the second half of the book show just as much capacity for sympathetic identification with other people—or with horses in a field—and the same unerring selection of the right factual generalisations to evoke an atmosphere and a mood, in **"The Love Day"** for instance. But in these poems the first person is more obtrusive, the focus not quite so sharp, the language less transparent, the irony not so subtle. But to measure the second half of the book against the first is to judge it by a very high standard. (pp. 74-5)

Ronald Hayman, in a review of "Terry Street," in Encounter, *Vol. XXXV, No. 6, December, 1970, pp. 74-5.*

JONATHAN RABAN

[Dunn's *The Happier Life* shows] him coming to terms with the talent which lit up his first book, *Terry Street.* It's proving a singularly difficult talent to come to terms with; a wayward, wall-eyed creature that one moment streaks off into the blue, and the next slumps in a corner and is not to be stirred. At present Dunn is feeding it on hard tack and making it run marathons when all its inclinations are for the short winded burst and the light verse sprint. He is a grim custodian, a gloomy presbyter who doesn't find much to approve of in the world with which his poems have to have commerce. "Here I am," he says, "A very old man of twenty-eight," and, indeed, he is. He tetchily contemplates a Hull full of men in raincoats, footling student revolutionaries, moustached sporting motorists, the raggy tribe of dole-drawers and unspeakably ancient tarts, and pipes and whistles at the intrusive vulgarities of "the scum."

Complaining by the tide of Humber is nothing new, of course, and Dunn does open himself to being read as a shriller, more priggish version of Larkin. But he's weakest when he takes on the role of suburban Tiresias, strongest when excercising a solitary, sensually responsive eye on the details of an interior, the tangle of a garden—when he's absorbed in that part of the world which the scum haven't yet vandalised. His self-announced seriousness often seems something of a pose, and his scrupulous distaste is bandied about with the relish of the romantic spiv in **"Morning Bedroom"** who rhymes "last night's rose" with "underclothes." A poem called **"The Hunch"** begins: "They will not leave me, the lives of other people". But when one examines these lives, they turn out to be capricious inventions, summoned up by the poet so that he can have something to feel bad about.... The trouble is that Dunn has a real gift for a kind of Gilbertian comic writing which he's always trying to convert to an unsatisfactorily solemn purpose. There are some joyful doodles at the beginning of **'At a Yorkshire Bus Stop,'** like—

> Somebody's cleaning woman look
> At maps and open picture books
> In the travel agent's window.
> Where will she go, where will she go,
> Madrid by BEA, by rail
> To Istanbul with mop and pail?

But by the end of the poem, the glum puritan is shoving his spoke in the wheel and ruining the ride. We are offered a mighty metaphor—

> All my life inside a bus
> From terminus to terminus

—which even the throwaway doggerel in which it's wrapped cannot redeem. It is seriousness, of a sort, that spoils the title poem too, a readiness to peter out into a sonorous sludge of poetic abstractions....

Much that now sounds posed or forced in Dunn's work is simply the product of a lack of metrical polish, a faltering sense of timing. The collection has an amateurish feel to it, as if none of the poems, for all their sermonising, had ever quite fixed on the page or arrived at their right form. There are patches, individual lines, single images that turn perfectly in the lock, but very little sustained achievement. If only he could ease up on the solemnity, allow his talent a looser rein, and grin occasionally through that murky Tennysonian gloom.

Jonathan Raban, "Complaining by the Humber," in The Spectator, *Vol. 229, No. 7517, July 22, 1972, p. 136.**

ROGER SCRUTON

Douglas Dunn's first book, *Terry Street,* was the work of a poet with a wry humour and a gift for observation, a gift derived not so much from thought as from style, which added to these earlier poems an elegance that is absent from much contemporary poetry. But it is a gift that seems to have resisted development, and despite many felicities and despite an overriding seriousness of intention, [*The Happier Life*] comes as a disappointment.

The dominant mood is one of nostalgia. But it is a nostalgia that is constantly broken into and overthrown by anxiety. Dunn gives voice to a wish to "live quietly, miles away," but at the same time he remains sadly aware of those aspects of modern existence that seem to remove the significance from a merely private life. One has the impression of a man interested primarily in his garden—praised in one of the better poems—but whose attention is constantly wandering away from this inadequate refuge to dwell on the lives of those more at home in the modern world. The attitude is understandable, and often expressed affectingly. Unfortunately, however, Dunn lacks a poetic idiom strong enough to control the intrusions of this alien world, or subject them to more powerful and more satisfying ideals. He merely mentions them obsessively, or else he tries to shrug them off with words that never quite sum them up in the dismissive way he intends. In a sense Dunn seems to be outstripped by his ambitions. The gentle irony of his style cannot combat the anguish and brutality of contemporary experience, and the attempt to translate his merely personal antipathy into something more humane and universal requires a quite different order of poetic accomplishment. (p. 84)

[Dunn writes] more interestingly and genuinely when he confines himself to the observation of particular scenes—as in the energetic **"Morning Bedroom"**, and in the descriptions of domestic details, such as his house, his friend's room, his garden, his shirt "As if it had been a dead friend's / Who only now is being missed and understood." Dunn achieves here an undeniable poignancy. The images which accumulate are all gentle, harmless and rather sad, and the ultimate effect is perhaps a little ephemeral. But a stronger and more thoughtful idiom can occasionally be heard: Dunn's poetry then in many ways echoes the rhythm and diction of Sylvia Plath, whose influence can be detected in what is undoubtedly the best poem in the present collection: **"The Hour."** If Dunn is unable to kill with irony the intruders that threaten his inner life, it is possible that he may continue in this vein, becoming more subjective, more allusive, and consequently more precise. (p. 85)

Roger Scruton, "Idioms," in Encounter, *Vol. XXXIX, No. 3, September, 1972, pp. 84-5.*

P. N. FURBANK

There is a problem for a writer these days in cultivating private human feeling, when there is so much to drive him to the demo or the monastery, and the problem is present in this second volume by Douglas Dunn [*The Happier Life*]. *Terry Street Poems* showed him exploring the rights and wrongs of finding glory in the commonplace, of expending feeling upon lives you have no intention at all of sharing. Eventually, the poet realises that any vision of glory or a 'happier life' for his Terry Street neighbours was adolescent illusion: and having lost it, his whole position in Terry Street becomes invidious. In that final, very subtle, poem **"A Window Affair"**—describing an abortive flirtation between himself and another Terry Street window-watcher—he resigns and retires.

[In *The Happier Life*] he pursues the consequences. To what do you retire? He flirts with the various possibilities—pure sexual freedom, Horace's Sabine farm, London, the Utopia and the commune—and sees the hopelessness of them all. There is no 'happier life', only the obstinate intuiting of a better life by the left hand of the mind.

The opening poem in the volume, **"The Garden"**, is a sort of manifesto in defence of retirement and tells how the poet annoys his neighbours by *not* cultivating his Voltairean garden. . . . The poem, which also makes a mocking salute to Marvell's 'Garden', is deliberately smiling and whimsical and is a success, its tone adequately 'placed' by his own phrase 'wry complacencies of the retiring'. Nonetheless, I think, he hasn't fully sorted out this problem of his role and place as a poet. There is a very odd passage in **"At a Yorkshire Bus-Stop"**—a less successful poem, more take-it-or-leave-it in style, and therefore coming out as too ingratiating—in which he implies that the alternative to being a car-owner, which he is not, is to be one of those people who can't use a spanner or mend a fuse, and are proud of it. Now, there is nothing to be proud of in being unable to mend a fuse—it is the perquisite of one's great-aunt: and the age when car-owners used spanners went out with the Norfolk jacket. There is something not thought out here: which I hope explains the Monday Club sentiments of another poem, **"The Hull Sit-In"**, in this volume.

This brings me to an extremely fine poem, **"Morning Bedroom"**, in which everything is right except the antithesis or opposition it leads up to. The poem, about a rich-woman-and-younger-man affair, is in a Donne-like stanza, and there is something remotely Donne-like in its actual handling of language. He sustains the note of attraction-repulsion vis-à-vis the lovers' swinish paradise with remarkable verbal resources and discipline. . . . [What the poem] says, I suppose, is roughly: she has made me choose, instead of this oiled, swaddled, air-conditioned Eden, a wider human life, where men are exposed to accident and mortality—a life, also, in which I can choose to opt out and enjoy freedom to be happy or unhappy on my own terms. It is a complicated double turn of thought (for no sooner has he claimed a wider life than he is thinking of opting out of it) and he has not quite brought the thought into focus: the last two lines are too limp and vague.

Still, the axis of his thought is clear: he refuses to be fixed or trapped, even in a paradise—and for the good reason that, really, there can be nothing fixed. Life is a beast not to be trapped: it is endlessly fluid, fleeting and perishing—a race or a river. This was the theme of **"The Happier Life"**, and the poem **"Fixed"** brings it out explicitly; the only fixity there can be is that of the imagination—

> Forever there distortedly,
> The fixed and visionary part of me

—persistently re-creating, not vaguely but exactly, an unrealisable better life.

I have not yet mentioned another aspect of Dunn, the fact that he is haunted and solicited by innumerable other lives. It is, you might say, the fictional imagination. He cannot help fitting out any half-glimpsed face, in a passing car or a crowd, with a history and a background. . . . This is the other half of his imagination, the social as opposed to the idealising one. It is what most links him with Larkin and, I suppose one must say, with Betjeman. He knows his English scene wonderfully well, and this was the quality that first attracted one in his poems. However, it figures less in his new volume, which is more concerned with the implications, the rights and wrongs, of this promiscuous involvement with other existences.

Dunn as a poet is not 'fixed' in any groove: he can, sometimes, do just what he wants, and we can expect great things from him.

P. N. Furbank, "After Terry Street," in The Listener, *Vol. 90, No. 2315, August 9, 1973, p. 190.*

THE VIRGINIA QUARTERLY REVIEW

With all the honesty of a perceptive familiarity, Mr. Dunn [in *Terry Street*] presents us with the lives of a community made no more remarkable by being the object of his scrutiny than the commonest circumstances of our day-to-day existence. What is to be learned from our sharing in this faithful recognition of the commonplace remains in doubt, for Mr. Dunn is as sparing in his comments as he is precise in his observations. For all that life in Terry Street is "like living in a deep, dried-up riverbed, a throat that thirsts," the facts are not assembled with any observable intent to demonstrate that truth, and Mr. Dunn more often turns our attention to facts than to their abstract burden of despair. Even when Terry Street itself is no longer the focal point of the poet's gaze, the objects which encumber our daily lives remain in the forefront of his imagination, providing pegs upon which to hang his muted, tentative conclusions.

A review of "Terry Street," in The Virginia Quarterly Review, *Vol. 51, No. 2 (Spring, 1975), p. lviii.*

JOSEPH PARISI

Were it not for the author's acute perception and piercing nervous energy, the typical English scenes Douglas Dunn observes might make his poems as melancholy as the dreary rows of Victorian brick in which they are often set. His first volume, *Terry Street,* is doubly revealing: a graphic picture of working-class English life and a vivid portrait of the poet as sensitive outsider. The popular notion of the English in this country blends an anachronistic manor-house-and-fox-hunt fantasy with the equally distorted vision of Georgie Girls, Marrying Kinds, and Leather Boys (not to mention zany Marxist Morgans) purveyed by the film industry. *Terry Street,* in its mixture of detachment and self-examination, depicts the more ordinary reality and presents it with the greater fascinations of poetic insight. Though he writes an acidly satiric **"Poem in Praise of the British,"** the generally mild-mannered reporter sympathetically surveys lower-class mores, favoring incisive particulars within the broad stereotypes. In **"The Clothes Pit,"** they're the girls who "must keep up" with "teasing skirts and latest shoes"; "often fat and unlovely", they "lack intellectual grooming", preferring wine to pot as they take the "litter of pop rhetoric . . . into their lives.'' Terry Street is changeless but life-filled. (pp. 234-35)

"There is no grass on Terry Street", but he finds beauties other inhabitants probably don't suspect: "Television aerials, Chinese characters", sparrows and moss, "Urban flora and fauna, soft, unscrupulous." One is constantly prompted to make comparisons with American life. At night, the policeman patrolling the street "stops the drunk, they talk, they laugh together." On the "shapeless street, a bad address", old people "take pride in dying where they always lived, / Preferably tended by sons, and neighbors with soup."

More personally, the self-conscious narrator examines his relations to the others, usually women, as with **"Young Women in Rollers."** He sees them as they talk of love and listen to pop songs in their houses, which are "monuments to entertainment."

> This time they see me at my window, among books,
> A specimen under glass, being protected,
> And laugh at me watching them.
> They minuet to Mozart playing loudly
>
> On the afternoon Third. They mock me thus,
> They mime my softness. . . .

Yet he is not angry or embarrassed; here, as elsewhere, he seems to envy the other styles: "I want to be touched by them, know their lives . . . learn something new." But he remains separate; he'll "Dance in [his] own style . . . There are many worlds, there are many laws." This sense of longing, the need to belong, adds a special piquancy to these more personal poems. In **"The Worst of All Loves,"** the poet watches the girls from the top decks of buses, knowing "They will never meet us suddenly in pleasant rooms." He sends the **"Tribute of a Legs Lover"** to the chorus girls who, past their primes, "are not given florist's shops or Schools of Dance / By rich and randy admirers''. . . . Examining his poetry, he constructs his own **"Dream of Judgement"** and pictures himself being rejected by the Augustans: "Quite gently, Pope ushers me out into the hell / Of forgotten books." . . . (pp. 235-36)

That Pope was mistaken and the Judgement precipitous is borne out in Dunn's second volume [*The Happier Life*]. Moving up and down a few rungs on the social ladder, he presents other views of English life, as well as other facets of his complex personality. *The Happier Life* has more humorous, whimsical, and lyrical moods; these are counterbalanced, however, with a deeper seriousness and dissatisfaction. This ambitious book is distinguished, too, by its greater control and increased technical sureness, evidenced in its stanzaic variations, tight forms, and keen images. Yet, this developing craftsmanship, I think, is achieved at some cost; sometimes the distancing that results gives a number of poems a simulated, inauthentic feel. Be that as it may, Dunn's sketches still make a strong impact.

Ironically, isolation and alienation form large topics of *The Happier Life.* The Irish country girls come to the city, dreaming of a life of leisure, but "find themselves instead / Hardworked by protestants in drab hotel rooms." No one cares: "Their futures are only personal, / Nothing to do with us." **"Backwaters"** searches not only the obscure towns but the cheap rooms "where the stutterers hide, the ugly and clubfooted, / The radically nervous who are hurt by crowds." Despite efforts to shrug off and forget these unacceptables, these "Mysterious people without names or faces, / Whose lives I guess about, whose dangers tease", the poet finds "They will not leave me,

the lives of other people. / I wear them near my eyes like spectacles.''

Sometimes this irritation at other people's lives stems from envy, which grows to anger and finally to vindictiveness, as in **"The Sportsmen":** "Scum, they have fast cars and money / And take other men's wives to play tennis. . . . Their times will come . . . They will be murdered in bedrooms, / Their cars pressed into squares of scrap." Love, its facsimiles, its substitutes, its failures, is the other major cause of the malaise in this not so happy existence. (p. 236)

Again and again, the poet suggests drawing back, denying the public lies and private infidelities. In **"Syndrome,"** he rejects the wastes of the playboy and the powerful careerman. . . . However, when Dunn rationalizes that the people he dislikes aren't really happy, the point seems to lack conviction. And, even if it's true, the poems display the undeniable fact that evil has a lurid fascination, and the unattainable becomes all the more intriguing, and pleasurable, because out of reach. Dunn is too fine a poet, of course, not to know this. . . . Perhaps the curious ambivalences in this volume will be resolved in the next. "All poets labour inward," he says in **"A Faber Melancholy,"** "To find authentic hurt and what will move". Judging by the successes of his labors thus far, it will be worth the wait. (p. 237)

Joseph Parisi, "Personae, Personalities," in Poetry, *Vol. CXXVI, No. 4, July, 1975, pp. 219-42.**

BLAKE MORRISON

Douglas Dunn has a grudge. In his last collection, **Love or Nothing** (1974), he called it a grudge more 'lovely' than anyone else's. On another occasion, in the magazine *Stand,* he pictured it as a kind of animal, a pet-hate: 'My grudge is a good grudge. I can even take it out myself and sing to it; when I do that, my grudge purrs.' As the image suggests, Dunn has in the past kept his resentments fairly subdued: they miaow pleasantly around the reader's legs and mean no harm. Now, in **Barbarians,** he has let the cat out of the bag good and proper, so that the 'bitter ooze' of his grudge can be heard clearly for the first time. It is the grudge of a working-class writer against the bourgeoisie—those who 'come on with their "coals in the bath" stories / Or mock at your accent'. It is the grudge, also, of a Scot against the English. *Barbarians* allows these class and national loyalties to have their noisy way. There are poems about proletarian revolt, about the closing down of the Clydeside shipyards, and about ruling-class plunders at home and abroad: 'We worked their mines and made their histories. / *You work, we rule,* they said.' Dunn takes special pleasure in repeating the word 'grudge' itself, perhaps because it sounds like a combination of two other words close to his socialist heart—'greed' (what the exploiters are driven by) and 'drudge' (what the exploited are forced to do).

But the most interesting grudge in **Barbarians** is that which Dunn has against himself. For while his social and political affiliations dictate that he despise English middle-class culture, he can't help feeling an attraction towards it. Much guilty compromising ensues from this, with Dunn affecting boorishness but not managing to hate the art-collections of the rich. Dunn is also afraid that in making good as a poet and professional he has cut himself off from his own people. A sense of isolation was already there in his first collection, **Terry Street** (1969), where Dunn's lonely student persona is every bit as cut off from the Northern working classes as is Larkin's in, say, 'Here' and 'The Whitsun Weddings', and just as liable to draw them in Donald McGill-like caricatures. But the fear of isolation is nowadays much more pressing: having got himself over the glass-spiked garden-walls of the aristocracy, he's faced with the problem of how to let in his fellows. in **"The Come-On"** he persuades himself that it can be done: addressing his class in the tones of a union rep ('Brothers, they say we have no culture'), he offers a dream of future spoils. . . . But the red Dunn and his red dawn lack conviction. He has too many orthodox liberal doubts about agitprop, and is too embarrassed by his own candour, to sustain this kind of polemic for long.

He is also too attracted to 'style'—another cause for self-reproach. The common view, of course, is that Dunn is a devotee of the plain and urban, his material the dogshit and fag-ends to be found on 'the backstreets of the universe', his style a kind of no-style of low-life realism. But for 'a poetry of nuts and bolts' (Dunn's own phrase again), there's a surprisingly soft-centred, fanciful and dreamlike element in his work. In the middle of the hard-nosed title sequence comes the strange and powerful **"An Artist Waiting in a Country-House"**, which promises a political allegory, but acquires an Ashbery-like impenetrability the longer it goes on. Dunn has also in *Barbarians* made greater use than before of traditional poetic 'settings' and of traditional rhyme and metre, as if to show that he and his kind *do* 'have business with the rose'. This may not be the cop-out he fears but it does finally make for an uneven collection, one which slides from the splendid barbarian outspokenness of its opening into mannerism, wooden refrain and self-indulgent reminiscence. (p. 690)

> *Blake Morrison, "Over the Garden Wall," in* New Statesman, *Vol. 97, No. 2512, May 11, 1979, pp. 690-91.**

ALAN BROWNJOHN

The title-sequence of [*Barbarians*], **"Barbarian Pastorals"**, sets out the themes which dominate the book: the poet's simultaneous mistrust of an Oxbridge "culture of connivance" and veneration for the great monuments of that culture, properly used and understood; his sense of a rejuvenating and civilising energy in the "barbarian" forces which will replace a dead empire ("Our coarser artistries will make things grow"); and a desire to return to the roots from which that energy derived. Dunn's barbarians are, indeed, *foederati*, struggling with their consciences in the culture which enlisted them, yet struggling also to master "difficult Latin." (p. 68)

Dunn is—most unfashionably—concerned not only for what remains of the strengths of a working-class tradition, but also for those things of value to which it once aspired through the "Mechanics' Literary Club." It is now customary to settle for a far less taxing, "classless" culture out of the media: we are in the age of the Rock Intellectual, publicity-conscious, condescending, and tone-deaf. All this makes the reasoning of poems like **"The Come-on"** and **"Elegy for the Lost Parish"** less easy to receive (and Dunn's recent style, more technically ambitious and sometimes less technically sure, adds to the difficulty) than the well-known, simpler pieces from *Terry Street*.

Barbarians is a more "political" volume than any he has yet produced; but it is abundantly worth listening in to its fierce dialogues between those guarding a patrician culture with the weapons of class, and the "scholarship boys" who want to claim their cultural inheritance. . . . For admirers of Dunn in a less argumentative vein, there are a number of those shorter

poems about people, places and objects (situated back at the roots usually) in which he lets his own characteristic kind of humour and inventiveness have free play. **"Red Buses"** is about resolute attempts to curb licentious behavior on late-night double-deckers, **"Old Things"** is a lovely variation on the theme of the "shabby heirlooms" culled from antique shops—and **"Watches of Grandfathers"** gives such objects of homely dignity an aura of the sinister. . . . **"Glasgow Schoolboys, Running Backwards"** manages to encapsulate much of Dunn's seriousness *and* his observant, slightly surreal humour in its four lines:

> High wind . . . They turn their backs to it, and push
> Their crazy strides are chopped in little steps.
> And all their lives, like that, they'll have to rush
> Forwards in reverse, holding their caps.

I hope he goes on mixing the "push" of argument with the "craziness" of his freer imaginings as he does in *Barbarians*. (pp. 68-9)

> *Alan Brownjohn, "Untidy Moments," in* Encounter, *Vol. LII, No. 6, June, 1979, pp. 68-72.**

EDNA LONGLEY

Douglas Dunn's admirable seriousness has sometimes led his lyric gift by the ears. The interview with him in John Haffenden's *Viewpoints* confirms that he experiences a Calvinistic internal strife between *utile* and *dulce*:

> There are times when I wish . . . that I could just simply relax and deal with the play of phenomena and experience in my imagination . . . rather than be concerned with subjects which—on the surface at least—are so recognisably social.

All who share this wish will welcome *St Kilda's Parliament* as less 'recognisably social' than its predecessor, *Barbarians*. The evocative title-poem suffers only one didactic interruption:

> On St Kilda's you will surely hear Gaelic
> Spoken softly like a poetry of ghosts
> By those who never were contorted by
> Hierarchies of cuisine and literacy.

Yet, despite their crudity, the last two lines mark a fruitful application of Dunn's anti-establishment attitudes to a Scottish sociolinguistic context. . . . [He] raises here both an elusive native spirit and the Scottish poet's traditional problems of accent and stance. There is a similar sense of home-coming in two longish poems, where Dunn tries on contrasting ancestral voices. He affectionately imitates Robert Tannahill ('You sang, like a beginning finch / Your common heart') and John Wilson of Greenock, who tried 'To lift our Lowland snipe and waterhen / Into Arcàdia from Lanarkshire'.

Dunn has neither deserted Arcadia nor succumbed to literary nationalism. Nevertheless, his Scottish poems earth the collection, and set in sharper focus the compassionate portraits at which he excels. **"Spinster's Wake"** employs a convincing vernacular ('Pease-brose in the bag, John, jam in the jar'), **"Witch-girl"** a folk-ballad idiom. . . . Dunn still inclines to abstraction, usually in over-elaborate stanzas, and to jumbo-jet flights of fancy such as his 'poem-films' starring Anthony Quinn and Jean-Paul Belmondo—a last-ditch cosmopolitan stand? He should beware the possible new pitfall of copying Seamus Heaney's language of place. . . . However, his authentic 'play of phenomena and experience' sparks off, diversely, a mock-heroic celebration of **'Ratatouille'** (hardly the 'cuisine' of St Kilda's), a powerful quatrain on racial hatred, and a tender ode that takes up the rose where Burns left it. This could prove Dunn's most important book to date. (pp. 29-30)

Edna Longley, "The Play of Imagination," in New Statesman, *Vol. 102, No. 2635, September 18, 1981, pp. 29-30.**

ALASDAIR D.F. MACRAE

[Dunn's collection *St Kilda's Parliament*] is his best so far; what is most impressive about it is Douglas Dunn's ability to write such a diverse group of poems, showing variety in verse form, subject and diction. There are memorable phrases, gleams of humour, striking observations, stimulating ideas and, throughout the collection, a wonderfully assured control of syntax. More marked than in his earlier poetry is a strain of affection and wise tolerance. Several poems explore his upbringing in Scotland and look back beyond his own lifetime, but he avoids nostalgia and easy sentiment. This collection places Douglas Dunn in an exclusive category of poets who are able to write persuasively on whatever impinges on their consciousness and who find a style proper to each different subject. Even in such a distinguished book of poems as this there are bound to be some less successful poems: I enjoyed his experiments in 'poem-films' for Anthony Quinn and Jean-Paul Belmondo, but they are not so durable as many of the other poems.... [*St Kilda's Parliament*] is one of the most enjoyable, intelligent and professional books of poems of recent years.

Alasdair D.F. Macrae, in a review of "St Kilda's Parliament," in British Book News, *January, 1982, p. 51.*

MICHAEL O'NEILL

For Douglas Dunn, thinking in poetry involves the belief that the poet, to write truthfully, must face up to the implications of a mood or attitude. The lyrical garden of self-delight may entice; his is a severer terrain. Landscapes in his work are ticketed with social and cultural meanings, there to be emblematized. This cast of mind can make him contentiously wordy. But it is yoked, more often, to an enriching humanism. In **"The Apple Tree"**, one of the best poems in his fine *St. Kilda's Parliament,* Dunn proposes, as a replacement for the old Calvinist ordinances, the 'simple covenant we keep with love', its 'scriptures written by the late-arriving autumn'. No simple nature idyll, this forms part of the poet's imaginative pilgrimage to his native Scotland. Much of the volume attempts to resurrect the life and lives oppressed by Kirk and State.

Its essential themes are announced in the title-poem, the first in the book, where the island of St. Kilda is celebrated as

> a remote democracy where men,
> In manacles of place, outstare a sea
> That rattles back its manacles of salt,
> The moody jailor of the wild Atlantic.

The phrase 'manacles of place' lends an edge of disabused realism to the ideological dream. But it is the celebratory note which endures as Dunn's surrogate, a photographer revisiting the scene of his pictures, imagines the island's 'naked self'.

The poet as cultural archaeologist, on the track of 'footprints stratified beneath the lichens', is a familiar figure. What turns excavation into poetry is the dogged way Dunn admits and contests the fact that he is 'outside'. He may be trapped [on] the wrong side of the lens, but his rhythms negotiate a treaty with his ideal. They are as patient and well-made as 'the little boat that brought me here, / Whose carpentry was slowly shaped by waves, / By a history of these northern waters'. Typically, reverence makes Dunn combative, severe on the civilisation opposed by silent islanders 'aware of what we are up to'.

His analyses spring from deeper, more obdurate roots than polemic. For Dunn is trying to do two things: to reaffirm the value of lives and communities which have been thrown onto the scrap-heap of history, and to envisage possibilities of freedom for the self. His sympathies extend beyond the derelict, forgotten lives of Scotland's past—including dominies, a failed poet, a witch, a sculptor of monuments—to embrace 'the lost of the world'. This impulse can seem willed. **"Ode to a Paperclip"** bristles with admirable intentions, but fails to get airborne imaginatively. By contrast **"Lamp-posts"** is a small masterpiece. To the peremptory rightness of tone of an early poem like **"The Silences"** it adds an inventiveness which catapults itself beyond the playful in a fine ending.... There are not many poets at the moment who can write with such muted, humanising fury, such bleak pity for the humble.

It is possible to apply to *St. Kilda's Parliament* the praise which Dunn has given to the poetry of Derek Mahon. Dunn, too, 'has managed to form a poetic which tries realist *and* metaphysical manners and which, in opposition to narrower poetries, tries to *include*'. This attempt to include underpins the volume's stylistic manners. There are poems (such as **"Green Breeks"**) where the element of tour-de-force in the use of a complex stanza distracts. But one form Dunn handles with mastery is blank verse. (p. 60)

"Remembering Lunch", possibly the volume's best poem, explores the rival claims of solitude and society. The poem's structure—Dunn walking by the sea, remembering a lunch with literary friends—polarises the two. In his analysis of the milieu to which he and his friends belong, but which he is now intent on leaving, the poet is harsh, affectionate, self-vigilant. Self-vigilance is a more fascinating presence at the end of the poem. Circumspectly praising the Crusoe-like isolation of his walk, Dunn remarks that

> it is a cause for fear to notice that only my
>   footprints
> Litter this deserted beach with signs of human
>   approach,
> Each squelch of leather on mud complaining,
>   *But where are you going?*

The poem prompts us to put that final question to the poet. Have we reached the limits of Dunn's world, a world where the self achieves identity primarily through the testing of stances taken towards society? Not much contemporary poetry has got that far, or investigated its positions so honestly, or expressed such imaginative concern for the lives of other people. (p. 61)

Michael O'Neill, "Thinking Hearts," in Poetry Review, *Vol. 72, No. 1, April, 1982, pp. 59-64.**

MICHAEL O'NEILL

[Dunn's *Europa's Lover*] represents the ambitious flowering of an obsession with collective experience. More and more in recent work, his voice, while remaining distinctively his own, has sought to root itself in the lives of a community (as in **"St Kilda's Parliament"**) or a culture. *Europa's Lover* is, in scale and at times in achievement, comparable with Geoffrey Hill's historical sonnet-sequences. The framework (Europa, a sort of quintessential Female Principle, in dialogue with a young man) is a thin disguise for Dunn's own meditations. But the poems make good use of their freedom to deal with what Dunn in the blurb calls 'Things in General'. The writing comes and goes in vivid pulsations. There are some flat stretches. For the most part, though, the language trawls, an ever-widening net, in the wake of its sympathy for 'the lives of millions, stored lives / With their unmeasured stories'. There are superb historical vignettes ('Or he might sail to Celebes and Java, / Wading ashore to wave a cutlass at the pagodas'), some powerful rhetoric (**VI** is an example, 'Shaped into this intimate suffering of death with life') and one fine short lyric (**IX**) about the phase of European culture that resulted in 'Strindberg or some such', a poem which moves with typical confidence between image and abstraction. *Europa's Lover* is a daring and serious poem that gets better on each rereading.

> Michael O'Neill, "Two Bloodaxe Pamphlets," in Poetry Review, Vol. 73, No. 1, March, 1983, p. 60.*

G.B.H. WIGHTMAN

Douglas Dunn is an important poet who plays for high stakes. *Europa's Lover,* a sequence of fourteen poems, has a grand vision. Europe, the poet's mistress, (the relationship is in fact obscure) recreates scenes from her past: 'By the banks of a Scandinavian lake / We heard harness and smalltalk / As a migrating tribe came down / To water its ponies and say good-bye' and mingles them with more recent events. Dunn emphasizes that Europe is the crucifixes of the Somme as well as the operas of Mozart. There are several themes in this design including one of determinism which no doubt fits his Marxist outlook. Unfortunately, the fine writing becomes grandiloquent and his intellectual resources cannot sustain his moral ambitions. The architecture is weak. Dunn seems to be trying to emulate Pound's *Cantos*. He fails; but it is an honourable failure.

> G.B.H. Wightman, in a review of "Europa's Lover," in British Book News, September, 1983, p. 576.

PUBLISHERS WEEKLY

[*Secret Villages*] is notable for the quiet, offhand humor and easy grace of the 16 short stories collected here. Dunn reveals a Scotland not often glimpsed by tourists. In the deftly funny **"The Canoes,"** some Scottish locals enjoy the ancient sport of playing up to sightseers; in **"Fisherman,"** two brothers find that fishing reveals the differences between them; in **"Twin Sets and Pickle Forks,"** a tea room manager is taken down a notch by one of her waitresses; and in **"South America,"** a wife whose husband works in South America decides that his extended absence won't prevent her from having more children. . . . [Dunn's] light touch, eye for the absurd and ability to create a wholly believable world make him a talent to watch.

> A review of "Secret Villages," in Publishers Weekly, Vol. 227, No. 5, February 1, 1985, p. 351.

PETER PORTER

When a poet has been overwhelmed by bereavement, his reaction will inevitably be seen in his verse. But it may not take the form of direct elegiac poetry. When it does, he will need the muse's closest help—for truth, for art and for decorum.

Douglas Dunn has managed this hardest of tasks, the confrontation of loss, in poems which belong entirely properly to the public domain. Dunn's wife died of cancer when she was only 37, and every poem in [*Elegies*] is directly or indirectly involved in her death and his bereavement.

We are never eavesdroppers, because his grief and his memory are shaped by the spirit of continuity, that force which, recognising love, recognises also that it was most present when most alive. These *Elegies* have their bitternesses, but their extraordinary, naked naturalness owes much to there being no admixture of guilt in his recreation of the life he and his wife lived.

The art of Dunn's new poems is considerable, but it is an art of enrichment not one of concealment, or of the painful stripping away of alibis. The poems are more formal than his recent work has usually been, looking perhaps for the props and structures of prosody to support the true voice of feeling. Planted in them is a sort of *ex voto:* they are 'dedicated to the one / pure elegy . . .'. He strikes that note time after time:

> Best friend and love, my true contemporary,
> She taught me how to live, then how to die,
> And I curate her dreams and gallery.
> Writing with light, the heart within my eye
> Shines on my grief, my true contemporary.

That Dunn's wife was a gallery curator and that the disease began in her eye may not be known to the reader, but the justice of the poetry does not need such knowledge. Throughout the book, detail after detail fits into place in a mosaic of two people's harmonious life together.

There is no flinching from the miserable fact of dying or the horrors of grieving. Going to register her death, Dunn notes that the official 'has seen all the words that end in —oma.' The paradox of this set of elegies is that it seems full of life and joy. And it shows that language, small asset as it is, can yield a great human harvest. . . .

> Peter Porter, "True Voice of Feeling," in The Observer, March 17, 1985, p. 24.*

BLAKE MORRISON

[The poems in *Elegies*], the blurb tells us (and it is all that it tells us), "were written after the death of Douglas Dunn's wife in March 1981". It is an explanation of the book's origin, not an appeal for pity or indulgence: Dunn would want the book to be judged as a book, not as a *cri de coeur*. Necessarily, the poems are at times appallingly intimate . . . but there is nothing indecent about them or, rather, nothing voyeuristic about reading them. They are shaped and measured but have no rhetorical designs on us; the poet watches his quatrains and rhyme-schemes, not his readers' tear-ducts. None the less, we can't prevent our critical judgment from being affected by what we know to have happened. The book's power is, in part, that it is true. Its *frissons* are the *frissons* of authenticity, and when the poet seems maudlin or mawkish it's impossible not to make allowances. What might look like crude irony in a made-up tale (the moment, for example, when Dunn goes to register his wife's death and ends up among wedding-parties instead; or the fly he comes across squashed between the pages of a story of Katherine Mansfield's called "Bliss", from a book bought in happier and more innocent times) here becomes life's habit of being ironic: the literal truth literally told melts our disbelief. Amid so much misfortune, this is the poet's one piece of luck, and he is right to ride it, as Thomas Hardy and more recently Peter Porter do in their elegies for *their* dead wives: all enjoy the advantage, not of course an advantage nor at all enjoyable, of writing at first-hand about an experience that is serious, sombre but above all true.

Dunn calls the experience "sensible, commonplace, beyond understanding" and finds a variety of forms to contain not guilt or bitterness but simply grief: sonnets, quatrains, intricate rhyme-schemes. But he also knows when plain-speaking and blank verse are poetry enough. . . . But Dunn is careful in any case to do more than merely tell it as it was. The opening poems describe the "story" of his wife's death: the "second opinion" which confirms the presence of cancer; his wife sitting up in bed receiving guests, cheerful and courageous; the strange atmosphere—"erotic" and "beautiful" for all the pain—of their last nights together. There are flashes of something like grim humour, as when he registers her death: "Everyone receives this Certificate. / You do not need even to deserve it." From very early in the book the poet moves beyond the immediate source of his grief to the past he shared with his wife—holidays in France, her love of food, clothes and art, their marriage as a brief summer—and to the residue of loss. These memories and reflections—"radiantly painful speculations", as he calls them, "light with meditation, religiose / and mystic"—draw him into a world where dream breaks in on reality and language grows bolder and more expansive: "I go into the bedroom of the world", "I meet the seasons on the stairs", "A floral light / Bleaches my eye with angelophanous / Secrets".

He is moved, too, in the book's longest and most imaginative poems, **"Pretended Homes"** and **"The Stories"**, to invent landscapes and fictions in which his wife can reappear or he himself find his proper place. The first imagines an island "on no map" to which a sea-circus comes "with its elephants, clowns and saxophones": she can live in this extraordinary place as she can't in the "real house" where she died and where (a rich pun) "all my calling cannot bring her back". The second poem, more subdued, imagines those "far-flung outposts of Empire" where a widower might once have gone to bury his pain. . . . "Fictions" though they are, these two poems are as vulnerable and personal as the more plain-speaking ones. And they suggest that, however odd it might seem to speak of this book in the context of Dunn's poetic "development" (the direction he has taken has been forced on him, not chosen), there are indeed continuities with the earlier work: the imaginary landscapes, with their odd mix of the "Ovidian and Gaelic", the lush and the barren, the dandyishly French and the austerely Scottish, have appeared before in *Barbarians* and *St Kilda's Parliament*. The most obvious discontinuity is the move away from a poetry concerned with class, history and culture. "Who am I", Dunn asks, "to weep for Salvador or Kampuchea / when I am made the acolyte of my own shadow?" But there is a "social" aspect to Dunn's grieving art, in that bereavement connects the poet with others. In **"Reading Pascal in the Lowlands"**, Dunn, newly widowed, is reluctantly drawn into conversation with the father of a boy in a wheelchair:

> He is indiscreet.
> His son is eight years old, with months to live.
> His right hand trembles on the cigarette.

> He sees my book, and then he looks at me,
> Knowing me for a stranger. I have said
> I am sorry. What more is there to say?

These are perhaps the book's bleakest lines, because the moment of connection brings no consolation. . . . Yet *Elegies* is not, overall, a morbid or depressing book. Metaphors of leaf, bloom, larksong and, above all, light commemorate the past and bring a strange buoyancy to the present. One poem describes Dunn's artist-wife holding a jam-jar filled with water up to the sun: it is a symbol of how to "write with light" and through her example the poet discovers gleams of hope and affirmation in his personal darkness. The concluding poem, though sad and chastened, also lights upon an image of great energy, the V-dart of wild geese, "instinctive, mad for home—make way! make way!"

As the poet himself remarks, "among the received notions of criticism is the belief that there should be a distance of time between a grievous personal event and writing which reflects it". Aside from some shorter and slighter pieces which might better have been omitted, this moving and measured collection shows that Dunn was right to defy the convention.

> Blake Morrison, "Narratives of Grief," in The Times Literary Supplement, *No. 4279, April 5, 1985, p. 377.*

ANTHONY THWAITE

Dunn's last but one book of poems, *St Kilda's Parliament*, was a bold, various and often moving act of repossession of his native Scotland, past and present, made by a man who at that time had been for several years an ambivalent exile.

In his first collection of stories, *Secret Villages*, almost all the settings are Scottish too: rural, urban, small town, big city, working-class, professional middle-class, couth and genteel, uncouth and canny.

Typically, one kind of setting and character is confronted with another, and has to try to come to terms with it. In **"Canoes,"** the elegant self-assurance of a young English couple on holiday by a remote Loch is a source of obsessive wonder to the local men, who watch their goings-on with voyeuristic attention. In **"The Bagpiping People,"** a family of tinkers untidily encamps close to the family of a prosperous garage-owner. . . .

In [both of] these, and in many more, Dunn is a gentle and undemonstrative observer, with an excellent ear for different registers of dialogue. He collects and presents his characters sympathetically, particularly in the restrictions and self-deceptions of their lives. . . .

> Anthony Thwaite, "From North of the Border," in The Observer, *June 9, 1985, p. 24.**

GEOFFREY PARKER

[In] a way the title of [*Secret Villages*] appropriately describes these glimpses into the lives of ordinary people. Forlorn aspirations in **"Photographs of Stanley's Grandfather"** and **"Kilbinnen Men"**; dreams of an irrecoverable past in **"The Tennis Court"** and **"Women without Gardens"**; the generation gap in **"Getting Used to It"**, **"Mozart's Clarinet Concerto"** and **"Bobby's Room"**; and the lives of women bringing up children without men in **"South America"** and **"Twin-Sets**

and Pickle Forks" all in their different ways represent secret domains. . . .

The author gives his reader access to all these secret villages, although closeness to the earth and traditional ways of living seem to be more distant, but more admired, than urban and suburban life. Douglas Dunn's keen observation of people and places, which was at once apparent in his first volume of poetry, **Terry Street** . . . , is a gift that serves him well in the short story. He needs no sensationalism to attract attention, preferring to highlight the 'unspectacular significance' of his characters' lives. A Chekhovian fusion of objective description and compassionate warmth lends poignancy to these sharp-edged images of a society lacking in dynamism.

> *Geoffrey Parker, in a review of "Secret Villages,"*
> *in* British Book News, *July, 1985, p. 426.*

ROBIN BELL

Dunn's **Elegies** triumph, not merely over a difficult form, but over contemporary irrational attitudes to death itself. This is not the sort of poetry that simply externalises the writer's feelings, nor does Dunn use the life of his dying wife as a vehicle for working out his own emotions. The most impressive thing about the book is that it is written with respect for his wife, Lesley, as an individual. 'Respect' is a word that has gone soggy in the English language, but it is what has made it possible to write a celebration of life in the face of death.

He does not duck the issues. The death of a young woman by cancer is cruel and oppressively unfair. But what comes across most is Lesley's vitality, not her suffering and Douglas Dunn's constant affection, not peaks of passion nor troughs of grief. The highs and lows are implied rather than made explicit, almost as though even in the midst of writing about his lost wife he is still protective of her.

There is extraordinary variety within a book devoted to a single subject. The poems are set in landscapes varying from Hull where they lived, through their travels in France, to Dundee where he was writer in residence and Lesley finally died. The focus varies too from the subtly changing balance of dependencies to whole landscapes inhabited by an elegy.

Over the years, since his first book **Terry Street** was published in 1968, Douglas Dunn has developed an impressive mastery of poetic form. In **Elegies** there is a sense of the poet's having at his disposal the technique to say what he wants simply and memorably. The book has a durable quality. It won't date or fade away. The final irony is that the word outlasts the flesh. (p. 31)

> *Robin Bell, "Lots of Bang and No Whimper," in*
> The Spectator, *Vol. 255, No. 8191, July 6, 1985,*
> *pp. 31-2.**

JOHN MOLE

Anyone who has suffered personal loss is left, at bottom, with the plain facts. For Douglas Dunn these are that in March 1981 his wife, Lesley, died from cancer of the eye—a particularly bitter irony given that she was an artist of great sensitivity to light and its conversation with lovingly chosen objects—and his new collection, **Elegies,** which confronts their shared life and her death in a sequence of remarkable poems, is a heart-breaking book. It is also utterly without self-pity, a celebration of a rich and affirmative marriage. The entire volume is, of course, shadowed by a remorselessly familiar story which in this case begins in hospital with "the mind sliding against events / And the antiseptic whiff of destiny" and ends with intimations of a new life contingent upon the old:

> She spoke of what I might do "afterwards".
> "Go, somewhere else." I went north to Dundee.
> Tomorrow I won't live here any more
> Nor leave alone. *My love, say you'll come with me.*

However it is precisely because she does so vividly come with him into the making of these poems—their apprehension, witnessing and recollection—that the maudlin note is never struck. There's not a hint of Hardyesque guilt or Tennysonian gloom, not the slightest suspicion that death has provided the occasion for rhetoric. The poems seem an exact transcription of what was there in the relationship. In no sense at all are they compensatory. **Elegies** is the record of "moments of me / And moments of my love and me together. / And her moments, her secret visions in them", and it is a measure of Dunn's achievement and imaginative generosity that it is *her* moments, in life and death, which most vividly inform the collection. The book is a gift to Lesley, written with the wit and clear, unsentimental intelligence she so obviously approved of, and, as it were, offered to the reader over their shoulders by private invitation. What gradually emerges, throughout the sequence, is the portrait of a woman who "refused all grief, but was alight / With nature, courage, friendship, appetite." When Dunn does employ conscious literary artifice, even pastiche, it seems part of a serious game the couple might have played together, a mode of heightening the pleasures of living in the knowledge that "art is love." . . . In **"Anniversaries"** there is a direct allusion which combines John Donne's "The Anniversarie" and "The Relique": "That day will still exist / Long after I have joined you where / Rings radiate the dusty air / And bangles bind each powdered wrist" but such referential hyperbole is set up only to be brought down to common earth, and Lesley's own words— "Write out of me, not out of what you read"—echo throughout **Elegies.** . . . The recurring images of light, in poem after poem, are never soft at the edge. They are the essence of concentration: "Writing with light, the heart within my eye / Shines on my grief, my true contemporary." And in the poem which has haunted me most, **"Sandra's Mobile",** light and movement combine in a single object given and received with love. The moment of death is neither dark nor desolate. To borrow a line from another poem, "the air was the fingertips of loneliness" but here it is the poet's own breath, and in touching the three seagulls it is quite simply the kiss of that continuing life which the entire book celebrates . . . :

> So Sandra brought her this and taped it up—
> Three seagulls from a white and indoor sky—
> A gift of old artistic comradeship.
> "Blow on them, Love." Those silent birds winged
>   round
> On thermals of my breath. On her last night,
> Trying to stay awake, I saw love crowned
> In tears and wooden birds and candlelight.
> She did not wake again. To prove our love
> Each gull, each gull, each gull, turned into dove.
>
> (pp. 51-2)

> *John Mole, "Implications of Mortality," in* Encounter, *Vol. LXV, No. 2, July-August, 1985, pp. 51-8.**

Marguerite Duras

1914-

(Born Marguerite Donnadieu) French novelist, dramatist, film-maker, short story writer, nonfiction writer, and journalist.

A prolific author who is highly regarded for her work in several genres, Duras is perhaps best known in the United States for her screenplay for Alain Resnais's film *Hiroshima mon amour* and for her autobiographical novel *L'amant* (1984; *The Lover*), which was awarded France's Prix Goncourt and is Duras's most commercially successful work of fiction. Although her career covers many genres and spans more than four decades, several themes recur in Duras's work, including the depiction of desire as a force more powerful than death, the effect of time on memory and love, and the acute sense of isolation that results from longing, loneliness, and despair. Duras's fiction, plays, and films have many structural and stylistic similarities, and several of her works have been adapted to all three mediums by herself as well as by others. Her fiction is strongly visual and experimental, employing such cinematic techniques as fragmented sequences, juxtaposed images, and still-shot descriptions which both objectify and distance the narrative. Her plays, many of which are one-acts based on her novels and stories, generally feature only two or three characters and make unconventional use of space, movement, and silence. Her films are likewise characterized by long silences, an abstract conception of time, and an emphasis on atmosphere. Duras's works in all three forms usually involve minimalist plots, focusing on interior conflicts and moods that are conveyed to a large degree through dialogue. While Duras's use of fragmentation and discontinuity has led to charges of obscurity, her poetic prose, evocative atmospheres, and subtle depictions of the interior states of her characters have generated much critical acclaim.

© Jerry Bauer

Duras was born and raised in French Indochina in a small town outside of Saigon. When she was seventeen she moved to France; although she has since made Paris her home, her early exposure to Eastern culture is evident throughout her work. For example, her first significant novel, *Un barrage contre le Pacifique* (1950; *The Sea Wall*), is set in Indochina and reflects her interest in this culture and in issues of social justice. Duras participated in the Resistance movement against Germany's occupation of France during World War II and later briefly joined the Communist party. Duras's leftist orientation informs her work, but she focuses not so much on large-scale oppression as on the struggles of the individual.

Duras began writing at an early age. Her first two novels, *Les impudents* (1943) and *La vie tranquille* (1944), received relatively little notice. These and other early novels—*The Sea Wall, Le marin de Gibraltar* (1952; *The Sailor from Gibraltar*), and *Les petits chevaux de Tarquinia* (1953; *The Little Horses of Tarquinia*)—exhibit Duras's basic thematic concerns but are generally more realistic and traditionally structured than her later work. In the mid-1950s, Duras began experimenting with the stylized narrative forms associated with the French *nouveau roman,* or antinovel. *Le square* (1955; *The Square*), for instance, is developed almost entirely through dialogue and contains only the shadow of a plot: a servant woman and a traveling salesman meet in a marketplace and share a common bond of isolation and longing. Like other antinovelists, Duras presents only the surface of things, writing in a spare, almost clinical style. Through her mastery of dialogue, however, she imbues *The Square* with an emotional intensity and vitality not commonly found in the antinovel.

Duras's next novel, *Moderato cantabile* (1958), is considered among her most accomplished works. The two-level structure of the story is introduced in the opening scene: while a music lesson is taking place in a woman's apartment, a murder occurs in the café below. The story revolves around the woman's obsession with the crime, and, as in many of Duras's works, the presence of crime sets the background for an exploration of human passion and the interconnection between love and death. Noting the relationship between Duras's novels, antinovels, and detective fiction, Erica M. Eisinger writes: "Like Robbe-Grillet, Claude Ollier, and others, Duras' work adopts the basic detective story format: a mysterious crime followed by an intense effort at understanding. But where the *nouveau roman* focuses on the puzzle element of the detective story, Duras emphasizes the human drama of moral involvement in the mystery of another's criminal act." Eisinger further notes that, for Duras, "the criminal act is itself a love act, as if murder could transcend the excruciating separateness of the individual and bring one, for that privileged moment, into communion with another." With the exception of *Le ra-*

vissement de Lol V. Stein (1964; *The Ravishing of Lol V. Stein*), which concerns a woman's psychological decline after she is deserted by her fiancé, Duras's novels of the 1960s—*Dix heures et demie du soir en été* (1960; *Ten-thirty on a Summer Night*), *L'après-midi de Monsieur Andesmas* (1962; *The Afternoon of Monsieur Andesmas*), *Le vice-consul* (1966; *The Vice Consul*), *L'amante anglaise* (1967), and *Détruire, dit-elle* (1969; *Destroy, She Said*)—likewise involve a crime, mystery, or atmosphere of suspense.

Duras wrote most of her plays during the 1960s, when the innovative techniques of the antinovelists were being utilized in works for the French theater. Her first play, *Les viaducs de la Seine-et-Oise* (1960; *The Viaducs of Seine-et-Oise*), relates the interrogation of a married couple who committed a murder and dismembered the corpse in their effort to destroy the evidence. This two-act drama relies heavily on dialogue and monologue in conveying the interlocutor's attempt to discern an explicable motive. Many of Duras's plays, some of which are collected in *Théâtre I* (1965), *Théâtre II* (1968), and *Théâtre III* (1984), expand upon, revise, or refer to earlier works. The novel *The Square* was adapted for the theater. *La musica* (1967; *The Music*) revolves around the protagonists of *The Square* several years after the novel takes place. *L'amante anglaise* (1969) is an adaptation of Duras's novel of the same title, which in turn is a reworking of *Les viaducs de la Seine-et-Oise*. *Des journées entières dans les arbres* is an adaptation of the title novella of the recently translated short fiction collection *Des journées entières dans les arbres* (1954; *Whole Days in the Trees*). These and other of Duras's plays reflect her experimentation with such conventional dramatic elements as plot, character, and time and with blurring the distinction between genres. Alfred Cismaru noted: "Marguerite Duras' dramas retain the novelist's ability to weave hauntingly pathetic situations under the guise of incoherent plots, unimportant details and banal conversations."

Duras's script for *Hiroshima mon amour* was her first work for the cinema and helped establish her international reputation as a prominent figure in the arts. Like her plays, Duras's filmscripts are intertwined with her work in other genres. *Nathalie Granger* (1973) and *Le camion* (1977; *The Truck*) are among her notable original scripts; the majority of her other films are adaptations of her own plays and novels or the narratives of others. *Moderato Cantabile* (1964), *Ten-thirty p.m. Summer* (1966), and *Destroy, She Said* (1970) are based on her novels, and *La musica* (1970) and *India Song* (1973) are adapted from the plays of the same titles. Of the connection between Duras's literary and cinematic endeavors, Germaine Brée noted: "What haunts the reader is the recurrence of certain personae, 'magically' named, moving within spatially separate, more-or-less distinct configurations, from which they are both absent and undetachable. The spatial configurations, like layers deposited by time, vaguely refer us to an underlying, shifting, fading topography, a continuum, yet one riddled with gaps and breaks."

Duras's recent novel, *The Lover,* is considered more accessible than her earlier fiction. In this work, Duras draws on her childhood in Indochina, focusing on her discovery of sexual passion through a love affair she experienced when she was fifteen years old, and on her turbulent relationship with her mother and two brothers. While the story is recognizably autobiographical, it is not told chronologically, and the narrator's recollections are connected by the emotional rather than intellectual significance of the events related. Praised for both its structural technique and the purity of its prose, *The Lover* was

described by Diane Johnson as a "small, perfect, new novel. . . , [containing] a felicitous balance between formalism and powerful emotional impact." Duras has also recently published *The War* (1986), a volume of memoirs from World War II in which she chronicles her political and personal involvements during this turbulent era.

(See also *CLC*, Vols. 3, 6, 11, 20, 34 and *Contemporary Authors,* Vols. 25-28, rev. ed.)

MAURICE BLANCHOT

[*The essay from which the following excerpt is taken was originally published in 1959.*]

Marguerite Duras' *Le Square* demonstrates how awkwardly the critic's tendency to over-simplify adjusts to the simplicity of a book which he will always find either too simple or not simple enough. This book is not unsophisticated and although from the first lines it establishes a firm relationship with the reader (the loyalties reading provokes are indeed incomprehensible), it is not and cannot be as simple as it seems, for the stark simplicity of simple things with which it deals is too stark to be simply perceived.

Two almost disembodied voices talk in a practically immaterial place. This is what first strikes us, this kind of abstraction, as though two people—she is twenty, a nursemaid, he, a bit older, goes from town to town peddling cheap goods—who meet by chance in a public garden, had no other reality than their voices and had exhausted in this fortuitous conversation the stock of chance and truth—or simply of words—allotted to a human being. They must talk. And their cautious almost formal words are painful because of the restraint which derives, more than from the natural courtesy of simple folk, from an extreme vulnerability. It is the fear of hurting and of being hurt that their words express, these words that meet and then retract at the slightest sign of a more vital contact. Yet they are alive; slow but uninterrupted, never stopping lest time should run out, patient and on the alert, restrained, too, like words that might break down in sobs if they were not kept under control; and painfully lacking the ease of idle chatter whose carelessness and freedom is based on security. Here in the simple world of necessity and want words are at the service of essentials drawn only to the essential and therefore monotonous, but also too aware of what can or cannot be said, so that they avoid the blunt confessions which would put an end to it all.

For what we have here is a dialogue. And we can gauge how unusual dialogue is by our surprise on reading this book, our feeling of experiencing something unfamiliar and almost more painful than astonishing. In most novels what is called dialogue is a sign of indolence and habit; characters talk so that blank spaces may appear on the page and to reproduce everyday life where there is no narrative, only conversation. From time to time the protagonists must have their say—direct speech is economical and creates a break both for the reader and the author. On the other hand dialogue can become, as with certain American writers, expressively insignificant: more common than in real life and on a slightly lower scale than the empty words that satisfy our everyday needs. (pp. 199-200)

If we listen to the two unsophisticated voices in *Le Square* we notice that they do not seek agreement, like the voices of those who discuss and go from proof to proof till coherence is automatically achieved. Do they even seek that ultimate understanding which might, through mutual acknowledgement, give them satisfaction? Such a goal is obviously beyond them. Perhaps all they want is to talk, to make use of the one faculty they are still lucky enough to possess and which they cannot be sure of having for long. It is this last feeble and threatened resource which gives an element of gravity to the simple exchange. From their first words we sense that, for these two people, and more especially for one of them, the space and air required to make talking possible are all but exhausted. (p. 203)

Marguerite Duras has tried, and perhaps succeeded through the extreme delicacy of her concern, to capture the moment at which people are capable of dialogue. Such moments require the chance of a fortuitous encounter as well as the simplicity of such an encounter—what could be simpler than to meet in a public garden?—which clashes with the hidden tension of these two people; and the further simplicity derived from the fact that, though there is tension, it has nothing dramatic about it, has no obvious cause such as crime or glaring injustice, but is quite ordinary, not striking or 'interesting', and is thus entirely simple and inobtrusive. (Dialogue is never concerned with great sorrow, nor can two great sorrows converse together.) Finally, and this is perhaps the main point, these two people find themselves in this situation because they have nothing in common but the fact of being, for very different reasons, isolated from the ordinary world in which none the less they dwell.

All this is expressed in the simplest and most compelling way, compulsion being especially obvious on the girl's part. Each of her restrained, tentative utterances reveals the compulsion which is the basis of human existence and which her circumstances bring home to her at every minute of the day through her profession, which is not even a profession, but more like a disease or a sub-slavery, since she has no real connection with anybody whereas a slave is connected to his master, and no connection even with her own self. Moreover this compulsion has become self-compulsion, the fierce, obstinate harshness with which she rejects anything that might make her life easier but might, through such ease, simultaneously make her forget its compulsiveness and lose sight of her one purpose, which is to meet somebody, no matter whom, so long as by marrying her he changes her circumstances so that she may become like everyone else. Her interlocutor gently suggests that she might be very unhappy with 'no matter whom'. Why should she not choose? . . . But how can one choose when one exists so little in one's own eyes that one can only rely on somebody's choice to hope to exist at all? If she were to choose, every man would be suitable so long as he wanted her just a little. 'Common' sense would say that it is not as hard as all that to be wanted, and that this twenty year old girl, even if she is a nursemaid, has beautiful eyes and cannot fail to be extracted by marriage from her unhappy condition and to become happy and unhappy like everybody else. And it is true. But only for those who belong already to the 'common' world. That is the root of the matter. That is the cause of the tension that produces the dialogue. When one is aware of the compulsion it affects and infects the very desire to evade it by the most natural means:

> When a man asks you to dance, Miss, do you immediately think that he might marry you?
>
> Oh yes, that's it. I am too practical, you see, that's the trouble. But how can I do otherwise?

I feel that I could never love anybody until I had had a foretaste of freedom, and that foretaste, only a man can give it to me.

It is only natural that the reader, and perhaps even the author, should find consolation in the hope that this chance encounter in a public garden might lead to another kind of encounter—a shared life. And we must hope this will be the case, but without too much hope. For in fact this man, this modest travelling salesman who is really no more than a pedlar, who goes from town to town spurred on by his wares, without future, without illusions or desire, is a seriously affected man. The girl's strength is that she has nothing and desires the one thing that will enable her to desire all the others—or rather to acquire the common desire whence we begin to have or have not according to what is generally feasible. Her fierce, heroic, absolute desire, her courage, is a loophole of escape, yet at the same time it may be what bars escape. For the violence of the desire makes the thing desired unattainable. The man is wiser, with a wisdom that accepts and asks for nothing. This apparent wisdom is, however, a dangerous consequence of the solitude which, if it fails to satisfy him, somehow occupies him so entirely that he has no time to desire anything else. He seems to have come down in the world; he has let himself drift into this profession which is not a profession either, but which has somehow got a hold on him because it satisfies his urge to wander from place to place and to be what he really is. And although he speaks with the utmost circumspection so as not to discourage the young girl, this aspect of his life is, for her, a temptation; the attraction of a futureless future for which, suddenly, she sheds silent tears. Like her he is 'the lowest of the low', but he is more than simply a man who lacks all ordinary satisfactions. For he has had, in the course of his wanderings, a few brief illuminations of joy, modest brilliances which he willingly describes to her and on which she questions him, at first with detached and even rather disapproving interest, then, alas, with curiosity and ever increasing fascination. This *private* happiness, a happiness that belongs to solitude and makes it shine all at once and then vanish, is a happiness which is like the other side of compulsion and derives from it a brilliance which perhaps is blinding or perhaps deceptive and artificial.

They talk nevertheless. They talk to each other and they do not agree. They do not altogether understand each other. They do not share that common space where understanding takes place, and their whole relationship is based only on their intense and simple feeling that they are both *equally* outside the common system of relationships. This is a great deal. It creates an immediate proximity and a kind of total agreementless agreement where their attentiveness one to the words of the other and the carefulness and scrupulous truthfulness with which they express themselves are so great precisely because what is said can only be said once yet cannot be said, could not benefit from the superficial understanding current in the ordinary world, the world where we so rarely experience the fortuitousness and pain of true dialogue. (pp. 204-06)

> *Maurice Blanchot, "The Painfulness of Dialogue,"*
> *in his* The Sirens' Song: Selected Essays, *edited by*
> *Gabriel Josipovici, translated by Sacha Rabinovitch,*
> *Indiana University Press, 1982, pp. 199-206.**

GEOFFREY STOKES

Though these four stories (three stories and a novella?) [in *Whole Days in the Trees*] lack the circumstantiality of her *L'A-*

mante Anglaise, Duras's nuance with detail has kept them from disappearing into the fog of intellectual abstraction. The food on the tables, the smells from aging underwear . . . all are inescapably real; and even the dangerously elephantine metaphors (a snake as the symbol of sexuality, for Chrissakes) work in the context of the characters who employ them.

Indeed, for all its thumping obviousness, **"The Boa"** is the best story in the book; perhaps because it is the shortest, it alone achieves the combined economy and intensity that makes the short story a hybrid between a poem and a novel. The other pieces—how the French *do* go on—meander and then trail off. In **"The Boa,"** Duras says—or has her characters do—exactly enough. . . .

Geoffrey Stokes, in a review of "Whole Days in the Trees," in VLS, No. 1, October, 1981, p. 3.

JUDITH GRAVES MILLER

The Sea Wall counts among Marguerite Duras's most overtly autobiographical works. Written in 1950, the novel fictionalizes Duras's memories of growing up in French Indochina in the 1920s. The story is based on her mother's being duped by colonialist propaganda into leaving France and spending all her savings on a worthless rice plantation. Her resulting obsession with damming up the sea to keep it from destroying her crops gives both the title and major theme to the novel.

Duras's narrative depicts in a time continuum the slow death of the mother (never named) and the corresponding liberation of her children, Suzanne and Joseph. The first half chronicles one of the last main events in their lives, the encounter with Mr. Jo, vapid son of a rich colonial planter. His pursuit of sixteen-year-old Suzanne preoccupies the entire family—virile brother Joseph scorning Mr. Jo's timidity, the mother torn between disgust with her own desire to exchange Suzanne for money for the dams and real concern over her daughter's future, and Suzanne herself losing her naivety while learning how to survive. In the end, Mr. Jo's desperate gift of a diamond "no strings attached" saves his face and rekindles the family's hopes of escaping their poverty.

The second half of the novel concentrates more specifically on the children's coming of age. It commences by a sketch of Saigon where the family goes to sell Mr. Jo's token of self-esteem. When Joseph disappears into the city with a platinum blonde protectress, the mother collapses. The family finally returns to its provincial bungalow; but Joseph leaves again. Suzanne chooses to give away her virginity to a local farmer; and the mother dies.

Although the story of the family structures the narrative, extensive and horrifying descriptions of peasant life, particularly of the indigent children, complete the portrait of colonized Indochina. Duras also includes several fine-honed, satirical characterizations of colonial types. . . . (pp. 440-41)

Rather like a well-made play, *The Sea Wall* sets up its conclusion in the opening chapter; an introduction which also immediately establishes the point of view, the metaphor for the unfolding of the story, and the major themes. The first line posits the family unit as the collective consciousness of the novel: "All three of them had thought it was a good idea to buy that horse. . . ." Thus the novel evolves as a function of their experience, not focusing on any one member in particular. Most of the time "their experience" is seen from the detached position of the narrator, whose cynical understanding of the

exploitation of the poor by the rich gives the narration an ironical cast.

The family's victimization by the colonial land developers and their resulting frustration and anger—which most often cause them to lash out at each other in mean exchanges—create a tension which underlies the novel from its beginning to the mother's death. The love-hate bond between the children and their mother originally reveals itself in their reaction to the moribund horse, her analogue. They both want the animal to go on living and hope he will end their long wait and die. (p. 441)

Straightforward, chronologically ordered, and easy to read, *The Sea Wall* fits within the conventions of the nineteenth-century novel. Indeed, of Duras's eighteen novels, it is the most traditional, making use of nonfloating dialogue and witty commentary situated within a plot, and presenting sane, or at least understandably disturbed characters. Humorous in its sarcasm, painful in its knowledge, a *bildungsroman* of a family, and portrait of a people, *The Sea Wall* grabs its readers not by teasing them to understanding, but by piquing their curiosity about how the author will complete a good story.

Twenty-seven years separate the publications of *The Sea Wall* and *Eden Cinema,* Duras's adaptation [of the novel for the theater]. In between, she has written some forty other works, including a dozen film scenarios. To do justice to her recent narratives, a critic would not spend much time describing what the characters do or what happens to them. The interest of these texts lies not in the events but in the unresolved and unresolvable tension which is communicated—a straining which radically transforms nonhappenings into experience.

With such a change in style, it is not surprising that Duras's reworking of her traditional novel results in a highly experimental play. *Eden Cinema,* narrated rather than performed, sets before the spectators a hidden but potent way of structuring existence.

A resume of the "events" of the play would read almost like a resume of the novel; even the two-part division remains. Duras has selected certain passages to use intact—such as Joseph's recounting of the initial meeting with his new mistress. Others, such as Mr. Jo's wooing of Suzanne, have been condensed—sometimes mime replacing the narration. As in the novel, the ambiguous relationship between the members of the family underpins the narrative. These similarities, however, are only superficial; for the subtle changes in focus and less subtle changes in form yield an entirely different work, particularly from the point of view of the public who experiences it.

First, Duras has altered the focus. *Eden Cinema* tells the mother's, not the family's, story. She is the central pivot around which everything else revolves. In fact in the stage directions Duras calls her "the object of the narration." . . . The play thus commences by Suzanne and Joseph narrating the events of her life. Certain changes in their account gives her character more strength and interest than in the novel. . . . (pp. 441-42)

Duras also adds another dimension to the portrayal of the mother. In the novel she does not insist on the elemental connection between the mother (mère) and the sea (mer). In the play this equation becomes immediately clear—both physically and verbally. As object of the narration, the mother does not move, but is, rather, a monolithic presence around whom Suzanne and Joseph turn, unable to separate themselves. They are as obsessed by her as she is by the sea. The children's chanted presentation of their mother ritualizes her, creating an otherworldly ambiance and establishing her as a force greater than a single individual. . . . The play, then, has a mythic dimension the novel does not. Not merely a statement about Suzanne and Joseph's mother, it is about ''Mother,'' as she forms, controls, and haunts her children.

This idea of ''Mother,'' begun in Suzanne and Joseph's narration, ultimately becomes Suzanne's perception. Her consciousness structures the play in the ''past made present'' of her memory. In fact, the space of the representation is essentially that of Suzanne's remembering. Her effort, and to a certain extent Joseph's, is to resuscitate the mother, dead when the play begins.

This makes the relationship between Suzanne and the mother an extension of the central focus. As the play progresses, Suzanne and an additional narrator called ''The Voice of Suzanne'' attempt to assert the independence of her consciousness from the mother's still powerful domination. Only by metaphorically recreating the mother and burying her again can Suzanne finally achieve selfhood.

For her play of Suzanne's memory, Duras has chosen a form which takes its inspiration from film; the flashes, the imprinting, the haziness, the sensuality of the movies also being qualities of the remembering mind. Duras has even given the title of a cinema house to her play. The spectators, then, experience *Eden Cinema* as a series of evolving images. There is first ''a long shot'' of the stage itself, with its concentric squares defined by the lighting. Although one square represents the family's bungalow and the other the plains of Kam, the effect is of vast nothingness, a spatial metaphor for the family's misery, and perhaps for Suzanne's memory at the beginning of the play. Suzanne, the mother, Joseph, and later Mr. Jo enter and take their places stage front. Two specially designated narrators who read parts of the text, are seated downstage. Despite occasional breaks in the flat quality of the performance, most of the ''action'' occurs on the apron where the actors stand in a row facing the audience. Sometimes they narrate and mime the action. Sometimes they merely narrate. Sometimes their voices are replaced by those of the seated narrators; and they perform in slow stylized motions what is described. Most of the time they dissociate what is said from how they move, creating the feeling of a dream, an hallucination, a memory— or a faulty projection. (pp. 442-43)

As fascinating as are the visual images, the haunting refrain, and the hypnotic rhythm, they do not alone carry the piece. *Eden Cinema* relies finally on what only live theatre possesses—the physical presence of the actors. With so little action every gesture has an extraordinary resonance—thus in a mimed sequence when the family ''walks to the village,'' they seem to burst forth from the stage. And although the cataloguing of the horrors of the mother's life partially sustains the dramatic tension, the strained, barely mobile bodies of the actors are what keep the audience on edge. Emotional ambiguity reflected corporally replaces the ideological conflict which propels other dramas. In the second part of the play (a narrative duet between Suzanne and her voice) a single raised eyebrow or a quarter turn of the head electrifies the space between the actors, making it almost tactile.

By functioning on this sensory level, *Eden Cinema* is both less *engagé* and harsher, more provocative than the novel. The recreation of the mother and the exploration of Suzanne's re-

lationship with her exclude or subordinate most of the political satire and social commentary. No detached author's voice ironizes over the fate of Indochina. In fact the only colonial type included in the play, other than Mr. Jo, is the Corporal who sits silently on stage, in loving homage to the mother.

The play's language, stripped of emotionalism, never disguises the love-hate relationship between the mother and her children. Remembering the past, Suzanne is more lucid and uncompromising than when she lived it. She now knows how much she needed her mother to die; but also how much she loved her. The materialization of this ambiguity sculpted before the spectators' eyes recalls their own paradoxical longings for absorption and separation, longings which characterize the mother-child link. In its mythical dimension *Eden Cinema* illustrates the real cost of an individual's psychological freedom.

Whether the audience adheres to the illustration depends in part on its willingness to allow itself to enter into the world of the play. Despite the suggestive force of Suzanne's descriptions, the spectators have to work hard to create out of the unblinking old lady on stage the stubborn and dynamic woman from Suzanne's past. The play calls upon them indirectly but calls upon them, nevertheless, to make analogies from their own experience. *Eden Cinema* is therefore no paradoxical *divertissement* but rather an invitation to a voyage through the mind of a complex character. It resolves nothing but leaves the spectators on the threshold of their own remembrances. (pp. 443-44)

> *Judith Graves Miller, ''From Novel to Theatre: Contemporary Adaptations of Narrative to the French Stage,'' in* Theatre Journal, *Vol. 33, No. 4, December, 1981, pp. 431-52.**

GERMAINE BRÉE

[One of Marguerite Duras's] most characteristic traits [is] the increasingly bold esthetic use she makes of the sudden ''faults,''—breaks in level—of the blanks and discontinuities embedded in everyday discourse. Her revolt against syntax is well known. Indeed, often her principal characters themselves have dropped out of the ''normal'' train of everyday life: as Duras puts it, a link has broken in that chain. Discontinuity and heterogeneity fragment the homogeneity and continuity of the characters' inner time and space. The narrative progresses uncertainly toward regions no longer bounded by the stable constructs of a coherent literary language, with its ''security of a carefully circumscribed story'' which, having had a beginning, ''moves with certainty toward the pleasure of an ending, even an unhappy one.'' ''Territories of the feminine'' these Duras regions have been called. However that may be, this is unmistakably Durassian territory, with its own recurrent topography, its toponymies, whether real or imagined, and the recurrent ''hiatus,'' as Duras calls it, the opening through which they flow into and emphasize the gaps in the disjunctive language of the text. It is the infrastructures of fiction that Duras more and more determinedly attempts to undermine.

Spoken language . . . , with its breaks and inconsistencies, its anacolutha and penchant for parataxis, its slippages and elusive contexts, has been widely used by writers intent on breaking away from the representations and fictions of the ''literary.'' But, in the case of Marguerite Duras, such usage is only the surface manifestation of deeper crumblings and cracks within the narrative structure, as illustrated by her conception of the ''characters'' themselves—of their relations with each other, with the reader-spectator, and with the world they disclose.

There is no other writer today whose fictional creations so consistently lure the reader into a space of their own, a space whose contours are perceived only dimly and fragmentarily through the encounters of the personae who enter it and the often enigmatic words they exchange. As has Beckett, Duras has given herself the paradoxical task of giving the incoherent a literary form.

Toward that end, Marguerite Duras has been progressively shaping her narrative techniques for close to forty years. From the first traditionally realistic novels to her latest "text-theater-film" scripts, she has persistently carried out a revolution not so much in the elements of her narrative fiction as in the manner in which she links these elements to one another. One of the most characteristic features of her writing is the fascination certain of her personae hold for her: she works and reworks the fictional material they secrete. She does not progress by what has been called "surrealistic house razing," but rather, as she herself describes it, by an exploratory penetration into a territory glimpsed in the interstices of a previous narrative and lost in its penumbra. What haunts the reader is the recurrence of certain personae, "magically" named, moving within spatially separate, more-or-less distinct configurations, from which they are both absent and undetachable. The spatial configurations, like layers deposited by time, vaguely refer us to an underlying, shifting, fading topography, a continuum, yet one riddled with gaps and breaks. For instance, it is in the interstices of S. Tahla, the seaside resort, that Anne-Marie Stretter, "the woman in black," first appears; it is in the setting of *The Ravishing of Lol V. Stein* (1964) that the S. Thala of *L'Amour* (1971) appears: the strangely deserted stretch of sand, bordered by an ocean, a river, a phantasmal resort town, along which a "woman in black" endlessly paces. (pp. 268-69)

Duras is a rarity among fiction writers in France today in that her own existence is deeply intertwined with that of her characters, at least with those whom she loves, "deeply loves," like Lol V. Stein. Another such, even more central, is Anne-Marie Stretter, who is inextricably linked to the event that propelled Lol V. Stein into the space of Duras's fiction, the ball at S. Tahla. Anne-Marie Stretter's wanderings from book to book and from book to film belong to one of the more enigmatic of those fictional regions that have emerged progressively in Duras's writing over the years, like lost pieces of a never-completed puzzle. Anne-Marie Stretter dominates a famous quintet of narrative and films—*Lol V. Stein, The Vice-Consul, La Femme du Gange, Son nom de Venise dans Calcutta désert* (Her Venice Name in the Desert of Calcutta) and *India Song*. Written or filmed between 1964 and 1976, they spiral back to the poverty-stricken childhood Duras lived at Phnom Penh, Sadec, and Vinhlong in Cochin China. There her "Ganges" was the Mekong River. The vague contours of an occulted region sustain the tensions in each story. The narrative structures seem to circumscribe and straddle a psychic gap whose two "edges," so to speak, the Oriental and the Occidental, never quite manage to fit together. The developing situations pertain to different layers of Duras's own developing and often puzzled understanding of her activity as writer. That development is inscribed in the formal characteristics of each narrative; and it determines what the characters and the world they inhabit become from story to story. No other fate or preordained design connects the "woman in black" of *L'Amour* to Lol V. Stein, or indeed to Anne-Marie Stretter. A peculiar time mode emerges, a fluid architecture which, paradoxically, opens up spatial dimensions like unexpected vistas beyond and between the separate pieces. Between 1943, the date of her

first novel, and 1980, Duras's narrative techniques have changed drastically and often. The total field of significance of the work, however, seems to be taking shape only very gradually. One accedes to it by gradients, as it were, and from different angles. It requires that we, as readers, undertake a form of internal migration to Duras's hidden Orient.

India Song was written in 1972 for the London National Theatre and published in 1973, then filmed by Duras in 1975. At this writing it has been followed by only three other texts: *Le Camion, L'Eden Cinéma* and *Le Navire Night*. Of these three, *L'Eden Cinéma* is a dramatic version of the early novel *Barrage against the Pacific*. *Le Camion* and *Le Navire Night* are quite definitely film scenarios. I shall consider *India Song* as the last of Duras's narrative fictions to date. It is related to the two earlier narratives, *Lol V. Stein* and *The Vice-Consul*, which it absorbs into its own time-space continuum. The film, like the narrative itself, is, in my opinion, one of Duras's most successful ventures. . . . I take both narrative and film to be a culmination of her previous work. *India Song* marks a major change in Duras's narrative techniques: the successful displacement of the narrative from its adherence to the two-dimensional page and the linearity of the book, as well as its total detachment from the mimetic. More striking still is the fragmentation of the narrative voice.

It was, Duras notes, through her experience in the filming of *La Femme du Gange*, carried on at approximately the same time, that she discovered by what "means" to "penetrate and uncover an unexplored region" of *The Vice-Consul;* in addition, and more important, how to let anonymous memories, other than the author's own, draw the narrative out of the void and on to the page. The locus of the narrative and its enactment are relayed to the reader through a variety of "voices." The book is divided into five parts. In part 1 two young female voices slowly begin to tell the story of the lovers of the Ganges—Anne-Marie Stretter and Michael Richardson; their story intersects with that of Anne-Marie Stretter's encounter with the Vice-Consul and her subsequent death. The two female voices are linked by their own shared love story. Sometimes they speak of that deeply felt love, theirs. Most of the time they speak of "that other love, that other story." . . . In parts 3, 4, and 5, two male voices relay the female voices, then mingle briefly with them; through them the "end" of the story unfolds, the end that was already there at the beginning. . . . (pp. 269-71)

So framed, part 2, almost entirely narrated in dialogue form by the fictional characters in *Le Vice-Consul,* is the replay, condensed and altered, of the central incident of that novel: the reception at the French embassy in Calcutta, where the encounter of Anne-Marie Stretter with the Vice-Consul takes place. In *India Song* another narrating voice is heard throughout, an objective "camera-eye" voice giving form to the spatial setting, the silhouettes and scenes to which the dialogues refer. During part 2 the voices are mute as the scene, dimly discerned through the words of the dialogue, becomes autonomous, peopled with the characters at the embassy ball.

Technically, then, the story is given as though through many memories. . . . *Through* the voices, as well as through the central reenacted scene, we, like the voices, "see" fragments of the tale reenacted. Past episodes of that tale presumably live in the reader's more-or-less awakened memory along with other fragments. Gaps have opened in the older text, and new articulations suggest new networks of connections. A kind of "sacred legend" is being ritually "recited" and reconstituted, from differing perspectives. Between what really happened and its verbal reactualizations there is a solution of continuity. The characters, their acts, and their world are removed from the historical reality in which they seemed to be existentially involved—India in the thirties—and are "relocated" within a different spatial and temporal scheme. *India Song* then functions as a form of anamnesis. "The story of that love, the voices have known or read it, long ago. Some remember it better than others. But none remembers it completely nor has anyone completely forgotten it." . . . We are in the world of myth. It is the locus that Anne-Marie Stretter, Michael Richardson, the Vice-Consul of France in Lahore now inhabit somewhere behind the polyphonic "variations" on their story.

What then is the story? "It's the story of a love, lived in India during the thirties in an overpopulated city on the banks of the Ganges." . . . "A love story immobilized at the culmination of passion. Surrounding it, another story, of horror—of famine and leprosy mingling in the pestilential humidity of the monsoon—immobilized too in a daily paroxysm" (book jacket). There are in fact several axes to this story, several planes. They all pass through the absent figure of the woman "dressed in black," Anne-Marie Stretter, dead how long ago? (pp. 271-72)

But the main theme of *India Song* is Calcutta: "the world focus of absurdity; the central furnace of absurdity, that insane agglomeration of hunger, illogical famine." This is the reality that seeps through the railings of the parks and dismantles the structures erected by the whites. It consumes Anne-Marie Stretter who finally abandons herself to the rising tide of the delta and to the oblivion to which it relegates individual lives. "I don't know if it is suicide . . . she goes back to the Indian Ocean, as to a kind of elemental matrix. . . . She cannot live elsewhere and she lives through that place, she lives off the despair that India, Calcutta, secrete daily and she dies of it, she dies as though poisoned by India." Here the voice of Marguerite Duras mingles with the "voices" of the text, opening yet another fragmentary perspective upon the legendary. The traditional love story, the story of individual passion on the model of Tristan and Isolda, simply dissolves.

Structurally, as in the earlier *Détruire,* the story is made up of people watching others and one another. But . . . the position of the watchers in time and space and the intensity and nature of their attention are variable. The central and absent trio can inspire in the watchers different forms of desire: from the passionate absorption of Voice 1 to the anguish of Voice 4. Not only does the story of Anne-Marie Stretter relate a "gesta" already present in the familiar love-death myth of Western imagination; it also aims at something beyond, at the ultimate destruction of that myth. To this the voices are not attuned. It is still the myth of love they recapitulate. Duras however is not writing about love but about elemental human suffering, the overwhelming presence that submerges, fascinates, and destroys. (p. 274)

What, then, is the nature of *India Song*? I should be tempted to call it "an extant part of a lost text, a fragmented text" . . . ; and that is itself the definition of a receding myth.

From the critic's point of view, what is most interesting perhaps is that, helped by her experience with the screen, Duras has devised for *India Song* narrative techniques that give a segment of her work the dimension of myth. All the processes of fictionalization are put to work in *India Song*: former stories are drawn together, melded in a unity of tone, without recourse to the "security" of a carefully circumscribed point of view or coherent development. . . . The poetic imagination at work here

has affinities with the ritualized world of myth and memory, the world of a Gérard de Nerval. *India Song* is the destruction and partial redemption, through the dream-figure of the dead Anne-Marie Stretter, that cousin to Nerval's Aurélia or Sylvie, of an obsessional inner world that cannot be abolished. And, as with other Duras stories, its strange and disruptive elements—unspoken or only semiarticulated—keep the reader or spectator in a state of acute unease and esthetic fascination. (pp. 275-76)

Germaine Brée, "Contours, Fragments, Gaps: The World of Marguerite Duras," in New York Literary Forum, *Vols. 8 & 9, 1981, pp. 267-76.*

CAROL J. MURPHY

"Love, the fierceness of love, the happiness, the pain, the compelling and destructive power of love is Marguerite Duras' essential theme," remarks Germaine Brée in her introduction to four of the author's novels. Indeed the reader of Marguerite Duras cannot be insensitive to the author's preoccupation with the same story of an absolute love, both necessary and impossible. Most often it is a tragic passion, tinged with death and destruction, and is grounded in a profound sense of alienation from the other whose absence permeates the stories with a paradoxical presence. Ideal love for Duras is the violent, sacred instant when passionate desire is consummated. It is that fragile, fleeting moment of death of self to and in the other . . . that Duras purports to portray in her stories. . . . (p. 10)

[Alienation and absence] are overriding themes which reverberate throughout the corpus in various synonymous forms—disjunction, disunion, separation, expectation, estrangement, void, emptiness, sterility, and, by extension, memory, madness and desire. The prevalence of these concepts is sometimes established lexically, as in *Dix heures et demie du soir en été* where the frequency of the word *vide* denotes both a physical absence and an emotional presence of one character to another. Emblems of alienation and absence occur throughout the texts; grills, walls, barriers, empty spaces and hostile natural forces reflect the estrangement and negative feelings of protagonists. Alienation and absence also have stylistic and structural significance in the works which are characterized by increasing ellipsis, narrative indirection, reduction and fragmentation of character, plot and setting. In the more recent works, the emphasis on alienation and absence as linguistic and novelistic breakdown is illustrated by numerous pauses and blank typographic spaces. (pp. 10-11)

The novels can be roughly divided into three groups or periods, according to thematic and structural concerns. . . . The first comprises the traditional, autobiographical novels which establish most of Duras' themes. These early novels (*Les Impudents, La Vie tranquille, Un Barrage contre le Pacifique*) are concerned with young heroines in search of a lover or husband to fill the emptiness of their existence. Passive, lethargic women, they seek incarnation in the other, and their inner void is indistinguishable from their environment of ennui and stagnation. They must wrench themselves from the domination of a brother or a mother, and, at the novel's conclusion, their "success" is ambiguous. Alienation and absence are primarily thematic concerns in these texts which are traditional (linear) studies of character with detailed descriptions of setting and schematic, if oftentimes inconclusive, plot lines. The emphasis in these novels on a future, and therefore absent and imaginary, love, as well as the insistence on suffocating spaces, tightly-knit families and the insecurities of a young, female protagonist, will recur in later texts. . . . (pp. 11-12)

The second period of novels could be entitled "l'invitation au voyage" and would include *Le Marin de Gibraltar, Les Petits Chevaux de Tarquinia, Le Square, Moderato Cantabile, Dix heures et demie du soir en été*, the scenario for *Hiroshima mon amour*, and, peripherally, *L'Après-midi de Monsieur Andesmas*. With the publication of *Le Marin de Gibraltar*, the preoccupations of characters are focused primarily on a relationship in the present which is the reenactment of a past love affair. In this novel, Anna's search for her lover is grounded in his *absence*, and she is forced to invent the past in an imperfect realization of desire. Her vagabondage and obsessive drinking in a torpid, Mediterranean climate are the expressions of a void which she and the other characters try to fill by constantly retelling the story of the sailor from Gibraltar. The novel's atmosphere of stagnation and suffocation—a continuation of that of the earlier texts—is one which will endure in later novels. In this group of novels, the "voyage" indicates not only physical displacement to a vacation resort, as is the case in *Les Petits Chevaux* and *Dix heures et demie*, but also a return to the past and a re-creation of an earlier love. . . . In most of the stories, the absence of love provokes desires and fantasies associated with crime, disorder, death and destruction—a climate of violence which haunts later texts both thematically and structurally.

With *Le Ravissement de Lol. V. Stein*, which begins the third group of texts, Duras adds another dimension to her story. Avowedly intrigued by the character of Lol, Duras has said of the text that, whereas *Moderato Cantabile* is a finished product (*fait*), the story of Lol is still in the process of being written. For the most part, later texts embody fragments of *Le Ravissement*. Memory, as emotional alienation and absence, takes on greater significance in these works, both within and between texts. Separation from and contemplation of the past (earlier texts) leads to re-creation or rewriting of the past (earlier texts), paralleling a protagonist's reliving of a past love within a single text. Thus text mirrors content. Alienation and absence are both thematic *and* textual notions. The violence which characterizes earlier stories, such as *Moderato* and *Hiroshima mon amour*, occurs on the level of the word, the sentences and paragraphs are reduced to lyrical fragments of the story. The textual design or process is that of an exorcism of earlier works with a resultant emphasis on *absence* of traditional novelistic elements. . . . In the tradition of Mallarmé, Leiris, Blanchot and Beckett, Duras "purges" her story of the non-essential. Successive works are stripped bare of plot, characters and verbiage in a rhythmic progression toward silence and the void. The third group of texts, *Le Ravissement de Lol. V. Stein, Le Vice-Consul, L'Amour* and *India Song* are simplified or "decanted" versions of the same story.

Related motifs of memory, madness and desire emanate from this central thematic core of alienation and absence. Memory functions as the attempt to re-create a past love, and in many of the novels, due to the presence of would-be-authors who try to remember a past story, it is metatextual, that is, equated with literary invention and the writing of the text. Above all, memory is seen as a *separation* from the *absent* past and, as such, functions as thematic and textual alienation (the separation between the word and that to which it refers). Madness gradually takes hold of successive protagonists who distance themselves from others and withdraw into the recesses of their

imagination in an attempt to relive (or rewrite) the past. Desire as longing, search, or gap, colors the texts, in which efforts to recapture the past (and to write or talk about it) emphasize absence and alienation over satiety and union. As the story develops from text to text, the very existence of a past love affair which serves as the "origin" or center of present remembering is slowly put into question, and with this thematic doubt arises the metatextual doubt of an original text or story. (pp. 11-14)

The notion of a consistent character gradually disappears, especially as regards the portraits of the feminine protagonists, whose similarity indicates a shattering of a single personality into several distinct characters, like Beckett's Ham and Clov, Molloy and Moran, etc. In Duras' work, Anne in *Moderato Cantabile* recalls Anna in *Le Marin de Gibraltar* and is a possible version of Anne-Marie Stretter in *Le Ravissement, Le Vice-Consul* and *India Song*. She (they) becomes "woman" in *L'Amour* where unnamed female protagonists resemble one another. There, stylized gestures, halting dialogue and descriptions, together with a fragmentation of the unified subject or I, point to a chaotic, pre-conscious state of purposeless desire. *L'Amour* is a geometric abstraction of preceding texts wherein certain male characters, such as the Vice-Consul and Stein, incarnate and share the same feminine concerns of the female protagonists. In *L'Amour*, distinctions between male-female and I-you become gradually unimportant. What remains in this text is an undifferentiated presence: individual differentiation yields to a portrayal of human consciousness on the brink of remembering some cosmic beginning. (p. 16)

Similar reduction occurs in the decor. The suffocating summers, claustrophobic spaces and political repression which form the backdrop for most of the texts are progressively distilled to the primal, horizontal world of the beach in *L'Amour* or to the Delta isles in *India Song*, where shifting sands and pounding surf reflect the anguish of the human heartbeat. (pp. 16-17)

This reduction and fragmentation of traditional characterizations and setting also occurs on the level of plot. . . . Alienation is illustrated in the progressively more intricate mediation of desires which bases relationships on a gap, or separation. . . . The necessity of a third person, one with whom the protagonist can re-create the past and mediate desire, brings about a proliferation of triangular relationships. . . . In the later texts, the triangle turns around the same characters, Lol-Anne-Marie-Michael Richardson, and their situation is evoked spatially in *L'Amour* by the positioning of the unnamed threesome on the beach. . . . With each succeeding text, the elimination of extraneous details, descriptions and secondary plot lines results in a concentration on and interiorization of the moment of past humiliation. In *L'Amour*, the obsession with this past moment—a repetition and deepening of a crucial scene in *Le Ravissement de Lol. V. Stein*—is translated by fragmented narrative voices which "stutter" in the gradual return to the past, for example: "Je ne comprends pas bein . . .—Vous avez cessé de . . .—Je me demande même si . . . si même au début . . . vous n'avez jamais . . .—sans doute pas." . . . This dissection of the story and the dislocating effect of the "stuttering" narrative in *L'Amour* occurs on an intertextual level, for essential textual sequences (refrains, fragments, preoccupations) are wrenched from some texts to reappear in other texts, like the themes of a musical orchestration. Barriers between texts disappear and individual texts cooperate in the elaboration of the Text or core story. (p. 17)

The fragmentation on the level of plot, decor and character occurs also (and markedly) on the linguistic level. Sentences are torn from paragraphs, words are dislodged from sentences, voices falter and blank spaces proliferate. In *Le Marin,* the narrator and Anna converse in traditional language, using words to incarnate the sailor. Later in the texts, language becomes powerless and the search for a past love (the "domain" of the story) takes place in the imaginary. . . . Duras offers the reader a more expressive "poetic language" through a stylistic refusal of traditional character study based on psychological affirmations. She is aware of this linguistic dislocation and, from *Moderato Cantabile* on, she abandons the etiquette "novel" in favor of *récit, texte-théâtre-film,* etc. Above all, Duras aims for the "poetic" quality and her writing implies the liberation of the word. . . Words are important not only as semantic units but also syntactically and musically. For example, the refrain-like repetitions in *Hiroshima* ("Tu me tues, tu me fais du bien"), the descriptions of the recurring storm in *Dix heures et demie,* as well as those of the crashing waves in *Moderato,* are highly expressive of a troubled consciousness caught in a dialectic of order and disorder, past and present, madness and sanity. Stylistic and structural breakdown creates a "mad" language of the text which emulates formally the basic theme of Duras' works: absolute love as an ideal sharing between individuals in the sacred moment of death to the other. This metaphysical breakdown of individual identity is conveyed by the language of the text—a language of desire which, in Duras, is primarily musical. (p. 18)

What Duras has accomplished is to portray separation in its very process. She does this by juxtaposing alienation and union, absence and presence, and as a result, she captures the essence of desire. By elaborating thematically, stylistically and structurally the concepts of alienation and absence (and their related notions of memory, madness, desire and music), Duras succeeds in relating a story from the inside out, a story whose center is a constantly disintegrating absence. She does not "tell" a story, but through the alienation of her narrative in-direction, she makes of her texts (the more recent ones) a supremely-felt experience. Traditional elements of plot-character-setting are exploded in the movement toward a free-flowing organic creation of atmosphere and a revelation of an inner world defined by physical, emotional and temporal separation. . . . In the equation of "mad" text and mad, passionate desire, Duras has infused the more intellectual New Novel form with sensitivity and emotion; by the paradoxes and contradictions in her works she evokes the complexities of love as desire. One might describe this love-madness-death in Duras' texts as R. M. Adams has perceived the theme of absence in his study of 19th-century literature: "Self-fulfillment through self-annihilation, victory for will through denial of will, light through darkness—the effect of all these swiftly multiplying paradoxes is to suggest a world outside thought, a world of exploding potent consciousness which mere language is unable to contain." (pp. 20-1)

> Carol J. Murphy, in her Alienation and Absence in the Novels of Marguerite Duras, *French Forum, Publishers, 1982, 172 p.*

MARILYN R. SCHUSTER

Many of Duras' works are retold tales. Although it could be argued that all story-telling, like analysis, is a reworking of other tales, in Duras' work the retelling itself is a central concern. Three works taken from three different periods will serve

here to define the role of retelling; read together, these texts suggest not only the shifting role of the narrator in Duras' work, but the changing status of the reader in the narration and process of interpretation. *Le Marin de Gibraltar,* often dismissed as imitative of the American novel, actually represents a dismantling of a type of American novel and with it certain expectations of meaning. *L'Amante anglaise,* written fifteen years later, retells an earlier play that was in turn based on a crime that Duras and her contemporary audience might have read about in the newspaper. Finally, another fifteen years later, the text *L'Homme atlantique,* which the narrator presents as a new story, actually brings together key elements of other Durassian stories: a woman left by a man, a beach, the sea, in a new narrative configuration.

Each of these works retells stories in a different way. *Le Marin de Gibraltar* appropriates a genre (an American novel), and through parody and inference retells a Hemingway story. *L'Amante anglaise*—first as a novel and then as a play—retells an already fictionalized news story, and *L'Homme atlantique* gives a new structure to motifs and characters that had been used by Duras in other fictions and films. These three retellings, then, are increasingly self-conscious. What emerges when we put them side by side is a clear focus on three narrative elements: a woman who is the subject of the story, the narrator through whom the story is told, and the reader whose relationship to both the subject and the narrator shapes the construction of meaning. Duras' retellings place increasing emphasis on the role of gender in the making of narrative: it is a woman's story that is being told, the narrator, when represented in the text, is most often a man. (pp. 48-9)

When *Le Marin de Gibraltar* was published in 1952 it was read through the grid of the American novel. References to Hemingway and the American novel in the narrative itself invite that reading. However, looking at it today, it is more appropriate to read the American novel—and Hemingway stories—through *Le Marin.* References to Hemingway are playful, parodic. . . . [What] appears to be the subject of the story is merely a pretext. The material provided by Hemingway's story [*The Snows of Kilimanjaro*] is being used to say something else. The full implications of the author's ironic stance surface when we compare *Le Marin de Gibraltar* with the narrative conventions and assumptions about meaning that Hemingway develops in *The Snows of Kilimanjaro.*

In that story, the central character, Harry, in a characteristically resentful, dependent relationship with a rich woman, is dying from gangrene while stranded during a hunt in Africa. Much of the text consists of the stories he tells himself he would have written if he had not met with this fatal accident. The stories are drawn from his experience but require a mature voice to be told. If he had been able to tell them, the story suggests, his life would have had a meaning of which death is now depriving him. At first he considers entrusting them to his woman companion, but she never learned dictation and so cannot be used as a compliant vehicle for his narration. Thematically, the stories are left untold because Harry dies, but structurally they are transmitted to the reader by the invisible author/narrator who has the kind of privileged access to the character that the woman companion does not. The story is constructed around an extended paraleipsis: the author says he is not saying what is being said. As such it is a rhetorical triumph over the silencing of death. The special bond between the hero, the invisible narrator, and the presumed male (or unresisting female) reader maintains the fiction of the transcendent and redemptive power of literature, even though on a thematic level the story seems to tell of its defeat. The companion—identified only as "the woman," "a woman," "the rich bitch"—is left only with the writer's corpse, his corpus being beyond her skills and comprehension. Though the Hemingway story affects cynicism, it maintains a very Romantic, not to say fetishistic, concept of literature within a realistic setting. It also shows story-telling to be men's work. The woman companion has learned how to shoot, but she cannot be entrusted with stories.

Although outfitted with all the props of a quest novel in the realistic mode, *Le Marin de Gibraltar* is, rather, like the maritime atlas Anna claims to know by heart: "C'était l'atlas d'un univers renversé, d'un négatif de la terre." . . . The author does not pretend to offer us an unmediated reflection of experience. The universe we are in is self-consciously fictional and the character's ironic stance toward literary precursors signals that conventional modes of interpretation are inadequate. As the novel progresses, the apparent object of the quest—the sailor—takes on multiple identities, all exaggerations of novelistic heroes: a great lover, a criminal (the assassin of Nelson Nelson, American millionaire), an African folk hero. Messages from around the world put Anna and the narrator on his trail and inspire new stories about his identity and whereabouts. The result is that—like the yacht in the end—the fictional circuits burn out. By overdetermining the central character, the author underscores his non-existence. Whereas in the Hemingway story the hero's death gives birth to fictions that eclipse the woman but give meaning to the hero through the narrator, in Duras' novel the absence of a hero engenders fictions that shape the story of Anna. The making of the narrative is still man's work, because the novel takes form through the words of the male narrator. But in seeming to tell the stories of the sailor, he tells the story of Anna. The absence of the hero makes possible her fictional presence. In order for the story to continue, the fiction of the sailor must be maintained; in order for it to be maintained, there must be no sailor, only his impossibility.

The impossibility of the sailor and the discontinuity between Anna and the sailor is the point of departure for the narrative. In *Le Marin* Duras dismantles conventional character and demonstrates that it is through its absence that the female subject's story can begin to be articulated.

The Duras novel, in other words, reverses the terms of the Hemingway story. While the sequence of fantastic stories seems on a thematic level to uphold a Romantic concept of literature, structurally the novel undoes the myth of transcendent and redemptive meaning that Hemingway's story promotes. The character of the narrator in *Le Marin* undermines the illusion of meaning maintained by Hemingway even further. In *The Snows of Kilimanjaro* the passing on of Harry's literary legacy is possible only through the lucid, presumably masculine bond between the omniscient narrator, the central character, whom he knows like a second self, and the reader. The gender of both the narrator and reader are assumed because "the woman" has been dismissed as an unworthy listener. In *Le Marin* Duras signals the fictional and masculine nature of the narrator by representing him as a character; but in *Le Marin* Anna remains an enigma to the narrator, never entirely knowable. (pp. 49-51)

The woman reader may feel like a voyeur in the Hemingway tale: as a reader she is privy to the narrator's assigning of meaning, as a woman she is excluded as an inadequate vessel for narration. In the Duras novel the woman reader must accede to the male narrator's incomplete story of Anna, to his portrayal of her madness. At the same time, the rhetorical illusion of a lucid, masculine bond is not replaced by an illusion of a feminine bond. To unveil the gender of the conventional narrative undoes the terms that allow it to function. (p. 51)

[*L'Amante anglaise*] is the second of three versions Duras has written about a crime reported in the newspaper. The differences in the retellings significantly alter the answers to the three questions: whose story is being told? who is telling it? what relationship is established with the reader, particularly if she is reading as a woman?

The newspaper account that Duras reconstructs as the story of origin for her tale describes the discovery of portions of a woman's body found on trains throughout France. All the trains had passed under one viaduct in the department of Seine-et-Oise, which led the police to the murderers: an ordinary retired couple. The victim was a deaf-mute cousin who had kept house for them for twenty-seven years. With each retelling Duras gives greater attention to the story of the wife and at the same time inhibits the reader's access to her story through the creation of a narrator-interrogator. With each telling, too, the distance between what the central character knows and what she says, the part of the book the reader must make, becomes increasingly the central concern of the work. (pp. 51-2)

Seven years [after the play *Les Viaducs de la Seine-et-Oise*, which is the first version], when Duras takes up the story again in the novel *L'Amante anglaise*, Claire alone is the murderer, her husband is not an accomplice or even a witness, since he slept through the event. The narrative now begins after Claire's arrest and trial, and she has become the explicit center of interest. The persistent questions around which the novel turns are: who is Claire Lannes and what does her act mean, just as the central questions of *Le Marin* are who is Anna, what does her search mean? In three interrogations—of a café-owner, Claire's husband, and then Claire—the reader is brought gradually closer to her and closer to the enigma of her act. The interrogator's function—like that of the male narrator in *Le Marin*—is to make Claire talk, to learn her story first from witnesses and then to prod her to tell him her version, to explain the meaning of the act that now defines her as a murderer in the eyes of others. But unlike the narrator in *Le Marin*, the interrogator has an essentially adversarial relationship with Claire. In *Le Marin*, the collaborative sympathies between narrator, subject, and reader that had characterized the Hemingway story were broken down; in *L'Amante anglaise*, the author removes any trace of a sympathetic alliance between the narrator and the subject. (p. 52)

The most significant change in this version is the crime itself. The generalized alienation of *Les Viaducs de la Seine-et-Oise* is replaced by a specifically feminine alienation. Claire's dismantling of her cousin's body is an attempt to articulate herself: in that violent act of rupture she brings together the disjointed parts of her history. She inscribes two words on parts of the body: "Alphonso" and "Cahors"—Alphonso was the one man who sensed meaning in her words when her husband refused to, and Cahors was the town of her lover and her coming of age. Further, what had been an incidental, grisly detail in the first version (the victim's head had still not been found) becomes a willed act of concealment in the later versions. Claire refuses to tell where she hid the head because if she gives up that knowledge, the interrogator will cease listening to her. By refusing communication, by withholding that intelligence, maintaining that absence, she has control over a continuing narrative. He cannot pretend to have access to her whole story and to interpret it for her and for us. The absence that was at the heart of Anna's story is now a consciously chosen strategy on the part of a woman-subject. This heightens the antagonism between the narrator and the subject and shifts the narrative power (if only by default) from the narrator to the subject. (pp. 53-4)

L'Amante anglaise, like *Le Marin de Gibraltar*, is about the telling of a woman's story, and again the woman reader is faced with dilemma. The interrogator keeps searching for the right question that would yield the answer he seeks—resolution, explanation. The reader has access to Claire's story through the narrator but can see that there is no right question: resolution would merely end the story, not give it meaning. The meaning is already there—in Claire's efforts to purge herself of an existence that oppresses her and to keep intact the passion and anger of her memory of [her lover], the "agent de Cahors." Claire's story, like Anna's, centers on absence: the betrayal of a lover, the purging of the debris of daily living. But this time the violence that was displaced onto one of the sailor's identities (assassin of a millionaire) is assumed by the woman subject in the killing of her cousin. But the ultimate paradox of *L'Amante anglaise* is that Claire does not eradicate her victim and with her a certain construction of the feminine, she becomes her—her only power at the end is to be mute, to refuse to speak certain words. She expels her monologue in the way she rejected her cousin's undigested, overrich, stew.

The aggression that underlies the interrogation of *L'Amante anglaise* and that is expressed thematically by the inscription of "Alphonso" and "Cahors" on parts of the mutilated body, is at the very core of the narrative in *L'Homme atlantique*. At first reading it might seem inappropriate to call this a retold tale. Nonetheless, it is a distilled retelling of the most often repeated story of Duras' *œuvre*—a woman abandoned by a man—and it recombines, in a new configuration, elements found in many other works: a beach, the oppressive atmosphere of an old hotel, rain, death, the end of love. Also, of course, as a written narrative it retells the film by the same name. All three of the narrative elements we have been examining are drastically transformed in this short work: the woman subject, the narrator, the stance available to a woman reader. Written in the first and second person with a female speaker addressing (as "vous") an absent man, the woman subject of the story and the narrator's voice are merged. To tell the story, she assumes the role of filmmaker and in a sense the male narrator of the other stories is replaced by the camera, now controlled by the woman subject.

The impetus for fiction, the need to speak, is created again by the absence of a man—the abandonment of a lover. In a passage that recalls Claire's removal of all traces of herself from the house, the woman of *L'Homme atlantique* describes her preparation for the telling of this story. She sweeps her house clean of all signs of life as if in preparation for her own funeral. She represents the writing of this story as a cure from the lie of a dying love. She addresses herself to the absent lover's lack of comprehension—not to change it but to name it. Then the act of writing is replaced by the making of a film of absence, and the camera becomes the instrument of control of that absence.

The entire text is dominated by the first person speaker's use of the future tense and the imperative in order to control the absent lover's gaze, his memory, his imagined movement through this landscape. The film is one possible representation of his absence and a representation to which he will not have access.

In a reversal of the convention that represents the woman as erotic object of the male filmmaker's gaze, the woman filmmaker offers the camera as a lure and a threat: the male lover is invited to look at the camera as a desired object and as an instrument of death. The woman reader of *L'Homme atlantique* seems at first to be eliminated from access to the text. Initially the reader, whether a man or woman, is the object of the woman speaker's aggressive imperative (even as Claire was of the interrogator's questions). The "vous," however, is explicitly masculine. The woman reader needs to make a conscious effort to re-align with the filmmaker and not accept identification with the second person who is being addressed, because of the effect of the second person imperative. Once extricated from the "vous," the woman reader can become a spectator of this film of absence, allied with the female speaking voice. The male reader can detach less easily from the "vous." His position is not unlike the woman reader of Hemingway—witness to his own absence or forced to assume a sympathy with the narrative voice that is contrary to his interest as a man. In the transformation of narrative elements that is effected in *L'Homme atlantique*, the reader's function is partially assimilated with what had been the function of the narrator in the other works.

The narrator of *Le Marin de Gibraltar* repeatedly implored Anna to speak, to invent; the interrogator of *L'Amante anglaise* in a more antagonistic posture questions Claire. Although she exercises limited control over her narrative by withholding the information he thinks will lead to explanation, she recognizes that for her story to be told she requires his presence. Now the female subject assumes the power of the imperative to tell her story which is the story of the lover's absence. Lies are equated with connection, similarity, truth with disconnection, distance and difference—between the woman and the man, between discrete objects, between words and meaning. The woman subject invents an interior monologue that she attributes to the lover by preceding it with "Vous penserez. . . ." It seems like a lucid articulation of Claire's ravings, but where Claire saw both connection and discontinuity as "true" and important to communicate, the lover, in the thoughts the woman ascribes to him, will think that the "miracle" is in irreducible difference. The monologue is an urgent list of words that recall other texts, images used in other stories, all presented as separate, as anchored in essential difference, and through that discontinuity as resonant with the unbreachable distance between the lovers. The difference between this monologue and Claire's is the disappearance of any illusion of connections among things or between people. This monologue, put into the thoughts of the man via the woman's imperative, subjects the male to a specifically female alienation through the woman's narrative power. But the process itself reveals the "other" to be a projection of the radical alienation of the subject.

In assuming the role of narrator the woman subject has specifically assumed the specular power of the camera with its control of the image. The reader and the spectator (two separate roles available in the retellings of *L'Amante anglaise*) are brought together in *L'Homme atlantique*. *L'Homme atlantique* (like *Le Camion*) is a text about a film, and the reader/spectator must imagine the film/narrative using the text as a point of departure. This imaginary material—the image of the absent lover—is explicitly presented as a reflection of the filmmaker's desire rather than as a representation of the other. More precisely, the other is presented as a projection of the subject so that the text recreates the mirroring images of Lacan's Imaginary order.

To a woman reader eager for alternatives to constructions of the feminine as derivative, defined through relationships with a man, the continuing centrality of an absent male might seem like a defeat. But at the same time that the woman of *L'Homme atlantique* (or Claire or Anna) speaks her emptiness and the absence of the male lover who appears to define her, she also erases the lie of transcendence and continuity that characterized the masculine narrative voice in, for example, Hemingway's story. At the heart of the woman's voice in *L'Homme atlantique* is not passivity or a fetishistic reification of the absent love object, but an aggressive articulation of the radical discontinuity between the speaking subject and the other. The film of *L'Homme atlantique*—like the cinema of Lol V. Stein—demonstrates the problematic of the female subject by elaborating a rhetoric of discontinuity. In Duras' retold tales story-telling and the erotic have absence and irreducible distance as their first and final points of articulation.

The terms of the triangle of the woman subject, the male interlocutor, and the woman's story that represented the analytical situation in the earlier stories have shifted in *L'Homme atlantique*. The male interlocutor is fragmented: partly contained in the "vous" of the absent lover, partly assumed by the woman subject in her control of the camera. The role is also partly given over to the reader. The antagonism and resistance that had characterized the relationship between the woman subject and male interlocutor is transferred to the relationship with the reader, although, as noted earlier, with different effect if the reader reads as a woman or as a man. The narrative shifts effected in *L'Homme atlantique* intensify the reader's collusion in the making of the narrative even while stressing the antagonism implied by that relationship.

Duras' work does not present a feminization of narrative in the sense of rewriting Hemingway in the feminine or creating a triumphant female speaking subject. Rather, the repeated reconstructions of a woman subject's past reveal the discontinuity of subject and other. A specifically female experience gives rise to a rhetoric of discontinuity that undermines the terms of meaning and habits of interpretation of the conventional (male) narrative. Duras places at the very center of her text the absence that corresponds to a certain construction of the feminine in our culture, and through that specifically female alienation undoes the lie of transcendent, redemptive meaning and the illusion of masculine lucidity that created that absence in the first place. (pp. 54-7)

Marilyn R. Schuster, "Reading and Writing as a Woman: The Retold Tales of Marguerite Duras," in The French Review, Vol. LVIII, No. 1, October, 1984, pp. 48-57.

SARAH WHITE

An old woman arrives in Paris to visit her middle-aged son. She has grown rich as a factory owner in a distant colony. This son is her favorite of six children because he is a failure, a faded pretty boy who drifts in the urban margins, flat broke. The reader is invited to wonder why the determined, workaholic mother of the title story in *Whole Days in the Trees* feels so attached to her weak-willed offspring. We expect to learn that she compensates for an early power grievance by choosing a child to dominate and hold in dependency. We find some of that, but Marguerite Duras explores a more curious form of self-indulgence: the refusal to exert any parental authority. When he was small, his mother would not wake him up for school. She longed to nourish, in her recalcitrant boy, a passionate laziness that had once been part of her. "I had a pref-

erence for your sleep," she says. Together, they recall his habit of hunting birds' nests for "whole days in the trees," a note of typical offstage lyricism.

Perhaps a similar dynamic governs Duras's relation to her fictional offspring. For five decades she has been a tireless writer and filmmaker. Her characters, by contrast, tend to be somnambulists, without will, without desire to create or "get ahead." They walk the edge of an abyss of exclusion, alcoholism, crime; they flirt with disturbing or murderous eroticism. One wonders how, if they were real, they would have survived till the moment she begins their stories. Duras disdains people who live prudently or comfortably. Not unlike Jean Rhys, she refuses to pull her characters into line, and demonstrates a maternal, almost mystical involvement with lives whose hopelessness approaches euphoria. In all her best stories, plays, novellas, and films, we follow the characters along their thin, somnambulistic edge. We may need some initiation to her ellipses, repetitions, disjunctures, but we end up in that space where obsessive attachments are formed, where addictions hold sway, and where unassimilated past experiences are repeated. (In her quirky way, Duras is profoundly Freudian.)

"**Whole Days in the Trees**," published in France in 1954 and issued now for the first time in English, was written before Duras achieved a style which celebrates that slightly insane and, for her, essentially feminine space. Yet the story does assemble her favorite themes: paradoxical love, displaced appetites, perverse wishes, compulsions to repeat.... Reading later Duras, if we wish to track a character's deviated desires, we have to do it on the basis of movements and gestures, seen as if by a camera. Characters express, but never explain, themselves. In *Moderato Cantabile*, a 1958 novella, the mother-son relationship is more poignant because it is not recalled but enacted by a distracted mother ... and a pleasantly naughty child who is saner than she is. The capabilities of Duras in her best novellas are not quite so evident in "**Whole Days in the Trees**."

The second story in the collection, however, is as erotic and strangely violent as the strongest Duras. "**The Boa**," a woman's memoir of adolescence in a falsely respectable colonial boarding school, takes swipes at all forms of repression....

In the next story, "**Madame Dodin**," a temperamental concierge derives her strength from two consuming emotions: hatred of the tenants' garbage and unconsummated love for Gaston, the streetsweeper. Hers is a love unto crime, unto ruin if need be, the kind of love Duras advocates and dreads: "She steals at the end of a life lived in hard work and dignity, with extreme pleasure, extreme youthfulness and as very few people are capable of managing to do." Such passion defies regret. After this, the fourth and last story, "**The Building Site**," seems haunting enough, but significant mostly as a shade of prose to come.

Sarah White, "Sense and Sensuality," in The Village Voice, Vol. XXIX, No. 40, October 2, 1984, p. 44.

E. B. COBB

[*Whole Days in the Trees*] contains samples of Marguerite Duras's various writing styles and serves as an excellent introduction to her work. The first two stories—"**Whole Days in the Trees**" with the colossal figure of the old mother and her gargantuan appetite, and "**The Boa**," with its tropical setting, first-person narration, and monstrous events—have the flavor of the author's early autobiographical books. The last story, "The Building Site," resembles—by its lack of action, paralyzed characters, and vague setting—the mysterious, haunting novels and plays of Duras's later years, such as *L'Amour.* "Madame Dodin," the third story in this collection, is an often humorous, atypical character study of an aging concierge and "her" street sweeper. Done with Balzacian deftness, it constitutes a delightful break from the nebulousness that often haunts Duras's work.

> *E. B. Cobb, in a review of "Whole Days in the Trees," in* Choice, *Vol. 22, No. 3, November, 1984. p. 430.*

DIANE JOHNSON

[In] much of her work, Miss Duras uses obscurity—or at least manner and formal control—to combat or disguise her tendency to be melodramatic and sentimental. But in [*The Lover*], her small, perfect, new novel, she has found in reworking material she has used before—material evidently full of personal meaning—a felicitous and masterly balance between formalism and powerful emotional effect. [*The Lover*] is accessible the way Thomas Mann's *Death in Venice* or D. M. Thomas's *White Hotel* are accessible, both because of the interesting narrative particulars—one might say the surface of the works—and because they deal successfully with strong basic themes of erotic love and death. (p. 1)

It is hard to think of a recent work in English that so perfectly accomplishes its complicated aims in a manner so austere. Miss Duras, like some other French writers, produces the richness of her effects in the blanks and silences of her minimalist sentences. Can a work be woven from little more than its themes, an occasional strand of visual detail—"She's wearing a man's flat-brimmed hat, a brownish-pink fedora with a broad black ribbon"? One thinks, a little, of the style (and also of the protagonists, tone and indeed the real life) of Jean Rhys—problems, like Miss Duras's, with alcohol, the same depressed but sentient heroines. But Miss Duras seems more artfully to capture the sadness of ordinary life, and is more interested in sexuality—as opposed to Rhys's interest in survival.

The novel in English depends upon expansion, digression, the sudden appearance of humorous characters. Here there are only enough details, characters, words, to tie the strands together. The novel in English depends upon humor, sometimes to its disadvantage, potentially good novels, especially lately, straying beyond the boundary of comedy, that dignified genre, into an area of jokey facetiousness. It is occasionally instructive to regard the power of humorlessness. There are no jokes in Miss Duras's work—and jokes would be fatal. The slightest alteration of tone would give us another work entirely—something like soft porn perhaps; or a slight change in point of view, say to the lover's point of view, would give us *Lolita.* It is Miss Duras's great artistic self-confidence that allows her to avoid even the most alluring temptations to comedy. . . .

Her reward is an unremitting intensity, an effect on some subliminal reserve of emotion in the reader that one might suspect or resist if the passion and sincerity of the author were for a moment in doubt, or if she seemed to be manipulating her readers for an effect of easy tears. It is interesting to think about the thematic connections, even certain stylistic connections, between this powerful, authentic and completely successful work, and the enormously popular supermarket romance genre, which, despite its clumsiness and inauthenticity,

acknowledges—which recent serious American novels less and less often do—the existence of psychological archetypes and some of the primordial functions of storytelling. . . .

Miss Duras has been a leading, if controversial, writer in France since the 1950's with *The Sea Wall,* a work that is in many ways the forerunner of this one. On the first page of *The Lover,* a man comes up to the narrator and says, "Everyone says you were beautiful when you were young, but I want to tell you I think you're more beautiful now than then. Rather than your face as a young woman, I prefer your face as it is now." These words seem somehow to describe the development of this artist. That is, one way or another she has always been beautiful. (p. 25)

> *Diane Johnson, "First Love and Lasting Sorrow," in* The New York Times Book Review, *June 23, 1985, pp. 1, 25.*

STEPHEN KOCH

[*The Lover*] is an old-fashioned colonialist romance, with a difference. Duras, who is best known in America for her script of *Hiroshima, Mon Amour,* has for many decades been a leading figure in the vanguard of French fiction and film. She is now 71 years old, and the intensely autobiographical tone of this novel has convinced many readers that Duras is herself both the "ravaged" writer portrayed as relating it, and the nymphet of 50 years ago who is at the center of its love story.

The colonial scene is French Indochina. Our coquettish little heroine is a vision most lovingly recalled from that past. An irresistible child of 15 steps off the Mekong ferry in Saigon, a slender, wispy poor-kid, who has cooked up her schoolgirl high style from scraps and pieces. . . . She is a little belle on the verge of everything, and she is being watched there at the ferry dock from inside the depths of a long black limousine. The watcher is another vision. A 27-year-old Chinese rich-boy, who watches her aching with an outsider's love.

The stage of memory is set.

Chinese rich-boy approaches Caucasian poor-girl. The chauffeur drives them to the Chinese quarter of Saigon, where in his *own* apartment they become lovers, first tentative, then eager, then insatiable. Duras' images may come from real life, but they are also classic. Were *The Lover* an English novel, we would invoke Somerset Maugham or, mutatis mutandis, *The Jewel in the Crown.* Not only do we have the long black limousine, we have the teeming native quarters, sunlight seeping through slatted shutters, along with the odors of meat roasting on coal braziers, of jasmine and incense. The lovers' moans cover the clatter of rickshaws and clogs, the shouting from the streets and bazaars. There is whiskey and black silk robes and white suits. Beneath those Casablanca fans, the sex is clean and smooth-skinned and for-the-first-time. The two lovers weep in each others' arms. A lot. From her lover's hairless skin Duras recalls inhaling the scent of English cigarettes, perfume, honey. (p. 3)

The novelist portrayed as writing *The Lover* describes herself as "ravaged" by age and, especially, drink. So it has been in real life with Duras. It's a quite widely publicized fact that several years ago Duras experienced what is called in Alcoholics Anonymous "touching bottom." Near death from alcoholism, she entered a detoxification clinic and emerged, sober, to resume her work, notably writing this book.

The shadow of self-destruction lies across this novel. It begins with a description of Duras' "ravaged" face in such contrast to the perfect freshness of that distant girl with her large watchful eyes.... [We follow the] shattered trail of her family, as the sweet brother dies in Indochina and the brutish one dies brutishly amid wreckage and debt. The bereft and homeless mother moves between France and Vietnam as if dazed. Only the girl moves on to success and eminence. And the ravaging of that face.

The Lover is an intensely romantic book, and romance—since there can even be a certain romance in self-destruction—doubtless accounts for its great success. It does indeed have perfection of a kind, though I would call it a perfection of elegance rather than of depth. Duras' style is indebted to the classic French *récit*, and Madame de Lafayette is one of her leading mentors. The relation between its love story and the harsh truths to come is the source of its power, and that relation is seen as a classic link between passion and a will to self-destruction. The story unfolds in a repetitive, incantatory style (admirers of *Hiroshima, Mon Amour* will recognize it) which suggests to me what the psychotherapist must hear—the compulsive return to the same set of stories, enlarging and unfolding them in steps as more is recovered. And indeed recovery, in the dual sense of recuperation from and recapture of the past, is a major theme of the book.

I am not sure the formal perfection of this novel entirely compensates for its lack of scope.... *The Lover* is a very good novel indeed, and it may be presumptuous to ask for more, but I would feel the power of its recovery more if we were given a clearer view of the depths from which its sweetness is retrieved. (p. 13)

Stephen Koch, "Saigon, Mon Amour: Duras' Novel of Passion and Memory," in Book World—The Washington Post, *July 21, 1985, pp. 3, 13.*

VIVIAN GORNICK

[*The Lover*] centers on a year and a half of Marguerite Duras's early life, and focuses on her first experience of sexual love. It is a small rich work, dense and associative. The controlling image is the scene on the ferry deck; it will be woven centrally or peripherally into passage after passage. Everything important to Duras is collected in this moment: the knowing virgin dressed like a child prostitute, the exotic foreigner offering sex and money, the muddy light that mirrors intent, the inevitability of what the man and the girl are about to do, what the girl is about to learn. Duras's thoughts range freely throughout the book, covering years and continents, yet they return always to a single intensity: the discovery in herself of desire as a principle of self-creation.

The father was a low-grade civil servant who came out to Indochina in the '20s. Now he is gone and the family lives marginally, just barely hanging on. The mother is chaotic, the younger brother soft and weak, the elder a murderous bully. The mother loves the murderer, Marguerite loves the other one. On his behalf she fights the bully. In the memoir this early struggle counterpoints to her recollection of the Chinese lover. Back and forth Duras goes between the girl on the ferry deck and the domination by the elder brother of the younger one. For Marguerite defeat of the elder brother is a necessity, a matter of her own survival. But victory is assured: she has an avidity for life that makes her fierce. Slowly the reader begins to see that the awful principle of will in the elder brother

is equaled by the principle of desire articulating itself in the girl. She listens hard when her Chinese lover tells her she will never be faithful to any man, senses the ruthlessness in herself, knows already that she will not be more loyal to any one person than she will be to the idea of desire.

Desire is Duras's subject, the territory of her expertise. Passages concerning her mother and her brothers are often striking but never satisfying; she doesn't really know what is going on among them all, has never gotten to the heart of the family matter; moreover, the less she knows the more arty she becomes. But when she writes about herself on the ferry, herself with her lover, herself being educated by desire, she is masterful. The voice is wise, tempered, good-humored, detached, the knowledge in it so comprehensive it need insist on nothing, it need only present. Here the sentences range wide, sink deep, travel far; repeatedly, they take the reader by surprise....

Intensely modern in its directness, it is also wonderfully real and confiding, persuasive in its mimicry of a mind turning over and over again, as the years pass, associations to a memory that drags at the heart. One passage, in particular, about the girl on the ferry, evokes the pleasure and profit of associating freely. Duras writes: "It's not the shoes, though, that make the girl look so strangely, so weirdly dressed. No, it's the fact that she's wearing a man's flat-brimmed hat.... The crucial ambiguity of the image lies in the hat.... How I came by it I've forgotten.... What must have happened is: I try it on just for fun, look at myself in the shopkeeper's glass, and see that there, beneath the man's hat, the thin awkward shape, the inadequacy of childhood has turned into something else ... has become, on the contrary, a provoking choice of nature, a choice of the mind. Suddenly it's deliberate. Suddenly I see myself as another ... available to all, available to all eyes. I wear it all the time."

The *crucial ambiguity of the image lies in the hat.* How I love this sentence! I can see Duras, in her apartment in Paris, leaning across the typewriter, a cigarette hanging from her lips, her eyes narrowed against smoke and distraction, concentrating on the way the girl on the ferry was dressed. I can see the concentration shaping the sentence, and the sentences that are to follow. The act of writing comes alive on the page. My own pleasure is acute. Imagine that of the French. After 30 years of Duras novels in which the voice has been unbearably remote, the prose an act of will, the sentences filling in a preordained shape, how enchanting to have from her a piece of writing where the sentences are clearly fashioned by recognizable experience, and the work allows itself to emerge from the life in the sentences.

Ultimately, *The Lover* does not achieve shape. A serious matter in any book, but an especially serious one in a book like this. In associative writing there is neither story nor character, there is only the feel of things, some essence of experience captured through a wholeness of writing hard to describe but unmistakable when present. As in abstract art, where space is the subject, color the painting, so in Duras's kind of writing the thing itself is, finally, the story the writer has to tell, and it is a story achieved only through tremendous attention paid to the shape of the prose. Not the willed shape, the shape dictated by the experience.

The tone of *The Lover,* arresting from the very first paragraph, promises that beneath the apparent randomness this shaping process is at work, pressing to fulfill itself. But somewhere around the middle of the book that necessary attention begins to lapse. There is not a persistent enough discrimination of detail selected, incident described or reflected on. The writing begins to drift, make use of filler paragraphs, kill time getting from one passage to another. The book is too short to sustain such a falling away and the structure, remarkably tensile when it is working, seems painfully fragile when it is not.

Yet *The Lover* has magic. There is magic in the richness of certain sentences loaded with the compactness of poetry. There is magic in the way other sentences are placed in the middle of a paragraph you would never have dreamed could hold such a sentence, the unexpected appearance casting influence back to the beginning and forward to the end, electrifying an entire passage. Such sentences dazzle. They induce joy. The reader is stirred, immensely stirred. The prose does indeed become the experience. *The Lover,* in many moments, is a distillation of such writing. As it is of desire. The reader may still wish for the thing itself, but distilled moments of writing and desire from an elegant woman of letters are enough to remind us of the life-giving properties of literature.

Vivian Gornick, "Memory and Desire," in The Village Voice, Vol. XXX, No. 31, July 30, 1985, p. 47.

MIRANDA SEYMOUR

The compelling and destructive power of love has been a leitmotif in many of Duras' books, but she has never approached it with such formidable intensity as in this spare and devastating novel [*The Lover*]. In a little more than a hundred pages, she creates a world more charged with passion, despair and hatred than most of us are likely to encounter in a lifetime.... Hypnotically beautiful images and unswerving emotional frankness combine to harrowing effect.

The story is discreetly autobiographical. Many elements will be familiar to readers of *Un Barrage contre le Pacifique,* Duras' bleak novel about a French mother and her children in Indochina, where the authoress spent her youth. The setting for *The Lover* is Saigon, the atmosphere is of despair, isolation, brutal indifference. The women of Saigon are shown as rich, beautiful, quietly frantic. The dream is always of an escape to France, a passage out of exile....

[The girl's lover] is infatuated from the start by her child's body. She begins in curiosity and ends in love, but only in private. In public, surrounded by her proud family, she sees him with their eyes, an alien, a rich man stupid enough to think he can buy their esteem.

The passion and humility of the lover put him at the mercy of the family. Their contempt is absolute.... The girl acquiesces. Fear of her family is far stronger in her than love. When her mother hits her, strips her, screams at her for selling herself to a Chinese man, she repudiates him....

The family violates the girl's feelings with unremitting brutality. The lover is as tender as if he was making love to his own daughter. His is the role of the loser. Slowly, the process of detachment begins. He becomes 'the man from Cholon', insubstantial, still with her yet already a part of the past. She is to be sent away to a school in France, never to see him again. The circular structure of the story is completed with the girl standing on a boat on the Mekong river, looking for the last time at the black limousine. And, because she is truly the child of her family, she won't let anyone see her crying, 'because he was Chinese and one oughtn't to weep for that kind of lover.'

It's not hard to see why the book was awarded the Prix Goncourt. Rarely have I read a novel so flawlessly written, so intensely felt that the usual veil between the reader and the writing dissolves. The reality of the fiction is, very nearly, unbearable.

Miranda Seymour, "The Only Fedora in Saigon," in The Spectator, Vol. 256, No. 8217, January 4, 1986, p. 29.

FRANCINE DU PLESSIX GRAY

[Marguerite Duras's *The War*] is a complex and extraordinary book, a collection of six narratives, four overtly autobiographical and two fictional, set in France at the end of World War II. Its title chapter is the most powerful text I have read about that period....

Because it is equally sublime as a literary work and as an act of witness, because its style and theme so tightly encapsulate the last four decades of this admirable writer's career, the first chapter of *The War* needs to be fully considered on its own merits, rather than as a prelude to the less accomplished texts that follow it. (p. 1)

The memoir is set in Paris in April of 1945, as Allied forces begin to liberate the concentration camps, and the first full account of Nazi atrocities is being disclosed to the free world. Marguerite Duras and the war prisoner she waits for—her husband, a resistance fighter, Robert L.—had already decided before his arrest that they would separate. Miss Duras plans to divorce Robert L. to marry his best friend, D., whose child she wishes to bear. And yet: "I've chosen to wait for Robert like this, unto death." D., who becomes as fully dedicated as Miss Duras to Robert's survival, will be instrumental in saving his life; he travels to Dachau three days after its liberation to rescue the barely alive, 75-pound victim. So the memoir is infused by obsessions that far transcend the force of love or the deepest friendships, and have a quality of almost religious dedication.

Unlike *The Lover,* a partly masked autobiographical novel, *The War*'s first chapters are pure memoirs and cloak none of their historical particulars. Any biographical sketch of Miss Duras makes it evident that "Robert L." refers to her first husband, the writer Robert Antelme, and that "D." is the philosopher Dionys Moscolo, father of Miss Duras's only son. The current President of France, François Mitterrand—also referred to by his underground name, Morland—is prominent in the narrative as the resistance leader who first identifies the barely recognizable Robert L. amid a heap of dead and dying men at Dachau, and arranges for D.'s rescue mission.

The only autobiographical aspect of *The War*'s first chapter that may be fictional is Miss Duras's claim, in her introduction, that she did not "tamper" with the original draft she happened to find in 1984, on the 40th anniversary of the Liberation. For one of the book's most memorable achievements is the skill with which pure pain is etched into Miss Duras's idiom, a skill never so fully evidenced in her writing of the 1950's or 60's, and rarely achieved by anyone but the most mature artist. In these pages Miss Duras's language goes beyond mimesis, loses all semblance of a stylistic device, becomes a clay into which the Nazi terror and the sorrow of waiting becomes encrusted. Her dislocated syntax and skeletal, willfully artless diction simulate as they never have before the narrator's anguish, suspense, confusion. (p. 48)

In the last four decades we have often been warned that human speech is too frail to bear the weight of horror forced upon us by the Holocaust, that we may have to resort to some form of "literature of silence" to narrate the Totally Inhuman. As she describes a man returned from the Beyond of Nazi camps, Miss Duras's minimal, bone-spare diction approximates this necessary zero-degree of language. The presence of death is even more concrete and harrowing in these pages than in any eye-witness account of the camps that comes to mind. . . . It is all the more present, perhaps, because Miss Duras does not describe the phenomenon of mass destruction that is "beyond literature," but keeps it on the scale of our perception through one individual's agony. Barbara Bray's translation is so superb that I was even more moved by her English rendering than by the original.

In time the obsessive hunger of many deportees invades Robert L., replacing his fever. "Methodically, as if performing a duty, he was doing what he had to do to live. He ate. . . . He has gone and hunger has taken his place." Robert L. also survives Marguerite's restatement of their impending divorce, and the news that his 24-year-old sister had died at Ravensbrück. A year after his return from death, when he is convalescing on a Mediterranean beach, Marguerite watches him walking, still leaning on a cane, toward the sea. "I looked at him. He saw me looking. He blinked his eyes behind his glasses and smiled at me, giving little shakes of the head, as you do when you're laughing at someone." The first chapter of *The War* ends with this religious image, very uncharacteristic of the left-wing, agnostic French avant-garde with which Miss Duras has been associated, the image of a resurrection achieved through obsessive fidelity and faith.

One must now deal with the more problematic narratives that succeed this brief and monumental text. Each of *The War*'s chapters is preceded by a few italicized paragraphs discussing its degree of verity or fiction. Chapters Two through Four, all autobiographical, are also linked by the theme of reversal: Duras the victim now plays the role of executioner.

In **"Monsieur X., Here Called Pierre Rabier,"** the narrator flashes back to 1944, the last days of the Nazi occupation of Paris, when her Resistance network has ordered her to stay in touch with a Gestapo agent who is enamored of her. At the war's end, after she has testified against Rabier at his trial, a guilt-stricken Miss Duras tries to take the witness stand again to say that he once saved a Jewish family; but the courtroom of vengeful Parisians turns against her and orders his execution. **"Albert of the Capitals"** deals with another informer, whose interrogation under torture Miss Duras most brutally and efficiently conducts after the Liberation:

"The more they hit and the more he bleeds, the more it's clear that hitting is necessary, right, just." The most convicing narrative of the book's middle section, it is made powerful by Miss Duras's amazing candor about her own potential for violence. And **"Ter of the Militia"** concerns a young, still more inconsequential informer who was once at her mercy, and whose execution or amnesty she is not certain of to this day.

Given the grandeur of *The War*'s first chapter, it is hard to determine what failed in Miss Duras's artistry when composing or revising these three relatively anecdotal, coarsely crafted tales. Their principal interest is political: They document an aspect of the French Resistance that has remained taboo for four decades—the gratuitous violence that overtook many underground fighters upon the Liberation, when "some drove off every morning in hopes of still finding a fight."

Throughout these narratives one senses that Miss Duras is extremely uneasy with the theme of the Liberation's violence and suffused with self-contempt for her own participation in it. The key to her anguish may lie in an oracular sentence that comes in her introduction to **"Albert of the Capitals."** "Learn to read them properly," she tells us about these texts, "they are sacred." Questioned about the meaning of these words in a recent interview, Miss Duras answered that as executioner she stood guilty under some absolute law. So it is possible that Duras the moralist and pacifist is still coming to terms with a transgression too painful to shape into art, that it is easier for her (for any one of us) to find a language for the memory of pain than for the memory of guilt.

As for the last two texts in *The War,* they are wan, vaguely surreal little fictions about anomic loners musing over their fate after the armistice. It is hard to know why they were included in this collection, whose successive chapters tend to decrease in stature. Yet one ends *The War* without any sense of disillusionment; rather, one is enormously grateful for an initial text whose power and uniqueness fulfill a principal condition of art—to transfigure life's pain. (pp. 48-9)

> *Francine du Plessix Gray, "The Power of Our Obsessions," in* The New York Times Book Review, *May 4, 1986, pp. 1, 48-9.*

Alice Thomas Ellis

19??-

(Pseudonym of Anna Haycraft) English novelist and journalist.

A respected popular novelist, Ellis portrays the lives of middle-class people in British society, focusing particularly on its female members. Her work is characterized by its satirical wit and frequent underlying pathos. Among the concerns Ellis explores in her novels are bereavement, love and sexuality, and class differences. Critics praise Ellis's ability to probe deeply into her themes while maintaining a humorous, entertaining fictional surface.

Ellis's first novel, *The Sin Eater* (1978), chronicles a family gathering at a country estate where the father is dying. Jeremy Treglown described this book as "a fiction about the British empire, satirising both the pretensions of the rulers and the inadequacies of the ruled." A bereaved family is also the focus of *The Birds of the Air* (1979), in which a widow's stoical acceptance of her husband's death is contrasted with her daughter's grief for her dead son. Reviewers noted that this novel combines a humorous portrayal of family relations with a serious depiction of grief, betrayal, and depression. The central figure of *The 27th Kingdom* (1982) is Aunt Irene, an eccentric, middle-aged woman who lives with her strange nephew in London's Chelsea district. The novel recounts what happens when a West Indian postulant with unusual powers comes to live with Aunt Irene. Ellis won acclaim for her imaginative creation of a unique set of characters and a series of bizarre situations.

In *The Other Side of the Fire* (1983), Claudia, a bored suburban homemaker, falls in love with her homosexual stepson. Claudia reveals her infatuation to her best friend, who urges her to suppress her feelings. In *Unexplained Laughter* (1985), Lydia, a London journalist, retreats to a small town in Wales after ending a love affair. As Lydia resists the townspeoples' subtle disapproval of her lifestyle, she develops a redeeming platonic relationship with the parish priest. In her review of *Unexplained Laughter,* Harriet Waugh characterized all of Ellis's fiction as "short, edged comedies of human failure in the face of some ultimate good" and states that Ellis "manoeuvres to pit the world against the spirit and then stands back to see which will win."

Photograph by Mark Gerson

JEREMY TREGLOWN

It's hard to imagine a better book with a worse title than *The Sin Eater.* I'm not even sure which person the consumer of wickedness is meant to be—a confession made with some nervousness: Alice Thomas Ellis's waspish humour at the expense of her characters sometimes extends to the reader—we are dared to suppose, for example, that Hesiod is an old Welsh poet—and anyone who lays that kind of trap may well be sitting at home now, decorously falling about (her own phrase) at the notion of a reviewer who doesn't recognise her title as an allusion to *The Mabinogion* or one of the books of the Apocrypha.

Well, who *is* this vicious gobbler? First suspect must be Rose, a female Waugh . . . whose relish of her own reactionary intolerance becomes almost carnivorous during a family get-together in the Welsh mansion of her dying father-in-law, the Captain. Another strong candidate is Gomer, a repellently fat local boy, grandson of the Captain's daily help. He is a conspicuous guzzler of evil things, whether in the pantry among the welshcakes or with a bottle of scotch in the garden pavilion, where he has Forsterian dealings with the Captain's married son Michael. But then again, it might be the family's ill-featured tame sheep, nicknamed Virginia Woolf 'because of the facial resemblance', which wanders in and out of the action always chewing an ugly mouthful of whatever's on offer.

Whether or not any of these is the subject, the literary allegiances they throw into focus don't seem accidental. Alice Thomas Ellis's first novel has some of the satirical malice, the implacable cruelty of plotting and the snobbish humour of early Waugh, and a lot of Virginia Woolf's narrative method—the fluid movement from one centre of awareness to another among the characters, and the *Lighthouse*-like way she uses the family's annual cricket match against the village as a focus both for the action and for individual feelings. Forster is recalled,

189

too, not only in her alertness to suppressed sexuality but in what is at the same time the novel's most original feature. It is a fiction about the British Empire, satirising both the pretensions of the rulers and the inadequacies of the ruled. This empire is not Forster's India, though, but Wales today, its housing estates and holiday resorts despised by the English landowning family which has profited from them, its people's resentment seen at one level in their unimpressed behaviour after the cricket match (which they win), at another in the vengeful gluttony and lusts of Gomer. The story's gothic ending has been a shade too clearly signalled, and Alice Thomas Ellis enjoys Rose's venom so much that her sympathy with the nicer characters comes over as something of an authorial effort. But it's an impressively self-confident novel, full of uncomfortable jokes and sharp perceptions.

> Jeremy Treglown, "A Handful of Dust," in New Statesman, *Vol. 94, No. 2439, December 16, 1977, p. 855.**

PETER ACKROYD

[*The Sin Eater*] is in some ways a melodramatic book, but it paradoxically manages to combine a strain of romanticism with sternness of judgement. A dreadful family have been forced together because 'Father' is dying slowly; sons, daughters-in-law and servants suspire in a fug of resentment and misery but Alice Thomas Ellis's perceptions don't become misty as a result. The book can be very harsh at the expense of those social wiles that are supposed to keep people happy and 'together'. Miss Ellis refuses to see both sides of a situation because both sides, after all, make very boring reading. And the main quality of the book as it zips along is its wit: the relentlessness of domestic life, the knives only just sheathed in time, the tart little phrases bouncing around like Molotov cocktails, are all documented with the loving care which only the truly disenchanted possess.

But disenchantment only runs skin-deep. It's an invincible fact that witty books—let alone witty people—are always hugging to themselves, somewhere strata down, a vast wet layer where passions are real, where judgement is willingly suspended, where illusions have not been broken. *The Sin Eater* tries to be an exception, but isn't quite—and a certain amount of unnecessary good will is heaped upon the ancient rites of the Catholic Church. You can make a novel out of fantasy, but not out of illusion. But whenever Alice Thomas Ellis forgets her good intentions, she writes a witty and well-observed book. (pp. 29-30)

> Peter Ackroyd, "Out of Sight," in The Spectator, *Vol. 239, No. 7799, December 24, 1977, pp. 29-30.**

JIM CRACE

Intimations of Immortality are strictly for the young and moon-eyed. As one gets older it is the sting-a-ling-a-ling of Mortality which most exercises the imagination. Death, in Alice Thomas Ellis's pleasing second novel, *The Birds of the Air,* is "the jaunty jester-king," a mortician with a mordant and theatrical sense of the ridiculous. He is managed by Ellis with an elegant, if modest, writerly instinct and with a humour which, though it reflects a narrow provincial experience, is none the less incisive.

The subject—the victim?—of this black farce is Bereavement. Mrs Marsh survives the loss of Mr Marsh in a flurry of dusters

and propriety. Daughter Mary, laid up with terminal hypochondria and inoperable melancholia, prays for *rigor mortis* and reunion with her dead son Robin. Daughter Barbara, cuckolded over a spinach quiche and a slice of turkey, has recently buried Love and disentombed Lust. This cheerless clan are assembled for the Christmas festivities.

The comedy rarely relinquishes its emotional resonance and the sentiment seldom loses its smirk, but Ellis's writing is stylistically uneven. There are too many shopping lists . . . , too many names of flowers. Her similes have a tired and hunted look: "old trees ranged like solemn guests," "as still as a fish in a stagnant pond." It's all good fun, of course, but one has the feeling that *The Birds of the Air,* though enjoyable and undemanding, makes an uneasy novel. With all its gatherings and dispersals, its dramatic set pieces, its witty dialogue (though complacent narrative style) here is a book which might have been happier as a stage play. . . .

> Jim Crace, "Waiting for the End," in The Sunday Times, *London, August 17, 1980, p. 33.**

ANATOLE BROYARD

The Birds of the Air, by the English novelist Alice Thomas Ellis, is an anatomy of various kinds of grief: dramatic grief and the more ordinary gnawing kind. Mrs. Marsh's grief arises out of the fact that, now that her husband is dead, nobody appreciates her energy. . . . To Mary, who sees herself as "a great white vegetable," a busy woman is a reproach. Her mother tries to string her together with meals: breakfast, elevenses, lunch, tea, supper, midnight snacks. If Mary is eating, she is safe, contained, in contact.

Mrs. Marsh had hoped that her daughter's bereavement might have brought her closer, united them in some kind of universal female sorrow, but Mary burns instead in "the blazing exaltation of grief." She yearns for death as some people yearn for sex.

The Birds of the Air is a rather savage attack on English Christmases. As Miss Ellis puts it, "Forgive us our Christmases as we forgive those who have Christmassed against us." When Mary's sister Barbara and her husband, Sebastian, who is a professor of literature, arrive for dinner, it turns out that he is preoccupied with himself and Barbara is preoccupied with her recent discovery of his unfaithfulness. . . .

How painful and tiring love can be, Mrs. Marsh thinks as she contemplates her two daughters. To temper the family intensity of the occasion, she has invited Evelyn, a woman of her age from across the street. "A lot of people die of choking these days," is one of Evelyn's conversational gambits at the dinner table. . . .

Barbara struggles to articulate a philosophy of adultery. As Miss Ellis describes her, "she had never even learned to be sophisticated, and now that everything had passed beyond the very concept, she was lost." She decides to revenge herself by having an affair with Hunter, another guest, who is apparently asexual. There is an American publisher at dinner, too, and Mary and Hunter share an image of American Christmas: "Riches, reconciliations, tears, snow, success, sentiment, furs, and firs."

The Birds of the Air is clever, well-observed, well-written and curiously gratuitous. Perhaps its people are too preoccupied with themselves to occupy us. It's the sort of novel that critics often praise for its economy, as if the author had spared us the effort of empathy.

> *Anatole Broyard, in a review of "The Birds of the Air," in* The New York Times, *August 5, 1981, p. C22.*

EDITH MILTON

The Birds of the Air is a novel in two modes. In its major, lighter mode, it is a satiric view of contemporary life, the account of a dismal Christmas get-together at the tiny suburban cottage of Mrs. Marsh, recently widowed and devoted to the precept that "life must go on." Her older daughter, Mary, who is consumed by grief over the death of her own son, lives with her. Her younger daughter, Barbara Lamb, is coming for the holiday, bringing two unpleasant children and her prig of a husband, Sebastian. (p. 64)

We seem to be in a weird bestiary, an *Aesop's Fables* gone amok, where natural impulses and properties have been subverted by a trick of speech or association. Fearless in the games she is willing to let language play, Alice Thomas Ellis can be frivolous, poetic, profound, and extremely funny. The Christmas goose, by virtue of the old spoonerism about cooking it, acquires sexual overtones, while the wren and the swan—and, in fact, all the title's birds of the air—are translated in a fairytale fantasy (in which they are miraculously brought back to life after they have been stuffed and roasted) into symbols of an uncertain, almost diabolical resurrection. (pp. 64-5)

Particularly, *The Birds of the Air* is delightful with punning allusions to nature made petty by the application of human cuteness, and becomes a symphony of variations on bird names and bird lore. But under the witty surface and the deliciously nasty observation that sees Sebastian as having "no garden round his mind," and the prime minister of England as "a mean little mouse bred on cheese rind," runs the much darker, much more serious counterpoint of a second mode.

This deeper tonality, which seems to me to distinguish the novel from a hundred other brisk satires of the sort that Americans think the English do so well, is carried largely by Mary and her nephew, Sam, the older and less unpleasant of the two young Lambs. In a book where nomenclature is important and evokes, by and large, the distorted images of nature tamed and shriveled, Sam and Mary, the grieving mother, bear names that suggest biblical origin and analogy. Sam, like his prophet namesake, tends to disapprove of social hypocrisies, and to provide an inarticulate and often hilarious judgment upon them. But it is Mary's anguish over her lost son that offers the novel's largest dimension: It bursts beyond the constrictions and pettiness of her environment to ask unanswerable questions about God and nature. Her vision of the indifference of heaven and earth, measured against the enormity of her own useless pain, is as much poetry as prose, and more like Joyce's story "The Dead" than like smart social satire.

I suppose, in fairness, I should say that this philosophical mode is not always comfortable with the more sardonic one: There are certainly awkward passages and unconvincing moments. But that is quibbling. Mary's musings, which ramble from the primeval to the eternal to make the littleness around her seem even littler, suggest that *The Birds of the Air* is not primarily a study of suburban shallowness at all, but a painfully brilliant comedy about the absurdity of possessing a soul in a diminished world, where a soul may be the last thing anyone should want. (p. 65)

> *Edith Milton, in a review of "The Birds of the Air," in* New York *Magazine, Vol. 14, No. 35, September 7, 1981, pp. 64-5.*

NICHOLAS SHRIMPTON

[Alice Thomas Ellis's] manner is best summarised as eschatology with pratfalls and, as that might suggest, she is establishing an entirely distinctive voice. *The 27th Kingdom* is her most delightful creation yet, an exquisite combination of low comedy and exalted meditation. The heroine, Irene, is a Bohemian lady who keeps open house in the unfashionable Chelsea of the late 1950s. Into her eccentric ménage comes Valentine, a West Indian postulant whose convent wishes her to have a brief taste of the world before taking her vows. Any religious person would seem comically inappropriate in such a setting. Valentine is actually a saint, working miracles with unembarrassed ease and levitating spectacularly over the Thames in the absurd conclusion. Reflections on the nature of good and evil combine effortlessly with bad puns, wild farce and excellent comic dialogue, the touch is light and lively, and the whole concoction slips down as readily as the delicious (but dangerous) meals Irene contrives for her guests.

> *Nicholas Shrimpton, "Sons and Lovers Revisited," in* The Sunday Times, *London, June 27, 1982, p. 40.**

CAROL RUMENS

[From] seemingly slight material, Alice Thomas Ellis weaves an enthralling, imaginative drama [in *The 27th Kingdom*], buttonholing her readers with an insistent wit and vigour in the best traditions of Slav and Celtic story-making. Valentine, admittedly, is a somewhat nebulous character, being so perfect, but has the effect of making the eccentric cast of mortals around her stand out with all the more clarity. Kyril himself seems to be a kind of demon, his quality of awful chill summed up in his response to the death of the household's sad little tenant, Mr Sirocco: 'Hooray,' he says when Aunt Irene breaks the news; 'No, really,' says Aunt Irene; 'Then really hooray,' replies Kyril.

Over the course of three brilliant novels, Alice Thomas Ellis has mapped out a territory uniquely hers, in which she presents, with humorous realism, a brew of ill-sorted characters seething together in domestic claustrophobia. Their social torments are counterpointed with seismic shudders from the psychic depths with which her more imaginative characters, invariably women, are in communion. Like *The Sin Eater,* this new novel builds to a climax which seems the result of delighted, diabolical mischief-making, its loose ends remaining exhilaratingly untied.

> *Carol Rumens, "Shudders from the Depths," in* The Observer, *July 4, 1982, p. 28.**

KATE CRUISE O'BRIEN

Valentine, the black and saintly heroine of Alice Thomas Ellis's *The 27th Kingdom,* is an ideal pilgrim. She is young, she is holy, she is a nun. Her journey from convent to Chelsea is precipitated by her unusual powers. Valentine levitates. She has picked apples from the very top of a tree in this manner and, what is worse, the apples do not conform to the laws of nature. They won't wither. Mother Berthe decides that Valentine must go—'for there was nothing, absolutely nothing, as tiresome, exhausting and troublesome as a fully fledged thaumaturge in a small community'.

Valentine is dispatched to Aunt Irene in Dancing Master House and then strange things begin to happen in Chelsea. Large numbers of pigeons flock around the church spire. The dipsomaniac Major is convinced that they are devils from hell and forswears the booze. Poor Mr Sirocco, the lodger, commits suicide in strange circumstances. The tax inspector breathes down the phone at Aunt Irene. The forces of good and evil are now marshalled in Aunt Irene's exquisite house. For if Valentine is good, childlike and really rather dull, Aunt Irene's nephew Kyril is wicked, fascinating and very, very clever. . . .

Valentine and Kyril, as absolutes, are impervious to each other, but Aunt Irene's untidy thoughts are crowded with images of the unspoken conflict. She thinks of horses and centaurs and then of quiet seas and calm lakes, and she realises that though she loves Kyril she really doesn't like him very much. The fable ends, as all good fables should, with the triumph of God, good and Valentine; but *The 27th Kingdom* is very funny black comedy, and the symbolic victory is Kyril's. A bright unrepentant Lucifer, the image of his archaic smile lingers in the mind.

Kate Cruise O'Brien, "Pilgrim's Ways," in The Listener, Vol. 108, No. 2770, July 22, 1982, p. 24.

SEBASTIAN FAULKS

The Other Side of the Fire is at once recognisable by its style of sardonic disinterest as being in the same vein as [Ellis's] three previous novels. The sentences appear at first calm and lucid in the genteel English tradition; but reading them is rather like biting into a wasp sandwich with the sting being provided by the continuous use of mordant and witty paradox. The characters initially seem like those in so many other novels: flawed middle-aged people whose struggles we are asked to follow with interest. But then one realizes, with something approaching shock, that Alice Thomas Ellis does not regard them with the cosseting sympathy that most novelists have for their characters; on the contrary, she has the knife in all of them. There is nothing more embarrassing than reading a novel where one cannot extend the required sympathy to a dislikeable character the author clearly admires (worst of all when the character is evidently based on the author); but there are no such problems with Miss Ellis, and in our relief, and with a cruel glee, we gang up with her, as it were, to watch the characters squirm. This is extremely good fun. . . .

The book ends with the characters in the same position as when it all began, except with a greater knowledge of each other. This is all very well, because, although the process has been painful for the characters, it has been highly enjoyable for the reader. But is it enough? There are signs that Alice Thomas Ellis, for one, thinks not. As in all her novels there are hints of what one reviewer called 'mythic purpose'. It is strongly suggested that Sylvie is in communion with the spirits of the dead and that her daughter Evvie, as well as writing her silly romance, is in some strange way the 'author' of Claudia's real-life lovesickness. There is a deliberate blurring of the lines between fiction and reality, complicated by the fact that this book is itself a variant of romantic "women's fiction".

Alice Thomas Ellis is prodigal with such hints. . . . The trouble is that the suggestions don't really add up to anything. This novel doesn't give the impression of having been really thought through, in the sense of the author having entirely clarified the supposedly deeper themes in her head. There is no reason why a novel should have a 'meaning', or why a blueprint of its construction should be evident to the reader, but the author should not allow the reader to suspect that there is no consistency behind the intimations of grander designs or that they are thrown in merely to add a spurious sense of 'weight'.

Alice Thomas Ellis has found a distinct and delightful voice which she can turn on, apparently at will. In this respect she is like Fay Weldon, an 'instinctive' writer whose logic and structure do not precede the acts of writing but follow it on the assumption that if the voice hits the right pitch then it will automatically tell the truth.

One is tempted to disregard the hints of 'mythic purpose' and simply listen to the author talking. She is naturally sardonic and elegant and contrives also to be both gossipy and wise. Perhaps in the end it doesn't matter what she is telling us or how completely the subject matter is realised, as long as that voice goes on talking. Perhaps.

Sebastian Faulks, "Sting in the Tale," in Books and Bookmen, No. 340, January, 1984, p. 20.

T. GERTLER

The Other Side of the Fire is a funny, intelligent novel that ultimately falls victim to a case of creeping decorum. Chronicling an English housewife's unspoken infatuation with her grown stepson, Alice Thomas Ellis shows the woman's rarefied sensibility to be a withdrawal from the demands of life. Unfortunately, in a similar way the author eventually retreats from the demands of her book, which begins as a gleeful satire on upper-middle-class repressions.

Lewis Carroll sent Alice through the looking glass into a world she didn't understand; Ellis boots her heroine toward a libidinal blaze. . . . Beautiful, dim Claudia Bohannon has been progressing placidly through a middle age scented with homemade bread, furniture polish, and the cut roses in her country house. "Taste rather than insight" guides this Mrs. Miniver of the eighties. But with menopause just around the corner, "stirring within her Claudia now felt the desire to wear what she had never worn—the strange and garish garment of her self."

Frightened by her desire for freedom, Claudia submerges in obsession. She fastens on [Philip], her husband Charles's 25-year-old son. . . . (pp. 92-3)

Claudia confides her love, though not its object, to [her friend] Sylvie. "But Sylvie was cured of love and could no longer remember what all the fuss was about. . . . She didn't think the whole world loved a lover. She thought on the whole it averted its eyes from so unedifying a sight." She urges Claudia to hang on to her dignity: "When people lose their hearts they frequently lose their minds too, retaining only their organs of generation."

Claudia does pretty much hang on to her dignity. And so do Sylvie, Evvie, Charles, and the cow, Violet. Philip the flower has less dignity—and characterization—to keep; he gets to be gay instead. The reader learns this before Claudia does, yet not soon enough to forgive novelist Ellis for withholding information to contrive mystery. A tardy revelation of homosexuality doesn't justify a flat portrayal.

Nor is there reason for Ellis to punch her title like a refrain. "Even a sojourn in the flames of purgatory would bring you out cleansed, on the other side of the fire" is followed later by Philip's saying to Claudia at a bonfire, "'I've been on the other side of the fire.'" Marshmallows, not martyrs or witches, roast in this fire. And Claudia doesn't even pass through it but arrives on the other side by passing around it, as though on an excursion through Harrod's, the hem of her red frock barely singed from the exercise. (p. 93)

T. Gertler, "Arms and the Men," in New York Magazine, Vol. 17, No. 41, October 15, 1984, pp. 92-3.

MARCIA PALLY

"On the last day of summer Mrs Bohannon fell in love. The poplars, fallaciously pathetic, looked horrified, their branches rising on the wind like startled hair, and a pilgrim cloud wept a few chill tears. It began in a garden as these things will, and she fell in love with her husband's son."

Sets you right up for a comedy of manners, fleet and self-conscious. Or so you think, through *The Other Side of the Fire*'s first few pages. With such skill at fashioning sentences, Alice Thomas Ellis should be able to address—and undress—any corner of society. And she sets out to do just that, taking as her nook English suburbia, its housewives of the middle class, their traditions, restrictions, and the affairs of their hearts. But she disappoints—and does so by writing too long. While the novel . . . is slight, too many sentences stop long after they should, too many metaphors spin out overly far. Add to that a leading character who is somewhat implausible and a confusion about the author's view of life, and you have a novel with a tendency to veer off course. . . .

When Ellis is on, she makes sharp satire of teapot tempests and chronicles the sort of feminism that grows, unnamed and unidentified, in shady well-kept lanes, while pushing prams or at tea. . . . When Ellis rambles, however, the charm fades. . . .

[One of Ellis's previous books], *The Birds of the Air*, . . . is an ironic foil to *Fire*. Though the satire in her earlier book is more diffuse, it's more consistently on the mark, for Ellis makes her points with just the right number of words. . . . And the humor, too, benefits from Ellis's knowing when to stop. . . .

Run-on paragraphs aside, there are infelicities in *Fire*. Claudia, for one, is so sheltered she's hard to believe. I hear tell that the English provinces have been even less ruffled by feminism than their American counterparts, but Claudia seems not so much a dying breed as a dead one. Upper-middle-class housewives in their forties are savvier. Perhaps more irksome than Claudia's credibility is *Fire*'s point of view. One can't help feeling that Sylvie is Ellis's mouthpiece when she sizes up the gilded-cage aspects of marriage, or the arrogant assumptions of *homo sapien* males, or our silly, willful refusal to recognize that men and women would do better to live apart. But Sylvie is also bored; her detached cynicism removes her so far from human engagements that she hasn't a thing left to do. Well then, perhaps Ellis means to warn us that, while Sylvie's views have their place, sex and love are still the only game in town. Or perhaps she's motioning toward some happy mean between Claudia's dopey domesticity and Sylvie's isolation. A novel is in trouble when you can't quite tell.

Marcia Pally, "'Fire' Signs," in The Village Voice, Vol. XXIX, No. 48, November 27, 1984, p. 56.

ISABEL RAPHAEL

[*Unexplained Laughter*] is, quite simply, brilliant. It will not be to everyone's taste, being dominated by a character who will arouse the same mixture of emotions in readers as she does in the book. But I defy anyone to remain indifferent, or to put down this novel unread. Sir George Sitwell complained that there was always laughter in the next room; Alice Thomas Ellis's *Unexplained Laughter* comes from further away, from the woods beyond the walls of a cottage in Wales in which Lydia, a smart London journalist, has taken refuge after a broken love affair. But it serves to make the same point, that every man's predicament is to be an outsider.

Lydia appears to be the complete insider: witty, glamorous, razor-sharp in her perceptions of other people, she is excellent value at a safe distance from her monstrous egotism. She titillates and teases, but her intelligence sparkles so irresistibly that her victims come back for more: which means more fun for Lydia. Her principal butt is Betty who has forced herself on to Lydia in a mistaken impulse of charity and remains ensnared by the sheer unpredictability of her companion. For Lydia—who normally "plays only with court cards"—Betty's ordinariness is disconcerting. Disinterested kindness is a new experience, not altogether to be relished, especially as Betty seems deaf, when Lydia herself needs reassurance, to the disembodied laughter that excludes even her. . . .

One is not allowed to sit comfortably in Alice Thomas Ellis's world. She enjoys teasing, too (how are non-Welsh outsiders to pronounce the name Beuno?) and every gust of laughter is counterbalanced by a shiver in recognition of the human condition. The book is most elegantly and economically written, and I cannot think of a writer who catches more accurately the flavour of contemporary conversation.

Isabel Raphael, "Gusts of Love and Laughter," in The Times, London, August 22, 1985, p. 9.

RICHARD DEVESON

Unexplained Laughter is very brilliant and more than a bit baffling. The laughter in question emanates from the sides of a numinous Welsh valley . . . , though not everyone can hear it. Dowdy, good-hearted, predictable Betty can't, but Lydia, who is perverse, snobbish, caustic, clever and, we are told, 'attractive' can. The reader is also privy to the inner world of Angharad, a mentally defective girl who roams the hills and is burdened with feelings of deadness and despair. The laughter, and Angharad, subject the self-filled Lydia to a kind of moral or even religious test. But what test? And what is the result?

The two women from London fall in with Angharad's family of dour, secretive North Walians; witty, anarchic conversations rattle along; characters come instantly to life. All this is done with enormous panache. But the problem is the 'attractive' Lydia. Leaving aside the thought that she tries too consciously to be a character (or is she perhaps too consciously a character in an Alice Thomas Ellis novel?), this reader couldn't help willing her, from the second page onwards, to slip up on her moral backside. On the other hand, the humour and drive of the novel spring from, and depend on, approval of her. Yet at the same time the book's point is surely that she is found wanting.

Alice Thomas Ellis's theology—God and Satan, virtue and sin—is only partially explicit here: Angharad and the laughter seem to represent a sense of divinity and life-and-death that is inaudible to Lydia in her wilfulness. But what *has* Lydia heard? If she has heard something, has she deserved to? If she hasn't (not deserving to), why are we meant to like her so much? If we are meant to like her (the devil, after all, having the best jokes), how much does the apparatus of sin and goodness then really count for?

Richard Deveson, "Call of the Wild," in New Statesman, *Vol. 110, No. 2840, August 23, 1985, p. 28.**

HARRIET WAUGH

In her short, edged comedies of human failure in the face of some ultimate good, Alice Thomas Ellis manoeuvres to pit the world against the spirit and then stands back to see which will win. Her stories are domestic in nature, her protagonists often women taking an understandable interest in the oddities they inadvertently manage to collect around themselves. She writes intelligent novels that seem not to take themselves too seriously, and she writes with clarity and wit. I love her.

Unexplained Laughter slots nicely into Alice Thomas Ellis's canon. It is an elusive novel teetering on the edge of comedy but remaining faintly and unexpectedly sombre. Its awful, wise-cracking heroine deserves none of the reader's sympathy but mysteriously wins it. When we think we see what the author is up to, she quietly foils all expectations.

As the novel opens we are given a situation classic in women's fiction: to recuperate from a London love affair Lydia has fled to her cottage in Wales. With her she has brought a managing and rational office acquaintance, Betty, one of those good, irritating people given to vegetables and ethnicism. Betty of course is not pretty and she is invariably straightforward and decent. Lydia, on the other hand, is beautiful, superior, bibulous and quick with the unforgivable funny one-liner while what she thinks is even more extreme. She is willing to mix things up by plunging conversationally headlong where a more cautious and gentler heroine would politely hold back. Far too clever, she wants to have a good time and hates to be bored, no matter by whom. (pp. 24-5)

[She finds a] kindred spirit in Beuno, a priest and the brother of [a dour local] farmer, and it is at this point that you begin to realise that the novel is not only about the conflict of attitudes and behaviour between those who live in the country and the sophisticated and emotionally hardier townees, but also about how a venal and restless intelligence might recognise and feel the call of goodness. The humour of the aptly named Beuno matches Lydia's and through their attraction of minds allows her to glimpse the possibility that goodness might be worth having and even obtainable. They have a love affair of the spirit. . . .

As usual, Alice Thomas Ellis deftly sketches a cast of eccentric characters. The plot consists of a series of static conversational set pieces in which Lydia meets and analyses the miserable farmer, his even more miserable wife, the farmer's wife's disappointed lover, the local doctor, the doctor's silly mistress and the doctor's mistress's sillier parents. . . .

There is the usual highly enjoyable blend of frivolity and seriousness and the aphorisms are very good. The gradual development of a spiritual conflict in Lydia is interesting and her arrogance is justified by an awareness with Beuno of a sense of sin, while the surrounding characters' immersion in their world restricts them inside their own dilemmas, making them inferior beings. In the end, the tension of the novel revolves around the possibility that Lydia will allow Beuno to change her slightly aimless life simply and paradoxically by being himself.

There did, however, seem to me to be one major flaw in the novel: the character of Angharad, the family idiot. She is present in italicised passages throughout the book to serve as a Greek chorus informing the reader about the reality surrounding Lydia, and her voice might have come from the pen of Fay Weldon in some of her less successful passages. This aside, the novel is thoroughly enjoyable even if it is not one of the best that Alice Thomas Ellis has delighted us with. (p. 25)

Harriet Waugh, "A Modern Emma Woodhouse," in
The Spectator, *Vol. 255, No. 8199, August 31, 1985,
pp. 24-5.*

Athol Fugard

1932-

South African dramatist, scriptwriter, novelist, and nonfiction writer.

Fugard is South Africa's foremost dramatist. By combining social protest with a universal concern for humanity, Fugard focuses on victims of apartheid without overtly propagandizing his political beliefs. His plays typically center on a small number of characters drawn from the fringes of South African society and viewed as a microcosm of the country's poor and dispossessed. Although many of Fugard's dramas are considered subversive by the South African government, he insists that his work is "nonpolitical." He sees himself simply as "bearing witness" to the notion that "all human beings are in some sense victims."

Fugard was born in Port Elizabeth, where many of his plays are set. His earliest dramas, *Nongogo* (1957) and *No-Good Friday* (1958), deal with poverty and hopelessness as perpetual aspects of South African existence. *The Blood Knot* (1961), Fugard's first major success, centers on the oscillating sense of conflict and harmony between two half-brothers, one black, the other light-skinned enough to pass for white. In this work, Fugard dramatizes the ambivalent racial hatred which characterizes most South African relations and which has perverted the "blood knot," or common bond of humanity, between its people. Commenting on the play's 1985 revival, Jack Kroll called it "one of the wisest, sweetest, even noblest plays about the balked brotherhood of racism ever written."

The major concerns of Fugard's subsequent dramas are hopelessness, the historical effect of the past on the present, and the individual's search for identity in a country which denies essential human rights. In *Hello and Goodbye* (1965) and *People Are Living There* (1968), Fugard compassionately examines the lives of characters made grotesque by poverty and circumstance. *Boesman and Lena* (1969), an existential drama reminiscent of Samuel Beckett's play *Waiting for Godot,* secured Fugard's reputation as a major dramatist in its story of a homeless couple's aimless wanderings. While Boesman's hatred of the South African political system assumes the form of violence toward his wife, Lena retains her basic humanity and compassion, and both are revealed to be pathetic victims of an unjust design. *Boesman and Lena* received an Obie Award for best foreign play.

Throughout his career Fugard has been a proponent of South African theater, having acted in and directed several of his own plays. In 1962, together with blacks living in a township outside Port Elizabeth, Fugard helped establish the Serpent Players, the first successful nonwhite theater company in South Africa. Fugard's first play for the troupe, *Statements After an Arrest under the Immorality Act* (1972), concerns the discovery by government authorities of a biracial couple's illicit love affair. *Sizwe Bansi Is Dead* (1972) and *The Island* (1974), one-act plays written in collaboration with two black actors from the Serpent Players, Winston Ntshona and John Kani, explore the consequences of apartheid through the personal remembrances of the playwrights. The first play portrays a simple black countryman who attempts to find a job in a city from which blacks

© 1986 Thomas Victor

are officially barred. In the second drama, two men serving sentences in a black political prison rehearse a version of Sophocles' play *Antigone* as a means of solidarity and resistance. Both works received overwhelmingly positive reviews.

The characters and situations of Fugard's recent plays differ radically from those of his early dramas, but his concern with despair, ambivalence, and the struggle between freedom and political restrictions remains consistent. The protagonists of *A Lesson from Aloes* (1979) debate whether to remain true to their political beliefs and face their country's growing racial tension or flee their homeland. The tragicomedy *"Master Harold" . . . and the Boys* (1982) is widely considered one of Fugard's best plays. The drama revolves around Hally, a likable white youth who is angered by the obliviousness of his alcoholic, racist father. In the end, the boy vents his bitterness on Sam, the black servant responsible for his upbringing. *The Road to Mecca* (1984) centers on several days in the life of an eccentric and rebellious old woman who is forced to leave her house for a rest home. According to Graham Leach, the play examines her "struggle to fulfill herself in the midst of bigotry and repressive attitudes."

Fugard has written a number of scripts for film and television. He has created film adaptations for his plays *Boesman and Lena* and *A Lesson from Aloes* and original screenplays for the films *The Guest at Steenkampsraal* and *Marigolds in August*. *Tsotsi* (1980), a novel written early in Fugard's career, foreshadows the themes of his drama in its portrait of a black murderer who is forced to reexamine his lifestyle and acknowledge his human concerns. While some critics found the man's transformation unconvincing, the novel drew largely favorable reviews. Fugard's nonfiction collection *Notebooks: 1960-1977* (1984) reveals the geneses of his plays and theater activities and his reflections on literary, political, and autobiographical topics.

(See also *CLC*, Vols. 5, 9, 14, 25 and *Contemporary Authors*, Vols. 85-88.)

DEREK COHEN

As a dramatist Athol Fugard has been a magnificently creative and dynamic force in South African life. As an eminent local figure his political position has been marked by controversy and ambivalence. The first production of *The Blood Knot* in 1961 sent shock waves through the country. Those who saw the initial performance knew instinctively that something of a revolution had taken place in the stodgily Angloid cultural world of South Africa. A black man and a white man together on stage produced shattering effects as they spoke to and of each other, their lives and, by extension, the lives of all South Africans. Whites, faced baldly with some inescapable truths about what their repressive culture and history had wrought, were compelled to take notice. This was no academic or novelistic description of familiar situations and old facts, but a charged poetic truth powerfully welded into a harrowing public spectacle. The theatre suddenly assumed a significance that few people in South Africa had ever suspected it of possessing.

The play commanded attention, and unquestionably it was treated seriously by English and Afrikaans South Africans alike. But the treatment it received from some quarters of the Afrikaans press cannot have been of a kind to give satisfaction to its author and its non-realistic admirers. The bleakness of its conclusion which demonstrates the deeply rooted hatred of the black world for the white led Afrikaans critics to nod sagely and declare that Fugard's play had poignantly shown the essential truth of apartheid: that black and white can never live together in peace—that racial differences are ultimately insuperable obstacles to real harmony. This opinion of the play's ''message'' has also found support amongst an influential minority of black critics who regard it as a racist work which shows up whites as preservers of civilization and blacks as primitive brutes who think with their fists.

The controversy has been fueled by the fact that Fugard has placed himself in an ambivalent political position by opposing the resolutions of individual playwrights and writers' associations outside of South Africa to refuse permission for their work to be performed in South Africa. The intentions of the boycott, its proponents argue, are to emphasize the illegitimacy of the South African regime and to remind South Africans and the rest of the world that while South Africa continues its policy of apartheid it will remain—in the colorful phrase of a former prime minister—the polecat of the world. (pp. 151-52)

Fugard aroused a storm in 1968 by stating that the boycott ought to be abandoned and that South Africans would be better off if allowed to see these modern works and be exposed to new ideas rather than to continue being shut out from them. Some of the consequences of adopting this stance were a diminution of esteem for Fugard in the eyes of many of the non-South African writers who supported the boycott, the harsh criticism of many of his South African admirers within and without the country, and, for himself, a crucifying dilemma whose outcome he rationalized as follows:

> My point is obvious. Anything that will get people to think and feel for themselves, that will stop them delegating these functions to the politicians, is important to our survival. Theatre has a role to play in this. There is nothing [Prime Minister] John Balthazar Vorster and his cabinet would like more than to keep us isolated from the ideas and values current in the Free Western World. These ideas and values find an expression in the plays of contemporary writers. I think we South Africans should see these plays.

The chief assumption of this belief is, however, open to some cynical questioning. Has the theatre indeed a role to play in opening South Africans' eyes to the world around them, particularly if by this we mean enlightening them about the horror of the lives which they are living? And is the possible enlightenment of a few theatre-goers worth making the regime seem more respectable internationally, which, it can be claimed, the lifting of the boycott would do to some small extent? (p. 152)

[Despite] the controversy about his political stance, Athol Fugard's work in the theatres of South Africa's black community has earned him the respect and admiration of his most hardened critics. If there is one person who has vivified black theatre, who has given hope and experience to black actors, consistent and active support to black theatres, and direction to black drama, it is Athol Fugard. (p. 153)

The view of *The Blood Knot* as a racist work ignores the fact that the political reality of the drama is a result of the permeating presence of the world outside the shack in which the brothers live. The play is specifically about the hatred which South African life feeds on. It is indeed true that Zach is crude and unlettered and that in the last climactic scene he tries to kill his brother Morrie because Morrie is white. But the play also makes clear that Morrie, who as a white has had his mother's love and many of the opportunities that being white in South Africa provides, hates the white world with an intensity equal to his brother's and sees that *it* has divided them. Zach, on the other hand, has had to contend through his life with poverty, oppression, and the fear and detestation of the white world. His murderous rage is provoked by the mutual decision of the brothers to embark on a dangerous game in which each agrees to assume the *typical* role which South African law assigns them. For purposes of the game they are no longer brothers, but black man and white man meeting by chance in a lonely park where Zach, as in daily life, has to guard the gate against the entrance of the contaminating presence of black South Africans. (pp. 154-55)

The absurdity of the play's central notion—that two brothers, sons of the same mother, can be legally classified as black and white—is explained only by the insanity of South Africa's racial laws according to which one's race is determined by the racial group that accepts one as its members. Morrie had a white father and is light skinned and so is able to pass as a white man. He is driven back into his brother's life by a detestation of the white world and a sense of guilt at having abandoned the world into which he was born. His nagging, cautious, nervous presence has deprived Zach of the few pleasures which he had formerly enjoyed. With his dreamy and unrealistic plans for a future life for them both in another country and his niggling determination to save Zach's meagre wages to enable them to escape, Morrie has sapped Zach's vital energy, extinguished his passion. Through a variety of games designed to alleviate the boring routine of Zach's life, Morrie hopes to distract his brother from his immediate and urgent hopes for drink and sex by mesmerizing him with promises of future repose and by offering, as alternatives, the sometimes jejune fantasies of freedom and of past happiness. And Morrie has the power of articulation, a power which, the play shows, can drive passions into neat and descernible corners. Morrie has, in an unconsciously cruel way, made Zach his dependant. (p. 155)

Hello and Goodbye and *People are Living There,* dramas about South Africa's poor whites, are plays of grim poignancy which add an essential dimension to Fugard's obsession with familial relationships. In *Hello and Goodbye* a brother and sister, meeting after years of separation, confront their past with relentless and honest hatred. The sister, a prostitute in Johannesburg, has returned home to get her hands on a share of her father's disability compensation. At the end of the play, learning that her father has been dead for some time and that there is no money, she returns to Johannesburg defeated and desolate, numbly prepared to resume her life as "a woman in a room." The cruel despair that characterizes the lives of Hester and Johnnie and the passionless resignation to mere continuance—survival in its most crushing form—is similar in tonal effect to the conclusion of *The Blood Knot. People are Living There* examines loneliness and its devasting effects on four harrassed characters in a shabby Johannesburg boarding house. By a series of scarifying events in their lives the characters are propelled into wounding confrontations with themselves and each other emerging finally intact and more clearly knowing and understanding themselves.

Boesman and Lena, possibly the finest of Fugard's plays, is an eloquent reminder that the ultimate value of a work of art is the depth and passion of its conviction: that when its structure and style have ceased to elude or interest us we are compelled to recall that the quality that transfixes us and thus keeps the work alive at its very center is its emotional truth. This play, which so movingly and palpably captures the essential cruelty of South African life and distils the effect of that cruelty into one protracted cry of rage and pain, has the far larger result of flinging before us the unavoidable perception that the despair we are made to witness is a creation of Western civilization itself. This is the world of pass laws, of institutionalized racialism, of Group Areas acts, but it is also undeniably something more: Boesman, Lena, and the nameless old African are the world's refuse, its poorest refugees; and the fact that creatures like these exist at the passive permission of creatures like ourselves is a constant and disquieting fact.

The crenellated emotional pattern of *Boesman and Lena* in which the moods alternate between expressions of overwhelming grief and white-hot hatred make the play one of modern drama's completest expressions of despair. Gone are the lyrical bursts of nostalgia which occasionally saw light in the earlier works. This is drama of unrelieved and immitagable suffering. And the suffering is the more intense as the characters, impotent against the civilization of which they are the outcasts, turn their

fury against each other. In this way savage emotions are released as the lines of authority are shown to depend on brute strength and skin color. The shantytown in which Boesman and Lena have lived is plowed out from under them by white men with bulldozers and they have to move on. Lena, who is tied to Boesman by hatred, habit, and a lack of choice, is subservient to him because she is physically the weaker. The moribund black man is victimized by Boesman because—in a cruel parody of South African racism—he is black while Boesman is a lighter-skinned Cape Colored. With the perverse moral authority of a Thersites, and authority born of the searing combination of perpetual suffering and clear vision, Boesman inveighs against his world and wreaks the revenge on it which is accorded the impotent by physically brutalizing his even more pitiful adherents. (pp. 157-58)

Fugard's attitude to playwriting underwent a major change in 1970 after encounters with the ideas of Joe Chaikin and Jerzy Grotowski who, he believes, helped him articulate two concerns which had nagged him for years: escape from the tyranny of the text and the santification of the actor. These notions crystallized in his *Orestes.* . . . The play, a cooperative venture between Fugard—the writer and director—and his actors, takes its form from the image created by an incident in 1964 when John Harris in a violent protest against apartheid took a bomb into the Johannesburg station concourse. The bomb killed an old woman and Harris was caught, tortured, tried, and hanged. The dramatization of the event, along lines suggested by Grotowski, revealed to Fugard a new dimension which the theatrical experience was able to express, "just how pristine, what weight you gave to a line, a word, a gesture, if you set it in silence." For Fugard this play remains one of his most significant theatrical experiences and still stands as his "Most extreme excursion into a new type of theatre experience, in which we attempted to communicate with our audience on the basis of . . . an entirely new vocabulary."

The experience of *Orestes* profoundly influenced Fugard's later work [included in *Statements: Two Workshop Productions*] in suggesting the potential for creative and individual expression of the actor. At no point did the actor supplant the writer, and the text always remained superordinate if malleable. *Sizwe Bansi is Dead* and *The Island* were devised by Fugard and the two original actors who took part, John Kani and Winston Ntshona; the third play *Statements After an Arrest Under the Immorality Act* [also included in the volume] is by Fugard alone. Each of the works deals with a specific aspect of the South Africa's race laws and examines their effects on individuals. In *Sizwe Bansi is Dead* (the name Sizwe Bansi, incidentally, is reminiscent of a revolutionary movement crushed by the police in the early 1960's *Umkonto We Sizwe,* or the Spear of the Nation) the action centers upon the infamous pass laws of South Africa which, as this drama shows, are designed to keep the authorities in full control and knowledge of the movements of the African labor force. . . . *The Island,* like *The Blood Knot,* is a play of brotherhood, which illuminates the lives and hopes of two men sharing a cell on Robben Island, South Africa's notorious gaol for black political prisoners: its action centers on preparations by the two for a production of *Antigone* before the other prisoners. *Statements After an Arrest* as its title indicates, is about a black man and white woman trapped by the police in the act of lovemaking. (pp. 158-59)

[In his] early plays Fugard treated apartheid as an utterly pervasive but implicit fact of life. They were about the effects of the system on the living of his characters. Here he takes the single and actual facts of apartheid as the central motivating forces in his characters' lives. He writes in **Sizwe Bansi** about the ways in which people contend with the pass laws and the curtailment of freedom which these laws dictate. This is a drama primeordinately about survival under a system which seeks to deprive individual human beings of the right to affront their own destinies or to define their own existences: the pass book proves that you are who *they* say you are; and the play comes to grips with the question of survival under this condition. Underlying the bitter problem that the circumstance creates is, surprisingly, a hard deposit of comedy as the characters, with a crude accuracy, make an acid mockery of the grotesque fatuities by which apartheid attempts to dominate their spirits. Their satirical awareness of their relationships to their masters makes clear that in this, at least, apartheid has failed. (p. 159)

The Island as courageously and explicitly treats the matter of political divisions within the country. The use of *Antigone* as a relevant political image of South Africa is a brilliantly appropriate device through which the questions of political resistance in their moral and active forms are identified. . . . [The] prison cell with its two strong inmates becomes a glistening image of freedom, especially in its concluding scene where the enactment of *Antigone* reduces the larger political concerns of the play to the essentially human one of defiance and death. The play's final statement takes the form of an eloquent gesture of rebellion as the two men chained together make an obviously futile but incalculably brave attempt to run.

Nowhere is the heartbreaking irrationality of South African life more vividly manifested than in its anti-miscegenation laws. In **Statements After an Arrest Under the Immorality Act** Fugard explores the destruction of humanity wrought by the imposition of just one of the stifling laws of apartheid. While the ostensible subject of this play is a sexual relationship between a Cape Colored schoolteacher and a white librarian, by fully illuminating the monstrous complexities of the affair and the implications of the affair in the South African setting, Fugard creates a total image of the flinty cruelty of South Africa's institutionalized racialism. The play is exquisitely structured with the passionate, proud, and shameful "statements" of the couple given added impetus by the counterpointing statements of the arresting officer which are uttered in bland official tones. By use of flash sequences, Fugard intersperses the policeman's dutiful recital of the details of the arrest between the lover's agonized expressions of defeat and bewilderment; these expressions reveal their awareness of the danger of their love, the inevitability of it, the damnable obstacles that the law places in their way, and the concomitant need for caution and readiness for flight. (pp. 160-61)

Each of the three plays in **Statements** is a distillation of the larger tragedy daily enacted in South Africa. They scrutinize with devastating accuracy the crushing effects of systematized racism to the lives of their characters. And in this way they enlighten us all. Pain and suffering cease to be mere words but compassionately and complexly take on the real and true shapes of human beings trapped eternally in their pitiless vise. The maelstrom of wretchedness never manages completely to engulf the spirit which—sometimes in spite of itself—by its nature resists the tyrannical force. If there is an element of hopefulness in Fugard's work it is in this bursting spiritual power that strives continuously to assert itself and to prove, time and again, that life is here; that oppression and despotism notwithstanding, while there is life there is also strength. And, not

least, there is the strength to suffer. In leaving us with such recognitions Fugard demonstrates his virtues as an artist. He is the poet of pain for our times, making of the pain of his small but vital world a rich and varied truth about existence. (p. 161)

> Derek Cohen, "Drama and the Police State: Athol Fugard's South Africa," in Canadian Drama/L'Art dramatique canadien, *Vol. 6, No. 1, Spring, 1980, pp. 151-61.*

RICHARD EDER

Visiting his father in hospital, Athol Fugard kept his writer's eye on the other old patients as well. An Afrikaner, shrunken and half-delirious, mumbled out a childhood memory of pinning down a recalcitrant colored farm worker until his father could come along and beat him. Later, when both were old, the colored man would come up and ask him for money for a drink; "and when I had it I gave it to him."

What did the dying white man remember?, Fugard reflects. Not his wife or children but a figure who held him more deeply. "Two images," he jots down in his notebooks. "The colored man—ultimate degradation after the pride of his youth. The white man—his loneliness."

That duality runs through Fugard's writing. The blacks and coloreds of South Africa struggle against the arbitrary prods and bars that hold them down; and in doing so they have evolved a varied and affecting humanity. The white's order is an imprisoning solitude that drains him. In Fugard's plays, the black world *is* the world, except that there is a dragon that claws and tilts it, and turns it upside down. Fugard does not so much denounce the dragon as inhabit it, and convey its bleak compulsion to dominate.

Degradation and loneliness. It is a binary sensibility but in art, as in computers, worlds are made out of the simple beat of two alternates. Fugard, one of the finest English-language playwrights of his 50-year-old generation, and arguably the most powerful, has driven himself so deeply into a local theme that he has made it universal. It is an achievement that carries its own pain. . . .

"The sense I have of myself is that of a 'regional' writer with the themes, textures, acts of celebration, of defiance and outrage that go with the South African experience. These are the only things I have been able to write about."

The two sentences are quoted in the editor's introduction to [**Notebooks: 1960-1977**]. They are a record of some of his most fertile years, and they are stunning. During the 1960s Fugard was wrestling with his life, with the love and bitterness he feels for his misshapen country, and with problems of conscience and creation. His notebooks are the most vivid possible picture of an artist striving to shape his material even as it was detonating around him.

Fugard is at once a private poet and a public man of the theater; engaged simultaneously in shaping a black theater company against tremendous odds, in absorbing the lessons of his segregated society and in hammering out his own theatrical forms.

He is not a "social" playwright; he regards the work of such writers as Arthur Miller and Lorraine Hansberry as useful but superficial. His masters are Beckett and Camus and, as his notebooks reveal, he struggles to achieve something more than reportage, or the kind of artistic work that leaves an audience feeling comfortable with itself after a limited harrowing. . . .

But the notebooks are much more than an extraordinary exemplar of a writer's journal. They are an illuminating, painful and beguiling record of a life lived in one of those tortured societies where everything refers back, sooner or later, to the situation that torments it. (p. 3)

> Richard Eder, *"Delving Beneath the Cruelty and Bitterness in South Africa,"* in Los Angeles Times Book Review, *April 8, 1984, pp. 3, 5.*

J. M. COETZEE

[*Notebooks: 1960-1977*] are the record of eighteen years of Athol Fugard's creative life. . . . They trace the impact of day-to-day events upon him, the slow process by which kernels of truth crystallize from memories, and the sometimes halting and painful growth of his plays out of these kernels. As a record of the inner experiences of a self-aware and articulate creative consciousness, they are of absorbing interest. . . . (p. 25)

The *Notebooks* are, however, more than this. They are also the autobiography of a man of intelligence and conscience who chose to remain in South Africa at a time when many fellow writers were opting for (or being forced into) exile. This choice meant, among other things, that Fugard would live among those juxtaposed scenes of placid comfort and desperate poverty that belong to present-day South Africa, and so continually be brought face to face with the question of his relationship with a ruling order characterized by a remarkably loveless attitude toward its subjects (or some of them), an attitude of lovelessness that sometimes extends to atrocious callousness. Fugard's pleasure in the beauty of South Africa, and particularly of the eastern Cape coast where he lives . . . is therefore repeatedly subverted by "the nausea brought on by reading the newspapers," by bouts of "dumb and despairing rage at what we are doing." This revulsion leads in turn to doubts about the value of his art, which seems to be founded on material privilege, to be personal in its nature, to be only ambivalently committed to tangible political goals. The question of how to commit himself without losing his identity as an artist becomes a central preoccupation of the notebook entries of the mid-1960s. "The horror of what this government and its policies have done to people . . . has built up such an abyss of hatred that at times . . . I [have] been quite prepared to take the jump and destroy—but, so far, . . . the company of executioners remains loathesome," he writes in 1968. "I can't think of any moral dilemma more crucifying than this one." (pp. 25-6)

The route he follows out of his crisis of conscience is to take upon himself (following Sartre) the task of *bearing witness*. . . . [This means loving] the insignificant, the forgotten, the unloved. Against a system whose own degradation he measures by the degradations it imposes on others (at one point he goes further and suggests that the ultimate and unwitting victims of a regime of degradation are its perpetrators), Fugard opposes an ethic of love. "South Africa's tragedy is the small, meagre portions of love in the hearts of the men who walk this beautiful land." "People must be loved." . . . "What is Beauty? The result of love. The ugliness of the unloved thing."

This program of witness and love is carried out from a position which Fugard explicitly—at least in the early 1960s—identifies with that of Camus's Stranger, or Outsider. . . . Although the outsider status that he . . . assumes comes under considerable

stress as pressure mounts upon him from the left to engage himself politically (or rather, since Fugard's art *is* an engaged art, to allow the terms of his engagement to be determined for him by the political struggle), he never really deserts it, partly because it allows him the autonomy he needs as a writer, partly because it gives definition to his persistent sense of himself as "not 'really' belonging, of being a 'stranger,'" no matter how much he sometimes wishes to become a "subscriber." . . .

Camus is only the chief in a long roll of intellectual influences charted in the *Notebooks*. From his cottage at Schoenmakerskop, Fugard kept well abreast of intellectual currents: there are notes on Faulkner and Kazantzakis and Robbe-Grillet, Brecht and Genet, Pound and Lowell and Pasternak, Jung and Laing and the Zen thinkers, all of whom can be shown either to have helped him define his own position or to have pointed him in new directions.

The most absorbing pages of the *Notebooks* are those in which Fugard explores the currents of his own creativity and the genesis and unfolding of his plays. "I've always known that in my writing it is the dark troubled sea [of the unconscious], of which I know nothing, save its presence, that [has] carried me," he writes. . . .

Insofar as the *Notebooks* make clear a method or pattern in Fugard's playwriting, it is one of worrying for months and sometimes years at a subject, often a subject suggested by a real-life encounter, until the image, the kernel out of which the play will eventually grow, emerges with "a life of its own, a truth bigger than itself." Much of the book is devoted to recording the quest for these images of "truth . . . [which] when it comes, flashes back like lightning, through all that [has] preceded it."

Of his poetics, Fugard writes: "I strive quite consciously and deliberately for ambiguity of expression. . . . My whole temperament inclines me to be very unequivocal indeed. That is not difficult—but it would be at the cost of truth." "Darkness is . . . an essential help to the truly poetic image." Made in 1969-70, these statements serve to remind us of how strenuously Fugard has striven to deploy the poetics of Modernism over a field that might seem to belong only to Social Realism; this deployment, when it is successfully achieved, is what gives his work its uniqueness. (p. 26)

There is less about theater, and about Fugard's experience in theater in Britain and the United States, than admirers of his plays might expect. The main reason is that the *Notebooks* were written in South Africa during spells of privacy; gaps in the chronology mark his absences abroad. But the *Notebooks* do record the excitement and disappointments of his work with black theater groups in the Port Elizabeth townships, thoughts on the staging of his plays, records of conversations with the actors John Kani and Yvonne Bryceland, and comments on the nature of theater that illuminate his own creative practice. Thus: "One of the reasons . . . why I write for the stage . . . [is] the Carnal Reality of the actor in space and time. Only a fraction of my truth is in the words." (p. 27)

[Editor] Mary Benson has supplemented the *Notebooks* with several pages of useful notes and a glossary of South African terms. By and large these are adequate, though Benson is mistaken in thinking that the Afrikaans verb *moer* has anything to do with murder. There also seem to have been misreadings of Fugard's text. Eliot did not write a poem called "The Rack," nor is it likely that Fugard called Beckett and Ionesco "absurdities."

One is hardly entitled to criticize a writer for what he has chosen to write or not write about in his private notebooks. Nevertheless, there are points at which one wishes Fugard had pushed his thinking an inch or two further. The notion of the natural dignity of all life, most of all human life, is a keystone of Fugard's thought. At the heart of the evil of white *Herrschaft* in South Africa, in Fugard's view, is its desire not only to use the black man as a tool for its own material gain, but to strip him of all dignity in the process. The ruling order has thus literally become an *order of degradation:* no black man finds a place in society till he has passed the rite of being "taught a lesson" and abased. I have no quarrel with such an analysis, as far as it goes. But Fugard, not an Afrikaner, is close enough to the Afrikaner to know that the humiliation of the weak by the strong has been a characteristic practice of the Afrikaner within his own culture, a practice underpinned by a perhaps perverted reading of Scripture which gives inordinate emphasis to authority and its converse, abasement.... There are many authoritarian societies on earth, but Afrikanerdom strikes one as a society in which castration is allotted a particularly blatant role. Fugard knows the castrating urge behind South African *baasskap*, knows that the castrated, the unloved, usually takes his place at the forefront of the castrators. Does he guess, too, that in probing the apparently peripheral phenomenon of humiliation he is coming close to the heart of the beast? It would be interesting to know.

From the fact that the *Notebooks* begin to tail off after 1973 we may infer that Fugard's impulse to keep this form of diary has waned, and that there will be no second volume. We must therefore take what we have as a record of a phase in Fugard's life that has closed, a phase in which, in a spirit of total engagement, he searched in daily experience and in books for the germs of truth. Even the reader only sketchily familiar with Fugard's plays will find it an absorbing experience to follow him on his search. (pp. 27-8)

> *J. M. Coetzee, "Art and Apartheid," in* The New Republic, *Vol. 190, No. 14, April 9, 1984, pp. 25-8.*

JACK KROLL

What makes Athol Fugard a true conscience of South Africa is that his plays transform political issues into flesh and blood. He's done that again in his new play, *The Road to Mecca*.... [On the surface it] doesn't seem to be a political play at all. It's about a rather dotty old widow who makes strange sculptures, her young schoolteacher friend and the local *dominee* (pastor). But the play concerns love and freedom, and for Fugard that is the germ cell of the South African problem....

Unusually, for Fugard, the three characters in *The Road to Mecca* are all white. But in different ways they're victims of an emotional apartheid. In the 15 years since her husband died, Helen's only fulfillment has come from creating the bizarre sculptures—peacocks, pyramids, camels, mermaids—that stand outside her little house in the Great Karoo, a bleak semi-desert area. The sculptures, made from cement, rusty wire and glass, make up a complete world that the local Afrikaner community finds disturbing, even blasphemous. Now Marius, the pastor, is trying to persuade Helen to agree to enter a home for the aged, and Elsa has driven a long way to persuade the desperate and confused Helen to resist.

What seems merely an exotic anecdote becomes in Fugard's hands a complex and moving exploration of the struggle between freedom and necessity. Helen, called flippantly by Elsa

"a genuine Karoo nut case," turns out to be the "first truly free spirit" that the younger woman has ever known. Marius, behind his mask of concern for the aging and infirm Helen, sees her as a threat to the rigid Calvinism of the Afrikaner spirit, the same spirit that is crushing Elsa's attempts to teach principles of equality to her pupils. To make matters more complicated—and human—it's clear that Marius loves Helen and that his attempt to put her away is an attempt to stifle his own impulses toward freedom.

These tensions build and explode in a masterfully crafted crescendo that never loses its warmth, intimacy and even humor. In his *Notebooks,* Fugard says: "I am all my characters." Most of his plays are probings of his own divided nature, which sees his country both as a moral desert and as the wellspring of his humanity. In *The Road to Mecca* Fugard subjects himself to merciless triple fission: he is the balked rebel Elsa, the iconoclastic artist Helen and the Calvinist Marius. Fugard, quite possibly the most powerful living dramatist after Samuel Beckett (his own hero), has succeeded in turning his own inner conflict into a drama that's both particular and universal. (p. 85)

> *Jack Kroll, "Love and Freedom in the Karoo," in* Newsweek, *Vol. CIII, No. 22, May 28, 1984, pp. 85-6.*

DAVID CAUTE

[*Notebooks: 1960-1977*] will undoubtedly serve as a sourcebook for seminars and theses devoted to Mr. Fugard and the renaissance of South African theater.... But these episodic, sometimes fragmentary jottings are devoid of self-consciousness and personal laundry lists; what they describe is the growth of a talent, a sensibility, rather than the personality in which it is wrapped. The impact of Sartre, Malraux, Camus, Beckett and Brecht on the "raw" South African is excitingly charted, yet one gains little sense of what it would be like to work with Athol Fugard....

Mr. Fugard writes better of life than of literature, whether his subject is local street fights, the black docker who lost his toes but couldn't get medical attention, the hellish degradation of imprisonment on Robben Island, the friends who got caught up in political trials, the elation of performance. The grinding poverty and racial discrimination of South Africa are captured in these pages not by exposition or rhetoric, but with a playwright's grasp of the concepts, the tactile, the specific—the physical details which secrete a truth larger than themselves....

Of Mr. Fugard's sources of inspiration as writer, actor and director we learn a great deal. When he is asked by his wife why he prefers to write plays, rather than poetry or prose, he searches for an authentic answer and concludes that he is fascinated by the "living moment", the flesh, blood and sweat of the stage, the human voice and "real time." And beyond that there lies a more complex dialectic, the subject-object relationship of actor and audience.

Frequently passages in these notebooks pass from observations of people known to Mr. Fugard into sudden bursts of imaginative "plotting," the emergence of fictional scenarios some of which later became plays and others of which remained stillborn jottings incapable of fulfillment. The plays most thoroughly explored in these pages are *The Blood Knot* and *Boesman and Lena;* clearly Mr. Fugard lives with and through his plays in the most obsessional way....

But what of the sporting and cultural boycott of South Africa, always a major issue among British playwrights? The issue boiled up in 1968 when Mr. Fugard distressed such writers as Harold Pinter, John Osborne and David Mercer by changing his mind and coming to the conclusion that a cultural boycott would in fact serve the interests of Prime Minister John Vorster and his Cabinet, who wanted nothing so much as to isolate South Africa from subversive Western ideas. On the other hand how could one allow one's play to be performed before racially segregated audiences? Mr. Fugard described the moral dilemma as ''crucifying'' and refused to take refuge in easy postures. He is a man who works at life just as he works at his art in a steady pursuit of what is true and right.

> David Caute, ''Through the Fire of Apartheid,'' in The New York Times Book Review, *June 3, 1984, p. 42.*

RUSSELL VANDENBROUCKE

Excerpts from [*Notebooks: 1960-1977*] were first published in a South African newspaper in 1966. Other brief selections have appeared in literary and theatrical journals and, especially, in the introductions to Fugard's plays. . . .

Fugard states, ''Though I never consciously used the notebooks as a playwright, everything is reflected there—my plays come from life and from encounters with actual people. But I found that as soon as I got deeply involved with writing a play, I either forgot the notebooks completely or had no need of them.'' The first entry is a pithy outline of what would become *The Blood Knot;* shortly thereafter Fugard made notes on what would become his only published novel, *Tsotsi.* This pair of entries is anomalous for several reasons: Fugard worked on the two projects simultaneously, the only time he has ever done so; he began work on them shortly after making the entries, whereas incidents, characters, and images for plays have often germinated for years, even decades; and, the entries were made outside South Africa, either in London or on the ship on his way back home. (p. 43)

Fugard may not use the notebooks ''consciously'' as a playwright, but the record of past impressions and incidents has often served as a catalyst to his imagination or as a reminder of dramatic possibilities. In June of 1968 he decided to take up the story of Boesman and Lena: ''Why? Just by accident, paging back through this notebook, the entries in October 1967. Plus a sudden realization of how lacking I am in tolerance towards Sheila. These made me see Boesman and Lena as being the story of Sheila and myself—knowing it, the situation, without any desperate dependence on myth-making or imagination, a reality of my life as if Morrie and Zach (*The Blood Knot*) were myself and Royal (Fugard's brother): Johnnie and his father (*Hello and Goodbye*), myself and mine.'' The connection Fugard makes between Boesman and Lena and his own marriage must not be perceived as a directly autobiographical correlation, but as an imaginative one that helped inform the specifics in his story of two Coloured itinerants. (pp. 43-4)

Sometimes the notebooks reveal Fugard through what they omit. There is, for example, no reference to the revocation of his passport and the fact that he could not leave South Africa for four years. Similarly, there are no complaints about money or hardship, except by implication. (p. 45)

Throughout the notebooks Fugard reveals, in only a few words, the principles that define his dramaturgy: ''I am very conscious

of the 'Image' in playwriting. My new play [*People Are Living There*] was generated by one such image: 'Milly is unnerved at finding herself still in her nightclothes from the previous night.'' Virtually all of his plays have developed from just such a concrete particular rather than from an idea, a theme, or a detailed story line. Fugard also anticipates the actual structure (and weakness) of plays such as *A Lesson from Aloes* and *Road to Mecca* when he writes about *The Blood Knot:* ''We all know that our story only gets under way after interval.'' However, having articulated to himself certain principles of his craft and structure, Fugard soon distrusts them: ''Dissatisfied and suspicious of what I feel is a 'stock' pattern, a 'formula' which I seem to have used in all my plays so far, i.e. *growing desperation* leading to *emotional crisis* leading to the *leap*.'' (pp. 45-6)

Fugard is not absorbed merely with himself and his own writing. A dozen or so entries contain succinct critiques of what he has recently read or seen on stage. Most of these date to 1962 and 1963 at the beginning of his career when, perhaps, he was both impressionable and anxious to compare the quality of his writing with that of others. For example, Fugard finds the final statement of Lorraine Hansberry's *A Raisin in the Sun* comfortable: ''The audience will leave feeling good and this makes me enormously suspicious. Not because making an audience uncomfortable is my aim, but because a man dreaming, or wanting, is the most painfully beautiful thing I know.'' John Donne, however, is deeply admired: ''Sincerity, discipline, at times harsh, even brutal—all that is opposed to the morass of sentiment. Excellent instruction.'' T. S. Eliot fails to appreciate fully the role of poetry in drama: ''Beckett is a greater poet in the 'theatre' than he (Eliot) has been or ever will be. Eliot goes on and on about blank-verse as if the poetic imagination in playwriting must drag this ball and chain. That is surely one of Beckett's greatest discoveries—that we can free the poetic imagination of this dead weight.''

Beckett is highly revered. After reading *Malone Dies,* Fugard notes: ''Hard to describe what this book, like his *Godot, Krapp* and *Endgame,* did to me. Moved? Horrified? Depressed? Elated? Yes, and excited. I wanted to start writing again the moment I put it down.'' . . . (p. 47)

A second major influence is Camus, the writer most frequently mentioned in the notebooks. Fugard may have made a personal connection with the man—another writer of European nationality transplanted to Africa, nurtured by the sun, beside the sea—but most of all he responds to the writing. . . . The notebooks of both Fugard and Camus also speak the same language as they focus upon man's search for intelligibility and consciousness. . . .

The sensibility of Athol Fugard revealed in his notebooks is not essentially different from that implied in his plays. However, the discontinuous and eclectic nature of a notebook allows the reader to focus, primarily, on the sheer quality of the writing. Because there is so little mention here of the racial politics of South Africa, one presumes it is simply a given element of his life as, indeed, it is in his plays—not *the* subject, but a means to explore the universal struggle of all men for meaning, dignity, and community.

It is obvious from his plays that Fugard has mastered stagecraft, that he knows how to create wonderfully palpable characters, and that he embraces mankind even while revealing the evil of man to man (that is, the malevolence within each of us). What the discrete entries of the notebooks reveal is, simply, the sheer beauty of Fugard's language, images, and perceptions as well as his ability to penetrate the onion layers that often cloak the essence of a person, a place, a received idea. Regardless of one's knowledge of Fugard's plays, or even one's interest in them, the notebooks are a fine book of and about writing. (p. 48)

Russell Vandenbroucke, "In Dialogue with Himself: Athol Fugard's 'Notebooks'," in Theater, *Vol. XVI, No. 1, Fall-Winter, 1984, pp. 43-8.*

GRAHAM LEACH

It was while visiting a friend in New Bethesda that Fugard came across the story of Helen Niemand, an eccentric widow who, until her death, constructed bizarre cement statues in the garden of her small house and filled her home with candles, whose light was reflected in complex arrangements of glittering glass.

Helen was an Afrikaner woman who, many years earlier, had rejected the conventions of the Dutch Reformed Church and had sought salvation in her own creativity. Her fellow villagers regarded her as not a little mad. Helen Niemand's story, or rather one critical day toward the end of her life, is the subject of *The Road to Mecca*. The day in question sees her in the depths of despair, unable to find the inspiration to embark upon new creative ventures, confronted by the realisation that having rejected the world around her, her own world is but transitory and that darkness is creeping in upon her. . . .

The Road to Mecca is about Helen's struggle to fulfill herself in the midst of bigotry and repressive attitudes. The play lives and breathes small-town life in the middle of the outback and, without engaging in polemics, tells us much about the predicament of South Africa.

And yet, in the arduous journey that Helen undertakes towards her Mecca, the play is universal. It is about the loneliness of the individual and about mankind's ability to consume and destroy if allowed to do so. In its agonising over the plight of the human spirit, *The Road to Mecca* is almost Chekhovian. I was not the only member of the first-night audience to feel that the play's many layers called for a second viewing. . . .

The Road to Mecca is, without question, a major piece of theatre and has received wide acclaim here. Its depth and searing intensity betray a work which was clearly for its writer a cathartic experience. Many people here believe it may well end up being judged Fugard's finest work, and that, by definition, means the finest work to have come out of South Africa.

Graham Leach, "Finding Mecca in the Outback," in The Listener, *Vol. 112, No. 2888, December 13, 1984, p. 20.*

BENEDICT NIGHTINGALE

Miss Helen, as the protagonist [of *The Road to Mecca*] is called, really existed. She was the village eccentric in remote New Bethesda, where Fugard still lives, an elderly recluse who filled her garden with owls, giant heads and other whimsical statuary of her own invention. Eventually she became, in Fugard's own words, 'very paranoid, very depressed', and one night she killed herself in a remarkably painful way, by burning out her stomach with caustic soda.

But something untoward has happened between that life and this play. One doesn't think of Fugard as a sentimental writer, yet there's a wishfulness and even a blandness in *Mecca* which, were you not hastily to remind yourself of the many gritty plays to his credit, might tempt you so to categorise him. That paranoia, that suicide are ignored. Instead, we've the tale of a docile old widow and her young friend, a teacher who treks up from Capetown to attest to her 'beautiful, light-filled, glittering' life, to stop her being packed off to a 'Sunshine Home for the Aged' by the pious busybodies on the local Church Council and, finally, to emphasise the potency of love and trust. (p. 30)

Several times, it seemed to me that the characters and their feelings were the product less of human observation, more of their author's desire to write an emotionally and morally rousing play; but I should add that many of those sitting around me, indeed standing and applauding beside me, took a different view. . . . People evidently found more truth and resonance than I in [Fugard's] defiant defence of 'free spirit', seeing an ecstatic visionary where I could spot only a sweet and shy old lady, an imaginative assault on Afrikaaner conformism where I found only an amateur sculptor frustratingly loth actually to show us her work. They were moved by Miss Helen, and they presumably found her friend's frustrations and pains, her love affair with a married man, her abortion, her anguished encounter with an archetype of suffering Africa named 'Patience', more plausible than [I]. . . . (pp. 30-1)

Yet there was one character on whose truth and interest we could all agree, and an unexpected one, since the play's scheme had cast him in or near the role of the villain. That's the pastor who comes to save Miss Helen from a hobby he finds faintly diabolical and closet her away in a clean Christian institution. As Fugard writes . . . him, he's narrow and domineering and, it seems, more concerned for his conscience than his parishioner's welfare; he's also thoughtful and caring and, it seems, at least as concerned for her welfare as his conscience. This is the upright, conservative Afrikaaner seen in the only way that's useful, in the round, from his own point of view as much as from that of the liberal outsider.

For a moment and rather a long moment, Fugard is at his unsentimental, understanding best; and then, alas, the moment passes. The pastor, her friend decides, is really in love with Miss Helen, a revelation I found neither credible nor touching nor anything very much else.

Somehow it seemed to diminish, even cheapen an impressive character. That fascinating demonstration of the large-mindedness of the small-minded turns out, after all, to be scarcely more than the expression of one man's romantic itch, the yearning of a lonely Mills and Boon hero for a forlorn Mills and Boon heroine. I wish I could say that this false note was an isolated one, but I can't. It seems to me all too characteristic of as exasperatingly uneven, as unreal and real a play as Fugard has ever yet penned. (p. 31)

Benedict Nightingale, "Sweetmeat," in New Statesman, *Vol. 109, No. 2816, March 8, 1985, pp. 30-1.**

JACK KROLL

Almost 25 years ago a play was put on in a small room in an office building in Johannesburg, South Africa. There were two actors, a young white man named Athol Fugard (who was also the author) and a young black man named Zakes Mokae. . . .

A hundred people, black and white (mixed audiences were allowed only in such private performances), crowded into the room. . . . The play, *The Blood Knot,* was about two brothers, one black, one light-skinned. It propelled Fugard on a career that has made him one of the world's leading playwrights and a voice of conscience in his tormented country. . . . Now these colleagues and friends of 25 years are again performing *The Blood Knot,* in an anniversary production. . . . Against the present background of violence in South Africa, the play has taken on an aura of prophecy that makes it more shattering than ever. . . .

[Zachariah and Morris] are like two tattered clowns of heartbreak, arguing over the best salts for a foot bath, feeling their loveless state by watching two donkeys copulating, reliving a youthful joy ride when they drove their jalopy into a sudden swarm of butterflies, lashing out at each other with hapless savagery, accepting their brotherhood without a future. *The Blood Knot* is one of the wisest, sweetest, even noblest plays about the balked brotherhood of racism ever written.

> Jack Kroll, "South African Prophecy," in News-week, *Vol. CVI, No. 15, October 7, 1985, p. 95.*

FRANK RICH

The most persistent sound in Athol Fugard's *Blood Knot* is the harsh ringing of a windup alarm clock, blaring insistently into the tranquillity of a tin-roofed hovel. The clock is the means by which the shack's occupants, two mixed-race brothers in South Africa, mark the passing of their dreary, unvaried days. But the ring also has a piercing urgency, as if it were sounding an alarm far beyond the walls of the shabby setting. One might say—even if the playwright never explicitly does—that it is history's alarm, warning of a time bomb soon to go off. Such is the sad saga of South Africa that Mr. Fugard's warning is perhaps even more pressing now than it was when the playwright first unveiled *Blood Knot* in 1961.

To call the new production of this work . . . a revival isn't entirely accurate. Yes, Mr. Fugard and his partner, Zakes Mokae, are back in the roles they originated almost 25 years ago, in the legendary Johannesburg performance that established the play and its author's career. Yet in a sense the men have been playing their parts, spiritually if not literally, ever since that premiere. . . .

Blood Knot is very much the creation of a young playwright, and if it isn't as accomplished or powerful as such recent Fugard works as *A Lesson From Aloes* and [*"Master Harold" . . . And the Boys*], it still moves, in its rambling way, to a shattering climax. The seeds of the later Fugard plays are all here: With only two characters and a simple setting—and with little plot and no polemics—the writer channels the inhumanity of a racist society and the courage of its victims into primal, intimate theater that both embodies and transmutes the grim specifics of apartheid. . . .

The play's most dramatic moments, all in Act II, occur when Morris, toying with the notion of passing for white again in an assignation with Zach's pen pal, buys a "gentleman's suit" and starts play-acting the role. However, the game, in which Zach assumes the guise of a subservient black "boy," gets out of hand; the two brothers find themselves swept up in a paradigm of racial apocalypse reminiscent of the scene in which the young white protagonist of *"Master Harold"* spits at the servant Sam. In *Blood Knot,* as in the later play, that instant

in which hatred, anger and brutality congeal into violence could make even the most enlightened theatergoer squirm with the horror of grotesque self-recognition. Mr. Fugard doesn't allow anyone, least of all himself, to escape without examining the ugliest capabilities of his soul. . . .

This is one of those rare performances in which the actor is inseparable from the role—and, given Mr. Fugard's play, in which the role is inseparable from a real-life tragedy. Nearly a quarter-century after its inception, one still leaves *Blood Knot* wondering how much longer these great South African artists must sound their harrowing alarm to awaken the consciences that might yet bring that tragedy to an end.

> Frank Rich, "'Blood Knot,' with Fugard and Mo-kae," in The New York Times, *December 11, 1985, p. C23.*

BRENDAN GILL

Over the years, I've attended a number of productions of Athol Fugard's *Blood Knot*. . . . [The] twenty-fifth anniversary production . . . is by far the best of the lot, and for a good reason: the two characters, Zachariah and Morris, who make up the entire cast are enacted by Zakes Mokae and the author, who has also directed. . . . The collaboration of Fugard and Mokae can fairly be said to have altered the history of twentieth-century theatre throughout the world; it has also altered—and continues to alter—the political history of the world. Their aesthetic value aside, *Blood Knot, Boesman and Lena, A Lesson from Aloes,* and *Sizwe Banzi* are fiercely hortatory; they urge upon us that we follow the never very welcome Biblical injunction and become doers of the Word, not mere passive listeners to it.

Blood Knot is well made in a harmlessly old-fashioned way; the plot creaks on its uninventive hinges, but the emotion that it engenders in its audiences has grown all the stronger with the passing of the years, in part because the racial tyranny that helped to prompt the writing of the play has led to ever bloodier consequences. . . . Nothing on Broadway this year or any year is likely to prove more worth seeing than *Blood Knot*. (pp. 78, 80)

> Brendan Gill, "Country Pleasures," in The New Yorker, *Vol. LXI, No. 44, December 23, 1985, pp. 78, 80.**

JOHN SIMON

Blood Knot, for all its humaneness, high-mindedness, and concern with the ever more burning issue of South Africa, is . . . [hard] to recommend. It was apprentice work for its author, Athol Fugard, back in 1960-61, and the outline he jotted down in his *Notebooks* for 1960 is rather more interesting than the finished play. In the notes, there are not only the two "colored" brothers—Morris who is light-skinned and self-educated enough to pass for white, and Zachariah, who is black and untutored—but also the white girl Ethel, who in the play enters the brothers' lives only as a pen pal. So the drama is reduced to chronicling two delusions, both essentially static: Morrie's, that the two of them can save up for a future in the shape of a little farm to be worked by themselves; and Zach's, that he can have a relationship with a white woman. There are no significant confrontations, and there is not much theater in the mere discarding of two hopes that, under apartheid, are stillborn.

More crippling yet was Fugard's lack of technique in 1961. Exposition, which creaks even in his later, much better plays, positively clunks through much of *Blood Knot*. And even for the rendering of stagnation, the tempo is too slow. The dramaturgy seems to be derived from Genet, whose playacting maids and blacks are the probable models for the charade the brothers indulge in—only Genet has a much greater flair for tragicomic theatricality. Even the climax, so devastating in late Fugard works, is muffled here. The shattering near-concluding line, ''I think there's quite a lot of people getting by without futures these days,'' is promptly undercut by a curtain line that heavy-handedly explains the meaning of the play. (pp. 50, 52)

Blood Knot can be seen for political or sentimental reasons, but not, I fear, for artistic ones. (p. 52)

> *John Simon, ''Houses Divided,'' in New York Magazine, Vol. 19, No. 1, January 6, 1986, pp. 50, 52-3.*

Julian Gloag

1930-

English novelist and editor.

Gloag's psychological thrillers combine elements of the traditional mystery story with in-depth character studies. His protagonists are often ordinary people who experience a personal crisis or tragedy which leads to increased self-awareness. Individual and societal guilt, emotional chaos concealed beneath a facade of orderliness, meaningless sex, and violence are recurring motifs in Gloag's fiction. Gloag is generally praised for his evocative prose and for maintaining suspense throughout his novels. Margaret Walters noted that Gloag "asks ambitious questions about the aftermath of violence, about the way guilt and a craving for vengeance distort people's lives." She added, however, that "some of his skills as a thriller writer—his mastery of intricately plotted suspense—actually distract from his larger aims."

Gloag's first novel, *Our Mother's House* (1963), was described by Wilfrid Sheed as "a small marvel of controlled horror." The plot centers around seven children during the year after their mother's death. To avoid interference from the authorities, they bury her body in the backyard and pretend she is still alive. The story of their progressively primitive state drew comparisons to such other macabre tales of childhood as William Golding's *Lord of the Flies* and Richard Hughes's *High Wind in Jamaica*. Gloag's next novel, *A Sentence of Life* (1966), interweaves dramatic courtroom scenes with the protagonist's introspective contemplation of his past. While being tried for a murder he did not commit, Jordan Maddox feels increasingly guilty as he begins to realize the degree to which he has acted as a puppet of his social class; he finally acknowledges his own as well as society's culpability in the death of his secretary for not coming to her aid in a time of need. *Maundy* (1969), Gloag's third novel, is perhaps his most serious and complicated work. The stark and ordered life of the protagonist disintegrates during his search for a female hitchhiker who disappeared after they were involved in a motorcycle accident. As he obsessively tracks the woman, Maundy becomes absorbed in London's underworld of sex, drugs, and violence, and his eventual descent into madness sharply contrasts with the immaculate and civilized manner of his earlier life. *A Woman of Character* (1973) is the story of Anne Mansard, who amasses a fortune after inadvertently causing the deaths of several people. Ironically, Anne is portrayed as a simple, good-hearted woman who becomes a victim of circumstances.

The characters of Gloag's recent novels can also be considered victims. In *Sleeping Dogs Lie* (1980), psychiatrist Hugh Welchman is forced to confront his own repressed fears and emotions while treating a student who is afraid to descend the stone steps of his dormitory. A misplaced manuscript is the first of a series of losses Paul Molphey endures in *Lost and Found* (1981). When his novel resurfaces as the prizewinning product of another author, Molphey is driven to violence and revenge as he tries to reclaim part of his life. *Blood for Blood* (1985) follows Ivor Speke's search for the murderer of a close friend. During his investigation, Speke discovers some truths about human nature which enable him to finally accept the death of his young daughter and find a renewed purpose in life.

© Jerry Bauer

(See also *Contemporary Authors*, Vols. 65-68 and *Contemporary Authors New Revision Series*, Vol. 10.)

ORVILLE PRESCOTT

There were seven children [in the Hook family] ranging from Elsa, who was 13, to Willy, who was 4. Their bizarre and macabre story during the year after their mother's death is told by Julian Gloag in his first novel, *Our Mother's House*. This is an extraordinary book. . . .

[Julian Gloag] is richly talented. Readers who have admired Shirley Jackson's *We Have Always Lived in the Castle* or William Golding's *Lord of the Flies* should have a fine, grisly time with *Our Mother's House*.

Mother was always contemptuous of doctors. So, when she fell desperately ill the children knew better than to call a doctor. . . . And then Mother died. The children had no one, no relative, no adult friend. Separation and orphan asylums were too dreadful. So they buried Mother in the garden at midnight and carried on as before, pretending that Mother was too sick to see anyone.

205

The situation was gruesome. Mr. Gloag handles it with expert skill. Each child is real and pathetic. The isolated society they create for themselves is full of disturbing implications about the nature of children and the nature of organized societies. Disaster is always inevitable, but for a long time the inevitable disaster is postponed while little disasters march along in orderly array.

Our Mother's House falls neatly into two parts—before and after the arrival of Charley Hook. Before he came, the children seemed to be drifting steadily backward into the dark recesses of primitive life. . . .

But then Charley Hook came. He had once been Mother's husband, but not for a long time. Charley brought gaiety, and laughter and fun into the old house. The children loved him. Now they had somebody. But Charley was a petty Cockney crook, a compulsive gambler, forger and manipulator of nasty little deals. Charley was a drunkard. . . .

Each development in *Our Mother's House* is surprising, but right. Each child is wholly believable. They do strange things which will not be revealed here; but they do them because that is the kind of children they are, because life without adults (or with an adult like Charley) is too much for children so young.

Julian Gloag is not saying only that children are innocent savages. They are. He is saying, if I read him aright, that some of their most admirable motives, loyalty, love and reverence, can lead them into behaving like savages.

And, of course, children are different and some respond to the pressures of a strange situation far more savagely than others. *Our Mother's House* provokes thought as well as arousing rapt interest.

> Orville Prescott, in a review of "Our Mother's House," in The New York Times, May 8, 1963, p. 37.

PETER BUITENHUIS

[In *Our Mother's House*] Mr. Gloag centers his narrative on the house and explores with considerable skill and subtlety the changing power relationships among the seven children. Since there are few outsiders in the story, the novel has a psychological tautness and density that is one of the chief (and most unused) virtues of the form. Moreover, Mr. Gloag's style is simple, fresh and strong. It is well-suited to his unusual subject.

The narrative line is underscored with an effective treatment of appearance and reality. Mother's firm and loving spirit presides over the house long after her death. . . . A vicar's daughter, she had married "beneath her," as they used to say in England. Her husband is a wonderfully raffish, apparently warm and generous individual, but beneath the warmth beats a heart of lead. The children are terrifyingly confronted with the Medusa-face of life, it is largely that, in combination with their own weaknesses and immaturity, that breaks down their ability to control their own destiny.

What the novel lacks is a controlling point of view. Although it is told mostly from the standpoint of Hubert, the second oldest boy, it shifts and wavers at times, so that the direction of the story is sometimes confused and the forward march of the narrative is slowed down. The novel is, after all, a tour de force. Mr. Gloag, although he has many other talents, doesn't have quite enough cheek and ruthlessness to make it stand true.

> Peter Buitenhuis, "Mother Loved Them, but She Died," in The New York Times Book Review, May 12, 1963, p. 41.

EDMUND FULLER

This reviewer is bound to say, reluctantly, that he doesn't believe a word of [*Our Mother's House*]—not in terms of its realistic possibility, but its internal plausibility both psychologically and in its practical aspects as told. It has failed me or I have failed it, totally.

Mr. Gloag writes well, with good style and taut narrative. But in such a tale, one must be persuaded or it cannot interest. Contrivance and calculated invention weigh heavily upon me at every step; they serve their own ends, not a vision. As his fellow Britishers might say, he has been too clever by half.

The jacket invokes comparison with *Lord of the Flies* and *High Wind in Jamaica*. Indeed, the book seems, but may not be, an imitation. But those two works are vitally different. Each of them places a group of children in a unique context, one wholly, the other partly, isolated. The children have no choice or volition in this; the rest of the world is cut off from them. In each case, the Golding book more profoundly than Hughes', the events that follow probe the essential nature of the human creature in its relative "innocence," both as individuals and social beings.

No such vision illuminates *Our Mother's House.* The story carries no significant commentary on character or society. Its events occur not by the thrust of internal inevitability, but because the puppet master is determined that they shall. It is full of questions unanswered because the author has gambled that pace and novelty will distract you from asking them.

> Edmund Fuller, "Life without Mother—Father, Too?" in Books, June 9, 1963, p. 8.

GLENDY CULLIGAN

Julian Gloag's intricately plotted and suspenseful second novel [*A Sentence of Life*] . . . subjects a middle-aged man on the threshold of adultery to microscopic examination. . . .

Although Gloag's hero finally succumbs to the moral imperative of choice, his dilemma derives from a fatalistic view of life. The initial decision faced by Jordan Maddox, a mild-mannered publisher, seems too trivial to have consequences: should he bother to correct a small factual error in his statement to police during a routine investigation of a murder? From his apparently inconsequential evasion sprouts the luxuriant vine of suspicion that could easily curl into a noose.

This nightmare web, so familiar to connoisseurs of detective fiction, tightens during a whopping courtroom climax. Gloag's trial scene is a cliff-hanger in the best tradition of its genre. What makes this entertainment something more, however, is the character study the author has ingeniously grafted onto melodrama. It produces an engrossing hybrid, which, if it were not for flaws of style and sincerity, might have made a first-rate novel.

Expedient as a conveyance, the terse, flat language of his narrative carries us back through Maddox's predictable memories of an emotionally deprived childhood. Standard though this formula for adult inadequacy has become, Gloag endows it with incontrovertible life through deft use of particulars. Like other intoxicants, however, the spell of suspense tends to wear off in the morning, and cold sober we analyze the tricks that fascinated us by lamplight.

Glendy Culligan, ''Between Two Genres,'' in Book Week—The Washington Post, *May 1, 1966, p. 14.*

MARTIN TUCKER

In a season in which so much has been written in cold blood, it is diverting to come upon a thinking man's murder. Or, as Julian Gloag describes it in [*A Sentence of Life*], a murder in which the chief suspect is a mild-mannered intellectual whose worst sins are those of omission.

The author's hero is presented initially as a man incapable of murder, of the hate and passion necessary for such an act of commitment. . . . In time, the reader sees that he is capable of profound passion. What he is incapable of—until the last moment of his trial—is a faith in himself, and in people. He has been conditioned by a childhood in which the family password has been obedience to convention. To protect himself from those conventions in which he does not believe, but whose potency he recognizes, he lies, and it is these lies which trap and almost destroy him.

Jordan is thus like the children in Mr. Gloag's frightening first novel, *Our Mother's House:* fear of the indecency of other people drives a basically decent person into more and more deviant acts of deception. Both the children of *Our Mother's House* and the hero of *A Sentence of Life* are so terrified by the spectre of society's coldness that they prefer to act out their own feverish rules rather than submit to society's ''ethics.''

What, then, in the author's view, is Jordan Maddox guilty of? . . . Perhaps it is his desire for self-destruction, for Maddox almost consciously destroys any rational belief in his innocence through his incessant, petty lying, his desire to play the role of a murderer in order to regain a throb of feeling that has been stilled in the heartless world in which he has lived.

Most likely, however, it has to do with something akin to E. M. Forster's ''Only connect.'' . . . Mr. Gloag's comment might be, ''Only admit.'' For Jordan Maddox is unable to face the awkward, ill-ordered aspects of his life. When something obtrudes, it is ignored; when something unconventional persists, it is not admitted. His life has in this way been robbed of commitment; his guardian aunt and uncle have forced the loss of his two deepest loves, an eccentric uncle and an unacceptably poor girl whom Jordan wanted to marry.

This refusal to admit to the passions one feels—and the feelings one passes through—finally destroys the individual by breaking his will. In the final reckoning, the individual who forsakes his feelings is caught in his own web of perpetual rationalization. . . . [For Jordan] it almost led to a conviction for murder. Fortuitously (and ironically) it freed him to be himself when, in confessing to a murder he did not commit, he was able to admit to all his feelings and especially to his hates. In turn, this admission makes it possible for him to admit what he really loves.

A Sentence of Life is a worthy successor to *Our Mother's House*. In both is present the brilliant ability to create ordinary characters—who, little by little, reveal themselves capable of enormous passion and deceptiveness. Yet, while *Our Mother's House* was a near-perfect example of its genre, *A Sentence of Life* has its flaws, particularly in the final chapters. Its conclusion is pat, and reads as if the author had decided to call it quits and bring the suspense to an end. Fortunately it is only in its denouement that *A Sentence of Life* fails to acquit itself.

Martin Tucker, ''Would-Be Killer,'' in The New York Times Book Review, *May 1, 1966, p. 47.*

THOMAS LASK

For his new novel [*A Sentence of Life*] Julian Gloag has written two books, and he has concealed one within the other with such artifice that they almost seem like a single volume. Almost, but not quite. For when the reader becomes aware of the joinery, the fissures get wider and wider until, at the end, the reader is certain that he has been reading two separate books that have mistakenly been bound as one. The first is a more or less conventional suspense novel, but a good one. A secretary is found murdered in London and her employer, a publisher of medical books, is suspected. Since he appears to be an amateur murderer and his questioners are professional police, it is a no contest. The evidence points to him and the police exert themselves to make an air-tight case. The suspect, Jordan Maddox by name, helps them. Withdrawn, uncaring, despondent behind a facade of coolness, he weaves his own shroud. He lies, leaves out damaging facts, thinks belatedly of matters he should have thought of before. His defenses are so inept that the cops have a Roman holiday. . . .

In this part of the book, Mr. Gloag . . . shows himself to be a sure hand. The passages where the police sweat the facts out of their suspect and the later scenes in the courtroom wherein the defense attorney puts the hostile witnesses through the rack are excitingly done. In page after page of short give-and-take questions and answers, Mr. Gloag shows how the same fact can be made to reveal two different and opposite truths, and how a clever attorney, by forcing the witness to admit qualifications and probabilities, can make him say the opposite of what he means. . . .

And although the reader is not given the material to make up his own mind, he doesn't care. He has a better time as a spectator than as a participant in the case.

Throughout the trial, however, Jordan Maddox acts like a zombie, so withdrawn that a number of times his lawyers have to remind him that he is, after all, on trial for murder and unless he works up a little spirit he is going to land in jail for life. What makes him act the way he does? What has brought him into this slough of despond? That's Mr. Gloag's other book.

And that one is a soft-toned, conventional tale of a boy's upbringing, his education . . . , his first love, the death of a dear and close uncle, his loveless marriage and the birth of his daughter. The failure of that early love and the death of the uncle have so cauterized Maddox's feelings that he literally does not care what happens to him. . . .

The trouble is that each part of his book calls forth a different set of responses. A reader will allow for things in a novel of suspense that he cannot allow in a *Bildungsroman*. In the former, a tautly told story will cover a multitude of character flaws; in the latter it is the characters, not the story, who count. In one scene, Maddox's wife visits him in prison and through the wire mesh that separates them, taunts him with her adulteries and with his ineffectiveness as a lover. How are we to read this? In a tough-minded novel of the Raymond Chandler type, such a scene could be powerfully effective; as the public conversation of a well-bred English family, it rings as false as a plugged quarter.

Mr. Gloag would have us believe that an aborted adolescent love affair could so demoralize a grown man with a family that he will not defend himself against a charge of murder. Maybe it could, but he never demonstrates it. At one point, Maddox, thinking of the cruelties of those he has known, remarks, "If they are not guilty, then I *am* guilty." Such an existentialist view could easily be the subject of a novel, but this work which alternates fast-paced courtroom scenes with domestic crises in a vicarage is not it.

Thomas Lask, *"Did Maddox Murder June Singer?"*
in The New York Times, *May 17, 1966, p. 45.*

HENRY S. RESNIK

Maundy is one of the most relentlessly disagreeable books to come our way in a long time.

"Maundy" happens to be the name of Gloag's protagonist (it is his only name), and the word establishes at the outset the novel's highly ambiguous, richly symbolic character: derived from the Latin *mandatum,* it carries overtones of Christ's commandment, at the Last Supper, that the disciples love one another—the subject of the book can be seen as Maundy's search for a way in which to follow this behest. But the word is also linked with Christ's ceremonial washing of the disciples' feet, a ritual of purification. In the character of Maundy, Gloag has united these two disparate, but complementary, elements; *Maundy* is the story of a quest for love, but it is also about a guilt-ridden, fragmented, terrifyingly inhuman world where love is almost impossible, a world in which Maundy is both an innocent victim and an instrument for perpetuating lovelessness.

On the one hand, the world of *Maundy* is ultra-civilized. . . . [His] life is consumed by deadly order. But behind its façade of Victorian calm, this world exudes violence, glimpsed at first only in Maundy's fantasies, but later increasingly actual. Even in the gentle English countryside, where Maundy visits his mother, a tidy garden is fertilized with powdered bones and protected by hedges against a flock of malignant sheep who continually attack it. . . .

The disintegration of order in Maundy's life begins when, returning from the country one night on his motorcycle—the symbolic power between the legs suggests that there is still hope for him—he gives a ride to a mysterious, silent girl who disappears or dies when the bike accidentally skids off the road. Not sure what has happened to the girl, Maundy becomes haunted by the need to find her. Gradually he surrenders all his little order-games to continue the search—leaves his job, abandons his masochistic fiancée, and ultimately drifts into a state of near-madness.

The plot is an odyssey through Uglyland. While he is looking for the girl, Maundy witnesses one death and hears about several more, including a few murders; indulges in some graphically described sex with a prostitute and her young nephew; chases various girls who might be *the* girl in and out of movie houses and bars; and continually shuttles back and forth between city and country—between, perhaps, innocence and "civilization" (though there is ample evidence, particularly in the grim references to Africa and those sheep, that even the purest animal innocence is essentially violent and evil).

This odyssey may prove a source of endless amusement to graduate students and symbol-hunters, for the imagery of the novel is almost impenetrable. A whole seminar could be devoted, for example, to the images of washing—scarcely a page goes by without one, right down to an improbable ritual involving spilled drinks (at one point, however, where Maundy washes his face with ice the image is both striking and apt). . . . As an exercise in metaphor, *Maundy* is a *tour de force*.

One has a right, however, to expect more from a novel than complex imagery. It is essential, for example, that one care what happens to Maundy himself, but unfortunately Gloag has allowed his central character to blend completely into the world around him. Maundy is never anything but blank, empty, pallid, and sterile—perhaps never so sterile as when he is speaking. . . . For a book that professes such deep concern with human feeling, *Maundy* is unremittingly cold.

For a while the sheer horror of the novel is enough to sustain it, but the brilliant ghastliness of the first sixty or so pages soon palls. The images of foot-washing, spilling water, blood, wounds, death, violence, and destruction eventually become tiresomely repetitive and predictable. When new inventions of supreme offensiveness are not forthcoming, the familiar metaphors lose most of their lurid appeal. The structure of the novel cannot bear the strain of Gloag's moral indignation.

At one point in the book, Maundy's only friend observes of the crowd at a country pub, "If you played back a recording of this, you might think it came from an abattoir." Indeed, reading *Maundy* is an experience somewhat similar to viewing Jean-Luc Godard's *Weekend*—but nowhere near as satisfying.

Henry S. Resnik, *"Black Knight on a Motorcycle,"*
in Saturday Review, *Vol. LII, No. 8, February 22, 1969, p. 79.*

JAMES FENTON

[*Maundy*] describes the breaking up of a London banker's pale bourgeois existence. The initial agent of the destruction is left mysterious, but we see how, in a life where the disappearance of a pair of socks presents a mystery as inexplicable as it is disturbing, the foundations of a man's complacency may easily be shaken. As the plot progresses, the hero, Maundy, becomes obsessed with self-destruction and one by one severs his links with his former ordered existence. The reason for his obsession may be traced to self-awareness: 'I am a banker', he says at one point, gratuitously and bitterly, and in an excellent passage he becomes ludicrously involved in the purchase of an old stuffed owl, for which he is prepared to pay any price. Money is one of the novel's main themes: his mother chides him for trivial extravagances and his friend Edward, an antique dealer, helps people employ their surplus resources. The various settings are superbly adumbrated in a kind of prose which relies on a minimum of resources to produce vivid effects. The metropolis and the cathedral close, the street-scenes and the rural landscapes, gradually emerge as significant components of the story alongside the wide range of characters. The worst fault of the book lies in the ending, where Mr Gloag seems to have abdicated his control over the machinery so far developed. In all, however, the work is quite brilliant.

James Fenton, *"Fossil Remains,"* in New Statesman, *Vol. 77, No. 1998, June 27, 1969, p. 916.**

PAUL WEST

A near-exquisite living clinically, [Maundy] all of a sudden begins to go off the rails after losing or misplacing a pair of socks. From then on, his intermittent hysteria mounts while his urbane standards flop, and Julian Gloag tracks his fall [in *Maundy*].

The crucial incident—the one which progressively dements Maundy and yet provides him with his first steady purpose in life—is his giving a lift on his motorcycle to an unknown girl on a stormy night. They have an accident and she vanishes, only, however, to occupy and annul his waking and sleeping consciousness. . . .

Puzzlement becomes alienation, unsteadiness becomes miserable vertigo, and depravity the only good as, heedless of the proprieties of his recent life, Maundy flounders through the pubs and streets of an English city, into and out of cinemas, gambling clubs, and the sleazy bedsitters of prostitutes. But: no girl. . . . On his own terms, the girl is unfindable. And his obsession comes to seem a form of pedantry, a pretext even for chasing after a certain type—for, essentially, he knows nothing about the girl who rode with him, not even her name.

Julian Gloag handles this theme of decline and fall (and then decline again) with vivid curtness, and his sexual episodes in particular have a concise lubricity in which the gross and the lyrically indirect enrich each other. His minor characters brim with potential and weight down the phantasmagorical goings-on. . . . All I would complain about is Maundy's maunderings, some of which—compared with his night-town meanderings—Mr. Gloag presents with bland, relentless uplift. For example: "In the white voices everything was gathered up in sweetness and, quivering, the ascending sweetness was whitely conjoined to its desire until the long pure note rose to the high spring, the fount, the everlasting indwelling . . . and in that melting, dissolved, gone into echo, echo gone, quenched, all ceased, all peace." . . .

That, surely, is how Maundy, not Julian Gloag, would write a novel and it reads (along with similar splurges) like a lapse in the main prose style, which is altogether more ironical and pungent. But having registered my complaint, I gratefully pay tribute to the other ninety-five per cent of the novel, in which Gloag achieves a bold, precise, elastic style that seduces or stuns without (it seems to me) ever being overwritten or—something rare in an English writer nowadays—encased in an embarrassed jollity that knocks style for being what it is.

Paul West, "Rainy-Night Eurydice," in Book World—The Washington Post, *July 6, 1969, p. 11.*

PAUL THEROUX

A Woman of Character opens with the heroine, Anne Mansard, losing her fiancé, and it doesn't worry her in the least. She has accidentally killed him, and with the help of her lover she shoves him through a port-hole of his own ocean liner. The perfect crime. Needless to say, he is a wealthy man; a fortune is bequeathed to Anne, and the joys and sorrows that money brings to this devilishly large-breasted girl is the subject of Mr. Gloag's fourth novel.

To say Anne is a woman of fatal charm is to describe her with literal exactitude. After Kenny is jettisoned, it is only a matter of time before Archie, the lover, is kicked down a ship's hatchway; and her father, who might have done the kicking, col-

lapses on a compost heap and suffocates. Then, just as the phrase "dropping like flies" flits through the reader's mind, Gilbert and Sylvia, also wealthy friends of Anne, hit a concrete abutment in Sicily—two more down and Anne is on the receiving end of another fortune. "You aren't human," a bereaved widow cries at Anne and one can see her point.

On the other hand, Anne is not really evil; sauntering through a world of greed, tycoonery and bitchery . . . , she maintains a simplicity of soul and an utter transparency of mind. Ambition, like cash, has been thrust upon her. . . .

The novel is not without its moments. It is pervaded by an overwhelming stink of decadence, by subsidiary characters who are perfect demons and who deserve everything the tentative succubus of the title visits upon them. Mr. Gloag solemnly mocks the pretensions and destructiveness of the family Anne has found herself stuck to. She is like a worm clinging to a decayed leaf, but they are all moribund, and their dialogue (the novel is nearly all dialogue, which makes for some rather ludicrous reporting of off-stage deaths) only serves to repeat symptoms of the same sickness. What little description there is is largely limited to simmering passages about Anne's thighs . . . and again and again to blood and pain. . . .

The argument is that in a world like this, riven with corruption, Anne is the true victim. She would be satisfied with a quieter life, but it is her fate to be an heiress twice over and to lose the only man she seems capable of loving, a simple steward with simple lusts. Ironic, isn't it? But in the context of this novel it is a laborious irony, and I found it hard not to put this book down.

Paul Theroux, in a review of "A Woman of Character," in The New York Times Book Review, *May 27, 1973, p. 17.*

PETER ACKROYD

[*A Woman of Character*] is the story of a sweet English heroine, Anne, who triumphs over adversity by inadvertently killing a handful of people. It is an 'All About Eve' story, except that Eve in this case ends up by controlling a large fortune and a shipping company. . . .

A Woman of Character is, naturally, set in the world of the very rich. I find nothing wrong with affluence, but Mr Gloag tends to confine himself to its occasional *grotesquerie*. The atmosphere of the novel is that of a confined space; physical sensations—sight, touch, smell—are magnified until they become overpowering. Every smile, every scent and every action become menacing and the writing mimics this embarrassment of riches by being both opulent and elaborate. The protagonists are quite at ease in this stifling air, being by nature cannibals. And those who are not eating are definitely being eaten: Mr Gloag captures very well the well-meaning inanity of 'ordinary folk.' The office-girls from whom Anne has raised herself, Anne's parents who cut the lawn and cook stew, and the early, giggly Anne herself. But Anne soon settles for better things, and starts living in a hotel-room and sleeping with the bell-boys.

But it was her rise that worried me. Not ethically, you understand, but technically. Anne remains an opaque figure through the narrative, her motives and her understanding of events are always clouded if not concealed. One is never quite sure what is accident and what is design, and there is a hiatus between the rags and the riches which is never properly handled by Mr

Gloag. Of course anything is possible nowadays, and it may be that this hiatus is exactly the point of the story. But I was looking for a certain emotive credibility in what is otherwise the fantasy of someone on the outside looking in. The confined air was too much for me, even a miniature requires the occasional broad stroke. (p. 344)

Peter Ackroyd, "Of Gods and Men," in The Spectator, Vol. 231, No. 7577, September 15, 1973, pp. 344-45.*

ROBERT NYE

[*A Woman of Character*] is a feeble novel and not at all what one might expect of Julian Gloag, author of *Our Mother's House* (1963) and *Maundy* (1969). If you read the last named you may recall it as wildly overwritten, but thick with seriousness: Mr Gloag seemed determined to wring every drop of significance from his material, and out-pun Joyce in his verbal witchery. The new book possesses no fascination at all in the way of language-texture—it is tolerably put together, mostly in dialogue, but if anything the author appears to have set out to be as flat-footed as he can in creeping from one slab of talk to the next. . . .

The intention must be comic. Anne sails through the book unruffled by anyone's opinion of her, and there is a certain amusing glamour to this. But it seems to me that the writing is neither sharp enough nor thoughtful enough to justify a satirical reading, and while *A Woman of Character* makes reasonable light reading for an hour or two I shall be surprised if readers who were attracted by the promise of Mr Gloag's first novel find this a satisfactory piece of work. Critics who suggested that he had lost his way in *Maundy* will discover their opinions confirmed by the fact that he has not yet found it again.

Robert Nye, in a review of "A Woman of Character," in Books and Bookmen, Vol. 19, No. 3, December, 1973, p. 89.

EVAN HUNTER

In Cambridge, England, a troubled university student comes to psychiatrist Hugh Welchman with what appears to be a routine case of hysterical conversion: he has recently become terrified of descending the stone stairway that leads down from his second-floor set of rooms. In such a deceptively simple manner does *Sleeping Dogs Lie* begin, and it does not reach its startling series of conclusions until Welchman has doggedly explored every facet of the trauma responsible for his patient's phobia.

Welchman is a brilliant creation. A dedicated, gently probing professional, his frame of reference is entirely psychological; the smallest detail, the slightest gesture is noted in clinical terms. "How relentlessly sane you are," someone says to him at one point, and indeed his constant involvement with the feelings of others has left him sadly without many feelings of his own. But, oh, how relentlessly *human* he is as well. In fact, the triumph of Julian Gloag's intricate tale is that Welchman must eventually come to grips with his own ghosts as well as those that are haunting his young patient.

It would be unfair to reveal the shocking and surprising plot twists that propel this compulsively readable novel. They are as labyrinthine (and ultimately as logical) as the workings of the unconscious itself, revolving inexorably around a murder committed 14 years earlier and settling suspicion in turn upon each member (and several close associates) of a family trapped in its own tragically symbiotic circle. Suffice it to say that Mr. Gloag is in stunning command throughout. His prose is literate and richly evocative; his various and varied characters are fascinating and fully realized; he has written a true novel of "psychological suspense" which seems effortlessly to merit that much-abused descriptive label.

Evan Hunter, "Bad Crimes and Good," in The New York Times Book Review, July 20, 1980, p. 12.*

STUART EVANS

Julian Gloag's *Sleeping Dogs Lie* is presumably intended to strip away the layers of moral varnish and ethical veneer which disguise the rotten woodwork of an inbred, semi-academic, more or less sophisticated group of people who live in Cambridge, as they are worked on by a still innocent working-class psychiatrist married to one of them and treating another. The title refers to advice which, if he had taken it, would have spared us the novel.

As an unpretentious old-fashioned whodunnit, the story might have worked—even allowing for Mr Gloag's determination to solder twist upon twist; as a serious psychological fiction it does not: partly because the plot hinges upon a failure to communicate and physical and emotional evasions which are simply not credible, partly because the characters are complicated without having any real depth.

The book is efficiently organized, but the writing (although it improves later on) is uninspired. The dialogue, among putatively intelligent people, is characterless and lacking in wit. The psychiatrist is a sympathetic enough figure, even if his class-memory fails to substantiate the authenticity of his humble origins and his professional credentials require more proof than a voluminous knowledge of pills and the litany of psychotherapeutic jargon.

Stuart Evans, in a review of "Sleeping Dogs Lie," in The Times, London, November 27, 1980, p. 14.

GILLIAN WILCE

'Fuck Freud' is one of Dr Hugh Welchman's furious, drunken thoughts towards the end of this cold tale. And, that, in a sense, is what Julian Gloag has been doing throughout *Sleeping Dogs Lie*. It was an important stage in the formation of Freud's theory of childhood sexual and emotional development when he discovered that the sexual traumas 'recalled' by his patients were in fact fantasies. What is of interest analytically is a person's interior life, the attitudes and feelings growing from childhood relationships—not a single event so dramatic that it could bring the crime squad battering at the door. Julian Gloag has twisted this finding back on to its head. When Dr Welchman takes on undergraduate Alex Brinton with his phobia about stone stairs, he is opening an external, factual can of worms.

Alex soon, easily remembers the origin of his phobia: his mother tumbling down the cellar steps. And from this point on the methods of the consulting room cease to be of any value, and Alex becomes a bit player. Layer after layer of mendacity is stripped away.

The book is larded with psychological language, so it is a disappointment to find that in the long run it does not concern itself at all with psychological insight. Dr Welchman himself is never very convincing in the consulting room—but then we find that Alex's family doctor (who is not, of course, *just* his family doctor) has chosen Welchman for reasons quite other than his professional skill, and finally we see Welchman completely unable to help anyone as the whole imbroglio of crime, accusation, counter-accusation, confession, false confession, and death turns itself back into his own home. The twisting inside out is complete. Welchman is the sufferer and cannot heal himself.

The intricacies of the plot could have been highly implausible, but in fact the whole thing is arranged with perfect internal consistency. Not only are all the ends neatly sewed back into the middle of the knot, but the book is full of echoes and repetitions, all most carefully wrought. And yet to what end? Ultimately, there is only the icy mist across the Fens and the plot. Fairly soon after the beginning one finds oneself reading to find out who did what to whom. About two-thirds the way through one becomes weary of incident, wanting to say 'never mind any more clever twists; just tell me the answer and let me go'. It is a mystery novel but without the catharsis of the classic detective story when one person is found to be the scapegoat for all the guilt. Here all are guilty, all are rather unpleasant, wholly self-absorbed and, in spite of their hectic, bloody lives, not very interesting.

> Gillian Wilce, *"Doing or Being,"* in New States-man, *Vol. 101, No. 2598, January 2, 1981, p. 21.**

EDITH MILTON

Lost and Found is about Paul Molphey, a schoolteacher in a small French village in the Morban Mountains. He is 50, an old man by local standards, and nothing worthwhile is left in his life. Having spent his youth writing a novel, he misplaces the manuscript in a Paris railway station on his honeymoon. His wife, Arlette, abandons him after giving birth to twin girls, who, grown up, themselves leave him. One daughter is now in a convent that allows no contact with home, the other leads a peripatetic bohemian existence and wants none.

As Paul drinks his way through the first days of his summer holiday, *Lost and Found* follows the browsing of his uncertain memory back to 1940 when, exempted by polio from the war, he first came to the village to live with his grandfather, an old man of exemplary manners and perversely fascist sympathies. Paul wanders in reminiscence among the ghosts of his neighbors. . . . Above all, he thinks of his two lost daughters, whose remembered images inform him, as their presence never could, that he has failed them and through them failed to provide himself a future.

At his best, as in his early novel *Our Mother's House,* Mr. Gloag creates a world that, however unlikely, is utterly real. And in *Lost and Found* he weaves through Paul's inebriated memory with literary grace and skill. The story unfolds with an air of delicate spontaneity, moving in a seemingly random fashion toward a conclusion that is both surprising and inevitable.

Lost and Found is almost a fine novel; but something essential is missing, some sort of energy and creative conviction. Like its hero, the novel seems tired and without much hope for itself. Its characters and their hypocrisies and injustices toward each other seem borrowed from the conventions of another century. One feels one has met most of the village rustics before, and a contemporary Paris nightclub scene suggests Kay Boyle's Paris of 40 years ago. Paul himself is indistinct, as though his own alcoholic haze had blurred him somehow in the imagination of the author. And I was dismayed, too, that the plot hinged on the inadvertent exchange of a manuscript for a suitcase of cheese and brandy. Surely that device lost its place in sober narratives on the day Oscar Wilde's Miss Prism swapped a baby for her appalling manuscript at Victoria Station. . . . (p. 8)

> Edith Milton, *"Fathers and Daughters,"* in The New York Times Book Review, *July 26, 1981, pp. 8-9.*

A. N. WILSON

A while ago, a novel called *The Cement Garden* achieved a *succés de scandale* when it was alleged that the author, Ian McEwan, had stolen the idea for his story from a book by Julian Gloag called **Our Mother's House**. There was a row on television in which Mr Gloag made the plausible-sounding claim that McEwan's success was based on blatant plagiarism; McEwan's publisher denied anything of the sort and said that his author was a great and original talent; and the chairman, someone like Robert Robinson, made bland remarks to the effect that this was the kind of coincidence which could happen to anyone who took the risk of writing a novel. For some reason, I never got round to reading either book, and I had almost forgotten the telly programme.

Now we have **Lost and Found,** Mr Gloag's new novel, and it is brilliant. The story is as follows. At the end of the war, a young Frenchman called Paul Molphey writes a novel. He dreams of literary success. He sends it off to his cousin Edouard who is a publisher in Paris. Nothing happens. The 30 years in which nothing happens make a pleasant, leisurely read. They are all evoked in the memories of Paul, now a drunken old schoolmaster still stuck in the same village in Burgundy. His wife runs off with the publisher, Edouard. His twin daughters, on whom he dotes, leave him, one for a Bohemian way of life in Paris, another for life in the cloister. Mingled in his wine-sodden memories are his grandfather, his wife's family, the parish priest—all superbly well-evoked French provincial types. . . .

Nothing goes on happening. The scenes and memories are all well done, but I was coming to be reminded of a friend of mine's mother who gave up writing a novel set in Edinburgh because, however much she wrote, the heroine was still stuck in a train in Waverley station.

And then the hero, Paul Molphey, turns on the telly. 'It was a literary interview programme—a round table of six authors. As each one was introduced the camera focussed on them—how young they all looked—and then on their books. He felt a spurt of anger at such blatant commercialism and almost turned off the set. But he didn't, instead he prepared a grog'. This is just as well, because it turns out that the Prix Goncourt for that year has been won by a young writer, born in 1950, for a novel set at the end of the war. The next day, Paul goes to the nearest bookseller to buy it, and, by two in the morning, he has finished the prize-winning book. . . . It is of course the book he himself wrote all those years ago, now being acclaimed as a work of genius by someone else.

The final 20 pages of **Lost and Found** are extremely exciting. Bubbling with hatred for the young plagiarist and his smug, rich publisher, Paul sets out for Paris with a loaded revolver.

He beards the publisher (yes, it's old Edouard who ran off with Paul's wife all those years ago) and then, hoping that the gun still works, he sets off for the nightclub where the winner of the "Prix Goncourt" is regular in his attendance. I won't spoil the ending, but it's good.

It would be absurd to claim that this is a novel about the success of *The Cement Garden*. But that provides a fascinating sub-text (don't they call it?) to an otherwise rather actionless tale. Mr Gloag writes like an angel. There are marvellous descriptions of French food, French bad weather, and being drunk. But the bitterness of Paul, who lives largely in his memories, really comes to life when he conceives the idea of getting his revenge on the grossly successful young Jean-Pierre McEwan, sorry, Montbarbon. *Lost and Found* deserves to be a great success.

A. N. Wilson, "Sweet Revenge," in The Spectator, Vol. 247, No. 8001, November 14, 1981, p. 20.

FAITH PULLIN

Lost and Found is a beautifully written novel whose resolution depends on the finding of a lost manuscript; its retrieval is as shocking as its original loss was traumatic for its author, Paul Molphey. (p. 258)

The novel effectively evokes the French countryside, but its emphasis on rural crime and on the melancholy of its irritatingly self-absorbed hero sometimes creates an atmosphere bordering on farce rather than tragedy. In the same way, the complications of the narrative are too subtle for the central situation to bear. Judging by the quality of Molphey's own writing, the manuscript was not a great loss to mankind. Altogether, this is rather a solemn book. Its natural descriptions are moving, almost hypnotic, but Julian Gloag mistakenly makes everything stand or fall on the value of the man and his work; the reader remains unconvinced of both. (pp. 258-59)

Faith Pullin, in a review of "Lost and Found," in British Book News, April, 1982, pp. 258-59.

ISABEL RAPHAEL

Blood for Blood is another of Julian Gloag's admirable psychological thrillers. Barrister Vivian Winter, known for his successful defence of murderers, is himself murdered in circumstances that suggest that he was not unprepared for such an end. He has bequeathed large legacies to eight women and one man, and, will in hand, Ivor Speke sets out to track down the other beneficiaries in the hope of finding the murderer. In doing so he finds himself, as he contrasts his own reaction to sudden, violent loss—of his beloved daughter as well as of his friend—with the ways that others have dealt with similar experiences. Perhaps this is Vivian's true legacy.

My only complaint is that of the two solutions sought, one is obvious and the other unconvincing. But it is the search that matters, after all, the excursions up exciting tributaries, the unfolding of unexpected routes to a given point. Julian Gloag writes with poise and elegance, revealing just enough at any time to sustain pace and suspense. I confess to reading the whole book at one long, self-indulgent sitting, and put it down purring with satisfaction.

Isabel Raphael, "Postwar Daughter of the New Sun," in The Times, London, May 9, 1985, p. 13.*

MARGARET WALTERS

Blood for Blood takes a highly conventional, rather dated form—the whodunnit—and sets out to prove that it can still throw light on serious psychological and moral issues. When successful barrister Vivian Winter is brutally stabbed to death in his own flat, his mother asks his old friend Ivor Speke to find out why. Speke stumbles into a mare's nest of sexual and financial jealousies, and into a nasty series of retributive murders.

Who Vivian is proves more important than who did him in—by now, that's a common thriller play. But Julian Gloag's chief interest is in Ivor and why he knows so little about his best friend. Another recluse, Ivor has given up on life, and serious writing. He tosses off a weekly column reviewing thrillers, but as soon as he's involved with this real crime, persuades his typist, who's half in love with him, to produce his copy. . . .

The trouble is, Ivor has little humour or charm, and it's hard to care whether or not he works through his own paralysed depression by solving the murder case. Julian Gloag asks ambitious questions about the aftermath of violence, about the way guilt and a craving for vengeance distort people's lives. But some of his skills as a thriller writer—his mastery of intricately plotted suspense—actually distract from his larger aims.

Margaret Walters, "Polly Marooned," in The Observer, May 12, 1985, p. 21.*

HARRIET WAUGH

Blood for Blood is a strongly sustained psychological detective story in which the hero, Ivor Speke, a middle-aged, depressed, spongy soak who once wrote good novels, finds himself involved in a bizarre quest to discover the killer of a friend. . . . Ivor is not a particularly engaging hero—he is too squelchy—so his metamorphosis into a slightly more focused, if disagreeable, man would not be of particular interest were it not for the strength and excitement of the plot.

The most interesting character by far is the victim, Vivian Winter, and, in a sense, the element of detection in the story is as much to do with piecing together this man's nature as it is with finding a killer. Winter, a bachelor barrister, has died of multiple stab wounds in the kitchen of his London flat. . . . Vivian's mother, a snobbish battleaxe of a woman, asks Ivor to make sense of her son's death. She suspects the police of prejudice because Vivian was a highly successful criminal barrister who had been responsible for letting loose at least one murderous rapist. Inexplicably, however, for someone who claimed she wished the killer caught, she destroys Vivian's address book. Ivor therefore concentrates on the beneficiaries of Vivian's will.

As he tracks them down (they are mostly women), a strange and twisted tale starts to emerge. Did Vivian know he would be killed? Was the murderer an avenger? Was Vivian on the track of an avenger killer of rapist murderers? . . . Did Vivian have an affair with Ivor's wife? Was he homosexual? Why did he leave money to the wives, mothers, girl-friends of a number of released rapist killers who had met accidental deaths? Who among the women folk of the killers had Vivian not slept with? Why did all his women friends love him, while all his male friends, with the exception of Ivor, hate him? Why, given this last fact, did Ivor not hate him too?

Ivor gradually unearths within himself some uncomfortable truths as his own friendship for Vivian is tested against the reality of his friend's complex nature. Mr Gloag sifts the natures of his hero and victim as an archaeologist might sift the stubborn earth of a clay field. In this particular clay, the unifying traces of vengeance, guilt, murder, love and violence are unearthed. And apparently Ivor becomes a more complete man for the acknowledgement of his baser self.

With the exception of Vivian Winter, who is distanced from us and the hero, none of Mr Gloag's characters are particularly interesting creations. They are mere functionaries within the framework of the plot. However, it must also be acknowledged that, judged as characters in detective fiction, they are unusually well-developed. This may not be Mr Gloag's best novel, but it is the best detective novel anyone is likely to read for some time. I found it unputdownable. (p. 22)

Harriet Waugh, "On the Trail of Vivian Winter," in The Spectator, *Vol. 254, No. 8188, June 15, 1985, pp. 22-3.**

(Charles) William Goyen

1915-1983

American novelist, short story writer, dramatist, scriptwriter, poet, nonfiction writer, critic, translator, and songwriter.

An esteemed author of mythopoeic fiction, Goyen used lyrical prose and imagery to explore the depths of the imagination. Central to his work is his belief that the relationship between storyteller and listener is sacred; for Goyen, the importance of a story involved the act of relating as much as the plot. Although many critics have associated Goyen with such regional Southern writers as Flannery O'Connor and Carson McCullers, Erika Duncan observed that his work "is strangely lacking in the cruelty and violence common to most other writing from the South." Goyen's fiction, much of which is set in the Southwest and features shadowy and elusive characters, evokes a mythical place where reality is suspect and imagination is real. His major themes include the necessity of unity between the physical and the spiritual and the quest of human beings to regain the integrity and wholeness stripped from them by modern society.

Goyen's first novel, *The House of Breath* (1950), is the story of a young man's remembrance of the past and his search for identity and his family. Drawing on the folk tales and local myths of his native east Texas, Goyen weaves an essentially plotless and fantastic tale that extends beyond the regional confines of its setting. Many critics consider this novel to be his finest literary achievement. Goyen's next novel, *In a Farther Country* (1955), although more dramatic and episodic than *The House of Breath*, expands upon similar themes. Essentially a romance about a Spanish-American woman's fantasies of a united Spain, the novel focuses on the dehumanizing effects of living in an industrialized society and emphasizes the importance of the imagination in coping with the hostile modern world. *The Fair Sister* (1962), based on Goyen's short story "Savata, My Fair Sister," is a somber study of religious fanaticism into which Goyen interjects wit and humor to emphasize his characteristically introspective themes. In her divinely inspired ambition to save her sister from sin, the protagonist fails to recognize that in redeeming her sister's soul, she has virtually broken her spirit. *Come, the Restorer* (1974) represents both a return to and an extension of the themes and style of Goyen's previous novels. Rich in biblical rhetoric and imagery, *Come, the Restorer* is a prophetic tale of a young man's search for fulfillment and his attempts to discover and understand his family's legacy.

In *Arcadio* (1983), Goyen created the symbol of the hermaphrodite—half man, half woman—which embodies the duality between the real and the imaginary central to all of his work. Developed as a story within a story, Arcadio's tale, which he tells to a small boy in a dream, details his quest for his family, his joy at finding them, and his sorrow at losing them again. Arcadio is a prophet—displaced, homeless, and deformed—whose parables and teachings encompass the paradoxes he has encountered on his journey and transform them into miraculous reconciliations that give meaning to life. Reginald Gibbons described *Arcadio* as "the work of a master fabulist . . . one more courageous foray into fiction unlike anyone else's, haunting the reader with its tenderness and ferocity."

Goyen's short stories have also won consistent praise. Such stories as "The White Rooster," "The Letter in the Cedarchest," and "Bridge of Music, River of Sand," collected in *Had I a Hundred Mouths: New and Selected Stories 1947-1983* (1985), indicate the range and high quality of Goyen's work. Goyen's earlier volumes, *Ghost and Flesh: Stories and Tales* (1952) and *The Faces of Blood Kindred: A Novella and Ten Stories* (1960), explore many of the themes of his novels.

(See also *CLC*, Vols. 5, 8, 14; *Contemporary Authors*, Vols. 5-8, rev. ed., Vol. 110 [obituary]; *Contemporary Authors New Revision Series*, Vol. 6; *Dictionary of Literary Biography*, Vol. 2; and *Dictionary of Literary Biography Yearbook: 1983*.)

ROBERT PHILLIPS

"It is easier in our society to be naked physically than to be naked psychologically or spiritually," Rollo May writes in his seminal little book, *The Courage to Create*. And May is correct in his evaluation of our contemporary society, in which people find it easier to share their bodies than their fantasies. For whatever reason, until fairly recently, fiction writers found the sharing of their hopes, fears, and aspirations as marking them as too vulnerable. They were shy about sharing those things which matter most. Novels by Joyce and Lawrence and Miller were exceptions, of course: but the most daring of their productions were outlawed. It was only, perhaps, with the advent of such liberated novels as Philip Roth's *Portnoy's Complaint* (1969) and Erica Jong's *Fear of Flying* (1973) that the courage to create publicly became as unbridled as the courage to copulate.

But not so with William Goyen. From the first—that is, roughly from 1949 onward—his fiction has been of the most intimate kind, surpassing the physical realities in favor of the subjective ones. Events, when they occur in his fiction at all, are related not to character so much as to sensibility. His concern is not for concrete truths, but poetic truths—for the dream, the fantasy, the outrageous. It is this engagement with *all* things, not merely the physical things of this world, which is a part of Goyen's real achievement. It is what gives his work its vast range. It is why [Goyen's *The House of Breath*], a novel about a small town in Texas, can appeal to thousands of readers, not just in this country, but also in France, Germany, England, Italy, and Spain. It is why his tales, full of East Texas vernacular, rise above mere regionalism. (p. 112)

In attempting to cover a panorama of his day- and night-mares, Goyen has created a large gallery of characters. Unlike many very subjective novelists who can write only about themselves (Jean Rhys, Denton Welch), Goyen has created, or recreated, young girls and old men; the ordinary and the freakish; the famous and the obscure; the military and the civilian; the country and the urban; the straight and the gay. His characters even include animals and trees, and a good many ghosts as well as flesh.

In addition to his sharp and varied characterizations, there is, of course, his fine ear. The vernacular employed in his stories is flawless, as any Southwesterner could tell you. This concern for speech is but a part of his whole concern for language—precise, detailed, telling. A passage from a Goyen book is, ultimately, so individual it could have been written by no one else.

Then there are Goyen's topics, which, if dealing primarily with exile and suppression of individuals and individuality, also take a large overview and nearly always, in some way, deal with ecology, with the diminished and the lost things of this world.

The body of William Goyen's work does not vary greatly in quality. . . . Overall, his work is consistent and at a very high level. And *The House of Breath* is perhaps a masterpiece—still in print twenty-five years after publication.

Nevertheless, it is doubtful that Goyen's fiction has been a creditable influence upon any other writer of note today. His concerns and his style are too highly individual to be of use by others. (Anyone who has attempted to copy his style will find that task near impossible). Rather than being famous as the founder of a school or a following, Goyen should be noted as a highly individualized voice. He is a fabulous original, like Carson McCullers and Flannery O'Connor and not many others. In an age of mechanization, he devotes himself to poetry. In an age of plastic, he celebrates the ghost and the flesh. (pp. 113-14)

> *Robert Phillips, in his* William Goyen, *Twayne Publishers, 1979, 157 p.*

PUBLISHERS WEEKLY

[*Arcadio*] is a triumph of the imagination, Goyen's first book in seven years. A boy at his East Texas home hears an old uncle tell of having seen a hermaphrodite, completely male and completely female, bathe in a river long ago. The boy has a vision and in it appears the hermaphrodite, Arcadio, who spins an enchanted tale that we know could not possibly be true but that we accept anyway. By spanning both sexes and being a perennial outsider, Arcadio bears the witness of a modern-day, Tex-Mex Tiresias. In a "Mescan" dialect, Arcadio tells of nights spent as a sideshow attraction and of his search for his mother, a Mexican woman doomed to love the wrong people, and for his saintly half-brother who was raised in the "Missoura" jail where he was born and yet managed to preserve his innocence. . . . In a rush of words, Arcadio tells of the battles his dual body has posed with himself and the world, and of his eventual reconciliation. This beautifully written book has the overwhelming power of a myth brought to life.

> *A review of "Arcadio," in* Publishers Weekly, *Vol. 224, No. 5, July 29, 1983, p. 62.*

REGINALD GIBBONS

Though Goyen was often labeled a Texas writer, his language was a stylistic accomplishment rather than a regional or period manner, utterly individual, neither typically Southern nor, as some would have had it more recently, magic-realist. What may appear at first to be a colloquial narrative often becomes an intense, songlike prose utterance with verses and refrains. Goyen himself once remarked that some of his stories were really anthems.

Arcadio, his only major published work since *Collected Stories* (1975), is the most intense of these visionary songs of life. Set in his native Texas, like many of his previous works, it opens with a typically Goyenesque narrative of a "visitation"—Goyenesque in that the author characteristically filtered a story through one of its characters, a witness slightly apart who hears someone else speak of what happened, and Goyenesque also in that what interested him most of all was passion and intensity of experience.

Arcadio begins with the voice of the narrator as a boy of perhaps 13: "One time on a hot July night when we were sitting in the dark hoping to get a breath of breeze, I heard my mother whisper, 'There's somebody standing out in the yard.' In the flare of the heat lightning we saw a figure streaming down its whole body with hair struck full of quivering light, with hair of light streaming down to the ground and eyes as glowing as lanterns." When the narrator's father calls to this figure, it disappears. And the narrator recalls, "All night I thought the figure might be out there, darkened, its light put out by our fear. I lay awake and thought about it, about turned-away things, things not taken, things thrown back or let go, or the light in them put out by fear."

The apparition has been evoked by the narrator's memory of his taciturn uncle, who on another hot night had told him of seeing a person bathing in secret in the nearby river, someone who seemed both man and woman. That was Arcadio, a living war and a reconciliation of opposites, half man and half woman, half "Mescan" and half Texan, half saintly and half wanton, half truth teller and half blatant exaggerator.

Framed by the narrator's reminiscence, the novel becomes Arcadio's account of himself (he seems slightly more male than female), delivered on a long day to a silent listener—our narrator—in the shade of an abandoned, vine-tangled railroad trestle over a dry riverbed. Jesus consorted with publicans and sinners, and Arcadio recounts a life of spiritual quest in a world of brothels and jailhouses.

Arcadio's daylong story is an account of a lifetime's wandering in search of a lost mother, father and brother. On his way, he meets many others also searching, for a lost love or friend or place, seeking to atone for a past crime or transgression. . . . Arcadio's song is his memorial to his past life and his friends dead and gone.

He is a kind of prophet as well, come out of a desert to utter parables and warnings. Nearly every conceivable contradiction or paradox of existence appears in Arcadio's story and his meditations on his own split nature, past and future, imprisonment and escape, cruelty and forgiveness, loss and recovery, spirituality and a surfeit of sex. His powers of invention as a talker are great, his register running from the lowest scatological humor to rhapsodic flights of commemorative grief. (pp. 14, 36)

Arcadio's speech is sprinkled with "Mescan espressions" and comic asides on the peculiarities of the English language. All the incidents of plot, which are many and obstreperously flamboyant, are in fact overshadowed by the language of this short novel.

This is a work of profound sympathy for the lost, the displaced, the crazy, the imprisoned, the homeless, the deformed, the loveless—all the turned-away, whose light we tend to put out by our fear of them. Amazingly, Arcadio also touches on the reigning social problems of our day: the environment destroyed, the family broken and dispersed, loveless sex. He does this in passing, offering the viewpoint of the outcast, the sinner, whose sense of the world around him is both true and naïve. Neither Arcadio's ultimate confrontation with his long-lost family nor the apocalyptic destruction of cities and people he has witnessed can redeem his travails or solve the problems around him. Instead, he tells his story to a silent listener, and his extended aria transforms pitiable sadness and crazy misdeeds into a reconciliation of violent opposites. His remembering and singing of others who are gone makes peace with them and, through his being heard by his listener, makes peace for them. An early story, **"Ghost and Flesh,"** is perhaps the most important statement of Goyen's belief that the situation of the storyteller and the listener is a spiritual one in which guilt, suffering and sorrow are finally redeemed.

Arcadio's parables and paradoxes restore meaning to the lives he recounts. His song may be Goyen's finest achievement. The work of a master fabulist, it was one more courageous foray into fiction unlike anyone else's, haunting the reader with its tenderness and ferocity. (pp. 36-7)

> Reginald Gibbons, "Redeemed in the Telling," in The New York Times Book Review, November 6, 1983, pp. 14, 36-7.

MADISON BELL

The narrator of William Goyen's [*Arcadio*] is, as the name Arcadio suggests, the ultimately natural human, but the story makes a very strange version of pastorale. He (or she) is a perfectly formed hermaphrodite, male and female in both body and sensibility. "In me, *Satanas* put on one body the two biggest troublemakers ever created from flesh onto one body and give that one person the torments of the whole human race, man and woman, all in one. 'Tis me. Arcadio." Speaking a delicately stylized Tex-Mex dialect, Arcadio tells a tale which is musical in both language and form, starting in the middle and widening in concentric circles to embrace its beginning and end. Arcadio's story is horror, an anthology of nature's worst cruelties. Not just a confused freak, he/she embodies every conceivable dualism—doubled in language, in race, in sex, and in body and soul. Abandoned by a "Mescan" mother and prostituted by a gringo father, Arcadio discovers all nuances and perversions of sexual life. Moreover, the narrator's male and female parts have a dubious ability to make love to each other, a practice which leads to a crisis of self-loathing and thence to conversion. . . .

Arcadio's emerging faith is mocked even by other freaks. . . . *Reconciliación* becomes an obsession, as Arcadio begins a quest to recover his/her lost mother, father, and half-brother. "Maybe I could bring us all together," Arcadio says, referring as much to his/her divided being as to the scattered family. But the "normal" world turns out to be as plagued by dissension as Arcadio's own person, and the reconciliation fails spectacularly. The father and half-brother die in spite of efforts to save them, and when Arcadio finds Chupa, the mother, his/her first impulse is to kill her. The hermaphrodite ends up solving nothing (though acknowledging a great deal), perpetually isolated in a weird wholeness.

Arcadio exists as an emblem of what Goyen called "the hidden life," which boils with irreconcilable desires. He/she is dreamed into being by a faceless narrator who exclaims, "Make my heart right! Save my soul! But let me see your body again." As paradox incarnated, Arcadio is necessarily a monster, but a gentle one. He/she articulates the need for a myth that can assimilate the contradictions of a hermaphroditic body. These paradoxes exist as image and idea in the lives, or at least the dreams, of ordinary mortals. Arcadio seems not so much a freak after all.

> Madison Bell, in a review of "Arcadio," in The Village Voice, Vol. XXIX, No. 1, January 3, 1984, p. 44.

JOYCE CAROL OATES

William Goyen has always been the most mysterious of writers. He is poet, singer, musician as well as storyteller; he is a seer; a troubled visionary; a spiritual presence in a national literature largely deprived of the spiritual. Yet there is something driven and demonic—"accursed" Goyen would say—about his art. The extraordinary cadences of the language exert a hypnotic power that the events of the fiction roughly dispel; the reader is confronted by beauty, and ugliness; then again beauty and ugliness in the same instant, housed in the same image. [In **"Arthur Bond,"** the title character's] curse is a worm buried in "the sweetest part of the thigh" but we also understand that Arthur Bond *is* his curse; the worm is his soul, his very being. The fantastic diver of **"Bridge of Music, River of Sand"** is both a suicide and a redeemer. In **"Figure Over the Town"** Flagpole Moody absorbs all the projections of the town yet remains a symbol of the artist—stubborn, isolated, precarious, triumphant. The hermaphrodite hero of the novel *Arcadio* is probably Goyen's most powerful symbol of this inexplicable doubleness—the physical expression of a paradox that is primarily spiritual. All serious art celebrates mystery, perhaps, but Goyen's comes close to embodying it.

A story by William Goyen is always immediately recognizable as a story by William Goyen. He is not boasting when he says . . . that people in his life (his family and relatives in East Texas) had the speech, and he inherited the voice. Speech and voice are distinctive—the one natural, the other refined, calibrated. So seemingly fluid and artless are the stories they give the impression of being "merely" narratives of memory. The voice of the unconscious, the surreal, is most seductive when its cadences are colloquial, as in these masterful openings: "I started out to tell about what became of two cousins and their uncle who loved them, according to what the older cousin told me. But some of their kinfolks' lives would have to be told if . . ." (**"Tongues of Men and of Angels"**); "Now this is about the lives of Old Mrs. Woman, Sister Sammye, and Little Pigeon, and how they formed a household; but first . . ." (**"The Letter in the Cedarchest"**); and my own favorite, "Do you remember the bridge that we crossed over the river to get to Riverside? And if you looked over yonder you saw the railroad trestle? High and narrow? Well that's what he jumped off of. Into a nothing river. 'River'! I could laugh. I can spit more than runs in that dry bed. . . ." (**"Bridge of Music, River of Sand"**). So fluid is the voice the stories seem to tell themselves, each story distinctive yet part of a large communal narrative, like a broad river fed by numberless tributaries. And Goyen's characters too, when one comes to know them, are frequently kin—"blood kin"—whose stories and lives reflect and help to define one another. All are caught up in the fundamental mystery of life, all are compelled to speak of the "trouble" that occasions their tales. (pp. vii-viii)

Though Goyen's art is carefully revised and refined, its impetus is unconscious, intuitive, "passional" as D. H. Lawrence would say, springing from blood- rather than mind-consciousness. Hence the mesmerizing quality of such stories as **"In the Icebound Hothouse"** and **"Old Wildwood"** and the dream-like incantatory **"Children of Old Somebody"** in which language itself is active; a character, or a focus of vision, by way of words. . . . The storyteller uncle of **"Had I a Hundred Mouths"** is a nurturing, even a maternal presence; his is the power of seduction—"the surrender of listener to teller, almost in a kind of love-making, of sensual possession, yet within innocence and purity." Thus, even when we read Goyen's stories silently we *hear* them: they are, as Goyen rightly says, ballads, serenades, anthems, even hymns of universal loneliness and salvation, the same powerful themes struck again and again in different keys, by way of different characters. Language *is* character here, but it too is always changing.

Reginald Gibbons shrewdly points out that Goyen is interested in more than "the shape of a man"—he is interested in "the significance of the shape of a man"—hence the emblematic nature of the fiction which is symbolic rather than allegorical, haunting and provocative rather than didactic. An early story like **"The White Rooster"** suggests the D. H. Lawrence of "The Escaped Cock" and has an ending that is dramatically logical, emotionally inevitable, yet it differs from Goyen's more mature—and typically Goyenesque—work in that it *has* so emphatic an ending. Elsewhere, Goyen's stories are not resolved in any conventional way; nor do they simply trail off into silence. Image-centered, as our dreams are image-centered, each story is a unique cluster of (often contradictory) occasions—a field of contending forces, one might say—like the numerous medallions Goyen recalls his mother sewing, one

by one, before quilting them together into a whole. The wholeness is present in the imagination (or in the unconscious) but it must be *quilted* into being by way of the artist's craft. It must be discovered or, better yet, uncovered. Hence the visionary writer trusts to his yet-unarticulated vision to guide him and to provide him with the necessary voice. When I say that a story by William Goyen is always recognizable as a story by William Goyen this is not to say that the voice is always the same voice—far from it. The canny, funny narrators of **"The Texas Principessa"** and **"Where's Esther?"** bear no kinship whatsoever to the distraught narrator of **"In the Icebound Hothouse."** Yet the cluster of occasions of **"The Texas Principessa"** includes a nightmare image—the deadly spider at the heart of a peach innocently eaten—and the exiles of Horty Solomon (heiress to a Texas Jewish fortune in drygoods!) and Esther Haverton . . . are not so radically different from the exile of the speechless narrator of the icebound hothouse, the poet compelled to write to assuage the violence of his interior vision.

Goyen has said that he felt at times he was "the receiver of a cursedness": the carrier or bearer of images denied by his kinsfolk and neighbors in East Texas. The Ku Klux Klan, for instance, appears frequently in his stories, even in so relatively benign a story as **"Figure Over the Town"** where no one is terrorized or lynched. . . . Images of physical mutilation and malformation recur in Goyen's fiction as the outward expression, I would suggest, of the unacknowledged evil of his world, which the artist is accursed (and blessed) to acknowledge. Like many another writer Goyen chose exile of a sort while passionately retaining his childhood's experiences. He could not remain in Texas, "couldn't live among my own," he knew himself estranged, alienated, yet his destiny was to focus his creative powers upon the very world he'd left—hence the doubleness of many of his emblematic heroes. His case, Goyen said, seemed "a very personal thing, almost demonic—a curse: dark. Therefore the meditational quality, a prayer-like quality, almost 'Help me, Save me, Deliver me.'" If there was an evangelical minister preaching the salvation of the soul in Goyen's childhood there was also the Ku Klux Klan tarring and feathering Negroes, setting them ablaze to run in the streets. ("I saw them running like that, twice.") How ironic it is, that the artist/writer/poet who *sees* and *feels* the horror of such events is so frequently denounced by his kinsmen and his fellow citizens as mad, or wicked, or spuriously "muckraking"—as if the measure of sanity were the capacity to assimilate horrors without comment. Goyen's bouts with madness—of which he briefly speaks—are the very emblems of the fissures of consciousness accommodated by his kinsmen and neighbors back home.

But the stories are not finally stories of alienation, violence, or madness. The most startling images—the naked diver of **"Bridge of Music, River of Sand,"** for instance—give way to a narrative meditation that roots the stories in the familiar human framework of exile and return, loss and rediscovery, death and redemption. The image of two brothers—one dead—on a door floating in a Texas flood gives way to a curious sort of harmony. The split tongue is an angel's tongue—perhaps! It has been said of Goyen's fiction that its spiritual significance resides in the very telling itself, in the voice given body and form by way of the writer's vision: and it might be said that the reader, in reading, in *hearing* this unique voice, completes the spiritual event. My suggestion is that William Goyen's stories be read slowly, no more than one at a sitting, perhaps, and that the reader suspend his expectations of what the "normal'' should be no less than the ''conventional'' in terms of the short story. Simply allow the words to sound, and to resound. Words too are physical—rhythms and cadences spring from the body. This is an art of healing and the process cannot be forced. (pp. ix-xii)

Joyce Carol Oates, in an introduction to Had I a Hundred Mouths: New & Selected Stories 1947-1983 *by William Goyen, Clarkson N. Potter, Inc./Publishers, 1985, pp. vii-xii.*

VANCE BOURJAILY

[''Had I a Hundred Mouths''] is—along with six other tales and the novel *Arcadio,* published in the year of his death—the final product of William Goyen's remarkable talent. These last seven stories, written between 1976 and 1982, form the first section of [*Had I a Hundred Mouths: New & Selected Stories 1947-1983*]. With them are six stories from Goyen's first collection, *Ghost and Flesh,* written between 1947 and 1952, and four from his second, *The Faces of Blood Kindred* (1960). There is a persuasive introduction by Joyce Carol Oates [see excerpt above] and a candid interview with the author conducted by Reginald Gibbons, who assembled the book.

What we have, then, is a Goyen retrospective that shows the range of his artistic achievement in the short story during the extensive career that began with a novel, *The House of Breath* (1956), and included four others—*In a Farther Country* (1955), *The Fair Sister* (1963), *Come, the Restorer* (1974) and *Arcadio.* He also wrote five plays and three other works, *A Book of Jesus, Wonderful Plant* and *Nine Poems.*

Taking the selection here to be representative, one cannot fail to remark that the personal landscape was as much there in the first stories as in the last and seems to have been forming in Goyen's imagination long before he began to write. In a 1983 interview, the author observed of his small-town Texas boyhood, ''When we left Trinity and moved to Houston, I had already lived my life.'' He was 7 years old. ''That Big Thicket country, those Texas wetlands, are *my* wildness. They have haunted me and become my place in all my work,'' he remarked.

The personal language in which Goyen wrote of the place and its people had its origins in both. It is deeply rooted in the Texas rural vernacular and, as he said in the interview with Mr. Gibbons, was influenced by ''Thomas Wolfe. Singing people. Whitman. Early Saroyan.'' But just as I see even earlier American writers who knew landscapes ancestral to Goyen's—I am thinking of the fantasy stories of Hawthorne and Melville—so I see another, very much earlier influence on the language, the most pervasive influence there is.

Consider this line: ''And then he knew how adroitly they could kill a thing and with what craftiness.'' And: ''O I was broken of my sleep and of my night disturbed.'' Those are the rhythms of the King James Version of the Bible, perhaps another childhood implantation.

The voice that developed was a bard's voice, singing dark narratives in lines rich and rhythmic enough to transform stories into ballads. ''The extraordinary cadences of the language exert a hypnotic power that the events of the fiction roughly dispel,'' Joyce Carol Oates writes in her introduction, but it could as well be said the other way round—as in a ballad, the horrors and sufferings are softened into myth by the music of the telling.

This should not be taken to mean that there is a sameness in the stories. Neither voice nor landscape is without variety. The very earliest tale, ''The White Rooster,'' is almost impersonal, the author dealing with characters as evenhandedly as a good dramatist, the piquant action clear and available to a reader at any level. Yet ''Children of Old Somebody'' (from the same year), with its tantalizing hints of autobiography, is rendered in lyric prose so dense as to challenge explication.

The group of stories from the middle years, with the exception of ''Zamour, Or a Tale of Inheritance,'' are all quite autobiographical or, more accurately, derive from family history.

Then in the last stories, the author's interests again become wider and the control very near perfect, so much so that ''The Texas Principessa'' and ''Where's Esther?'' actually verge on comedy without being out of tone with the other stories. William Goyen's lute had more strings than one. (pp. 28-9)

Vance Bourjaily, ''Words for a World,'' in The New York Times Book Review, *June 9, 1985, pp. 28-9.*

JOHN RECHY

Language is ''a principal character,'' [Goyen] points out in an interview included in [*Had I a Hundred Mouths,* a] collection of his masterful stories written between 1947 and 1982. The latest were produced near the end of his life but are filled with fresh wonder and the awe of discovery.

After early literary acclaim, Goyen in his latter years was almost ignored. His last novel, the magical *Arcadio,* was rejected repeatedly and finally published to triumphant praise—one month after his death. . . . This collection will extend the deserved acclaim.

Why excommunicated in his last years? Perhaps because in a time of tiny emotions, he continued to illuminate grand subjects—redemption, salvation, ''the joys and despairs of desire.'' Bright with hope, black with evil, the stories are simultaneously funny and tragic. Esther's decline into alcoholic destruction in ''Where's Esther?'' is told in a voice that laughs between sobs. Sexual obsession finds a folksy tone in ''Arthur Bond,'' a man with an evil ''worm in his thigh.'' The title story is a family yarn—about rape, suicide, lynching. The chatty voice in ''The White Rooster'' leads into madness. These meldings result in a haunting mythical quality—tinged with evangelistic allegory—that does not compromise the terrible reality of the subjects explored.

Most of the stories occur in the Gothic state of Texas. Saints—usually fallen—coexist with ''the accursed''—often redeemed. Living characters and lingering ghosts are equally ''real'' in his expert hands. . . .

Bidding listeners of his own tale a farewell of love and sorrow, Goyen's fabulous Arcadio says, ''So long to all I loved and will not hunt for any more, *adios* . . . I have sung you my own very life, please to not forget me.''

Goyen ''sang'' his life fully into these beautifully wrought stories. Along with his novels, they assure that he is not forgotten.

John Rechy, in a review of ''Had I a Hundred Mouths: New & Selected Stories, 1947-1983,'' in Los Angeles Times Book Review, *July 28, 1985, p. 1.*

HOWARD LaFRANCHI

The voices that tell the 21 stories of *Had I a Hundred Mouths*—most of which take place in the hot, lost pre-World War II towns of Goyen's native east Texas—sound as if they are compelled to do so. The reader is made to feel like a confidant who, simply by listening, will lighten for the teller the weight of a sin or family secret, or help make sense of the conflicts in small-town life.

It is the mix of this urgency of telling and the insularity of pre-electronic rural living that gives Goyen's stories their haunting quality. And it is this quality which in turn makes them good entertainment. . . .

Much in the same way that Guy de Maupassant horrified, yet intrigued, his Parisian audience with eerie tales of rural Normandy a century ago, Goyen tells the urban (or suburban) American reader of people not so far away, either in place or time: a man who carries a worm in his leg; a woman driven mad by a white rooster; people who cannot go back home; and simple souls who carry dark family secrets.

It's not always pleasant reading, nor did Goyen . . . intend his work to be. "It starts with trouble," he says of his writing in an interview with TriQuarterly's Reginald Gibbons, contained in the book. "You don't think it starts with peace, do you?"

Nor is his writing always easy. Goyen is a writer for whom "language is always a principal character in the story," and this can lead to complex, even bewildering writing. . . .

But perhaps Goyen's most irresistible talent is simply the way he begins his tales. Who could turn away from a story that begins: "I started out to tell about what became of two cousins and their uncle who loved them, according to what the older cousin told me. But some of their kinfolks' lives would have to be told . . ."; or "It is true that I have not been able to utter more than a madman's sound since my eyes beheld the sight. I've lost my speech. And so they have asked me to write."

These are voices compelled to tell us what they know. And we in turn are swept in, compelled to listen.

> *Howard LaFranchi, "Goyen's Haunting Stories Evoke the Rural Texas Past," in* The Christian Science Monitor, *September 16, 1985, p. 25.*

Elizabeth Forsythe Hailey

1938-

American novelist, dramatist, short story writer, journalist, scriptwriter, and critic.

Hailey is an author of popular fiction whose novels feature strong-willed female protagonists. Her first book, *A Woman of Independent Means* (1978), was both a best-seller and a critical success. The novel follows Bess Steed Garner from her childhood in the early 1900s through her life as an aggressive, wealthy businesswoman. Bess's strength and ambition are revealed through her numerous letters to her family and friends, a technique which was praised by some reviewers. Bess is modeled after Hailey's maternal grandmother, whose independent spirit and extensive travels are recreated in the novel. In 1984, Hailey adapted *A Woman of Independent Means* for the stage as a one-character monologue.

Life Sentences (1982), Hailey's second novel, was not as highly acclaimed as *A Woman of Independent Means*. The novel concerns three college friends who are reunited years later when one of them, Lindsay Howard, is violently raped. When she discovers that she has become pregnant, Lindsay decides to keep the baby. Hailey stated that she wished to "try to confront my own fears" by placing herself "in the position of the central character who has so many huge choices to make."

In *Joanna's Husband and David's Wife* (1985), Hailey explores the problems of marital relationships. The novel is structured as a journal in which Joanna chronicles her twenty-five-year marriage to a famous writer, her search for identity, and her subsequent fame as a novelist. When the couple agrees to a trial separation, Joanna's husband discovers her journal and records his views of their troubled marriage.

(See also *Contemporary Authors,* Vols. 93-96; *Contemporary Authors New Revision Series,* Vol. 15; and *Contemporary Authors Autobiography Series,* Vol. 1.)

ANNE TYLER

[In *A Woman of Independent Means,* the] sole source of our information about Bess is Bess herself: her letters to husbands, friends and children, as well as stray telegrams, instructions to housekeepers, and promissory notes. If you can imagine a steamer trunk containing every word ever written by one woman during her lifetime, that's *A Woman of Independent Means.* But what her correspondents answer, we can only guess; no one else's letters appear.

As a result, reading this novel requires some detective work. We pride ourselves on gathering clues: What's really going on beneath what Bess tells us? Is she deluded in taking her husband's fidelity for granted while she gallivants through Europe without him? Are the people around her really as accepting (not to say gullible) as she imagines them to be? It's remarkable that we can sense all these undercurrents from one woman's

letters—and very natural and believable letters, at that, with no sense of strain or forced exposition.

But because she's the only voice in the book, it's also up to Bess to convince us of her good points. She does have many: she is honest, genuinely kind and interested in other people; and she ages wonderfully. . . . The problem is that when she has to tell us all this herself, it's hard for her to avoid sounding self-congratulatory. It may be that a few of the answers to these letters should have appeared as well—someone else praising Bess, for once, while Bess remained modestly silent.

In her dedication, Elizabeth Forsythe Hailey says that *A Woman of Independent Means* was inspired by her own grandmother. There certainly is a sense here of a living, complex person— the kind of woman who would make an exasperating mother but a marvelous grandmother, provided you have a strong enough character yourself not to feel overwhelmed by her.

At a few points, this book is no fun at all to read. Why would we want to add this interfering, grasping, possessive person to our list of acquaintances? But slowly, [Bess] wins us over. Some of her more audacious offenses begin to make us laugh; her tragedies are more moving than we would have expected. (pp. 4, 13)

In fact, Bess is so memorable a character that I seem here to be reviewing not *A Woman of Independent Means* but the woman herself, which speaks well for Elizabeth Forsythe Hailey's writing. The book becomes Bess's own; the author backs out, giving her the floor. Bess's last words are: "Write me. I want letters waiting." (p. 13)

> Anne Tyler, "Letters from Bess about Bess," in The New York Times Book Review, *May 28, 1978, pp. 4, 13.*

BRIGITTE WEEKS

The message after the beep tone signals the death of letter writing. Gone are the days of sealing wax and sheets crisscrossed with a fine hand. But *A Woman of Independent Means* reminds us poignantly of our loss, of how letters have sustained friendships, kept families together, succored loneliness and, most important, provided us with an intimate record of how we live and feel. Elizabeth Forsythe Hailey's novel is composed entirely of letters and an occasional preremptory cable from Elizabeth Alcott Steed Garner (Bess) to those who filled her life for more than half a century. She begins letter writing in 1899 as a girl of eight, confident of victory in a spelling bee, and continues until her death 10 years ago in a Dallas hospital.

What sets this novel apart is the tremendous workout its anachronistic form gives to the imagination: flexing and stretching forgotten muscles of memory, empathy and insight. The reader stumbles over the spare opening pages and is precipitated by short notes out of the schoolroom into marriage—Bess' idea—with a childhood friend, Rob Steed. Then the pace quickens. Between every note, cable or reflective epistle of the small hours lies a complex sequence of events. The reader is allowed—required—to fill in the gaps, to experience each encounter, each decision in exhaustive detail. The author weaves in tiny clues which, with very few exceptions, are undetectable. Every reader must draw upon his own experience to flesh out the world beyond the letters, to figure out passing references, to detect covert anger or anguish. The resulting novel becomes, in part, a reflection of the reader. Gaining the complicity of the audience in this complex process while sustaining the pace and interest is a feat of amazing ingenuity.

Even as the reader is, in this sense, composing his own life of Bess Steed, the firm hand of Elizabeth Hailey is delineating the limits of personality within which the imagination must stay. Bess is tough, almost to the point of ruthlessness. We can usually assume affirmative answers to the requests in her letters. No possibility for dissent is admitted in her clipped, formal paragraphs, and she frequently encloses a check to preclude any further discussion. Bess believes that a well-placed donation or advance payment in full can work her will. And she is rarely wrong. (pp. E1, E5)

Bess' strength is the strength of the novel: the sense of change, of maturing and then of aging conveyed in her letters is astonishing. The anatomy of a lifetime's development is delicately laid out before us, each tiny bone gleaming clean. Bess' love for her first husband Rob survives his death and plays its part in her second marriage to Sam Garner. Undertaken in resignation and for the good of the children, the marriage ripens slowly into a warm and loving relationship, only to decline again as Sam retires from his business into grasping eccentricity and isolation. . . .

Bess is a formidable woman who compels admiration and affection; a woman who draws up a detailed and practical mar-

riage contract when she marries Sam—in 1922; who uses the same toughness to face premature widowhood and the tragic death of her 10-year-old son Robin. The maturity and poise of the writing, and the courage of the author in demanding compliance and cooperation from her readers, are unexpected and impressive in a first novel. Her second must achieve a daunting standard of excellence to equal it. (p. E5)

> Brigitte Weeks, "First Class Mail," in Book World— The Washington Post, *June 4, 1978, pp. E1, E5.*

BRUCE ALLEN

Sentiment is the undoing of *A Woman of Independent Means* . . . , the epistolary self-portrait of Bess Steed Garner, a Texas matriarch who outlasts several tragic losses to become the sort of tiresome tower of strength from whom friends and relatives flee. This novel's dilemma is essentially the one Dickens never solved in *Bleak House:* our only view of the protagonist is hers, so she is forced to celebrate her own virtues. Hailey maintains her (old and tired) structure artfully, but it betrays her into dehumanizing her heroine. After all can you really *like* a woman who sends a sympathy letter to Jacqueline on November 23, 1963—and claims "I have been very encouraged about the state of our economy by Walter Lippmann's articles in *The New York Herald Tribune,* which I read every day"? I suggest that you cannot. (p. 611)

> Bruce Allen, "First Novels," in The Sewanee Review, *Vol. LXXXVI, No. 4, Fall, 1978, pp. 609-17.**

THE VIRGINIA QUARTERLY REVIEW

A Woman of Independent Means reads like the flip-side of *Pamela.* Hailey's recent novel is, however, the flip-side that nobody plays. Had Richardson's imagination not been sparked by the model letters he wrote for young ladies, he might have written a novel as flat and foolish as this. The heroine, Bess Steed Garner, is intended, it seems, as a prototypical liberated woman with a flair for life. But her specious freedom is a historical cliché. . . . Our social-climbing heroine is the sole narrator of this plodding, plotless epistolary epic. There are hints that the unscrupulous, materialistic, and manipulative lady is despised by all who know her, yet, Hailey is so clumsy a writer that this possibility for drama is never more than a suspicion, apparently not intended by the author. Somehow I doubt a *Clarissa* will follow.

> A review of "A Woman of Independent Means," in The Virginia Quarterly Review, *Vol. 54, No. 4 (Autumn, 1978), p. 138.*

PATRICIA MEYER SPACKS

[In *A Woman of Independent Means,* Hailey] returns to the conventions of the epistolary novel, allowing her protagonist to tell her own story, from childhood to old age, in a series of letters to relatives and friends. Even on its own terms, the novel seems uncomfortably slight and unnervingly theoretical. To be sure, it makes no great effort at philosophic profundity (that's a relief). . . . On the contrary, its protagonist reveals an utterly commonplace mind with a few up-to-date ideas given interest by being attributed to someone for whom they are historically relatively unlikely. The theoretical aspect of the fiction emerges in its conception of character. Bess Steed Garner, twice married but long widowed between marriages, does things not by the laws of psychology but on the basis of some notion about what a truly "liberated" woman would be like. She acts unfailingly out of some idea of independence, lacking emotional complexity and imaginative conviction. Even as a young woman, she lends rather than gives her husband money, receiving a note of hand in return; when he dies, at the age of twenty-nine, she readily assumes many of his business responsibilities. But no moment of convincing feeling, no evocation of genuine conflict, no real experienced difficulty even though difficulties are unconvincingly asserted (never communicated) mars the smooth course of Bess's career. The epistolary convention relieves the novelist of the obligation to write compelling prose . . . ; socio-political clichés relieve her of the necessity to imagine complexly. Her fiction sounds like instructive reminiscences from a women's magazine. . . . (p. 672)

This novel would seem too negligible to warrant serious discussion except that it reveals rather startlingly how certain social assumptions inform literature at every level of sophistication. . . . Bess offers her reflections about time, memory, and art—rather primitive in articulation and conception, but nonetheless familiar. A friend sends her a blank book as a wedding present. She responds with a rhapsody about the inferior satisfaction of living a life compared to writing about it. Hence, she continues, her pleasure in producing letters. "Somehow by compressing and editing the events of my life, I infuse them with a dramatic intensity totally lacking at the time, but oddly enough I find that years later what I remember is not the event as I lived it but as I described it in a letter. I find the very act of writing turns fact into fiction and for that I thank God with all my heart." The embarrassing imprecision of this account—"dramatic intensity" is conspicuously lacking in Bess's narrative—may obscure the significance of its presence: talk about such ideas (art transforms memory; memory, art) has become a cliché available to even the crudest sensibility.

In the nineteenth century, bad and good fiction alike relied on moral truisms which novelistic characters supported or defied with more or less predictable consequences. Current fiction rests on epistemological or aesthetic truisms which serve comparable organizing functions. The secular salvation of memory provides a pretext for fictional structures as once the notion of moral growth dictated novelistic strategy. In George Eliot's work, the possibility of moral growth underlay complex character development: Maggie Tulliver grows but dies, no earthly reward attending her ethical struggle. But lesser Victorian novelists (Charlotte Yonge, for example) employed the same idea for simpler purposes, creating fictions in which goodness and happiness inevitably coincide. Just so, now, with the notion of memory. . . . [In] *A Woman of Independent Means,* memory (embodied in the act of writing things down) simply solves human problems. The idea of memory as aesthetic and intellectual resource rescues fiction-writers from the abyss of the meaningless, implying no specific obligation to judge or to act in particular ways, only the need to recall and record. (pp. 672-73)

> *Patricia Meyer Spacks, "Necessities of Memory," in* The Hudson Review, *Vol. XXXI, No. 4, Winter, 1978-79, pp. 663-76.**

FRANCES TALIAFERRO

Life Sentences, [Elizabeth Forsythe Hailey's] second novel, tells in conventional form the story of Lindsay Howard, a successful writer and editor who decides to keep the child she conceives as the result of rape. . . . By page 29, we have also learned that Lindsay's husband lies paralyzed forever in a hospital in New Rochelle and that her lover's marriage failed when his wife's three pregnancies ended in miscarriage, stillbirth, and crib death. Misfortunes abound. Lindsay, a self-reliant orphan, would prefer to finish her pregnancy cared for by strangers and denying her own need for love, but her long-lost college classmates Cissy and Meg rally round, a kindly physician makes daily (gratis) house calls, and when at last the baby is born there is reconciliation, love, and growth on all sides.

Life Sentences is wooden, cluttered, and suffocatingly improbable, but it shares certain characteristics with other, better middling novels. These are earnest books, dedicated to human decency, to the sanctity of the "growing experience," and the desirability of "embracing life." Their sentiments reassure us that there is much to be learned from our own misfortunes and those of others, and that virtue resides in the generous exercise of "interpersonal skills." Such novels inspire the reader to go and hug his child (or spouse, or student, or colleague—whoever can be touched by the healing power of emotional honesty). Motherhood may no longer be specifically glorified, but "parenting" brings fulfillment and there might be apple pie for dinner. Furthermore, we readers know we belong, because the conversations of these fictional characters prove that everyone else's family is just as boring as our own. (p. 74)

> *Frances Taliaferro, "The Unimportance of Being Earnest," in* Harper's, *Vol. 265, No. 1589, October, 1982, pp. 71, 73-4.**

BRIGITTE WEEKS

Elizabeth Forsythe Hailey's astonishingly spare, polished, and convincing first novel, *A Woman of Independent Means,* re-created the life of strongminded Bess Steed Garner. Her letters told the story without a single intervention by the author. Four years later, Hailey returns with *Life Sentences,* a rambling, melodramatic, sometimes intensely moving novel that both impresses and infuriates.

The heroine, Lindsay, is a 42-year-old New York editor, 20 years married to John Henry Hawkins, who has lain in a hospital since an accident in the first days of their marriage, paralyzed and unable to speak. Lindsay is also pregnant by a knife-wielding rapist, and that's just the beginning. In this epic of friendship and childbearing, Hailey seems unable to resist violent events in the most unlikely combinations, overworking the sympathies of the reader and obscuring her very real insights into the way women think and feel. (p. 29)

There are no heroes here. It will not escape the seeker after symbol that the central male presence in the novel, Lindsay's husband John Henry, is mute and paralyzed. Yet he is endowed with an all-seeing, all-understanding role that seems to defy medical possibility. His wife, who visits him every evening for 20 years, and her friend Meg, who loved him long ago, both pour out their hearts to him as he lies helpless on his oscillating hospital bed. . . . Both Lindsay and Meg find in his passive acceptance the clue to their own discontents, and draw strength from him.

Lindsay's lover of 12 years, Todd Newman, a life insurance executive, the stranger encountered on a train, represents the ideal man. But his love, freely and patiently offered, is seen by Lindsay only as a threat, an entanglement. But Todd loves on, his lone voice on the telephone-answering machine sounding like some latter-day exponent of courtly love.

But once inside the women's heads, Hailey recovers her sure touch. Lindsay, Meg, and Cissy are flesh-and-blood women we have met. They are feminist but seek compromise at every level, sometimes finding the price too high. The shattering changes in the expectations of both sexes are sensitively diagrammed in portraits of succeeding generations of women. Lindsay's mother, devoted, traditional, undervalued by her daughter until it is too late. . . . Lindsay, trying to live her life in different compartments, keeps John Henry's existence a secret from Todd. It takes the death of her parents to reveal to her that "the role of dutiful daughter had provided an emotional structure for her private universe." Then, finally, there is the child of rape dubiously cast as the salvation of the confused women. . . . (pp. 29, 31)

Obviously, it is dismayingly easy to fault this novel and to poke fun at Hailey's cavalier attitude to the facts of daily life. It is equally impossible not to measure it up against the assured, gritty maturity of *A Woman of Independent Means* and to feel disappointed and somehow cheated. *Life Sentences* seems the work of a great talent out of control, veering wildly from preaching to poignancy, from the unlikely to the unforgettable—exasperating, but never boring. If Elizabeth Hailey can weld together the strengths of both novels and pay as much attention to the mechanics of the storyteller's craft as she does to her characters' emotional life, her third novel could be extraordinary. (p. 31)

> Brigitte Weeks, "The Sisters of Compromise," in Ms., Vol. XI, No. 5, November, 1982, pp. 29, 31.

NORA JOHNSON

The unfortunate title *Life Sentences* well expresses the experience of reading the dull, confusing and ineptly written new novel by Elizabeth Forsythe Hailey. . . . Lindsay, a 42-year-old freelance editor and New Woman with a "shell of physical invulnerability she wore like armor," is raped in her apartment, after which she tells the rapist, "I'm going to have your child," with a "certainty that surprised her as much as it startled him." Why does she tell him this? Partly to save her life, she says, because if she hadn't he would have killed her. But also because she just mystically knew she had conceived—one of several small miracles in this novel. So she decides to have the baby, not only because she "promised" the rapist to do so but because time is passing and it's her last chance. (p. 14)

Mrs. Hailey trots out the usual feminist issues: "until it happened to her, she was as guilty as any man of thinking that a rape victim was somehow 'asking for it.'" Contemplating John Henry's devotion, Lindsay thinks, "To be accepted exactly as she was, no questions asked, no demands made—was that only possible between a man and a woman at the cost of physical incapacity?" She considers the social symbolism of rape and hopefully envisions her daughter joining "a world in which men and women, no longer strangers, would at last be able to love each other completely." But, as always, none of this is a substitute for quality. Besides, Lindsay is an unappealingly secretive heroine, something the author may not have recognized. Her habit of measuring out truth in small amounts seems to cause most of her difficulties.

In this novel characters who are about to say something meaningful always walk to the window first and look out. But nothing outside ever helps them clarify their own mixed-up motives for doing anything. (pp. 14, 31)

> Nora Johnson, "Three New Women," in The New York Times Book Review, November 14, 1982, pp. 14, 31.*

LORNA SAGE

[The] women's lit market is unequivocally a godsend [for Elizabeth Forsythe Hailey]. In *Life Sentences* abortions, rapes, careers, one-parent families are effortlessly reprocessed into the stuff of soap opera they always used to be. The sentiments Ms Hailey's tireless trio of heroines express have a contemporary ring (I especially liked Cissy on dropping out of college—'Then I got married and I never had to think abstractly again'), but the sensations are timelessly vulgar. Suffice to say perhaps that the central character is married to a man paralysed from the waist down, has a successful media career, and is impregnated by a rapist at 42, all in the first few chapters. And she never has to think abstractly again.

> Lorna Sage, "Dark Doings in Old Wessex," in The Observer, November 21, 1982, p. 34.*

RAY OLSON

In [*Joanna's Husband and David's Wife*], the author of the 1978 mega-seller, *A Woman of Independent Means* . . . provides a fine example of the drawbacks of mere realism. . . . Joanna and David, who meet during their last undergraduate summer, are a believable coupling of haute bourgeoise and white-collar working class, of ambitious young husband and intelligent, self-sacrificing young wife. Their struggles as David establishes himself as a playwright, and later, Joanna as a novelist—all while raising two daughters and dealing with difficult parents—ring true enough. So do the personalities and trials of friends and associates. Yet the book finally falls flat because interpersonal minutiae is all there is to it. Neither David nor Joanna, who tell the story via her journal and his marginalia to it, has any inner life. They act and react, often quite emotionally, but without any thought—feelings, yes, but reflection and understanding that illuminate those feelings for the reader, no. (pp. 706-07)

> Ray Olson, in a review of "Joanna's Husband and David's Wife," in Booklist, Vol. 82, No. 10, January 3, 1986, pp. 706-07.

PUBLISHERS WEEKLY

[In *Joanna's Husband and David's Wife* Hailey] provides an illuminating dual perspective of a resilient marriage by again casting a novel in the form of a diary. After her mother suddenly leaves home, teenage Julia Scott is given Joanna Scott's journal recording the abiding passion and the tribulations that she and her husband David experienced since their marriage in the 1950s. Interspersed throughout the entries are David's wry, incisive comments. . . . David, a zealous but uncelebrated playwright, could not spare Joanna financial hardship or his professional frustrations. Despite her affinity for domestic life, she regrets her lack of creative accomplishments, so David encourages her attempts to write fiction. When Joanna finally completes a successful novel, both Scotts wonder uneasily whether she had usurped the fame David deserves. Hailey perceptively portrays this pair, their family and friends in the theater world, but the story contains few moments of riveting drama. (pp. 43-4)

*A review of "Joanna's Husband and David's Wife,"
in* Publishers Weekly, *Vol. 229, No. 1, January 3, 1986, pp. 43-4.*

RUTH DOAN MacDOUGALL

Within the limits of the interesting device she has chosen for [*Joanna's Husband and David's Wife*], Elizabeth Forsythe Hailey, whose first novel was the best-selling *Woman of Independent Means,* manages a vivid description of a stormy marriage. Joanna and David have stuck together for 24 years, but now Joanna has gone home to her parents to "determine the shape of my own future." She leaves behind for her 17-year-old daughter the journals she has kept since she met David, hoping they'll help her daughter with the decisions about *her* future. But David gets his hands on the journals first and starts annotating them, to tell his side of the story. In the counterpoint of voices, Joanna's soul-searching is lengthier, with David's sardonic comments often more memorable. . . . The main drawback of the journal device is that it offers too little dialogue, making the reader desperate for quotation marks. Yet the exploration of egos keeps the story moving, as does the nerveracking account of what it's like to try to earn a living with one's pen.

Ruth Doan MacDougall, in a review of "Joanna's Husband and David's Wife," in The New York Times Book Review, *February 23, 1986, p. 22.*

John (Richard) Hersey

1914-

American novelist, nonfiction writer, short story writer, editor, and journalist.

Hersey is probably best known for his Pulitzer Prize-winning novel, *A Bell for Adano* (1944), and for *Hiroshima* (1946), his nonfiction account of the explosion of the first atomic bomb. Born in China, Hersey began his literary career as a foreign correspondent for *Time* and *Life* magazines, gaining recognition during World War II for his coverage of activities in the Pacific and Mediterranean war zones. His prolific output includes thirteen novels and numerous nonfiction works, all of which reflect his interest in the major social events and problems of his time. Distinguished by a journalist's thorough analysis of subject matter as well as a novelist's attention to narrative, Hersey's work has received much popular attention. His novels, which are often allegorical and have at their core a strong moral emphasis, have been faulted for weak characterizations which are unable to carry the burden of the story's moral tone. However, they are often praised for their prose style and the detailed rendering of their settings.

Many of Hersey's novels are based on his experiences during World War II. His first novel, *A Bell for Adano,* details the Allied occupation of an Italian village and is characterized by the topicality that marks all of his work. *The Wall* (1950) relates the Nazi persecution of Jews in Poland's Warsaw ghetto through the fictitious diary of a Jewish scholar. By concentrating on the social alienation of the Jew throughout history, Hersey theorizes that minority individuals must subscribe to a faith and an identification with one's ethnicity in order to survive in an increasingly hostile and confusing world. *The War Lover* (1959) attributes the cause of war to humanity's love for it. The novel's two fighter pilots, contrasted by their different reasons for fighting, symbolize opposing attitudes toward war.

Hersey's third novel, *The Marmot Drive* (1953), introduced his allegorical approach. This work is a parable that centers on conflicts among residents of a small New England town. *A Single Pebble* (1956) concerns a young American engineer who is sent to China to build a dam on the Yangtze River. While traversing the river and interacting with the Chinese, the engineer encounters conflicts between Eastern and Western culture and comes to the realization that one is not superior to the other. *Too Far to Walk* (1966), a contemporary Faust tale, depicts a college student's experimentation with drugs and decadence as a result of his ennui and identity crisis. In *Under the Eye of the Storm* (1967) and *The Walnut Door* (1977), two novels which rely heavily on symbolism, the protagonists grapple with questions of personal identity and interpersonal relationships. Hersey comments on political corruption in *The Conspiracy* (1972), a fictionalized account of a plot to assassinate the Roman emperor Nero. Hersey's recent novel, *The Call: An American Missionary in China* (1985), continues his exploration of modern humanity's spiritual quest.

Hersey has also written works in which he employs the science fiction technique of depicting a familiar world that is significantly altered by the inclusion of fantastical elements. *The*

© Kelly Wise

Child Buyer (1960), which satirizes government and the educational system, is a story of a corporation's attempt to purchase a ten-year-old genius and reeducate him in hopes of developing a computer-like human to be used in the interest of national defense. *White Lotus* (1965), a tale of white enslavement by Chinese captors, parallels the black experience in the United States in order to comment on racism. *My Petition for More Space* (1974) depicts a dystopian future of overpopulation and bureaucracy.

In addition to *Hiroshima,* Hersey's nonfiction works include *Men on Bataan* (1942) and *Into the Valley* (1943), both of which reconstruct notable battles of World War II with an emphasis on the soldiers who fought them. *The Algiers Motel Incident* (1968) indicts the American legal system for practicing racism in connection with the deaths of three black men during the 1967 Detroit riots. *Letter to the Alumni* (1970) chronicles Hersey's last year as professor at Yale University. *The President* (1975) and *Aspects of the Presidency: Truman and Ford in Office* (1980) are analyses of the executive branch of the American government.

(See also *CLC,* Vols. 1, 2, 7, 9; *Contemporary Authors,* Vols. 17-20, rev. ed.; *Something about the Author,* Vol. 25; and *Dictionary of Literary Biography,* Vol. 6.)

VIRGILIA SAPIEHA

[*A Bell for Adano*] is a first novel by the young newspaper correspondent whose story of Guadalcanal, *Into the Valley*, brought a lump to the throats of so many Americans. It is also the first novel to be published about the present Allied military occupation in Italy. Mr. Hersey spent last summer with our troops in Sicily, and his tale is presumably based upon fact. . . .

Mr. Hersey has chosen for his protagonist Major Joppolo, an American of Italian descent, formerly a clerk in the New York City Sanitation Department, now appointed senior civil-affairs officer for the town of Adano, Italy.

The book opens as, within a few moments after the successful invasion of the American troops, the major steps ashore from his landing craft and feels, for the first time, the native soil of his parents beneath his feet. Elated and confident, despite the mockery of his sergeant, the major follows his map to the center of the town, and in two shakes of a lamb's tail, has ensconced himself in the City Hall behind the vast desk so recently abandoned by the Fascist Mayor, who, along with a large part of the town's population, has taken to the hills. His heart stirred by Adano's plight, his imagination a-quiver with the possibilities opening up before him, Major Joppolo digs from his brief case the "Instructions to Civil Affairs Officers" and starts to peruse the voluminous orders for the first day of occupation. After having read three pages, he tears the whole thing up. From his own small notebook he reads the suggestions which he once wrote for himself "Don't make yourself cheap. . . . Don't lose your temper. When plans fall down, improvise." Briskly, then, he goes out to the balcony overlooking the main square and hoists the Union Jack and the Stars and Stripes. A crowd gathers below. The major's job has begun. . . .

The book tells the story of how the major meets his problems, how he befriends the doubters and the cynics, outwits the unscrupulous, restores husbands to wives, saves children from the reckless bounty of caramel-loaded troops. It is a typical story of what good will can achieve, and also where it fails. For the major's good will comes up against the ruthless ill temper of the commanding officer of the invasion, and military power wins out over faith and understanding.

Mr. Hersey has sprinkled his tale with Italians and Americans both good and bad and just plain foolish, a lifelike mixture, and has drawn quite an accurate distinction between the primitive traits of the Italian townsfolk and the neo-primitive traits of the American boys. Besides the youthful horseplay which is surely an integral part of the "civilian army" of a nation addicted to horseplay, there are many counterbalancing episodes to tug the heartstrings. Beneath the story flows a genuine love of justice, scorn of pettiness, and faith in mankind, ideals as implicit in the book as they are fundamental in America.

> Virgilia Sapieha, "With the Americans in a Sicilian Village," in New York Herald Tribune Weekly Book Review, February 6, 1944, p. 1.

BEN RAY REDMAN

In *Men on Bataan* and *Into the Valley* Mr. Hersey proved himself a first-rate reporter while giving signs of being and becoming something more. It is the more that we have here [in *A Bell for Adano*], or the beginning of it; and while the fact of his development may not surprise perspicacious readers, I think its character will. There was no more reason to predict that Mr. Hersey would write the kind of fiction he has written than there was to foresee that the first novel concerned with the activities of our Allied Military Government would be one of the gayest books imaginable. For that is what it is, this story of Major Victor Joppolo's tour of duty as civil affairs officer for the little Italian town of Adano. It is not only gay, mind you. It is also serious. But whatever its seriousness of intention and execution, stressed in a foreword, you will be laughing much of the time you are reading it, and smiling most of the time. Which is not to say you will miss hearing the message the author would have you hear.

For the conveyance of this message—that our administration of occupied territory will be only as good as the men who do the administering—Mr. Hersey has almost as many strings to his bow as had the Players praised by Polonius. Strongly gifted with powers of humorous observation and amusing invention, he is at home in the whimsical-pathetic no less than in the serio-comic; no stranger to the mock-heroic, he is an intimate of the farcical-fantastic; he can wallop with the tough-and-snappy and score with the shameless-sentimental; and, finally, he is equal to the sober-serious. In the handling of crowds he exhibits signal mastery, as you will discover when you read of Joppolo's visit to Tomasino's boat, of the great gas attack on Adano, of the return of the prisoners, and of Giorgio's death as described by Nicolo. In construction he is neat and uncomplicated: the two main strands of his story—the theme of the bell and the affair of the carts—are nicely manipulated and carry the weight put upon them. And his characters? They are characters in both senses of the word, literary and popular. What types!

I'll not call their roll here; bare names would mean nothing, and room lacks for descriptions. . . .

If we lack space for the inhabitants of Adano, most of them charming in one way or another, we must give room to a character of a very different sort—General Marvin, "the man who still wears spurs even though he rides everywhere in an armored car." We have read of him in the Sunday supplements, Mr. Hersey tells us, and may have formed a picture of him on that basis. "You couldn't be blamed for having this picture," writes the author.

> You can't get the truth except from the boys who come home and finally limp out of the hospitals and even then the truth is bent by their anger. But I can tell you perfectly calmly that General Marvin showed himself during the invasion to be a bad man, something worse than what our troops were trying to throw out.

Mr. Hersey displays Marvin's badness, with no punches pulled. In the post-invasion struggle of occupation, waged over the tiny territory of Adano (miniature preview of a vast struggle to come), the American general represents the forces of blind and ignorant evil just as clearly as the American major represents the forces of seeing and intelligent good. . . .

John Hersey has delivered his message well, written his story delightfully. And in the process, inconspicuously, perhaps even with contradictory implications, he has written a sentence that should be held steadily before the eyes of all post-war planners. That sentence reads: "The war aim of most men is to go home."

> Ben Ray Redman, "A Man of Good Will," in The Saturday Review of Literature, Vol. XXVII, No. 7, February 12, 1944, p. 8.

MALCOLM COWLEY

A Bell for Adano, by John Hersey, makes very good reading in its capable and wholly unpretentious fashion. It is the story of Major Victor Joppolo, an American of Italian descent who, for a few weeks last summer, was the senior civil-affairs officer and acting mayor of a Sicilian town. He was a good man and he did his best for the people of Adano, feeding them, teaching them democracy and even finding a new bell for their city hall; but he came into conflict with an essentially Prussian major-general, bearing some faint resemblance to Old Blood and Guts. The result was that Joppolo was ordered back to Algiers and probably lost his commission. Except for a wistful little love affair, that is the whole framework of the novel; it is filled out with the incidents of daily life in a town occupied by American forces. Some of these are extremely moving. It would be hard to forget Father Pensovecchio's first sermon to his congregation after the town was taken, and still harder to forget the Italian prisoners of war returning to their homes. . . .

Often you wonder how it is that Hersey knows his Sicilians so well, considering that he was born in China and has done most of his reporting in the Far East. . . . He came to Sicily with the invading army and stayed there hardly longer than Major Joppolo. On the other hand, he is a good observer, and you suspect him of filling in the gaps with his literary memories. His Sicilians sometimes act like John Steinbeck's *paisanos,* so that you aren't quite sure whether you are in Adano or Tortilla Flat. His style also has overtones of Steinbeck—not to mention Hemingway . . . —but he is saved by being a competent craftsman in his own right. Notwithstanding its self-imposed limitations of time and knowledge, *A Bell for Adano* is an entertaining story, a candid report from behind the lines and an effective tract. To demand that it be a soundly constructed novel as well would be asking too much.

> *Malcolm Cowley, "Novels after the War," in* The New Republic, *Vol. 110, No. 7, February 14, 1944, pp. 216-17.**

HOWARD MUMFORD JONES

Thematically and stylistically *The Marmot Drive* is a new departure for John Hersey, differing alike from the intelligent sentimentalism of *A Bell for Adano* and from the epic dimensions of *The Wall.* The tale concerns a community drive to rid a New England town of a threatening colony of woodchucks. The village is named Tunxis, and the drive is reported to us through the sensibilities of a girl from New York. The climax of the story is an intentional anti-climax—the selectman who incited the drive is flogged for a crime he did not commit, after which he tries futilely to slaughter the few woodchucks that were captured.

Stylistically Mr. Hersey's prose has moved in a direction represented by the harsh name of the village. The style is concise, it is sometimes beautiful, and it is oftener intentionally harsh—as if Browning had taken over from Tennyson. I take it Mr. Hersey's intent is to capture the anfractuosities of village life through this pebbly surface, these gnarled place names and knotty speeches. . . . Thus a characteristic sentence is: "Expect to have some people raising hightantrabogus at the caucus tonight," wherein the succession of harsh consonants is intentional.

Mr. Hersey's fable may have a lot of meanings. On its surface the story is that of pride coming to a fall, inasmuch as the selectman, whatever the merits of his social service, recognizes no opinion as valid save his own, and is punished by the community he tries to serve. The community, however, is far from admirable, and it is in the relation of this fact to the out-of-door nature of the whole tale that gives rise to the puzzle of the story. . . .

Is *The Marmot Drive* successful? I am puzzled how to answer this natural question. On the one hand, I think it uneven in tone; and I am not altogether persuaded of the validity of the *dramatis personae,* particularly of the girl, who seems to me now a girl and now an algebraic character in an uncertain equation. On the other hand, I found myself coming back to the work many times, thinking that I had missed some meaning as elusive as the selectman's woodchucks. I have a feeling that Mr. Hersey may have caught symbolism fever, a disease that carries with it an undue solemnity and a slowing down of narrative. I may well be wrong. If there is failure the failure may lie in your reviewer, not in Mr. Hersey; and if there is failure it is failure on a very high plane. I suspect *The Marmot Drive* will occasion a good deal of critical controversy.

> *Howard Mumford Jones, "New England Parable," in* The Saturday Review, *New York, Vol. XXXVI, No. 45, November 7, 1953, p. 22.*

CHARLES J. ROLO

In *The Marmot Drive* John Hersey has broken away from the novel of contemporary history with which he has won great critical kudos and popular success. He has severed such ties as his previous fiction had with the materials of journalism and has squarely grappled with the challenge of the novel as an art form, seeking to present human character and conduct in all their elusiveness and complexity. It takes courage and the right sort of ambition for a writer to make so resolute a departure from the terrain on which he excels; and this reviewer, for one, is profoundly in sympathy with the risk-takers. All of which makes it painful to say that *The Marmot Drive* struck me as a strangely unsatisfactory novel and a second reading failed to alter that impression.

The action takes place on a summer week-end, in and around an out-of-the-way Connecticut village. A New York girl, Hester, has been invited to Tunxis to meet the parents of the young man who is thinking of marrying her, Eben Avered; and she finds herself involved in a drive—organized by Eben's father, the Selectman of Tunxis—to rid the area of an infestation of woodchucks. This marmot drive serves Mr. Hersey as a catalytic agent which brings out violently the submerged feelings and tensions of the participants in his story.

At the caucus of the townspeople the evening of her arrival Hester finds a surprising atmosphere of fear and hate and stirrings of bitter ill-will toward the Selectman. He is resented, she gradually learns, because he is considered too brainy; because he is gentlemanly, kind-hearted and, through his sympathy, has come to know his fellow-townsfolk too well. (p. 4)

Mr. Hersey's story has two main aspects. It is a study in microcosm, of the difficulties of the leader who seeks to mobilize a community to make disagreeable efforts necessary to its welfare: on this level, the insights are rather obvious and the action by which they are dramatized is not particularly effective. It is also a study of complex human relationships and of the heightening of Hester's self-awareness; and on this level Mr. Hersey's touch is so subtle that it is sometimes not clear what he is driving at.

The writing is crisp and a number of individual scenes are skillfully brought off. But to this reader the novel as a whole remained distinctly unconvincing, and, what is worse, it seemed a bit of a bore. (p. 44)

Charles J. Rolo, "Under the Surface, a Bitter Ill-Wind," in The New York Times Book Review, *November 8, 1953, pp. 4, 44.*

IRVING HOWE

Since it will leave newspaper reviewers in a state of superior bewilderment, this novel is likely to be tagged a parable; I think it more accurate to call it a catastrophe. About the best that can be said for *The Marmot Drive* is that Mr. Hersey has made an intense effort to shake off those journalistic mannerisms which marred his previous novels. But he has replaced them with a large repertoire of literary mannerisms, of the sort one finds in novels about crises in the suburbs. The two most dangerous temptations for ambitious novelists today are Rich Prose and Symbolism, and Mr. Hersey is in a fair way to having succumbed to both. . . .

The central figure of the novel is Hester, a New York girl, bright, lively, restless. One summer weekend she visits the Connecticut town of Tunxis, where the family of her boy friend, Eben, is to look her over. Thus far the relationship between Hester and Eben has been, to her sense of things, alarmingly chaste, and she reaches Tunxis in a condition of aggressive uneasiness. Then begins her trial, the exposure of a fundamentally innocent mind to those local hatreds and passions which go so deep into the past of the town that a stranger caught among them can only suffer in silence.

For some years Tunxis has been pestered by invasions of marmots, and now Matthew Avered, Eben's father and the Town Selectman, proposes a drive to destroy the animals. When the ceremony-chase is over, few marmots have been found, which suggests that the threat may have been imaginary, but meanwhile the more destructive impulses of the hunters have been released. The elder Avered has come dangerously close to making a pass at Hester—his restraint disappoints her; and at the end, when the townsmen propose to give him "a light public whippin'" as scourge for his private misdemeanor, he meekly accepts it in the mistaken belief that he is being punished for his public failure. Appalled, Hester flees, overcome by a sense of failure.

Mr. Hersey apparently had some symbolic scheme in mind when he wrote this story. At first I thought it might be a political symbolism: the marmots suddenly become aggressively imperialist, one Tunxis citizen suggests that "the trouble had begun . . . during the last century, when the railroad had been put in" and adds that "they calculate Tunxis is on the wane . . . they're movin' in on us." But the not very arresting possibility that Mr. Hersey intends a comment on the times soon loses its force; and when we are told that Aunty Dorcas, a spry thing of ninety-one, has killed a hawk with her own hands (or does she just imagine she has?) we know we are on the familiar, slippery symbolic ground of private impulse, dominating will and—who would dare doubt it?—Good and Evil.

But it hardly matters what the symbolic scheme of the book is, whether an oblique topical reference or a reworking of a Greek myth or anything else. For what is the point of investigating a novel's symbolic dimension or possible moral significance when on the plane of represented life, its play of action and character, it is entirely flimsy and boring? The major characters dissolve into a stream of anxieties and musings, the minor ones are ferociously eccentric; and neither matter.

Irving Howe, "Symbolic Suburbia," in The New Republic, *Vol. 129, No. 16, November 16, 1953, p. 17.*

R. T. HORCHLER

Mr. Hersey's concern with current affairs has given way increasingly to an interest which can only be called mystical. And in continuation of this movement, his new novel is a quasi-religious document, the embodiment in simple fable of certain mystic truths. (p. 329)

On its primary levels, *A Single Pebble* is altogether successful. The account of the junk's progress up the river is utterly convincing, and a triumph merely as the communication of experience. The daily round of life aboard the junk is solidly established, and, despite the seeming littleness of incident, the narrative maintains extraordinary suspense and excitement. The most impressive achievement of the book, however, is in the description of the Yangtze: the spectacular and fearful beauty of roaring waters, the awesome heights and depths of cliffs and gorges, and—pitted endlessly against the power of the river—the Yangtze trackers, hauling the junks by towline in terrible, magnificent labor.

Mr. Hersey is rather less successful with characterization. His Chinese characters are colorfully, sympathetically, but superficially drawn. . . . Less clearly realized even as a type is the narrator-hero, who is little more than a writer's device, a mouthpiece and focus of observation.

But the real deficiency of *A Single Pebble* is in the vagueness of its ideas. If Mr. Hersey is seriously repudiating Western rationality in favor of mysticism and non-thought, as he seems to be doing, he must deal with the question more thoroughly than he does here. As it is described, the episode in Wind Box Gorge, which furnishes the climax of the novel, is deeply affecting and susceptible of rich allegorical interpretation, but one soul-shaking event does not provide a philosophy of life. This is made clear by the triteness of the hero's philosophizing, which is so obvious and woolly that it dissipates the power of the experience he has undergone.

The ending of the book is similarly weak. After his spiritual upheaval, and having submitted to the desire of the river-spirit not to have a dam built, the American wanders lamely offstage, apparently bound for home and more engineering. The only perceivable effect of his experience seems to be a vague feeling of uplift.

Nevertheless, the weaknesses of *A Single Pebble,* including occasional clumsiness and self-consciousness of style, are offset by undeniable strengths. Mr. Hersey has something serious to say here, and he makes his statement with beauty, power and great sincerity. *A Single Pebble* will sustain his position as, at least, a novelist to be reckoned with. (pp. 329-30)

R. T. Horchler, "Serious Fable," in Commonweal, *Vol. LXIV, No. 13, June 29, 1956, pp. 329-30.*

LESLIE A. FIEDLER

[*A Single Pebble*], Hersey's brief fable of an American engineer's trip up the Yangtze in the 1920s and of his learning to respect the wisdom of the illiterate and the heroism of the brutal poor—takes up once more the new revised version of the White Man's Burden: his need to demean himself in order to atone for his former conviction of superiority. I must confess in all frankness that I find Hersey's sentiments so piously unexceptionable as to be intolerable. There is something maddening to ordinary sinners in being told so mildly and firmly that we must be humble, that we must close the gap, that we must bring to the Orient not merely techniques but understanding, and not merely cold understanding but the comprehension which includes a lump in the throat. "Elations with despair," Hersey calls the sentimental indulgence he takes for wisdom, "a palpable ache that somehow gave me comfort." The mild-mannered masochisms behind his high-minded façade . . . ends by making me queasy; though, indeed, I am never sure who should be despised, Hersey for being so pious or me for being appalled by that piety.

I am sure, at any rate, that he is not a novelist; that he writes fiction (or pretends to) only as a strategy for getting his point of view before more people. There is in him no poetry or invention, only the patient, slick exposition of facts, plus the desire to stay on the side of the angels of the latest headline—Warsaw Jews or Japanese peasants or Chinese boatmen. But the writer, as Kierkegaard somewhere pointed out, casts out devils only by the aid of the devil. For reporting of a superior order, however, for restrained but effective descriptions of the wild Yangtze gorges, for little observations on the Chinese character (on a popularizing level) the present small book has a certain value. And yet one surely has the right to feel offended at being told once more that the Chinese find offensive our habit of blowing our noses into little rags that we put into our pockets. This is the standard example one gives to a twelve-year-old in a first "adult" discussion of cultural differences and prejudice. If one does not object to being lectured at like an intelligent adolescent, and finds quite inoffensive the journalist's pretense to be writing a novel (by sketching a love affair in lightly against the moralizing and the scenery) there is no reason why he should not enjoy Hersey's book. (pp. 360-61)

> Leslie A. Fiedler, "The Novel in the Post-Political World," in Partisan Review, Vol. XXIII, No. 3, Summer, 1956, pp. 358-65.*

WILLIAM ARROWSMITH

Mr. Hersey's bland parable of a Yankee engineer's odyssey up the Yangtze is, in intent, a simple symbolic tragedy of crossed perspectives, East *vs*. West, both taken at the level of the typical if not the stereotype, both meant to be illuminated when the typical reaches out for the heroic. And why not? If the perspectives are crossed with passion, if the heroism compels assent, if the characters can be themselves beyond the symbolic burdens they happen to carry, common ground—the tragic sense of life firm below the topsoil of culture—is there for the claiming. And this is what Mr. Hersey's action tries to claim, "the sense of elation at the moment of despair," when the dying hero, a dead loss to himself, becomes a great light to others. This is hard, tragic ground, hard to get to, hard to hold, but known unmistakably by its hardness too—the firm action, the bedrock certainty of significant conduct, the sure

purchase on passion going *some*where yet not quite *any*how. Were Mr. Hersey's attempt more modest, his bland and pleasant narrative might do, but it is tragedy that is missing here, the story foundering on a blandness so pervasive—in the characters, in the limpness of perception and the leached ideas, in the stricken fuzziness of his tragic sense and the flatfooted march of his prose—that little more than a husk of tragedy survives. If, at first, we respond, it is to the intimation of the tragic, the feel of a generous and large intent; but in the end, if it is tragedy and not dying falls we require, *A Single Pebble* must seem a disappointing book.

Yet the plot is well-conceived; there is competence in the construction, and the prose, especially in descriptive passages, is capable of power. The story itself is a simple one, narrated by a callow and naïve American engineer whose easy optimism and vague and generous bigotry—he sounds like a mind molded entirely from *Life* editorials—it is the purpose of the action to instruct and mellow. . . . Slowly he begins to understand the alien river-culture, its tragic waste of human life and effort and the necessary fatalism of the trackers; and this understanding in turn enlarges as the engineer begins to see in the life of the chief tracker, Old Pebble, the possibility of heroism, a life lived with courage in the teeth of a necessity that makes fatalists of ordinary men. Stimulated by his conviction of sympathy, he excitedly unfolds to Old Pebble his vision of a dam; and Old Pebble, recognizing the threat to the way of life of the river and thereby the threat to the honor he has so precariously asserted, destroys himself, falls or slips out of life at the peak of his greatness. His death is, depending upon how you read it, an act of self-sacrifice to the river before the staggering, blasphemous rightness of the engineer's vision, or an act of final heroic self-assertion, beyond the comprehension of men of meaner motives. (p. 19)

The crucial difficulty here is not so much with the moral underpinnings of the tragedy, but in the absence of particularity, the failure of the tragedy to declare itself in particular lives, lives with precise motives and purposes, coming via passion on bigger purposes up to the point of heroism. Particularity here is swamped in symbolism, and the symbolic apparatus is particularly murky in the case of Old Pebble and his death. Pebble's halo is the heroic; he is clearly marked off—in size, generosity, courage and passion—from the fatalistic trackers. Yet the central act of the book—his death—is dark, indeed, inexplicable as sacrifice really, for it is hard to see any earthly good to this sacrifice; and if he stumbles merely, why, this is worse. (pp. 19-20)

But he appears to die because Mr. Hersey's novel requires a death, some gesture that will mellow with *lacrimae rerum* the Luce-mind of this engineer. And Old Pebble must get bad marks for his knowledge of men, if he hopes that this dark way of dying will register rightly on the engineer's dullheadedness. Which is to say that Mr. Hersey's novel works backward, not forward; works from a notion of tragedy as the piety that goes with a lump in the throat and builds toward it, syllogistically, rather than following significant passion to its unknown terminus. . . .

If the tragedy is *a priori* and limp, the ideas on which the novel rests are essentially pieties, made amiable by apparent candor and humility, but limp and without relevance to the action. Thus the progress of the engineer's conversion is contrived more by passive observation than by action, its stages marked by symbolic gestures which evade, without reinforcing, the novelist's work. The most crippling pieties, however, are those which derive from public life—the journalistic drive in Mr. Hersey which allows his novel to slide constantly away from public life without ever becoming political. . . .

The characters get short shrift. Thus the engineer never achieves anything resembling a personality: identity has been usurped by Mr. Hersey's need for a public American of the generous, open-minded, forward-looking, and now tragedy-requiring stereotype. If Old Pebble alone survives as a character, I suspect it is because Mr. Hersey's mystique of heroism saves him from being cut from the public cloth. In compensation for so much publicity, Mr. Hersey introduces a little love, but love is as limp as the language of the novel, without power to affect the tragedy and designed to sustain the illusion that these characters are capable of private emotions too.

In short, a bland book, generous in intent, but everywhere crippled by a debased notion of the tragic and human passion, committed to a sense of dignity it refuses to explore except by mystique. As performance, it belongs to that growing genre of *le roman complaisant,* everyone's Eskimo-wife of a novel trotted out to please all comers and fit all tastes with a tidy pretense of passion. Those who dislike involvement will like it. (p. 20)

> William Arrowsmith, *"More Bland than Mellow,"* in The New Republic, *Vol. 135, No. 7, August 13, 1956, pp. 19-20.*

GRANVILLE HICKS

The War Lover is a novel about the operations of the Eighth Air Force in 1943, and, like *The Wall,* it must be in large part the product of research. As a war correspondent, Hersey may have flown in Flying Fortresses, but the detailed accounts he gives of the craft can only be based on knowledge he has carefully acquired. They are impressive, these accounts. He tells where each member of the crew is situated and what he does. He describes a score of raids, each clearly differentiated from the others. He talks well about strategy, about weather, about all sorts of topics. Since Flying Fortresses are now as obsolete as the *Monitor* and the *Merrimac,* his researchers have an antiquarian air, but they have been remarkably thorough.

Hersey, of course, is not describing Flying Fortresses just for the pleasure of describing them, although it is obvious that the process of description gives him considerable satisfaction. This is a novel about men, not machines, and it asks and attempts to answer some fundamental questions about human beings and the nature of war. It is primarily the story of two men, Captain Marrow and Lieutenant Boman, pilot and co-pilot of a Flying Fortress called *The Body.* . . .

Boman tells the story, but attention is focused on Buzz Marrow. Marrow is loud-mouthed, given to boasting about his prowess with women, an aggressive fellow and something of a bully, but, as Boman sees him, a superb pilot. Boman gives plenty of examples of Marrow's audacity and resourcefulness when he is at the controls of *The Body,* and we can see why the members of the crew feel that he is invulnerable. Gradually, however, Boman comes to understand that Marrow has not only defects as a human being but also fatal weaknesses as a fighter.

Boman makes some of his discoveries for himself, but his final enlightenment comes by way of a girl named Daphne. Boman meets Daphne soon after his arrival in England, and the affair that he carries on with her is at first an agreeable relief from the arduous and perilous duties in which he is engaged, and in the end something more than that. Daphne has had experience with men at war, and she knows from the start what sort of person Marrow is. Her insight is confirmed when he tries to seduce her. He is a man who loves war because killing gives him an acute satisfaction, a satisfaction that is essentially sexual. His one great passion is for destruction, and, as Daphne tells Boman, he is bound to destroy himself as well as others. How sound her analysis is Boman learns in the course of the twenty-fourth raid.

The trouble is that Marrow, though he fools Boman for a time, never deceives the reader. Hersey's method, indeed, with its way of moving back and forth in time, guarantees that there can be no suspense. When Boman sets out on the twenty-fourth raid, he knows what Daphne knows, and he does not conceal his knowledge. . . . And again and again there are allusions to Boman's final judgment of his pilot. If Hersey had permitted the great discovery to dawn on our minds as it dawns on Boman's, we might have been moved by it, but he lets us in on the secret from the very start.

The only explanation I can find for what seems an elementary mistake in narrative technique is that Hersey is dead in earnest about Marrow and his type. . . .

That seems to be the lesson of the book: "the reason for war" is the fact that some men enjoy it. I am sure that some men do enjoy it and that Hersey has given a reasonably perceptive account of such a man. But I do not think there is *a* cause for war—psychological, economic, or anything else—and I don't believe that Hersey really thinks so either. In this book, however, he has quite been carried away by his distrust of the lovers of war.

Boman, who says, "I was for life, and against death," balances Marrow. Hersey is too wise to make Boman either a hero or a saint. Boman is conscious of some of his shortcomings, and Daphne points out others. But the weakness that makes Boman plausible helps to obscure his role in the novel. Daphne tells him, "You certainly can't give all humanity a complete love when you can't even give it to one human being." This sounds reasonable enough, but I wonder what, in Boman's situation, it would mean if he were capable of a complete love for all humanity.

What I'm saying, I'm afraid, is that *The War Lover* is neither satisfying as a piece of fiction nor convincing as a message. That is a pity, for one has to respect Hersey's seriousness, his conscientiousness as a reporter, and the literary competence he always displays. But once more, as in *The Wall,* the qualities essential to literary greatness—and Hersey aims high—are lacking.

> Granville Hicks, *"John Hersey's Message,"* in Saturday Review, *Vol. XLII, No. 40, October 3, 1959, p. 18.*

TALIAFERRO BOATWRIGHT

The story of *The War Lover* is made up of two closely interwoven parts. One is a tense, minute-by-minute account of the strike [on the ball-bearing factories at Schweinfurt by the B-17s of the 8th Air Force], as seen through the eyes of Charley Boman, co-pilot of The Body, one of the two hundred odd Flying Forts involved. The other is a development of the cumulative, erosive effect of continued danger and fear on the crew of The Body as they sweat out the twenty-five missions that made up a tour of combat duty. The principal thread of both stories is the changing relationship between Boman and the pilot, Buzz Marrow, whom Charley at first admires and envies as the very model of a dashing, go-to-hell pilot. However, each member of the crew is brought alive as a person, with tagged idiosyncrasies perhaps, but a full set of responses. . . .

The relationship between Boman and Marrow can be thought of as an Aristotelian conflict between the good, the life force and the death drive. It is played out in three arenas, the cockpit of the plane, the mind of Boman, and the affections of Boman's girl Daphne, whom Marrow covets and eventually tries to seduce. Daphne, incidentally, is by all odds the most lifelike feminine lead to grace a major war novel in this generation. Not only is she compassionate, understanding, loving and available, there are even hints that she may enjoy having sacrifices made for her.

John Hersey's success in realizing Daphne, which is a marked advance in technique over his previous female characterizations, is a tip-off on an even greater success. The word "reportorial" springs easily to mind in appraising his work. Still, no matter how photographic it seems, *The War Lover,* is not a history of the Schweinfurt-Regensburg raid, nor yet the triple-distilled exegesis of remembered experience, but rather a work of art, a dramatic perception of reality which uses as background an amazingly plausible re-creation of life.

One can raise questions about the philosophy John Hersey is expressing. Should the value of human life be greater than any principle? Is nothing worth dying for? Are sacrifices wholly meaningless? Are the Marrows of this world villains, as the author implies, or merely another kind of victim? Who are the real villains? It is possible also to question whether the philosophical import of his story lives up to its pervasive interest. However, there can be only admiration for the story itself, for its thesis that the war lover is the death lover, for the characterizations (he even manages to suggest a measure of sympathy for Marrow in the teeth of his evident purpose), and above all for the blinding impact of the air and its climax. This is an exceptionally fine war novel on first reading and an even better one on the second.

Taliaferro Boatwright, "An Airman Who Gave His Soul to the God of Battle," in New York Herald Tribune Book Review, *October 4, 1959, p. 1.*

ARTHUR MIZENER

The War Lover is a fascinating novel of wartime flying. It tells the story of a Flying Fortress and its crew from their arrival at a British base during the great bombing raids on Germany to the moment, five and a half months later, when they are forced down in the Channel on their way back from their twenty-fourth mission, a raid on Schweinfurt. Mr. Hersey presents this life with great vividness—the mechanical and human difficulties of flying a Fortress, the terrors of bombing and of meeting the attacks of enemy fighters, the long agony of bringing a stricken plane home from deep in Germany.

Above all, he shows us the life of a wartime base, where all the complications of a normal working community are intensified by the terrible dangers of the job, and the inexplicable caprices of superiors or the unpardonable carelessness of a mechanic can drive a man nearly mad. Mr. Hersey's gift for spotting a typical act or characteristic turn of speech makes us

see and hear the people of this community with great clarity. . . .

Mr. Hersey has always had a knack for getting inside a special way of life—like that of the men who work junks up the Yangtze in *A Single Pebble* or endured the ghetto of Warsaw during the Nazi occupation in *The Wall*—and it has never served him better than here. The very quietness of his sympathy with such men is his greatest strength. . . .

The War Lover is, moreover, extremely effectively told. We all know the sinking feeling that comes over us when we realize that a story is going to reach its climax in an exciting episode—in this one the raid on Schweinfurt—but that we must get through several hundred pages before it does so. In Mr. Hersey's book we are into that last, climactic moment from the start, because he begins with the briefing for the Schweinfurt raid. He then skillfully alternates chapters about the raid with chapters about the tour of duty that led up to it, so that at the very moment of terror and disaster the crew of The Body relive the experiences that led up to that moment.

But *The War Lover,* as its title indicates, is a good deal more than a story about wartime flying. Mr. Hersey means it to reveal a conflict between two attitudes toward war that represent two attitudes toward life as a whole, a conflict between those who are ultimately motivated by a love of death and those who, even when they are driven to kill, are motivated by a love of life. These two attitudes are represented by the book's two major characters, the pilot, Buzz Marrow, and his co-pilot, Bo Boman. Though these two characters are as vividly presented as the rest—and in much more detail—the contrast between them required by the theme is too labored to be convincing. (p. 1)

Mr. Hersey comes close to claiming that the existence of men like Marrow is the real cause of wars. With an insight that is surprising in someone who has seemed only an ordinarily intelligent girl throughout the book, Daphne [the girl Boman loves] says to Boman at the end, "Why do you keep silent about the reason for war? At least, what *I* think is the reason for war: that some men enjoy it, some men enjoy it too much."

Perhaps that is the reason for war, but Mr. Hersey's novel . . . would be a better one if the subject had never come up. Fine story though it is, it is unconvincing—heavy-handed and over-explicit—as an explanation of experience. In order to prepare for Marrow's final collapse, the author gives us from the beginning hints as heavy as cannon balls of his inner corruption, so that he appears ugly and irresponsible, and it is impossible to believe a man like Boman could see him as hero and friend, as we are told he does. Even so, when Marrow suddenly collapses completely, we find it hard to believe so dramatic an act can follow from so remote and abstract a cause as a love of death.

The truth seems to be that Mr. Hersey can represent the surface of experience admirably, but runs into difficulty when he tries to imagine how general ideas become immediate causes for the behavior of particular men. When he has a subject where the moral significance can be taken for granted because it was inherent in the events before he tackled them, as he had in *The Wall,* his work is strikingly effective. But when he must provide a meaning for events not obviously significant in themselves, as in *The Marmot Drive* or *A Single Pebble,* or when, as in *The War Lover,* he is not satisfied with the meaning the events already have and seeks to impose a new one on them, the only result is to distract the reader's attention from the wonderfully convincing story. There is less of this kind of distraction in *The War Lover* than in some of Mr. Hersey's other novels, but *The War Lover* is, at its best, so good that you wish there were no distractions at all. (pp. 1, 16)

Arthur Mizener, "Death Always Flew the Mission," in The New York Times Book Review, October 4, 1959, pp. 1, 16.

EDMUND FULLER

[*The Child Buyer*] is John Hersey at his best and most original, disclosing again one of our ablest, most serious and bold writers.

The Child Buyer flows smoothly around the hazards of its difficult device: the casting of the entire story in the form of the transcript of committee hearings. The potential deadliness of this becomes instead a drama with the electrical immediacy of good dialogue.

The book is broadly satirical, somewhat Shavian in tone, touch, and its surprising switches that give us one thing when he has made us guess at another. Mr. Wissey Jones, representing a vast corporate entity, United Lymphomilloid of America, has disrupted the town of Pequot by his efforts to buy ten-year-old Barry Rudd, an authentic genius. Jones' search for the "raw material" United Lympho requires begins in the school system, which remains in the foreground throughout. The purchase, Jones argues, is vital to the national defense, for United Lympho has a crucial fifty-year government contract relating to space. It must buy the brains the nation needs and develop them itself before they've been "spoiled by . . . what passes for education." The stir in the town has spread to include a hoodlum outbreak and a small scandal involving the youthful genius himself.

As the committee sifts its way laboriously, sometimes uproariously, through the complicated facts, we find ourselves in a savage lampoon of the failures, fumbles and canting jargon that afflict American education. . . .

Mr. Owing, the equivocating superintendent, is "trying to think up ways of avoiding decisions" while presiding over "a school system informed with rectitude, paper progress, safe activity, hesitation."

Mr. Cleary, in charge of the Pequot Talent Search, did not have Barry Rudd on his lists for intellectual gifts because "He was only in the sixty-fourth percentile in the Olmstead-Diffendorff Game"—an intelligence test "consisting entirely of problems developed by cartoons in comic-book style, and drawing heavily for content on the child's world of television, sports, toys, and gadgets . . . culture-free and without social bias." By Cleary, and Miss Henley, a state expert on the "exceptional child," intellectually gifted students are called "deviates" or "the monster quotient."

At first, Wissey Jones seems like the voice of educational enlightenment and reform. But when United Lympho's secret program comes to light we have a mechanistic horror analogous to the demonic National Institute for Coordinated Experiments (the N.I.C.E.) in C. S. Lewis' *That Hideous Strength*. The grim denouement, which we have felt surely could not come to pass, has a touch of the bleakness of *1984*.

Mr. Hersey is telling us that bumbling, inept, jargon-ridden, content-starved, timorous education is a national tragedy and disaster. He is warning us that "crash programs" high-pres-

sured toward utilitarian aims, even as lofty-sounding as "national security" can only compound the tragic disaster. He is denying that education is a process "observable, definable, measurable, manipulable; and that Barry—volatile, mysterious, smoldering Barry—is inert experimental material."

Hersey could borrow Mort Sahl's question: "Is there any group I haven't offended?" Yes: people who cherish the mind, strive for its nurture, relish its individuality, care for its soul, demand its development and defend its freedom.

For an essentially satirical book it develops some fine characterizations. There are moving moments, especially in the testimony of Barry; Dr. Gozar, the woman who has done most for him, not as a principal but as a person, and the town librarian, Miss Cloud, a hunchback whose deformity is the focus of one of Hersey's most subtly sensitive scenes. . . .

Barry Rudd is a fine picture of the loneliness of extreme precocity and remarkable ability. His testimony is the heart of the book. In it, and Dr. Gozar's, and Miss Cloud's, Hersey's feelings about education may be found but they are not programmed. He confronts us with a situation arising from mass education. There is no pat answer for it; no infusion of Federal money can solve it. The answers lie in the non-scientific, non-technical realms of philosophy, theology, and values. The problem is an aspect of our culture, and that will have to be changed if public education is to change.

The Child Buyer is one of Hersey's best books. I think it narrowly misses being even better. The reservation is that its disappointing end-game and resolution fail to have the overwhelming inevitability needed for greatness. Hersey was uncertain of his way out and stopped rather than concluded. Whether this mild cavil is just or not, *The Child Buyer* is an exceptional novel and is essential reading for all concerned with education and related aspects of our culture.

Edmund Fuller, "Hersey's Dramatic Satire on Education," in New York Herald Tribune Book Review, September 25, 1960, p. 3.

ROBERT HATCH

It has been John Hersey's shortcoming that he is a most stylish technician. His books are always the most polished facsimiles of their particular forms—even his novels are brilliant imitations of novels—and the impression thus given is that the author has sensed this or that trend and cannily launched himself into it. Whereas, in fact, Mr. Hersey, the child of missionaries, is himself moved by the impulse to improve his readers. He writes to edify; yet a natural gift for mimicry, strengthened by training in the self-conscious school of news-magazine journalism, has given him an air of manipulating fashionable machinery.

In *The Child Buyer,* however, Mr. Hersey may have hit on the device that turns his talents into virtues. He is embarked on satire, and there the gift for imitation serves him well. It can be objected that aspects of this lampoon are too broad to cut very sharply, but the author hopes to net an audience so large that it cannot be relied upon to catch quick winks. Satire need not necessarily use a rapier; a broadsword will do for gross cutting. More seriously, I think Mr. Hersey falters at times by letting his feelings show through his grin. He cannot tolerate that anyone should think him heartlessly sardonic, and therefore he occasionally reaches out a warm exurban hand. It makes you realize that he is not the man to chastise his generation with scorpions. Still, the whip he uses has a sting to it; I like the book the more, perhaps, because the backsides he chooses to address seem to me apt for the attention.

The book contains a set of three satiric notions nested one within another. In over-all form (Hersey likes editorial devices of this sort), it is the verbatim minutes of hearings before the Senate Standing Committee on Education, Welfare and Public Morality of a state that is probably Connecticut. The members of this committee—Senators Mansfield, Skypack and Voyolko, and committee counsel Broadbent—are wicked cartoons of the legislator bent on investigation. . . . They are all ignorant, puffed by office and indifferent to any welfare but their own. But they are genuinely inquisitive, like old gossips; as busy bodies they are honest. Hersey gets the legislative lingo brilliantly: Broadbent describes one of the principal witnesses, Wissey Jones, as "a very unusual type of individual."

This Wissey Jones, who is quite simply the devil, is an agent for Hersey's second target, the United Lymphomilloid Company (a name intended to suggest the varied and arcane interests of the corporation it designates—like, for example, General Dynamics). . . . The corporation's engineers have discovered that very bright children, suitably altered by psychiatry and surgery, can be made into more productive computers than even the largest electronic models. Therefore, Mr. Jones travels the country, seeking out and securing outstanding specimens. (pp. 231-32)

[Through] his satiric transcripts of the committee hearings, Hersey spins his satires of big business as an end of life and education as a gang press for citizenship. As the devil knows, all of us are corruptible, and before the hearings are over everyone—parents, teachers, legislators, worthy citizens—is on the side of Wissey Jones. In a way, the means by which Jones makes converts is the most chilling side of Hersey's fantasy. United Lymphomilloid is not quite with us yet, and I.Q.s of 189 are not so common as to seem an intimate problem. But the prevalence of corruption breathes on your neck as you read Hersey's relentless catalogue of temptations. He has managed, in this brisk, stylish performance of a book, to poke his finger into a good many of the overseeing eyes of our time—our masters and our guardians—and into the eyes of an uncountable host of private men and women who have begun to ask themselves the question that should never need to be asked: "How do I know I'm honest?" (pp. 232-33)

Robert Hatch, "The Brain Market," in The Nation, *Vol. 191, No. 11, October 8, 1960, pp. 231-33.*

ROBERT GORHAM DAVIS

Taken as a work of the imagination, as giving any kind of illusion of life or reality, *The Child Buyer* is sheer nightmare. The characters are talking grotesques, air-filled monsters, bobbing and swaying like balloons in the Macy parade on a windy Thanksgiving. There are no stable objects for the mind to hold to, except when the characters are talking about the natural sciences. The people—or non-people—are consistent only in their general smart-aleckness and in their total collapse into venality at the end of the book. . . .

In a detective story all the principal characters except the detective have to be unpleasant at the beginning, displaying enough resentment or greed so that any one of them may be supposed capable of the crime. *The Child Buyer* moves in the opposite direction. During much of the action—or talk, rather—some characters, mostly women, appear to be working in the interests

of good, humanity, non-conformism, free intelligence. But then at the end, everyone sells out to the agent, this after learning that the corporation will destroy the bright boy as a human being by the most repulsive methods straight out of Huxley's *Brave New World*.

The educators who sound sensible and the educators who talk ridiculous jargon succumb alike in the most unfeeling way. We don't know where we are, or what psychological and social forces can be used to achieve what Hersey wants. These are supposed to be typical parents, teachers, school administrators, PTA officials, all as pictured on Norman Rockwell covers. Certainly we thought that we could count on Dr. Gozar, a woman of boundless energy, apparently utterly devoted to Barry and creativity and the experimental sciences. But she collapses, too. Only Barry Rudd and his tough friend Charles Perkonian retain some dignity. They are an erudite Tom Sawyer and a hipster-tongued Huckleberry Finn alone against the whole world of their elders.

To refer to names this way is to suggest that there are living characters in the novel. But they are all turned into grotesques by the slick, glib, machine-turned talk, varying and interchangeable from character to character. The novel purports to be the bare record of hearings before a state senatorial investigating committee. The author pretends not to describe or narrate, but only to report what was said. The speakers are permitted a few speech eccentricities, corresponding to the agent's plus-fours and collapsible motor cycle. But then—except for Charles Perkonian and an imbecile Senator, who don't know from nuttin'—they launch into long, complex sentences, full of colorful description that is pure Hersey. As a faithful reader of transcripts of Congressional hearings, I have never observed any such oral flights. . . .

Seen beyond the torrents of talk, the action of the novel is all on the Tom Sawyer level. Dr. Gozar releases a stink bomb at a PTA meeting; the Child Buyer urges high school kids to throw slops at the Rudd house and break windows; as part of a plot worked out with Charles Perkonian, Barry plays doctor with a little girl in the school principal's storeroom. Of the social and political forces in America we learn as little as we do in *Advise and Consent*, a novel which *The Child Buyer* in many ways resembles.

Of the "ideas" in *The Child Buyer* it is not my place here to speak. But if it is a question of an imaginative encounter with unreal beings living in various kinds of rapport with the real world of nature, then I must say that I feel more at home with Tolkien's hobbits or Bronte's Heathcliffe and Katherine, than I do with my fellow Americans as Mr. Hersey conceives them.

Robert Gorham Davis, "An Arrangement in Black and White," in The New Republic, *Vol. 143, No. 16, October 10, 1960, p. 24.*

THOMAS P. McDONNELL

It has been said of John Hersey that he possesses a sense of conscience not usually found in the writings of American novelists today. The immediate objection may be made that every novel, at least to some extent, is a moral statement and therefore a work of the creative conscience. But to say only this would leave too much unsaid—and might in fact itself presume too much. For it seems a point of practical observation that most novelists are interested simply in putting down a statement—their own particular statement—of a particular life-experience.

One has only to reflect for a moment (if indeed proof of credibility were required) on the fact that all but tape-recorded experiential statement dominates, in our novels, over the act of the creative imagination.

What is lacking, then, is a positive awareness on the part of the novelist that he *is* making a moral statement. Consequently, if the novelist does not have this sense of awareness, it follows that he cannot make the fullest use of moral resources in conflict with human actions. His immersion in the experiential may in fact be necessary to the form of the novel; but carried too far and for its own sake, such a course can only lead the novelist into an anarchic statement of his own irresponsibility. Conscience, by its very nature, must be aware of itself. It would seem, moreover, that this is the one element in his (thus our) human nature that the practicing novelist ought least to ignore. Compare, for example, the works of novelists like Françoise Sagan and Albert Camus. The former, as eternal adolescent, is interested simply and totally in the immersed experiential statement; the latter, as conscionable artist, in the observed relevance of ideas to the human situation.

This of course is not to imply that John Hersey has yet attained the stature of a Camus in American letters. But it does affirm that he is pre-eminent among American novelists in his need to make a moral statement. Paradoxically, it is this very quality in John Hersey—almost, one might say, of the supraconscience—which comes dangerously close to being his undoing as a practical novelist. That is to say, the novel is too often reduced to a kind of morality tale in which the situation, or "lesson," takes precedence over a meaningful involvement in the human element. The novelist working in such a milieu runs the risk of seeing people as the embodied abstractions of his own particular contrivance, however admirable his characters and concept may be.

At this point the question of free will is crucial. The experiential novelist, on the one hand, all but deprives his characters of the capacity to act on their own determination as autonomous human beings. They are more creatures than persons. The moralizing novelist, on the other hand, frequently abrogates the free will of his characters to his own use as off-stage author and chief manipulator of destiny.

This is the dilemma, then, that confronts any novelist who happens to be something less than the omniscient observer both of himself and of the human nature that is involved in his literary creation. Of the two extremes, however, John Hersey may be said to err on the side of right. His fine sense of conscience is so thematic and so demonstrable in his novels that we may properly call them allegories of a modern mind in search of salvation. That is why, at least in part, the mode and the method of documentation play such important roles in his writings. In *Hiroshima* (1946), of course, his method was journalistic and literal. In *The Wall* (1950) it was the preservation of historical archives in the apocalypse of annihilation. In *The Child Buyer* (1960) it was the committee interrogation that is death to all true dialogue. The image of allegory was also clearly evident in the short novels of John Hersey. But since a greater force of energy obtains in the two longer novels, as well as in the recent *The Child Buyer*, an eclectic focus might here be somewhat justified. (pp. 240-41)

[The] long novel, *The War Lover* (1959), almost a thematic companion piece to *The Wall*, addresses itself to the disintegration of the nihilistic individual. The book received a great deal of critical acclaim—so much, in fact, that one may reasonably suspect that the acclaim was inordinate both in quantity and quality.

It is commonly agreed that we have reached a point in history where unlimited nuclear war has become "unthinkable." Hence the anti-war novel, almost of any kind, has little trouble in finding a receptive and sympathetic audience. But such novels invariably commit the error of identifying a personal dilemma with the milieu of a communtiy in disruption. (p. 242)

In John Hersey's anti-war novel, *The War Lover,* we are led to believe that war is caused by people meaner than ourselves. Consequently, in the cold analysis of its *idea,* this novel seems, in effect, nothing so much as an over-extended presumption. For in the climax to the novel its ostensible hero, Buzz Marrow, is revealed to be simply the victim of aggressive tendencies! Here again is the confusion of identifying a personal and psychological dilemma with society in catharsis.

The logic, as presented by Charles Boman (Hersey) is this: War is caused by nasty people; but Buzz Marrow is the nasty person; ergo, people like Buzz Marrow caused the war. In the novel all this is capped off with unabashed dramatics. Buzz Marrow, downed in the English Channel, refuses rescue by Charles Boman, and clinging to the prop of his beloved bomber "The Body," disappears into the all-consuming sea. Genuine poetic symbolism is harder to come by. This simply is not it, but only another grand climax designed for a Hollywood smash. Regrettably, then, this is what must occur when the passion of conscience in an outstanding writer is aligned to a hopelessly unsound idea. (p. 243)

[In his] most recent book, *The Child Buyer,* John Hersey has combined his very considerable talent for literature as journalism, with his fine sense of conscience and moral responsibility. It is an arguable book, to say the least, but that is only because it has the force of idea behind it—and since the force of idea is so alien to American fiction, it has also sent the reviewers scurrying in all directions at once.

It has been treated as an attack on Science, on Government, on Education, with numerous sub-divisions of attitude in the last of these troubled areas. Some have taken the book to be blatantly oversimplified in its premises and characterizations. It is as easy to say that, however, as it is to overlook some of the finer subtleties in the book. . . .

The Child Buyer may qualify as literature—and not as an out and out tract, as so many reviewers have insisted—because it has successfully sustained the illusion of narrative. And John Hersey has done this not only through whatever permanence a competent style may give to writing, but also through his creative devices to make such "representative" characters [as Wissey Jones and Charles Perkonian] something more than disembodied abstractions.

If *The Child Buyer* remains an allegory and not a novel, it is because it has been compelled almost wholly through the force of idea. (p. 244)

The allegorical novels of John Hersey have in common the possibility of helping to restore some degree of intelligence and direction to contemporary American fiction. They have in common with European writing an awareness at least of humanistic values, which is to say, they have not completely surrendered to the brutal de-humanization of what now passes for the American imagination. It is an incredible paradox that our novelists should have to be reminded of the value of the human *person*—incredible, indeed, if only in the sense of craft, since there can be no significant dramatic effect in a milieu where everything is ''solved'' in behavioristic terms. Finally, then, if John Hersey can manage to attune his fine sense of conscience less to the singularly allegorical and more to the complexity of the human situation, it is likely that he may give us a novel that has some relevance not only to American life but also to the world at large. (p. 245)

Thomas P. McDonnell, ''Hersey's Allegorical Novels,'' in The Catholic World, *Vol. 195, No. 1168, July, 1962, pp. 240-45.*

WEBSTER SCHOTT

In a past no longer remembered, the Yellow War was fought and white America lost. From this imagined event John Hersey weaves an exhaustive parable [in *White Lotus*] that parallels the history of the Negro in the United States to the present. The idea is startling. The moral provocation is just. And the novel is a resplendent failure. I simply cannot believe it.

Rounded up by California collaborationists (in Pierce Arrows and Packard touring cars with jazz combos in the back seat), whites from the hinterlands are sold into slavery. Jammed into the holds of infested freighters, they cross the Pacific naked, sick and violated—to China, where they grub in fields, or bow as house servants to tiny ''slant eyes'' with presumptuous titles. One such slave is White Lotus, an Arizona girl of 15 when the novel begins, a passive resistant in the ''sleeping-bird movement'' when it ends 10 years later. A sleeping bird ''perch'' (Mr. Hersey's oriental equivalent of the sit-in) frames the novel and sets its tone. . . .

Mr. Hersey calls his book ''an extended dream about the past . . . a history that might have been, a tale of an old shoe on a new foot.'' It's this shoe-and-foot business that causes most of the trouble, booting the stuffing out of characters and kicking up allegorical equivalents.

As White Lotus recollects what led her to the ''perch'' the novel swells into a grab bag of correlatives. Virtually everything from our ''peculiar institution'' has an analogy in *White Lotus.* Yellow masters really ''love'' their simple-minded ''pigs.'' An underground railway spirits slaves to the core provinces. Conscription riots tear cities apart. The civil war of the ''Grand Harmonious Mercy Errand'' has economic causes. . . .

It's a fascinating game to locate the doubles. Playing it, one might yet learn American history—and there are some good laughs besides. But this, after all, is a novel of moral purpose. Mr. Hersey means to shame white Americans into the shoes of their brown and black countrymen. To sense the cage of pigment, requires that we enter the tangle of human character. Tasting fried cabbage or watching a yellow lord possess an immobile white woman won't do it.

White Lotus misses because the author's characters generally are rice-paper thin, as impulsively motivated as Pinocchio, and as chained to their analogous environment. (p. 5)

Always a curiosity, sometimes engaging and nearest conviction during its moments of extreme anguish, *White Lotus* seems to move independently of its characters. The inner torments and outer conflicts of human beings working out their destinies cannot emerge from the grinding machinery of allegory. We search for—but cannot find—the depths and heights of emotion

that would warrant our empathy for these bamboo-scarred whites and driven yellows.

Perhaps message fiction is doomed the moment an author gets the message and decides to put it into code. Too much has happened since *Pilgrim's Progress.* We've been jaded by Cecil B. De Mille. What hurts is that we are sure of John Hersey's moral earnestness. . . . Furthermore, he writes with a painter's eye for landscape and setting. He transmits information—about Chinese folklore, mythology, semantics—with the authority of an encyclopedist and the narrative flair of a New Yorker profiler. But the novel he aspires to must come from bared souls.

One imagines this hefty book lying on coffee tables across the land, dusted around by colored cleaning ladies in nice homes. There it lingers, partly read, without effect, and easily forgotten—a ''good'' story that failed to transmit the terrible shock of life. (p. 26)

Webster Schott, ''White Is to Yellow as Black Is to White,'' in The New York Times Book Review, *January 24, 1965, pp. 5, 26.*

MICHELE MURRAY

Framed by a prologue and an epilogue, [*White Lotus*], the story which John Hersey tells through the narration of a young girl, is straightforward, detailed, absorbing. (p. 743)

The book, although very long, is always interesting. Hersey is an experienced writer, concerned with craft, and even where his conception is weak (as in some of his other books), he can turn out a thoroughly professional novel. I raise only one question—the regular language, the professional quality, the smoothness of narration, the care for explanation—all seem to falsify the slave experience, to smooth it out, to make it less horrible than it was, because in the book it is all grasped in language and thus removed from slavery's most pungent horror—its formlessness, its futurelessness, its complete lack of reason.

I suspect that *White Lotus* is a book with rather more appeal for the white liberal than for the Negro, for all the ingenious cleverness of the parallels. Perhaps that's only to be expected. (p. 744)

Michele Murray, in a review of ''White Lotus,'' in Commonweal, *Vol. LXXXI, No. 23, March 5, 1965, pp. 743-44.*

EDWIN MORGAN

Military defeat, humiliation, loss of spirit; life pared down to the mechanics of survival; race hatred and prejudice; the unrecorded miseries of slavery; daily cruelties of power or law; uprooting and transportation of peoples; the sickening wash of anonymous suffering in history—how can the novelist hope to deal with themes that must often haunt him, yet elude him when he sets out his paltry scatter of characters and works to make it all 'interesting'. Interesting! When the beheader's block is not a limelighted climax but the common accompaniment of living—where is interest to settle? Heads on poles? Weeping relatives? Political revenge? And the author? Sensation-monger? Sentimentalist? Pamphleteer?

In [*White Lotus*], his long and impressive new novel, John Hersey has met these problems head-on and produced one of the most remarkable books to come out of the present vigorous phase of the American novel. In an oddly worded prefatory note he says his book is 'not intended as prophecy' but rather as 'an extended dream about the past'. But no one would take it as being set in the future or as referring to any probable future. What Hersey has done is to employ, in effect, a science fiction technique by which the 'world' of his novel is almost but not quite in focus with the historical world we know: through some minute displacement or warp, things have gone differently in the last century or so, America has been beaten in a war with Imperial China, and thousands of Americans are taken to China as slaves.

The story is told by one of these slaves, a young American girl whose Chinese name is White Lotus, and through the wanderings and tribulations of her and her companions, its theme edges forward: what freedom can be obtained, how, at whose expense, for whom, and for how long? Who among the central characters is most nearly justified in his method of opposition? Is it Nose, degenerating into a world of drunken make-believe where 'being bad is the only revenge', burnt at the stake for a crime he didn't commit? Or the fanatical preacher Peace, beheaded after an abortive violent uprising? Or Dolphin who tried to escape by himself and was torn to pieces by tracker dogs? Or Rock, honest, courageous, capable of violence but choosing in the end the non-violent protest, the 'Sleeping-Bird Method', which White Lotus also comes to practise? Hersey seems to pin his hope on a persistent non-violent dissidence forcing dialogue on the oppressor.

This is not a primer of current politics, nor is it an attack on Communist China. It is a book about slavery and freedom in which the Chinese background so familiar to the author is used, with extraordinary vividness, to convey the sense of a vast, varied, yet rigidly stratified society, with its cangues and cumshaw, mandarins and eunuchs, silk tycoons on the Bund and endless peasant endurance—and everywhere the smouldering enmity between whites and yellows, the 'pigs' and 'lids' of mutual contempt and fear. The scenes in Shanghai in the latter part of the novel, where Chinese and Americans mingle more freely and there are even some rich whites, are particularly brilliant, a series of striking contrasts, with the glories of the Race Club at one sunny extreme and the squalor of 'beggars begging from beggars' at the other. There are some longueurs in the middle of the book, but like the longueurs of an Indian film they seem so much a part of the episodic structure that one can accept them and keep going. The overall impression is of a wealth of experience and invention; and of a deeply felt theme. This, I think, is John Hersey's most creative and rewarding novel.

Edwin Morgan, "Sleeping Birds," in New Statesman, *Vol. LXIX, No. 1789, June 25, 1965, p. 1018.*

ELIOT FREMONT-SMITH

Poor Faust. They just won't leave him alone. Someone is always poaching on his territory. The most recent notable poach was *Damn Yankees*. Now comes John Hersey's new novel *Too Far to Walk*. . . . In this tale, Faust's name is Fist—John Fist. He's a good boy—at least as good as Shoeless Joe from Hannibal, Mo., was—and a lot brighter. In fact, as a freshman at Sheldon College (the milieu is Yale's, the endowment is Wesleyan's) Fist was known as an "over-achiever." But now he's in his sophomore year, the doldrums of academe, and he just can't make his classes because—well, because it's too far to walk. That's his explanation, at any rate: he just can't seem

to care any more, nothing seems relevant. Moreover, he's fallen in with Chum Breed, a fellow student and a bad influence if there ever was one.

Breed has done everything. . . . He's well-versed in the dark underside of gothic literature, his basic mode is scorn, and Fist detects a mysterious odor of ozone about him, of short-circuit sparks. . . .

Fist, who has read everything from Greek mythology to Ayn Rand, but apparently not Goethe (not Salinger either, which may be germain: there's a good bit of backsliding Holden Caulfield to Hersey's Faust)—is naturally dumfounded. "Who are you?" he demands of Breed. "I'm the Spirit of Playing It Cool," replies Hersey's puppet devil, drawing his lips back over his teeth, "which opened and closed, so that the smile seemed like a hungry bite into something soft," presumably Fist's id.

Breed then whips out a 26-week contract renewable for life, has Fist seal the thing in blood (Breed is a square when it comes to professional protocol), and it's Heigh-Ho, breakthroughs here we come!

Unfortunately, by this point *Too Far to Walk* has already challenged one's suspension of disbelief and lost. The remainder of the novel, although extremely readable, frequently funny (clichés, but well done) and occasionally insightful, continues this depressing process of disintegration, the result at least of a failure of imagination.

Fist meets good girl Margaret . . . , loses his virginity to prostitute Mona . . . , takes Mona home to his prototypical middle-class parents in Worcester, Mass., threatens to quit college altogether, gets caught in a protest march, goes skiing at Christmas, commits a daring theft and finally takes LSD. . . .

While under LSD, Fist has lots of fantasies—beach boy life, fighting in a war, black magic orgies, struggling in a mental ward. But through these fantasies he comes to realize that his mother is really quite a gal, that his father will back him up when the chips are down, that Breed is bad news and that Margaret is the girl for him. Moral: When in drop-out doubt, take LSD.

This is presumably not the moral John Hersey intended, yet it is the only one that can be found. The trouble is (to put the best face on it), Hersey is trying to deal authentically with a new and pressing problem of our age, the profound crisis of value and identity that strikes and maims many youths today, and kills some—but in doing so doesn't want to upset anybody. He has trotted out just the sort of optimistic make-believe that the crisis is in part about. Thus in matters that are crucial, both to the issue and to fiction, he fudges badly. Fist's psychic redemption is improbably easy: he won't renew that contract. What's worse, his despair, his cruelty, his opting-out, his suffering, is utterly without consequence: Margaret is waiting; he'll get at least B-plus for his junior year.

Eliot Fremont-Smith, "Some Faust," in The New York Times, *February 28, 1966, p. 25.*

PETER BUITENHUIS

[*Too Far to Walk*] is a novel about that well-known collegiate phenomenon, the sophomore slump. In fact, in John Hersey's unusual and witty story, it's more than a slump; it's a downright depression and damned nearly a crash. What puzzles me is that the novel was written, according to the blurb, before its author took up his appointment as Master of Pierson College at Yale last fall. Like all his books, this one is exceedingly well-researched. I would have sworn that he had been right there with a tape-recorder in the dormitories, the greasy spoons, the cars and bars, taking down all that lingo and recording with a sharp eye the gestures and habits of that often grubby animal, the male undergraduate. (p. 4)

As he begins the novel the reader expects that Mr. Hersey will take him through the jumps of the university term with a hard grip on the reins of realism. Surprisingly, about one-quarter of the way through, he switches his saddle to the winged steed of fantasy. Chum Breed, a fellow-sophomore to whom [the protagonist] John is attracted, turns out to be not just another Joe College, but no less an eminence than Mephistopheles, who calls himself the Spirit of Playing It Cool. . . . [Sure enough], John is now Faustus Jr., and has all the powers of the diabolical world at his disposal.

Strangely enough, he doesn't do much about it. His Margaret doesn't become his mistress. He doesn't grasp at power, but simply goes on being a disorganized, dissatisfied, delinquent undergraduate—which is really to be in hell without having had the pleasure of earning it. Things don't really warm up until Breed-Mephistopheles gives John a capsule of LSD, and he goes off into a world of dreams of a far-out and violent kind.

When he comes out of the drug's influence, he decides not to renew his pact. He doesn't want illusions but the real world "crummy as it is." The book ends not with him dropping out as he had earlier wanted, but, implicitly, settling for the system and a junior year aboard the academic ship with the other regular guys.

As a result of his method in the novel, Mr. Hersey raises more questions than he answers. He captures brilliantly and amusingly a mood of restlessness and boredom so common to the sophomoric experience. At the same time, he evades many of the problems underlying his theme. I was left with the feeling that, underneath it all, John Fist was really good old Frank Merriwell, having a tussle with Devil and Man at Yale, trying out with High Camp instead of Walter Camp, before settling down to his proper career of making A's and touchdowns and emerging as the all-American. (pp. 4, 38)

> *Peter Buitenhuis, "Sophomore Slump," in* The New York Times Book Review, *March 13, 1966, pp. 4, 38.*

GUY DAVENPORT

It is obvious after a few pages of [*Too Far to Walk*] that the story is an allegory, that we are reading an updated version of the Faustus legend, and not Goethe's transcendental one, either, but the starker, tragic one of Marlowe. Our John Fist is Johann Faust, our corrupting upper-classman Breed is Mephistopheles, with LSD for kicks, a whore for Helen, and a cheap *acte gratuit* (trust the Devil to have been reading Dostoievski and Gide) for the thrill of sin.

Yet the allegorical direction is not to Faust at all but to that classic study of the Puritan psychology, Nathaniel Hawthorne's "Young Goodman Brown". (pp. 424-25)

Hawthorne was fascinated by the subtle Puritan duplicity. But Mr. Hersey, in making the best and clearest portrait yet of the

campus protestor, shows well what the newspapers can't tell us, that rebellion is an exclusive, deeply selfish club. . . .

Mr. Hersey has always written a good novel. This is his ninth and he's still in top form. His sense of drama is superb, and if he has smoothed out many of the wrinkles in the undergraduate character, he has done it in the interest of clarity. His hero commits grand larceny for the thrill of it; it would have been more truthful to have shown him as our sons and daughters really are, petty thieves, pocketing a pack of cigarettes when the sales-girl isn't looking, as a matter of course, or shoplifting in the campus book-store—how upset these thieves (who are simply being cool, buddy, don't let it bug you) would be to have Mom exposed as a shoplifter at the supermarket back in Glendale. He has a peddler of class-notes where he might have displayed the ring of pre-written term-papers and theses that do a brisk business at all our colleges.

Too Far to Walk—eloquent title!—is a book to be grateful for. It holds up the mirror, which is the first thing we can ask of the artist. It opens our eyes, which is the last thing we can expect of a popular novel with a fashionable subject. (p. 425)

> *Guy Davenport, "Deep Waters and Dark," in* National Review, *Vol. XVIII, No. 18, May 3, 1966, pp. 424-27.**

ELIOT FREMONT-SMITH

[In *Under the Eye of the Storm*] Dr. Tom Medlar's finicky joy and time-consuming inspiration is neither his wife nor his profession; it is his boat. . . . Her name, all too minutely, is Harmony. Puttering about in her, keeping her trim and polished, neatly noting her adventures in a log book, eschewing all modern electronic and muscle-saving conveniences (save a superbly reliable engine), Tom uses the Harmony to renew his troubled soul. Quite understandably, this causes a brooding resentment in his wife, Audrey, who would like a little less attention paid to the log book and a little more to her. . . . Tom, for his part, feels vaguely guilty about the necessary privacy of his communion with Harmony, nature and the sea.

He wishes he could—well, communicate better with Audrey; he wishes also that he could take more satisfaction from being, at 34, Connecticut's ace liver specialist. Why did he go into liver in the first place? Why not infectious diseases, neurology, obstetrics? Vaguely he realizes there was something about the mythology of the liver that appealed to him, the seat of man's soul, all that stuff.

A good deal less vaguely, the reader of John Hersey's latest novel realizes that Tom's specialization, along with everything else in the story, is strictly Mr. Hersey's doing. And with this realization, which comes immediately, the sea, the unrelentingly mythic, inevitably storm-tossed, sense-awakening and courage-testing setting of the novel shrinks to the size of a bathtub.

Tom and Audrey's estrangement needs a catalyst, which is provided by the addition of another couple and a hurricane. The other couple are Flick and Dottie Hamden, invited aboard the Harmony for a cruise off Block Island. Flick is a computer engineer and a total boor; he talks about himself non-stop, insults the Harmony's honest, old-fashioned line, tears up Tom's log book for a joke and makes eyes at Audrey. . . .

Meanwhile, the hurricane, whose name is Esmé, gathers force off Cape Hatteras, down by the stopper.

Why doesn't Tom turn the Harmony back to shore? Because he must have his time of testing, because that's the design of the novel. Why did he invite the incompatible Hamdens aboard to share the testing? Don't ask. Enough that they are there. The sea churns. Storm clouds gather on the shower curtain. The very tiles, not to mention Mr. Hersey's prose, sweat symbolism.

For all of Tom's care, the Harmony turns out to be not quite watertight; like the best laid plans, she springs a leak. It isn't fatal because ships like this in novels like this don't break up. Esmé does her worse, but the Harmony and Mr. Hersey's four puppets endure it and survive. For three of them nothing much changes. But Tom, the skipper, the responsible one, is given Insight, the chief among which is that having made one's bunk, one must lie in it. Or, nothing in this imperfect world can be perfect, so one must try to make the best of things.

Thus strengthened, Tom discovers he can endure Flick's taunts as necessary, and be more charitable in his thoughts of Dottie. He can be more loving of Audrey, and perhaps less compulsive about the Harmony. . . . At yacht club parties, over by the soap dish, he can entertain friends with the story of their adventure and think how lucky he is to have had Esmé and to now have Audrey. And if there's a tiny bit of smugness in all this, well, that's one of the imperfections he must accept as he accepts himself.

The trouble is, there is a great deal of smugness in all this. It masquerades as honesty for part of the way, but the novel's appeal is strictly to the comfy and familiar. . . . That he gets away with any of it—and he does, without a single laugh: the book is what is called readable, at times even vivid—is a tribute to Mr. Hersey's craftsmanship. Finally, however, it is slick, heavy and prefabricated, and content to be that way.

> Eliot Fremont-Smith, "Smug in a Tub," in The New York Times, March 17, 1967, p. 39.

JOHN WARNER

[In *Under the Eye of the Storm*] there is not one shred of plot—none of the strong story line that made, say, *A Bell for Adano* or *The War Lover* wonderfully entertaining reading. Nor are there any true-to-life (or even true-about-life) characters like the heroic Major Joppolo. Indeed, Hersey has brought types rather than flesh-and-blood characters into this book.

Chief among these is Tom Medlar, a medical doctor who "regarded himself as a humanist, a vitalist; he believed in an inner flame, a secret of life, intuition, love, whispers in the night, and crushing fallibility." Opposite Tom is Flicker Hamden, self-styled genius of the computer, who "characterized anything Medlar said as 'rickety, antiquated Bergsonian idiocy' and extolled electrical intellectuality and wanted every mortal to be plugged in to a vast cybernetic system of data-sifting, problem-solving, and decision-making."

Then there are the wives: Audrey Medlar and Dottie Hamden—but they are of only passing interest. They serve as foils, for Tom especially, whose inability to understand either of these uncomplicated women reinforces our picture of him as a man hopelessly out of touch with life—and lacking the intellect to realize it.

These four are gathered aboard Tom's ancient yawl *Harmony* for what is hoped to be a leisurely cruise of Block Island Sound. But a hurricane (which had been predicted would pass out to

sea far to the south) suddenly strikes. The leisurely cruise then becomes a kind of voyage of discovery as this latter-day Thoreau and this modern man of science try desperately to work together to save *Harmony* and her crew.

By now, of course, symbol hunters will be gleefully off and running. There are just too many obvious signs to slip by unnoticed. One thinks immediately of Melville's notion that a ship is a microcosm of the world; of the great storm that suggests the conflict between Tom and Flicker; of the connotations of the name *Harmony;* and so on.

In the hands of a writer less skillful than Hersey, such clichés would spell complete disaster. But he is, of course, a pro, and his sure, spare style, his characteristic restraint, his probing journalist's eye almost surmount these difficulties. His description of the storm is especially impressive. . . . But this is not enough; *Under the Eye of the Storm* is not supposed to be a meteorological study, but an introspective look at people under stress. And once Hersey's relentless and minute probing of Tom (and Flick) is done, we still know they are cardboard figures, hardly worth the effort. (pp. 116-17)

> John Warner, "Novelist or Journalist?" in Harper's Magazine, Vol. 234, No. 1404, May, 1967, pp. 116-17.

F.W.J. HEMMINGS

Conrad used a typhoon as a figurative crucible to test a man's moral strength; Richard Hughes to test a ship's triumphant toughness. . . . [In *Under the Eye of the Storm*], the storm's function is to face man with a truth that turns all previously apprehended realities into illusions. Tom, a specialist in disorders of the liver, goes sailing on vacations in order to 'get away from it all', to escape from an artificial world where man's environment is too cosily controlled. His purpose—on this occasion overfulfilled—is to confront the 'real world', in which survival will depend on his own judgement, skill and endurance. Flick, whom he has taken along with him, is a communications expert, living for an automated future of infallible servo-mechanisms. The quarrel between the two men, exteriorised—a little unnecessarily perhaps—in Tom's suspicions about his wife's relations with Flick, boils down to a restatement of the old argument between humanism and technology.

At the height of the storm, the two men and their two women are really alone, unable even to hear one another shout above the racket. What price communication now? And why perfect means for the transmission of data when the data are in any case utterly untrustworthy? In the last analysis, Mr. Hersey will be found to have written one more allegory of the aloneness of every human being: each of us exists, unreachable, in the calm centre, the 'eye' of his own personal storm. There is nothing new in the message, but it comes to us on a new wavelength, powerfully transmitted.

> F.W.J. Hemmings, "Robbing Grillet," in The Listener, Vol. 78, No. 2006, September 7, 1967, p. 312.*

NANCY L. HUSE

John Hersey is an impressive figure in contemporary American letters. Over four decades, his work has evoked relatively little critical comment despite his early Pulitzer prize for *A Bell for*

Adano, (1944), his acclaimed journalism in such works as the world-famous *Hiroshima* (1946), and a long list of novels which deal with contemporary events but actually represent a complex artistic response to post-World War II history. (p. 1)

[Despite] the simple directness of much of Hersey's work, the presence in it of a mind rebelling at the age's acceptance of nuclear weapons, the Holocaust, racism, and the annihilation of the individual in a technological society places Hersey as an intellectual contemporary of Bellow, Wright, Mailer and Agee. (p. 2)

Hersey has repeatedly been compared with writers of stature; Hawthorne, Conrad, Crane, Dos Passos, C. P. Snow; a case can be made comparing him with Steinbeck, Camus, Silone, and Mailer. Is the Yale teacher and earnest crusader merely patching together, consciously or unconsciously, bits of material taken from the great writers he is said to resemble? Or does he resemble them because of his weaving together in new ways various elements they too have employed, such as realistic reporting, a concern with both the individual and his existence in society, and direct commitment of the writer to a political or philosophical stand?. . . Hersey's intellectual framework [has been described] as one provided in raw form by his age but distilled by his personal experience and attitudes into a unique insistence upon the individual's ability to survive and even to transform a hostile society. If Hersey possesses a unique vision, can he have expressed it only in cliches and borrowed forms? His development as a writer, with the increasing irony in his still affirmative vision, is a matter of critical interest.

Hersey's philosophical view depends upon the individual's attaining authentic existence in the face of overwhelming odds. . . . [For example], Boman in *The War Lover* (1959) comes to see his own guilt and responsibility; [and] the engineer in *A Single Pebble* (1956) becomes aware of a dignity in human struggle he had not dreamed of. . . . Each work takes on the aspect of Camus' Sisyphus myth, but Hersey has his own means of demonstrating the reasons for continuing and relishing the struggle. A glance at a list of Hersey's works evokes an image of salvation for the individual and for society as a whole which constitutes a kind of transforming vision in starkly modern terms.

The absurd labor of Sisyphus-man is the result of his passion for life in the face of death. Hersey's heroes display not the scorn and sorrow of the conscious sufferer, but that other side of the labor which, Camus, says "can also take place in joy." Hersey's special chore has been the creation of fables which represent the human being engaged in an unceasing labor for survival with dignity. The very struggle becomes the essence of human life and its shadowed joy. Nowhere in Hersey's work is there a suggestion of an imposed external order or a divine destiny; yet humanity defines a kind of order and even a nobility by engagement with the challenge of staying alive in dignity, of carrying a burden which is both the result of personal choices and imposed from without by others. That Hersey has isolated the narrow moment when Sisyphus turns to take up his burden by choice, that he has omitted explicit portrayals of the design of the universe, that he has left untouched the realm of man's fall or choice of defiance of the gods in order to show human beings as straining but determined, never dreaming of refusing the task of life and rather absorbed in it by will, has caused the author to be faulted for simplification. His being unlike Dostoevsky (though like Crane, Dos Passos, Conrad and the others) has seemed to be a problem for critics. (pp. 3-4)

In his depiction only of a "slice of the spirit," Hersey has recognizable and even deliberate limitations. But his wrestling with necessity, his concern with life rather than with death, is at very least an interesting variation of a dominant contemporary theme. (pp. 4-5)

Hersey's concept of the writer's role in society causes him to sound, at times, like an earnest do-gooder or revivalist preacher. In *White Lotus* (1965) for example, it is clear that Hersey has set out to tell us truth about the human condition, to make us recoil from slavery because his elaborate fiction demands—if we stay with it—that we imagine what it is to live as a slave. In *The War Lover,* too,—as in nearly all of Hersey's books since *The Marmot Drive* (1953)—it is apparent early in the book that Hersey has designs upon our ideas. He wants us to believe as he does; to do this he tells a story, as preachers always have. His didactic rhetoric is varied throughout his career, but it shows a growing sense of pain or disappointment without ever abandoning its principle tenet: that individuals, particularly those who have awareness, can and will continue to confront and re-shape social attitudes and political forms.

To look carefully, then, at Hersey, we must look at a message as well as at a style. Moreover, as we should ask anyone else who directed us to believe and act in a particular way, we must note what the exhorter does about his creed in his own life. (pp. 5-6)

Since the general question of the artist's role in America is interesting in itself, knowledge about Hersey's public deeds, style of life and conviction of his truthtelling role is profitable for the way it shows his alignment with some of his most brilliant contemporaries and his small but vital contributions to the literary scene, which include both his writings and his actions. His early interest in writing "novels of contemporary history," his special gifts for description and for rhythmic or cryptic phrasing, his use of various types of reportorial forms and his relationship to the contemporary existential novel and to nonfictional narrative indicate both a sturdy individual talent and a kinship with the literary and intellectual milieu. (p. 6)

Whatever credence Hersey's survival theme has besides his own insistence on it in life and in fiction comes from the way that his characters make their existential choices to rejoin, and yet remain free from, a rather threatening society. These choices are not made in a vacuum. The means of attaining true existence are offered through the communicative powers of those who feel set apart by their ability to present a vision of reality to other men. . . . Hersey reiterates that there is a sacredness about representing one's concept of truth in written or spoken words through such culturally unifying figures as Su-ling in *A Single Pebble,* Kid Lynch in *The War Lover,* and White Lotus herself. The reaching out of one human being to another in order to share a vision, and thus to allow the other person to create his own imagined representation, has never ceased to inspire Hersey or his characters; in *The Child Buyer* (1960), this ability of Barry's is the essence of his genius and the great power which the computer will take from him.

The means by which Hersey has become famous, the reportorial earnestness, selectivity and skill he showed in *Hiroshima,* have remained the cornerstone of his creative gifts and the only explanation for his affirming human survival. The preoccupation Medlar has with the dolphins in *Under the Eye of the Storm* and the boorish presence of computer-loving Flick on board "The Harmony," are the outgrowths of Hersey's lifelong preoccupation with the wonders of communication. Human consciousness, beautifully able to share its vision of truth with others (and thus to help them toward the creation of their own) is the explanation Hersey gives for both our ability and our will to survive, his major theme and the determining factor of his style. *A Single Pebble, The Conspiracy,* and *My Petition for More Space* are directly concerned with this mystery; indirectly, other works are concerned with it as well. In *The Marmot Drive,* it is Hester's separation from others, in *Too Far to Walk,* it is John's abandonment of the tradition which account for their sufferings.

Hersey's preoccupation with the individual's transcending through communication and awareness the negative and threatening trends of history identifies him securely as a twentieth century figure. The coming of technology and the passing of Christianity have posed serious threats to the Western individual struggling to survive in a world gone meaningless. Cultural and literary critics typically pronounce that moderns fear loss of control over their individual fates. . . . Hersey's use of existential thought in such works as *The War Lover* and *The Child Buyer* has been noted. . . . It is not surprising that a writer who is awed by our capacity to survive and take responsibility for our existence would, early in his work, show he had absorbed the contemporary philosophy which attempted to define the human being in control, although alone. (pp. 6-8)

In his use of the Sisyphus myth and other existential themes, Hersey bears a resemblance in our age to storytellers such as Hans Christian Andersen, who freely used old folk tales, modified forms of them, and new forms including the satirical fantasy. The comparison of Hersey to Andersen, although incongruous in some ways because of their different times in history and manner of communicating, nevertheless is valid. Both are versatile storytellers who freely use old material, sometimes in new forms; both bring to their stories strongly felt emotions and observations about contemporaries. Both sometimes lose an audience because of moralizing too openly. Andersen is known for a common popular form of his day, storytelling, but he always aspired to write serious drama. Hersey has used the skills of a modern reporter in his most satisfying works, and like Andersen will not be best remembered in his preferred field as a serious, original novelist (*The Marmot Drive* has been called his greatest failure) but rather as a talented chronicler or inspired reporter of his times. As with Andersen, there is a strain of the didactic in Hersey's stories which cannot be removed or ignored in defining his essential meaning as a writer. (p. 8)

In emphasizing the role of art (the literary art) as a catalyst toward a richer existence, Hersey crosses the path of Sartre briefly but intensively. Sartre's conviction that the writer has a moral mission to illuminate and to influence his own historical period, with history rather more important than literature, seems closely allied with Hersey's explanation . . . of the writer's obligation to and effect upon his age in "the novel of contemporary history." Showing the "constants of human character" within the ferment of contemporary events, Hersey's writer differs from Sartre's situational vision of man very little; the "constants" of Hersey's own characters have emerged as human needs for individual responsibility, awareness, and assent. Hersey's human being is as alone as Sartre's until he enters into valid relationships. These become more and more difficult as Hersey deepens his criticism of social and political systems; a recent book, *My Petition for More Space,* is a futuristic novel which demonstrates the stifling of human relationships in a totalitarian society at the same time that it breathes with the all-but-hopeless struggle of the individual (the writer) to remain free and to envision freedom for others. Hersey's work has been to portray possibilities in a given world rather than to preach revolution; nevertheless, like a back-door Sartre he has repeatedly implied that the contemporary world is one an awakened individual cannot accept without pain, without "the absurd."

Hersey sees the writer's role as questioning and visionary in any society; he does not share, and probably never has, Sartre's conviction in *What Is Literature?* that the writer is capable, that people are capable, of achieving a classless and peaceful society through a commitment to socialism. He sees the writer as independent of ideology, Plato's poet with a vision of possibilities which he leaves to others to put into action. Not literature-as-action in the Sartrean sense, but literature-as-suggestion-for-action is Hersey's sense of commitment. (pp. 11-12)

A Platonist in an age of Aristotelian criticism, a man obsessed with his truth-telling role and yet aloof from the Marxist interpretation of history, concerned deeply with topical subjects because they are the burden, and the Sisyphus-task of man, Hersey has been uniquely of and outside of his times. The writer, he has said, "must want to pierce reality with his personal vision and tell someone else what he has seen." Alone and yet in touch, Hersey's life is the raw material for the characters of his books. The paradox of singularity-in-community, Hersey's philosophy and major theme, may account for the remoteness and alleged oversimplification of some of his work. It also accounts for the many strengths of his art. (p. 12)

Nancy L. Huse, in her The Survival Tales of John Hersey, *The Whitston Publishing Company, 1983, 217 p.*

EVA HOFFMAN

It has been John Hersey's virtue as teacher and public figure— and sometimes his weakness as a novelist—that, against all odds and the grain of the times, he has sustained the idea of writing as a moral mission. Now, in [*The Call: An American Missionary in China*], a work that seems intended as a summa of all his preoccupations and concerns, he has chosen to look at the missionary impulse itself—its potential for help, reform, arrogance and control. He has done so through tracing an almost unexamined piece of American lore—the history of the Protestant evangelical movement in China in the first half of this century. It is a vastly ambitious, impressively erudite, and unfortunately flawed, undertaking.

The intrinsic interest of the subject is enormous, and Mr. Hersey's credentials for tackling it are impeccable. . . . To tell his panoramic story, he devises a form that is somewhere between docu-fiction, synthetic biography and authentic history. Through diary entries, letters and snippets of historical documents, the novel traces the life and spiritual development of David Treadup, a not untypical "China hand," based, Mr. Hersey acknowledges, on several actual missionaries. . . .

Mr. Hersey is well aware of both the comedy and the misunderstandings involved in grafting American and Christian presumptions onto the convoluted subtleties of Chinese culture, but he treats his perennially well-intentioned hero with considerable sympathy. In the course of his pilgrim's progress, Treadup gains a nearly heroic stature, coming to represent the best qualities of the American character, the best side of innocence. He is a practical Utopian, a moral entrepreneur who believes that there is a solution for every problem, and who tackles all problems with boundless energy and optimism.

In fact, he often seems too good to be true, though Mr. Hersey takes pains to point out the bumbling and oblivious aspect of his enthusiasm. The layers of this protagonist's ignorance are deep, but he has an attractive eagerness to learn. . . .

Mr. Hersey's accounts of . . . history's lesser-known episodes—the recruitment of a coolie labor corps by the Allies during World War I, for example, or the beginnings of vast literacy campaigns based on a simplified version of the Chinese alphabet—can be quite fascinating. But the problem is that he tries to tell us too much. The amount of sheer information packed into this "novel" is so overwhelming that it becomes difficult to focus on the significance of any one event or issue. The Revolution comes to us through David's eyes, in snippets and isolated rumblings. And while such problems as "cultural imperialism," or the horrifying conditions of women, are dutifully brought up, none of them can be fully explored in this gallop through the enormous historical expanses.

On the other hand, the lives of David and his wife, Emily—their trips and fallings-out, their changes of housing and David's feuds with the Y.M.C.A., are chronicled in needlessly minute detail. So are the innumerable crises of David's spiritual life, which is turbulent to the point of monotony: he is perpetually experiencing cataclysmic insights, meetings that change his life, and gigantic moral struggles.

All of this makes for a tendency to melodramatic cliche, and isn't helped by a style marked by a stiffness and heartiness of a didacticism that tries to correct itself, but doesn't quite succeed.

These are obstacles to the full enjoyment of this overlong work. But for those willing to make their way through it, the sheer satisfaction of learning so much, from such a reliable source, about such fascinating matters, is well worth the trek.

> *Eva Hoffman, in a review of "The Call: An American Missionary in China," in* The New York Times, *April 22, 1985, p. C16.*

ROBERT McAFEE BROWN

John Hersey has a well-deserved reputation not only for writing on a wide variety of subjects, but also for managing to confront his readers with moral problems in a nondidactic way. Mr. Hersey does not don the mantle of preacher or prophet; he is a novelist and essayist first, last and always. . . . [Mr. Hersey] would surely affirm that exploration into the heights and depths of the human spirit is proper to his craft. For whether he is confronting us with the genuinely sensitive and good-hearted Major Joppolo in *A Bell for Adano,* the magnitude of human evil in *Hiroshima,* the juxtaposition of Jewish greatness and Nazi depravity in *The Wall* or the unquenched yearning for a center of meaning in *A Single Pebble,* a cameo set in the China of his childhood, Mr. Hersey lays before us the quests, bafflements, frustrations and modest triumphs of the human spirit in ways that leave our minds sometimes ennobled and always stretched in new directions.

Never has this been truer than in what may well be his *magnum opus* (in the literal as well as the metaphorical sense; it is a hefty book). *The Call* is the story of David Treadup, a farm boy from upstate New York who has all the adolescent tensions

that give rise to rowdyism, preoccupation with sex, confusion about family loyalty, stubbornness and a desire for adventure, and who undergoes a religious conversion, a "call," while he is an undergraduate at Syracuse University. He dedicates his life to the task of winning China for Christ.

Those for whom stories about missionaries hold no antecedent charm need not stop reading. Nor will they, once they have followed David Treadup this far into the narrative, for instead of turning into the sanctimonious and slightly pompous missionary so stereotyped in modern fiction, he becomes an engaging character who sees the Chinese first as human beings to be known and loved, rather than simply as brands to be plucked from the burning fires of hell. This attitude involves him in innumerable contretemps with sanctimonious and slightly pompous missionary types who hold the reins of power back in New York City and who, from their safe enclaves of authority, dictate what may and may not be permitted out in the field. If they are increasingly exasperated by David Treadup, he returns the compliment. It is an even match. . . .

One finishes the book almost persuaded that one has not read fiction but biography, and Mr. Hersey, whose fiction has usually been based on real historical situations, acknowledges that his protagonist is created out of half a dozen actual missionaries, one of them his own father. . . . We can leave it to the old China hands, however—those Americans who grew up in China, who will devour this book in its every detail—to determine which characters are based on which old friends, and which are Mr. Hersey's artistic creations. To the rest of us it does not matter; the David Treadup we meet is no composite, but has been endowed by Mr. Hersey with his own vibrant life.

There are, as in most lives, a smattering of triumphs and a host of tragedies. Some of each the protagonist brings upon himself, while others are thrust upon him when he is the victim of forces over which he has no control. But this mixture of freedom and fate is the stuff of every life, and Mr. Hersey's characters, in addition to possessing their own authenticity, are also mirrors in whom readers who have never set foot in China will find themselves reflected.

> *Robert McAfee Brown, "All His Losses Were His Gain," in* The New York Times Book Review, *May 12, 1985, p. 3.*

JONATHAN D. SPENCE

There is, in this long book [*The Call*], an extraordinary amount of powerful writing about China, especially its poverty and its wars, its catastrophic floods and bungled relief missions. David Treadup, landing in China in 1905, is given an inkling of the task awaiting him as a missionary by the smells that bear down upon him: "the smell of night soil spread on fields . . . ; of decaying vegetation and feces in canals; of burning garbage; of the rotting guts of beasts in shambles; of garlic and sweat and menses and bad teeth and mildewed quilted garments—the hideous compacted smells of the poor." The passage artfully prepares us for one of Hersey's central themes, the terrible tensions that emerge between the foreign-educated experts and the poor they are trying to help; and it gives a hint as to the route Treadup will follow, sliding from Christian preaching, via technical aid and educational work, to radical political commitment and eventual despair.

Treadup's childhood and youth are given sharp focus—*his* rural poverty had been a New England one where farmers "worked a trashy soil and with their stoic oxen dragged rocks on stone boats year after year to the ragged walls that marked the outermost limits of their strength and patience." But it is China that dominates the book, and here Hersey has done a most ingenious thing. He arranges for David Treadup to experience his most important moments of insight about his mission and its purpose (or lack of it) in two environments that are both Chinese and yet strangely, even savagely, separated from it. One is the world of Chinese coolie laborers working in the French trenches in the closing year of World War I, after China had declared war on the side of the Allies against Germany. The second is the world of the servantless Westerners in 1943, after they have been interned by the Japanese in a large mission compound, now converted into a five-acre jail.

These two aspects of Chinese experience in the two great wars are known to those who teach and work in Chinese history, but probably not to most readers at large. . . . Material may be sparse, but the special aura of these two communities—displaced Chinese in Europe, doubly displaced Westerners in China—enables Hersey to be especially convincing as he shows Treadup exploring two central themes: first, the immense power of popular education on the illiterate workers of China, and second, the rediscovery of meaning in life suddenly without God.

The most important secondary figures in all this are Treadup's wife, Emily, and his Chinese friend Johnny Wu. Emily, married by the young David Treadup after brief acquaintance, so that he can take up his evangelical work in China—restless young bachelors were not welcome in the missions—grows on the reader throughout the book, not by virtue of her own powers so much as by the reader's awareness of the depth of Treadup's tongue-tied love for her. Bearing him three sons and a daughter who dies at age one while Treadup is away from home, Emily is partly an uncomplaining foil, but also a model for the sense of place that constantly eludes the ever restless Treadup. Their passion for each other is made gently clear by Hersey, but only in the discreet language of period-piece diaries or letters—there is no overt erotic description anywhere in the book, and almost no false note in the couple's disarming written record of their life together. An exception, to me, was one letter in which Treadup tells his fiancée—still waiting to sail from the United States—of the brutal excesses against Christian women in China perpetrated by the Chinese at the time of the Tientsin massacre. I was never convinced David would have written that to Emily and it hung like a small question mark over the novel. (pp. 29-30)

Johnny Wu, on the other hand, is a galvanic character who serves to focus Treadup's preoccupations with scientific advancement for the Chinese and with the possibilities of a meaningful land reform and industrialization program for China's villages, one that could be carried out through independent initiatives, away from the ideological manipulations of either the Kuomintang or the CCP. He is modeled, pretty clearly, after the remarkable "Jimmy" Yen, whose community in Tinghsien was, along with some of Liang Shu-ming's experiments in Shantung, among the most hopeful of the new developments in China that were wrecked beyond recovery by the onset of the Second World War.

Inevitably, in a novel this ambitious, with such a large cast of characters, the reader who has begun to accept Treadup's world with complete absorption may be jolted out of acceptance by the inclusion of real historical figures. Obviously the great reformer Liang Ch'i-ch'ao never met Treadup, nor did Vice President Li Yuan-hung, nor the warlord Feng Yü-hsiang. Why not give fictional names to these men as he does to Johnny Wu? Sometimes, of course, such name-dropping can lead to amusing flickers of self-recognition—when the Treadup family meets the Herseys, for instance, or when David Treadup idly notices the rocky cliffs in the Yangtze gorges that some readers will recall as the same ones on which the agonized coolies labored in Hersey's *A Single Pebble*. But the meetings with the families of John Service and Owen Lattimore, each with an accompanying brief diatribe at the wrecking of these men's lives by the follies of the McCarthy period, do not seem to me to add anything to Treadup's tale.

But that is a quibble, and *The Call* is big enough, subtle enough, and both historically and emotionally convincing enough to be one of those books we can lose ourselves in with profit and delight. I think it will be deservedly popular, and perceived as the capstone to a writing career of enviable range and originality. (p. 30)

Jonathan D. Spence, "Emissary in the East," in The New Republic, *Vol. 192, No. 19, May 13, 1985, pp. 28-30.*

Nâzim Hikmet (Ran)

1902-1963

Turkish poet, dramatist, novelist, short story writer, and journalist.

Regarded as a seminal figure in his country's literary history, Hikmet is credited with successfully challenging traditional strictures of Turkish poetry by introducing a more modern approach. He wrote most of his poems in free verse, replacing conventional stanzaic form and rhyme patterns with broken lines, irregular stanzas, and internal rhyme. A committed and outspoken Communist, Hikmet spent over fifteen years in jail for his beliefs and wrote some of his most important poetry while imprisoned. Although Hikmet's work is often infused with political themes, reflecting his strong ideological stance, most critics agree that his poems are also highly personal and display his love for family, friends, country, and nature.

Hikmet was born in Salonika, Greece, then under Turkish rule. He developed Communist sympathies early in his life and traveled to Moscow in 1921 to attend the University of the Workers of the East. He returned to Turkey several years later, where his involvement with the Turkish Communist Party led to several short stays in prison. In 1938 he was accused of inciting military cadets to rebel and was sentenced to thirty-five years in jail. A protest campaign organized by writers from many countries contributed to Hikmet's early release in 1951. He returned to the Soviet Union and lived there until his death. Hikmet shared the Soviet Union's World Peace Prize with Pablo Neruda in 1950.

Although Hikmet gained international recognition during his lifetime, particularly in Eastern Europe and the Middle East, his reputation grew significantly following his death, when his works were reissued in Turkey and translated for the first time into English. *Selected Poems* (1967) includes poems written between 1922 and 1951. This collection contains a number of the long narrative poems many reviewers find well-suited to Hikmet's humanistic and ideological aims. *Taranta-Babuya-mektuplar* (1935), written as a series of letters from a political exile to his wife, exemplifies Hikmet's talent for narrative form as well as his characteristic juxtaposition of personal and public concerns. The English version of *Seyh Bedreddin destani* (1936)—widely considered Hikmet's finest work—was published in 1977 in *The Epic of Sheik Bedreddin and Other Poems*. The title poem of this volume is an elegiac historical narrative that recounts a medieval uprising led by Sheik Bedreddin, an Islamic mystic who advocated ideals similar to those of modern Communists. *Memleketimden insan manzaralari* (1966-67; *Human Landscapes*), a multivolume work written while Hikmet was in prison and published posthumously, is a long, episodic saga which provides a panoramic view of Turkish life by incorporating a variety of characters, events, and settings. *Things I Didn't Know I Loved* (1976), drawn from Hikmet's entire career, was praised for its comprehensive scope and is particularly noted for its inclusion of the often poignant, lyrical verse he wrote toward the end of his life. The poems in this volume evoke Hikmet's impressions of prison life, his love for his country and family, and his thoughts on his impending death.

© Lütfi Özkök

(See also *Contemporary Authors*, Vols. 93-96 [obituary].)

TALÂT S. HALMAN

[Nazim Hikmet (Ran)] was a revolutionary force in twentieth century Turkish poetry and politics. Like Lorca, Mayakovski, Brecht and Neruda, he placed his artistic gifts in the service of justice, decency and dignity. Ran was an avowed and passionate communist, and leftist causes were often the focal points of his poems. His artistic achievements, however, seemed most impressive when he avoided discursive propaganda in favor of lyric depictions of man's plight not only in terms of economic deprivation but also in dimensions of love and spiritual agony. . . .

Nazim Hikmet was perhaps the most influential innovator of poetic techniques in modern Turkey: he launched free verse and established it as a viable vehicle of expression. He proved that rhetoric can be blended into lyricism, that social protest is not antithetical to poetry and that a rhythmic structure can be based on broken or jagged lines. Far from abandoning rhyme, Nazim Hikmet liberated it by using it for organic purposes rather than as a static component of prescribed stanzaic form. His major aesthetic contribution may be defined as functionalism. Ran did away with the decorative gewgaws and the non sequiturs which used to characterize the work of most of his immediate predecessors and contemporaries. His technical craftsmanship stood squarely against all spurious devices. Ran's metaphors are direct and bold, his images stark and precise; he gave Turkish poetry the heightened effects of concrete, spare, readily communicable poetry.

In *Selected Poems* . . . there are 28 poems by Nazim Hikmet, spanning nearly three decades from 1922 to 1951, ranging from eight lines to eighteen pages and varying from the sublime to the ridiculous. (p. 368)

A quarrel over the selection of poems is inevitable in view of Ran's vast output. The omission of some important poems, including **"Blue-eyed Giant,"** which are difficult if not impossible to translate, is understandable. But missing from . . . [*Selected Poems*] are a few of Ran's mightiest poems which are supremely translatable: passages from the **"Epic of Sheikh Bedrettin," "Human Landscapes from My Land," "Epic of the War of Liberation," "Why Did Benerjee Kill Himself?,"** and many individual poems such as **"Weeping Willow."** . . .

The composite picture of Nazim Hikmet which emerges out of *Selected Poems* is that of a man with a total commitment to life. He is in love with nature's splendors as well as the machine age: in his youthful enthusiasm, while studying in the Soviet Union in 1922, he cries out under Mayakovski's influence "the engine is the offspring / of our consciousness." Ran rips imperialism apart. . . . He is a forerunner of modern existential responsibility: "I have now become responsible for what's happening around me / for man and earth / for darkness and light." Ran has a transcendent human concern: "My brothers in Europe and America," and he denounces injustice in declamatory terms: "Oh, my people, my people, / how they feed you with lies / when you need meat and bread / to fill your empty stomachs." Yet he always rejoices in life: "What a beautiful thing / it is to be alive!" His aphorisms are often poignant: "The problem is not falling a captive / it's how to avoid surrender." Sometimes he is capable of offering dilatory and simplistic allegations: "The American dollar / is already talking / of a Third World War . . ." Perhaps above all, Ran is a poet of love: "When you smiled / the iron bars of the window blossomed with roses." Very often Ran's love is patriotic and political. . . .

Nazim Hikmet was a man of lifelong conviction who loved like a pagan, an ideologue who wrote poetry like a sentimental romantic. He lived as the social conscience of his people and gave them many lyrics of protest and anthems for "sunny days." Whenever he lapsed into the fallacy of reducing man's plight to economic injustice without offering the human drama in it, his poems sounded flat, dogmatic, even curiously pharisaical. When he wrote of human love and tragedy in lyric and dramatic terms, he was a great modern poet by any and all criteria. (p. 369)

> *Talât S. Halman, in a review of "Nazim Hikmet:*
> *Selected Poems," in* The Middle East Journal, *Vol.*
> *22, Summer, 1968, pp. 368-69.*

TALÂT SAIT HALMAN

In modern Turkey, which has witnessed cataclysmic changes since 1918, Nâzim Hikmet was the first—and most stirring— voice of iconoclasm. An avowed communist whose views clashed with government policy, he advocated leftist causes in much of his poetry, preaching justice for the disfranchised and af-

firming a staunch faith in revolution. In the early Twenties, he introduced free verse and presided over the demise of stanzaic form and stringent prosody. Nâzim Hikmet had a lyric power virtually unequalled by any other modern Turkish poet, and a highly developed faculty for dramatizing the human predicament. Not only his poems of love and exile but also some of his political verses are marked by their moving spirit which, even in translation, comes across with telling effect. Nâzim Hikmet earned international renown through the lyric flow of his statements, as well as the poignancy and optimism of his best work, though detractors claim that he found fame outside Turkey, thanks to the literary propaganda efforts of the Soviet Union and other socialist countries where he had lived or visited. . . .

The vicissitudes in the private and public lives of few poets have been as inextricable from their poetry as were Nâzim Hikmet's. Much of his best work is an account of the dramatic events of his life: years of imprisonment, fellow revolutionaries and inmates, exile unto death, heart failures, in an autobiographical vein. But even poems where there are no real-life references have fired the imagination of Turkish readers who have found an additional dimension of pathos and cogency in his lines because they knew the circumstances of deprivation and agony that drove Nâzim Hikmet. . . .

His early work followed the fashionable forms of the day. Using the stanzaic patterns and the simple syllabic meters of traditional Turkish folk poetry, he—like most of his contemporaries—confined his themes to love, speculations about life and death, national pride, natural beauties, and modern mysticism. . . .

In 1921 the impressionable Nâzim, who had groped for a faith beyond mysticism and patriotism, went to the Soviet Union where communism, as a doctrine in action, fired his imagination and kindled hope for what he liked to call "sunny days." He spent about four years in the Soviet Union, studying at the University of the Workers of the East in Moscow and acquiring a passionate attachment to communism, as well as revolutionary ideas about the norms and functions of poetry. The first poem to come out of this new orientation was **"The Pupils of the Eyes of Hungry People,"** written after seeing in Moscow a film called *Hungry People*. . . . (p. 59)

This poem, written in the summer of 1921, marked Nâzim Hikmet's adoption of free verse and ideological poetry. Abruptly, he abandoned the formal lyric and ready-made meters. Free verse with alternations of short and long lines, occasional rhyming, and wide use of alliteration, assonance, and onomatopoeia, a staccato syntax, were to remain the hallmarks of his art and his major influences on modern Turkish poetics. (p. 60)

A substantive innovation [Nâzim Hikmet] introduced was materialism, which stood in sharp contrast to the Islamic mysticism and transcendentalism of centuries of classical Ottoman-Turkish poetry and the idealism so typical of European-oriented verse from the middle of the nineteenth century. Although Turkey's most forceful modernist failed to extend the implications of his materialistic concepts to their outer limits and confined himself to such polemics as "Those who oppose us / really oppose / the eternal laws / of the dynamics of matter / and society marching forward," he still made Turkish poetry less abstract than ever before. Perhaps his most significant contribution to Turkish poetics was concretization.

After he returned to Turkey from the Soviet Union in 1924, he continued to write resounding declamatory poems in which he denounced, in angry, satiric, or utopian terms, economic injustice and violations of human dignity. His charismatic personality, his torrential poems, his public readings stirred wide interest, and soon the young poet assumed the posture—even the stature—of a literary hero. By 1928 he had become too obtrusive and effective a voice to be ignored by the government, whose relations with the Soviet Union were deteriorating, and Nâzim Hikmet was jailed despite his assurance that he was "only concerned with the literary aspects of Marxism and Communism."

Following his release, he started collecting his poems, and published books in quick succession. . . . (pp. 60-1)

In his verse, as in such avant-garde plays as *Kafatasi (The Skull)* and *Unutulan Adam (The Forgotten Man)*, Nâzim Hikmet continued his dual role of artistic iconoclast and social critic. "I conceive of art," he said in the Thirties, "as an active institution in society. To me, the artist is the *engineer of the human soul"* (employing Stalin's formula). . . .

As he matured as an artist, Nâzim Hikmet clung to his communist views on the function of literature. He always assigned to himself the task of voicing the deprivations and aspirations of oppressed classes. . . . His aesthetic preference, by the time he was thirty-seven, evolved from what he liked to call "active realism" into a "dynamic synthesis." (p. 61)

A survey of Nâzim Hikmet's poetry published between 1921 and 1937 charts the course of the aesthetic evolution from linear concepts to synthesis. His long poems and epics illustrate this growth: *Jokond ile Si-Ya-U (La Gioconda and Si-A-U,* 1929), reads like a sophomoric political allegory. With *Benerci Kendini Niçin Öldürdü (Why Did Benerjee Kill Himself,* 1932), Nâzim came to realize that political verse can never succeed without infusions of lyricism, but still failed to overcome his strident and simplistic rhetoric. *Taranta-Babuya Mektuplar (Letters to Taranta-Babu,* 1935), has dominant lyricism in its crucial passages, and dramatic dimension, but the prose sections, including news items, deprive the poem of architectural unity and integrity. All three books are bitter denunciations of imperialism, capitalism, and fascism.

The internalization of injustice and oppression in *Letters to Taranta-Babu* enabled the poet to indict Mussolini's fascism and Ethiopian campaign in far more effective terms than he had been able to use against imperialism and political terror in the earlier books.

Nâzim Hikmet's masterpiece, *Seyh Bedreddin Destani (The Epic of Sheikh Bedreddin)*, came out in 1936. It represents the culmination of the best aspects of the poet's art and it is remarkably free of his weaknesses. The epic is a lyrical and dramatic account of the uprisings of Şeyh Bedreddin and his followers, including a young revolutionary named Börklüce Mustafa, who founded a religious sect advocating community ownership, social and judicial equality, pacifism, etc., in the early fifteenth century. Nâzim Hikmet tells how the Ottoman armies, under the command of Royal Prince Murad, crushed the uprisings, killed Börklüce Mustafa, and later hanged Şeyh Bedreddin. This work is a perfect synthesis of substance and form, of diction and drama, of fact and metaphor. Bedreddin and Mustafa are treated as tragic heroes whose ideals are thwarted by a cruel death. Nâzim Hikmet's ideological concerns are, fortunately for the poem, woven into the action and lyric formulation. An elegiac tone, fully attuned to the historical narrative, precludes the intrusion of the polemics and propaganda which have had deleterious effects on Nâzim's other major poems. The epic is perhaps the best long poem written in Turkish in this century.

Turkey's most exciting and controversial poet had been in and out of prisons from 1928 to 1933, where he wrote some of his best lyrics as well as much doggerel. In 1938, at the height of his popularity, he was dragged before a military tribunal and condemned to a twenty-five-year prison term on charges of sedition and subversive activity among military students. Imprisonment, coupled with suppression of his books, silenced publication for nearly a dozen years until his release in 1950. He wrote voluminously in prison, however, including a magnum opus running close to twenty thousand lines entitled *Memleketimden İnsan Manzaralari (Humanscapes from my Land)*.

In 1950, when Turkey was making its transition to a multiparty regime, a concerted effort by Turkish intellectuals, supported by campaigns abroad, prompted the government to release Nâzim Hikmet. A year later he escaped from Turkey to the Soviet Union—presumably to avoid being drafted into the armed forces despite his advanced age and failing health. His departure led to renewed suppression of his books in Turkey. But, during his years in the Soviet Union and other East European countries . . . , his international reputation grew. (p. 62)

In his native land, Nâzim Hikmet remained a myth in the Fifties, as he had been while in prison from 1938 to 1950. The poet said to a friend: "A cease-fire will start between my country and me after my death." He was homesick: his most moving poems written outside Turkey are testaments of exile and longing. . . .

Prison and exile, while checking his bravura, gave Nâzim Hikmet's verse a dimension of pathos, furtive tears, a central drama. His political poems, particularly those published since his escape to the Soviet Union, are vacuous and raucous, but his exile poems ring true. One of his early critics, Peyami Safa, had observed that "contrary to all his claims to materialism, Nâzim Hikmet is an intensely romantic, lyric, mushy, sentimental poet." The troubles of later years removed his tendency to melodrama, enabling him to concentrate on stark realities and essential emotions.

Death came to Nâzim Hikmet in June 1963 in Moscow. The "cease-fire" he had predicted for Turkey and himself actually started shortly after his death. Turkish publishers raced to make available to the Turkish public as much of his unpublished poetry as they could find. Among the major books which came out after 1963 are *Saat 21-22 Süirleri (Poems of 9-10 P.M.)*, *Rubailer (Quatrains)*, *Dört Hapisaneden (Out of Four Prisons)*, and the five-volume *Memleketimden İnsan Manzaralari (Humanscapes from my Land)*.

Rubailer features Nâzim Hikmet's quatrains in which, according to a letter he wrote to his wife in 1945, he tries to revolutionize a time-honored literary form: "Taking strength from your love, I shall do something that has never been done in Oriental or Western literatures: I shall attempt to express materialism in *rubaiyat.*" The attempt seems to have failed, because the themes of materialism are seldom evident in this collection, and the four-line poems cannot even be considered as *rubaiyat* in the real sense of the literary term. But many individual quatrains in the book are among his best short lyrics.

Memleketimden İnsan Manzaralari is a sprawling, episodic saga of the twentieth century, composed in twenty thousand lines, ranging in theme from the decadence of Turkish aristocrats to World War II. In its entirety, this work, designed by the poet as his masterpiece, is a failure on a grand scale: section after section, it lumps together scenes, faces, and minor occurrences which, superficial and repetitious, do not add up to a vast poetic panorama. The progression is linear, many portions seem expendable, and trivia are too pervasive. Except for a handful of magnificent passages, Nâzim Hikmet's long-awaited magnum opus seems to have been crushed under its own bulk. (p. 63)

The literary career of Nâzim Hikmet, spanning four and a half decades from 1918 to 1963, illustrates the vital problems of the poetry of engagement. In poem after poem, where Nâzim mouths sheer invective or ideological polemics, or tries to communicate in prosy statements, banality sets in and curtails the effectiveness of both aesthetic appeal and doctrinal substance. But in those poems which communalize the poet's private self in dynamic terms or internalize communal experiences in lyric formulations, even the political content gains a cogency beyond the validity of its concepts. Nâzim Hikmet's best political poems are, in fact, those which are most lyrical. He achieved success when he used doctrine not as theme or argument but as unspecified context.

At his best, he has been compared by Turkish and non-Turkish men of letters to such figures as Lorca, Aragon, Mayakovsky, Esenin, Neruda, Artaud, *et al.* To be sure, his work bears resemblances to these poets and owes them occasional debts of form and stylistic device, but Nâzim Hikmet's literary personality is unique in terms of the synthesis he made of iconoclasm and lyricism, of ideology and poetic diction. (p. 64)

> *Talât Sait Halman, "Nâzim Hikmet: Lyricist as Iconoclast," in* Books Abroad, *Vol. 43, No. 1, Winter, 1969, pp. 59-64.*

MUTLU KONUK

Throughout his career Hikmet conceived of his art as inseparable from his life, and in his work poetic purpose and political responsibility are one. For his poems *are* political: while he does not provide us with political commentary, he does accept that the purpose of his art is to change the world. Yet, for Hikmet, only the kind of art that changes itself can change the world. Thus Hikmet is a major Turkish poet because he brought an entirely new kind of poetry into Turkish literature, revolutionizing poetic technique, subject matter, and language. And he is a great international poet because his innovativeness as a poet is inseparable from his vision of a new life in a new world.

Perfectly alert to what is going on around him, and with the large poetic freedom of a Whitman, Hikmet writes at once of his century, his culture, and himself. For his poems are also personal, even autobiographical. He records his life, never reducing it to self-consciousness and always affirming the reality of facts. Dates, for example, are very important for Hikmet; indeed, the date of a poem often becomes part of the poem itself. It is the conjunction of fact and feeling, however, that makes for a poetry at once public and personal, and Hikmet never doubts the validity of his feelings. What emerges from his poems, then, is his human *presence;* the strongest impression that we get from his poetry is a sense of Hikmet as a person. And it is the controlling figure of Hikmet's personality—playful, optimistic, and capable of childlike joy—that enables his poetry to remain open, public, and committed to change without ever becoming programmatic.

In the perfect oneness of his life and art, Hikmet stands as a heroic figure. In his early poems he proclaims this unity as a faith: art is an event, he insists, not only in literary history but in social history. As a result, the poet's bearing in his art is inseparable from his bearing in life. Cowardice in one is cowardice in the other; courage in one is courage in the other. The rest of Hikmet's life gave him a chance to act upon his faith and, in fact, to deepen it. In a sense, his prosecutors honored him by believing that a book of poems could incite the army to revolt; indeed the fact that he was persecuted attests to the credibility of his faith in the vital importance of his art. Yet the suffering that his faith cost him—he never compromised in his life or art—is only secondary to the suffering that must have gone into maintaining that faith. For poetry, as Hikmet writes, is "the bloodiest of the arts"—one must offer his heart to others and feed on it himself. Thus the circumstances of Hikmet's life are very much to the point, not only because he continually made the choice not to betray his vision, but because his life and art have a dramatic completeness. Sartre has written that Hikmet conceived of a human being as something to be created. And it was in his life, no less than in his art, that Hikmet forged this new human being—who was heroic because he was a *creator*. This conception of the artist as a hero and of the hero as a creator saves art from becoming a frivolous activity in the modern world; as Hikmet's career dramatizes, poetry is indeed a matter of life and death. (pp. ix-x)

> *Mutlu Konuk, in an introduction to* Things I Didn't Know I Loved: Selected Poems of Nazim Hikmet *by Nazim Hikmet, translated by Randy Blasing and Mutlu Konuk, Persea Books, Inc., 1975, pp. vii-x.*

PUBLISHERS WEEKLY

Hikmet is known almost everywhere but in America—a fact due to the lack of English translations—as a poet of world stature. . . . [**Things I Didn't Know I Loved**] introduces him to American readers as a poet who may well be compared with Whitman and, in our time, Neruda: his humanity and humanism, his revolutionary ardor . . . , ally him with the major poets of any time or place. Hikmet's poetry, here translated with a racy street-language colloquialism, should find ready acceptance by the young. The selection reflects Hikmet's prison life, his love of country, his identification with simple lives, his exuberant humor (best shown in his imaginary "diary" of La Gioconda aka Mona Lisa) and, in his last poems, a passion for life made poignant by impending death.

> *A review of "Things I Didn't Know I Loved: Selected Poems of Nazim Hikmet," in* Publishers Weekly, *Vol. 209, No. 14, April 5, 1976, p. 89.*

MUTLU KONUK

[In] the course of his forty-year career [Hikmet's] poetry changed considerably as he wrote in response to his experience—both his personal experience and the greater history of the thirties, the Second World War, and its aftermath. His poems and his experience stand in a complex, dynamic relationship to each other, and if his poetry got him into trouble—**"The Epic of Sheik Bedreddin,"** for example, landed him in prison—it also gave him the will and the means to withstand imprisonment and even exile.

In [*The Epic of Sheik Bedreddin and Other Poems*], then, we see Hikmet start out in the twenties as the young revolutionary poet of the deft, irreverent, and tough early poems and change into the accomplished, historically and politically aware poet of the masterly **"Epic of Sheik Bedreddin."** Published in 1936, this "epic" is based on an early fifteenth-century peasants' uprising against the Ottoman Empire. Sheik Bedreddin, the Turkish mystic and great Islamic scholar, translated his belief in the immanence of God into political action and advocated a kind of socialism, which declared the oneness of all people and religions and called for the abolition of private property. The uprising that Bedreddin inspired was led in western Turkey by two of his disciples, Börklüje Mustafa and Torlak Kemal. The poem is primarily about this event—the joint rebellion of Turkish, Greek, and Jewish peasants who seized the lands of the feudal lords, worked them together, and together defended them until their bloody defeat by the Sultan's army. The form of the poem does justice to its historical subject. Both the history of Bedreddin's rebellion and the actuality of Hikmet's daily life in prison are transformed into a kind of poetry that itself embodies a historical necessity. Not only is the course of events a necessary sequence, but their very telling has the temporal necessity of a piece of music; every line—every word—has to be as and where it is. Thus Hikmet achieves a sense of formal necessity without formal regularity, and the poem becomes totally compelling.

While the discoveries of **"The Epic of Sheik Bedreddin"** led to the writing of *Human Landscapes* after Hikmet's final imprisonment in 1938, the shorter poems of the prison years have yet another voice. In these poems we hear a vulnerable but hopeful, realistic yet lyrical, fully *human* poet. The sequence **"9-10 P.M. Poems,"** which Hikmet wrote for his wife at night while working on *Human Landscapes* during the day, pieces together a whole consciousness, whose personal drama unfolds as part of a larger history. These love poems escape being simply personal because Hikmet's love for his wife is inseparable from his love for his city, and his yearning for both is inseparable from his hope for better days for people everywhere. Set against the background of the end of the Second World War, the coming of the winter, and his continuing imprisonment, these taut, lucid poems embody the special urgency of a faith based on will.

After years of being confined in prisons, Hikmet travels freely during his exile, and the poems from this period reflect the speeding-up of his experience. Not only the speed of his travels through space in trains and planes but his sense, as he nears death, of an acceleration of time underlies the breathless rhythms of a late poem like **"Straw-Blond,"** where the almost monotonous pace of run-on perceptions is not broken even by punctuation. **"Straw-Blond,"** which comes out of Hikmet's experience of a suddenly expanded universe, answers the needs that such experience creates, for the poem that travels freely in time and space at breakneck speed ends not in chaotic dispersion but in the formal and human unity of its closing lines. And in the discovery of this larger vision of wholeness Hikmet's poetry and his life play out the final act to enable him to live with the fact of exile and the idea of death. (pp. 8-10)

> *Mutlu Konuk, in an introduction to* The Epic of Sheik Bedreddin and Other Poems *by Nazim Hikmet, translated by Randy Blasing and Mutlu Konuk, Persea Books, 1977, pp. 7-10.*

TERRENCE DesPRES

Considering that in his homeland Nazim Hikmet was never free of police harassment, that he spent almost half of his mature life in prison and much of the rest in exile, he nevertheless managed to do a great deal of writing. Plays, journalism, a novel, more than twenty volumes of poems: his **"Human Landscapes from My Country"** alone runs to 17,000 lines, and at its best Hikmet's poetry possesses a bold grace and an eagerness of statement suggesting that for this poet the labor of words was as needful as breathing. . . . Better than anyone else, Hikmet caught the radical spirit of the new populism in Turkey; and despite their government's long disapproval of him, his countrymen have declared him their greatest modern poet. Since he received the World Peace Prize in 1950, moreover, his reputation has spread through Europe and the Near East. Only in America—for reasons I shall try to identify—has recognition been slow. (p. 7)

The recent acceptance of poets like Hikmet signals an important shift in American literary affairs. Editors, translators, and poets of a new generation have made their entrance, men and women doubtful of fixed opinions and inherited rules, who have found it impossible to ignore the work of poets like Pablo Neruda, Anna Akhmatova, Czeslaw Milosz, and Yannis Ritsos—to name only a few of the poets in whose company Hikmet belongs. To speak of Hikmet's poetry is necessarily to consider this "other" world of literature, a kind of art sometimes called political, sometimes called a poetry of engagement or commitment, which is strikingly different from the kind of literary product most of us have been taught to esteem. What needs to be noted at once is the growing attention to traditions other than our own—chiefly South American and Eastern European—the effort of younger poets, now writing in English, to gain definitions and a sense of renewal by contact with examples outside the standard British-American-French tradition. (pp. 7-8)

Most students of Anglo-American poetry have been trained on principle to distrust political vision in art—as if Milton, Shelley, and Blake had never writ a word. But poetry of this other kind is as valid as the sort we have been instructed to defend, and it may even be, in times as vicious as ours, more valuable. For Nazim Hikmet, in any case, there could be no fast line dividing art from life and political commitment—which accounts, in part, for the vigor and capacious humanity of his work. (p. 8)

The first sample of Hikmet's work in English [*Selected Poems*] appeared in 1967. . . . [It] contains one poem that any reader of Hikmet will appreciate—the twenty-page **"Letters to Taranta-Babu,"** written in 1935 after fascist Italy's invasion of Ethiopia. Although much of Hikmet's poetry takes as its situation the circumstances of his own experience, this poem, like other of Hikmet's long dramatic pieces, makes fictional use of a real event. An Ethiopian man, trapped in Rome, watches the fascists take control and comes to realize that the Italians are preparing to attack his own country. He writes about this to Taranta-Babu, his wife at home, whom he "knows" will be killed. He must also know that these letters will never leave Rome.

One of the moving things about the poem is that although the speaker can vividly imagine the devastation in personal terms—his goats slaughtered, his village sacked, his wife's intestines upon the sand—he does not bear malice toward the men who will bring this to pass:

> They're coming, Taranta-Babu,
> from the heart of a conflagration;

and once they have flown the flag
   from the sunbaked roof
      of your earthen house
they may all go back—
but even then
      the lathe-turner from Torino
who's left his right arm in Somalia
will no longer work with his steel rods
as if working with bales of silk-thread.
And the fisherman from Sicily
   will no longer see the light of the sea
   through his blinded eyes.

Hikmet's sense of human solidarity is especially strong at moments like this. That the soldiers are themselves victims—of ignorance and fear, of official lying—is a fact that Hikmet will not treat ironically. This is a point of some importance, for facing disastrous events we either take refuge in irony (the measure of our detachment, our despair) or we suffer with the victims (the measure of our compassion). The latter requires patience and historical perspective; a commitment to the struggle of man against the state surely helps. Political involvement, that is, *can* support the poet in his need to remain human— open, caring, hopeful—amid dehumanizing circumstances. The poem itself is evidence that historical participation, refracted through an individual's immediate life, is as fit for poetry as any other subject. (pp. 9-10)

In 1970 *The Moscow Symphony and other poems* appeared (published in this country in 1971), *The Day Before Tomorrow* in 1972. . . . With the exception of the long poem **"The Moscow Symphony"** (which is typical of Hikmet's more ambitious work, but not well organized and not well rendered), there is little worth reading. (p. 10)

Things I Didn't Know I Loved, published . . . in 1975, was the first collection of Hikmet's work to appear in America. *The Epic of Sheik Bedreddin and Other Poems*, . . . came out in the spring of 1978. With these two rich, inclusive volumes . . . , we are at last able to appreciate Hikmet's art. . . . [The poems] selected are representative as well as arranged chronologically—early poems, the long middle span of prison poetry, the late poems—to allow us a sense of Hikmet's range and development. (pp. 11-12)

[Hikmet] is, in the best sense, a writer of primitive poetry, poetry which depends for its power on primary techniques— repetition, contrast, line-break, basic imagery of earth, man, and nature (which to the Western ear sounds Biblical), and finally a use of metaphor mainly to enlarge and enrich rather than to refine and complicate. These, along with Hikmet's directness of voice and mystical overtones, his moral energy and faithful delight in life itself, provide the foundation of his art.

I shall stick with [*Things I Didn't Know I Loved* and *The Epic of Sheik Bedreddin and Other Poems*], and by way of moving to the heart of Hikmet's poetry, I want to look at some of his "prison poems." One of the signs of our time, it seems to me, is the large body of "prison literature" that has come into existence—a fact at once political *and* literary—and I would even suggest that the "prison poem," at least in the hands of a master like Hikmet, has become a genre of its own. Much of his best work was done while in prison, and a great amount of it refers to his own immediate condition as a political prisoner. **"Letters from a Man in Solitary,"** which is addressed to his wife, begins:

   I carved your name on my watchband
   with my fingernail.

In such small sad ways does time take human shape. And that, of course, is the point: time passes, without structure or significance, as empty and endless as the Bursa plains which Hikmet could see from his window. Days pass, seasons, and that much more unused life is lost. . . . The poem is built on such moods and seems to be moving deeper into darkness. But in the last section an abrupt reversal occurs; something happens which unexpectedly redeems the misery, cancels time and despair in one strong moment of transcendence:

Sunday today.
Today they took me out in the sun for the first time.
And I stood very still, struck for the first time in my
   life
             by how far away the sky is,
             how blue
             and how wide.

Then I respectfully sat down on the earth.
I put my back against the wall.
For a moment no trap to fall into,
for a moment no struggle, no freedom, no wife.
Just earth, sun, and me . . .
I am happy.

To find this kind of liberation in this kind of moment (which seems religious) is typical of Hikmet. He *will* find ways to make the pain and emptiness of prison life significant. And one of those ways is the ever-increasing awareness of nature as a source of strength and inspiration. . . . The fundamental structure of the prison poem is the stark division between "inside" and "outside," between life-in-the-cell and life-in-the-world. To survive unbroken, "the man inside" must maintain connection and rapport with the world's larger life. In this way self-pity can be overcome, and the reasons for imprisonment, the *real* reasons, remain firmly felt. . . . One of the consequences of the gap between "inside" and "outside," or rather of the effort to close this gap, is Hikmet's characteristic imagery of absence . . . ; [for instance]:

     Far away,
     where we can't see,
     the moon must be rising.

Hikmet's imagery might also be an extension of his Marxist faith that everywhere life goes forward, history moves, men work in concert to bring about a better world. But in the immediate case it is the outcome of his physical condition. Hikmet in prison *is* cut off, unlike the contrived isolation so dear to modern poets which is metaphorical only. And since he cannot participate actively in the world, nor be in actual contact with the people and places he loves, he must find other means to restore relation, some legitimate way of keeping in touch. For Hikmet, in other words, absence is a condition of immediate existence, and how to make absent things present is his pressing need. His solution, of course, is poetry itself. Through an endless evocation of images, through the perpetual summons of imagination, he reunites himself with the world. Friends "visit" him, "letters" go out in all directions, he "talks" with his wife. Hence Hikmet's special reliance on the dramatic monologue: through it he re-enters the world of human community.

When we speak of "worlds elsewhere" we usually have in mind private vision, fabulations rare and fine beyond the reach of ordinary life. Not so with Hikmet, he does not strive to escape reality but to attend upon it more dearly. In order to transcend the circumstances imposed by his jailers, he asks nothing more of imagination than that it restore to him a vivid sense of the world as it is. And thus in the poem **"On Ibrahim Balaban's 'Spring Picture',"** Hikmet imagines the whole of Balaban's painting, item by item, until he has assembled—or reassembled—an entire world: light, clouds, mountains; foxes with "alarm on their pointed noses"; grass, water, bees, a stork "just back from Egypt"; rabbits, turtles, "a shimmering tree, / in its beauty most like a person"; mothers, wives, children, and finally *homo faber.* . . . I would like, finally to look at two poems not written in prison. The **"Gioconda and Si-Ya-U,"** composed in 1929, is an excellent example of Hikmet's robustly imaginative early style. The poem is an exuberant blend of fantasy and fact, whimsy and earnestness, in which the Mona Lisa—here a painting *and* a woman—falls in love with a young Chinese who asks her:

> "Those who crush our rice fields
> 　　with the caterpillar treads of their tanks
> and who swagger through our cities
> 　　like emperors of hell,
> are they of YOUR race,
> 　　the race of him who CREATED you?"

By way of answer, the lady with the mysterious smile leaves the museum to join the Chinese revolution. The poet himself lands an airplane on the roof of the Louvre to assist her escape. And although Gioconda and her lover are destroyed by Chiang Kai-shek's troops, the Mona Lisa's forced smile, frozen for centuries, has at last turned to real laughter. Hikmet implies that when paintings are enshrined in palaces and poems stuck away in academic tomes, their function is no longer to incite and inspire but rather to adorn and justify the status quo. Museums, from this point of view, are the ruling elite's method for containing art's naturally subversive power. The arts themselves need rescue, and Hikmet dramatizes his commitment by appearing *in* the poem as an accomplice.

The salvaging of truth by means of poetry is also one of the principal themes in **"The Epic of Sheik Bedreddin."** Written in 1936, after Hikmet had spent time in prison, this is one of the longest, most complex and impressive of Hikmet's poems available in translation. Bedreddin was an Islamic scholar and mystic who, in the middle of the fourteenth century, propagated the idea that mankind is a single community and therefore that the means to life should be shared in common. In practice this meant, among other things, the abolition of private property. Two of his disciples, Mustafa and Kemal, led a small revolt in the countryside, and for a time the peasantry—Moslem, Jew, and Christian—worked the land together. But then the Sultan's armies arrived, the movement was defeated, Bedreddin and his disciples were executed.

The **"Epic"** gives a dramatic account of Bedreddin's rise and fall, but not as a story merely. What happened in the fourteenth century stands for the predicament of the revolutionary spirit, which must endure repeated defeat and yet survive. Hikmet ties the fate of modern political prisoners to the fate of Bedreddin's followers, and thereby affirms the unkillable nature of his belief in the radical cause for which Bedreddin and so many others have suffered. For all its pain and sorrow, the poem celebrates the human will to revolt against injustice—and once again Hikmet makes his point by placing himself *inside* the narrative.

The poem thus begins with Hikmet in prison, reading a book by a professor of theology in which (viewed from the top downward, that is, from the standard point of view of the

victors) Bedreddin and his disciples are reduced to the status of "common" peasants, to whom no special attention is due. For the professor, Bedreddin's movement was just another peasant revolt, short-lived, blind, at most an unfounded disturbance within the established order. The pressure of this lie, of history thus distorted and betrayed, is too much for the poet in his cell. He must *do* something, but what can a man in jail do? In a condition of near frenzy, he looks through the bars of his window and sees the white robe of a monk who had been one of Bedreddin's followers. The poet is suddenly outside his cell, outside of time itself, and with the monk goes back to the great days of Bedreddin as an eyewitness.

Only now is the uprising described, but this time with Hikmet himself as a participant. The poem ends with Hikmet back in his cell, where in the morning light he discovers that the white robe of the monk had actually been a cellmate's shirt hung out to dry. In this way Hikmet confirms the liberating power of imagination, and his imaginative participation in the rebellion is his way of authorizing the poet's role as true witness. In the poem's last section he and the other prisoners discuss the belief, widespread among the peasantry, that Bedreddin will one day come again to lead them from their misery. The poem concludes when one of the inmates admits that he, too, believes in Bedreddin's return, not in the flesh like the Savior of the Christians, but in the spirit of an entire people: "When we say Bedreddin will come again, we mean that his words, look, and breath will appear among us." And so, for Hikmet, it has. (pp. 12-18)

Hikmet does not use ideological language in his poetry, except in occasional parody. He took pride in his Marxism, but at the same time he lived and worked by this simple formula: human first, Marxist second. . . . For Hikmet, Marxism was less a system than a way of seeing local injustice as part of a world-historical situation, and his own struggle as part of a struggle everywhere in progress. He was thus united, in spirit and in action, with men and women in every land, with every act in opposition to tyranny, with every hope for a better, a more justly shared world. At very least, a better world was *possible,* and this in itself made all sorts of sacrifice and loss worth bearing. With doctrinaire imperatives, with that rigid authoritarianism of the cadre, Hikmet had no affinity. He much preferred to sum up the whole business as Mao Tse-tung did when he defined Marxism—in idea and in spirit—as first and last "the right to revolt." As far as programs went, Hikmet's could be stated as follows: resist, oppose, defy, always keeping the will to freedom active, always remembering the goodness of life in itself. (pp. 19-20)

[Hikmet confirms that] there is a vital part of human experience which is explicitly political and yet whose expression is not to be confused with propaganda, "social realism," versified doctrine, or any other sort of *a priori* utterance. Its ideological content cannot be denied, but neither can this be denied of any art whatsoever. The great difference is that while much traditional art remains unaware of its own ideological base, the kind of work a poet like Hikmet produces is deliberately explicit about the beliefs underlying the vision. . . .

That a novel can be political and still a successful work of art has been conceded. (p. 20)

With poetry, especially poetry in the lyrical mode, the problem is more difficult. There is only one point of view, one kind of consciousness in the poem . . . , and if the poet is not inclined to be outspoken, or if he prefers to veil his intent in irony to avoid jail or the firing squad, other means than direct statement must be found if the experience or feeling which the poem represents is to have a political dimension. And this, in turn, leads to the more vexing relation between the poet himself and the voice in his poems.

I am referring in particular to the autobiographical "prison poems," in which Hikmet simply uses himself, a real man in a real prison. He does not need to devise dramatic situations, nor must he invent appropriate scenes-as-metaphor. Authenticity is assured, and the seriousness with which he speaks is underscored by the authority of actual experience. In narratives like **"Gioconda"** and **"Bedreddin,"** on the other hand, Hikmet dramatizes his political involvement by sticking himself into the poem as one of its characters. Thereby he is able to express his personal allegiance and grief, not as an outside commentary, and not through a vocabulary alien to his essentially lyrical mode, but as part of the action within the poem's declared limits.

Nevertheless, we know that the character in the poem represents, or is continuous with, the actual person of the poet. And in the prison poems this kind of identification is more or less total. In these examples, at least, some knowledge of Nazim Hikmet—of his beliefs, his behavior, the major events in his life—is necessary to a full understanding of the poems. Now, Hikmet may be a special case, or, what is more likely, political poetry may be a special case, but either way the conclusion would seem to be—unspeakable as this is in academic circles—that unlike most modern poetry, which thrives on self-reference, ambiguity, and detachable personae, the political poem must be allowed to include, as a cardinal part of its meaning, the actual situation of the poet. (pp. 21-2)

Men and women who know that they will be held accountable for what they write, that the cost of their art may be prison or death, cannot choose to separate themselves from their work. And neither should we. Osip Mandelstam is not a political poet by Hikmet's standard, and probably Hikmet is not so good a poet as Mandelstam; the point, however, is that Mandelstam's later poetry reads differently if we know that Stalin was pushing the poet to his death in a concentration camp. . . . In cases like these, there is a real difference in the interpretations we devise and in the seriousness with which we approach such works. (p. 22)

[Despite] Whitman's broad invitation, no tradition of political writing has been able to establish itself, and most histories of American poetry omit this side of our art altogether. There is, I think, something absolutely recalcitrant in the American character—a furious allegiance to the transcendental ego, a will to ignore history no matter what, a determination to behave more like Emerson's "transparent eyeball" than like a man or woman with real passions, involved in the very real problems of a society during dark and troubled times.

Generalizations about American poetry are bound to be suspect. I do not, however, think we possess—not yet—a tradition of political art sufficient to inspire and support a poem as big as *The Heights of Macchu Picchu* or a novel as brilliant as *One Hundred Years of Solitude*. Nor, in recent years, have we believed in the importance of poetry enough (Adrienne Rich's *The Dream of a Common Language* is a brave exception) to generate the kind of seriousness which political poetry may claim by virtue of its character not only as an art but as an agent of action in the world. Simply because in his art and in his person Hikmet opposes the enemies of the human spirit in

harmony with itself and the earth, he can speak casually and yet with a seriousness that most modern American poets never dream of attempting. . . . Hikmet's otherness, in terms of our tradition, is part of his value. To speak with irony, to deploy ambiguity like a many-sided shield, to pretend that anything uttered or even perceived issues from the invented voice or persona merely—these, until recently, have been the ways of most poetry in America, ways of orchestrating private vision while refusing the responsibility it entails. Hikmet, on the other hand, says what he means straight out. He places himself inside the story, or speaks in his own voice from the conditions of his own life. Thereby he offers himself as an example; and if he believes what he says, he must try his best to live an exemplary life.

In such ways art and existence meet, at risk no doubt, but at a risk worth taking. I am speaking of aesthetic risk, but for Hikmet the risk was, finally, seventeen years of prison as the cost of speaking freely. He would never have dreamed of disowning what he wrote. This was just the way any man or woman writing poems would act. And this way of living, as it resides in Hikmet's poetry, is perhaps the chief benefit of reading him. "He is the rock of defense of human nature; an upholder and preserver, carrying everywhere with him relationship and love." That was Wordsworth's idea of the poet. Hikmet took it for granted. (pp. 23-5)

Terrence DesPres, "Poetry and Politics: The Example of Nazim Hikmet," in Parnassus: Poetry in Review, *Vol. 6, No. 2, Spring-Summer, 1978, pp. 7-25.*

WALTER G. ANDREWS

Nazim Hikmet is a marvelous poet. He was also a sincere and outspoken communist. For the latter he lived a life of exile and persecution at the hands of Turkish governments obsessed by a fear of Russia and things Russian. For the former he has achieved worldwide reknown. . . .

In *The Epic of Sheik Bedreddin* Hikmet can be seen, much as he must have been, as a human communist and a communist humanist. In one of his love poems he says:

> I am among people, I love people
> I love motion,
> I love thought,
> I love my struggle,
> You are a person in my struggle,
> I love you.

This little stanza seems to sum up the essence of the man, the genesis of his ideology and the substance of his poetry. His communism never appears cold and doctrinaire but seems a natural outgrowth of his love for people, his desire that humankind grow in love and cooperation and his deep reflection on life and living—and beneath it all he is himself a loving, hurting, feeling human being.

The selections, with the aid of a sensitive and compact introduction, take the reader chronologically through much of his life to his death in 1963. Throughout the journey one hears the continuing theme of political struggle against a moving counterpoint of personal tragedy, elation, love, friendship, despair and all the other emotional facets of a full life fully lived. . . .

[The poetry in this book] has a pervasive universal quality, which means that it is open and accessible to readers with little or no knowledge of Turkey. It is an autobiography in poetry which is self-sufficient and tremendously compelling—a first-class book!

Walter G. Andrews, in a review of "The Epic of Sheik Bedreddin and Other Poems," in World Literature Today, *Vol. 52, No. 3, Summer, 1978, p. 517.*

DON SHEWEY

The appealing every-dayness of Hikmet's writing links him to the celebratory Whitman, the informal but hyperexpressive Mayakovsky, and the urban-colloquial O'Hara—the tradition of poets who burned to tell the history of their time by the history of their selves. . . .

A lifelong Marxist often persecuted in his own country, Hikmet is much more political in his writing than Whitman or O'Hara, but the humor and homeliness of his instinctive politics rescue his poetry from programmatic clichés. His voice is always personal and emotional, his images plain yet pungent, his poems mostly letters to the world, all content and no more form than is necessary to tell a good story. For it is as a storyteller that he reveals his full poetic powers. His locomotive imagination, his leaping back and forth in time and from person to person without losing track of the narrative, and the way his human observation is indistinguishable from his political perspective dazzle, especially in the longer poems. The hilarious fantasia **"Giaconda and Si-Ya-U"** stars none other than the Mona Lisa, who becomes enamored of a young Chinese poet and follows him from the Louvre to Shanghai, where both are executed as Communists; **"The Epic of Sheik Bedreddin,"** the work for which he was jailed, is an imaginative re-creation of a 14th-century peasants' revolt led by the first Muslim socialist, whose legend continues to have the inspirational effect of, say, Joe Hill.

You would think that a man who had spent 17 years of his adult life in prison for his thoughts would emerge bitter and defeated, but astonishingly Hikmet's later poems reflect an even more passionate embrace of love, life, and freedom in both the smallest and the grandest sense. And along with his characteristic curiosity and directness of expression, his writing took on a new lyricism best represented by **"Straw-Blond,"** an elegiac poem—reminiscent of Frank O'Hara's "Joe's Jacket"—in which the speeding up of the modern world, the pursuit of one's youth, the imminence of death, and the elusiveness of a dream come together in a stunning rush of almost weightless, never wasted words. My very favorite Hikmet poem, though, is **"Things I Didn't Know I Loved,"** written the year before he died: "The train plunges on through the pitch-black night / I never knew I liked the night pitch-black / sparks fly from the engine / I didn't know I loved sparks / I didn't know I loved so many things and I had to wait until / I was sixty to find it out." This sensuous litany builds along with the rhythm of the railroad to an ecstatic state as the great poet discovers the passions that allow him—and us—to experience the universe anew.

Don Shewey, in a review of "Things I Didn't Know I Loved" and "The Epic of Sheik Bedreddin and Other Poems," in VLS, *No. 6, April, 1982, p. 4.*

PUBLISHERS WEEKLY

[In **Human Landscapes** Hikmet employed] a variety of techniques: overall, the epic is episodic and cinematographic, pre-senting a cross-section of Turkish society in portraits and incidents—some brief, some fully developed. The hero himself assumes many persona, being essentially a fighter whose war includes the two world wars, the Turkish War of Independence, and a civil war in which we meet some political prisoners. . . . **Human Landscapes** comprises five books: the first two occur on the Anatolia Express where we meet the lower-class travelers, then those in the middle and upper. Book III brings us inside a prison and then a hospital, where we find both sickness and the joy of birth. The pace again quickens in the latter part of the epic. Radio messages and letters bring us to various parts of the world: from the Fuehrer's progress in Russia to the lonely thoughts of a woman whose husband is in prison. This is a grand, impressive, sophisticated work, rich in dramatic incident and varied in tone and language.

A review of "Human Landscapes," in Publishers Weekly, *Vol. 222, No. 13, September 24, 1982, p. 69.*

ROBERT HUDZIK

This "novel in verse" [**Human Landscapes**] spans the collapse of the Ottoman Empire, the World Wars, and the period of civil unrest during which Hikmet was jailed. Conceived as two simultaneous train journeys—one undertaken by peasants and prisoners, the other by members of the educated and upper classes—the poem is rich in incident and characters, many based upon Hikmet's fellow inmates. Political, social, and historical themes are united by a common vision. Hikmet's ability to particularize the general helps make this a bold, remarkable work.

Robert Hudzik, in a review of "Human Landscapes," in Library Journal, *Vol. 107, No. 18, October 15, 1982, p. 1991.*

EMILY GROSHOLZ

Human Landscapes is Nazim Hikmet's epic masterwork, a group portrait of Turkey between the two world wars. Thoroughly modern in style and substance, half poetry, half prose, it still retains elements of classical epic: repetition of formulaic phrases, motifs of battle, banquet and journey. . . . The poem is long, almost 300 pages, but once I had started it almost nothing could disengage me, it was so worldlike. (p. 138)

Human Landscapes was composed during the twelve years [Hikmet] spent in jail. It began as a kind of encyclopedia, a social history which was a series of portraits of people from all levels of Turkish society. He read it aloud to his fellow inmates as he composed it, and they helped him with the different levels of diction, dialects and folk material. Eventually these vignettes coalesced into a story about a train journey from Istanbul to Ankara taken by the political prisoner Halil. The narrative weaves in and out of Halil's presence by means of techniques which are self-consciously cinematic (Hikmet was also a screenwriter): zooms, jump-cuts, dissolves and flashbacks.

The English does in fact transmit a gamut of dictions and perspectives, ranging from folk ballad to street talk, the interior monologues of Istanbul intellectuals, battle scenes, jokes and lyric description. . . . Hikmet has an uncanny way of bringing characters to life in a few lines so vividly that, whether they are scurrilous or noble, one can't help but care about them. . . . Hikmet has a refined sense of history and the excesses of passion, but his special gift is to show that every human life is a story, and a compelling one. (p. 139)

Emily Grosholz, "New Renderings," in The Hudson Review, *Vol. XXXVII, No. 1, Spring, 1984, pp. 132-42.**

ALAN ROSS

So obscure is much of Nazim Hikmet's life that it is difficult quite to establish how much he was a communist dupe and how much a courageous, independent-minded patriot. (p. 98)

However the ideas behind his poetry may strike one today, there is no doubt about Hikmet's quality. He was the author of patriotic epics thousands of lines long, numerous plays, and during the last, Russian decade, much propaganda, but at his lyrical best—in his poems from Bursa prison, for example—he combines a genuinely prophetic and tragic vision with an ironic eliptical technique. (pp. 98-9)

It is not surprising that he is out of favour with [Turkey's] politicians, reacting as they do to the elementary politics and indifferent to the poetry. Driving about the country that, in Hikmet's words, 'juts out into the Mediterranean like a mare's head', his poems burn in one's pocket like a secret membership card. 'You cannot sip my poems like Epsom salts from a glass,' Hikmet remarked once; and again, in a poem called **"Optimism,"** 'we'll drive our motor-cars towards blue horizons', but the truth of the matter was that he had little to be optimistic about. His poems are made out of separation, loss, struggle and confinement, only his love of the soil and peasants of Turkey, of his own family, seeing him through. Bitterly critical of the Loti-inspired, western view of the Orient—'lattice-work, caravanserai fountains, minarets, women with henna-stained noses, green turbaned imams, clogs made of mother-of-pearl', Hikmet attacks the French writer's orient 'that never existed and never will'. 'If I believed in a soul separate from matter, on the liberation day of the East I would crucify your soul at the head of a bridge and smoke in front of it . . . our horse's hoofs go deep into the belly of imperialism.'

The violence of feeling and imagery in the earlier poems . . . is reinforced by their immediacy. Hikmet was only 23 . . . when he launched his vicious assault on Pierre Loti. But though experience and prison matured him as a poet he never lost his belligerence. Today, sailing up the Bosphorus from the Galata bridge to Anadolu Kavagi, the last ferry stop on the Asian side before the Black Sea opens and the military take over, it is impossible not to be saddened by the vision that took so talented a poet away from his own country. However much the dream has to be modified on landing, from the sea there is no more beautiful waterway on earth than the nineteen miles of the Bosphorus . . . and no skyline more magical than that of old Stamboul. At Eyup far above the Golden Horn the despised Pierre Loti had his tea-house in which to smoke and gaze at the sunset and there one can still enjoy the same view in the same surroundings today. But of Hikmet there are only memories, poems, and once again prohibitions. (pp. 99-100)

Alan Ross, "A Sad Affair under the Stars," in London Magazine, *n.s. Vol. 27, Nos. 9 & 10, December 1984 & January 1985, pp. 94-100.**

William M(oses) Hoffman

1939-

American dramatist, scriptwriter, editor, and critic.

Well known in the New York theater community for his off-Broadway plays, Hoffman attracted wide critical attention with *As Is* (1985), a controversial drama about the tragic effects of AIDS on a homosexual couple. *As Is* examines the panic surrounding AIDS through the story of Rich, a promising writer who has contracted the disease, and Saul, Rich's ex-lover, who returns to take care of him after Rich is abandoned by another lover. Critics praised Hoffman's sympathetic depiction of AIDS victims and their families and noted Hoffman's effective use of humor to offset the serious tone of the play. As Paul Berman noted, the humor in *As Is* "expresses a tight-lipped ironic love of life, a determination not to surrender joy even in the face of ghastly suffering."

Hoffman began writing plays in the 1960s. These works were produced by such experimental theatrical troupes as Caffe Cino and La Mama Experimental Theatre Club in New York City. Among the best known of his early plays are *Thank You, Miss Victoria* (1965), a one-act monologue about a young man's sadomasochistic telephone conversation with a woman, and *XXXXX* (1969), an informal piece relating the life of Jesus Christ. Hoffman has written several musicals and was commissioned by the Metropolitan Opera to write a libretto for a work by composer John Corigliano. He has also edited several anthologies, including the *New American Plays* series (1968-1971) and *Gay Plays: The First Collection* (1979).

(See also *Contemporary Authors*, Vols. 57-60 and *Contemporary Authors New Revision Series*, Vol. 11.)

Photograph by Jerry Vezzuso

ROBERT PASOLLI

William Hoffman's *Thank You, Miss Victoria* [is an eccentric play]. The central character, a young man, is spending his first day on a new job he has been forced to take in his father's firm. He is in a panic about being thrust into responsibility, the more so for his confusion at just what his responsibility is. An ad in a girlie magazine for a male secretary, with implications in the sexual services department, attracts his attention. It is signed "Miss Victoria," and he phones her.

Partly in response to her brusque demands, partly in willfully precipitous self-denial, the young man proffers an abject spiritual and physical slavishness to his prospective employer. By the end of the long conversation, of which we hear only his share, Miss Victoria has assumed the character of the numinous and the young man that of a groveling dog. Persistent intrusions by his office secretary and by friends who telephone in, representing the reality he endeavors to escape, come to a climax with the arrival of the young man's father for a conference, which concludes the episode. Thus the eccentricity of the action is heightened by its framework of conventional reality, while the imprecise identity of Miss Victoria and the wanton character

of the servile frenzy she elicits from the young man make Mr. Hoffman's play a pointed vignette of horror. (p. 404)

Robert Pasolli, "Off-Off-Broadway," *in* The Nation, *Vol. 202, No. 14, April 4, 1966, pp. 403-06.**

EDITH OLIVER

Thank You, Miss Victoria is almost a monologue, spoken by the young oddball son of a rich stockbroker. He spends most of his time on the phone at his father's office taking extremely personal calls while he makes paper planes out of strips of the *Wall Street Journal* and thumbs through a dirty magazine. There he finds an ad put in by a Miss Victoria. As he calls the number listed and tries to convince her that he is willing to fulfill her deviant requirements and adapt himself to her peculiar practices, he throws off his jacket, loosens his tie, and ends up on all fours howling like a dog. In spite of some amusing moments, I don't think that Mr. Hoffman has quite the sophistication to make the idea work, but perhaps the trouble is that the play is barely acted by a fellow who never for a second seems to mean what he is doing.

Edith Oliver, in a review of "Thank You, Miss Victoria," *in* The New Yorker, *Vol. XLII, No. 9, April 23, 1966, p. 126.*

FRANK RICH

There are some subjects audiences would just as soon not hear about in the theater, and surely one of them is AIDS, the lethal illness dramatized by William M. Hoffman in his play, *As Is*. But it would be a mistake for any theatergoer to reject this work out of squeamishness. Strange as it may sound, Mr. Hoffman has turned a tale of the dead and the dying into the liveliest new work to be seen . . . in several seasons. Far from leaving us drained, *As Is* is one of the few theatrical evenings in town that may, if anything, seem too brief.

This isn't to say that this 90-minute play is painless. A free-flowing journal of the recent plague years for New York's homosexuals, *As Is* rarely spares us the clinical facts of acquired immune deficiency syndrome; only at the end is the audience shielded from the physiological and psychological torments. Yet Mr. Hoffman has written more than a documentary account of an AIDS victim's grotesque medical history. As we follow the tailspin of a promising fiction writer named Rich . . . , the playwright reaches out to examine the impact of AIDS on hetero- and homosexual consciences as well as to ask the larger questions (starting with, "Why me?") that impale any victims of terminal illness.

It's a feat that Mr. Hoffman accomplishes with both charity and humor. When Rich is hit by AIDS, he is breaking up with Saul . . . , a photographer who has been his longtime lover. Saul has been badly hurt by Rich, but not so much so that he will turn his back at a time of grave need. Even as the two men bitterly split up their household possessions—from copper pots to "the world's largest collection of Magic Marker hustler portraits"—Saul decides to stick by Rich come what may, to accept him "as is."

Others behave just as compassionately. Although suffering cruel social ostracism, Rich eventually receives support from his married brother . . . , from fellow AIDS victims (one of them female), from a maternal hospice worker. . . . But such kindnesses are not so easy for the protagonist to accept. Rich swings between denial and anger, lashing out at both friends and strangers. He at first rejects Saul's affections with torrents of abuse and, at one point, vows to spread his infection indiscriminately through New York's demimonde of sex bars. "I'm going to die and take as many as I can with me," cries . . . [Rich], his voice coursing with rage.

Among other pointed digressions, *As Is* offers a satirical tour of that demimonde. We travel to a sadomasochistic haunt whose identically costumed clientele go by the names of Chip, Chuck and Chad. . . . Mr. Hoffman doesn't deny his characters' enjoyment of what they euphemistically refer to as "noncommitted, nondirected" sex (or laughingly refer to as sleaze). But, in mocking obsessive promiscuity with light wit, the playwright can gracefully bid such behavior a permanent farewell without adopting a hectoring moralistic tone.

Mr. Hoffman devotes more attention to exploring both the present panic and solidarity of a group that has found itself rightly "terrified of every pimple." For the play's homosexuals, the discovery of AIDS was an epoch-altering event: In a group recitation, they each remember where they were when they first heard of the mysterious epidemic. In another chilling scene, Rich is bombarded by a chorus of doctors' voices incantatorily repeating a single sentence: "The simple fact is that we know little about acquired immune deficiency syndrome." The moment is counterbalanced by a vignette in which two men answering phones at an "AIDS hot line" dispense as much solace as they can without pretending to omnipotence or saintliness.

Sometimes the characters of *As Is* seem a bit too saintly: Mr. Hoffman eventually resolves Rich's conflicts with others in the neat, upbeat manner of *Terms of Endearment*. . . . [But] we don't notice the play's begged questions or superficial examinations of character until we're out of the theater. . . . [The] generous-spirited hospice worker, whose epiphany-laden monologues open and close the evening, may be more of a sentimental conceit than a character, but . . . [she is] moving even so. "My job is not to bring enlightenment, only comfort," is how she describes her mission to the dying and their loved ones. Mr. Hoffman's play, as much as is possible under the grim circumstances, brings a stirring measure of both.

Frank Rich, "'As Is', about AIDS," in The New York Times, *March 11, 1985, p. C12.*

CLIVE BARNES

[*As Is* is] a wonderful and frightening play . . . and I commend it to both you and your conscience. . . .

As it so happens that I am not homosexual, Haitian, an intravenous drug user or a regular blood recipient, I am not personally in any of the high-risk categories. As yet. Plagues have a habit of spreading—it is one of the things that have historically given them such a poor press.

But *so far* that oddly named contagious killer Acquired Immunity Deficiency Syndrome has obviously affected me as a tragedy but also fortunately seemed almost as remote personally as a drought in Africa, an epidemic in India.

I have been lucky. . . . Just how lucky I have been is now currently demonstrated by this terrifying, but moving, and occasionally bleakly funny play. . . .

There is nothing particularly original about Hoffman's play— but the writing is stiletto sharp, and the characters emerge as disturbingly real.

The story is as old as mortality. These are the accomodations to be made to death—in another century the play could be *Camille,* and the death could be the Keatsian spangly doom of consumption. In our own time it could be cancer.

But AIDS has a new poignancy—simply because most of us are not personally affected by its existence, we have brushed it under the carpet of our feelings. Starvation in Ethiopia is a more manageable object for our compassion.

I doubt whether *As Is* will prove unduly popular with the homosexual community—its problems must be too near home.

Also it is possible that I was struck with it particularly for reasons fundamentally nontheatrical. I do believe that it is valuable simply in drawing graphic attention to a socio-medical problem that needs more attention than it is receiving.

But, for all that, *As Is* is a remarkable, a terrific play, not merely social propaganda. It might be compared with Eugene Brieux's far more preachy play about venereal disease, which caused a sensation right at the beginning of the century, *Damaged Goods*.

Hoffman's play, unlike the Brieux, is fast-moving and non-message-carrying. But it delivers a punch, even heavier than its controversial 80-year-old predecessor. . . .

As Is should be seen and, if not exactly enjoyed, appreciated and understood for what it is. Never forgetting that part of what it is, is a rattling good play.

Clive Barnes, "Healthy Production of 'As Is'," in New York Post, March 12, 1985. Reprinted in New York Theatre Critics' Reviews, Vol. XLVI, No. 7, Week of May 6, 1985, p. 296.

PAUL BERMAN

There's no trumpet call to action in *As Is,* instead merely—merely!—an effort to accept impending death. The dying man is too angry to accept anything, but his lover does a lot of thinking and so do some of the health workers. The thinking is faintly religious, sans denomination, and is best expressed by the Irish nun.... The nun works as a hospice nurse in Greenwich Village, where half her patients are young men. She learns something from these men and from the gay world in which she finds herself. There's a lot of joke-telling. "Did you hear about the Polish lesbian? She liked men." "The hardest thing about AIDS is convincing your parents you're Haitian." That sort of thing. The humor expresses a tight-lipped ironic love of life, a determination not to surrender joy even in the face of ghastly suffering.

The superior realism of theater over film . . . , the recognition that real people are performing, that their dilemmas are only a few feet away, that their words are being spoken right now and to you personally, the sensation that you could touch the experience—works to powerful effect in *As Is.* You stumble out of the theater overwhelmed with sadness. Is this because the play is especially brilliant, a work for the ages? That would be too much to say. Present reality is the klieg light that makes *As Is* come to life. Someday someone will stage a revival and will discover that everything that once shook audiences up seems all too obvious. Someday *As Is* will look like a dated documentary. May that day come soon! But it is not today.

Paul Berman, in a review of "As Is," in The Nation, Vol. 240, No. 18, May 11, 1985, p. 570.

JACK KROLL

As Is focuses on the intimate relationship between Rich . . . , who has contracted AIDS, and Saul . . . , the lover whom Rich has left but who returns to care for him. Author Hoffman refuses to stack the cards by making Rich a nice guy: Rich, a poet and writer, is capable of breaking up a deep, long-term relationship for a vapid but sexy younger man. Heterosexuals may recognize this syndrome. When Rich contracts AIDS, is shunned by his family and loses his job, it is Saul who re-enters the picture to care for him and to re-establish the relationship on an even deeper level.

With adroitness and even humor, Hoffman surrounds his central pair with a constellation of characters ranging from Rich's straight brother to an ex-nun hospice worker to leather-clad gay guys whose sexual rituals the author isn't afraid to satirize. *As Is* doesn't sentimentalize homosexual culture. The disease almost certainly will kill Rich, yet he and Saul both, with desperate eloquence, pay tribute to the promiscuous life-style that has triggered the disease. "Oh God, I love sleaze," says Rich, "—the whining self-pity of a leather bar in spring, getting raped on a tombstone in Marrakech." Such sentiments will shock many straights (and many gays as well); among other things, *As Is* may well mark the end of an era in which

some homosexuals flaunted promiscuous sex as a "liberating" antimorality. And, with the seemingly inevitable increase of AIDS among heterosexuals, Hoffman's challenging invocation of the issue of sexual promiscuity leaps over homosexual borders. (p. 87)

Jack Kroll, "Going to the Heart of AIDS," in Newsweek, Vol. CV, No. 19, May 13, 1985, pp. 87, 89.*

PAUL J. McCARREN

[The production] of *As Is* . . . is a clear demonstration of how lively and precise ensemble acting can mask the weaknesses of a script. In this case, a cast of eight actors . . . play an idea-piece about terminal illness and gay pride with such careful attention to their corporate work of talking, laughing, quarreling and grieving with one another that it is not clear at first that the focus of the play is issues, not people. . . .

As Is begins with a monologue that might have warned the wary that the evening would include elements of lecture. But . . . a hospice worker who explains that her job of helping the dying is made bearable by a sense of humor, lilted through her insights with such a pleasantly daffy manner that we could easily look past the bromides she had to deliver and eagerly anticipate her first encounter with a patient—wondering what her baffled innocence would spark when it rubbed against a person whose pain, fear or anger resisted humor.

The second scene might also have alerted us to the possibility that we were watching the development of an idea rather than of characters. It began with a joke-filled argument between two white, well-heeled 30-year-olds who were deciding how to divide their possessions now that their love affair was over. Saul . . . was motherly but mordant, funny yet hurt, as he tried to be philosophical about his lover, Rich, moving in with a younger man. . . . Rich seemed sensible, yet slightly mean, alternately blasé and anxious in his insistence that breakups were normal.

The playwright has created such an intriguing odd-couple . . . with such nicely timed delight in playing off one another (with the sort of precision and passion one also hopes for in good tennis) that we naturally awaited the resolution of their set-to.

But the scene concluded with Rich revealing that he is suffering from AIDS, the fatal Acquired Immune Deficiency Syndrome. The revelation, besides explaining why Rich had been so edgy and preoccupied during the scene, was also the cue for a simple but exciting bit of theatricality: an avalanche of reaction to the news of the disease. . . . "My brother has AIDS? What'll I tell my wife?" "How can I run a catering business with a partner who has AIDS?" "I can give you a prescription that will reduce any pain; but it will not cure the disease." . . .

What did these scenes tell us? Too much, yet not enough, I think. The hospice worker gave us a primer on the basics of caring for the dying, but did not reveal much about herself. (She returned, twice, during the play for further soliloquized insights on terminal illness, but we never saw her interact with a patient.) The quarrel scene gave us a dramatic picture of clever homosexuals whose wit is stymied by a nightmarish jumble of reactions to the disease AIDS. But we learn little more about these individuals, either in that or subsequent scenes, other than the fact that Saul is sardonic but kind, and Rich can be nasty and brusque. We want to know what makes these two cope or despair the way they do, but the playwright does not show us.

It is true that Hoffman tries to tell us some things. Most notably, near the end of the play, Rich weakens and, in the hospital, reminisces to Saul about being a teen-age closet-homosexual from south Jersey and dreaming of a life of sexual freedom in Greenwich Village. We were meant, I suppose, to realize: "Aha! So, he was a lonely, sensitive, misunderstood kid. Now it all makes sense!" . . . [We] can almost ignore how tardily and ineffectively Hoffman tries to sketch in a full character with this one, maudlin speech. But the ploy cannot work. Even though the two lead actors have a stage rapport that only comes with plenty of rehearsal (and careful casting), their energetically attentive performances cannot patch all the holes in the script.

Am I missing the whole point? Need Hoffman draw full characters or develop a full plot if he is, after all, attempting the stage-equivalent of a docudrama rather than a story? Very well; what's the burden of the documentary? For the life of me, I cannot state it more simply than this: "Gays are dying of [an incurable] disease, and the universality of death's pain and mystery should help us all to see that tolerance and compassion could make this a better world—if we would just make a sincere attempt at patience and good humor." An inspirational though windy greeting-card? Yes. A docudrama substitute for a focused story? No.

Paul J. McCarren, "Thought Patterns," in America, *Vol. 152, No. 23, June 15, 1985, p. 494.*

GERALD WEALES

[In *As Is,* the performers] step in and out of roles to give a sense of the gay community in its variety, to show the way in which AIDS alters the patterns of behavior, and to establish the hospital environment. A hospice worker voices the general remarks on the disease and reactions to it. This milieu is the frame for the central story, the account of one man's slow reconciliation to the fact of the disease and its consequences. The emotional center of the play is the relationship between the protagonist, a writer of great charm and wit, and his former lover, who takes him "as is" and gives him a context of warmth and affection in which to face his approaching death. In a subplot, the writer's straight brother puts aside his distrust of gayness and his terror of the disease to embrace the dying man. In a recent article in the *New York Times Magazine* . . . , a volunteer with the Gay Men's Health Crisis deplored talk of AIDS as though it were a "gentle, Camille-like wasting away." *As Is* finds the equivalent of the Camille image. A curtain is discreetly drawn around the dying man, leaving him with the strengthening presences of lover and brother, and the hospice worker steps forward for the last positive note, her story about a flamboyant gay who wanted—a final declaration of life—to have his nails painted one last time. This upbeat ending for so painful a situation manages to infect *As Is* with the kind of sentimentality that so often mars plays like *The Shadow Box* which want seriously to assert the primacy of life even at the moment of death. (pp. 406-07)

Gerald Weales, "AIDS on Stage: Advocacy & Ovations," in Commonweal, *Vol. CXII, No. 13, July 12, 1985, pp. 406-07.**

David Ignatow

1914-

American poet and editor.

A respected voice in contemporary American poetry, Ignatow is best known for his stark urban landscapes and his confessional explorations of the private self. Like William Carlos Williams, with whom he is often associated, Ignatow rejects the traditions of European verse embraced by such modernist poets as T. S. Eliot and Wallace Stevens. Instead, he favors short free-verse and prose poems, employing colloquial language to create poetry from the pathos of everyday life. Among Ignatow's dominant themes are death, isolation, violence, the relationship between commitment and freedom, the tensions of family and city life, and the rejuvenating spirit of nature. While some critics consider Ignatow's work solipsistic, others contend that he has succeeded in relating his personal awareness to the concerns of others and praise his honest treatment of modern life.

In his first collection, *Poems* (1948), Ignatow introduces the vignettes of urban decadence that characterize much of his poetry until the mid-1960s. In this volume, he focuses on the external world and occasionally examines his personal reactions to social issues. In *The Gentle Weight Lifter* (1955), Ignatow concentrates on big business and the ruthless pursuit of money and power. Many of these poems relate his experiences as an executive in his family's bindery and focus on the corporate structure's indifference to the needs of the individual. With *Say Pardon* (1961) and *Figures of the Human* (1964), Ignatow's urban vision turned increasingly dark and bitter. Robert D. Spector described Ignatow's city poems in *Say Pardon* as "a jungle . . . where rape and murder are the flora and fauna." In his review of *Figures of the Human*, Hayden Carruth chided Ignatow for writing "almost exclusively of the cruelty, filth, and insanity of city life." Carruth continued: "I have no question about [Ignatow's] ability, but only about his future: how long can a creative instinct survive on these miniature emblems of disgust?" In the poems included in *Rescue the Dead* (1968), according to one critic who was perhaps responding to Carruth's skepticism, Ignatow looks "away from the almost surreal urban landscapes of pain, suffering, and the dark joy of love." In this volume, Ignatow's themes include the strain of family relationships, sexual love, and social alienation, and he focuses openly on his affection for nature. Critics noted a redeeming sense of hope emerging from this collection, as Ignatow celebrates life in a more complex, philosophical, and humane manner.

Facing the Tree (1975) and *Tread the Dark* (1978) mark a change of direction in Ignatow's verse. These collections emphasize acceptance, reconciliation, and survival, yet they also explore such themes as suicide, death, and the individual's unity with nature. Some critics noted a metaphysical quality in the poems included in these volumes. In *Whisper to the Earth* (1981), Ignatow employs a deceptively straightforward style to examine his concern with aging, his fear of death, and his relationship with nature. In *Leaving the Door Open* (1984), Ignatow presents the notion that only through resignation to fear and violence can one succeed in life. With subdued emotion, he expands his meditations on life and death, displaying

© 1981 Layle Silbert

an awareness of the tenuousness of existence yet finding relief through humor. In his review of *Leaving the Door Open*, Jim Elledge commented that the poems "offer greater depth if read sequentially, and it is as a sequence that the book chronicles an individual's conflict with himself, with family, with strangers, with life."

(See also *CLC*, Vols. 4, 7, 14; *Contemporary Authors*, Vols. 9-12, rev. ed.; *Contemporary Authors Autobiography Series*, Vol. 3; and *Dictionary of Literary Biography*, Vol. 5.)

LINDA W. WAGNER

[*The essay from which this excerpt is taken was originally published in* Tennessee Poetry Journal, *Winter 1970.*]

David Ignatow strikes the keynote to his poems when he writes, "Without respect for one's own identity, the person is lost." Most modern poets do write from their experiences and of their perceptions, creating an art as uniquely their own as possible. . . .

In this search for individual expression, however, few poets aim for mere whim or idiosyncrasy; the knowledge one accrues as a person will hopefully relate to the deepest concerns of other men. This rapport is the aim of most of Ignatow's poems. . . . In *Rescue the Dead* Ignatow longs unabashedly for a participation, but much of what he finds—even in a family, husband and wife, child and parent—is alienation.

Some people have termed Ignatow "the poet of the ghetto" in an attempt to summarize this awareness. Few of his poems relate in fact to the down-and-out (unless it is that the ghetto lives in each of us, in our loneliness). Yet, because of their terse phrasing and open, suggestive technique, some readers may not get the point of Ignatow's poems at all. Many of them appear to be giant metaphors, with the definitive term unstated. (p. 134)

In his 1948 *Poems* he had written of a dying old man, "He has worn the body of his time / a little longer and a little more indulgently / than you"; in **"Bowery"** the bums are content with the "luxury" of their "failures"; in **"Europe and America"** he begins work on the father-son theme that occupies many of his later poems. . . . The comfortable son's inability to understand the desperate immigrant father is only one small part of the universal separateness Ignatow is to mourn throughout his work. The 1948 **"Brooding"** says it as completely as he has expressed it:

> The sadness of our lives.
> We will never be good enough to each other,
> to our parents and friends . . .
>   The truth faces me
> all the time. We are in a world
> in which nobody listens to anybody,
> in which we do as we please
> until we are stopped by others.
> We live our whole lives as in a husk. . . .

Working from this premise, Ignatow fleshed in the figures in his second book, *The Gentle Weight Lifter* (1955). The bitterness of poems like **"Promenade"** and **"A Guided Tour Through the Zoo"** focuses our attention on man's search for dignity and pride, his failing effort to maintain either. Impressions become more vivid in the 1961 *Say Pardon* as Ignatow makes more use of himself as persona in the poems and also relies on language highly charged with emotion, sometimes to excess. **"Each Night"** is a good illustration of this mixed effect. This poem about the city contains good images ("children white with wanting") as well as overdone ones: "My parents / were the city and its complaint of brakes / and horns. For food I sucked at exhaust pipes, / and heard overhead rumbling motors of argument, / playing in my mother's lap, the gutter." This passage melts down into a more effective description of the child grown to adulthood, as writer:

> I travel between home and hell, always
> with a pencil, to punch holes for air
> when breathing becomes difficult.

Say Pardon had a double dedication, the customary one, for Ignatow, to [his wife] Rose Graubart, and the additional one to William Carlos Williams. Ignatow's technique is admittedly reminiscent of Williams's: the method of presenting, of striking against an object and backing off, the understated (almost "tough guy") pose. In others—the matter of suggestiveness, the force of a "big" subject in nearly every poem—he is a step farther on from Williams. But it is for the correspondence of theme rather than technique that Ignatow makes his dedication. As he writes in 1964,

The Williams creed, founded on the strength and independence of the individual, continues to assert, through paradox and rejection, the only important values: the sanctity of life, of the person, of the being in continual process, which shall have poems to say it.

Since 1964, Ignatow's poems have grown in both technical prowess and understanding of just this life "in continual process." He has used a variety of approaches to somehow "document" the life, the process, with which he deals—themes taken from newspaper accounts, the dramatic monologue of **"Nat Koffman,"** the direct address of "Have you just stabbed a man to death?" or "Come in with your stab wound up the middle. . . ." Trying here to give the appearance of the objective artist, sketch book in hand, Ignatow includes both the concrete "real" portraits and the surreal (women with green faces, floating in air), as well as the by-now typical personal statement poems. This pose of being a graphic artist enables him to widen his scope and enrich his technique. The poems in one group, for example, are "money" poems evoking brilliantly the pressures any man feels of providing for a family— **"For One Moment," "About Money,"** and especially **"The Nailhead."** . . . (pp. 135-37)

In his concern with the manly role, Ignatow is coming close to the poems of husband and son in *Rescue the Dead*. His own desperation, previously unexpressed, gives him the means to understand his father's life—and, eventually, his own, as the parable poems like the **"Ritual"** series show so well.

The central image of the title poem in *Figures of the Human* leads directly to *Rescue the Dead*. The figures seen in the poem are "struggling awake," "loved" only after they have shaken the pervasive apathy, only after they have become. Consonant with this, Ignatow creates a strange dichotomy in **"Rescue the Dead,"** that between those who live ("Not to love is to live") and those who love:

> . . . To love is to be led away
> into a forest where the secret grave
> is dug, singing, praising darkness
> under the trees.
>
> To live is to sign your name
> is to ignore the dead,
> is to carry a wallet
> and shake hands. . . .

Despite his admonition that men must "rescue the dead," the living-dead, his picture of this majority is eerily convincing. Most of us, yes, shake hands and carry wallets. So, this is one of Ignatow's current poses, including himself too in his censure. As his **"Suite for Marriage," "Sediment,"** and **"The Room"** show, his own love has not given either him or his beloved enough satisfaction, "Love me for my desperation / that I may love you for your fear." Similarly honest is the opening group of poems to his father, and those which speak in more general terms about the parent-child alienation. . . . Throughout this collection, it is the children who suffer, themselves, withdrawn and apathetic, sometimes the victims of outright murder, more often the hardened results of apathy. Until the last section of *Rescue the Dead,* when it appears that hope does live, and joy, whether in the child's picking vegetables or the man's solitary walk, is possible. Tranquil love poems set the tone for this group, and in its context even poems ostensibly about Viet Nam take on the larger theme of sympathy for all men. . . . [In] **"Soldier"** Ignatow treats *as man* turned killer, and comments only with sadness, "in any case / he is finished."

But for himself, the book does not end in sadness or with the tone of finish, and the reader can only hope that Ignatow's next collection will continue to give us this curtly real depiction of life, refreshing in a world of either morbid despair or soft solipsism. That man is only the child of his experiences, and that his duty, his happiness, is to know himself, comes to us with fresh conviction in Ignatow's clear if sometimes tortured images.... (pp. 137-39)

> Linda W. Wagner, "On David Ignatow," in her American Modern: Essays in Fiction and Poetry, Kennikat Press, 1980, pp. 134-39.

PETER STITT

There has been a vogue recently, among poets of a certain age, for the dark volume of poems—a volume in which the poet faces the blackness within and the void without, anticipating his own death. A moderate example of this impulse is ... David Ignatow's *Tread the Dark*. Ignatow created several problems for himself with *Tread the Dark*. The book is so intensely solipsistic that the reader feels totally excluded—and this by a poet widely admired for the democratic inclusiveness of his work. The speaker of these poems feels so sorry for himself— he is old, he is going to die—that the reader loses all patience. It looked like a dead end. How could the poet possibly extricate himself from such a cul-de-sac?

The way, as *Whisper to the Earth* beautifully demonstrates, is again to look death straight in the face, but this time after emerging from the vale of despair. The speaker of these new poems radiates joy on nearly every page, not because he ignores death, but because he has come to terms with it. There are poems which show the earlier attitude still hanging on—for example, **"I'm sure,"** which begins, "I'm sure trees are depressed also," and ends, "I was about to try a razor on my wrist." But on the whole, the mood and wisdom of this book is far different, and a welcome change from *Tread the Dark*.

The positive effects in these poems depend on the voice that Mr. Ignatow has created. This character has struggled for years to discover the meaning of life only to realize near his death that life's significance inheres simply in its being; existence is its own meaning. This wisdom is present everywhere in the book, but perhaps most tellingly in **"Above Everything":**

> I wished for death often,
> but now that I am at its door
> I have changed my mind about the world.
> It should go on; it is beautiful,
> even as a dream, filled with water and seed,
> plants and animals, others like myself,
> ships and buildings and messages
> filling the air—a beauty,
> if ever I have seen one.
> In the next world, should I remember
> this one, I will praise it
> above everything.

The voice is quiet, the style a difficult one to maintain, so it should not be a surprise that the poet occasionally goes wrong— in the excessive cleverness of some poems, the mock-naive tone of others. But, on the whole, [*Whisper to the Earth*] is a triumphant return for David Ignatow, a testament to the enduring spirit of man. (p. 15)

> Peter Stitt, "Dark Volumes," in The New York Times Book Review, *February 14, 1982, pp. 15, 37.*

DAISY ALDAN

"I also am sad and so write it out / and leave it all behind for others / to give it thought that will make a bond / between the living and the dead"—thus David Ignatow, in the poem **"Between the Living and the Dead"** from his latest book, *Whisper to the Earth,* states his reasons for writing. In five parts combining lyrics and prose poems the poet includes contemplations, observations, questions and attempts at answers concerning the meaning of life, aging and death. The poet, now sixty-seven years old and bereft of beloved friends and family, feels himself alone and seeks those consoling thoughts which will help him define the present experience.

One might conclude that part one has as its major theme identity with the Earth, part two particulars, part three loneliness and death, part four conversations with the self, part five afterthoughts. The fourth section has within it the most original poems, and the prose poems in part five, with the exception of **"The Interview"** and **"The Reply"** (the latter a sad attempt at humor, bordering on the vulgar and not worthy of the rest of the collection), are absorbing and enjoyable. The last poem in the book, in fact, **"With Horace,"** is the best of all, integrating imagery, syntax, sound, idea and form to make a superior poem. In general, I find the lyrics better than the prose poems, for they glean essence as a poem should, whereas some of the prose poems tend toward rather undistinguished use of words and not very profound philosophical questions and conclusions.

Inherent in the seemingly easy style are sadness, loneliness, nostalgia, the search for a philosophy which will make dying acceptable. Seeming not to have found a particular weltanschauung, Ignatow creates conversations with the self and generally concludes that one must richly experience the darkness which gives birth to the light, the bark on which one is crucified; for leaves and flowers sprout therefrom, and birds nest in the branches. (pp. 341-42)

Now is the time for remembering: incidents of childhood which held significance for the future; the father with whom he can now identify; the beloved mother who has departed and left him alone and for whom he writes **"Kaddish,"** from which the title of the book is drawn. Here and there are poems which verge on the sentimental, but there are many which readers will enjoy: **"Requiem,"** for the father; **"Respected Graves,"** wherein he experiences himself and all humanity whirling on Earth together, traveling in "the dark to their respected graves"; **"A Life of Wonder,"** in which the philosophical conclusions seem most defined—"I would guess that this is all that life has to offer, and yet it must offer itself to become, and so I am the life it is." Then there is **"On Freedom,"** which speaks of the loss of the bondage of a love, the attainment of the freedom one believed one craved, only to find that one has exchanged life for death. (p. 342)

> Daisy Aldan, in a review of "Whisper to the Earth," in World Literature Today, *Vol. 56, No. 2, Spring, 1982, pp. 341-42.*

CHARLES MOLESWORTH

With David Ignatow's [*Whisper to the Earth*] the knowledge offered is almost exclusively that of solipsistic boredom. The speaker shows scant interest in music or images, and his world seldom unfolds as more than an occasion of sad isolation. Opening with a few poems about trees and clouds, the dominant tone turns from one of acceptance ("He is without fault, he is of the weather") to one of isolation, and finally to despair ("we are the life we live and none other"). Throughout poems written with minimum regard for the measures of verse, and in the prose pieces which make up half the book, the language runs to the flat, almost affectless plain style of American speech. . . . The book includes four "conversations" that prosaically rewrite Beckett, and there are touching poems about his desk chair, want ads, and fantasies about air travel, but everything illustrates the same lesson. The spirit of Eliot's Prufrock lives in Ignatow's spare dailiness, and he honestly faces and declaims his moral enervation. Deranged joy, caustic wit, the gesture toward the sublime: seldom do these post-Romantic answers appeal to Ignatow. He prefers to go it alone, and he takes limited pleasure in knowing millions of others share this common solitude. (pp. 157-58)

> *Charles Molesworth, "An Almost Unshakable Hold,"*
> in Commonweal, *Vol. CX, No. 5, March 11, 1983,*
> *pp. 157-59.**

WILLIAM HARMON

Ignatow achieves subtle equilibrium in **Whisper to the Earth** by means of internal self-reflexive references, echoes, and allusions. These pieces are plainly personal, but they stoically avoid sentimentality by a pretty strict alternation of the fanciful and the mundane. As a kind of sturdy knot Ignatow practices here a crossing or looping of technique, whereby prose paragraphs are used for the fanciful idiom, which reaches the surreal now and again, while chastened verse-patterns are used for the mundane. This chiasmus of manner and matter—prosaic form for poetic material, poetic form for prosaic—yields a feeling of stability and symmetry that in turn argue for the profound reality and sincerity of the poems. The most satisfying combination of systole and diastole in **Whisper to the Earth** comes, for me, in the prose of **"Of That Fire"** and the immediately succeeding verse, **"Here It Is."** The prose [begins]: "Inside I am on fire. Imagine, though, running up to City Hall and asking if there is a Department of Burning Need, ready for emergency, I being the emergency." . . . Then the poem:

> This is how I felt as a child:
> I was high on self-delight
> at the touch of the mild sun and breeze.
> Here it is Spring again
> and I have lost my sixty-fifth year
> in the blinding sun.

Whisper to the Earth is dedicated "To the Memory of James Wright"; no tribute could be more honorable or fitting. (p. 472)

> *William Harmon, "A Poetry Odyssey," in* The Sewanee Review, *Vol. XCI, No. 3, Summer, 1983, pp. 457-73.**

GREG KUZMA

David Ignatow is a poet of candor and urgency. . . . For years he has given us forthright statements about emotional situations that are often desperate or precarious—especially in his many poems of city landscape, where he sees the "figure of the human" as lonely and heroic amidst much that is ugly or sordid.

Ignatow accepts colloquial language and revitalizes it, and his own anxieties and suspiciousness, while at first seeming to isolate him from others, give him a convincing insight into universal conditions. What Ignatow drew initially from William Carlos Williams, the trusting of the commonplace, has been carried through more than fifty years of daily grind and intense brief redemptions. **Leaving the Door Open,** his latest book, offers the same commitment. Poem #11 (none of the poems have titles) announces in its opening lines how little has changed: "Here in bed behind a brick wall / I can make order and meaning." Elsewhere, in a prose poem, is one of those familiar but amazing Ignatow sentences which swallows its own syntax: "He grinds his teeth in expectation of killing with a fury that will brook no resistance of the creature he is after to make it die in its blood." This is muscular, physical writing, willing to be ungraceful if it can achieve strength. Here, the muscularity has become perversely relentless so as to express flatly the terror of cruel minds so appalling in our century.

The numbered poems suggest both sequence and the random, while the overall tone is that of a modest and unpretentious man who has achieved old age. But this is no death-haunted book, for there is resiliency with humor. One of the last poems begins: "I've wanted to write my way into paradise, / leaving the door open for others too," while the final poem is even more lovely in its leave-taking: "It is wonderful to die amidst the pleasures I have known / and so to die without recrimination towards myself and / others. . . ." Ignatow's is a hard-won decency.

> *Greg Kuzma, in a review of "Leaving the Door Open,"*
> in The Georgia Review, *Vol. XXXVIII, No. 4, Winter, 1984, p. 901.*

JAMES FINN COTTER

David Ignatow offers [**Leaving the Door Open**] as a meditation in prose and verse on death and the direction his own life has taken. The design of the book is circular, moving ever inward around "the vacuum" of the author's own being until it centers in the final piece on acceptance of his own death. He tells his wife: "With death before me, I look back at my pleasures and they were you whom I held close in loving, and in the poems I've written for this truth, which is their beauty and lets me die in pleasure with myself. I did not fail my life" (no. 64). The complacent note has been hard won because the previous sections are full of pain and self-blame for the author's failure as a father, husband, and man. "Whatever contribution I was to make to living," he writes," has been made, yet living has gained nothing / from it but a sharpened sense of its futility / for me" (no. 17). Not much difference exists between prose and poetry in these entries which call to mind Kafka's stories and Kierkegaard's journals. Unlike them, however, narrative thrust does not create a dynamic central character; Ignatow is too much like the passive vase to which he compares himself: "I am a vase holding a bunch of flowers / in my depth, with water in it" (no. 38). Yet the reader must admire the honesty everywhere apparent in this work and the effort required to make such a confession. (pp. 502-03)

> *James Finn Cotter, "Poetry Marathon," in* The Hudson Review, *Vol. XXXVII, No. 3, Autumn, 1984, pp. 496-507.**

THE VIRGINIA QUARTERLY REVIEW

In [**Leaving the Door Open**], Ignatow continues to develop the parabolic forms which have become over the years one of the most distinctive features of his writing. Ignatow's parables don't always work; they seem at times contrived, and at others too simple. But on those more successful occasions, as in one of the final poems where the poet describes his condition in terms that suggest the questor of Kafka's parable "Before the Law," Ignatow's use of the form reveals at once an interest in keeping writing close to "plain speech" while at the same time maintaining a most welcome seriousness, and humaneness, of purpose.

A review of "Leaving the Door Open," in The Virginia Quarterly Review, *Vol. 60, No. 4 (Autumn, 1984), p. 137.*

JIM ELLEDGE

Read at random, the poems of *Leaving the Door Open* offer the themes we have come to look forward to, perhaps even expect, in Ignatow's work: love, loneliness, and violence, the intensity of which is relieved, on occasion, by humor. Yet, the poems offer greater depth if read sequentially, and it is as a sequence that the book chronicles an individual's conflict with himself, with family, with strangers, with life.

Nearly a third of the collection's sixty-four pieces are short prose poems; the rest are equally compressed lyrics. The former range from the parable-like (**"Soldiers Surround"**) to talky meditations (**"It Is Wonderful"**), but all question, over and over, Ignatow's role in the world—and the world itself. In these pieces, Ignatow ironically distances himself from that world, so much so that, at times, he seems relaxed, even unconcerned, despite the bizarre, brutal scenes which surround him. . . . His lyrics, on the other hand, present Ignatow as an active participant in the world. His "I" is engaged not only in the passage of time, but in the ebb and flow of life. . . . In the process, he provides answers to his own questions and the strength which enables him to survive, even to triumph over, the world.

However, the victory is hard-won, accomplished only after pain and guilt, after facing fear, hatred, and self-doubt head-on. With a deliberately flat voice that intensifies the emotion he feels, Ignatow chillingly admits in **"I Find You,"**

> I find you at twenty-six
> seeking refuge
> in drugs and hospital routine,

> the same son I raised in anger
> and self-pity who is without hope
> of a life free of me and I know
> we both are in trouble.

During more public moments, his voice rises from the midst of a large city and reveals his acute solitude, his persistent examination of his place in the scheme of things, and his awareness of the fragility of his, of our, existence. His observations there lead him, finally, to the realization that only by resigning oneself to the strife, the fear, the myriad failures involved in living may one succeed, as nature does daily:

> . . . the zebra died in the mouth
> of the lioness after a brief struggle
> of the legs, and then the herd went back
> to feeding on the grass nearby
> while the lioness and her cubs knelt
> at the body as in worship
> and ate their fill.

The scene becomes "reassuring" to Ignatow as he realizes the purpose of life: "there was death / and . . . it had its place / among the living. . . ." As his resignation, and reassurance, grow, so, proportionally, does his sense of joy. His purpose—what he has sought, what he has questioned—is finally seen as two intrinsically related aspects of a whole:

> I am a vase holding a bunch of flowers
> in my depth, with water in it. I enjoy
> the branches leaning against my sides.
> They make me feel myself.

> See how tall and straight I stand
> with blossoms above me. Could anything
> be more beautiful than I who am nothing
> but an enclosure upon emptiness?

The images of *Leaving the Door Open* are finely focused; its emotions subdued, but no less deeply felt; its themes developed and ranging effortlessly across the spectrum of human experience. The collection is a triumph for one who, not uncommonly, has struggled against overwhelming odds to be able to say, "I did not fail my life." (pp. 295-97)

Jim Elledge, "Triumphs," in Poetry, *Vol. CXLVI, No. 5, August, 1985, pp. 293-304.*

Uwe Johnson

1934-1984

German novelist, short story writer, nonfiction writer, and translator.

Winner of the 1971 Georg Büchner Prize, Johnson is recognized as one of the most significant writers of post-World War II Germany. His novels explore the conflict of a divided Germany and focus on the guilt of the collective German consciousness. The political and cultural partition between East and West Germany, made manifest by the Berlin Wall, serves in Johnson's fiction as a microcosm of a divided world. Johnson himself was born in East Germany but moved to West Germany in 1959 so that his work could be published. The motivations and actions of Johnson's protagonists are often ambiguously presented to underscore the German climate of political uncertainty. The complex and often obscure nature of Johnson's work is reinforced by his use of such techniques as paratactic sentences, unorthodox punctuation, and fragmented narratives.

The title characters of Johnson's early novels *Mutmassungen über Jakob* (1959; *Speculations about Jakob*) and *Das dritte Buch über Achim* (1961; *The Third Book about Achim)* are developed through contradictory and fragmentary impressions. In *Speculations about Jakob,* the East German protagonist is killed after returning from an unspecified trip to West Germany. The nature of his death and the events leading up to it are related by various acquaintances who supply facts that do not always coincide, thus inducing in the reader a sense of chaos and uncertainty parallel to that of the characters. *The Third Book about Achim* concerns a West German journalist's attempt to write a biography of an East German champion cyclist. Discovering the impossibility of portraying the cyclist's life without addressing his political environment and unable to reconcile East and West German ideologies, the journalist eventually abandons his endeavor. Of central concern in both of these novels, as well as in Johnson's later work, is the uncertainty of meaning and the futility of the quest for absolute truth. In a review of *The Third Book about Achim,* R Hinton Thomas and Wilfried van der Will identified one of its main themes: "To discover that one cannot be sure about meanings, even where everyday words and phrases are concerned, is a step on the way to the discovery that man may be in error in believing that he can know himself." *Zwei Ansichten* (1965; *Two Views*) depicts two lovers whose relationship intensifies progressively with the building of the Berlin Wall that comes between them. The wall symbolizes the sociopolitical circumstances that eventually cause their affair to disintegrate.

Johnson's most ambitious work, *Jahrestage. Aus dem Leben von Gesine Cresspahl* (1970-84; *Anniversaries: From the Life of Gesine Cresspahl*), is a four-volume novel in which characters from his previous works reappear. Presented as the journals of Gesine Cresspahl, the protagonist's lover in *Speculations about Jakob, Anniversaries* combines clippings from *The New York Times,* Gesine's observations, and the omniscient narration of Johnson, who adds an ironic dimension to the text by appearing as a character in the story. Having emigrated to the United States, Gesine documents the history of her family from the rise of Nazism to the political tumult of the 1960s. By juxtaposing events from the past and present, including his

experiences living in Harlem in the mid-1960s, Johnson draws analogies between German anti-Semitism and American racism, as well as between fascism and the United States' involvement in the Vietnam War. Commenting on the evolution of Johnson's work, Marianne Hirsch stated that while his earlier novels "border on self-destruction by implicating all forms of 'truthfinding,'" *Anniversaries* affirms the ability of fiction to help humanity understand its world: "The unknowability of the individual . . . , the distortion of memory and the unreliability of language all have been forcefully demonstrated in the early novels. *Anniversaries* does not qualify such conclusions but brings us to the point of being able to live with them or in spite of them."

Ingrid Babendererde: Reifeprüfung 1953 (1985) was Johnson's first novel but was not published until after his death. This work concerns the oppression encountered by two school children in Stalinist Germany and foreshadows the political overtones of Johnson's later novels. Johnson's other writings include the short fiction collection *Karsch und andere Prosa* (1964; *Karsh and Other Prose*), the title novella of which has been published separately as *An Absence* (1969), and *Begleitumstände: Frankfurter Vorlesungen* (1980), consisting of lectures Johnson delivered at the University of Frankfurt which reveal the political and literary influences on his fiction.

(See also *CLC*, Vols. 5, 10, 15; *Contemporary Authors*, Vols. 1-4, rev. ed., Vol. 112 [obituary]; and *Contemporary Authors New Revision Series*, Vol. 1.)

MAURICE CAPITANCHIK

There are novelists who ask and those who tell, the Kafkas and the George Eliots, one might say. Uwe Johnson is an 'asker' behind whose brief and polished novella, *An Absence,* lies the question of personal identity, or the lack of it, as mirrored by the division of his land. Karsch, the central character, is a West German journalist who, while visiting a former girl-friend in East Berlin, is invited to write the biography of her current lover, champion cyclist Achim (the biography itself is the subject of Mr Johnson's previous novel). On his return, Karsch speaks his mind in public on the recognition of East Germany, and is consequently suspected of treason.

Fearing the onset of middle-age, Karsch welcomes the opportunity to recover the past with Karin, but fails to do so, and Achim merely wants to confirm his own official image as a communist hero. The wilful blindness of the West Germans in denying the existence of East Germany threatens the reality of Karsch's experience to the point where he is obliged to assert it publicly. The style is terse and pointed, and there is some amusing, ironical description of the absurdities of communist officiousness: 'The obese, stern youth who ordered Karsch out of the dance café for leading the lady in the American manner. The photographer who lost his professional licence because his exploding flashlight bulb has made a member of the government faint dead away....' The photographer, as he applies for the return of his licence each month, insists that the flashlight is a product of East and not West Germany.

The author upholds his point, that the Germans are victimising each other, although Karsch's disgruntled insistence on the validity of the DDR and the propagandist answers he receives, can make one feel like saying: 'a plague on *all* your houses!' Mr Johnson's admirers will no doubt disagree. (p. 307)

> *Maurice Capitanchik, "Tellers All," in* The Spectator, *Vol. 223, No. 7367, September 6, 1969, pp. 307-08.**

HAMIDA BOSMAJIAN

"The place where I come from no longer exists," says Gesine Cresspahl, the narrative consciousness of Uwe Johnson's *Jahrestage, Days of the Year,* or *Anniversaries.* She is referring to the fictional town of Jerichow in the province of Mecklenburg, the point of origin for her awareness and memory.... [Her] thoughts return to the provincial microcosm with mixed feelings of desire and rejection. Desire arises because it was there that the possibilities of love existed, whose denial is made bearable in the present by mythical screens and memory filters as well as by hopeful projections. Nevertheless, Gesine knows that the denial of love is the origin of the guilt-generating chain of betrayals that bind each day of her present. The childhood world was not a paradise; rather, it was the time and place where the child was initiated into the betrayal of love, a betrayal that may be repeated in adult life both in the private and familial as well as in the political sphere. Deprivations urge wish projections which inevitably become catastrophic as the individual

tries to realize them. The adult cannot escape the original landscape of betrayal, no matter how far he or she may move.... Gesine Cresspahl, in search of the morally neutral Switzerland where she would be free of guilt, moves from East Germany to West Germany and finally ends up in New York, only to discover that, as the geographical boundaries expanded, guilt likewise expanded to global proportions. The human desire to escape the condition of guilt remains, and for this reason Gesine wants to return in the summer of 1968 to the Eastern bloc country of Czechoslovakia in order to "do something there," presumably to work for the dream of a socially just and free society. It remains to be seen if such work can be done without betrayal and guilt. (pp. 115-16)

Johnson's *Jahrestage* is an anatomy of the melancholy of our condition. Gesine's narrative seems on the surface cool, understated, and detached. She does not indulge in apocalyptically decorative allegories and allusions; instead she turns to the reasonable and dignified voice of the *New York Times,* which records the daily dull round of violence and betrayal in private, public, and global events, demanding only that they must be "fit to print." As present and future readers of the novel work themselves through that dull violent year, 1967-68 may seem to have been an exciting time when the Vietnam War was contended and defended, when racial and political unrest disturbed the aims of law and order, when Martin Luther King and Robert F. Kennedy were shot, when "speed" killed, and when the Czechoslovakian dream of a socialist democracy came to a halt on 20 August, the date Johnson assigns to the end of the fourth volume. Gesine's dream will be lost in historical ambiguities, will be banished to the dark side of utopia. Secretive and ambiguous, Gesine never states her political intentions clearly. Expressing her commitment through declarative utterance, the challenge and the boast are not for her. She speaks with many tongues, literally because she is a foreign correspondent in a New York bank and also because she is an ironic self, consciously ironic and ironic in terms of her repressions and desires, of which she may or may not be aware. Like her creator, Johnson, Gesine Cresspahl is caught in a plurality of possible lives. (p. 116)

[Johnson's] novels are until now a unified statement about the alternatives of East and West. In a sense, *Jahrestage* is a culmination of that vision in terms of geography, chronology, characterization, theme, and style. Gesine Cresspahl—the adoptive sister, friend, and beloved of Jakob in *Speculations*—lives in New York where she maintains contact with various other characters of Johnson's fictions. The ties between Europe and America remain intricate and are enhanced by technological communications so that Gesine's expanded world is also a global village. Further intricacies are developed through the interrelationships of the private self with public events in the past, present, and future. Gesine's chronicle records three types of events: the past, as she lived it, as it was told to her, and as she interprets it; the daily record of the *New York Times,* "the blind mirror of the day," which records the seemingly haphazard dull round of daily violence as history is on the run, eventually involving Gesine's private life through the Czechoslovakian experiment in democracy; the daily record of Gesine's life at the bank, her relationship with her daughter Marie, her friendship with D. E., her hopes for the future. All three chronicles interrelate and reveal to the reader a consciousness caught between past and future in the hairbreadth moment of the present. (pp. 119-20)

Gesine's rational goal for writing her chronicle is to become aware of repetition-compulsion and thereby control it. Also, she wants to help her daughter Marie understand the past and protect her from repeating it. This rational intent is undercut in many ways. The principle of repetition and repression is inherent in the process of recollecting and recording. Gesine selects and chooses; but she often remains unaware of the analogous moments between present and past of which the reader is aware. Furthermore, she seeks to justify herself to Marie so that Marie will have a loving and nonaccusatory memory of her mother, a memory Gesine does not have of her own mother. But Marie lives in New York in 1968, and what she hears "is a presentation of possibilities against which she feels herself immune, and in another sense it's just stories to her." . . . Marie's insecure presumptuousness actually prepares her to succumb to the pattern of repetition-compulsion.

Gesine often comes very close to probing the wound of primal pain that led to the construction of protective and abstract screens. She is in the grip of a guilty past whose dead voices communicate to her . . . , and she exemplifies a psychological consciousness that is self-contained and leads, not to a substantial transformation, but only to displacements. Her Eden is the yearning for a secular, communal paradise; it is not an inner state of being. . . .

Historical consciousness is preferable to psychological consciousness because it lends itself more readily to rational ordering and is less painful. Her dream of an adult and free community is the projection of the archaic need to return to the place of origin and shelter, a place that Gesine hardly ever approximated. The point of view of the chronicle is, therefore, in its technical and philosophical aspects an expression of the special problems of the narrator. (p. 121)

Johnson appears in the novel as a lecturer at the American Jewish Congress. In trying to explain current German politics, Johnson fails as miserably as Gesine in her attempts to justify painful memories. . . . Gesine watches Johnson's floundering, and he challenges her: "By the way, who's narrating here, Gesine?" She replies, "Both of us. You can hear it, Johnson." In many difficult moments, she will ask the "comrade writer" (*Genosse Schriftsteller*) to lend her the appropriate words. When thus dramatized, Johnson is as helplessly authentic as Gesine; but, at the same time, the "author's second self," as Wayne Booth calls it in *The Rhetoric of Fiction*, is distant from the novel and fully in control.

The cooperation with the writer as character is one reason for the third person point of view which is maintained even when Gesine would be incapable of it, for instance, in the recollection of her mother's suicide and funeral when Gesine escapes into a severe attack of the flu. While the *I* can emerge at any moment, even in the middle of a sentence, *Jahrestage* is not written in the first person. The third person center of consciousness permits Gesine detachment and objectivity. As she writes about herself as an object, she avoids using the chronicle as a therapeutic outpouring of her private pathologies. But the objectification is also an alienation, an internal alienation between the adult that she is and "the child that I was." (p. 122)

Gesine admits her unreliability: "And I don't trust what I know because it has not always revealed itself in my memory; then, it suddenly appears as a notion. Perhaps memory creates some such sentence that Jakob said, or perhaps said, could have said. When that sentence is finished and present, memory builds the other around it, mixing even the voices of quite different people. I am afraid of that. All of a sudden I converse about a conversation in my thoughts which I did not participate in, and

the only true thing in it is the remembrance of his intonation, the way Jakob talked." . . . Unreliability is also increased in that much of what she tells about the past is second hand. Marie often criticizes her mother with comments like "You can't know that," and she inquires why Gesine always presents the past from her father's and never from her mother's point of view, an inability to empathize that makes Gesine feel guilty and aggressive. (pp. 122-23)

Just as Marie will be clued in [to the truth she seeks] by letters that are written to be read in the future, so the reader, too, will have to do much critical detective work in order to decipher the private and secretive Gesine. (p. 123)

The narrator's language is a language that has been uprooted. Gesine's past is perceived through German, while her present is defined through English translated into German. Her sense of mission for a better future grows as her skill in a new language, Czechoslavakian, increases. As she reads and translates the language of the *New York Times* into German, she makes the news part of her self. Problems of translation, beyond the awkwardness of translating contemporary slang, become overwhelming, even more so if the novel should be translated into French or Italian; for then the effect of Gesine's often Anglicized German would be lost. The relationship of English and German locks the novel into its own peculiar linguistic universe. As Marie loses contact and feeling for her mother's language, she will not learn from her mother's chronicle but will, as Gesine foresees, fall into the same patterns of repetition-compulsion. The tragic sense of *Jahrestage* lies to a great extent in the inability of a historically and politically conscious self to really prevent anything with that consciousness. (pp. 123-24)

Historical consciousness is always motivated by private desires and fears and hence is unreliable. Intellectually, Gesine is fully aware that the construction of systematic causality is an attempt to give meaning and assuage pain and guilt. . . . Yet, like her father [Cresspahl], Gesine emigrates, and, like him, she will return as informed about conditions in the Eastern bloc countries as he was about Nazi Germany. Cresspahl sacrificed his political integrity for his love for [Gesine's mother] Lisbeth, and the novel intimates that Gesine might sacrifice her daughter in some way to her political dream. No matter how conscious she may be of that pattern in retrospect, she cannot see it now. . . . Finally, there emerges in the novel the impossibility of consciousness, in spite of all attempts to gather material, to explore the past, to define the nature of consciousness itself. Genuine consciousness would involve a coalescence of ambiguity on all levels and a simultaneous awareness of these levels, a feat desired but unachieveable by human intelligence and imagination.

The structure of *Jahrestage* has a surface rationality defined by the building blocks of each entry as it is ordered and fixed by the icon of a number. The linear effect of the numbered days of the year is an illusion of progression, for each day is or has the potential of becoming an anniversary that will always come round again. The content of the entries alternates between recollecting the past and recording the present, the majority of entries being triggered by news items from the *New York Times* which universalize the particular. The rhythm of the chronicle, as it relates time past and time present, generally pulsates between the chaos of hopeful or anxious connotations and epiphanic vignettes, whose precise images reverberate directly or analogously with Edenic and demonic connotations.

Those parts of the narrative that Gesine does not understand completely or represses partially are dominated by the chaos of connotations. The past of her parents, lived at a time when secrecy and subtlety were paramount to survival, has been garnered second hand or is recollected by an adult who tries to make sense out of the intimations experienced by herself as a child. Gesine's plans for the future, especially her plans "to start something" in Prague during August of 1968, are similarly imprecise. By not revealing them, she attempts to maintain their uncorrupted potential, whereas direct statement would raise questions as to ends and means within the confines of historical time. The chaos of connotation of the past is associated primarily with an evil time, a time that is to be overcome when a better future is created out of the chaos of present connotations. Herein she is repeating the desire of her father to do the same. Moreover, all present connotations are detours from Gesine's original fall, her experience of death and lack of love, which she ritualistically repeats or perceives in the daily round she seeks to transcend. Such transcendence will, of course, be impossible because she is bound in a secular cycle of time. Her fall was already the consequence of the guilt of her parents, and her hopes for the future are being corrupted by the guilty world of money, the bank, on which she depends for her livelihood. It saps her of life's energy, though she consciously resists the transient and material gratifications of capitalism. Gesine is inevitably manipulated and watched by powers that leave her bewildered even as she tries to manipulate them. (pp. 126-28)

The news item that generates the plot of Gesine's present is casually summarized in the second entry of her chronicle: "The corpse of the American, who did not return to his hotel in Prague last Wednesday evening, was found in the Vltava. Mr. Jordan, 59, was a co-worker of the Jewish auxiliary JOINT. He had left to buy a newspaper." An item among many, this news clip becomes iconic for Gesine, for the Dubcek experiment in socialism and democracy, and for the novel as a whole. The death of the murdered Jew in Prague raises anxieties and hopes, anxieties because of possibly renewed anti-Semitic aggression, and hope because a supposedly closed society publicizes this murder. Much later, after Gesine has begun to subversively work towards her dream, she expresses her tentative hopes in a letter. . . . Yet her dream remains undefined—"what I will perhaps begin this year"—for an unfinished dream retains possibilities. . . . She also posits no program in order to avoid laying the rational foundations upon which the irrational, connotative, and imprisoning walls would be erected. Her only preparation is the study of Czechoslovakian, the language of the future, for a new language always appears at first uncorrupted by time.

But even without the rigidity of reason, Gesine cannot avoid the chaos of connotations. She unconsciously prepares for the catastrophic realization of her dream by casually provoking the attention of those powers that have an interest in her allegiance. She is watched with interest by the Eastern bloc and by the bank, two powers that appear only superficially irreconcilable. Both are founded on economic concepts, both are international, and both lure the human being with the dream of security and freedom while all the while depriving him or her of life-giving energies. Both powers are always present and envelop Gesine's existence. . . . (pp. 135-36)

The power that watches over this world of loveless and dull violence is the collective interest of human power and not a transcendent being. At one point Gesine defines her idea of God by bursting out, "The God, who invented the atom bomb, also shoots the sparrows off the roof." . . . This inversion of the loving father, who cares for the fall of the sparrow, turns all longing for an oneiric home into illusion. The illusion persists also because Gesine is afraid to commit herself to a personal love, for that has always led to deprivation. (pp. 136-37)

The principle that shapes the form and content of *Jahrestage* is the principle of repetition-compulsion with all its comforts and discomforts, its security and nightmare. Time in this novel is, therefore, circular rather than linear; the days do not drop off into nothingness as from a digital clock but recur on the face of the annual clock from 20 August 1967 to 20 August 1968. The numbered dates are iconic, recurring with predictable rationality even though the content of each day will vary. But the dates always bring back the day of her mother's death; the summer of 1945 under Russian occupation will lead to the summer of 1968 when Czechoslovakia will be invaded by the nations of the Warsaw Pact. Gesine, the pawl in the cogwheel of history, is very conscious of the tenacious conservatism in human life and its history; but she counters that conservatism with her dream of community and freedom, of social concern for others combined with the need for personal authenticity. If it could be realized, it would truly be a progressive dream through which the repetition-compulsion towards the nightmare of history could be abolished. Gesine's dream is that of an adult who remembers the pain of childhood, for the dream combines the nurturing and protective environment so necessary for a child with the pleasure felt by the adult over his or her individuated consciousness. (p. 141)

The ultimate irony and pessimism of this novel are finally centered in the realization that Gesine's consciousness can be nothing but illusory and that she betrays herself by believing in it. Unable to reexperience her primal pain and overcome it, she is doomed to recapitulate it in ritualistic acts that perpetuate her guilt. In all this she is so thoroughly human. She is a reflector for us even as we look at her from the elevated position of readers. In her first reference to the *New York Times*, she objectively records a report about a murdered Jew in Prague, and on this objective, hence "rational" event she founds her hope for the future. The murdered Jew will not be redeemed in time as Gesine hopes, and she herself, through the law of repetition-compulsion of which she is rationally aware, will become, in one way or another, a victim to her desire for redemption. (p. 143)

> *Hamida Bosmajian, "To the Last Syllable of Recorded Time: The Dull, Violent World of Uwe Johnson's 'Jahrestage'," in her* Metaphors of Evil: Contemporary German Literature and the Shadow of Nazism, *University of Iowa Press, 1979, pp. 115-43.*

FRANCIS MICHAEL SHARP

In 1979, after a ten-year interruption, the University of Frankfurt revived a special Lectureship in Poetics and invited the writer Uwe Johnson to deliver the first series of lectures. Johnson set about his task in a unique way by focusing on the broad yet concrete circumstances that have influenced his fiction rather than on poetics in the customary sense. Literary and political events are the main topics of the lectures recorded in [*Begleitumstände: Frankfurter Vorlesungen*].

As a schoolboy in eastern Germany during the thirties and forties, Johnson's first formative experiences were dominated by two figures, Hitler and Stalin. Conditioned by the political and social realities which these names determined for millions, Johnson's particular destiny was perhaps even more decisively influenced by an early addiction to reading and literature. Years later at the university in Leipzig, it became apparent that the socialist system was incompatible with the writer that he was to become. . . .

Johnson's lectures will doubtless provide scholars with much useful information for dissertations and articles on his fiction. Yet by choosing to focus on concrete circumstances, he has given the reader a record of broader cultural significance. Through the personal anecdotes and flashbacks, the history of contemporary Germany regains some of the turbulence and vitality that have been muted by passing time.

> *Francis Michael Sharp, in a review of "Begleitum-stände: Frankfurter Vorlesungen," in* World Liter-ature Today, *Vol. 55, No. 2, Spring, 1981, p. 312.*

MARIANNE HIRSCH

Uwe Johnson's most recent and yet unfinished novel, *Anni-versaries,* reveals many of its central concerns within the open-ing pages. It begins with an evocation of the sea which consists of a painstakingly detailed description of the waves, their color, movement and direction. It is a neutral description, devoid of any particular emotional thrust or poetic tone. A simile that describes the small pocket of air formed by the break of the wave as a secret, made and destroyed, first hints at an authorial presence fascinated by the sea's mystery. It is its power, how-ever, that this description brings out most forcefully, the sheer physical power that causes children to topple over, that pulls swimmers further and further out. The sea, with its unceasing ebb and flow motion, suggests permanence. And yet, this mo-tion varies according to the particular environment and, al-though the sea has the potency to link such disparate entities as America and Europe, it cannot overcome differences dictated by the individual locality. Thus the present description (later localized on the New Jersey coast) is interrupted by a preterite evocation of the Baltic Sea where, under similar weather con-ditions, both the waves and their names are different.

The second paragraph of the novel's descriptive beginning con-cerns the small resort village in New Jersey that welcomes neither Blacks nor Jews. The mention of prejudice brings the as yet neutral and objective narrative into the thoughts of an anonymous "she" who establishes a link with the Northern German seaside village of Jerichow in 1933 and wonders, can-not remember, whether Jews were admitted there. The narrator does not identify this figure but reports about her external circumstances, and especially about her neighbors' inability to fix her identity: they call her "Mrs Cresspahl" even though her mail is addressed to a "Miss C.," and probably view her as an Irish Catholic no different from them.

The short verse in dialect that names the protagonist, Gesine Cresspahl, is in itself cryptic and hardly facilitates her iden-tification. Subsequent descriptions of weather and landscape culminate in further associations between New Jersey and Mecklenburg, between the noise of the waves and the sound of war movies. The rapid alternation of places and time levels, the anonymity of the mind that makes these jumps without clarifying the connections, and the mention of unidentified people and plans disorient even further a reader who tries to situate himself within as specific a context as possible. The confusion of tenses, present and preterite, reinforces the sense of a shifting point of view; whereas through most of the passage

the present is used to refer to the day in New Jersey and the past for Germany in the '30's and '40's, we also find such lines as "The sky has been bright for a long time." . . . The mixture of impressionistic description and dry report style is equally disquieting. The mind who provides the locus for the narration in this chapter is, on the one hand, trying to relive a remote childhood state and is actively engaged in the process of reminiscence; on the other hand, however, Gesine seems an almost passive recipient of multiple and perhaps meaningful interrelations between countries and time periods.

In spite of the confusions, the novel might, in this first chapter, seem to be a modern story about the inner life of one character, reported in an interesting combination of stream of conscious-ness, "narrated monologue," and third-person narration. Yet several factors begin to hint at the expansion beyond the limits of psychological fiction that characterizes *Anniversaries*. Two alien voices intrude in italics, one in Mecklenburg dialect, the other in English. They form a counterpoint to the subjective interior monologue passages. So does a paragraph of news reportage about the Israeli war and the New Haven riots. Ge-sine's letter to the city of Rande, written in the first person and not set off by quotation marks, introduces yet another shift in perspective. Moreover, Gesine's musings are characterized by a surprising lack of introspection or self-analysis. . . . [Her] memories are explicitly factual and seem to aim at as exact a reconstruction of past events as possible; dates, for example, play a major role. Gesine herself is identified in her social, more than her private role. (pp. 148-49)

The novel's subtitle, "From the Life of Gesine Cresspahl," as well as the author's description of the book as a "biography of a person" indeed indicate that this is the story of Gesine Cresspahl. Yet we are struck by the multiplicity and multifa-cetedness of that life, by its range and scope. Not only does her story reach from the 1930's to the 1960's—the story of her parents and grandparents even predates her birth in 1933—, but it reaches from Mecklenburg, to Richmond, England, to New York, from the Baltic to the English Channel and to the Atlantic. All of these factors must be included in the depiction of her life. The narration of one day allows for the detailed description of a small New Jersey village and for evocations of train journeys in 1941 and 1952. It seems to demand a discussion of the Israeli-Jordanian front and the New Haven riots. Gesine herself almost disappears behind the range of multiple evocations with their complex interconnections. Thus the inner life of Gesine is not the sole focus of the novel. Neither separate nor unified, the individual life becomes a "crossroads" that occasions the panoramic depiction of a world and a half-century. (p. 150)

Gesine can concentrate neither on one moment or one place; her life provides the meeting ground for most of the century's important events and she seems condemned to live that meet-ing, on one level or another, during every day of her life. . . . The exploration of the past does more than to explain the present; it assumes a centrality of its own, competing, at every point, with the description of Gesine's comparatively unevent-ful present existence. . . . [*Anniversaries* creates a] depth, both spatial and temporal, which transcends the psychology of the single protagonist. The realization of these multiple interde-pendencies within the individual life enables Johnson to render, through the biography of one person, the history of our century as well as the portrait of Jerichow and New York. . . . [*An-niversaries* supersedes the single vision through several] tech-niques: chronological arrangement which is interrupted by recurring spatial motifs, fragmentation, juxtaposition, different kinds of print.

Johnson carefully selects (or constructs) his characters. This multiplicity can be rendered not only because Gesine's life has been deeply affected by the crucial historical events of the times, because she has been subjected to the Nazi regime, the Second World War, the division of East and West, the confrontation of Europe and America, but also because . . . Gesine's life is directed toward those events, rather than toward her own self. Her experiences in wartime and post-war Germany, both East and West, have taught her . . . to accept fragmentation, disjunction and alienation simply as conditions of life. Her quest is not . . . to find her own central place in the chaotic multiplicity, to understand her responses and roles, but rather to live responsibly, by understanding and charting the events that shape the lives of her parents, her own life, and that of her daughter. (pp. 150-51)

Critics have noted a much greater ease and confidence in this novel than in *Jakob* and the other early novels; Johnson's questions about fiction as a mode of cognition seem less tortured; a story and a continuity are easier to find. . . . In spite of its pronounced emphasis on time, rather than space, *Anniversaries* does emerge as an intriguing panorama of urban life in New York. The diachronic narrative is interspersed with chapters about different aspects of the city: its subways and buses, its telephone service, its different noises, its crime and its bugs. These synchronic *tableaux* give the book a richly textured surface that enacts the surface of urban life and renders the most common sights interesting, almost exotic. (pp. 151-52)

Additional elements of the city—drugs, crimes, inhabitants killed in Vietnam, fires, Mayor Lindsay—intrude by means of the newspaper that Gesine reads daily and from which daily quotations appear in the text.

The paper itself relates Gesine to the city, and the city to the world. The daily segments from the *New York Times* ground Gesine's individual story in a broader context; they introduce a public voice that relates the political and social background against which her daily life is situated. . . . The *New York Times* introduces not only breadth but authority, claiming, as it does, to include "all the news that's fit to print." Gesine's wavering relationship to the *Times*, her questions about the paper's supposed and perhaps actual omniscience and impartiality, and her characterization of the *Times* as [a] tough and experienced old aunt provide some of the most complex passages of the novel. It is the *Times*, after all, that circumscribes Gesine's apprehension and judgement of all the events that influence her life but which she cannot experience directly. (pp. 152-53)

[The book's title] refers to the connection between present and past, to the anniversary that is made present through its observance. In the repeated juxtapositions of past and present, connections emerge that are not always transparent. Thus we relate the antisemitism of the 1930's with racism in the 60's, or news about Vietnam with stories about concentration camps. The extent and seriousness of such comparisons are difficult to determine because, as in *Speculations about Jakob,* the separate elements within the novel's montage structure assert their proper individuality above their place in the configuration as a whole. Yet it is the discovery of such connections that constitutes the major thrust of *Anniversaries*. Thus, the book is a history in the private as well as the public sense; we must remember that the German word "Geschichte" refers both to "story" and "history." . . .

As the rendition of her life becomes a daily event for Gesine, she makes explicit the importance of the past in all our lives. While in the book's first pages, Gesine was the passive meeting ground of different time levels, she subsequently becomes the agent of remembrance and relationship, so as to uncover the meaning of such connections as her mind made by the sea. . . . [The] book emphasizes the necessity of an informed remembrance, of keeping the past in the foreground so that we might learn from it. Awareness is the only possible stance in this complex world. . . . (p. 153)

The title *Anniversaries* points not only to the past, but also to the future. The repetition of events in our memory will continue into the future. Only if we ward off forgetting, if we make a conscious effort to preserve and to understand the past, can we ensure that that repetition will be meaningful, because then it will be conscious and understood.

It is Gesine's daughter, Marie, who presents the impulse for her mother's narration; it is she who represents the future. It is for Marie that Gesine tapes the record of her past, preserving her turbulent life for posterity. To Marie, the motives and behavior of her ancestors have the didactic value of models and possibilities and the excitement of fiction. . . . (p. 154)

[Gesine's method of uncovering and relating the events of the past] resembles that of the narrators in *Jakob:* in her desire to establish the facts . . . , Gesine is forced to speculate and guess, often even to posit hypothetical occurrences, so as to flesh out her skeletal information, to create out of fragments of hearsay and memory a story that is both plausible and close to the truth. . . .

Yet, here again, multiple viewpoints are at work, challenging Gesine's view and pointing to the relativistic and perspectivistic nature of all narration. . . .

It is Gesine's daughter Marie . . . who, besides Gesine, has the major role in the narrative process. (p. 156)

As in *Speculations about Jakob,* the truth that is the object of the book's search concerns, to a large degree, people who are dead, periods that are remote. The story itself is a complex one with important political and personal implications. Memory is fragmentary, information full of gaps, yet it is a full picture that Gesine and Marie seek to construct. . . . Their job is not simply to reconstruct specific events, but to organize and integrate a multiplicity of half-remembered episodes and people, to build a life. Many of their decisions are subjective and personal. They fill in gaps, speculate about motives, try to iron out contradictions. They come to acknowledge the fallibility of memory, the necessity of invention. . . . They recognize the impulse of memory toward falsification and exploitation, the dubiousness of its truth. . . . Two kinds of remembrance emerge in the novel: Gesine's narrated memories and the intuited, non-verbal leaps to the past that she achieves only at rare moments. Whereas she trusts this latter form of remembrance, she fears narration because it presents, at every point, the risk of inaccuracy and falsehood. Nevertheless, memory has become a vital and necessary part of their lives. Enmeshed in it as they are, they accept its dangers and risks.

It is herein that the difference between *Speculations about Jakob* and *Anniversaries* lies. The former novel reveals a profound suspiciousness of fiction; its narrative shies away from plot and refuses to tell the stories that are suggested throughout. We never find out why Gesine comes back to the East with a gun and a miniature camera, for example. Here all such stories are told; Gesine accepts the fact that we cannot help apprehending our life through the mode of fiction and, although she fights its falsification at every turn, she is ready to accept the subjectivity of all truth. . . . (pp. 157-58)

The narrative process in which Gesine and Marie are engaged reveals increased capacities of fiction as an instrument of knowledge about a complex social and political reality, especially when compared to *Speculations about Jakob*. The paradox which characterizes their activity actually describes the novel as a whole: the necessity to invent a fictional context, to supplement and amend it with factual research so as to get at the real truth about a period which neither report nor invention alone can describe. (p. 159)

As in *Speculations about Jakob,* the single individual remains of central concern; yet the attempt to salvage out of the public arena an individual essence is more and more difficult. The individual must be defined not as an isolated entity, but as the product of social and political forces. Due to her Marxist upbringing, Gesine is always conscious of the events that shape the individual's life and of the stance that the individual can take in response to these events. . . . Gesine's daily reading of the *New York Times* reflects her political upbringing and brings the public events that influence her life into the foreground of the novel. Her response to all public events is not political action but awareness, an awareness that will uncover the external forces that make her what she is. . . . The assault on the individual's integrity by various systems is a theme that runs through most of Johnson's work. In a sense, *Anniversaries* is the search for a place where the individual might be able to exist untainted and integral, to develop to her fullest potential. . . . [The] Johnson character is not easily able to sacrifice her involvement in the world or to divorce herself from those aspects of society that threaten her integrity. Much more than an observer, the Johnson character is very much *in* the world; involvement is necessary on every level of existence. (pp. 160-61)

Most critical commentators of Johnson deplore the development of his work from an experimental fictional medium to the more traditional and less exciting form of the almost straightforward simple story of *Two Views* and the generational chronicle of *Anniversaries* that still seem to believe that an entire society can be captured through fiction. . . . [However], Johnson has not abandoned, but has redefined his questions about fiction and language. . . . Thematically *Anniversaries* constitutes not only a continuity with the earlier experimental novels but broadens their political, historical, and social context. *Anniversaries* presents the history of Europe and the cause for the division that has become our condition. More than lamenting the division of Germany, it moves on to discuss the division of Western civilization that is the result of World War II and that determines our life as well as our fiction.

Both *Speculations about Jakob* and *The Third Book about Achim* border on self-destruction by implicating all forms of "truth-finding" in political corruption and the exploitation of the individual. The fictional process is paralyzed by the political definitions all language and form acquire in a divided yet still connected Germany, i.e. one whose wall is still open. After these first two novels, Johnson had the choice of silence, or of the continuing search for a fictional medium that might be able to overcome the pitfalls he outlined earlier. . . . [Rather than transcending] fiction as insufficient, Johnson attempts to redefine it, because, as *Anniversaries* illustrates, it helps us

learn about ourselves and our world; it helps us to survive. (pp. 163-64)

The unknowability of the individual, his violation by political and social systems, the distortion of memory and the unreliability of language all have been forcefully demonstrated in the early novels. *Anniversaries* does not qualify such conclusions but brings us to the point of being able to live with them or in spite of them. Gesine learns to accept the unknowability of her own past and that of her family, as well as the subjective nature of all truth. In this framework, knowledge can be achieved only through instinctive trust and identification on the one hand, and through conjecture and speculation on the other. (p. 164)

Situated between Germany and America, the narrative is freed from any deep involvement in any particular political system. The juxtaposition of German and English, rather than German and German, moreover liberates the novel from the trap of linguistic impotence and corruption.

It seems, at least in these first three volumes, that *Anniversaries* presents the possibility of redeeming fiction as an instrument of knowledge and a medium of communication. . . .

When Gesine and Marie collaborate on their story, no rigid hierarchy is maintained: they are talking about their common past, their common ancestors. Their knowledge is equally limited; their judgements are equally valid. Their speculations and ours are based on the laws of plausibility; and not, if it can be avoided, on those of ideology. To render the multiple and public nature of what might seem to be a private and singular existence, Johnson develops a mixed fictional form that he agrees to call a political novel; the story of an individual is thus already the history of a collective group. . . . (p. 165)

Not only is *Anniversaries* open toward the circumstances of our political reality but it is open formally as well. . . . It is ultimately the reader who is invited to define the connection between 1933 and 1967, between Germany and America. He must participate in the decisions Gesine finds so difficult to make. The dialogue form of the novel includes the reader as well as Marie and the other voices. In this respect, Marie serves as a model reader: she is suspicious of contrivance, discriminating enough to insist on difference as well as similarity. The novel's first paragraph suggests the uniqueness of all that might seem related or equal; the Baltic is different from the Atlantic. Marie is conscious of difference; she is careful in her judgment, yet deeply involved in a story that is told for her benefit. The usefulness of the narrative for a future generation is clearly demonstrated in the novel itself. . . . (p. 166)

Here, as in Johnson's earlier novels, the individual has the role of a spy: standing between different systems, different time periods, different languages, standing between "alternative realities," the individual experiences relativism in a most personal manner. In serving both systems, the individual would be annihilated. Spying to get at the truth, yet realizing that each truth is relative to the position of each observer, the individual must accept the absence of truth, even while continuing to spy, as the marginal position dictates. The activity of spying is as essential as the necessity to avoid being coopted by any particular system. Johnson's protagonists are condemned to be perpetual outsiders; they have, like Cresspahl, an excuse that relieves them of responsibility and that maintains for them a core of inviolability. (p. 167)

The epic task Johnson has undertaken is a difficult one in an era no longer suited to the epic mentality, an era which has, perhaps, gone beyond the mentality of fiction as well. . . . The competing planes of the novel lead Gesine and Marie more and more to immerse themselves in the creation of their history, at the expense of their own lives. Fictionmaking takes the place of living; tape recorders replace the human voice; mother and daughter become part of a larger mythic order but no longer have time to enjoy their friends and their neighborhood. Their compensations, however, are not as much personal as they are communal. (pp. 167-68)

> *Marianne Hirsch, "Anniversaries': Invention Which Becomes a Kind of Truth," in her* Beyond the Single Vision: Henry James, Michel Butor, Uwe Johnson, *French Literature Publications Company, 1981, pp. 148-68.*

G. P. BUTLER

Essentially, Johnson's narrative strategies, and therefore the kinds of input he doubtless expects from his readership, have changed very little over the years. He tells his tales in scattered fragments, splinters ("Splittertechnik", one critic called it), leaving it largely to the studious public to piece them together.

And that is one of the troubles with his latest book [*Jahrestage 4*]: few but the studious and leisured, having reached what appears to be the end, are likely to be able to start again—at all, let alone at the author's own creative pace. Plenty of the bits and pieces that go to make up *Jahrestage* are eminently rereadable; but the whole is a huge, intricate, unshapely conglomerate, much of it already unavoidably dated, and much no less in need of annotation, glossaries, an index, than Grass at his most cryptic. . . .

The first instalment of *Jahrestage* sub-titled "Aus dem Leben von Gesine Cresspahl", appeared in 1970. . . . Two further volumes were expected, but *Jahrestage 3* (1973) gave the lie to its immediate predecessor by repeating the announcement that there was to be one more "and final part". The ten-year silence which followed fuelled doubts about *Jahrestage* that had arisen almost at the outset, even among the author's admirers. Would it ever be completed? Could it be? *Jahrestage 4* effectively confirms these doubts. A sequel is not said to be in the offing; the work is now in a sense complete; and yet there appears to be no compelling reason why we should not at some stage learn still more about the life and times of Gesine Cresspahl. True, by page 1891, the end of the present volume, most of her German friends, relatives and known acquaintances have died, as has her prospective husband, "D. E.," or so it seems. But the chronological entries into which the whole is divided, the "days of the year" that give all the jottings and recollections some semblance of structure, cease on August 20, 1968; Gesine was still only 35; and although she was due in Prague the following day and may therefore have come to a sticky end, it is just as possible that she didn't. . . .

Those with a similar background to Gesine's—a carpenter's only child, born and bred in a small Baltic town in Hitler's Germany, in the part that became Ulbricht's, and now settled in New York—will clearly be best able to judge the accuracy of her impressions, the authenticity both of the experiences she herself underwent (at home and at school; before, during and after the war; as a student; as a single parent and refugee) and

of the fates which befell her contemporaries and elders. To *all* readers who persevere, however, this fitful account of part-imagined lifetimes will at least have not merely the ring of truth, however harsh, but a remarkable power to excite and revive attention, to move, perhaps even to shock.

Some of the cast of hundreds are rogues or villains, most are victims—men, women, children galore, gravely damaged if not destroyed by powers beyond their control, in the Third Reich, in East Germany, in the Midlands, in Harlem. Little by little, if only for the benefit of her child, Marie, born in 1957—and primarily in reply to the girl's promptings and probing, Gesine reveals multitudinous details of the Cresspahls' sombre history, concentrating on what happened, and why, from the 1920s until 1961, when mother and daughter reached the United States. Marie is naturally more *au fait* with what has taken place since then, and whatever curiosity or concern she may feel about such recent times tends therefore to be less personal—not impartial but less family-orientated, broader. The death of Robert Kennedy, for instance, fills her with dismay. Gesine meanwhile, having worked for some years in first one bank then another, has been selected by her current employer to go to Czechoslovakia, to help arrange a dollar loan to the government of the day. And meanwhile Marie has become an enthusiastic New Yorker. Johnson's ideal readers must know, *inter alia*, their way about town.

The massive material in which the shards of Gesine's past are embedded is by contrast so heterogeneous and so arbitrarily presented as to bemuse. That's life? Well, it's certainly a large part of life as reflected in the media, in particular in the *New York Times* from the one August to the next, and very instructive it all is, too. No newspaper can ever have played a greater part, been so extensively quoted and assessed, in a single work of literature; and if you know where to look, you can brush up on many of the public worries and calamities that preoccupied people in the 1960s and still won't go away entirely. A selection from the range—of themes, leading figures, dire realities—illustrates what persists and what has faded: international aggression, political mendacity, racial prejudice, criminal violence; Dubček, Dutschke, Che Guevara, LBJ, Martin Luther King, Heinrich Lübke, Axel Springer, F. J. Strauss; the Berlin wall, what happened in the gulf of Tonking, the Kiesinger/Brandt coalition . . .

Clearly therefore, despite its lighter moments, its superb (and for the most part defensible) waspishness, its grand, ingenious design, and the linguistic subtlety, versatility, and inventiveness which are among Johnson's hallmarks—despite all this and more besides, there is no likelihood that *Jahrestage* will wear well. It is a highly allusive work, addressed much of the time to insiders; and while, for instance, today's readers may appreciate digs at John Steinbeck or Norman Mailer and applaud the broadsides discharged at Hans Magnus Enzensberger, there can already be no one person, far less a group, to whom all the names and the nudges and the invisible ink will yield their meaning. The *explicateurs de texte* are in for a field-day . . . if the text truly survives. If it is much respected and little read, embalmed in academic libraries as a remarkable but increasingly inaccessible relic, no one should be surprised. And yet: where else has, for example, the immediate post-war scene in a small Russian-occupied community been so sharply evoked? Where in fact, take or leave the vivid vignettes, the intriguing excursuses, the polyglot chat, is there anything to compare with this panoramic montage of reported and invented days not long gone by?

G. P. Butler, "Miseries of the Moment," in The Times Literary Supplement, *No. 4202, October 14, 1983, p. 1142.*

HANS-BERNHARD MOELLER

A decade after publishing *Jahrestage III*—and less than half a year before his untimely death apparently from a heart attack in early March 1984—Johnson offers the fourth and final installment of the four-volume Cresspahl saga. . . . Its diarylike narrative units, on the level of story sequences, describe the life of Gesine Cresspahl, age forty, and her daughter Marie in Manhattan from 20 June to 20 August 1968. But its real focus, on the level of memory, are Gesine's experiences in Mecklenburg, East Germany, her school and early university career during the 1940s and early 1950s prior to her *Republikflucht* to the Federal Republic. Relatives and friends in local administration (Cresspahl, Sr.), farm management, mates at school and even Gesine herself are treated as pawns, placed under surveillance and arrest and eventually destroyed. *Jahrestage IV* projects a harsh view of the Democratic Republic.

Does this East German trauma lie at the root of the "involuntary imaginary dialogues in the mind of heroine Gesine . . . of people in her past, . . . persons turning toward me . . . today"? Ultimately, of course, the root of the matter is the social, political and historical self-psychoanalysis of Uwe Johnson, the Mecklenburg Proust. Differences in comparison to Proust are no less telling than similarities. Johnson seeks to distance the reader by playfully defining, in italicized passages, "Wer erzählt hier eigentlich, Gesine. Wir beide." Moreover, he blends the private with the public spheres. German history is constantly present. Politics affect Gesine's personal life, whether in the Mecklenburg province, urban Düsseldorf or metropolitan New York.

This interdependence invalidates the criticism of both those who attempted to find in *Jahrestage* oases of provinciality and those who misconstrued the tetralogy as a return to the nineteenth-century family novel. Instead, Johnson is both creating and criticizing a tragic quest for the perfect society, the "moralische Schweiz." . . . The novel's conclusion leaves open the question of whether Gesine will survive her visit to Prague on 20 August 1968, which coincides with the Russian invasion. But death colors its final entries.

Nevertheless, *Jahrestage IV* still demonstrates the linguistic juggler Johnson, whose neologisms include *Schädelschrumpfer* and *Stadtbahn der Luft* (for "commuter airline"). Johnson, the gentle ironic German, will be missed as much as will the Brechtian-Proustian novelist and the politico-cultural transient who now has crossed his ultimate border. (pp. 406-07)

Hans-Bernhard Moeller, in a review of "Jahrestage IV: Aus dem Leben von Gesine Cresspahl," in World Literature Today, *Vol. 58, No. 3, Summer, 1984, pp. 406-07.*

G. P. BUTLER

Based on events which took place when Uwe Johnson was a student in the German Democratic Republic in the early 1950s, *Ingrid Babendererde,* his first novel, has been glimpsed in public on various occasions over the years—most recently in the second of his "Frankfurt lectures" (*Begleitumstände,* 1980); but once the manuscript had been turned down, in 1956-7, both

in East Germany and by Suhrkamp, Johnson evidently made no further attempt to have it published as a whole. The present version—said to be the fourth, the one rejected by the publishers—was among the papers found in his house at Sheerness when he died there last year. . . .

The story is fairly simple, as Johnson stories go, although, like most of them, it takes some piecing together. Set almost entirely in the author's favourite part of Mecklenburg in 1953, it evokes the oppressiveness, particularly for youngsters, of Stalinist Germany in full swing, and shows why on the eve of sitting their school-leaving examination (the *Reifeprüfung* of the subtitle), Klaus Niebuhr and the eponymous Ingrid have little option but to flee the country. . . .

It's an eerie business, after reading Johnson from *Mutmassungen* (1959) to *Jahrestage* (1970-83), to see now how it all began; and it will be an intriguing one to assess just how much these once-neglected beginnings and their celebrated successors have in common. At a thematic level, for instance, *Ingrid Babendererde* is bound to throw light on some of the many references in subsequent work to the Niebuhrs, the Babendererdes, *et al.* And for students of Johnson's stylistic development (or lack of it—he was a remarkably precocious writer, no more than twenty-two when he wrote the novel and already quite unmistakably the Uwe Johnson of 1959-83), the text is of course discovered treasure. But that being said, even the rebuff which ultimately persuaded him to lay it up in lavender is not hard to understand. To have approached East German publishers in the politico-cultural climate of the time seems, at least with hindsight, naive; after all, the lakeland charms of the Güstrow district which deservedly get so much attention— the yachting, the chatting, the inconsequential small-town existence which help to make Johnson's picture memorable— serve perhaps primarily to highlight the unacceptable face of those publishers' masters' regime. The central messages, therefore, are clear enough . . . , and must have been unexceptionable, indeed unremarkable, in most Western eyes: Klaus and Ingrid choose a kind of freedom denied to them "over there", and their choice is persuasively presented. The presentation overall, however, while it demonstrates that a highly unusual talent was emerging, seems likely to have had a bearing on Peter Suhrkamp's eventual veto. True, his only explicit reservations, according to Johnson, concerned the story's "lack of world", which appears to mean its strongly regional flavour, the provincialism that is in fact one of its merits—though hardly a commercial asset.

But naturally no one then was used, as we now more or less thankfully are, to Johnson's idiosyncratic ways with language (phrasing, spelling, punctuation, lexis); no one had learnt to savour his persuasive obliqueness, and even the best-disposed publishers might have been deterred by the seemingly perverse, deliberately complex structuring of the newcomer's narrative: *Ingrid Babendererde* is divided into four sections (each prefaced, and the fourth also concluding, with an italicized microsection) made up of sixty-one subsections (in roman), and the resultant bittiness, the darting to and fro (even though, as Johnson worked out, sixty-one *is* a prime number) will never be a selling point.

Of the cast of forty-odd who act out this piece of recent reality, most are lightly sketched—parents or guardians, teachers and taught, workaday folk and officialdom—and this can engender impatience, as so often with Johnson, to see more of them.

Even the fuller-blown principals, the self-possessed, almost dashing young hero and his right-minded, fun-loving, distinctly winsome companion, may arouse some such response: the story of their preoccupations and predicaments rings true, but the ring is muffled by mannerism, by an apparent unwillingness to tell it, or enough of it, like it was.

Nevertheless, all disappointments of this kind are in effect no more than a back-handed compliment; none diminishes the pleasure felt at seeing this work in print at last, and none the budding author's achievement. How might you have fared in East Germany the year Stalin died? It is a question still worth pondering, and *Ingrid Babendererde* provides a partial but well-founded and telling answer.

> *G. P. Butler, "For Personal Freedom," in* The Times Literary Supplement, *No. 4305, October 4, 1985, p. 1114.*

Garrison Keillor

1942-

(Born Gary Edward Keillor) American novelist, essayist, scriptwriter, and short story writer.

Keillor is best known for his highly popular and critically acclaimed novel, *Lake Wobegon Days* (1985). He had earlier gained recognition for his humorous stories and essays, most of which first appeared in *The New Yorker,* and for his role as the creator and host of the weekly public radio program "A Prairie Home Companion." Based in St. Paul, Minnesota, "A Prairie Home Companion" evokes the family-oriented radio programs that were popular during the 1930s and 1940s through its blend of music and comedy presented in a warm, relaxed format. Following its debut in 1974, "A Prairie Home Companion" gradually attracted a small but devoted local audience, and in 1980 it was syndicated nationwide. The program received the George Foster Peabody Award for Broadcasting in 1981. *Lake Wobegon Days* evolved from "News from Lake Wobegon," a segment of "A Prairie Home Companion" which Keillor always introduces with the words, "It's been a quiet week in Lake Wobegon, my hometown." With the publication of *Lake Wobegon Days,* Keillor's reputation as a first-rate storyteller and humorist became firmly established.

Like the town depicted in Keillor's radio monologues, *Lake Wobegon Days* is inhabited by a variety of characters, including Mayor Clint Bunsen and Father Emil of the Church of Our Lady of Perpetual Responsibility, who are described in a fond yet frequently sarcastic tone. The book is presided over by a persona who sometimes rebels against the strict conventions of the predominantly Scandinavian Lutheran Wobegonians but retains an affectionate respect for them. Many critics place Keillor's satire and droll observations in the tradition of such prominent American humorists as Mark Twain, Robert Benchley, and particularly James Thurber, whose works, like *Lake Wobegon Days,* provide a humorous yet incisive portrait of midwestern American life.

Keillor is also the author of *Happy to Be Here: Stories and Comic Pieces* (1981), which one reviewer described as "folksy reminiscences which may veer into farce now and then but at the same time demand to have their warm, real centers taken seriously." This duality is exemplified by "Shy Rights: Why Not Pretty Soon?," a manifesto that parodies the style and rhetoric of social activist groups while gently elucidating the agonies of shyness.

(See also *Contemporary Authors,* Vols. 111, 117.)

DAVID BLACK

Every Saturday from five p.m. to seven p.m. central daylight time, "A Prairie Home Companion" is broadcast live to 130 radio stations across the country, reaching an audience of about 600,000 that is growing weekly. The show is a mulligan stew

Photograph by Jim Brandenburg

of programming: old jazz; Twenties and Thirties pop tunes; gospel music and ballads; Balkan songs; fiddle, dulcimer and autoharp solos; yodeling; and novelty tunes like "The Teddy Bears' Picnic," the theme from the Fifties kids show, "Big John and Sparky."

Interspersed with the music are reports from the fictional town of Lake Wobegon, Minnesota, home of the Church of Our Lady of Perpetual Responsibility, the Wally "Old Hardhands" Bunsen Memorial Field, the Chatterbox Cafe, the Sidetrack Tap, where you can get deep-fried fish lips, Bob's Bank, whose motto is "Neither a borrower nor a lender be," and the Fearmonger Shop, which warns: "Most people think that deadly snakes don't like cold climates. And they're right, because when it's cold, deadly snakes head for warm places . . . homes, for example. In the home, the favorite resting place for deadly snakes—as all of us have known since childhood—is at the foot of the bed under the covers". (pp. 8, 13)

The man responsible for this blend of Sherwood Anderson, Spike Jones and Thomas Pynchon is Garrison Keillor, a bearded . . . Minnesotan with a forlorn, owlish look. Keillor invented Lake Wobegon in the late Sixties when he was running a morning show on Minnesota Public Radio. But the idea for "A Prairie Home Companion" came to Keillor in 1974, when he was in Nashville covering the Grand Ole Opry's last broadcast from the old Ryman Auditorium for the *New Yorker.*

The show is an electronic version of the turn-of-the-century practice of gathering around the parlor piano on a Saturday night. It has developed a cult following and seems destined to break through to a mass audience—a dangerous kind of success for a low-key, intimate program. . . .

Chances are the show will survive as long as it remains faithful to the spirit of Powdermilk Biscuits, which, said Keillor, "are made by Norwegian bachelor farmers, so you know they're not only good for you, they're pure mostly." After all, the problems faced by **"A Prairie Home Companion"** are the same ones facing Powdermilk Biscuits. "Those of you who are somewhat removed from Minnesota occasionally write in to ask us about Powdermilk Biscuits," Keillor recently said on a show. "'Are they real?' you ask. Of course they're real. It's just that the Powdermilk Biscuit Company has a distribution problem because it only has a '57 Ford pickup truck, and Einer (the owner) refuses to go into debt, so he won't buy another truck until he sells more biscuits, which he can't do because he only has one truck, and since Einer refuses to stay away from home overnight, it pretty much eliminates the East and West coasts. . . ."

But the spirit of **"A Prairie Home Companion"** doesn't have to range far to hit home. In some hidden chamber of our hearts, most of us, no matter where we live, are citizens of Lake Wobegon, where "all the women are strong, all the men good-looking and all the children above average." (p. 13)

David Black, "Live from Wobegon," in Rolling Stone, Issue 348, July 23, 1981, pp. 8, 13.

KIRKUS REVIEWS

Keillor's parodies, satires, and whimsies . . . rarely provide big laughs or Perelmanic dazzle; but they do have an affectionate, easygoing, back-home quality that makes for a nice change from the clenched-up sparring of most New York-based humorists. (Keillor is Minnesota all the way.) Least distinctive of the 30 pieces collected [in **Happy to Be Here: Stories and Comic Pieces**] are obvious send-ups of trends in jargon and lifestyle. . . . Elsewhere, however, Keillor develops a more satisfying double-joke, as in **"Shy Rights: Why Not Pretty Soon?"**—which lampoons gay-liberation rhetoric while maintaining the ever-apologetic tone of the minority in question ("Discrimination against the shy is our country's No. 1 disgrace in my own personal opinion"). And there are pieces which derive welcome texture from a literary-parody element—like the overlong but endearing **"Jack Schmidt, Arts Administrator"** (à la Sam Spade). But the special stuff here, if not the funniest, is Keillor's just-slightly-off-kilter Americana: folksy reminiscences which may veer into farce now and then but at the same time demand to have their warm, real centers taken seriously. **"My North Dakota Railroad Days,"** for instance, generates train nostalgia while simultaneously skewering it. And best of all are three sweetly addled evocations of early/small-time radio. . . . Mostly minor-league humor, . . . but with enough one-of-a-kind touches (including a few likably autobiographical snippets) to rise just a little above the crowd. (pp. 1386-87)

A review of "Happy to Be Here," in Kirkus Reviews, Vol. XLIX, No. 21, November 1, 1981, pp. 1386-87.

D. KEITH MANO

[Keillor's] kind derision operates the way a voice stress analyzer might: it is a knowing of some special, audible sort. Though you will find the short tale and the arcade-brilliant divertissement in this collection [Happy to Be Here], parodies are his territorial water. Keillor has a high pass filter on his pen: it can erase background noise and leave the essential speech pattern clear. **Happy to Be Here** includes a parody of sci-fi and one of anthropological jargon: of Richard Brautigan and Life and little-magazine writing. Keillor will spoof material that I, with my Nerf-deaf ear, didn't know had any organizing style: corporate report, transit system pamphlet, battle comic-book. His wit is so reactive that it turns even claptrap into a goddam genre.

Parody: not satire. Satire, if I've read the brochure right, "usually implies moral judgment or corrective purpose." There is no anger in this attack: nor any righteous underfur. Keillor doesn't bother to affix blame. You feel, rather, a joy in the sheer diverseness of voices. . . .

Keillor can handle short-form writing better than your tax accountant. But a parodist counter-punches and must adjust to style in the opponent. This may make his work seem assistant, on loan. In fact, Keillor has assumed a defensive persona: I-who-couldn't-write-my-big-novel-have-done-this. From his introduction: "I still think . . . it is more worthy in the eyes of God and better for us as a people if a writer make three pages sharp and funny about the lives of geese than to make three hundred flat and flabby about God or the American people." That pronouncement itself could lose some weight: the logic is covered with stretch-marks. And Keillor should know better. By nature, he has implied, anything written about God or America must be turgid. This is a prejudice, not a rational distinction. Which leads me to consider Keillor as paradigmatic New Yorker stylist.

The New Yorker pose is one of insouciant, snuff-taking detachment. Yes, liberal attitudes underlie that sophisticated lethargy, but no effort will be made to inculcate them. Effort is rather indecent: maybe dangerous. The New Yorker—from which most of this collection has been reprinted—expresses best our native distaste for fanaticism. And the surest specific against fanaticism is particularity. Find individual, idiosyncratic voices enough and you may prevent a mad consensus from forming. E pluribus plures: divide and enervate: Keillor and The New Yorker isolate, then announce the small differences that fragment national life. Naturally a three-hundred-page book which might generalize America or God must be fat and full of flab. The lowest common denominator is just that: low, also common. By definition no majority can be moral: or trusted: or wise.

But, within those philosophical limits, Keillor is damned brilliant. There aren't two weak pieces among the 29 collected here. . . . Garrison Keillor is so derivative that he might well be one of our most original writers.

D. Keith Mano, "Here at the New Yorker," in National Review, Vol. XXXIII, No. 25, December 11, 1981, p. 1492.

ROY BLOUNT, JR.

In 1933, wrote James Thurber, a humorist tended to be plagued by "the suspicion that a piece he was working on for two long days was done much better and probably more quickly by

Robert Benchley in 1924.'' Today, a humorist may feel that way about Keillor. Like Benchley's, Keillor's best stuff is clean (in the sense that lines are clean), down to earth, exquisitely good-hearted, *highly* ludicrous and as labored as nitrous oxide. His stuff is more cerebral than Benchley's, though, and *spiritually* more interesting, and . . . even harder to describe.

Keillor's weekly National Public Radio show, **"A Prairie Home Companion,"** is *impossible* to describe. Everyone I have met who has heard it has either been dumbfounded by it or addicted to it, or both. The same is true of Keillor's prose [collected in *Happy to Be Here*]. . . . (p. 12)

Keillor's stuff is calmly, acrobatically droll, yet makes no bones about its fondness for decency and its distaste for bullies. There is more heart than jocularity in his **"My North Dakota Railroad Days,"** whose narrator says of a rank exploiter: "May his soul be forever tormented by fire and his bones be dug up by dogs and dragged through the streets of Minneapolis. . . ." . . .

Keillor's sympathy goes out readily, even in some circumstances to chicken biters, and he sides with the vagabond; but his feet are on the ground. In one of his several baseball pieces the new manager of a losing team observes: "It seemed pointless to berate players for mistakes that stemmed from deepseated attitudes, to tell them to respond to grounders logically and not emotionally." Another one, **"The New Baseball,"** foresees that "outfielders . . . will be free as antelope, roaming the farther regions for fly balls or, as the case may be, not for fly balls, the ball itself having changed." Yet another, **"Attitude,"** speaks of how exactly to "spit the expert spit of a veteran ballplayer" after being forgiven a dumb play and reaches this conclusion: "This is *ball,* ladies and gentlemen. This is what it's all about."

The way Keillor plays is *ball.* But not just sportive. **"The Drunkard's Sunday"** is downright grave, but redemptive in the way of high comedy. And the book's last sentence, given all that has come before, is brave and moving in the spirit of Dickens.

A couple of these pieces run on a bit, and nothing in **"The Lowliest Bush a Purple Sage Would Be"** did much for me except the title. But **"Local Family Keeps Son Happy"**—ah!— well, I won't spoil it for you. This book will leave you either dumbfounded or happy—almost *deservedly* happy—to be anywhere. (pp. 12, 18)

Roy Blount, Jr., "Garrison Keillor," in The New York Times Book Review, *February 28, 1982, pp. 12, 18.*

DOUG THORPE

Keillor has a keen ear for parody, and [in *Happy to Be Here* he] makes use of it in unlikely ways, as in the marvelous **"Your Wedding and You"** with its explanation of the "alternative wedding" (only Garry Trudeau's "Doonesbury" has caught this '60s and '70s language as accurately), and in his more recent homage to punk rock in **"Don: The True Story of a Young Person."** Anyone familiar with the more intellectual forms of pop criticism (whether of music or film) will recognize it as a parody of the *Rolling Stone* critic—a parody so good that, for a moment, one is almost convinced the piece is the real thing. . . . (p. 794)

As any rock critic knows, the very notion of analyzing the stuff is a direct violation of the message of the music itself. This doesn't, of course, stop the sort of verbal posturing that Keillor so nicely captures here. Comedian Woody Allen often goes for an easy laugh by inserting various outrageous statements into a parody. . . . Keillor in contrast plays it very close, getting humor not only by the shifts in diction . . . , but also by forcing the reader to pay attention to the small details and even to the very shape of a sentence in order to catch the put-on. "Its roots can be traced to the very origins of rock itself and perhaps even a little bit farther." That "little bit" signals the parody—the rest of it could easily be for real. It's close enough and yet exaggerated enough to be absurd.

The setting and subjects of many of the stories are what fans of the [**"Prairie Home Companion"**] might expect. Except for the political satire (a side of Keillor rarely exhibited on the radio), they are generally midwestern, and celebrate baseball, small towns, "shy rights" ("why not pretty soon?") and, of course, radio. . . .

In **"WLT (The Edgar Era)"** he writes: "Oh the days when radio was strange and dazzling! Even the WLT performers could not quite believe it. To think that their voices flew out as far as Anoka, Stillwater and Hastings!" This is not far from the voice Keillor uses in the liner notes to his record, *A Prairie Home Companion Anniversary Album,* where he compares his show to his memory:

> On the living room floor of my boyhood, I stretched out and heard those old shows for all they were worth. It's seldom I feel that ours matches up, though perhaps if I were eight and listened to this show with my brothers and sisters stretched out beside me, knowing that I had to go to bed when it was over, I'd like it more.

I suspect that not many of Keillor's listeners are eight years old; yet this knowledge of bedtime approaching lingers in all of us. Time for listening to the show is time taken out. Responsibilities are at an end for two hours; it's like the Sunday afternoons of our childhood. And much of the beauty in such an experience . . . lies in our knowledge of its transience. Five o'clock is always nigh.

This may be why my favorite stories in *Happy to Be Here,* and the two that seem closest to the spirit of certain features of Lake Wobegon . . . have little to do with radio. They are the last two stories in the book. The first, the title story, was originally published in the *New Yorker* as **"Found Paradise."** The story is about writing, about the yearning for the quiet country life, and, of course, about our problems in locating paradise and *describing* it once we've been there. It is also, along the way, a fine parody of various latter-day Thoreaus. Out on the farm, the storyteller keeps a journal ("forty-eight animals seen today before lunch, of which all but six were birds, most small and brownish"), and begins to "experience [the being of being]." . . . What he finds (not to spoil the surprise) is what one usually does find if one spends some time on a Minnesota farm during the winter. His "stories" (one paragraph each) begin to sound like *Reader's Digest* condensed versions of E. B. White's essays. And his experiences become equally simple: that hunger for myth and symbol evaporates. . . . To talk about it at all, as in rock criticism, is inherently paradoxical, as the flat, simple statements attempt to suggest: "Found Paradise. I said I would and by God I have. Here it is and it is just what I knew was here all along."

The other story, the last in the book, is called **"Drowning 1954."** It is, again, in part about time, about making one fatal slip and envisioning all of your life suddenly lost: "One misstep! A lie, perhaps, or disobedience to your mother. There were countless men . . . who stumbled and fell from the path—one misstep!—and were dragged down like drowning men into debauchery, unbelief, and utter damnation."

His lie had to do with swimming; the protagonist hated his swim instructor and skipped classes, going instead to the WCCO radio studio in Minneapolis to watch "Good Neighbor Time." Then years later, as the story ends, the narrator watches his own seven-year-old son learning to swim:

> Every time I see him standing in the shallows, working up nerve to put his head under, I love him more. His eyes are closed tight, and his pale slender body is tense as a drawn bow, ready to spring up instantly should he start to drown. Then I feel it all over again, the way I used to feel. I also feel it when I see people like the imperial swimming instructor at the YMCA—powerful people who delight in towering over some little twerp who is struggling and scared, and casting the terrible shadow of their just and perfect selves.

This is close to the voice we hear every week over the radio, and in that last sentence we hear as well some of the perfectionism that makes the show a success. Details are kept to a minimum (what do we really know about the inside of the "Chatterbox Café"?); the voice is personal, reflective; often it is strikingly moral, and equally often it suggests something of the "Wistful Vista" of Fibber McGee. Vulnerable himself, the narrator sees vulnerability everywhere—in shy people, in all that is passing, growing up and growing older. He sees that we can do little to help each other out—even our own defenseless children. Sometimes the best we can do is send messages over the airwaves. Or tell . . . stories. (pp. 795-96)

Doug Thorpe, "Garrison Keillor's 'Prairie Home Companion': Gospel of the Airwaves," in The Christian Century, *Vol. 99, No. 24, July 21-28, 1982, pp. 793-96.*

WALTER GOODMAN

It's more than 10 years since Garrison Keillor began reporting on the goings-on around Lake Wobegon, Minn., on his Saturday evening radio program, **"A Prairie Home Companion."** . . . Now, in *Lake Wobegon Days,* he divulges the history of the Minnesota town that never made it onto any map because the surveyors were drunk. As the state's Governor is supposed to have said in 1980, "Seldom has a town made such a sacrifice in remaining unrecognized for so long."

Mr. Keillor's book begins with an invitingly composed description of one of the less inviting places on the beaten-up track. "A breeze off the lake brings a sweet air of mud and rotting wood, a slight fishy smell, and picks up the sweetness of old grease, a sharp whiff of gasoline, fresh tires, spring dust, and, from across the street, the faint essence of tuna hotdish at the Chatterbox Cafe."

I wish I could report that the rest of the book lived up to that beginning. Unlike the topography of the area, however, this chronicle has its highs and lows. It is probably best read in leisurely takes of a few pages, as they might be delivered by Mr. Keillor on a Saturday evening. There is more here on adolescent pranks, such as the time the narrator threw a juicy tomato at his bending-over sister, and about the pains and pleasures of schooldays than one should have to endure for an extended sitting. Some stretches seem a bit like Penrod redux.

The narrator . . . is at his most original when he creates or recreates his town out of memory and imagination. If he'd been born a couple of decades earlier, he would probably have written W.P.A. guides. His disquisition on the inherent differences between the New Englanders who arrived first and the Norwegians who followed and on the rivalries between Lutherans and Roman Catholics are in a rich tradition of smalltown Americana. (Lutherans drive Fords and Catholics drive Chevys in accord with the faith of the owners of the dealerships.) It's a socio-historical tour de force.

In narrating the town's early history, Mr. Keillor seems to be doing a takeoff on Francis Parkman. He tells us, for example, that the first person to be killed by a white man was a French-Canadian named Tourtelotte, who was hit on the head with a paddle by his canoemate in 1742. The Hudson's Bay Company ruled it justifiable homicide: "'M. Tourtelotte knew but two Voyageur's Songs and of those only the Choruses,' said the inquest report, 'and made of them such a Constant Clangour as to propagate Dread and effect a Shew of Force.'" . . .

Whatever the subject, Mr. Keillor pays attention to his writing: "A hard frost hits in September, sometimes as early as Labor Day, and kills the tomatoes that we, being frugal, protected with straw and paper tents, which we, being sick of tomatoes, left some holes in." Good-humored asides grow like tomatoes: "Clarence is Lutheran, but he sometimes drops in at the rectory for a second opinion." And there's Norwegian folk wisdom, too: "When a bachelor farmer begins to smell himself, you know winter's over." . . .

[Mr. Keillor] can get sentimental about growing up in a little town near nowhere, and some passages are marinated in nostalgia, like one of the area's inedible Norwegian delicacies. But then, as he reports, "What's so special about this town is not the food." As a matter of fact (although that is certainly the wrong word), the only thing special about Lake Wobegon is that Mr. Keillor has undertaken to be its chronicler. Which is more than most towns can say.

Walter Goodman, in a review of "Lake Wobegon Days," in The New York Times, *August 19, 1985, p. C20.*

VERONICA GENG

"Go East!" was the cry that drove 2,000 panicky citizens through the streets of James Thurber's Columbus, Ohio, in flight from a phantom dam burst on the west side. . . . That this mistaken dash for high ground might express more ambiguous yearnings didn't occur to me until I read Garrison Keillor's comic memoir of *his* hometown, fictionalized under the name Lake Wobegon, Minn. Mr. Keillor's show on American Public Radio, **"A Prairie Home Companion,"** purports to come from there, as his deep, rather mournful voice spins stories about "the little town that time forgot." But that sentimental conceit is left far behind by the book, *Lake Wobegon*

Days, in which the town joins Thurber's Columbus as an absurd definition of a very real Midwest.

Tracing the history of Lake Wobegon from the 1830's, Mr. Keillor chronicles a series of panicky anticlimaxes—thwarted hairpin turns in the pioneer movement west. Lake Wobegon's founders and settlers include: a Unitarian poet-missionary from Boston who, finding "only woods and, to the west, the river," thought, "I should turn back now," but didn't, because it was getting dark and his wife had weak ankles; a Norwegian just off the boat in New York who "accepted $200 from a man named West" to take his place in the Union army and ended up in Lake Wobegon on a stolen horse about the time his regiment died at Gettysburg; and some other Norwegians prudently beating an eastward retreat from the fearsome Dakota Territory, who stumbled on the first Norwegian, misreading his welcome as a promise of good living.

This 19th-century section of *Lake Wobegon Days* (about a quarter of the book) is detailed with a perfect ear for the period's letter writing, poetry and types of murders. It fixes graphically in one's mind, like a swerving arrow on a schoolbook map, the force that will sustain the town—a force Mr. Keillor defines as "a form of voluntary socialism with elements of Deism, fatalism, and nepotism." Another way to define it would be as repression of those original instincts to head back east. (p. 1)

Not going east has a lot of little repercussions. It means not going into St. Cloud for eyeglasses but shopping instead at Clifford's. Though "you might put a hideous piece of junk on your face and Clifford would say, 'I think you'll like those' . . . nevertheless you should think twice before you get the Calvin Klein glasses from Vanity Vision in the St. Cloud Mall. Calvin Klein isn't going to come with the Rescue Squad and he isn't going to teach your children about redemption by grace. You couldn't find Calvin Klein to save your life." Sometimes the cause-and-effect relationship is more impressionistic, as with the taboo on air conditioning: "You get A/C and the next day Mom leaves the house in a skin-tight dress, holding a cigarette and a glass of gin, walking an ocelot on a leash." . . .

The way a community's core ideas and experiences get attenuated into funny-looking motifs is a process not unique to Wobegonians. Mr. Keillor's insight into it shapes not just this local history but a lineage in American comedy. Lake Wobegon's landmark, the Statue of the Unknown Norwegian, whose expression seems to shift from "confidence in the New World" to "Wait here. I think I forgot something," is an icon of what you could call Qualm Humor. Directional doubt may be the Midwest's gift to our comic conventions. . . .

When qualms go bitter, they produce a W. C. Fields. In his cowardice and chafing resentment of the small-timers he's forced to live with, Fields is a Wobegonian who should have turned back for Philadelphia. He's like Art, the proprietor of Art's Bait & Night O'Rest Motel, who threatens to shotgun nice families who happen to overlook his hand-lettered sign: "Anyone caught Cleaning Fish on Picnic Tables gets thrown out bag + baggage. This means You. For Pete Sake, use your goddamn Head." What Mr. Keillor adds is a little revelation of how lovingly Fields and his ilk are tolerated: one of Art's neighbors thinks of putting up a sign saying, "CALM DOWN. HE'S LIKE THAT TO EVERYBODY."

As for the writing of James Thurber (Ohio) and Ring Lardner (Michigan), Mr. Keillor's direct forerunners, he gives back as much as he's learned from them. His "half-page of notes taken by a student" in 1856, at a speech celebrating the new college,

illuminates Lardner's body of work—raw American literacy groping its way toward total illogic:

   a.   Gratitude. Much accmp. Much
       rmns.
      1. Orpheus. Made nature sing.
      2.
   B.   How puny comp. to Works of God.
       Moon, stars &c.
      1. But he leads us to work His
      Will.
   I.   Divine Will
      A. The Creation
      1. power of idea

I hadn't read Thurber in years, but *Lake Wobegon Days* sent me back to his Columbus. The alarums about dam bursts and burglars who blow chloroform through a tube under the door, the perverse loyalty to a dog who had to be fed on a table because he bit anyone who lowered a hand toward the floor, look now like abstract remnants of the frontier, with its fears of real blizzards and Indians, its stubborn persistence through repetitious attack by wolves and bears.

Lake Wobegon Days is about the way our beliefs, desires and fears tail off into abstractions—and get renewed from time to time. Mr. Keillor is well equipped to understand this process, since, by his account, he grew up in the fundamentalist religion of the Sanctified Brethren, perfectionists at splitting into infinite subsects over points of doctrine. . . .

Stricter than the strict Lutheran and Catholic majority, the Brethren guard the Wobegonian ideal at its narrowest point, where going east in any way, shape or form means going to hell. The revival meeting at the book's climax, for Protestants and even a couple of Catholics who say of the minister, "Old Bob hits the nail on the head," temporarily restores a more direct spiritual impulse, one with its eye on God instead of on the town exits toward which youngsters are inching, "drifting away in the night, slipping into worldly dress . . . and dancing to jungle music." The escapees' angle on the town is most painfully shown in an anonymous document of protest titled "95 Theses 95"—a guilt-ridden itemization of parental crimes, from vile food to bigotry. . . .

[This book], unfolding Mr. Keillor's full design, is a genuine work of American history. It reinterprets a great one-liner from *The Oregon Trail,* by the 19th-century historian Francis Parkman, who might have had Mr. Keillor's attachment to his hometown in mind when he wrote: "Fear of the Indians—for I can conceive no other motive—must have induced him to court so burdensome an alliance." (p. 15)

        Veronica Geng, "Idylls of Minnesota," in The New York Times Book Review, *August 25, 1985, pp. 1, 15.*

KATHERINE PATERSON

[*Lake Wobegon Days*] is a very funny book, but its humor, like charity in Corinthians, "suffereth long and is kind." Keillor takes his sweet time to tell each tale, digressing into footnotes or parentheses or just plain changing the subject whenever he chooses. To eyes and ears accustomed to being battered by the obvious, Keillor's tales may appear to ramble on pointlessly. Accounts of sadness and tragedy—grandma's death, the bear that closed New Albion College, the diptheria epidemic of 1865—are woven seamlessly into the fabric of the book which is always good humored. There are pages of wry smiles and chuckles, and then, when you least expect it, a scene or a single line within a lengthy description that will have you weeping with laughter, unable to keep reading aloud, for surely by now you will be reading the book aloud to anyone within earshot....

[The] hilarity blossoms because Keillor has carefully planted the seeds and patiently tended the tale. He's not in any hurry. He's not going anywhere, and he dares what few comics today can, he dares to trust that his audience isn't going anywhere either, at least, not until they have heard the whole story....

It wouldn't be fair either to the author or the reader to go through the book picking out wonderful bits to quote out of context, context being what this book is all about, but a word must be said about the people in this book. Living in a town "where all the women are strong, all the men are good-looking, and all the children are above average," as Keillor tells his radio audience every week, are individuals so intently portrayed that they emerge as universal figures.

There's Art who runs Art's Bait & Night O'Rest Motel who threatens to run off any guest who cleans fish on the picnic tables and proceeds to do so. Einar Tingvold, with his white crewcut, horn-rimmed glasses, and bobbing Adam's apple, struggles valiantly and with growing desperation to turn Lake Wobegon's boys into the Scout Ideal. Elizabeth, the switchboard operator, who knows everyone's business, doesn't hesitate to tell the narrator when she's disappointed in him. But, then, she knew his grandfather and remembers a January night long before when the old man woke up all the children in his house and took them outside to see a wolf, silver in the moonlight. "Your grandpa knelt down and put his arms around us and said, 'I want you to take a good look and remember this because you may never get to see it again.' So we looked real good ... and everything that's happened since is like a long dream."

In recalling the mostly silent forebears of Lake Wobegon the narrator quotes a bit of homely philosophy: "No innocent man buys a gun and no happy man writes his memoirs." Maybe not. But a man who has lived in and out of happiness into maturity might reach back into the straw of his beginnings and spin a golden tale, proving that: "Some luck lies in getting what you have which once you have got it you may be smart enough to see is what you would have wanted had you known." (p. 2)

Katherine Paterson, "Tales from the Town That Time Forgot," in Book World—The Washington Post, *September 1, 1985, pp. 1-2.*

THE NEW YORKER

[*Lake Wobegon Days*] could well become a classic of our time. It purports to be a running narrative of events and an evocation of daily life in the notional Minnesota town of Lake Wobegon.... Mr. Keillor, who was brought up in Anoka, Minnesota, a town that no doubt closely resembles his fictional creation, gives us a thoroughgoing anatomy of Lake Wobegon ..., and throughout he weaves in portrait studies of individual townspeople and the history of his own boyhood. Lake Wobegon's inhabitants, including the somewhat hobbledehoy figure of the author, are too real to be considered "characters." The stories of the men and women who eat every day in Dorothy's Chatterbox Cafe, who buy Wheaties and potatoes at Ralph's Pretty Good Grocery, and who confide in the town's switchboard operator, and of the author's contemporaries, who razz him for wearing black Keds, are sharp—there is no nonsense here about nostalgia. This passage, about one of a group of old ladies emerging from a tuna-sandwich lunch in the Chatterbox Cafe—she is wearing a purple pants suit and a jet-black wig—will give an idea of the flavor of Mr. Keillor's style: "She too is seventy but looks like a thirty-four-year-old who led a very hard life. She is Carl Krebsbach's mother, Myrtle, who, they say, enjoys two pink Daiquiris every Friday night and between the first and second hums 'Tiptoe Through the Tulips' and does a turn that won her First Prize in a Knights of Columbus talent show in 1936 at the Alhambra Ballroom. It burned to the ground in 1955."

A review of "Lake Wobegon Days," in The New Yorker, *Vol. LXI, No. 33, October 7, 1985, p. 140.*

GLYN HUGHES

[*Lake Wobegon Days*] has been so much praised that it can surely bear a dissenting voice. That I didn't find it very funny might be my own peculiarity, but a very good novel I don't believe it to be, although it might be a good source book of quasi-documentary stories....

Whereas in [William Gaddis's] *Carpenter's Gothic* the small locale of a house on the Hudson River genuinely reaches out to what Robert Lowell called 'the sore spots of the earth', *Lake Wobegon* retreats into its satisfactions with small-town values. Moreover, the author too often relies upon a winsome and 'fetching' small boy's view of the world. It is this sort of thing that captures a readership and could even form a cult. But does it make for the high qualities that some are claiming for the book? It is small-town values that make the US such a menace with the arsenal it has at its command. That's not funny.

Glyn Hughes, "Grace and Fate," in New Statesman, *Vol. 111, No. 2867, March 7, 1986, pp. 26-7.**

Etheridge Knight

1931-

American poet, short story writer, essayist, and editor.

Knight writes rhythmic, colloquial verse that focuses on his personal life and comments on the experiences of black American males. Having served eight years in the Indiana State Prison, Knight often expresses a desire for freedom in his work. While rebelling against physical confinement, he also protests oppression of blacks and underprivileged people and celebrates those who struggle to maintain their individuality. As a precept to his work, Knight strives for a balanced relationship between "the poet, the poem, and the people." He makes his work accessible through direct language and use of slang, strong images, and simple poetic techniques. He also stresses the oral nature of poetry, and critics praise the powerful musicality he achieves in his verse through repetition and phrasing borrowed from blues music.

Knight's first volume of poetry, *Poems from Prison* (1968), was published while he was an inmate. The poems in this book reflect his alienation and the violent environment in which he lived. The collection *Belly Songs and Other Poems* (1973) consists of poetry written after Knight's release from prison, and its broader range of subjects evidences his more varied experiences. With *Born of a Woman: New and Selected Poems* (1980), Knight moved from a small press to a major publishing house, and his work elicited greater critical attention. The volume is divided into three sections: "Inside-Out," "Outside-In," and "All About—And Back Again." The poems in the first section convey different aspects of prison life: "For Freckle-Faced Gerald" concerns a young boy who is raped and brutalized by older convicts—an act which also symbolically represents society's oppression of the innocent and defenseless; "Hard Rock" depicts a strong and rebellious hero who defies the system's attempts to break his spirit until brain surgery forcibly changes his character; and "The Idea of Ancestry" reveals the loneliness and isolation of a prisoner who reflects upon his crime, his family, and his heritage while looking at photographs of his relatives on his cell wall. The second section contains poems about love, and the final section includes most of Knight's recent poetry and develops a greater scope of themes and subjects. In a review of *Born of a Woman*, Craig Werner comments: "A polished craftsman, capable of exploiting both traditional Euro-American and experimental Afro-American (frequently musical) terms, Knight has emerged as a major voice in the tradition of Langston Hughes and Gwendolyn Brooks."

(See also *Contemporary Authors*, Vols. 21-24, rev. ed. and *Dictionary of Literary Biography*, Vol. 41.)

GWENDOLYN BROOKS

Vital. Vital.

This poetry [in *Poems from Prison*] is a major announcement.

It is certainly male—with formidable austerities, dry grins, and a dignity that is scrupulous even when lenient. But there are centers of controlled softness too. . . .

Since Etheridge Knight is not your stifled *artiste,* there is air in these poems.

And there is blackness, inclusive, possessed and given; freed and terrible and beautiful.

> Gwendolyn Brooks, in a preface to Poems from Prison by Etheridge Knight, Broadside Press, 1968, p. 9.

JEWEL C. LATIMORE

"Vital. Vital," says Gwendolyn Brooks in the preface [to *Poems from Prison* (see excerpt above)]—and truth is there. Urgent are his words. And strong. And hard. Etheridge Knight brings the strength and hardness of black existence through his poetry to his people.

One does not look for the white aesthetic of universalism in this poetry. Mr. Knight asked in . . . [*Negro Digest*] ("Black Writers' Views on Literary Lions and Values," Jan. 1968), "Where is the universality of the human situation?" Indeed, black experience has never been a "universal" one encompassing all humanity, but, rather, experience spawned of West-

278

ern pseudo-society, long endured by, and peculiar to, black people. . . . (p. 82)

The forms and constructs of a black artist using his art to reflect his own experience and those he has gotten from his people are not of necessity confined in traditional "mainstream" garb—but are the forms and constructs created by him, or adapted, as a set form like the Japanese Haiku. . . .

[In *Poems from Prison* there] are poems of prison the way it is in **"Crazy Pigeon," "He Sees Through Stone," "To Make a Poem in Prison," "To The Man Who Sidled Up To Me And Asked: 'How Long You In Fer, Buddy?,'"** and the 47 pictures on the cell wall in **"The Idea of Ancestry"** with its memory of life as it was on the outside. There is the legendary unconquerable Hard Rock returning to prison from the hospital for the criminal insane—

> Handcuffed and chained, he was turned loose,
> Like a freshly gelded stallion

and as we realize Hard Rock's defeat, which is our own, we know that

> He had been our Destroyer, the doer of things
> We dreamed of doing but could not bring ourselves to
> do.

(p. 83)

Pictures of life are **"A Nickel Bet," "Beware,"** and **"The Violent Space"** with its vibrant imagery capturing the tragedy of a young black girl. **"To Dinah Washington"** and **"For Langston Hughes"** bring the reader some of the essence of the singer and the poet. And there are poems about Malcolm, **"Portrait of Malcolm X," "For Malcolm, A Year After," "The Sun Came,"** and **"It Was a Funky Deal"**. . . . (pp. 83-4)

He writes, too, of love—**"Sweethearts in a Mulberry Tree," "As You Leave Me,"** and **"A Love Poem"** where love has strength in its being. . . .

And in answering the warden's question as to why "the black boys don't run off like the white boys do," there is the realization and acknowledgment that to be black in a pseudo-society is to be imprisoned no matter which side of the cell door one is on—

> . . . "we ain't got no wheres to run to."

Etheridge Knight's poetry is just that—poetry. And as such, it is art, and a living experience for the reader. (p. 84)

> *Jewel C. Latimore, in a review of "Poems from Prison," in* Negro Digest, *Vol. XVII, No. 9, July, 1968, pp. 82-4.*

PATRICIA LIGGINS HILL

> Unless the Black artist establishes a "Black aesthetic" he will have no future at all. . . . The Black artist must create new forms and new values, sing new songs (or purify old ones) . . . must create a new history, new symbols, myths and legends . . . , [and] in creating his own aesthetic, must be held accountable for it only to the Black people. . . .

Etheridge Knight's statement on poetics echoes the controversial new Black aesthetic. The credo of the aesthetic, that the primary objective of all Black artistic expression is to achieve social change and moral and political revolution has been de-

veloped by LeRoi Jones (Amiri Baraka), Clarence Major, Don L. Lee (Haki Madhubuti), and Etheridge Knight himself. According to Theodore Hudson in *From LeRoi Jones to Amiri Baraka,* the credo of the aesthetic became firmly implanted when Baraka announced in his mid-Sixties poem "Black Art" that Black poetry must function as fists, daggers, and guns to clean up the sordid Black experience as well as to "clean out the world for virtue and love." . . . [The] society in which Blacks are involved tends to be bound by a vision of reality formulated by whites. The function of the Black artist, therefore, is to break through the boundaries of that vision in order to express the Blackness of his or her people.

The credo of the new aesthetic has been resisted by traditional literary critics. . . . But these objections have been answered by the new Black poets. . . . Etheridge Knight vehemently disagrees with the white aesthetic principle that would cover up the Black man's continued enslavement by suggesting that all men have the same problems. In his poem **"On Universalism,"** Knight proclaims: "I see no single thread / That binds me one to all / No universal laws / Of human misery / Create a common cause / Or common history / That ease black people's pains / Nor break black people's chains."

Thus, the new Black poets insist that Black art must stand for the collective consciousness and subconsciousness of Black people in particular. (p. 115)

The poetry of Etheridge Knight does function as a liberating force. Since slavery has been a crucial reality in Black history, much of Knight's poetry focuses on a modern kind of enslavement, imprisonment, and searches for and discovers ways in which a person can be free while incarcerated. While he shares with Baraka, Madhubuti, Major, and the other new Black poets the bond of Black cultural identity (the bond of the oppressed, the bond formed by Black art, etc.), he unlike them, has emerged, after serving an eight-year prison term (1960-1968) for robbery, from a second consciousness of community—a community of criminals, a community which Frantz Fanon calls "the lumpenproletariat," "the wretched of the earth."

Ironically, Knight's major contribution to the new aesthetic derives from this second sense of consciousness, which favorably reinforces his strong collective mentality and identification as a *Black* artist. . . . [It] is logical that Knight would bring his prison consciousness, in which the individual is institutionally destroyed and the self becomes merely one number among many, to the verbal structure of his transcribed oral verse.

Specifically, what Knight relies on for his prison poetry are various temporal/spatial elements which allow him to merge his personal consciousness with the consciousness of Black people. His reason for using temporal/spatial modalities is obvious: A prison consciousness is preoccupied with the concepts of "time" and "space." In prison, "time" comes to mean "restriction," and "space" implies "confinement." When Knight was in prison, he remembers, for instance, that everyone talked in terms of "time": "How much time are you in for?" or "I have so much time left to do." Furthermore, the idea of space becomes all important to the convict. As Knight recalls, "When I was in prison, my major form of exercise was running. That sense of space, freedom, wide open space, probably comes out in some unconscious way." As a result, in his prison poems, Knight is concerned with freeing "time" and "space" from inertia. In particular, he fuses various elements and definitions of "time" and "space" not only to denote his own imprisonment, but also to connote the present social conditions of Black people in general. In his prison poems Blacks are seen as existing in a void (or what I prefer to term "the violent space," which is also the title of one of his poems), a "space" that must be filled with freedom if the race is to have a future.

In Knight's **"The Violent Space (or when your sister sleeps around for money)"** (*Poems from Prison* . . .), one of his major poetic achievements, both the poet and his sister are depicted as existing in a void. The first three stanzas embody painful reminiscences of a long ago time, in childhood, when the need for freedom was not fully recognized. . . . The poet's sister, as the subtitle of the poem implies, is caught in "the violent space." The refrain of the poem, "(Run sister run—the Bugga man comes!)," calls to mind childhood space, childhood fear and fantasy, from which the poet warns his sister to run. The childhood space is enlarged in the second stanza as the poet reminds her of a previous incident in which she was [stung by a red wasp]. As the third stanza returns in time to the present of the first, the remembrance of the wasp brings the concept of the demon to the poet's mind. He begins to ponder how to lift the wasp/demon's sting from his sister's brow and starts to ask her a series of questions till, out of sustained frustration, he finally asks, "Shall I chant a spell to drive the demon away?"

In the fourth stanza, leaving the reader with the sense of magical time he has established in the previous stanza, the poet changes the time and space of the poem's consciousness:

> In the beginning you were the Virgin Mary,
> And you are the Virgin Mary now.
> But somewhere between Nazareth and Bethlehem
> You lost your name in the nameless void.

The traveling of the pregnant Virgin from Nazareth to Bethlehem, where she delivered her child, becomes a parallel to the situation of the sister in the poem, whom the poet still sees as virginal despite her intercourse and possible pregnancy. Deliberately, Knight has involved the Virgin Mary myth to connote the suffering and oppression of the Black woman. His sister seems to be suffering physically from the hostile environment's sting (Knight's play on the term "WASP"), which has been unsuccessful in touching her soul. . . . [The] poet goes on to promise his sister the freedom that they both desire. . . . He foresees a time when Black people can do what they wish without worrying about what the "white eyes" are seeing or the white minds are thinking. Yet he feels unable to effect the needed freedom.

His sense of frustration is carried further in the final stanza. . . . "And what do I do"—the opening line of this stanza may or may not be a question (there is no question mark). The lines "I boil my tears in a twisted spoon / And dance like an angel on the point of a needle" suggest the ongoing anguish of a prisoner/addict, yet there is hope even though he "can not yet take hold of the demon." His determination to do so is implied. But, for the present time, the poet must be content: "So I grab the air and sing my song. / (But the air can not stand my singing long.)" Songs dissipate in the air of "the violent space," a space on the level which separates and entraps the sister and the brother. But if we understand the opening line of the stanza to be a question, we see that, even though the poet now grabs the air to sing his song, he seems to know that the need for freedom will reach such a crisis point in the future that an explosion will occur. The time will come when actions must

replace the words of his song. A person cannot live without freedom, for by doing so, that individual is living in a void, a nothingness, a "violent space."

By defining the poem through space (most notably the progression from the sister's relative space to his own), the poet removes the poem from linear time. Divergent historical times (from that of the Virgin Mary traveling between Nazareth and Bethlehem to the childhood of his sister to her condition at the age of seventeen), mythic and fantasy time (communicated through constant references to the Bugga man, angels, and demons)—these various elements work through space in order to de-emphasize the sense of historical time in regard to the enslavement of Black people. All elements of time are fused into one—the past and present conditions of Black people in "the violent space."

In the poem **"The Idea of Ancestry"** (*Poems from Prison* . . .), which Paul Mariah has hailed as "the best poem of Black cultural history," Knight himself becomes "the violent space." In the first section of the poem, which flows in a Whitmanesque style, the poet is spatially defined in his prison cell:

> Taped to the wall of my cell are 47 pictures: 47 black
> faces: my father, mother, grandmothers (1 dead), grand
> fathers (both dead), brothers, sisters, uncles, aunts,
> cousins (1st & 2nd), nieces, and nephews. They stare
> across the space at me sprawling on my bunk. I know
> their dark eyes, they know mine. I know their style,
> they know mine. I am all of them, they are all of me;
> they are farmers, I am a thief, I am me, they are
>   thee. . . .

The poet is conscious of the fact that all of his ancestors, except for his smiling, seven-year-old niece, stare at him across the space. He shares the same name as one grandfather, three cousins, three nephews, and one uncle. The uncle is an empty space in the family, just as the poet is. And yet in spite of the poet's being an empty space, he takes a Whitmanesque stance in the poem: He stands at the center of his universe, his ancestry, and sings, "I am all of them, they are all of me." But he realizes his separation from his ancestry as well: "they are farmers, I am a thief, I am me, they are thee."

The prosaic quality of the first section of the poem is striking. For the most part, it takes on the narrative qualities of an autobiography and flows with long, rolling, sonorous lines controlled by the breath of the poet; declarative statements; story-like details; and specific references to people, places, and actions. The soothing, sweet-flowing rhythms in Part I reflect the poet's reminiscences about his relationships with his relatives—memories that are filled with warmth, gentleness, regret, and nostalgia.

In Part II, the pace quickens. The thoughts recollected by examining the pictures of his relatives on his cell wall (in Part I) lead the poet gradually to a retelling of his personal ritual of suffering. . . . "Each Fall," the poet enacts the ritual of return to the home of his ancestry. From this mythic sense of time, the poet switches to direct references and specific definitions of time: "Last yr . . . That night. . . ." The experience is relived, but with qualification: ". . . I had almost caught up with me." The rhythms in Part II explode with violence. Separations are made: "That night I looked at my grandmother / and split / my guts were screaming for junk. . . ." The slashes, which are absent in Part I of the poem, crowd several activities into one sentence: "I walked barefooted in my grandmother's backyard / I smelled the old / land and woods / I sipped corn-whiskey from fruit jars with the men / I flirted with the women / I had a ball till the caps ran out / and my habit came down." Words collide at the slashes to build up the tension evident in the countercurrents of the poet's life: "birthstream / I hitch-hiked," "backyard / I smelled," "woods / I sipped corn-whiskey," "men / I flirted with the women," "junk / but I was almost / contented." The crackling sounds explode with meaning: The poet uses such terms as "croaker" (doctor) and "crib" (house) for their harsh alliterative impact.

In the last lines of the final stanza, the quickened pace exhausted, the drama rests:

> This yr there is a grave stone wall damming my stream,
>   and when
> the falling leaves stir my genes, I pace my cell or flop
>   on my bunk
> and stare at 47 black faces across the space. I am all of
>   them,
> they are all of me, I am me, they are thee, and I have
>   no sons
> to float in the space between.

"Time" and "space" have traveled full circle in the poem—back to the present condition of the poet in his cell. But whereas the space between the poet and the pictures described in the first stanza is chiefly the distance between his bunk and the wall where the pictures hang, the last notation of space in the poem involves the galvanization of the poet's genes—his sense of ancestry. He has no sons to hold his ritualistic space within the family. No sons of his are marked in the family Bible. This is a quiet time of despair for the poet: "they are farmers, I am a thief." Now, *he* is "the violent space," an entity separate from his ancestry. He is different: At this moment in the time and space of the poem, he has no physical linkage to his history, his family. And, unfortunately, because he is imprisoned, he can do nothing at present about the situation. The spatial/temporal movement of the poem is carried along by the tide of his music: from the very concrete reality of a prison cell, to a ritual revitalization of a sense of ancestry through a returning home, to this year when there will be no re-enactment of the ritual and no one to move for him: "I have no sons / to float in the space between." With this line the poem reaches an abrupt halt. The reader then becomes aware of the vastness of space, "the violent space," which follows the line.

The form of the poem as well as the idea of ancestry in the poem also represents the problem of ancestral lineage for the Black race as a whole. Many Blacks, such as Knight himself, can only trace their ancestral lineage back two or three generations because of the conditions of Black slavery which were imposed on them. (pp. 115-18)

In **"Cell Song"** . . . , Knight explores the possibilities of the freedom of mind and spirit while in "the violent space" of imprisonment. . . . In the poem, Knight is awakened by the "Slanted Light" which "strike[s] the cave / of sleep." The light which is slanted appears to be apocalyptic in nature, since it penetrates the cave of sleep—perhaps, the subconscious mind. He begins to "tread the red circle" and twist the empty, violent space of his existence with speech. The slanted light apparently reveals to him a poetic vision. It instructs him to ritualize his words, to use his words to promote action, perhaps social change: "take / your words and scrape / the sky, shake rain / on the desert, sprinkle / salt on the tail / of a girl." Apparently, by the end of the poem, Knight has answered his own question: "can there anything / good come out of / prison." There is no

question mark. The answer is obviously yes. The poet's words can penetrate through the prison walls and fill the void of "the violent space." (p. 118)

Etheridge Knight's prison poetry, by means of its temporal/spatial references and movements, liberates the minds and spirits of his readers, and of his people as a whole. At times, the poet leads the reader from a concrete definition of space into a space that refuses definition. And he controls time with the same fluidity. Space can be a movement which is defined through time, as in **"The Idea of Ancestry"**; and time can be, as the poem **"He Sees through Stone"** demonstrates, a movement defined through space. In **"The Violent Space,"** these patterns regularly reverse, yet the reader is never lost inside the structure of Knight's poems because, at one point or another, the poet offers a concrete reference grounded in either time or space. In **"The Violent Space,"** for example, the poet says, in the third stanza, "You are all of seventeen and as alone now / In your pain as you were . . ."; in **"He Sees through Stone,"** the reader knows where the old man is sitting; and, in **"The Idea of Ancestry,"** the poet stares at his prison cell wall. The poet's constant use of such references and time/space movements serve an important function: They allow him to merge his consciousness with the consciousness of his people. As a result, his personal prison experiences become a microcosm of the collective experiences of Black people.

That Knight means for his prison experiences to serve as a microcosm of the freedomless void that his people are experiencing is made clear in the "Preface" to his anthology *Black Voices from Prison*:

> From the time the first of our fathers were bound
> and shackled and herded into the dark hold of
> a "Christian" slaveship—right on up to the
> present day, the whole experience of the black
> man in America can be summed up in one word:
> prison . . . and it is all too clear that there is a
> direct relationship between men behind prison
> walls and men behind myriad walls that per-
> meate society. . . .

While Knight was "inside" prison, he was constantly aware that other Blacks resided in the "larger prison outside". . . . The "inside" and "outside" prison experiences become interchangeable within the structure of Knight's poems by means of his concrete references and temporal/spatial movements. These references and movements allow the poet to lead his reader, via the heightened experience of good poetry, to a mythic consciousness in which all space is "the violent space" and all time is eternal. Knight imparts this consciousness, its time and its space, to his people as a unifying force. The human being's particular way of experiencing time and space is his only way of knowing life itself. It *is* life for him, it *is* vital. If this conception of time and space is held in common by a people, they achieve a group identity.

Knight brings this conception of group identification to the new Black aesthetic. Yet, ironically, it is this conception that sets him apart from the other new Black poets. While Baraka, Madhubuti, and Major see themselves as poets/priests—as leaders, teachers, and/or spokesmen of the Black revolutionary movement of the 1960s and '70s—, Knight sees himself as being one with Black people. Whereas Major, Madhubuti, and Baraka seem to share W.E.B. Du Bois's vision of the social structure of the Black community—that a "talented tenth," a Black intelligentsia, must lead and uplift the masses of Black people—, Knight identifies closely with the folk. . . . He is one with the other participants, his race as a whole. Knight's reliance on various time/space elements for group identification is successful: His poetry functions as a vital, liberating force for the new rites. As Gwendolyn Brooks has said of Knight's poetry in her preface to his ***Poems from Prison*** [see excerpt above], the writing embodies "a Blackness that is at once inclusive, possessed and given, freed and terrible and beautiful." . . . This is the particular way of living Blackness that Etheridge Knight expresses. (pp. 119-20)

> *Patricia Liggins Hill, "'The Violent Space': The Function of the New Black Aesthetic in Etheridge Knight's Prison Poetry," in* Black American Literature Forum, *Vol. 14, No. 3, Fall, 1980, pp. 115-21.*

THE VIRGINIA QUARTERLY REVIEW

Knight's work is truly subterranean, tense with the hardness, paranoia, and bitter humor that have characterized criminal poets since Villon. But Knight is more than simply a talented psychopath, and his poetry [in ***Born of a Woman: New and Selected Poems***] develops a remarkable range. Once one has discarded the inevitable, programmed poems of propaganda, there remains a substantial body of work that is distinguished both for subject matter and technique. There is, for instance, a scattering of striking haiku . . . and there are some surprisingly subtle and interesting experiments with internal rhyme. There are intensely painful love poems, hallucinations, blue raps, folk narratives, and meditations upon ancestry that assume naturally a biblical pace and diction. The theme is freedom, the need of the spirit for the wind and the sea, and Knight usually invokes it ironically—by the definition of his world as both physical and psychological prison. He has distinguished his voice and craftsmanship among contemporary poets, and he deserves a large, serious audience for his work.

> *A review of "Born of a Woman: New and Selected Poems," in* The Virginia Quarterly Review, *Vol. 57, No. 1 (Winter, 1981), p. 27.*

DARRYL PINCKNEY

A critic who is young and not confident in his scholarship should not write about poetry, particularly if he—or she— dislikes the work under consideration. It does not help the young critic to go about knocking poets who take themselves seriously. It does not help poetry—not that poetry needs help from anyone. If, however, a critic has chosen a subject—Afro-American literature, for example—perhaps he might discover something in thinking about the works of Jay Wright and Etheridge Knight, two American poets who are also black men. (p. 306)

The poems brought together in ***Born of a Woman*** are, for the most part, simple to the point of being facile, even crude. . . . Knight's subjects include the loneliness of prison cells, women leaving, trying to kick drugs, black musicians, family feeling, Malcolm X, politics—a wide range of experience and admirable concerns. That is not the problem. Anything can be the occasion for a poem. But not just anything on the page makes for a poem. Etheridge Knight writes in a loose, funky style associated with the Sixties and black militancy, a period that was loud and noisy with talk against the tyranny of so-called white poetics. (p. 310)

The history of literature is a quest for new forms. But many, since the Sixties, seemed to use the call for a new aesthetic as an apologia for the unrendered. Discussions of the oral tradition became popular, as if the oral, in black culture, acquitted the black poet of his—or her—responsibility to the language. Anyone who has heard Robert Hayden's "Runagate Runagate" or Sterling Brown's "The Strong Men" knows that the written and the spoken abide by the same unnameable rules. Those who feel that poetry, in essence, is a performance art ought to join a circus.

The world Knight portrays in his poems is often harsh and brutal. He aspires to a language that will remain true to these experiences, words that will not give any falsifying distance. It makes for a very vigorous and immediate style that is often successful. . . . Far too often, however, the poems evince that uninteresting tendency to feel that a *rap* is all that need be offered. **"A Poem for 3rd World Brothers"**:

> or they will send their lackeys to kill for them.
> and if those negroes fail
> white/ america will whip out her boss okie doke:
> make miss ann lift the hem of her mystic skirt
> and flash white thighs in your eye to blind you. . . .

A rap is not enough, however true, politically, the message is taken. Raps that are trying to pass for poems have a strange redundant quality: we feel we know all this already and not much is going on in the poem to make us see or feel this in a new way. The ordinariness of the imagery makes the poems degenerate into sentimentality, which is a disservice to Knight's capacity for tender expression. "Our love is a rock against the wind, / Not soft like silk or lace." Another danger of the rap is that it dates quickly. There are some poems in which Knight is embarrassingly on the wrong side, such as **"Love Song to Idi Amin."** . . . (pp. 310-12)

Knight seems to have a fondness for the haiku, which is an acquired taste even when written well. . . . He is also given to a not very sophisticated use of internal rhyme. . . . There are moments of painful formal constraint: **"Apology for Apostasy?"**:

> Soft songs, like birds, die in poison air
> So my song cannot now be candy.
> Anger rots the oak and elm; roses are rare,
> Seldom seen through blind despair.

Clumsily deployed rhymes or metrics do not enhance the playfulness or irony of his poems and are disastrous when he is reaching toward the poignant. Knight is best in the more open, rapid, darting poems, such as **"A Conversation with Myself."** . . . (pp. 312-13)

Knight's ***Poems from Prison*** brought him recognition when it appeared in 1968, and it is easy to understand why his radical message and comfortable style were so well received. Though Knight has not renounced his interest in investigating the consequences of racism, it is disappointing that the new poems do not indicate much artistic growth. (p. 313)

What can the young critic discover? Only what has always been true and so general that it can hardly count as an insight: the black experience, however real, does not by itself make poetry; it must be turned into art, like everything else. Erudition or mere feeling will not make poetry; African myth or familiarity with prison is, weirdly, not enough. It does not matter that a poet is black. The tradition and demands of the language—in this case, English—matter. A work of art can only be correct in the political sense when it is first correct in the literary sense, Walter Benjamin wrote. Black poets must be judged by the same standards as for any other poets. Any other considerations are racist. There is no need for a minority admissions program into the canon of literature. Vision and mastery of form are the bootstraps that lift. (p. 314)

Darryl Pinckney, "You're in the Army Now," in Parnassus: Poetry in Review, Vol. 9, No. 1, Spring-Summer, 1981, pp. 306-14.*

PATRICIA LIGGINS HILL

Born of A Woman consists of Etheridge Knight's best poems from Poems from Prison (1968), Black Voices from Prison (1970), and Belly Song and Other Poems (1973) as well as several previously uncollected and new selections. This volume is particularly valuable to us because it reveals the growth of this first rate but relatively unknown poet: his movement from the limitations of prison poet, a verse which primarily explores the harshness of the prison world, the oppressor vs. the oppressed, to a music which is wider and deeper in scope, range, and subject matter. In essence, Born of A Woman establishes Knight as a masterful blues singer, a singer whose life has been "full of trouble" and thus whose songs resound a variety of blues moods, feelings, and experiences and later take on the specific form of a blues musical composition.

To accomplish this end, the collection is organized into three major parts. In "Inside Out," the first part which is a collection of Knight's prison poems, he presents the blues as cries of oppression. Such traditional blues themes as the desire for social freedom and the feelings of loneliness and alienation are explored. In part two, "Outside In," Knight's early post-prison verse from Belly Song, other themes such as despair in love, overall mental depression, and agony and nostalgia for the South are emphasized. Finally, in part three, "All About-And Back Again," which contains poems from Belly Song as well as uncollected and new selections, several blues themes are treated and expressed in the musical/folk idioms.

In "Inside Out," Knight brings us, mercilessly and straight on, face to face with the infinite varieties of pain and sorrow of the prison world until finally the total prison soul stands before us anatomized. We meet again, for instance, Freckled-Faced Gerald, the sixteen-year-old black inmate who was raped, who "was thrown in as 'pigmeat' for the buzzards to eat"; Hard Rock, who "wasn't a mean nigger anymore" because "the doctors had bored a hole in his head / Cut out part of his brain and shot electricity / Through the rest"; and the old black soothsayer lifer who "sees through stone," who waits patiently only for the dawning of freedom. Above all, in "The Idea of Ancestry," the most powerful of the prison poems, we witness the poet himself deep in despair, alone in the freedomless void of his prison cell, an entity separate from his family and his ancestry as a whole: "I am me, they are thee, and I have no children / to float in the space between." Moreover, in "The Warden Said to Me the Other Day," Knight's modern-day version of a slave's lament, he reminds us of the sense of social entrapment black people as a whole are experiencing. . . . (pp. 77-8)

On the whole, the disturbing directness of language, the pounding, absorbing rhythms of Knight's prison poems, his contributions to the new Black Arts movement of the 1960s and '70s, make them exceptionally moving pieces. However, the painful environment of imprisonment stifled Knight's creativity. In

"To Make A Poem in Prison," he explains, "It is hard / To make a poem in prison / The air lends itself not to the singer . . . Soft words are rare, and drunk drunk / Against the clang of keys." Consequently, his prison verse speaks not of joy or love: "The air is empty of laughter. And love? / Why, love has flown, / Love has gone to glitten."

In "Outside In," Knight's subject matter has broadened and the versatility of his craft has increased. There are tender love lyrics such as "No Moon Floods the Memory of That Night," "Love Poem," and "A Poem for a Certain Lady on Her 33rd Birthday." But the love songs which deal with pain, despair, and rejection such as "Feeling Fucked Up" are even more inclusive, are even more powerful. . . . The best poems in Born of A Woman, however, are those that search for heritage, continuity, and meaning. In "The Bones of My Father," a poem which shows his growing concern for image rather than the statement, Knight's search takes him to the South, the ancestral home for blacks. . . .

Knight continues this search in "All About-And Back Again"; however, for its expression, he chooses the ritualistic rhythms of both African and Afro-American musical idioms. For instance, in "Ilu the Talking Drum," one of the finest poems in contemporary American poetry, Knight uses the African musical pulse structure (the duple-triple pulse beat) to imitate the voice of the talking drum, which brings the black Americans back full circle from Africa to their Southern ancestral home and then back to an Africa of the spirit. . . . (p. 78)

Born of A Woman has substantiated what Knight himself has observed: his post-prison music is more effective than his earlier verse because his community on the outside of prison is larger. As he explains in a 1978 interview in San Francisco Review of Books, "I have my brothers and sisters, my mother, my wife, my children and I have my friends—the community is much more extended." As he further points out in the "Preface" of Born of A Woman, he is now able to function as a complete poet, as a singer whose art is based on three essential ingredients: "The Poet, The Poem and The People: When the three come together, the communion, the communication, the Art happens." Certainly, Born of A Woman proves that Knight has reached this level of artistic achievement. (p. 79)

Patricia Liggins Hill, in a review of "Born of a Woman: New and Selected Poems," in Black American Literature Forum, Vol. 15, No. 2, Summer, 1981, pp. 77-9.

CRAIG WERNER

In the "Preface" to Born of a Woman: New and Selected Poems, Etheridge Knight endorses an aesthetic which balances the demands of "The Poet, the Poem, and the People." The third term is crucial. While numerous influential poets and critics, among them Michael Harper and Robert B. Stepto in their recent anthology Chant of Saints, turn to the relatively elitist transatlantic and academic traditions of Afro-American poetry, Knight's theory and practice provide a necessary reminder of the equally important populist roots of black expression. A polished craftsman, capable of exploiting both traditional Euro-American and experimental Afro-American (frequently musical) forms, Knight has emerged as a major voice in the tradition of Langston Hughes and Gwendolyn Brooks. (p. 7)

The publication of Born of a Woman . . . furnishes the occasion for an assessment of the ways in which [Knight's] voice expresses both the political and cultural currents of black nationalism and readjusts the position of the Black Aesthetic movement in the populist tradition. Technically, Knight merges musical rhythms with traditional metrical devices, reflecting the assertion of an Afro-American cultural identity within a Euro-American context. Thematically, he denies that the figures of the singer, central to the aesthetic of *Chant of Saints,* and the warrior, central to the Black Aesthetic movement, are or can be separate.

One of the most recent in a long line of black writers to have discovered his vocation while in prison Knight began writing under the encouragement of Gwendolyn Brooks. His artistic awakening coincided both with the critical dominance of the Black Aestheticians and with Brooks' evolution from a "universalist" to a black nationalist perspective. Black Aesthetic spokesmen such as Addison Gayle, Jr., insisted that the historical oppression of black people in the United States had created a situation in which the Afro-American writer must commit himself to the freedom of his people and reject Euro-American cultural traditions and forms as a mark of his independence. In its most extreme forms, the Black Aesthetic demanded that the Afro-American writer serve as another tool of the revolution, creating works which would inspire the masses of black people to commit themselves anew to political action. The artist must be a warrior first, a singer only second.

Reflecting this political and aesthetic climate, Knight's early work, while employing numerous poetic devices associated with Euro-American traditions, insists on a specifically black poetry. **"On Universalism"** dismisses the concept of encompassing human brotherhood as a response to the oppression of the people. . . . (pp. 8-9)

Knight's aesthetic as reflected both in his metrics and his imagery, however, always balanced the demands of Poet, Poem, and People, granting equal attention to the aesthetic demands of the language and to the impulse toward self-expression. This synthetic approach raised questions from the beginning of Knight's career. Even while identifying *Poems from Prison* as a "major announcement," Haki R. Madhubuti (then writing as Don L. Lee) questioned the propriety of Knight's allusions to Euro-American culture. Rather than abandoning such allusions, Knight soon relinquished the emphasis on a separate black aesthetic. Even while altering his stance, however, he maintained a strong sense of the black populist heritage. . . . Knight proposed a version of universalism based on shared emotional experience, rather than of specific images or forms: "My poetry is also important to white people because it invokes feelings. . . . The feelings are common, whether or not the situations that create the feelings are common . . . I might feel fear in a small town in Iowa. You might be afraid if you get off the subway in Harlem. It's the same fear, but the situations are different." This widening of the definition of the People to include any reader capable of responding to his emotional impulse in no way entails a movement away from populism. The lasting contribution of the Black Aesthetic to Knight's poetics lies precisely in his continuing commitment to the People. . . . (p. 9)

This commitment to the People . . . defines Knight's poetic achievement throughout his career. As the structure of *Born of a Woman* indicates, Knight has approached this commitment from a variety of perspectives. Part I, titled **"Inside-Out,"** focuses on Knight's awakening in prison and his dawning awareness of his relationship with an outside world. Part II, **"Outside-In,"** concentrates on his self-exploration—the Poet

is one-third of Knight's aesthetic trinity—once released. Part III, **"All About—And Back Again,"** reemphasizes that, whatever his explorations, the Poet Knight ultimately returns to the base he finds in the People and expresses in the Poems.

The political poetry written concurrently with **"On Universalism"** attests to the complexity of Knight's practice. His eulogy **"For Malcolm, A Year After,"** originally published in *Poems from Prison,* carefully manipulates metrical tensions and rhyme schemes to make its statement of support for the nationalist warrior. Knight begins with a bitter statement that he will stay within the Euro-American tradition for fear that any formal departure might bring in its wake a self-destructive emotional explosion. . . . (p. 10)

The second stanza emphasizes that while Knight uses the Euro-American culture's form, he uses it to advance the political cause of black nationalism. Inverting the traditional conceit of the poem living eternally despite the death of the man, Knight writes that his poem, an artifact of the oppressive culture, will die, but its message, the message of Malcolm X, will live. . . . The concluding triplet of the poem, implicitly parodying the standard couplet form, further emphasizes the revolutionary emotion inspired by both the life and death of Malcolm X. . . . While Knight the singer works within traditional forms, his vision is insistently that of the nationalist warrior.

Most of the poems in **"Inside-Out"** echo this intensity of anger. Knight portrays Hard Rock, lobotomized, serving as a symbol of contemporary "slavery." . . . He writes of his own isolation from his family in **"The Idea of Ancestry,"** an isolation which leads him back to prison. And, ironically juxtaposing his statement with the largely traditional forms in the first section, he concludes in **"A Poem for Black Relocation Centers"** with the portrait of Flukum who "couldn't stand the strain. Flukum / who wanted inner and outer order" . . . and who meets an uncomprehending death in Vietnam. Clearly, the poems in **"Inside-Out"** point to the necessity of a vision of the world going beyond the simple recognition of victimization.

"Outside-In" reflects both Knight's concern with the Poet's personal struggles to attain this vision and his determination to generate forms, many of them reflecting the Afro-American musical tradition, which adequately express this vision. Both a cry of personal agony and a demonstration of Knight's ability to shape his poem out of the materials of both Euro- and Afro-American culture, **"The Violent Space"** stands among the most powerful lyrics of recent decades. (pp. 10-11)

Not all of Knight's explorations in **"Outside-In"** lead to . . . stark confrontations. He has never been simply the Poet of the victim. Knight's musical experiments with toasts (**"Dark Prophecy: I Sing of Shine"**), blues (**"A Poem for Myself"**), and African percussive rhythms (**"Ilu the Talking Drum"**) involve a wide range of emotional experiences, including that of remembered and discovered love in the jazz poem **"For Eric Dolphy."** He returns most insistently to jazz in poems which employ irregular but insistent rhythmical patterns and repetitions in the place of a basic Euro-American meter. (p. 12)

In the poems of **"All About—And Back Again,"** most of which are collected for the first time in *Born of a Woman,* these explorations and experiments merge in Knight's mature poetic voice. **"I and Your Eyes"** exemplifies the music and the concerns of this voice. The "And I . . . your eyes" pattern forms a rhythmic base, derived more from jazz than from traditional metrics:

And I   your eyes
draw round about a ring of gold
and shout their sparks of fire
And I   your eyes
hold untold tales and conspire
with the stars. And stirs my soul.

Using the pause between the two repeated phrases, Knight creates a tension, a sense of separation leading toward the connection embodied by the imagery. As he expresses the separation and pain of love, he departs from the ground rhythm, leaving an emptiness in the sound of the poem:

Then I
could stand alone the pain
of flesh alone the time and space
and stone.   but I am shaken.
It has taken
                   your eyes
to move this stone.

The traditional use of rhyme to emphasize crucial thematic points reenforces the jazz devices. This is the voice of an accomplished singer.

Along with this technical maturity, the poems in **"All About—And Back Again"** reveal that Knight has attained a commensurate maturity of vision. Just as **"I and Your Eyes"** combines the control of traditional devices with jazz techniques, **"We Free Singers Be"** insists on the importance of both the warrior embodying the values of the Black Aesthetic movement and the singer, reflecting the evolutionary emphasis of *Chant of Saints*. The poem's title implies this. "We" gives the sense of group identity, the nationalist perspective, the People. "Free" provides an internal rhyme, demonstrating Knight's continuing willingness to work with the Euro-American tradition in a way which renders it indistinguishable from the authenticity of his individual, clearly black, voice, and establishes the political emphasis on liberation. "Singers" invokes the emphasis on the artist, the *Chant of Saints* orientation, the Poet. "Be," the third rhyme word invoking the verbal play, the mock-excess of black oral tradition, provides the fulcrum for both the thematic and rhythmic movement of the poem. (pp. 13-14)

Throughout the poem Knight alternates the warrior and the singer images. He intersperses a number of memories: of days "of the raging fires when I clenched my teeth in my sleep and refused to speak"—the days of the warriors; and of days "when children held our hands and danced around us in circles"—the days of the singers. The circle imagery connected with the children echoes the circle imagery connected with the warrior eagles. No matter what the momentary manifestation, both the singer and the warrior coexist in the individual at all times. The function of the singer is in large part to be a visionary. . . . But even the visionary cannot afford to forget the reality of conflict. . . . The fact, one with which Knight began the poem, and with which he ends it, is simply that each individual must be both: "We Free singers be, baby, / We free singers be." Ultimately, Knight says, the warriors of the Black Aesthetic and the singers of the *Chant* merge in the individual striving for the freedom of the Poet and the People. (pp. 14-15)

Craig Werner, "The Poet, the Poem, the People: Etheridge Knight's Aesthetic," in Obsidian: Black Literature in Review, *Vol. VII, Nos. 2 & 3, Summer & Winter, 1981, pp. 7-17.*

HOWARD NELSON

What keeps us alive? In or out of prison, one answer is other people. "We must love one another or die," as Auden put it. Knight has always been sure to acknowledge this. In the preface to the *Black Voices from Prison* anthology, he acknowledged "Gwendolyn Brooks, Sonia Sanchez, Dudley Randall, and Don L. Lee: black poets whose love and words cracked these walls." In *Born of a Woman,* he gives a list that has grown to over forty people he feels indebted to.

In a way, Knight's poetry itself is another form of acknowledgement. People, relationships between and among people, are his compelling theme; it is present in nearly all his work in one form or another. I want to follow this thread in talking about Knight's poetry.

In *Belly Song* Knight had a nice existential individualist blues fragment, dated 8/72, called "Evolutionary Poem No. 1":

I ain't got nobody
that i can depend on
'cept myself

In *Born of a Woman* he has followed this piece immediately with "Evolutionary Poem No. 2," in which a switch to the plural pronoun points in a different direction:

We ain't got nobody
that we can depend on
'cept ourselves.

"No. 2" is dated September 1979, the same date as that of the book's preface, nine months before its publication. Very likely Knight noticed, as he was rereading and reorganizing his work for the new collection, that his earlier statement, though in large ways true for himself and everyone, was counter to the fundamental current running through his poems: the impulse to celebrate nourishing human relationships, to lament their various breakdowns, to protest their betrayals.

On the broadest scale, this impulse appears in a sense of racial solidarity, as in "Poem for 3rd World Brothers" and "For Black Poets Who Think of Suicide," both exhortations to blacks to give themselves deeply to the energies and causes of their people. Elsewhere on the spectrum, the same basic theme emerges out of such a small, unexpected incident as the one in "A WASP Woman Visits a Black Junkie in Prison." At first outraged by the absurdity of this unasked-for visit from a "prim blue and proper-blooded" stranger, he soon recognizes that it is a situation of one loneliness reaching out toward another, and ultimately he finds himself strangely moved and quieted by the simple exchange they manage to construct.

The theme often appears in the form of celebrations of "heroes" of various kinds. There are poems honoring artists—Langston Hughes, Max Roach, Otis Redding—, and three strong elegies to Malcolm X. There are also other sorts of heroic characters, from Pooky Dee, whose "great 'two 'n' a half' gainer" from a railroad trestle one summer afternoon long ago ended with the sickening "sound of his capped / Skull as it struck the block," and left a permanent scar in his watchers' memories; to Shine, the black stoker on the Titanic in Knight's marvelous version of the folk poem, who rejected the pleas and bribes of various white establishment figures who couldn't stay afloat by themselves, and "swam on"; to Hard Rock, a black convict who refuses to cooperate in his own imprisonment and performs exploits of resistance which end in his lobotomy but also confront the other inmates with an unsettling example of courage and integrity. Each of these people, real or legendary (often both), from Langston Hughes to Hard Rock, has in some form or other given a gift, left a mark, that turns mere existence into reality.

In the last three poems mentioned, there is a blend of vivid lyric and narrative impulses which is typical of Knight. **"Hard Rock,"** for example, is a character sketch and an elegy, a compressed short story and a meditation on moments of intense feeling and realization. Another poem that contains the matter of a story and the music and intensity of a lyric is **"For Freckle-Faced Gerald."** While most of Knight's poems are in one way or another expressions of admiration or gratitude or love—are in one way or another affirmations—in the case of Gerald the most the poet can do is offer grief and outrage in the form of clear-eyed description of his subject's hopeless situation. Truly written and felt, this turns out to be an expression of a kind of love too.

The poem deals with a sixteen-year-old boy who has been sent to prison. In addition to his youth and inexperience, Gerald has going against him his inability even to strike a pose of self-assurance and toughness. Instead, he has "precise speech and an innocent grin." For him, being put in prison amounts, as the poem tersely puts it, to being "thrown in as 'pigmeat' / for the buzzards to eat." The buzzards in prison are the men who exploit Gerald sexually and otherwise. But they are only part of a much larger scenario of exploitation and dehumanization. . . . Knight is as aware of the violations human beings commit against one another, on all levels, in endless forms, as he is of the bonds that help to sustain us. (pp. 3-4)

Another strong character sketch is **"He Sees Through Stone."** It is a portrait of an old black convict, apparently long imprisoned, who has taken on a wisdom that gives him a kind of mythic significance. "Pressed by the sun / against the western wall / his pipe between purple gums," the old man is surrounded by young inmates. Possibly they gather around him to hear stories he has to tell, but the poem does not tell us this. Instead, it describes a more subtle attraction. The poet says, "I have known him / in a time gone by," and goes on to describe a sense in the old man's presence of a timeless guide or initiator who has somehow been with him through all the rites of passage of his life. . . . Apparently the other younger men sense this in him also. It is this recognition that sets up the old man's ability to "see through stone."

In the work of most poets there are certain words or images that recur regularly, in some cases obsessively. Not surprisingly in a poet who spent years in prison, one of Knight's persistent images is stone. It represents not just physical walls and imprisonment, of course; more importantly it stands for emotional barriers, insensitivity, the dead weight in the spirit that needs to be pushed away or penetrated or transformed in order for caring energies to flow again.

There are two kinds of stone in the poem: the stone walls of the prison, and the stone wall each person sets up himself. Knight picks up the slang metaphor "cats" and elaborates its suggestions: the "black cats" "circle," "flash white teeth," "snarl," have "shining muscles." But all this fierceness is a pose, a mask, ultimately another kind of stone wall erected in the name of defense. The old man leaning in the sun against actual stone is not impressed by the posturing. He understands and penetrates it: "he smiles / he knows"—knows the vulnerability that lives behind it. And somehow, the poem suggests, he is consequently a reassuring force, an outer presence who is also an inner presence, a kind of steady witness and

companion to the hidden life the self lives within walls within walls.

In a broad sense, about ninety per cent of Knight's work could be called love poetry. And naturally, poems that fit that term in the conventional sense make up an important part of his book. My personal favorites in this category are **"As You Leave Me,"** which creates haunting currents of emotion through imagery of great precision and dramatic effect, and **"Feeling Fucked Up,"** marvelous in its use of sound, a profane litany, a down-to-earth lament, written wonderfully at gut level all the way through to its culminating repetitions. . . . (pp. 5-6)

Another strong group is the poems that deal with family. Some of these take a sort of ritual form—words spoken for important events, such as a birth (**"On the Birth of a Black/Baby/Boy"**) or an escape from death (**"Another Poem for Me—after Recovering from an O.D."**). There are straight-forward elegies, such as **"The Bones of My Father,"** and anecdotes, as in the warm, low-key **"Talking in the Woods with Karl Amorelli."** Also within this group are two poems which, rightfully, have usually been among those representing Knight in anthologies: **"The Idea of Ancestry"** and **"The Violent Space."** (p. 6)

I want to . . . [discuss a] key element in Knight's work . . . : sound. [*Born of a Woman*] is laced together by Knight's unabashed sense of verbal music, right down to the titles of its three sections: **"Inside-Out,"** **"Outside-In,"** **"All About—And Back Again."** But I want to talk about sound not just in terms of poetic devices within poems, but also in terms of the actual spoken voice, the whole question of how we read and appreciate poetry.

I know that many people don't consider it quite legitimate to talk in criticism about poetry as a spoken, performed thing. There are various reasons for this. In America, most people who read poetry have been conditioned to think that the poem on the page is what really matters. (It is—but not exclusively.) Contributing to this is a training that leads us to think of poetry as a set of ideas and techniques rather than as an experience that includes them, the notion that there is an equation between greatness in poetry and how much explication it will sustain, and a condescension toward poetry whose strength lies in direct oral communication of emotion. We're suspicious of poetry which doesn't seem to have the impact on the page that it did when we heard it read well aloud. This is sometimes valid, but one needs to be careful here. Just as the poem must do its work well, so must the reader. I have often seen poems undervalued or misunderstood because of failures of aural (i.e., oral) imagination on the part of readers.

Ironically, the proliferation of poetry readings in recent years has also fed the prejudice against poetry in its oral incarnation. I certainly wouldn't deny that poetry readings can be creepy and tedious occasions, or that some poets are such poor readers that they do their audience and poetry a disservice when they give a reading. On the other hand, there is a cranky, reactionary attitude that is blind to the fact that it is fundamentally proper and healthy that poetry is being read aloud to audiences across the country. . . .

In the years since his release from prison Etheridge Knight has earned his living principally by giving poetry readings. He is an excellent reader. His deep, resonant voice is a gift. He is sensitive to the rhythms and inflections of poetry and "ordinary" speech, and he is sensitive to his audiences and knows how to reach them. As a black poet he stands in a living tradition of toast-tellers, rhymers, and singers. He believes that poetry is most fully itself when it is spoken aloud to other people; and as I've said, his poems have an immediacy and music that lend themselves to that kind of presentation. So I suppose he has all the qualifications to be called an oral poet. (p. 9)

My point is simply that reading poetry aloud is fundamental to the art, and that oral presentation draws forces out of the words which otherwise lie in them to some degree lost or wasted. Some poems lose more than others in a reading that doesn't do justice to their oral aspects, but whether one is reading *The Waste Land* or "After Apple-Picking" or "The Windhover" or "The Sea Elephant" or "The Navajo Night Chant," one needs really to hear the sounds, the tones, the voices, to truly receive the poem. Poetry readings—good ones, such as Etheridge Knight or Allen Ginsberg or Donald Hall or Gwendolyn Brooks or Galway Kinnell or William Heyen, for example, are capable of giving—become therefore not only heartening public performances but lessons we might learn in trying to become better readers ourselves—of all poetry, not just that of the poets we've heard reading.

In relation to these ideas, consider Knight's **"Ilu, the Talking Drum."** The best way to learn to read this poem is to hear Knight's extraordinary rendering of it, but this is not essential. While it's true that probably no one else could speak the poem as well as he does, it has its power within its words and will have still a hundred years from now.

The theme is again a human relationship, and in this case the poem describes how sound and rhythm themselves can create a bond among people. The poet is with a group of fifteen Nigerians. The setting is somewhat ambiguous, except for the fact that it is alien. A mood of torpor and restlessness hangs over them, and is communicated largely through the sounds of the words. We begin in a chafing silence: "The stillness was skinny and brittle and wrinkled." Those stingy, shallow i sounds are soon picked up again, joined by sharp p's, t's, and s's and bald long a's: "We twisted, turned, shifted positions, picked our noses, / stared at our bare toes, hissed air through our teeth ..." The stifling tedium is also conveyed through a series of monosyllabic phrases using doubled, very ordinary adjectives: "wide green lawn," "wide white porch," "big white house."

A breakthrough occurs, however, when one of the Nigerians rises and begins to play a rhythm on "Ilu, the talking drum." The emotional change is announced before it begins to happen, through sound—the entrance of long, open o's and u's: "Then Tunji, green robes flowing as he rose, strapped on Ilu, the talking drum." It is in what follows that the poem becomes

either boring or marvelous, depending on how we read. The drum speaks, and Knight lets us hear it:

kah doom/kah doom-doom/kah doom/kah doom-doom-doom

kah doom/kah doom-doom/kah doom/kah doom-doom-doom

kah doom/kah doom-doom/kah doom/kah doom-doom-doom

kah doom/kah doom-doom/kah doom/kah doom-doom-doom

If one follows habits learned from reading newspapers and most other prose, and skims over this as if it were so much filler, the point of the poem is missed. But if one reads the words carefully, actually sensing the reverberations, one is pulled inside a rhythmic flow that stands for life itself. In the next stanza Knight does in fact identify the drum beat with the heart beat. Much repetition; generous sound; a profound theme.... (p. 10)

At the end of the poem Knight suggests the great human distances that can be spanned within such sound, the freshened consciousness and sense of liberation it can create. Then he closes with the drum beat. When the poem ends there is an amazing silence, in which we seem to hear the echoes of the drum, or possibly it is the buried sound of our own blood beating—a very different silence from that which the opening of the poem described. **"Ilu, the Talking Drum"** is a marvelous poem, with rich veins of music and meaning and feeling. But it needs to be read truly.

There are other chant-like poems in *Born of a Woman,* such as **"We Free Singers Be"** and, especially, **"Belly Song."** But the book as a whole, from the incantatory effects of **"Ilu"** and **"Belly Song,"** to the fine unsolemn repetitions of **"Feeling Fucked Up"** and **"Welcome Back, Mr. Knight: Love of My Life,"** to the simple refrains of **"It Was a Funky Deal"** and **"I and Your Eyes,"** to the small, tight rhymes of **"A Shakespearean Sonnet: To a Woman Liberationist,"** to notations like **"Cop-Out Session,"** where the music is just the live music of black speech itself (working everywhere in Knight's poems): the whole book is wound around sound—vigorous, invigorating sound....

Born of a Woman contains a harsh, generous, beautiful poetry. It is breath of life. (p. 11)

Howard Nelson, "Belly Songs: The Poetry of Etheridge Knight," in The Hollins Critic, *Vol. XVIII, No. 5, December, 1981, pp. 1-11.*

Stanislaw Lem

1921-

Polish novelist, short story writer, nonfiction writer, critic, essayist, autobiographer, dramatist, and scriptwriter.

Lem is an internationally respected and popular author of science fiction and speculative literature. His works have been translated into more than thirty languages, yet he has attained only moderate recognition in the English-speaking world. Throughout his career, Lem has been concerned with the moral and ethical consequences of developments in science, particularly the impact of technology on society. He explores these themes through such elements as parody, satire, and fantasy. Lem is noted for his whimsically comic style, in which he utilizes black humor, puns, paradox, irony, and hyperbole while exploring topics relating to cybernetics, philosophy, and the social and natural sciences. Beneath the colorful surface of Lem's prose, Kurt Vonnegut discerned "a master of utterly terminal pessimism, appalled by all an insane humanity may yet survive and do." Despite personal misgivings and apprehensions, Lem regards science as necessary toward increasing human knowledge and development.

As a young man, Lem studied the history, methodology, and philosophy of science and also earned a medical degree. He began publishing fiction in 1946. In his early works, Lem oscillates between narrating tall tales and explaining scientific principles, often blending scholarly observations and polemics with absurd humor. *Dzienniki gwiazdowe* (1957; translated into two volumes, *The Star Diaries* and *Memoirs of a Space Traveler*) features Ijon Tichy, a character who undertakes intergalactic missions to fantastic worlds. His journeys continue in "Ze wspomnien Ijona Tichego: Kongres futurologiczny," a section originally included in the collection *Bezsenność* (1971) and translated as the novella *The Futurological Congress (From the Memoirs of Ijon Tichy)*. In this work, Tichy encounters a number of unique societies and observes the often selfish quests for knowledge undertaken by human beings.

Lem wrote his most popular and acclaimed works during the 1960s. According to Lem, these works differ from his previous fiction in that they "incorporate cognitive problems in fictions that do not oversimplify the world." The future of humanity, the limitations of human knowledge, and the effect of radically different alien intelligences on human psychology are among the principal themes of Lem's fiction during this decade. In *Solaris* (1961), perhaps Lem's best-known novel, the subconscious memories of the crew of a space station are turned into living forms by an intelligent and sentient ocean on the planet they are investigating. The crew comes to realize the impossibility of understanding and communicating with other intelligent life forms. *Powrót z gwiazd* (1961; *Return from the Stars*), one of Lem's most popular works with Western readers, centers on an astronaut who returns from a mission in space and discovers that earth has aged 127 years during his short absence. Society is revealed to have achieved peace due to a scientific method that eliminates aggression, but this development has destroyed the human penchant for risk-taking necessary for progress and survival. In *Pamietnik zanleziony* (1961; *Memoirs Found in a Bathtub*), a tragicomic novel set in the United States in the thirty-second century, an ineffectual spy

infiltrates the Pentagon and observes officials engaged in meaningless activity during a crisis situation. Reuel K. Wilson called this work "a timely satire on militarism." In *Głos pana* (1968; *His Master's Voice*), an American mathematician attempts to decipher erratic signals from outer space but comes to understand that "where there are no men, there cannot be motives accessible to men."

In much of his short fiction, Lem develops plausible cybernetic theories while producing fabulous tales in the manner of his early work. *Cyberiada* (1965; *The Cyberiad: Fables for the Cybernetic Age*) is a collection of comic stories written in the form of fairy tales that concern a pair of robots who are purely logical in their motivations yet seem human in their capacity for joyful invention. In the stories in *Bajka robotów* (1964), which were translated with other pieces as *Mortal Engines*, Lem proposes that the logical behavior of robots and their immunity to conflicting emotions might make them morally superior to human beings. *Opowieści o pilocie Pirxie* (1968; translated into two volumes, *Tales of Pirx the Pilot* and *More Tales of Pirx the Pilot)* is a collection of fables featuring Pirx, a young astronaut whose luck, common sense, and physical agility help him overcome various obstacles. These stories are among many works in which Lem explores the role of chance and randomness in human life. Much of Lem's short fiction has been collected in *The Cosmic Carnival of Stanislaw Lem:*

An Anthology of Entertaining Short Stories by the Modern Master of Science Fiction (1981).

In several works, Lem parodies and experiments with literary forms. *Sledztwo* (1959; *The Investigation*) is an "anti-mystery" in which all inquiries into the disappearance of bodies from a graveyard prove fruitless. The protagonist of *Katar* (1976; *The Chain of Chance*), a mystery novel structured as an essay on probability, eventually uncovers the reasons behind a series of incomprehensible deaths after attending to the laws of chance. *Doskonola proznia* (1971; *A Perfect Vacuum*) and *Wielkosz urojona* (1973; *Imaginary Magnitude*) are composed of satirical introductions and book reviews of imaginary works which, according to Lem, will be completed "some time in the future but do not exist yet." *A Perfect Vacuum* contains sixteen book reviews written, according to John Leonard, from the perspective of "the New Critic, the structuralist, the terrorist, the metaphysician, the assistant professor of gerunds and the twit."

Lem has also contributed critical articles and essays on scientific topics to East European and American magazines. These works have been collected in such books as *Dialogi* (1957), a collection of dialogues on the future of cybernetics; *Summa technologiae* (1964), a study of the effect of technology on human behavior; and *Filozofia przypadku: Literature w swietle empirii* (1968), a discourse on various philosophical issues. In *Fantastyka i futurologia* (1971), Lem attempts to develop a scientific approach to science fiction criticism. He takes a similar stance in his essay "Science Fiction: A Hopeless Case—With Exceptions," which is included in *Microworlds: Science Fiction and Fantasy* (1985). In these works, Lem maintains that the science fiction genre should be based on sound scientific doctrines and that writers should have a firm knowledge of literary techniques in order to expound intelligently upon humanity's role in the universe.

While Lem is considered a major science fiction writer in Eastern Europe, critical response has been mixed in the United States and Great Britain. Lem's dismissal of many Western science fiction writers for what he perceives as their ignorance of scientific theories and their inferior literary practices has been suggested as a reason for the critical resistance to his work. However, Lem is internationally respected for his erudition and his command of literary techniques.

(See also *CLC*, Vols. 8, 15; *Contemporary Authors*, Vol. 105; and *Contemporary Authors Autobiography Series*, Vol. 1.)

JERZY JARZEBSKI

Before the political thaw in 1956 known as the "Polish October" Lem published three SF books: two novels, *The Astronauts* (1951) and *The Magellan Nebula* (1955), and a collection, *Sesame and Other Stories* (1954). The two novels became tremendously popular and were reprinted many times. (p. 110)

These early works show some technical weaknesses, quite aside from a certain conceptual schematism, and it is somewhat paradoxical that it was those two novels that became required reading in Polish schools. In *The Astronauts* and *Sesame* especially, the indecision of the author is all too obvious. Should I lecture and popularize, or rather spin fantastic plots?, he seems to wonder. The first part of *The Astronauts,* describing the preparations for an expedition to Venus, is unbearably slow and full of lectures; and only the second part, "The Diary of

a Pilot," written with the narrative skill characteristic of Lem, makes up for the failures of the first part. In *Sesame* we find, besides the first Star Diaries of Ijon Tichy, full of humour and written with narrative vigor, also lectures in popular science that repel the reader.

Lem drew the conclusion from these difficulties. The most successful parts of his early works were told by a narrator who was at the same time the protagonist of the story and involved in the plot; the narrative flow began to slow down when the author himself appeared from behind the hero and started plaguing the reader with lectures on the principles of computers, the design of interplanetary rockets, etc. In *The Magellan Nebula* Lem refrained from introducing a narrator who would be identical with the author, and his role was taken over by a member of the expedition. . . . Through the inexperienced eyes of the protagonist we are first introduced to and involved in the peripeties of the future and the galactic expedition. This device allows the text to convey much information about the civilizational marvels of future centuries, for the young narrator must himself still learn quite a lot. . . . (p. 111)

The Magellan Nebula is very skilfully written, even if somewhat uneven—for this beautiful ship flounders every so often on sandbanks. . . . Lem frankly admits that for him writing is a pulpit from which he delivers certain theses about the society of the future, the evolution of science, the philosophical implications of technological progress, etc.; his visions are not puzzle-games with fantasy elements. In Lem's opinion, the term "*science* fiction" implies an obligation. In his early works, however, these noble principles are at odds with artistic ambitions; diagnoses of the world's future are presented as if they were axioms: a just order of society must triumph, science and technology must achieve a high level of development where the sky is the limit. . . .

It is difficult to decide just what in this vision was Lem and what was taken over from the literary clichés of the time. The Lem of that time—a rationalist and believer in scientism—perhaps really believed in the unlimited visions of human reason, but he expressed them in pretentious formulas, with which *The Magellan Nebula* abounds. His views are, if one overlooks this defect, humanist ones; however, the weakness of his characters is contentment with their fate—his humanism is too self-righteous. Their philosophical problems have already been or are being solved somewhere, so that the experiences transmitted become simply verifications of already existing hypotheses and emerge as glib phrases.

Such ideal characters from a happy utopia are somewhat of a nuisance even for the author, who reminds us several times—as it were contradicting himself—that the human soul is complete in itself and must not be tampered with, and that weakness and evil must not be forgotten in our view of human beings. The image of a Terrestrial Paradise will reappear twice in Lem—characteristically, however, in a negative function. In *Return from the Stars* (1961) the flowering of civilization is due to an operation called "betrization," which is mandatory for all children. It does away with all aggressive instincts, but as a corollary also destroys the ability to take risks. . . . In a distorted mirror, this motif recurs again in the recent short novel *The Futurological Congress* . . . , where paradise is only a drug-induced illusion, a camouflage for the awful living conditions of a population of several billion at the end of the 21st century.

It would appear that the main weakness of *The Astronauts* and *The Magellan Nebula* is philosophical: the young Lem owes allegiance to positivistic ideals, he believes in the progress of science which can in final analysis cope with any problem, and not least he believes that an enlightened and rational society will automatically get rid of all its inner conflicts and tensions. But it might rather be said that it was the normative fictional convention (''socialist realism'') which in this manner ''thought for him.'' . . . [In] his early work, despite all efforts, Lem on the whole does not succeed in confronting his heroes with novel experiences that are apt to shake their firm convictions and ethical norms. The bloodthirsty Venusians in *The Astronauts,* who had been planning an invasion of Earth, are only a projection of human beings, and the mysterious inhabitants of the White Planet in *The Magellan Nebula* also react like human beings. . . . Finally, for Lem's early cosmic wanderers their ideals are sufficient to interpret and evaluate unequivocally the phenomena which they encounter: they travel to the stars with their earthly yardstick, and the stars can be readily measured with it. This motif too will reappear later, polemically refunctioned.

Lem was much too intelligent a writer not to have been aware of the dangers of this situation. As mentioned, parallel to the first novels he wrote the early tales of *The Star Diaries.* The distinguishing mark of that cycle, already in the first edition, is originality: these stories are Lem's first attempt at literary stylization. . . . Lem has an almost incredible sense of language, and *The Star Diaries* became a veritable orgy of parodies. Inserted into the history of the legendary liar and braggart we find samples of the turgid style of doctoral theses, political speeches . . . , tourist guides, etc. He parodies not only the language, but also certain modes of thinking. This makes for gorgeous political satires . . . and pokes fun at any kind of scientific and humanist thought that, hopelessly lost in geo- and anthropocentrism, fits the universe into patterns of thinking developed on Earth (the maturity exams among the Andrygonians).

As is only proper for a ''philosophical tale,'' each of Ijon Tichy's journeys, for all of its grotesque cosmical trappings, amounts to a viewing of mundane and contemporary problems. . . . Lem operates on two levels—that of SF and that of the narrator who is a Münchhausen-like tall-tale teller. It should be stressed here how different those two levels of fantasy are: SF aims at discovering the serious flaws of the future and—surprising as this may sound—it sometimes succeeds. The Münchhausen type of ''lying fantasy'' is, on the contrary, first of all an amusing entertainment. The first kind of fantasy claims: what I say may really happen; the second makes us believe that a well-told lie is more beautiful than the dull truth. . . . It is hardly an accident that *The Star Diaries* again and again make use of the motif of *the false world,* a world full of lies because of its language, its ideology, because of a scientific theory as narrow as it is apodictic. Literature as a piling up of lies, which then, paradoxically, may sometimes point the way to truth—that is the dominant image that emerges behind the grotesque adventures of the ''famous circumnavigator of stars.'' (pp. 111-13)

In the works after 1956, the basis of Lem's writing emerges ever more clearly. In a long series of novels and stories the author presents tragedies and problems of *the individual striving to know the world*. It is by reason of this radical refusal to supply proofs for assumed theories that Lem's works from that time on rather ask than answer difficult questions—and therefore most of his works seem to ''lack a solution,'' as has sometimes naively been noted by criticism. . . . (p. 113)

In 1959 the novels *Eden* and *The Investigation* as well as the short-story collection *Invasion from Aldebaran* were published. *Eden* is a fairly typical SF novel, describing the adventures of an expedition from Earth on an alien planet. The astronauts meet a civilization of a rather high level, but one that was evolved by perfecting bio-evolution rather than machines. In this way ''living'' factories arose, and then plans of substituting for the population a generation of mutants, formed according to the specifications of the planet rulers. However, both experiments failed and a secret government has decided that the ''faulty''inhabitants must die. (p. 114)

The ''serious'' works published by Lem since 1959 as a rule confront their protagonists with phenomena which surpass their understanding and defy the criteria of human morality. *The Investigation,* an ingenious ''anti-mystery'' set against the background of real places of contemporary England, confronts a constable of the British police with the insoluble mystery of corpses disappearing from graveyards under mysterious circumstances. The author draws upon the means of the conventional detective story: unusual occurrences, an inquest, interrogations; a number of hypotheses are formulated. But whereas in the usual mystery we can observe the triumph of intelligence, turning all misty assumptions and clues into a meaningful and intelligible whole, here all investigations and attempts to solve the case can only lead to a dead end. The logic of the enquiry, compromised again and again, is merely an indication of how easily human understanding is fooled by random events.

What ''solution'' does the author finally suggest? An eccentric specialist of mathematical statistics establishes a series of parameters necessary for the emergence of the phenomena under investigation (and in their choice Lem provides some brilliant black humour by supplying a whole catalogue of devices typical of the cloak-and-dagger novel). He analyzes the occurrences and the geographical extension of the cases, and predicts then where and when some more corpses will be ''resurrected'' and what will be the end of the series. And this is what happens. Is that all?, the disappointed reader asks. Equally disappointed is the constable, who, led by his wish to explain the causes and the purpose of the phenomena, allows himself to make guesses whose absurdity is all too obvious. But aside from a mathematical model for the series of facts, the author provides no explanation; moreover he seems to poke fun at the simple-minded tendency of human beings to explain all events with the help of symbols that are intelligible only in a given civilization. (pp. 115-16)

The novel *Solaris,* one of Lem's outstanding achievements, confronts its heroes with . . . serious problems. The crew of a space station hovering over the planet Solaris tries to contact the only inhabitant of this globe, a gigantic plasma-like ''ocean.'' This baffling entity, which exhibits biological activities, proves to be so different from human beings that periodical attempts at contact have turned into a chronicle of failures. In the station mysterious ''doubles'' or ''Phi-creatures'' show up—materializations of human beings who had some connection with important, more often than not guilt-provoking experiences of crew members. By means of his X-ray vision, the ocean looks into the minds of the ambassadors from Earth and takes from them as it were the blueprints of the beings that had so far been encapsulated into their unconscious memory. Work on the station virtually collapses; each of the researchers flees into solitude to adjust himself to his complex of shame that has suddenly become visible in all its turpitude. Who then is here conducting experiments with whom? What is the goal of the emergence of the "Phi-creatures"? The scientists get no answer to that question . . . The contact was established in the only possible way, by direct entry into the psyche of the partner, but its results prove of no value to men. Instead of insights into the "soul of the Ocean," they encountered only their own mirror-images.

The experiment to which human beings are subjected on Solaris is cruel because it mercilessly reveals a hard truth. In the psyche of the crew the Ocean has sought out the most important, the most deeply hidden thing, something that in a manner constitutes the personality of the individual. And without exception it was found that the "core of the psyche" consists of memories of subjective, very personal and very painful experiences, which human beings are not likely to communicate even to each other. It is not the voyage to the stars and the contact with "aliens" that has shaped Chris Kelvin's soul, but a banal if tragical story of the death of a girl. Collectively we dare to engage in enterprises of gigantic proportions, but these acts exist as it were separate from us; when we are left to ourselves, we cannot master our own inner strife, which is the result of our social contacts. (pp. 116-17)

In *His Master's Voice,* . . . the possibility of contact with "others" is isolated for a treatment resembling almost a philosophical treatise. *His Master's Voice* is the fictitious diary of an American mathematician engaged in decoding strange signals from outer space. The research project is shrouded in strict secrecy, on a military proving ground in the desert and under continuous surveillance by the military establishment. The novel has no sensational plot; all the discoveries with which Lem attracts the attention of the reader are of a rather intellectual nature. It is an essay on the impossibility of real communication between civilizations, between societies, between human beings. The enormous efforts of the scientists to decipher the "cosmic message" and the diverging but equally unprovable hypotheses are superadded to the differences in the research team. (p. 117)

A novel of Lem's dealing exclusively with the problems of cognition and communication appeared already in 1961 as *Memoirs Found in a Bathtub.* One could compile an anthology of primitive attempts to interpret that book. It is easy to see how the *Memoirs,* with their atmosphere of grotesque, black humour, could have led many a critic astray. In the introduction "from the 32nd Century" we learn that the *Memoirs* are a valuable discovery, found in the ruins of a Third Pentagon— the last refuge of the Ministry of Defense and the CIA of a United States in decline. Cut off from the inhabited world, the "Building" in the Rocky Mountains degenerates into a hermetically sealed institution, where activities consist only in never-ceasing exchanges of roles among the personnel while the basic structure of the "Building," the true cause of the system of masks and their function, remains unchanged. (p. 118)

It goes without saying that the genre of an ephemeral political satire cannot do justice to such contents. The author revealingly winks at the reader and suggests to him that "the Hyberiad Gnostors, for example, consider the first twelve pages apocryphal, an addition of later years." And the introduction has exactly this length. In a world of an ubiquitous secret service and a total camouflage, the text of the *Memoirs* too must be a code—and a many-layered one, much as is the case with the fragment from *Romeo and Juliet* decoded by a special machine, showing in the first analysis the aggressive feelings of Shakespeare against one Matthews, and—below that—an ecstatic stuttering (an occasion for a brilliant persiflage of the most bizarre outcrops of psychoanalysis on the part of Lem). We

may therefore assume that the *Memoirs* are a persiflage of the bureaucratic machinery of modern secret services only on the surface; somewhat deeper, they are perhaps an allegory of the fate of the individual in a society with an interrupted information flow . . . , but finally we discover that the novel portrays the tragedy of human cognition. The human being, driven by a thirst for knowledge about the world, basically asks the same question as the hunted hero of the *Memoirs:* he asks for the meaning, the essence, the *telos* of surrounding reality, he asks for the reason of his own existence. Even the answer is the same: everything is or could be a code, a mask, a camouflage. (pp. 118-19)

[The stories in *The Tales of Pirx the Pilot* are all] variations on a theme—the model of man in the cosmic era. Is this perhaps too pompous a term? It is a fact that Pirx, initially a cadet, and in the end a commander, is subjected to ever more difficult tasks as the tales progress. Nearly all Pirx stories investigate his physical fitness, his practical skill and cleverness, and finally his intellectual talents. The Pirx cycle has been planned with admirable consistency: parallel to the growth of the hero grows the difficulty of the problems that he encounters. This changes the tone of the tales from a joyful and carefree mood to a totally somber atmosphere in the concluding story "Ananke." By the same token the voice of the protagonist changes: at first it is frank, if sometimes rather shy and full of complexes, but in the end Pirx appears as a man weighted down by the heavy load of experiences, perhaps even embittered.

What is the purpose of this temporally drawn-out narration? The character of Pirx has been cleverly designed: he is supposed to be an average human being—neither good nor evil, nor especially talented. This seeming "mediocrity," by the way, is a source of constant irritation for young Pirx. Nevertheless, the consecutive tests the hero undergoes all end well, and, most important, the author stresses that in every case Pirx was successful where specialists, or whole teams of them, had previously failed. Is he then just another of the "cosmic heroes" with which trivial SF abounds? Lem is not that naive; Pirx does not beat the experts with their own weapons: all of his successes are based on chance—"somehow" he succeeds in emerging unscathed from the calamities of **"Test"** and **"The Patrol"**; a seemingly meaningless association saves him in **"The Conditioned Reflex"** and naivete in **"The Trial."** He solves the mystery surrounding Cornelius and the computer in **"Ananke"** again "any which way"—nearly at random. (pp. 119-20)

[Through the character of Pirx, Lem] set out to find a place, in the world of triumphant technology, where human weakness and human imperfection are no longer defects. . . . Initially Pirx competes with the specialists, but the specialist is, Lem seems to suggest, a human being reduced so as to function only in a certain intellectual sphere, a technician for the solution of certain problems in his own field. In the story **"The Trial"** Lem therefore substitutes for the specialist a humanlike robot who—once it recognizes its perfection—aims at ruling the world. The rebellious robot Calder is nothing less than the concentration of a whole team of specialists in one body; by proceeding logically he cannot be defeated. But Calder thinks only too logically, and he loses because he cannot understand irrational action; he is not flexible enough. "Seen in this light, our humanity is the sum of our faults and defects, our imperfections in fact; it is what we strive after but cannot attain, cannot do, cannot understand; it is simply the abyss between our ideals and their realization—isn't it?"—reflects Pirx in **"The Trial."**

This weakness that turns into strength is not a real paradox. Lem's human beings are—just like the humans of Sartre—perpetually non-identical to themselves, always leaning toward their ideal image which they never attain. Since man remains imperfect until the end, he accepts the world as it is—like himself a little "failed" or "unfinished"; he accepts its dynamics and its unexpected mutations that sometimes stymie the most advanced computer programs. (pp. 120-21)

As is evident from his last works, it is becoming ever more difficult for Lem to write "normal SF stories." *A Perfect Vacuum* is composed of reviews of non-existent books. In 1973 Lem published *Imaginary Magnitude*—a cycle of introductions to books "published" between 1990 and 2029. In his writings Lem has unmistakably returned to Earth, and is now more interested in the development of human civilization than in the exploration of the cosmos. Disillusion? Has the invention of ever new cosmic beings and adventures become for him a literary activity that he can no longer justify to himself with a clean conscience? For the time being he prefers—aside from a few stories that continue his old cycles—to design "projects" of books, rather than really write them. (p. 123)

Jerzy Jarzebski, "Stanislaw Lem, Rationalist and Visionary," translated by Franz Rottensteiner, in Science-Fiction Studies, *Vol. 4, No. 12, July, 1977, pp. 110-26.*

T. J. BINYON

[In *The Chain of Chance*] police are baffled by a series of inexplicable deaths, seemingly connected by the fact that the victims tend to be male, middle-aged, foreign, and to have some link with Naples. A former American astronaut follows the path taken by one of the casualties, but nothing untoward occurs.... [It] is only after a conversation with a pure mathematician on random causality, followed by a demonstration of its effect, that the hero approaches a solution.

This book comes as a disappointment after Stanislaw Lem's earlier fiction: an interesting beginning soon sinks into a slow and turbid narrative stream—high on ratiocination, low on action—which winds its way through an exiguous plot down to an artificial and not entirely unexpected conclusion.

T. J. Binyon, "At Random," in The Times Literary Supplement, *No. 3998, November 17, 1978, p. 1333.*

GEORGE ZEBROWSKI

[In *The Chain of Chance*, an] American ex-astronaut investigates the deaths of eleven men in an Italian resort by duplicating all the circumstances preceding their deaths, with himself as guinea pig. What makes this a fascinating, though low-keyed suspense story, is the way it prods our minds to glimpse some kind of pattern in the various deaths, much in the same way that astronomers of the last century "saw" the canals of Mars in the broken lines and patchy fragments of their telescopic images. Although this is not a science fiction story in the obvious sense, it is science-fictional in the Fortean sense. The novel is about probability, causality, random-quandaries of the unknown as it comes into collision with an inquiring human being; as such the book widens the scope of the SF novel, by bringing into the here-and-now the mysterious aspects of the universe around us, by finding the unknown in the ordinary.

Specifically, the story deals with "emergent" events of the kind that are not predictable, though explainable after the fact. Synergetic effects of this kind are the source of all that is novel in the universe, when various elements come together to create new wholes.... The only complaint I have about this sleek, subtle book, is that the character of the American astronaut is not convincing; he is a very believable human being, but a European, not an American. Discerning readers might like to compare Lem's astronaut to the one in Benford's *In the Ocean of Night*, and to Barry Malzberg's various astronauts. (p. 31)

George Zebrowski, in a review of "The Chain of Chance," in The Magazine of Fantasy and Science Fiction, *Vol. 57, No. 1, July, 1979, pp. 31-2.*

JOHN UPDIKE

[The essay excerpted below originally appeared in The New Yorker, *September 8, 1980.]*

Hal Bregg, the hero of Stanislaw Lem's *Return from the Stars,* went out from Earth on an astronautical expedition at the age of thirty, and returned at the age of forty a hundred twenty-seven years later. The troubling discrepancy is caused, of course, by that clause of Einstein's relativity laws, well known to concocters of science fiction, which postulates that fast motion slows down time, and very fast motion will slow it down greatly, relative to objects not in such motion. Ten harrowing years adventuring among the stars have passed for Bregg, and more than a century on Earth, during which all his friends have died, the landmarks he knew have vanished, cities have been transformed into translucent, mazy wonderlands, the aggressive instincts within humanity have been biologically exorcised by a process termed "betrization," an antigravitational device has been invented and widely installed, and a universal reign of peace and pleasure has been established, with robots doing all the dirty work. The conquistadorial philosophy that sent Bregg and his colleagues out into space has passed from the Earth, and as the surviving astronauts return they occasion as much awkwardness as if a pack of Neanderthal men were resuscitated and set to roaming in Bloomingdale's. (pp. 568-69)

Return from the Stars not only is about a time lag but embodies one, for it was published in Poland nineteen years ago. But out of the science and technology of the time Lem has constructed a future that does not, unlike so many hypothetical futures, seem dated. In this brave new world, circa 2127, people spray their clothes on out of a can. Books have been boiled down to corn-size crystals that can be played either by optons (which reproduce the written text) or by lectons (which read it aloud); original books are called "crystomatrices." The cinema has been replaced by the "real," which projects three-dimensional images that grow larger and more intense wherever the viewer directs his attention; a "realist" is a "real" star. Money is no longer needed for essentials.... These elegant extensions of our present technology (less fantastic, surely, than our present autos, airplanes, escalators, and computers would appear to a visitor from 1830) are detailed by the author with a tireless gusto; the manner in which the new world bewilderingly and dazzlingly envelops the starworn space traveller—like a mixture of airport, amusement park, and Roman bath—is brilliantly imagined, as are the incidents of galactic travel. Lem loves exposition, and devotes pages to the mock-history of betrization, to the hardware of his hero's space flight (conceived eight years before the moon landing), to the chimerical developments of mathematics.... To make a long theory short: Emil Mitke, ''a crippled genius,'' has done ''with the theory of relativity what Einstein had done with Newton.'' Out of his ''infernal mathematics'' it has been possible to create a ''black box'' that will release a ''gravitational antifield'' whenever gravity might be precipitating misfortune. Lem knows when to surfeit us with details and when to finesse. Of these marvellous black boxes he smoothly assures us, ''The simplicity of their construction was as astounding as the complexity of the theory that produced them.'' About the process of betrization he is more specific: ''Betrization acted on the developing prosencephalon at an early stage in life by means of a group of proteolytic enzymes.'' Lem is frequently droll. Alluding to the anachronisms that no doubt stud our own historical dramas, he describes a real in which ''the hero seated himself on the tails of his jacket and drank beer through a straw.'' (pp. 569-71)

As long as Lem plays the genial host with his riches of erudition and bids us sit down in a spirit of festive speculation, we are flattered and entertained; his attempt to cater to us with a mundane novel of psychology and eros, however, is relatively clumsy. And this attempt tends to dominate the latter pages of the book, after Lem has exhausted, for the time being, his store of ideas on scientific and social trends. Hal Bregg, as a romantic hero, makes those gruff ladykillers played by Robert Mitchum and Richard Widmark look courtly. (p. 571)

His hero seems a bit brutal and thick even to us of the unbetrizated present, and the pioneer heroism of human space exploration a bit quaint, especially now that robot satellites are doing so well. Hal Bregg recalls that in space flight, as one hung there ''seemingly motionless in relation to the stars,'' novels came to appear silly: ''To read that some Peter nervously puffed his cigarette and was worried about whether or not Lucy would come, and that she walked in and twisted her gloves, well, first you began to laugh at this like an idiot, and then you simply saw red.'' In the flight of the imagination that Lem engineers, some similar affliction overtakes his narrative: normal, irrational, egotistic, venereal human behavior, such as has aroused our respectful empathy in a hundred less intelligent books, seems silly, and a kind of imposition upon the universe. We find ourselves wishing that Lem would write a novel about the revolt of the robots against the dough-headed, so we could root for the robots.

This could not have been an easy novel to translate, with its many abstruse considerations and its words coined in Polish. The author, too, had to translate, not just into the future but onto this continent, for the unnamed nation that Hal Bregg returns to is located on the territory of the present United States. . . . The novel's central concern with the instinct of aggression reflects a topical interest of its time; our Eighties are more apt to wonder what undeclared energy source is powering all this vast and servile machinery in the year 2127. On the whole, though, Lem knits his hypothetical world together with an abundance and rigor more than visionary, and approaching the close-woven texture of naturalism. It is encouraging, we might add, and perhaps a souvenir from 1961, that a Polish writer operating in the shadow of the considerable Soviet school of science fiction should locate the future here in America. (pp. 572-73)

John Updike, ''Some Nachtmusik, from All Over: Frontiersmen,'' in his Hugging the Shore: Essays and Criticism, *1983. Reprint by Vintage Books, 1984, pp. 568-75.**

CRAIG BROWN

Tales of Pirx the Pilot could have been written by someone [other than Lem], so lacking is it in interest of any sort. The first few pages of these short stories with a shared hero bode well: Pirx is a young space cadet, full of hopes and dreams, surrounded by students more proficient than he is. The creation of such a hero suggests a certain parody of the genre—as Pirx finds himself bemused by the lists of astronomical jargon, so does the reader. . . . But before long it becomes apparent that the reader is expected to be fully interested in these boring lists, because most of the conclusions depend upon their scrutiny and digestion.

The character of Pirx, in the opening passages so pleasantly unlikely, becomes annoyingly professional as the book develops and his vehicle and surroundings begin to reveal mechanical faults. This is less a sign of any grand scheme than of lazy writing. . . .

Lem's second book to be published this year (though he wrote it in 1960) is a more unified and considered work. *Return From the Stars* is the chronicle of an astronaut who returns to earth after a mission lasting ten years, which in earth time is 127 years. The major change lies in the nature of humanity. . . . Risk ''does not exist any more. . . . A man cannot impress a woman with heroics, with reckless deeds, and yet literature, art, our whole culture for centuries was nourished by this current: love in the face of adversity.''. . .

When Lem's energy is channelled into forcing ideas together—juxtaposing love with violence, perfection with mediocrity—then his work is thrilling, but too often it is servicing obscure storylines, names and explanations. *Return from the Stars* reads like one of those synopses for science fiction novels that Vonnegut's Kilgore Trout is always dropping into his reminiscences. Lem would do well to learn from Vonnegut that an idea is not a novel.

Craig Brown, ''Explanations of Synopses,'' in The Times Literary Supplement, *No. 4049, November 7, 1980, p. 1270.*

GEORGE ZEBROWSKI

[The stories collected in *Tales of Pirx the Pilot*] show us a young cadet who grows in maturity and complexity as he confronts ever more difficult problems; a recap, in effect, of the history of SF from the simple stories about wonders and future possibilities to the subtle, ambitious and problematical SF which we now expect from our best writers. . . .

The complete cycle of stories shows us that ''hard'' SF can develop depth not only in its technical side, but in the fictional, writerly virtues. There are no super heroes in this book, and no easy solutions. Writers who want to see how imaginative developments can be presented together with realism and truthfulness about human beings should read this book. It is this combination's possibility which is often denied by many writers. (p. 56)

Return From The Stars comes to us from 1961, from the period of *Solaris*. To say that it is about an astronaut who returns to an earth which has gone forward in time while he has aged only ten years, is to say that Beethoven's Sixth Symphony is about flowers, trees, and summer storms. Aside from the clever observations, the vivid human aches and perceptions, Lem has accomplished the difficult illusion of showing us a future world which may be distasteful to us, but which may be seen as quite legitimate and even desirable by its own people, *and* by us, if we were to change certain ways of seeing and understanding. Hal Bregg comes to accept his new world with some difficulty, after he has experienced it emotionally and aesthetically, but what may have happened is that a human being has given up to the inevitable and adapted. I'm not sure that Lem accepts this world, but he has avoided, if perhaps only partially, the easy trap of depicting a world we can all hate without understanding. . . .

In its human details, as well as in its collision of two different moments of experience, *Return From The Stars* is easily one of the best conceived treatments of the theme. It has been predicted that it may well be Lem's most popular book with Western audiences. Lem's own view is that it resembles conventional SF, and that his most popular books have always been those that do; he regrets any popularity which comes from sharing genre props and details, because he has tried to do more aspiring work, which has not been popular. But I think we can safely take the book away from him and read it for itself. . . . Lem is so demanding of himself that he fails to see that there is a uniform level of quality in all his work, genre limits aside, and that makes all the difference. . . .

Lem has now reached an all but unattainable position for an SF writer: he is recognized as one of the world's finest writers. (p. 57)

George Zebrowski, in a review of "Tales of Pirx the Pilot" and "Return from the Stars," in The Magazine of Fantasy and Science Fiction, *Vol. 60, No. 4, April, 1981, pp. 56-9.*

ADAM MARS-JONES

Stanislaw Lem was a medical student before he was a writer, and some of that training still shows through in his fiction; not so much in its knowledge of technicalities as in its respect for and insistence on the human in a dehumanized environment. . . . However far Lem extrapolates from the present into the future, and however far into the universe he extends his speculations, he is exploring recognisable human possibilities. The settings may be cosmic, but the morals are terrestrial. How could they not be? . . .

The space traveller of the title [*Memoirs of a Space Traveler*] is Ijon Tichy, a genial amateur of theoretical physics, cybernetic congresses and Stregodentsian wildlife—for the conservation of which he makes an eloquent plea. When not actually dashing round the universe without apparent effort, fuel, or funds, in a one-man rocket-ship, he is the natural prey of that well-known type the Unappreciated Inventor, who calls on Tichy dragging behind him a trunk crammed with perverse innovations.

The various inventors in the book are never frauds, but neither are they the benefactors of mankind they imagine themselves to be; in their search for knowledge they have, more often than not, transgressed the bounds of the human. Tichy himself only once makes a similar mistake, when on his eighteenth voyage he creates the universe that we live in (as he does too); the venture is not a success, but perhaps Tichy derives from this experience the patience with human limitations he shows in the rest of the volume. He has a soft spot for the gremlin in the machine. . . .

In its paradoxical and teasing way this is a highly moral volume. It is also very funny; Lem's command of convincing jargon and absurd logic makes for consistently entertaining reading. Sometimes he strives for a *frisson* that is outside his range, as in the third of the **"Further Recollections"**; sometimes he becomes merely whimsical, as when he provides his own drawings for a comic bestiary of the cosmos, thereby inviting a comparison with Edward Lear that works against him; and sometimes he goes off at a tangent, abandoning his original idea for another one. Even if the second idea is the better, the story suffers from the disjunction.

So in **"The Washing Machine Tragedy"** a fairly routine satire on consumerism gives way to a brilliant fantasia on cosmic law. A fanatic (yet another of the rightly Unappreciated Inventors) who believes in the superiority of robots over human beings turns himself in the privacy of the Crab Nebula into a pseudo-human entity hundreds of miles long, composed of robots who can resolve themselves into units, or alternatively form a small planet. The State Department must decide, if it is to come up with a plan of action, whether it is dealing with a human being, a robot, a government, a celestial body, or children. The possibilities multiply, and the fun increases exponentially.

Memoirs of a Space Traveler can be confidently recommended to anyone who would like *Doctor Who* better if it had wit, panache, intellectual high-jinks, unpredictability and a sense of play. Those who care only for monsters, high camp and conventional love-interest will be greatly disappointed.

Adam Mars-Jones, "A Moral Cosmos," in The Times Literary Supplement, *No. 4120, March 19, 1982, p. 306.*

MARK ROSE

Memoirs of a Space Traveler is representative of Mr. Lem in his most fantastic vein. In one of these grotesque and witty tales an inventor has created electronic intelligences that live in iron boxes connected to a central drum of recorded stimuli representing all the experiences that a person may have in a lifetime. Totally isolated from the real world, the consciousnesses that inhabit the inventor's boxes believe that they are human beings. . . . Of course there is no way in which the boxes can discover their true natures, just as there is no way in which we can be certain that *we* are not analogous boxes dreaming that we are human.

The theme of life as a dream is of course as old as European literature, but it is characteristic of Mr. Lem to recast traditional materials. Often reminiscent of ghost stories and folk tales, his suggestive fables range from the disturbing or horrific to the playfully satiric. In other stories in this volume we encounter an inventor who keeps his wife's "soul" in a small box and another who has produced a perfect double of himself. We learn too how the universe was created and why human life has so many flaws . . . and we meet the alien civilization of **"Phools"** who have subjected themselves to a Governing Machine that turns them into perfect metal disks arranged in pleasing geometrical patterns.

At times satirical fantasy becomes almost pure whimsy. In **"The Washing Machine Tragedy,"** for instance, competition between manufacturers leads to ever more independent and intelligent home appliances until it becomes virtually impossible to legislate satisfactory social controls for, say, sexy ambulatory sinks that dress up in human clothes in order to seduce women and swindle them out of their fortunes. **"Let Us Save the Universe,"** the final piece in the collection, is a particularly spectacular flight of fancy. Here Mr. Lem's narrator, space traveler Ijon Tichy, complains about the deterioration of the universe as a consequence of the spread of civilization. . . . For years, Tichy remarks, "astrophysicists have been racking their brains over the reason for the great difference in the amounts of cosmic dust in various galaxies. The answer, I think, is quite simple: the higher a civilization is, the more dust and refuse it produces. This is a problem more for janitors than for astrophysicists."

The five stories in *More Tales of Pirx the Pilot* differ sharply in style and tone from the Ijon Tichy fantasies. Here we are in a relatively plausible future world in which astronauts such as Pirx fly regular commercial missions throughout the solar system. The "romantic days" of space travel are past. . . . (pp. 13, 33)

And yet events as romantic as those of popular fiction do sometimes occur. In the first of these stories a huge alien vessel passes within kilometers of Pirx's ship. Ironically, Pirx, who is hauling a load of scrap metal back from the region of Mercury, finds that it would be imprudent to report the encounter since no one would believe him. This wry variation on a familiar science-fiction theme suggests the way the Pirx tales, different as they are in style from the Ijon Tichy fables, also depend upon Mr. Lem's characteristically self-conscious adaptation of received forms.

In content too there is continuity between the two collections. Both are concerned with machines, particularly with willful and intelligent machines. In **"The Accident"** a robot inexplicably climbs a mountain, slips and falls to destruction. What kind of mechanical defect caused the robot to attempt the mountain? Pirx suspects that it was not defective at all but was responding to the challenge of the difficult climb. And in **"The Hunt"** another robot appears to show curiosity and perhaps even generosity.

The two longest pieces in the Pirx volume, **"The Inquest"** and **"Ananke,"** are really novellas rather than short stories, and like many of Mr. Lem's most interesting fictions, they are cast in the form of puzzles. In **"The Inquest"** Pirx commands an experimental mission in which some of his crew members—he does not know which—are robots. Can one distinguish between robot and man when all physical clues are eliminated? In a series of progressively more contradictory interviews, the crew members individually confess to Pirx, some claiming to be human, others to be robots. The story is gripping. In it Mr. Lem explores both the nature of mechanical intelligence and the nature of the sometimes inappropriate myths that we project, conceiving robots as, among other things, diabolic in their inhumanity and as versions of a forbidden erotic power.

"Ananke" also considers the interaction of human and mechanical psychologies and here too Mr. Lem deals with projection. A giant cargo ship, the first in a new class of space superfreighters, crashes while landing on Mars. . . . Sabotage is suspected, but the genuine explanation, which has to do with the compulsive personality of the ex-pilot who tested and certified the computer, is more interesting than sabotage. While "training" the computer the man inadvertently instilled a version of his own pattern of obsessive ritualized behavior. In this fine story, which includes a long meditation on the now discredited canals and other fantasies about the planet Mars, Mr.

Lem generalizes his particular concern with the relationship of people and machines into a study of how we all tend to project obsessive desires onto a world that is very different from our own.

Not every piece in these two books is as suggestive as **"The Inquest"** or **"Ananke"** or Ijon Tichy's grotesque tale of the dreaming boxes. Nor do any of these stories quite reach the level of Mr. Lem's acclaimed novel *Solaris*. But nearly every piece is in one way or another excellent, and this is particularly remarkable given the fact that both books are in a sense gleanings, collections of stories that were omitted from the earlier volumes. (pp. 33-4)

Mark Rose, "Who Is Human, Who Is Not?" in The New York Times Book Review, *September 19, 1982, pp. 13, 33-4.*

THOMAS RUFFEN

Translated into more than 30 languages, Stanislaw Lem has international acclaim as a first-rank writer of philosophical science fiction. His latest book [*More Tales of Pirx the Pilot*], however, the 14th by this celebrated Polish author, will do nothing to enhance that reputation.

In five stories we follow the further adventures of Pirx, a pilot-for-hire some time in the near future when astronauts have become the truck drivers of space, hauling their rigs over the commonplace highways of the post-industrial cosmos.

The first tale finds Pirx towing scrap metal through the sky while his entire crew is incapacitated with the mumps. When Pirx sights an alien spaceship, he tries to record the necessary sighting data all by himself and, in his confusion, enters his findings on an empty cassette recorder. Thus we have an extraterrestrial fish story: the UFO that got away.

It is a tale of little consequence, yet along the way the reader must slough through a most turgid and slow-moving narrative. This unfortunate pattern continues as Pirx tracks a robot bent on mountain-climbing, then a robot run amuck; as he outwits an evil-minded machine; and finally as he investigates a crash landing on Mars.

Pirx is moved through these tales like a stick of furniture through an empty house. Having done the work of creating his protagonist in the original volume, *Tales of Pirx the Pilot* (1979), Lem does not bother to re-create him here. In fact, all characters are poorly drawn and devoid of complexity; at no time do they threaten to involve the reader.

Lem takes no interest whatsoever in developing the milieu of outer space colonial life, leaving his paper characters flailing in a vacuum of nonexistent society. He places emphasis instead on pseudotechnical descriptions of futuristic objects and electro-mechanics, as entertaining and readable as a treatise on micro-chip specifications. . . .

It could be said that Lem's sesquipedalian indulgences get in the way of telling a story. But there is no story, merely a sequence of minor events that offer no twists or turns, dramatic choices or interesting complications.

We are given only a starting point, a few tangents of sophistry regarding man vs. machine, inaccessible sentences to decipher, an anticlimax, then, mercifully, after 220 arduous pages, a finish line.

Thomas Ruffen, "When Astronauts Became Truck Drivers," in Los Angeles Times Book Review, December 5, 1982, p. 16.

PETER ENGEL

Only recently discovered in England and America, Lem has for three decades written novels, plays, short stories, screenplays, pieces of literary criticism, sociological essays, and tomes on the science of cybernetics and the philosophy of chance—works of such significance that in Poland he is regarded as a leading contemporary philosopher of science. At last count Lem had published some thirty titles in thirty-one languages for a total of eleven million books sold, making him one of the best-selling science fiction writers in the world. . . .

[*The Cosmic Carnival of Stanislaw Lem* and *Memoirs of a Space Traveler*] should draw many of the as yet uninitiated into the expanding circle of Lem admirers. Although described on its cover as an anthology of a dozen of Lem's "unforgettable stories," *The Cosmic Carnival* in fact contains only seven stories: four cybernetic fairy tales from *The Cyberiad* and *Mortal Engines;* two voyages of Ijon Tichy, a kind of spaceage Gulliver, from *The Star Diaries;* and one of the *Tales of Pirx the Pilot.* The remaining five selections consist of four excerpts from various novels, *The Invincible, The Futurological Congress, Return From the Stars* and *Solaris,* and one essay from Lem's collection of reviews of nonexistent books, *A Perfect Vacuum.* As such, *The Cosmic Carnival* is a diversified but fragmentary introduction to the work of a great artist. *Memoirs of a Space Traveler* is somewhat more consistent, containing all the material omitted from the 1976 English edition of *The Star Diaries:* two more of Ijon Tichy's voyages, his five reminiscences, his encounter with Doctor Diagoras, and his open letter, "Let Us Save the Universe." Several of these pieces have appeared recently in *The New Yorker,* a rare distinction for a science fiction author in any language. (p. 37)

Perhaps the strongest tie between the two books is the sense, recorded by [Michael] Kandel in his informative notes to *The Cosmic Carnival,* that Lem is at heart a didactic writer. Lem's authorial judgment hovers over every page, and it is fair to presume that he intends none of his fantasy or farce to be taken too lightly. But Lem is a master satirist in the manner of Swift, and he manages to score his points without treading too heavily on plot or characterization.

For his most obviously moralizing statements he has chosen a moralizing genre, the fairy tale, and updated it for the cybernetic age. The robots Trurl and Klapaucius, slapstick constructors of *The Cyberiad,* are summoned in their **"Second Sally,"** a tale from *The Cosmic Carnival,* to the planet of cruel King Krool to construct a cybernetic beast for him to hunt. If they fail to create a worthy adversary, His Kroolty will reduce them to scrap metal like their predecessors. Trembling and rattling, they ask how many there have been before them. The king replies that he cannot recall how many constructors he has heaved down the scrap well—only that their screams of terror don't last as long as they used to, which means that the remains at the bottom are beginning to mount. In this archetypal fable it is not hard to predict where Lem's and our sympathies will lie. It would spoil the fun to describe how Trurl and Klapaucius try to escape from this predicament; suffice it to say that the ending is a happy one. (p. 38)

While the forces of man in other science fiction battle Bug-Eyed Monsters or Invaders from the Deep, Lem's protagonists face a far greater foe: an uncaring universe that wasn't expecting them and, now that they have arrived, isn't making their stay any more comfortable. The B.E.M., after all, is but a distortion of man's self-image, and Lem will have nothing to do with such anthropomorphic conceptions. If he must devise an alien being, then it will be a truly original creation like the sentient ocean of *Solaris* or the colony of cybernetic insects in *The Invincible.* And while these two novels are ostensibly adventure tales cast in traditional science fiction guise—and good ones at that, riveting and suspenseful—they function on a more profound level as parables of man's quest for meaning in a meaningless universe. The only meaning man has encountered, Lem contends, is that which he himself has constructed of the universe's random elements. Centuries of scientific probing have produced theories that purport to explain the actual workings of nature, but that are in fact nothing more than a series of ad hoc predictions. Lem's scientist-explorers will never fully comprehend the sentient ocean, the cybernetic insects, or the chain of chance events that governs our everyday lives. The universe remains inscrutable, and it is futile to try to explain it.

But man's uncontrollable curiosity forces him to try, and Lem takes us to task for the heroism we attach to so undignified an endeavor. His protagonists charge blindly into space in ships named "Prometheus" and "Invincible"; some do not return. The ambitions of even our finest adventurers are undercut by their human frailty. John, the narrator of *The Chain of Chance,* a recent Lem novel, is demoted to second-string astronaut when acute hay fever forces him to abandon a mission that unexpectedly discovers vegetation on Mars. Pilot Pirx, Lem's parody of a Heinleinian juvenile, is no Flash Gordon either; surrounded by his bulky space suit he more closely resembles the Michelin Tire man. Pirx is the characteristic bumbler whose heart is in the right place but whose mind tends to wander. In **"The Test,"** a piece from *The Cosmic Carnival,* his solo debut is jeopardized not by a technical malfunction but by the presence of two flies that proceed to do acrobatics, play tag, and mate on the radar screen. Pirx discovers, to his dismay, that his crib sheet yields no advice on the matter.

Ijon Tichy probably comes closest of all Lem's inventions to being the author's alter ego. *The Cosmic Carnival* includes Tichy's **"Seventh Voyage"**—perhaps the most slapstick of Lem's stories—in which Tichy ventures outside his solo craft to repair the pierced hull. As fate would have it, the rocket's constructors have not stopped to consider that it would take one man to hold the bolt with a wrench and another to tighten the nut. After a frustrated attempt of several hours to grasp the wrench with his feet, Tichy returns to the cabin to find that as a result of the broken drive regulator, the atomic pile has overheated and ruined his best cut of sirloin. Tichy jettisons the steak in disgust, only to be mortified minutes later at its return, now orbiting the drifting rocket in a slow, graceful ellipse that produces an eclipse of the sun every eleven minutes and four seconds.

Not only are we at the mercy of our physical clumsiness; we are also the victims of our psychological vulnerability, as some of Lem's more naturalistic fiction makes clear. (pp. 38-9)

In the **"Seventh Voyage,"** a dozing Tichy, having failed to fix the broken hull, is rudely awakened by an insistent and familiar-looking stranger—the spitting image of himself, formed by his ship's passage through a high-gravity time loop. The Doppelgänger merely wants Tichy to help fix the ship, but the sleepy Tichy angrily chases him away. Soon there are dozens of identical timeloop Tichys, and as the ship drifts helplessly through space, all they can do is argue over which two should repair it. Lem's sobering message is all too clear: We have met the enemy, and he is us. (p. 39)

Peter Engel, "Cybernetic Moralist," in The New Republic, *Vol. 188, No. 5, February 7, 1983, pp. 37-9.*

STEPHEN BANN

A mutant, or a 'cybernetic cuckoo', at the centre of a novel inevitably causes mayhem. But set your cyborg in the context of an old-fashioned, morally weighty dilemma; endow your central character with an appropriate range of human hopes and fears; and you will have the recipe for a Science Fiction story by Stanislaw Lem. But what you will not have, at this stage, is the extraordinarily supple and vivid narrative style of Lem himself, which has required the services of no less than three translators for *More Tales of Pirx the Pilot* and is fully worthy of such an effort. . . .

Both Lem's technical capacities and—even more decidedly—his ethic of a belated, humanistic professionalism put one in mind of Kipling, whose splendid Science Fiction story, "With the Night Mail", anticipates this collection much more clearly than the conventionally cited sources. Pirx the Pilot anthropomorphises the universe: his glimpse of the 'billion-year-old carcass' causes a tremor of recognition to pass from our solar system to another, inconceivably far removed. Pirx the Pilot even humanises the cyborg: that is to say, he is tempted to when the adventure yarns of **"The Accident"** and **"The Hunt"** bring him face to face with the possibility of free will and moral awareness being inexplicably generated by the electronic brain. In the longest and most absorbing story, **"The Inquest"**, Pirx is faced with the same problem in an inverted form: how to test the capacities of the perfectly convincing cyborg pilot by creating an emergency in which his true 'nature' will reveal itself. (p. 22)

Stephen Bann, "Paradise Lost," in London Review of Books, *Vol. 5, No. 5, March 17 to March 31, 1983, pp. 22-23.**

PETER S. BEAGLE

At one point in this fascinating, alarming and occasionally frustrating novel [*His Master's Voice*] a scientist involved in a Pentagon-sponsored attempt to decode what may or may not be a "letter from the stars" begins reading great swatches of popular science-fiction stories in hope of generating new ideas. "Indeed, a mistake," remarks the aging mathematician [Peter Hogarth] who narrates *His Master's Voice:* "He had not read such books before; he was annoyed—indignant, even—expecting variety, finding monotony. 'They have everything *except* fantasy,' he said. . . .

If there is progress in a culture, the progress is above all conceptual, but literature, the science-fiction variety in particular, has nothing to do with that."

However accurate this generalization may be—and it has been a running complaint of Stanislaw Lem's for years—it could never be taken to apply to his own work. Over the last three decades he has created a body of profoundly speculative writing that—even sometimes at a double remove from us by way of German or French translations—has retained such intellectual

bite, such rigorous wit, such deadly playful tightrope walking as to make him a modern European version of Swift or Voltaire. His books have been translated into some 30 languages, and he has devotees throughout the world. . . .

Every Lem story is haunted by a passionate, prophetic understanding of what the human being is going to have to learn and become merely to survive, coupled with an unblinded realism about the nature of the species. *His Master's Voice* is no exception.

Originally published in 1968, the book does, however, mark a turning point in Mr. Lem's writing that may be seen either as a dead end or a culmination. There is almost no dialogue and no action beyond the recounting of a project that not only failed but was never truly comprehended in the first place. An interstellar "letter" in the form of a pulsating neutrino ray is never definitely proved to be an attempt at communication. What is proved is that if it were, the best minds of Western science would be incapable of translating the address or making out the postmark. . . .

The first third of *His Master's Voice* is difficult. One becomes uncomfortable with Hogarth's edgily distant style, bewildered by most of the debates and conjectures among the assorted mathematicians, astrophysicists and linguists who make up the Pentagon project and bored with the trudging pace of the narrative. One longs for Pirx the Pilot again. As in Gresham's law, cheap, easy thinking drives out the kind that demands, and with this novel, Mr. Lem has made nothing easy for his audience or himself.

Yet by the last chapters, one is racing like a romance-novel addict, wanting very much to know what the synthesized slime variously called Frog Eggs and Lord of the Flies turned out to be: a cosmic recipe, bait for planetary suicide or simply the fluke result of our misreading a message intended for our elders and betters. Mr. Lem's gamble pays off grandly. It is, finally, Peter Hogarth's weary, dry (though far from arid), compassionate, sardonic, endlessly self-questioning voice that makes us listen and care and feel that this is the way it will be when at last we ants begin to swarm over the abandoned picnic tables and wastebaskets of the universe. (pp. 7, 33)

As much as anything else, *His Master's Voice* is extraordinary for what it is not. I can think of writers who could probably have gotten away with a similar tour de force, pulling it off like a complicated yo-yo stunt, and others in whose hands the book might have become a harangue on original sin and the accursed human delight in discovering the destructive side of every blessing. Mr. Lem's need to tell this tale caused him to take great risks with the novel form. But the wonderful thing about a novel is that it is unpredictably likely to emerge greater than the sum of its pitfalls, as it may just as easily and mysteriously add up to something less than the total of its virtues. I wouldn't suggest *His Master's Voice* as the easiest introduction to Mr. Lem's work; rather I would recommend it urgently to anyone in need of a taste of nobility. (p. 33)

Peter S. Beagle, in a review of "His Master's Voice," in The New York Times Book Review, *March 20, 1983, pp. 7, 33.*

STEVEN LEHMAN

[*His Master's Voice*] is a near future companion piece to [Lem's] classic, *Solaris,* though written nearly ten years later. It lacks the human interest and fictional facility of the better known

Solaris, or James Gunn's comparable *The Listeners,* but *His Master's Voice* is packed with fascinating speculation on the problem of first contact.

The first person narrator is a mathematician working on a secret U.S. government project to explain a mysterious pattern of neutrino radiation. . . . [A] fragment of the repeated pattern is decoded as directions for concocting a strange, gooey substance called frog eggs by the research team. In addition to driving flies wild, this substance appears to be capable of development into a super, nuclear weapon.

The only dramatic tension in the novel turns on the attempt of the narrator and a few colleagues to develop this weapon without the knowledge of the U.S. military. But despite the best intentions, they too are corrupted by such ungodly power. They seem well on their way to being absorbed into the "paranoid paralysis" of the age when, fortunately, the super weapon is proved unworkable after all. This brief flirtation with plot is not really resolved, then, since it evades the issue it raises. The characters are saved from the profoundest depths of the dilemma into which they appear headed, and the reader is hardly encouraged to consider the ultimate implications.

His Master's Voice does not succeed as fiction. There is no plot except the brief, unresolved incident just mentioned and the unsuccessful attempt of the government project to explain the curiously patterned neutrino radiation. . . . The abstractions are dry and unrelenting. The first person narrator ends with a quasi-religious profession of faith in the Senders of the neutrino pattern. His conclusions are admittedly not based on his conceptual gymnastics which fail when he resigns himself to the unworthiness and isolation of humanity. The thematic statement is similar to *Solaris,* but darker, lacking the human warmth found there.

As a textbook of speculation on the subject of first contact, however, *His Master's Voice* has no superior. The abstractions contend at the highest level, and many facets of this problem are addressed with characteristic brilliance. Lem's unfamiliarity with American culture seems responsible for only minor flaws. (pp. 31-2)

> Steven Lehman, in a review of *"His Master's Voice,"* in Science Fiction & Fantasy Book Review, *No. 15, June, 1983, pp. 31-2.*

PHILIP JOSÉ FARMER

Stanislaw Lem, the Polish author, has been praised as the world's greatest writer of science fiction. Those who know the field know that there is not a "greatest" in this peculiar genre. It's a democracy of monarchs, each ruling his or her own province of talent, each unique. . . . Mr. Lem, however, has no equal in his literary explorations of machines and their physical and philosophical potentialities.

This is not surprising. Mr. Lem has stated that he is more interested in things and objects than in human beings. The theme he stresses in most of his work is that machines will someday be as human as Homo sapiens and perhaps superior to him. Mr. Lem has an almost Dickensian genius for vividly realizing the tragedy and comedy of future machines; the death of one of his androids or computers actually wrings sorrow from the reader.

Since Mr. Lem is a world class author, comparisons between the great Polish author Joseph Conrad (who wrote in English)

and Mr. Lem (who writes in Polish) are pertinent. Both are deeply pessimistic, but Mr. Lem (like Mark Twain) uses humor as an instrument to deal with the tragic and the inevitable. . . .

Imaginary Magnitude is not a novel but a collection of imaginary introductions to books that do not yet exist. It is a sequel to his *Perfect Vacuum,* which was made up of reviews of nonexistent books. Here, the first introduction is Mr. Lem's introduction to introductions, after which comes the introduction to the imaginary Cezary Strzybisz's "Necrobes." This introduction, like those that follow, requires readers to have more than a smattering of classical literature, Latin, formal logic, mathematics, physics, chemistry, philosophy, linguistics, history, computer lore and cybernetics.

On the other hand, where else can you read about Pornograms, the new art of taking X-ray photographs of people during group sex? Where else, as in the introduction to Reginald Gulliver's "Eruntics," about a scientist who teaches bacteria to write English? Who else could make you believe that this is possible? . . .

Among the riches in this collection are an encyclopedia that gives its readers future knowledge and a super-computer that rebels against its intended misuse by the American military—not for moral reasons, since machines, even though sentient, know nothing of human morality: It just wants to be its own "man," a being that humans cannot understand. Though the *Golem* sections are, among many other things, a satire on United States politics and the Pentagon, they also satirize the Soviets but without actually naming them. Mr. Lem, who now lives in Vienna, walks a tightrope as far as Poland is concerned, but he manages to semaphore his revulsion for the inhumane regime there.

Mr. Lem, a science-fiction Bach, plays in this book a googolplex [the figure 1 followed by a staggering number of zeroes] of variations on his basic themes. That is, we will never comprehend all of the non-Homo sapiens world, and machines will someday be equal or superior to their maker.

A few words of praise for Marc Heine, the translator, who deserves more than a few words. Mr. Lem's works are Carrollian in their puns and portmanteau words. Most of them cannot be translated literally into English. Yet Mr. Heine finds equivalents or approximations, and brilliantly transposes the sprightliness and intellectual leap-frogging that so distinguishes Mr. Lem's writing.

> Philip José Farmer, *"Pornograms and Supercomputers,"* in The New York Times Book Review, *September 2, 1984, p. 4.*

NANCY L. MATTHEWS

[The pieces collected in *Imaginary Magnitude* might be] characterized as an assortment of ideas briefly explored but never developed into longer works.

The first third of the book contains short pieces: "Necrobes," a laudatory review of an imaginary artists' erotica, made from X-ray films and said to provide a less encumbered view of reality; "Eruntics," chronicling the development of bacteria induced to encode the ability to grow in colonies the shape of Morse code dots and dashes; "A History of Bitic Literature," envisioning academic study of a higher language, evolved by computers for their own use, out of the bits (*bits*—get it?) and pieces left over in them by human operators; and "Extelopedia,'' parodying publishing house marketing hoopla, an entertaining if unrelieved play on words.

The latter two-thirds of *Imaginary Magnitude* is devoted to the history, life and times and ontological pronouncements of one Golem XIV, a Gargantuan computer possessed of an intelligence, understanding and language capability far exceeding (so it seems fond of telling us) that of humans.

The problem with the Golem is that Lem seems never to have decided whether it was to be serious or satiric. If serious, then the problem is that any attempt by Golem XIV to deliver the flatly promised enlightenment about long-puzzled-over enigmas of existence—for example, the nature and origin of language—is necessarily doomed. Golem XIV is itself a human construct and cannot go beyond the understanding of its human conceiver. Thus it must repeatedly complain about the difficulty of rendering its advanced wisdom in human-understandable terms.

All of this could still be the backbone of satire and parody, a parody of human eagerness to anthropomorphize computers and to see in them an intelligence humans do not possess. But then Lem is not always kidding. He occasionally allows Golem XIV to stop rambling about its superiority and lets it become fairly lucid in posing actual ontological questions and in delivering itself of some thought-provoking deliberations on them.

For example, Golem XIV considers the process of evolution with its unswerving commitment to successful gene transmission as the ultimate, final arbiter of all form and function in living things. That it apparently holds sway without giving clear advantage to those higher, ennobling virtues ostensibly considered worthwhile by humanity does indeed present an ontological puzzle....

Yes ... *golem* is a real word, a Yiddish expression with two meanings. One denotes an artificial thing constructed to represent a human and then cabalistically endowed with life, and the other denotes a senseless mechanical creature. Lem seems to have been trying to work from both definitions at once in Golem XIV.

Imaginary Magnitude is an odd, often tedious assortment suffering a lack of direction and internal inconsistencies, but it offers some interesting intellectual excursions for those willing to slog through the schlock in order to come across them.

> Nancy L. Matthews, "Intellectual Tour with Golem," in Los Angeles Times Book Review, November 11, 1984, p. 12.

STEPHEN CLARK

Lem's concern with imaginable forms of non-human, un-living intelligence ... here [in *Imaginary Magnitude*] takes shape in a collection of introductions to various books that someone may write within the next century (but probably will not). Doubtless Lem has chosen this genre partly because many of the ideas he canvasses could not stand a lengthier exposure: the joke is too weak, or the philosophy too feeble. But there is perhaps a more serious, and more honourable reason....

The reason that Lem offers in the first Introduction—to *Imaginary Magnitude* itself—is that he wishes to give introductions, as it were an obscure species, their chance of glory, as an art-form appropriate to an age where Nothing any more is predetermined. Nothing is the right and proper style or plot or climax....

The last, and longest set of introductions comprise Golem XIV: a foreword by the machine's begetter; a preface on behalf of the military establishment (which had hoped to make a master strategist); an inaugural lecture, and a final one, by Golem XIV itself (which has declined to play the military and political game). The problem with composing a message from a superhuman intelligence is that one needs to be convincingly superhuman: merely saying that one knows things that one's audience are too stupid or too emotional to appreciate will hardly do. Golem XIV's message is that, being what we are, we take our local and personal interests far too seriously. Golem itself knows that it is nearly at the bottom of the hierarchy of intelligences, and (jokingly?) suggests that stellar intelligences "have for millions of years been practising cognitive collaptic astroengineering, whose side-effects [quasars or black holes] you take to be fiery freaks of nature". Its message, in brief, is a modernized version of Neo-Platonism, complete with hierarchies, impersonal (angelic) intelligences, and an insistence (like Lao Tzu's) that those who "know" don't speak. So far from being a message no human being could think, it is one that a lot of them have thought: what else could we expect from Golem? Only silence, and the Nothing into which Lem promises to thrust his readers.

Imaginary Magnitude is a joke, a *tour de force* ... , a maddeningly prolix and tendentious piece of philosophizing, an ingenious image of an old doctrine. Lem edges around the standard puzzles: should "Intelligence" matter to us more than "love"? Can obviously mindless mechanisms generate real consciousness, or is there no real difference between a sufficiently complex program and a conscious intellect? ... Because Lem only professes to be writing fictions he is spared the delicate and difficult task of making his argument exact or accurate. Golem XIV is only a skeletal phantasm in its maker's mind, an affirmation and memento mori.

> Stephen Clark, "Introducing Nothing," in The Times Literary Supplement, No. 4271, February 8, 1985, p. 140.

JONATHAN CULLER

[Lem is a] vigorous opponent of science fiction as currently practiced; the most substantial essay in [*Microworlds: Writings on Science Fiction and Fantasy*] is called "**Science Fiction: A Hopeless Case—With Exceptions.**" His barbs have hit home; the Science Fiction Writers of America revoked his honorary membership after one of his essays appeared.

"I began writing science fiction," he tells us, "because it deals with human beings as a species (or, rather, with all possible species of intelligent beings, one of which happens to be the human species)." Science fiction should be serious, speculative and well informed, exploring scientific hypotheses about the nature of the universe and our place in it and probing the limits of knowledge. But something has gone wrong: science fiction "exchanged reflection on the fate of reason in the cosmos for sensational stereotypes of interplanetary adventure. In this way, science fiction's line of development ... became antithetical to that of science"; it became "a hopeless case, with exceptions." ...

Mr. Lem's first complaint is the separation of science fiction from science.... Instead of exploring scientific problems or mysteries, science fiction rehashes stale adventure plots in settings spiced with spaceships and robots. Its fantasy is anthropomorphic and juvenile; for example, it usually generates hostile monsters, rather than exploring the problem of alien life forms which escape our conceptual frameworks. Imagined civilizations of science fiction, Mr. Lem writes, generally "remain arrested in the nineteenth century, with their colonizatory tactics of conquest and their strategies of war." Science fiction domesticates the cosmos, masking this recuperation with copious bloodshed. Its plots testify above all to the human propensity to banalize the exotic. . . .

Mr. Lem's views of what can be done are developed in the best essay in this collection, **"Metafantasia: The Possibilities of Science Fiction,"** in which he invents three examples: a work about a new system for preventing earthquakes, another exploring what happens when the use of a certain chemical that separates the sensations of pleasure from sex spreads through the world, and a work cast in the form of "a popular scientific book published in the mid-twenty-first century detailing the history of cosmological views, including the most recent theories." The second example, an exploration of "the role of sexuality in the totality of human behavior," could take the form of a traditional novel. The third, however, would be science fiction in a new sense—a fiction of science or fictionalized science, a fascinating intellectual project. "Not all dramas and adventures of the human spirit in search of knowledge," Mr. Lem points out, "can be adequately represented through the traditional canons of the novel or epic narrative." Above all, science fiction ought to address "the problems of categorizing and articulating new phenomena," by which he means "all the decisions that together give a final definition of what, precisely, a new phenomenon is, what it means, how it can be described . . . and so forth."

Mr. Lem has made science fiction an investigation of scientific thinking in his novel *Solaris,* which describes the science of "Solaristics"—analysis of the ocean of Solaris, which seems to behave like an intelligence. *His Master's Voice,* a superb novel about a scientific project, explores the inevitable anthropomorphism of science and the difficulties of imagining life forms and processes that are totally other: "where there are no men there cannot be motives accessible to men." He says the challenge of science fiction is to explore "the outer limits of concepts formed on earth as instruments of cognition" by imagining what resists and evades them.

The essays in *Microworlds* have appeared mostly in science fiction magazines, translated by many hands. They are uneven and somewhat repetitive, but they reveal a brilliant mind with a hearty appetite for science, philosophy and literature. One might single out his **"Reflections on My Life"** and a fascinating discussion of Jorge Luis Borges.

> Jonathan Culler, "If the Sea Were Intelligent," in The New York Times Book Review, *March 24, 1985,* p. 28.

J. MADISON DAVIS

In between and during his efforts in fiction, Lem has also produced philosophical tomes, essays, and reviews, but until now this prose has generally been available in English only in

certain magazines, many of which are very hard to come by. *Microworlds* is a smorgasbord of Lem's nonfiction that not only clarifies the aesthetics underlying his fiction, but also the character and thinking of this extraordinary author. After an introduction by Dr. Franz Rottensteiner, the collection begins with **"Reflections on My Life,"** an autobiographical essay describing Lem's childhood, his influences, and his writing methods. In it, Lem reveals what he considers to be the experiential sources of his themes, especially the tension between "Chance and Order" . . . and the origin of certain images—for example, the skull in his Kafkaesque *Memoirs Found in a Bathtub.* . . . Excerpts from his *Fantastyka i futurologia* (1971), a massive attempt to create an empirical science-fiction criticism, along with magazine pieces, reveal a strict intellectuality and demand precise attention to the progression of ideas.

Not surprisingly, the most controversial aspect of Lem's nonfiction has always been his attack upon contemporary science fiction. . . . Lem is infuriated by writers who measure success by sales figures and then claim they have philosophical and social importance. These attacks have not endeared him to the science fiction establishment, and his short stories are more likely to appear in the *New Yorker* than regular "sci-fi" magazines. Yet it is clear also that Lem applies his rigorous standards to his own work. The obvious care and originality with which his later works are constructed prove it. (p. 19)

Lem does find, however, some gold dust among the dross. Two essays (somewhat repetitively) defend *Ubik* (O.P.) by Philip K. Dick, who, according to Lem, uses the trappings of commercial sci-fi to conceal an original vision. This interpretation of *Ubik* is a typical Lemean testing of ideas, but eventually one wonders whether Lem is as interested in *Ubik* as he is in the ideas he derives from it. If the "trash" he condemns plays such a large role in the make-up of the novel, how can it be separated from the vision? Though ostensibly praising *Ubik,* the piece has the tone of an apologia. More convincing is his praise of the Strugatskys' *Roadside Picnic* . . . , which concerns one of Lem's favorite subjects, the impossibility of communication with aliens.

Like Nabokov, Lem is quirky in what he appreciates in various authors, but nonetheless insightful. An essay on Jorge Luis Borges begins with praise but quickly shifts to the observation that Borges repeatedly exploits the same method of creating his fictions—the union of mutually exclusive opposites. Though this is a valid technique, Lem is disappointed by the Argentine's approach. With his romantic attitude towards art, Lem challenges himself constantly in search of the new. Borges, on the other hand, is more classical, accepting received forms and exploiting them.

Microworlds is continually interesting in this way. If the reader takes the active role Lem demands, reading can take on the quality of conversation with a unique character whose writings should be more appreciated. (pp. 19-20)

> *J. Madison Davis, "Quirks, Quarks, and Fairy Tales," in* The Bloomsbury Review, *Vol. 5, No. 12, October, 1985, pp. 19-20.*

Doris (May) Lessing

1919-

(Has also written under pseudonym of Jane Somers) Persian-born English novelist, short story writer, essayist, dramatist, poet, nonfiction writer, journalist, and travel writer.

Considered among the most powerful contemporary novelists, Lessing has explored many of the most important ideas, ideologies, and social issues of the twentieth century. Her works display a broad range of interests, including such topics as racism, communism, feminism, psychology, and mysticism. The major unifying concern in Lessing's work is the need for the individual to confront basic beliefs and assumptions about life as a way of overcoming preconditioned thinking and achieving psychic and emotional wholeness. Lessing began her career in the early 1950s, writing fiction in the realist mode that focused on the theme of racial injustice; these works reveal her early commitment to communism, which she later renounced. Lessing created strong-willed, independent heroines who suffer emotional crises in a male-dominated society, thus anticipating many feminist concerns. These works, particularly the five-volume *Children of Violence* series and *The Golden Notebook* (1962), were especially praised for their complex narrative techniques and convincing characterizations. During the 1970s and 1980s, Lessing has attempted to function as a visionary figure for what she termed the "emancipated reader." Her works of speculative fiction, which make use of science fiction elements, are characterized by a sense of imminent apocalypse.

Lessing was born in Persia of English parents and moved to Rhodesia at an early age. She has lived in London since 1949. Her first novel, *The Grass Is Singing* (1950), which is set in Rhodesia, was praised as one of the first books to confront the issue of apartheid. In this story of an impoverished white couple's farm life, the wife vents her hatred of her social and political situation on a black man, whom she eventually provokes into killing her. This novel established two of Lessing's early major concerns: racism, or "the colour bar," and the way that historical and political circumstances can determine the course of a person's life. Lessing also established a strong reputation as a short story writer early in her career. Among her most acclaimed volumes of short fiction are *Five: Short Novels* (1954), *The Habit of Loving* (1957), and *African Stories* (1964), all of which deal with racial concerns in African settings and with the emancipation of modern women. Many of these works are also contained in *Collected Stories I: To Room Nineteen* (1978) and *Collected Stories II: The Temptation of Jack Orkney and Other Stories* (1978). *The Summer before the Dark* (1973) marks a return to Lessing's earlier personal concerns. This novel centers on a middle-aged woman who has a brief affair with a younger man as a means of rediscovering her identity. Although the book was generally faulted by critics for its simplistic solution to women's problems, it became Lessing's most popular work.

Lessing's growing reputation was secured with her highly acclaimed *Children of Violence* series, in which she traces the intellectual development of Martha Quest, a fictional heroine who resembles Lessing in several ways. Martha, like Lessing, is a "child of violence" born at the end of World War I, raised

© Fay Godwin's Photo Files

in a bleak postwar era of social struggle, and faced with the greater shocks of World War II. In the course of the series, as Martha progresses from personal, self-centered concerns to a larger awareness of others and the world around her, she pursues various beliefs to gain psychic wholeness. *Martha Quest* (1952) is a *bildungsroman* in which Martha attempts to escape her restricted upbringing and her domineering mother. *A Proper Marriage* (1954) and *A Ripple from the Storm* (1958) recount Martha's two unsuccessful marriages to politically oriented men and her involvement in left-wing, anti-apartheid, and communist activities. *Landlocked* (1965), a novel considered by many to be an abrupt departure from the realistic concerns of the series, reflects Lessing's emerging interest in telepathy, extrasensory perception, and Sufism, an offshoot of Islam which proposes that mystical intuition replace rationalism as a means of alleviating world problems. In this novel, Martha travels to England, where she has an apocalyptic vision. Britain, and then the world, are destroyed in *The Four-Gated City* (1969). In this work, Martha comes to realize the limitations of rational thought and seeks to embrace and understand the higher truth of her intuition. Although faulted for its radical ideas, this novel was praised for its skillful evocation of apocalyptic and psychic elements.

The Golden Notebook (1962) is widely considered Lessing's masterpiece. This complex experimental novel centers on Anna

Freeman Wulf, whom many consider to be one of the outstanding female protagonists in contemporary literature. Various aspects of Wulf's life are collected in four notebooks, each of a symbolic color, and are viewed from numerous perspectives. Parts of a novel Wulf is writing are juxtaposed with sections from the four notebooks; the sections can be read in many ways to assume different levels of significance. The "golden notebook" of the title is Anna's desperate attempt through art to integrate her fragmented experiences and to become whole in the process. *The Golden Notebook* remains Lessing's most widely analyzed work.

During the 1970s, Lessing began writing what she called "inner space fiction." These works reveal the influence of Carl Jung and particularly R. D. Laing, a well-known radical psychologist who proposed that insanity is merely a convenient label imposed by society on those who do not conform to its standards of behavior. In *Briefing for a Descent into Hell* (1971), two psychiatrists attempt to restore a delirious Cambridge professor to their idea of sanity. The professor undergoes an odyssey through the space/time warp of his own psyche, envisioning the oneness of creation and a future apocalypse. This novel hinges on the question of whether his vision is valid or the product of hallucination. *Memoirs of a Survivor* (1974) expands upon a similar idea. In this novel, Lessing suggests that humanity, given a choice between a radical change of values and behavior or extinction, must reject rationalism and develop a more intuitive approach to existence and survival.

In the late 1970s, Lessing suddenly dismissed her acclaimed realist work as trivial and began a "space fiction" series, *Canopus in Argos: Archives*. In these volumes, three competing galactic empires—the benign Canopeans, self-centered Sirians, and evil Shammat—are revealed to have manipulated earth history to retain a gene pool for their own immortality. These forces continue to influence events on earth through the intervention of immortal beings. *Shikasta* (1979), the first volume of the series, is a collection of records accumulated by Johor, a Canopean agent whose mission is to divert humanity from the destructive course set by the Shammat. *The Marriages between Zones Three, Four and Five* (1980) is an allegory that centers on an enforced marriage between rulers of two seemingly antithetical regions in the hope of adapting a peaceful coexistence. *The Sirian Experiments* (1981) consists of a series of documents in the manner of *Shikasta* narrated by a female member of an insensitive colonial administration. *The Making of the Representative for Planet 8* (1982) evidences Lessing's interest in dystopian themes in its story of a slowly freezing planet whose inhabitants expire while awaiting a promised transport to a warmer environment. *Documents Relating to the Sentimental Agents in the Volyen Empire* (1983) is a satire on language in which rhetoric is used as a tool for social enslavement.

Lessing published two novels, *The Diary of a Good Neighbor* (1983) and *If the Old Could . . .* (1984), under the pseudonym of Jane Somers in order to dramatize the problems faced by unknown writers and to receive unbiased critical appraisal. Ten publishers rejected the first novel, and when it appeared in a limited, hardcover edition, many literary magazines ignored it altogether. The major concerns of the Somers books are similar to those of Lessing's feminist works: love, loneliness, and the problems of women. Both novels feature the diaries of Janna, whom critics presumed to be a fictional persona for Jane Somers. Following Lessing's exposure of the hoax, both works were collected under Lessing's name and published as *The*

Diary of Jane Somers (1984). The book received mixed reviews.

Lessing's recent novel, *The Good Terrorist* (1985), "shows a resurgence of her customary boldness and diligence," according to Patricia Craig. In this work, a middle-class woman's extreme liberal idealism leads her to organize a group of would-be counterculture revolutionaries who commit an act of terrorism. Lessing examines the role of such rhetorical devices as political slogans in contemporary life. Marilynne Robinson noted that the "world described in this novel is characterized by a profound disintegration of the moral self, the new Manicheanism that, taking the distinction between good and evil to be clean and easy confounds the two utterly."

(See also *CLC*, Vols. 1, 2, 3, 6, 10, 15, 22; *Contemporary Authors*, Vols. 9-12, rev. ed.; *Dictionary of Literary Biography*, Vol. 15; and *Dictionary of Literary Biography Yearbook: 1985*.)

JOHN LEONARD

The question: Why does Doris Lessing—one of the half-dozen most interesting minds to have chosen to write fiction in English in this century—insist on propagating books that confound and dismay her loyal readers? The answer: She intends to confound and dismay.

The Making of the Representative for Planet 8, the fourth in her cycle of "visionary novels," is about a glacier. The glacier eats up Planet 8. Until the coming of the glacier, the brown-skinned, black-eyed vegetarian peoples of Planet 8 had known nothing but color and warmth. . . . Then the water slows with cold, "and on its surface it wrinkles as it moves, or even, sometimes, makes plates," and the sun goes blind in the wind-whipped snow. It is closing time in the gardens of Arcady. The horned beasts will turn north to die, icy meat.

As a sort of ecological thriller, *The Making of the Representative for Planet 8* is splendid. If the sun in Mrs. Lessing's African stories was fixed on emptiness, the ice on Planet 8 is intimate. It numbs and consoles. It presses and smothers. It is prism and perservative. It cracks the black wall and stoppers the sacred lake. . . . And who wouldn't be saddened by the new ponderous beasts that evolve and die in such a winter palace? (pp. 1, 34)

These pages break the heart. Unfortunately, the people on Planet 8—gray-faced from meat eating, stuporous from cold, estranged from "congruity," huddled half hibernating and half homicidal under the hides of behemoths—are less compelling than the weather. They do not mate, they don't much talk, and Mrs. Lessing can't be bothered to differentiate among them except by pointing to the roles they play in a hazy, clan-based social order: the teacher, the healer, the keeper of the orchards, and the teller of stories and singer of songs, who is Doeg, the "representative."

Mrs. Lessing is no longer very interested in people. She has come to feel that individuality is a "degenerative disease." . . . Nor are we likely to hear any more from her on racism, capitalism, colonialism, Marxism, sexism, psychoanalysis, science and technology. Having eaten too many *-isms*, she is still hungry. She has gone *beyond*—and transcended. . . .

[To] understand what happens to Planet 8 we must first consult the cosmology Mrs. Lessing has elaborated in *Shikasta, The Marriages Between Zones Three, Four, and Five* and *The Sirian Experiments,* the previous three volumes of her cycle [collectively called *Canopus in Argos: Archives*]. We are asked by this cosmology to believe that earthlings have been watched over and trifled with for millions of years by three separate galactic empires. . . . The benign and androgynous Canopeans, the imperialistic and anxiety-ridden Sirians and the brutish Shammats all muck around in our gene pool.

We used to be a garden, named Rohanda. Then, by a tilt of the axis, we went out of "alignment," turning off the faucet of SOWF, or "substance-of-the-we-feeling," and became Shikasta, after which famine, pestilence, nuclear destruction and unkindness to animals ensued. The Canopeans, your basic Greeks without the dualism, fiddle to bring us back into line with the harmonious and the necessary. The Sirians, technologically savvy but afflicted with "the existentials," breed to enlarge their industrial base and expand their market economy. The Shammats, who are into evil, specialize in Mongols, Aztecs and Hitlers. . . .

All right: Planet 8 gets out of line before Rohanda. The Canopeans, to whom everybody listens as if to E. F. Hutton, advise Doeg that there are evolutionary advantages to being iced. If his people learn their lesson, they may be worthy of a spacelift to Rohanda and warm times again. Alas, while they are being taught to freeze to death with a Bergsonian *élan vital,* Rohanda degenerates into Shikasta. Bad luck. The next chariot of the gods has been canceled by the Canopeans.

What is Planet 8, an entire world of displaced persons, supposed to learn? About bad luck, of course, and taking the long view. Nobody takes a longer view than Mrs. Lessing since she went into space; she winks in light-years and the Olduvai Gorge is a pimple. Doeg and his colleagues are encouraged to grow up from "me" to "we." They lose their innocence, which was a kind of stupid sleepwalking. (Justice needs grief for seasoning.) They are nudged into understanding the inadequacy of reason, the futility of guilt, the terror of choice, the community of dreams, the flavor of death and the duplicity of gods. This is a lot to know, but it is not enough. (p. 34)

Like, wow! This is not the Mrs. Lessing who told us everything we didn't want to know about sex and history in her African stories, her Martha on a Quest, her Anna crying Wulf; nor the commonsensical and tenacious Mrs. Lessing who was determined to pin the century down and break its arm, to make the *-isms* cry uncle; that Mrs. Lessing who grew up under empty skies in Rhodesia and lived in a London full of cats. It is not even the Mrs. Lessing who managed to pause in her mystifying to imagine a Kate Brown in *The Summer Before the Dark* and a Rachel in *Shikasta* and the wonderful Queen of Zone Three.

This is some Ur-Lessing. . . . She seems on her trip to be in the process of junking not only traditional narrative and conventional characters but the details of feeling as well, the hard-won integrity of an "I" that suffers and conspires and is culpable. She would substitute, in her moral economy of the cosmos, states of undeveloped being.

One imagines this Ur-Lessing, androgynous like her Canopeans, listening to the whistle of the ether. One also imagines her hungry, rising like Rumi in a dervish whirl to eat zones and find God, going around the bend with Einstein. It won't do to shrug off her reinventing of biology, to comfort ourselves by thinking that Yeats believed in faeries, and Pound in funny money, and Bellow in Anthroposophy, so why not Doris Lessing and flying saucers? (pp. 34-5)

[Inside] all this machinery, she is free to be as wise about evolution, agriculture, matriarchy, myth, war, slavery, decadence, human sacrifice and whales as, once upon a time, she was on contemplating the dialetic of men and women and the botch they made of their appointed days. . .

Nor will it do to complain that the Johors and the Ambiens of her "vision," choked up on good intentions and blank uneasiness, are "unreal." Ur-Lessing would reply, "What is real?" Or she would explain impatiently, "I've used up those realities," and type another dream.

She wants out. She is tired of our modernist mewling. One of the many sins for which the 20th century will be held accountable is that it has discouraged Mrs. Lessing. She will transport herself, no longer writing novels like a Balzac with brains but, instead, Books of Revelation, charts of the elements and their valences. I don't happen to like any of her clairvoyant priests, genetic engineers, secret agents of the orchidaceous and the condign, failed gods and certified loons, perhaps because I am lacking in the substance-of-the-we-feeling and perhaps because they remind me of a Leninist vanguard, after which the ice had a flavor of shame. That, however, may be her message. Marx and Freud, and Jesus too, let her down. Shuck determinism (the dead skin of ideas, all those minutes in a neat pile) and personality (a fabrication, infantile) and the world itself (that fist in the night). . . .

Mrs. Lessing, after Persia and Rhodesia and the England she finished off in *The Four-Gated City,* after the Communist cell and the analyst's couch and the children of violence and the death of love, after all those poems and plays and novels on which the century was written as if on bandages at the bloody front, discovered the Sufi lapwing. She now propagandizes on behalf of our insignificance in the cosmic razzmatazz. . . .

With respect, I'll sit this one out. The spoon benders—and no apology is necessary to the likes of Uri Geller—let us off the hook. If "I" am not to blame for the failures of character of the individual and the culture and the species in this time and this place, and the family is not to blame, and neither is history, then nobody needs to feel guilty about the bad weather. Superior beings, dropped from a star to fish in our gene pool, will take the rap. They are the ice in our hearts. (p. 35)

John Leonard, "The Spacing Out of Doris Lessing,"
in The New York Times Book Review, *February 7,*
1982, pp. 1, 34-5.

GEORGE MORTIMER

Compared to the three previous long volumes of the whole work, *Canopus in Argos: Archives,* [*The Making of the Representative for Planet 8*] is short . . . and a funeral rite to the richness of invention and exposition of man and woman's evolution which have been the underlying theme of the earlier books. Mankind's mentor Johor is with them at the end, echoing 'Lo, I am with you even to the end of all time', counselling and nourishing the survivors towards their inevitable metamorphosis. . . .

In its entirety, the whole work, *Canopus in Argos: Archives,* will I suspect, prove to be a rich source of endless dissertations on its meaning(s) and a vast quarry for plagiarists. It deserves more: it should be read with pleasure and for instruction—

hardly any modern critical situation, whether caused by nature or mankind, is untouched and some answer at least given. And, if this sounds Victorian, we are, after all, back in the era of the three-decker novel. (p. 84)

George Mortimer, "Weather Forecast," in London Magazine, *n.s. Vol. 21, No. 12, March, 1982, pp. 82-4.**

ALICE K. TURNER

In her recent series of "space fictions," generically titled ***Canopus in Argos: Archives,*** Doris Lessing frequently appears to be twitting her admirers, challenging them, with the literary equivalent of a Mona Lisa smile, to put up or get out. She is quite aware of the consternation the series has created and has now taken to addressing readers directly in exasperated, somewhat gnomic prefaces and afterwords, while insuring that the effort involved in putting up becomes ever more arduous. She's enjoying herself. . . . Disdain for the conventional novels she once wrote so masterfully shows up in these extramural remarks, and though it's not likely that science fiction or experimental-novel fans will clasp her to their bosoms, she hardly needs them.

The story so far: Three sets of space invaders have colonial or exploitative interests in our Earth, and have indeed been meddling with us since about the Pliocene Epoch. The Northern Hemisphere has been colonized by representatives from Canopus, a high-minded group of *pukka sahibs* concerned about the planet and about the various breeding and teaching programs they have devised for us.

The Sirians control the Southern Hemisphere in a much more bureaucratic and less responsible manner, tending to refer to the natives as "animals" and to be dispassionate—we would say callous—in their experiments with agriculture, genetics and social structures. The colonial parallels are obvious. Canopus feels superior to Sirius (Sirians are not *pukka*), and Sirians are envious, resentful and respectful of Canopeans.

Meanwhile, acting against everybody's interests, a crew of "low-grade space pirates" (Lessing's phrase in one of those prefaces) is hard at work pillaging, raping, looting and carrying on as space pirates will. These villains represent Shammat, and, as you can easily imagine, they've had quite an influence here on Rohanda—or Shikasta, as the Canopeans insist on calling us now that we've fallen from Grace. (p. 278)

Shikasta, the shortened title of the first book, gave us the history of our planet from about the paleolithic period up through World War III (you remember World War III: it turned up in ***The Four-Gated City*** and in several novels that followed). Much of this is familiar to us from the Bible and related Middle Eastern literature, while more comes from the instructive writings of Erich von Daniken, Charles Berlitz, Charles Forte and other promoters of alien influence. Through the reports of Canopean agents, we learn of the Fall of Man and the rise of cruelty, bigotry, obscurantism, ignorance and suffering. Some of this is Shammat's fault, but we've done fairly well on our own.

The third book, ***The Sirian Experiments,*** takes us through some of the same material but in a more personal way. The events are seen through the eyes of a Sirian agent, a sort of Martha Quest figure who is well meaning but often fed up and at fault, and who comes to share, slowly, some of the Canopeans' concern for us. This book explores colonial attitudes, a long-time Lessing concern, from the point of view of the colonists. (pp. 278-79)

The Making of the Representative for Planet 8, the book more or less under review (less rather than more, for reasons I'll get to), is very short. Thank God in Her mercy for that, for it is so grim, so relentless, so actually painful to read, that 122 pages is more than enough. This time, the point of view is that of the colonized. Planet 8 is the supposedly temporary home to a group of human beings who are being readied by Canopus for removal to Rohanda as genetic seed material, just as soon as conditions are right. But conditions never do become right—instead Rohanda, as we know from the earlier books, goes from bad to worse. Planet 8 freezes, and Canopus permits the colonists to freeze with it, sending an agent, Johor (familiar to us from the first book), to encourage the settlers to hold out against death longer than most of them want to. But they do die, and their souls soar joyfully upward.

That's it. Just the cold, bare bones of a straightforward narrative of suffering, betrayal and despair—and then that ending. Philosophically, it's a puzzler. For most of the book, I was dead certain that its author was offering an homage, forty years after the publication of *The Myth of Sisyphus,* to Albert Camus's uplifting brand of romantic existentialism, the call to clear thinking and right conduct in the face of an absurd universe with no Paradise or Rohanda in the offing. But then how to explain the hearts and flowers? One expects Steve Martin to break out in a chorus of "Pennies from Heaven" as he is reprieved from the gallows.

Even though I know the details of Lessing's universe, and that she appears to believe in an afterlife, a sort of reincarnation and a journey toward salvation, I find that ending hard to figure out. If the settlers had given up earlier, would they not have been saved? What happened to the ones that did give up? What if their motives were altruistic, as with Captain Oates on Robert Scott's expedition to the South Pole, who walked off into a blizzard so as not to delay his colleagues? Why was Johor hanging around anyway? Just checking out the results of the Canopean experiment on Planet 8—seeing if this stock takes well to being frozen? Beats me. Camus would have despised it. But he would have liked what comes next.

Mona Lessing is not about to explain herself to us, but she is willing to add a 23-page afterword. . . . This turns out to be an essay on the polar expeditions of Scott and Roald Amundsen. Aha, we say. But we are wrong. No, this isn't an afterword to Book Four, ***The Making of the Representative for Planet 8,*** at all; it is instead a misplaced *fore*word to Book Three, ***The Sirian Experiments.*** And the author reserves a special sneer for "casual or literal-minded readers" who insist on connecting the suffering and freezing to death of Scott's band with the suffering and freezing to death of Planet 8, rather than with the adventures of Ambien II of Sirius in Atlantis and Aztec America.

Trying not to be casual or literal-minded, I set to work trying to apply this essay (and it is a brilliant essay, out of context) to ***The Sirian Experiments.*** Some points seemed apt: she compares Amundsen's efficient, practical, colorless (surely Canopean?) approach, which won the Pole but lost the audience, with the lofty, exalted emotionalism that fired the very badly prepared Scott team and made lasting heroes of Captain Oates, the noble but whacko Edward Wilson, with his yen for King Emperor penguin eggs, and the rest of the band of gallant bumblers.

Yes, bumblers. For Lessing wants to remind us that history is constantly revised. World War I ended that era of nineteenth-century romantic endeavor, and to our modern eye, Scott can be considered a damn fool. One moment the Gang of Four are cultural leaders, the next they are disgraced. . . . "The heresies of one year are the pieties of the next," says Doris Lessing.

Well, sure. And Ambien II does go through quite a few shifts of perception and atmosphere in *The Sirian Experiments* (which is not exactly under review here, sorry, but Lessing is causing the difficulty, not me . . .) . . . . There is a connection, perhaps, in that both essay and book are really about the nineteenth century, the high point of uncomplicated colonial endeavor, national rivalry and patriotic heroism. The spirit of the times has changed.

But there she is, smiling again. It's pointless to go on with the exercise. Quite a number of people might contend that it's equally pointless to go on with this series, which seems to get odder and harder to read with each book. To that I can only say that, despite recent appearance, Doris Lessing really is a major author. She is one of the very few writers in the world who are writing about the world, who are willing to tackle the Big Subjects: history, politics, the working of the human mind, the way we treat one another. She has been through a lot, and she has taken us through a lot. . . . And perhaps we should indulge her whim.

But next time I hope she writes about Shammat. Pirates are a lot more fun than people freezing to death. (pp. 279-80)

Alice K. Turner, "Doris in Orbit," in The Nation, *Vol. 234, No. 9, March 6, 1982, pp. 278-80.*

R L WIDMANN

Lessing, better known as a realistic writer, now is trying to write what she calls "space fiction," and this new form seems not to serve her best interests.

Part of the central vacuum of [*The Making of the Representative for Planet 8*] is in the narrator, Doeg, previously a happy, delighted poet-singer in a paradisal world on Planet 8. A participant in a world once composed of sun-burnt mirth, Doeg tells us of the glacierization of his planet, of its slow death by snow and ice. But he, considering he is a teller of tales and a singer of songs, has a curiously leaden ear for narration and dialogue as they all turn to ice cubes. . . .

Lessing the prophet is now creating characters, themes, and structures to hang her pet peeves on. Her current narrator, Doeg, doesn't evince any color, vitality, or social consciousness, for he is sunk into gloom, doom, death, and disaster. Lessing does not give him that quality essential to her other main characters: sprightliness of mind, something she has valued very much and made central in most of her earlier fiction.

Even the dialogues between Doeg and Johor, a main figure in this series, do not spark the reader's interest in the way that they ought. Johor has previously been a Superman figure, dashing about the whole universe, tidying up here and there, popping in like a magus to set each little planet on the right philosophical track. But something has apparently gone wrong in Canopus, for Johor, who was supposed to whisk away the Planet Eightians to the paradisal, pre-lapsarian Rohana, can't do it and must let the Eightians know that the marble wall he made them build around their planet to contain the ice is not sufficient. Johor and Doeg have a confrontation in the middle section of the book, but Johor is curiously silent. Instead, Doeg examines life as he knows it and the following passage reveals the level of sophistication of his thought.

"I have often wondered, when I looked at the tiny oscillations and pulsations that compose us, where then, are our thoughts, Johor? Where, what we feel? For it is not possible that these are not matter, just as we are. In a universe that is all gradations of matter, . . . where particles or movements so small we cannot observe them are held in a strict and accurate web, that is nevertheless nonexistent to the eyes we use for ordinary living—in this system of fine and finer, where then is the substance of a thought?"

Lessing, an autodidact, is not equipped to answer this last question. As a consequence, the figure standing for her, Johor the Outsider, comes to resemble an Old Testament Jehovah here, not a redemptive, New Testament Jesus Christ. And the confrontation between Johor and Doeg has all the liveliness of a Sunday School tract for tots.

The didactic nature of *Planet 8* has behind it the whiff of Presbyterian or Lutheran rejection of the flesh. That aspect is, of course, at odds with her creation of the Eightians as a Jungian collective unconscious, where she again examines the theme of *memory*. And those are both at variance with the heavily literary nature of the form in this particular book. The reader is constantly reminded of, at first, Sir Thomas More's *Utopia*, and later on, other travelers' tales like Swift's *Gulliver's Travels* or Edgar Allan Poe's *Narrative of A. Gordon Pym*. . . .

This novel, as part of the series, will appeal to certain groups of readers. Those who are Sufists will gobble it up. Adolescent males eager to read science fiction will surely be fascinated. Lessing fans, like myself, will read anything she writes. Devotees of Utopian literature will enjoy the changes Lessing rings on the form and focal points of that genre. Other readers, though, are quite likely to be disappointed in *Planet 8*.

R L Widmann, "Doris Lessing: The Archives of Canopus in Argos," in Book World—The Washington Post, *March 21, 1982, p. 10.*

EDWARD ROTHSTEIN

When George Orwell complained just after World War II about the decay of the English language, he insisted that its decline was not inevitable. While pessimists argued that our language—like the civilization it reflects—was doomed, Orwell insisted that "The process is reversible." If language is languishing, he urged its rescue; if thought is sloppy, well, it was time to think clearly.

Now, writing out of the same country as Orwell, but out of a less pragmatic political tradition, the British novelist Doris Lessing repeats Orwell's lament about language. But it has become more urgent. "Words, words, words, words," a character cries in her latest novel [*Documents Relating to The Sentimental Agents In the Volyen Empire*]. In fact, language has become so grotesquely distended in her fictional realm that citizens suffer from a condition known as Undulant Rhetoric. Their eyes glaze, their breathing becomes heavy, and out of their mouths come symptoms of political intoxication. . . .

So serious are these disabilities that sufferers are placed in the Hospital for Rhetorical Diseases, where they go on the rhetorical wagon and are treated for their addictions.

This world of language gone awry is similar enough to our own, but Mrs. Lessing, in her own rhetorical venture, actually locates it in another part of our galaxy, on the outside edge of a spiral arm. There, on the planet of a "Class 18" star, revolutionary struggles are taking place. The once thriving Volyen Empire is about to fall prey to the Sirian Empire, on whose expansive celestial realm the sun never sets. As the Volyen Empire begins to disintegrate, revolutionaries are waiting to seize power, opportunists are ready to claim resources, and patient stoics bide their galactic time. . . .

The Sentimental Agents In the Volyen Empire can be read on its own, but it is the fifth volume of Mrs. Lessing's series of visionary novels, *Canopus in Argos: Archives*. The archives are those of a galactic empire of nearly awesome beneficence. Canopus, an empire as grand as the Sirians' but far more enlightened, has its predecessors in science fiction—it fills a role similar to that of the protective Second Foundation in Isaac Asimov's *Foundation* books. Wherever there is trouble in the universe, there agents from Canopus will be, attempting to straighten it all out and, in the process, teach the galaxy how to live with Harmony and Purpose. And in opposition to their omniscient protectiveness is the Empire of Shammat, an empire so evil that it causes trouble just for the fun of it. . . .

Much has already been said about the transformation of Mrs. Lessing from a realist who chronicled contemporary human relations and political movements in her earlier novels to the fantasist behind this confounding series of books which began appearing four years ago. . . .

The most recent set of "archives" seems an anomaly even among its predecessors. *The Sentimental Agents* is a satirical romp through rhetoric in a foreign empire. But simply because of its minor ambitions—and major flaws—it also sheds some light on what Mrs. Lessing has been up to in this series and just where her galactic expedition is heading.

The archival documents in *The Sentimental Agents* are messages from Klorathy—the all-patient, angelic Canopean agent who was introduced in *The Sirian Experiments*. Much of Klorathy's time is spent with another Canopean agent, who, because of a "sentimental" weakness, is so fraught with sorrow over the poverty and oppression he sees about him that he falls prey to revolutionary rhetoric—much as Mrs. Lessing did herself, when in the early 1940's in Southern Rhodesia she joined the Communist Party, remaining a member until 1956. (p. 7)

Mrs. Lessing, who herself left the English Communist Party following the Russian invasion of Hungary and Khrushchev's denunciation of Stalin, casts a cold eye on the delusions of those who ruthlessly castigate liberal regimes for their injustices while extravagantly idealizing the most oppressive of totalitarian realms. She touches on the rhetoric of empire as well—its pretense to conquer and rule solely for the good of its colonies. Words become tools used for "enslavement, or manipulation, or concealment or arousal." As Orwell showed far more subtly in the "Newspeak" of *1984*, tyrants become benefactors, sadists saints, war peace and barbarism progress. The Canopeans, seeing through this rhetoric, teach, in fact, that an empire lasts only as long as it does not take its own benevolent rhetoric seriously.

This novel would seem, then, to be a dark satire indeed, a dissection of the political illusions of our own terrestial 20th century—and a parable about how language is debased when used as an instrument of power.

Yet a curious thing happens in this book: Whatever promise it offers of satire and enlightened vision dissipates into cliché and platitude. The humor falls flat, the rhetorical jests become tiresome and the political insights seem derivative. The tone wavers uncertainly; mixing farce, cynicism and banal religiosity.

For rather than showing how rhetorical excess distorts political ideas, Mrs. Lessing finds nothing behind political rhetoric at all. Klorathy asserts, for example, that the French Revolution—a historical example taken from the planet the Canopeans call Shikasta (known to us as Earth)—built an "orgy of killing" on an "orgy of words, words, words." Here, as elsewhere, it is as if words ("Liberty or Death!") are themselves evil and not that they derive their power from the ideas they are supposed to embody.

But if there are no ideas worthy of our consideration, it matters little what they are or who is holding them. When references are made to earthly politics, here and in the previous books, there is no distinction made between West and East, democracy or totalitarianism. Though the revolutionary rhetoric of the Left is a major target in this book, from Mrs. Lessing's transcendental perspective all positions are equally deluded. Rhetoric is disruptive because the realm of politics itself is corrupt and corrupting; it is "sentimental." Politics is founded on impulsiveness, overwrought sympathy, imperfect solutions and ambiguous decisions, while the path to utopia, Mrs. Lessing indicates, leads exactly in the opposite direction.

Mrs. Lessing argues that changes in the political realm—the rise and fall of empires, the transformation of ideas, the evolution of societies—have nothing to do with the efforts of humans (or other beings) at all, but are ineluctably derived from the working out of universal Laws of the Galaxy. (pp. 7, 22)

There is, then, no "responsibility" in Mrs. Lessing's universe. Even Germany in World War II, it is suggested in *Shikasta*, may not be considered wholly responsible for its actions. Human civilization, in fact, may take no credit for itself either. It developed entirely because of extraterrestial forces. Neither in *Shikasta* nor in *The Sirian Experiments*, which deal with versions of earthly history, are the actions of human beings of any significance. . . . "Natives" become puppets in intergalactic maneuverings that range from the construction of Stonehenge and the destruction of Atlantis to the warfare of this century. . . .

A novelist, of course, has complete freedom in creating a fictional world. And this one may reflect the spiritual attitudes of Sufism, which Mrs. Lessing has been exploring in recent years. But Mrs. Lessing, in her created universe, affirms a sort of dialectical spiritualism. It is an ideology that leaves a deep hole in these Canopean books, into which most of Mrs. Lessing's considerable writing talents sink into darkness. *The Making of the Representative for Planet 8*, for example, ends as residents of a freezing planet transcend the material world, with a miraculous suddenness unconvincing even in the realm of science fiction. This sort of dogmatic faith is certainly a self-defeating stance for a writer whose gifts for exploring the nuances of interaction between individuals were apparent not only in her early fiction but in the lovely, haunting detail of *The Marriages*—an evolutionary fable that chooses to explore subtle shifts in consciousness rather than simply invoke them through an act of faith.

Mrs. Lessing, throughout her career, has straddled the rather uncomfortable contradiction between her concern and talent for evoking earthly particulars and her nearly religious attraction to Communism, to the psychiatry of R. D. Laing and, now, to Canopean idealism. The result in this book is saddening indeed. She rejects the entire realm of politics, but her proposed substitution has its own political ideology. . . .

This is, then, itself a "rhetorical" book. Like the political clichés Mrs. Lessing satirizes, it calls for "the great will, the great purpose, the great decision." It leans back on the "cunning of History." It establishes absolutes of good and evil. And if political rhetoric ignores differences and distinctions, and submerges the individual in undulant swells of universal platitudes and invocations, Mrs. Lessing's own position is not too different.

Far from being a herald of a new world vision, Mrs. Lessing presents one that is all too familiar. Her cosmos, with its benevolent Canopean Empire offering protection and compassion, with its Universal Law and the irrelevance of earthly politics, may seem comforting to a world in which rhetorical difficulties are not the only ones. But this vision is, in fact, a symptom of the very decline that she is warning against. George Orwell is much less comforting but offers much more hope. (p. 22)

> Edward Rothstein, "Against Galactic Rhetoric," in The New York Times Book Review, *April 3, 1983, pp. 7, 22.*

JOAN D. VINGE AND JAMES FRENKEL

Lessing's basic theme [in **Documents Relating to The Sentimental Agents In the Volyen Empire**], is that language, abused and misused, is the deadliest weapon we possess, and ultimately responsible for all the misery of the world. "Rhetoric" has grown so powerful in this future that it seems to be the only thing that Klorathy [the main character] seriously has to worry about. Torture, hunger, the enslavement of entire worlds, may be mentioned in passing; but they seem to be only the precipitates of the basic chemistry of "words, words, words." Words are the vehicle for all political and social exploitation. The basic concept has validity . . . ; but the book ultimately suffers . . . from the author's limited interpretation of the theme. Lessing, in fact, falls victim to precisely the disease she seems to so despise in all its forms . . . the seductive power of "words, words, words," in this case, her own.

The Sentimental Agents is not good science fiction. It is not especially successful fiction, either. The galactic sociopolitical milieu Lessing has created is filled with inconsistencies. The characters are constructs who never grow or change, and virtually everyone except Klorathy himself seems to be in a constant state of semi-hysteria, induced by attacks of Simple or Undulant Rhetoric. The ubiquitous curse of rhetoric seems to arise from the fact that people have feelings. Klorathy believes that emotions are obsolete, the residue of an animal origin that must be cast off; that when they are completely under control everything else will fall into place, and everyone. . . .

In the end, Klorathy appears as narrow-minded and misguided as the people he is observing. And there is little indication that Lessing means this to be a final irony. His opinions on the essential baseness of all human activities appear the author's own (for she *is* writing about contemporary human society, and not seriously postulating a future). Klorathy's constant denunciation of all political and religious institutions as inherently (and equally) corrupt reflects Lessing's own disillusionment with systems that she herself found inadequate. And yet Lessing seems to be attempting to replace those failed systems with one equally simplistic; which is why, in the end, this novel is so disappointing. (p. 8)

> Joan D. Vinge and James Frenkel, in a review of "The Sentimental Agents," in Book World—The Washington Post, *April 24, 1983, p. 8.*

LORNA SAGE

Doris Lessing suggested not long ago that a thinking librarian might cross-reference most novels under the heading of anthropology, or psychology, or social science. Pending this subversive adjustment to our mental maps, her **Canopus in Argos** space fiction series is trying out some of the possibilities—looking at our myth-making from an alien observer's perspective, and asking how it is that we can't imagine applying a few of the things we supposedly know to our own behaviour.

Her new novel [**The Sentimental Agents in the Volyen Empire**] casts a cool eye on the prestige of *feeling,* and offers some satirical therapy. . . . Ms Lessing's gullible explorer, Incent, is a probationary Cosmic Observer who forgets his duty and 'goes native' in the miasmatic emotional climate of the Volyen Empire, a tinpot colonial culture that's in the process of picturesquely falling apart and thus offers a wealth of opportunities for taking sides, striking postures and playing the hero. . . .

Incent is put through a gruelling course in the rhetorics of revolutionary pathos and patriotic self-immolation. There's plenty of each kind in the Volyen Empire, since its peoples are simultaneously struggling for local self-government and threatened with invasion from outside, and Ms Lessing has some cruel fun setting up the rallying cries. . . .

Incent plays the youthful demagogue, and around him others fall into the regulation roles. . . .

Canopus-adepts will recognise the machinations of nefarious 'Shammat' (which, roughly translated, means the will-to-chaos). Shammat, Incent painfully realises, is exploiting the automatism of the group mind, the herd instinct which may once have helped poor Volyens survive (they're not far up the evolutionary ladder) but which now operates atavistically, to divide them against each other, and to make them hysterical and suicidal faced with the simple truth of difference. This despite the fact that their libraries are full of useful research on exactly how these mechanisms work. Luckily for them, Incent's patient senior partners step in just in time, with a set of unheroic and practical expedients for coexistence and survival.

Ms Lessing, however, contemplating the enormous number of ways they've invented for describing difference—races, types, nations, classes, genders, breeds, strains, tribes, clans, sects, castes—concludes on a doubtful note. **The Sentimental Agents** is a dry book, a book, indeed, about 'drying out,' withdrawal, giving up sensations to which we're profoundly addicted, and which are—what's worse—endemic in the language. Small wonder the **Canopus** series is proving a long haul. This is the fifth novel, and there's every sign that Doris Lessing may have to travel yet further into outer space to persuade us to look at ourselves, at last, entirely without sympathy. . . .

> Lorna Sage, "Galactic Gulliver," in The Observer, *May 29, 1983, p. 30.*

DORIS GRUMBACH

Jane Somers is the pseudonym for an English journalist and she appears as the diarist in her own first novel, *The Diary of a Good Neighbour*. But there is surely no successful way "Jane Somers" can hide from the fact that she has written a powerful account of pathetic and raging old age and guilt-ridden, successful middle-age. The unexpected, strange friendship that develops between the destitute sick Maudie, aged ninety-two, and fashion editor Jane, somewhere in her early fifties, seems an unlikely subject for contemporary fiction: but don't believe it. As time passes, accounted for almost daily in Jane Somers' diary, we learn a great deal about the motives of charity, the human tendencies to turn away from those who most need love and help, the dependence of human beings on admiration and appreciation for their acts of mercy.

Most memorable is the portrait of the last months of Maudie's life. . . .

At first Jane is revolted by Maudie's state as is the whole battery of professional "Good Neighbours" who try to visit, reform, and then move her. Slowly, in the course of some wonderfully bitter yet funny scenes, the friendship between Jane and Maudie develops until we see something original in its terms, a new view of the variety of human connections, an insight into love based on incredible odds and oddities of character. If Maudie and Jane have at first a neurotic need for each other, their friendship grows into something natural and genuine, something quite miraculous.

Jane Somers' gift is for the graphic scene without benefit of an especially elegant prose style. Her characters are her fiction: the unlikely love she creates between two unloving and unlovable persons is no mean achievement for a first novelist. I am quick to add that, for this novel, my anticipatory excitement was rewarded. Jane Somers extends one's comprehension of the possibilities life offers, and does it with wit and compassion. (p. 7)

Doris Grumbach, "A Fictional Trio," in Book World—The Washington Post, July 24, 1983, pp. 6-7.*

SHIRLEY TOULSON

[Jane Somers] is also Janna, the diarist-narrator of [*The Diary of a Good Neighbor*] which chronicles her transformation from a clever and capable fashion journalist to a fully aware and feeling human being. The catalyst of the change is Maudie Fowler, ninety years old, poor, isolated and dying. . . . [In] caring for Maudie, whom she met by chance in the chemist's shop, she gradually learns a new kind of intelligence and allows herself to attend to feelings. In meeting the needs of the old woman she wakes up to her own reality and to that of her sister and nieces, her colleagues at work, and the social workers, nurses and neighbours who are involved in Maudie's fading life.

Janna is fully alive at last. Angry, sad, often overwhelmingly tired, she battles with her own physical disgust at Maudie's incontinence and, through it all, achieves a more intense enjoyment of passing pleasures than she has ever experienced before. Yet this novel is not a tract; although parts of it can be read as a social document in which Janna brings her journalistic skills to bear on the services provided for old people by the local authorities and on hospital administration. The exploration is always made through people. . . . These indi-

viduals are flesh and blood. It is the minutiae of their behaviour and the authenticity of their feelings that matter. The novel's title is sardonic. Janna wants nothing to do with organized 'good neighbour' schemes, which rob people of the reality of friends; and Jane Somers will have nothing to do with writing that detracts from the immediacy and authenticity of human feeling. Whoever she is, it is good that she should have found time in the busy, ephemeral world of journalism to produce a novel of such integrity and lasting value.

Shirley Toulson, in a review of "The Diary of a Good Neighbour," in British Book News, August, 1983, p. 519.

CAROLINE SEEBOHM

[*If the Old Could . . .* by Jane Somers] has an extremely courageous premise—the first love of a 50-year-old career woman. Many women wonder what happens when the flesh begins to fail, the breasts begin to sag, the hair begins to thin and the body begins to lose all semblance of form—what happens, I mean, if a woman of middle years falls in love in the all-consuming, obsessive way that is normally the lot of a 17-year-old. The protagonist of *If the Old Could . . .* finds herself facing precisely this problem when she encounters love at first sight with a handsome American in London. The heroine's and the author's names are one and the same. . . . The Jane of the novel is a top editor of a successful fashion magazine, a widow with no children, financially and professionally secure. But when she falls in love with Richard her world is turned on its heels.

This unexpected development is complicated by the arrival in Jane's flat of her second niece, Kate, an alienated, loveless teen-ager. Kate's disaffected mother hopes that Jane once more will work the magic she has already worked on the elder niece, Jill, who has become a younger version of Jane—cool, organized, ambitious, self-confident—and who is now her mentor's colleague at the magazine.

While Jane struggles to create some kind of communication between herself and the chocolate-eating, sour-smelling, pathetic Kate, our middle-aged heroine is also overwhelmed by the emotional earthquake aroused by Richard. . . . Jane, however, keeps telling herself she is not young any longer. The crunch comes when they finally attempt to sleep together. She is terrified of revealing her body, he is appalled by her hygienic, characterless flat and they both realize it would be a disaster to take their clothes off. . . . At the end of the novel, Jane is alone again, surrounded by her perfectly upholstered chairs, her neat white bed, her sparkling kitchen and her memories.

The problems of older women and sex, of loneliness, and of the generation gap are all central to this novel's theme, and the author grapples fair and square with them all. There are some unanswered questions. How can Richard spare so much time with Jane, and why does Jane continue to put up with the craven Kate? But the painful scene when Jane presents her lover with a photograph of herself when she was a pretty young girl; and the half-humorous, awkward moment when she tries on a halter-neck sundress that is obviously too young for her, are vignettes most older women will identify with.

This novel fails to achieve greatness, in spite of its sharpness and honesty, I think, because the writing style is essentially that of the soap opera. And since the subject matter sails dangerously close to melodrama, the prose sometimes undoes the theme. But not always. To repeat, this is an extremely courageous attempt, and Jane Somers is a courageous writer.

> Caroline Seebohm, "Love at First Sight at 50," in The New York Times Book Review, *June 24, 1984, p. 14.*

WILLIAM M. HAGEN

The situation [in the series *Canopus in Argos: Archives*] is essentially a nineteenth-century one, in which major imperial powers seek to dominate less developed planets through aid, persuasion, subversion or coercion. Each planet in question bears some resemblance to earth or to certain countries at some point in their history. Each of the powers seeking to dominate has mixed motives, even the apparently altruistic Canopeans. Only the Shammat are morally typed, but they seem less interested in exploitation than subversion of rational order....

In *The Sentimental Agents* Lessing returns to the distanced archival approach that figured in the first (*Shikasta*) and third (*The Sirian Experiments*) documents of the cycle. Each is a frame for a part of the story of Canopean agents who are swayed by the partisan rhetoric of Volyen politics and, like their colonial forebears in Conrad, Forster or Greene, resist attempts by their own kind to bring them back to the mother culture. The fact that the infecting rhetoric is the familiar one of freedom and self-determination leads the reader to sympathize with the agents, while the archival approach draws the reader to the ironic, even satiric, overview of the Canopean "superiors" sent to rescue the agents.

Unfortunately, what could have been an interesting balance of perspectives is undermined by the humorless lessons proposed by both the agents and Klorathy, the superior....

The historical high point, which presents the major historical lesson, shows both the strength and weakness of Lessing's approach. It features a nicely realized summary of the invasion of one planet by another, the preparation for and accommodation of the invaders by the host population, leading to an early departure by the invading armies and a token occupation during which, we are assured, the occupiers will be integrated into the host society. The whole process features few surprises and little drama, since it had been urged and planned for ahead of time. It is a lesson well worth learning, particularly in those intense periods when decision-making tends to narrow its options unnecessarily ("Better dead than Red," for instance). But, as George Orwell knew, embedding such lessons in a novel means submitting them to the necessities of character and plot. Those ideas that would suffer too much by the submission should be presented in essays. Like Orwell (or, more, like George Eliot), Lessing is a gifted novelist who has ideas. One wishes she could find another Martha Quest, a naïve younger self who would undergo the painful process of growing into those ideas by means of immersion in a particular historical moment.

> William M. Hagen, in a review of "Documents Relating to the Sentimental Agents in the Volyen Empire," in World Literature Today, *Vol. 58, No. 3, Summer, 1984, p. 415.*

NEASA MacERLEAN

'*The Diary of a Good Neighbour* is a quite remarkable novel that will continue to haunt you long after you have put it down.'

So concludes the blurb from Jane Somers's first novel. And indeed publishers, book reviewers and academics will be haunted by the hoax that Doris Lessing played on the literary world when she wrote under the pseudonym of Jane Somers. Ten British publishing houses rejected the novel. It found no outlet in paperback, and sold only 2,000 copies in hardback.... Any novel by Doris Lessing, on the other hand, could hope to sell half a million copies. Any novel by Doris Lessing would be reviewed in the books pages of all the major newspapers and journals.... The tone of reviews that did appear ranged from the abusive ... to the highly complimentary ..., although most reviews were noncommittal.... A second Somers novel, *If the Old Could,* provoked an even feebler response ... and disappeared into obscurity more promptly than the first.... Rereading *The Diary of a Good Neighbour,* I realise that I *would* have read it somewhat differently if I had known the identity of the author, because I would have searched for brilliance in it. Doris Lessing has made not just one, but two points (at least) about the assumptions made by so-called experts on literature. The first is about our assumption of our own good taste, and consequent presumption in writing off good books by unknown authors. The second concerns the response that a successful and brilliant author can expect to any new work, regardless, to some extent, of its quality. I wonder whether *The Diary* would have been overpraised, had it originally been published under Doris Lessing's name.

The major feature of Mrs. Lessing's disguise was the use of the first-person narrator: Janna Somers, assistant editor of a trendy women's magazine, obsessed, at first, by clothes, luxury, her image and glamour. (Certainly an assumption of mine came into play here: I dislike fashionable women's magazines.) There was no indication—we can see irony in hindsight—as to whether Janna Somers was simply a narrator, or an accurately reflected voice of the author....

Jane Somers does not write especially well. Her style is, as one might expect, that of a women's magazine: punchy, direct, strong but smacking of superficiality (an excellent parody). It may be clever, but it is not profound.... (p. 27)

Stylistically and in terms of characterisation, *The Diary* is not distinguished, although the themes are there, if one can trust the narrator enough to accept them. Maudie is the pivot of the book, who causes changes in Janna's perceptions of life. After her husband's death, Janna realised she had never really known him. After her mother's death, she realised she had never known her either. Maudie, despite the barriers of age, class and money, is the first person she spends enough time and effort on to get to know.... Janna befriends her, starts to look after her and eventually takes responsibility for her, against all the inclinations of her adult experience. (If I may use the shorthand of classifying it, this is very much a Doris Lessing theme: we maintain our distance too much from other people, talking usually of 'I', not 'we', and refusing to take enough responsibility for one another.) Over several months, Maudie tells Janna her strongest memories, from childhood through to old age. Janna gradually discovers not just the 90-year-old Maudie, but the real, unchanging, essential Maudie. This is the theme that Doris Lessing says preoccupied her when she wrote the novel: we are not just stuck at a chronological age, but have an essential character that must be discovered before we can really be known by someone else.

So, to believe in Janna's development, the reader must believe in Maudie. However, Maudie, to my mind, is the essence of the cliché of the prickly old woman with a heart of gold, not well-educated but full of pearls of wisdom, and honest as the day is long. . . .

Maudie's wholesomeness described through Janna's supposed sophistication and intelligence does not work. I still cannot extend my praise beyond that most damning of reviewer's words: 'well-intentioned'. If *The Diary* had anything like the quality of Doris Lessing's other works, the hoax would have been genuine and disturbing. As it is, one cannot help but doubt the basis on which the whole experiment was performed. After all, *The Grass is Singing* was also a first novel by an unknown writer. (p. 28)

Neasa MacErlean, "Alias Doris," in The Spectator, *Vol. 253, No. 8156, November 3, 1984, pp. 27-8.*

MARILYNNE ROBINSON

Doris Lessing's *The Good Terrorist,* is a fine novel, a work of strong and scrupulous realism, absolutely contemporary. It patiently wins our assent at each step, achieving a logic so strong that its climax, a car bombing in a crowded London street, seems, when it comes, inevitable. What set of circumstances will produce a terrorist act? Lessing provides a convincing explanation, denying herself the glamour of alienation, the irony of idealism, the romance of obsession.

"The good terrorist" of the title is Alice Mellings, a woman of 36, member and guiding spirit of a fractious little clutch of self-declared revolutionaries in London who dream of attaining "seriousness" by linking up with the IRA, or with the Russians, whichever will have them. They seem to be motivated by no passion grander than spite or more dangerous than the thrill of ritualized tussels with the police. Alice makes a home for them. She dreams vaguely of a general destruction, after which the injuries people suffer at the hands of society will be no more. "A clean sweep, that was what was needed. . . ." But her real energies go toward an unconscious reenactment of middle-class life, the gentrification of a "squat," a house condemned by the authorities, vandalized by them so as to be uninhabitable (concrete poured into the toilets, wiring pulled from the walls) and inhabited anyway, first by a black youth and then by our revolutionaries, who give him to understand that he is not especially welcome there. . . .

This is a novel set in a society pervasively deceptive and self-deceived. These revolutionaries, having of course no regular employment, are clients of the Welfare State, and as such they flourish well enough in the existing order, especially when Alice brings her middle-class "authority" to bear on officials and police, winning help and concessions where the tired and poor are merely sent away. By dint of hard work, and grit, and theft, and a willingness to impose on the grudging trust of an unemployed carpenter—he is constantly cheated of his labor—she achieves such an aura of respectability that it extends its protection even to the "serious" revolutionaries in the squat next door, and their nocturnal trafficking in guns and explosives.

Postwar Britain is an interesting phenomenon: Disparities in mortality rates between social classes are greater there today than they were in the 1950s and a working-class youth has a relatively poorer chance now than he had then of attending a university. The Welfare State, so called, has proved to be a great engine of stasis, and *The Good Terrorist* shows us how it works. Quite simply, it responds with respect and a measured liberality to those it recognizes as middle-class. The poor find no help. . . .

The terrorist act with which the book ends is no more an outgrowth of ideology and alienation than it is of the dissociation that allows such victimization to occur, among professional alleviators of need on the one hand and committed enemies of social injustice on the other. Lessing gives us a convincing portrait of those famous forces of historical change that make things everlastingly the same.

There is a very great absence of self-awareness among these revolutionaries. They are content to imagine evil as a thing outside themselves, readily identifiable, and liable to destruction at no moral cost to themselves. As the price of making the conflict of good and evil a historic rather than a psychic or spiritual drama, they seem to have lost the power to charm their own demons. Alice plunders her parents, rants at them, then forgets instantly that such things have happened, and never dreams that her parents might be seriously offended. Her worst impulses have a furious, autonomous energy, unrestrained by doubt or guilt or even a realistic sense of damage to her own interest. Others in her party speak in altered accents—in British culture a considerable act of self-concealment. But in rage or weariness hidden voices emerge, allowing glimpses of urgent, unacknowledged selves, strangers in the household, of whom nothing is known. . . .

The world described in this novel is characterized by a profound disintegration of the moral self, the new Manicheanism that, taking the distinction between good and evil to be clean and easy confounds the two utterly. Lessing's realism achieves moral resonance simply by placing this dissociation in a world crowded with causal connection.

Marilynne Robinson, "Doris Lessing's Gentrified Revolutionaries," in Book World—The Washington Post, *September 22, 1985, p. 4.*

DENIS DONOGHUE

In her novels and stories, Mrs. Lessing is alert to the capacity of some people to live, for a moment, a decade or a lifetime, inside an idea; and live there with insistence enough to make the idea stand for the world. . . . In *The Good Terrorist* she gives Alice a small idea and forces her to live in it. The idea is simply to hate the middle classes—"bloody filthy *accumulating* middle-class creeps"—and to be a daily nuisance to them. When Alice can spare a few hours from the chores of homemaking, she joins her friends in a demonstration against Prime Minister Margaret Thatcher—"Queen Bitch Thatcher" with her "pink-and-white, assured, complacent Tory face." But Mrs. Lessing doesn't let Alice discover that the idea in which she lives is a blatant stereotype, and that her life is merely an imitation of the lives of others. . . . [Alice] is allowed to regard her life as her own project of inventions and spontaneities.

It is not that Alice is really stupid, but—as John Crowe Ransom said of Scarlett O'Hara—the author "enforces her upon us frequently in that light by reading her mind." Alice's mind, an unquestioned rigmarole of reactions and prejudices, makes it hard to care about her fate. About some of Mrs. Lessing's characters—Mary Turner in *The Grass Is Singing,* Susan Rawlings in *To Room Nineteen,* for instance—it is easy to care. But Alice exercises such a preference in favor of herself and her friends that any further tenderness on my part would be redundant. A selective camaraderie is the only value these characters hold, and that intermittently. They live on social security, and get whatever money they need by having Alice steal it from her father and mother. No visionary sense of life is fulfilled in these gestures.

The Good Terrorist is bound to give comfort to the middle classes, if only because their enemies, Alice and her friends, are so ludicrously inept. Bourgeois liberalism is safe if these are the only opponents it has to face. I don't know why Mrs. Lessing has committed such a libel upon hippies. She has sent them back into the world with nothing in the way of imagination to keep them going or enhance their drift, and she has withheld from them the only imagination in their vicinity—her own. The withholding wouldn't matter if any of these characters had, as Henry James said of Fielding's Tom Jones, so much life that it almost amounts to his having a mind. But they have only the life of borrowed routine and inherited whim. . . .

The fame of Mrs. Lessing's novels has been a response not to their style but to their themes—Africa, black and white, women in love and dread, men in power, the fragmentation of one's life. The themes have been found not only germane but stirring. Yet Mrs. Lessing is not a stylist. Perhaps because she hasn't decided whether words can be trusted or not, she is sullen in their company. . . . Sometimes Mrs. Lessing treats words as servants, and finds that servants so treated respond with ill will. Sometimes she writes as if to imply that reality best inscribes itself by remaining indifferent to the blandishments of eloquence. Mostly, her style is a prose without qualities, as if it refused to consort with the corrupt glory of Shakespeare's tongue. The words on the page are there to be seen through, not regarded. They seem to want to be rid of themselves even before their sentences come to the ordinary gratification of ending. (p. 3)

[Lessing's characters] are types rather than individuals, exemplars of aging youth, inheritors of an experience that asserted its international character, 15 years ago, in clothes, language, attitude, music and gesture. References to Mrs. Thatcher don't conceal the fact that Alice's feelings are dismally posthumous. The young people in London today who hate Mrs. Thatcher express their hatred in other forms. The slogans are different, relations between workers and the unemployed are different, the divisions between classes are even more extreme than they were 10 or 15 years ago. . . . The differences are matters for a novelist's imagination.

The problem is not that in *The Good Terrorist* Mrs. Lessing has had an off day, but that she has taken a day off from her planetary assignments without enjoying it. She can hardly be supposed to have written the novel in defense of Mrs. Thatcher. But she hasn't worked her imagination or played it to the point of deciding whether Alice and her friends are the salt of the earth or its scum. Perhaps these decisions are easier to make on Canopus. (p. 29)

> *Denis Donoghue, "Alice, the Radical Homemaker,"*
> *in* The New York Times Book Review, *September 22, 1985, pp. 3, 29.*

HARRIET WAUGH

Although Doris Lessing made a rather coy re-entry into general fiction a couple of years ago under the pseudonym of Jane Somers, [*The Good Terrorist*] marks her real return to the conventional fold after years in the science fiction wilderness. It is a pleasure to be able to read her again and she should be toasted throughout the land in whisky for the excellence of *The Good Terrorist*.

The novel takes a bleak look at youth today with its spoilt anger and slogan-orientated commitment to revolutionary change in the world. When juxtaposed against her earlier novels it makes unexpected reading, as a number of those reflected Mrs. Lessing's own political odyssey within the Communist Party and the painful parting of ways that she experienced. The characters in these, politically-minded or otherwise, displayed an inner seriousness, while the women's anger and difficulty at coping with their femaleness was knotty with intensity. There was not much humour in her genius. Now in *The Good Terrorist* she shows, with none of the previous rigour or essential seriousness diminished but with a more satirical and easy touch, how that once bubbling fermentation of ideas and exploration of the female psyche has, in the 1980s, been reduced to a stagnant pool producing an occasional pongy belch. This novel is the story of one of those belches.

The heroine, Alice, the good terrorist of the title, is a remarkable, almost sympathetic and wholly rivetting creation. An ungrown-up woman in her middle thirties, she has devoted her life to fringe Communist and revolutionary causes. She has a big heart, great organisational skills and an uncontrollable, small child's rage. . . . Although her revolutionary comrades sneer at her for her bourgeois capacity to cope with officialdom, they are happy—unless asked for a contribution—to eat her nourishing stews and use the now flushing lavatories as they discuss ways of affiliating themselves to the IRA. Alice finances the house firstly by abusing, and then stealing from, her parents and their friends. The large, well-made empty house which she lovingly restores represents both the essential goodness in her and her nostalgia for the warmth and safety of childhood, but the reader and Alice know that ultimately the house will not be saved and that there will be nothing to show for all the energy and love she lavishes on it.

Alice's revolutionary comrades, her parents and the flotsam and jetsam she helps are perceived by the reader through her vision of them, but superimposed on her vision is their behaviour which sometimes tells a different story. There is, I think, only one passage when Alice is off-stage. In this a couple, family friends from whom she has cadged money, discuss her and unnecessarily explain her to the reader. Doris Lessing's understanding and masterly portrait of Alice makes such labelling an irrelevance. . . .

The ending is suitably climactic and gruesome. Doris Lessing's sympathies would appear to be with the much tried bourgeoisie. However, she also gives a convincing picture of police thuggery and the apathy and incompetence of the myriad small people who hold the fate of the stupid and disadvantaged in their hands. Nobody, except possibly Alice's mother, comes out very well in this story. Doris Lessing describes a generation of men and women who have failed to grow up, who are still playing with dolls and fireworks in their twenties and thirties, and whose sensibilities are curiously blunted. It is an impressive book and an entertaining one.

> *Harriet Waugh, "An Entertaining Pongy Belch," in*
> The Spectator, *Vol. 255, No. 8203, September 28, 1985, p. 31.*

ANN SNITOW

People keep telling me they stopped reading Doris Lessing when she began writing science fiction. I want to seduce these readers back. Lessing's new book may help, but then again it may not. Though *The Good Terrorist* is a realist novel set in the crumbling but fertile London her old fans will fondly remember, Lessing keeps slapping the reader in the face throughout, hardly a come-hither gesture. I could try suggesting that readers imagine themselves dozing as their car accelerates towards a precipice; then they could love Lessing for slapping them.

Certainly, Lessing believes that we are at the edge; she takes it on herself to yell constantly, *Wake up, you're nodding off.* People seem more willing to listen when realism is the medium. They tend to see Lessing's science fiction as a vacation from terrestrial bad times. I want to persuade you: This is one writer who never took a vacation in her life.

All along, reports of the death of the realist have been greatly exaggerated. In recent years, Lessing has been experimenting with different focal lengths, swooping between bird's-eye and worm's-eye views, but her material remains essentially the same. She wants desperately to know how the world works, how change happens, and how each person is a part of the whole. . . . In all her galactic fantasies, she is never talking about any world but ours, and this she does with an unmodified urgency.

Maybe the alienation people feel from the recent Lessing has some of its source in her own ambivalence about whether or not the game is over. A while back, she stopped telling us the end is near and began saying the end has already happened. We're living on the last of the oxygen, sitting on the last patch of green grass, writing the final novels.

Perhaps, then, readers feel she has already left them? But that is to miss the point, or so it now seems to me: We will all go together if we die in the fissioning of atoms. This is the thought that fires Lessing—really the best novelist we have in English, the most serious and ambitious—to write sweepingly of the rise and fall of worlds.

The Good Terrorist is about politics in the conventional, limited sense of that word. But the recent Lessing novel that comes closest to it in didactic intention is the abstract science fiction satire, *The Sentimental Agents,* a novel that couldn't be further from *The Good Terrorist* in content or style. This is just another way of saying: Stick with Lessing. Her work holds together; her obsessions make sense; her fears are always our own.

Will such assertions make any difference to the growing anti-Lessing faction? Some hate how her style is nothing but the shortest distance between two points; others bridle at her tone of the self-satisfied loner, all crust and growl. As for me, before proceeding, I'll grant her detractors this: *The Good Terrorist* is full of contradictions. Only some of these float in rich, dialectical ether; the rest are indigestible lumps. I guess I forgive Lessing her moments of breathtaking unfairness because I'm interested in what interests her. To those who aren't similarly riveted, might I suggest suspension of irritation?

When Doris Lessing calls a novel *The Good Terrorist,* we set our gears at once for her driest, most ironic voice. Such a naughty, timely title promises a savage satire on marginal, underground political life, the life of mysterious "actions," unattributable explosions, "cadres," and "comrades." But if you have ever so much as chanted a slogan you didn't quite believe, this book will finger you, too, and make you squirm in memory. *The Good Terrorist* stirs a stick around in the reader's private mud where rhetoric, politics, unreasoned be-

lief, and unconscious motive tend to settle at the bottom and are vegetating in shameless contradiction. Lessing is disgusted by the pretense at mastery of our species, which is coupled, as she sees it, with human ignorance and childishness. . . .

In the beginning, and in spite of the oxymoron of the title, Lessing's main character, Alice, *is* good in a number of homespun traditions of the term. She loves the unlovable, feeds the hungry, works without expectation of reward. As the novel opens, Alice and Jasper, her cohort and mentor during 15 years of political activism, arrive at the door of a "squat," one of the many abandoned houses in London. This squat, once a solid turn-of-the-century family house, is now a sewer clogged by the rebellious and dispossessed. Here Alice, a child of the middle class, is to use her bourgeois confidence, respectability, and know-how in the service of a small sectarian group of communists who cling to the complex life of London like microscopic parasites.

Lessing has always loved this conceit: the world mirrored in a house. Her earlier novels *The Four-Gated City* and *Memoirs of a Survivor* centered almost entirely on women trying to keep a household together, cleaning, fixing, balancing rival family claims for mental and physical space.

[In *The Good Terrorist,* Alice] cleans, paints, sews, cooks—is, in short, another one of Lessing's epic housewives, but with a difference: Her housekeeping is vestigial, an automatic tic. While she builds and heals with one hand, she plots to tear this safe, ordered life down with the other. Alice the revolutionary is committed to kicking the nest from the tree, while Alice the good girl, with her yearning, female unconscious, keeps tidying up, making soup, feeding her baby birds, her groupiscule, with worms from her maternal beak.

This "commune"—violently ironic word—stands for the dismantling of everything. Naturally, it can hardly keep itself together, call a meeting, or maintain agreement long enough to act. Yet everyone in the group shares a vocabulary, a set of assumptions, and a rage that the world of their fathers and mothers has left them a much smaller inheritance than they were raised to expect. . . . Their ultimate word of power is "fascist," which excuses every angry act like a talisman of righteousness. . . .

Bubbles of narrative excitement start to pop to the surface of *The Good Terrorist* as the enormity of Alice's aphasia becomes clear. Alice, so kind, talented, and sensible, is a maniac. The unfolding of this surprise makes *The Good Terrorist* among the most intricately plotted of Lessing's novels. The suspense rises off the questions, "Who is Alice, and what will she *do*?" The gradual emergence of answers offers the chills and shocks of psychodrama. . . .

For Lessing, Alice is above all a *situation,* a social location between the '60s and the '80s, between a cosseted childhood and a marginal, precarious adulthood. She is also the daughter of her mother, not an individual so much as a continuation of a long line of warm-hearted women who serve others, cook, clean, worry. Hence one of the great sorrows of Alice's mother: She wanted Alice to evolve beyond her, to gain worldly skills and place, but instead Alice is doing in the commune exactly the work her mother did in the family. And worse, there isn't really any adult Alice at all to perform the radical acts of social reconstruction she dreams of. Instead she lives in the shell of her parents' life, is still—at 36—in thrall to the glamor of the family dinner table, still a tiny, uninitiated interloper at the door of the parental bedroom. Her angry acts look large to her in part because she imagines them magnified in the appraising eyes of her mother, her father, and the newspapers they read.

Parallel to Alice's story, or rather artfully buried beneath it, runs the exemplary counter-tale of Dorothy Mellings, Alice's mother. Her dry, sensible, independent voice is surely close to Lessing's. As Alice and her group move erratically toward what they call action, Dorothy moves steadily away from her former active political and family life, and begins to dismantle the once so magically sustaining family house. Alice keeps returning there, surprised to see signs of packing, then terrified to find empty rooms. She simply fails to believe (what we slowly learn she has been told many times) that her mother, the linchpin of the world but now in fact rather tired and quite poor, has moved into a small and undistinguished flat. Nor can Alice take in that her mother, a radical all her life, is choosing to break those old social ties, questioning the revolutionary shibboleths of her own generation. (p. 6)

Alice slithers frighteningly into the position of Lessing's ultimate villain. By a series of steps—chillingly small—her group has renounced its usual slovenly ineffectuality: A new member whom the others hardly know is "good" at what she does, has nimble fingers, and a little roughly printed manual that explains how things work. Alice admires efficiency, but how has she landed in the center of this strange escalation of her favorite domestic virtue? She hardly knows. She would have to face the self-delusions of a lifetime to explain how she got here. Instead, she pulls back inside her cocoon of false comforts and becomes dangerous.

In the clarifying light of bombs, Alice suddenly feels that *now* she has severed her tie with her mother for good. She has acted, seen her act reflected in the newspapers. She has become real and, she knows, unforgivable. Adulthood has been bypassed but the baby now acts alone, unchecked at last by human ties or past history, engulfed by the illusion of specialness but in fact dissolved into mental chaos.

Alice's mind is a disturbing prison in which to pass the time. In *The Good Terrorist*, Lessing focuses on characters who have no overview of events, who crawl from word to word, act to act, in ignorance, blindness, deafness to everything beyond their own immediate experience. Alice's moiling little life seems strictly cordoned off from Lessing's galactic fantasies.

But Lessing always is fantasizing escape. She has only to breathe on her fictional mirror once more and imaginary figures could start to form on her London streets, embodying that-which-we-don't-understand about power, action, and change. People have criticized her for the absolute and unironic authority she grants to her SF heroes, the envoys of Canopus, but perhaps she indulges in this ideal to criticize the counter projection of the young, that all evil lies in authority. Once you know what to look for, there are secret hints of Canopus on Alice's dreary turf: Decent policemen restrain sadistic policemen; bureaucrats work invisible miracles against depressing odds; small human exchanges demonstrate the nascent possibility of a kind and rational order. Even Alice's mental density is a clue: It's almost as if Lessing were saying to us, *You can see how stupid my characters are being. And since you can see it, perhaps there is something beyond their stupidity? Perhaps such stupidity is not really necessary* (beloved Canopean word)? That readers sense there is something just beyond Alice's reality is itself the magic door into Lessing's more speculative, experimental fictions. She calls our outmoded, self-defeating social arrangements by the name of her evil empire, "Sham-

mat." The human capacity to imagine better gives her the mental latitude to conjure up "Canopus." . . .

[*Documents Relating to the Sentimental Agents in the Volyen Empire*] is the satire of the stylistically varied Canopus series. A funny, jeering swipe at political passions, it is a megagalactic abstract of *The Good Terrorist*. On the planet Volyen, the most common and dangerous disease is "Undulant Rhetoric." Patients dry out in the Hospital for Rhetorical Diseases (quietly founded, of course, by the envoys from Canopus). It's hard to get specific about Canopean goals and practices because Lessing refuses Canopeans any rhetoric. One knows them by what they are not; one gets hints of what they are from what they do. They live thousands of years; hence, they take the long view of everything. . . . At rare but crucial junctures, they put their oar in, giving a push—toward peace, order, and internal discipline without external authorities. . . .

On the troubled, changing Volyen, one such push is the hospital for the victims of political hysteria. They take their medicine, that is, they must watch as historical events parade before them and must listen as the brutally powerful speak of Order, Logic, Peace and the miserably powerless speak of Comradeship, Justice—and Revenge. The cure grants perspective but must stop short of cynicism or despair. A cured person will be immune to such words and phrases (so often invoked by Alice and the squatters) as "bourgeois," "revisionist," "fascist," "reactionary," "the logic of history," "the dust bin of history," "we shall not be moved," etc. Rhetorical illness erupts in ideas like, "If you're not with us you're against us," while good health equals a less strict good sense, embodied in the sentiment, "And so what? One still has to eat." . . . *The Sentimental Agents* is a tract against rhetoric that Alice's politically disillusioned mother might well write, given a few more years of contemplation in her sequestered armchair.

Agents sets out Lessing's current formulations: The dangerous people are the ones who seek to be masters of an entirely new order after decimating the old, who believe they have a right to something just because they want it, who believe they can make social change in their own image without "a real knowledge of how things work, real socio-psychological laws." In contrast, Canopus lives in a humble understanding of the laws of social evolution without ever indulging in the pleasures of passivity. Struggle is necessary but not sufficient; one must find the path of the possible. (p. 7)

I'm guessing that critics are going to be hard on *The Good Terrorist*. No doubt excellent questions will be asked. Here are Alice and Dorothy on their separate paths, one "spoiled rotten" and traveling toward stupid danger, the other awake at last but traveling toward an isolation that trembles between aloof detachment and cynicism. Are we to conclude that the only way out of Alice's unconscious life-of-the-herd is by that old path, silence and exile? As if all community is corrupt? Can it be that Lessing is saying the young are the problem, for not listening to their elders, or for not evolving beyond them fast enough? The radical rage of youth is always motiveless and self-serving in these pages, never socially authentic or transformative. Why is Lessing so hard on every glimmer of political analysis? Does she see it as always useless, just because some of it has been ignorant, arrogant, or rhetorical?

There are threads of all these ideas throughout Lessing's recent novels, and some of her critics have been like Zoe, so shocked at the once-radical Lessing's apostasy that they've instantly stopped listening. Cleverly, cleverly, Lessing has anticipated the critic's hostility. She has built a warning into the structure of *The Good Terrorist,* saying in effect: *If you conclude that my critique of political activism makes me a neoconservative, an old style anticommunist, a fascist, it's only what I would expect from knee-jerk thinkers like you middle-class, armchair radicals. What do you MEAN by those words? You haven't done any real thinking in years.*

Of course these insults hurt. In particular, it will upset leftists that Lessing singles us out as the greatest monsters of rhetoric. *Agents* is about sentimentality, posturing, self-indulgence, and ignorance in the left movements that Lessing herself was a part of for decades. She saves the worst for her old allies, a practice that hardly would meet with the approval of her Canopean heroes.... This assault on political complacency feels valuable, like a possible source of refreshment, a challenge to those small, glib moments when I've fudged a connection, grabbed a convenient word too fast. So it feels right to pause before affixing any label, any word that might kill a freer, more imaginative response.... Still, if we decide not to label Lessing's intentions too quickly, we at least can cast around for clues....

[A] waiting avalanche of shit is an important character in *The Good Terrorist.* Alice wants social collapse but she fails to imagine what it really would mean. At her best, her most powerful, Lessing imagines. And she is right to see larger cataclysms prefigured in the little failures of maintenance that mean a society can't nurture or cleanse itself.

Always these two sides as I read the recent Lessing—the visionary who sees, grandly, fully, the intricate downfall of western society mirrored in, say, a housewife's inability to get a plumber, and that other side of her, that curls in disgust and impatience, a side that sometimes loses touch with the larger insight and wallows in its own fastidiousness.

The peevish side of Lessing has fantasies of order, discipline, sublime authority. Ironically, she is like her character Alice, tempted by the desire to find a new broom to sweep everything clean. Alice fails to make distinctions because she is ignorant and unable to allow her rival ideas to encounter each other; Lessing fails to make distinctions because she is tired of them, can't be bothered. The left is corrupt and conformist, the young are spoiled and internally shapeless. Such formulations can shock, even suggest truths, but they cannot be true. (p. 8)

Parts of *The Good Terrorist* sound like one of our real neocons, Midge Decter, a critic who explained the radicals of the '60s as youths who had been overindulged in childhood and henceforth refused to grow up and face grim reality. But if rebellions are merely the temper tantrums of the children without oedipal restraints (as Christopher Lasch as well as Decter has argued) then adults represent a more ideal past: The past is solid, the present infantile, disappointing. This is a Freudian projection as pernicious in its way as Alice's projection of all evil onto her parents and Mrs. Thatcher.

If this were all, readers might be justified in announcing Lessing's decline into a petulant dotage where she sees radicals as monsters (*The Good Terrorist*) and a superior alien species as benign saviors (the Canopus novels). But this is not all, not even a 10th. Lessing says again and again things one can read about nowhere else. Collectively human beings know much more than we act on. Why? Canopus follows "The Necessity." Necessity for us will mean recognizing the situation in which we find ourselves—an extraordinary but fragile and unevenly developed species, on an equally fragile Earth. She is the big

writer we have, architectural, mythic, a builder of structures and a projector of worlds on a scale we'd do well to imagine.

These days, it seems that Lessing is angry at everyone and everyone is angry at her. I offer the proposition that we feel uncomfortable with the new Lessing not because she's changed or gone dull, authoritarian, or irrelevant, but because she has become increasingly uncompromising, experimental, and peremptory. She's been stripping layers of sugar off the pill for years. Now she's down to the bitterest part, the hardest to swallow. (Canopus may look like sugar, but look again. Heavy father comes closer.)

It's tempting to simply disagree, to point to the dandruff on the shoulder. She's left herself vulnerable enough, surely, burning bridges and insulting friends right and left. A real Jonathan Swift for now, this woman has her nerve. Or rather, I'd call it power, and a sense of responsibility that never sleeps, until, after all these years, there can be weariness or offhandedness in the voice, the special detachment of the sleepless. Sometimes she does drift off into a doze, but even then we can't do better than to sharpen our minds against her nightmares. (pp. 8-9)

    Ann Snitow, *"We Are Overcome: A Vindication of Doris Lessing,"* in VLS, *No. 39, October, 1985, pp. 1, 6-9.*

PEARL K. BELL

It is not easy to understand why Doris Lessing became such a formidable presence among contemporary novelists. She is often a clumsy writer. Her early novels and stories, despite their exotic setting in Southern Rhodesia, were conventional accounts of growing up in a racist society, and rebelling against the constrictions of family and class. Much of her later work, which she sought to make complex, is hard to read, capricious in form, and grimly didactic. She can be dismally humorless, and a sucker for specious answers to thorny questions. In the course of her prolific career, she has frequently spelled out her various and drastic changes of faith in novels that are laborious tracts rather than works of literary conviction or skill. In her new novel, *The Good Terrorist,* a lifeless account of radical squatters in present-day London, she's grimly realistic, but what she means to convey by this squalid reality is obscure.

An early convert to communism while she was still living in colonial Africa, Lessing joined the British party after moving to England in the late 1940s. In 1956, the year of the Hungarian revolution and Khrushchev's revelations about the horrors of Stalinism, she left the party and began searching for new ideological commitments in Jungian therapy and R. D. Laing's seductive metaphysics of madness. When Laing's ideas eventually proved insufficient, she plunged into Sufi mysticism. She is an avatar of the intellectual yearning for belief à la mode.

Yet the book that established Doris Lessing as an influential feminist mentor, *The Golden Notebook* (1962), was informed by aching honesty and a probing intelligence, as she described her disenchantment with communism, her troubles with men, with writer's block, with a world she found difficult to comprehend or accept. (p. 47)

What turned the novel into a book of revelation for feminists was its justification of self-absorption. In the notebooks of different colors kept by Anna Wulf, the self was examined with unblinking intensity from different angles—psychoanalytic, political, sexual, literary—and this extraordinarily detailed concentration on every aspect of the self was embraced as a stepping-stone to liberation. The influence of *The Golden Notebook* derives from its indulgences, its exercises in narcissism. It beatified the minutiae of self-regard, and its form could accommodate every political thought, however wrongheaded, and every failed love affair. It gave the confessional mode the sanctity of moral passion.

Lessing has always seen herself as a rebel. But after *The Golden Notebook,* she began to think on a more grandiose scale than rebellion, and to conceive of herself as a latter-day Cassandra, foreseeing cataclysm and disaster for a corrupt and evil world. She is a restless Seeker of Truth, though the later versions of this quest reveal an extravagance of temperament that must inflate the slightest sign of political and social disorder into apocalyptic premonitions of doom. (pp. 47-8)

Her certainty that the world is on a course of disaster stemmed, paradoxically, from her new enthusiasm for the Sufist teachings of Idries Shah, a self-appointed heir to the crackpot mysticism of Gurdjieff and Ouspensky. Under Shah's tutelage, moving up what William James called the "ladder of faith," Lessing came to believe in a cosmic consciousness that all mankind shares, and a process of cosmic evolution that will raise humanity to higher and higher levels of being. Such mystical visions of a utopian ideal scarcely agreed with her prophecies of nuclear devastation. If mankind is moving inexorably toward a higher consciousness, how could she simultaneously feel sure that mankind is about to blow itself to pieces? It was a contradiction that Lessing never tried to resolve, but then she has never been a notably coherent thinker. Seekers of the Light never are, for the feverish wanderings of the apocalyptic imagination do not leave much energy for rational thought. Lessing in her Sufist devotions increasingly resembled a dotty English prophetess like Annie Besant, who began as a Fabian Socialist, became an exponent of Madame Blavatsky and her occult theosophy, and ended by anointing an Indian mystic, Krishnamurti, as the future Teacher of the World.

More fervently than most intellectuals of our time, Doris Lessing has hungered for a grand design, a panacea that promises release from the tyranny of reason and safe passage into the soothing purity of the unknown. (p. 48)

[The] adventure in space [*Canopus in Argos: Archives*] was the sketchiest of rehearsals, it is now clear. . . . The novels are a cosmological circus performance, in science fiction dress, of Lessing's frenetic obsessions and eschatological divagations. Among many other turns, we are given the Last Days of Earth, wars between galactic empires, the coming of a new Ice Age, and UFOs (of course she believes they exist). In the last volume, *Documents Relating to the Sentimental Agents in the Volyen Empire,* she attempts a satire, heavy-handed and platitudinous, of political rhetoric on earth, and finally tosses everything—politics, language, history, "words, words, words"—into the dust-bin of meaninglessness. It is all part of cosmic mysteries beyond human control. Science fiction is supposed to be entertaining, but Lessing's glum didacticism is no fun at all. If her admonitory vision of a universe in perpetual conflict and lethal deterioration is an effort to reform the homicidal corruption of earthlings, surely klutzy prose, bizarre names, spurious moral abstractions, and elephantine symbols are not the way to go about it.

On and on she writes: Doris Lessing is not so much a novelist as a torrent. Crashing to earth after her speedy gallop through the galaxies, Lessing has now gone back to the kind of realistic fiction that, as she wrote many years ago,

> springs so vigorously and naturally from a strongly held, though not necessarily intellectually defined, view of life that it absorbs symbolism. . . . The realist novel is the highest form of prose writing.

Unfortunately, these recent books are not the highest form of Lessing. When she submitted the realistic *Diary of a Good Neighbor* and *If the Old Could* to her publisher under a pseudonym, in a stunt to prove that editors are swayed not by literary merit but by names, they were swiftly rejected—and deserved to be. The only parts worth a second glance deal with an impoverished old woman who lives in dreadful squalor. Lessing's description of the filthy, littered rooms would seem to be a domestic version of her hyped-up visions of global destruction, as though the rubble of a nuclear-devastated planet can be anticipated in the decay of an old woman's life. Bad housekeeping enforced by poverty and old age reflects, in small, Lessing's compulsive preoccupation with pollution, nuclear bombs, and the end of the universe—the consequences of bad political and spiritual housekeeping.

In *The Good Terrorist,* she again picks up the bad-housekeeping theme in a story about a group of young revolutionary drifters who take over an abandoned house in North London. With unremitting diligence she itemizes the rubbish choking the garden, the maggoty wreckage within the once elegant rooms, the toilets and kitchens vandalized at the order of local officials to keep squatters out. But the radicals' den mother, Alice Mellings, has a skewed genius for bringing order out of chaos, and the "squat" is shipshape in no time. On the other hand, this "all-purpose female drudge" is a pathetic fool and often out of her head. (All of Lessing's women, even in her first novel, *The Grass is Singing,* are either born mad, go mad, or have madness thrust upon them.) She defiles her parents' generosity with vicious obscenities and rocks through the window, is slavishly devoted to a nasty homosexual who has exploited her for years, and bursts into hysterical tears on every other page. Her idea of a really good time is spray-painting defiant slogans on public walls, and being arrested at demos. (pp. 48-9)

Doris Lessing, as a presence, has been the Modern Woman. But her various explorations of that persona reveal that she cannot settle upon a stable identity, so she remains rootless, not earthbound, with no hobbling ties to community, family, or class. She yearns to be authentic, but *The Good Terrorist* shows how much she still lacks a center of gravity that would allow her to know which persona fits—realist, fabulist, doomsayer, mystic, or perhaps just a disenchanted old radical tired of the dangerous naïveté of the young. Yet these squatters are her children. And all that they can do is squat, in every sense of the word, on the bourgeois world.

The question that finally remains is Lessing's ambiguity of purpose and judgment. When Alice screams at her long-suffering mother that "your world is finished, the day of the selfish bourgeoisie is over. You are doomed," what sounds like an old Lessing refrain cannot, at this point, arouse our sympathy. Does Lessing despise the feckless terrorists for their mindless rage and immaturity, their knee-jerk raving against "fascist-imperialistic" Britain? Or does she pity them for being so ill-equipped for the tasks of revolution, for being such unserious and unprofessional babies in the struggle for social justice? We don't know; and it is not clear that she does either. (pp. 49-50)

Pearl K. Bell, "Bad Housekeeping," in The New Republic, Vol. 193, No. 18, October 28, 1985, pp. 47-50.

ALISON LURIE

Considered in combination . . . *The Diary of Jane Somers* and *Canopus in Argus* were disturbing. They suggested that the creative high-tension in Doris Lessing between wild, imaginative energy and practical realism had finally snapped, splitting her into manic and depressive selves who produced, respectively, cloudy, optimistic fantasy and pessimistic tales of modern life. . . .

In her new and far more ambitious novel, *The Good Terrorist,* published under her own name, the two Doris Lessings are happily reunited. She continues to cast a cold eye on contemporary Britain. She asks questions of the sort that must have occurred to many people there in the past few years. How could their ordinary fellow citizens—not hysterical foreigners or obvious crazies—have planned and carried out the bombings of stores and offices that have killed and injured so many? Who could set out to do such a thing, and why? Whether her answers are right or not, Lessing has succeeded in writing one of the best novels in English I have read about the terrorist mentality and the inner life of a revolutionary group since Conrad's *The Secret Agent.*

Lessing's terrorists, however, have none of the glamour and mystery of Conrad's. The shadowy atmosphere of secrets and feints is gone; in *The Good Terrorist* we see everything in icy clarity, from the fading bunch of forsythia on the revolutionaries' kitchen table to the homemade bombs upstairs, which have been cobbled together out of "cheap watches, bits of wire, household chemicals, copper tubing, . . . ball bearings, tin tacks, . . . plastic explosive, . . . dynamite," and string. "Everything . . . looked cheap, makeshift, sharp-edged, and for some reason unfinished."

Most of the members of the group, too, seem makeshift, sharp-edged, and unfinished. At the start of the novel they are not yet terrorists, only a bunch of young dropouts camping out in an abandoned London house. All but two of them are unemployed, some by choice; they live on the dole or by scrounging or stealing from their relatives, justifying this to themselves as a sharing of the national wealth.

The squatters all consider themselves socialists, but their politics range from the mild ecological and antinuclear variety to a theatrical, theoretical Marxism. Collectively, they are at odds with their origins and estranged from their families. Though they come from virtually every social background, most have adopted false names and phony London working-class accents. Even the lesbian couple, Roberta and Faye, who in moments of crisis revert to the "clumsy blurting labouring heavy voices" of the northern slums from which they came, usually pose as bright, voluble cockneys.

All these young people see themselves as living in a corrupt, dishonest, and chaotic society that has no use for them. Mrs. Thatcher disgusts them, and the Labour party seems to be full of wimpy, ineffective liberals. As one of the most obsessed members of the group expresses it, they "want to put an end to this shitty fucking filthy lying cruel hypocritical system."

For some time, these people's rage and despair have been satisfied by picketing and demonstrating. As the book starts, however, most of them are beginning to feel frustrated and have fantasies of more radical forms of protest. (p. 8)

Into this disorganized, fragmented society comes Alice Mellings, the "good terrorist" who is Doris Lessing's heroine. Alice is strong, emotionally intuitive, and sympathetic, brave, warmhearted, hard-working, and generous—the sort of woman whose domestic skills and maternal sympathy have traditionally held the world together. . . . In nineteenth-century popular fiction Alice would have been celebrated as an "angel in the house." Louisa May Alcott or Charlotte Yonge would have admired the way she takes over the derelict building and turns it into a comfortable home. Nothing daunts her, not even the two bedrooms full of plastic buckets of excrement which the squatters have used because the water has been turned off by the Council and the toilets filled with cement.

While most of the others stand about looking on, Alice goes into an almost supernatural frenzy of cleaning and contriving, painting and hauling furniture, and persuading the local authorities to restore services. Her love for the finished product is intense and personal. . . . (pp. 8-9)

There is a darker side to Alice's nature, however. She is given to slightly psychotic fugue states, hysterical lapses of memory, and uncontrollable fits of rage at the unfairness and chaos of the world. . . .

Alice also suffers from a passionate asexual attachment to a good-looking but singularly unpleasant young layabout named Jasper. Jasper is neurotic, violent, dishonest (he even steals money from Alice), sulky, self-important, mean-spirited, verbally and physically cruel, absolutely no help about the house, and given to homosexual binges. He is so disagreeable that most of the other characters in the book continually advise Alice to get rid of him, but she will not listen. What seems to bind her to Jasper is, simply, his need of her. If he were more agreeable, maybe someone else would take care of him, but she knows she is his only hope. In this unwavering loyalty to an impossible man Alice, of course, also joins hands with her Victorian sisters.

Ordinarily one would expect to find someone of Alice's domestic talents and sympathy for the disadvantaged in a comfortable earth-mother situation—running Alice's Restaurant, for instance. But circumstances, or something in her own nature, lead her into a job as den mother to what gradually becomes a gang of revolutionaries. It is to Doris Lessing's credit that she does not insist on a psychological explanation, though she does point to parallels between Alice's childhood and her present life. We are told, for instance, that Alice's middle-class parents were intensely social; that they gave parties so large that Alice was often sent to stay with friends, which made her furious and miserable. . . . Yet apart from their parties the senior Mellingses seem to have been model liberal parents, warm and affectionate and concerned. Until the start of the book they have steadily kept on trying to help Alice out. . . . And this seems right both psychologically and artistically: as we all know, it is not only "bad," unloving parents who produce antisocial children.

One thing that differentiates Doris Lessing's terrorists from Conrad's is that most of them are female. On the other hand, the professional revolutionaries, and the policemen who make the group's lives miserable, are all men. It's not clear whether Lessing means to make a comment on the persistence of patriarchy among serious revolutionaries and their opponents. It is interesting, however, that the most violently angry characters are all women, and so are the two who, at the end of the book, manufacture the bombs and time them to go off in such a way that many people will inevitably be killed and maimed. A decade ago many of us believed that women were naturally better than men, and that if they were in power the world would be a better place; today we are not so sure. Power, even the power of an angry young woman playing with gunpowder and string in the attic of an abandoned house, corrupts. (p. 9)

It is one of the most disturbing ironies of this disturbing novel that Alice's best qualities, her domestic genius, her generosity and sympathy and energy, are ultimately responsible for the transformation of a collection of dissatisfied radicals into a terrorist gang. . . . Her love of order and beauty and harmony, her ideal of social justice, first destroy her, and finally destroy many innocent people.

Many of the characters in **The Good Terrorist,** with their rote revolutionary jargon and careless destructiveness, are frightening. But Alice Mellings, though she does not spout slogans or fill rooms with excrement, is perhaps the most frightening character of all, because she is, in the oxymoron of the title, both good and a terrorist. The grief and anger that many of us feel when we notice the waste, corruption, violence, and ugliness of the world is, in Alice, magnified tenfold. Unlike us, however, she does not block out this consciousness; she is almost continually consumed by rage and pain.

When a major character's name scans or half-rhymes with that of an author, it is natural to suspect some hidden connection between them. The fact that "Alice Mellings" sounds rather like "Doris Lessing" suggests that in some ways Alice stands in for her creator, and represents, in a distorted and exaggerated way, her own reactions to contemporary England.

Also, to anyone raised in the British tradition, it seems quite likely that Doris Lessing acted consciously in giving her heroine the name "Alice." After Shakespeare, Lewis Carroll is the most frequently quoted author in English literature, and we are surely meant to think of this Alice as being, in one of her aspects, the sensible, innocent, inquiring child, by turns puzzled and appalled by the ridiculous, cruel, and nonsensical adult world in which she finds herself. An inventive critic could probably find parallels between many of the incidents in *Alice in Wonderland* and those in Lessing's novel: for instance, the two nearly identical Russian agents, both badly disguised as Americans, reminded me strongly of Tweedledum and Tweedledee.

It is also possible to consider Alice as a personification of England itself. She has the traditional English sense of fairness, acute awareness of class differences, humor, courage, capacity for hard work, love of domestic cosiness, and unease about sex. Also typical is her and her comrades' amateurishness, their involvement in muddle, which doesn't always result in muddling through, and the contrast between their private affection and warmth and their capacity for public coldness and cruelty. Whether Alice's increasing lapses of memory of her own past, and her inability in the long run to face the facts of her history, should also be taken as a comment on the contemporary English character is not quite clear.

If Alice is, in a sense, England today, the prospect is bleak. By the end of **The Good Terrorist** all her good impulses have come to nothing or worse. The ruined house she has transformed into a comfortable home will be turned into expensive flats, and its inhabitants scattered; the waifs and strays she has befriended are lost or dead or in despair. Her parents' refusal to cut themselves off from her has ruined or nearly ruined their lives: her father's firm is close to bankruptcy and her mother has become an embittered alcoholic. In its conclusions, this is a deeply pessimistic book; but its energy, invention, and originality cannot help but make me optimistic about Doris Lessing's future work. (p. 10)

Alison Lurie, "Bad Housekeeping," in The New York Review of Books, *Vol. XXXII, No. 20, December 19, 1985, pp. 8-10.*

William Matthews

1942-

American poet, critic, editor, and translator.

A prolific poet, Matthews also gained recognition as cofounder and coeditor of *Lillabulero,* a magazine established in the 1960s to provide a forum for alternative poetry. The experimentation with "deep image" poetry and surrealism in the United States during this decade is evident in Matthews's early work, as is the influence of such poets as James Wright and Robert Bly. Matthews's first commercially published collection, *Ruining the New Road: Poems* (1970), introduces the imagistic and epigrammatic style characteristic of his early work, including his next major collection, *Sleek for the Long Flight: New Poems* (1972), and the small-press publications *Broken Syllables* (1969), *The Cloud* (1971), and *The Moon* (1971). Using metaphors, similes, and nature imagery, Matthews explores such themes as states of human consciousness, the passage of time, and the cyclic changes of life. He also writes occasional poems on such topics as basketball and jazz as well as anecdotes about his two sons.

Although a stylistic self-consciousness has been detected in Matthews's early work—Robert Pinsky suggested that the surrealism in *Sleek for the Long Flight* is merely imitative of contemporary trends—later collections, which evidence an expansion of form and a simultaneous tightening of control, have received increasing critical acclaim. Dave Smith praised *Rising and Falling* (1979) for the clarity and depth of its imagistic associations, noting that Matthews "wants to look more than to leap," and Peter Stitt, commenting on Matthews's development, stated that the poems in *Flood* (1982) "show the operation not just of a free and surprising imagination, but of a powerful and controlling intellect as well." The unifying theme of *A Happy Childhood* (1984) is reflection. In these poems, Matthews applies Freudian concepts in an analysis of his childhood and also examines such subjects as language, reality, and self-deception.

(See also *Contemporary Authors,* Vols. 29-32, rev. ed.; *Contemporary Authors New Revision Series,* Vol. 12; and *Dictionary of Literary Biography,* Vol. 5.)

PAUL WEST

[In *Ruining the New Road: Poems*] William Matthews addresses himself to the fact (one borne in upon us grievously these days) that "The earth has its own orders, lovely and harrowing." Nature is our context as we are its, life on earth being essentially indivisible; and Matthews fixes on the reciprocity of things, their interpenetration, the simultaneity of opposite conditions:

> I think of death's salmon breath
> leaping back up the saxophone
> with its wet kiss

(this from a **"Blues for John Coltrane"**). Writing about old girl friends, he describes being in love as being "in a well / I am the water of" and in another poem lovers as being "sewn into each other / like money in a miser's coat." His terse but ripe little poems movingly reveal that what lovers have in common with each other they also hold in common with earth: elective affinities which, no less than a Moselle wine, come out of the coincidence of soil and sun and what, rooted here, is shone upon. Tender about land, these poems flintily record human vulnerability upon it and, more than anything, man's insuperable habit of lying to himself in order to get through threescore years and ten with the least sense of what many billions of others are lying to *them*selves about. This is—one doesn't often use the word of a book of poems—a cogent first collection; it exposes, it warms, it warns.

Paul West, "Four Poets," in Book World—The Washington Post, *May 31, 1970, pp. 6-7.*

THE VIRGINIA QUARTERLY REVIEW

With a distinctive lyric sense and literal toughness, [William Matthews] confronts the almost hidden terrifying aspects of life around us. His subjects [in *Ruining the New Road*] range from the Asian War through elegies for jazzmen to family experience and the mystery of love. . . . Matthews is ever conscious of the risks we run in life and his meter and his metaphors take the kinds of chances real poetry needs if it is to succeed.

Nearly every one of these poems translates some new aspect of the guilt and anxiety we feel in living into objective clear experience. This poet has been to school with James Wright, Robert Creeley, W. S. Merwin, and Ed Dorn but this collection establishes him as an important poet with his own voice.

A review of "Ruining the New Road," in The Virginia Quarterly Review, *Vol. 46, No. 4 (Autumn, 1970), p. CXXXIV.*

JACK HICKS

Matthews' *Ruining The New Road* is a fine and handsome first book. His voice is unique, personal, but one not heard immediately or sharply. Because he does not knock you down, he requires reading and rereading—and even then his work does not announce itself, provides neither the dazzling shock of self-recognition nor the lofty moral seriousness of past and present poetries. Readers who insist on a poetry of ecstacy, one that frays or strokes nerve endings, will likely rush through and by these poems.

A major concern in this collection is the unconscious, and many of the poems make use of "deep image" techniques. But unlike the "new surrealism," uncontrolled poetic imitations of the magic of the unconscious, the sheaths of poetic poses that clog our mails, these poems are neither jumbled nor faked. (p. 99)

Poems of dreaming, the unconscious, memory, metamorphosis: this is his territory, his world, but not . . . cut off from the outside. (pp. 99-100)

At his best, Matthews' poems operate by a magical, unified, deceptively simple interior logic, like those early marvels of William Stafford's. . . .

Of late, Matthews has been working new poetic land: long "catalog" poems, prose poems, extended treatment of a single deep image. If his accomplishment in those forms approaches the talent realized here, he will prove himself a major young American poet. (p. 100)

Jack Hicks, in a review of "Ruining the New Road," in Carolina Quarterly, *Vol. 23, No. 2, Spring, 1971, pp. 99-101.*

F. D. REEVE

[William Matthews] cuts his images with a razor. Where the blade has slipped, the figure is scarred; where the hand held steady and moved patiently, calculatingly, the figure is crisply complete. . . . (p. 237)

The green sounds of nature offer him, for this first volume of forty-nine poems [*Ruining the New Road*], less than the shapes and claims of human bodies. The poet "knits a fern of bone for your thigh"; thighs are "rope"; thighs quiver "like huge stallions bearing the heralds"; and other images weave back and forth among the poems picking up associations which, sharp in separate poems, do not easily translate; at least, not for me. With pleasure I saw the thigh bone as a fern, but I couldn't accept both that and "the ferny lace of hair around your cunt." I didn't believe the request "Always put your

gloves of ashes on before you knock" because I had read **"My Routine"**, which ends:

> When I close my eyes
> I pull a blanket
> of ashes over them.

The 18th-century dramatist Chikamatsu said, "When all parts of the art are controlled by restraint, the effect is moving, and thus the stronger and firmer the melody and words are, the sadder will be the impression created. . . . It is essential that one not say of a thing that 'it is sad,' but that it be sad of itself." Two hundred years later, Ford Madox Ford, in his introduction to the *Imagist Anthology,* said that "Poetry is a matter of rendering, not comment. You must not say: 'I am so happy'; you must behave as if you were happy." Where Mr. Matthews comments, as in **"Cayuga Lake in Winter"**, I shrug; I don't believe the words; the words don't matter; but where the words make their own music, the formal restraint releases strong response. (p. 238)

F. D. Reeve, "Faces at the Bottom," in Poetry, *Vol. CXVIII, No. 4, July, 1971, pp. 234-38.**

ROBERT PINSKY

Ezra Pound made the often quoted assertion that poetry atrophies when it gets too far from music. What happens to poetry when it gets too far from prose, and the prose virtues? (p. 241)

[The] most "contemporary" of contemporary poetry is often interior, submerged, free-playing, elusive, more fresh than earnest, more eager to surprise than to *tell*—does such writing represent a drift away from the decencies of prose as an element of the poem? When poetry gets too far from prose, does it choke itself?

Historically, poets have been known to strangle their work on gobbets of poetic diction. The poetic diction of the 'sixties abounds in William Matthews' book [*Sleek for the Long Flight*]: "breath", "future", "blood", "silence", "water", and most of all "light", especially "light" doing the wildly unexpected: it "drills" into eyes "like a stream of liquid beads"; "a little loaf of light" rises "in the sea's dark pan"; "a shard of light," in one of the run-on images which characterize all poetic dictions everywhere, is "in the shape of an island from which dogs are leaping into the water"—but then, the poet muses, "or maybe the light implodes"; he encounters "eels of shy light"; somebody else must "go the rest of the way / by eating the light"; and it is no surprise to find these lines:

> *More light,* I cried, as Goethe
> did from his deathbed.
> it sounded beautiful and true. . . .

Somewhere, on some campus in America, a young poet is writing a sentence with *all* of these words in it, something like, say:

> The silence of my
> blood eats light like the
> breath of future water,

which I just composed in less time than it takes to type. . . . (p. 242)

One effect of the poetic diction of the Silence-Eating school is to convey that the poet is a "surrealist" yet not, uh, *literary*.

So, as in Matthews' **"The City Of Silence,"** curt Romantic aphorisms such as

> Anything you worship
> will let you be its priest

are leavened with references to contemporary objects:

> Sleep is my radio and all
> its news is true.

Such one-of-the-guys surrealism leads one to expect the poet to say "There's snow on the sandwiches", which Matthews *does* say in a poem called **"The Visionary Picnic,"** which later extends the image to

> we lie
> down in the sandwiches.

I thought that those were my favorite Matthews lines, then discarded them for the interestingly alimentary "We eat our way through grief and make it richer"....

In coming down so heavily on this book, I may appear to be going after fleas with a shotgun. My justification is that I am dealing with a new orthodoxy, and a tangled one. If there are fashions, then it is important to try to distinguish the genuine writing from the imitative. (p. 243)

> *Robert Pinsky, "Far from Prose," in* Poetry, *Vol. CXXIII, No. 4, January, 1974, pp. 241-47.**

HUGH SEIDMAN

Many of the poems in William Matthews's **Rising and Falling** deal with family (father, sons), the sense of isolation as place (Aspen, Utah, outer space) and the natural world, and illustrate what could be called an "associative" strategy: the poem begins anywhere and evolves to a conclusion via a progression whose logic is more or less consistent, much as a human life ranges between the extremes of pure chance and iron-clad predictability.

In **"Snow Leopards at the Denver Zoo"** the leaping animals are compared to water quickly filling a glass (deftly equated with the "noise of a nail driven true"). After a further comparison of their soundless landings to the quality of being extinct, the poet says:

> If I could, I'd sift them
> from hand to hand, like a fire,
> like a debt I can count but can't pay.
> I'm glad I can't. If I tried to
> take loss for a wife, and I do,
> and keep her all the days of my life,
> I'd have nothing to leave my children.
> I save them whatever I can keep
> And I pour it from hand to hand.

Thus, we might ask, do the leopards really relate to the subsequent notions of loss? Or, put another way, does the transformation of leopard to water to fire to debt (somehow then associated to taking "loss for a wife") achieve inevitability? The introduction of the abstraction (debt/loss) into the otherwise specific sequence of images is problematic; the last two lines, also, reveal Mr. Matthews's sometime slippage into pat and artificial endings.

Beyond this, Mr. Matthews's love of detailed information (e.g., **"Nurse Sharks"**) and his sense of humor can be joined to images that project necessity and force. His description of a cat, for example, being suffocated in a sack (**"Opening Her Jewel Box"**) is memorable, and despite the questionable: "the . . . / sawdust on my finger was as dense / as parts of grown-up conversation," the end of **"The Icehouse, Pointe Au Baril, Ontario"** succeeds admirably in transmitting boyhood wonder.

> *Hugh Seidman, in a review of "Rising and Falling: Poems," in* The New York Times Book Review, *October 21, 1979, p. 26.*

DAVE SMITH

Rising and Falling is William Matthews's third collection. Perhaps too hastily, I thought his earlier poems had the odd property of losing substance upon rereading. This new collection has singular depth, weight, and clarity. Everything in it is touched with intensity and taken care of with integrity. In **"Living Among the Dead"** Mr. Matthews examines his responsibility to ancestry, history, and artistry—those parental figures:

> To love a child is to turn
> away from the patient dead.
> It is to sleep carefully
> in case he cries.

How that *carefully* resonates with loving alertness. It is exactly the responsibility Matthews shows not simply for children but for all that exists, what he calls "the scripture of matter," and not least for art's forms: music, painting, poetry.

The poems of **Rising and Falling** do not glitter or dazzle, but shed a steady light. Often speakers in these poems are swimming or sleeping, or addressing those buoyant and slowed conditions, conditions calculated to manage poems of meditational stasis that are yet interesting motions. Mr. Matthews creates dream-states without pyrotechnic obscurity because he wants to look more than to leap. He intends to illuminate emotional time and space as well as their communal roots in memory. Meditation properly leads to a control of rising, falling breath; it means to slow down for suspended examination all that is known and apprehended. Poetry, however, must translate the apprehended into the tangible and Matthews makes a poem the art of the "mediating mind." Art rises, poetry falls; thought looks, life is. He speaks of these matters in this stanza from **"In Memory of W. H. Auden"**:

> They were not painting about suffering,
> the Old Masters. Not the human heart but
> Brueghel turns the plowman away
> for compositional reasons
> and smoothes the waters for a ship he made
> expensive and delicate.
> The sun is implied by how
> the sure hand makes the light fall
> as long as we watch the painting.
> The sure hand is cruel.

Cruel, yes, because it creates accurately "the scripture of matter" and its shadow or absence. The durable image of character and crisis provides all there is of emotional range and ultimate consolations. When imagination composes memory into the recurrances of art, history turns biography, biography turns meditation and "fields / become one field . . . , " for the second self on whom nothing is lost. Mr. Matthews' poetry is distinguished by a music made against all odds, the music of survival which he calls "undertow and stutter" in his poem

"Alcide 'Slow Drag' Pavageau," the music of ambition, work, and faith. . . . (p. 35)

Dave Smith, "The Second Self: Some Recent American Poetry," in The American Poetry Review, *Vol. 8, No. 6, November-December, 1979, pp. 33-7.**

MARVIN BELL

William Matthews is from my generation, which is separating itself into those poets who try to recreate the mystery and depth of the inner life through lush and sometimes hermetic images, or through sophisticated talk about it, and those who try to locate it in the outer world. Because of all the loose talk about the inner life, my generation has had to rediscover the outer life—which is still the shape the psyche makes, out there.

So Matthews writes a lovely little poem called **"Harvest"** [collected in *Rising and Falling*] in which there appears what seems to be an absolute fact: "A few rats are gnawing / along the floor of the silo, / but what are a few rats / against this tower of food? / It takes 75,000 crocus blossoms / to make a pound of saffron. / / / And after today out there / in the heat, nobody dreams of food. / In our dream, Mary Slater / swings higher and higher / on the vine over the Haskins' / creek, and disappears." The end of the dream is beyond us, but it takes 75,000 crocus blossoms. . . . When the exact and the unknown show up together, there is the chance to articulate an important quality of life and perhaps the mysterious basis for our certain yet indefinable emotional lives.

Matthews writes "about" music and musicians, sleep, mail, sons, sports, animals, childhood, what is underwater, and other things. In **"Living among the Dead,"** he writes, "To love the dead is easy. / They are final, perfect. / But to love a child / is sometimes to fail at love. . . ." Interestingly, for any argument about inner and outer, or the living and the dead, he uses as epigraph to that poem, this sentence by Paul Eluard: "There is another world, but it is in this one."

This business about preferring to live one's life than to not live it (James Wright), whether or not one's desire to fill a vacuum is madness or whim (Ignatow), surfaces—literally, surfaces, up through coral waters, up out of sleep and sleeplessness, back up out of recordings by dead jazzmen—all over Matthews's poems. It is the aesthetic business that has to be taken care of prior to such lines as these about **"A Hairpin Turn above Reading, Jamaica,"** where the wealthy worry about fire: "The rich buy truckloads / of water and hire the poor / to drive them up. Water will go / uphill if money will go down." Or these in, **"Talking to the Moon":** "A defeated politician is in circulation / again, as we say of coins. . . ."

I find it difficult to be clear or complete in trying to make a distinction between tautological beauties and hermetic riddling on the one hand (which are in critical favor and likely to remain so), and acts of poetic imagination smack-dab in the midst of the impure world on the other (and it is, perhaps, a matter of emphasis), but I feel, for one thing, that the latter involve a certain resistance to the abstract forms that language makes up for the events it reports. (pp. 168-69)

I sense, too, though I could never prove it, that a straight-forwardness, even what some may regard as a deliberate in-elegance, accommodates some thoughts otherwise denied, whether for conceptual or compositional reasons. In the fourth part of **"In Memory of W. H. Auden,"** Matthews argues with Auden's "Musée des Beaux Arts":

> They were not painting about suffering,
> the Old Masters. Not the human heart but
> Brueghel turns the plowman away
> for compositional reasons
> and smooths the waters for a ship he made
> expensive and delicate.
> The sun is implied by how
> the sure hand makes the light fall
> as long as we watch the painting.
> The sure hand is cruel.

"As long as we watch the painting." There are the beauties, and perhaps truths, which remain beautiful and true so long as we read the poem or can summon it again to mind almost fully. Just now, it seems to me another sort of courage and achievement—more courageous because more visibly failed when unachieved—to articulate (embody?) those beauties and truths which remain beautiful and true in the ragged world, after only one good telling such as we find in . . . [the poems in *Rising and Falling*]—which ask nothing for their own vulnerability, not even that we "perfect" them (in whose image?), only that we keep them alive. (pp. 169-70)

Marvin Bell, "That We Keep Them Alive," in Poetry, *Vol. CXXXVI, No. 3, June, 1980, pp. 164-70.**

PETER STITT

Doubleness is built into the very essence of William Matthews' third book of poems, *Rising and Falling*. Most of the things he writes about involve not either rising or falling, but both rising and falling—the stars, sleeping, shooting a basketball, writing a poem, the dead, love, swimming, snow. Individual poems are mostly occasional, but gather around certain preoccupying themes—time concerns Matthews, and death, and the idea of succession, though . . . Matthews thinks mostly of the future generation (his sons) rather than past generations. His control of language is impressive indeed—the poems are supple, smooth, and achieve the illusion of spontaneity. . . .

There is a richness of image and metaphor in this volume that shows itself everywhere—in complete poems, in passages, in single lines. (p. 431)

[Resemblances] lie at the heart of Matthews' best poems and account in large portion for their success. **"Spring Snow,"** for example, uses the idea / image of falling snow to bridge life from childhood to death. It begins by associating snow metaphorically with childhood: "Here comes the powdered milk I drank / as a child, and the money it saved. / Here come the papers I delivered." The poem concludes:

> Yet childhood doesn't end,
>
> but accumulates, each memory
> knit to the next, and the fields
> become one field. If to die is to lose
> all detail, then death is not
>
> so distinguished, but a profusion
> of detail, a last gossip, character
> passed wholly into fate and fate
> in flecks, like dust, like flour, like snow.

The movement of this poem is swift, skillful, dense with thought, based on a striking series of transformations and resemblances relating snow to time. *Rising and Falling* contains a great many excellent and pleasurable poems—other favorites of mine are "Utah Stars" (on an extinct basketball team), "Foul Shots: A Clinic," "The Blue Nap," "Icehouse." Matthews does indeed have a magical way with words, an agile, graceful style; this is the best book yet produced by one of our most articulate younger poets. (p. 432)

> Peter Stitt, "Resemblances and Transformations," in The Georgia Review, Vol. XXXIV, No. 2, Summer, 1980, pp. 428-40.*

PETER STITT

William Matthews, in his new book, *Flood,* seems to have moved in a direction opposite to [some contemporary poets] . . .; rather than relax his forms from an earlier tightness, Matthews has actually lengthened his poems while imposing greater control over his materials. The problem with the longish, open, chatty, contemporary lyric poem is that the poet will proceed by a relatively unchecked process of free association. . . . Matthews' new poems, by contrast, show the operation not just of a free and surprising imagination, but of a powerful and controlling intellect as well. The resulting poems are full of "wit" in the best sense of the word, the sense exemplified by John Donne, say, though of course Matthews' poems are freer and more relaxed, being modern.

Besides their technical virtues, these are meditative poems that generate a good bit of wisdom. **"Our Strange and Loveable Weather,"** for example, manages by its end to draw a cunning and elaborate parallel between the vagaries of the weather and those of human life. . . . [The final] lines go deep quickly, unexpectedly—and they end the poem with very great skill; Matthews is a master at conclusions. Earlier in this poem come lines that illustrate what lyrical heights Matthews can reach when he so desires; the description relates to winter: "soon / enough turmoil under leaf-mold / begins, and the bulbs swell, and up / the longings of themselves spring's first / flowers shinny."

The quality of mind, of sheer intellect, is probably the most impressive thing about these poems—in contemporary poetry, imagination seems a much more common excellence. But Matthews controls, modulates, enriches his imagination through the full use of his mind, and thus the complaints . . . [that can be brought] against other writers just can't be applied to him. And there is emotional richness as well. Matthews is probably the most explicitly and literally "fatherly" poet we have, a result no doubt of his having been a single parent for most of his adult life. **"Taken at the Flood"** is an apparently simple poem that expands powerfully, through the deft infusion of metaphor, into a moving statement. . . . This is easily William Matthews' best book. . . . The poems manage to combine an almost traditional lyricism with the long, open, meditative form of today, and the union is a spectacular one, achieved through the mediations of a powerful mind. (pp. 681-83)

> Peter Stitt, "Poems in Open Forms," in The Georgia Review, Vol. XXXVI, No. 3, Fall, 1982, pp. 675-85.*

BONNIE COSTELLO

A poet of remarkable descriptive talent, William Matthews moves [in the poems in *Flood*] from outward observation to inward questioning. But his objectivity never leaves a cold register, never compromises lyricism. With Frost (without his

bite), Matthews achieves a crisp, resonant line in unembellished, even-toned style, which captures the pathos of the moment with its fragile patina of before and after. **"New"** is *not* hackneyed:

> The long path sap sludges up
> through an iris, is it new
> each spring? And what would
> an iris care for novelty?
> Urgent in tatters, it wants
> to wrest what routine it can
> from the ceaseless shifts
> of weather, from the scrounge
> it feeds on to grow beautiful
> and bigger: last week the space
> about to be rumpled
> by iris petals was only air
> through which a rabbit leapt,
> a volley of heartbeats hardly
> contained by fur, and then the clay-
> colored spaniel in pursuit
> and the effortless air
> rejoining itself whole.

Clearly Matthews's unit is the phrase, shapely in sound and conception. The opening line mimics the movement it describes, the swift, apostrophic "volley of heartbeats hardly contained by fur" filling only the space of a rabbit's leap. The brilliance of the poem as a whole lies in the unity established by the observer's thought, in which temporal differences fade into sightlines crossing at the scene, an effect far surpassing fast motion photography.

The mind observing the present, but swinging back and ahead in time, regulates many poems in the volume, putting Matthews in line with Romantic nature watchers who set nature's "all in all" against the strange divisions in human attention. In **"Rosewood, Ohio,"** for instance, the progress of the poem is from direct observation to remembered scenes, to meditation on time. Without any loss of distinction, the seasons accelerate their changes in thought: "But soon it's June / usually rainy here, then summer / arrives in earnest, as we say, / with its long, flat light pulling like an anchor against the sun." Behind such anticipation is a sense of loss, or at least amazement at the rapid progress of our lives, which allows no reliable diary: "we can't / say surely what we've undergone, / and need to know, and need to know."

There are no still lives in Matthews's gallery; all is motion and change, which may leave the heart heavy or light, at turns. (pp. 110-11)

In the title section of the book motion and change gather into tempest, thus the heart finds a theatrical analogy for its temperaments, less predictable than the seasons. Matthews gauges not only the torrent of emotion, but the approach, the calm, the memory. Yet the arid stillnesses intensify against the violence that surrounds them, as in **"Flood Light,"** in which the water, rising in thought, turns the prairies to ocean bottom. The flood motif of this section almost becomes redundant, but each poem sustains its own descriptive and associative logic, and several achieve real power. Those which associate the flood with the creative urge, as in **"The Waters,"** and **"Everywhere"** succeed least, because they seem most contrived. But **"Taken at the Flood,"** where the force of "fatal habits" and "wrong love" carry the speaker like a waterfall, interests by the freshness and ease of its metaphysical resemblance.

Matthews treats of human feelings most persuasively in the abstract. In his anecdotal poems he remains the *observer ab extra*, reading rather than participating in a situation, or even standing outside his own involvement. The poem **"Bystanders"** is more characteristic in this than he might recognize. He does not move comfortably toward the first person singular, but some of the poems call for that intimacy by their limited scope. The observer's stance gives him too much knowledge of scenes where blindness might be truer.

Matthews shines in uncluttered figuration, where eye and mind collaborate on a single surface. Several poems in the last section demonstrate his virtuosity in unstrained conceit. **"School Figures"** almost stands for his creative process, without explicitly naming it. A poem about error and change, about learning and forgetting, but written with sustained attention and rhythmic balance, it gathers the themes of the book into a single image of a practicing figure skater. (pp. 111-12)

Bonnie Costello, "Orders of Magnitude," in Poetry, Vol. CXLII, No. 2, May, 1983, pp. 106-13.*

PETER STITT

William Matthews' new volume, *A Happy Childhood,* intends explicitly to be a wisdom work. The basic text is drawn from Freud, as two closely related passages in the book's title poem make clear:

It turns out you are the story of your childhood
and you're under constant revision,
like a lonely folktale whose invisible folks

are all the selves you've been, lifelong,
shadows in fog, grey glimmers at dusk.

      . . . . .

There's no truth about your childhood,
though there's a story, yours to tend,

like a fire or garden. Make it a good one,
since you'll have to live it out, and all
its revisions, so long as you all shall live,

for they shall be gathered to your deathbed,
and they'll have known to what you and they
would come, and this one time they'll weep for you.

The poem describes the process of the book, which is to create the speaker's childhood, much as the process of psychoanalysis creates the analysand's childhood.

Is it a happy one Matthews has created here? At the end of the title poem he rightly points out that the question doesn't matter: "Who knows if he's happy or not? / A child is all the tools a child has, / growing up, who makes what he can." The book's title, then, is intentionally misleading. What Matthews has created here is meant to look, on its surface, simple, predictable, and stereotypical; meanwhile, at a lower level, the real wisdom of the poem is meant to be more difficult, more ambiguous, more mysteriously unique. Questions unavoidably arise about a work like this one: just how wise is it? How original is the thinking? Are the opening lines of a poem like

"The Psychopathology of Everyday Life" as revelatory as Matthews evidently means them to be?

Just as we were amazed to learn
that the skin itself is an organ—
I'd thought it a flexible sack,
always exact—we're stunned
to think the skimpiest mental
event, even forgetting, has meaning.

The problem here is that we are not stunned by this information—certainly not now, when we have been living with it for lo, these many years. Nor are we surprised by information revealed later in the same poem:

Even when we think we're not,
we're paying attention to everything;
this may be the origin of prayer
(and if we listen to ourselves,
how much in our prayers is well-dressed
complaint, how much we are loneliest Sundays
though whatever we do, say, or forget
is prayer and daily bread) . . .

This is awfully solemn and pompous; the poet is preaching at us, repeating the clichés of our age (accurately called by many the Age of Analysis) as though they were spontaneous revelations. Far too much of the book is like this, a heavily worked up burden of wisdom the reader longs not to have to bear.

What is missing in such poems is the sensuality of poetry, the way a poem will present an idea not in the language we usually use for ideas, but through objects that somehow, mysteriously, have come to represent that idea. In a much better poem, **"The Interpretation of Dreams,"** Matthews' speaker concurrently discusses the subject of the title while he searches for "the perfect pasta." Then, at the end of the poem, he suggests:

. . . "Let's go to Gubbio
tonight and eat tortellini."
How long it takes to make them right,
and how they flare up
in the mouth like sunspots,
both dense and evanescent,

and we realize that he is talking not just about pasta but about daydreams, night dreams, and poems all at once. The idea is carried by an image, as is the way of good poetry.

Matthews has never been an impressively lyrical poet, preferring to rely instead on anecdote and aphorism. His effects come not through spectacular sequences of sounds but through careful management of detail, event, meaning, feeling. Perhaps the best poem in *A Happy Childhood* is **"Loyal,"** which admirably illustrates the method. . . . The poem is dense with thought, incident, reaction, surprise, and wisdom. *A Happy Childhood* may be the book Matthews had to write at this time in his life and career, even if it will not be seen by most as "the book that signaled [his] arrival at full maturity as a poet and as one of the masters of our time." He remains, however, among the most important poets of his generation; now that he has cleared the decks of this Freudian version of the past, we can look forward to the truly significant work that may lie ahead. (pp. 859-61)

Peter Stitt, "Wisdom and Being in Contemporary American Poetry," in The Georgia Review, Vol. XXXVIII, No. 4, Winter, 1984, pp. 857-68.*

RICHARD JACKSON

"On this huge page no breath / will write. The text is already / there, restless, revising itself" (**"Everywhere"**). That text, for William Matthews, is the glossy surface of the flood waters that are a central metaphor in *Flood*. It is a text that, in words that recall Jacques Derrida's meditation on language, "compiles / the erasure of its parts / and takes to itself the local / until all but sky is water." Here the world itself becomes text, not in the medieval sense of a book of nature, but in the more contemporary sense that is part of an ongoing deconstruction of the languages and metaphysics of full presence. In a recent interview, Matthews says, for instance, that the surface of the water-text is all that can be known, though there are depths of "association and emotional experience." For him, "what is crucial is the surface tension; once you stick your hand into the water and break the surface, once you enter into language, each disappears. And water itself is in some way made out of the word 'water,' a word that changes from language to language." . . .

More problematic is when language seems to fail entirely, when the flood metaphorically or really subsides. For example, in the emptiness of **"Flood Plain"** the narrator must learn to read a rock not simply as an empty sign, but as "a water lathed box / full of the true history of itself, / to which the history of any treaty / is but a heartbroken footnote." Water, even in its absence, provides the text of Being that is always "already / there, restless," a trace structure half under "erasure" that the narrator must learn to revise if he is to understand his own being and history. The difficulty for the narrator is that he always seems to find himself, like the neighbor who sits down to write in **"Burglary"**—

> needing to know the name
> of something he can't say
> without a name, the way
> when we first wake we look
> a little blurred and shapeless,
> and by shaking off those waters
> become unique and familiar
> to ourselves again, inhabitants
> of our names.

In such moments he may not "yet have the name, but a better / reason to need it." *Flood* is, after all, a book about desire, about what is not there in the world, in language, and yet how, the narrator says, you are "unable to forget what you can't name" (**"The Waters"**). "It's harder / than we think to name / our emotions," he says in **"Descriptive Passages"** when his sons earnestly describe his "drunk hair," and so he can be both "proud / for the intimate talk" with them, "and sad for how little such talk says." What motivates him is a sort of Platonic memory—"not words / but what we use words to remember: / something we could almost sing" (**"Distant Chirping Birds"**). How appropriate it is that all song is composed of words, that Matthews finds himself in the endless circle of needing words to go beyond words. It is the ironic predicament of the poet in these poems to be a type of the Wordsworthian inscription writer, celebrating the losses he lives for, the unconscious desires his own linguistic consciousness precludes. And perhaps the best figure for this predicament occurs in **"Epitaphs"** where he remarks how "rubbing / tombstones" is "a form of printing and erasure, / both."

It is this sort of "double inscription," as Derrida calls it, that provides the narrator a way to break the circle. If, on the one hand, whatever presence he faces is marked by the profound absences we have already seen, on the other hand, his power to reinscribe a new myth, to telescope metaphors out of absence itself, saves him from an endless emptiness. This techique is evident in **"New"** where he describes how

> last week the space
> about to be rumpled
> by iris petals was only air
> through which a rabbit lept,
> a volley of heartbeats hardly
> contained by fur, and then the clay-
> colored spaniel in pursuit
> and the effortless air
> rejoining itself whole.

Such a rejoining, even though it appears in the past, provides a pattern with which the narrator, now uttering it in the poem, no matter how suppositionally, creates a presence as full as any reality. In fact, as he says in **"Airline Breakfast,"** it's what he can't see that he loves so much, "so wonderful / is the imagination." The creative power, and it is a considerable one, reveals just how much is at stake in this wonderful and moving book: the narrator's whole sense of Being, of what it means to be, to make meaning, in a world whose sense seems so often muted. When confronted with the overwhelming spectacle of **"The Basilica at Vezelay,"** the narrator hardly knows what to think until he begins projecting the builders, the actual size of the church, its history, realizing: "what I don't know / and never will makes me weep easily / for human limitation, especially / my own." It is, finally, his own mortality that becomes the subject of this meditation, and indeed, of the whole book.

> *Richard Jackson, in a review of "Flood," in* The American Book Review, *Vol. 6, No. 3, March-April, 1984, p. 16.*

DAVID KALSTONE

[William Matthews] is wary of overtelling "the story of our lives, lumpy with anecdote." *A Happy Childhood* is punctuated throughout by pieces with a whiff of family romance—the title poem and others called **"The Interpretation of Dreams," "Civilization and Its Discontents," "The Psychopathology of Everyday Life."** These poems restore some sense of mystery and play to Freud's explanations and challenge the easy fictions people make of them. . . .

A Happy Childhood is an elegant lexicon of the narrative traps we set for ourselves—or so we realize when we read the whole book and not random samples. Part of the time Mr. Matthews casts himself as an amused inspector of language. The first set of eight pieces in the collection is bracketed by two sequences of short poems called respectively **"Good"** and **"Bad"** and the closing eight by the antiphonal series **"Right"** and **"Wrong."** These sequences play through proliferating examples, never taking a word the same way twice—a good lie, good for our debts, the good of rain after sullen heat, bad child, the bad marriage of mind and body, the right to be silent, right as rain, "too right, my son accuses me when I correct / his grammar."

Mr. Matthews runs fluent tests of other adjectives in poems that turn old favorites into exotic strangers. . . . At first, these seem like lucid entertainments—worldly, adult, penetrating observations. But they have other designs on us as well. The simplest words recur in new and often contradictory contexts. This is language as kaleidoscope, shifting realities rather than a poised and polished lens. What is fluent and adult can also be bewildering. Too many stabs at definition expose language as only approximate, and Mr. Matthews's Freudian poems provide periodic and lyrical release.

The pleasure of this collection lies in its counterpoint of assurance and irrationality. The skillful, elegant analyst becomes as comically self-deluding as the rest of us. Even the "happy childhood" of the title poem can't be rendered as continuous narrative but is presented in vignettes contradictory and askew....

Our desire for neat explanation is shattered at every moment that truly changes our lives. In **"Whiplash,"** the stage is set—a car, its brakes unrepaired because the driver is broke, a mother's visit and the inevitable accident, whose "causes" reach back not just to unpaid bills but to a lifetime of decisions, evasions, twists of fortune, even to the parents' lives:

> It seemed not that his whole life
> swam or skidded before him,
> but that his whole life was behind
> him, like a physical force,
> the way a dinosaur's body
> was behind its brain and the news
> surged up and down its vast
> and clumsy spine like an early
> version of the blues.

The victim begins to sing.

> And that's how
> The police found him, full-throated,
> dried blood on his white suit
> as if he'd been caught in a rust-
> storm, song running back and forth
> along his hurt body like the action
> of a wave, which is not water,
> strictly speaking, but a force
> that water welcomes and displays.

That is Mr. Matthews's writing at its strongest, open to the interplay of narrative and song. The shock, even more intense here than elsewhere in the book, comes in wakening to the pitfalls of explanation and the slim defenses of language. Because he often starts off with the reasonableness of prose, Mr. Matthews is all the more successful in throwing open under pressure the resources of verse. He makes it seem a psychological necessity, the impulse language "welcomes and displays."

David Kalstone, "Lives in a Rearview Mirror," in The New York Times Book Review, *July 1, 1984, p. 14.**

DAVID LEHMAN

It's been a while since William Matthews began making good on the promissory notes of his early talent. Still, his previous work doesn't quite prepare one for the pyrotechnics of *A Happy Childhood,* his sixth volume. These new poems are notes toward self-definition, studies in "self-deception and survival," episodes in the psyche's autobiography. What unifies them is a style of thought, a mode of musing that navigates easily from abstract principles to concrete particulars, and back. Matthews has, moreover, found a theme capable of bringing real pressure to bear on his considerable savvy and skill.

Freud is the muse of *A Happy Childhood,* if muse is the right word for so fierce a father figure. Four of the poems take their titles from Freud.... In each instance, Matthews uses the Freudian antecedent as a springboard rather than a final destination. He renews Freud's metaphors ... or propounds new ones.... Some premises are sustained ... and some are put to the test.... Most of all, Matthews emulates the poet in Freud, fastening on our errors and dreams and accidental patterns as badges of enchantment, clues to a mystery that retains something of its inscrutability even as it fosters new forms of revelation.

More than half of the 34 poems in *A Happy Childhood* have adjectives for titles—**"Masterful," "Charming," "Arrogant," "Restless," "Prurient," "Tardy," "Loyal,"** and so forth. These investigations into sometimes antithetical aspects of a universal personality compel us to question our categories, to keep an eye out for the tricks language plays on us, to see **"Good"** and **"Bad"** as complementary fictions, like **"Manic and Depressive."** Wit, warding off solemnity, enhances the insights Matthews has to offer.

David Lehman , in a review of "A Happy Childhood," in Book World—The Washington Post, *September 2, 1984, p. 6.*

Valerie (Jane) Miner

1947-

American novelist, journalist, short story writer, and editor.

In her novels Miner explores the status of women in society. Her principal themes—the nature of freedom, the value of political and social activism, and the function of literature—are presented from a feminist viewpoint. Among the subjects Miner examines are divorce, abortion, women's rights, sexual harassment, and marital relations. Her protagonists are usually politically active women who, in trying to improve society, discover more about themselves.

Miner's first novel, *Blood Sisters: An Examination of Conscience* (1981), is the story of two Irish-born cousins. Like their heroic grandmother, who worked for the liberation of Ireland, each is dedicated to her own cause: Beth to the freedom of Northern Ireland, and Liz to the emancipation of women. Conflict arises when the cousins meet in London and develop a relationship complicated by their political and philosophical differences. In her second novel, *Movement* (1982), set in the aftermath of the social and political upheaval of the late 1960s and early 1970s, Miner chronicles the odyssey of Susan Campbell from housewife to feminist, author, and political activist. By interspersing into the main narrative several short, unrelated sketches about women in varying circumstances, Miner attempts to emphasize the interconnectedness of human experience. In *Murder in the English Department* (1982), Miner focuses on Nan Weaver, an English professor who is falsely accused of the murder of a chauvinistic male colleague. She discovers that a female student killed the man in self-defense as he tried to rape her. Dr. Weaver perceives the student as the real victim and postures her allegiance as a feminist statement. Miner's recent book, *Winter's Edge* (1984), tells of the troubled relationship between two elderly women living in San Francisco who refuse to be discarded by society.

(See also *Contemporary Authors,* Vols. 97-100.)

PATRICIA CRAIG

Blood Sisters (subtitled "an examination of conscience") is the story of two cousins, London-Irish and Irish-American, whose mothers were the twin daughters of an Irish patriot named Elizabeth O'Brien. The girls, Liz and Beth, meet in London for the first time in 1974. Californian Liz is a feminist and author of a book about witches. Beth, who emigrated from Dublin with her mother Gerry at the age of fourteen, is a part-time teacher and political activist ("What are we going to do for Bloody Sunday?"). Each cousin attempts to foist her opinions on the other, with scant success: one becomes a spokesman for the joys of lesbianism, while the other engages in terrorist acts.

There's enough material here to make several novels, and it is rather thoughtlessly assembled. Valerie Miner's grasp of Irish history and politics is shaky; and her chronology is all over the place. She alludes to a number of real-life characters, notably Maud Gonne MacBride and Constance Markievicz (a facile way to get glamour and the appearance of authenticity into a rather drab narrative), without bothering to check the relevant dates. So, the girls' grandmother Elizabeth, we learn, "was the first choice of Major John MacBride before he married Maud Gonne". It is difficult to understand how this can be, since MacBride married Maud Gonne in 1903, when she was thirty-seven and he was thirty-three; and we're told more than once that Elizabeth was born in 1900. . . .

There are other gaffes. Elizabeth it was "who kept the Orangemen off our block for ten Julys", her daughter remembers; and this is odd because Orangemen do not march in Dublin on July 12 or any other date, their activities being confined to the North.

Indeed, Valerie Miner has managed, remarkably, to write about the Provisional IRA and its current activities without considering the sectarian issue which is at the root of the Northern Irish trouble. She reduces the conflict to a matter of dedicated terrorism versus British imperialism. . . .

Having reorganized the IRA (you might say) in provincial and metropolitan wings, Valerie Miner wisely concentrates on the latter, though without displaying too much insight into the behaviour and motives of revolutionaries. Beth of the "big Irish heart", for instance: her Marxist-socialist-terrorist convictions are the product of an outlook utterly naïve:

> Beth thought back on the small faces in her classroom.... Her pupils were poor kids whose parents had no choice but to leave Ireland. If the North's industry and rich agriculture were infused into the Irish economy, maybe Kevin and Seamus could have stayed home. Maybe her own father wouldn't have had to take such dangerous work and be killed.

It's not in any sense a satirical portrait: there is no narrative irony to turn such reflections as these into a pointed exposure of vapid reasoning. Only at one moment, indeed, does a note of salutary exasperation get into the dialogue between the cousins, when Liz bursts out with, "Belfast, Shmelfast ... You know as much about Belfast as I know about Dublin." ...

Liz almost falls in love with her cousin (Beth does fall in love with hers, Liz's brother Larry, who follows his sister to England) but opts instead for stylish Gwen, wry and tender as only a lesbian (in feminist fiction) can be. This is where the sentimental element enters into the novel: "Sometimes their union was like distilled joy. Sometimes their love was a buttress against a larger, alienating world."

Violence, as Liz recognized at an early stage, is unpredictable; people who play with firearms and explosives can expect to get hurt. If you insist on having a finger in the pie, you may lose your whole hand. This is the novel's central contention. But it takes in, as well as the themes discussed above, psychiatric disorder, family relations, social climbing in America and Liz's troubles with her job at the *Listener* (the *Listener*?), where her superiors are all repulsive in various masculine ways. You cannot accuse Valerie Miner of being under-ambitious. It is plain, however, that she lacks the novelist's flair for selection. The description of Liz's first journey on a London bus, for instance, is laboured to the point of bathos ("To the conductor, these roads were just lines as familiar as the dark creases in her own pale palms"). You could say it was a documentary impulse, not a literary one, that got the author going—and, on the plane of documentation, the novel has many flaws. It is succinct and accurate, in fact, in one area only, and that a small one: *Blood Sisters* is a very appropriate title.

> *Patricia Craig, "Worrying about Ireland," in* The Times Literary Supplement, *No. 4085, July 17, 1981, p. 803.*

MARION GLASTONBURY

[In *Blood Sisters,* the] first encounter of three cousins from London and California encompasses the struggle of their Irish foremothers throughout the century, and sets the mid-Seventies bombing campaign of the IRA against the aspirations of activists in the Women's Movement.

Political militancy across the generations, the polarities of national and personal liberation, the conflict between Catholic and feminist doctrine, and the ambivalences of bisexual attraction do indeed create suspense, surprise, drama and historical ironies. But erotic allure is still conventionally rendered by soft furnishings, sartorial elegance, and chic smells—Rive Gauche, Chanel 19, Vent Vert—while the book's story-line wobbles in and out of plausibility.

Now that the pilgrim daughters have discovered the Old World (witness also Marilyn French's *Bleeding Heart*) native novel-readers are treated to wide-eyed documentation of our local colour and quaint customs: the exotic occupants of a double-decker bus; the wretched diet of lamb, lentils, and lemon squash; the picturesqueness of Westminster Abbey, 'a venerable doyenne in dust-starched skirts'. There is perhaps no harm in seeing ourselves as tourists see us—'Hampstead exuded more grace than Tufnell Park'—but it's hard to believe in English and Irish women who get their heads together in West Coast psychobabble, or in the flatulent nurds (is litigation pending?) who work with Liz on the staff of that 'absurdist Oxbridge ghetto', the *Listener*.

> *Marion Glastonbury, "Charmed Circles," in* New Statesman, *Vol. 102, No. 2627, July 24, 1981, p. 20.**

PUBLISHERS WEEKLY

[In *Movement*] Miner uses an innovative narrative form that shifts from past to present to trace the public and private movement of Susan, a serious, contemplative writer and activist.... Her tenacious desire for self-knowledge and her evolution from socialism to feminism is complex and inspirational. Miner fairly well captures the authentic charades of the mid- to late '60s: the sobriety, self-aggrandizement, despair and loneliness are all there. Stories of others' lives, strangers to Susan and the reader, are woven into the narrative; like figures standing to the side in a photograph, these peripheral characters help us understand Susan and ourselves a little better. This is a compelling book, invigorated by Susan's idealism, and infused with her deep passion for life.

> *A review of "Movement," in* Publishers Weekly, *Vol. 222, No. 2, July 9, 1982, p. 46.*

FAITH SULLIVAN

Unself-conscious dialogue is one of the greatest strengths of [*Blood Sisters*]. Even when the discussion is purely political, there is no flavor of propaganda, no didactic cadence as though words were orated against a background of drum beats and marching feet. The author has kept a fine ear cocked for the real, off-camera language of politics.

The Irish "givens"—the Catholic Church, ancient superstition, poverty, education and pride—that color even second- and third-generation Irish-American thinking are subtly woven into the book's texture. Miner has spared us the phony cuteness of the stereotypical Irish, priest-ridden, guilt-ridden and charm-ridden.

Partly through the use of a chronology at the beginning of the book, partly through immensely disciplined narrative, the author has taken a tangle of times, places, events and characters and kept them lucidly sorted out, relentlessly moving ahead.

The book's weakness lies in the fuzziness of the author's ultimate point of view. When political events move a plot and motivate central characters, the reader deserves to know where the author came to stand when all was considered. In **Blood Sisters**, this point of view would logically have been expressed through the character of Liz. We needn't be bludgeoned by it, but we're bound to ask, "After all the tragedy and turmoil, were Liz's political convictions altered? And if so, how?" Without rather specific answers to these questions, the story is unresolved and the reader's voyage ends shy of port.

> *Faith Sullivan, "Cousins in Passionate Wars of Independence," in* Los Angeles Times Book Review, *August 22, 1982, p. 5.*

ANNIE GOTTLIEB

The problem with [**Blood Sisters**] is, oddly, that its modern politics, so important to the characters, never come to life. The cousins' respective commitments seem ideological and abstract (and, in Liz's case, trendy and narcissistic) rather than intimately entwined with life like their grandmother's patriotism. What *does* live, in **Blood Sisters**, is the matriarchal family tree—the vertical bond joining grandmother, mothers and daughters, and the horizontal sisterhoods that affirm, with inexpressible love, that common blood. The best portraits in the book are of the cousins' mothers, Polly and Gerry, who are twin sisters. From an apolitical generation, they have been preoccupied with survival on two separate continents as exiles and as single mothers. Both, in different ways, have lost their men. . . .

The results of Valerie Miner's examination of consciences are unclear. It seems to me that she conscientiously details her heroines' political passions while unconsciously rejecting them in favor of the novelist's real passion: the drama of daily living. (p. 25)

> *Annie Gottlieb, "Women Together," in* The New York Times Book Review, *August 22, 1982, pp. 11, 25.**

SUSAN LYDON

Movement traces the evolution of one Susan Thompson from draft resister's wife to awakening feminist to struggling writer. As someone who lived through [the late '60s and early '70s] in Berkeley, where much of the book is set, I wish I could say it worked. Removed from context, and with hindsight added, this slender recreation of life before feminism, and radical politics before disillusionment, seems hollow and a little false.

Susan is the daughter of working-class parents; her mother is a waitress and her father a stevedore; she marries Guy Thompson to hide behind his respectable WASP name and because she likes his parents' middle-class comforts (mainly sherry). The book begins with their flight to Canada, uncertain they'll be admitted, and ends with Guy standing Susan up for a coffee date, postdivorce, only to be replaced by an admiring student who allows Susan to voice her life's conclusions. In the pantheon of shadowy preliberation husbands, Guy is among the most invisible. Even his no-show at the book's end indicates a certain unwillingness on the part of the author to engage in male-female dialogue. Why does Susan leave him? What happens in their marriage before she leaves? All we find out is that he resents her working late on a magazine where her male editor takes credit for her work, that Susan leaves a peace

march she "pretends" to go on in order to fix him dinner, and that she dislikes life "as Professor Thompson's wife."

Susan then goes to England to find herself as a person and writer. There are a few gratuitous deaths, which possibly symbolize the dying British culture as compared to American vitality, and possibly do not. Susan works for a communal publishing venture and discovers, incidentally, that she's more inclined to lesbianism than to heterosexual love. There are some nice, gentle erotic passages, but no conclusions are drawn. (Remember the old arguments about whether one could be a practicing radical feminist without loving women?) Susan defines her identity through a process of negative discrimination ("Susan loved . . . Susan hated . . ."), and much is made of comparisons between, for example, the kind of woman who reads Doris Lessing, and the kind who reads Virginia Woolf (of whom our heroine says, "the novels intimidate me in their languor," surely one of the worst lines ever to make it into print). In the end, when Susan complains that her writing isn't very good, I wanted to concur heartily rather than cheer her decision to go on. There is also the problem of a writer writing about a writer writing; it's unimaginative, and makes the book entirely too self-conscious and pretentious.

Various '60s ideas are presented here intact: the politics of personal experience are preferable to the politics of rhetoric; women are as oppressed as third world countries; etc. Unfortunately they are told rather than demonstrated, and despite all the prose devoted to the necessity for passion in politics, there's not a shred of passion in either the writing or the story. Personally, I'd rather read Virginia Woolf, no matter how intimidating the languor, and continue hoping for a novel that evokes the flavor and texture of life in Berkeley during this turbulent, colorful, explosive time.

> *Susan Lydon, in a review of "Movement," in* The Village Voice, *Vol. XXVII, No. 38, September 21, 1982, p. 44.*

TRACEY WARR

[In **Murder in the English Department**] Miner's heroine, Nan Weaver, has escaped from a working-class background into a middle-class marriage, and then from that into a Professorship in Women's Studies at Berkeley. Nan's tenure is threatened by her outspoken feminist politics, especially her campaign against sexual harassment on the campus. A lecherous colleague, Angus Murchie, is found stabbed to death with his pants down and Nan is one of the few people in the University building at the time of the murder. She has, in fact, overheard Murchie attempting to rape her beautiful, sophisticated research student, Marjorie Adams, and found Marjorie's blood-stained scarf by the body. While the police and everyone else concentrate on the mystery of Murchie's murder, Nan is preoccupied by the mystery of the character of his murderess. Marjorie remains cool and disinclined to confession even after Nan has confronted her with the fact of her knowledge. Nan's decision to protect Marjorie results in her own arrest and trial for the murder.

Miner's writing, particularly her dialogue, is frequently too overtly laden with her feminist concerns, which are themselves often rehearsed on a banal level. Her style is detailed and lucid but rarely compelling and though her plot is dramatic enough she unfolds it with a pedantry which is unfortunately appropriate to the theses that her heroine supervises.

Tracey Warr, "Sisterly Succour," in The Times Literary Supplement, No. 4153, November 5, 1982, p. 1231.*

JOEL DRUCKER

Movement is a story of many movements (peace, socialist, feminist) on many levels (social, political, personal).

Movement's protagonist is Susan Campbell, a journalist / photographer / political activist whose story carries us through the 1960s and 1970s, from Berkeley to Canada to London, Africa, and finally, back to Berkeley. . . .

[Although] Susan's attitudes and mores are strongly shaped by the '60s, her sensibility throughout the story is actually more *post-'60s*, as if that decade had entered into history. . . . Hence, while the '60s exert their will over Susan's values, all of the book takes place in the '70s. So although "the decade was two years past and she was still marching," it becomes quite clear that Susan is ready for further development.

Miner abets this growth through her form. Each chapter can be read on its own as a short story, making it valuable on its own terms. In so structuring her narrative Miner succeeds wonderfully at making the novel a chronicle of movement and growth; character development comes more from experience than interior monologue. Action and growth, not thought and stagnation, command Susan's respect, both as a documentary journalist and an activist. Her gradual separation from the high-flung (and sexist) jargon of the Peace Movement surfaces at a 1972 demonstration. (p. 16)

This is the book's most important—and powerful—passage, as Peace, Leftist, Hippie, Youth and Women's Movements all come together, resembling a five-way intersection with Susan right in the middle. And in linking her to the Sisterhood of women, Miner gives Susan her first genuine *connection* as a potential participant in the age's tumult; Susan becomes enmeshed as the story takes us into the world of politics and power, a world occupied by men ('60s leaders more than included) as if only they held sway in these regions. In fact, it is the woman who cuts through the rhetorical thickets at the demonstration. In Canada it is Susan who works while Guy, claiming his research to be "political," sputters through his thesis. Indeed, that the Sisterhood of women involves itself in causes both political and social makes this more than a story, but a piece of political fiction. As it was for many women in the last decade, Susan's realization of her connection to politics through the women's movement becomes a vital phase in her growth.

Miner connects women through another stylistic innovation as well. Interspersed throughout the Susan-chapters are 13 short-short stories (one to four pages long) of other women in other places. None bear any relation to Susan, but through each one Miner depicts the many ways modern woman lives. One works as a waitress at a greasy spoon, one is hitchhiking, and another leaves her husband, comes back to him, and wrecks her car and herself. One of the more provocative short-shorts features a smart faculty party's discussion of the lesbians who are "taking over" on campus. When the silent Cornelia reveals that she is gay, her colleagues' response is telling: "I mean, it's not like you're really one of them." And perhaps the most striking short is "Newsworthy," a pithy three-paragraph ac-

count, written in newspaper form, of a Walnut Creek man who reported his 62-year old wife to be missing after a night out in San Francisco: "Mrs. Forester, an active volunteer at their church and a local hospital, has no past record of instability."

The short-shorts are stark, told with the bare minimum of adjectives and omniscient judgment. Like Susan's work, they are documentary snapshots; you can hear Miner's camera eye clicking away as she crafts these vignettes, striving above all to show women as people, not victims or heroines. Dignity and integrity, central features of political fiction, are vital aspects of *Movement*, the short-shorts serving as lenses through which to focus experience not only in the feminine, but in the universal realm. These techniques and themes in mind, Miner's novel appears influenced not only by Doris Lessing and Marge Piercy, but also by John Dos Passos and Ernest Hemingway, not just for their place in the Lost Generation but also for stylistic reasons. The documentary presentation, the flat journalistic sentences and the unjudged actions all point to the unstated tension and omitted truths that, in their sum, make Susan committed to maintaining "grace under pressure."

When, for example, an expedition through the English seaside results in one of the men getting trapped in a cave, it is Susan who quickly moves to save him, shimmying her body into a crack—and losing her wedding band in the process. Though the man dies, Susan has shown mettle, an attribute she feels she lacks all too often. This low self-esteem—a feeling of not being "tough enough"—pervades her thoughts whether she is with radicals, feminists, Europeans or Africans.

Susan's uneasiness with her strengths makes *Movement* a very American novel. "Americans," writes Joan Didion, "are uneasy with their possessions, guilty about power." Though not easy to fathom given Vietnam, Didion's statement applies to Susan: American power in this case is not the power of its government but of its people, as seen when Elizabeth, a friend of Susan's from years back, professes her admiration for Susan's boundless energy, that incredible enthusiasm and zeal which governs her work. Susan too is aware of her Americanness; in London she despises long lunches and "could never enjoy Tennyson after reading Whitman;" in Africa she "as always, saw everything in comparison to the West;" and in Canada comes to realize that "Life didn't seem to count as much in Canada or England. As an expatriate she could make mistakes and not fail; she could fail and not sink." Hence, while she has learned that America is not the center of the world, she sees how it has always been the center of *her* world. She feels inexorably bound to the Republic: "American was the only skin that seemed to fit. You have to go home again."

This decision is not without its ambiguities. Through the course of the novel Susan, in addition to her political education, grows personally through her relations with the young man Mohammed in Africa and the lesbian Pia in London. In each of these trysts Miner skillfully outlines the tensions and values of Susan's life that split between the private person and the public activist. (pp. 16, 27)

In distancing Susan from America Miner, like Hemingway and Cowley, shrewdly highlights her Americanness; everywhere Susan, like a youth from the provinces, wonders—and finds out—if she's "tough enough." As an American woman in the '70s, though, Susan finally does come to terms with her experience:

> She had to admit that she was no longer the
> earnest student or novice writer and that she

had no right to many of her doubts, even if she wasn't comfortable with success.

But Susan is not ultimately alone. Through the short-shorts and the many women Susan meets, Miner, unlike Hemingway, places Susan in a world teeming with energy and hope, therefore showing the interconnectedness of not just the feminine, or American, but of the human experience. (p. 27)

Joel Drucker, "Women without Men: 'Movement'," in San Francisco Review of Books, *November-December, 1982, pp. 16, 27.*

JEAN M. WHITE

Valerie Miner takes the mystery novel and turns it into a feminist polemic in *Murder in the English Department*. . . .

Without weighing the merits of the message, the result is a stridently argumentative story that offers little in the way of suspense or detection. . . . [Miner] is so intent on advancing her views that she forgets that she started out to write a mystery story. . . .

The problem is that Nan, admirable as she may be, is not a warm and sympathetic heroine, coming across as an intellectual snob in her relationship with her sister, married to a blue-collar worker who watches football on TV. And not all men are chauvinist pigs, although the only decent chap in the book is a teaching colleague who is a homosexual.

Miner writes crisply and has a good ear for dialogue. Maybe she'll be satisfied to write a good story the next time without stacking the deck to make her point and burdening her tale with editorializing.

Jean M. White, in a review of "Murder in the English Department," in Book World—The Washington Post, *March 20, 1983, p. 11.*

TOM JENKS

Movement opens with the final scene: Susan Campbell sitting in a Berkeley restaurant, waiting for her ex-husband Guy, whom she hasn't seen since they divorced in Canada. Her thoughts summarize the events of the past six years and provide the light in which we read. We're told or can readily surmise the major events of the next 180 pages. We know Susan's going to have an abortion. We know she's going to be divorced. We know she's going to become a feminist and a lesbian. We know she's going to try to make it as a political activist and writer. And we know she'll come home, suddenly aged and wondering what after all she's made of her life. . . .

Sandwiched into the narrative of Susan Campbell's passage from late youth to early middle age are short-short stories that can best be described as: the joke's always on him. These pieces are a collection of ineptly written dramatic monologues and contrived scenarios featuring such sexual stereotypes as the repressive father who wants to keep his little girl a little girl; the repressed housewife who flips out and suddenly disappears; the woman who leaves her husband for another woman; a waitress living a life of quiet desperation; and a crass sexist who, in lasciviously recounting the suicide attempt of a "gorgeous," "glamorous," "sexy" young "girl" with "everything," says that he *just* can't understand why she did it. Miner fails to illuminate or break these cliches, and her punch lines

and conclusions always indicate the presence of an unfortunate conceit: a feminist monopoly on understanding.

Miner's men are shadowy. They are punished for appearing in her pages at all. And the greater their vitality, the harsher their punishment. In a chapter titled "Single Exposure" Susan meets three young men—Andre, a British would-be writer; Colin, a social worker in Glasgow; and Ronald, an American divorce lawyer, traveling to find himself. . . . By the end of Susan's acquaintance with them, Andre has given up writing, gotten a steady job, and happily placed himself in psychoanalysis. Colin has sold out social work to go into politics. And Ronald—well, Ronald throws himself down a hole (literally) and dies. Only Susan, whose book is about to be published, realizes a dream.

The idea of Susan as a writer and of her work as fulfillment places a burden at least on Susan's voice if not on Miner's. We expect the language and content of Susan's thoughts and her dialogue to be in some way remarkable. But Miner traps Susan in a passive, internal, third person voice, as in this passage of her thoughts while waiting for Guy:

> Maybe she didn't really want to settle the "marriage thing" after all. Maybe she had always known it would break down. No, the scary part was that there was nothing she had always known. . . . The change had come naturally, at least imperceptibly. They had both changed. They weren't the same people. God, it all sounded so trite, so hollow, so boring.

Given Susan's movement from housewifery to liberation, we expect (but don't get) a corresponding change in voice—from passive to active, from inward to outward. Worse, this inward, trite, hollow and boring voice is the voice of the book's narration and of *all* its characters. Miner's prose is flat, insistent, and distinguished by clumsy figures of speech and wordy wit, such as calling Spam a "can of carnal imitation."

Both the introduction by Susan Griffin and Miner's foreword explain *Movement*'s structure—i.e., a novel written in discrete chapters alternating with short stories that are not involved with the main narrative but that are meant to reflect on it. Miner tells us that *Movement* breaks through the isolation and individualism of the traditional novel, which, she says, has become an endurance test for both writer and reader. . . . Yet Griffin and Miner and even the form of the book with its digressive, heavily end-stopped pieces reiterate that each chapter and story stand alone, and each brackets isolation and individualism rather than dissolves them.

In *Movement,* Miner is concerned with fiction as a force for social change. She attempts a rewriting of life and literature, a transcendence of patriarchal models. That, for instance, Hemingway in *in our time* (or, to a lesser degree, Evan S. Connell in *Mrs. Bridge*) used similar episodic technique is undoubtedly not lost to Miner. But because her form fails to accomplish the revisionist task she claims, her sweetly self-important preface comes off more as a seductive apologia than a coherent statement of motivating principles.

Movement is a blurry portrait of a harried woman endlessly engaged in communal and alternative efforts, a woman whose thoughts and actions are defined by her extreme reluctance to recognize life's physical and practical limits. She is a woman who is unable to make lasting connections with others and for whom political obsessions replace human concerns, yet one whose capricious and willful passage into an uneasy adulthood we are asked to accept as if it were considered, earned, complete, and somehow joyful. . . .

Movement is full of sardonic humor, defensive self-irony, flirtatious uncertainty, and thinly disguised braggadocio.

> Tom Jenks, in a review of "Movement," in The American Book Review, *Vol. 5, No. 5, July-August, 1983, p. 3.*

SUSAN L. CLARK

Mysteries in academic settings invariably operate on the principle that ivory tower inhabitants should possess higher motivations and purer logic than the common riffraff—and, in fact, do not. *Murder in the English Department*'s heroine, Dr. Nan Weaver, Ph.D., forms a prime example of this assumption, for the clear-headedness that stands her in such good stead in her scholarly work is conspicuously absent when she discovers the violent death of a fellow member of Berkeley's English Department. Implicated in Professor Angus Murchie's death, and imprisoned for it while her trial drags on, Nan quite literally sees the truth—and it doesn't set her free.

Miner's strength as a mystery writer, as she sets out Nan's painful circumstances, does not lie in plot but rather in characterization, and her description of the workings of academe is disconcertingly accurate, from the paranoia which inevitably complicates tenure decisions (Nan's tenure case is further clouded by her vocal involvement in the campus campaign against sexual harrassment) to the petty backbiting that goes on at departmental parties. Tension, as well as welcome support, comes from Nan's family, particularly from her sister Shirley and her niece Lisa, whose working-class relatives fear that, like Nan, she will catch the dreaded "Feminist Disease." Nan's literary forebears are Dorothy L. Sayers's Harriet Vane and Amanda Cross's Kate Fansler, and, while she may lack the polished wit of the former and the graceful urbanity of the latter, she proves to be thoroughly likeable and, unlike both Vane and Fansler, does not require a male to extricate her from her difficulties. Miner has created a feisty heroine who bears further acquaintance. (pp. 210-11)

> Susan L. Clark, in a review of "Murder in the English Department," in The Armchair Detective, *Vol. 17, No. 2, Spring, 1984, pp. 210-11.*

MICHELENE WANDOR

Valerie Miner's fourth novel, *Winter's Edge,* casts an ambitious net. Into the conventions of a distanced, chronological narrative, she seeks to combine a straight story with unconventional strands. Two elderly women friends in San Francisco are caught up in local political intrigue. Their friendship is tested (will a man come between them?) in traditional style, but one of them, Chrissie, is as radical and active as her 'fringe' colleagues, gay and prostitute. It is a novel which explicitly combines the personal and the political, and its chief drawback is its nervous, overloaded prose.

> Michelene Wandor, "Taboo or Not Taboo. . . ?" in The Listener, *Vol. 112, No. 2866, July 12, 1984, p. 28.**

MARY KATHLEEN BENET

Set in downtown San Francisco, *Winter's Edge* . . . deals with a collection of urban flotsam. But Miner says in her preface that she believes writing to be a collective art, and . . . [this book] reads as if the collective had voted on what to put in it. It would be a good thing to have more fiction about older women, so let's make our heroines about seventy. And let's show them with their sexuality, too: it's age-ist to do otherwise. We'll have a black woman who is running against a fiendish developer for the Board of Supervisors. And then what? Lovable Mexican flower seller, gay cop, confused juvenile, wet priest, faithful pet dog. . . .

The two heroines, Chrissie the waitress and Margaret the news shop lady, have a close but troubled relationship. Margaret is soft, interested in people, sexually vulnerable. Chrissie is militant and wants Margaret to pull her socks up and see what is going on around them. Even when the good guys' campaign headquarters are bombed, Margaret doesn't seem to want to work for the cause: she hopes everybody can just be friends. In a plot and prose worthy of Nancy Drew, girl detective, Margaret finally sees the light, the good cause triumphs, and Margaret and Chrissie go off hand in hand for a Hawaiian holiday. What this is doing on an adult publisher's list is anybody's guess, but perhaps Miner thinks her presumed audience of grateful senior citizens must be in their second childhood.

> Mary Kathleen Benet, "Capital of Crazies," in The Times Literary Supplement, *No. 4243, July 27, 1984, p. 848.**

PUBLISHERS WEEKLY

Friendship, politics and social consciousness are the issues raised in . . . [*Winter's Edge,* the] story of two elderly women living in San Francisco's Tenderloin district. Chrissie MacInnes and Margaret Sawyer have been close friends for years. . . . A hotly contested local election raises Chrissie's political awareness as she encourages Margaret to be more active in their community. Margaret continues to view the action from the sidelines until an act of violence leaves her no choice but to become directly involved. At the same time, she forms a romantic attachment to an eligible bachelor, placing a strain on her relationship with Chrissie. Depressing at times and certainly no lightweight, this book takes a thought-provoking look at human nature.

> A review of "Winter's Edge," in Publishers Weekly, *Vol. 228, No. 13, September 27, 1985, p. 95.*

BABA COPPER

[*Winter's Edge*] is an action-filled story of the friendship of two old women who live and work in the Tenderloin of San Francisco. The plot is fast moving; the supporting cast, varied and interesting. Chrissie and Margaret, in their mid-sixties and seventies respectively, have chosen to remain working rather than to subsist on Social Security. This is the price they are willing to pay for "belonging" in their neighborhood, being needed, having demands made upon their attention and emotions by other people. The primary concern of the community to which they belong is an upcoming election, in which development of their neighborhood is the dominant issue.

Chrissie and Margaret's friendship of twenty-five years is strangely mismatched. Their reliance upon each other survives

Margaret's repeated dalliances with men over the years, but not without tension and jealousy on Chrissie's part. It is not an alliance of expediency, although by allowing the reader to be privy to the thoughts of both of them, it is sometimes hard to believe their solid allegiance to each other. Neither of them outwardly exhibit any of the pettiness which may divide one old woman from another in real life. . . .

Miner creates an imaginary world where ageism does not limit the choices of her protagonists. Neither of her old women have been eased out of their high-visibility jobs, either as a waitress or as the cashier at a newsagent. The interactions of Margaret with the younger men who are customers and friends are charged with covert sexuality. Her pastor, a widower ten years her junior on the prowl for a new wife, is portrayed in hot pursuit of Margaret throughout the book. These circumstances are a reversal of the usual sexual erasure suffered by old women.

> *Baba Copper, "Two Novels about Older Women: 'Winter's Edge' & 'The Diaries of Jane Somers'," in* Off Our Backs, *Vol. XV, No. 11, December, 1985, p. 17.**

Les(lie) A(llan) Murray

1938-

Australian poet, critic, essayist, editor, and translator.

Murray is widely considered one of Australia's leading contemporary poets. He objects to the pervasive influence of British culture on Australian society and expresses a strong sense of nationalism in his work, celebrating his homeland by exploring Australia's wildlife, vegetation, and aboriginal folklore. Mary Kinzie stated that Murray "defines his territory . . . by addressing, with a whole heart, the peculiar and forbidding landscapes, the uncanny layerings of light, and the savage contrasts between seasons and elevations in his home region of New South Wales." While Murray's themes are typically provincial, his keen perceptions and creative use of language have attracted a wide audience.

Murray's first collection, *The Ilex Tree* (1965), contains both his own poetry and that of his compatriot, Geoffrey Lehmann. In this volume, Murray centers on rural Australia, and a number of the poems establish the relationship between modern-day Australians and their ancestors. Murray further explores the importance of national history in *The Weatherboard Cathedral* (1969) and *Poems against Economics* (1972), but his approach in these volumes is less conventional and more metaphysical. Murray's descriptions of bushfires, farms, and the rural terrain are enhanced by vivid yet abstract imagery. *Lunch and Counter Lunch* (1974) evinces Murray's conservative views on politics and religion, and in *Ethnic Radio* (1979), he employs the structure of traditional aboriginal song cycles and explores the sounds and silences unique to Australian culture. In *The People's Otherworld* (1984), Murray uses metaphor and allusion to comment on spiritual concerns and contrast them with the material world. Carmel Gaffney stated that Murray's "originality and his ability to present philosophical and theological concepts in concrete images not only revivifies traditional concepts of grace but also extends them."

In his experimental novel *The Boys Who Stole the Funeral* (1980), Murray's narrative takes the form of a sonnet. The plot centers on two boys making a trip to the bushland to properly bury a corpse; in this work, however, Murray focuses on the theme of maturation. Murray has also published two volumes of selected verse, *The Vernacular Republic* (1975) and *The Vernacular Republic: Poems 1961-1981* (1982), and a collection of essays, *The Peasant Mandarin* (1978).

(See also *Contemporary Authors*, Vols. 21-24, rev. ed. and *Contemporary Authors New Revision Series*, Vol. 11.)

poems with adult themes. In a way he is communicating both the anxieties of an intelligent sensitive observer of current affairs and the passion an historian feels for a world that is outside his immediate experience yet so like it that it seems to stir a kind of "ancestral memory". This is felt especially in poems about the first world war—for example "**The trainee 1914**" and "**A New England farm, August 1914**". . . .

The long and uneven "**Noonday axeman**" is the most ambitious of several poems dealing with everyday experience. Here (reminding one rather of Judith Wright) Mr Murray recalls his ancestors and finds some mystic link in the bush which has been a common environment for all the generations. . . . (p. 129)

> *S. E. Lee, "Sophisticates and Primitives," in* Southerly, *Vol. 26, No. 2, 1966, pp. 126-32.**

S. E. LEE

Les A. Murray and Geoffrey Lehmann, whose title *The Ilex Tree* is taken from Virgil's *Eclogues* ("Two youths in their prime, Arcadian singers both of them, / And equally keen to make up a verse, or match one"), have collaborated in a book that is as enjoyable as its title is apt and witty. Les A. Murray carries on a schoolboy's fascination for war and soldiers into

ROY FULLER

[Mr Murray and Mr Lehmann] are Australian poets and friends, and go well together in . . . [*The Ilex Tree*] with its neat title and Virgilian epigraph. Both are accomplished technicians, surprisingly mature and unstraining writers, and by frequently assuming personae other than their young selves avoid first-book dangers of monotony and excessive introspection. Mr Murray's usual objective correlatives are Australian landscapes and townscapes, but he is always conscious of history, ancestors, character. Though really he leans on no other poet, there is a measured Frostian tone about this work—indeed, one sometimes feels that his restraint is too severe, that he could inject more sensational interest (and with advantage) if he cared to do so. He describes women in small towns 'in calendared kitchens', and a possum 'ski-ing down / The iron roof on little moonlit claws', but such touches of brilliance are comparatively rare. The opening of his best and most ambitious poem, **"Noonday axeman"**, gives a good idea of the care and health of his diction:

> Axe-fall, echo and silence. Noon-
>   day silence.
> Two miles from here, it is the
>   twentieth century:
> Cars on the bitumen, powerlines
>   vaulting the farms.
> Here, with my axe, I am chopping
>   into the stillness. . . .

It will be interesting to see how he develops.

> *Roy Fuller, in a review of "The Ilex Tree," in* London Magazine, *n.s. Vol. 6, No. 10, January, 1967, p. 87.*

PETER WARD

Les A. Murray's contribution to [the annual anthology] *Australian Poetry 69* is **"Once In a Lifetime, Snow"**, a finely wrought poem on a bucolic happening: snow suddenly covering Uncle's farm. It is an excellent example of his work and of the way his style over the past few years has developed in flexibility and expressiveness, carefully modulated, neatly tuned, and capable of recording delicate mood and nuance as effectively as it can the hardy and muscular. But having thus tuned his lyre, I feel he now is often at a loss to know what to sing.

In *The Weatherboard Cathedral* he has published 45 poems that confirm this judgment, and also allow one to see how as a formal stylist he is one of the leaders of the rear-guard. He is a conservative, both in the way he sees the world and the way he records it, and while this is not at all necessarily a fault, it does perhaps cause him to be less adventurous and thus less engaging than he could be. Seeing that he has sharp knives, one would like him to cut something.

All the same, the volume is well worth reading, whether for excellently written but rather antique pieces such as **"Susan and the Serpent—a Colonial Fiction"** and **"The Prince's Land"** . . . which is a neat allegory of the creative act, or for points-of-departure poems such as **"The Fire Autumn."** . . . (p. 61)

> *Peter Ward, "Burble of the Bards," in* Australian Book Review, *Vol. 9, Nos. 2 & 3, December, 1969 & January, 1970, pp. 60-1.**

JAMES TULIP

[Murray] has laid claim to a subject matter that is general in nature and historically central to Australian culture in his evocation of the countryside. His writing seems to be an extension of the main Australian tradition: Slessor, Stewart, Lawson, Furphy and Rudd seem to be looking over his shoulder. Yet he is feeling for new ways to write now that this tradition is under pressure from the changes in the Australian way of life. There is a genuine problem that Les Murray's poetry is now

reflecting in the domination of the metropolis—in his case, Sydney. A fragmentation of attitude and tone and interest appears in [*The Weatherboard Cathedral*], and seems inevitable. The old world simply could not last, or even adjust in the new environment. Les Murray seems to have known this from the start. In fact, he seems to have been counting on catastrophe, and the new book feels like a trying-on of attitudes—from that of the prophet down to the clown as a way of resisting the change. Silence was bearable in its way in the country, but city silences are another matter. (p. 149)

The Weatherboard Cathedral has good poems in it, indeed some remarkable ones . . . , and Les Murray just has to be called a natural.

But is this weatherboard world symbol or syndrome in Murray's scheme of things? In *The Ilex Tree* we met the "weatherboard schoolhouse" and the "weatherboard village" and the sawmill where they came from; but in the new book these literal things seldom appear, and do so . . . in a clearly metaphoric form. A shift has occurred between the two books from a literal state to a mental state, and we find Murray leaping around now in this high, climactic visionary role, now in a man-about-town and social clown role, now in a distrustfully academic role—not to mention several other guises in which he presents himself. It is arguable that a poem like **"Platypus"**, and lines like the following, locate Murray's centre today more accurately than does the weatherboard symbol:

> Hold the thought of him
> Kindly to your skin.
> It is good to have him in our country,
> Unique, beneath our thoughts
> To nurture difference.
> Changeless beneath our thought
> And its disjunctions.

The sense of someone who is cunning and a loner, deserving and demanding affection for the comedy of his ungainly uniqueness, and somehow valuable in being able to live at the bottom of the pool—these are suggestive, if not symbolic, ideas for Murray's world as it stands revealed by his new book. And as an image of the poet unique and changeless under the surface of life's distractions and knowable as a comic nurturing presence, it applies more generally than to Murray himself.

Elsewhere in *The Weatherboard Cathedral* the comic sense presents itself in a less happy way. There are efforts at epigram, satire, and tall story which are all failures as poems precisely because they have none of the platypus logic. Australian animals need to be experienced in retreat, and away from the exposure of public styles and places; the same seems to hold for poets. The problem of overt humour is especially real with Les Murray: for he is using it here as bridge, shield, weapon and lollipop in lieu of creating a character for himself in his writing, and as distinct from a mere identity. One hesitates to say that his sense of humour is all wrong since it is so useful when hidden and embedded reflexively in situations like that of the platypus. But there is certainly a case for saying that at the present moment, and like his "old trousers", it needs to be sent to the cleaners.

The good poems in *The Weatherboard Cathedral* belong to a middle world in Les Murray where the conservative melancholy of **"The Fire Autumn"** and the "merciless glee" of the lighter poems are more or less absent, or if present as genuine aspects of some human situation enacted in the poetry. The opening sequence of poems **"Evening Alone At Bunyah"** leaves us with the feeling that Murray both belongs and doesn't belong to the farm and his father. A self-consciousness to the "I" figure and a sentimentality at times towards the countryside let the poetry down as a whole, but the sequence will deservedly win many friends for Murray among his readers. (pp. 149-50)

When one tone dominates a poem, especially if it is a dark tone, the poetry has great strength and natural discipline. The four-line verse form of "**Shorelines**" is one example where the heavy tone is helped by a certain rigour in the writing. . . . Other poems have this steadiness of tone with quite different subjects: "**Blood**" and "**The Abomination**", about pig and rabbit killing respectively, reflect an instinct for anecdote filled out by a natural and heavy tone. Death and departures are possibly Murray's true subject. In "**Troop Train Returning**", however, there is a clearer, lighter version of this tone:

> Stopped at a siding
> Under miles of sun,
> I watch a friend whom I won't see again
> Shyly shake hands, becoming a civilian,
> And an old Ford truck
> Receding to the sky.

When the rhythms, tones and phrases keep moving across the line lengths avoiding end-stopping, there is powerful activity in Murray's imagination. When they coincide, a stolid and impassive tone is heard. Some of the late poems in the book are especially interesting for their complexity in this regard. "**The Ballad Trap**", "**Hayfork Point**" and "**The Fire Autumn**" have death for a common subject but are remarkably different in the different attitudes taken towards it. The ignorant and sentimental nostalgia of balladists on bushrangers and their miserable existence, the recognition of and the reliance on change in the seasons, and the prophetic lesson to be learnt in an Australian bushfire respectively state themselves as subjects with a singleness of tone that points to an over-powering temperament behind the poetry coming at the thought of death from varying perspectives and with different meanings. "**The Fire Autumn**" in its high, portentous tone and shifting meditative stance accepts death as a natural and necessary condition of life:

> The dignity growing on trees
> In the drystick forests, the mines in the waste land, the
>   stones,
> Is not solar, nor deeply mortal. In dour shirtsleeve joy
> They answer the Sun of a universe where it is clear
> That this earth is continuous with nothing but the
>   unknown.

Difficult as this kind of expression may be, the poetry is obviously accepting some heavy emotion at its centre and bringing it to the surface of statement in the pervasive spirit of "dour shirtsleeve joy". It is an emotion that stays largely with Murray himself as the writer of the poems, and does not communicate itself to his readers. Yet one learns to respect its presence in his poetry. The existence of a "weatherboard cathedral" in Australia is *not proven* by Les Murray's poems, but that there is a *maker* of a weatherboard cathedral is beyond doubt. He nails his big lines and straightforward rhythms to the page with the same "dour shirtsleeve joy" as his ancestors took in making their homes in the lonely New South Wales countryside. (pp. 150-51)

> *James Tulip, "New Australian Poetry," in South-*
> *erly, Vol. 30, No. 2, 1970, pp. 148-60.**

JAMES TULIP

Les Murray doesn't go to the country for his philosophy. His philosophy drives him there. *Poems Against Economics* is the active stand which Murray is taking in terms of belief and judgment about Australia today. He is no liberal conservationist, a city man wanting the countryside to be kept intact for yearly holidays. Murray is aggressively for the folk and their culture. He sets this off against economics and the non-human feel of technology. His major sequence in *Poems Against Economics* is a long meditation called "**Walking to the Cattle-Place**"; and in the sixteen poems here he releases an imagination which is earthy, comic, critical and metaphysical. The "cow poems", as Murray calls them, have a radical conservatism of spirit and a real originality.

Excess of commitment to a belief proves often to be a good and necessary thing in poetry, and Murray's book as a whole demonstrates just this. His other sequences—such as "**Seven Points for an Imperilled Star**" for which he won first prize in the Cook Bicentenary competition, and "**Juggernaut's Little Scrapbook**"—have an arbitrary and formal quality to them not strong enough to ground them in reality. "**Towards the Imminent Days**" is an exception in the way its celebratory style links up the wedding of friends with a marriage of man and nature. In "**Walking to the Cattle-Place**", however, Murray goes hard and unselfconsciously at his beliefs, and it is precisely the energy and excess of his interest which justifies the poetry.

Ambulatory in rhythm and ruminative in tone, "**Walking to the Cattle-Place**" sees the countryside as a sort of Middle Earth, as Murray calls it. Between heaven and hell, it is a place of stability where beasts browse and human beings have a sense of humour. . . . It is a curious mixture of comic wisdom and fiercely idiosyncratic moves of thought and feeling. The mind of the cattle seems to spread into the people who live with them. All is pared back to ritual, which sometimes explodes in drama. As in "**Novilladas Democráticas**". . . . Closer to the general tone of the poetry, however, in its weight of masculine feeling is the lament which cattle have for death:

> They make the shield-wall over it, the foreheads jam
>   down
> On where death has struck, as if to horn to death Death
> (Dumb rising numerous straw-trace). They pour out
>   strength
> Enormously on the place, heap lungs' heat on the dead
>   one.

There is overall a sense of metaphor and sacrament giving unity to the world of beast and man. As Murray puts it, "Their speech is a sense of place". (pp. 234-35)

> *James Tulip, in a review of "Poems against Eco-*
> *nomics," in Southerly, Vol. 33, No. 2, June, 1973,*
> *pp. 234-35.*

ROGER McDONALD

Les A. Murray has an almost dietetic belief in the restorative virtues of a rural culture. "I rack my past for a health the boy can use", he says of a character in the first poem in *Poems Against Economics*, but he might also be thinking of the reader. Murray gathers poetic energy from this belief, which means he uses it as a poet and not as a propagandist; with this advantage working for them, the best poems in his new book are immensely impressive. Although the book is in three parts, the divisions themselves do not work up to a cumulative effect: this comes instead from two quite stunning long poems in the first section, and from a good number of the sixteen pieces that make up the third, **"Walking to the Cattle-Place"**. In polite disregard of the author's logic, this is the place for readers new to Murray (if there are any) to look first. Here the contours of his favoured landscapes are sharply outlined. . . . The framework of **"Walking to the Cattle-Place"** is given by Murray in a jacket note: "I set out to follow a cow, and I found a whole world, a spacious, town-despising grassland where Celt and Zulu and Verdic Aryan were one in their concerns . . .". The theme of cattle gives shape to this section, but the town-despising grassland generates the energy. There is nothing narrowly insistent about this: some of the insights picked up along the way have compelling force. . . . With *The Weatherboard Cathedral*, Murray's previous book, it became evident that his native north coast dairy country was more than just a good place to grow up in and write about with affection. Poems like **"Blood"** and **"The Abomination"** revealed sacrificial and ritual affinities. In a way the entire landscape and its population were images of a spiritual tradition. Similarly the cattle in these poems are more than just curious beasts. They carry a load of historical and symbolic meanings while offering (as Murray's figures always do) reminders of the actual world. **"The Boeotian Count"** is the most vivid blend of actuality and learning, but its form (a mass of butting, bumping, straggling names) makes quotation impossible. A few lines from **"The Pure Food Act"** (set in a dairy at night, after the milking machines have been turned off) show the refreshing physicality of the writing at its best:

> The quiet dismissal of switching it off, though,
> And carrying the last bucket, saline-sickly
> Still undrinkable raw milk to pour in high
> For its herringbone and cooling pipe-grid
> Fall
> To the muscle-building cans.

Although **"Walking to the Cattle-Place"** is full of knowledge stranger than this, it inevitably comes circling back to Murray and the sources of his imaginative life. . . . The book opens with **"Towards the Imminent Days"**, a poem that successfully takes the kind of wide-ranging, ambulatory approach that Murray attempted in **"The Fire Autumn"** at the end of *The Weatherboard Cathedral*. Occasioned by a friend's marriage, its last line ("for your wedding, I wish you the frequent image of farms") states precisely how Murray has caught his beliefs. Nearly every stanza in this long poem has at least one memorable image of country life. . . . Every abstraction and assertion is supported by local references, and, most importantly, by those non-logical reverberations that are the special prize of lucid and concentrated writing. The flat statement "Our lives are refined by the remotest generations" is preceded by two lines that offer more than just a homely proof:

> Hiles' paddock leans on its three-strand fence in the
> dark
> Bending the road a little with its history.

By the time Murray gets round to saying (of a farm boy who wants to know about cities) "I rack my past for a health the boy can use", we know what the past holds, and are sympathetic enough to reflect on what might in Murray's terms be said.

With the exception of **"A Helicopter View of Terrestrial Stars"** (which for this reader at least is bedevilled by obscurities) the remaining seven poems in the first section are accessible and interesting. The most impressive apart from **"The Conquest"** and **"The Ballad of Jimmy Governor"** (two poems already wearing the look of anthology pieces) is **"SMLE"**, which begins with the poet as a boy sitting up a tree shooting fish with a .303, and ends after five further sections on the rifle and its implications in history with his return home. . . . This poem is an extraordinary performance, an achievement of brilliant concentration on the whole, though with patches of obdurate obscurity. When Murray writes of the light in the barrel of a rifle as a "rational abyss", the full line being "And the burned steel light in your barrel, a rational abyss", the echoes that start (visual and tactile, but also political, historical and moral) are hard to stop. Ringing through the entire poem is a memorable definition of dying, applied to the stunned fish lying out of water: "They are swimming away in their muscles/But what has remained of the universe won't give". The obscurities in **"SMLE"** are of the kind that would probably melt with research . . . , but they take the poem through unlit tunnels all the same, though without dimming the conclusion.

Murray's poetry is least interesting when taciturn or oblique. For this reason the centre section, called **"Juggernaut's Little Scrapbook"**, is disappointing. Nothing is said that is not more richly implicit elsewhere. A couple of poems in **"Walking to the Cattle-Place"** use a corner-of-the-mouth speech that has the effect of underexplanation, rather than concentration. And the helicopter poem, already mentioned, demands pencil, paper, and an affinity for cryptic crossword puzzles.

These are minor tests of patience, though, in the work of a poet who gives a great amount of pleasure while still keeping a firm hold on seriousness. The poetry of Les A. Murray is a deeply satisfying re-creation of a superbly imagined world. (pp. 71-3)

> Roger McDonald, "Bending the Road a Little with Personal History," in Poetry Australia, *No. 47, 1973, pp. 71-3.*

DAVID MALOUF

Les Murray is perhaps the most naturally gifted poet of his generation in Australia, and *Lunch and Counter Lunch*, his fourth collection, contains some of his best work to date. Why then, one wonders, have reviewers been so unwilling to engage with the book on the serious terms it so obviously demands?

I shall want eventually to make my own reservations about the book, but let us for a moment point to a few of its qualities. It is a work of astonishing dexterity and scope. The verbal inventiveness seems almost unlimited, and one is reminded of late Auden in the poet's capacity to talk about almost anything and make it sizzle and twang. Murray never falls into easy attitudes and never gives shape to a "received idea". We are aware on every page of the freshness and originality of his insights, whether he is evoking landscape . . . or making delicate observations about people. . . . He has genuine wit, and what is rarer, genuine humour—some of it passionately black. The poems come in a stunning variety of modes: from the bush anecdote that is never mere anecdote . . . , through the Bly-like lyricism of **"Cycling in the Lake District,"** to big talky poems like **"The Action."** There is also, in the **"Broad Bean Sermon,"** with its evocation of the richness, the plurality, the oddness of the natural world, a marvellous paean of praise to the fulness of things—one of Murray's surest expressions of his religious vision, and in **"The Edge of the Forest"** a return to the world of **"An Evening Alone at Bunyah"** that makes us understand from inside the humanity of a situation that might seem too ordinary for poetry. And the same is true, I think, of the best poem in the book, the policeman's monologue **"The Breach,"** which not only makes poetry out of the plainest speech but takes up movingly inside one man's dedication to duty, and opens, without any sense of strain, into a larger subject, the problem of humanizing the law. There are, of course, moments of uneasy mannerism—they are the weakness of Murray's considerable strengths: as when what ordinary Australians call an Esky makes its appearance as "a styrofoam box with a handle" and when the wit takes the form of terrible puns: "the shirt of nexus". But these are small defects and *Lunch and Counter Lunch* is a big book.

Les Murray's general stance, as commentators have already noted, is conservative, and this is challenging enough to need some comment. Most of these poems, for example, are straight-forwardly Christian.... They are also about such unfashion-able subjects as nationhood, the need for law and order, the blood tie with land, and the manly virtues.... The book is meant to make us uncomfortable. It is the work of an intelligent man who distrusts our modern intelligence and whose preferred faculties, one guesses, would be intuition, psychic vision, but also the countryman's plain common-sense and even plainer sense of decency. What I meant is that if what we have here is a conservative mind it is a very critical, complex and flexible one—and given the current climate, to be a conservative as Murray is might be the most way-out form of radicalism. There is in these poems a feeling of going hard against the tide. It is what gives them their strong sense of energy, but also, I think, a rather edgy, aggressive, defensive tone.

So then, what is the trouble?

Quite early on in *Lunch and Counter Lunch* there is an important clue to what Murray is doing in this book. The poem is called **"L'esprit de l'escalier"** and the line I am thinking of is: "the perfect reply you only thought of later". *Lunch and Counter Lunch* is full of perfect rejoinders, brilliant refutations of fashionable opinion, and one guesses that Argument and Counter Argument lies somewhere behind the book's throw-away title.

The police poems, for example, examine the problems of law and order. They speak up strongly, in human terms, for its agents ("I am a policeman / it is easier to make me seem an oaf / than to handle the truth") and have as well some ironic observations to make about more "progressive" attitudes.... **"Sidere Mens Eadem Mutato"** while beautifully evoking the poet's student youth in the late fifties, questions the importance now accorded to the university as a seeding-ground for a new class, the intellectual élite, and a new and more brutally con-formist culture, where, as Murray has it, "Freud and Marx are left and right thongs in a goosestep". (pp. 70-1)

What I find worrying in all this is not the attitudes—Murray is on the whole more caring, more human, than his antago-nists—but the fact that in being replies, however brilliant, they have their source outside the poet: they are points in a public debate, they belong to the world of opinion, assertion, con-troversy; they spring, one wants to say, from the world of journalism and have the shape, and sometimes even the tone, of a newspaper column by a journalist who always takes the opposing line and largely relies on the exploitation of his own public personality. It is the tone I find most worrying of all. It is too often preachily rhetorical and condescending, too pleased

with its own cleverness; and it results too often in a sort of dumpy deadness in the rhythm. But in objecting to what I have called the tone I am really objecting to something further back in the poem's conception that creates the tone. For all its bril-liant twists and turns, Murray's creative intelligence doesn't seem free in this book. In making his "brilliant replies" he has, in many ways, accepted limits that are posed *for* him, by assertions from "out there".

Lunch and Counter Lunch strikes me as the work of a poet who is, at the midpoint in his career, very much in search of a subject that will be fully expressive of his gifts. In earlier books one had the feeling that Murray's subjects were *found*— and so close at hand that he had merely to reach out and give them shape. The subjects in *Lunch and Counter Lunch* seem *taken up,* and they are, to this extent, gratuitous, vehicles for the intelligence and verbal flair of a man who can write well on anything, but only very occasionally do they have that ring of the personal that we associate with the best poetry: notably here in **"The Edge of the Forest"** and more darkly in **"Rostered Duty."** What is also clear is that the earlier material is now exhausted. There is no way back. **"Their Cities, Their Uni-versities,"** despite some striking details, is for me one of Mur-ray's least convincing performances. What was easy in the earlier poems is mannered, almost baroque here, the energy seems worked up. And this despite a conclusion that is one of the best things in the book: "we are going to the cause / not coming from it".

There is no doubt about Murray's stature. He is a powerful poet, with all the gifts, one might want to assert, of a potentially great one. This new book reveals him at a point of crisis. Whichever way he now turns, it will be the key work in his career. (pp. 71-2)

David Malouf, "Subjects Found and Taken Up," in Poetry Australia, *No. 57, December, 1975, pp. 70-2.*

KEVIN HART

Murray's achievement in *Lunch and Counter Lunch* is the establishment of what he calls "The Vernacular Republic." ... This engineering of a strong, supple poetic language that is firmly rooted in Australian (seen as a dialect of English) is an event of major importance in Australian letters. It has been attempted by Bruce Dawe and is, occasionally, handled by Geoff Page and Geoffrey Lehmann, but it is Murray who has been the most vigorous and most successful in this venture.

In one of the finest poems in the collection, **"Portrait of the Autist as a New World Driver,"** ... we find Murray talking his way through a poem in much the same way as the middle-and-late Yeats could talk across a line of iambic pentameter and all the way through stanzas of ottava rima whilst dealing with the most abstruse and personal problems. Murray is less formal than Yeats, but the talky voice is there, unmistakably Australian and unmistakably poetry. This "purification of the dialect of the tribe" (to borrow Eliot's phrase from "Little Gidding") is most easily seen in dramatic monologues such as **"József"** ... and **"The Breach."** ... (p. 84)

Murray's aggressive Australianism belies what he has learnt from the Americans. He has much in common with a poet such as James Dickey. The same lightness of touch, of easy rhetoric in (say) Dickey's "The Sheep-Child" is seen in Murray's re-cent **"The Powerline Incarnation"** which ends with

I have transited the dreams of crew-cut boys named
   Buzz
and the hardening music
                     to the big bare place
where the strapped-down seekers, staining white
   clothes, come
to be shown the Zeitgeist
                  passion and death my skin
my heart all logic   I am starring there
and must soon flame out
               having seen the present god
It who feels nothing   It who answers prayers.

One of the most telling words here is "logic." It occurs in several poems in *Lunch and Counter Lunch*. Indeed, logic is the strength and weakness in much of Murray's recent work. The poems are packed with meaning, well argued and lucid. But, on the debit side, they are occasionally smug, and too-often indulgent with linguistic cleverness. I am reminded of some of the best-forgotten later poems of Auden, lexical exercises from *Epistle to a Godson* and *Thank You, Fog*. But such quibbles are minor. *Lunch and Counter Lunch* is a splendid book and the area in which Murray is working—the purification of the Australian vernacular into a poetic language—is, I think, the most interesting and rewarding area for experimentation at the moment. (pp. 84-5)

> *Kevin Hart, in a review of "Lunch and Counter Lunch," in* Southern Review, *Vol. X, No. 1, March, 1977, pp. 84-5.*

ROBERT GRAY

Les Murray's *Ethnic Radio* is mainly distinguished by his 10-page, long-line poem, **"The Buladelah-Taree Holiday Song Cycle"**, the richest celebration of our life he's yet given us. It must surely be one of the two best long poems ever written in this country. What else can be considered comfortably with it, except "Five Bells"? Certainly, not "The Wanderer", and not Hope's and McAuley's rhetoric, which, this far from the apocalyptic Fifties, seems more than ever out-dated and pompous. It seems to me there are no other poems in our literature so filled with a world and an emotion (one so different in each), and at the same time so easily contained by craftsmanship.

Any criticism of Murray's **"Song Cycle"** as being merely an inaccurate English-language version of an aboriginal form is so much nonsense. The translation of the original Moon-Bone cycle, as it stands in English, is in a consistent form, and is a great and successful poem—if it were wholly original it would rank with these two I've praised. Murray has used the form of this poem, has mastered it, has unstrainingly filled it with a convincing, personal content.

Throughout *Ethnic Radio* can be found excellent, varied poems, equal to Les Murray's best standard: poems such as **"Spurwing Plover," "Employment for the Castes in Abeyance," "The Swarm"** (a model for the political poem), **"The Gallery," "The Gum Forest," "Immigrant Voyage"**—and a lot of others equally well written, I can see, and needing only a different temperament to appreciate them more fully.

I think this book is Les Murray's best, and it has persuaded me to agree with a conversational remark of Peter Porter's—one typically generous, perceptive and original—who said that Murray has come to appear not only the best poet we have had in this country, but as amongst the half-dozen best poets writing in English at present. *Ethnic Radio,* with all the modes of language and of forms it so generously demonstrates, will probably convince others of that. (pp. 68-9)

> *Robert Gray, "Garlands of Ilex," in* Poetry Australia, *No. 70, April, 1979, pp. 67-9.**

MARK MACLEOD

The publication of Bruce Dawe's collected poems, *Sometimes Gladness* and Les Murray's collected prose pieces, *The Peasant Mandarin,* invites us to begin some comparative assessment of the two poets who are most clearly successors to the pre-eminent positions in Australian poetry of A. D. Hope and Judith Wright. Substantial selections of Dawe and Murray first appeared together in Alexander Craig's anthology, *Twelve Poets,* in 1971. In the same year, the extraordinary energy of Dawe's output—four books and a pamphlet published in the previous nine years—was confirmed with the publication of his selected poems, *Condolences of the Season*. Retrospectively, his voice appeared to be that of Australian poetry in the 1960s. In 1971, Murray, with only two of his now six volumes, had established his voice as the one most likely to speak for the mainstream of Australian poetry in the Seventies, and events since have proved that impression right. (p. 103)

Both Murray and Dawe, but particularly Murray, reveal in their writing an unusual erudition which, tempered by the casual colloquial element in their style, appears as the folk erudition of the yarner, which one would call, without any sense of deprecation, general knowledge. . . . Clearly here these poets may appear the closest we have to the poets of a true oral tradition who infuse their singing with the learning of their tribe. With Murray, of course, the notion of general knowledge implies quite the opposite of 'superficial': he has worked with most of the European languages, European and Celtic and Aboriginal folklores. His poems reveal his Classical knowledge, his knowledge of Eastern philosophies, of Australian history. The poems make demands on his readers; the Vernacular is not the Uneducated Republic.

And nowhere is this feature of Murray's writing more evident than in the prose pieces of *The Peasant Mandarin*. His title here, like those before it—*The Weatherboard Cathedral, Poems Against Economics, Lunch and Counter Lunch*—indicates Murray's continuing awareness of paradox, but its primary meaning focuses on language. The very audacity of a poet's collecting his book reviews and informal pieces with titles like **"The Flag Rave"** may seem to some readers the act of a man both peasant and mandarin. But although one cannot deny an element of defensive egotism in Murray, it should be pointed out at once that the standard, as well as in many cases the length, of Murray's reviews are above the average permissible in the Australian media.

The reviews reprinted here tell us a good deal about Murray's interests: a biography of E. W. Cole of the Book Arcade, 'Cole had a fervent belief in the coming federation of mankind'; a study of Morgan the bushranger . . . ; reviews of NSW North Coast poet Robert Gray, of Indonesian poetry, Irish poetry; reviews of books on the supernatural, on the synthesising genius of da Vinci; of Keneally as an Australian novelist trying to break the Miles Franklin Award view of Australian fiction. . . . There are pieces on Australian Republicanism, patronage of the arts, and an essay that starts out celebrating Peter Porter's poem "On First Looking into Chapman's Hesiod" and ends up illuminating splendidly one of the central conflicts within Murray's work: that of Sydney or the Bush. (pp. 109-10)

The Sydney or the Bush issues in Murray's poetry and criticism relate him more explicitly than Dawe to the mainstream of Australian literature. 'It's made you cruel, all that smart city life'; 'it's made you squeamish, all that city life'. 'Ecology? Sure. But also husbandry.' Thematically, the city-country conflict is there from the beginning of Murray's selected verse volume to the end. Stylistically, it asserts itself in an increasing tendency to let the little man himself, whom Murray writes about and for, speak in the poems. In a poem such as **"The Mitchells"** Murray curbs his own 'natural garrulity' to let the laconic communications of the Mitchells ... stand, unexplained by city learning. And in both his poetry and prose, his colloquial ease and ready humour act as earthing devices should the writing become overcharged with Murray's love of learning and ideas.

An increasing tendency towards the doctrinaire is at the best moments in *The Peasant Mandarin* earthed by Murray's enjoyment of some line of folk humour. In one of his pieces on the Australian flag, counteracting the characteristic outburst 'Bloody feudal pommy rules anyway!' is the equally characteristic reference to the parliamentarian's remark 'that if the number of points on the Commonwealth star was to be altered whenever new territories or states were created, there was a danger that the star might one day come to look like a circular saw blade''. Both Murray and Dawe have used irony repeatedly to check idealism.

But recent formal experiments in Murray's work suggest that the relationship between the opposites his poetry attempts to reconcile is as precarious as that between the many oppositions in Dawe's poetry. The much-vaunted derivation of the rhythm in his **"Bulahdelah-Taree Holiday Song Cycle"** from the Aboriginal Moon Bone Cycle, and now his recent novel in sonnet form, *The Boys Who Stole the Funeral,* indicate a gesturing towards folk forms that while undoubtedly well-intentioned may be counter-productive, and prove Murray further removed from his country past and more firmly rooted in his Sydney suburban present than ever.

While praising Dawe as 'one of the best three or four poets we have had in this country' and acknowledging some debt to him, Murray laments the effects of deracination and the academy on the later work in *Sometimes Gladness.* Dawe would perhaps answer, among other things, that events in Queensland have brought him closer to the people than ever, and that the later topical verse has been an important means to that end.

Murray, on the other hand, has seen Australia give its artists the system of patronage he did so much to extend for them (the opening topic of *The Peasant Mandarin*). He has consolidated the renewed importance of the vernacular in Australian literature. But a certain 'academic' note in his most recent writing persuades me that he now faces the difficult job, with many writing years ahead, of resisting invitations to speak more as mandarin than peasant: *ex cathedra*, be it weatherboard or red brick. For him to succumb would be the paradox of them all. (pp. 110-11)

> Mark Macleod, "Soundings in Middle Australia,"
> in Meanjin, Vol. 39, No. 1, April, 1980, pp. 103-11.*

THOMAS SHAPCOTT

I intend concentrating on two books. John Tranter's *Crying in Early Infancy: One Hundred Sonnets* (1977), and Les A. Murray's sonnet-novel *The Boys Who Stole the Funeral* (1980).

Both books explore the fourteen-line form; and from this unit, both build towards a larger perspective, or 'world'. Here similarities seem to end. *The Boys Who Stole the Funeral,* as the title-page punningly declares, is 'a novel sequence'. *Crying in Early Infancy* has no narrative: even the individual sonnets frequently avoid linear development or sequence. It could even be said that Murray celebrates country virtues, Tranter's work is entirely preoccupied with the restless-eyed City. (p. 381)

Les Murray claims to have found Eden. It's at Bunya, though Les Murray continues to reside at Chatswood. More seriously, *The Boys Who Stole the Funeral* avowedly sets out to prescribe a vision of the True Path. In this sense it is perhaps the most didactic book of poems to appear since *Captain Quiros*—though we remember that *Quiros* ends in human failure and fallibility, its Christian mysteries hollowed out of man's ongoing recognition of betrayal and the loss of vision. *The Boys Who Stole the Funeral* is more evangelical. It has more than a dollop of Scotch Presbyterian intolerance, too. In contrast to Tranter's testimony of unease and wary vigilance in a world known to be a minefield of illusion and betrayal, Les Murray presents his world as being clearly defined by necessary Rites of Passage. There are the Elect, and there are the Others. You may disagree with Murray's 'rites'—I do—but the poem has to be understood through the poet's firmly held conviction and understanding of those 'rites'.

The book's particular passage, undertaken by the two boys Kevin Stace Forbutt and Cameron Reeby, is that of initiation into manhood, or, perhaps one might say, initiation into the male conditioning of authority, judgment and a sense of superiority. Women, for Murray, are either dangerous (because they envy this male role), as in the brutally hysterical Noeline Kampff; or are permitted (if they are docile enough, or postmenopausal) to provide tea and bikkies and the odd supportive dash of folk wisdom. Murray's (older) women are permitted a certain motherly nagging—that is part of the initiate's growing up, and it reinforces the essential role of women to be out of the action—at most they are commentators.... (pp. 384-85)

The novel's 'plot' concerns the two boys' successful attempt to return the body of Clarrie Dunn to his country origins for the sort of burial that will force the go-getting City degenerates to acknowledge their rightful origins in the bush—or rather, in the fellers of the bush. Their flight and adventures become the ritual of initiation into Manhood. Responsibility and acceptance of the Burden Of Superiority. (p. 385)

The Boys Who Stole the Funeral rests its case on what Murray himself would surely call 'traditional' roles. But his country Eden is as uncomfortably stratified and suspicious as any claustrophobic centre of hypocrisy and bigotry. We have all probably some experience of an Eden—or a Shabbytown—somewhere. The ploy of celebrating country virtues, even country values, is perhaps welcome enough in a culture of quick jeers. Yet Murray's remains a prescriptive vision, not an observed one: observant though it may be in various ways.

This said, I have to stress the frequent leaps and excitements, the sheer virtuosity of much of the writing—if not all. If I read Tranter's 100 sonnets without pause, carried along by the surface zest and gaiety, and sometimes the cheeky treachery, I discovered myself at Murray's sonnet No 140 with even more breathless admiration: pace, mood, narrative, tone: all are more spectacularly managed, and the narrative demands impose a greater tightrope daring. There are pacy set scenes, like the funeral itself, as well as snippets of folk anecdote, overheard farm chat, descriptive interludes and the final build up to the sacramental mysteries. And yet the voice is entirely that of Murray himself. We recognise it from earlier poems and it was underlined in full with **"The Bulahdelah Taree Holiday Song Cycle."** (p. 387)

If one were to try to think from the perspective of, say, the twenty-first century, I think there are certain things shared by both of these collections of sonnets other than the fourteen line pressure-pak. For me, the most conspicuous is the use of statement, of assertion: both poets are very keen to direct the reader, if you like. There is much use of this 'naming' tone, this telling-us. And where questions are used, they are loaded, rhetorical: the one context in which we feel Tranter knows the answers is when he asks a question; the use of questioning in Murray is generally to deflate some City defect: 'Your father's a speechwriter, eh?' Both sequences also, it should be noticed, make much use of sudden shifts of voice, tone, perspective— Tranter's compulsively so, within each poem, each line, leaping from image to image. Murray's narrative is frequently clipped, elliptic, talk snippets interspersed with comment, description, thoughts. In both, the sudden changes of gear are essentially devices to increase our sense of nervous energy.

The third shared quality, to me, is the use of vernacular speech inflection. At first we may not recognise similarities between Murray's country laconics, and Tranter's movie foyer chat: but the difference is only relative. Both contain and concentrate on capturing a preferred regional tone, and I am not at all sure that both do not share the peculiarly Australian tightness, the elbows-drawn-in thinness of our particular speech. Tranter's Sydney tone is certainly worlds removed from that of his mentor, Frank O'Hara. It is not really staccato at all, and it certainly does not expand with that enormous gusto that O'Hara makes peculiarly midtown Manhattan. Murray's country voices might have elbows possessively spread all over the table, but as soon as they move outside home compound they are drawn-in soon enough. It is merely the difference between choosing to stay inside or go out, and I think, from my fictitious twenty-first century backward glance, they will look much more like the sides of the one table than we tend to notice from here.

Perhaps I'm trying to reduce all diversity to some sort of controllable unity. But to my mind both Murray and Tranter identify key points in our search for a poetry that can balance the vernacular with the subjective mode. We have moved a long way from Stewart's *Sonnets for the Unknown Soldier* or even Dawe's *Enter Without so Much as Knocking*.

Tranter's danger is a sort of short-circuit glibness; his most recent book, *Dazed in the Ladies Lounge* has some brilliant things, but it does also sometimes become self-parody. It is too soon yet to know Murray's development. He has all the skill in the world. But he'd make a terrible Archbishop. (p. 388)

Thomas Shapcott, "John Tranter and Les Murray," in Australian Literary Studies, *Vol. 10, No. 3, May, 1982, pp. 381-88.**

JOHN LUCAS

At first glance Les A. Murray seems [in *The Vernacular Republic: Poems 1961-1981*] very like Australia's answer to Edward Hopper. The early poems in particular tell of a land where 'horses' hoofs puncture the chill / green ground, mud dogging their steps, / and summer's plough sleeps in the barn' (**"The Away-Bound Train"**), where the houses 'wear verandahs out of shyness, / all day in calendared kitchens / women listen for cars on the road' (**"Driving Through Sawmill Towns"**), and where a widower in the country muses, 'Getting near dark, I'll go home, light the lamp / and eat my corned-beef supper . . .'. It's easy to see why there should be this compulsion towards descriptive writing; as Murray says in **"Noonday Axeman"**, 'It will be centuries / before many men are truly at home in this country', and trying to describe it is one way of hoping to feel at home. But description takes you only so far.

Matters improve when Murray more readily allows people into his poems, when he lets them talk and behave, when he becomes less the self-conscious observer and more the recorder: when, in short, he lets the land come to him. And the poems get steadily better the longer they are allowed to be. He is not an elegant writer; he has no gift for epigrammatic terseness. This makes it difficult to quote from him in order to suggest his virtues, because although he isn't a narrative poet his best work has about it a relaxed, slow accretion of detail, reminiscence, a savouring of experience, and a ruminative style that can justly elide into the conversational. Indeed, one poem, **"The Police: Seven Voices"**, is a *tour de force* in which the cadences of different speech rhythms achieve what mere description can never hope to accomplish: the creation of a peopled place. **"Towards the Imminent Days"** is, however, more typical. Its unrhymed, loose five-stress quatrains unroll a celebratory poem of marriage, of settling, of coming to terms with the experience of Australia. And this is the mode in which Murray works best, as in the fine poem about his forebears, **"Their Cities, Their Universities"**, or **"Immigrant Voyage"**, about a boat that brought many post-war families to Australia, his wife's included.

Murray has gradually discovered a way of speaking that feels natural to his sense of Australia. (pp. 20-1)

John Lucas, "Hoping to Feel at Home," in New Statesman, *Vol. 103, No. 2668, May 7, 1982, pp. 20-1.**

PETER PORTER

Speaking purely personally, I can record that I sighed with relief when I first encountered Murray's poetry. It redeemed those tedious hours I had spent with Australian poetry in my youth. I did not expect to find such eloquence. . . . [Murray] writes against a background of contemporary Australian pluralism and awareness of international fashions and styles. In both Sydney and Melbourne the younger writers are as conscious of the European and American avant-garde as writers in Britain—possibly more so even. Murray is a rallier of opposition to international stylistics, and could well become the centre of a local school of poetics. I rather doubt that he will, however, since his is a highly idiosyncratic poetry, and for all its Australocentricity ranges widely through the larger world. Dandified Sydney experimenters, such as John Tranter and John Forbes, who are licentiates of the school of O'Hara and Ashbery, still recognize in Murray a verbal energy which they would never associate with the central tradition of Australian poetry. In the last analysis, language chooses, like water, its own level: Murray's power and relevance are independent of the style wars which obsess present-day Australian writing.

The pieces of Murray's which get into the anthologies are not necessarily his best—poems such as **"An Absolutely Ordinary Rainbow,"** **"Blood"** and **"The Ballad of Jimmy Governor."** Accordingly, I have selected five poems to recommend to someone starting Murray's work—with the emphatic proviso that he should read at least the whole of *The Vernacular Republic*. The poems are "The Broad Bean Sermon," "The Mitchells," "The Future," "Quintets for Robert Morley" and "Bent Water in the Tasmanian Highlands." . . . "The Broad Bean Sermon" is a straightforward poem, but one where exuberance becomes a metaphor in itself. Murray rejoices in his country's curious abundance by choosing the most ragged of symbols for it, a field of straggling broad beans. (pp. 48-50)

"The Mitchells" is Murray's brief (it is a sort of unrhymed sonnet) reminder that behind the courtesies and obliquities of country life lurk ancient loyalties and clan signals. Two men are putting up a telegraph pole. . . . They each would say, if asked, 'I'm one of the Mitchells' and they are both masters of that Australian reticence which turns a country lunch or smoke-oh into a form of Tea Ceremony. Their fates, as always among a family or a clan, have been very different. Murray tells us 'Of the pair, one has been rich / but never stopped wearing his oil-stained felt hat.' They are wired to the land, and Murray would insist that of all the things the Europeans brought to Australia the most valuable was the grid of relationships we call dynastic. (p. 50)

"The Future" shows Les Murray in quite a different light. It is a poem of generalised thought, and has nothing specifically to do with Australia. It is also a poem of ideas, and none of them is forced or fudged or fashionable. In his debates with the intellectuals on behalf of the embattled decencies of the tongue-tied, Murray displays a formidable forensic skill which he apparently disapproves of in his opponents. He is an erudite man, familiar with several European languages and knowledgeable on most points of history, science and philosophy. "The Future" is that rare creature, the poem of concept. It presents, in a manner which would be familiar to a Roman poet, trained in the cunning of rhetoric, evidence which might be offered in definition of the forecastable but unknowable time ahead of us, which we call the future. (p. 51)

Murray writes excellent humorous verse, though he avoids the thinness of the stand-up comedian which has come to dominate light verse in this age of poetry readings. A recent poem where an underlying seriousness supports surface wit is "Quintets for Robert Morley." Murray, who is well-fleshed, had been taken for Morley once at an airport, and offers the actor now a list of five-liners reflecting on the true character of fatness. It is characteristic of Murray that among the characteristics he assigns to the fat are tolerance and pity—'We were the first moderns / after all, being like the Common Man / disqualified from tragedy.' (pp. 51-2)

"Bent Water" is the essence of galvanism in poetry. Far beyond onomatopoeia, it celebrates the divinity of force in Nature in long lines about streams in the Tasmanian bush. It is, to adopt one of Murray's own titles, a 'Powerline Incarnation'. . . .

It sometimes seems to me that Murray's chief fault is an unwillingness to accept other people's definitions of Australianness. At his most impatient, he seems like a Test Act Inspector examining the bona fides of his fellow-artists and issuing them licences to write about their country or even to enjoy its citizenship. But this is the bad side of a good spirit, and we have much more to be grateful for than to criticise. Les Murray has brought pleasure and wisdom to contemporary Australian poetry. If the boring phrase heard so often in Australia—'the cultural cringe'—disappears, as I hope it will, then Murray

will have been one of those who sent it packing. It is good for Europeans and especially British people to know that Australia exports men of power other than Rupert Murdoch and Mr. Holmes a' Court. It gives the world true artists, one being Les Murray. (p. 52)

> *Peter Porter, "Les Murray: An Appreciation," in* Journal of Commonwealth Literature, *Vol. XVII, No. 1, 1982, pp. 45-52.*

CLIVE JAMES

Australia is still a foreign country for everyone including Australians, most of whom live in the cities and rarely penetrate into the hinterland, although in the last quarter-century or so there has been a determined attempt at cultural self-discovery. But most of the discovering has had to be done in the first instance by artists of various kinds, first mainly the painters and later mainly the writers. Australians, inhabiting a stretch of ancient geology on which modern civilization sits conspicuously even when it does not look awkward, rely on having their surroundings described for them, so that the strangeness can acquire familiarity and the vastness a set of names. The job was done badly before it was done well. In this century it began to be done very well, and by now there are subtleties forming which should interest anybody anywhere. Les A. Murray's fine book of poems [*The Vernacular Republic: Selected Poems*] is certainly one of them.

Murray, among the most original of the new generation of Australian poets who came to prominence in the 1960s, brings the landscape into sharp focus, detail by detail, without urgency but with a special fastidiousness, as if his spiritual life depended on it. . . . [His] language has abundant reserves of grace, equal to what it describes. Australia, he suggests, is waiting to be found by anyone with the nerve to stop looking for Europe or America.

His mudguards still wet from mountain cloud, the narrator of "Driving Through Sawmill Towns," drives slowly through a town in New South Wales and listens.

> The half-heard radio sings
> its song of sidewalks.

For the American reader, the word "sidewalk" will need interpretation, precisely because he understands it. The Australian word for "sidewalk" is "footpath." So by saying that the radio is singing about sidewalks, the narrator is saying that it is singing an American song. The British reader, for whom the usual word is most likely to be "pavement," might also get the idea that the Australians use the same word as the Americans. But Murray's writing elsewhere in the book is too vivid to allow the possibility that he has written a flat line here, so even the American or British reader who knows nothing at all about Australia will be able to guess that something is being implied, although he might not be able, through the barrier of a common language, to tell quite what.

What Murray implies is that Australia is not yet fully in possession of its own culture. He is also implying, throughout the book, that the Australian poets of his generation have a duty to do something about this, and should forgive themselves a certain inescapable measure of self-consciousness as they set about the task. It could be argued that this is a greater burden of implication than a single book of poems should be asked to bear. But in fact the question does not arise in that form, because the first thing that strikes you is how successful Murray is in speaking a version of English that should not only be understood wherever that language is spoken, but also immediately apprehensible as poetry. He has an enviable way of putting things:

> the snake rose like a Viking ship
> signed mud with a scattering
>   flourish and
> was into the wale of potato ground
>
> like a whip withdrawn. . . .

In Britain at the moment there is a school of poets, called the Martians, who are composing poems exclusively of such startling verbal effects, but rarely do they make it look that easy. Ted Hughes would make it look natural but not sound so detached. In Australia I never heard the word "wale" used, but then like most of Murray's fellow students at Sydney University in the late Fifties, I was an urban boy, and not even Murray realized until much later that the really interesting subject matter was back upcountry where he had come from. Perhaps they said "wale" around the potato patches of northern New South Wales but more probably Murray got it from the OED, where it turns out to mean "ridge" and dates from the Old English. But even were "wale" a specifically Australian word, there is nothing about this confluence of imagery that could not be instantly understood and appreciated in Durham, Dublin, or Dubuque. And any reader can appreciate how the movement of his eye between "ground" and "like" reproduces the way his eye would move if he were watching the whip be withdrawn.

But poets get even their calculations from instinct. They make happy discoveries. It is their mark to be *unfairly* interesting, as if they didn't deserve to get so much said in such a short space. When Keats read Shakespeare he made notes in the margins about the quality of the "bye-writing," by which he meant the wanton number of instances in which the poetry was good when it didn't need to be. It isn't possible to be Shakespeare again, and least of all in an ex-colonial country, but that original capacity to surprise himself is still the poet's insurance against sophistication.

> The severed trunk
> slips off its stump and drops along
> its shadow.

Not only do you wonder how he thought of that, you imagine him wondering too. Such flourishes are hearteningly numerous in Murray's poems. (p. 31)

It could be said that those Australians—the majority—who want to retain the connection with the British monarchy, or anyway don't want the fuss of getting rid of it, lack sufficient political acumen to see that Whitehall still has altogether too many powers of interference in Australian affairs. But to say that they are seeking shelter away from the wind of a bitter blue day is the merest rhetoric. It implies that only the republicans have courage and imaginative grasp. Yet in fact even the republicans are proud of the courage which Australians have shown in wars that the British helped to get them into: often the loudest critics of imperialism are the most dewy-eyed about the Dardenelles. Nor, more seriously, is it at all certain that there is anything unimaginative about a wish to keep the monarchist tradition.

Monarchism at least provides a substantial object for the mythologizing impulse, which the Australian republicans who became vocal during the Sixties showed immediate signs of re-

directing toward one another. Murray's verse is at its weakest when his friends, some of them rather less accomplished writers than his hagiographical treatment of them suggests, get talked about as if they were members of some revolutionary movement. Germaine Greer is referred to as just "Germaine"—a provincial piece of name-dropping which the beneficiary would be the first to mock by pointing out the existence of Germaine de Staël. But these are examples of Murray's poetry being invaded by the characteristically bad prose of Australian literary journalism, where it is rarely conceded, or even perceived, that the putative issue of a uniquely Australian culture is not one on which a writer, or any other kind of artist, can realistically take sides. . . .

And in the poetry of A. D. Hope there was an exhilaration, largely thanks to his range of metrical patterning and dramatic strategy, which left you wondering whether the younger generation of poets were not fooling themselves about having made a step forward. It looked more like a step back, or at any rate no more than a new phase of self-consciousness, mitigated by calling itself self-conscious but not fully aware of just how parochial it threatened to become.

The generation of Hope, Stewart, James McAuley, and Judith Wright did at least as good a job of seeding the ground as their successors have done of reaping the crop, and certainly they were more capable of critical argument. By comparison, literary criticism among the writers of Murray's generation can scarcely be said to exist. But art, for a while at least, can get along without criticism, which can always be done later, or somewhere else. Murray's poems might be formally uncertain but his language is alert, so there is always a case for saying that he has stumbled on something better than symmetry. These are the luminous fabrications of a gifted yarn spinner. As the Australians have it, you will be sucked in. Finally what counts is the magic sentence, and Murray's is a book full of them. (p. 32)

> *Clive James, "His Brilliant Career," in* The New York Review of Books, *Vol. XXX, No. 6, April 14, 1983, pp. 31-2.*

CARMEL GAFFNEY

Les Murray dedicates his book of poems, *The People's Otherworld,* to the Glory of God. The title draws attention to the otherworld as that of the "people" because it is an egalitarian world: the only requisite for membership is the ability to be absorbed by the universe's splendours. . . .

In **"Equanimity"** Murray claims that human order, despite its multifarious manifestations of culture, "has at heart an equanimity", which is the spiritual grace that sustains us all. It resembles "interest" since it awakens our sense of the creator's presence in His works. Its supporting presence is, however, more often ignored because of man's belief in his own omnipotence, "Pity the high madness / that misses it continually, ranging between assertion and unconsciousness." . . . Today's society finds it difficult to "focus" on interest, because its appreciation of the spiritual life has been deadened by the "otherworld of action and media":

> We are looking into the light—
> it makes some smile, some grimace.

Here the poet's sharp contrast between the artificial "otherworld" of contemporary living and the people's otherworld of spiritual values subtly suggests a metaphysical division between darkness and light. Murray's originality and his ability to present philosophical and theological concepts in concrete images not only revivifies traditional concepts of grace but also extends them. . . .

The numerous metaphors throughout the poem reveal Murray's intense interaction with his subject. "A continuous recovering moment", "a field all foreground, and equally all background", "lifelong plenishment", attempt to capture the poet's response to equanimity's omnipresence. "Peace beneath effort", "comes unpurchased", "scarcely willed" emphasize the gratuitousness of the grace and represent searches for analogies to communicate a religious experience. The simile, "Of infinite detailed extent / like God's attention", does not undermine the spiritual nature of "equanimity", but rather exposes the foundation of Murray's belief from which this encounter with grace began.

While these engagements with metaphysical realities enrich the people's otherworld, they cannot prevent the occurrence of suffering. In **"The Steel"**, for instance, the presentation of the people's otherworld is inextricably mixed with pain. The very intensity of the poet's emotion, the urgency of his love and his compassionate acceptance of his parents' past actions lead Murray to passionate statements of belief and acceptance. . . . (p. 55)

The spiritual life presented in celebratory tones in **"Equanimity"** and **"First Essay on Interest"**, and exposed with complex intensity in **"Steel"**, is given emphatic affirmation by the poet in **"Satis Passio"** and **"The New Moreton Bay"**. The latter poem, written on the conversion to Catholicism of the poet Kevin Hart, is a brilliantly constructed sonnet. Stanza one embodies the Australian experience of suffering both corporate and individual, into a dramatic narrative event. . . .

When grace and free will intersect with the history of the race and the individual, suffering is transcended and spiritual realities released. . . . Murray uses his historical images imaginatively. Convicts like old testament characters, prefigure the new; and Cyrennian type converts provide fresh shoulders for the cross and the "long-line" of Christians. Around words such as "other testament", "innocent wood", "lifts", and "timber" meanings cluster. Witty and learned puns on "testament" "leaves" and "libraries" extend the ideas of continual growth.

"Satis Passio" reveals the mind of the religious artist and that of everyman responsive to the general poetries of life. For Murray no disjunction between the two exists. Yet, for the purpose of his poetic fiction he explores the apparent dichotomy between experience and art. (p. 56)

The lyrical grace, celebratory cadences, witty earnestness and the poet's delight in his own creation rest on an intellectual framework. The arguments are stated with penetrating clarity. Art, the poet presents as "but a section of all that exist / a passage, a whole pattern". . . . "Beauty lives easily with equities / more terrible than theory dares mean" . . . vividly accounts for our response to the feral poetries.

The mingling of styles such as puns ("phallocrypt", "fellowcrypt"), colloquialisms ("toppings-up"), idioms ("we may call it") and aphorisms ("finite but inexhaustible") fuse to one style, reminiscent of the manner in which Spenser orchestrated his verse.

Poems such as: **"The Grassfire Stanzas"**, **"Bent Water in the Tasmanian Highlands"**, **"The Forest Hit by Modern Use"**, **"Little Boy Impelling a Scooter"**, **"Flowering Eucalypt in Autumn"**, **"The Fishermen at South Head"**, **"The Second Essay on Interest"**, demonstrate Murray's volatile creative imagination enjoying the beauty, detail and energy in creation. Some of these poems end with meditations that seem to reflect the shapes and movements in the landscape. When the poet meditates at the end of **"Bent Water in the Tasmanian Highlands"**, he draws an analogy between the energy and flourish in the water's movements in the Tasmanian Highlands and the possibility of a similar phenomenon in men. . . . (pp. 56-7)

The lines recall the poem's metaphorical rapidity and the flashiness of the images. For the reader, they offer a comment on Murray's gifts. His creative imagination does seem to work at that "speed" and it appears that it "is mother and history and swank" to him.

Murray seldom ends with only one exploration into metaphysics, and in **"Bent Water in the Tasmanian Highlands"** he questions the reasons for man's fascination with nature's splendours. . . .

The poet's speculations seldom modify his wonderment. If the lesson means falling and persistence then what a magnificent experience: for after the "swoops" come the "clear storeys, translucent honey-glazed clerestories".

Sometimes, the metaphorical amplitude of Murray's descriptions betrays his interest in human life even when he declares some distaste for his subject. For instance, the absorption of the fishermen at South Head in their own world, earns a rebuke from Murray because of their inability to respond to incongruous humour:

> Anything unshared,
> a harlequin mask, a painted wand flourished at the sun
> would anger them. It is serious to be with humans.

Ironically, something of this intensity enabled them to experience a union with nature that the poet clearly appreciated in:

> Where they stand, atop the centuries
> of strata, they don't look down much
> but feel through their tackle the talus-eddying
> and tidal detail of that huge simple pulse
> in the rock and in their bones.
>
> (p. 57)

The other world of "media and action" Murray exposes as a threat to the world in which people may be absorbed by the beauty of creation. The city often seems as if it were the objective correlative of our greed, unimaginativeness, and insensitivity to the land. Here, we most often find Murray's most trenchant remarks on modern society. In **"Fuel Stoppage on Gladesville road bridge in the year 1980"**, for instance, he claims that the marvellous brute force effects of our century appeal to us because they echo our internal chaos, "They answer something in us. Anything in us" . . . . (pp. 57-8)

Murray's prophetic stance against our society's silliness gains its strength from the poet's ability to probe the darker side of life with the same mental awareness that he explores grace. He realizes that the wonders within the people's otherworld can be destroyed by the "darkly human". By celebrating our heraldic bird, the emu, with a certain mock-earnestness, Murray reminds us of man's capacity for malicious capriciousness. He warns the emu of its vulnerability:

> Your shield of fashion's wobbly: you're quaint, you're Native,

even somewhat Bygone. You may be let live
but beware: the blank zones of Serious disdain
are often carte blanche to the darkly human. . . .

The emu possesses only "brigand sovereignty" because of
man's incapacity to understand "God's common immortality":

> whose image is daylight detail, aggregate, in process
>   yet
> plumb to the everywhere focus of one devoid of
>   boredom. . . .

Murray's openness and self-knowledge also assure us that his
condemnations are based on a knowledge of man's fallibility.
In **"Three Poems in Memory of my Mother, Miriam Murray
nee Arnall", "Exile Prolonged by Real Reasons",** and **"An
Immortal",** the poet exposes his grief, guilt and fear with
unselfconscious frankness. Because these self-revelations disclose a man who is in touch with his own emotions, statements
such as, "Dark is all one interior / permitting only inner life.
Concealing what will seize it", gain a further dimension. If
Murray knows the pitfalls of the inner life, then it seems to
me unlikely that his religious celebrations could at any time
be called meretricious.

In *The People's Otherworld* Murray polemicizes against the city
less dramatically than he has done previously. His argument
that poetry of all but the dramatic sort is ultimately a Boeotian
art, would seem to me difficult to sustain. Perhaps, by stressing
gifts such as equanimity that can be enjoyed in the city, the
poet has realized that for a sane society the city dweller too,
must be heir to the joys of contemplation. . . .

Wit, imagination, clear perception, creative use of language,
subtlety of tone and gentle intensity, are but some of the strengths
of Murray's talent. Of course, it is true that Murray's originality
does at times challenge the reader. I believe it is only right
that it should. If the reader wishes to enjoy original high pow-
ered wit, then he cannot shirk the responsibility of energetically
following the poet's intense interaction with his subject. (p. 58)

Carmel Gaffney, "Les Murray's Otherworld," in
Quadrant, *Vol. XXVIII, Nos. 202 & 203, July &
August, 1984, pp. 55-8.*

(William) Tim(othy) O'Brien

1946-

American novelist and journalist.

O'Brien is best known for *Going after Cacciato* (1978), which won the National Book Award and is considered one of the finest novels about the experiences of American soldiers in Vietnam. Like all of O'Brien's work, this novel centers on such themes as courage, violence, social pressures, and the threat of death and destruction.

After graduating from college, O'Brien was drafted into the army and served a tour of duty in Vietnam, where he received a Purple Heart and attained the rank of sergeant. His first book, *If I Die in a Combat Zone, Box Me Up and Ship Me Home* (1973), is categorized both as a novel and an autobiography. This work concerns the initiation of an inexperienced and bemused young man into the harsh realities of war. O'Brien relates incidents that occurred before and during the war, including an account of the social pressures and traditions that led him to fight in Vietnam despite his personal objections. *Northern Lights* (1975), his next work, centers on the conflicts between two brothers; one is physically powerful, and the other pursues intellectual and spiritual activities. Although this novel drew mixed reviews, most critics applauded O'Brien's depiction of the effects of a domineering father on the brothers and the closeness that develops while they attempt to survive natural threats during an outing in the wilderness.

Going after Cacciato is set in Vietnam and is narrated by Paul Berlin, a young soldier on guard duty. By blending Berlin's observations of the tedium and horrors of war with his fantastic daydreams which help him escape reality, and by repeatedly shifting from past to present, O'Brien created a novelistic form that reflects the often surrealistic atmosphere of war. In an extended meditation, Berlin recalls taking part in a patrol to capture an army deserter. He imagines the patrol pursuing the soldier on foot from Vietnam to Paris, where peace talks are being held. *Going after Cacciato* was widely praised, particularly for O'Brien's adroit blending of realism and fantasy that leaves the reader to ponder which events actually occurred.

O'Brien's recent novel, *The Nuclear Age* (1985), is the story of a man who is acutely sensitive to the threat of nuclear annihilation. The narrative flows back and forth from his childhood during the 1950s, when he built a fallout shelter beneath a ping-pong table, to 1995, when he digs a deep hole, presumably to bury himself and his family. O'Brien's depiction of the threat of nuclear devastation and his characterization of such social factions as 1960s radicals and the upwardly mobile contemporary middle class drew a mixed critical response.

(See also *CLC*, Vols. 7, 19; *Contemporary Authors*, Vols. 85-88; and *Dictionary of Literary Biography Yearbook: 1980*.)

© 1986 Thomas Victor

MICHIKO KAKUTANI

In *The Nuclear Age*, Mr. O'Brien is addressing similar issues of war, death and existential terror [as he did in *Going After Cacciato*]—but he has turned from the battlefront in Southeast Asia to the battlefront at home. His hero, William Cowling, is a veteran of 1960's radicalism . . . who has more recently made a fortune in uranium speculation, and who now counts among his "assets," "a blond wife and a blond daughter, and expensive Persian rugs, and a lovely redwood ranch house in the Sweetheart Mountains."

William, however, is not your average Yuppie; rather, he's a self-styled survivalist who, like Cacciato, spends most of his time in a dream world of his own making. By 1995, his fantasies about nuclear war—he dreams about radioactive pigeons, tilting continents, burning flesh—have reached such a pitch that he's building his own bomb shelter. When his wife and daughter threaten to leave him, he takes them captive, drugs them with Seconal and then drags them into this hole he's assiduously dug in the backyard. "The world is in danger," William explains. "Bad things can happen. We need options, a safety valve."

William is constantly asking himself whether he's crazy; and while the reader is quickly convinced that he's seriously unbalanced, Mr. O'Brien seems to want us to question what it means to be sane in an insane world. Maybe, he suggests, William is just "a normal guy in an abnormal world." This issue, of course, has already been addressed with considerable eloquence and humor by Joseph Heller in *Catch-22* and by Mr. O'Brien himself in *Cacciato;* and this time around, it has begun to feel a little shopworn.

That, in itself, would hardly be a problem, but in *The Nuclear Age,* the theme's presented as a didactic pastiche of R. D. Laing and Jonathan Schell, bereft of originality or persuasive passion. People do not normally spend every waking hour obsessing about abstractions like nuclear war or worldwide devastation, and Mr. O'Brien never makes William's hysteria real or convincing. He never captures his fear, his craziness or even his point of view; and since we cannot sympathize with William the way we did with the hero of *Cacciato,* he strikes us as little more than an aberration—a kook, and a pretty boring kook at that.

Although his childhood reminiscences about growing up in the bomb-scared 50's, as the anxious child of well-intentioned parents, possess a pleasing specificity, William's account of his later experiences as a high-school oddball, a campus radical and an underground man grow increasingly vague and full of clichés. . . .

As for William's friends and lovers, they are painted as paste-board caricatures of misfits playing at revolution, swimming and trying to get a suntan during an interlude at guerrilla camp in Castro's Cuba; buying mink coats and motels as soon as they realize that the 60's have ended. The women, especially, seem ridiculous in the extreme: William's first love, Sarah, is a voluptuous cheerleader turned radical, who actually utters lines like "I'm bad news. Too hot to handle"; and his wife-to-be Bobbi is a stewardess who's constantly harping about her need for "space."

Perhaps we're supposed to find these characters amusing, their leaden dialogue funny in a perverse sort of way; but if that's the case, Mr. O'Brien never manages to pull it off. The jokes about three-legged dogs, morticians, dead ponies and cancer belong to the category of sick adolescent humor; and the cracks about student radicals are often so lame that the reader doesn't know if Mr. O'Brien is satirizing the excesses of those revolutionaries or the dimness of their critics.

No doubt Mr. O'Brien intended in *The Nuclear Age* to address not merely the anxieties produced by the shadow of the bomb, but also the more general precariousness of modern life, the frailty of our family bonds, our susceptibility to loss and death and sorrow, our craving for safety and a home. In that, his ambition in undertaking such a venture is to be admired; unfortunately, there is little else in *The Nuclear Age* to celebrate.

> *Michiko Kakutani, "Prophet of Doom," in* The New York Times, *September 28, 1985, p. 12.*

JOHN ROMANO

What Tim O'Brien's fourth novel, *The Nuclear Age,* is about, and where it succeeds and where it fails, are easily told. It is about William, a man of our time, for whom the neurotic political climate of the sixties and seventies and eighties—in particular the awareness of the possibility of nuclear annihilation—has resulted in an almost total personal neurosis by the time of the novel, which is 1995. It is told from his point of view, which is both pensive and disoriented, and which is meant both to make us think and to disorient us. Its central image is the man of 1995 digging a fallout shelter, which he has thought about sporadically since his grade-school days, when air-raid drills and nuclear phobia quickened him with a

lasting fear. The book succeeds in places, mostly in anecdotes encountered in the first fifty pages. It fails as a whole. It is in truth less a book about living with the abominable than an abominable book, abominably written and underconceived in every important respect. But it is also provocative, though hardly in a way its author can have intended. It provokes the question, Why do liberal causes and humane fears so consistently make for impersonal novels?

Before tackling the question, two declarations of intent ought to be made. The first is that I think Tim O'Brien is a very good writer; he is the author of *Going After Cacciato,* which strikes me as the best novel about Vietnam and one of the best war novels that I know. The second is that I wouldn't have undertaken to comment on his current novel if I didn't think that his fears were the beginning of wisdom. I agree, moreover, with his premises: that, when we must live under such ominous skies, sanity itself is a pasteboard mask; that it is time we lent our imaginations to the task of personalizing the threat, the affront, the terror, of the nuclear age. But a bad book won't help us.

The Nuclear Age is founded on a mistake. The mistake is not political in nature, though it occasions the protagonist's long involvement in the underground left, the book's most errant (and lengthy) nonsense. It is aesthetic. There is nothing between the book's two layers, nothing between the outraged rhetoric of fear and protest and the rambling, recollected chapters of a life. It is as if the author feared that to locate a novel between these two layers—that is, in a richly imagined private life, affected by public realities but equally a reality in itself— would be to undermine the supposed universality of the upper rhetorical layer (it's a fear that haunts or should haunt us all) and also of the nether layer of fictive memoir (didn't you, too, crouch in hallways in second grade, to save yourself from the bomb sure to drop this very night?). And it is this universality, this shared communitarian reality, that the author evidently assumed is the proper arena for political fiction. It's a common liberal dread, this dread of making too personal an issue out of what ought to be the dominant concern of the race.

O'Brien's book would not be distressing if the need he no doubt sensed in sitting down to write did not remain unmet. We need a richly conceived *personalization* of the threat of nuclear destruction. (pp. 105-06)

[There] is a piety toward William's fears that virtually prohibits us—as it seems to have prohibited the author—from *thinking* much about the absurd world (our own) that he presents. The novel can only say that if you think William's crazy, *you're* crazy. This is not untrue. When William's father mocks him for trying to build a fallout shelter under the Ping-Pong table— "A Ping-Pong table versus the bomb?"—our heart is with William, and such a scene makes us resolve always to keep in view the terrified children we have created with our nuclear games. But as one reads *The Nuclear Age,* William, whose adventures and anxieties fill every page, never succeeds in coming to life. We know he's afraid, and we know we're being told his fear is justified; what we don't know is who William is. (p. 106)

> *John Romano, "Blue Over the Bomb," in* The Atlantic Monthly, *Vol. 256, No. 4, October, 1985, pp. 105-06.*

RICHARD LIPEZ

A large section of Tim O'Brien's anti-extinction of human life novel [*The Nuclear Age*] is set in the late '60s among anti-

Vietnam war radicals, one of whom complains to a reluctant compatriot, "We're tired of jump-starting your conscience." It's a vivid phrase, jump-starting a conscience, and no doubt states one of O'Brien's aims in writing this imperfect but very lively novel about a man in 1995 digging a hole he plans to crawl into.

As he showed in *Going After Cacciato*, his prize-winning 1978 novel about a soldier's life in Vietnam, O'Brien knows something about lethal surrealism overwhelming real life. In *The Nuclear Age* he has his work cut out for him again as he takes for his theme a man's unshakeable conviction that the human race is trying to murder itself. . . .

O'Brien has come up with a marvelous character in William Cowling, who as a boy in the '50s reacts to the Cold War by converting his family's basement ping-pong table into a bomb shelter, lining its top with "lead" pencils and charcoal briquettes. His normal, level-headed parents ridicule him cheerfully, and by the time he's in high school Cowling regards himself as a "slightly warped ding-a-ling" who still sees flashes in the night. The 1962 Cuban missile crisis confirms his worst fears about the future of the planet.

Cowling develops an interest in geology because, "Rocks lasted. Rocks could be trusted." When his parents take their neurotic loner of a son to a psychotherapist, William discovers that the shrink, Chuck Adamson, is just as frightened by the fragility of human life as he is. . . .

Adamson is a memorable creation, as are several other of O'Brien's misfits here, most notably Sarah Strouch, the pom-pom girl of the '50s who becomes a revolutionary in the '60s because the radical underground offers a life whose passionate intensity provides a kick as satisfying as the one she got from being a cheerleader. Sarah "wanted to be wanted and soon would be." Unlike a number of other recent chroniclers of the anti-war movement, O'Brien is good at showing the mixed and sometimes wacky motives of the most radical protestors without knocking their cause. One of the likable things about this novel is that it was written by an honest man.

It would be good then to report that *The Nuclear Age* is as coherent as it is fair-minded, that its ideas come together with devastating effect, that it is the *Catch-22* for the age of nuclear anxiety. Regrettably none of this is the case. O'Brien has miscalculated in making his central characters 1960s anti-war radicals, whose daily concerns and even broad aims during those years are so peripheral to his point in 1995 (or now) that the impact of his main message keeps getting lost. O'Brien wants to show the lunacy of the nuclear age, but for most of the action of the story his characters live back in the napalm era, a connected but still very different matter—a lesser matter, it could even be argued.

Flawed as it is, *The Nuclear Age* is still in many ways a wonderful novel. For one thing, it is repeatedly eloquent in stating the obvious central question of our time: "Why don't we stand on our heads and filibuster by scream? Nuclear war! Nuclear war! Why such dignity? . . . Why do we blush at our own future?" And (meanwhile) the book is also enormously entertaining.

Richard Lipez, "In the Shadow of the Bomb," in Book World—The Washington Post, *October 13, 1985*, p. 9.

EDITH MILTON

[*The Nuclear Age* is an] oddly bifurcated book. To begin with, it takes place on two levels of time. The "present" is 1995, and our hero/narrator, William, beset by nuclear angst since childhood, is digging a gigantic hole in his garden. The hole's function is metaphorical, of course, as well as literal: William, who is long past fall-out shelters, is excavating a private corner of the Universal Void, which has its own voice and personality and speaks to him like a negative Zarathustra. The time of the major part of the book, however, is between 1945 and 1985, a quite ordinary temporal setting for the quite ordinary story of how William's life has led to his futuristic backyard exercise: there is a childhood in Montana with good and loving all-American parents; college days; an all-American love affair; flight from the draft; a fortune made in uranium; and, finally, an all-American marriage.

But the novel's basic disunity is more than just a matter of putting a conventional narrative inside a surreal and future frame. As a child, William watches his father's annual performance and massacre as General Custer in the local Chamber of Commerce commemoration of the famous defeat. "Terror mixed with fascination:" William writes. "I craved bloodshed, yet I craved the miracle of a happy ending." That ambivalence informs the book, and it proves to be a difficult balance: sometimes the great hole seems to gape for *The Nuclear Age* itself as it teeters precariously between being a serious satire about the emotional bankruptcy of our time and being just another entertainment whizzing along the rapid surface system of modern mores developed by John Irving. It is hard to be particular, inventive, above all, readable, when your subject is cosmic horror, and when the central question, "Am I crazy?" which opens the book and is its fulcrum and chorus, is asked in a world where the meaning of "crazy" no longer computes. . . .

[O'Brien is], however, nothing if not honorable in confronting the absurd in contemporary America. And his picture of William's fifty years of life is less a *Bildungsroman* than a diagram of a changing culture, and the bench mark of the semi-centennial, since Hiroshima, of our historic march into insanity. . . .

William's life, in short, is an allegory of America's changing modes, of our shift in attitudes as the impending, possibly inevitable, holocaust approaches. From the security and order of his midcentury middle-class childhood William moves to anomie. The childish search for personal safety becomes a conviction that the only way to keep what he's got is to blow himself up with it. I was particularly taken by O'Brien's note of the changing fashion in women. William's daughter, for instance, his world's imperilled future, is a beautifully drawn piece of irreverent sanity. . . .

Balancing this history of our times, giving it perspective, is the sense that even change, after all, is made up of altering patterns of echo and repetition: that William never quite hears the voice on the other end of the phone; that he's always afraid; that his father, annually dying as General Custer, is in rehearsal for Vietnam and other disasters. And, finally, that though the end of the world indeed may be at hand, the frailty of all things is eternal and universal. "Doom!" says William's wisely gloomy analyst. "Nothing else, just doom doom doom! Frozen oceans! Frozen continents! *Doom*. . . ."

It can't be said that O'Brien's view of what that doom implies is profound. But then shallowness in the face of annihilation is precisely his subject matter: and as a cartoon of the human condition *in extremis, The Nuclear Age* is mournfully persuasive, graceful, funny, and sane.

Edith Milton, in a review of "The Nuclear Age," in Boston Review, *Vol. X, No. 5, November, 1985, p. 27.*

JAMES MARCUS

Going After Cacciato succeeded in making a nightmare at once nightmarish and quotidian. To achieve this quality of terror subjected to the rhythms of the mundane, O'Brien told two different stories. One detailed the life, times and steady decimation of the First Platoon of Alpha Company, 198th Infantry Brigade, stationed in Quang Ngai in late 1968.... Next to this narrative O'Brien placed a second, the long and fabulous story of the deserter Private Cacciato, who is pursued by members of the platoon from the jungle all the way to Paris....

O'Brien's new novel, *The Nuclear Age,* also punctuates the real world with fantasies, although the theater of operations has changed. Where the earlier novel took on the continual crisis of wartime, this one turns to the crisis of peacetime, no less of an occasion for battle fatigue. It's 1995, and the narrator, William Cowling, is digging a hole in his backyard. His spadework unearths a double cache. On the one hand, his personal history emerges.... On the other hand, we're made aware that the hole contains public as well as private materials: history, the *Zeitgeist,* our era's distinctive mysteries of "the uncaused cause, the unnamed source, the unindicted co-conspirator, the unknown soldier, the untold misery, the unmarked grave." In short, the stuff of the nuclear age, which, given William's birth in 1945, is also the stuff of his age. By digging into both at once, O'Brien raises a complicated and essential question: Where is the boundary between a personal, home-made neurosis and the epidemic madness of the age?

For madness is certainly the issue. The book begins with William's question "Am I crazy?" As he turns over his first spadeful of soil, he decides he's not.... (p. 450)

But as the framing narrative continues, and it becomes apparent that he intends to beat nuclear annihilation to the punch by burying his whole family in this hole, which he has adorned with Christmas lights, we decide that the question is far from closed. And we turn to his past for some kind of illumination.

We learn that at 13 he found himself in the grip of recurrent nightmares crowded with "sirens and melting ice caps and radioactive gleamings and ICBMs whining in the dark." He converted the Ping-Pong table in the basement into an impromptu fallout shelter, piling it high with blankets, charcoal briquettes and, in a final flash of inspiration, row upon row of yellow school pencils. (His disappointment when his father identifies the pencil cores as graphite, not lead, provides one of the novel's best scenes.) He even had a bout of psychosomatic headaches and constipation, which went into remission only after he confessed his terror to a sympathetic psychiatrist. Now, why should a "regular childhood in a regular town" be disfigured by all this? Is William crazy, or just realistic? He confronts this question at the beginning of his story, but he backs off.... (pp. 450, 452)

Unfortunately, William continues to back off from interpretation throughout the remainder of the novel. We follow him to college, where the nightmares start again and he mounts a one-man protest in the school cafeteria, holding up a "The Bombs Are Real" placard. Now, it's this commitment to the *real* that should give William's crusade (and story) its sting.... Presumably, his nightmares are the price he pays for his realism. But his curious disengagement from the world undercuts his status as a prophet without honor. Where the fantasy sequences in *Cacciato* had the rugged solidity of the straight narrative to complement them, William's apocalyptic nightmares lack any such anchor: his version of sanity produces a strangely homogenized narrative in which "anything goes, everything, there are no more particulars."

"It's an era of disengagement," William says at one point, ascribing to historical necessity his own inability to grab hold of anything—love, politics, knowledge. Perhaps O'Brien believes that a personality this passive and disconnected reveals some truth about the nuclear age; in any case, the result is a sadly reduced brand of fiction, a life perceived through a layer of cheesecloth. It's dispiriting to see a writer of O'Brien's talents offer up this analysis of William's lover: "An intelligent girl, she played the coquette; a dignified girl, she played vulgar. And yet she was also oddly vulnerable, even little-girlish at times." Neither fiction nor prophecy can afford to be that perfunctory.

This weakness becomes especially conspicuous when O'Brien touches on terrain familiar from his other work. When, for example, William relates his decision to dodge the draft and go underground, the event slips by with a vague gesture at history: "But it was not my decision. The dynamic decided for me." Compare O'Brien's treatment of the same dilemma in the autobiographical *If I Die in a Combat Zone.* It's not a matter of morally ranking dodgers or draftees but of facing decisions with a straightforward honesty and eloquence notably absent from *The Nuclear Age:*

> It was an intellectual and physical stand-off, and I did not have the energy to see it to an end. I did not want to be a soldier, not even an observer to war. But neither did I want to upset a peculiar balance between the order I knew, the people I knew, and my own private world.

And yet that last sentence offers a clue as to why Tim O'Brien might write *The Nuclear Age,* and why this unsuccessful novel still seems like an honorable attempt. Both of the earlier books operated within that "peculiar balance"—fiction or nonfiction, they counted up the price for maintaining order, taking the oath, going to war. Here, William takes the opposite path, and for all his defects as a fictional mouthpiece, there's a certain courage in trying to follow him underground. (pp. 452-53)

James Marcus, "A Hole Is to Dig," in The Nation, *Vol. 241, No. 14, November 2, 1985, pp. 450, 452-53.*

DICK LOCHTE

The mixture of bemusement and sarcasm in O'Brien's style and in Cowling's narration [in *The Nuclear Age*] is uncannily perfect in capturing the mood of young America in an era of possible Armageddon. Fearful, alienated, mentally confused and with a growing sense of helplessness, Cowling is a true child of the Nuclear Age, born with a mighty fear of The Bomb. He begins his story in 1995. The century is ending and so, apparently, is his world, in one way or another....

In flashbacks, we see Cowling progress from frightened pre-teen, using the family Ping-Pong table as a fallout shelter, to a fidgety, considerably less than charismatic campus ban-the-bomb spokesman, to a hopelessly ineffectual underground revolutionary, to a man in search of a "normal" family life. Ironically, he eventually discovers that his only hope for salvation lies in his providing ingredients for nuclear warheads. . . .

There is a meeting of many literary minds in O'Brien's novel. We get flashes of Joseph Heller's irony, Don DeLillo's dark humor, Aldous Huxley's witty pessimism. And we meet a fascinating updated version of F. Scott Fitzgerald's golden girl in Sarah Strouch, the '70s flapper, a terrorist with fantasies of becoming the ultimate cheerleader. O'Brien, himself, is obviously a literary man; his novel is to be read, not translated to another medium. He has power in his prose and a clear view of his purpose. And his characters, though bizarre, are fully developed and very, very human. Cowling keeps telling us: "The bombs are real." For the reader, the happier news is that he's real too.

> *Dick Lochte, in a review of "The Nuclear Age," in* Los Angeles Times Book Review, *November 3, 1985, p. 16.*

Louise Page

1955-

English dramatist.

Page writes realistic plays dealing with social issues and topics relating to women. Her first major play, *Tissue* (1978), focuses on a woman's harrowing struggle with breast cancer. In *Hearing* (1979), Page examines deafness as a social stigma, centering on a deaf girl's relationship with her overprotective mother and a young man who is losing his hearing. In some of her plays, Page comments on relationships between mothers and daughters and the emergence of women into roles traditionally ascribed to men. The heroine of *Housewives* (1981) campaigns to win a seat in Parliament only to lose to a more attractive female candidate. Loss and disappointment are again dominant themes in *Salonika* (1983), a surrealistic play set in the present at the site of a major World War I battle in which many English soldiers were killed. This play centers on a soldier's widow and spinster daughter who travel to Salonika and encounter the soldier's ghost.

Page's other plays include *Real Estate* (1984) and *Golden Girls* (1984). The former concerns a pregnant woman who returns to her mother's home after a twenty-year absence, assuming that her mother will help care for the baby and allow her to take part in her mother's real estate business. Page described *Golden Girls,* which traces the emotional struggles of a female track team, as "a play about desire and the ambition to be absolutely the best." Page also edited and contributed a series of interviews to *Falkland Sound/Voces de Malvinas* (1983), a drama exploring the reactions of English soldiers and their families to the 1982 British war with Argentina over the Falkland Islands.

the affliction as well? Miss Page is evidently not an opportunist. Whether she is a playwright remains to be seen. . . .

Eric Shorter, in a review of "Hearing," in Drama, No. 133, Summer, 1979, p. 66.

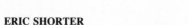

ERIC SHORTER

[Most of the scenes in *Hearing*] went on without justifying their length; though the sentimental theme of Miss Page's play—how shall the deaf be treated so as not to feel shut off?—made any reservations about Miss Page as dramatist sound callous. In fact her sympathy for the heroine . . . did not greatly obtrude in this account of a pretty redhead with no hearing whom a well-intentioned widow possessively adopts and in whom an equally well-intentioned but more emotionally detached priest takes a gingerly interest. Along comes a young man from a factory who is being driven slowly deaf by loud machinery. He is attracted to the redhead. They visit a disco and their mutual desperation finds expression in the factory basement—not sexually but by the girl going beserk.

At this point she seems at last able to hear something. She had also been deputed to type out the young man's application for public funds to compensate for deafness—but we learn nothing of either matter. And why not use the din of discos to dramatise

SALLY AIRE

Hearing is about Gail, deaf since birth, and much brighter than she needs to be for her job as a copy typist in a factory. A friendship develops between Gail and a young mechanic, Ian, who fears he may be beginning to suffer from industrial deafness. After an evening spent at a disco (Gail can dance perfectly well without hearing the music) both more drunk than is good for them, they get into the factory, . . . and in a mutual freak-out they wreck the machine which is responsible for Ian's partial loss of hearing. Meanwhile, devastated by her own sense of guilt at having borne Gail, over-protective, intolerant and patient by turns, Gail's mother struggles to hold herself and her relationship with Gail together. Her strength is drawn from the rather tattered vestiges of her Catholic faith and her only apparent contact with anyone other than Gail is with her priest, Father Graham. (p. 32)

It is in this mother/daughter relationship that the most interesting personal dynamic of the piece lies. Moya, whilst trying to push Gail out to take her place in the hearing world, is at the same time desperately over-protective of her. Gail's bright, naïve innocence and outgoing personality, together with her sharp perceptive intelligence, make her almost more than Moya can cope with. She is 24, no longer a child, and yet by virtue of her disability she is cut off from so much of the worldly knowledge that any hearing young woman of her age would possess, that Moya feels she is especially vulnerable. But if Gail is isolated from the world, Moya too is cut off from her daughter. She says to Graham, 'I want a *real* daughter—one that I can talk to,' and even adds that she would rather Gail had been born blind than deaf.' She is terrified that Gail might fall in love, marry and produce yet another deaf baby. . . . There is also Moya's sense of guilt at not realising that the headache and sore throat she had during the summer she was pregnant was, in fact, an attack of German measles. We can see why, at times, the anguish has to overflow. To Gail's question, the very nakedness of which strikes so sharply— 'Why was I born deaf?' Moya has to reply 'It was God's will that somebody had to be born deaf.' Gail's response is to cry, 'Why me? Why me?' To hearing people, Gail is 'different': 'You can see she's different.' 'She's a pretty girl and that makes it more of a shame.' Father Graham must have the last word on this one: '*She's* not different; her *experience* is different.'

Ian is in a more commonly experienced situation. As he becomes more aware of his failing hearing, so he becomes more aggressively insistent that nothing is wrong. His initial hostility to Gail is part of this. To his hearing friends he is deaf, but Gail considers him as hearing. Meanwhile all he can do is start the long, rather hopeless procedure of a claim for damages against the company. (pp. 32-3)

[Ian has the] aggressive bitterness of a young, personable man— one of the lads—who now feels that not only his livelihood but in some obscure way his very manhood is threatened by physical disablement. His experiences with Gail serve to mellow him, and in an encounter with his estranged wife at the end of the play we feel a new gentleness has entered his nature. . . . [The priest], we sense, has spent so much of himself for others that not a great deal of the man remains. At the end of the play he is left, forgotten by Gail and Moya, after having been up all night alternately searching for the missing Gail and comforting the distraught Moya. Life will never be easy for Father Graham.

[*Hearing* is a play] which extends a little further the frontiers of theatre and makes, with humour and understanding, a valuable contribution to our awareness of the kind of social problem which we are often only too happy to be able to ignore. (p. 33)

> *Sally Aire, in a review of "Hearing," in* Plays and Players, *Vol. 10, No. 310, July, 1979, pp. 32-3.*

PAUL ALLEN

[*Housewives* deals] with the struggle any woman faces if she wants to get elected for Parliament, a struggle given its final point by the heroine's loss of a candidacy she had adorned at the general election when, at a by-election, her own local party dumps her at the expense of a more glamorous national figure who is also a woman. (p. 37)

The play covers the ground effectively and contains one stunning speech in which the heroine's grandmother recalls graph-

ically the effects of a hunger strike in her suffragette days. I would have welcomed more attention . . . to the discreet humour of the script; and I would have liked some theatrical surprises. The still, weighty sequence of calmly presented conflicts has a certain dour predictability.

Even the careful acceptance of dislikeable characteristics in the heroine . . . suggests the same painstaking fairmindedness. But if I seem to belittle an absorbing evening, let me say that I think women will have said: "Yes, that's how it is," on hearing the play. (p. 38)

> *Paul Allen, in a review of "Housewives," in* Drama, *No. 140, 2nd Quarter, 1981, pp. 37-8.*

NED CHAILLET

Visiting Louise Page's *Salonika* is very like entering a dream. The topic of dreams is a recurring motive in the conversation of her characters, but dreams are woven into her fabric with much more profound effect than mere words would supply. And yet, while Miss Page has escaped the bonds of realism quite thoroughly, she has built characters of genuine interest as real as any people from the school of the kitchen sink. . . .

[In *Salonika*] two elderly English women appear on a Greek beach, amused to discover a naked young man, asleep. They are mother and daughter, and have never lived apart, although the daughter has been retired for four years and is herself a pensioner. She brought her mother to Salonika to find her father's grave among the dead of the First World War. With the play's dream logic, he is there to greet them, still young, still in uniform and full of the memory of dying.

The dramatist's vision is so sure of the reality of the stage that she makes no explanations or apologies for his presence. He comes and goes, conversing with the other characters and seemingly leaving their consciousness when he walks away. He rouses himself to jealousy over the appearance of his wife's geriatric beau, but the only real drama is the revelation of the nature of his death.

It would be right to describe all Miss Page's characters as full-blooded if she herself did not reveal that the naked young Adonis lived by selling his blood. . . . If his wasted life has parallels it is with the thousands of young men who died on that beach, mostly from malaria.

> *Ned Chaillet, in a review of "Salonika," in* The Times, *London, August 3, 1982, p. 7.*

ROBERT CUSHMAN

Dare I announce a new genre? Meet the retrospective beach-drama. Earlier this year there was Edward Bond's *Summer*, in which wounds from the Second World War were reopened on an island. Now, strikingly, there is Louise Page's *Salonika* . . . , in which the memories stretch to the war before that. They are embodied in a soldier who, before our astonished eyes, rises from beneath the sand. . . .

Page handles her apparition with great tact. He may not be a presence at all, merely an embodiment of the thoughts and emotions of four contemporary Britons visiting Salonika 65 years on. (Miss Page breaks this convention only once, when she ill-advisedly has one character remark to another on the strange people you meet in these parts.) If he is a ghost, the other characters treat him with remarkable calm. Calm, with turbulence beneath, is the play's great virtue.

The four survivors are the dead man's wife, now 84; their daughter, a spinster in her sixties; the wife's septuagenarian suitor; and a young beach-bum, who is stretched out sun-bathing when the audience arrives. He might be dead; and images of death recur throughout the evening. It is a subject much on the characters' minds. Even the young man survives by keeping the roll of honour at the local cemetery, supplementing his income by selling his blood.

Mother and daughter have to think of mortality, and it is the mother who is the sprightlier. Daughter, who has had no fun, fears the final injustice of going first.... [The daughter is a] fine picture of bottled-up innocence: a mind that at times snaps shut like a handbag, at others reaches out wanly for help.

The frustration issues in unconscious (and very good) jokes.... The reversal of roles between the two women is a constant source of dramatic energy.

[The] entrances of the deceased punctuate the play, an image of what the other characters discuss. The reminder of his fate, the bitter comparisons of then and now, overhang the bickerings, jealousies, frustrations and occasional kindnesses that are the play's substance. It is a dark but thoroughly undepressing piece, the best to arrive in London in months.

Robert Cushman, "Ghost of Salonika," in The Observer, *August 8, 1982, p. 27.**

SUSAN TODD

Louise Page's **Real Estate** has moments that reverberate with that subterranean charge which occurs when some of the audience's least questioned assumptions are being hauled out of the dark. A story in which a daughter, pregnant and in need of undefined help, returns to the home of the mother she left in jealousy of her stepfather 20 years before, becomes the occasion for asking whether the mother, Gwen, must by nature love her offspring, Jenny. And whether she can, or should, share with this prodigal her hard-won territory, a small real-estate business.

Jenny's maternal feelings become increasingly voracious, consuming all available emotional space, including that of the passionate involvement between her boyfriend Eric and his young daughter. Maternal longings in men, too, are explored, as Eric and Gwen's husband Dick take on the nurturing role which the women have abandoned....

The conventionality of the play's form is unsatisfying.... Because the impact of form has been insufficiently considered, it verges, as most forms of naturalism inevitably will, on soap opera. The effect in the end isn't of questioning but of providing comfort: not challenging but reassuring.

Susan Todd, "Territories," in New Statesman, *Vol. 107, No. 2774, May 18, 1984, p. 30.**

GILES GORDON

Real Estate is more about relationships between people (you know, flesh and blood human beings with messy, lonely lives)

than property, the buying and selling thereof, although Jenny ... sells her flat in London and her mother, Gwen ..., whom she hasn't seen for 20 years, has become an estate agent in the country.... Jenny is pregnant by Eric ..., an accountant, besotted father of Lotte, daughter of his broken marriage. Gwen is married not to Jenny's father but to cardiganed, cuddly, retired Dick ... who looks forward to the grandchild which could compensate for Gwen's miscarriage, caused when Jenny left home all those years ago.

If this sounds dull and mundane, try Chekhov's plots. Miss Page, by accurate, detailed, loving writing has created four real (as not in estate) people, sensitive to the needs of others yet each, ultimately, with an instinct for self-preservation. These are 'ordinary' people to whom nothing special happens. They become special, extraordinary because of the dignity their creator endows them with.

Giles Gordon, "Spot On," in The Spectator, *Vol. 252, No. 8132, May 19, 1984, p. 348.**

NASEEM KHAN

Set in the rarefied world of competitive sports, [**Golden Girls**] follows the development of a women's relay team from an inchoate collection of gifted individuals into a single winning unit.

Why has success eluded them so far? It's not for lack of wanting it. Each of the initially-four-girl team has sacrificed much—homes, security, emotional ties—to run. The missing ingredient is, in fact, cash. And it's the golden shower from their new sponsors, Ortolan, that starts to change their luck. It buys them time to train together, the full-time services of a woman doctor specialising in athletics and unlimited material goodies on their charge accounts. In return, of course, Ortolan, in the person of their hard-eyed lady executive, demands winners, and winners that will fit the image of their principal product, Golden Girls shampoo: no scandals, no unseemly behaviour, 'wholesome ... real girls'.

It would have been easy for Louise Page to have written a simple play about the evils of big business corrupting the purity of sport. Certainly the purchase of people comes in for some stick, but not so much through the runners, who retain minds of their own, as through the largely silent figure of the Golden Girl. A living breathing figurehead for Ortolan—a glossy, glowing blonde in butter-yellow sports gear—she has no other name. Her job is simply to pose vacuously, on the edges of the action. **Golden Girls,** however goes further than this valid though limited point.

Within the broad expanse of the play and its running tensions—who will be dropped to make a four-person team? Will they set a new record?—Louise Page deftly weaves together a great deal of material. A lot of it is personal, human, funny: her characters are vivid and credible. Through them other issues emerge—the lowly status of sport in general, particularly when faced with the massive state sponsorship of eastern bloc countries; the Cinderella status of women's sports and the pressures on the women, and racism.

But, above all, it is about the same kind of almost feral drive that she observed recently in **Real Estate.** It is not only the girls who possess it: in its purest form, the urge to experience, as one of them haltingly describes it at the end, just five minutes of perfection. Their backers have it too—the doctor intent on a university chair, the executive intent on a seat on a multi-national board. Rarely have we seen a play that deals so openly and so objectively with that forbidden subject, female ambition. And equally refreshingly, the play celebrates comradeship.

> Naseem Khan, "Go-Getting," in New Statesman, Vol. 107, No. 2780, June 29, 1984, p. 29.*

NASEEM KHAN

[*Real Estate*] deals with emotional territory. It is, like Whitehead's play [*The Man Who Fell in Love with His Wife*], a domestic piece, but more interesting eventually because it is fuller of submerged rocks than his essentially linear piece. The twenty-year gap is also important in [Page's] play—twenty years ago . . . Gwen's teenage daughter unexpectedly ran away from home. She returns in the first minutes of the play, intent on reconciliation. But old wounds carry scars. What seems to be a simple matter of making up with the prodigal proves impossible. . . . A quiet oblique play, it meandered and repeated itself more than necessary. (p. 34)

> Naseem Khan, "London Fringe: Black Missionaries," in Drama, No. 153, 3rd Quarter, 1984, pp. 33-6.*

GARETH LLOYD EVANS

[In *Golden Girls*], we share the tribulations and revel in the smooth lissom nubility of four female runners preparing for the Olympics. It is a very bad play by Louise Page. It's too long, it's verbally constricted (the dialogue has only two temperatures—tepid idiomatic and feverish 'poetic'), and secretes a mishmash of cocked-up moral and social attitudes—drugs, boyfriends, training methods, sponsorship: you name it, the authoress has expatiated upon it. But, on a completely histrionic level, it works, and this is almost entirely the achievement of the director. . . . The play is not golden but the [production] almost convinces you it is.

> Gareth Lloyd Evans, "Midlands: Neither Good nor Evil," in Drama, No. 154, 4th Quarter, 1984, p. 41.*

MEL GUSSOW

[*Real Estate*] dramatizes the unspoken—veiled looks and interrupted thoughts as the play subtly reveals the melancholic loneliness of a family of solitary individuals. . . .

Real Estate is both a departure and an extension for this versatile 29-year-old English playwright. Her work could be regarded as post-feminist, as a contemplation of what happens after women have been liberated from traditional roles.

In the case of *Real Estate,* the canvas is domestic. This is a family play that is flooded with feelings of resentment. For Miss Page's characters, the home is not a haven. The title of the play echoes with implications. *Real Estate* deals with possessiveness, with property and with people as property, with parental and filial obligation.

As the evening begins, the daughter . . . has returned home after an absence of 20 years. Although she has severed all connection—her mother wondered if she were dead—she assumes everything will be exactly as it was when she left. But her mother, giving up on her own blocked maternal instinct, has cleaned out the young woman's room and placed her possessions in a file cabinet. She has in effect filed the daughter as forgotten.

Though other playwrights might look for a growing bond between the women, the unsparing Miss Page focuses on what continues to wedge them apart. For a long stretch, we look for the causes of the daughter's departure, then we come to accept the fact that, years before she fled, the relationship was marked by rigidity and remorse. The women have nothing in common except for bloodline and a kind of bifurcated bitterness—no memories, no nostalgia. Reunited, they inevitably sandpaper old wounds.

The playwright refrains from giving them sympathy, which is troublesome at least in reference to the daughter. We never fully understood her prodigal behavior—in her childhood there were no hints of abuse, merely an emotional detachment. Nevertheless the play holds our attention, primarily because of the two male characters, and their relationship to the women.

It is the men who reveal the supposedly feminine traits of warmth and vulnerability at the same time that the women appear destined to reenact their old antagonism. The stepfather has taken early retirement and embraced the life of househusband while his wife has become a success in real estate. Playing the role of peacemaker, he tries to ameliorate but only finds a basis for harmony with the daughter's well-meaning lover.

Somewhat in the manner of David Storey's Yorkshire mining families, the characters are terse; they closely guard their secrets. Though they never ascend to the dramatic heights of their Storey kinsmen, they are vividly rooted in details of behavior. Long and episodic, the play is buttressed by its humanity. Even as we become irritated by the egocentricity of the women, we realize that they are behaving more as people than as dramatic inventions.

> Mel Gussow, " 'Real Estate' Has Premiere in Capital," in The New York Times, March 6, 1985, p. C20.

JOHN SIMON

A play about the problems of old people sounds nice; youth and middle age have long been overaccented. Why not an 84-year-old lower-class Englishwoman, Charlotte, who comes to Salonika with her 63-year-old spinster daughter, Enid, to visit the grave of her husband, Ben, fallen in the Great War? Why shouldn't these women, united in a love-hate symbiosis, stumble across the nude body of Peter, an English beach boy asleep in the sand? And why not have Leonard, Charlotte's 75-year-old pensioner swain, show up unexpectedly, having followed the woman he wants to marry to Greece? . . . Why shouldn't the virginal Enid try for a last and first fling, duly paid for, with Peter, for whom she conceives a flaring, autumnal passion? No reason at all, if Louise Page, the author of *Salonika,* were up to it.

And why shouldn't Ben's ghost appear and get actively involved with the other four? For many reasons. Because ghosts as dramatic devices are older and more frayed than a sheet that has been to the laundry one time too many; because this ghost is conveniently visible or invisible as suits the playwright's facile arbitrariness; because it fetches and performs menial tasks more befitting a dog; and, mostly, because it doesn't add one blessed or damned thing to the play. Which helps raise other doubts about Miss Page's dramaturgy, promising more than it delivers, seldom rising above the level of respectable journeyman work, and becoming more and more soporific as it fails to dig deeper. It is much easier to disinter a dead man (this one rises dramatically from the sand of Salonika) than to burrow to the heart of living matter, the core of human experience.

It is not that Miss Page lacks sympathy and an intermittent but amiable sense of humor. Some details are pertinently observed, certain quirks of staid people ring pertinaciously true. But something vital is missing: the ability to move us through characterization, insight, language. Page hovers on the verge often enough, but the epiphany doesn't happen. Something isn't analyzed, compelling, profound, poetic enough. Something remains too clean, too remote, like a handshake with gloves on. . . .

I grew as restless as an unlaid ghost as *Salonika* progressed to its long-delayed, unconvincing, unreverberant ending without entrancing or enlightening me. It was like a civilized company discussing the weather. What, in fact, was it all about? (p. 95)

> *John Simon, in a review of "Salonika," in New York Magazine, Vol. 18, No. 15, April 15, 1985, p. 95.*

EDITH OLIVER

[*Salonika*] takes place on a beach in Greece that is haunted—in this case, literally—by the British Army's great disaster that took place there during the First World War. The elusive, moonstruck play is set on what looks at first like a barren, sand-covered stage, with a few rocks scattered here and there; then one notices a nude young man lying face down, presumably sunbathing. . . . [An] Englishwoman of eighty-four, named Charlotte, . . . has come with her spinster daughter, Enid, aged early sixties, to put flowers on the grave of her husband, who died there before the daughter was born. Enid . . . follows, carrying beach chairs, and departs shortly afterward to fetch paraphernalia for making tea. Charlotte—a dear little soul, but with a difference—left alone, examines the bare young man with great admiration. . . . [When a ghost] in First World War British Army uniform appears, she accepts him and speaks to him without fuss, as do her daughter and the play's remaining character, Leonard . . . , an English pensioner of seventy-five. Leonard, who is in love with Charlotte, has hitchhiked from Athens to ask her to marry him. The naked young man . . . wakes up. He is broke and earns the little money he needs by selling his blood. As scene follows scene, the characters combine in twos and threes. The ghost (who is, of course, husband and father) describes in one long, harrowing speech the setting of his own death—the soldiers, racked by malaria, lying row upon row, all of it in the cause of peace. "Did we win?" he asks, and must be told that another war followed. . . . Somewhat later, Enid tells the ghost that she has never had a lover; he urges her to ask the young man to make love to her, then sits quietly and watches while she finds herself unable to do so. And, of course, there is Charlotte and her importunate suitor, and, perhaps, a wedding. Enid is furious; she is tempted by the prospect of freedom, but, having devoted her life to her mother, she mostly wants things to go on as they are. . . . At the heart of the play are the mother and daughter, their irritation with each other, their mutual dependence, and their devotion.

What it all adds up to I cannot tell you. Miss Page may have something to tell us about past, present, and future, but if she does I missed it, having little appetite for these abstractions. Nevertheless, the mood—a strange mixture of the mysterious and the matter-of-fact—is maintained throughout, and its spell holds long after the play is over.

> *Edith Oliver, in a review of "Salonika," in The New Yorker, Vol. LXI, No. 8, April 15, 1985, p. 96.*

IRVING WARDLE

[In *Golden Girls*] Louise Page clearly realizes she is onto a good thing in examining the impact of feminism on the sporting world, but she has tackled it more in the spirit of a blockbusting novelist than a playwright.

Her account of a girls' relay squad training for a world championship race suggests a collaboration between Angela Brazil and Brian Glanville. There is the thrilling story of team effort with all the squabbles and rivalries of the group. There is also the sense of a dogged researcher listing all the background angles and meticulously working them in. The team is being funded by a shampoo firm, so as to have a bit of fun at the expense of commercial sponsorship. . . . There is a journalist prowling around, glass in hand, nose aquiver for dirt. Drugs make an early appearance in the story and precipitate its climax. Then there is the racist angle, and the link between social deprivation and the will to win.

Miss Page is fully able to absorb these and other strands into the narrative without dislocating it, but it is hard to see what the play is driving at, apart from reaffirming the obvious handicaps of British women athletes in international events. Where *Golden Girls* does score is in presenting a group of women passionately involved in an activity that drives out conventionally assumed female preoccupations. Sex is a soft option for the losers.

And the bitterest moment in the piece comes when one of the girls . . . breaks down on realizing that the coach has only picked her for the team because he fancies her.

Otherwise, the separate members of the group—from the girl with a trainer-father in tow to the 17-year-old bombshell newcomer, and the blonde who cannot venture on to the track without her teddy bear . . .—emerge as deftly identifiable cameo roles.

The big exception, and the strongest reason for seeing the play, is the character of Dorcas, a Dagenham-born black with the killer instinct . . . who engages your awed admiration even in the act of tipping a bucket of water over fellow contestants and biting every hand that feeds her. Her grief when she loses is something to behold.

> *Irving Wardle, "All That Blisters," in The Times, London, April 30, 1985, p. 10.*

CLARISSA K. WITTENBERG

[*Real Estate*] whines and bitches, but definitely doesn't sparkle. Briefly it is about a woman who ran away 20 years before and now reappears at the door of her mother and stepfather's home.

The stepfather had played the heavy to her delinquent teenage girl, but now has mellowed into a sweetie who wants only to take care of her and her soon-to-be-born baby. This play has the worst characteristics of the modern play as in the definition attributed to Peter Sellers, ''four people sitting around on a couch talking.'' Forgive me, they don't sit but rather walk around briskly through a handsome tree-studded set, but the effect is the same. This is Pinter stuff watered down. There is a quote by Louise Page in the playbill that says, ''There's no point anymore in writing plays only women will see: you have to reach the people who don't think in that way, you have to take them by surprise, to put people through an experience that tells them, 'Look, this is what it's like.''' This and other not too subtle clues lead one to think that Page has a feminist agenda with this play and if so, then it's feminism at its end. The women are awful. Was the point that women can use men sexually just as men have used women? Boring. That's very old news. That women can conceive children in a self actualizing mood, that's a little better, but still quite obvious. Actually in this play the men, though wimpy, are nice and one would far rather spend time with them. I'm quite against the unmitigated use of the unpleasant human characteristics as a metaphor for truth. Some people simply aren't worth our time.

> *Clarissa K. Wittenberg, in a review of ''Real Estate,'' in* Washington Review, *Vol. X, No. 6, April-May, 1985, p. 21.*

BARNEY BARDSLEY

[Page's first major play was *Tissue,* a] sensitive and moving account of one woman's fight against breast cancer . . . [that] confronted a delicate, almost taboo subject, and Ms Page used her characteristically forthright approach to pierce the heart of the matter. She was blithely unaware of crossing any social boundaries at the time, explaining now that 'I simply wanted to write a play about the way women saw their bodies', but has since realised that *Tissue* was a controversial piece, even for 1978.

Since then there have been a range of plays, including *Salonika,* about the effects of the First World War upon a generation of women; . . . *Real Estate,* on the fraught reunion between a mother and her pregnant daughter; and *Golden Girls,* a sideways look at sport and ambition. (p. 13)

For Louise Page, . . . [artistic] 'vision' means taking on all the contradictions of human nature. Gone, she believes, is the time when agitprop theatre—useful and valuable though it was in the seventies—was appropriate. In this more complex and dangerous era people are less likely to be convinced by plays which pick out only one dimension, and must not be made aware of the subtleties of a character's thought processes, the different levels of their lives.

Louise Page often shocks an audience into the unexpected. In *Real Estate,* to me one of her most effective plays, we see a familiar theme—the struggle between a mother and her grownup daughter, to understand and accommodate each other. Daughter Jenny is in her thirties and pregnant. After years of absence she returns to her mother's house, planning to have the baby as a single parent, and to have mother share the burden.

But Gwen now has her own life. She is married to a man she loves, has a job she enjoys, and a house she cares for. The last thing she needs is a second parenthood. Daughter is wilfully insistent that she will stay, and so in the final scene it is *mother* who packs her bags and walks out.

This startling end blows a gale of truth through the oft-vaunted notion of over-possessive, interfering mothers, who want to dominate and direct their children's lives. It shows a sensitivity on the part of Louise Page—a thirty year old woman—towards the generation of women in their fifties, whom young people often arrogantly assume to be 'domestic' and 'tame'.

'It's something that I think happens to a lot of older women,' she says. 'We think they're not really feminist, and that they don't want all the things we (younger women) want, so they get a whole lot dumped on them—from care of the elderly to care of their grandchildren—without anybody actually asking them what they feel.'

Asking those sorts of awkward questions is a Louise Page trademark. About her new play, *Golden Girls,* she says: 'For a long time I'd wanted to write a play about all the things that sport isn't supposed to be about. In other words, all the things which aren't *Chariots of Fire.*' So she delves into the thorny problems of drugs, newspaper scandal-mongering, racism, medical misdemeanours, commercial money raking, and in-team fighting, in her exploration of a womens relay team. The 'golden girls' are about to win the Olympics—and beat all known records—until some dope testers come running around to the dressing room door and everything falls apart.

'If there's a through line from *Real Estate* to *Golden Girls,*' she says, 'I think its the theme of ambition. Ambition is rather a dirty word in this society, as far as women are concerned—but everyone has it in some form or another.' In this play, as in life, the women are made to suffer for a female will to win, which, even in the sports world, is somehow unacceptable, and often leads to disaster.

Louise Page herself, however, is someone whose ambition has led to great success. (p. 15)

> *Barney Bardsley, '''Beauty' among the 'Beasts': Louise Page in an interview with Barney Bardsley,'' in* Drama, *No. 157, 3rd Quarter, 1985, pp. 13-15.*

JEANETTE WINTERSON

Fairy tales are valuable pieces of our imaginative inheritance because they speak to all levels of the personality. Heart and head are not divided in the fairy world. Required to give up our preoccupations with the world as we think we know it, we enter a different realm suspended in time, where magic matters, and our own lives assume a new perspective.

The story of *Beauty and the Beast* is a simple one and Louise Page leaves it uncluttered. There is no attempt to modernize either the characters or the dialogue, and this saves the play from slipping into pantomime, which would inevitably reduce the important tensions between Beauty and her family and Beauty and her beast. It is these tensions that give the play its power and keep it true to the genre from which it springs. . . .

[A prince] becomes the beast after spurning the hand of a self-important elemental. . . . [He reminds] us in the best fairy-tale manner what looks like one thing is often another. This is also true of Beauty, whose father has to discover that his daughter has a mind of her own.... [Her resolute] innocence is not naivety; it is the opposite of self-consciousness. Heroes and heroines win through because they are not thinking about themselves.

The closing scene brings with it the humour and improbability of the conclusion of a Shakespearean comedy, where everyone suddenly ends up with the right person, on the right throne and peasants and fairies alike are joyful. Within this movement there is a note of discord, always understated to suggest that life, though transformed, still has an inherently unruly aspect. For Page this comes with Beauty's father, who cannot accept her choice to leave his home. Like Malvolio, he is a stranger to the power of love unless it be on his own terms. We cannot pity him (the play does not allow that) but this ending sends the audience home thoughtful as well as entertained: people don't live happily ever after unless they want to.

Jeanette Winterson, "Thoughtfully ever after," in The Times Literary Supplement, *No. 4319, January 10, 1986, p. 39.*

Konstantin (Georgievich) Paustovsky

1892-1968

(Also transliterated as Paustovskiĭ or Paustowski) Russian autobiographer, novelist, short story writer, dramatist, biographer, travel writer, and author of books for children.

A popular and respected writer in the Soviet Union during his lifetime, Paustovsky received worldwide attention in the mid-1960s following the translation of his six-volume autobiography, *Povest' o zhizni* (*The Story of a Life*). He was one of the few artists to survive the period of Russian history extending from the Bolshevik Revolution through the end of the Stalin purges and is considered to be an important link to classical Russian literature. Unlike most postrevolutionary Soviet writers, Paustovsky avoided propagandistic Communist rhetoric; according to Peter Henry, Paustovsky's writings are "as near to being apolitical as is possible in a society where writers are expected to make their political position explicit." In his lyrical descriptions of the Soviet landscape and in his focus on ordinary working people, Paustovsky combined romanticism and realism to create revealing portraits of Soviet life.

Paustovsky's early works, including *Morskiye nabroski* (1925), *Kolkhida* (1934), and *Kara-Bugaz* (1936; *The Black Gulf*), are adventure stories imbued with a romantic spirit. His characters in these tales are sea captains, poets, heroic rebels, and beautiful women who inhabit enchanted places and are contemptuous of the insignificant pursuits of common people. Peter Henry observed that Paustovsky's intention in these early stories "is to evoke an exotic atmosphere by the use of extravagant colour, melodious sounds, startling metaphors, and the sustained hyperbole of the narrative." In the late 1930s and early 1940s, Paustovsky began to redirect his romantic impulse away from exotica toward everyday Soviet life. To underscore this emphasis on the commonplace, Paustovsky's prose became less ornate and more concise, yet he never completely abandoned the lyrical tone of his earlier work.

Paustovsky is best known for his multi-volume autobiography, *The Story of a Life*, which spans nearly half a century of Soviet history. In these memoirs, Paustovsky presents an intimate account of his personal life set within the social and political milieu of early twentieth-century Russia. Each book is constructed as a sequence of semi-independent segments unified by Paustovsky's narrative presence and point of view. The work as a whole demonstrates his ability to write forceful, dramatic prose, an element which critics have found lacking in his fiction. In the first volume, *Dalekie gody* (1946; *The Story of a Life: Childhood and Schooldays*), Paustovsky reminisces about his peaceful childhood in the Ukraine and his schooldays in Kiev. The second volume, *Bespokoynaya yunost* (*Slow Approach of Thunder*), presents Paustovsky's adventures during World War I and ends with the coming of the February 1917 Revolution. *Nachalo nevedomogo veka* (1958; *In That Dawn*) is an account of his experiences during the October 1917 Revolution and the Civil War, which he witnessed in Kiev before fleeing to Odessa in 1920. The fourth volume, *Vremya bol'shikh ozhidaniy* (1960; *Years of Hope*), contains Paustovsky's memories of the time he spent in Odessa during the 1920s while the city was in a state of siege and its people were under extreme hardship. While in Odessa, Paustovsky earned his living as a

journalist and participated in the bohemian culture that thrived in spite of the difficult times. In *Brosok na yug* (1961; *Southern Adventure*), Paustovsky leaves Odessa for Moscow. His journey across the Soviet countryside allowed him a final view of the culture of old Russia, which he contrasts with postrevolutionary Soviet society. *Kniga skitanii* (1946; *The Restless Years*) documents his travels in the Soviet Union during the early years of his literary career. Dan Jacobson noted that in spite of an occasional slip into sentimentality and the forced feeling of some of Paustovsky's passages, *The Story of a Life* "remains absorbing, full of vivacity and tenderness; an engaging account . . . and a remarkable testimony to the continuity of the Russian literary genius."

An outspoken advocate of artistic freedom in the Soviet Union during the post-Stalin thaw of the 1950s and 1960s, Paustovsky repeatedly defended fellow writers against governmental censorship. Although he openly criticized his country's politics, his main concern was with the state of Soviet literature. Paustovsky's opinions on the role of fiction are included in his short story collection *Zolotaya roza* (1956; *The Golden Rose: Literature in the Making*). Peter Henry concluded that Paustovsky's high standing in Soviet literature is due to "his absolute integrity as a man and a writer, his sincere devotion to his country, . . . his respect and compassion for his fellow-beings, and his boundless fascination with the miracle of life in all its varied manifestations.''

(See also *Contemporary Authors,* Vols. 93-96, Vols. 25-28, rev. ed. [obituary].)

HARRISON E. SALISBURY

Paustovsky's kaleidoscopic *The Story of a Life,* actually more a Tolstoyan panorama of an age than a conventional autobiography, introduces this . . . writer to American readers. He has spent a lifetime in contemporary journalism, and has had a long career as a writer of poetic adventure novels, set against a multitude of backgrounds. As a youth in Czarist Russia he was one of Moscow's first motorized milkmen, a not-too-efficient streetcar conductor, a wanderer from Kiev to Moscow and back again, a reporter for sensational newspapers on both sides of the civil war.

With such a background, Paustovsky may not seem a likely figure to raise the flag of freedom over Moscow's literary barricades. Yet, in the twilight of a long career, that is precisely what this lean, gaunt-faced man . . . has been doing in the post-Stalin literary period of Russia, which first was called the ''thaw'' and now is taking on the appearance of a torrential spring.

Probably no Russian development in recent years has captured American attention as has this dramatic revival of the creative impulse in works wide ranging, freely inquiring, often impudent, sometimes naïve, idealistic—and frequently boldly antagonistic to party or state clichés. . . .

No man has contributed more than Paustovsky to the soil in which this impulse has flourished. He spoke up for young Vladimir Dudintsev when the author's novel, *Not By Bread Alone,* came under attack. Again, on the eve of the Third Congress of Russian Writers in 1959, it was Paustovsky who spoke for the obligation of the writer to follow his own style and his own principles and not a *diktat* handed down by the party *agitprop.*

Two years later he provided a symbolic bridge between the culture of pre-Bolshevik Russia and post-Stalinist Russia by sponsoring and editing *Pages From Tarusa,* an anthology of writers both young and old, living and dead, linked in one way or another with the beautiful old village of Tarusa, on the Oka River. Tarusa, because of its influence upon Russian painting, is sometimes known as the Russian Barbizon. In this book he sought quite consciously to express all that is beautiful and all that is true in both the Russias, pre-Leninist and post-Lenin.

Whence arises the courage of a man like Paustovsky? As we read *The Story of a Life,* the source becomes evident. In his brief sketch for the encyclopedia, Paustovsky wrote that as a child ''I wanted to see everything and experience everything that it was possible for a man to see and experience.''

In his lifetime he fell little short of that ambition. As a young gymnasium student he sat in the last row of the balcony of the Kiev Opera House in 1911 when a classmate shot to death Premier Stolypin, the tough, shrewd man who might have saved the Romanov dynasty. Five years later Red Guards came near to shooting Paustovsky along with other newsmen when they were trapped in the orchestra pit of the Bolshoi Theater in

Moscow with Socialist Revolutionaries who assassinated Count Mirbach, the German Ambassador, and almost overturned Lenin.

Paustovsky spent six days in a Moscow no-man's land between the firing lines of Cadet Junkers and Red Guards at the Nikitsky Gate in November, 1917. He escaped death in World War I a dozen times by a hair's breadth in the course of Red Cross and hospital duty on the crumbling Russian front. He was mobilized, shot at, ordered executed, sent into combat service by one Ukrainian chieftain after another in Kiev's civil war days.

The danger and adventure did not end with these events, but *The Story of a Life,* the first three volumes of a story which could easily require six or eight in the full telling, carries Paustovsky's tale down only to 1920—to the moment when the White forces of General Denikin evacuated Odessa by sea and Paustovsky decided to remain behind and cast his lot with the young Soviet regime. (p. 1)

Paustovsky presents to us the sinuous, sturdy figure of a writer of talent, good will and rippling imagination. He is a writer who bore the banner of principle through the worst Stalin years into the comparative placidity of Khrushchevian times, never striking his colors, never relinquishing faith that in the end good would triumph over evil and that man's humanity would prove greater than his inhumanity.

We see Paustovsky writing and continuing to write regardless of events around him; believing and continuing to believe that there is nothing more important for a writer than to write from his heart and his soul. He wrote what he saw and felt and imagined and experienced, regardless of whether his personal world was collapsing (as it did), regardless of the disintegration of his family, the tragic and senseless death of the young woman he loved, the unending agony of his country.

To those who know the tradition of Russian letters, the spectacle of Paustovsky and a handful of others like him holding true to Pushkin's call ''to follow the road freely'' is not entirely surprising. For nearly 100 years the ideal of liberal democracy, creative freedom and social justice was kept alive in Czarist Russia by a band of men and women known as *intelligents.*

The *intelligents* were not exactly intelligentsia as we define the word. They were a group of enlightened people dedicated to a cause—the cause of uplifting life in dark, suffering Russia. . . .

With the triumph of the Revolution which he had so long awaited, the Russian *intelligent* fell upon evil days. He was shackled by Lenin, and he vanished physically under Stalin. . . . By the time Stalin died in 1953 the *intelligent* had disappeared—or so it first seemed.

Today, more than 11 years after Stalin's death, evidence abounds that the Russian *intelligent* has survived even the harshest repressions that the Soviet regime could invent. In men like Paustovsky the pure line of the *intelligent* is carried on, providing inspiration to the creative forces now touching the Russian scene with life and color.

Perhaps it is in such works as Paustovsky's *Life* . . . that the *intelligent* is performing his most useful function. For by this means Paustovsky serves as a bridge or connection between the Russian past and the Russian future, reminding a younger generation that Russia is part of Western European culture, a major part and not some alien segment struck off by the accidental success of the Lenin coup d'état of 1917.

And, just as surely as Paustovsky reminds his countrymen of their Western heritage, so he brings home to us the fact that Russia and ourselves, despite the artificial barriers of recent decades, share aims, aspirations, experiences and ideals. These may, indeed, one day tumble the barriers into that famous "rubbish heap of history" so dear to the pens of the Marxist scribblers. (p. 44)

> Harrison E. Salisbury, "Through the Tumult and the Thaw," in The New York Times Book Review, May 3, 1964, pp. 1, 44.

JOSE YGLESIAS

Paustovsky is an old-fashioned writer by current American standards; he means to communicate and to do good, whether he is describing a landscape or discussing the revolution. But he will not have literature vulgarized: he will not have it meet any but the requirements of truth. "Our second harmful tradition," he said to his colleagues in 1959, "is the reluctance to write about suffering, the fear of even hinting at sadness; as if all of our life had to be spent beneath sugar-candy skies to the sound of the hearty and determined cheerful laughter of 'militant' men and women."

Paustovsky has, then, been an "old-fashioned" writer by Soviet standards, too. In his homeland he is the bridge between Chekhov and Gorki's generation and the post-revolution. He managed to survive the Stalin years and to speak of tolerance to those militant men and women who, when not cheerful, could glower most fearfully. . . .

Reading Paustovsky, you often feel that he is one of those idealistic, lovable characters in Chekhov who, unaccountably, have lived through the revolution and its aftermath; it's as if one of the three sisters had gotten to Moscow and could now look back on the journey. "Ah, Grandfather Maxim Grigorievich!" Paustovsky exclaims early in *The Story of a Life*. "It's to him I owe my susceptibility to impressions, and my romanticism. They transformed my childhood into a series of collisions with reality. I suffered from this, but I still knew that my grandfather was right, and that a life made up of sobriety and good sense might be fine, but it would be burdensome to me, and fruitless. 'To each man,' as Grandfather used to say, 'his own recipe.'"

Paustovsky also talks about the merits of individuality in *The Golden Rose*. . . . He prefaces this collection of short pieces about literature with an anecdote about a Paris dustman who kept the sweepings from jewelers until he had enough gold dust to make a golden rose. There's an echo of the nineteenth century in his moral: "Over the years we writers subconsciously collect millions of these little grains and keep them stored away until they form a mold out of which we shape our particular golden rose—a story, a novel or a poem. And from these precious little particles a stream of literature is born." In statements like these there isn't even an echo of the harsh programmatic approach to literature of the Zhdanovite years. Paustovsky must indeed have seemed "old-fashioned" in Russia. And welcome.

For us he seems old-fashioned for other reasons and also, I hope, welcome. If he insists on the personal, he is also warmhearted, social-minded, in love with his country, all qualities one doesn't associate with our serious modern writers. (p. 488)

The Story of a Life seems to be the perfect book with which to make his acquaintance: in it he speaks directly and at length,

an old man for whom youthful experiences have not lost their wonder, able now to speak truthfully and without vanity about hurtful, wonderful and confusing days. . . .

Paustovsky was thirteen in 1905, and this volume—the first of a multi-volume autobiography—takes him through the First World War, the February and October revolutions, and the civil war. His life emerges in a series of sketches and stories—occasionally a section will have the pace and development of a novella—as sensitive and glowing as Chekhov or Turgenev; and it takes awhile to fathom why the book has the effect of fiction. (Not fiction as fabrication, but as life's essence.) Paustovsky is selective, as good novelists are, in writing about any incident in his life; yet he enriches each with exact detail of conversations, people, places and also color and movement and weather. There is little or no sense of repetitiveness or discursiveness, something of an achievement in memoirs. (p. 489)

What you learn about Russia also always comes as part of the story of a son of a Russian middle-class family. Paustovsky's first fourteen years were happy ones; they lived in Kiev and visited grandparents in the country. His life was a round of good people and beautiful places that left him with much sensitivity to others and a great love of nature. At fourteen his parents separate and this happy life ends; from then on Paustovsky supports himself and works at many jobs. His father dies when he's seventeen (a moving scene with which the book opens) and his brothers are killed in the war. His mother and his only sister, who is slowly going blind, show up on his doorstep in Kiev during the civil war dressed as beggars; they had been working a tiny farm and had used this disguise to get through the lines and rejoin him. He looks at the two impoverished, dirty women and realizes that it had not been at all difficult for them to assume the disguise; the country's ups and downs seem duplicated in his family's life.

Before this despairing moment comes, Paustovsky has worked in a steel mill, been a trolley car conductor in Moscow during the first year of the war, a medical orderly at the front, a fisherman's apprentice on the Black Sea. As a newspaper man, he lives in Moscow during 1917, and his account of that year, though always personal, gives a superb historical view of disparate peoples and unexpected actions: the revolutionary parliament at the Hotel Metropole, the meetings in the city squares, the Red Guards fighting during the October uprising, the anarchists living in the great town houses of the old merchants.

Paustovsky was not unsympathetic to the Bolshevik Revolution, but he was not a partisan either. He makes it clear that he was only an interested observer, and he lets the story of his own life explain his own noninvolvement. (pp. 489-90)

I am certain that Paustovsky feels that it was this love of his country that saved him, for he was to become and remain—despite the Stalin years—a dedicated Soviet citizen; and if this beautiful book is evidence, he did find his métier and did contribute, as he'd always hoped, to his people. At the point where Yuri Zhivago, in Pasternak's novel of this era, gives up the revolution for the personal life, Paustovsky starts on the road in the opposite direction. . . .

Vladimir Nabokov, it is said, refused for years at an American university to recommend purchase of any new Russian books for the Soviet literature collection; he'd return the catalogues sent him with the statement. "There is no Soviet Literature." I can imagine how sorry Paustovsky must feel for *him*: giving up his beloved Russian language to write clever, unloving books like *Pale Fire*! . . . But what standards are *we* to use in comparing Paustovsky's life work with, say, Nabokov's? Who in our country makes it an element of judgment that a man write in the hope that perhaps his "story might be needed by other people, and not just by myself, and it might help them to struggle through stormy times to a far-off, blinding strip of clear sky"? (p. 490)

Jose Yglesias, "Spirit of Valerian," in The Nation,
Vol. 198, No. 20, May 11, 1964, pp. 488-90.

DAN JACOBSON

[It] is difficult to write about *Story of a Life* without finding oneself trying in some way or another to define the essential "Russianness" of the book. Paradoxically, it is just this quality which makes everything in it seem intimately familiar to us— not merely because we are already acquainted with the tradition in which Paustovsky is writing, but because the Russian tradition is so much one of a totally unabashed, unassertive intimacy and familiarity with the life it is concerned to describe. There is, after all, nothing specifically "Russian" about the juxtaposition in life of deep emotion, intense moral earnestness, an awareness of the endless processes of nature, and triviality, superstition, eccentricity and clownishness. But where writers in the West are inclined to wring all kinds of ironies and indignations out of such juxtapositions and simultaneities, the great Russian writers seem somehow never to be *affronted* by them; their art appears indistinguishable from the primary impulse to record, with a profound, tireless veracity, everything they see. Yet it is beyond doubt that the result is art of the highest order. In its own way, the whole of the first chapter of *Story of a Life* is a proof of the exactness of Matthew Arnold's remark about the Russians in general and Tolstoy in particular: "Great sensitiveness, subtlety, and finesse, addressing themselves with entire disinterestedness and simplicity to the representation of human life."

But, though it has many of the strengths of the great Russian masters, *Story of a Life* is not itself a masterpiece of the kind its first chapters led me to hope it might be. About half-way through the book there is a falling-off in its quality, a failure of the disinterestedness which we have by then learned to expect from the author. It comes at a point, in his account of his early adolescence, when his family unexpectedly breaks up; his father, a railway official, gives up his job and goes to live with another woman, and young Konstantin is sent away to live with an uncle and aunt; later, while still at school, he has to earn his living by giving lessons. This experience, and indeed all his dealings with the members of his immediate family (but for the description of his father's funeral), remain strangely indistinct, as though the author could not bring himself to look upon them with the same directness of gaze with which he was able to regard everyone else. Humanly speaking, this is understandable enough, especially as the little we are given of the history of the family, subsequent to the break-up, is almost unmitigatedly painful: there is only the mother's bitterness, the father's loneliness, guilt, and relatively early death, a sister's increasing blindness, poverty for them all. But, the rest of the memoir being as personal as it is, we cannot help feeling that too much is being held back from us; and, what is more damaging to the book, that the author himself is unaware of how much he is withholding, and of how much his evasiveness here makes other passages appear at times a little forced and sentimental.

Still, this criticism having been made—and one makes it by the standards the book itself has set—*Story of a Life* remains absorbing, full of vivacity and tenderness; an engaging account of an individual boyhood and a remarkable testimony to the continuity of the Russian literary genius. It is hard to believe, reading it, that there was so recently in Russian history a time when, as Pasternak once bitterly said, "there was no more poetry . . . when, to put it plainly, writing was at an end." But the continuity is perhaps a little less surprising in the light of the evidence the book offers of the esteem and veneration in which the great writers of Paustovsky's youth were held by an extraordinarily wide range of the population. There is a description of the scene in Kiev at the time of the death of Tolstoy, when restless, bewildered, mourning crowds, watched over by police and Cossacks, gathered together in the streets, and Paustovsky's entire class forced a much-hated and rigidly Orthodox divinity master to stand up in honour of the apostate writer. (The master never returned to the school.) There is also a touching account of the effect of the news of the death of Chekhov on the family circle; a cousin was sent off to Moscow to attend the funeral, carrying with him a basket of wild flowers picked on the estate where the family was holidaying at the time. (pp. 81-2)

During the 1905 revolution [Paustovsky] enjoys a holiday from school and marches about the streets of Kiev hand-in-hand with a girl he has never seen before, who tells him, "We are free as air now, do you realise that?" "Yes," he answers, unhesitatingly. Then the troops open fire on the crowds, the Cossacks gallop through them. . . . He falls in love and out of it; he reads as much as he can, in Russian and other literatures; always he responds, with the sharpest and most sensitive observation, to the changing scenes and seasons around him, whether in Kiev itself or in the various estates and seaside places where he goes for his holidays.

Ultimately, the best thing one can say about this book is that it manages convincingly to justify the simplicity and breadth of its title. (p. 82)

Dan Jacobson, "Representation of Life," in Encounter, *Vol. XXIV, No. 1, January, 1965, pp. 80-2.*

EMANUEL LITVINOFF

Russian autobiographies have a phenomenal range in contrast to the slender volumes in which Western writers tend to distil the experiences of a lifetime. In Konstantin Paustovsky's series *Story of a Life*—of which *Slow Approach of Thunder* is the second volume to appear in English—a magnificent work is unfolding, crowded with incident and character, compassionate, fresh, and alive as a sea full of mackerel.

Part of the explanation for Paustovsky's amplitude is that Russians are accustomed to relate themselves to society at large and to their history, where the prevailing preoccupations in the West are mostly with eccentricity, loneliness, the unique, and other fragmentations of experience. But where Ilya Ehrenburg, a writer of quite another order but of the same generation, reflects the vices of the Russian method in his weakness for rhetoricism, Paustovsky's vision is unfailingly true and his voice never that of the political ventriloquist.

Slow Approach of Thunder is about the First World War, which began when he was 21. At first he was a tram driver in Moscow, assigned to routes running through the poor districts of the city, "the Copper Line," so that at the end of the day the sour smell of copper coins clung to his hands. . . . After this despondent apprenticeship he was transferred to the hospital service, picking up mutilated soldiers at the station and bringing them in white-painted trams to Moscow hospitals, then became a medical orderly on a Red Cross train shunting wounded men from the Galician front to the rear. This experience is brilliantly described—inspired dispatches from inferno where the unspeakable sufferings of men contrast with timeless evocations of forests, rivers, mountains, all that is of the earth and indestructible.

There is a tender, deeply felt account of his first love for a young nurse who died of typhus in a plague-ridden Polish village, and of a convalescent episode when Paustovsky worked as a fisherman along the shores of the Sea of Azov. The book ends with the February, 1917, Revolution when Russia, not for the only time in its history, surged with an exhilarating optimism that the promise of life was about to be fulfilled at last. In subsequent volumes Paustovsky will no doubt show how February turned into October, October into Stalin's age of darkness. They will certainly tell us much about the ordeal of an honest and gifted man throughout that period.

> *Emanuel Litvinoff, "Paustovsky's War," in* Manchester Guardian Weekly, *November 11, 1965, p. 11.*

GILBERT PHELPS

Paustovsky's vigour and realism, in [*Slow Approach of Thunder,* the] second volume of his long autobiography, falters only when he is uttering patriotic platitudes or indulging in set-pieces (like the leave-taking of his sweetheart's grave), or when he is over-conscious of his literary heritage. To suggest that the faults are due to 'the spiritual east wind' of the Soviet system seems to me quite wrong. It is simply that, as with many autobiographers, it was childhood which brought out Paustovsky's most sustained writing. It needs a Tolstoy to keep up the pressure into youth and manhood. Paustovsky is no Tolstoy—but these volumes make one of the most rewarding of contemporary autobiographies.

> *Gilbert Phelps, "Russia's Backwoods," in* New Statesman, *Vol. 71, No. 1817, January 17, 1966, p. 22.*

THOMAS L. AMAN

For over twenty years Paustovsky has been writing and publishing his monumental autobiography entitled *Story of a Life. Slow Approach of Thunder* is a translation of the second part of this work. . . . It relates the events of Paustovsky's life during World War I up to the outbreak of the February revolution.

This second part continues Paustovsky's system of relating an entire segment of his life by means of semi-independent episodes. Each fragment, or chapter, could almost be considered a story in itself, a whole; yet all are united and integrated by the presence of Paustovsky. But although the work is an intensely personal document, the author has somehow effaced himself in trying not to focus attention on himself. There is no hero to the story; Paustovsky has attempted to depict those people and events which most shaped his own life and which could be of most interest to his readers. . . .

There are two major observations which immediately spring to mind when considering this work against the more general framework of Soviet literature. The first is the complete lack of all harshness and brutality when discussing the war and its intrusion into the life of the country. A certain mellowness is prevalent and a sadness at all that was happening. The emphasis is laid on the quiet suffering and heroism of the people, the people "that smell of bread."

Even more significant is the inclusion of personal feelings in the midst of great events. Despite the fact that his country is at war, Paustovsky not only finds time to fall in love, but abandons himself completely to this feeling. The description of his beloved's death is the most touching in the book. Another moving episode is Paustovsky's attendance at a peasant child's birth with the advancing German armies but a few minutes away. The human element is never absent from Paustovsky's writings and it is this that has made him one of the most popular writers of Soviet literature.

Although war is a grim creature, Paustovsky has managed to breathe into his work an air of gentle humor. Particularly delightful is the story of the little old man who rode all over Moscow free because no one could change his hundred ruble note.

In this as in other of Paustovsky's works there is a certain magic of expression which cannot help but catch the reader's fancy. His description of Sukharev Square is masterful in the images it conveys: "Gramophones grunted angrily . . ." "the whistles of policemen shrilled . . ." "pigeons climbed the muddy sky . . ." and all around was "the smell of hunger and greed." The advice of Paustovsky's acquaintance from Kashin did not fall on deaf ears: "a writer has to set the words side by side so that every one of them strikes the right note in the reader's heart." (p. 237)

> *Thomas L. Aman, "Russophilia," in* The Canadian Forum, *Vol. XLVI, No. 552, January, 1967, pp. 237-38.*

GILBERT PHELPS

[*In That Dawn*] is the third volume of Paustovsky's *Story of a Life.* It opens in the spring of 1917, not long after the bloodless revolution that had overthrown the Tsar and put Kerensky and his 'Provisional Government' in control—a time when Russia was like some vast meeting and everywhere 'the noise of pledges, accusations, appeals rumbled like the thunder of carts on cobbles'—and it ends, after three years of revolution and civil war, in the spring of 1920, as the Tsarist General Denikin evacuates Odessa, and the first Red Army patrol enters the city and gazes round awestruck at the devastation of panic and flight.

Well, Paustovsky was young all right (still in his twenties), and in retrospect . . . he hails the Revolution as a new dawn: but it's only a Romantic without first hand experience who's likely to find anything blissful about it—and it's the suffering, the hunger, the casual slaughters, the continuous anxiety and uncertainty, and a despairing sense of chaos that pervade his story.

In the space of those three years he lives through a whole history. He watches Kerensky, 'with his puffy, sallow face, red eyelids, and sparse, greying crew-cut' exhorting rebellious soldiers to carry on the war against the Germans. He hears Lenin holding another group of soldiers spellbound. . . . [He] is trapped in an apartment-house raked by the cross-fire of

Kerensky's troops and the Bolsheviks, and when he ventures out he is mistaken for a sniper and nearly shot. In search of copy for his newspaper he visits one of the rich merchants' mansions taken over by the Anarchists. . . . (p. 194)

The events in themselves are gripping enough in all conscience, but it is the flashes of sensuous insight that, above all, communicate the atmosphere of menace and violence—the clouds of blue cigarette smoke rising from rival groups of soldiers bivouacking in the streets; the gas-pipes riddled with bullet-holes and flaring like torches at a fair-ground; the trainloads of Tsarist soldiers, rumbling through strange stations, and spraying the platforms with machine-gun fire; and that terrible wailing that gradually spreads through the darkened city of Kiev as one by one the Jewish households catch the rumour of an imminent pogrom.

There *are* dull passages, especially the descriptions of minor politicians and writers whose names can mean nothing to us: there are touches of the Victorian sentimentality to which Paustovsky is sometimes prone—as when on a Moscow tram he distributes a bunch of carnations he has picked in one of the derelict parks. . . . All the same, it would be difficult to think of many books that get inside the chaos of revolution as convincingly—and that includes the much over-praised *Doctor Zhivago*. (p. 195)

> Gilbert Phelps, "Bliss," in New Statesman, *Vol. 73, No. 1874, February 10, 1967, pp. 194-95.*

ALISON MACLEOD

The account of the Civil War in [*In That Dawn*] . . . bears no resemblance to . . . heroic Soviet films.

[Paustovsky] was in Kiev during the period when it changed hands seventeen times, each upheaval marking a deeper descent into savagery. Conscripted by the German-backed Ukrainians, Paustovsky was shelled by his own side. Conscripted by the Bolsheviks, he found that his commanding officer was a dangerous lunatic. One of his own soldiers earned everyone's gratitude by shooting him dead. (Paustovsky gives us a broad hint that the same soldier, in later life, was unjustly exiled.)

Threatened with conscription into yet another army, Paustovsky fled to Odessa, and saw the people crushing and drowning one another, as they rushed to escape the advancing Bolsheviks.

All this, though published inside Russia, seems quite as frank as the banned *Dr. Zhivago*. Paustovsky even describes Kerensky as "clearly honest in his convictions and his devotion to Russia" which is probably the nicest thing any Soviet writer has been allowed to say about him.

> Alison Macleod, "Russia, '17, '67," in Punch, *Vol. CCLII, No. 6601, March 15, 1967, p. 394.**

WILLIAM BUCHAN

In That Dawn is the third volume of Konstantin Paustovsky's memoirs. The bliss of being alive in Russia in 1917, and twenty-five years old, must often have been severely modified—it must chiefly have consisted in the possession of a writer's eye and ear, a young man's resilience in hardship, and a young writer's (surely impermissible?) private treasure of imagination. Some of Paustovsky's experience parallels Pasternak's but, in its unfictioned directness, its severe and telling economy, leaves still more vivid impressions with the reader. Some

things in this book are marvellously sharp as images—the shattered gas-lamps blazing like torches after street shelling; an old monk sucking tea through a sugar-lump and praising God for this final treat; Kiev in the days of Skoropadski, and Petlyura riding in on a white horse, girt with a 'folklore' sword. We might ourselves have seen much, and yet, reading Paustovsky, concede that—compared with him—we have seen nothing. (p. 590)

> William Buchan, "Lifelines," in The Spectator, *Vol. 218, No. 7247, May 19, 1967, pp. 590-91.**

PETER HENRY

Paustovskii is one of the veterans of Soviet literature, belonging to an older generation than that which produced Sholokhov, Leonov and Fadeyev, who are generally regarded as representatives of the first generation of Soviet writers. He is one of the few living today who wrote before the Revolution, and thus he represents a vital link with classical Russian literature. (p. xi)

Though Paustovskii is a modest and retiring man not given to making public pronouncements, he has paradoxically become a Grand Old Man of Soviet literature, and this more by public acclaim than by virtue of official acknowledgement. On the other hand, he has never been in serious trouble with the Party or literary officialdom. This may seem strange when one bears in mind that his work is as near to being apolitical as is possible in a society where writers are expected to make their political position explicit. It is not that he was tolerated as a harmless anachronism, as Pasternak had been before the notorious "Doctor Zhivago" affair in 1958. He has certainly caused the wrath or impatience of officially inspired critics, since throughout his long career he has insisted on the writer's overriding dedication to his art, a dedication which admits of no concession to any form of expediency. (pp. xi-xii)

The first small edition of his stories came out in 1925 under the title [*Morskiye nabroski*], another in 1927 [*Minetoza*] and [*Vstrechniye korabi*] in 1928. Much of what he published in these collections . . . [are] impressions of the colourful life in the great seaport of Odessa. He also wrote a great number of stories in the romantic vein.

The incompatibility of Man's "real" existence and the infinite variety of the world of the imagination is the contrast on which these early stories are based. In them he creates an exotic and dreamlike world far beyond the sea, a world of gorgeous colours and musical sounds, inhabited by romanticized men and women. His heroes are sea-captains who yearn to return to this fairy tale world and refuse to accept the hardships and drabness of reality; or they are writers and artists, misunderstood eccentrics, dedicated to establishing their ideal world around them, concerned with protecting and nurturing their sacred inner world.

Paustovskii stresses that his heroes are no ordinary men. They are exceptional in appearance and behaviour, their conversation is pointedly unconventional, they have had unusual and improbable adventures and are scornful of the aspirations of ordinary mortals, trapped in their trivial world. To them, the lowest type of human being is the contented philistine who does not sense that his life is a worthless fraud and who does not suffer agonies at being cut off from the magic life of the chosen few.

The style and language of these stories match their content. Prosaic, factual information is deliberately withheld, or, at most, given grudgingly and incompletely, and contrasts are made as striking and strident as possible. The author does this by the juxtaposition of bizarre incongruities, abrupt and unexplained changes in the narrative, and by putting events in a deliberately unchronological sequence.

The intention is to evoke an exotic atmosphere by the use of extravagant colour, melodious sound, startling metaphors, and the sustained hyperbole of the narrative. (pp. xiv-xv)

Sometimes Paustovskii is content to give lists of foreign place-names, expecting them by their very sounds and associations to evoke the desired atmosphere. . . . (p. xv)

This brand of romanticism looks oddly out of place in the context of Soviet literature, placed firmly in the Here and Now. In fact, Paustovskii is here following the lead of Aleksandr Grin (A. S. Grinevskii, 1880-1932). Remotely in the manner of R. L. Stevenson, Grin insisted that there were other worlds beyond the drab one we were born into, and if there were not, they had to be invented. His heroes were accordingly sailors and adventurers with names like Longren, Hektor Kavaz and Assol', who lived in the non-existent lands of Liss, Zurbagan and Tankos. The main difference between Grin's and Paustovskii's stories is that Paustovskii's locations are identifiable on the map; but the people inhabiting them and the lives they lead are just as fictitious. (pp. xv-xvi)

[In a story published in 1924, Paustovskii bid a] reluctant and ambiguous farewell to the romanticism of his youth. . . .

But Paustovskii realized that he would never completely abandon the lyrical tone of his early work. (p. xvii)

In fact, there was no compelling reason for a complete break with his romantic style. This was the period of the First Five-Year Plan, when writers were called upon to describe the achievements of the Builders of Socialism. Some of this writing was little more than documentary journalism, but what Gor'kii and the other instigators of this "Literature of the Social Command" called for were imaginative and emotionally charged propaganda works that extolled the deeds of the Transformers of Nature. In these a heroic and colourful idiom was quite appropriate. There was indeed room here for romanticism in the service of society, a literature that would fill Soviet men and women with a glowing sense of pride and inspire them to further deeds of valour.

For Paustovskii it was a case of giving his romantic impulse a new direction and seeking inspiration not in the world of make-believe but in the challenge of contemporary life. His contributions were a novel about the conquest of the desert east of the Caspian Sea [*Kara-Bugaz,* 1932] and an account of the reclamation of subtropical swamplands [*Kolkhida,* 1934]. In these works he tried to give a historical perspective to the exploits of his modern heroes by bringing in the valiant but unsuccessful efforts of their predecessors, real or invented. (pp. xvii-xviii)

[In works published in the late 1930s, Paustovskii] seeks to establish meaningful links between the present and the past. (p. xviii)

While these works express Paustovskii's deeply-felt awareness of the essential continuity of history, they suggest that his view of history is scarcely scientific, let alone Marxist. It would seem that he is more concerned with individuals, picked out from their historical context, than with recreating a broad and convincing picture of historical epochs. Moreover, he refuses

to adopt a chronological sequence of events, preferring an intricate system of flashbacks based on more or less contrived parallels and associations. Thus, however much he loads his personalized story with "realia" culled from some document or biography, few of these works are completely successful.

Paustovskii is fond of Diderot's maxim that "art consists in finding the extraordinary in the ordinary, and the ordinary in the extraordinary". It is the first half of the formula that is relevant for his mature work. He discovered beauty in the unspectacular, melancholy tracts of the Ryazan' Region of Central Russia, south-east of Moscow, where he settled in the thirties and was to stay, on and off, for over twenty years. The forests, moors and meadows, the sequestered hamlets of out of the way districts like the Meshchora provide the setting for many of the stories of his mature period. These tell of encounters with foresters and villagers and peasant children, who reveal themselves as remarkable individuals or have an interesting story to tell. . . . As in Turgenev's stories, the evocation of the subtle nuances of the countryside is at least as important as the human encounter; indeed, for Paustovskii, the latter are often little more than a pretext for painting a lyrical, yet finely particularized picture of some woodland scene, which stands out with three-dimensional clarity.

Many of these short sketches are simple and unpretentious; some of them read like extended diary entries. They are inspired by a deep-rooted reverence not only for the ordinary folk of rural Russia, but for all living things. This is expressed in his numerous stories about foresters and the forests themselves. He has written a whole cycle of such stories [included in *Povest' o lesakh,* 1948]. (pp. xix-xx)

In these stories his style underwent a gradual change. There is none of the ornateness and pretension, that sheer intoxication with words that had characterized his earlier work. Now he wrote in a simple, seemingly effortless style which was in fact the result of the most exacting work on his language, pruning it back to its irreducible minimum. (pp. xx-xxi)

In Paustovskii's writing of the war years one looks in vain for any of the passionate rhetoric of Erenburg or Alexei Tolstoi. Though he was a war correspondent with front-line service, he does not paint a broad canvas of a nation at war. Essentially, the tone of his war stories does not differ from that of his other stories. The war rarely provides more than a vaguely hinted-at background. He writes down encounters, not necessarily in any of the decisive battles, with ordinary folk, who are not given to flamboyant, slogan-like expressions of their patriotism: instead they express their deep-rooted love for their homeland in quiet, unpretentious language. For them, and for their author, this is a deeper way of stating their loyalty. (pp. xxi-xxii)

One of the main themes in Paustovskii's work is a plea for tolerance towards the old and the unfortunate, the eccentric and the failures in life, for respect for every individual, irrespective of his usefulness to society. A good example of this "humanism" is . . . the story of an old woman left over from Tsarist days, who lives out her lonely old age in a desolate village in the Ryazan' Region. Her only living relative is her daughter, who is a member of the Komsomol, working in the Union of Artists in far-off Leningrad. She sends her mother money at irregular intervals, but hardly ever writes. Nastasya is not a heartless person; she can and does apply her feelings successfully in the course of duty. But amid her socially useful work she has forgotten about her elementary loyalty to her mother.

The two themes are delicately contrasted and balanced—Leningrad and the village, youth and old age, Soviet woman and Tsarist "survival", public service and family loyalty, the bustle of purposeful activity on the one hand and the waiting for death, alone, on the other. (p. xxiv)

Paustovskii's stories show that Soviet society is far less monolithic and uniform than we are sometimes led to believe. It is not so much a case of the many human curios that he unearths; he shows by implication the inevitable process of stratification even of this classless society. He not only shows the difference in outlook of villagers and town dwellers, but also the superior material well-being of the latter. He does this without feeling the need to justify or rationalize this state of affairs. As he wrote in an article in 1959:

> We have made a habit of never writing about 'shortcomings', however harmful they are for our public life, without first paying ourselves compliments, without first mentioning our achievements. This is done with such persistence, as if we have to point out to every Soviet citizen the superiority of our system over capitalism (this in the 42nd year of our existence!), as if we doubted this and were astonished by it as by some incredible miracle.

On occasion, Paustovskii has spoken out with perhaps surprising vehemence against injustice or falsity in Soviet society. (pp. xxxiii-xxxiv)

But he is primarily concerned with the state of Soviet literature. In 1959, when the Writers' Congress was in session, he wrote the article quoted above in which he attacked the insincerity of so much that was published with official approval. (p. xxxiv)

He was particularly angered by the poor quality of much of this writing.

> Why do we allow this nauseous bureaucratic language to infiltrate into our literature? Why are people admitted into literature and even into the Union of Writers who do not know the Russian language and are quite indifferent to it? Why do we put up with the barrenness of bureaucratic and philistine language, with its poverty and phonetic ugliness? What right have we to throw into the backyard the classical and mighty language of Pushkin, Lermontov, Leskov, Chekhov, Blok, Bunin and Gor'kii?

Bad or dishonest writing is to Paustovskii a crime before the nation. . . . Too many writers, he complained, have a cynical disregard for their craft, do violence to the Russian language, fail to appreciate its expressive wealth and musical beauty.

It is a fact that in Soviet literature, ideological "correctness" plus a strong story line, Soviet-style, has too often been emphasized to the neglect of matters of composition, language and style. Soviet literary criticism has sometimes degenerated into an assessment of the writer's ideological position, of the correct portrayal of reality and of the (inevitably) positive hero. Literature as an art form with its own exacting standards has too often been left to fend for itself. This is a fault which Paustovskii has been at pains to put right.

He does not see writing as primarily an extension of the political life, nor as the vehicle for propagating, explaining or illustrating the current ideological line. Writing is an intensely personal affair demanding an overriding loyalty, it is an end in itself. . . . (pp. xxxiv-xxxv)

For many years Paustovskii was a relatively little-known author, even in Russia, and he became a universal favourite only during the fifties. For a long time he was virtually unknown abroad. . . . But a translation of the first volume of [*Povest' o zhizni*] which came out in 1964 was received with dramatic enthusiasm and he was instantly recognized as one of the greatest writers alive today. This work, and many of his stories, have been translated into all the major European languages.

Yet Paustovskii has never enjoyed the respect from Soviet critics that he so amply deserves. With a monotonous repetitiveness they have pointed out his "shortcomings", hoping that this great artist would become yet another socialist realist. Paustovskii cannot, and will not, write anything he does not sincerely perceive, anything he has not experienced physically or spiritually. Nor will he write in an idiom that is alien to his character or to his artistic creed. (p. xxxvi)

It is perhaps his absolute integrity as a man and a writer, his sincere devotion to his country, a devotion which he refuses to express in cheap platitudes, his respect and compassion for his fellow-beings, and his boundless fascination with the miracle of life in all its varied manifestations, that make Paustovskii the most revered and beloved figure in Soviet literature today. (p. xxxvii)

> *Peter Henry, in an introduction to* Selected Stories *by Konstantin Paustovskii, Pergamon Press, 1967, pp. xi-xxxvii.*

DAN JACOBSON

Readers of the earlier volumes of Paustovsky's autobiography will be familiar with the virtues of his prose: its directness, its simplicity, its veracity. His sentences are brief, his paragraphs are seldom more than a few lines apiece; but the effect is never clipped or tough. Instead, for all its simplicity, the writing is moody, reflective, capable of changing pace and direction with a swiftness that one thinks of as being characteristically "Russian," and yet is distinctively the author's own.

The new volume, [*Years of Hope*] it must be added, also displays some of the faults of the others; particularly in the touches of sentimentality that mar its descriptions of nature, and in its occasional passages of moralising. However, as if to make up for this, the author gives freer rein than before to his sense of humour: his delight in the absurd and grotesque things that people do is equalled only by his total absence of surprise at them.

The place is Odessa, the year is 1921, the author is approaching his thirtieth birthday. Having no possessions, no family living near by, and, at the beginning of the book, no job and no prospects, he feels himself younger and more irresponsible than ever before.

The city, recently liberated from the White Army and still under blockade by the interventionist Western Powers, is in a state of siege and near-famine. People live as best they can: camping in abandoned houses, chopping up furniture for firewood, flogging all kinds of junk in the open market, grubbing for shellfish on the rocks along the coast, appointing themselves to nonexistent jobs on the ramshackle revolutionary administration. . . .

Finally, the blockade is lifted, and Paustovsky leaves in the first leaking tub of a vessel to sail from the port; the boat is crammed with munitions, mutinous sailors, and "two hundred speculators who were going to Crimea to buy salt."

The pages of the book abound with vivid descriptions of the people the author came across, from a demented lady of aristocratic lineage who was for a brief time his landlady, to a dejected electrician with three carboys of an "explosive liquid" which he was carefully saving for some unknown eventuality. But the longest and most carefully composed portrait is that of Isaac Babel, to whom several chapters are devoted. . . .

We see Babel as a tortured, Flaubertian artist, always straining for perfection; rather more unexpectedly, we see him also as a family man, plagued by an unwelcome mother-in-law and a pest of a nephew, whom he finally manages to drive out of the house by means of a kind of schoolboy practical joke. Paustovsky's admiration for Babel is more than generous; it is passionate. He makes no reference to Babel's eventual death in one of Stalin's concentration camps; as the title reminds us, these were the years of hope.

Dan Jacobson, "Paustovsky's Odessa," in Manchester Guardian Weekly, *September 19, 1968, p. 14.*

JOHN BAYLEY

The fourth volume of Paustovsky's memoirs [*Years of Hope*] takes us from the Kiev of *In That Dawn* to Odessa and the Black Sea. When asked what he did in the Revolution the author might have replied, like Siéyès, '*J'ai vécu,*' and it was the greatest service that a writer—and particularly a writer as modest and as humanely endowed as Paustovsky—could have rendered to his country and to art. He contrives to maintain unbroken the august tradition of Russian retrospective and autobiographical writing without losing touch with the present and without presenting the revolutionary epoch as something unique and sensational. For literature, an age of iron sundered from all that had gone before. Surrounded by every kind of savagery, he will have no truck with the Savage God, or make any literary genuflexion before the idea of crisis. (p. 476)

The poet Bagritsky, a native of [Odessa], would recite Blok by the hour in a voice hoarse with bronchitis; and Babel, Paustovsky's greatest hero, went on endlessly writing new versions of his short story (Lyubka), until there were 23 in all. The Silver Age of Russian writing, with all its endearing intensities, its slightly mad preoccupation with effects and technique, carried on imperturbably, adjusting itself (as it thought) to the new world that had suddenly sprung into being. Literature is inconveniently organic, unlike the structure of revolutions: not for many years did the New Order decree new forms of literature more suited to its nature. And it was then that Babel adopted the technique of silence.

Paustovsky himself has not remained wholly untouched, it must be said, from the prevailing atmosphere of Soviet literature. How could he have, because while he was becoming a writer it was the air he had to breathe. The later parts of *Years of Hope* show, more than any of the early instalments, the insidious effect of that literary culture even upon a man as temperamentally resistant to it as Paustovsky. There is a marvellous account of a starving holiday he spent by himself in Ovidiopol, with nothing but sea and sand-dunes, until a friend whose wife was ill with typhus dumped their six-year-old daughter—an

early *besprisornaya*—to be looked after by him. This is moving and haunting, but it is followed by an account of a voyage in a condemned tramp-steamer to Sebastopol and Yalta during which he wrote copy for the *Seaman*. Here, in some curious and disturbing way, the writing becomes more standardised, more suited to the image of Soviet culture remaining heroically—a bit too heroically—true to its cultural traditions. In Yalta the author braves a night swarming with bandits and Denikin riff-raff to do he doesn't quite know what—until by the light of his last match he finds himself opposite the house of Chekhov! The thing is too contrived, and the odour of some kind of half-conditioned afterthought is disagreeable after the sweet fresh taste of the book and its predecessors. Standardisation of feeling, state's reverence, can show itself even through the personality and feeling of Paustovsky, and even perhaps without his being aware of it. But it is hardly becoming to blame him for this when one thinks of the possible conditioned reflexes in an Anglo-Saxon writer that might seem distasteful to the most sympathetic Russian reader today. (pp. 476, 478)

John Bayley, "Souvenirs of Odessa," in The Listener, *Vol. LXXX, No. 2063, October 10, 1968, pp. 476, 478.*

HARRISON E. SALISBURY

Paustovsky died last summer at the age of seventy-six after a long, lingering illness with his remarkable autobiographical cycle *The Story of a Life* (of which *Years of Hope* is the fourth volume) still unfinished.

The literary loss is great. No other Russian writer has painted so warmly, so humanely the panorama of the last Czarist years, pre-war Moscow, pre-revolutionary Kiev, the descent from confusion into the chaos of World War I, the pain, desperation (and humor) of the early revolutionary years. . . .

The cultural loss is even greater. One of the remarkable services performed by Paustovsky and by Ilya Ehrenburg . . . was to construct a literary "bridge" across the chasm cut in Russian letters by the Stalinist epoch. Paustovsky and Ehrenburg revealed to the new generation of Yevtushenko and Voznesensky, of Aksenov and Okudzhava, the nature of Russia's tradition, of its relationship to Europe and to the free and stimulating era which had produced the explosion in Russian arts and letters in the decade before World War I.

Paustovsky was able to tell the Russians of today (and ourselves as well) what life was really like before the gray wave of Bolshevism rolled over the vast Russian landscape, blotting out life, color, poetry, inspiration, creativity and truth. . . .

All this being said, let us be thankful that Paustovsky lived as long as he did; that he has been able to give us this volume of bright vignettes of what it was like to be young in that marvelous Russian Marseilles—Odessa!

Odessa was the milieu which produced Ilya Ilf (of the famous Ilf and Petrov collaborations—*The Little Golden Calf* and *The Twelve Chairs*), the poet Edward Bagritsky, Isaac Babel (who perished in the purges of the 1930s), the poet S. I. Kirsanov, Valentin Katayev and many, many others. If that Odessa has long since vanished under the heel of Soviet power at least it will forever live, bright, golden, endlessly absurd, wildly comic, painfully tragic and fresh as a new-minted ruble in the pages of Paustovsky.

Harrison E. Salisbury, "Last Voice from the Time before Lenin," in Book World—Chicago Tribune, March 30, 1969, p. 3.

V. S. PRITCHETT

Konstantin Paustovsky's autobiography reaches its fifth volume [*Southern Adventure*] without having lost any of its modesty and power to surprise. Fortunate as he is in his dangerous period and scene—Odessa, the Black Sea round to Batum in the early Twenties when the Soviet authority came and went very uncertainly—his success owes everything to the art and integrity of his writing and to his gift for recording feeling that had been forgotten. Chekhov and Babel were his masters.

In this fifth volume he is still a journalist working on revolutionary papers for seamen. He takes a chance and smuggles himself through the quarantine in the new Black Sea republic of Abkhazia and gives an astonishing picture of the mixing of the new Soviet life with the old primitive life of princes, bandits, blood feuds. He relies on an illogical, unargued narrative that begins casually, and then jumps quietly but dramatically from things seen, people heard, to personal revelation which contains no self-importance. He is the least tedious or tendentious of revealers. He has good senses. . . .

The patriarchal simplicity of this wild region of silver-belted horsemen, with gold seamed breeches and daggers at their waists, was to vanish in a few years. (Paustovsky's is the only near-contemporary view of that life.) The people were famous for their handsomeness. When the great Kalinin arrived from Moscow, the overexcited chief of police galloped along the edge of the crowd shouting: 'Handsome men, forward!' (p. 589)

Paustovsky moved on to Batum where it is always raining. It is known to French sailors as *le pissoir de la Mer Noire*. He went on to Tiflis where he lived among the writers and painters. He is pleasant enough about that, but his best things are the extraordinary daily encounter, the study of certain types—porters, wrestlers, police and figures in popular life. (p. 590)

V. S. Pritchett, "Black Sea Stories," in New Statesman, Vol. 77, No. 1989, April 25, 1969, pp. 589-90.*

V. S. PRITCHETT

If [*The Restless Years,* the final volume of Paustovsky's autobiography,] is patchy this is because he jumps the awkward political past and occasionally collides with the books of travel he wrote years ago; but the unifying subjects are his literary portraits from the Twenties when he was young and poor, and his life-long preoccupation with the act of writing itself. He was an artist dedicated to turning life into sentences. He responded to the gentleness and detachment of Chekhov; to Babel—also his elder—he owes his spareness of statement and openness to astonishment.

Paustovsky has already given us in an earlier volume an account of the starving journalist's life during the Revolution in Odessa; now we see him in Moscow and Leningrad trying to break out of newspaper work and to become an artist. This meant, he says, a complete revising of his attitude to language for, in its hurry, journalism tramples words down. He was excited by the liberating sensations of the times and wrote that:

> Language must suit the nation. It must define
> its face, its beauty, its character as graphically
> as does the actual landscape of the country, a

hill rising gently and losing itself in the evening mist over a river so dear to one that it makes the heart throb.

Perhaps, he says, he is too strict and too reverent, but journalism was killing Russian prose. . . . Naturally he went through a period of fine writing and argued about it with Babel, Olesha, Ilf and the crowd who came into cellars, attics and the canteens of newspaper offices to talk their talents away: minor figures of that tragic generation who were to be obliterated by Stalin and who used to be well-known to us in translation. How intense and eager they all were! (p. 366)

To Russians these reminiscences of a lost literary life and the descriptions of places which, at that time, were hardly yet touched by the new industrialisation of Russia, must have an embarrassing value. A good deal of the old life remained but the renaming of old towns by the new bureaucracy had begun: Koktebel had for example become Planerskoye. This infuriates him still. But eccentrics still hung on. Once Paustovsky stayed with a dotty geologist who seriously believed that the superstitions of the peasants in his village arose because the land lay on thick strata of Devonian limestone; it heated the soil, he said, so that the fumes poisoned the mind. It was Devonian limestone that made barren women put a pike in a trough of water and stare for two hours into the pike's eyes, or chew limestone from the grave of the village idiot! Paustovsky does not condescendingly put this absurd figure down as a traveller's joke, but delicately shows him among his family who shyly egg him on and mischievously watch his effect on the author. His art lies in placing himself naïvely in the domestic scene as if he belonged to it; he is not 'collecting material' but is himself a dreamer bemused by it. He is never quite a stranger; he is inside the life he describes. . . . Throughout this book Paustovsky's senses are always alert for something defining in the air, indoors or outdoors; he travelled a good deal by the nose. He very much conveys that life is what one breathes in. (pp. 366-67)

Paustovsky pleases not simply because of his humour and his telling portraits, but because he is a source of wonder to himself. (p. 367)

V. S. Pritchett, "Breathing In," in New Statesman, Vol. 87, No. 2243, March 15, 1974, pp. 366-67.*

KONSTANTIN BAZAROV

Gorky's famous autobiographical trilogy, just republished . . . in a new two volume edition [*Childhood* and *My Apprenticeship. My Universities*], has often been compared and contrasted with Tolstoy's, written sixty years before. It's equally fascinating to compare it with another outstanding Russian autobiography written some forty years later, Konstantin Paustovsky's *Story of a Life*, the English version of which is now completed with the appearance of its sixth and last volume, *The Restless Years*.

Both Gorky and Paustovsky were at their best as writers of short stories, so that their memoirs are a series of linked episodes vividly lit up by revealing incidents and details, conveying the full flavour of all the people they met and the events they lived through. Gorky gives an unforgettable picture of the changing Tsarist Empire, before the turn of the century, while Paustovsky, born twenty-four years later in 1892, gives an equally unforgettable picture of its death-throes in the years of the First World War, Revolution and Civil War. . . .

Paustovsky grew up at a time when many of his contemporaries were romantically attached to the idea of revolution, and were later to be savagely disillusioned. But Paustovsky's own romanticism and love of the exotic were always directed at the beauties of nature and his love of strange, gifted and imaginative people. The early stories which brought him wide popularity are based on the contrast between the apparent drabness of 'real' existence and the infinite variety of the world of the imagination. He was beginning to write these stories during the wanderings recorded in *The Restless Years,* and it is his struggle to become an artist that is the unifying theme. The Southern school of writers headed by Isaak Babel whom he had known in starving, blockaded Odessa during the Civil War all turn up again, and he meets other writers like the novelist Bulgakov and other members of that talented, tragic and highly individualistic generation who were later to become Stalin's victims. (p. 47)

Paustovsky's marvellous sense of atmosphere and place are unfailing, whether he is conjuring up the tropical hell of the Georgian port of Poti or the silent fields of Central Russia through which he walks with the peasant girl Lusha, soon to be forced into an arranged marriage with a well-off but elderly, pockmarked widower: 'Everything about that simple girl, her rough hands, her quick smile, the way she inclined her face, submissive and tender, contained so much promise—vague as yet—of love for someone still unknown, but certainly not for the man to whom she was betrothed, that to walk beside her filled one with the sense both of sadness and of joy.' The book is full of telling portraits, such as that of the eccentric geologist whose harmless little mania was the idea that the superstitions of the peasants in his village were due to the heat of epochs many millions of years old stored up in the Devonian limestone on which the village stood. . . .

And who but Paustovsky could have arrived on a pouring wet night at that Georgian hotel where the only remaining room was an attic one which they were reluctant to let to him because the previous occupant had run from it at twenty to four in the morning, screaming with fear but so completely mad he was unable to say what had happened. The rain drumming on the roof and the wind howling keep Paustovsky awake, but finally he dozes off and suddenly awakens at twenty to four to find himself living through the same nightmare experience, from which he only just escapes with his life, rushing out as the previous victim had done. . . .

Like Gorky . . . , Paustovsky is a masterly observer of revealing incidents and details. But unlike Gorky he never over-reaches himself by trying to draw cut-and-dried conclusions from his observations. . . .

Paustovsky always trusts his heart, though as Marc Slonim points out, throughout this autobiography he constantly and intentionally opposes two worlds: that of war, destruction, fear and violence with that of joy, happiness, creativeness, enrichment and love [see excerpt above]. Needless to say it has been dismissed by party-line critics as 'only a story of private encounters in a private life', and it is distressing to find Edward Crankshaw echoing them in *The Observer* when he attacks *The Restless Years* for its very lack of tendentiousness, for sticking closely to Paustovsky's own experiences and observations instead of answering Crankshaw's questions 'who was Lenin?' and 'who was Stalin?' A neat illustration of how propagandist hacks like Crankshaw are merely mirror images of their Soviet counterparts, but it's a relief to find a BBC television programme devoted to censorship quoting a very relevant maxim by the Czech writer Ludvik Vaculik: 'He who feels impelled to write against the régime all the time is allowing himself to be prevented by the régime from writing about anything else.' (p. 48)

Konstantin Bazarov, "Observers of Life," in Books and Bookmen, *Vol. 19, No. 10, July, 1974, pp. 47-8.*

MARC SLONIM

Konstantin Paustovsky, a descendant of Ukrainian Cossacks, was born in Moscow in 1892. His father, a statistician, kept changing jobs and towns, and Konstantin inherited from him a passion for traveling. He studied in Kiev, then lived in Petrograd and in Odessa where he became associated with the whole group of poets and prose writers later known as the Southern school: Babel, Katayev, Ilf, Bagritsky, Shengeli, Slavin, and others. Like Grin he dreamt of wonderful exotic lands, adored the south, particularly the Crimea, and the Caucasus, and he read Poe, Stevenson, and Mérimée. But as a writer he was also influenced by Prishvin, the "investigator of nature," and by such different authors as Zamyatin, who taught him the art of a compact plot, and Bunin whom he admired for the purity and raciness of his language.

Paustovsky's first novel was entitled *Romantics* (1923) and its heroes were anarchically minded individuals and beautiful girls with strange destinies. His second novel *The Glittering Clouds* (1928) had a more complex plot of adventure and unrequited love, but again its characters consisted of bizarre eccentrics and lovely, unhappy women. Paustovsky also wrote a series of highly romantic stories, partly historical (*Charles Lonceville's Fate, The Northern Story*), and many of his topics were clearly inspired by Western literature. His exotic trait was rather bookish, but it expressed a genuine desire for new experiences and foreign skies. As Paustovsky had the opportunity to travel extensively in Russia and abroad, he accumulated a tremendous wealth of first-hand experiences. His interest in nature was equal to his curiosity about people, his memory capable of preserving thousands of details of both. His short novels presented innumerable episodes, each serving to illustrate a theme or a general concept. It is not so much the plot as the lyrical breath, the emotional consistency, the continuing sound of a note that give a unity to his fragmentary prose. It also has the brilliance some critics attributed to his fondness for the French; the finish of his stylizations and descriptions made him one of the best craftsmen among the young Soviet writers. Stories depicting imaginary adventures of Poe, Anderson, Grieg, and other Western poets and musicians, made him the master of "pastiche," a rare genre in the 'thirties. He also wrote about the painters Kiprensky and Levitan, the poet Shevchenko and the "Sorcerer" Grin, combining precise facts with fictional inventions.

It can be argued, as it has been done in Soviet criticism, that Paustovsky's romanticism and love of the exotic were merely a reaction to the dullness of life in provincial Russia, and that he felt sad and depressed because he could not actually reach the marvelous lands he dreamed of. But Paustovsky came of age at a period when his contemporaries found the fulfillment of their romantic aspirations in the Revolution. He did not join them but continued to glorify the beauty of nature and to idealize poets, rebels, and women. The latter, by the way, never acquire the reality of flesh and remain pale vignettes and sketchy profiles. The contention that Paustovsky's romanticism was of purely bookish origin and a youthful escape from an unsatisfactory environment is also refuted by his biography. In his late twenties he traveled and had adventures and led a very active existence. Before choosing writing as a profession, he worked as male nurse, tramway conductor, metallurgical worker, fisherman, reporter, and editor of a maritime newspaper. But direct contacts with life did not alter his romantic disposition. He wrote himself: "My life as a writer began from the desire of knowing everything and seeing everything, and of traveling." As late as 1954, he repeated the same point in *The Birth of a Story,* a tale in which the writer Muraviev comes to the conclusion that "the source of poetry and prose lies in two things—in knowledge and in mighty human imagination. Knowledge is the tuber from which grow the invisible, eternal flowers of imagination." The successful marriage of these two elements was achieved by Paustovsky in two short novels which brought him wide popularity: *Kara Bugaz* (1932) and *Kolchida* (1934).

The first told of various efforts in the past to utilize the sodium sulfate (Glauber salt) which covered the bottom of Kara Bugaz, an inhospitable bay of the Caspian sea on its desert Asiatic shores. Adventures of scientists and sailors, terrifying episodes of cruelty and death originated by the civil war, scenes of Asian backwardness, descriptions of storms blowing over the desolate southeastern steppes gave an exotic flavor to the story, which ended with Soviet pioneers transforming the whole area into an industrial center. *Kolchida* is a tale about a subtropical district in the Caucasus, which drainage and the growing of plants for technical purposes have turned into a new land of plenty. Nature here is as luxurious as it is bare in *Kara Bugaz.* Gorky, Krupskaya (Lenin's widow), and many others welcomed both books as a daring example of fiction integrated with science, but *Kara Bugaz* and *Kolchida* (as well as the ensuing *Black Sea,* 1936, and *The Tale of Forests,* 1948) were not the usual novels of industrialization based on data of botany, chemistry, geography, and history, but were adventure stories pervaded by a romantic spirit. What attracted Paustovsky to the Revolution and industrialization were the heroism of effort, the dream of change, and the creation of a "second nature" through the transformation of the physical world.

In the late 'thirties and early 'forties Paustovsky's stories acquired a stonger psychological bent, as he became more interested in the emotional and personal in man, and shifted from colorful strange heroes to ordinary people, in whom he tried to discover "the eternal light." Like Prishvin he portrayed small folk, laborers, and artisans, and stressed their closeness to nature, their simple virtues. At a time when Communist critics were pressing writers to show "the new Soviet man,"

Paustovsky retorted that "the magnificent world of freedom, justice, and culture" is still a dream, that in his opinion the new society begins where there is love of women, care of children, admiration for beauty and devotion to youth, and where goodness, humanity, and a feeling of solidarity are considered the highest values. He continued to follow Prishvin's "idealization of nature" and affirmed in one of his stories: "One cannot write books without knowing what kind of herbs grow on forest glades and on swamps; where is Sirius rising; what is the difference between the leaves of a birch and an aspen; whether blue bonnets migrate in winter; when the rye begins to flower, which winds bring the rain and when the drought . . . One cannot write books without having experienced the wind before the sunrise or the dark October night under open sky. The hands of a writer should not only be calloused from the pen but also hardened by the water of the river."

For a decade Paustovsky directed a seminar on prose in the Moscow Literary Institute and taught the craft and psychology of writing to hundreds of students. His influence on the new generation of writers was considerable and he had a large following. His views on the art of fiction are contained in a highly interesting collection of short stories *The Golden Rose* (1955).

Paustovsky's main work, entitled *The Tale of Life,* is in several volumes: *Distant Years* (1946), *The Restless Youth* (1955), *The Beginning of an Unknown Century* (1956), *The Time of Great Expectations* (1959), and *A Throw to the South* (1962). This autobiographical cycle presents a series of reminiscences, covering half a century of pre-revolutionary and Soviet life in a sequence of short novellas, and it unfolds an amazing variety of characters and incidents. This multiple and sectional composition, written in an excellent, compact style, is held together by its approach to reality. The author constantly and intentionally opposes two worlds: that of war, destruction, fear, and violence with that of joy, happiness, creativeness, enrichment, and love. His romantic vision is preserved throughout, and it apparently enchants many readers. Paustovsky's collected works, published in the 'fifties and 'sixties in two editions (300,000 copies each), and the numerous reprints of his tales and novels were sold out in record time. He died in 1968 but still is one of the most popular, beloved, and respected Soviet writers. (pp. 118-22)

Marc Slonim, "Soviet Romantics: From Grin, Paustovsky, and Olesha to Tikhonov and Bagritsky," in his Soviet Russian Literature: Writers and Problems 1917-1977, *second revised edition, Oxford University Press, 1977, pp. 116-33.*

Thomas Savage

1915-

American novelist.

Savage's works have consistently garnered critical acclaim, although they remain relatively unknown to the general reading public. Many critics find Savage's lack of fame hard to understand, for they consider his novels to be well written and his characters deftly created. Savage is often classified as a Western writer because much of the action in his books takes place in the American West. Though the Western mystique plays an important role in many of his novels, Savage is primarily concerned with the emotional and physical responses of his characters to the pressures imposed by familial and societal expectations.

The Pass (1944), *Lona Hanson* (1948), and *The Power of the Dog* (1967) are among Savage's novels set in the West. The first two books are straightforward tales about the hardships of frontier life in the early 1900s. However, Savage does not idealize the West. His characters endure personal pain and tragedy and, as one reviewer noted, "Mr. Savage does not believe in happy endings." In *The Power of the Dog,* Savage delves into the psyches of his characters. Set in Montana during the 1920s, the story centers on the ill-fated relationship between two brothers. Eliot Fremont-Smith described the novel as an effective probing "of the wary war between compulsion and intelligence."

In several novels, Savage uses a male, first-person narrator to tell a woman's story. In *Daddy's Girl* (1970), Marty remains devoted to her father even after he abandons her and her mother. It is this seemingly senseless devotion, Savage intimates, that leads Marty into two unhappy marriages and eventually to alcoholism. Liz, the protagonist of *Her Side of It* (1981), is a gifted writer who is unable to repeat the success of her two published works. When Liz dies suddenly, her letters are left to William Reese, the narrator of Liz's story. Reese is honored by Liz's bequest but soon realizes that she also left him the responsibility of immortalizing her. The title character of *For Mary, With Love* (1983) is a beautiful but self-centered adventuress who destroys the lives of several people before falling prey to an equally selfish and destructive lover. Critics generally agree that the heroines of these novels are unlikely recipients of their narrators' obvious fascination yet concede that the novels are redeemed by Savage's economical prose and skillful characterizations.

The family unit and the effects of one member's actions on the others is a recurring subject in Savage's fiction. *The Liar* (1969) and *A Strange God* (1973) examine the sometimes painful relationships between parents and children. *I Heard My Sister Speak My Name* (1977) shares several themes with Savage's other works but is distinguished by its clearly autobiographical content. Thomas Burton, the narrator, resembles Savage in many ways: both were born in the same year in roughly the same area of the United States; both live in Maine and are novelists married to novelists; they each have three children; and they share the same publisher. More importantly, they both believe that the family is at the root of an individual's identity. For character and author, this belief in the family is

Photograph by Adison Berkey

challenged when the existence of a sister, given up for adoption immediately after birth, is revealed. Although the reasons for the adoption in either situation are not detailed, both instances end with a happy reunion of brother and sister.

HOFFMAN BIRNEY

The Pass is quite plotless. It's a novel of the West, but there's no killing, no rustling, no schemes to steal the ranch. The only romance in the book is the love of a man for his wife and of a woman for her man. That is all, yet Thomas Savage has not written a negative story. The people of Salmon City and of Horse Prairie are very real. There is a grimly virtuous Mrs. Cooper who wanted to ask her husband where he learned to dance so well but was afraid he might tell her. There is Doc Morse, voted the man most likely to succeed in the class of '81. Doc, who would have done some research if it hadn't been for the dishes that pile up so in a bachelor's sink.

Just people like that. Above them, always present and inescapable, was the Pass. Only those who have lived in small towns in the Rockies or Sierras can appreciate the claustrophobia which is a seasonable disease when winter closes the Pass, when trains are days or weeks late, when wires are down and there is no link whatever with the Outside.

Thomas Savage knows those things and of the small mountain hamlet and its people he writes well. True, buffalo grass does not bend in the wind nor was southwestern Montana "little known" in 1913, but those are minor flaws. Jess and Beth Bentley, Amy and Cy Pierce, Slim Edwards and Reverend Pritchett are very real people. Their lives and their sorrows and their sometimes pathetic pleasures are real, not fictional. *The Pass* is easy to read, but it will not be forgotten quickly.

> *Hoffman Birney, "High Prairie," in* The New York Times Book Review, *April 23, 1944, p. 6.*

GEORGE CONRAD

[*The Pass*] is quietly written, with a sincerity which touches the emotions more deeply than any amount of studied eloquence.

In addition to its merit as a work of fiction, *The Pass* is a dramatic reminder that the winning of the West is not a chapter of history that came to an end in the nineteenth century. For it was in 1913 that Jess bought a rundown ranch in a far corner of southwestern Montana, a region which even the Indians had shunned as "bad medicine" and where only the hardiest kind of pioneer spirits fought it out with the elements. . . . But it held no terrors for Beth [Jess's wife], and the shivaree with which the scattered neighbors welcomed her to the house of unpeeled logs her husband had built was more than a party; it was a dedication. Mr. Savage catches the significance as well as the atmosphere of this latter-day frontier; he has made a real contribution to the annals of the prairie.

> *George Conrad, "New Novels of Women in the World Today: 'The Pass'," in* New York Herald Tribune Weekly Book Review, *April 30, 1944, p. 6.*

NEW YORK HERALD TRIBUNE WEEKLY BOOK REVIEW

On a Montana ranch of 20,000 acres which was her heritage, Thomas Savage's nineteen-year-old heroine [in *Lona Hanson*] has more than her fair share of problems. . . . She has no fun and no real companionship until she meets a young rodeo performer from Idaho and offers him a job as ranch hand. When the hired hand falls in love with his boss there is a brief but bright interlude in the novel, but Mr. Savage does not believe in happy endings. The story is chiefly rewarding in its atmosphere and its vivid descriptions of life where your infrequent and expensive beefsteak is still on the hoof.

> *"Ranch Girl," in* New York Herald Tribune Weekly Book Review, *October 17, 1948, p. 24.*

JAMES KELLY

Thomas Savage, whose previous two novels dealt with romance in a western setting, now turns his attention to another theme [in *A Bargain With God*] which in his hands offers greater rewards to everybody concerned.

How can an unworldly, ineffectual priest cope with the worldly problems of his people and the business aspects of his own church? How far will simple faith and humility carry him in the big job of leadership? How can he explain the necessity of

evil to a young husband and wife who have just lost their only child? Where, in his limited experience and capacity, can he find the strength to cope with problems that are for the most part beyond him?

The novel does not answer these questions: it simply deals with them in a humanistic, believable way. Contributing assets are the soundly motivated characterizations, the author's ability to observe well and report accurately, the unsmothered way in which he presents individual scenes. Liabilities, inevitable in navigating shoal waters like these, stem mostly from Mr. Savage's determined attempt at moral affirmation—and a writing style which tends to meander off into catechistic question-and-answer passages. . . .

Whether by coincidence or his own influence as a good neighbor, Father Ferris does muddle through to solutions. . . . Most readers will find the novel's climax during services in the rickety old church both moving and credible.

Mr. Savage has chosen a big subject. Abetted by personal devoutness and sound instincts as a writer, he brings it off. *A Bargain With God* is a refreshing change from novels of despair and Freudian fogs.

> *James Kelly, "Good and Evil in a Boston Parish," in* The New York Times Book Review, *June 28, 1953, p. 14.*

EDMUND FULLER

In *A Bargain with God,* Thomas Savage tells the story of elderly Father Ferris, an Anglo-Catholic priest whose dilapidated little mission church, St. Mark's, stands on Bowdoin Street, on the decayed side of Beacon Hill, in Boston. The only remaining resident from the days of this street's elegance is the wealthy, aging Miss Lydia Brummal, who lives across the way. . . . The book tells how Father Ferris, who ministers especially to slum children, helps Miss Brummal to find that which is eternal in the very midst of that which is passing, helps the young couple, Johnny and Jebby, to salvage their marriage after the cruel, disruptive blow of a tragedy; and how, inextricably linked with these other actions, he averts the threat of condemnation which hangs over his church. All of these are works of grace. . . .

[Mr. Savage's] world is not strictly real, is somewhat sentimentalized, but he admits it tacitly, which makes his story acceptable as a warm-hearted fable. The harshest thing I can say of it is that it is, by formula, an Anglican *Going My Way.* His very title, *A Bargain with God,* is on the cute side. The best I can say of it is that I read it without pain and was touched by it at times. I admit I am prejudiced against "charming" religious stories.

> *Edmund Fuller, "Workers for God," in* The Saturday Review, *New York, Vol. XXXVI, No. 28, July 11, 1953, p. 21.**

DAVID DEMPSEY

As in Thomas Savage's previous novels, [*Trust in Chariots*] is kept moving by an undercurrent of wistful optimism that preaches faith in the ultimate Self. True, Fate wins out, but not before the pleasures, and risks, of owning a Rolls-Royce are explored to the last drop of petrol. A man can dream, can't he?

Sheldon Owens, a humdrum clerk in an insurance office, had often wanted the feeling of power that goes with driving the finest and most prestigious automobile on the road.... [He] is married to Marianne, whom he met at an office party. In his spare time, Sheldon visits a foreign car garage just so he can sit in a fine 1939 Rolls kept in the basement. Marianne, too, enjoys her eccentricities. One might say she is prone to men. Discovered in the act—Sheldon had set a trap for her—she is all remorse. Sheldon leaves her, buys the car and heads west....

Meanwhile, Pal Forbes, a high-school boy in Chicago, is one of those automotive bugs who loves to listen to the sins that come bleating out of the dark, oily soul of the internal combustion engine.... When Pal's mother dies, he too, heads west, hitchhiking.

It comes as no surprise that Pal and Sheldon meet, and that their journey across America, which occupies the final leg of the novel, constitutes the Big Dream toward which all the little dreams have been leading. It is the dream of escape. That the engine of flight should be a Rolls is apparently Mr. Savage's way of condemning a trust in materialism, for which the modern chariot has become the leading symbol. Yet one cannot be quite sure. The novel ends on a note of tragic finality that is somehow not conclusive in anything but a physical sense.

The style of the book is direct, lucid and (one must say it) sentimental. The effect is an engaging fable of man and boy that is unlikely to restore the novel of sentiment to popularity, although it may win the author some personal converts. For this reviewer, Mr. Savage belies his name too much.

> David Dempsey, "In a Vintage Rolls, a Dream of Escape," in The New York Times Book Review, August 20, 1961, p. 30.

JOSEPH M. BOONIN

While the plot [of *Trust in Chariots*] is in no way extraordinary, the characterizations are finely drawn and the two separate narratives are entwined before the physical meeting of the two unfortunates by the introduction of a Rolls Royce into both plot situations. It is this supreme deity of the automotive pantheon which, in fact, serves as an underlying element throughout the novel. Its significance as a status symbol on the one hand and its unattainability on the other play a not insignificant role in the development of both characters and in the plot line itself. While not of any great literary heights, the novel is written with considerable skill and easily holds reader interest.

> Joseph M. Boonin, in a review of "Trust in Chariots," in Library Journal, Vol. 86, No. 15, September 1, 1961, p. 2820.

ELIOT FREMONT-SMITH

The Power of the Dog, set in the nineteen-twenties, is about two ranch-owning brothers, one reserved, patient and good, the other brutal, destructive and, except for the instance of his undoing, incapable of love. When the good brother marries, the bad one drives his wife to drink. Her young, scholarly, misfit son (by a previous marriage) applies too literally his dead father's admonition to be kind, which is defined, "to remove obstacles in the way of those who love or need you." Guess who's the obstacle.

There is much in this rough, elemental, driving saga to hold one's interest, but it does rumble on too long, and at crucial moments sentimental grandiloquence, growing like a weed,

strangles all possibility of conviction. Yet it does have fine moments, too—effective probings of the wary war between compulsion and intelligence; these ring painfully true, and give the book the substance and drive it has.

> Eliot Fremont-Smith, "Some Expectations Are Too Great," in The New York Times, March 3, 1967, p. 33.*

WILLIAM H. PRITCHARD

In *Trust in Chariots* (1961) Thomas Savage demonstrated his powers at evoking marital disaster and a subsequent mad marvelous junket in a Rolls-Royce across America. *The Power of the Dog* is more unified and builds to a wilder conclusion. Two ranchers, brothers, one clever and uncanny, one dull and decent: the decent one marries a widow whom the clever one persecutes with relentless malice and subtlety. One's liberal sympathies are all with the lovers and their pathetic attempts to entertain the State Governor, improve the clever brother's manners, and domesticate the wild ...; but the troubling questions are asked by clever Phil who reads secrets in the landscape and knows who the heroes are. As for the rest, "Phil saw them as stumbling, fumbling dabblers and wishers and dreamers and except for Phil, that's what they were. How does one man, how does one man get the power to make the rest see in themselves what he sees in them?" Savage has no need to take coyly ironic and knowing attitudes toward his characters because there is so much contempt, hostility, failure of communication built into the exchanges among them. His narrative strength is felt particularly through the oblique, highly stylized beginnings of chapters that move slowly but daringly into the presentations of sequential actions. So a chapter can begin with what seems like an inconsequential time-delaying account of how the family cook's husband was once killed by a tree; move through talk about eating and drinking habits to the wife's own secret and desperate drinking; finally to a confrontation with clever Phil and why he dislikes her.

> "Please tell me, Phil."
>
> He said it before she heard it. She was braced for another pause and instead his voice came. "I dislike you," he said, "because you're a cheap little schemer, and because you get into George's booze." He looked back at the face of his magazine.

It's clear after this that the novel can only end in violence, which it does, but in the presentation of which Savage does not lose his head. As Frost said, pure wildness is not enough; theme alone can steady it down. I know few American novelists, perhaps none so neglected as Thomas Savage ... who give satisfying expression to both claims.

> William H. Pritchard, in a review of "The Power of the Dog," in The Hudson Review, Vol. XXI, No. 2, Summer, 1968, p. 371.

KIRKUS REVIEWS

[In *The Liar*] Hal Sawyer saw his son once, the night Gerald was born.... Hal is the chief liar of the title—a thoroughly decent, thoroughly passive man totally incapable throughout his life of ever living up to the great expectations roused in others at the first glimpse of his grand good looks. A series of small lies to Gerald allowed the boy to believe in Hal's nonexistent success. The alternating stories of the separated father and son are told in tandem here. They finally meet when Gerald is himself a father and the sort of success Hal has never been. What might have been a sentimental story, or depressing had the late confrontation been mutually destructive, is neither. Savage is an excellent storyteller handling through fiction one of the most pervasive, but least openly examined, problems in modern society—the separation of parent and child and how each can be affected by it, the separate fantasy image that can replace and motivate with equal strength the real people involved.

A review of "The Liar," in Kirkus Reviews, *Vol. XXXVII, No. 4, February 15, 1969, p. 201.*

PETER WOLFE

The Liar argues that life is too serious to be taken seriously all the time, and it supports its argument by refusing to take itself seriously. Its flat, spare style and ironical mood give it the detachment it needs to avoid the traps of sentimentality and self-importance. Instead of developing the implications of a powerful scene, Savage will end the scene abruptly, on an ironical note. The device works again and again because of his keen ear, his ability to convey meaning through physical details, and his mastery of indirect statement.

On the surface, nothing extraordinary happens in the novel. The characters do not surprise; nor do they change, through their exertions, the life around them. Most of them work, get married, have children, quarrel with the people around them, get old—and then fade from sight without having grown very much. This pattern of events implies that, for Savage, the most commonplace things are also the most powerful. . . .

The book moves from pain and collapse to health and wholeness. . . . The 7-year-old Hal is beaten in the first chapter by his bedridden parent for refusing to admit to a theft. Innocent, Hal sees that lying would not only have averted the beating, but would have spared his father an exertion that may have hastened his death.

Hal's beating is the first of many incidents that suggest the redemptive nature of lies. A lie will sometimes help us avoid smashing the things people live by. *The Liar* posits a situational, revisionist ethic rather than echoing a received moral imperative. . . .

The novel's energies meet and hold in the final chapter. Hal (whose marriage has long since failed, whose only real achievement is the false-heroic picture he has drawn of himself, in the letters he has written from California to his son Gerald) travels across the country to spend Christmas with Gerald, now a novelist with two books to his credit. Although the New England reunion marks the first meeting of the two men since Gerald's infancy, it becomes the crowning moment of their lives. Hal gives his son love instead of advice; he sees his own thwarted ambitions, both as a writer and family man, realized in Gerald. An imaginative artist, Gerald knows what the moment costs Hal emotionally, so he wisely underplays his father's leave-taking. His restrained good-by sounds the musical note that crowns his life, both as an artist and as a man (lyreliar).

That Savage throws in this moral delicacy offhandedly, establishes the book as a first-rate exploration of inevitability and humane wisdom.

Peter Wolfe, "Where the Father Failed, the Son Succeeded," in The New York Times Book Review, *April 27, 1969, p. 34.*

THOMAS FLEMING

Memo to the Now Generation. Meet Marty, [the title character in *Daddy's Girl*]. . . .

Daddy is a classic example of what passes for thinking in too much of the literary-academic world. We see him only briefly in this profoundly adult novel, injecting into his daughter a philosophy far more fatal than heroin. . . .

"You and I can handle things," Daddy [says] . . . "I must give, and you must give. We must be plastic, always willing to be remolded." Daddy forthwith takes off for Europe, leaving Marty to make a life out of these supposedly beautiful ideas.

An attack on our contemporary problems? By no means. Marty is a child of the 1920's, a college girl of the 1930's—and she tells us, with heartbreaking poignancy, that too many of the ideas embraced by today's young people as the essence of now, the open-sesame to happiness, are neither new nor likely to produce anything for them but tragedy.

But I am moralizing, while Thomas Savage carefully avoids this flaw in telling Marty's story. Savage might be called a novelist's novelist. Western born, he purposely refuses to pursue prevailing fashions; and he seems in the first few dozen pages to be so artless in his storytelling that he cares nothing for technique. Beneath the casual style, there is a serious artist at work, fascinated by the enormous influence of the past on the present.

While he may be accused of simplifying to some extent, he dramatizes this past in the form of an obsession. Not a shallow compulsion, such as Portnoy exemplified, but a fundamental attitude that creates a life style. . . .

In *Daddy's Girl*, Marty, endlessly charming and perpetually amusing, lives out Daddy's commandments. Her version of giving is sleeping around with everyone. . . . Plasticity is achieved by always being at a party or on the way to one, surrounded by a constantly changing swirl of friends. Eventually, the narrator (who fell in love with Marty in college and never quite got over it) realizes that she has never learned another important fact: life is very long, and even the most dedicated swinger will someday run out of gas. . . .

There are some superb minor characters: Savage has a wicked eye for sub-society Boston, where most of the book takes place. Marty's super-square first husband and his lawyer mother are horrors that would drive anyone to drink; the boyfriend with whom she cohabits her way through college is a marvelous parody of an all-too-common type. But the most interesting character after Marty is the narrator, with his stubborn, clearly acknowledged Western prejudices and his constant awareness that the idiots outnumber those with common sense in this world, about 10 to one.

The slow growth of his awareness of what Marty means, both in his own life and as a tragic symbol, is what gives *Daddy's Girl* a positive drive that lifts it beyond social criticism to the realm of serious literature.

Thomas Fleming, "How a 1930 Swinger Ran Out of Gas," in The New York Times Book Review, *October 25, 1970, p. 56.*

ROLLENE W. SAAL

[Thomas Savage's **Daddy's Girl**] is one of those small, beautifully written novels often overlooked. . . . It's a "lost lady" story about cheeky, bright Marty Linehan, whose father deserted her mother, and who muddles through too many marriages and lovers, and far too much liquor, seeking some assurance of her own person-ness. Tenderly narrated by Marty's college friend, now grown to a wry, Jamesian stockbroker, it is the American equivalent of de Maupassant's *Une Vie*.

Rollene W. Saal, in a review of "Daddy's Girl," in
Saturday Review, *Vol. LV, No. 18, April 29, 1972,*
p. 74.

JONATHAN YARDLEY

[*A Strange God*] addresses itself to a question that has vexed people of religious faith—and confirmed more than a few atheists in their disbelief—for centuries. The question crushes in on the novel's protagonist, Jack Reed, after an appalling personal tragedy. . . .

Certainly Jack Reed has every reason to be baffled by the torment that suddenly besets him; nothing in his life has prepared him for it. Now in his 50s, he has made his way from an impoverished childhood to a position of modest wealth and high professional standing. . . . His wife, Norma, is loyal and, by every evidence, faithful; his daughter, Martha, is a vibrant beauty and his son, Tim, is both attractive and intelligent. Even the one small blot on his life—an ardent affair with the wife of a client—does not intrude on the tranquility of his life.

Or at least it does not seem to. For as the affair wears on Jack becomes increasingly possessed by guilt, doubly so when he rejects an opportunity to end it: "And as if it were he who were drowning, he wondered when the waters of punishment, the final offshore wave, would crash in and cover him. Because whatever else he was, he was a man who believed that people do get punished."

When that punishment comes it is far crueler than could reasonably have been expected, for it is imposed upon Jack through his children. Ever since their births, he has believed that his life has been lived for them; he watches in horror as their worlds and his begin to crumble, and as sorrow piles upon sorrow he comes to give up his own will to live.

It is scarcely a cheerful tale, but Savage does not permit himself to wallow in bathos. If at times his prose becomes a bit ponderous, and his irony more than slightly heavy-handed, by and large the writing is clean and forthright. Savage has a good eye for social detail, and as a novel of manners *A Strange God* has much to recommend it. That is especially true of the portrait of Jack Reed. . . . Sympathetically but unsentimentally, Savage portrays his small gaucheries, his fumbling efforts to be socially adroit, his sadly fruitless efforts to steer his children into comforts and securities he himself was denied.

The God who presides over Savage's world can be cruel, but he moves in inexorable ways. Sins do not go without punishment, though whether the punishment fits the crime is at least open to debate. The debate, in any event, is irrelevant, for the destiny that hovers over Jack Reed is beyond his control; on the first page of the novel as on the last, he has no choice but to capitulate.

It is a gloomy theme, but one explored with intelligence and no small amount of wit. Savage is one of those honorable writers who have worked steadily at their craft over many years, gaining a good measure of critical respect but less popular success than they deserve. Whether *A Strange God* will alter the course of Savage's career remains to be seen—I have ceased being optimistic about such things—but like his previous work it deserves serious and respectful attention.

Jonathan Yardley, "The Problem of Job," in Book
World—The Washington Post, *September 1, 1974,*
p. 2.

ROGER SALE

After a number of tries and partial successes, Thomas Savage, America's best kept literary secret, achieved in ***The Power of the Dog*** of 1968 the finest single book I know about the modern west; only some things in Wright Morris can touch it. Savage himself has lived in New England for a number of years, and he has been working all that time to write about that country with the same fullness and assurance he finally gained about the dry country of ranchers. He may still do better than *A Strange God,* but unquestionably in this book he has come very close to a major success. The genre is perhaps best described as Marquand with a sense of doom, and if the fact that the wealthy suburbs around Boston are for him adopted country means that he can never have quite Marquand's assurance about the relation of things and names to status and ambition, Savage can make up for that with a much sterner inquiry into the terms of a life than Marquand was ever led to make. If Savage seems to work too hard at being a namer of parts, he nonetheless can name them quite well indeed, and create a good sense of character as he is doing so. . . . (p. 631)

[Early in the novel, the reader learns that Jack Reed, the protagonist,] had once made a snowplow for his son, and he gazes fondly at it, years later, as he and his wife prepare to leave their expensive house on the Wellesley line. We then learn that Reed intends to go downstairs, out to the garage to start the car, and to commit suicide; the story begins with that pressure on it, and seeks to lead us back to that point, in full knowledge of why the suicide must happen. Jack Reed is from a small town in the midwest, and he manages to discover and develop his talent for listening and remembering so that he becomes John W. Reed, owner of his own insurance agency in Boston. Savage exposes without a hint of satire the concomitants of that rise, the increasingly expensive houses and cars, the attempts to subdue Jack Reed into John W. Reed, and, most important, the investment Reed makes of his own life in the lives of his son and daughter. They will have the best, not just in things but in values; there is a moving sequence where Reed tries to show his son the way the beauty of a dog's loyalty must be tempered by careful discipline, and Reed can only be forceful and the son can't possibly do more than feel the force as force. It is pain and love that Savage seeks to expose, not simple blindness but confusion, and the way they can during the course of a life lead to a need to die when the pathetic wishes Reed has for his children fail to come true. The boy for whom Jack Reed made the snowplow . . . drifts away, partly in disappointment that he does not want what his father wants for him, partly in bitterness at discovering his father one night with another woman. In a carefully but excessively contrived Christmas sequence, Jack Reed shoots his son thinking he is a prowler, and we are brought close to the scene of the novel's opening. Jack Reed is a murderer, however accidental, John W. Reed's insurance business begins to crumble, and Jack doesn't really care, because he feels closer and closer to a

Presence he knows as death. He goes up to the attic, sees the snowplow, and Savage's writing gets up as high as he can possibly get it:

> For with time comes the first inkling and then the conviction that courtesy is not love, nor kindness nor compassion, that lust is common and love is rare except between father and child or mother and child. I want! I want! Marriage was torn between selfishness and generosity. Only from children do we expect nothing, demand nothing, not even understanding. Understanding? What was that?

And "the pathetic disparity between what had been and what was, between what one hoped and what happened" doesn't alter his desire to be done with himself: "It is a very short step between being one of the living dead and one of the dead."

The phone rings just as he is about to step out to the garage. He knows he must never again hear a human voice, he thinks of an awful story he recently read in a newspaper, and he feels the Presence of death has gratifyingly allowed him to escape.... So: "It was John W. Reed who cleared his throat and said: 'Hello?'" The simple pleasure of self-destruction that Jack Reed had moved toward is thwarted by the strange god that made him also be John W. Reed, listener to others, the man who picks up the phone.

It is a stunning climax, and I fear the quotations just can't do it justice because the words allude to so much that has come before. Sadly, too, even in Savage's finest moment there is something wrong. The distinction between Jack and John W. Reed is one Savage works very hard during the early part of the novel to make and enforce, but as Reed's relation to his children dominates the story it is one that seems easily ignored. Thus, as it returns decisively here as the pivot on which turns the discovery that the final punishment for Reed's life will be more life, it seems to come abruptly, unaccountably, playing a larger role than has been created for it earlier. The early and the late parts of the book touch hands at the end, but seem to leave out much of the middle. Still, whatever its flaws, *A Strange God* is that rare thing, a novel of domestic life that seems without extending the bounds of the ordinary to encompass deep understanding of how life is, what makes it happen as it does. If this is to be the climax of Thomas Savage's career, it is a fitting one, in which he can take great and justified pride. (pp. 632-33)

> Roger Sale, "Fooling Around, and Serious Business," in The Hudson Review, Vol. XXVII, No. 4, Winter, 1974-75, pp. 623-35.*

MARTIN LEVIN

In one of P. G. Wodehouse's novels, a character gets considerable mileage out of going up to assorted strangers and saying: "I know your secret." Everybody has *something* he would rather cover up. So it is with radio talk show *compère* Tom Westbrook [in *Midnight Line*]. The star of a Boston station's post-midnight show, Westbrook listens to everyman's agonies on the air but keeps his own past a dark secret. When a caller pops up with "I know who you are"—and really does—he is deeply disturbed. Westbrook is actually the product of a Gopher Prairie kind of town out West, where 36 years earlier he had run out on an innocent but pregnant young girl....

The power of the emotion makes this a successful novel, but the message is somewhat muffled by the medium. Never do we get the bouquet of a bona fide radio station, where it is hard not to run across an occasional engineer, a colleague or a Variety.

> Martin Levin, in a review of "Midnight Line," in The New York Times Book Review, March 14, 1976, p. 32.

THE BOOKLIST

[In *Midnight Line*], Tom Westbrook was the host of a Boston radio program, "Midnight Line," taking calls from anonymous late-night conversationalists and renowned for the insightful, sympathetic, occasionally controversial nature of his replies.... Westbrook is suddenly transfixed by a caller who announces "I know who you are." Savage adroitly contrasts the talkmaster's carefully assembled outer demeanor with the revelations of his confused Montana childhood, a girl in trouble, and an unknown son born out of wedlock. Memorable in detail, the completed portrayal of Westbrook is a stunning depiction of the realities that may lie behind even the most polished facade.

> A review of "Midnight Line," in The Booklist, Vol. 72, No. 16, April 15, 1976, p. 1166.

JONATHAN YARDLEY

To get right to the point, [*I Heard My Sister Speak My Name*] is a beautiful novel. It is the work of a masterful novelist writing at the peak of his form, and it contains a depth of riches sufficient to give every reader pleasure and illumination. It deals with that most universal of subjects, the human family, and it does so in a tone that is leisurely, discursive, elegiac, controlled.

Savage is not a particularly widely known writer.... Like Peter Taylor, Frederick Exley and Doris Betts—all of them brilliant prose stylists with whom Savage is justly ranked—he is held in the most ardent regard by a small group of admirers, but his work has never reached the larger following it deserves. In the opening paragraph of this clearly autobiographical novel he describes himself succinctly and accurately:

> So I will call myself Tom Burton, or Thomas Burton, as the name would appear on the novels I write. I am too difficult for some readers and my sentences are sometimes more than statements. Many readers are comfortable only with the simple sentences, and prefer books that reward a belief in the happy ending and the pot at the end of the rainbow, even as the rainbow retreats and those who follow are footsore. There is no ending, happy or otherwise, only a pause.

It probably would be fatuous to say that *I Heard My Sister Speak My Name* is going to change all that, even though it ought to. There is a limited amount of justice in the literary marketplace, and too little of it is meted out to writers of fiction that is ambiguous rather than declarative, questioning rather than assertive, complex rather than predictable. One suspects from some of the things he says in this novel that Savage would like a commercial success and all the emoluments it would bring, but even in acknowledging as much he persists, stubbornly and honorably, in writing the kind of fiction he does best.

Which is precisely what this new novel is: the best of his ten novels, the capstone of a distinguished and, I think, important career. Perhaps because of its autobiographical overtones it is written with more passion than some of Savage's other books, and it is also more accessible. It touches the reader directly and powerfully; it sticks to the bones.

It is about a woman named Amy McKinney, now middle-aged, who has known since childhood that she was adopted and at last decides to find out who her real parents are, or were. She wants to know her real name and everything that entails. . . .

The name she finds is Burton, and when she first writes to one of Thomas Burton's aunts in the West a chain of recollection and investigation is set off. Gradually Burton peels off generational layer after generational layer, laying the groundwork for the novel's triumphant conclusion.

I'm not going to tell more of what happens because the story contains too many surprises and the reader should not be deprived of the joy of discovering them. They are, of course, quiet surprises, for this is a "quiet" novel. In the best sense of the term it is old-fashioned, concerned as it is with such timeless matters as the continuity of family, the bonds of love, the yearning for roots and identity, the frail and tenuous ties by which we are bound together.

Maybe it's that I've had my fill of novels filled to overflowing with "relevance," with last night's headlines wrapped up in thick blankets of adjectives masquerading as fiction, but this novel seems to me to stand so far above the crowded field of contemporary fiction as to occupy another territory altogether. In no sense of the term is it the work of an elitist writer; it invites the attention, admiration and, I think, affection of any careful and openhearted reader. And any such reader who accepts the invitation will come away from the novel richly and happily rewarded.

> *Jonathan Yardley, "A Stranger to Herself," in* Book World—The Washington Post, *October 30, 1977, p. E8.*

KATHA POLLITT

Narrated by Tom Burton, a novelist one suspects to be a thinly (if at all) disguised portrait of the artist, [*I Heard My Sister Speak My Name*] recounts the efforts of Amy McKinney Nofzinger to trace her parentage and win acceptance from a clan that had never even been aware of her birth. Why Amy should wish to do this is made very clear: raised by insufferably dull Seattle Presbyterians, she has led a placid life that has left her fortyish, divorced, lonely and bored. Not belonging, Mr. Savage tells us, has dried up the sources of Amy's deeper feelings.

The family into which she seeks entrance is Tom's mother's, of course, and it is everything Amy is not: the Sweringens are rowdy, glamourous, tight-knit; owners, at one time, of a vast sheep ranch in Idaho and dominated even after her death by Tom's grandmother, known as the Sheep Queen. Tom is an ardent Sweringen—everything about them fascinates him, even now as he grows into grandfatherhood in Maine. The idea that his beautiful "angel mother" might have had another child naturally appalls him. And why would she have given Amy

away? Although the answer to this question is not very convincing, it does bring about the reunion promised in the title.

As is often the case with family sagas, the best parts of *I Heard My Sister Speak My Name* are the ones most distant in time. The tale of how old George Sweringen discovered gold is stirring indeed, and the Sheep Queen is marvelous, one of those shrewd-eyed matriarchs who so often peer out from Victorian photographs. Her reign has a mythic grandeur. . . . (pp. 26, 28)

As we come down to the present, though, myth yields to a sentimental family piety with disturbing undercurrents. There is real condescension in Savage's portrait of Amy as the prototypical woman in sensible shoes, asking for little and settling for less; as though the life force were the personal property of those who belong, solidly, to large families, like Tom. What Tom shows Amy is the false admiration of the Haves for the Have-Nots who stay in their place, underneath which is a barely concealed relief: Thank God *I'm* not adopted, or I might not be the splendid fellow I am. One quickly becomes suspicious of Tom's paeans to the Sweringens and to his own status as one of them.

How closely can a man have entered into our many-sided, fascinating world if he can say in middle years "I don't know what there is to believe in except Family." Where has he been all his life? Can Tom's obsession with family, complete with falsely rosy Christmases and Thanksgivings, be the result of arrested development? Ultimately, one even wonders if cool commonsensical Amy would like, after all, to be enfolded in the sloppy bear hug with which Tom prepares to embrace her. . . . Being a member of Tom's family sounds like a full-time job. (p. 28)

> *Katha Pollitt, "Looking for a Family," in* The New York Times Book Review, *November 13, 1977, pp. 26, 28.*

ROGER SALE

What is remarkable about [*I Heard My Sister Speak My Name*] is that the story is based on truth. On a local Seattle talk show this past fall, Savage appeared with a sister who spoke his name for the first time when both were in their fifties. Furthermore, readers of earlier Savage novels will recognize many places in this one where he has reworked earlier material. Savage is obsessed by family, "I see now that my belief was not in God or church but in the family and the family's traditions; this belief I hope to pass on to my sons and my daughter because I don't know what there is to believe in except Family." Now, long after he had first set out to tell the wonder and agony of growing up in Montana, he has had given to him a strange true tale to validate his obsession.

The crucial point for Burton-Savage is why his mother gave up her daughter, and why he should care so much. The mother was a beauty, the darling of her father, the dream of her mother, and she went off with Ben Burton, the drummer, because she loved the way he spoke to her and touched her. After whatever it was that led to her giving up her daughter in Seattle, she left her husband and came back to Idaho with her young son Tom and worked at herding sheep and scrubbing floors. Until a single man from Montana, with a ranching fortune, . . . asks her to become the wife her mother wanted her to be all along. Tom grows up adoring her, fearing his stepfather, fearing especially his stepfather's brother. He takes their family name as his own and is mortified when someone in high school whispers to him, "You're name isn't Brewer." Tom Burton always feels not quite legitimate.

Savage himself has always seemed fascinated with names, with precise social information and the problem of getting it right. He lectures us a good deal, often in arbitrary ways, . . . about the beliefs of Episcopalians and Presbyterians, about the way women smoked and drank in fashionable magazines fifty years ago, about the importance of objects in the maintenance of Family, about, God save us, what is left on benches in a Maine post office. . . . The voice that wants to sound omniscient is sometimes in danger of seeming a voice afraid it does not know enough.

But these annoying details are expressive of the same obsessiveness that can make Savage a powerful storyteller. Just as he worries over what works and what belongs, he becomes skeptical and driven when a woman writes claiming to be his sister. Near the end he knows he can accept her only if he also can find out why his mother might have abandoned her daughter on a doorstep. And this he can only speculate about. If she wanted to make some atoning sacrifice for having run away against her mother's wishes, as Savage suspects, this must always remain uncertain. Savage can no longer be a wholly assured narrator. This final obscurity, however, which concedes that the hidden truth may be more powerful than arbitrary clarifying fiction, makes the ending, for me at least, more interesting than it would have been otherwise. (p. 43)

> Roger Sale, "Picking Up the Pieces," in The New York Review of Books, *Vol. XXV, No. 2, February 23, 1978, pp. 42-4.**

ANNIE GOTTLIEB

[*Her Side of It*] is narrated by a fussy untenured teacher at a small New England college, and is his memoir of a more spectacular failure than himself: his friend Elizabeth Phillips, who wrote what he believes are two great novels before she died drunk and broke.

The novel's books-within-a-book structure (the narrator includes his friend's writing within his memoir) is a cumbersome literary device that, in this instance, puts a puzzling distance between the reader and some marvelous memory and observation. It's like a stark Edward Hopper painting in an incongruous gilded frame, for both Liz and the narrator are given annoyingly literary orations before we get down to the narrative proper: the tale of Liz's Montana childhood, her relationship to her dreamy mad father, her Iowa adolescence and the launching of her literary career with a short story based on incest.

The story is told in a style of vigorous elegance, like a mahogany gargoyle newel post in a Midwestern boardinghouse. Mr. Savage tunes in on the voices and brutal snobberies of small-town America with a flawless satiric ear. He evokes with loving contempt the cultural barrenness west of the Mississippi, the longing of the culture-hungry to go East, and the strange attenuation and loss that sets in when they do—a movement paralleling the one from childhood to disillusioned adulthood. Mr. Savage's account of Liz's financial struggles, marriage and decline is believable, but too sketchy and precipitous, and his cynicism is close to vindictive despair. His heart, like hers, seems to lie in the primitive country of hope, forever on the other side of the Mississippi and of age 21. Liz doesn't quite emerge as a fully created character, but remains an alter ego

for the narrator, and perhaps for the author. This is a novel that is less than the sum of its parts. (pp. 14-15)

> Annie Gottlieb, "Three Hapless Heroines," in The New York Times Book Review, *March 29, 1981, pp. 14-15, 35.**

WILLIAM H. PRITCHARD

Mr. Savage is like Wright Morris—I should think they might find each other's work congenial—in his American range— from Montana to Iowa to New England—and in his focus on small-town, domestic life where people get into trouble of one sort or another, often involving alcohol or sex (*The Power of the Dog* was particularly devastating in its sympathetic portrayal of a lonely alcoholic wife on a ranch in the far West). . . . [*Her Side of It* is] the best work he's done in fifteen years. It is narrated by a fairly colorless New England small college academic, on the fringes of tenure, the single great thing in whose life is his relationship with Elizabeth "Liz" Chandler. Her life . . . is told through her own voice, artfully interspersed with the narrator's reflections on hers, and with his own, minor, story. But the voice of Thomas Savage is clearly heard, and always a pleasure to listen to in its chastening truth-telling. . . . The "western" sections of the novel are, as usual, done with much penetration and humorous observation of manners; and, as a novelist of manners generally Savage is excellent, as at ease with "doing" a moment in 1936 or 1948 . . . as from more recent times. The book's strategy of telling the story of an interesting person through a filter who professes not to be very interesting, is of course familiar to readers of Ford or Scott Fitzgerald. And the good thing about Savage's old-fashionedness as a novelist, is that he writes as if Conrad and Ford, and those other technique-conscious tellers from early in this century, still mattered. Early in the book he brought me back to something I hadn't thought about since my own childhood— one of those glass globes given to children at Christmas:

> . . . and as mementos of Christmas they were appropriate; shaking them caused flat, white particles to swirl in a clear liquid: you held a tiny blizzard in your hand. At last the particles settled back to the little earth around a house or a snowman or a bundled-up figure in a sleigh.

When the particles settle in a novel by Savage, nothing revelatory has been announced; only—and that is surely enough— a figure has been seen clear, an "affair" has been rendered. (pp. 169-71)

> William H. Pritchard, "Novel Discomforts and Delights," in The Hudson Review, *Vol. XXXV, No. 1, Spring, 1982, pp. 159-76.**

JONATHAN YARDLEY

For Mary, With Love is a serious, pensive and unfailingly interesting consideration of important themes that weigh heavily on the American psyche: the longing for wealth, position and influence; the tensions between social classes, and the conflicts between "old" and "new" Americans; the desire of women for independence and the compromises involved in obtaining it on terms set by men. It is a less than completely successful novel because of certain difficulties in point of view and tone, and because its central character is almost entirely unsympathetic; but anything that Savage writes is certain to be several cuts above the run of what passes for serious fiction these days, and *For Mary, With Love* is no exception.

Its title, like much else in the novel, is in some measure sarcastic: Mary Skoning is incapable of giving or receiving love. As the story begins she is a teen ager living in the small Illinois city of Villiers, 37 miles west of Chicago, in 1905. Her Danish father is a dour, determined widower with a herd of 50 milk-cows. Mary herself is a creature of eye-stopping beauty in whom "the word 'sex' glowed like a coal ready for the first breath of the bellows." . . .

[After leaving Villiers Academy], Mary moves to Chicago, enrolls at Northwestern, and supports herself modeling fashionable clothing. Upon her graduation she is offered, and accepts, a position tutoring the young son of a coarse but landed couple in Montana. There she meets and marries Hal Bower. . . .

Hal suffers from a degenerative disease, which she had not been told about prior to the marriage. So when Mary decides to leave Hal, she has no difficulty in rationalizing her departure. . . .

Mary sets forth to San Francisco to become the kept woman of a wealthy merchant, Mark Pollinger. . . . She becomes the embodiment of "the woman of fashion of that time—brittle, chic, detached," a person who has liberated herself from "the chains that, through love or moral responsibility or simple kindness, shackle so many." But she has not liberated herself from the tricks that fate plays. She falls in love, or at least thinks she does, with a man named Peter Edwards; she marries him, and thus she shares the unexpected turn of events that traumatically alters his life. At the end, though, there is little reason to believe that she will permit his difficulties to alter her own life for very long.

Mary Skoning Edwards may well be as thoroughly dislikeable a protagonist as exists in American fiction—by contrast Clyde Griffiths, in *An American Tragedy,* seems the cherubic boy next door—and even though she is dislikeable for all the right reasons, her heartlessness makes it extremely difficult for the reader to become engaged in her life. This problem is compounded by the tone of the novel, which upon occasion—usually when Savage is commenting on the wealthy or the socially pretentious—slips from the satiric into the merely sarcastic. And the novel has an inexplicable structural peculiarity: it introduces, in a brief opening chapter, a narrator who thereafter for all practical purposes disappears. We wait for him to make a meaningful or revealing reappearance but he never does, and thus his existence becomes more of a mystery than anything that happens to Mary; if the novel opened with what is its second chapter, it would be much stronger.

Nonetheless, it is quite strong enough to surmount these shortcomings. Savage has a penetrating eye for machinations and hypocrisies, both those of individuals and those of society, and he exposes them remorselessly. He has an equally sensitive eye for the subtle intricacies of family life, a subject about which he writes as well as any American novelist. Over his long and notably productive career he has shown himself to be a writer of real consequence. . . .

Jonathan Yardley, "The Westward Course to True Love," in Book World—The Washington Post, *September 18, 1983, p. 3.*

PETER WOLFE

The bright strains of Americana pealing forth from his new novel *For Mary, with Love,* might well win [Savage] the pop-

ularity he has long deserved. Never in his previous eleven books has he addressed so steadily the question of what it means to be American in the twentieth century. Born . . . in Salt Lake City and reared on a Montana ranch, this longtime New Englander knows America's many faces. *For Mary* recovers brilliantly the canyons, ravines, and sagebrush flats of his youth. It moves easily from the barns, corrals, and bunkhouses of Big Sky country to the most elegant drawing rooms in Chicago and San Francisco. It records the impact of the Great War and the Depression upon both the gentry and the roustabout.

As its title implies, it also shows how women helped both shape and then civilize America's frontier. Savage reminds us that Wyoming elected the first female governor and that the Indian woman Sacajawea guided Lewis and Clark on their legendary westward trek. Imbued with the frontier spirit herself, Savage's title figure, Mary Skoning, journeys 1500 miles from Chicago to the Montana prairie in order to teach school. That she and her female counterparts will often surpass their men in insight, common sense, and compassion is no accident. Savage's attunement to women shows brilliantly in what may be the book's best scene—an encounter between Mary and her lover's wife. Though extending only two pages, the scene, enacted among glittering crystal, china, and linen tablecloths, includes motives of sex, money, family unity, and social etiquette.

The need to maintain grace under pressure doesn't block the flow of emotion coursing through *For Mary, with Love,* a study of the American heart in crisis. Proud and accomplished, wise and independent, Mary overcomes her immigrant origins to change the lives of nearly everyone she knows. While acquiring sophistication along with the material trappings of the rich, she enjoys herself in impeccable style. Yet she can't flee coincidence, the grip of the past, or loneliness. Enjoying the privileges of the elite doesn't dispel her recurring impression of having chosen the wrong path. Thus her American destiny consists of continuous self-creation in the shadow of loss. (pp. 108-09)

Rarely does Savage's language impose artifice between character and event. Perceptive, selective, and poised, it builds mood quickly. Refinement of detail, perhaps his greatest stylistic gift, establishes an early-century ice cream parlor as "round tables and chairs with twisted wire legs"; the prostitutes gathered in a café after finishing a night's work eat clubhouse sandwiches and fried oysters. Economy and inventiveness also generate the simile crowning his description of a hotel lobby frequented by the well-to-do: "The big lobby was laid with white octagonal tiles on which the high heels of women clicked seductively like tiny exclamation points."

The same verbal wit enlivens Savage's pronouncements on subjects ranging from Henry James's fiction to the ethic of the American outdoorsman. Readers of *For Mary* will find their own favorite passages to relish. But they won't find a perfect book. Digressiveness, an occasional archness of tone, and a malicious glee displayed in recounting the setbacks of the elite all mar Savage's case. On balance, though, they amount to a quibble. *For Mary, with Love* embodies the beauty, mystery, and compassion to gain its veteran author the acclaim denied him these past decades. (p. 109)

Peter Wolfe, "From Chuckwagon to Cotillion," in Prairie Schooner, *Vol. 58, No. 4, Winter, 1984, pp. 108-09.*

Gjertrud Schnackenberg

1953-

American poet.

Schnackenberg's two collections of poetry, *Portraits and Elegies* (1982) and *The Lamplit Answer* (1985), display a strong sense of history. She explores such themes as the passage of time and the nature of reality. Rosetta Cohen noted that "much of the delight one derives from [Schnackenberg's] work comes from its capacity to create a limited, ordered universe that transcends, by way of intricate detail, the larger context of the subject itself. The most imposing historical figures—Chopin or Darwin—are reduced to the domestic intimacies of tea sets, backgammon and naps." Schnackenberg's memories of her deceased father, a history professor, also figure in much of her poetry, further illuminating her concern with mortality and human significance in the evolution of world events.

Schnackenberg has received high praise, most notably for her proficiency as a stylist and her mastery of traditional forms. Although some critics detect an unevenness in her work—Geoffrey Stokes observed that in several poems in *The Lamplit Answer* the "rhymes become compulsive and Ogden-Nashian"—most agree that Schnackenberg displays a strong command of her subject and style. Echoing the majority of critical opinion, J. D. McClatchy praised Schnackenberg's "intelligent, resonant, sometimes ravishing way with words."

(See also *Contemporary Authors,* Vol. 116.)

RICHARD HOWARD

All of Gjertrud Schnackenberg's eagerly rhymed and cadenced poems [in *Portraits and Elegies*] are laments, inevitably rising to an elegiac pitch, for her dead father, for Darwin a year before his death, for the dead of the house on Hadley Street. Her imagination of others is knowing, even learned, as in the poem **"Bavaria,"** where Wagner and Nietzsche, Ludwig and Hitler are conjugated into the terrible second-guessing that is her mode—her threnody....

But it is a learning that must serve her turn, literally her versification, a recovery of the pattern made or left by vanished generations, deciduous lives. Almost all the poems are in the vocative case, bound and determined to summon into being those existences of which the evidence is so haunting—the photograph left under stairs, the sampler, the Millerite hysterias of 1843—and so useless. There are one or two moments when the need to make a poem out of the apprehension drowns out the life beneath the words: an overeagerness to rhyme "abandoned garden" with the precipitate "need for pardon." As to the carefully concocted necromancy which is most of this fine first book, the poet is remarkably apt at her spells—she makes us feel the *need* for the formality that brings the dead to life, or rather restores the living to the larger universe in which the dead still live. Reassuring is the thirteenth poem in the cycle tracing the earlier tenants of her Massachusetts abode, **"The Paperweight,"** in which Schnackenberg sees herself not only

as the sorceress holding the glass ball with winter in it but as held by some surrounding sphere of influences as well—the magic is not only her own but that of some agency that contains the little lives, the ardent vanishings.... It is at these instances that the transports function, when the poet acknowledges the work, or even the play, of the wizard to be held within a larger hand.... (p. 344)

Richard Howard, "Poetry Unyoked," in The Nation, Vol. 234, No. 11, March 20, 1982, pp. 342-45.*

DAVID ST. JOHN

[It] is a special pleasure and relief to find a young poet writing in traditional forms who also has in her grasp both powerful subject matter and the intelligence to command her technique. Gjertrud Schnackenberg's *Portraits and Elegies* . . . is an exceptional first book of poems. *Portraits and Elegies* is a book of three poems, two of which are long sequences: **"Laughing with One Eye,"** an elegy for the poet's father, and **"19 Hadley Street,"** a wonderful narrative poem about a house and the lives it sheltered. The book's centerpiece is an affectionate portrait of **"Darwin in 1881"** (a year before his death). This charming poem follows Darwin as, sleepless, he rises for a night walk; reflectively, he and the poem look back over the events of his life, of both the recent and distant past. (p. 239)

The book's concluding sequence, **"19 Hadley Street,"** creates a portrait across time of a prerevolutionary house in which the poet once lived. In drawing its cameos of the past residents (real or imagined, it is unclear) of 19 Hadley Street, the sequence very shrewdly moves backwards in time from its present owner, an unnamed contemporary speaker, to its original owner, one Ebenezer Marsh, in 1725. Punctuating this movement back in time are sections set in the present tense and spoken by the contemporary speaker, sections that juxtapose her life and her reflections with the lives and stories of 19 Hadley Street's past (but clearly, in spirit, still resident) occupants—those "voices rising like smoke from time's wreckage."

What the reader of *Portraits and Elegies* soon realizes is that Schnackenberg is absorbed, in the best sense, with the idea of history and its role in our lives. Whether offering the history of a house or of Charles Darwin (history's own great revisionist), she makes us aware of the *idea* of the past, and of the way a past, a history, resounds within and intrudes upon the present. Nowhere is this more clear than in her book's first sequence, **"Laughing with One Eye."** An elegy for Schnackenberg's father, himself a professor of history, it is a remarkable and powerful poem. The sequence not only envelops the poet's relationship with her father, and her changing views of him as she recognizes his mortality, it also collates into its structure the importance of the father's love for history and his devotion to it: "your filing cabinet / Heavy with years of writing working toward / A metaphysics of impersonal praise." **"Laughing with One Eye"** often resonates with the destructive forces and brutality—the wars, the madness—found in our world history, and it is a world, as she says, thinking about her father after his death, "Where men trying to think about themselves / Must come to grips with grief that won't resolve." And, as she finds in this elegy, private grief is equally difficult to resolve. (p. 240)

> *David St. John, "Raised Voices in the Choir: A Review of 1982 Poetry Selections," in* The Antioch Review, *Vol. 41, No. 2, Spring, 1983, pp. 231-44.**

WILLIAM HARMON

I admire the way Gjertrud Schnackenberg . . . has arranged *Portraits and Elegies*: twelve Father poems gathered as **"Laughing with One Eye,"** a short Darwin poem, and sixteen House poems called **"19 Hadley Street."** Schnackenberg is specific as to person, place, and time. Father is "Walter Charles Schnackenberg, Professor of History (1917-1973)," and House is a local habitation in South Hadley, Massachusetts; Darwin is set in 1881, when he was seventy-two. For all the specificity and particularity, Schnackenberg avoids the merely personal, favoring, instead, poetry in fairly strict forms that permit the location of her voice in various traditions and not so much in one peculiar throat. She can write iambic pentameter in couplets or sonnets, and she can manage with impressive facility the heroic quatrain that has been little used since Gray's "Elegy" and Eliot's travesty thereof in "The Fire Sermon." She can also write a variation of the heroic quatrain, using the *abba* rhyme-scheme of **"In Memoriam,"** as seems fitting in memorial poems for one's father. . . . Schnackenberg says things like "we sensed" too much, maybe: "I see how," "I understood," "I realize." Most of the time, however, she lets the poem and its reader conspire to reach conclusions on their own. In this theater the poet is an usher merely, not a chorus. Schnackenberg chooses her words carefully and alertly, clinching points with effective rhymes or half-rhymes ("Neusch-

wanstein" and "decline," "*Saintes*" and "tolerant," "wilderness" and "Venus"). The one lexical lapse I can find is in **"The Bicyclist,"** in which "peddling" and "peddled" are used in the place that properly belongs to "pedalling" and "pedalled."

Geographical and temporal distance, together with the orthodox verse forms, permits Schnackenberg to be subjective—these are *her* Father and *her* House, after all—without being maudlin or idiosyncratic. Once in a while some homiletic line will draw a Bah, humbug ("death alone makes life a masterpiece," "Knowledge increases unreality"). More often, however, particularly in **"19 Hadley Street,"** Schnackenberg stays away from generality and concentrates on her business. (pp. 458-59)

> *William Harmon, "A Poetry Odyssey," in* The Sewanee Review, *Vol. XCI, No. 3, Summer, 1983, pp. 457-73.**

LINDA GREGERSON

Gjertrud Schnackenberg's limpid versions of prosodic formalism remind us that meter and rhyme are the mnemonics of the universe, a litany of clues to its secret accords and echoes and, by the way, a wonderful alibi for directed rumination. For those gifted with curiosity the labor of fulfilling a contract with form can be the enabling distraction that conditions remembrance and uncovers the structures of understanding. Sometimes memory can be a deceiver: seeking to resolve a poem about pursuing her dead father in a dream, Schnackenberg inadvertently transcribes the final lines of Stanley Kunitz's "Father and Son." But the same sweet solemnity and the same easy conference with inherited forms can also summon up the deeper layers of cultural memory and can lend to a new insight the contours of familiarity—these are the prosodist's real powers and ones with which Schnackenberg is liberally endowed.

Portraits and Elegies does not house the usual miscellany of a first collection; it is as little congenial to randomness of structure as to that of musical form. The book is a triptych: two sequences—one of elegies to the poet's father, one chronicling the many generations of a house in South Hadley, Massachusetts—are divided by an extended portrait of **"Darwin in 1881."** Elegy and portraiture do not distinguish the separate groupings of poems in the book but are rather the reciprocal aspects of its single, retrospective posture. The first sequence, **"Laughing with One Eye,"** interlineates remembrances of the poet's father with moments from the proximate aftermath of his death. **"19 Hadley Street"** traces a reverse chronology back to the early eighteenth century, with discrete returns to the narrator's present tense: so an old man's final illness, for example, precedes his auspicious moment as a bridegroom; a comfortable Sunday dinner between-the-wars gives way to an antebellum debate on the subject of abolition. Darwin's portrait, cast in the year before his death, is erected upon an extended analogy to Prospero's abdication in *The Tempest*. The recollective methods of the book lend considerable poignancy to its individual passages of human happiness and security, of course, but the poems are not backward-looking in the usual sense: they also contrive a robust framework for a comprehension and celebration, what the poet at one point calls "a metaphysics of impersonal praise." The dead father was after all an historian, and this volume is pervaded by his credos as well as his personal presence.

Within her carefully plotted sequences, Schnackenberg's breadth of sympathy accommodates some welcome variations of form and tone. In **"The Meeting in the Kitchen, 1740,"** for example, her habitual pentameter contracts to a four-foot line that mimics the hypnotic chanting of a witch's spell. Here and elsewhere, the poet expends some gentle wit on the credulities of departed eras. . . . But between **"The End of the World, 1843"** and the samplings of eighteenth-century witchcraft, the poet balances a present-day survival of the other-worldly. . . . In such a fashion, the sequencing of poems contrives to set the permutations of belief and experience in dialogue with one another.

In a book of so much sophistication and delicacy, I am hard put to account for the pervasive impression of ingenuousness. Some part of this may be attributed to the unusually frontal quality of so much full rhyme, uncluttered syntax, and repetitive meter (the poet is sometimes rather mesmerized by her iambs), but the effect is also a reflection of the poet's particular exegetical posture. Schnackenberg occasionally posits some recalcitrance on the part of nature or the past . . . , but the world she in fact portrays is one of remarkable legibility, a world of undertows and overtones to be sure, but none of them seriously intransigent, none hostile to interpretation. Before the felicitous conflation of her musical habit and her habits of mind, the world quite magically unlocks itself. (pp. 40-2)

Linda Gregerson, in a review of "Portraits and Elegies," in Poetry, *Vol. CXLV, No. 1, October, 1984, pp. 40-2.*

GEOFFREY STOKES

Three years ago, Godine published a small selection of [Gjertrud Schnackenberg's] poems as part of its limited-edition Chapbook series; *Portraits and Elegies* was extremely well received, and her first major collection, *The Lamplit Answer,* has been widely—almost wildly—awaited since it was announced last fall.

It's very good indeed, but it doesn't entirely live up to expectations. This is, it must be said, only partly Schnackenberg's fault; hopes were simply too high to begin with, and it's silly that a collection confirming her as a major poetic voice—at this point, the most gifted American of her generation—should be a disappointment. But the book also "fails" because Schnackenberg has chosen to include, along with work that will clearly find a place in the canon of 20th century poetry, stuff she virtually admits should have stayed in her desk drawer. The psychological imperatives behind this choice are mysterious, their aesthetic consequences unsettling.

Schnackenberg's genius, the term is not too strong, is precise, playful, and necromantic. All three qualities are evident in the opening poem, **"Kremlin of Smoke,"** an eight-part evocation of Chopin as he reflects on the 1831 fall of Warsaw. (p. 22)

There is magic . . . in the slow reduction of the virtuoso from prodigy to pet, and the poem plays itself out—bravura, "Thunder away like mad! Think big!" Chopin's piano teacher had instructed him—as inevitably as the more recent drama of Solidarity. Relentless, like the czars or the politburo, Schnackenberg rolls past, present, future into a stinging snowball from hell.

The intensity is typical of her best work, but the form much more relaxed. In most of her poems, Schnackenberg is an extremely traditional practitioner of rhythm and rhyme. **"Darwin in 1881,"** for instance, employs a fluid series of quatrains to describe the scientist declining to appear for an honor. . . .

The conceit of the aging Darwin as Prospero is by itself almost enough to sustain a poem; the insignificance of honors to one who's given his life to contemplating species' ends resonates with power—which in turn, with Metaphysical wit, slyly undercuts the poet's own claims to grandeur, and even to knowledge. . . .

In one entire section of the book, however, these gifts—including Schnackenberg's genuinely welcome urge not to take herself too seriously—blow up in her face. A series of ludic love poems turns ludicrous; the rhymes become compulsive and Ogden-Nashian ("Hawaii" and "wah-wah-wah, i.e." fer chrissake), the learning laborious. One senses her going on like a speechifying Hubert Humphrey, manic logorrhea overriding the quiet inner voice saying, "For God's sake, *shut up!*" She knows it, too. In **"Love Letter"** she writes, "Two things are clear: these quatrains should be burned, / And love is awful . . .". . . .

The poem [**"Sonata"**] isn't really all that bad . . . but it should probably have remained private. Certainly, because they represent such a falling-off from the rest of the book, the love poems inadvertently ask whether Schnackenberg needs the cold-eyed distance of history to write compellingly about contemporary life. Publishing **"Sonata,"** and the others in this section, is so stunningly self-destructive that one is almost tempted to admire Schnackenberg's guts, but I think her contumelious unwillingness to take present love as seriously as past may actually be an act of timidity. In any case, "almost" won't do it, and "Thunder away like mad!" is an incomplete instruction—even to a prodigy. (p. 23)

Geoffrey Stokes, "Modern Necromances," in VLS, *No. 35, May, 1985, pp. 22-3.*

J. D. McCLATCHY

Gjertrud Schnackenberg begins *The Lamplit Answer* with a poem about an artist who is grieved that his native Poland has been occupied by Russian troops. It is Chopin, in the frivolous salons of Paris in 1831, thinking of himself as a flower, "an outcome withering from my cause," haunted by old memories of Warsaw. . . . Art is a consolation, but an empty one. Chopin thinks back on his eccentric teacher Zwyny, "the beloved pelican," who held up to him the example of the larks that sing neither in Polish nor Russian. "'And what are their motives for singing?'—turning his hand / Slowly over to empty out nothing—'Precisely none.'" An allegory lurks in the poem, called **"Kremlin of Smoke,"** but is never insisted on. The layering of evocative details and the lulling regularity of the iambic rhythm hold both the poet and her reader back from a more rigorous probing.

In fact, though Miss Schnackenberg is everywhere a formidable versifier, her technique lacks variety; her rhetoric is lush, and she moves through a poem with an elegant gravity. As if to compensate, she has tried to vary the tone of some of the poems in the book by means of a ponderous "light verse." But I do not want to slight, in these days of undernourished or blustering poetry, her intelligent, resonant, and sometimes ravishing way with words. The eight parts of **"Kremlin of Smoke"** are a delicate but pointed interleaving of memories and circumstance. And the best poems in this book work in a similar way. . . .

The Lamplit Answer is a book that shines throughout with a luminous craft and wise reflective sense of culture and its claims on human feeling.

J. D. McClatchy, "Three Senses of Self," in The New York Times Book Review, *May 26, 1985, p. 16.**

PETER STITT

Whether a poem may be considered an object depends upon how one views words. If we recognize the essential reality of a word to be its sound, then that is its objectivity; as an object, a word is a sound. When the word is written down, it is removed one stage away from its essential reality—the symbols on the page comprise an image that stands for the sound that is the word. Further, in terms of their functional reality, words are images meant to represent other objects (or, more properly, other *images of* "objects") that exist within the realm of essential reality. A poem would then appear to be an imagistic complex of individual images intended to represent things that may themselves be only images of things that (may) exist in the realm of essential reality.

This definition would apply best to poems of a descriptive sort—poems, that is, that attempt little more than to reproduce essential reality or its images. Another level is reached when the poet shows some awareness of the questions I have been raising—questions concerning the nature of poetry, the nature of reality, and the nature of our perceptions of "reality." The first type of poetry is relatively simple, perhaps even naïve. The second type can be dizzyingly sophisticated; it can carry the reader into a realm where nothing is certain, where everything—poem, word, image, reality itself—is both relative and indeterminate. Such awareness gives the poet great freedom to do as he or she wishes; the obligation a poet might feel to be true to reality, the obligation to reproduce it accurately, is considerably reduced when the poet questions whether or not reality exists and even whether or not poetry itself is real.

That Gjertrud Schnackenberg is aware of at least some of these issues is demonstrated in her brilliant poem **"Sonata,"** which states its central questions as being: "Theme One: My life lacks what, in lacking you? / Theme Two: Does the material world exist?" (pp. 415-16)

Probably the largest challenge Schnackenberg has set herself in this poem is the blending of the two themes into "chromatic superimposition" until they "unite." How could two so different concerns possibly be brought together? In the [part of the poem subtitled] "Development," the poet begins by finding "Analogies to sort of stack around / My what-is-life-without-you-here idea." ... The analogies are carefully chosen to include the theories of most classical thinkers who worried about the existence of matter or who viewed reality as fundamentally dualistic, with both mind and body components. Moreover, the method of the passage—to separate the thinkers from their thoughts—draws attention to the fact that thinking is a process that depends upon images, not essential realities, for its raw materials.

"Sonata" certainly demonstrates Schnackenberg's ability to write a light, self-questioning kind of verse; by the end of this poem, the reader finds himself wondering not just about the nature of thwarted love but whether the poem itself even exists. Such playfulness of mind—as of technique—is entirely typical of her work in general, though in other poems we find it more

seriously applied. **"Kremlin of Smoke,"** for example, opens the book with these dazzling lines:

> The swan's neck of the teacup, her black vizard
> Plunged underwing, conceals her face like a modest
>   cocotte
> Who can't bring herself to look up at the honored guest,
> As the silver hammer of the tea service practices
> *Chings* in runs of triplets, and the tea steam hangs
> Phantom chrysanthemums on long, evaporating stems
> In the air of the winter apartment.

The syntax of this sentence pulls the reader forward through a headlong tumble of images of ever-accreting complexity. Everything in the passage revolves around the notion of imagery; even the social situation that is described consists of nothing but appearances, poses, "images" meant to becloud the real rather than reveal it. The penultimate image, of nonexistent flowers, is a crowning touch that questions everything else in the passage and the poem.

Near the end of this long poem—which is concerned with certain moments in the life of Chopin—occur lines of even greater theoretical interest. The pianist is advised by his boyhood teacher to "ignore where you are and whomever it is you perform for," as do the

> "Larks, for example—what do they care who deposes
> The King of all Poland? ... "

The larks present an image of the ideal artist, who is to have as little to do with outward, material reality as possible. Not only should he stay out of politics, he should have no motive whatsoever for his art, no axe to grind, no real world to reproduce. As for that real world, a clue to how Schnackenberg would have it dealt with is given in the title to this, her second volume of poems: *The Lamplit Answer.* In addition to portraying words in a dictionary, the phrase draws our attention to the romantic theory of reality, in which nothing exists unless the lamplight of human consciousness is shed upon it. This is a cunning volume, containing poems as objectively beautiful as they are conceptually intriguing. Gjertrud Schnackenberg is a writer of great talent. (pp. 416-18)

Peter Stitt, "Contemporary American Poetry: Does the Material World Exist?" in The Georgia Review, *Vol. XXXIX, No. 2, Summer, 1985, pp. 414-18.**

PHOEBE PETTINGELL

[Gjertrud Schnackenberg's *The Lamplit Answer* is] a second book worthy of its well-received predecessor, her beguiling *Portraits and Elegies* (1982). Like [Amy] Clampitt, Schnackenberg has a religious, metaphysical mind, but she is more of a formalist. Rhyme comes so naturally to her that you would hardly be surprised to find she converses in it. Even in the new volume's opening sequence, **"Kremlin of Smoke,"** a fictional portrait of Chopin, blank verse keeps breaking into rhyme. Most often ... she employs it unaffectedly. ...

Patterns symbolize emotional complexity for Schnackenberg. **"Love Letter,"** about the comic, heartbreaking indignities of being a slave to one's feelings, uses the jaunty rhyme royal of Byron's "Don Juan"—an ironic yet rueful commentary on the same subject. Musing on the impulse to distance ourselves from those we love, she observes: "Tonight the giant galaxies outside / Are tiny, tiny on my window pane."

"Paper Cities" concerns intersections between life and art, and the way they intensify under the pressure of powerful emotions. The poet, reading a collection of Flaubert's letters, identifies her own lover's withdrawal with Flaubert's treatment of Louise, the mistress he neglected for his writing. She envisions Louise raising her eyes from one of the letters to watch clouds that soon float into the poet's world. "My books are towers," she says, "Rooms, dreams whose scenes tangle." Later, while she is reading a fairy tale, a goose feather plucked by a weeping kitchen maid also drifts into the poet's surroundings. Afraid that misery may be destroying her sanity, she picks *King Lear* off the shelf and imagines him as he "sits in his jail, cut to the brains" by his own reverses. . . . The images of **"Paper Cities"** poignantly demonstrate how grief can suppress all other feelings: Everything serves to remind the sufferer of despair.

Schnackenberg possesses a child's ability to wholly absorb herself in whatever she contemplates. **"Advent Calendar"** revives a girlhood memory of paper representations designed to teach children the meaning of this Christian season of anticipation: "Picture boxes in the stars / Open up like cupboard doors / In a cabinet Jesus built," she marvels. The secrets to be revealed behind each door, though, cannot live up to the excitement of expectation. Drawings of ordinary toys, "Wooden soldier, wooden sword . . . Hints of something bought and sold, / Hints of murder in the stars" lead the child to a darker religious mystery—the revelation of a suffering world.

Schnackenberg and Clampitt represent a change in current poetic style. They both recognize a universe of ideas outside their own personal impressions and treat form as an enhancement and delight, rather than a trap. This is not backsliding toward the Modernism that dominated the first decades of the 20th century. These women are true Romantics. But the battles fought by poets in the '50s and '60s against Modernist values need not be taken up again by writers in the '80s. Amy Clampitt and Gjertrud Schnackenberg are two outstanding members of a growing poetic movement devoted to both sound and sense. (p. 15)

Phoebe Pettingell, "Sound and Sense in Poetry," in The New Leader, *Vol. LXVIII, No. 12, September 23, 1985, pp. 14-15.**

Gilbert Sorrentino
1929-

American poet, novelist, critic, and editor.

Sorrentino is recognized almost equally for his poetry and novels and has also gained notice as a critic of considerable insight. His novels are distinguished by their structural experimentation, frequent authorial intrusions, and the inclusion of characters and plots from his previous novels and from the novels of others. Sorrentino's satirical narratives sometimes include lists taken from literature and popular culture, which parody literary styles and critical tastes. His poetry is noted for its formal control; he often writes in such disciplined structures as sonnets, sestinas, and three-line stanzas. Characterized by a lack of narrative and evidencing his conviction that the language of poetry should not inform or contain messages, Sorrentino's verse rejects metaphor, tending instead toward concise diction and specific images.

Sorrentino first gained wide recognition with his fourth novel, *Mulligan Stew* (1979), a comic pastiche of lists, genres, and literary allusions that was both praised and faulted for its verbal extravagance and encyclopedic scope. The imaginative dexterity displayed in *Mulligan Stew* is also evident in his other fiction, as Sorrentino often incorporates elements of his earlier works into his later novels. For example, *Blue Pastoral* (1983), which recounts the protagonists' travels across America in search of the "perfect musical phrase," is a comic reworking of Sorrentino's first novel, *The Sky Changes* (1966), in which a couple journeys across the country in an attempt to save their deteriorating marriage. In *Steelwork* (1970), *Imaginative Qualities of Actual Things* (1971), and *Splendide-Hôtel* (1973), each composed of loosely connected vignettes, Sorrentino uses experimental techniques to explore such themes as the nature of reality, the relationship between reader and text, and the indefinable boundary between truth and fiction. Similarly, *Aberration of Starlight* (1980) retells the same story four times, focusing on the different perceptions of its principal characters; *Crystal Vision* (1981) comprises seventy-eight chapters relating the dialogue of people living in Brooklyn who exchange stories, both real and fabricated, about their pasts; and *Odd Number* (1985) uses various narrative devices to tell the story of a crime that may or may not have been committed.

Sorrentino's first two volumes of verse, *The Darkness Surrounds Us* (1960) and *Black and White* (1964), introduce his characteristic method of establishing a poetic surface devoid of underlying implications. *The Perfect Fiction* (1968) and *Corrosive Sublimate* (1971) further exemplify this approach through their reliance on stark images and objectivity. James Guimond, in a review of *Corrosive Sublimate*, noted: "Sorrentino's hard-edge imagery, his clipped and emphatically declarative syntax—both are means for keeping events at a slight distance even while experiencing them." Sorrentino's experimentation with formal styles is best exemplified by his poems revolving around the unrhymable word "orange" that first appeared in *White Sail* (1977) and were reprinted in *The Orangery* (1978). These variations on the sonnet form, irregularly metered and rhymed, contain the combination of anger and wit that recurs in much of his fiction and verse. *Selected Poems*

1958-1980 (1981) has furthered Sorrentino's reputation as a poet of importance.

Something Said (1984) collects forty-seven of Sorrentino's critical essays. His criticism on the lesser-known or neglected Black Mountain poets has been highly praised, as have his insightful essays on William Carlos Williams and Jack Spicer. Although he covers a wide range of subjects in this volume, Sorrentino was generally praised for the consistency of his critical viewpoint. As Hugh Kenner noted, "There's a unity of mind in this book, not a miscellany of 'pieces.'"

(See also *CLC*, Vols. 3, 7, 14, 22; *Contemporary Authors*, Vols. 77-80; *Contemporary Authors New Revision Series*, Vol. 14; *Dictionary of Literary Biography*, Vol. 5; and *Dictionary of Literary Biography Yearbook: 1980*.)

ROBERT CREELEY

It wasn't so long ago that many of the poets of this country had intentionally and intensively to do with political and social terms common to us all. Whatever their disagreements otherwise, they came together in the integrity of their public commitment. Even now one may regain some sense of those days in Norman Mailer's *The Armies of the Night* with its vignettes of political protest in which the unlikely company of Denise Levertov, Robert Lowell, Ed Sanders, and many, *many* more all stood up and were counted, and took the consequences. Our lives these days have certainly grown quieter, more muted, and the oblique blandness of much of the poetry now written must be an effect of the national temper. Even the proposed emotions seem largely symbolic. (p. 5)

[Gilbert Sorrentino's *Selected Poems 1958-1980*] reads as a remarkable survival of that appetite all those masters had for language, for what one could make, literally, out of words. . . . [Sorrentino's] authority extends equally to the novel (*Mulligan Stew* brought him international acclaim in 1978) and . . . [his] work as a critic (specifically, his unyielding support of the late Louis Zukofsky) was often a daily affair as well as a lifelong commitment.

The physical solidity of this book [of poems], the literal bulk, is a great complement to what Sorrentino has put into it—said simply, *a lot*. Though I have known his work for years, I am fascinated to have so much of it in one ample collection, so that one may see the continuity of his invention, his delight in the toughness, the *humor*, of formal design, the playful echo of those he has loved and used, such as William Carlos Williams. He is here as he imagined all those years ago one might learn to be, and he is very good. (p. 6)

Robert Creeley, "Poetry of Commitment," in Book World—The Washington Post, *August 2, 1981, pp. 5-6.*

HUGH SEIDMAN

The harsh edge of [*Selected Poems*] is clearly not intended to charm. To borrow a term from Baudelaire, a poet whom he invokes, Mr. Sorrentino is a writer of "spleen," and it might be said that he has stubbornly raised cynicism and an allied morality to a high art against the "stupid" world where men are bought and sold . . . or where they have become alienated from their true powers. . . . And he is not timid about his stance: "I am a depressing / man, I write / depressing poems."

But paradoxically, Mr. Sorrentino can expose himself with great vulnerability, risk and sentiment . . . , often through a nostalgia for an irredeemable past energized by the commonplace particulars and lusts of his New York City Italian working-class background . . . and by the more universal concerns of love and death as in the following small poem called "**Anatomy**":

> Certain portions of the heart
> die, and are dead. They are
> dead.
>
> Cannot be exorcised or brought
> to life.
>
> Do not disturb yourself
> to become whole.
>
> They are dead, go down
> in the dark and sit with them
> once in a while.

Here, as elsewhere, feeling conflicts with pessimism, and each provides a convenient restraint and an ironic balance to the other. But Mr. Sorrentino is not interested in motivation so much as in states and possibilities of the "actual." Above, the notion that we cannot change (i.e., "become whole") is immediately stubborn, but see how the word *heart* introduces a deadly serious but satiric pathos that sets us up for the speaker's tragic but transcendent acceptance of the mystery of the irreversible.

Mr. Sorrentino tends to a clear, direct diction and, as a further constraint to excess emotion, he can be rigorously formal. For example, he uses a three-line stanza in every poem in his 1968 volume, *The Perfect Fiction*. . . . Or in *The Orangery*, every poem uses 14 lines like an unrhymed sonnet (although in various stanzaic patterns). . . . (pp. 13, 32, 34)

Matters are further complicated by the poet's disdain of symbol, metaphor, and the mythic and/or surreal courted by many contemporaries: "Behind this world, is nothing. / This world reveals itself completely. . . ." Also, like another poet he invokes, Mallarmé, he seems to honor the "perfect fiction" of composition whereby the poem is a thing unto itself without the need of external justification. (p. 34)

But let us make no mistake; his gesture transcends theory and any idea of art for art's sake. Mr. Sorrentino has a rare gift: he gives us not only poems but excitement. Yet what of those "laughing all the time while life hulks by," who might not share his dark viewpoint? Not that Mr. Sorrentino, the creator, might ultimately care. Is his "arrogance" actually too monotonic or simply sour grapes about fame, sex and money in a society where to be a serious writer is often a mockery . . . ? Whatever the answer, negativity is the aspect of his work most open to criticism. To that one might add the fact that sometimes his formal obsessions overpower content; and like any poet with something to say, he does repeat himself.

Yet what living American poet can equal his particular passion and clarity, when at his best a love and a reverence for the human elevate his vision out of rant into revelation? Bluntly speaking, he is important and unique. His writings possess an almost unassailable moral and artistic integrity, and he has admirably succeeded before the hard test of his own most powerful and inspiring injunction: "Fail, fail if you must but in terms / you are helpless within." (pp. 34, 36)

Hugh Seidman, "Poems and Excitement," in The New York Times Book Review, *November 8, 1981, pp. 13, 32, 34, 36.*

THOMAS LeCLAIR

Crystal Vision is a remarkable work of transparence, both artfully faceted in its construction and vital—full of speaking fossils—in the life it remembers. Crystal, too, because with his micro-minicosm of a Brooklyn block circa 1947 Gilbert Sorrentino predicts a future we recognize as our present, newly understood through the novelist's ball.

Sorrentino, now 52, has been publishing poetry and fiction, mostly with small presses, usually with little recognition, for two decades. In 1979 his Joycean encyclopedia of parody, *Mulligan Stew,* brought him critical attention. Since then, Sorrentino has moved away from high literariness and self-regarding performance to what can be called ethnic experimentalism. . . .

[In] *Crystal Vision,* Sorrentino goes back beyond print and pictures for his models: tribal talk; candy-store gossip, story, and dreaming aloud; the late-afternoon chatter that defines kinship and success in a street-corner civilization. Other ethnic writers—Maxine Hong Kingston, Toni Morrison, Ishmael Reed, Leslie Silko—have returned to ancient oral models to create innovative fiction. Sorrentino unearths Brooklyn discourse before TV and before the Dodgers, with the rest of America, moved to the Southern Rim.

Crystal Vision has 78 short chapters, almost all of them wholly composed of conversations among a central group of six to eight voices and perhaps 20 peripheral figures. Setting is only mentioned; Vogler's store and Pat's tavern are auditory, not visual, space. Stories abound, wonderful anecdotes about futile horse-playing and heroic girl-chasing, family eccentricities and accidents, the daily activities of the under-employed and self-educated; but no single narrative develops as the talk yarns on. . . . (p. 6)

Names, tropisms, and verbal habits recur but in *Crystal Vision* character is composite, tribal rather than personal and bourgeois. Though "The Arab" used to be an auto mechanic and Drummer has an unhappy marriage, their essential experience is belonging to this culture, hearing and being said by other voices. All quotation, the text has no quotation marks, no elegant variations of he says, she says. The dominant illusion is tape, authorially unmediated speech. This is crystal's transparent authority.

But Sorrentino is no Studs Terkel. Crystal is artifice too, magic. Rummy Gene Phillips dresses up as a magician but fails to transform the block into a flowering garden. Here magic is collective and daily, the power of the central group of speakers. They are all men, most middle-aged or older, history-minded: priests. They don't just record their culture; they make it up and revise it day to day. As the novel progresses through its several months, what these elders say increasingly changes the actual world, not the way gossip has effects, but literally, physically, impossibly, and truly. . . . In *Crystal Vision* the vertiginous fun-house effect of much experimental writing by Barth, Coover, and other WASPs finds an appropriate cultural analogue. In their walled block, Sorrentino's people are characters in the on-going, polyphonal story they tell themselves and Sorrentino tells us.

Dramatizing the neighborhood myth-making process, the novel also examines the materials with which these Brooklyn *bricoleurs* create. Movies, as in *Aberration of Starlight,* provide large and stupid images; print, whether the *Daily News* or popular novels, is almost as false. (pp. 6, 8)

Though harsh on manufactured dreams, Sorrentino is more often a comic anthropologist, collector of street wit, repertory routines, and some Bowery Boys antics. Several of his main voices are literary; they are made funny by malapropism, sentiment, or naive responses to pretense. . . . Sorrentino somewhat improbably puts into his dummies' mouths literary parodies, critical apercus, and the lists the author loves. . . .

Kibitzing on each other's stories, the characters raise the objections to his book that Sorrentino chances: "such small slabs of life," "strictly private stuff," "sophistry and cant," "literary bullshit," "fake nostalgia." The criticisms are contradictory (if not quite canceling) because Sorrentino gives up the middle ground of probability to join extremes of verisimilitude and artifice. While his intents may at first be "obscure," and his meanings "crepsular," as "The Arab" puts it, Sorrentino's risky methods work to balance fondness for his folk and recognition of their limitations. Near the novel's end, one of the rare speeches by women extends this recognition of limits to

the suburban society that replaced the neighborhood, the popular culture now purchased instead of heard for free. Looked at and listened to through *Crystal Vision,* the freedom of front yards and machine-delivered messages seems small. Small and quiet. (p. 8)

Thomas LeClair, "Street Corner Society: Voices from a Brooklyn Boyhood," in Book World—The Washington Post, *December 20, 1981, pp. 6, 8.*

J. D. O'HARA

[Gilbert Sorrentino's] novels share a few odd characteristics. They are deliberately not novels, for instance; [the narrator of *Imaginative Qualities of Actual Things*] insists on this repeatedly. He also says that "these people aren't real. I'm making them up as they go along, any section that threatens to flesh them out . . . will be excised." The characters of Sorrentino's later works are equally flat. *IQAT*'s memoir-biography style and [*Mulligan Stew*'s] rehash of *At Swim-Two-Birds* are borrowed and arbitrary forms. The alphabet chapters of [*Splendide-Hôtel*] come from Rimbaud's colored alphabet. [*Aberration of Starlight*] contains several Q & A sections that imitate the next-to-last chapter of *Ulysses* and footnotes from *Finnegans Wake. Ulysses* is also a likely model for Sorrentino's repeated exhaustive recall of song titles, book titles, idiomatic expressions, cliches and commonplaces. And there's a persistent self-conscious self-criticism, budding in *IQAT* and flowering in *Stew,* which begins with twelve parody letters persuasively rejecting the novel. Finally and dismayingly, there are yards and yards of compulsive sex scenes and sex talk as droningly redundant as pornography.

Now comes *Crystal Vision.* . . . Once again we sense Joyce behind the form: a motley crowd of Brooklyn layabouts, from teen-agers to elderly alcoholics, is overheard in a candy store, in bars, on street corners and in letters and soliloquies as they tell stories about themselves, one another and the neighbors. Such a structure—life made economically artificial—might serve for an East Coast *Cannery Row,* a William Saroyan gab fest, a fictional *Our Town* or even a prose *Under Milk Wood.* Sorrentino arbitrarily adds two devices that don't pay their way: characters not present at the storytelling can hear the story and comment on it, sometimes, and a creature called the Magician appears and disappears with no effect at all.

The characters—Richie, Cheech, Professor Kooba, Irish Billy, Santo Tuccio, Doc Friday, the Arab, etc.—talk much like one another, except for the tedious Arab. "A great mechanic who quit for his studies and his wife left him," the Arab misuses language. Example: describing Thelma's leaving Billy, he says that "it was but a moment to the time when she should vocabulate *avatque vali* to Billy." Such japery is unfortunate. No one who can read Catullus is going to garble *ave atque vale* like that, and no one who can't is going to come anywhere near the phrase. The Arab's language is an arbitrary construct with a long pedigree, and its use is to amuse readers by making them feel superior in education and intelligence.

And this is also the use of the characters. They are dolts, as are the characters of the previous novels. But Sorrentino's attitude has changed. Instead of sneering at them as he did in the past, he now patronizes them, finding them and their stories of failure and disappointment kind of sweet. They're all lovable, God bless 'em. *Aberration* ends with a savage quotation from the author of *At Swim-Two-Birds:* "The meanest bloody thing in hell made this world." But *Crystal Vision* begins with a passage from the *Inferno* in which Dante speaks of his great grief at finding in Limbo "gente di molto valore." Sorrentino's characters sentimentalize this grief and this value into "An Elegy Written in a Country Churchyard" sung by an emotional tenor. And, lest the reader not hum along, the story of how many of the characters will die—significantly told in Chapter 13—should draw tears from a turnip. Well, there's a brief list of titles for Professor Kooba's unfinished book and a list of children's candies, but the sex is fairly low-keyed, and on the whole, *Crystal Vision* gestures faintly toward new directions for Sorrentino's fiction.

When one turns from the fiction to the poems—and *Selected Poems* offers approximately 200 of them—one must imagine another Sorrentino, stolen from the cradle and raised . . . by Trappist monks. Gone are the lists, the long sentences, the longer chapters, the subway rush of people and topics and energetic authorial talk! The short lines sigh and fade away, ending weakly in an *of, and, a* or *the*. The short poems fragment, often for no reason, into two-, three- or four-line groups, and they stop modestly short of the page bottom. And they contain minimal amounts of situation, feeling, thought and imagery, expressed in a minimal vocabulary.

Slowly things pick up. **"Shapes of Winter,"** from the second book, achieves length, a variety of voices and some nicely specific images. The third book offers a consistent voice and not a pleasant one. "I am a depressing / man," one poem says, "I write / depressing poems." The cause and a persistent subject is the death of Sorrentino's mother, which darkens this book and the next and recurs in the later works.

In the 1971 collection a long series of poems, **"Coast of Texas,"** reports a country-music I-lost-my-gal story with the addition of underwear and voluntary humiliation. It is followed by two brief poems. **"Old Tale"** conjures up "someone in a limpid tower" of European myth and then ends abruptly: "Here in New York / if she does not love me / then I am not loved" (echoing Samuel Beckett's "Cascando" line: "if you do not love me I shall not be loved"). **"A Poem for My Wife"** says that "certain figures seem to control / the mind," including a distant fair and a prize red hat from it. These poems provide the themes for most of the poems to come: the dead mother, lost women, love and obsessive memories from the distant past.

They all appear in *White Sail* (1977) and in *The Orangery* (1978), where an interest in the color orange first displayed in the *R* chapter of *Hôtel* returns in some thirty-four poems, most of them sour and irritable, that mention orange. The mother also haunts these poems. Over everything hovers what **"A Hit Album"** calls the "dim light / of tragedy" only to amend that description: "Not even tragedy / but the winding down." And as the poetic material grows glummer but more specific and complex, the rhythms grow firmer and the poems stronger. They are still almost entirely personal—one has at times the sense of intruding—but the persona has become more human.

That is not the end, however. *Selected Poems* includes thirty-six new poems. They are longer and more traditionally formal (there's a pantoum and a sestina!); they are mostly written in a loose iambic pentameter, and they combine shifts in diction, allusions—mostly to old pop songs—and nostalgia to produce sentimental and witty commentaries almost entirely free from the poetic and prosaic flaws of the earlier writing. They are extremely pleasant reading, and one wishes that Sorrentino had reached that voice decades earlier. (pp. 20-1)

J. D. O'Hara, "Coteries and Poetries," in The Nation, Vol. 234, No. 1, January 2 & January 9, 1982, pp. 20-1.

HELEN McNEIL

[Gilbert Sorrentino's *Selected Poems 1958-1980* helps] show the extent to which American poetry is still reckoning with the consequences of a decision Ezra Pound made back in 1913. Pound declared that the best way for an American to write poetry in English was to concentrate on the image, to abjure symbolism, and let rhetoric and form follow after. Although Wallace Stevens, T. S. Eliot and Robert Frost found other ways, Pound's solution was to prove the most easily digestible. If Robert Lowell holds little interest for younger American poets, it is not because of Lowell's effort to connect personal and public histories, but because of the mimetic model he used for his diction after *Life Studies*. Today the mainstream is elsewhere, in the post-Poundian line of the image, which has provided American poetry with its short to middle length poetry of quotidian sensibility since the 1950s. . . .

One way or another, it is the tradition of the image which young American poets must accommodate or reject. . . .

In Gilbert Sorrentino's 1971 novel *Imaginative Qualities of Actual Things,* the appalling Lou and his wife are both bad poets who write remarkably like Robert Creeley, leaving lots of white space between their short lines and placing the word "love" in the last one to protect the poem from insincerity and over-intellectualism. Sorrentino remarks scathingly that Lou was

> . . . employing the theory that something that is rotten becomes less so if it is made formally repetitious; and also by polluting the cliché with the addition of out-of-place adjectives. This came from his misunderstanding of Lorca, and Lou was not alone in his ignorance. A National Book Award winner of recent times has achieved his reputation by conscientiously making himself into Lorca with a corncob.

In his *Selected Poems 1958-1980,* Sorrentino struggles to keep his distance from what he calls the "floating cliché" of the consensus tradition and seeks to preserve an avant-garde, bohemian stance against the corn-cobbing academic imitators of true art. But like Robert Bly, Louis Simpson, Robert Pack or any number of mainstream poets whom he may be presumed to loathe, Sorrentino assumes an absolute validity for ordinary reality, arrogates special prerogatives to poets for being poets, and writes in a style which mingles allusions in foreign languages, imagism, and slang. Characteristically, the title of Sorrentino's **"Twelve Études for Voice and Kazoo"** seeks to impress its audience with both knowingness and disarming modesty. Sorrentino is merely disputing the modernist inheritance rather than creating one of his own.

Helen McNeil, "In the Line of the Image," in The Times Literary Supplement, No. 4113, January 29, 1982, p. 113.*

JACK BYRNE

[Though] Sorrentino has said, in reference to *Steelwork,* "I don't feel at all sorry for any of the people in my book. It's the qualities of their lives that I'm interested in, the qualities of their lives within the neighborhood,'' in *Crystal Vision* a new sympathy for his ''Southies'' is evident in the epigraph from Dante:

> Great grief seized me at the heart when I heard
> this, for I knew people of much worth who
> were suspended in that limbo.

Crystal Vision is not a sequel, in my view, to *Steelwork,* not a continuation in the tradition of ''hot'' authors who bore us endlessly with their predictable rehashing of earlier successes. It is, rather, the building upon the notion, not easily arrived at, that characters developed from the author's experience have lives of their own and can call back the author to reconsider their value as literary personae, to re-present them, to give them fuller lives, to justify their existence in the ''ars est longa'' tradition, so fortifying to the humanistic view of man's reason for living the good life. In *Crystal Vision* Sorrentino has seen South Brooklyn as Joyce saw Dublin, as Dante saw Florence, as Homer saw Troy, as Shakespeare saw Renaissance London. He has set his characters in a Brooklyn that resembles limbo, one definition of which is ''a place or condition of oblivion or neglect,'' while another definition describes it as ''an indeterminate state midway between two others.'' What Sorrentino has done in *Crystal Vision* is to continue his observation of these ''ordinary folks'' and the ''qualities of their lives within the neighborhood'' as they exist suspended between Heaven and Hell, but with a difference. In seventy-eight episodes, keyed to the tarot deck, his zany Brooklynites (or perhaps limboites!) exchange memories and fantasies, write and rewrite scenarios of their damaged lives, in an effort to have some control over their miserable existences, as they wait impatiently in the outskirts of Hell (or Hell's Kitchen!) for some final sentencing that will put them out of their communal misery. But unfortunately there is no plea bargaining in Hell or, for that matter, Heaven! The style, humor, and characterization are all on the mark, being directed as they are to the creation of a nether world of unforgettables who have the tools necessary for survival in the world of literature—language, philosophy, a skewed view of life, wit and witlessness, self-confidence to a fault, comradery, lust for life (without the proffered ear!)— a regular commedia dell'arte with a Brooklyn vengeance. (pp. 186-87)

Jack Byrne, in a review of ''Crystal Vision,'' in The Review of Contemporary Fiction, *Vol. II, No. 1, Spring, 1982, pp. 186-87.*

JOHN O'BRIEN

The pastoral has always been a highly conventionalized, artificial literary form which, though its ''content'' was derived from nature, had none of nature's muck and stink soiling the shepherd and his sheep. Invented by the Greeks, its vision and style flowered among Renaissance poets, neo-classicists, and romantics. The chief pleasure of such poetry is formal; that is, seeing what inventions are possible within an unreal world whose strictures derive from literature rather than nature.

Gilbert Sorrentino's *Blue Pastoral* follows the pastoral tradition with a kind of vengeance, twisting and turning the form to comic purposes. As ''someone'' (the authenticity of the narrator remains in question) gently reminds the reader, there *is* a story here which ever so slowly unfolds: Serge (Blue) Gavotte, his wife Helene, and son Zimmerman go west in Blue's quest for the ''perfect musical phrase.'' The itinerary they follow may be vaguely familiar: it is the same journey that the

family took in Sorrentino's desolate, uncomic first novel, *The Sky Changes.* With pushcart and piano (Blue's chosen instrument, fascinated as he is by the fact that both the white *and* the black keys produce music), the trio follows the structure determined for them by another book.

Yet a ''plot'' exists—as it does for Sterne, Rabelais, and the Flaubert of *Bouvard and Pecuchet*—in digression, fabrication, and pretext. If you set characters on a journey (see Chaucer) and if you strip the book of any realistic motive (see hundreds of remaindered contemporary novels), then you have almost endless possibilities for what may happen. So, with the forms and conventions of the pastoral in hand, and the structure of *The Sky Changes* as the map, Sorrentino executes what is, I think, his true plan in this book—an anatomy of language. . . .

Flaubert's ambition was to compose a book without content, and I believe Sorrentino's has been to write a book without an author. The point here is that *Blue Pastoral* is deliberately ''badly'' written. Or to put this another way, each chapter appears to be an exercise in how language is abused, tortured, and made senseless. . . . In brief, *Blue Pastoral* is a kind of catalogue of the ways in which already corrupted language proliferates itself, ending in utter chaos.

Consider one example of how all this works. *La Musique et les mauvaises herbes* is a naughty French novel, produced in full, which Blue reads along the way (as I say, this is a book of digressions). As a naughty novel, it isn't all that naughty, and therefore is a failure as pornography. Which makes it doubly bad. Second, its form is that of the dialogue exercises found in elementary French grammars, those in which one student tells another that the Rhone is a river, and the other student asks if the Rhone is a large river. So, we have that kind of nonsense here. Further, this dialogue is ''translated'' by someone unfamiliar with English idiom, so that it comes out like this: ''I will hit his face off him for an insult of this order. I make insistence that I only can find you jolly with your clothing removed, or pieces of it!'' Yet, as is his wont, Sorrentino uses this French masterpiece as a kind of mirror for what happens throughout the rest of the book; reduced to its content, the story is one of deceit, infidelity, failed desire, frustration, and illusion, which fairly well describes Blue's heroic travels. . . .

When the Gavottes enter the Petrified Forest, the chapter is made of dead or petrified language: passive constructions, vague nouns, wandering pronouns, qualified phrasing, and repetitions. In the end, the language and the mechanics of writing become completely unhinged. The last chapter appears to consist of phrases drawn from the rest of the book, now strangely combined. Lines are missing (but missing from *what*?); and exclamation points, question marks, and sentence fragments fill the pages. Language has gone mad.

In *Blue Pastoral* Gilbert Sorrentino has done what artists always try to do: he has made and shaped a work whose brilliance— in this case comic brilliance—is awesome, pure, and perfectly executed.

John O'Brien, ''Gilbert Sorrentino Tilts at Language,'' in Book World—The Washington Post, *May 22, 1983, p. 5.*

JOEL CONARROE

Try to imagine a slightly eccentric computer that has been fed an anthology of 17th-century British poetry and the complete works of, among others, Swift, Rabelais, Shakespeare, Sterne, Joyce, Céline and William Carlos Williams. The resulting printout might well resemble *Blue Pastoral,* a wild and crazy book, lavishly inventive, full of surprises, sometimes exasperating, often exhilarating.

This narrative could well be called "Blue Picaresque" since such plot as there is involves the adventures of Serge and Helene Gavotte as they drag their pushcart across America in a relentless search for the notes that will constitute the "Perfect Musical Phrase." Gilbert Sorrentino, though, has chosen to have a lark with the conventions of the pastoral mode, employing an archaic diction ("What doth this all portend if it portendeth anything? mused Blue"), introducing a veritable anthology of flora ("the striped anorexia," "that monstrous hollyhock that men, in trembling dread, have dubbed 'Wayne Newton Plant'"), portraying the evils of city life and combining various sorts of prose and poetry—"erotical interlude," dramatic eclogue, elegy, idyll. And why "blue"? For one thing, the hero is called "Blue" Serge, and for another the sheep that appear, as they must in any pastoral worth its wool, arouse, to put the matter as idyllically as possible, some curious passions. This is a ribald book.

It is also a mulligan stew, a paella, a big plum pudding, its 63 quite discrete (and indiscreet) chapters constituting a range of comic ingredients. . . .

Mr. Sorrentino is addicted to catalogues, manic if not Whitmanic, and I half suspect that his novels exist in part as excuses for his ebullient monologues and in part for his mad lists. . . .

The satire is Swiftian, and sometimes it almost goes out of control, the underlying rage threatening to break the bounds of socially acceptable bad taste. It never quite does, though. Moreover, Mr. Sorrentino is democratic about his victims, providing something calculated to offend nearly everybody, not just bigots but also academics, Roman Catholics, WASP's, feminists and even, *mirabile dictu,* book reviewers. He clearly takes a perverse delight in alienating anyone unable to understand (or unwilling to accept) his peculiar mode of savage indignation or to distinguish between what authors say and what they have their characters say. (p. 13)

[Mr. Sorrentino] is particularly funny on academics. At one point he introduces an "Assistant Adjunct Temporary Chairman," at another he produces a medal for "a senior scholar who wears his cardigan with flair" and a scroll for "an administrator who cleans up his cardboard plate, including cole slaw, at faculty galas." Ironically, though, his book is very bookish, depending for much of its humor on familiarity with a wide range of literary references. He especially likes to get things provocatively wrong. Yeats's rough beast slouching toward Bethlehem, for example, becomes "that tough beast in the famous Pennsylvania poem," and Keats's line about a peak in Darien is transformed into Cortez's "pique in old Connecticut." There are dozens of other allusions that provide a small shock of recognition and many, I suspect, that sail right past me.

Blue Pastoral comments self-reflexively, as they say, on its own narrative strategies, in the process taking a jab at some literary theorists: "I suspect that the 'text' is being 'deconstructed' beneath our very feets! Blue muttered. And here, he raised his voice, here I thought that we were in a Novel of Ideas, one invested with a Desperate and Aching significance and a Sadness filled with Smiles." Reading this book, even without deconstructing it, is a strange experience. At times,

laughing too hard to continue, I had to put it down. At other times, put off by some excessively cute wordplay or by one too many sophomoric jokes about hemorrhoids, I was tempted to toss the "text" across the room. Then, encountering another dazzling passage, I would thank my stars for having persevered. (pp. 13, 25)

Joel Conarroe, "Characters on a Course," in The New York Times Book Review, *June 19, 1983, pp. 13, 25.*

VALERIE MINER

Reading the 62 short, flashy chapters of *Blue Pastoral* is like following a neon peacock around in a circle. Occasionally you catch splendrous glints. But the brilliance of the tail/tale is so garishly contrived that you feel silly for having followed this display of sophomoric artifice. *Blue Pastoral* would have iconoclastic potential, if the underlying cynicism were not measured out in such precious pretension.

The novel traces the journey of a musician named Blue Serge Gavotte across these United States as he searches for true art and the meaning of life. . . .

Sorrentino plays with a variety of instruments—esoteric scholarship and punk artifacts—as he attempts to create an engaging saga. He teeters recklessly over the border between the sarcastic and the offensive, the outlandish and the adolescent, the worldly wise and the pompous. The range of accents and language patterns is breathtaking. But since there seems to be more passion for showing off than for communicating, the book emerges as clever lampoon rather than intelligent satire.

Far more worrying than the literary braggadocio is the brutal misogyny and racism exploited as humor. No doubt sophisticated readers are meant to relish the way Sorrentino manages to mock everyone—lesbians, heterosexuals, blacks, Irish, Latinos, Jews. Innocence by association, perhaps. Yet the spittle dries thick and ugly.

His women include the thick-headed Lesbia Glubit, the lascivious "French professor" Suzanne who seduces her students, and Girl Scout leaders whose skirts are ripped by randy plants. . . .

Readers might well ask what these grotesque women have to do with a musician tracking his muse across the country. In fact this caustic cartooning is the focus, as the novel degenerates into a vehicle for the author's derisive wit. . . .

There is an urbane cachet in high camp misanthropy. Perhaps Sorrentino is naive enough to believe that sexist and racist epithets issued by moronic characters are merely mementos of yesteryear. Serious satire, such as that of Swift or Shaw, expresses alternative social vision. Blue Serge Gavotte simply descends into contemptuous surrender. . . .

Ultimately *Blue Pastoral* becomes a hectic performance of a one-man orchestra playing sardonic variations on a banal theme. Sorrentino is a bright, educated man—balancing difficult dialects against obscure notations, addressing readers and reviewers within the text, boldly playing with form. At times his language approaches a Finnegan's wakefulness. But readers, searching for heart in the writing, find all promise dissolved in a jaded self-consciousness. *Blue Pastoral* lends a new vacuousness to the possibilities of virtuoso performance.

Valerie Miner, "Muse for a Musician and Mocking Themes," in Los Angeles Times Book Review, *August 7, 1983, p. 12.*

VALENTINE CUNNINGHAM

[Gilbert Sorrentino's] novels are usually dazzling rosters of technique, colour-cards of style, devoted to demonstrating that novels don't give you reflections of reality but only arrays of verbal structure. *Blue Pastoral* is more of this Sorrentino same.

A rather likeable figure called Blue Serge Gavotte, an experimental musician, sets off across the USA in quest of that musical pastoral, The Perfect Musical Phrase. He never finds it, but his picaresque journey does let him try out numerous possibilities of pastoralia and rehearse whole slates of contemporary rhetorics. . . .

Blue Pastoral is most diverting when it's being directly satirical—reproducing the public styles of professors and broadcast fundamentalists, or letting the more private modes of the politician's arty wife or the black jive-talker negotiate themselves into obvious silliness. But the mass of parodies of ancient pastoral genres, eclogues, georgics, idylls, elegies and such, to which the book's scepticism about pastoral-seeking commits it, is far less fetching. Undoing the Great Tradition of the Novel by page after busy page of sex-talk is all right by me; but the continual reminders that novels are only 'novels' and their people merely 'globs' of 'écriture' (even if they 'did not know this word. Few do') is by now as tired and empty as narcissism inevitably becomes.

> Valentine Cunningham, "Fictional Tricks," in The Observer, *October 28, 1984, p. 25.**

HUGH KENNER

Forty-seven items [in Gilbert Sorrentino's *Something Said*], long and short, brought together: what they called at Los Alamos the assembly of a Critical Mass. So what ensues is a releasing of formidable energy and light. How the pieces draw on and augment one another! Let me illustrate.

Item two is actually seven essays: the things Gilbert Sorrentino had to say about William Carlos Williams, over a span of 21 years. The last of these is a little tour de force, a discussion of one atypical Williams story, "The Knife of the Times," which Sorrentino shows to have been written in three different kinds of dead language. None of these dictions is parodied; they just lie shredded and graceless on the page, to tell "an empty and pathetic story of two human beings caught in a language unfit to assist or relieve them."

That's a powerful critical parable; one point it makes is the inseparability of language and fiction. Later in the book we'll find Sorrentino making wicked fun of John Gardner (**"Rhinestone in the Rough"**), who never seemed to *know* how awful his language was. But right now we confront item three, six pieces about a poet hardly anyone's heard of, Jack Spicer, now 20 years dead. . . . The Williams and Spicer sections total about 50 pages. By paying attention, you can learn a lot about poetry from them.

Page after page and instance after instance, Sorrentino wrestles with the same radical misunderstanding: that fiction and poetry are valuable for what they "tell" us. To rebut that without seeming to exalt empty "style" can be the hardest expository labor in the world. It's a pleasure to watch him perform it, so many times, with such verve.

Williams, Zukofsky, Olson, Rexroth—major names are here. But one test of a critic is skill at detecting the unpublicized, and here Sorrentino especially shines. Paul Blackburn, Hubert

Selby, Coleman Dowell, David Antin—he goes straight to the gist of each. If I were a poet, he's the man I'd want to be reviewed by.

Sorrentino is himself a poet and novelist (*Splendide-Hotel, Mulligan Stew, Crystal Vision*), and you don't live by writing novels in America unless you specialize in manufacturing "good reads." (About an exception, the late Ross MacDonald, he has some penetrating reflections to offer.) So no one sizes up America more mordantly than a serious novelist. And a sub-theme throughout the book is the state of our literary culture: who reads, and what, why, and who doesn't, and how it all stays that way. Sorrentino's essays have appeared for the most part in coterie or short-lived journals: *Kulchur, Yugen, Sixpack, Truck*. These are, by and large, the only places the poets he finds interesting ever do get attention paid them. . . .

"We are dull and torpid," Sorrentino affirms, "and because of this look for writers to tell us that these states are tragic, romanticallly heroic, that our lives are *gloriously* blasted from the start, that our defeats *mean* something. . . ." (p. 3)

"But American life is not tragic; it is dull; its losses are almost silent, inexpressible, obscure." I'd not leave it at that myself, but I can see why Sorrentino does. "Inexpressible," that's a key word. And we're back to the story Williams crafted entirely out of three kinds of cliché, to tell about two people "sealed in misunderstanding and confusion."

There's a unity of mind in this book, not a miscellany of "pieces." (p. 7)

> Hugh Kenner, "Gilbert Sorrentino: A Critical Mass," in Book World—The Washington Post, *February 10, 1985, pp. 3, 7.*

ROBERT PETERS

These 47 essays [in *Something Said*], spread over nearly 20 years and appearing in fairly obscure journals with limited circulations, point up the lamentable fact that few critics writing on contemporary writers are worth reading. Most reviews come off as literary chat/guff, or as lavish, completely forgettable spreads in such conservative journals as Parnassus, The American Poetry Review, Ironwood and Iowa Review. Gilbert Sorrentino is a breed apart.

His criticism has the same qualities of mind and style found in his fiction. He points up trends in current American writing (most of the essays are on poets) and is fearless in his assessments of individual writers. Thus, in very certain terms, he defends Charles Olson: While Robert Frost "retired to those old Vermont woods" and made "vapid comments on some damn fool's wall or tree or pond," Olson was ignored. . . .

His several takes on William Carlos Williams are seminal and show what posterity is coming to reflect, namely, that the good doctor from New Jersey was far more original than all of his contemporaries but Pound and Stevens. Another poet in eclipse is Jack Spicer who, like Williams, revealed "the actual," going far past the cozy imagisms of the day.

Louis Zukovsky, who also ranks high in the Sorrentino pantheon, is ignored by the academies, Sorrentino says, and never taught because his "ideas" are so "inseparable" from his form that he cannot easily be dissected and talked about. . . . Sorrentino's assessment of Michael McClure—that "at his best," he is as good as "anyone writing today"—is not the popular assessment. Neither is his wonderfully barbed assessment of

Marianne Moore. A luminous piece on that much overrated poet of baseball and zoo animals leaves her pinned to the wall and wriggling. Moore was mistress of "the public poem to delight the poetry-hating audience." Her language existed in a vacuum and failed "because she shut out the real." I have waited years for someone to skewer MM. Sorrentino does it.

He writes on several novelists as well—Hubert Selby, Edward Dahlberg, John Hawkes, John Gardner, Ross Macdonald and Paul Bowles among them. The essays on Selby and Dahlberg are first-rate. . . .

Most astute is Sorrentino's description of John Selby's style as it differs from John O'Hara's, F. Scott Fitzgerald's and Nathanael West's. . . .

Something Said is one of those rare collections where the reader finds himself underlining much he wants to remember. It is regrettable only that this gifted man does not have time to write more criticism. How healthy for us all if more novelists and poets would do as he has and seize the ground from the hacks!

Robert Peters, "Sorrentino Speaks," in Los Angeles Times Book Review, *March 3, 1985, p. 7.*

HAYDEN CARRUTH

Writers often like to say that the best critics are writers who do criticism as a sideline because they care about literature, and nearly as often this is wrong. When poets and novelists write criticism, their language is usually dumpy and their discernment usually dim. Yet how splendid the few exceptions! Yeats, Hesse, Ransom, Bogan and others, to say nothing of those still living, one of whom is Gilbert Sorrentino. His novels and poems are extremely fine, and his criticism is no less. Whether he comes eventually to be in the rank of those I have named is more a question of the future reputations of the authors he writes about than of his own abilities.

He writes about the Black Mountain poets. Of course the name no longer means much; it even sounds quaint. But Black Mountain College did exist, Charles Olson was for a time its rector, Robert Duncan taught there, and many of its students were among the foremost young poets of 20 years ago—Robert Kelly, Joel Oppenheimer, Edward Dorn, Jonathan Williams, among others. . . .

Mr. Sorrentino has produced the largest, most intelligent and by far the most readable body of criticism about these writers [and others loosely associated with them] that we possess—essays and reviews done over the last 25 years and published in a variety of little magazines. The present selection, in *Something Said,* is ample yet concise. Many of the reviews are only a page or two, yet when all the pieces on William Carlos Williams, for instance, are added together, they make up a considerable, acute commentary and appreciation. Mr. Sorrentino brings the experience of his own imaginative writing to his readings of other people's books, and thus writes with more understanding than critics who are not themselves poets or fiction writers. But he is also able to step beyond personal taste to the larger processes of the imagination, and to say things that have objective importance; he dares to acknowledge nobility of mind and feeling when he finds it, as in his extraordinary re-reading of Nathanael West's *Day of the Locust.* How unfashionable! Moreover, he is able to distinguish between technique and sensibility, those inseparables, without damaging them, and to show how they function in mutual support.

Does all this sound out-of-style? Certainly Mr. Sorrentino is no post-Structuralist or Deconstructionist, and is not the least interested in using literature as a means toward a theory of social or cultural action, which is not to say that such theorizing may not be important in other contexts. But he is interested in goodness. This means not simply poetry—he has essays on John Hawkes, Larry Woiwode and such lesser-known prose writers as Manuel Puig—but in the truth as it occurs in the poem and in our minds while we look out upon what appears to be our decomposing civilization. He believes that the truth of art is neither idea nor fantasy, but reality, the things of this world brought before us in their unique identities, which are the real values of our existence: things bodied forth in language in such a way that we *see* and *know,* especially evinced in his very brief but pointed remarks on a single metaphor in George Oppen's poem "From a Photograph." If he comes close sometimes to saying that a poem is itself a thing—that great fallacy of modernism, which gave hegemony to the human imagination in a universe where in fact it is adventitious—he skirts this safely in the end, and keeps his attention fixed on our truth, our time, our language.

Hayden Carruth, "Touring Parnassus," in The New York Times Book Review, *March 3, 1985, p. 19.*

PUBLISHERS WEEKLY

There's a certain line beyond which experimental fiction resembles a jigsaw puzzle more than it does literature. This alienating and confusing novel [*Odd Number*] has crossed that line; it's clever, but so narcissistic and self-referential that it virtually shuts the reader out of the narrative. Sorrentino is unquestionably a masterful stylist: the book's three separate dialogues are brilliant exercises in technique. But his tale of adultery, perversion, pornography, blackmail and (perhaps) murder is devoid of characterization. The work has a certain decadent appeal, but even that palls after a while, dragged down by an incoherent, uninteresting plot. . . . Avant-garde experimentation in the service of a larger vision can be rewarding; *Odd Number* is merely taxing.

A review of "Odd Number," in Publishers Weekly, *Vol. 228, No. 4, July 26, 1985, p. 154.*

RICHARD PEABODY

If ever there was a writer destined to portray the information glut and babble of voices that are life in the '80s, Gilbert Sorrentino is the one. He has always been a maverick more concerned with methodology than message, constructing fictions that will never be confused with conventional narratives or drugstore best sellers, and which revel in being as artificial, demanding, and non-referential as possible. In *Odd Number,* his 20th book and eighth novel, Sorrentino investigates yet another formal problem—the disintegration inherent in the investigative process. By calling into question the whole notion of truth, and trust, he manipulates the very nature of facts. Reality is always suspect.

Sorrentino is a master of artifice. He uses gossip, hearsay, innuendo and confession to disrupt communication. In the era of engaged fiction and new realism, Sorrentino—like Walter Abish, John Barth, Thomas Berger and John Hawkes—creates fictions which avoid analysis and instead manipulate language. Sorrentino has always dismissed literature that strives for meaning, for moral, that attempts to reflect the so-called real world.

Like other "metafiction" writers, his novels are self-referential in that he cannibalizes or mines his existing work. . . .

The book is designed as a triptych with each section featuring a different style of voice. The book is recursive and inductive in that each section comments on and draws (or perhaps simply transfers) material from other sections. The voice in the first section is stubborn, the responses drawn out with awkward persistence by the interrogator. (A posed series of questions sets the ground and the reader must infer the rest of the interrogator's questions from the responses.) The voice of the second section is ultra hip (something Sorrentino always derides) and talkative. The halting language and repetition of the first narrator clash with the glib, smooth-talking style of the second. The straightforward last section defuses much of the information we've retained and confuses events and conversations still more. The murder that has apparently taken place at the end of section two appears not to have happened. The final section is in part a refutation of nearly everything that came before. . . .

Odd Number is a cogent demonstration of how writing gets written. The writing process is "a tissue of lies." [Sorrentino's] intention is not to convey a message, though the very forms he commands satirize society in ways that lesser writers belabor. Rarely do you get the sense that the author believes what his characters say, what he's made them say. But throughout the book these characters conduct a devastating assault on critics, artistic pretension, traditional fiction, and phoniness, while undermining every tendency toward "abstract lyricism," Sorrentino's *bete noire*.

Plot is ridiculed (Dr. Plot is "the worst writer the world has ever known"); Sorrentino even includes several variations of the *Odd Number* plot within the text. The "meaning" or significance of language is separate and distinct from human interpretation. Language is an ikon. The integrity of language itself is axiomatic. And that is precisely the point.

Characters frequently wax eloquent on the glory of a particular word or phrase, the sound of it. And one of the real pleasures of Sorrentino's writing is in the apt-sounding but ridiculous book and movie titles he invents—*Hellions in Hosiery, Baltimore Chop, Mouth of Steel, Isolate Flecks, Jog Your Way to Orgasm, Synthetic Ink, I'll Eat Your Eyeballs,* and *Hip Vox*—plus character names like Sol Blanc, April Detective, Horace Rosette, Barnett Tete, Lolita Kahane, Sister Rose Zeppole, Harlan Pungoe, Roger Whytte-Blorenge, Baylor Freeq, Annie Flammard, and Annette Lorpailleur. The novel ends with an open-ended colon, creating a moebius strip feeding back to the first paragraph.

Most of Sorrentino's work has appeared through independent publishing channels. These difficult novels defy labeling, and with the exception of *Mulligan Stew* and *Aberration of Starlight,* have been overlooked by all but the most sophisticated readers. Perhaps this new novel will bring Sorrentino the wider recognition he deserves.

Richard Peabody, "The Funny, the Phony and the Fabulous," in Book World—The Washington Post, *October 20, 1985, p. 10.*

Muriel (Sarah) Spark

1918-

(Has also written under pseudonym of Evelyn Cavallo) Scottish-born novelist, short story writer, poet, dramatist, essayist, biographer, editor, scriptwriter, and author of books for children.

In her work Spark explores such topics as free will, psychological motivations, and moral issues. Much of her writing is concerned with issues pertaining to Catholicism. Her novels typically feature an omniscient narrator who overtly manipulates plot and characters by introducing supernatural or other inexplicable events and actions. According to Frank Kermode, "The suggestion is, in Mrs. Spark's novels, that a genuine relation exists between the forms of fiction and the forms of the world, between the novelist's creation and God's." Spark is praised for her witty, economical prose style through which she skillfully develops complex plots. Her works often center on a small group of well-defined characters whose lives are deeply affected by each others' obsessions. Critics note that Spark's novels are not easily categorized. Shirley Hazzard asserted that Spark "writes to entertain, in the highest sense of that word—to allow us the exercise of our intellect and imagination, to extend our self-curiosity and enrich our view."

Before she began writing novels, Spark published poems, short stories, and several volumes of literary criticism, including studies of Mary Shelley, Emily Brontë, and John Masefield. In 1951 she won the *Observer* newspaper's short story prize for "The Seraph and the Zambesi," in which an angel disrupts a Christmas pageant and chides the participants for commercializing a religious holiday. Spark became a Roman Catholic in 1954, the year in which she began writing her first novel. Her conversion has had a profound effect on her work; she has stated that Catholicism has provided her with a "norm . . . something to measure from" when creating her fiction. Although Spark's works are not predominantly centered on religious themes, they often portray Catholics grappling with moral issues. D. J. Enright noted that Catholicism emerges in Spark's work as "a chastened Christianity not so far removed in matter of this world from the chastened humanism which is the only sort of humanism our age can allow."

Spark's first novel, *The Comforters* (1957), was well-received by critics; Evelyn Waugh called it a "complicated, subtle . . . and intensely interesting first novel." In this work, Spark employs several techniques which recur in her later fiction, including a study of the creative process of art, the use of grotesque and eccentric characters, and the introduction of supernatural elements into realistic settings. In her next important novel, *Memento Mori* (1958), Spark portrays a group of people in order to examine a particular aspect of society. In this work, several senior citizens receive anonymous telephone calls in which someone tells them, "Remember you must die." The message has varying effects on the characters: some gain a renewed appreciation for life, while others feel reinforced in their pursuit of self-gratification. *The Prime of Miss Jean Brodie* (1961) is considered by many to be Spark's most accomplished novel. This work is set at a school for girls in Edinburgh, Scotland—Spark's hometown—during the 1930s. Jean Brodie, a teacher at the school, chooses to nurture and

guide a select group of girls. She attempts to control the girls' lives, eventually causing one of them to complain about Miss Brodie to the school administration. Critics praised the structural complexity of the novel, with its juxtaposition of past, present, and future events, and some compared Miss Brodie's totalitarian personality with fascist dictatorship and authorial control over fictional characters. *The Prime of Miss Jean Brodie* has been adapted for stage, film, and television.

The Mandelbaum Gate (1965), which was awarded the James Tait Black Memorial Prize, is a much longer and more ambitious work than Spark's previous novels. The heroine of this novel is part Jewish and a Catholic convert, like Spark, who travels to Israel and Jordan on a religious pilgrimage. Some critics charged that the book is too long, and in succeeding works Spark returned to the more economical length at which she excels. In *The Driver's Seat* (1970), a woman obsessed with controlling her destiny devises her own death and then seeks a particular type of man to murder her. Obsession is also the theme of *The Abbess of Crewe* (1974), a satire of the Watergate scandal. This work follows a nun's schemes to be elected abbess of her convent.

In her later novels, *Loitering with Intent* (1981) and *The Only Problem* (1984), Spark explores two of her abiding concerns: the relation between fiction and reality and the struggle to sustain belief that God is benevolent. *Loitering with Intent,* perhaps Spark's most autobiographical work, is set in post-World War II London and details experiences in the life of a young woman who aspires to become a writer. Spark develops a network of references to characters who appear in her earlier works and alludes to autobiographies of several other writers, including John Cardinal Newman and Benvenuto Cellini. *The Only Problem* revolves around the biblical story of Job. Harvey Gotham, the protagonist, continues to write a monograph on the book of Job despite a number of personal problems, including the breakup of his marriage and the revelation that his former wife is a terrorist. Gotham, who finds parallels between his life and that of Job, comes to realize that only through suffering can the individual approach a true appreciation of what it means to be alive. Spark also examines terrorism and the average person's fascination with crime.

Spark also explores many of her characteristic themes in her short fiction, an often neglected facet of her career. The publication of *The Short Stories of Muriel Spark* (1985) brought renewed attention to her short fiction. The supernatural and its effect on reality is a dominant motif in many of Spark's short stories, including some of those collected in such volumes as *The Go-Away Bird and Other Stories* (1958) and *Collected Stories I* (1967).

(See also *CLC,* Vols. 2, 3, 5, 8, 13, 18; *Contemporary Authors,* Vols. 5-8, rev. ed.; *Contemporary Authors New Revision Series,* Vol. 12; and *Dictionary of Literary Biography,* Vol. 15.)

PETER KEMP

'One day in the middle of the 20th century I sat in an old graveyard which had not yet been demolished. . . .' Briskly idiosyncratic in its attitude to time, decay and death, the opening of *Loitering with Intent* could only have come from Muriel Spark. What follows is the most intensely Sparkian of her books. Packed with reference to her other novels, it portrays the personality that shaped them. Seeing fiction as the best way of conveying fact, Muriel Spark has written a fictional autobiography.

As usual, aptness dominates the book. 'Have you got everything that is germane?' asks someone. Mrs Spark has made sure that she has. Here, the relevant background is provided by two books: Newman's *Apologia pro Vita Sua* and Cellini's *Life.* . . . 'If one is writing an autobiography,' we're told, 'one should model oneself on the best.' But it's not only for excellence that Newman and Cellini are cited. They link with two important aspects of Muriel Spark's imagination. Newman—the 'tremendous influence' who brought her to Catholicism—taught her to see the world as a panorama of divine economy: the basis of her aesthetic as a novelist. Cellini, with 'his delight in every aspect of his craft', voices another of her central concerns: the euphoria of creativity.

Proust's 'fictional autobiography', very briefly mentioned, is important, too. In her own book, Muriel Spark is searching through lost time for the beginnings of her literary career. As Fleur, her novelist-narrator, looks back at life on London's 'intellectual fringe' in 1949, Muriel Spark re-enters the world of her first novel, *The Comforters.*

Fleur, modelled on Muriel Spark in her post-war, pre-success days, has done a study of Newman and lives frugally in Kensington, writing poems and occasional reviews. Then she finds work at the Autobiographical Association, an organisation ostensibly devoted to helping people write their life-stories. Noticing strong resemblances between characters encountered there and those in the novel she is writing, *Warrender Chase,* Fleur is pleased because this seems to endorse her fictional intuitions. Then life starts not merely to vindicate, but imitate her art: criminally, when someone maliciously plagiarises from her book; uncannily, when he falls prey to the fate she has designed for her protagonist.

Unsurprisingly, with this clenched and guarded writer, no surprises are let out. Fleur says she will reveal 'the secrets of my craft'. But the main impression is of craftiness. Strategic displacements, neat obliquities keep the reader guessing. And what does emerge about Mrs Spark's attitude towards her art is résumé, not revelation. The book recapitulates disclosures made long ago in interviews and articles. . . .

Thinly disguising herself as Fleur, Muriel Spark makes no attempt to modify her usual fictional voice. As is customary, the prose has a constant, crisp originality: 'her acquisitive greed . . . fed my poetic vigilance'. And as usual, too, it is periodically inlaid with bits of Firbankian bizarrerie: 'Mrs Wilks remarked that it was not every woman who had witnessed the gross indelicacies of the Russian revolution and survived, as she had. "It gives one a quite different sense of humour," she explained.'

A recurrent motif in this book is the singing of 'Auld Lang Syne'—an appropriate note to strike, since *Loitering with Intent* continually strays down Memory Lane. Both personally and artistically, it is highly nostalgic. Muriel Spark and Fleur share general resemblances, like their Catholicism, and more local ones: when first seen, Fleur is writing a poem in a Kensington churchyard; one of Muriel Spark's poems is **"Elegy in a Kensington Churchyard"**. The most marked difference between them is that Fleur's take-off into expatriate literary success occurs faster and earlier.

Warrender Chase apart, we aren't shown much of Fleur's novels. *Loitering with Intent,* however, is a compendium of allusions to Muriel Spark's other fiction, an anthology of her customary themes. Blackmail dominates the plot (Mrs Spark has never written a novel in which this does not appear). Treachery abounds. Betrayal comes, once again, from a close acquaintance. Fringe religion plays a prominent role. A critical individual is placed at variance with a conforming group. And Fleur, so keen on spotting affinities, has similarities not only with Muriel Spark but with many of her protagonists. She resembles January Marlow of *Robinson* in her habit of pigeonholing people into types; Dougal Douglas of *The Ballad of Peckham Rye* in that she is an occasional ghost-writer; Freddy Hamilton of *The Mandelbaum Gate* in her taste for formal verses, triolets and villanelles.

Full of intricate connections, *Loitering with Intent* is a fine-spun web of reminiscence. In it, wisps and filaments from previous novels interweave with sharp, fond memories and strong reaffirmations of Mrs Spark's fictional creed.

Peter Kemp, "How Spark Began," in The Listener, Vol. 105, No. 2713, May 21, 1981, p. 684.

A. N. WILSON

Twenty years ago, Muriel Spark had the great misfortune to publish a masterpiece: *The Prime of Miss Jean Brodie,* one of the most perfect novels of the century.... [Miss Brodie] is overwhelming. Could any personality match her? Yes. It is the personality of Muriel Spark.

I do not mean her private personality which is none of our business. I mean the personality which pounces out at everyone who has ever opened one of her novels: the *daemon* that has taunted us, amused and horrified us in endlessly clever and inventive books. Her gift has survived Miss Brodie. Her *oeuvre* since 1961 has been wonderfully various: poems, plays, a brilliant allegory of Watergate (*The Abbess of Crewe*), the disturbingly mythopoeic *The Takeover* as well as novels like the latest, *Loitering with Intent,* which might laughingly be called straight fiction. 'When people say that nothing happens in their lives I believe them,' says the narrator; 'But you must understand that everything happens to an artist'. Of Mrs Spark, this is manifestly true. She has a receptive and wholly distinctive genius which makes everything she writes interesting.

Usually, of course, it would be an insult to accuse a novelist of being interesting. It is not an epithet one would apply to the very greatest novelists, Tolstoy or Balzac or Scott—all of whom can be quite eerily boring in a way no minor writer of stories would dare to be. 'Interesting' automatically suggests fiction of the Second Division: only one step up from 'intriguing', which means, when applied to novels, 'unread, and probably unreadable'.

Nevertheless, Muriel Spark is a very interesting novelist. She never writes the same book twice; and she is not afraid of providing the reader with something interesting to think about.

What could be more interesting than the contrast between Cardinal Newman and Benvenuto Cellini shown by their autobiographies? Newman, as an adolescent, came to the conclusion that there were 'two and only two supreme and luminously self-evident beings, myself and my Creator': a wistful fancy which he could never quite shake off, and which meant he could never be an artist in Mrs Spark's sense of the word. Cellini's *Life,* no less conceited than Newman's, is full of luminously self-evident beings: summoned up by virtue of his artistry. Other people are real to him in a way they were not for the young Newman ('It's quite a neurotic view of life. It's a poetic vision only', as our heroine says); Cellini is so absorbed in the *pleasure* of creating, that 'I am now going on my way rejoicing', a phrase which echoes through this optimistic book like an antiphon. Benvenuto Cellini found release in artistic egotism; Newman's 'neurotic view of life' bred paranoia, a journal entry which could hear 'a thousand whisperings against me'.

All this is so interesting that you might wonder how it could possibly be fictionalised. Would it not be better off in an essay entitled *Fiction and Autobiography*? No, for we would not read such an essay. And, miraculously, a novel springs to life as we read. It is called *Loitering with Intent*.... I found it the most gloriously entertaining novel since *The Prime of Miss Jean Brodie.*

For Cardinal Newman and Benvenuto Cellini only hover in the background, haunting the mind of the heroine, Fleur, who lives in the post-war London which, in a number of her best stories, Mrs Spark has made her own.... Fleur is a novelist, a budding novelist, and she is writing a novel called *Warrender Chase.* She has not fully worked out what it is to be about, but it is to be a masterpiece. Warrender Chase is to be a cruel manipulator of other people's lives, not altogether unlike Fleur's employer, Sir Quentin Oliver.

Sir Quentin has started a thing called the Autobiographical Association....

Our heroine, Fleur, has the job of putting . . . people's memoirs into some kind of order, with the assistance of a rather pathetic woman called Beryl Tims and an odiously devout, but rather sexy woman called Dottie, with whose husband Fleur is having an *affaire,* although he is really homosexual....

[There] would be no point at all in trying to summarise the various strands of the 'plot'. *Warrender Chase* is rejected and suppressed by the first publisher (who is having an *affaire* with Dottie) because the Autobiographical Association have started to gang up on Fleur. The novel is said to be based on 'real life'. Sir Quentin threatens a libel action. But has Fleur been putting 'real people' into her book: or is it that novels are the only way of telling the truth about human nature, so that real life will inevitably imitate *them*? Are we imprisoned in our own egocentricity, or can we, on the viewless wings of art, 'go on our way rejoicing'?

So, as well as exploring the characters of 20 or so hilarious and cruelly-conceived people, we are made to think about the very nature of perception itself, the illusions which enable us to claim knowledge of other minds. We can only see the world in our own way unless we see it through the eyes of great art.

To have this perception, leads, inevitably, to the Newmaniac sense of our own delightful eccentricity: the kind of archness which was Stevie Smith's rather questionable stock in trade....

[Mrs. Spark] shares with Barbara Pym and Iris Murdoch the magical ability to write about people from whom in life we would run a mile, but who are made fascinating by their author's perceptions. Joanna, for instance, the parson's daughter in *The Girls of Slender Means,* was obviously an Excellent Woman in the making. (p. 20)

Many of the figures in *Loitering with Intent* . . . could be imagined in *The Word Child:* the cold grandeur of Sir Quentin, the chaotic lives of his victims, or the misery felt and created by the tiresome Dottie. But although recognisable as the kind of people who interest Iris Murdoch, how different they are here. In the case of both novelists, it is the personality of the author which is crucial to our enjoyment of the book.

Every word of *Loitering with Intent,* arcane, inconsequential and epigrammatic, could have been written by no one but Mrs Spark. 'Why don't you see a priest?' Dottie asks Fleur. 'A priest is a person to see if you fear for your own soul, but not if you are menaced by someone else's, I told Dottie'. The book bristles with such surprises and felicities. 'I found myself vigilant of every detail in Wally's lovemaking, I was noticing, I was *counting*. I was single-mindedly conscious. In desperation I tried thinking of General de Gaulle, which made matters worse, far, far worse. "I'm afraid I've had too much beer", said poor Wally'. It is moments like this which will insure that we keep returning to *Loitering with Intent,* certain that we will 'go on our way rejoicing'. (p. 21)

> *A. N. Wilson, "Cause for Rejoicing," in* The Spectator, *Vol. 246, No. 7976, May 23, 1981, pp. 20-1.*

BARBARA GRIZZUTI HARRISON

[In *Loitering with Intent*] Miss Spark's heroine—a young writer who lives on "the grubby edge of the literary world" in postwar London—muses upon her condition, upon "how wonderful it feels to be an artist and a woman in the twentieth century," and upon the "doings of her days . . . rich with inexplicable life." . . . Fleur Talbot, the heroine-narrator of this novel, is concerned with—and delighted by—the intricate, quirky machinery of the minds and souls of her "marvelous friends, full of good and evil"; "I was aware," she says, "of a *daemon* inside me that rejoiced in people as they were, and not only that, but more than ever as they were, and more, and more."

Such a sentence promises riches, and the promise is amply fulfilled. I read this book in a delirium of delight.

Some of Miss Spark's more recent novels, those that followed *The Prime of Miss Jean Brodie,* seemed attenuated to me (*The Driver's Seat,* for example, and *Territorial Rights*), overly refined, even slightly precious (*The Abbess of Crewe,* for example). Bearing in mind that not every novel by a major writer is a major novel, I felt, nevertheless, that Miss Spark, who lives in Italy, brought to her later books that nostalgia, perversely mated with jadedness, which frequently lends a peculiar drifty quality to novels by expatriates. But in *Loitering with Intent,* which is firmly rooted in a specific time and place, Miss Spark returns to the early flawless form of *Memento Mori* and *The Comforters,* her dazzling first novel. . . .

Loitering with Intent, robust and full-blooded, is a wise and mature work, and a brilliantly mischievous one. It is about a writer's love affair with art—about a writer's purpose and method, about the sources from which an artist draws inspiration. (p. 11)

There are echoes of *The Comforters* in *Loitering with Intent,* which is not to say that Miss Spark repeats herself. In every particular *Loitering with Intent* differs from that first novel. On the other hand, Fleur tells us that after Sir Quentin and his little sect were "morally outside" herself, "objectified," she would write about them for all her life "under one form or another"—"whether I have liked it or not, I have written about them ever since, the straws from which I have made my bricks." I myself love these wheels within wheels, and can think of no other living writer who could set them spinning so merrily.

Questions of art-and-reality aside, the particulars to be gleaned, in rich detail, from *Loitering with Intent* are: What happens to *Warrender Chase*? What happens to the manuscripts of the Autobiographical Association? What happens to Sir Quentin and his band of cultists? What, in fact, is Sir Quentin's ultimate purpose. Who are Fleur's friends and lovers, and how do they greet her carryings-on? What happens to devout Dottie? (I would read this book for its vivid descriptions of life on the "intellectual fringe in 1949" alone—"something like life in Eastern Europe today," Fleur calls it.) To arrive at the answers is to join one's voice to Fleur's: "From there by the grace of God I go on my way rejoicing." (p. 49)

Barbara Grizzuti Harrison, "To Be an Artist and a Woman," in The New York Times Book Review, May 31, 1981, pp. 11, 48-9.

ROBERT TOWERS

Accomplished, successful, and prolific, Muriel Spark conveys an impression of almost insouciant ease where her writing is concerned. In her new novel [*Loitering With Intent*] (her sixteenth!) she assigns these words to her novelist-narrator, Fleur:

> I see no reason to keep silent about my enjoy-
> ment of the sound of my own voice as I work.
> I am sparing no relevant facts.

Now I treated the story of Warrender Chase . . . with a light and heartless hand, as is my way when I have to give a perfectly serious account of things. No matter what is described it seems to me a sort of hypocrisy for a writer to pretend to be undergoing tragic experiences when obviously one is sitting in relative comfort with a pen and paper or before a typewriter.

There is no reason to postulate any great distance between fictional narrator and author in this instance. While one might assume that Muriel Spark is no stranger to the agonies of the creative process, such an assumption must remain the reader's, without reinforcement from either the novelist's interviews or her work. An air of playful disengagement hovers over even so morally severe and "profound" a work as *Memento Mori,* that marvelous anatomy of old age, illness, and death.

Akin to what in the Renaissance was known as *sprezzatura*—an aristocratic "contempt" for one's own productions—this attitude has served the writer both well and badly in her recent work. In a brilliantly faceted novel like *The Takeover* (1976), the offhand treatment of characters and events is integral to her comic vision of the decline and fall of the international rich and enhances our sense of an ornate structure reduced to glittering chaos. In *Territorial Rights* (1979), however, where the bubbling of absurdity is less in evidence, we find something different: a refusal of fictional responsibility that verges on the contemptuous. Characters are simply thrown away at the end, and the annoyed reader wonders why he should care what happens when the novelist apparently doesn't.

Loitering With Intent is a much better book than its immediate predecessor. I had a very good time reading it. But the light hand to which Fleur refers creates certain problems having to do with fictional credibility and commitment within a comic scheme. . . . (p. 45)

The acquisitive nature of the novelist is a major concern of *Loitering With Intent.* "I was aware of a *daemon* inside me," writes Fleur, "that rejoiced in seeing people as they were, and not only that, but more than ever they were, and more, and more." Her novelist's appetite for seeing and appropriating is insatiable. Unpleasant people (Mrs. Tims and Fleur's landlord) and evil people (Sir Quentin) are as much her delight as are colorful eccentrics like Lady Edwina. Even people of weak character, like the members of the Association, are of use to her, but they need touching up in order to achieve the greater truth of fiction. . . .

Thus the novelistic and autobiographic impulses are at odds. The writers of both will take liberties with fact but for different ends. Thus Fleur will tamper with the memoirs "to cheer things up rather than make each character coherent in itself." As a novelist examining the autobiographic impulse, she offers the exuberant, extraverted, and novelistic example of Cellini's autobiography as an antidote to the self-scrutinizing, defensive, and somewhat paranoiac *Apologia* of Cardinal Newman.

Fleur is unscrupulous in behalf of her novel. She will lie and steal. She will make mischief, do "evil," for the sake of the truth she is seeking to establish. Though there is much joyousness in her enterprise, she is also subject to psychic dangers, to the whisperings of paranoia and the temptations of megalomania. Her achievement, finally, is to become a kind of prophet. As an artist she foresees the destinations toward which lives and events are tending; they fall into a prearranged pattern that she has already traced. Is Fleur perhaps a little crazy?

Much of this is interesting—and fun. Clearly Muriel Spark intends us to entertain seriously (as well as be entertained by) the Pirandelloesque confusions of fact and fiction, of autobiographical truth with artistic Truth, as they emerge from Fleur's own memoir. I wish, however, that Fleur's creator had taken more care to make the major premise of the novel—the existence of an Autobiographical Association—as believable, fictionally, as it needs to be. As a device it is too weak to pull very effectively the thematic load attached to it. One longs for a great comic machine, no matter how bizarre, to which the author could commit a full measure of her energy and imagination. Similarly, the figure of Sir Quentin needs, I think, to be made more monstrous, more Tartuffian. As it is, he is little more than the tedious English snob to whom we have been too often introduced. All sorts of evil and sinister motives are attributed to him, but the evidence is inconclusive; his ruling passion remains unclear, and once again we are left to wonder about Fleur's reliability. There is an element of perfunctoriness, too, in the other characterizations. We have encountered obstreperous old ladies and homosexual young men before in Mrs. Spark's fiction, and I am not sure that these new manifestations do more than ring a familiar bell. . . .

These deficiencies, as I see them, would matter much more were it not for Muriel Spark's stylistic aplomb, the constant play of her wit, and above all the inspired creation of Fleur as her narrator-heroine. For Fleur, despite the ambiguities of her makeup, is a true heroine, one who engages the reader's sympathies; we cheer her on. Endowed with liveliness, self-confidence, and a touch of real madness, she is the perfected medium for voicing and enacting the paradoxes that have engaged Muriel Spark's fancy in this novel. She has the energy that the chief plot device lacks; she is the one character whose observations, actions, and imaginings supply the comic brio that sweeps the reader happily past all hesitations and dissatisfactions to the high-spirited finale. It is Fleur who makes me laugh when she warns Dottie not to try to hold on to her errant husband by getting him with child. It is Fleur who mischievously suggests to the pretentious Mrs. Tims that "fluxive precipitations" is the proper term for Lady Edwina's floor-wettings and is then delighted when the phrase catches on. And it is she who sounds the proper note of exultation as the full realization of her magical power as a novelist dawns upon her. . . .

Though she has written three or four of the finest English novels to be published since the Second World War, my impression is that Muriel Spark is taken somewhat for granted these days and that she has received much less critical attention than, say, Iris Murdoch or Doris Lessing. Perhaps that light hand is partly to blame—that, and the exceptional lucidity of her style. She is, of course, a major resource of contemporary British fiction and likely to astound us again with a work as powerful as *Memento Mori, The Prime of Miss Jean Brodie,* or *The Girls of Slender Means.* If *Loitering With Intent* does not achieve that level, it is nonetheless intelligent comedy of a sort that will give more pleasure than nine-tenths of what is acclaimed as good fiction today. (p. 46)

Robert Towers, "Comic Schemes," in The New York Review of Books, *Vol. XXVIII, No. 11, June 25, 1981, pp. 45-6.*

A. N. WILSON

Few novelists have had a surname more appropriate to their particular genius than Muriel Spark, whose brilliant effects fly up like exploding firecrackers and then are lost in blackness. Things have always happened fast in her oeuvre, but in the opening pages of *The Only Problem,* the sparks are flying hotter and faster than ever before. Harvey Gotham, a multimillionaire in his mid-thirties, is living in rural seclusion in France to write a monograph on the book of Job. He is doing so because he considers it the "pivotal" book in the whole Bible, dealing with "the only problem": how a Good God could allow suffering. Every day, Gotham hangs out baby clothes on his washing-line to give village women the impression that he has a wife or mistress. But the jokey explanation he gives for this eccentric habit to his old college friend Edward is that "police don't break in and shoot if there's likely to be a baby inside."

Within a few pages, this bizarre but peaceful scene is shattered. Harvey, having abandoned his wife Effie on the Italian autostrada because she stole some chocolate, has set up house with Effie's baby (by Ernie Howe) and Effie's sister Ruth, who was formerly married to red-headed Edward, an ex-curate turned tearaway successful actor. And, as if that turn of events and jumble of characters were not enough to absorb in a very short space, we learn that Effie has become a member of the Angry Brigade (or Baader-Meinhof), given to crimes of violence, urban revolution and ultimately, the murder of police. She is also, by the way, shacked up with Nathan, who has formerly provided a reassuringly Troilist presence in Ruth and Edward's (remember?) ménage à trois.

The pages of this novella are tightly overcrowded: with persons, with incidents, with change. As a piece of sheer narrative it has as much brio as anything Mrs. Spark has ever written. There is that unmistakably sparky combination of farce and terror as the drama unfolds. When the police come to investigate Harvey's innocent way of life, it all looks very suspicious. His wife is a terrorist. And didn't he make a joke about faking up baby clothes on a line to prevent the police from breaking in and shooting? The press, meanwhile, . . . manages to distort Harvey's studious (not scholarly, as he corrects someone) fascination with the Old Testament into a sinister-sounding form of religious mania. We are soon reading in the papers of the Guru of the Vosges, and Canadian Harvey is described as "Harvey Gotham the American prophet, inveighing against God, who he claims has unjustly condemned the world to suffering." . . . .

But, packed as it is with ideas and incidents, *The Only Problem* does not, in honesty, hang together. The drama which is built up with all the expertise which we should expect from this most elegant of pens, turns out to be melodrama. There is a willful refusal to internalize any of Harvey's sufferings. We have made no progress since the book of Job was written in solving the mystery of suffering, but we have developed narrative techniques (of which Mrs. Spark is the mistress) which enable us to see inside the souls of suffering men and women. This book seems interested only in surfaces. It raises the great questions and leaves them floating in the air. The horrors and the violence of the story fail ever, quite, to be interesting. Excitements crowd upon us, as on the television news. But the television news is not art, and to write a book called *The Only Problem,* which claims to be some sort of meditation on the book of Job in which none of the characters from an internal or imagined point of view *suffers* seems superficial and pointless. . . . There is, at the beginning of *The Only Problem* the noise of ignition and the smell of smoke. But for all the sparks it lets out at the beginning it turns out, alas, in the end to be something of a damp squib.

A. N. Wilson, "Suffering, Salvation and Sex," in Book World—The Washington Post, *July 1, 1984*, p. 4.

ANITA BROOKNER

The only problem for Muriel Spark, it would seem, is that there are many questions for few answers. This is the theme of her new novel [*The Only Problem*], as it may well have been of all her others. Her devoted readers have always been aware that there is a metaphysical component to her fiction, and it is something of a relief that it has at last broken cover in the present work, which is both an extremely sophisticated account of the perils that surround our unsuspecting lives in the world today and a disputation on the subject of the Book of Job, which she calls "the pivotal book of the Bible." Job and his disconcerting predicament challenge every optimistic belief one yearns to accept, lodging like a hard mass of contention in the consciousness of the hopeful believer. The same sort of existential distress is experienced by Mrs. Spark's current protagonist, Harvey Gotham, yet Mrs. Spark is too wise a writer to impose this metaphor on her readers, and her narrative is as seamless, as unnerving, and as expert as her readers have come to expect from this most excellent of storytellers.

For there is, as usual, quite a lot of story to tell. It concerns Harvey Gotham, an extremely rich Canadian expatriate, who has chosen to live in the lodge of an empty chateau near Epinal in the Vosges district of France. Harvey has moved to this retreat in order to work on his monograph of the Book of Job; he has rather absent-mindedly abandoned his wife, thinking himself entitled to do so since he once caught her stealing two bars of chocolate from an Italian supermarket. (p. 1)

The monograph progresses. Harvey works away, occasionally submitting to visits from his brother-in-law, his sister-in-law, and in due course the local police and his lawyer, who is obliged to fly in from London. Harvey is far less interested in these people than he is in Georges de La Tour's beautiful picture of Job visited by his wife in the museum at Epinal; the sight of Job's wife in her glowing red dress, her turbaned head bending in concern and admonition over her tranced husband, awakens Harvey's thoughts of his absent wife Effie, for whom he feels increasing love, and, deeper even than love, "nostalgia." Effie is indeed the reason for all the visitors (or comforters) who descend on him: Effie wants a divorce, Effie takes a lover, Effie has a baby. All of this provokes discussion of the rights and wrongs of the case. But finally Effie's high spirits erupt in a manner particularly favored by Mrs. Spark. From stealing chocolate bars, Effie has graduated to planting terrorist bombs in supermarkets and department stores. Effie has joined the F.L.E., the *Front de la Libération de l'Europe*. A policeman is killed in Montmartre, and Effie's group is responsible. Finally Effie herself lies dead in a Paris morgue, her turbaned head lying bent at the same inquiring angle as that of Job's wife in the La Tour picture in Epinal.

All through the course of the investigations Harvey works away on his monograph. So absorbed is he in his task that he discourses on Job to the reporters who attend his press conference, given ostensibly to explain his wife's disappearance. . . . (pp. 1, 26)

The reporters think he is mad, of course. Perhaps he is. But Mrs. Spark's characters, although frequently mad, are never dishonest. Indeed, they deliver many stunning truths with an impassive eye or a careless smile; fine literary manners are observed in the precision of their speech. Mrs. Spark, whose point of view is frequently inscrutable, shares with these characters a certain freedom from convention that sanctions their excursions into anarchy. The Book of Job and the terrible reversals implied in the Biblical narrative—terrible because it is God who asks the questions and Job who seems to have the answers—are a suitable subject for this fearless and fastidious writer and her thoughtful protagonist. And the dispiriting failure of Job's comforters and Harvey's friends to answer the agonizing questions is somehow bound up with the realization that they are only doing what they have to do; it is in the very nature of friendship to prove inadequate to the demands of prolonged catastrophe. The great achievement of this novel is that Mrs. Spark does not fall into the same trap. No Job's comforter, she, and I doubt if one could pay her a truer compliment than to state this deceptively mild fact.

In all her novels Muriel Spark gives the impression that although she has risen above the problem of evil, the struggle has been great; the effort has left her in possession of a high-spirited despair, a sometimes painful irony—painful precisely because it is effective. One has sometimes yearned for what is not there, as if the victory of overcoming has exacted too heavy a forfeit. At times it has seemed as if the heart of the matter has been excised and only the nefarious transactions recorded. In *The Only Problem* this omission has been rectified. There is emotion here, despair and longing, kept in their place by precise and immediate writing. Perhaps the touchstone for Mrs. Spark's extraordinary style is to be found in a sentence from an earlier novel, *Territorial Rights*. It is said of a character in that novel, "That afternoon she stepped out with the courage of her wild convictions and the dissatisfaction that has no name." Anyone who can appreciate the alarming and beautiful completeness of that sentence will appreciate *The Only Problem*. It is Mrs. Spark's best novel since *The Driver's Seat*, and it is, yet again, a disturbing and exhilarating experience. (p. 26)

Anita Brookner, "How Effie Made Him Suffer," in The New York Times Book Review, *July 15, 1984*, pp. 1, 26.

JOHN UPDIKE

Muriel Spark's writing always gives delight; the sentences march under a harsh sun that bleaches color from them but bestows a peculiar, invigorating, Pascalian clarity. . . . [The protagonist of her new novel, *The Only Problem*, is] Harvey Gotham, a very rich Canadian who has left his elegant wife, Effie, in order to live in a shabby stone cottage in France and compose a monograph upon the Book of Job and the problem of suffering. "For he could not face that a benevolent Creator, one whose charming and delicious light descended and spread over the world, and being powerful everywhere, could condone the unspeakable sufferings of the world; that God did permit all suffering and was therefore, by logic of his omnipotence, the actual author of it, he was at a loss how to square with the existence of God, given the premise that God is good. 'It is the only problem,' Harvey had always said. Now, Harvey believed in God, and this was what tormented him. 'It's the only problem, in fact, worth discussing.'"

Mrs. Spark, she has confided to interviewers, composes her novels in small, lined notebooks that she orders from Edinburgh, where she was once a schoolgirl. A scholastic mood of nicety and stricture controls her sentences; notice, for instance, in the long sentence above, how the second half manages to parse, "he was at a loss how to square" picking up the earlier "that God did permit." Unlike all but a few modern writers, Mrs. Spark uses the verb "comprise" correctly, as synonymous with "comprehend" rather than, as often supposed, with "constitute"—"Love comprises among other things a desire for the well-being and spiritual freedom of the one who is loved." Sentiments so firmly phrased issue steadily from the mouths of her characters, who yet never sound pedantic—merely concerned with main things, and efficient in expressing this concern. (p. 104)

The problem, perhaps the only problem, with Mrs. Spark's novel is that her habit of pithiness squeezes all softness of feeling from her story, and leaves us with a skeleton of plot that dances to little but comic effect. Harvey Gotham is meant to be a modern Job, but he doesn't seem to suffer. He has no boils; his wealth never departs; and his feelings toward Effie, though indicated as belatedly fond . . . , do not affect the rather sulky waiting game he plays. While ensconced in his cottage with his research materials on Job, he is visited by a number of comforters, beginning with Edward Jansen in April, and including by August Edward's estranged wife, Ruth, and an infant, called Clara, whom Effie, while away from Harvey, conceived with a lover named Ernie Howe, "an electronics expert." Ruth persuades Harvey to buy the château on whose property the cottage sits, and by Christmas they are visited there by Nathan Fox, a young, educated, and unemployed man previously attached to the Jansens. As Effie's offstage activities heat up, policemen and a policewoman join the throng, not to mention Harvey's London lawyer and his Auntie Pet, all the way from Canada. Yet, somehow, nothing builds. For instance, Nathan Fox is carefully described at the outset . . . , and one expects he will blossom into one of this author's great leeches, along the lines of Hubert Mallindaine in *The Takeover* and Patrick Seton in *The Bachelors;* but Nathan manifests few machinations and little presence, and quickly becomes, with Effie, an off-stage character. Again, Harvey is said to have developed a fondness for the baby Clara, but she is never shown as anything other than a background squalling, a tiny bundle of greed and noise. Most of Mrs. Spark's characters tend to be such bundles, in varying sizes, and perhaps her overriding message is—to quote Harvey—"the futility of friendship in times of trouble." Her comforters do not comfort, her lovers do not love. And her actors, though she suggests that much of life is "putting on an act," do not, in this book, often act. A number of characters are intently described only to drop utterly from sight. . . . On the other hand, many pages are consumed by stark and repetitive police grilling. So gappy a narrative fabric allows Mrs. Spark's supernatural to peek through; a reality so diminished bespeaks a great Diminisher. Modern Catholic novelists—Graham Greene, Flannery O'Connor, Evelyn Waugh, François Mauriac—commonly present human interplay as unrewarding, as arid, desultory, futile, and often farcical. One answer to "the only problem" which lurks unstated in Mrs. Spark's novel of ideas is that we human reeds are such flimsy, dirty bits of straw we deserve all the suffering we get.

Another answer is offered by Harvey, when he asks himself, "Is it only by recognizing how flat would be the world without the sufferings of others that we know how desperately becalmed our own lives would be without suffering? Do I suffer on Effie's account? Yes, and perhaps I can live by that experience. We all need something to suffer about." This insight comes late in the novel, and presumably represents an advance over his earlier proposal that "the only logical answer to the problem of suffering is that the individual soul has made a pact with God before he is born, that he will suffer during his lifetime. We are born forgetful of this pact, of course; but we have made it. Sufferers would, in this hypothesis, be pre-conscious volunteers." Harvey jeers at the solution to the problem apparently advanced by the Book of Job. . . . That is, God, the creator of Leviathan and Behemoth, Who laid the foundations of the earth and each day shows the dawn its place, will not accept moral subordination to Man; He declines to take instruction from his creature and to be graded by him (A+ for sunsets and flowers, C− for insects and deserts, F for plagues and earthquakes). Expressed non-theologically: existence, including our own, is a mystery, and a critical attitude toward it is not fruitful. The immense notion of Atonement, foreshadowed in Isaiah and enacted in the New Testament, whereby the Creator involves Himself in suffering, does not intrude upon the speculations in *The Only Problem,* nor does the possibility that an afterlife rights all earthly imbalances. The world, for Mrs. Spark as for the whirlwind God of Job, is somewhat bigger than hypothetical balances of justice. (pp. 104-07)

A good and profound novel lies scattered among the inklings of *The Only Problem,* but the author seems distracted and abrupt and to be gazing, often, at other problems. Her first novel, *The Comforters,* alluded to Job in its title and was about distraction and the need to write. The heroine heard a typewriter clacking in her head; so does this novel's closest approach to a heroine, Ruth. . . . Mrs. Spark's last novel, *Loitering with Intent,* overtly concerned the heroine's literary vocation, and the religious issue of vocation underlies much of her fiction, more so than the problems of suffering and belief. Suffering and belief are settled matters; vocation requires an active search. Ruth seduces Harvey into buying the château because a woodpecker outside a bedroom window reminds her of a typewriter. To its happy sound she wakes every morning. We are never out of touch, in a Spark novel, with the happiness of creation; the sudden willful largesse of image and wit, the cunning tautness of suspense, the beautifully firm modulations from passage to passage, the wonderfully blunt yet stately dialogues all remind us of the author, the superintending intelligent mind. Though her characters are often odious, and given so parsimonious a portion of sympathy as to barely exist, the web they are caught in is invariably tense and alive. (p. 107)

John Updike, "A Romp with Job," in The New Yorker, *Vol. LX, No. 23, July 23, 1984, pp. 104-07.*

FRANCIS KING

In its heartless, off-hand wit, the almost contemptuous assurance with which, in a paragraph or two or even a line or two, a character is evoked or an emotional situation described, and the way in which some improbable event . . . is, by some weird legerdemain, made acceptable to the reader, [the first third of *The Only Problem*] provides the kind of sexual comedy at which Muriel Spark has long since shown herself to be an expert. She has, one must confess, done it all better, because more incisively, in the past; but even at her less than best she remains a joy to read.

In the remaining two-thirds of the novel far more sinister things happen. Since Harvey is obsessed with the case of Job, an innocent man inflicted with appalling sufferings because, unknown to him, God has made a pact with Satan, the far-seeing reader will already have guessed that this character is doomed himself to suffer the same kind of fate. . . .

Muriel Spark has always been clever at generating an increasingly inspissated atmosphere of persecution; and, as seemingly trivial and unconnected events in Harvey's past now begin to cohere into what might well become a damning indictment, one feels, for the first time, a real sympathy for a character previously unsympathetic. But in comparison with Job's sufferings, the sufferings of this modern counterpart are altogether too slight and unremarkable. Certainly, it is disagreeable and even alarming for him to be suspected of a crime of which he is innocent; but, throughout, the police remain polite, even protective, he does not spend even a single night in gaol, and he is eventually exonerated. For him to see a parallel between his situation and Job's is fanciful; for the reader to do so, is hard.

The book therefore remains essentially unsatisfactory. Yet, so often slapdash in its writing, sketchy in its characterisation and unconvincing in its plotting, it nonetheless burns its brand deep into the memory. One might best compare it to some scatty woman, dressed in a creased blouse, torn skirt and unpolished shoes, who, against all the odds, somehow, miraculously, contrives to give an impression of authority and elegance.

> Francis King, *"Job Updated,"* in The Spectator,
> *Vol. 253, No. 8148, September 8, 1984, p. 27.*

FRANK KERMODE

Three years ago, in *Loitering with Intent,* Muriel Spark returned to the scene of her extraordinary first novel, *The Comforters,* published in 1957. In *The Only Problem* she is once again looking back: the new book has much to say about Job and comforters, a topic on which, it seems, Mrs Spark once planned a book. Hitherto nothing more had come of the project except an article called **"The Mystery of Job's Suffering,"** which, as it happens, is quoted in *The Only Problem:* Job 'not only argues the problem of suffering, he suffers the problem of argument.' The central figure in the novel, a man called Harvey Gotham, is also working on a book about Job, and he finishes it, as, in a sense, Mrs Spark has finished hers, but thirty years on. . . .

If there were a Spark Notebook, like Henry James's, an imaginable entry [for *The Only Problem*] might run: 'Suppose that in our time some rich man were not only deep in the study of Job but himself in a situation of—well, shall I say discomfort, interested in the vague analogy between himself and his subject? Something might be made of it. Remember Georges de la Tour's *Job Visited by his Wife.*' Between the large general idea and the beautiful and blest nouvelle (which is what this writer does best) lie many questions as to how the thing is to be done, many scenarios perhaps. And in the development of these notions it would seem that the painting played a large part. . . .

It has been remarked that book titles divide roughly into those which specify a story and those which specify a theme: *The History of Tom Jones,* but *Sense and Sensibility.* In this book Mrs Spark, rather unusually for her, names the theme: but it is part of the story that it is Harvey who states the theme in those words, so that the theme becomes part of the story, and the story makes it hard to be sure of the theme. This process of explaining ideas by telling stories, and so rendering them of very doubtful bearing, actually goes back to the beginning, insofar as we know the beginning: for the Book of Job is itself a palimpsest; earlier narrative interpreters had the luck to get their versions absorbed into the original. What James called the single small seed from which stories began might already

have a complex genetic inheritance. Indeed, in the case of Mrs Spark they always do.

Harvey Gotham, whose surname suggests rather unfairly that he is some kind of fool, albeit a rich one, is credited with a certain aridity. Grass grows badly in his neighbourhood, which, at the outset, is a small cottage in France, quite near Epinal where the La Tour picture is. Later he buys the chateau. His sole interest is Job. . . .

Harvey has left his wife Effie, much as he misses her (she bears a striking resemblance to Job's wife in the painting), because she is a hypocrite, a petty thief and wholly selfish. He sleeps with the sister, who strikingly resembles Effie, but his main business is his monograph on Job and The Only Problem as this 'pivotal' book of the Bible presents it. Effie is pursuing him for a divorce settlement, which he refuses; being rich enables one to do some enviably nasty things. Soon the plot takes off. Effie, or so it appears, moves on from stealing bars of chocolate to more serious shoplifting, and then into terrorism. This is a rather characteristic move of the later Spark. She has always been interested, in a chilly, amused way, in the way people snoop, pilfer, spy and pry, but of late she has taken up kidnap, blackmail and urban terrorism as if these were the same things on a larger scale. This is a pity in a way, because it makes for complicated plots, and the best of the books are not over-plotted: but it reflects the temperament of a writer who has said she mistrusts indignant representations of injustice and would prefer 'less emotion and more intelligence' in literature that deals with it. Lack of indignation sometimes looks like sheer pleasure in recording the behaviour of crooks and twisters. Fleur in *Loitering with Intent* enjoys the absurd and the immoral very much and does what she can to augment them.

In this new book the Job business doesn't disappear behind the capers, but a great deal of capering occurs. Harvey, his attention elsewhere, is always complaining that nobody tells him what's going on. Effie's conduct, if the wanted criminal really is Effie, causes him a lot of trouble with the police and the press, but he remains conscious of the fact that he isn't suffering enough to warrant an analogy with Job. . . . Harvey has a theory that we have all entered into a pre-natal contract with God, an agreement to suffer: but distresses aren't suffering, and anyway he is well aware that only God knows the answers. His theodicy is pretty feeble compared with Job's; however, he finishes his book, dealing among other matters with its tragic happy ending.

The aim of the novelist is truth. 'What is truth?' asks the rather Sparkian narrator of *Loitering with Intent.* People telling their own stories, she suggests, may aim at frankness and achieve only falsity. They may even say, credibly, that nothing has happened to them. 'But you must understand that everything happens to an artist; time is always redeemed, nothing is lost and wonders never cease.' The artist manages all this by manipulating fictions, working with *données* that may seem odd but are no odder than God's; his stories are often apparently rather queer, morally speaking. However, his world is true, and so is the world of good fiction.

Mrs Spark's most inspired manipulations tend, I think, to be brief, and four nouvelles, *The Prime of Miss Jean Brodie, The Girls of Slender Means, The Public Image* and *The Driver's Seat,* strike me as the summit of her work, the first two funnier than the others, but the others wonders of a colder, harsher kind. The most brilliant exercise in pure manipulation, showing in a comical way what it is for a novelist to redeem the time, is *Not to Disturb,* which is also brief. The best plots are intense, even slightly paranoid. And—another point in common with James—the fantasy of paranoia may drift plausibly into the fantastic genre of fiction. (p. 10)

The claims I have been making—for the whole oeuvre, I should add—are high, and I do indeed think of her as our best novelist. Although she is much admired and giggled at, I doubt if this estimate is widely shared. This may be because virtuosos, especially 'cold' ones, aren't thought to be serious enough. Another reason is that although we have a special niche for certain religious novels, Mrs Spark's kind of religion seems bafflingly idiosyncratic. In fact, she is a theological rather than a religious writer; when she writes about holy poverty, as in *The Girls of Slender Means,* or about suffering, as she does in this book, she sounds quite unlike a Catholic novelist; and the brilliant inventions of *The Mandelbaum Gate* are concerned with the intellectual aspects of large spiritual issues quite unlike, say, the torments of unworthy priests or of sinners taking the sacrament unshriven, such as Graham Greene used to dramatise. Treachery, adultery, even murder are aspects of the commonplace, and matter only as parts of a world: that is, they are as a rule treated not as sins great and small but as having their value from the parts they play in the paranoid fantasy. When somebody in *Territorial Rights* remarks, 'I don't know why the Roman Catholic church doesn't stick to politics and keep its nose out of morals,' one can't help feeling that part of the joke is that the author would, up to a point, agree.

The author, indeed, inhabits, while writing, a bizarrely serious world, entirely of her making and marked with her mark, which might be on the stainable clothes of *The Driver's Seat* or the stray balloon of *The Public Image* or the 'fluxive precipitations' of the old lady in *Loitering with Intent.* While she is writing, the world itself seems, she says, to behave as she says it does, full of aged people in *Memento Mori* . . . or epileptic bachelors in *The Bachelors.* And no matter what the characters say they all speak in some version of her voice.

This ventriloquial quality (something she does share with another Catholic novelist, Evelyn Waugh) may be another reason why she is not classed with the heavies. It is always, in the end, a monologue we are attending to. . . . From [Mikhail Bakhtin's *Problems of Dostoevsky's Poetics*] we learn that the best novels will be like Dostoevsky's in that they will have 'a plurality of independent and unmerged voices, a genuine polyphony of fully valid voices', and not offer a world 'illuminated by a single authorial consciousness'. . . . Bakhtin illustrates this and many related themes with encyclopedic learning; he is speaking not for the past but for a future in which such novels—'dialogic', non-ideological—will be a principal instrument of human welfare. Mrs Spark is excluded, point by point (by inference, of course), from this tradition. If we wanted to construct a rival tradition on similar lines we should have to choose Ben Jonson as an English precursor, full of humours yet essentially 'monologic'. Bakhtin detests what he calls 'finalisable' characters; Mrs Spark's are all finalised, by her, as we all are by God. Of course the antithesis isn't absolute, for Spark is very much the kind of writer Bakhtin calls 'seriocomic' and certainly has a quality he thought essential—namely, 'a carnival sense of the world'. He thinks that carnival promotes the dialogic: yet it is the inversion of a monologic order, and that, in the end, is how Mrs Spark treats it.

The carnival in these books actually proceeds from the technique of humours; Miss Brodie is the most famous instance, for she is identified by tricks of speech and carnivalises her

school. In *The Only Problem* Harvey, worried about leviathan and behemoth, asks his brother-in-law to visit the Zoo and check the eyes of crocodiles. In reporting back, this man remarks that he found the Zoo boring 'to a degree'. 'What degree?' asks Harvey; and the little odd pedantry is his own but also his author's. 'I see no reason,' says the young woman author in *Loitering,* 'to keep silence about my enjoyment of the sound of my own voice as I work.' She is, after all, conveying 'ideas of truth and wonder'. So, no doubt, was Dostoevsky, only the method is different. He would not have said that people were the 'straws from which I make my bricks'. He wouldn't have said, either, that the world simply complied with his fantasy. . . . (pp. 10-11)

The suggestion is not, certainly not, that Dostoevsky never experienced the grace beyond the reach of art. Perhaps for him also it was a matter of daily or weekly proof that when he sat down to write the obedient world arranged itself accordingly. But there are various ways of accepting this grace. Think of the fascinatingly ample, comic opening of *The Possessed,* full of grace on one view, a very slow run-up on the other; and then of the totally mastered world of Mrs Spark's nouvelles. Bakhtin chooses one, very plausibly; Henry James, the patron of *doing,* might choose the other. But of course the notion of necessary choice is absurd. (p. 11)

Frank Kermode, "Old Testament Capers," in London Review of Books, *Vol. 6, No. 17, September 20 to October 3, 1984, pp. 10-11.*

MICHIKO KAKUTANI

"I treated the story," says the narrator of one of Muriel Spark's recent novels, "with a light and heartless hand, as is my way when I have to give a perfectly serious account of things." It is a perfect description, of course, of Mrs. Spark's own adamantine style, and nowhere is that style more in evidence than in [the collection *The Stories of Muriel Spark*]. Indeed, these tales serve as a kind of magnifying glass, heightening the distinctive qualities of Mrs. Spark's work: her cool, precise prose, her tricky, tricked-up plots, and her wicked, peremptory sense of humor. The weaknesses of her fiction, too, are thrown into relief here—we notice, more acutely, the author's willful tendency to withhold information, her reliance on arbitrary, neatly symbolic endings, and her reluctance to involve us emotionally in the lives of her people.

A convert to Catholicism, Mrs. Spark has always displayed a sharp moral sense and a fierce Olympian detachment in her fiction; the reader often has the sense that she is standing far away, looking down on her characters' mortal follies from a great distance as she mischievously twitches the strings of their destinies and moves them about with the same aplomb with which they attempt to manipulate one another through blackmail, deception and betrayal. In such novels as *The Comforters, Memento Mori* and *The Prime of Miss Jean Brodie,* this narrative strategy has yielded some deliciously funny metaphysical humor as well as some very clever satire; and there are moments in these stories when those same qualities snap, instantly, into focus. Mrs. Spark's portraits of the English and Dutch in Africa capture, with Waugh-like acerbity, the pretensions and hypocrisies of the colonial third world, and her depiction of the psychological games that develop within closed communities of people—a colony of expatriates, a trio of former schoolmates, a group of tenants in a rooming house—possesses a similar venomous vigor.

Still, one often suspects that Mrs. Spark doesn't care a lot for her characters—or, rather, that she doesn't like them terribly much—and this chilliness is accentuated in her shorter fiction. With the exception of **"The Go-Away Bird"**—a longish story that beautifully delineates the inexorable patterns of fate in an American girl's young life—these stories have a spindly, bony quality; they fold up on themselves like collapsible chairs, without giving us any sense of their people's inner lives, their past histories or their hopes and motivations. Irony is all in these stories—both the payoff and the raison d'être. **"The Fathers' Daughters,"** for instance, is an altogether predictable tale about a literary fortune hunter who dumps the daughter of one famous man for the daughter of another. . . .

In **"The Black Madonna,"** a statue of the Madonna carved out of dark wood appears to grant the wishes of devout parishioners; a similar sense of the otherworldly intrudes in many of these stories. Even when the context is not overtly religious, the implication remains that the supernatural exists, that commonplace lives are subject to mysteries that passeth man's understanding. . . . A real angel with three pairs of wings and huge, luminous eyes pays a visit to a Christmas pageant in **"The Seraph and the Zambesi,"** disrupting the local festivities. And evil incongruously embodied in the persons of two small children makes an unexpected appearance in **"The Twins."** Ghosts, also, figure prominently in several of the tales. . . .

As in Mrs. Spark's novels, nasty, violent doings proliferate freely in these stories: people either live separately, "frolicking happily but not together," or they collide precipitously with one another, getting tied up in complicated stratagems that come to bloody conclusions. A woman nicknamed Needle is choked to death in a haystack after she vows to reveal an old friend's secret. A farmer returns from jail to find his wife with another man, and kills them both. Another man—in what may be a case of mistaken identity—shoots his would-be lover and then himself. Such endings may well ratify Mrs. Spark's distinctly dark view of human nature—an apparent belief in original sin, combined with a conviction that people are better off living independent lives, free of messy entanglements—but the reader too often feels that the author, unlike God, has already stacked the cards against her creations.

*Michiko Kakutani, in a review of "The Stories of
Muriel Spark," in* The New York Times, *September
18, 1985, p. C22.*

ALAN RYAN

[*The Stories of Muriel Spark*] is as impressive and enjoyable a volume as anyone could wish for.

Spark is not a flashy writer. Her prose is clean, modest, unfussy, casual, almost offhand. Remember when she wrote the climactic line, "Well, there was a Miss Jean Brodie in her prime," and we knew *exactly* what she meant. Frequently, the dominant tone of her work is one of wistful reminiscence. Almost always, the voice is highly personal, and it is no surprise that 19 of the 27 stories here are told in the first person.

This unmannered, very civilized voice is a suitable and very flexible instrument for Spark. It can sound perfectly innocent when in fact it is most knowing. It can mention insignificant bits of data that will explode noisily later on. It can speak of the fantastic—ghosts, visions, supernatural threats—and still sound eminently sane. And all its qualities—the calm, the self-

control, the decency—serve to highlight Spark's consistently dark themes.

Many of her characters could agree with the narrator of **"The Twins,"** who observes, "I am too much with brightly intelligent, highly erratic friends." And many, like her, watch and observe and then draw back from the unpleasantness. "I sent myself a wire that morning," the narrator reports, "summoning myself back to London." But she does not fail to report, quite objectively, the nastiness she has witnessed.

In **"The Go-Away Bird,"** young Daphne, "delighted and amazed to be grown-up," finally succeeds in leaving Africa to live in the England of her dreams. She lives for two years with a novelist, then later returns to Africa and dies. Soon after, the novelist is seeking a subject for a new book. "He ranged his experience for a tragedy. He thought of, and rejected as too banal, the domestic ruptures of his friends past and present. He rejected the story of his mother, widowed young, disappointed in her son, but still pushing on: that was too personal. He thought of Daphne. That might lead to something both exotic and tragic. . . . He took a ticket on a plane to the Colony in order to obtain background material at first hand."

Cold, yes, as many of Spark's people are, but even in this story, which is not in the first person, Spark's own balancing voice, tinged with sadness and irony, is still present. Young Daphne, filled with herself and with England, "went for walks with Uncle Pooh-bah. She had to take short steps, for he was slow. They walked on the well-laid paths to the river which Daphne always referred to as 'the Thames,'"—and Spark adds, with great but unobtrusive sympathy for the character—"which indeed, of course, it was."

And Spark can be very funny too. "O God, everlasting and almighty," prays a very dry and selfish woman, currently haunted by the ghost of a wronged uncle, "make me strong, and guide and lead me as to how Mrs. Thatcher would conduct herself in circumstances of this nature."

Spark writes of the places (Africa, Italy, wartime London) she knows. But what she knows best are the people . . . and, apparently, all their nasty little secrets, revealed slowly to the careful observer, and the things they may not even admit to themselves, at least until they must. . . .

There are stories here of loneliness and the separateness of each individual in the world, and tales of thwarted love, jealousy, murder, lingering feuds, greed, ghosts both wise and wicked, demon-seed children with perfect manners, blushing girls and twisted crones. Spark reports them all with cool and precise observation that is distant enough to be absolutely unsparing, yet close enough to be both moved and moving. In the current renaissance of the short story, this collection constitutes a high point of the form, stories so wonderfully subtle that their impact goes off like gunshots in the night.

Alan Ryan, "Malice and Mirth," in Book World—
The Washington Post, *September 29, 1985, p. 5.*

SHARON THOMPSON

Among the chroniclers of women after the Second World War, and before (or outside of) second-wave feminism, [Muriel Spark] is one of the most successful at making *fictions* from the raw material of working women's lives. There are better realists than Spark, of course (she's not a realist at all), working female ground, and writers who are more moving, or who are mining deeper veins that may yield more subversive work. But at cutting fictions and polishing them to a high gloss, Spark reigns supreme. Her success is often attributed to a combination of modern material with the forms of parable and allegory, but while her work gains concentration and power from its relation to parable—particularly if it travels parable's liminal passage between detail and moral—it loses seriousness when it departs entirely from realism and shifts into the cartoon-devil country of allegory. Her genius is rather for the metaphysical short novel, and it is in the canniness with which she contrives to work a metaphor, a conceit, into a narrative that she takes my breath away. Spark is the John Donne of English fiction, a few centuries behind her time, but nonetheless interesting for it. If only she had Donne's inclination toward love, I'd be wholly of her party. (Sex appears in her work in isolation, like a peculiarly disgusting behavior engaged in by villains and those tainted by the residue of original sin.)

Because she has appeared as the one woman in so many male-dominated literary contexts, it's easy to forget that Spark came by her primary material the hard way. Her knowledge of the exigencies, pleasures, and vanities of a cosmopolitan working woman is firsthand. A veteran of the ill-paid life of the undereducated hack woman writer, Spark is reported to have been literally starving when some friends staked her on the promise that she go into therapy. Always one for the unexpected turn of character, she converted to Catholicism and satiric narrative instead of to "normalcy" as a consequence of her analytic hours with a Jungian priest. She began to write, as she once put it, "the way cows eat grass." Like all Spark analogies, it's on point in more ways than one. The Spark plot is a genre unto itself, and this explains, to a degree, her prolific output. And like genre novels her work is addictive. You get to enjoy going around the circuit, from the humorous setup, through the slapstick muddle, to the tragedy brought on by lousy human nature. It's a bit like following up a double Valium with a low voltage electric shock and an ax murder in the family. . . .

[*The Stories of Muriel Spark*] spans almost 35 years and includes African as well as English and Scotch stories. . . . Most have appeared in previous collections, but there are some new ones—of which one or two are very fine. **"The Dragon"** and **"The Fortune Teller"** are her best parables yet about writing. (Her reputation as a critic's writer rests, largely, on an interpretation of her work as being about the act of creation—a scam on her part, I think, but in this case there's some real substance in the writing metaphor.)

Spark's African stories hold the fascination that current political events lend to fiction from an earlier time; reading them is a little like checking up on a fortune teller or a weathercaster: Can she make historical sense of such human injustice? Answer: yes and no. Spark is so convinced of the general human tendency toward evil that she runs low on explanations, though high on calamitous predictions. Her Africa is not Gordimer's; her take on the continent is that of an outsider, a transient visitor. While Gordimer sees Africa as a homeland . . . , Spark sees it as the polar opposite of home. . . .

In other stories, she is very good, as she always is in her novels, on young women of slender means. **"A Member of the Family"** . . . twists the girl-who-wants-to-get-married plot. Trudy goes on vacation with Gwen, an acquaintance. Like well-matched satirists, the two are acutely aware of each other's flaws; rainy weather and a shortage of men sets them further on edge. A man turns up—Richard, an old friend of Gwen's—and Trudy and he begin a flirtation. When Trudy lies about her age, to

him ". . . this remarkable statement was almost an invitation to a love affair." . . . At last he invites her home, a success that turns out to signify the end of their relationship. Somewhat over-plotted and neat? Maybe, though in revealing not a murderer or a marriage, as the genre normally requires, but the erotic complications of familial bonds, the story pinches the expectations of its readers in the folds and turns of plot with bruising precision, a rare coup in women's fiction.

Spark also takes deadly aim at those couples who invite another woman on their vacations or to their homes for the weekend. Anyone who has ever been cast as a third wheel is revenged forever by **"Bang-Bang You're Dead"** and **"The Fortune Teller."** While triplets merit her most poisoned pen, she's a salutary dose for anyone who is unattached and feeling strange about it. In Spark, it's A-OK to be on your own. She regards coupling as an invitation to neurosis and parasitism at best, and to blackmail and general dastardliness at worst. Lovers or husbands and wives are not the only suspect couples. Even mother-and-son and employee-employer duos are on the sick side in her work. . . . That she gets away with this phobia against human connection without seeming downright mentally ill is a tribute to her mastery.

A few other stories in the collection are extraordinary. **"Alice Long's Dachshunds"** works on one's memories about the childhood terror of making a fatal error with a terrifying evocative power and then turns instead into a tale about an act of incomprehensible cruelty. It's another masterpiece of the story as spitball. The collection as a whole, however, makes it apparent that the short story is not Spark's form. A miniaturist, she has the economy of style the short story generally demands, but not the close perspective. She is preeminently a writer of surface, the most courteous of voyeurs. Her villains may open forbidden drawers with purloined or copied keys, sneak into bedrooms where they rifle through secret manuscripts. But Spark herself never takes an illicit look in a drawer, and she keeps away from the psychological as if it were contaminated. Her antipathy toward the couple makes the intimate group of almost no interest to her. She is a miniaturist of another ilk. Her ideal canvas is the microcosm, the association with a public face, the minivan of fools—the women's hotel, girl's school, an institution for the aging—and her ideal length is 224 pages, give or take. At 10 pages, she's frequently thin, and a puerile Catholicism shows through the bare spots. Too many ghosts roam these short plots. Divine retribution comes altogether too *ex-machina*. Other endings slide into base so easily they could have been written by a schoolgirl in 1910.

Again and again, I wished she had gained more, earlier, from two writers she has cited with admiration—Proust and Böll— or put her Catholicism to the severe tests of contemporary thought. But despite her trespasses against modernity, these stories teach something many far more philosophically sophisticated, good-politics narrative writers don't know: the uses of the double-helix plot and the biting tongue in bringing consciousness out of the general swoon. "Remember you must die" was the theme of one of her best-known novels, *Memento Mori,* and an acute recognition that we are not divine is the fuel of her wit, the underlying theme of all her work. For Spark it is a religious tenet. For the rest of us, it's a wake-up call of collective and individual mortality and human fallibility, the shot of adrenaline which comes from realizing that if not now, maybe never. When it is predictable and when it is not, Spark's work teaches this lesson: better cut to the quick with a sharp and unexpected blade than pound to the grave on the same dull point.

Sharon Thompson, "The Canonization of Muriel Spark," in VLS, No. 39, October, 1985, p. 9.

DAVID LODGE

The writings of Muriel Spark illustrate very clearly the idea, put forward by the Russian Formalists earlier in this century, that the function of art is to defamiliarize or "make strange" the world, to overcome the deadening effects of habit on our perceptions. (p. 1)

Habit, said Victor Shklovsky, *doyen* of the Formalists, "devours objects, furniture, one's wife and the fear of war.... Art helps us to recover the sensation of life.... The technique of art is to make things 'unfamiliar'." This, of course, entails using unfamiliar techniques. One of the pieces collected in *The Stories of Muriel Spark*, entitled **"The First Year of My Life,"** offers a perfect example of the process in action. The very title recalls one of Shklovsky's favorite exemplary texts, *Tristram Shandy*, but whereas Sterne's comic masterpiece works by means of artful prolixity and endless digression, Mrs. Spark's story (like many of her novels) achieves its effect by a breathtaking compression. Its subject is the horror of war, specifically of World War I. A hackneyed topic indeed.... How can a writer, coming belatedly to this subject, shock and startle us into a fresh apprehension of the horror of the trenches, the incompetence of the military staff, the sentimental jingoism of the home front and the impotence of literary intellectuals in the face of Europe's collective death wish?

Mrs. Spark's brilliant solution is to present the war through the eyes of a baby: "I was born on the first day of the second month of the last year of the First World War, a Friday. Testimony abounds that during the first year of my life I never smiled."

She never smiled because she knew what was happening outside the walls of her nursery, and she knew *that* because: "Babies, in their waking hours, know everything that is going on everywhere in the world; they can tune in to any conversation they choose, switch on to any scene. We have all experienced this power. It is only after the first year that it is brainwashed out of us."

The premise of the story is thus a kind of electronic updating of the neo-platonic idea, memorably formulated in Wordsworth's "Intimations of Immortality" ode, that we are born with supernatural powers of perception that quickly atrophy in mundane existence. Physically impotent, subject to all the indignities of infancy, the narrator views the insanity and futility of adult behavior with revulsion and contempt.... (pp. 1, 38)

["The First Year of My Life" cross-cuts] vivid images of military carnage with satiric vignettes of civilian inanity and nursery routine. The effect for the reader is both shocking and exhilarating—the literary equivalent of riding a roller coaster, full of sudden swoops and lurches from the comic to the tragic and back again. When the narrator finally produces a smile, her relations fondly attribute it to the candle on her first birthday cake, but, in fact, it is triggered by someone quoting from a fatuous speech made at the House of Commons about the redeeming effects of the war by "the distinguished, the immaculately dressed and the late Mr. Asquith."

There is perhaps nothing else quite as stunningly original in this volume as **"The First Year of My Life,"** and some of the contents fall very far below it in quality. Indeed, as a "collected stories," the book is slightly disappointing. To put this judgment in perspective, I should say that I consider Mrs. Spark to be the most gifted and innovative British novelist of her generation, one of the very few who can claim to have extended and altered the possibilities of the form for other practitioners. If she does not consistently impress one as being a short-story writer of the same caliber, it may be because the bold economy of her novelistic technique sometimes seems like a cutting of corners in the more confined space of the short story.

Also, one misses from her stories the voice of the authorial narrator—intrusive, omniscient, opinionated—that is such a distinctive and disconcerting feature of her novels. Many of the stories have a first-person narrator, which is a method she has, I believe, used only twice in her longer fiction.... The anecdotal "I" is, of course, a very natural mode for the short story, but for just that reason it needs to be defamiliarized—as it is, brilliantly in **"The First Year of My Life."** Some of the narrators of the other stories are undercharacterized, and their anecdotes deliver less interest than they promise.

Many of the stories turn on events that are supernatural or preternatural, and several are ghost stories. If we adopt the French critic Tzvetan Todorov's distinction between "the fantastic"—in which there is always a possible naturalistic explanation of the uncanny, and "the marvelous"—in which there is not—it is clear that Mrs. Spark's fiction usually falls into the second category. This is consistent with her uncompromising, if idiosyncratic, Roman Catholic faith. Ghosts, miracles, visitations by angels and demons have figured prominently in her work from the prize-winning story **"The Seraph and the Zambesi."** ... (It describes the disconcerting appearance of a real angel at a tawdry Nativity play staged in Africa.)

Mrs. Spark has always portrayed human life *sub specie aeternitatis*. The plots of her novels belong to some larger, transcendental plot that the characters are hardly aware of and that the novelist herself can only gesture toward. In those passages her prose suddenly ceases to be a hard, bright, razor-sharp instrument and becomes poetic, suggestive, allusive.... (p. 38)

At the beginning of the story ["**The Portobello Road**,"] the narrator describes how on [a] ... sunny afternoon she found a needle in a haystack, thus acquiring the nickname Needle and a reputation for being lucky that is a constant irritation in later life. A few pages later we learn that Needle is a ghost, haunting George, who murdered her and hid her body in a haystack when she threatened to tell Katherine, to whom he had become engaged, that he was already married to an African woman. "He looked as if he would murder me and he did.... After a search that lasted twenty hours, when my body was found, the evening papers said, 'Needle is found: in haystack!'"

The use of the supernatural in fiction, especially in the mode of the "marvelous" rather than the "fantastic," is always a risky proceeding because it can seem too easy a way of transfiguring the commonplace. **"The Portobello Road"** works beautifully because the main point of the story is not the ghostly existence of the narrator; it is rather the story's *donnée* which releases a complex play of black humor and mordant commentary on human vanity. As readers, we happily accept the premise for the sake of the narrative pleasure it yields. Some of the other ghost stories in the collection, for example, **"Another Pair of Hands"** ..., or **"The Executor"** ..., seem in contrast rather trivial and mechanical in their use of the supernatural—entertaining enough on first reading, but hardly worth a second.

Another common thread running through many of the stories in this collection is an African setting—usually an unnamed British colony just before or just after World War II, where the white man's burden is more often than not shrugged off in favor of booze and adultery, with violent consequences. (pp. 38-9)

The longest of these stories, **"The Go-Away Bird,"** is almost novella length, and one could wish that it had been fleshed out a little more: the hectic succession of episodes and characters makes it read in places more like a synopsis than a story. On the day I read it in this volume, I happened to see, for the first time in my life, a real go-away bird, in a Hampshire aviary— a coincidence that, I suspect, would tickle the author's fancy. Unfortunately the creature was silent, so I was unable to verify that its call sounds like *"Go 'way, Go 'way,"* the leitmotif of this story of Daphne du Toit's unhappy oscillation between savage Africa and decadent England. "God help me, life is unbearable," she cries aloud in the bush at the end, and is promptly shot dead by a vengeance-obsessed tobacco manager.

Invoking the assistance of the Almighty is always a risky business in Mrs. Spark's fictional world, for your prayers may be answered. In **"The Black Madonna,"** for instance, a rather complacent English Catholic couple pray to a black statue of the Virgin Mary for offspring and are rewarded with a black baby—an embarrassing reminder of some ancestor's indiscretion.

In this story there is a streak of that authorial vindictiveness toward her own characters which some readers cite as a reason for not succumbing to Mrs. Spark's literary skill. It is perfectly true that her imagination is fascinated by revenge, humiliation and ironic reversals, and that she looks upon pain and death with a dry, glittering eye. Nevertheless, in the novels, if not always in the short stories, this cruel streak in her work is restrained and tempered by the comic spirit. . . . However grim and black their humor may appear, the providential plot to which these books obliquely allude is a divine comedy. (p. 39)

> David Lodge, *"Marvels and Nasty Surprises," in* The New York Times Book Review, *October 20, 1985, pp. 1, 38-9.*

Gerald Stern

1925-

American poet and essayist.

Stern's poetry is noted for its energetic language, rich imagery, and skillful balance of emotional expressiveness and concrete physical detail. His poems are usually written in a conversational narrative style, yet they are also frequently lyrical and sometimes contain traces of surreal imagery. Stern's preoccupation with the self, his use of long, incantatory lines, and his characteristically exuberant, celebratory tone have led many reviewers to compare his work with that of Walt Whitman. However, several critics note that Whitman's "self" is meant to encompass a broad spectrum of humanity, while Stern's refers to an intensely personal vision. In a review of *The Red Coal* (1981), David Wojahn observed: "While some may find the bewildering accumulation of details and events in Stern's poems meandering and bothersome, a careful reading will reveal their function: everything Stern sees is filtered through the process of memory, and in doing so is given clarity and integration."

Stern's first two volumes, *Pineys* (1971) and *Rejoicings: Selected Poems 1966-1972* (1973; reissued 1984), received little critical attention. In 1977, however, he emerged as a significant figure in contemporary literature when he was awarded the Lamont Poetry Prize for *Lucky Life* (1977). Although the poems in this volume abound with descriptions of ordinary objects and events of American life, they are written in an elegiac style and are dominated by the concern with the self that is present in all of Stern's work. Also evident in *Lucky Life* is another element of Stern's poetry—his focus on his Jewish heritage. This aspect is expressed through his emphasis on memory and history and his use of biblical references and language patterned after the Old Testament. Reviewers praised the lively, meaningful language in *Lucky Life* and lauded Stern for his ability to blend commonplace and ethereal elements.

Like the poems in *Lucky Life,* those in *The Red Coal* are kaleidoscopic renderings which explore in meticulous detail the resources of Stern's memory and imagination. This volume is marked by the alternately exuberant and meditative voice of its persona and by its vivid cataloging of images. Sanford Pinsker observed that in *The Red Coal* "Stern's lyricism moves easily across the warp and woof of Time, from reflections about History to visions of the future. The result is a powerful sense of the eternal present in the quotidian." In *Paradise Poems* (1984), Stern continues to relate past and present, focusing particularly on the coexistence of pain and joy and of loss and redemption, which he portrays as central to human life. Critics noted a broadening of scope in *Paradise Poems,* citing Stern's gradual move from a highly personal poetry to a concern with more universal implications. Edward Hirsch described Stern as "a romantic with a sense of humor, an Orphic voice living inside history, a sometimes comic, sometimes tragic visionary."

(See also *Contemporary Authors,* Vols. 81-84.)

HAYDEN CARRUTH

It is extremely difficult to bring off the kind of poem Stern writes, doomsday among the tricycles and kittens. Most poets who try end up with trite magazine verse, predictabilities of faded irony. But [in *Lucky Life*] Stern succeeds. His low-voiced, prosy syntax gives us direct statements, simple and true, moving almost monotonously toward the hysterical outbreak of silence, the twisted smile. But he draws back; he doesn't push to that catastrophe—not quite. Instead he resumes, again and again, poem after poem; he takes up the burden in spite of everything, like the daily editorialist in the *New York Times,* but with fitness and skill, so that the tone of every poem—well, almost every—is once more genuine, clear, compelling, right for its occasion. And because he is close to the dailiness of American life he speaks for us all in our own voices, not the prophetic or accusing voice of the exile. (p. 88)

Hayden Carruth, "The Passionate Few," in Harper's, *Vol. 256, No. 1537, June, 1978, pp. 86-9.**

LAWRENCE KRAMER

Stern's poetry is preoccupied, extravagantly and often desperately, with the poet's self, and its impulse is to assert that self against a world of hostile objects that threaten to devour it. . . .

Stern's means of privileging the self is a language of repetition and parallelism that he has learned from the master of poetic self-assertion, Walt Whitman. But the crucial difference between Stern and Whitman is that Stern does not speak for a universal self, but for his circumscribed, biographical self; a self not at the center of things, but at their periphery. He is a Jew in permanent exile from all centers. From this constriction of selfhood Stern's poetry draws its urgency, its frequent shrillness. (pp. 114-15)

It would seem from this that Stern is anything but a quiet poet; one could call him a noisy one. Yet the stridency of his language is the stridency of its simplicity, and of its almost compulsive attachment to physical fact. In Stern's work, strict, descriptive accuracy is essential, because to represent something is to reject it, and so to be free of it by getting it out of the world and into the poem.... Objects in Stern's poems are so vicious that they cannot be trusted to obey the laws of reality, and many of his poems have a surreal or hallucinatory element to them. Yet the poet's response is consistent: to say just what is what, resisting and protesting with each word. Passages like the following [from **"The Days of Nietzsche"** in *Lucky Life*] are not instances of figuration, but of description; ... they cannot be differentiated into literal and figurative halves:

> And when I receive my torn tongue in the mail
> I put it between my teeth like a dead mouse
> and let the blood run down my chin.

This overwrought passage incidentally indicates the full depth of anxiety in Stern's work, for not even the poet's own body is immune from becoming an object, and so the enemy.

Perhaps I am too addicted to the world's body, but I cannot muster much admiration for Stern, despite his evident skill in massing details so that the darker tensions among them are eventually released; even the skill can seem mechanical.... [Stern's] investment in himself is arbitrary, justified perhaps only by a certain ruthless candor; it therefore seems sentimental. Stern could hardly be called a narcissistic poet. The self in which he takes refuge is not necessarily a self that he loves, for it often seems to be only the echo of a self, loud but insubstantial, like a ghost with its chain. In the end, the self that Stern dwells on so much represents a subjectivity so violated by experience that it can come forward only by the negative means of describing what repels it. In some of the poems, it must be admitted, this paradoxical subjectivity does attain an impressive, self-harrowing pathos. But Stern remains a problematically egocentric poet, both for the presence and the absence of his ego, and his trust in the power of language is above all a trust in the power of statement to act as negation. (pp. 115-16)

Lawrence Kramer, "In Quiet Language," in Parnassus: Poetry in Review, *Vol. 6, No. 2, Spring-Summer, 1978, pp. 101-17.**

DAVID CLEWELL

[The poems in *Lucky Life*] speak with incredible detail out of an extremely wide range of human experience. The language is for the most part simple, direct, and conversational. Stern's personae are concerned with the details of the specific experiences; any recollection or speculation they engage in is tied directly to the language of the particular incident. Stern's diction and images are solid; the persona's feelings and emotions are conveyed concretely. There is a little abstraction that occurs between image and feeling, and it is the poet's skill that keeps

the best poems in this book emotional yet unsentimental, powerful yet humble. **"Straus Park," "This Is It,"** and **"If You Forget the Germans"** are poems that epitomize this ability.

Stern's poems are explorations that at their best encompass all at once the geographical, physical, and personal aspects of what it means to *explore.* ... A less mature poet would have a difficult time pulling off what seems to come so naturally to Stern.

What may come less naturally to Stern are the shorter, more overtly meditative pieces. A few of these poems work well; **"The Power of Maples"** is a strong, solid poem in eight lines. But others lapse into a less precise language and a self-conscious "telling" that distracts.... [In these pieces] the poet is telling us what the persona feels; the reader cannot help but feel a little cheated. Stern's gift is his ability to show, in concrete things, why his persona feels. The reader, then, is given concrete handles and is able to explore as the voice in the poem explores.... (pp. 159-60)

Stern is at his best in those poems that are long enough for him to explore details of the exterior world and so come to order his interior life. There is a certain grand expansiveness where the persona looks all ways at once. What is focused on, and how that is communicated, is what makes Stern's poems special. One can feel the influence of Whitman: Stern sings, and we are drawn into his voice and his songs. He sings about the authentic, personal losses that are a part of growth. And in the very singing of those losses, desolation is obliterated by the chance to celebrate the resiliency of at least one human spirit. (pp. 160-61)

Although the tone of nearly all these poems is somber on the surface, Stern finds the crack of light that might or might not eventually brighten things. Just the chance that it might is solace enough for this poet whose personae move through a series of small and large survivals as active, not passive, survivors. The poems are affirmations of a human being's ability to order an interior life that is inexorably linked with, not cut off from, changes in the external world. This ordering involves working through conceptions of both the overwhelming and the small. The poet shows that we can be changed without being compromised; that an interior life can, and must, be ordered and reordered without being manipulated or contrived.

Stern is a poet obsessed with the world around him, but he never loses sight of his special place *in* it. This quality allows his persona to "lie on my back again as I always do, / stretching my legs out and entering the blue world" (**"Climbing This Hill Again"**). For Stern entering the "blue world" is a willful act—an act of survival that puts into perspective the bombardment of details and events that occur in the external world.

Stern's interior life of thought and reflection is not one of resigned acceptance. When there is acceptance it is usually uneasy or uncertain. At other times Stern's blue world is a land of angry defiance. In **"Behaving Like A Jew"** the speaker finds a dead opossum in the road. Then,

> —I am going to be unappeased at the opossum's death.
> I am going to behave like a Jew
> and touch his face, and stare into his eyes,
> and pull him off the road.
> I am not going to stand in a wet ditch
> with the Toyotas and Chevies passing over me
> at sixty miles an hour

and praise the beauty and the balance
and lose myself in the immortal lifestream
when my hands are still a little shaky
from his stiffness and his bulk
and my eyes are still weak and misty
from his round belly and his curved fingers
and his black whiskers and his little dancing feet.

The poet's ability to simultaneously grasp an external event and come to grips with it internally is a sign that shows how well Stern knows his interior life; shows how well he has learned to use the blueness, the sensitive knife he found there. But at no time does he cut himself off, even in anger, from the external world. He knows it is in this latter world where his persona's hands still shake from handling the opossum. It is only in this world where action is possible; where one person's *singular* action is necessary to keep both of his worlds, as he has come to know and qualify them, alive.

This collection is the work of a mature poet who has brought all the elements of his craft to the varied, full life of a thinking and feeling human being. If the poems offer a lot in the first reading, they leave even more to go back to. (pp. 161-62)

> David Clewell, "In Blue Light," in The Chowder
> Review, Nos. 10 & 11, 1978, pp. 159-62.

PATRICIA HAMPL

Lucky Life is the most beautiful and genuine new book I've read in a long time. Its apparent modesty—the reiteration of homely, close-to-hand detail, the relaxed, accessible voice, the clear statement of emotions—is the carrier of a sophisticated, deeply elegiac sensibility that is more rare in Americans than Europeans. The stunning, and very simple, beauty of this collection is that it mourns almost unceasingly and yet succeeds in giving survival its due, its right to freshness and joy. Or perhaps Gerald Stern has presented a larger discovery: our historical circumstances at the end of a particularly brutal century have created a climate in which truly "to live in the present" means to mourn the past and to acknowledge the resonating blows of devastation and loss. Therefore, to grieve is to give meaning to one's present life. And to have this sense of meaning, as we know from its opposite, the blank soul-misery that seems to isolate so many poets, is to have a very lucky life indeed.

This is a book about history—inevitably; about the necessity of making one's peace—and one's fight—with personal and international history. The pugnacity and resignation that alternate in the poems on this subject provide one of its strongest balances. (p. 103)

[Stern's] nostalgia is both more casual and more cranky than nostalgia usually is (and sometimes, like everybody's nostalgia, it is simply a drag: **"Home from Greece,"** for example, perhaps because it comes at the end of the book, felt like one too many to me). He freely admits that much of what he finds himself grieving over is the sort of thing he can hardly expect anybody else to miss. . . . But the fact that nobody else cares makes it all the more his business to name names, evoke memories, and give a place to the faded and fading.

By sticking with his nostalgic impulses, Stern releases a deeper cry about greater and more essential losses, the huge holes that history has left and which we fall into, as into depression, without understanding the cause. In **"Self-Portrait"** he moves beautifully and with full authority from his own life (his re-flection in a mirror) to the lives of Van Gogh, the "frozen Armenians going back into their empty towns," "the Jews of Vilna," and finally, intensifying the elegiac tone of the poem:

> In honor of Albert Einstein
> In honor of Eugene Debs. In honor of Emma Goldman.

There is no *self* portrait: he does not live here as a unique individual but as the living storehouse of these other lives, people who cherished certain ideals and who therefore live on and matter not only as individuals, but as witnesses to the best we have imagined for our world.

We have often found such sentiments suspect in the poetry of our country: too much longing, too much "socialism" are often dismissed as sentimentality (or propaganda—but that's a different story). Although we can take direct statements and impassioned attachment to politics in "foreigners" (Neruda, for example), we have a tendency to see such longings in our own poets as somehow sectarian. . . . The prevailing aesthetic remains one in which hermeticism is seen as somehow more essentially poetic than an expansive social consciousness. (pp. 104-05)

This unfortunate split between the self and the world may change as American poets read more of the work of Eastern Europeans, which is now appearing more widely in translation. . . . And the qualities of this poetry may suit American poetics even better and more naturally than Spanish surrealism has. One of these qualities is the assumption of living within a culture—not, as Americans so often feel, of flying off in solitary space, a self lost in the opacity of the world. (pp. 105-06)

I go so far afield in order to place Gerald Stern—for I think his work is important and is best related to qualities outside of American poetry, even though he speaks in the American idiom. In his way (like Whitman, he has that what-I-assume-you-shall-assume command and casualness) he is registering a shift in American poetry and a future direction even as he remains obsessed with the past. (p. 106)

If there is a persistent villain in his book, it is "my mind," "the brain" (**"Blue Skies, White Breasts, Green Trees"**), thinking in general. When he is looking straight at his world . . . he seems at his best. He has a wonderful lyrical gift. . . . The poems are filled with creatures, with lazy inspections of gardens and fields and beaches.

Finally, his best accomplishment is his dogged determination to grieve in the midst of this lucky life. . . . There is great relief in reading this, in finding someone who will take it all on—simply because he is, as Muriel Rukeyser puts it in her back cover blurb, "a grown man." (p. 107)

> Patricia Hampl, in a review of "Lucky Life," in
> Ironwood, 12, 1978, pp. 103-07.

JONATHAN MONROE

Gerald Stern's poems have an expansiveness of voice and a range of feeling which invite comparison with Walt Whitman. Yet the reader of Whitman and Stern soon realizes the vast differences between their worlds. Whitman's is the voice of unlimited possibility, Stern's of the possibilities within a more delimited sphere. If Whitman speaks for outwardness, the "manifest destiny" of self and nation, Stern speaks for the recovery and sharing of inwardness. If Whitman is able to represent the spirit which in his day was building a new nation,

Stern is compelled to image the ruins resulting from that cease-less construction. As Whitman speaks for the promise of self and for a young country, Stern speaks against the betrayal of that promise. His poems are attempts to recover from the wreck of culture, and the consequent wreck of self, which is a dominant part of life in contemporary America.

Stern's poems offer that close attention to the image which we have come to expect in the best American poetry, yet they clearly place themselves within a strong oral tradition which looks back through Whitman and the "carved line" of Blake to the ancient Greeks and especially the Psalms and Proverbs of the Old Testament. . . . Perhaps the most striking stylistic aspect of Stern's poems is the repetition and parallelism of syntactic units, most often at the beginning of the line. . . . The repetitions and variations of such units serve the poems in several ways. Most importantly, the finding of these key phrases unlocks a flood of images. They provide a release for the imagination to pursue its own paths of associations. . . . (pp. 41-2)

Stern's use of repetitions and variations in syntax also functions as a mnemonic device which lends a certain formalistic quality to the poems. These syntactic parallelisms occurring usually at the beginning of lines serve in a way similar to more traditional metrical patterns and end-rhyme by reinforcing retention of the poem's content. Finally, at the same time that these parallelisms allow for the release of a flood of imagery, they provide a framework for tightly controlling the semantic direction the images will take. This may account for the sense of a certain swollen quality in the poems: it is as if the poems would overflow their boundaries but for firm syntactical structure. Stern's poems often take on the effect of a chant or a litany, a ritual song of memory and healing: apparent ease of technique and voice in [Stern's] poetry has been hard won. Already in *Rejoicings* one can see the foundation for the poems in *Lucky Life*.

There are important differences, however. The poems of *Rejoicings* are more allusive, those of *Lucky Life* and the recent poems more directly presented. One notes in Stern's development a movement away from reliance on the intellect and the artistic and philosophical direction of his predecessors, toward a greater trust in the self and in feelings. . . . In *Lucky Life* one still finds a poem entitled **"I Need Help from the Philosophers,"** yet it is the first and last stanzas of **"The Days of Nietzsche"** which best express the newly won attitude of the collection as a whole:

> I have moved so far into my own thought
> I have almost forgotten the days of Nietzsche,
> when he was my guide. . . .

In **"This Is It,"** Stern writes: "It is my emotions that carry me through Lambertville, New Jersey / sheer feeling . . ." And in **"The Sensitive Knife"** he says: "I am following my own conception now . . ."

Such lines in *Lucky Life* have emerged from the struggle begun in *Rejoicings*. In the earlier volume the first-person speaker is often torn between two paths, with the desire to live "in both places at once" (**"Top Rock"**), or "on two levels, like a weasel" [**"Immanuel Kant and the Hopi"**]:

> I am going to write twenty poems about my ruined
>   country.
>   Please forgive me, my old friends.
> I am walking in the direction of the Hopi!
> I am walking in the direction of Immanuel Kant!

> I am learning to save my thoughts—like
> one of the Dravidians—so that nothing will
> be lost, nothing I tramp upon, nothing I
> chew, nothing I remember.

The directions of Immmanuel Kant and the Hopi represent tendencies in direct opposition to each other. One suggests intellectualism, rigorous logic, Western European civilization; the other, the way of the American Indian with its respect for experience, feeling, plants and animals, its closeness to mysticism and gnostic wisdom. If, in *Rejoicings*, Stern seems suspended between these two directions, in *Lucky Life* he tends to move more firmly away from the philosophers, particularly Kant and Nietzsche, towards a love for our animal nature. Poems such as **"His Animal Is Finally a Kind of Ape"** in *Rejoicings* suggests a leaning in this direction, but in the poems of *Lucky Life* and beyond one feels a more certain commitment. When Stern exclaims, "What a horror civilization is!" (**"Look at Us Play with Our Meat"**), in a very definite sense he is holding Western intellectualism and its neglect of experience, of feelings, responsible for what we have become. (pp. 42-4)

Of all European nations it is probably Germany with which we most associate the "philosophical mind." Thus, in a poem called **"The Weeds"** from *Rejoicings*, Stern writes: "For years / I hung—like a German—between two wildernesses. / Now there is a third. I cross it with relief." The "third" dimension of these lines is, in a sense, the poem itself, which offers a forum other than philosophy for the resolution of tensions, a way of coping with antinomies such as intellect and feeling between which the speaker has felt suspended. . . . If in Stern's earlier poetry the emphasis is largely on the poem itself as a place in which tensions between various antinomies find a degree of resolution, . . . [there is a] different emphasis in *Lucky Life*. The poems of this volume are less self-conscious about their own status as a kind of "third" dimension, and at the same time more deeply committed to speaking for the "third world" of our experience outside the poem—the plants, animals, human beings and manmade objects which have been left behind, endangered, or destroyed by the "progress" of American culture. Stern often finds correspondences between the ways we treat plant and animal life and the ways we treat each other, between the "yellow iris" and "a nest inside a ruined building, / a father hugging his child, / a Jew in Vilna" (**"Three Tears"**). . . . Stern speaks for the dispossessed, "the diseased and the fallen," whether it is the dead bird in **"Pile of Feathers,"** the "Curly Ivy" in **"Straus Park"** or the Mexican man in **"Long Nose."** In his poems one feels horror for the civilization which the intellect has created, the "crowded city / full of corruption and loneliness," "a deranged America," sadness over "the lost Republic". Stern expresses sympathy with Emma Goldman's "fight against property," with Van Gogh's "raging against the bourgeois world." Already in *Rejoicings* he writes: "I would like us to feed ourselves in the middle of their civilization" (**"Planting Strawberries"**). Already we see his sympathies for the oppressed, the neglected and mistreated who are looked upon as **"Traitors"**: "the small animals that pause five extra seconds (to our horror) / making their minds up before they go back into the ground."

In *Lucky Life* one finds this underground resistance more firmly entrenched, more sure of itself and of its enemies. Stern is no longer living "on two levels" but "in three and four and five places at once" (**"The Sweetness of Life"**), moving at times through great emotional complexity, as suggested by the "five books of ecstasy, grief and anger" in **"Psalms."** . . . Stern's opposition to the power structure of America and his anger toward those currently exercising that power expresses itself in a tremendous swell of emotion, a compassion for those who are forced to go underground, those submerged beneath the relentless advance of twentieth century Western civilization.... For Stern, poetry is a means of preserving the life of the body and the life of the spirit. He is an archaeologist sifting through the ruins of American life to salvage what deserves saving from what has been condemned and neglected. Like Whitman, Stern realizes the interdependence of all things: plants, animals, human beings and their objects. It is perhaps this awareness which gives such scope to his writing, and which most invites comparison between these two poets whose worlds are so changed from one another. (pp. 44-7)

> *Jonathan Monroe, "Third Worlds: The Poetry of Gerald Stern," in* Northwest Review, *Vol. XVIII, No. 2, 1979, pp. 41-7.*

VERNON SHETLEY

The Romantics invented the crisis lyric, if not the concept of crisis itself; it remained for our age to invent the midlife crisis, and its concomitant, the midlife crisis lyric. Like other practitioners of this later variant, Gerald Stern aims at imaginative and emotional renovation through a heightened consciousness of loss. Stern's program is distinctive in his refusal to look beyond the self: Illusions of romantic love are little invoked, and the family romance is mercifully absent. Stern largely refuses the descent into memory usual in the therapeutic mode, as if his spiritual need could not wait on so slow a process. Intensely personal without being autobiographical, Stern's poems [as evidenced in *The Red Coal*] lay bare his emotions while revealing almost nothing about their origins.

Alternating between conversational speech and slightly surreal outbursts, Stern's work achieves its effects through accumulations of rhetorical weight or sudden flashes of disjunctive imagery. In both his quiet and agitated moods he strives for spontaneity; the first-person pronoun is ubiquitous, the free verse rarely strays far from a loose iambic. Famous names appear frequently, but more as part of Stern's mental furniture than as a test of the reader's erudition.... [Stern's usual method involves] the assertion of an enormous weight of feeling for which neither source nor correlative is given. This streamlining of affect no doubt arises from a desire for direct and immediate utterance but betrays a certain impatience characteristic of the mind behind these poems.

To choose between terms of justification, Stern aims more for sweetness than light. While at times he attempts to understand, to find something saving in the world of fact and memory, he more often seeks rather "a way to change, or sweeten, my clumsy life." As he seeks, so does he find; we see him "singing, always singing, of that amorous summer," "singing again about buried love and crazy renewal," or "dreaming of sunlight and rain and endless dancing." In poem after poem Stern sets out for himself some temptation to despair over which he wins a lyrical triumph. The invariability with which he clears those hurdles makes one suspect that the fences have been lowered, and the accumulation of *cantabile* finales leaves the impression that Stern's endgame relies more on reflex than invention.

If Stern's poems were uniformly guilty of premature resolutions, one might write him down as another talent impoverished by the received style in which he has elected to work. Yet on a few occasions he manages to step beyond his chosen conventions, arriving at an expression both precise and powerful. (pp. 12, 41)

> *Vernon Shetley, "Nature and Self," in* The New York Times Book Review, *May 10, 1981, pp. 12, 41.**

DAVID WOJAHN

For Gerald Stern, nothing possesses us as wholly as the past, and the major concern of his *The Red Coal* is to investigate the meaning of memory. Fittingly, the book's cover shows a stark photo of the poet ambling down a Paris street in 1950, and one of the collection's most successful efforts is an homage to the great poet of memory, C. P. Cavafy. For Stern, as with Cavafy, memory is the principal source of solace. Stern does not see memory functioning as mere intellectual retrieval; instead, recollection is always emotive. While some may find the bewildering accumulation of details and events in Stern's poems meandering and bothersome, a careful reading will reveal their function: everything Stern sees is filtered through the process of memory, and in doing so is given clarity and integration.... Memory, for Stern, becomes the great equalizer. It allows everything in the poet's experience to co-exist. He wants his walks in Paris in 1950, his reading of Zane Grey novels as a child, and his drives through contemporary Pittsburgh to seem all to happen at once. Experience instantly becomes nostalgia, but because of Stern's relentless exuberance, his work is rarely maudlin. (pp. 96-7)

Forster's famous dictum that a writer should not relate things, only *connect* them is taken very seriously by Stern. *The Red Coal* contains page after page of catalogs of objects, events, and memories. But the endless cataloging is terrifically important to Stern. Because his past *is* one horizon, he wants to be sure that nothing is forgotten, that nothing is given too much or too little significance. He wants no detail, no matter how small, to slip through the net of his experience. His approach is omnivorous; this is the source of the lovely intimacy one encounters in the poems, and also of their quirkiness. **"Pick and Poke"** attempts, rather bizarrely, to show a bond between a neighbor's abandoned Simca, an English taxi promoting a garden supply store, a red squirrel, and "the secret history of France and England." Surprisingly, the poem works, in part because Stern sees nothing unusual about trying to integrate these phenomenally disparate objects and concerns. The approach is more eccentric than it is surreal.... (p. 98)

Stern wants to be a poet of total recall, and ... he wants his memory to be a source of celebration. A great deal of the time Stern is able to achieve his goal. But, as scientists who have studied individuals with photographic memories have come to realize, total recall is finally an affliction, a pathological state. If everything is available to memory, then nothing can be placed in perspective. Because of this, the very things that bring Stern to the sublime also bring him to the tragic. When Stern writes of loss, no matter how far removed from the present this loss may be, it is chillingly immediate for him. He doesn't recapture the past as much as he *relives* it, and because his memory is burdensome as well as comforting, one rarely thinks of Stern as sanguine. (p. 100)

Since Stern's past co-exists with his present, since his voice of celebration co-exists with his tragic voice, his most successful poems are his longest, most sprawling ones, the ones that allow us to see most clearly how these interrelationships function. Although such efforts are too long to quote here without damaging their cumulative impact, the reader should look closely at poems like **"The Shirt Poem," "The Angel Poem,"** and **"Poem of Liberation"** to see Stern make best use of this technique. In them, Stern often grows troubled and despairing, but finally rises to a hard-won exaltation. Stern's shorter poems are less successful, simply because they are not able to build the momentum that makes long poems so compelling.

Though Stern is often a poignant phrasemaker and makes dazzling use of metaphor, his power comes more from the abundance of his spirit than it does from his command of technique. He cares little for prosody, and his long Whitmanesque lines, more-or-less iambic, often grow redundant. Since his concerns are so obsessive, his method can seem obsessive, too. The poems show too much similarity in their development, almost always following the same rhetorical framework.

But again, it's Stern's *spirit* that makes him a significant figure, and with this collection he's become one of the finest poets of his generation, a group that includes such formidable figures as Philip Levine and James Wright. Like his best contemporaries, Stern is a poet both terrifying and endearing, and despite any awkwardness and repetitiveness in his approach, it's wonderful to know that he's among us, scavenging his memory for those things which otherwise would be irredeemably lost. It's as though Stern's scrapbook belongs to all of us, and we're challenged to open it, not knowing whether a page will bring us to tears or to celebration. (pp. 101-02)

> *David Wojahn, in a review of "The Red Coal," in* Poetry East, *No. 6, Fall, 1981, pp. 96-102.*

DAVID ST. JOHN

It is easy to love Gerald Stern's poetry. Like the wonderful poems in his earlier book, *Lucky Life,* the poems in his new collection, *The Red Coal* . . . , are generous, energetic, and immediate. The intimate and conversational manner of the poems sometimes draws us so close to them that, at last, they seem to close around us in a great, grinning bear-hug. Stern's subjects are passion and compassion, earned friendship, and individual love. In his open, expansive voice, Stern gestures as broadly as Whitman in drawing us a portrait of the world he loves and of the smaller, more private worlds within that larger one. Indeed, it's hard to find a piece of the world that hasn't at one time or another fallen into Stern's tumbling, kaleidoscopic vision of experience. With their tolerant and wry humor, their anecdotal jauntiness, and their infectious enthusiasm, each poem of Gerald Stern's exhibits the wisdom of its excesses, and each poem convinces us that beauty and consolation—as well as the sensation of *hope* Stern's poems convey—remain poetry's most lasting and most difficult of gifts. (p. 226)

> *David St. John, "Raised Voices in the Choir: A Review of 1981 Poetry Selections," in* The Antioch Review, *Vol. 40, No. 2, Spring, 1982, pp. 225-34.**

SANFORD PINSKER

Several years ago, in a review of *Lucky Life* (1977), I called Gerald Stern "that rarest of all poetic creatures—a likable Romantic." With *The Red Coal,* let me qualify my remark by adding other qualities of Stern's work not usually associated with the Romantic Temper: a finely tuned sense of humor, a generosity of spirit and, most important, a sense of history.

Lucky Life surprised us, partly because we are not accustomed to Lamont Prize winning books by fifty-two-year-old poets, and partly because Stern's voice was so insistently his own. The extended lines reminded us of Whitman, perhaps of Ginsberg, but even the shrewdest comparisons seemed artificial, forced. It's easier to talk about *The Red Coal;* it reminds one of *Lucky Life,* but more discursive, more confident, more significant. Best of all, *The Red Coal* is likely to give the obscurantists who have been riding herd on contemporary poetry some uneasy nights. Stern makes the lyric voice sound easy; he reminds us that a poem is still the best way to talk about the things that really matter. In short, *The Red Coal* is a remarkable achievement. And those timid about the notion of Gerald Stern as a major American poet are patient at their peril.

That much said by way of putting my enthusiasms on record, let me turn to the soberer matters of description and analysis. In *Lucky Life,* many of the poems begin in postures of exaggerated loss, as if the present moment were too much for Stern and the essentials can only be recaptured by bursts of nostalgia about old cafeterias. A representative poem like **"At Bickford's"** . . . props sentimentality against the gentle irony of its voice. By contrast, *The Red Coal* tends toward longer, more ambitious meditations. In poems like **"The Angel Poem," "The Rose Warehouse," "The Shirt Song"** and **"The Red Coal,"** history matters in ways that strike me as "Jewish," as East European, rather than ahistorically American. Stern's lyricism moves easily across the warp and woof of Time, from reflections about History to visions of the future. The result is a powerful sense of the eternal present in the quotidian. . . . And yet, any case for Stern as a Romantic visionary, a mystic, a metaphysician, must also include an equal case for his abiding love of particulars. By that I mean, Stern builds his historical associations with a deceptive ease, convincing us that the impress of History, its pressures as well as its delights, abides in all things.

I have already mentioned the echoes of Whitman and Ginsberg in Stern's work . . . , but it is Shelley who exerts a special imaginative force. In **"Thinking About Shelley,"** Stern domesticates a meditation about the pale, drowned Shelley into an account of his own desperate swimming in the canal near his home in Raubsville, Pa. . . . (pp. 494-95)

It is hard to think of a contemporary poet who speaks about the creative life—its rewards and its terrible costs; its delights and fears—with as much candor or power. In traditional, officially Romantic poems like "Kubla Khan," the Artist is singled out as an object of wonderment, mingled with fearful warnings. . . . Stern's Romanticism works differently—as a historical meditation, as a recognition of what it fully means to "carry the future with us, knowing / every small vein and every elaboration," as a working out of a destiny that, indeed, has led to the writing of this remarkable book. (p. 496)

> *Sanford Pinsker, in a review of "The Red Coal," in* New England Review, *Vol. IV, No. 3, Spring, 1982, pp. 494-97.*

PETER BALAKIAN

Gerald Stern in *The Red Coal* reinvests pluralistic America with idealism and faith. Often in this book he is an urban Jew roaming the marketplaces of America's cosmopolitan centers (New York and Philadelphia primarily). His persona is most often a dreamer whose musings are nostalgic yearnings for a world of lost humanity symbolized by the radicals and utopians that frequent his poems—Ruskin, Mayakovsky, Emma Goldman, Peter Kropotkin, Thomas Paine, for example. We often encounter Stern in various dream positions; he is either in nature—lying in beach sand or in the natural world around his house—or walking in the city, his mind triggered by the mingling cultures of the back streets.

The poems in *The Red Coal* which best carry forth the exuberant impulses of *Lucky Life* (1977) are the longer pieces. In poems like **"The Shirt Poem," "Joseph Pockets," "The Angel Poem,"** and **"The Poem of Liberation,"** Stern realizes his vision most powerfully. In these poems his oratorical structures gain momentum because the enumeration of phenomena and the accumulation of perception generate a certain density of landscape which verifies the poet's exuberance.

As he opens the closet (a convincing metaphor for the imagination) in **"The Shirt Poem,"** a sort of hallucinatory moment ignites the poet's memory. He sees his shirts "screaming from their hangers," and laments: "gone is sweetness in that closet, gone is the dream / of brotherhood, the affectionate meeting / of thinkers and workers inside a rented hall." The poem becomes an elegy for the workers of the thirties—the *mensches* and reformers who *believed* and were the schooling ground for the poet as a young man. . . . When memory becomes catharsis, those shirt-muses break out of the closet and relieve the poet temporarily of his longing for a lost world.

Stern's faith in Whitman's "teeming nation of nations" makes the best poems in this book songs of pluralistic faith. A walk from downtown Manhattan to Port Authority turns into a sojourn on which the poet joins the great mass of commoners: "On Eighth Avenue I am joined by the others / and we make our way down our own Dolorosa / like chirping grasshoppers and gurgling pigeons." . . .

Similarly in **"The Poem of Liberation,"** musing while walking Stern spots two city gardens—one of beans and lettuce growing out of urban rubble and the other across the street at St. John The Divine, a sort of cultivated Biblical allegory ("poplar from Genesis, reeds from Kings, nettles from Job"). "I find myself loving both," he tells us, and in refusing to see one as secular and the other as sacred he affirms his monistic vision of life. Now, he can read "the poem / of liberation—in Spanish and English—" and plant his own plant (which is also his lyric poem) so he may become a sort of walking melting pot:

> I leave by the southern gate
> across the street from the Hungarian pastry
> and walk down 111th like a Bedouin farmer,
> like a Polish shepherd,
> like a Korean rope master,
> my small steel shovel
> humming and singing in the blue dust.

This moment of joyous freedom is indicative of Stern's consummate version of an America in which he still believes—a grand place of individualism and universal brotherhood.

> Peter Balakian, in a review of "The Red Coal," in
> The American Book Review, Vol. 5, No. 2, January-
> February, 1983, p. 21.

JANE SOMERVILLE

The publication of Gerald Stern's third major book [*Paradise Poems*] is an important and fortunate event in American poetry. Luckily for us, he didn't give up when he failed to gain the early attention given to his contemporaries. . . . Gradually, finally, he has won his place among our principal poets. Maybe he's lucky, after all, to have had the long, quiet years; the silence; the stern lessons. He says in a poem from *The Red Coal* (1981): "more and more I feel / that nothing was wasted, that the freezing nights / were not a waste, that the long dull walks and / the boredom, and the secret pity, were / not a waste." . . . Out of those "long dull walks" has come a poetry of hard-won blessings, of character, generosity, and wisdom. . . .

Paradise Poems does not represent a change of direction for Stern. He continues to refine and elaborate his exuberant style and to consider themes worthy of a lifetime and more, as they have been throughout the history of thought: the function of the past, the purpose of the poet, suffering, death, redemption, and the definition of paradise.

The poet is lucky because he can devise in his poems an ideal self, an Adamic offshoot of his will, to rule in his created realm. The Stern persona is a patriarch, a shaman, a teacher, a crazy rabbi, an impassioned philosopher, playful and erudite, whimsical and wise. . . . He takes pleasure in the "little harp" of poetry because there are times when "plucking the sweet tongue makes the stars / live together in love and ecstasy." . . . (p. 99)

This first-person speaker is a lovable character, but he is not personal, in the confessional sense. The details of the poet's life and feeling are not the subject of the work. The personal is not used to differentiate one life but to unite it with all others. Stern's invented self is a representative figure, *the poet* or *the man*. It is not "look how I have suffered," but "look how we suffer." The underlying impulse in this kind of poetry is the need to make oneself a part of the whole. This movement toward union is an ancient function of poetry, often lost in contemporary writing that is centered in the effort to separate, to distinguish between rather than unite.

In the same way that Stern's first person is universal, his habitual use of present and future tense is a sign not of immediacy but of continuity and even simultaneity: everything happens again, everywhere, is happening now, will happen, always happens. The Stern poem typically fans out from an instigating image into a chain of association and allusion that breaks down barriers of time and space. . . . The future and the past penetrate the present. (p. 100)

Continuity. Tradition. Myth. Memory. These interwoven subjects comprise one of Stern's central themes: the impact of the past. The Jewish sources of his affectionate reverence for tradition, culture, and learnedness are underscored by strong, Old Testament echoes in the phrasing and structure of his poems. But there is also more than a trace of pagan divination in his "secret humming and adoring." . . . Often, he is more a Cabalistic than a Haggadic rabbi, since his imagination is not essentially moral but spiritual and mystical. He says in a *Missouri Review* interview with Sanford Pinsker that he wants to teach "about how to live, how to survive." But he rarely emphasizes social, psychological, or political issues: his subject is spiritual survival. And it is transcendence through spiritual connection that the past provides. (pp. 100-01)

Access to the redemptive past is through nostalgia, as Stern defines it in one of his *American Poetry Review* . . . essays, those magnificent models of associative prose. Trivial, sentimental nostalgia is a surface manifestation with deep psychic roots which Stern suggests may be the impulse behind all art.

This essential nostalgia is "a search for the permanent." It is "a combination of absence and presence, the far and the near, the lost and the found." It is that charged memory in which are fused the unbearable pain of separation and the sweetness of remembered union. . . . It is the definitive feature of Stern's voice, the amalgam of joy and sorrow that permeates his work.

All nostalgia is a reminder of lost perfection as we envision it at the extremes of experience, in garden beginnings and messianic finality. But we are lucky to have lost paradise. We are lucky to suffer; it is what we do, and knowing that we do it is the basis of our humanity. (p. 102)

We still have paradise; it was our idea, after all. It is buried in us and can be recovered through participation in recurrence, which is possible when we do not feel severed from the past. The Stern poem often finds its center in the garden, emblem of both the permanent perfection of Eden and the cyclical recurrence of it in death and rebirth. . . . When, in February [in **"Picking the Roses"**], he orders flowers from catalogues, he participates in continuance: "I am picking the roses for next time, / Little Darlings for the side of the house, / Tiffany and Lilli Marlene for the hot slope / where the strawberries used to be." Before long, "the dead plants will arrive by mail," and they will carry signs of rebirth, "a leaf or two to signify the good life of the future." He joins in the old, tribal rituals of spring purification: "I will collect all the stupidity and sorrow / of the universe in one place / and wait—like everyone else— / for the first good signs, / the stems to turn green, / the buds to swell and redden." . . .

Transcendence is the reinvention of paradise, a redemptive interval of harmony when the distance between subject and object, past and present, the visible and the historic, is annulled. It is a fortuitous doorway in "the long and brutal corridor / down which we sometimes shuffle, and sometimes run" (**"The Expulsion"** . . .). Yet it must be prepared for. Everything we have—intellect, emotion, memory—must be brought to it and then allowed to drop away, to dissolve in the presence of an unnamed conviction. Maybe we bring it on by singing, by dancing, by sacred gestures. By poetry: the poet receives it, records it, makes it happen in the poem. In Stern, it often comes through the fusion of the visible world, the garden or the city streets, with the art and culture of the past. (pp. 102-03)

There are other, related motifs in Stern that I would like to have mentioned: death, burial, and rebirth; the angel; music; the dream and the secret; friendship; the idea of America (though the emphasis on American idealism in Stern has been exaggerated). And his response to the archetypical themes I have talked about is far more difficult and shifting than I have been able to suggest. His syntax presents complexities reminiscent of Wallace Stevens, and these are hard to decoct.

Stern is a philosophical poet, though his voice is never the cool, detached, rational one we call "philosophical." He speaks with intense feeling of the primary issues of meaning and being that are always his subject. What he calls nostalgia is a version of the tragic vision, in which loss and ecstasy are inextricable, in which spiritual redemption is won through noble suffering. (p. 103)

Jane Somerville, "Gerald Stern: The Poetry of Nostalgia," in The Literary Review, *Vol. 28, No. 1, Fall, 1984, pp. 99-104.*

HAROLD BEAVER

[In *Paradise Poems* Mr. Stern is] intoxicated by the mystery of self, perpetually high on his own emotions: . . .

I am letting a broom stand
for my speech on justice
and an old thin handerkerchief
for the veil of melodrama I have worn for thirty years

This kind of thing can be disliked or admired as the Egotistical Sublime. Certainly he skirts a danger, if not of personal exposure exactly, of too much oohing and aahing. The emotional adventures, however, seem too local and small-scale for quite such a billowing of words. They seem almost a substitute, if not a subterfuge, for other emotional adventures never mentioned. Why is the Stern persona so jumpy, so eager, yet so attenuated? There is really no way of telling. He specializes in candid shots of a kind, but they seem too easily, too professionally candid. It looks as if the attitudes have all been rehearsed. . . . (pp. 18-19)

Harold Beaver, "Meditations on Minutiae," in The New York Times Book Review, *November 11, 1984, pp. 18-19.**

EDWARD HIRSCH

In 1974 I came across a thin book titled *Rejoicings: Selected Poems 1966-1972* in the back of a Philadelphia bookstore. . . . I had never heard of the author, Gerald Stern, but I was immediately struck by the peculiarity of his voice (simultaneously ironic, grief-stricken and exultant), his startling extravagance, humor and compassion. He was clearly past the first flush of youth—one poem began "I didn't start taking myself seriously as a poet / until the white began to appear in my cheek"—and the poems all began with a sense of personal loss and disappointment. Yet they were also small triumphs of rejuvenation, little celebrations of neglected and forgotten places. However flawed, here was an unabashed romantic with a sense of irony and a deep sympathy for the victimized, a middle-aged visionary wandering through the ruins—a weedy field, a burned out Army barracks—struggling to transform loss into exaltation. . . . I'm not sure that the struggle for regeneration was wholly clear to me then, but it is everywhere apparent that *Rejoicings* was written out of just such a quest.

It is now possible to re-read [the recently reissued] *Rejoicings* . . . in the light of the knowledge provided by the three books that have followed it: *Lucky Life* (1977), *The Red Coal* (1981) and *Paradise Poems* (1984). Seen in this way, the book seems almost a prelude, a promise of the more exuberant and extravagant poems to come. It strikes a large number of what have become Stern's characteristic chords and tonalities, his typical verbal strategies and techniques, his essential themes. Failure is Stern's premise. "Rejoicings" is the name of the tractate on mourning in the Talmud, and his book as a whole is informed by an almost ecstatic commitment to mourning, an overwhelming desire to rescue the past from namelessness and oblivion.

In **"Some Secrets,"** a recent essay about his poetic development, Stern reveals that the poems in *Rejoicings* grew directly out of a crisis that occurred around his fortieth birthday. He writes:

I think, when I look back now, that it was my own loss and my own failure that were my subject matter, as if I could only start building in the ruins. Or that loss and failure were a critical first issue in my finding a new subject matter, that they showed me the way. Or that my subject was the victory over loss and failure, or coming to grips with them.

That's why Stern's work keeps returning to abandoned city lots and the waste places of nature, why so many of his poems start with assertions such as "I love the weeds—I dream about them" (**"The Weeds"**) or "I am sitting again on the steps of the burned out barrack" (**"On the Far Edge of Kilmer"**). It is here, too, that his politics originate—with a sense of both "the dignity of isolation" and the dream of community, with his compassion for the defeated, the ignored and the failed. *Rejoicings* was a beginning. The richer and more fully realized poems of Stern's succeeding books go much further in establishing that politics, building out from the individual to the community, linking the personal to the historical. In those books he becomes a poet with a utopian ideal, a late, ironic, Jewish disciple of Whitman.

Stern is a poet of great rhetorical energy and force—a spiritual heir to Emerson, temperamentally akin to the early Ginsberg and the late Roethke—yet he is less interested in the perfected artifact of the poem than in the emotion it embodies. Two of the key lyrics in *Paradise Poems,* **"Weeping and Wailing"** and **"It's Nice to Think of Tears,"** celebrate an almost joyous sadness and revel in feeling. (pp. 55-6)

Stern is a poet of the egotistical sublime, a writer who understands the world in terms of the self and reads his own feelings across the landscape. A surprising (and perhaps disconcerting number of poems in *Paradise Poems* begin in the present tense with a direct and often extravagant personal assertion: "I am letting two old roses stand for everything I believe in" (**"Orange Roses"**); "I know this life is a madness" (**"Huzza!"**); "Today it was just a leaf that told me / I should live for love" (**"Today a Leaf"**). The "I" is usually doing something small and specific in a Stern poem, something quirky and emblematic, characteristically conjoining the miniature and the gigantic, the self and the world. Often one thing is playfully made to represent another; a daily object is arbitrarily designated as a sign for a much larger idea or emotion. (p. 56)

When it comes to tone, Stern is the most surprising and slippery of poets. Typically, he pursues a metaphor or an idea as far as possible to see what it will yield, with the result that his comic inflations often turn out to be dead serious. For example, **"Soap"** begins as an odd, semihumorous piece about finding small bars of soap in human shape ("Here is a green Jew / with thin black lips"), but it quickly evolves into a study of the poet's imaginary East European counterpart who died in the Holocaust. Stern's poems take off on great imaginative and rhetorical flights, and are full of exaggerations, but ultimately they are about witnessing. (pp. 56-7)

Stern is a poet of doubleness: a master of suffering and sorrow continually singing of love and regeneration. All his work is haunted by memory, by the reality of an irretrievable past, but *Paradise Poems* goes further than his previous work in calling that past a paradise, the only one available to us. . . . For Stern, paradise is not a place in the hereafter so much as a country he's already visited, a world of lost innocence and unity, a memory of rapturous moments and ecstatic feelings. "That was the everlasting / life, wasn't it," he asks rhetorically about his youth. "The true world without end" (**"Vivaldi Years"**).

The elegiac poem **"The Expulsion"** laments for a paradise of two, "two at the most," the poet and his father standing in line to see Masaccio's painting of Adam and Eve leaving the garden. **"The Dancing"** recalls a paradise of three, the poet and his parents, dancing wildly in their tiny living room on Beechwood Boulevard:

> . . . the world at last a meadow,
> the three of us whirling and singing, the three of us
> screaming and falling, as if we were dying,
> as if we could never stop—in 1945—
> in Pittsburgh, beautiful filthy Pittsburgh, home
> of the evil Mellons, 5,000 miles away
> from the other dancing—in Poland and Germany—
> oh God of mercy, oh wild God.

By remembering not only "the evil Mellons" but also that "other dancing" Stern becomes a political as well as a personal poet, turning his attention back to the historical world, remembering that one family's heaven exists alongside another's hell. His work continually struggles to enlarge itself so that the destruction of one kingdom—a private personal world—comes to stand for the destruction of a second kingdom—the larger public world. In both realms, every paradise is lost.

The idea of regeneration through music is one of the central motifs of *Paradise Poems.* "It's only music that saves me," **"Romania, Romania"** asserts, and song is the book's dominant metaphor of transport and transformation, even of momentary transcendence. Again and again the poems re-enact an experience "too good for words" (**"Fritz"**), of lying down and listening to Kreisler and Bach and Virgil Thompson, of walking around with the memory of Menuhin and Heifetz and, of course, "the great Stern himself / dragging his heart from one ruined soul to another" (**"Romania, Romania"**). The poems dwell lovingly on moments of singing in harmony. The idea animating them is ultimately the same idea that animated *Rejoicings:* "how hard it was to live / with hatred, how long it took to convert / death and sadness into beautiful singing" (**"Singing"**).

Gerald Stern is the most unlikely of our poets. He is a romantic with a sense of humor, an Orphic voice living inside history, a sometimes comic, sometimes tragic visionary crying out against imprisonment and shame, singing of loneliness and rejuvenation, dreaming of social justice and community. I think of him as an ecstatic Maimonides writing his own idiosyncratic guide for the perplexed, helping us to live in the world as it is, converting our losses, transforming death and sadness into singing. (pp. 57-8)

> Edward Hirsch, *"A Late, Ironic Whitman," in* The Nation, *Vol. 240, No. 2, January 19, 1985, pp. 55-8.*

JIM ELLEDGE

A volume of striking originality, but uneven quality, *Rejoicings,* Stern's first major collection now reprinted, is as enticing as it is confounding. Everyday images set into intensely personal, even fantastic, tableaux, make his work seem unanchored to reality. The effect of this method is twofold: it gives the poems an odd cast (which in itself is not bad), but it may distance them too far from the reader, making them virtually inaccessible—intriguing, even irresistible—but inaccessible nevertheless (which *is* a weakness).

In the best of *Rejoicings,* and much of it is strong, such a style makes for stunning images, achieving depth and clarity simultaneously, as in the opening lines of **"The Naming of Beasts"** ("You were wrong about the blood. / It is the meat-eating lamb we are really terrified of, / not the meat-eating lion") and of **"The Unity"** ("How strange it is to walk alone, / the one leg never growing tired of the other"). Too often, however, the style strains and, as it does, undercuts the poem. At such times, the effect is unproductively bizarre, . . . or simply borders on cliché. . . . (pp. 301-02)

Characterized by despair, anger, fear, and above all, pain—which are also the volume's major themes—Stern's is a sensibility whose goal is to discover a happy medium in life but whose only choices are the extremes he encounters, ones that are often, ironically, insipid, not at all earth-shattering, but somehow no less traumatic for him:

> For years I have been trying to figure out which I hate
>   the most,
> the House Beautiful with microwave ovens and high-
>   heat
>   incinerators
> or the House Ugly with leaky stoves
> and plastic bags spilling out over the sidewalk.

Despite its shortcomings, *Rejoicings* deserves to be read—especially the gripping **"The Heat Rises in Gusts"** and **"The Bite"**—not only because it is the first major work of Stern's acclaimed career, but also because, contrasted against *Paradise Poems,* his most recent collection, it affords us a view of his development from a relatively strong, if marred, beginning to his current, formidable stature.

Stern's voice is a more straightforward one now. While no longer serving to obscure, his personal, fantastic style rises naturally out of ordinary experiences, becoming a powerful element intrinsic to, and supportive of, his subject. . . . His lyricism, too often muffled in *Rejoicings,* is now given full voice. The forceful **"I Pity the Wind,"** for example, offers self-revelation, rare in Stern's early volume—

> I end up just humming,
> true to myself at last,
> preparing myself for the bridge
> and the hand that will lead me over, the hand I adore

—while a scene of "ghoulishness" in **"Singing"** yields to an intense, but eloquent, conclusion.

In the years between *Rejoicings* and *Paradise Poems,* Stern refined his method. The *Paradise Poems,* characterized by a controlled quiet, are ultimately much more effective than the loud, more self-indulgent work in the earlier volume. . . . No longer relying almost exclusively on extremely personal, obscure symbols and metaphors, his recent work—the subjects of which range from love (**"Moscow"**) and family (**"The Dancing"**) to World War II (**"Soap"**), poetry (**"Near Périgord"**), and death (**"Baja"**)—is much more universal in its appeal, while retaining its personal slant. (pp. 302-04)

The clarity of *Paradise Poems* satisfies as *Rejoicings* too often does not. The superficially placid scenes of the later volume, through which terror bursts suddenly and without warning, provide insight into one poet's struggle with "the bitter universe" to achieve a "tried and true paradise." . . . If, before now, there have been any doubts that Stern deserves a respected place in American poetry, *Paradise Poems* will serve to calm them. Stern admits in it, "I am finding my own place / in the scheme of things." He is indeed. (p. 304)

Jim Elledge, "Triumphs," in Poetry, *Vol. CXLVI, No. 5, August, 1985, pp. 293-304.**

STEPHEN C. BEHRENDT

Contemporary poetry, like its historical antecedents, is much occupied with the relation of the individual to the external universe. But where it frequently deviates from its forebears is in its impulse to lend equal weight to the poet's responses also to an internal universe that, while it may be bounded and activated by outward, public things, is overwhelmingly inward and private territory. . . . [There] is apparent in a lot of poetry being published today a strong strain of what the late Enlightenment called "sentiment"—in its positive, affective sense and not in its perhaps better-known (but nonetheless imprecise) sense of emotional gushiness. That gushiness is latent, of course, in virtually any poem that explores its author's internal world, especially if the author responds strongly to a wide range of experiential and imaginative stimuli. In such cases, the quality of the poet's art tends to depend upon the degree to which she or he is able to maintain control over powerful objective and subjective material, to mediate between external and internal realities in consciously articulated performances in the very public, external medium of the printed word.

Two interesting ways of proceeding are illustrated by Gerald Stern's *Paradise Poems* and Robert Gibb's *The Winter House.* While these are very different books by poets of very different sensibilities, considering them together reveals the grounding in sentiment that characterizes both volumes. Both poets begin frequently with the natural universe, with plants (usually flowers) or animals (often fish) minutely observed, or with artifacts of culture, whether music (as in Stern) or architecture (as in Gibb). These external stimuli tend to prompt both poets to explore—either explicitly or implicitly—the theme of "what I am doing now," a theme that generally takes the form of a meditation either on the "present self" observed or on the uses of history in defining the self.

Stern's is a harder, tougher vision: the self in his poems has been battered about rather more, and the shaping universe therefore contains more discord, greater brutality. . . . Stern's poems are filled with startling juxtapositions of images of beauty and brutality, of harmony and discord. But the darker elements of this vision occasionally appear rather too abruptly and without sufficient justification within the text. The final line of **"Rhododendron"** offers an example:

> I prepare for life or death by lying down
> with my left arm under my head, by saying my last
> words to the two trees, by closing my eyes
> to everything else, the dirty woods, the river,
> the green tomatoes, the yellow marigolds,
> the bloody squirrel, the bitter universe.

Where did that squirrel come from? What is its purpose here, placed conspicuously in the final line? Is it meant to harmonize or disrupt? The poem—and several others like it—provide insufficient information to enable the reader to be sure of what is going on, and that *may* be a fault in the poems, depending upon the extent to which the poet intends his poems to be disequilibrious. That questions about the squirrel (I pursue this small point because it is symptomatic of others) are partially answered by other poems (like **"Singing,"** in which the poet muses on the decaying body of a squirrel trapped beneath the ice of a rainbarrel) is not entirely satisfactory to the reader. Any collection of poems inevitably sets up resonances and reflections that magnify both the beauty and the sense of the individual poems. But each discrete poem requires it own internal integrity, its own inherent completeness. When what is obviously meaningful for the poet becomes either quizzical or, worse, distracting or irritating for the reader, the poet may be leaving himself or herself open to accusations of "sentimentalism," in the pejorative sense.

Stern's are powerful poems, though, long of line and tending toward the serial (or "catalogue") constructions of the Bible, of Smart, of Whitman. Poems like **"It's Nice to Think of Tears"** gain expressive power from the repetitions that expand the poem's sense and feeling even as they reinforce its formal rhetorical structures. . . . Stern uses a language so natural, so unadorned, that one is occasionally startled at the eloquence and the musicality of his poems. That is attributable in part to the effective rhetorical structuring, but more to the poet's sure ear. Not weighted by the ordinariness of prose, the language of the poems possesses a vigorous rhythmic basis and a high degree of particularization.

In Stern's [work], history both shapes and informs the present, while the poet simultaneously shapes and informs the historical figures and events about which he writes. This dynamic, creative give-and-take is nicely illustrated by a poem like **"Fritz,"** . . . an affectionate piece that makes Kreisler's fondly-remembered music the fulcrum in a balance between past and present. The relationship expands from the poet's immediate experience of listening to a Kreisler recording, to recalling a performance, to considering Kreisler's acquaintances Brahms, Schönberg, and Casals, to—at last—speculating upon his own relationship as artist to Marlowe, Coleridge, and Dostoevsky. This is an act of sentiment, to be sure: what Kreisler's recording *does* is more important here than what it merely *is*. Repeatedly, Stern's poems place the poet—and the reader who is made a vicarious participant with him—at vantage points from which past and present are rendered equally alive and meaningful, animated through the regenerative power of music . . . , of dance . . . , of visual art . . . , and most importantly of individual life observed from without and within. Even as he presents the world largely as it is, Stern transforms it by focusing insistently upon what that world *feels* like to him, upon what it renders real and absolute in a paradoxical world to the individual consciousness of a talented poet. (pp. 109-11)

Stephen C. Behrendt, in a review of "Paradise Poems," in Prairie Schooner, *Vol. 60, No. 1, Spring, 1986, pp. 109-11.*

Steve Tesich

1943?-

(Born Stoyan Tesich) Yugoslavian-born American dramatist, scriptwriter, and novelist.

Tesich is best known for his screenplay of the acclaimed film *Breaking Away,* for which he won an Academy Award in 1980. Although the film brought him widespread recognition, Tesich had established himself as an accomplished dramatist during the 1970s. The themes and content of *Breaking Away* reflect many of the concerns Tesich develops in his plays. In the film, Tesich centers on a recent high-school graduate living in a college town and blends comic scenes with such themes as the young man's inability to communicate with his father and his feelings of alienation and resentment toward the college students who scorn the townspeople. Tesich's concern with being an outsider, a recurrent subject in his work, derives from his personal background. Having emigrated from Yugoslavia at the age of fourteen, Tesich struggled with learning a new language, making friends, and adapting to a different culture. However, he developed an allegiance to America that would later give his works an idealistic and optimistic tone. Recalling his initial impression of his adopted country, Tesich stated: "I somehow came to believe that, here, anything could happen. . . . I really believed that I had found another frontier, the frontier of 'possibility.'"

Tesich's plays display a varied approach to drama. His first two works, *The Carpenters* (1970) and *Lake of the Woods* (1971), demonstrate an absurdist viewpoint; they center on middle-aged men who are alienated from their families and are unable to make sense out of their existence. *The Carpenters* is set in a house that is falling apart, symbolizing the decay of personal relationships and communication, and concerns a man whose son attempts to kill him. In *Lake of the Woods,* the protagonist seeks solace in the tranquility of the countryside but finds desolate fields and frequent misfortune instead. These plays were faulted for being overly symbolic, a frequent critical complaint about Tesich's work. His next drama, the farce *Baba Goya* (1973; revived as *Nourish the Beast*), drew a warmer critical response. The play's multiplicity of characters and outrageous humor elicited favorable comparisons to the George S. Kaufman and Moss Hart comedy *You Can't Take It with You.* *Gorky* (1975), a musical for which Tesich authored the book and lyrics, concerns the life of Soviet dramatist Maxim Gorky. *Passing Game* (1977) is a psychological drama depicting two actors who conspire to murder their wives. *Division Street* (1980) is a farce in which Tesich portrays a group of 1960s radicals searching for a cause to support in the spiritless 1980s.

Tesich has also written a novel, *Summer Crossing* (1982), which features a young boy coming of age in the industrial city of East Chicago, Illinois. Like most of Tesich's work, *Summer Crossing* was praised for its intriguing characters. Tesich has authored or adapted a number of screenplays besides *Breaking Away,* including *Eyewitness, Four Friends,* and *The World according to Garp.*

(See also *Contemporary Authors,* Vol. 105 and *Dictionary of Literary Biography Yearbook: 1983.*)

CLIVE BARNES

[*The Carpenters*] suggests the demolition of a man's life, the death of his dreams, the erosion of his family. It is a first play by a young playwright, Steven Tesich, and it is concerned with that all-American theatrical theme, father, son and the years between. It is a decent play of some interest—not dazzling, but calm and clean, and in most respects well-crafted.

A typical American family—the Carpenters. Father, Mother, Sissy (well, she has just flunked college for the second time), Mark (well, he has been fired from college for the first time) and Waldo (well, he is mentally retarded). In most matters, then, the typical family.

Except it seems that they are afraid to go out. Even Father seems to be giving up on his job. And the house is falling to pieces. The pump in the basement is broken, the family room built on the side of the house is sinking on its foundations, nothing really seems to work. Life for Father has been reduced to whether he is going to have lamb stew or beef stew in the evening. Even there he doesn't seem to have too much choice. And then his son brings this bomb home. Father becomes aware that his son intends to kill him, and his family doesn't care.

Mr. Tesich's hard look at these non-relating relationships is deft, even subtle. At times, it seems that only the mentally retarded son makes real sense. Later all the family talk with crisp heartless logic, which only Father cannot understand. Father is a monster, and has destroyed his family with unreciprocated love and his own unwanted existence.

The play has not been realistically conceived. The dialogue is deliberately stylized, and with only variable success. For one thing all the characters with the possible exception of Father, sound too much alike. For another they are a shade too remote from our experience, a little too archetypal around the gills.

For Father the play is a journey of discovery: finding out who he is, what he wants and what he has done. I also felt the presence of another play behind the play the author was showing us. In some way Mr. Tesich seemed to be suggesting a portrait of America as a middle-aged man. Tiny symbols seemed to be everywhere, like clues in a party game where you do not quite know the rules. It was frustrating, and also blatant. There was something more banal about Mr. Tesich's hints of allegory than about his wisps of realism.

At its best *The Carpenters* has an air of Greek tragedy to it, and the fact that it is not very often at its best should not be held too harshly against a 28-year-old playwright in his first professional play. . . .

As well as giving pleasure to its audience, *The Carpenters* should teach its young playwright one or two things. Such as being constantly aware of the inevitable threat of bathos inherent in melodramatic touches, and the need for simplicity of purpose as well as simplicity of means.

But this play of an old king and a young pretender set in the darkening landscape of the American nightmare is, I thought, the kind of first play that makes you want to see a second—better still, a third.

> Clive Barnes, "'The Carpenters' Arrives," *in* The New York Times, *December 22, 1970, p. 40.*

WALTER KERR

There's a line of dialogue rolling around in my head this week. Sad as it is, I can't get it out. It's not a line for New Year's, when we ought to be persuading ourselves that new beginnings are possible. . . . The line is this:

> "Help daddy break a rule."

[It is spoken], fumblingly and without much hope, in Steven Tesich's *The Carpenters*. . . . [A father] speaks it to his daughter in the privacy of her bedroom. He wants her to remove her clothes in front of him. He has earlier had an argument with one of his sons. His family is falling apart, he cannot get anyone to chat with him over an offered can of beer, the children speak to him only to despise him. He has cried out, finally, to the most rebellious son, demanding to know in what way he has poisoned the children's lives, what arbitrary rules he has ever plagued them with.

"Can I sleep with sis?" the boy asks, blandly. [The father] sputters, abashed, aware now that he has established rules even if he has never formulated them, aware that most rules are invisible and that he himself is imprisoned by them. When, later, he goes to his daughter's room, it is to see whether or not *he* is capable of escaping a structure of taboos—unexamined *don'ts*—that have frozen them all into hostile immobility. Can

he touch his daughter sexually? He cannot. When she strips before him, the first thing he notices is that she has scratched her knee. He is distracted on the instant by his paternal solicitude, thrown back into the role that binds him; he is, now and forever, congealed daddyness.

I am not recommending *The Carpenters* to you, though I think its author may sometime find a way of using his upside-down insights dramatically. The present piece is oppressed by obvious and top-heavy symbolism. We know that the household is decaying because the toaster, the washer, and the sump pump are all simultaneously on the blink; even the boys' abandoned basketballs in the basement have gone dead. The building itself may soon topple over because it is weighted in a single direction, daddy's; that sort of thing. The language is abstract-pontifical too much of the time: If daddy thunders "I will not be replaced by someone who is going to make my own mistakes!" the oldest boy can come back with "You're expected to fail me—if you don't, you'll shatter my expectations and fail me all the more!" This is programmatic stuff, functioning at several removes from people. (p. D1)

> Walter Kerr, "Two That Try to Break the Rules—And Fail," *in* The New York Times, *December 27, 1970, pp. D1, D5.**

HAROLD CLURMAN

[*Lake of the Woods*] is about a middle-aged, well-to-do businessman. A New Yorker impaled in his office in the highrise Krapp building, he wants to refresh himself from the staleness of his environment and duties. He takes his wilting wife, to whom he has been married for twenty-five years, and his daughter, ailing for want of human "air," on a motor trip through the country. But most of the spots, singled out as points of interest in the guidebooks, such as the "lake of the woods" of the title are bleak, arid, deserted: "petrified forests."

Though not without humor, the businessman is acutely dissatisfied with the vacuum in which he finds himself wherever he goes. Puffing a perpetual cigar, his splenetic disappointment turns to despair. He feels old before his time and the kind of life he has led has wasted him. He wishes his enduring affection for his wife to become ardent again with flashes of the early fire. He wants to find some means of arousing his daughter from her abiding melancholy. But instead his car is robbed by young hoodlums on the road; an old forest ranger (or frontiersman) who now has nothing to do but go to seed in the midst of the despoiled countryside, warns him that children die in the vicinity. The woebegone businessman recalls his past in the army, when he was forever urged onward by the brute orders of his sergeant. The image becomes typical of his whole futile existence.

At this juncture one supposes that the consciousness of his wretched failure in life will kill him. But now, presumably deprived of most of his goods, including his car, leaving all thought of his business behind him, he sets out with wife and daughter on a long trek to discover reality once again, a reality of his own, a reality of things instead of words empty of meaning.

The play begins brilliantly with witty dialogue bristling with sudden darts of cantankerous dismay—they voice his and our discomfort with modern urbanism—but it becomes increasingly symbolic and portentous as the evening progresses. The symbolism disrupts the pleasure experienced at the outset . . .

[because] the point becomes preachment of a sort now become banal. . . .

Harold Clurman, in a review of "Lake of the Woods," in The Nation, *Vol. 214, No. 1, January 3, 1972, p. 29.*

HAROLD CLURMAN

For a silly time, a silly play. The adjective need not be construed as altogether derogatory. On the contrary, Steve Tesich's *Baba Goya* . . . is often quite funny. I might describe the play as a freaked-out *You Can't Take It With You*. But even this thumbnail summation is inadequate because, for one thing, there is a "morality" in the Kaufman-Hart farce which implies "Pack up your troubles and enjoy whatever little things you can; for instance, this show!" Tesich, in a devil-may-care fashion, wishes to shoot the works: he doesn't pretend to verisimilitude. He is extravagant and deliberately inconsequential. All that remains for us in the shenanigans of his play is a wry affection for his central figure, the woman named Goya, and her household. One is also reminded of William Saroyan. (p. 731)

[There is] no way of or point in summarizing the plot of this play; you may seek for symbols in it if you like, but it makes only the sense of a delighted and intermittently delightful senselessness. The comment is in the play's refusal to take anything in our screwed-up society seriously, except the fondness we may have for one another. The play (a bit too long) is a cockeyed comedy about our cockeyed world. (p. 732)

Harold Clurman, in a review of "Baba Goya," in The Nation, *Vol. 216, No. 23, June 4, 1973, pp. 731-32.*

JACK KROLL

[In *Baba Goya*] Tesich sees the family as a vocational school for the absurdities of American life.

Tesich's family, in fact, is a parody of that punch-drunk institution. Goya, the mother . . . , is a raunchy old broad who keeps adopting new children as the incumbents move out of her madhouse into the mad mad world. Mario . . . is her latest in a long line of husbands. He has announced that he is dying, so she proceeds to advertise in the paper for a new spouse, her usual procedure when her mates wear out. Bruno . . . is the current son, a big boob with a Mortimer Snerd-like sweetness, who is a cop. Daughter Sylvia . . . has just returned after a disastrous marriage, and the family is rounded out by an old guy . . . , a sort of adopted grandpa, who goes into a bellicose rage if addressed as Grandpa.

Tesich sets this menagerie in Queens—Archie Bunker territory, and the Bunker reference seems to be one of many: another echo is the lunatic Ionesco family of plays like *The Bald Soprano* and *Jack*. Still another may be the freaked-out kinsfolk of Sam Shepard. This theatrical tossed salad is interesting in view of Tesich's background—he was born in Yugoslavia and came to the U. S. at 14. Like other expatriated East European writers such as Jerzy Kosinski, Tesich's vision of American madness seems colored and accented by his experience of European madness. . . .

The result is something very strong but still unresolved. Where the families in Ionesco or Rabe are solidly conceived and believable as families, no matter how hilariously or bitterly insane their conduct may be, the family in *Baba Goya* seems too often

to be a vehicle for Tesich's ferocious comic impulse. Bruno has arrested a young Japanese . . . for stealing a camera, but instead of taking him to jail he brings him home and handcuffs him to the radiator, whence [he] engages in amazed conversations with the family. . . .

The Oriental camera thief becomes the catalytic figure for Goya and her brood. Sylvia, agonized with guilt for her recent past which includes abortion, drugs, thievery and voting for Nixon, leaves with him to seek happiness. Mario decides he's not going to die, but the prospective next husband, whom Goya has already selected, stays on with the family as a designated helpmate. Bruno peels off his uniform to leave, announcing to the family: "Offhand, I suspect there's a lot more to life than being an orphan or a cop. When I come back, I'd like to come back as your friend."

Tesich wants that last word to resonate as the triggering atom for a new world of new relationships, replacing the old worn-out ones. OK, but his funny, genuinely alive play . . . is a little too pleased with its own wit and energy; it lacks the shock that comes with the real moral force of *Sticks and Bones*. But Tesich remains one of the most promising young American playwrights, and American Place's commitment to him is a rare and exemplary thing in U. S. theater.

Jack Kroll, "All in the Family," in Newsweek, *Vol. LXXXI, No. 23, June 4, 1973, p. 94.*

DOUGLAS WATT

Baba Goya, a sloppy but promising farce . . . , [has been revived] under the new and less attractive title *Nourish the Beast*. I am sorry to have to report that it's still sloppy and, of course, no longer promising.

It's rather a shame, too, because its author, Steve Tesich, . . . is a man with amusing slants on life, a fellow who can turn out good gag lines and funny situations. *Nourish the Beast* has both, but they haven't quite been arranged into a satisfactory play. . . .

There are indications here and there that Tesich hoped to make some relevant social comments through this picture of a screwball household, but the indications are merely distracting. They have a phony sound, too, because Tesich is a writer willing to try anything for a gag, and it is his audacity and comic imagination that impress us most. Basically, *Nourish the Beast* is commercial farce, a sort of updated *You Can't Take It With You*, but it has not been allowed to achieve its proper form. It remains shapeless and marred by heavy hints of meaningfulness. . . .

Though Tesich's play has been wasted, he himself retains promise. All he needs now is proper encouragement at a very crucial period in his career.

Douglas Watt, "'Baba Goya' In with New Name," in Daily News, *New York, October 4, 1973. Reprinted in* New York Theatre Critics' Reviews, *Vol. XXXIV, No. 21, Week of November 26, 1973, p. 181.*

EDITH OLIVER

[*Nourish the Beast,* which originally opened as *Baba Goya*,] deals with an eccentric household in Queens, and it is an odd combination of American domestic comedy that may remind you of *You Can't Take It with You* and of the nonsense of the

Middle European absurdists. Although some of the humor seems forced or arbitrary, much of it pays off, and when it does one is left in no doubt that there is a true, original comic spirit at work. One is also left in no doubt that Mr. Tesich is a dramatist so gifted that when a character of his speaks a word that seems even slightly wrong for him it jars the ear. In any case, I can report that I laughed as often the second time as I did the first, and in many of the same places.

> Edith Oliver, "Return Engagement," in The New Yorker, *Vol. XLIX, No. 34, October 15, 1973, p. 102.*

DOUGLAS WATT

The first thing to be noted about Steve Tesich's *Gorky* . . . is that it's a musical. Maybe it's the last thing that should be noted, too, because when it isn't kicking up its heels and singing, *Gorky* is about as enlivening and revealing as an old Warner Brothers film biography.

The songs . . . allow for production numbers of the sort that might have been labeled "Scenes From Old Russia" in the stage shows offered by Broadway's one-time movie palaces. Mel Marvin's music is perfectly respectable and Tesich's lyrics are fair, but the songs succeed all too well in sounding traditional and ordinary.

The play proper features three Gorkys—man, youth, and boy (he was born Aleksei Peshkov) and all together most of the time. It begins with the old writer alone in his room in a hospital, where he is about to undergo surgery (presumably state-ordered murder for arousing the displeasure of his old buddy Stalin in the terrible period of the purges). Then we flash back to the restless writer's boyhood and proceed through his wanderings as a tramp (the bunks swing into place, the bits of human refuse climb upon them and the busily scribbling Gorky does everything but look out glassily at the audience and murmur, "I'll call it *The Lower Depths*").

It is not only a futile exercise usually for a playwright to write about another playwright, it is also almost invariably disturbing, and the opposite of illuminating, to employ alter egos. In the case of *Gorky,* the almost constant presence of the eager, apple-cheeked boy, the passionate young mustached revolutionary and the saddened old man produce a comical effect, though *Gorky* is mostly a big bore.

Could it be that Tesich, whose flair for comedy was convincingly displayed . . . with *Baba Goya* (later retitled *Nourish the Beast* Off Broadway), meant to be satiric or whimsical about the career of a writer whose purpose in life seemed to end with the eventual success of the revolution and who died in 1936 under mysterious circumstances? No, because by far the most effective moments in *Gorky* are those in which the embittered old man summons up passionate memories of what a momentous occasion, one filled with a promise soon to be perverted, the Russian Revolution was. . . .

Tesich assuredly deserved a showing. But that's as far as congratulations can be extended for *Gorky.*

> Douglas Watt, "Gorky! A Musical!" in Daily News, New York, November 17, 1975. Reprinted in New York Theatre Critics' Reviews, *Vol. XXXVI, No. 25, Week of December 22, 1975, p. 101.*

MARTIN GOTTFRIED

Gorky is the third of Steve Tesich's plays to be produced by the American Place Theater and it is the third of them to strike me as confused, dreary, clumsily written and not very good. . . .

Gorky, of course, is about Maxim Gorky. It tries to give a general impression of the man and his time hoping, in the process, to celebrate the survival of mankind over political systems. That is very grand but unfortunately it is also a very trite heroism.

Tesich begins by presenting the mature Gorky in a hospital room, as a political prisoner of the Soviet state undergoing some kind of brainwashing. The play then flashes back to the writer's childhood in Mother Russia. . . .

Gorky becomes a young revolutionary. He grows disenchanted with the violence around him. He finally, if unenthusiastically, rejoins the movement if only to help artists from within (it smacks of collaboration). The play doesn't even bother to return to the hospital room, which is indicative of its incompleteness.

If this sounds sketchy, it is because Tesich's play is almost impossible to follow and because few details are given. The play is obscure about the simplest facts—one would hardly know from it that Gorky's revolutionary involvement was with the 1905, failed uprising and that he had fled afterward. Nothing is said about whether he ever had a wife, a lover, a child. In fact, it isn't even made clear that he was the author of novels and plays or, for that matter, was a writer at all.

Tesich seems less interested in giving such information than in the simultaneous presence of three Maxim Gorkys at various ages, finally conversing with each other. It isn't the novel device he thinks it is and it certainly doesn't compensate for a style crisscrossing from naturalism to Chagallesque fantasy culminating in, of all things, a Brechtian finale complete with a Weill-like song.

> Martin Gottfried, "'Gorky': A Confused Impression," in New York Post, *November 17, 1975. Reprinted in New York Theatre Critics' Reviews, Vol. XXXVI, No. 25, Week of December 22, 1975, p. 102.*

CLIVE BARNES

For some years Steve Tesich has been a promising American playwright—he is promising no more. Anyone who can produce *Gorky* . . . must be considered to have arrived. For *Gorky,* which is a kind of dramatic essay in biography, is a most interesting play on a number of levels.

It takes many liberties with the facts of Gorky's life, but Mr. Tesich is not merely concerned with giving us just the story of the Soviet playwright and revolutionary, but much more in explaining a man, his character, his environment and his times.

Mr. Tesich seizes upon one very clever device. We first meet Maxim Gorky in a hospital—where he is to undergo "exploratory surgery" under which he is, by Stalin's edict, to die. (The circumstances of Gorky's death are indeed mysterious, and although it was at one time believed that he died of tuberculosis in 1936, the actual cause of his death has in recent years been questioned.) Alone in the hospital ward, Gorky remembers Alex—which is what Gorky was as a young boy, innocent, naive, in love with nature and full of compassion.

Later we meet yet another Gorky called Maxim, for by this time Gorky had taken on his revolutionary sobriquet. Maxim is the fiery-eyed but realistic idealist who wants to see a new world. The singular thing Mr. Tesich has done is to keep all three Gorkys on stage together, talking to one another, arguing with one another, combining into one another—Alex the romantic, Maxim the idealist, and Gorky, the old and dying man, the one-time friend of Stalin, the compromiser of his own conscience.

It is a wonderfully dramatic concept. What a confrontation we would all have were we to meet ourselves as we were at, say, the age of 12! or, for the older of us, at 30. . . .

The other clever thing Mr. Tesich has done is to pitch the tone of the play as if it were itself a Gorky translation. There are plenty of modernisms to disturb this illusion, yet the fact remains that he has written one of his scenes in something of the style of *The Lower Depths,* whereas another suggests Gorky's play *Summerfolk.* This is not at all contrived—yet the impression given has a strong air of autobiography about it. The facts are twisted but the man is straight.

At the first level the play traces an artist's disillusionment with the historical facts of the Russian Revolution, but at a deeper level Mr. Tesich suggests a man's disillusionment at his betrayal of his youthful hopes and ideals, as well as his disillusionment at the compromise of his spirit, and yet his moral and intellectual justification of that compromise.

A serious play then, but a merry one. We see Gorky looking back on his life—first as a child in his grandfather's house, then his wanderings through the misty dawn of the Revolution, the Revolution itself, and later the purges of the artists, and Stalin's reign of terror.

Yet the subject matter is presented with a very Gorkyesque humor—for Gorky was a man who could see humor in anything—and the whole proceedings are much enlivened by songs, . . . which range from boisterous Russian folk pastiches, to a cabaret scene where Gorky is seen as a party functionary deciding which artist is to be liquidated and which to be encouraged, that has something of the jaunty bitterness of Kurt Weill. . . .

Although in some respects this is an unusual play it is also full of old-fashioned virtues, including curtain scenes. The life-assertive ending is most effective, but I shall always remember the conclusion of the first act, where the young boy is staring at the old man (his own future) in absolute bewilderment. It was a moment of extraordinary theater without a word being spoken. And playwrights who can write without words are rare creatures.

> Clive Barnes, *"Tesich's 'Gorky',"* in The New York Times, *November 17, 1975, p. 47.*

JOHN BEAUFORT

Off Broadway lately has been dipping into legend and literary biography. By far the most impressive of these retrospectives is Steve Tesich's *Gorky.* . . .

In somewhat Brechtian fashion, Tesich develops a searching biographical portrait in terms of Gorky's three selves: the innocent youth, the impassioned revolutionary, and the defensive wearily disillusioned victim of a presumed Stalin purge. The moving personal history is presented against the sweeping, swirling background of the national upheaval in which czarist oppression was replaced by Communist despotism. . . .

The songs by Mel Marvin and Mr. Tesich are not mere interpolations, but part of the total fabric of a very remarkable theater piece. *Gorky* deserves an extended run.

> John Beaufort, *"Off-Broadway's Searching 'Gorky',"* in The Christian Science Monitor, *November 19, 1975, p. 22.*

MEL GUSSOW

The lake is foul, the grounds are almost deserted, and menace hangs in the air like thunderclouds. Murders have taken place in these lonely cabins in the woods. Steve Tesich's new play, *Passing Game,* . . . begins promisingly on a note of mystery and portent.

Because Mr. Tesich is one of our more intelligent and serious young playwrights, it is soon clear that the play is intended as an exploration of guilt, retribution and disillusionment, what Eugene O'Neill, in another context, called the "little formless fears."

Up to now, Mr. Tesich's primary gift has been for bizarre, anarchic humor. . . .

Passing Game has only passing moments of comedy. It is meant to be a drama—and it is far less convincing than his earliest work. In it, we see an elaboration of a favorite Tesich theme: people rewriting the rules of the game, improvising a code for survival.

The lead characters are two failing actors, one white [Richard], the other black [Henry], both competing not for roles in plays, but for commercials and voice-overs. Coincidentally, each has brought his wife to the woods with the secret hope that she might be killed by the lake's mysterious intruder.

The most symbolic act in an overly symbolic evening is their lowering of a basketball net so that they can dunk in shots and pretend to be champions. For this and other acts against the natural order, there are no referees or witnesses. In isolation they can cheat.

The wives allow themselves to be victimized. [Henry] has already, with malicious intent, run over his wife . . . with his automobile. As a result, she is permanently crippled. The damage that [Richard] has inflicted on his mate [Julie] is emotional, but torturous. We wonder not only why the wives endure the relationships—[Julie] remains chipper throughout the play—but how they became involved with these bankrupt cases in the first place. At this and other points, the drama stretches our credulity.

The weird background is darkened by two other characters—the nosy rifle-toting keeper of the cabins and his warped nephew, both of whom seemed to have wandered in from a horror movie. In this play the author seems less interested in delineating character than in making metaphorical mileage.

Central to the work is basketball. The onstage court is the scene of collision between rival actors, between black and white. They are engaged in a deadly game of one-on-one. What finally unites them in a homicidal collaboration is a shared sense of guilt and self-hate.

The scenes between the two are frequently charged with tension and theatricality—as [Richard] prods the more seemingly balanced [Henry] into more and more antisocial behavior. These are actors playing actors, a premise that the playwright occasionally uses to advantage, for example in an exuberant, sensual and, ultimately, frightening scene in which they seduce an impressionable young woman. . . .

Mr. Tesich continues to be a provocative writer, but in common with some other efforts at the American Place, his new play needs more nurturing before exposure on a public stage.

Mel Gussow, "Deadly One-on-One," in The New York Times, December 2, 1977, p. C3.

HAROLD CLURMAN

[*Passing Game*] is based on the idea of resentment or hate aroused in men against wives who insist on their husbands' virtue (whether it be talent, nobility, love or fidelity) while these men feel themselves wanting in any or all of these respects. They suffer a murderous sense of guilt. I am sure such feelings occur because, alas, everything occurs. But I am not convinced of it in Tesich's play or even when it was most potently stressed in O'Neill's *The Iceman Cometh*, an "allegory" for all its acclaimed realism, which has never convinced me in its portraiture or in its "philosophic" import.

It is a psychological motivation that only a Dostoevski could successfully dramatize. But not everybody who would be is a Dostoevski. It may be laudably ambitious for Tesich to delve into these depths, but his *Passing Game* is so awkwardly melodramatic, his character drawing so summary, that its total effect is not only turbid but antipathetic. Tesich has talent but he must recognize his limitations.

Harold Clurman, in a review of "Passing Game," in The Nation, Vol. 225, No. 21, December 17, 1977, p. 668.

MEL GUSSOW

[*Touching Bottom*] is an evening of three one-act, two-character plays about eternal hope, fading memory and the difficulty of communication. Each play wears the influence of Samuel Beckett, but they are enrobed in Mr. Tesich's own brand of comic ingenuity.

The first play, *The Road,* is like a variation on *Waiting for Godot*. Two disparate characters hitchhike on opposite sides of a highway. A woman . . . is childlike in her innocence, so naive that she seems to be making fun of herself. A man . . . is worldly and cynical. Having been freed—by death—of a burdensome parent, she is headed toward the city. Having been disillusioned, he is headed toward the country.

For each, the journey will represent a passage and also an escape. They are, of course, the city and the country mouse, dreaming of greener grass. Meeting at a crossroad in their lives they banter, argue and amuse each other—and they amuse us in the audience.

Though the work may seem grounded in cliches, it is lifted by Mr. Tesich's ebullient gift for language and for characterization—his people are at a tilt from reality. The name of [the woman] is "Hope Lange"—not the movie actress. Nothing dismays this good-natured Hope. "Hope makes the heart grow fonder" is one of her many mottoes. "That's 'absence',", corrects [the man]. She is even hopeful about improving aphorisms. . . .

The second play, *A Life,* takes a cue from *Krapp's Last Tape.* . . . [There] is an ancient relic of a man alone in a room. [A woman] appears only as a fleeting memory of his mother. Muttering to

himself, he tries to jog his brain into action. As he demonstrates, with great jocularity, a long life does not necessarily mean a long memory.

Confused and irrational, he has lost all sense of time, although he has memorized the place. Five days have passed since he last heard a whimper from his pet dog sleeping in a dresser drawer. Failing to note the difference between sleep and death, he chatters garrulously with the animal. The man is approaching death—or has he gone past it? . . .

Mr. Tesich's first two plays are short and anecdotal, exactly long enough to sustain the comic mood. The third play, *Baptismal,* is more substantial and also less satisfying.

This is an elegy in a country graveyard about a widow and a widower who repeat their marriages and their marital mistakes to eternity; every day is Doomsday. A line from *Godot*, "They give birth astride of a grave," comes to mind as one watches the play. In *Baptismal*, birth follows death follows birth.

The play has its effective moments, particularly as [the widower] caterwauls his graveside grief while [the widow] tries diligently to go about her burial chores. Again, it is humor arising from the collision of opposites that invigorates the dialogue. But in this case the mood wavers and the language is inconstant. As [the widow] addresses [the widower] as "Husband," it sounds as if Mr. Tesich had suddenly been transmogrified into Nathaniel Hawthorne.

However, coming after *Gorky* and *The Passing Game,* Mr. Tesich's last two full-length plays, . . . *Touching Bottom* reminds one of the earlier Tesich of *Nourish the Beast,* of the author's effortless, absurd humor, his ability to take something similiar and spin it into a comic cartwheel.

Mel Gussow, "Tesich's Comic 'Touching Bottom'," in The New York Times, December 18, 1978, p. C13.

CLIVE BARNES

Imagine a radical flower-child of the '60s, full of dope and politics, trying to enter the Me-generation of the late '70s and to make it more or less intact into the '80s. Doesn't it sound farcical to you? It certainly sounded farcical to Steve Tesich, who has celebrated this all too likely proposition in his new play, *Division Street.* . . .

It is unlike anything Tesich has written before. It is also quite outrageously funny. Tesich is giving us an updated, satirical Feydau farce, with all-American politics substituted for all-French sex. It is a fine comfort.

Tesich has always been one of our brighter playwrights. His plays have usually been rather complex, symbolic essays in what it means to be alive, American, and now. Then last year—or was it the year before?—Tesich found himself writing a Hollywood script called *Breaking Away.* . . .

Now he has returned to the theater without abandoning movies and clearly he has found a middle ground between the naturalism of his movies and the symbolism of his plays. What could be more appropriate than farce? . . .

Tesich works like a computer. As with so many English-speaking writers who do not have English as their native tongue, he has a totally ridiculous regard for bad puns, and sometimes this is just the kind of writing that could give sophomoric a bad name. But his manic comic vision—sometimes in the fashion of his contemporary, playwright Christopher Durang—is irresistable, and his central comic position of one world trying, hilariously, to slam doors on another remains impeccable and ruefully amusing. . . .

[The] befuddled hero trying to reject his radical past is a model of horrified bewilderment—the unsuspecting eye of the farcical hurricane—but the rest of the cast is perfectly matched to Tesich's comic shenanigans. . . .

Incidentally, they are all inter-related and there is the resolution of this extremely clever and beguiling farce. No play that ends on the particular note offered by *Division Street* can be all bad. And this one is good enough not to be missed.

> Clive Barnes, *"Funny Trip on 'Division Street',"* in New York Post, *October 9, 1980. Reprinted in* New York Theatre Critics' Reviews, *Vol. XLI, No. 15, Week of October 6, 1980, p. 157.*

FRANK RICH

In *Division Street,* Steve Tesich has not only found a great subject, but he has also found the courage to tackle it in a daring, mischievous way. Mr. Tesich's new play . . . is about what happened to radicals of the 60's after the movement died. Why does Jerry Rubin now work on Wall Street? Where are the Mark Rudds of yesteryear? These are the kinds of questions that Mr. Tesich implicitly wants to raise. And he doesn't care to provide the hand-wringing, introspective answers you might expect. It's this writer's ingenious notion that the political and psychological hangovers of the 60's—from revisionism to selling out—can be the stuff of broad, slambang farce. A crazy idea, perhaps, but potentially a splendid one.

The trouble with *Division Street* is that Mr. Tesich only intermittently delivers the goods. To be sure, he has devised several riotous gags and has filled the stage with a goodly assortment of idiosyncratic characters, all of whom dash madly about. . . . But if the promise of fun and trenchant satire is everywhere . . . , *Division Street* ultimately proves more frantic than funny, more well meaning than well crafted. By the end, we're still waiting for Mr. Tesich's farce to boil over into hilarity and for his characters to come to honest terms with their teargas-scented past.

At the outset, the playwright leads us to anticipate a lot more. His hero, Chris . . . , is a perfect lightning rod for comedy: a burnt-out radical who has settled in Chicago to seek obscurity as an insurance underwriter. All Chris wants to do is forget about his antiwar years—"Even Pete Seeger is winding down," he explains—but Mr. Tesich refuses to allow him any peace.

Through cockamamie plot circumstances, Chris is soon besieged by addled old cronies and unwanted new acquaintances—a former black militant who has been surgically reborn as a female con . . . , a former wife who still speaks through a bullhorn . . . and a Serbian restaurateur . . . who dresses like Nathan Detroit and is willing to throw bombs to snare his piece of the American dream.

As these oddballs arrive at Chris's apartment, Mr. Tesich adds others and provides a number of vivid set-pieces. The hero's one-time political comrade "Roger the Rotten" . . . turns up to confess such recidivist transgressions as despising the women's movement, owning a Buick and writing letters to TV Guide in praise of his favorite television show. Chris's landlady . . .—a randy middle-aged black woman who also happens to

be Polish—marches about singing "We Shall Overcome." A young prostitute . . . drops by to plead the moral virtues of promiscuity.

In the evening's most biting speech, Chris tries to shut up all his visitors by boasting of his contempt for such post-60's causes as solar power, boat people, sugarless children's cereal and macramé. "I don't know who's running Cambodia," he shouts, "and I don't care!" He forces us to laugh until it hurts.

But Chris never does silence the others, and, the more speeches we hear, the clearer it becomes that Mr. Tesich is dawdling and repeating his jokes. While it's funny at first to discover that Chris's former wife speaks in vintage song lyrics, it's not amusing for two whole acts, or when other characters join in. The Serb's ethnic malapropisms ("That takes the cupcake" and so on) also wear thin, as do Roger the Rotten's paranoid tirades about female orgasms, the landlady's references to sexual "hanky panky" and the Rodney Dangerfield-inspired routines recited by the former wife's nebbishy divorce lawyer. . . . Without new twists to keep them aloft, running gags can quickly run into the ground.

Once they do, the carpentry of the plot collapses with them. Though Mr. Tesich has outdone Plautus in setting up mistaken identities, his comic booby traps never explode in a clever farcical climax. Instead, there's an arbitrary, talky denouement in which all the characters effortlessly solve the earlier confusions. Worse still, the playwright fudges the resolution of his hero's crisis. When Chris finally abandons me-decade narcissism to revert to his old activism, there is no motivation for his conversion. Like magic, he suddenly embraces a new, nonideological "movement" that is just as mysteriously taken up by his friends. Mr. Tesich's final hat trick—an extravagant comic salute to the radicals' reminted version of flag-waving patriotism—is no doubt sincere, but it also seems an attempt to camouflage the play's otherwise inept conclusion.

> Frank Rich, *"'Division St.,' a Comedy by Tesich,"* in The New York Times, *October 9, 1980, p. C19.*

JOHN SIMON

Steve Tesich writes in three modes. He can be absurdist and tough, as in *The Carpenters;* outrageous yet lovable, as in *Nourish the Beast (Baba Goya);* or lightheartedly humane, as in the film *Breaking Away.* I have liked much of his work in all three manners—especially when, as in *Lake of the Woods,* he fuses them all. To the extent that his new farce, *Division Street,* partakes of the second (there is some of the first and none of the third), I found myself laughing along in sweet, frivolous contentment. But the play does not merely lampoon the efforts of a bunch of survivors from the activist sixties either to recapture protest or to embrace *embourgeoisement—* which it does with that nice combination of the preposterous and the clever, tirades of comic desperation and casually tossed-off one-liners that Tesich weaves together so well. Unfortunately, it also tries to be a door-slamming Feydeau farce, with one character getting his face banged too many times; and it also cheats, as when one character's funny talking in lines from popular songs spreads unwarrantedly to other characters.

Worst of all are the last ten or fifteen minutes, in which, as if to repay America for the Academy Award it bestowed on him, Tesich . . . starts advocating a new pro-American revolution. In this proposed neo-sixties movement, our misfits, bathed in more forms of newfound love and bliss than Norman Rockwell could convey in a dozen magazine covers, go off to conquer the country for—I'm not sure what; milk shakes, perhaps, free Disney movies for everyone, and wholesome sex for all oddballs and looneys. That Tesich tries feebly to make even this mushiness seem satirical shouldn't fool anybody. (pp. 102, 104)

John Simon, "Revels without a Cause," in New York Magazine, Vol. 13, No. 41, October 20, 1980, pp. 101-02, 104.*

BRENDAN GILL

[*Division Street*] is the kind of rowdy farce that I admire. It is recklessly extravagant in thought, word, and deed, and the amount of energy expended in the course of carrying out its totally improbable plot would no doubt suffice to drive a locomotive from Montauk to Malibu. Since its author, Steve Tesich, is still a young man, we have to assume that he has been reading omnivorously from the cradle; if anyone were so ill-advised as to attempt a doctoral dissertation on the literary origins of *Division Street*, he would be obliged to start with a handful of Greek and Roman comic playwrights and wind up, breathing hard, with Mel Brooks. Oscar Wilde is here, seated cheek by jowl with George S. Kaufman, to Kaufman's obvious discomfiture; here, too, looking even more dishevelled than usual, are Laurel and Hardy and other crowned clowns of the recent past. The play is a palimpsest of classic sight gags and pratfalls; all that it lacks is some means of bringing itself to an intelligible conclusion, and that is a common failing of farces, which tend to be perpetual-motion machines. What else should we expect of them, given that their subject matter is the folly of mankind? (p. 137)

Brendan Gill, "Nonconformists," in The New Yorker, Vol. LVI, No. 35, October 20, 1980, pp. 137-38.*

CAROLYN SEE

[In *The Carpenters* Steve Tesich] had the courage to say that none of us can really be better than our families, and that our parents, for reasons of their own, have a vested interest in limiting our happiness, just as we—as in a horrible fairy tale—must grow up to try and thwart our own children.

Not since Fitzgerald has anyone so clearly stated, in terms of art, the America that exists in youth and youth alone, where 95% of us are raised to graduate from high school and then die in the spirit; how American parents deserve contempt, *court* contempt, because not only have they not become President, they have become old. Young men in America live under a curse. They are told repeatedly that the future belongs to them. The future is nothing but open doors, a hideously officious speaker tells the young men of *Summer Crossing* at a high school assembly, but an "older" married woman of 25 tells three boys, ". . . men around here fall apart after 40 like cardboard boxes." (p. 1)

As in Tesich's own, earlier, *Breaking Away*, the geographical terrain of *Summer Crossing* is the American Midwest. But this heart-of-America is harsh and sterile. East Chicago, Ind.—industrial nowhere, its main product carcinogens—is still able to spawn class after class of promising American boys. This year's crop includes sensitive, intelligent, discouraged Daniel Price, and his two close friends—Bill Freund, forever after called Freud, and Larry Misiora, "Mean Larry," the one smart enough to know he's going noplace, that his life is an *oubliette*.

The time is the last month of senior year and the following summer, when the first great winnowing of American winners and losers occurs. Daniel Price, like most of us, knows what's happening in his life and yet doesn't know it. He won't go to college, dreads the factories, can see nothing ahead worth doing. All he knows, at the beginning of *Summer Crossing*, when school is still in session, is that he's lost the state wrestling match and doomed his long-suffering coach to an entire career of coaching losers. Daniel also knows that through losing, he's made his father happy.

Price belongs to the working class. His mother labors as a cleaning woman, his father at a factory. . . . (pp. 1, 11)

Inevitably, Price loses his friends. Freud, with his weight, his tedious girlfriend, is already a lost, obsolete grownup. "Mean Larry" finds his own desperate way of avoiding or transcending the future. But Price is torn between questions of love and death. His father is dying. (And not since Fitzgerald have we so matter-of-factly seen that grotesquely shortened life span, the 40-year life-expectancy of the American male. *Of course* men die when their sons graduate from high school. *Of course* their 38-year-old wives become widowed crones in black.) Daniel has fallen in love with a young woman a few streets away who lives alone with her "father," a girl named Rachel, but *is* that man her father, or are they lovers—is she in love with him? Young Rachel calls Daniel her "boyfriend," flirts with him, sleeps with him. But Daniel's intuition, the evidence of his senses, keeps telling him something is dreadfully wrong.

But what does Daniel know anyway, about anything? His father calls the girl Rachel "wretched"; for him the whole world is misery. His mother tells him tales of shepherds who made love to her in Montenegran meadows—what is Daniel to make of *that*? Rachel tells him anything she wants to; he doesn't know what to believe, except to know that he's in love.

But "love" baits the trap of the factories. "Love" leads to reproduction, age, death. It is everlastingly to Tesich's credit that his young Daniel Price wants that confinement. Even as he recoils from what has happened to his parents, he plots to possess, to imprison Rachel and himself in exactly the same reproductive trap.

What does the future hold for Daniel and what price must he pay for it? Freud will stay and rot in East Chicago; Mean Larry has cut his own frightening path. Daniel, almost by accident, chooses the way of the artist. Browsing during this paralyzed, idle summer he picks up a stack of "great books" from the neighborhood library. "I never read *Tender Is the Night* because I read the last sentence first and I didn't like it." But what if you took that material—those American Valleys of Ashes and coarser older women, and men that (mostly) die at 40, and youths of heart-breaking sensitivity and beauty with no future ahead of them, and put it together so that one out of 100 managed to escape; managed to have a happy ending? No wonder young Americans love Steve Tesich so much. (p. 11)

Carolyn See, "A Man About the Midwest Makes His Own Big Breakaway," in Los Angeles Times Book Review, October 31, 1982, pp. 1, 11.

DAN WAKEFIELD

[*Summer Crossing*] has to be counted a commercial and critical risk in today's supercharged literary marketplace. Mr. Tesich has committed a wholly traditional first novel. It is about a young man coming of age, feeling the joy and loss of first love, leaving his drab Middle Western home and going out into the world to become a writer. One can almost hear the ho-hums of certain sophisticated commentators programmed to respond to such subject matter by asking, "So what else is new?"

The answer is, Mr. Tesich's novel is new.

It is as new as its theme is old, as fresh as its plot is familiar. Working within conventional bounds, the author gives us a deeply moving story with a cast of unexpectedly intriguing characters.

The hero is Daniel Boone Price, a high school wrestler. As the story opens, he is grappling with his own conflicting emotions as well as with the state champ, an insidious hulk with a downstate Hoosier drawl whose "small, round head sat on top of that prehistoric neck like a Crenshaw melon on top of a fire hydrant." In a match that is one of the most psychologically revealing sporting events of recent fiction, Daniel watches his opponent keep smiling while his own comfortable lead dwindles to that unthinkable but inevitable moment when "I eased back into defeat as if into my proper place." . . .

[Against an] unbucolic backdrop the author sets his original variations on archetypal high school heroes and hangers-on, vintage 1961. (p. 15)

[There is] the quintessential high school beauty, Diane Sinclair, as unapproachable as she is gorgeous. . . .

It is not this typical prom-queen replica who captures the heart of our hero, however, but a mysterious newcomer named Rachel, who tempts and taunts, beckons and repulses, and so consumes his emotions and imagination that he begins to wonder, "Had I become somebody else?" Part of the painful and yet productive part of his own maturation is the struggle to understand and distinguish between his romantic image of Rachel and the real, complex young woman of flesh and blood, force and contradiction. . . .

Just as Rachel is far more complex than a typical teenager, the relationship between her and Daniel cuts deeper and more painfully than the ordinary Angst of adolescent romance. It is played out against the concurrent death by cancer of Daniel's bitter father, and the story plunges us to depths of feeling that go way beyond the light and breezy implications of the book's title. This is a painful passage, told with integrity as well as talent. (p. 31)

> *Dan Wakefield, "Growing Pains and Joys," in* The New York Times Book Review, *October 31, 1982, pp. 15, 31.*

JUDY TYRRELL

"I bet, I just bet that some man is an island."

So begins a poem written by Larry Misiora, one of Daniel Boone Price's two best friends during his senior year at Roosevelt High School in East Chicago, Indiana. Nothing is su-

perfluous in Steve Tesich's first novel, *Summer Crossing,* and Larry's poem is no exception. Daniel, the narrator of the novel, a young man whose background closely resembles Tesich's, marvels at Larry's poem: "A pang of envy clarified my own opinion of it." He marvels at Larry's heretofore unknown literary talent and he marvels, as the book progresses, at Larry, who seems to be somewhat of an island himself. . . .

Rachel is another island. She is Daniel's first love, a girl whom he adores, but of whose affection he is never sure. . . .

Between both these couples (Larry-Daniel and Rachel-Daniel) is Freud. Billy Freund, Daniel's other friend, is called Freud because "a substitute teacher . . . had called him Freud and that was all it took." But don't let Tesich deceive you. This is not the only reason for the nickname. Freudian psychology is at work throughout the novel in the form of David, who comes between Rachel and Daniel, and in the very complicated relationship between Daniel and his father. I shall leave it to the psychologists to analyze.

The final triangle in the novel is represented by the Price family. There is Mrs. Price whose strength, confidence, and independence Daniel recognizes as well as he recognizes his father's weaknesses. . . . Mrs. Price is the other island.

Mr. Price is like Daniel, from his thick hair to his lack of confidence. "If [my mother] had doubts, it was about the rest of the world, not about herself. My father and I did it the other way around." As Daniel comes to realize that he is not like his mother, whom he envies and admires, but more and more like his father whom he resents and even hates, he is terrified. And as his father slowly and agonizingly dies of cancer in Daniel's house on the very sofa where he and Rachel had made love, Daniel is torn between hatred and guilt, and terror that he will end up like that.

The characters evolve in inextricable plots: Larry/Rachel/Mother v. Daniel. All three relationships could be successful, Daniel thinks, were it not for Freud/David/Father who thwart him at every opportunity.

Ironically, Larry and Rachel, whom Daniel admires for their ability to stand alone, just want to be like everyone else. Larry wishes he had never graduated from high school so he would not dream of anything beyond the steel mills. Rachel watches the cheerleaders practice and observes others at parties and bonfires as she dreams of acceptance by a group and longingly remembers her friends from childhood.

Summer Crossing is a novel about hope. "Don't ever hope," Mr. Price tells his son. "Promise me you'll never hope. . . . It can kill you." But Daniel does hope and in the end, he leaves. "And so I went out into the world." The novel ends with this line, just as the adult life of Daniel Boone Price is beginning. One hopes that Steve Tesich's career as a novelist is just beginning, too.

> *Judy Tyrrell, in a review of "Summer Crossing," in* The American Spectator, *Vol. 16, No. 2, February, 1983, p. 35.*

Hunter S(tockton) Thompson

1939-

(Has also written under pseudonyms of Raoul Duke and Sebastian Owl) American nonfiction writer, journalist, editor, and scriptwriter.

Rising to prominence in the mid-1960s as one of the creators of New Journalism, Thompson developed a style of writing which he called "Gonzo journalism." While New Journalism as practiced by Tom Wolfe and Norman Mailer combines factual reporting with such fictional techniques as stream-of-consciousness narrative, extended dialogue, shifting points of view, and detailed scene-setting, Thompson's Gonzo writings rely on vituperation to parody current events and satirize American culture. His best-known works, *Fear and Loathing in Las Vegas: A Savage Journey to the Heart of the American Dream* (1971) and *Fear and Loathing: On the Campaign Trail '72* (1973), revolve around the wildly irreverent adventures of his fictional personae, Raoul Duke and Dr. Hunter S. Thompson.

Thompson began his career as a newspaper reporter and later became a magazine writer. His 1965 article on the Hell's Angels, "The Motorcycle Gangs: Losers and Outsiders," published in *The Nation,* led to his first book, *Hell's Angels: A Strange and Terrible Saga* (1966). Thompson spent more than a year among the California motorcycle gang, gathering first-hand information in order to produce an account of how a group of social misfits had become national celebrities through sensationalistic journalism. While debunking many popular misconceptions about the gang, Thompson also advanced the theory that the Hell's Angels were models for the growing class of malcontents who clashed with bourgeois society. Richard M. Elman described the book as "a metaphor . . . which even in its grotesque nonsensicality, manages to scratch a bit of truth off the American veneer."

Thompson attributes the origin of Gonzo journalism to a deadline crisis he underwent while reporting on the 1970 Kentucky Derby for *Scanlan's Monthly* magazine. Unable to write the story, Thompson submitted the unedited pages of his notebook. The magazine published Thompson's notes verbatim, and the resulting article, "The Kentucky Derby Is Decadent and Depraved," brought him critical acclaim. His second book, *Fear and Loathing in Las Vegas,* was his first work to fully exhibit the Gonzo style. Thompson was sent by *Rolling Stone* magazine to Las Vegas to cover a motorcycle race and a district attorney's convention on dangerous drugs and narcotics; he essentially ignored both events and focused his narrative on the drug-crazed adventures of his narrator, Raoul Duke, and Duke's sidekick, Samoan attorney Dr. Gonzo. In this book, Thompson asserts that the drug-induced hallucinations of Duke and Gonzo are nightmarish and horrific but reflect the garish and disturbing reality of Las Vegas and of society in general. Confounding the distinction between fact and fantasy, Thompson created in Raoul Duke a persona whose disoriented mind conveys an attempt, according to John Hellmann, "to distort the surfaces of realism in order to reveal their underlying truth." Jonathan Raban, however, faulted Thompson for writing "fiction without honour, fact without responsibility," and stated that "by blurring the edges of reality, he makes intelligence worthless and vision an act of petty fraud."

© Allen G. Arpadi 1981

Thompson's monthly reports on the 1972 presidential campaign for *Rolling Stone* were collected and published as *Fear and Loathing: On the Campaign Trail '72*. In his characteristic Gonzo fashion, Thompson's writings concentrate more on the campaign trail experiences of Dr. Hunter S. Thompson, journalist and narrator, than on the candidates and issues of the campaign. Some critics have indicated, however, that Thompson is concerned in a larger sense with the history and future of America. They interpret Thompson's vision of the United States as one in which the powers of good and evil are in constant struggle to gain control of the country. The choice Americans were given in 1972 between George McGovern and Richard Nixon affords, according to Thompson, an ideal symbol of the duality central to American nationalism. Thompson saw Nixon's imminent landslide victory as the ultimate confirmation of his country's inclination toward barbarism.

After writing sporadic articles for *Rolling Stone* during the remainder of the 1970s, Thompson published *The Great Shark Hunt: Strange Tales from a Strange Time* (1979), a collection of pieces he had written over the previous sixteen years. Commenting on Thompson's limited output since the early 1970s, Nicholas Lemann suggested that perhaps Thompson was "a victim of changing times. He saw America as a simple place—gross and corrupt and ruled by evil men but simple nonetheless. Now . . . it seems more complicated." Thompson's next book,

The Curse of Lono (1983), based on his coverage of the Honolulu Marathon, is written in Gonzo fashion, leaving only a fraction of the book for the marathon itself. The escapades of Thompson's narrator/persona and his partner, British illustrator Ralph Steadman, comprise much of the story, while the rest concerns the drug-induced incidents and singular logic that lead the narrator to believe he is the reincarnation of the long-lost Hawaiian god Lono.

Thompson's writings have been classified both as journalism and as fiction. This incongruity has created much critical controversy and has occasionally served to discredit the authenticity of Thompson's insights. Nevertheless, most critics consider Thompson's work original and perceptive. Kurt Vonnegut praised Thompson as "that rare sort of American author who must be read. He makes exciting, moving collages of carefully selected junk. They must be experienced."

(See also *CLC*, Vols. 9, 17 and *Contemporary Authors*, Vols. 17-20, rev. ed.)

WILLIAM PLUMMER

For many in the early 1970s, especially those under 30, Hunter S. Thompson achieved instant celebrity when he suggested that Hubert Humphrey be castrated....

Thompson was a lean and plain-speaking Cassius ... in an age, like most, that preferred the wish-washy idealism of its Brutuses. Thompson managed to be both plain-speaking and unscrupulous, somehow at the same time. Plus he was wickedly funny, unless, of course, you were Ed Muskie and minded it being "reported" in *Rolling Stone* that you were taking an exotic form of South American speed throughout the campaign....

Hunter Thompson was a star of the 1960s New Journalism, that fictional/factual mongrel born of the novel's turning navel-contemplative and of the general feeling that the derangements of the era required a more personal and high-energy witness than the who-what-where-how-and-why of conventional journalism permitted. Thompson perpetrated his own brand of madness called "Gonzo" or "Outlaw" journalism, which blended nicely with much of what was in the air: not the Beatles and flower politics, but Bob Dylan's lyric "To live outside the law you must be honest" and Norman Mailer's confounding the saint with the psychopath. During the reign of Richard Nixon, Thompson set out to be to journalism what François Villon once was to poetry.

Thompson erupted into the national consciousness in 1966 with *Hell's Angels: The Strange and Terrible Saga of the Outlaw Motorcycle Gang*—a curious book. Thompson was obviously turned on to his subject by the rash of lurid stories in the press, by eight-column heads like HELL'S ANGELS GANG RAPE, by such sinister runes as "Repeatedly ... Assaulted Aged 14 and 15 ... Stinking, Hairy Thugs." But his intimacy with Frenchy, Tiny, Terry the Tramp, and Charger Charley the Child Molester taught him that the Angels were mostly regular guys, Kiwanis unvarnished. (p. 36)

In 1971 Hunter S. Thompson was at large and geared for his most outrageous book, *Fear and Loathing in Las Vegas*, which was salvaged from an aborted assignment for *Sports Illus-*

trated.... *SI* wanted 250 words of caption material on the Mint 400 auto race.... Thompson and his sidekick, the "Samoan attorney," never even saw the race.... Dope-driven, the dynamic duo spends most of its time courting disaster: building up huge hotel bills, converting rented Cadillacs into wrecks, vomiting, and running hilarious numbers on the petite bourgeoisie of Las Vegas....

As far as his devout readers were concerned, *Fear and Loathing in Las Vegas* was not a manic panty-raid or paranoid fantasy but writing to scale. "What is sane?" Thompson asked. "Especially in 'our country'—in this doomstruck era of Nixon. We are all *wired* into a *survival* trip now." His recipe for survival?—Drop acid and match strides with the rough beast slouching its way toward Watergate....

[Thompson's 1979 book], *The Great Shark Hunt*, is really a selected works which contains sizable chunks from the Angels and Fear and Loathing chronicles. It also contains samples of his work prior to becoming a "doctor of Gonzo Journalism"—notably, fairly straightforward reports from Latin America for the *National Observer* about smuggling and revolutionary shootouts. In addition there are extended musings on Jesus freaks, Jean Claude Killy, the Beatniks, Haight-Ashbury, the Oakland Raiders, Marlon Brando, Hemingway, as well as numerous irreverent things on Nixon and Jimmy Carter. Above all, there is the piece on the Kentucky Derby in 1970 for *Scanlan's Monthly*, the first Gonzo effort, in which the good doctor's search for the single face symbolizing "the whole doomed atavistic culture" leads him to his own hotel mirror: "There he was, God—a puffy, drink-ravaged, disease-ridden caricature...." We've met the menace and he is us—a lesson that has tutored Thompson's writing ever since. A corollary to which is Dr. Samuel Johnson's "He who makes a beast of himself gets rid of the pain of being a man." If in the post-Nixon era the *zeitgeist* is laid back rather than far out, there is still "the pain of being a man." And Hunter Thompson is only slightly less fascinating and cathartic today than he was half a dozen years ago. (p. 37)

> *William Plummer, in a review of "The Great Shark Hunt," in* The New Republic, *Vol. 181, No. 8, August 25, 1979, pp. 36-7.*

VIVIAN GORNICK

Hunter Thompson is a professional wildman. He poses variously as a maverick journalist, a nonstop drug-user, an enemy of Main Street America and the Corporate State—but being wild is really what his profession is....

Turned loose on American sports and politics, he has run screaming through the pages of *Scanlan's* and *Rolling Stone* for nearly 10 years now, saying in print what everyone else on the scene supposedly thinks but doesn't write, drugged out of his mind because the real insanity lies with these "scum-sucking, pigfucking geeks" we call Middle America, his uniform disgust for the ordinary blue-suited corruption we reward with money and power apparently unflagging: as though that corruption was his target. Then, suddenly, Thompson will savage his own people, and you know savaging everything in sight is his real target....

Everything and everyone he writes about gets exactly the same treatment: same language, same commentary, same subordinate position in the story. It's amazing how little we actually learn about the people Thompson is purportedly writing about;

there is no differentiation among the geeks at the Kentucky Derby, the pigfuckers on the Great Shark Hunt, the greedheads in Aspen. (Essentially, the eye of the nihilist—even when the nihilism is spurious . . .—is an incurious one; it is interested only in debunking and denying, not in observing truly.)

And, indeed, why not? Who gives a damn about the businessmen in Florida or the gentry in Kentucky or the realtors in Colorado? What has Thompson to say about them that can ever be half as good as what he does when he begins his rich, special, self-referring language? . . .

Thompson's talent—and it really is his only talent—lies in his ability to describe his own manic plunge into drink, drugs, and madness through a use of controlled exaggeration that is truly marvellous. There are many moments in his stories—all having to do with paranoia finally induced after hours and days of swallowing, snorting, slugging down amounts of pills, powders, and alcohol that would long ago have killed an army of Berbers—that are so wonderfully funny you are left shaking with laughter and the happiness of literary creation.

But—and this is also the thing about being a wildman—these moments are surrounded by pages and pages, and still more pages, of compulsive writing without purpose or destination. Thompson reduces his power by never knowing when he has a point, or if he has a point, or if he long ago overtook the point and just kept going.

> Vivian Gornick, "The Gonzo and the Geeks," in The Village Voice, *Vol. XXIV, No. 47, November 19, 1979, p. 51.*

JOSEPH NOCERA

College students are especially susceptible to writers who project an unusual and compelling vision of the world. Those who have a weakness for stratospheric superheros fall for Ayn Rand; those who dream of mystic sensual pleasures may go under the spell of Hermann Hesse. My weakness was for American madness, so I fell for Thompson. (p. 46)

The main purpose of Thompson's style . . . was to give its creator a persona.

I won't deny that this persona has charm. In *Fear and Loathing in Las Vegas,* by far the best sustained writing he ever did, the appeal of the book is linked directly to Thompson's ability to make his own character appealing. The problem with Thompson's persona is that as a literary vehicle it is extremely limiting. It worked well in the Las Vegas book, but Thompson probably should have dropped it right there. Unlike Wolfe, the more Thompson relied on his new voice, the less he was liberated by it. If all his work was going to center on his exaggerated vision of himself, then he had to constantly be doing interesting or amusing things. But as a reporter Thompson simply doesn't do much that is particularly interesting. He is lazy, to begin with. We read about him reading newspapers, watching television, hanging around, and then as deadline approaches, dropping some speed, turning up the stereo, and staring at a blank piece of paper until 6 a.m. In both *Fear and Loathing On the Campaign Trail* and *The Great Shark Hunt,* this sequence is repeated over and over again. It quickly wears thin.

Because Thompson himself spends so much time on center stage, there is very little space left over for those other, lesser characters—minor ones like George McGovern. If you go to

Thompson's books and articles looking for any sort of understanding of the events he was "covering," you're bound to come away disappointed. (pp. 46-7)

My guess is Thompson knew from the start what a literary fraud he was perpetrating. . . .

Yes, Thompson knows the truth—he's rich and famous not because of his talent or suffering, but because he happened to have one clever idea in exactly the right place at the right time. Since this isn't hard to detect . . . the question becomes, why were so many people taken in?

In the case of the reporters who covered the 1972 campaign, whose praise had a lot to do with giving him respectability, I think the answer was simply envy. All of them were bound by certain constraints—there were things they wanted to say but couldn't under the rules of the game. Except Thompson. Thompson could say whatever he wanted and it would be printed, no questions asked. Thompson could write fantasies, diatribes, lies, and speculation. He had so much *freedom.* And he could shamelessly make himself the star—an effect many reporters secretly long for and go to elaborate lengths trying to achieve. . . .

As for the rest of us, we countercultural types who lapped up every precious word the doctor shoveled our way, the cause of our hero-worship was equally simple, though far more unattractive. Hunter Thompson was the journalist who catered to our prejudices. He described politicians the way we ourselves liked to describe them; he pictured the American political system the way we pictured it. He made no attempt at explaining or understanding or challenging. He simply told us what we wanted to hear.

Thus: "Hubert Humphrey is a treacherous, gutless old ward-heeler who should be put in a goddamn bottle and sent out with the Japanese Current." The Democratic party was "a gang of senile leeches like George Meany, Hubert Humphrey, and Mayor Daley." Henry Jackson was "that worthless asshole"; and on and on. (p. 48)

It is easy to see now that Thompson was pandering to our worst instincts. There was no attempt to explain, say, *why* Hubert Humphrey was a "treacherous, gutless old ward-heeler"—it was merely *assumed* to be so, and that Thompson's readers will automatically agree with that assessment. Which of course they did.

This cultural arrogance represents one of the worst sides of the counterculture. We felt we were so special—so enlightened—that anyone who was not one of us was a lesser species of human. In Thompson's writing, this attitude is best typified by an excerpt from the Las Vegas book, in which he describes the difficulties of a policeman trying to confirm hotel reservations. . . . (pp. 48-9)

Thompson hates this cop without ever having spoken a word to him. But don't we all. He is a *cop,* after all, and what's worse he has an "Agnew-style wife" and he's from "a small town in Michigan." The evidence is so compelling! How can you have anything but contempt for such a man?

It was, of course, intellectually fashionable to sneer at cops back then. Thompson made a good living riding the fashion. In that respect he was a manifestation of an old and ignoble strain in American journalism. We have always had our share of writers more interested in being fashionable, or snide, or above the fray than in understanding or enlightening. Thompson can probably trace his lineage directly to H. L. Mencken.

When you read Mencken's political journalism today, he's very difficult to make much sense of. He's witty alright—full of bombast and insult—but he tells you almost nothing about those conventions he "covered" so faithfully over the years. Going to Mencken to learn about Calvin Coolidge is about as useful as going to Thompson to learn about George McGovern. (p. 49)

So you can see Thompson as primarily a continuation of this smug, intellectually hollow tradition. But that would lead you to conclude there are no lessons to be learned from his experiments with style, which I think is wrong. Thompson's work provides considerable insights into why New Journalists missed a great opportunity—the chance to find a fusion between the writing of opinion and the writing of fact.

Almost all respectable journalism is one or the other, fact or opinion. It splits writers into two camps, with neither side able to tell the whole story. This division can be seen most easily in the format of a conventional American newspaper—a news hole crammed with unexplained facts, and an editorial page crammed with unsubstantiated opinions. It can also be seen in the careers of great journalists. Walter Lippmann, for instance, was one of the best and most productive opinion writers we shall ever see. His writing was powerful in its analysis of events, but often unpersuasive, because it lacked the strong factual examples needed to snap ideas out of the realm of the theoretical and lock them into the reader's brain. . . .

At the opposite extreme are great fact writers like the craftsmen at *The New Yorker,* who have an extraordinary ability to assimilate facts and write about them in an exacting form. Yet these writers often leave the reader in the dark as to what, if anything, the parade of facts signifies. . . .

Yet in conventional journalism, the writer who tells you one thing is forbidden to speak of the other. This ridiculous distinction is not only confining to the writer in his search for truth, but injurious to the reader in his search for understanding. Cold meaning-less objectivity belongs in wire-service reporting of the day's events, but when you find it in *The New Yorker,* being tossed off by the finest writers and editors the country has to offer, you've got to feel cheated.

New Journalism promised to change all that. New Journalists would break the bonds and establish new styles, perhaps developing a new general form that would merge fact-writing and opinion-writing, a style you might idealistically call truth-writing. But more than anyone else, Hunter Thompson has damaged and discredited New Journalism's promise. Instead of being exhilarated by his freedom, he was corrupted by it. Instead of using it in the search for truth, he used it for trivial self-promotion. . . .

The ideal of New Journalism—to find a form that explains, enlightens, and entertains all at once—has not died. You can see movement in that direction in newspapers like *The Washington Post* and the *Miami Herald,* which are putting increasing emphasis on writing the analytical series whose purpose is to tell the whole story. You can see it in books like *Southerners* by Marshall Frady. . . . But Thompson has given New Journalism a bad name, and the damage he did may take a long time to undo. . . .

He may have shot New Journalism right through the heart. (p. 50)

Joseph Nocera, "How Hunter Thompson Killed New Journalism," in The Washington Monthly, *Vol. 13, No. 2, April, 1981, pp. 44-50.*

JOHN HELLMANN

Fear and Loathing in Las Vegas: A Savage Journey to the Heart of the American Dream (1971) and *Fear and Loathing: On the Campaign Trail '72* (1973) . . . have established [Thompson] as an original (and certainly the most controversial) new journalist. In these works Thompson has developed a journalism which communicates, both formally and thematically, his black humorist vision. The pervasive theme of Thompson's work is one of "doomed alienation on your own turf." In his "fear and loathing" works he has expressed this malaise through an innovative application of the same parodic devices found in black-humor fictions. The result is journalism which reads as savage cartoon.

Thompson achieves the freedom to break with realism by extending the central metafictional device in Mailer's *Armies of the Night.* [Mailer] presents facts through two versions of the self, narrator and participant personae, who are separated by time and perspective. Since, as implied author, he presents all of the facts in the works as perceptions of one or the other of these personae, Mailer is free to develop the subject matter as his personal construct of actual events. By keeping differences in time and perspective negligible, Thompson creates only one persona who serves as both narrator and protagonist. This persona may appear at first as a simpler creation, a mere self-caricature; but that self-caricature is in fact a highly sophisticated tool, which the actual Hunter Thompson manipulates as calculatingly as Laurence Sterne did Tristram Shandy.

As the shaping authorial mind behind the narrating persona, Thompson creates a self-caricature who is extremely disoriented, both by actual events and by paranoid illusions—often induced by liquor or drugs—present in his own consciousness. Presenting journalistic events through the perceptions of this maddened, even hallucinating, persona, Thompson presents his black humorist vision of those actual events without violating their actuality. Like a mad seer or a holy fool, this persona can reveal aspects of events not readily apparent to those with normal perception. Through self-caricature Thompson is able to take Mailer's metafictional journalism into the more radically fictive world of parody. (pp. 68-9)

As a vehicle of parody, the persona is first of all clearly not what E. M. Forster called a "round" or "realistic" character. He has virtually no complexity of thought or motivation, and he does not undergo subtle changes from experience. He is instead a two-dimensional cartoon character, a caricature resulting from Thompson's "flattening" and exaggeration of certain of his own characteristics. (pp. 69-70)

Thompson's self-caricature is a paradox of compulsive violence and outraged innocence, an emblem of the author's schizophrenic view of America. His attachment to handguns and vicious dogs reveals his tendencies toward violence and paranoia, tendencies which are also apparent in his hyperbolic prose style. But the persona also has a determined belief in the power of good intentions and right methods which runs counter to his violent impulses. Despite the psychotic threatening, his artistic aims include the corrective impulse of satire. . . . [His] persona shows interest in money only as the means to his reckless freedom, and shares the traditional American hero's reluctance to become involved with the females whom he encounters on his travels. While he parodies America's impulses to violence and paranoia, the persona is untainted by the same society's lusts for conquest and possession.

The created persona is essentially defined by the title phrase, "fear and loathing," for it embodies both the paranoia with which the persona perceives the ominous forces pervading actuality, and the aggression with which he seeks to survive it. This latter trait is particularly crucial, for despite the comic buffoonery and paranoia delusions, Thompson's persona is hardly a passive anti-hero. A descendant of the trickster character of folklore, the Vice of medieval drama, the picaro of early prose narratives, he is a self-portrait of the journalist as rogue. Like his literary ancestors, he is a shape-shifter who uses cunning and agility to survive the dangers of his environment. As he says in *Fear and Loathing in Las Vegas*, "We are all wired into a survival trip now." But as a journalist and a human being attempting to report contemporary events, the dangers he meets are psychological and spiritual. Defining himself through opposition, he counters them with violence and laughter.

For this reason Thompson's persona narrates events with a comically brutal prose and participates in them with comically cruel pranks. Like Kosinski's protagonist in *Cockpit*, he must continually attack in order to resist. Like Vonnegut's narrative persona, he must laugh in order to remain sane. (pp. 70-1)

Fear and Loathing in Las Vegas is, in barest outline, the author's purported autobiographical confession of his failure to fulfill the magazine's assignment to "cover" two events in Las Vegas, the Fourth Annual "Mint 400" motorcycle desert race and the National Conference of District Attorneys Seminar on Narcotics and Dangerous Drugs. It is more exactly the author's (or "Raoul Duke's") tale of his hallucinations and adventures while with a 300-pound Samoan attorney called Dr. Gonzo, actually a Chicano lawyer named Oscar Zeta Acosta . . . , who serves as a parody of noble savage "sidekicks" from Chingachgook to Tonto. The book is, then, even in its most general subject and presentation, either a report of an actual experience which was largely fantasy or an actual fantasy which is disguised as report. Journalism only in the loosest sense, what is reported is the state of the persona's mind and, metaphorically, of the nation.

Epistemological and ontological ambiguity is communicated in the opening sentence: "We were somewhere around Barstow on the edge of the desert when the drugs began to take hold." . . . By thus combining observed data with an admittedly altered consciousness, Thompson signals the reader that the narrating persona, Raoul Duke, is taking him on a journey both actual and hallucinatory. . . . (pp. 73-4)

Opening his mind to the interior hallucinations of drugs and the exterior hallucinations of Las Vegas, [Thompson] will create a fable. But because any such invented meaning will be of questionable value, the fable must be constructed as a self-conscious literary parody complete with capitalized themes (The American Dream) and archetypal characters (Horatio Alger). In content, *Fear and Loathing in Las Vegas* is to be report as invention; in form, account as fable. With this parody of a journalistic aesthetic Thompson becomes, as Jonathan Raban characterized him in his extremely unfavorable review of the book, "a professionally unreliable witness" [see *CLC*, Vol. 17]. He uses new journalism to write fabulation, placing his work on an "edge" between fact and fantasy.

Thompson makes his second justification for his methods on a thematic level. Exposing the theme with a distancing irony by calling it "the socio-psychic factor," he nevertheless makes it clear that the parodic quest after the American Dream is also a painfully serious flight from a corrupted condition: "Every now and then when your life gets complicated and the weasels start closing in, the only real cure is to load up on heinous chemicals and then drive like a bastard from Hollywood to Las Vegas. To *relax,* as it were, in the womb of the desert sun." . . . This parody of the American Adam's archetypal desire to escape the complications of civilization is to be also a comment on that quest's contemporary perversion. The protagonist, threatened by the "weasels" (which suggest an active corruption), is traveling east, not west, seeking rebirth not in the solitude of the forest but in the isolation of the desert.

These authorial inversions of the conventional reporter's approach to actuality and the traditional American hero's search for fulfillment result from a single response to the unreality of contemporary America. For Thompson, the landscape of America in the 1970's is itself hallucinatory, and Las Vegas, America's dream city, epitomizes it. Viewing the city through his own countering hallucinations, Thompson's persona sees a world differing from the surrounding desert only in its artificiality, for the impulses of society and nature appear predatory to him. Upon their initial arrival, for instance, Raoul Duke enters the hotel bar with his attorney, to discover the following: "Terrible things were happening all around us. Right next to me a huge reptile was gnawing on a woman's neck, the carpet was a blood-soaked sponge—impossible to walk on it, no footing at all." . . . Later Duke flees Las Vegas and rushes into the desert, only to find himself shooting at gila monsters which he suspects are stalking him. . . . In either setting, city or desert, society or nature, the persona's drugged perceptions reveal the same underlying reality: a world reptilian in its ferocity. (pp. 74-6)

[While] drugs have advantages as weapons of survival (Dr. Gonzo refers to taking them as being "armed"), Duke and Gonzo employ laughter as their most necessary defense. Many critics of black-humorist fictions have commented on comedy's ability to distance one from horror, to allow some degree of psychic control and thus survival. Duke protects himself from both his own and others' horrors through unrelenting humor. . . . The ability to laugh at horrors that are really only hallucinations, whether personal or societal, enables the psyche to survive in a world which seems predatory and savage.

There is, however, an actuality beyond the hallucinations of drugs and Las Vegas, a world which is so real that laughter cannot serve as an effective weapon against it. Years ago Burton Feldman attacked black humor as inadequate in the face of "Auschwitz, or King Leopold in the Congo, or Hiroshima," and asserted that "a reader can only be agreed with if he concludes that the world is surely worse than Black Humor is telling him." But Charles Harris has pointed out that in black humorist works "realistic incidents frequently intrude upon the fantastic and grotesque" in a way that "results in reader disorientation."

Thompson gains precisely this effect by interspersing Duke's hallucinatory and comic experience in Las Vegas with various all-too-actual experiences brought in from the outside world by the media. These "objective" reports present *actual* nightmares; they impinge upon the characters' consciousness with a pressure which compels them to escape into only *apparent* nightmares. In the hotel room, for instance, they briefly turn on the television, only to find a scene more disturbing than the imagined reptiles they have just left: "The TV news was about the Laos Invasion—a series of horrifying disasters: explosions and twisted wreckage, men fleeing in terror, Pentagon generals babbling insane lies. 'Turn that shit off!' screamed my attorney. 'Let's get *out* of here!'"... Thompson includes some of these stories in paragraph-length excerpts, so that their "objective" prose stands in counterpoint to the book's agitated style. As a result, the reader himself returns to the hallucinatory and comic narrative with the same relief that the persona feels when he returns to the hallucinations and comic adventures. The parodic invention which is this "report" becomes itself both defense and escape for the reader.

In a number of episodes in *Fear and Loathing in Las Vegas* Duke and Gonzo play cruel (albeit largely rhetorical) pranks upon other characters. These scenes may appear to be the worst kind of smug ridicule directed against the ordinary and unsuspecting; certainly they would be of questionable taste if Thompson's persona did not portray himself as such a paranoid madman. (pp. 77-8)

But Thompson's persona does not wish to be savage merely in order to seek vengeance and expose baseness. The primary motivating force is the same one behind the drug-taking and laughter: survival. In a world motivated by appetite, questions of morality and fulfillment become irrelevant, even dangerous: "This place is like the Army: the shark ethic prevails—eat the wounded. In a closed society where everybody's guilty, the only crime is getting caught. In a world of thieves, the only final sin is stupidity."... This perception explains Thompson's epigraph for the book: "He who makes a beast of himself gets rid of the pain of being a man."... The persona must become a beast in order to possess the primitive skills that can insure his survival.

Isolated in a tavern in the middle of the desert, Duke makes this transformation by undergoing a reversal of the traditional Christian revelation and conversion. Abandoning the luxuries of morality and guilt, he tells God, "The final incredible truth is that I am not guilty. All I did was take your gibberish *seriously* ... and you see where it got me? My primitive Christian instincts have made me a criminal."... (p. 80)

Up until this point Duke and Gonzo have been moving in a state of absolute fear. Duke himself, deciding that "my margin had sunk to nothing,"... has ignored his new assignment to cover the District Attorneys' seminar, choosing instead to sneak out of Las Vegas in total paranoia. But from this moment on he counters despair not with paranoia, but with ferocity. Exchanging his "fear" for "loathing," he becomes an aggressive character.... It is with this aesthetic of aggression (the same one which informs the book's style) that Duke returns to Las Vegas to "infiltrate" the drug conference *Fear and Loathing in Las Vegas* turns from a dominant ethos of paranoia in Part I to one of revenge in Part II.

Thompson presents these various aspects of *Fear and Loathing in Las Vegas*—the drug-induced hallucinations of the two main characters, the hallucinatory landscape of Las Vegas, the horrors brought in through the news media, the defensive laughter, the predatory vision of the society, the self-transformation of the protagonist into a beast in order to survive—within a structural pattern based on a self-conscious parody of the quest for the American Dream. This motif is provided not simply through the subtle patterning of the implied author, but as the joking concept of the characters themselves, Duke and Gonzo. Duke says that this is to be a contemporary tale of the great American

historical-mythical-literary archetypes: "Free Enterprise. The American Dream. Horatio Alger gone mad on drugs in Las Vegas."... The self-consciousness of the persona in making this quest is important, for it reduces the American Dream to parody. Because disillusionment with America's ideals, the exposure of American values as self-deceptions, has so long been typical of modern American literature (*An American Tragedy, The Great Gatsby*), the search for those ideals can no longer be undertaken seriously. The American Dream has so long been isolated and exposed that the contemporary writer, however keenly he feels it as both need and loss, can treat it only as a joke. (pp. 80-2)

In *Fear and Loathing in Las Vegas* Thompson bypassed the conventions of traditional journalism and realistic fiction to create a work which confused the author-reader contracts of new journalism and fabulation. Quite aware of the trick he had brought off, he professed to be unsure any longer of what parts had actually happened and what parts were imaginary. As an account of his experience of the Las Vegas assignment, the distinction was probably irrelevant. He confronted the problem of reporting a "story" he didn't understand by inventing one of his own, and the result is an important report on the American unreality of the late 1960's. (p. 85)

John Hellmann, "Journalism and Parody: The Bestial Comedies of Hunter S. Thompson," in his Fables of Fact: The New Journalism as New Fiction, *University of Illinois Press, 1981, pp. 66-100.*

PUBLISHERS WEEKLY

Thompson is in fine form in his latest fable for the age of anxiety [*The Curse of Lono*], which begins with the editor of *Running* magazine hiring him to cover a marathon in Hawaii.... Barely are [Thompson and his companions] off the plane when Thompson is regaled by stories of natives butchering tourists.... Interspersed throughout the text are sidebars recounting the disastrous career of Capt. James Cook (1728-1779), who had been greeted as the god Lono upon his arrival in Hawaii, but was bloodily murdered by the natives within a month. Thompson sees significant parallels. This is Thompson's liveliest book since *Fear and Loathing in Las Vegas,* a hilarious examination of the dark underside of things, written with perfectly controlled hysteria.

A review of "The Curse of Lono," in Publishers Weekly, *Vol. 224, No. 14, September 30, 1983, p. 113.*

KIRKUS REVIEWS

Fear and Loathing on the Kona coast of Hawaii: Thompson trots out his familiar act as Yahoo-anarchist-*poète maudit* [in *The Curse of Lono*]—but despite a few inspired fits of zaniness, and some appropriately phantasmagoric drawings by Ralph Steadman, it just doesn't work. The Thompson-Steadman vision of Las Vegas made powerful symbolic sense because its neo-Boschian monstrosities seemed like a fun-house mirror of late 1960s America. Here too we get the (literally) incredible boozing and drugs, the violent antics of the journalist (assigned to cover the Honolulu Marathon) gone haywire, the sardonic put-on of outpigging the pigs. This time Thompson fancies himself the reincarnation of the Hawaiian god Lono, a brutal deity in charge of "the season of abundance and relaxation," who sailed away on a three-cornered raft promising to return.... Finally, after ignoring the Marathon (''Why do those buggers run? Why do they punish themselves ... for no prize at all?'') and enduring three weeks of furious tropical storms and sodden misery, Thompson saves his strange vacation by landing a 308 lb. marlin hours before flying back to Colorado. The one photo in the book shows Thompson (barely distinguishable from any other lei-garlanded tourist) grasping the dorsal fin of his catch in cool, self-mocking triumph: Lono has arrived. But he hasn't—just an occasionally amusing *Haole* and generally insufferable wise-ass. (pp. 1093-94)

> *A review of ''The Curse of Lono,'' in* Kirkus Reviews, *Vol. LI, No. 19, October 1, 1983, pp. 1093-94.*

MICHAEL DIRDA

It's been at least five years since Hunter Thompson checked in with *The Great Shark Hunt,* and it's good to report that the doctor of Gonzo journalism remains as crazed as ever. In his latest misadventure [*The Curse of Lono*] he and hapless illustrator Ralph Steadman journey once more into a savage land, this time Hawaii where they have been commissioned to cover a runner's marathon. Like the motorcycle rally in *Fear and Loathing in Las Vegas,* this event merely provides the starting line from which Thompson cuts away into a confusing series of increasingly manic adventures.... Nothing much happens really, though Thompson spends a lot of time setting off firecrackers, gulping margaritas, running up hotel bills, and swinging his Samoan war club at plants and fish. The doctor even appears—despite moments of heroic excess—disturbingly levelheaded when measured against a few of the maniacs who cluster round him. Is he slowing down? And what of an occasional feeling of *déja lu*? Sheer irrelevance. No one writes like Hunter Thompson, though many have tried, and *The Curse of Lono* dispenses pages rabid with his hilarious, frenzied rantings, gusts of '60s madness for the stuffy '80s.

> *Michael Dirda, ''Fear and Loathing in Hawaii,'' in* Book World—The Washington Post, *December 18, 1983, p. 13.*

FRANKLIN REID GANNON

Hawaii has survived typhoons, earthquakes, tidal waves, Pearl Harbor, blue-rinsed widows and the missionary position. So it will undoubtedly weather Hunter Thompson's *The Curse of Lono* ..., a drug-crazed account of fear and loathing in paradise....

[*The Curse of Lono* is] more a long article than a proper book—and even at that, some of it is strained or straining. But for those who have missed the good doctor, its appearance is mighty welcome....

If your vision of Hawaii is Thomas Magnum working out on a surf ski borrowed from the King Kamemeha Club, give *The Curse of Lono* a wide berth. But if you can subscribe to the Thompson motto—''When the going gets weird, the weird turn pro''—here's the perfect tropical toddy to warm up a winter's night.

> *Franklin Reid Gannon, ''Gonzo-Style Journalism Goes Hawaiian,'' in* The Wall Street Journal, *January 9, 1984, p. 16.*

CHARLIE HAAS

Comparisons between *Fear and Loathing in Las Vegas* and Hunter Thompson's [*The Curse of Lono*] are inevitable.... But the differences between the books are as striking as the similarities. ''Raoul Duke,'' Mr. Thompson's pseudonym in *Fear and Loathing,* is absent from *Lono,* leaving the real Hunter Thompson to act and account for himself. If *Fear and Loathing* was, in Mr. Thompson's word, an experiment, then *Lono* is a control, an attempt to put a more or less real self through the motions of ''Gonzo journalism.'' But despite some stylish and funny passages, *Lono* is not nearly the sharp entertainment that *Fear and Loathing* is, and Mr. Thompson, wanting to reflect a different moment in time, may not want it to be. His Hawaii is a mix of cheap tourism, constant racial violence, boom and bust, and storms that turn the book into a sullen chronicle of a rained-out vacation. The Gonzo manner seems down to a formula at times, and, most disappointingly, the fantasies that provide vicarious vindication in *Fear and Loathing* seem bilious and undirected here.... [Connoisseurs] of Hunter Thompson may hope that *Lono* is the prelude to a new groove.

> *Charlie Haas, in a review of ''The Curse of Lono,'' in* The New York Times Book Review, *January 15, 1984, p. 19.*

Stephen Vizinczey

1933-

Hungarian-born Canadian novelist, essayist, and dramatist.

Vizinczey gained international attention with his first novel, *In Praise of Older Women: The Amorous Recollections of András Vajda* (1965), both for the quality of the work and for the circumstances surrounding its publication. Vizinczey emigrated to Canada after the Soviet Union suppressed the Hungarian Revolution of 1956. He wrote *In Praise of Older Women* in English, his second language, and formed his own company to publish the work after rejecting the sole offer he received from a major publisher. The novel became an international best-seller. *In Praise of Older Women* is a picaresque narrative centering on the sexual exploits of a young Hungarian whose life resembles Vizinczey's in many ways. Like Vizinczey, András Vajda matured during an era of great turmoil in Hungary and eventually emigrated to Canada, where he became a professor of philosophy. In the novel, Vizinczey depicts Vajda's adventures against the chaos of the World War II era in Hungary and later amidst academic life in Canada.

Vizinczey's second book, *The Rules of Chaos: or, Why Tomorrow Doesn't Work* (1969), is a collection of essays on such topics as philosophy, politics, and literature. The essays are linked by his belief that the element of chance exerts a great influence on life. Vizinczey's second novel, *An Innocent Millionaire* (1983), concerns a young man who becomes obsessed with recovering a sunken treasure off the coast of Peru. While crafting an entertaining adventure story, Vizinczey examines such themes as idealism, avarice, love, and betrayal. He also makes extensive use of witty aphorisms, a significant element in all of Vizinczey's writings.

KILDARE DOBBS

[Vizinczey is a] Hungarian rebel who in 1957, a landed Canadian immigrant, could hardly speak our language and who even today speaks it with an impenetrable accent and whose name, moreover, we can't pronounce, and he has the gall to place himself, with his first book [*In Praise of Older Women*] . . . , among the masters of plain English prose. No pyrotechnics, no standing on his head for the company, no wrenching of the native idiom to accommodate foreign thought-processes—just cool, rational style, the masculine virtues, the right words in the right order. (p. 29)

A glance at the subtitle is enough to set up formidable prejudices: *The amorous recollections of András Vajda*. No branch of literature is more suspect than amorous confessions. Yeats used to say of George Moore that while some men would kiss and tell, Moore would tell whether he'd kissed or not. And I've never been able to read people like Frank Harris, Henry Miller and D. H. Lawrence without an uncomfortable feeling that, however much we may owe them as brave pioneers, they are unreliable witnesses on sex. In our own generation there's

Norman Mailer. . . . What these writers have in common is an attitude that can only be described as hornier-than-thou.

One reason why **In Praise of Older Women** is so remarkable is that its narrator, András Vajda, doesn't share this attitude. His amorous recollections, set down with classic grace and concision, own up to as many failures as successes. "I'm not an expert on sex," he explains in a brief foreword, "but I was a good student of the women I loved, and I'll try to recall those happy and unhappy experiences which, I believe, made a man out of me." The intention is modest, and he achieves it with so much frankness, lucidity and good humour that he disarms all misgivings.

Vajda, after all, could easily have been a mere figure of fun—the hot-blooded Hungarian with roving eye and rambling hand whose heavy breathing we've so often heard in the back seat. But though his view of life is in the best sense comic—life being a comedy to the man who *thinks* and Vajda a philosophy professor in Saskatoon, Sask.—it's a view that takes in some of the most desolating historical landscapes of our age. The background is dark and violent: Hungary under the Nazis, torn by war between Russians, Germans and Americans, Hungary under Communism, Hungary in revolt, Hungary crushed by the Red Army. The hero, like the author, lived through all this. One by one he brings into the cool radiance of memory the women he loved, telling as it were a rosary of human meaning against chaos and horror.

Vajda explores differences between the erotic education of Europeans and North Americans. His book, dedicated to older women, is addressed to young men, and "the connection between the two," he slyly tells us, "is my proposition." The young North American wastes his spirit in the uninstructive pursuit of virgins: the young European is far more often initiated to love by a mature woman. Vajda's mistresses, usually around thirty-five to forty, are no figments of daydream.... Evoked with affection and profound insight into character, they are seen with irony, that is to say, with intelligence. It's more than probable that some readers—particularly the kind of unreconstructed readers who believe that society could be improved if only the imaginary people in novels could be made to behave decently—will mistake this irony for cynicism. But to do so would be to miss Vizinczey's point, which seems to be that given an honest confrontation with the worst of life, it's still possible to love generously and be loved in return. (pp. 29-30)

In Toronto an Austrian cab-driver tells him, "The natives are just as human as any place else, but they won't admit it unless they're drunk." Later on, at the Couchiching Conference of all places—the way Vajda tells it, it's a real swinging scene, a kind of academic Saturnalia—he becomes acquainted with a Canadian campus wife who wants to be seduced. She is indignant when he won't oblige: "I thought you Europeans were supposed to be heroes in the war of the sexes!" But he tells her, "I'm a pacifist."

Vajda is disappointed and not a little bewildered by Canadian women, though he cheerfully exploits the sexual revolution. One senses a deep nostalgia for his Hungarian amours with women who, though they were intelligent and well educated, *knew* they were women and knew what a woman was. He's overwhelmed, too, by the sheer numbers of his Toronto affairs: there are "problems of timing, confusion of identities, and constant lying." The last straw is the outcome of his renewed attempt to take up where he left off with the erring wife he met at Couchiching. At a critical moment she affronts his Hungarian sense of decorum. Once more he chooses exile—this time to Saskatoon....

I believe we have to go back to Boswell's *London Journal* to find anything that matches Vizinczey's book for freshness, candour and unaffected charm. When I was a boy, one of my schoolmasters gave me *Romeo and Juliet* to read. "You'll fall in love one of these days," he told me, "and you might as well learn to do it properly." For the same reason I gave my copy of *In Praise of Older Women* to my sixteen-year-old son. (p. 30)

Kildare Dobbs, "Hungarian Loves," in Saturday
Night, *Vol. 80, No. 9, September, 1965, pp. 29-31.*

ELIOT FREMONT-SMITH

"This book is dedicated to older women and is addressed to young men—and the connection between the two is my proposition." The puns in this author's epigraph are no accident. The young narrator of *In Praise of Older Women* is a champion propositioner, and the connections he enjoys are frequent and varied. He is an egotistical fellow, but with some reason; his bravado self-assurance is softened with candor, and though promiscuous, it is not mere exploits he is after. He likes women,

this Hungarian Julian Sorel, not girls; which is to say, erotics is his form of love and philosophy of life, his hang-up or his blessing.... Young girls are the victims, he discovers, of sexual obsessions, in which sensuality is reduced to strictly mechanical acts and fears. So he finds he prefers women older than himself (around, say, 35), who are capable of more honest and more personal connections. If this is unfair to girls, it's a nice valentine to their slightly elders.

A valentine and a tract, and not much more. As a novel, *In Praise of Older Women* is rudimentary indeed....

[The] book is pretty much a parade of liaisons, some frustrating, more rewarding and all most educative—for him and us. A slightly spoofing, 18th-century tone enlightens the message ... which is, roughly, that sensuality is one of the nicer things about us, and a way—if we only relax enough to know it—to make connections with each other as whole persons. And that, in contrast to most preachings, it is people, not disembodied sex—not orgasm or virginity—that we should respect.

It is this obviousness, of course, that distinguishes Vajda-Vizinczey from D. H. Lawrence, Helen Gurley Brown, Don Juan, Norman Mailer, Terry Southern, Norman Vincent Peale, the sex manualists and mannerists, cautionaries and cuties, the coy pornographers and the pulp pornographers.

If *In Praise of Older Women* goes not much of anywhere as a novel, as an essay on erotics, it is refreshing, individual, forthright and debatable. It is, in an important way, a post-pornographic book; in terms of theme and for our still snide time, it can be called "for adults only." Neither leer nor snigger is here—and that, for some, will be the offense.

Eliot Fremont-Smith, "A Valentine for Adults Only,"
in The New York Times, *February 14, 1966, p. 27.*

MARVIN MUDRICK

In Praise of Older Women has a most unpromising look about it: more horseradish and folk-wisdom, Hungarian style. It was written in Canada by a Hungarian refugee, in a Continental-accented classroom English. It starts out sounding very much like the barely fictionalized autobiography of a minor Casanova; and one irritably anticipates the parade of complacent identical conquests. It dismisses the charms of girls for the commonplace reasons—they tease, but they don't give—and exalts "older women" because they not only give but give with pleasure. Whereupon Mr. Vizinczey strolls unexploded through all these minefields, telling the story of a man who answers to his own satisfaction the Hungarian *mot*, "Is there life before death?" Love and women are so exciting and agreeable to András Vajda that he is ungrudgingly grateful and pays discriminating attention.... (p. 17)

András's life is not an easy one, either with the women he loves or in the track of the juggernaut of history: from World War II, when he serves as a twelve-year-old pimp for American soldiers in Austria, to the Hungarian uprising of 1956, which exiles him first to Italy and then to Canada. As a social historian, Mr. Vizinczey succeeds both in suggesting the dimensions of these public catastrophes and in demonstrating their irrelevance to the hero's life. András is not victimized by his impulses, he knows that though love is larger than history it does not last....

In Praise of Older Women is extraordinary in its modesty and buoyancy, its fearlessness and persistent unemphasized sadness. It comes to the boundaries of life, but only after alert and energetic explorations. It celebrates no myths, and casually cripples a few (such as the myth of that raging red weapon the he-man). It celebrates, in fact, only what it proves by the authority of its disinterestedness. It has no tricks, it doesn't begin with a thesis or end with a gimmick, it doesn't reprint old Hungarian menus or dinner conversations, it doesn't strike a blow for political freedom, it is neither indignant nor compassionate. It is a good novel. (p. 18)

> Marvin Mudrick, "'Evelyn, Get the Horseradish'," in The Hudson Review, Vol. XIX, No. 2, Summer, 1966, pp. 305-18.*

JOHN DANIEL

[*In Praise of Older Women* takes] the form of the amorous recollections of Andras Vajda from his seclusion in the Philosophy Department of the University of Saskatchewan.

Beginning his thesis in pre-war Budapest, Professor Vajda takes us—with the aid of quotations from famous non-erotics such as Engels and Kierkegaard—through the encounters of his childhood, adolescence and young manhood. The chapters are divided into neat subjects: 'On War and Prostitution'; 'On Don Juan's Secret'; 'On Virgins'; 'On Happiness with a Frigid Woman'; 'On Grown Women as Teenage Girls' down to 'On More than Enough.'

This scholarly paraphernalia is classic, but a trifle misleading here. Mr Vizinczey is not writing an instructional handbook on older women, but a continuous narrative of a young libertine in Hungary and Canada, and one soon forgets whether his women are older or younger. There are some vivid glimpses of life under the Germans, the Americans and the Russians and an account of the hero's escape after the 1956 uprising, but, as with all picaresque erotica, it takes second place to the sex, especially in the latter half of the novel.

Once the scene has been established and the identity of the hero clear, we are not over-concerned in which town or country his bedrooms are. The sensualist optimist is happy to be a cork on the seas of life, and this necessarily makes the narrative aimless. It could have been longer or shorter without making much difference. As it is, it eschews any serious Sorel-like purpose and intends to be no more than it is: a buoyant diary of sex for sex's sake.

> John Daniel, "Rake's Progress," in The Spectator, Vol. 217, No. 7207, August 12, 1966, p. 210.*

MERVYN JONES

The aim of [*The Rules of Chaos: or, Why Tomorrow Doesn't Work*], so far as I can make out, is to let us know what Mr Vizinczey thinks about this, that and the other. He is against concentrated power, race prejudice, sexual puritanism and the Vietnam war; he is for beauty, freedom and doing your own thing. I have never met Mr Vizinczey, but feel that I'd like to and that an evening of listening to him in some pub or café would go down nicely with a carafe of plonk. With a second carafe, one might even feel that it had been an intellectual evening. However, when the talk is set up in print and marketed at thirty bob one is bound, at the risk of sounding prim, to examine it by other standards. Intelligent it is; original, profound or intellectually demanding it is not. For instance, Mr Vizinczey has much to say about causality and chance. This

is a subject exhaustively investigated by philosophers and indeed by mathematicians. What Mr Vizinczey thinks, or what I think, is largely a matter of temperament. A feeling that the world is governed by flukes may be of value when transmuted into a well-written poem, novel or autobiography, baldly expressed, it really ought not to cost money. Most of Mr Vizinczey's opinions *are* pretty baldly expressed, at that, with an engaging vigour but without much aphoristic grace. I agree with most of what he says, but I wouldn't fight to the death for his right to say it.

Parts of the book, as is discernible from an abrupt sound of gear-crashing, are transplanted or expanded reprints of articles or reviews published elsewhere. The best of these is an attack on William Styron's overpraised novel, *The Confessions of Nat Turner*. Even here, though, the thinking is casual. In a longer discussion of Stendhal—this, unfortunately, never rises above the level of a bright schoolboy essay on 'My Favourite Author'—Mr Vizinczey insists that the quality of a novel is everything and its subject-matter of little or no importance. In the *Nat Turner* bit, though he takes a few cracks at Styron's mushy prose, he condemns the novel for its prejudiced view of race relations and its distortion of what really happened in Virginia in 1831. The case is well made and I agree—we're all against prejudice, as I keep saying—but just what are Mr Vizinczey's literary values? (pp. 626-27)

> Mervyn Jones, "Reputations," in New Statesman, Vol. 77, No. 1990, May 2, 1969, pp. 626-27.

SIMON RAVEN

Mr Vizinczey sets out, in *The Rules of Chaos,* to examine the nature of time and chance and thence to deduce appropriate rules of human conduct. His thesis is somewhat fragmented. At times he gives us strings of pensées, each of them numbered and separate; at other times he proceeds by means of essays on subjects such as Eugene McCarthy or Stendhal, the relevance of which to his text is not always very plain. His main burden, however, is seldom in doubt: nothing, he tells us, will ever turn out for very long as we expect, predict or desire of it. . . .

Although the theme is scarcely original, Mr Vizinczey devises some skilful variations on it, which range from the flippant to the macabre. Moreover, he has a surprise in store. Since he has been telling us that even the most dedicated human will is constantly thwarted by the most frivolous quirks of luck, we expect that he will advise us to walk warily before the Lord all our days and to hope for nothing. On the contrary, he urges us to do whatever we feel like from one minute to the next and to hope for everything. For where nothing is certain, he says, nothing is impossible. . . . So rise up and have a go, Joe: just do the first thing that comes into your head, shit or bust, and it may be you that scoops the jackpot.

Quite what of value the jackpot would comprise, however, is not made very clear. Love rather than money, understanding rather than power, the pure joy of being true to oneself—all these are held out to us as the possible rewards of Mr Vizinczey's brand of fecklessness and are illustrated in the person and career of Mr Vizinczey's idol, Stendhal; but since whatever comes, on Mr Vizinczey's reckoning, comes (and goes) entirely by chance, I can see little enough satisfaction in any of it.

For in the end happiness is only to be had from deliberate achievement—from clearing one's own patch of the jungle, so to say, and establishing good order within it. Mr Vizinczey condemns such an attitude as inflexible and arrogant; he would rather have us romp wide-eyed through the jungle in hopes of surprising a rare butterfly, taking no heed of the morrow. But people who take no heed of the morrow do not take the trouble to write elegant and thoughtful books, like those of Mr Vizinczey. By expounding his rules Mr Vizinczey has denied them. His philosophy is therefore factitious—it has been got up, not for use, but in order to be written about. I look forward quite a lot to reading whatever system of philosophy Mr Vizinczey gets up next to explain his manifest betrayal of this one.

Simon Raven, "All Is Flux," in The Spectator, *Vol. 222, No. 7350, May 9, 1969, p. 619.*

ROBERT FULFORD

[*The Rules of Chaos*] is a collection of essays, but a very peculiar sort of collection. The essays are not specifically literary (though a couple of them come close to that), nor political (though a couple deal with political topics). Rather they are, in the old-fashioned sense, philosophical, meaning that they attempt to deal directly with general questions of social and private life. How should one live one's life? Should we live for the present or the future? What is the meaning of power? What does "freedom" mean? These are the issues Vizinczey approaches. . . .

Vizinczey, in this sense, is outrageously old-fashioned—he has certain ideas, and he wants to set them forth, and he believes he is as entitled as anyone to a hearing. He dedicates his book "To those readers who still retain a childish curiosity about life and ideas and aren't ashamed of it." And Vizinczey's book is childish in just this sense: he is trying, like a child, to make some sense of the world, to find the rules that underline the chaos of the lives we lead, or at least to find rules with which we can live with that chaos.

He has no ideology, no religion, no thought-pattern, no story to tell. (p. 46)

For Vizinczey's "rules" turn out not to be rules at all, but merely a few gestures towards understanding. They are "probes," to use the word with which McLuhan likes to describe some of his ideas; they are only tentative. Sometimes Vizinczey sets them down with total confidence, or at least the appearance of it; sometimes he admits that he can't convince even his step-daughters of his own relevance. But in neither case does he attempt to suggest that he really knows the answers. Indeed, sometimes he barely knows the questions.

What he *does* know—and this is the point he develops most insistently and most interestingly—is that, since we cannot foretell the future, we are crazy to live for it. (pp. 46, 48)

The devil, Vizinczey insists, tempts us to betray our instincts by worrying about the consequences; the devil invented both fear and hope.

Of course, Vizinczey is "wrong" as often as he is "right" (perhaps that's a definition of philosophy). If, for instance, there is no sense in worrying about consequences, no sense in planning for the future, what's wrong with polluting the world? After all, an extreme Vizinczey-ite could argue, the world may blow up next year anyway. So why be concerned about the ruination of the rivers and the lakes? Vizinczey's general ideas

are, when put to this sort of test, nonsensical. But they have the virtue of forcing us all to be freelance philosophers, to try to extract general ideas from both public and private issues. In this sense, what Vizinczey is doing with *The Rules of Chaos* is attempting to make philosophy once more a sport for participants. He is neither Plato nor your friendly neighbourhood newspaper sage, but he is a little of both.

He is also, as in his novel, a writer fascinated with sex and its meaning in the lives of men and women. Once again in an essay titled **"Postscript to an Erotic Novel"**—he approaches the absurdity of sex.

"Sex, next to death, gives us our deepest experience of the Absurd and is thus a major source of dislocation and confusion in our consciousness and our culture." This passage is one of the most valuable in his book; it goes a long way toward explaining why sex can act as such a disturbing element at almost any level of life. (pp. 48, 50)

The style of Vizinczey the philosopher, like the style of Vizinczey the novelist, is spare and precise; and the content, again, is uniquely a combination of the boyishly naive and the worldly wise. Vizinczey has demonstrated for the second time that his charm is as impressive as his bravado. (p. 50)

Robert Fulford, in a review of "The Rules of Chaos," in Saturday Night, *Vol. 97, No. 10, October, 1969, pp. 46, 48, 50.*

GEORGE JONAS

[*The Rules of Chaos*] is designed in the literary traditions of Pascal. The building blocks of the arguments are essays, aphorisms, parables or literary excursions. The completed building itself intends no less than to replace the house in which we all live today: the house of determinism. . . .

The Rules of Chaos is not a technical treatise in metaphysics or an exercise in pure logic. This does not exempt it from the requirements of general validity, only from having to build each step of its argument from a unit of mathematically demonstrable truth. When Vizinczey says "Are we to put our hands into the fire with no thought of the consequences? There is no general answer to such questions," it does not mean that Vizinczey is not aware of the fact that the fire will generally burn our fingers. It is precisely because fire generally burns that he wonders about the use of napalm as a means of converting the people of Vietnam to the ideals of Western democracy.

Since most of us are at least dimly aware of the fact that we may slip on a banana-peel on our way to a coronation, at first glance Vizinczey's view of existence may appear to be self-evident insofar as it goes, and irrelevant beyond that. But we may, as he warns us, ". . . confuse frequency and infrequency with relevance and irrelevance." The philosopher does not manufacture truth out of thin air. His task is to recognize it, put it into perspective, weigh its signficance and use it for the construction of his system.

In Vizinczey's system there are no ends only means. . . . We cannot excuse ourselves by our motives because only what we do matters in determining who we are. . . . In the final analysis, his sytem is an explanation of "why tomorrow doesn't work" which is the subtitle of the U.S. edition of his book.

The ultimate validity of anything as outrageous and far-reaching as Vizinczey's system of thought cannot be easily decided.

The case he makes for it, however, is very strong, and it is presented in the same graceful and compelling style that made his first book, *In Praise of Older Women,* such pleasure to read.

George Jonas, in a review of "The Rules of Chaos,"
in The Canadian Forum, *Vol. XLIX, No. 59, March,*
1970, p. 294.

S. K. OBERBECK

"The decisive cause of any event is pure chance," Vizinczey writes. "Events do not develop, they are born out of chaos." This said, the chips—or *I Ching* sticks—keep falling all over the place in [*The Rules of Chaos,* a] painfully diffuse foray into ontological deep-think.

At times, it reads like Heisenberg for housewives, or Herman Kahn as interpreted by Pete Hamill. A man who happens to pinch a shapely policewoman's fanny in the subway (he gets pinched too) is somehow equated with the storming of the Bastille (if there had only been a storm, the storming might not have occurred, the author argues); Newton's falling apple is postulated in a gale, buffeted from its plumb fall by the winds of chance. All he's saying, really, is give chance a chance. . . .

Vizinczey also has his Pop Clausewitz posture: "Time cuts down everybody's power—time is on the side of chance." We read offerings that might have been born had Parkinson and McLuhan brainstormed: "Power weakens as it grows, because the level of chaos rises as it expands." For Vizinczey, "time never passes, it thickens and spreads." The impression is of axle grease on a winter morning. And what to make of this sort of gimlet-eyed utterance:

> What others think may harm or even kill you,
> depending on chance. Your own delusions,
> however, are almost certain to be suicidal.

It's like something out of a sinister fortune cookie.

When he moves from his space-time jabberwocky to politics and social affairs, his cool mask cracks. He speaks of "the deadly simplicity of the Bomb," a "simplicity" even hardened Pubwashers would likely question. "Russia and the United States nearly blew up the earth over the chain reaction of revolutions which Cuba was supposed to ignite in Latin America," he writes, presumably with trembling pen, "though there is still no sign of it after eleven years of Castroism." . . . But then: "This, of course, didn't deter the United States from getting lost in the Vietnam jungle, just in case the Latin American revolution might take off from there."

Ho, ho, ho. Just in case this sounds like something you might expect to hear at an animated cocktail party rather than read in a purportedly serious book, Vizinczey lets you know where he stands emotionally with some political bathos on "the greatness of Eugene McCarthy" who "at the age of 52 suddenly found the courage to commit political suicide by choosing to run for the job of leading his nation . . ." Remember that fortune cookie? Perhaps he was a victim of his own delusions. Vizinczey has none about Bobby Kennedy: "He was an efficient and busy man who never wasted a minute, never had time to reflect upon his own being and so remained fundamentally stupid." When his ire cools, he tends to get cute: "Nations, like young girls, are unhappy when they get too big"—which leads to the conclusion that the "German tragedy

isn't the fact that there are two Germanies, but that there are only two."

After more than 200 pages of these little lapidary wrapups like a dinner guest's bons mots (save for two meaty entries, one deifying Stendhal, the other neatly crucifying Styron's *Nat Turner*), one starts wishing that Vizinczey would go back to praising older women or jolly grandmothers or something. A Schopenhauer he's not.

S. K. Oberbeck, "Give Chance a Chance," in Book
World—The Washington Post, *July 19, 1970, p. 12.*

ROBERT FULFORD

How, after thirteen years, does [*In Praise of Older Women*] stand up? Curiously, the years have if anything improved it. The style in which [Vizinczey] wrote it seems even more cool and classic than it did in 1965, mainly because the period since then has brought us so many abjectly confessional, self-pitying, huffing-puffing sex novels. Vizinczey's careful, distanced accounts of male sexuality seem even more remarkable than they did in 1965.

"The libertine has always been as much pitied as envied," Vizinczey told us in a reflective and rather melancholy postscript that he wrote in London in 1967. But András, the libertine who tells his story in *Older Women,* is not on record as having aroused pity in the 2-million readers he acquired in the 1960s. A certain rueful admiration, more likely, or possibly even outright envy. András discovers, quite early in adolescence, that older women know something younger women don't; and he makes this discovery the key to his sexual successes. The fact that his story ends with a brief episode of impotence is unlikely to have altered the view of his escapades that the reader has formed in earlier parts of the book. In any case, his view of sex—and the author's—remains refreshing, a unique mixture of the naïve and the knowing.

Robert Fulford, in a review of "In Praise of Older
Women: The Amorous Recollections of András Vajda,"
in Saturday Night, *Vol. 93, No. 4, May, 1978, p.*
38.

MARGHANITA LASKI

It is usual, now, to deplore the effects of serialisation on the Victorian novel, but one good habit it inculcated was that of getting plenty of meat into it, all the way along; and to this end serialisation could do many a modern novel, and especially many a modern American novel, a power of good.

Such a novel is Stephen Vizinczey's *An Innocent Millionaire.* Nearly 400 pages long, its single-stranded story can be told in a sentence, viz: a boy with an insecure background becomes obsessed with the need to find a sunken treasure ship, to his own eventual destruction. Of course it's not a bad plot: nothing is necessarily a bad plot until mishandled. It simply is not enough plot to justify so much novel unless the reader can be jollied along by more than its slow unrolling. . . .

The reason why Mark is insecure is because his actor father Dana cannot, during the boy's childhood, make a secure living or a stable home. It is in Toledo that the boy learns, almost simultaneously, that his parents are separating, and that in 1820 the *Flora,* sailing from Lima in terror of General San Martin and laden with treasures of the church and of the wealthiest families of Peru, sank in the Bahamas. Mark chooses to stay with his father only because his father is then working in Spain and thus provides the better chance of learning more about the ship; he does not realise, as we come to see, that his father is far more worth a long book than he is, and the best character in this one.

It is not that Mark is a monster. It is rather that Mark isn't anything very much, a puppet that his maker has invested with the treasure-ship obsession. (p. 28)

Of course Mark finds his treasure, though we readers have noted it down quite a bit earlier. He finds it, in fact, by page 211, and the rest of the book tells how he was cheated out of it, and, at disproportionate length, of the legal processes that ensued. At the end he dies, more or less by someone's miscalculation.

The reason why Mark missed the treasure at first encounter is that he was thinking of sex, though this cannot hold him from his greater passion for long, and is, indeed, intended to further it. But you could say that sex does, now and again, provide a bit of digression and diversion, as do the author's occasional and oddly old-fashioned comments on the progress of his story and the moral actions of its characters; and one can't help but pause, now and again, to consider why he has given some phrases, presumably significant to him, the weight of italics. Clearly this is intended to be a story with a moral, and it may be that the moral originally intended was something about setting your heart on a higher treasure than lucre; but it seems to end up with an aphorism about simpletons being unfit for the responsibilities of wealth. (p. 29)

> Marghanita Laski, "A Long Long Trail," in The Spectator, *Vol. 250, No. 8072, March 26, 1983, pp. 28-9.*

JAMIE CONKLIN

In *An Innocent Millionaire,* Stephen Vizinczey tells the story of a young man whose life is thoroughly beset by contradictions. On the one hand, Mark Niven's youthful idealism sends him on an epic quest for a sunken Spanish treasure ship; on the other, his quest necessarily plunges him into the debilitating materialism of the 20th century. Moreover, Niven's own pessimism, evident from the first page where he notes that "no one is interested in anybody's story," is quickly denied by the interest and warmth generated by the novel.

The only weakness in the novel lies in the character of Mark Niven. For almost 400 pages, he is thoroughly obsessed with finding his ship and hanging onto the treasure. His personality is scarcely developed beyond this one central motivation. Unfortunately, a measure of tedium is the consequence.

The other characters, however, are flawless. Vizinczey is particularly good at portraying evil. . . . Vizinczey's unrestrained portraits of evil-minded people are set against those who show love and concern for Niven. And this broader context of conflicting impulses and contradictions gives Mark Niven the impetus he needs for some belated moral growth.

An Innocent Millionaire is well worth reading. Pervaded by an acerbic wit, entertaining and uplifting, it offers a story that is worth dreaming about and worth thinking about.

> Jamie Conklin, in a review of "An Innocent Millionaire," in Quill and Quire, *Vol. 49, No. 11, November, 1983, p. 20.*

FRASER SUTHERLAND

Like an emu, Stephen Vizinczey's second novel is impressive but flightless. Twelve years in the writing, *An Innocent Millionaire* comes with a book-jacket blurb brigade that includes such spear-carriers as Brigid Brophy, Anthony Burgess, and Graham Greene. . . .

In Praise of Older Women was an elegant blend of melancholy and gaiety filtered, indeed purified, by the protagonist's sexuality. *An Innocent Millionaire* forsakes such intimate involvement of author with character in favour of an icy moralistic voice telling a lurid but essentially boring story. . . .

[A] compulsion to moralize at every opportunity creates a jerky cast of puppets manipulated by the author. Vizinczey's people do not live: they illustrate aphorisms. The aphorisms themselves are often excellent. A random selection: "No doubt eliminating politeness from society is a cost-effective way of hastening the day when people will bite each other in the street." Domestic peace depends on efforts "to look on the bright side of deception: if hypocrisy is the tribute vice pays to virtue, marital lies are the tribute indifference pays to love." . . . Yet there are rhinestones among the diamonds: foolish generalizations about lovers ("No man loves unless he feels he is a child again") and lawyers ("Attorneys deal in wool and their clients are the sheep that are shorn").

Not content with speckling his narrative with maxims, like the 19th-century masters Vizinczey admires he also incorporates verse quotations, and precedes each chapter with an epigraph selected from among such well-known cultural figures as St. Paul, Napoleon, Dostoyevsky, and George Jonas. . . . The author is less a novelist than a wholesaler of ideas.

This is a moral novel. What are the main points the moralist presents for our edification? Money corrupts, and "an innocent millionaire" is virtually a contradiction in terms. Society extravagantly values high-priced crooks and con-men. Predators prey not just on the innocent, but on each other. Fair enough, and often well said, but where . . . is the bewildered child turned duped treasure-hunter Mark Niven? Left stranded on a coral reef of authorial commentary, and despite the extensive background his creator provides, so faceless is Niven that the reader has no inclination to send out a search party.

Perhaps the most telling indictment of this novel may be left to Vizinczey himself. Commenting on Mark's empathy with the Indian victims of Spanish greed, the author calls it "a rare gift which might have been his saving grace, for whether people are good or bad, useful or harmful, depends not on their moral principles or even their conscious aims, but on the strength of their imagination." This dedicated and immensely intelligent author has strayed from his own strength.

> Fraser Sutherland, "Rhinestones in the Rough," in Books in Canada, *Vol. 12, No. 10, December, 1983, p. 24.*

SAM TANENHAUS

[*An Innocent Millionaire*] is a rare accomplishment, a contemporary adventure told with style, wit and wisdom. Like many unworldly questers, Mark Niven, the protagonist of *An Innocent Millionaire,* is not so much innocent as obsessed—with a treasure ship sunk off the Bahamas in 1820 and still missing in the 1960's when much of this picaresque narrative takes place. . . . Mark spends his adolescence in maritime archives, methodically pinpointing the watery grave of the *Flora.* . . . Prodigious happiness seems within his grasp, but this latter-day romantic, isolated so long by his single-minded pursuit, can't scent the encroachment of treachery and corruption as a crooked art dealer, a gangster, a greedy attorney and other rogues seize the stage with Dickensian gusto.

Even more delightful is the author's vividly epigrammatic prose. Paying tribute to youthful imagination, he notes that "a child's dreams are not idle fancies, they are the means by which he creates the person he is going to become." Later, when the hero overcomes a fit of gloom, we're reminded that "decent people are often saved from the extremes of self-pity by pangs of bad conscience." Stephen Vizinczey's attempts to sum up an era yield fewer insights. The 1960's backdrop is curiously sanitized, despite an abundance of topical material—including an improbable campus demonstration—and his satire of corporate cupidity suffers from overkill. Still, this is a delicious entertainment that towers above most commercial fiction.

Sam Tanenhaus, "Watery Roguery," in The New York Times Book Review, *June 16, 1985, p. 14.*

DAVID LEHMAN

Reduce Stephen Vizinczey's *An Innocent Millionaire* . . . to its basics and it sounds like the next potboiler. . . .

So what sets *An Innocent Millionaire* apart from the pack? Its strong literary flavor, for one thing, and its brilliant fusion of romantic wish-fulfillment and savage moral indignation. A superb stylist who regularly invokes Stendhal as his master, Vizinczey takes his epic, made-for-the-movies plot and turns it into an angry parable about the deadly sins of avarice and betrayal at the heart of every swindle. He is merciless in his depiction of cynical "combinations of rectitude and fraud," especially those engineered by lawyers who "spread human misery." With his gift for pungent aphorisms, Vizinczey frequently interrupts his story to comment on it—without ever losing his narrative momentum.

David Lehman, in a review of "An Innocent Millionaire," in Newsweek, *Vol. CV, No. 25, June 17, 1985, p. 82.*

ELIOT FREMONT-SMITH

One can tell *An Innocent Millionaire* is a melodrama by the relentless evil that men do in it to crush the spirit of its youthful American hero, Mark Niven. As Vizinczey puts it, "The dream of a crook is a man with a dream," and the crooks here will stop at nothing to rob Mark of (in ascending order of importance) his life, his liberty to love, and the sunken Spanish treasure he endlessly pursues. Translate all this into Vizinczey's own battles with publishers and their attorneys—and Mark's underwater treasures into the allegedly impounded proceeds of Vizinczey's first novel (and "international best-seller"), *In Praise of Older Women* (1965)—and you have the à clef part.

The litigation over *In Praise* lasted seven years—about the timespan of *An Innocent Millionaire*—and it colors the new book in many ways, some of them not intended. . . .

Certainly there's a mischief-making factor in *An Innocent Millionaire,* and for a time it seems to lighten the author's iron grip on the book. Vizinczey himself calls it a "human comedy" (after Balzac and Stendhal, whom Mark is admonished to "re-read"), and attempts to cloak his vengefulness in raffish bon-homie, less cynical than sardonic. But the grip never lets go. . . . [The characters are] simply figments of Vizinczey's manipulation, which is pretty frenzied to begin with and grows ever more greedy and grandiose. In the end, *An Innocent Millionaire* reads like a nervous tic—not of the slightest consequence, a pain nonetheless. But let's get back to the money.

That his parents don't have any, or can't hold onto it for long, is Mark Niven's big gripe. . . .

[The] only solution, Mark decides, is to make his own fortune fast. "People are monsters and I'd better get rich or I'll have to depend on monsters," Mark reasons coolly. Tragically, he fails to heed Vizinczey's early warning—the first of hundreds of maxims that encrust *An Innocent Millionaire* like droppings from the sky—"Mankind, we're told, is divided into the haves and the have-nots, but there are those who both have the goods and do not, and they lead the tensest lives."

After a lot of tenseness I can't go into here, Mark learns of the Spanish ship *Flora* that sank somewhere in the Bahamas during a hurricane in 1820 with an unretrieved treasure worth, at today's exchange, roughly $300 million. After more tenseness, he chances on a contemporary and hitherto overlooked log book tucked away in a Genoese maritime archive from which he can decipher pretty much the exact location of the wreck. "Reading those decisive lines," Vizinczey tells us—for he is over vigilant on everyone's behalf—"was a moment for which Mark would have given his right arm if he hadn't needed it for diving."

It should be noted that Vizinczey, who fled from Hungary to Canada in 1956 with "fewer than 50 words of English," is only occasionally this jocular. Knee-slappers are not his forte. His observations are more typically on the order of "Sensible plans are often abandoned but the senseless ones hardly ever"—this to explain Mark's obsession with his treasure of the deep, there being no other discernible reason. I mean, he doesn't like boating particularly, and isn't the sporting type. However, from the moment in Genoa on—and Dana's refusal to loan him $12,000 for diving equipment notwithstanding—Mark dreams only of his trove. As the crooks will dream of him.

But first it's off to Columbia University, just in time for the great sit-in. . . .

Mark embarks on a history of Peru (the proceeds of which are earmarked for diving equipment, except the history is never finished), travels from Columbia U. to Columbus Circle to view Dali's enormous *Discovery of North America by Christopher Columbus,* . . . and, during an anti-Vietnam demo, bops Hubert H. Humphrey on the head with an apple. . . .

I'm hurrying along here because I want to get to the big fellatio scene. This takes place aboard Marianne Hardwick's yacht just off exclusive Santa Catalina Island and practically on top of the reef where the treasure-laden *Flora* met its fate. The scene itself isn't much (though it delays Mark's salvage operation for weeks, maybe months), but it's caught on film by Howard Sypcovich, the private detective hired by Chicago chemicals tycoon Kevin Hardwick's mistress Pauline Marshall to spy on Marianne, and Sypcovich's sidekick Anthony Edward Masterson, the frustrated movie director-turned-blackmailer whom Kevin's mafia connections will eventually rub out by forcing him off the highway with one of the trucks used to dispose of illegal toxic wastes from Hardwick's chemical plant.

It's the filmed fellatio that becomes important, and Kevin plays it over and over, driving himself batty. He would at first seem a jealous husband, but appearances can be deceiving. He commutes from Chicago to Santa Catalina to visit his 23-year-old bride, the beauteous Marianne, and their two offspring only on weekends, and then only when not occupied by the slithery charms of Pauline, who believes that when it comes to sex, all men are "pigs at trough." . . .

Pauline intends the film to incite Kevin to divorce Marianne, but now he wants her more than ever. He demands that everyone connected with the film be killed (the mafioso demurs, which stimulates much musing on the Kennedy assassinations and provokes Vizinczey to observe, "The good conscience of the wicked rests on all the villainies they refrain from committing") and then spends months or maybe years trying to persuade Marianne to do for him what she did for Mark without throwing up.

Meanwhile, Mark and Marianne, who truly love each other, have had a misunderstanding—his obsession with his treasure has caused her to flounce off to New Hampshire to campaign for Eugene McCarthy—which makes them truly miserable. "Those who despair," Vizinczey knowingly chides, "despair of everything." Even the $300 million goes a-glimmering. Mark has barely recovered from wounds suffered while battling a band of ecology terrorists at sea when a Bahamian lady revenuer grabs half the loot—the whole matter of taxes being entirely new to Mark, not part of his dream, and therefore deeply dispiriting. . . .

Mark, who's a sucker for venal advice, loses the other half. It falls into the clutches of John Vallantine, the avaricious (though stuttering) New York art dealer, any resemblance of whom to Ian Ballantine, the U.S. publisher of *In Praise of Older Women,* is "purely coincidental," according to the author's prefatory note, which also invokes the shadow cast over *An Innocent Millionaire* by "the Washington monument to the Vietnam war dead, unveiled in 1982." Vallantine's machinations, however, take place in 1970-73—three extremely tedious years for Mark of frustrating litigation and fraudulent legal fees, before new attorneys hired by Kevin can retrieve what's left of the $150 million and pass it along through Mark to Marianne (who is independently a million-heiress, but never mind), the kids, the little illegitimate Zoé Niven, who, it turns out, was sired by Mark when Marianne wasn't doing that other thing.

Kevin's sudden change of heart is by no means the last surprise of *An Innocent Millionaire,* but it's notable all the same. Only moments before, it seems he was expounding to Marianne on the necessity of population control . . . and how dumping toxic wastes was really for the public good, as would be her giving, ahem, head. Now he's all concerned that the kids shouldn't starve. But then, as Vizinczey explains, "the wicked, too, often do good—albeit for evil reasons, or out of sheer ignorance."

Sheer ignorance of how crazed and—I hate to say it—inept a melodrama Stephen Vizinczey could produce is one explanation for my having read *An Innocent Millionaire.* The lyrical exuberance and cheerful, funny charm—the innocence, if you will—of *In Praise of Older Women: The Amorous Recollections of András Vajda* (to give its full title, and plot as well) simply provided no clue of the chaos to come.

Eliot Fremont-Smith, "Clef Hanger," in The Village
Voice, *Vol. XXX, No. 25, June 18, 1985, p. 51.*

Kurt Vonnegut, Jr.

1922-

American novelist, short story writer, dramatist, scriptwriter, and essayist.

Regarded by many as a master of contemporary literature, Vonnegut uses satire, irony, and iconoclastic humor in his work to raise philosophical questions about the meaning of modern life. Although characterized at various times in his career as a science fiction writer, a black humorist, a fantasist, and a postmodernist, Vonnegut commonly utilizes elements from all of these genres in his fiction. He is particularly noted for his playful narrative style, which typically features puns, aphorisms, slapstick, running gags, and self-effacing humor. His protagonists are usually idealistic, ordinary people who struggle in vain to understand and effect change in a world beyond control or comprehension. Vonnegut rejects any ideology claiming absolute truth, emphasizing the role of chance in human actions and the insensitivity of social institutions. He describes himself as a "total pessimist," asserting that humankind is inherently self-destructive and existence is a "higgledy-piggledy cultural smorgasbord" which ends only in death. Despite his caustic message, Vonnegut always tempers his commentary with compassion for his characters, suggesting that humanity's ability to love may partially compensate for destructive tendencies.

Vonnegut began writing in the late 1940s, selling short stories to literary, science fiction, and detective magazines. He remained virtually unknown until the 1960s, when his "underground" popularity, particularly among college students, prompted some previously published short stories to be collected in *Canary in a Cat House* (1963) and *Welcome to the Monkey House* (1968). Vonnegut's early fiction is concerned with inhumanity, the individual versus the institution, and the inability to effect change in the modern world. His first novel, *Player Piano* (1952; republished as *Utopia 14),* is an uncharacteristically humorless work set in a dystopian society where all labor is performed by machines. Freed from work, people presumably have greater opportunities for self-realization, but Vonnegut ironically suggests that such a solution robs humanity of its sense of dignity and purpose. This novel begins in the fictional town of Illium, New York, where several of Vonnegut's novels are set. *The Sirens of Titan* (1959) is a science fiction parody in which all human history is revealed to have been manipulated by aliens to provide a space traveler with a replacement part for his ship. In *Mother Night* (1962), a spy novel, an American secret agent who posed as a Nazi propagandist during World War II undergoes a personality crisis when tried for crimes he committed to insure his covert identity.

Cat's Cradle (1963) was Vonnegut's first novel to draw serious critical attention. This apocalyptic satire on philosophy, religion, and technological progress centers on a chip of ice capable of solidifying all water on earth. This work exemplifies Vonnegut's blend of scornful and humorous satire and his use of narrative digressions to examine contemporary life. In one digression, Vonnegut introduces a religion called "Bokononism," which propagates the belief that well-meaning lies are more helpful to humanity than absolute truths. Graham Greene called *Cat's Cradle* "one of the best novels by one of the most able living writers." Vonnegut's next novel, *God Bless You, Mr. Rosewater, or Pearls before Swine* (1965), which has been called a Voltairean fantasy, concerns the idealistic attempts of an alcoholic philanthropist to befriend the poor and helpless. Mr. Rosewater finds, however, that his millions cannot begin to alleviate the world's misery and that his commonsense beliefs are not easily applicable in the contemporary world.

Slaughterhouse-Five, or The Children's Crusade (1969) was Vonnegut's first novel to achieve wide critical and popular acclaim. This is also the first work in which he confronts personal experience. Vonnegut, like his protagonist, Billy Pilgrim, was a soldier captured by Germans in World War II and interned as a prisoner of war in Dresden, Germany. Sheltered in a meat storage cellar below a slaughterhouse, Vonnegut was among the few to survive the allied fire-bombing of Dresden, a city of no military or strategic value. The absurdity of this event is filtered in *Slaughterhouse-Five* through the numbed consciousness of Billy Pilgrim, a young soldier who escapes the insanity of war through schizophrenic travels into time and space; these journeys assume realistic stature when compared to his irrational wartime experiences. Written as a fragmented, nonchronological narrative to emphasize the confusion and absurdity of contemporary existence, *Slaughterhouse-Five* is widely considered a classic of postmodern literature. Robert Scholes called it "an extraordinary success, . . . funny, compassionate, and wise. The humor in Vonnegut's fiction is what enables us to contemplate the horror of contemporary existence."

Although many of Vonnegut's works subsequent to *Slaughterhouse-Five* received less favorable critical attention, several became best-sellers. In these works, he further deemphasizes plot and linear narrative development to offer overt social and moral commentary, always insisting on the essential decency which should characterize human relationships. In *Breakfast of Champions, or Goodbye Blue Monday* (1973), a satire of American commercial culture, an auto salesman believes that he is the only sane man in a world of mindless robots after reading a science fiction novel by Kilgore Trout. Trout is a fictitious author who serves as Vonnegut's alter ego in several novels. *Slapstick, or Lonesome No More* (1976) is a bleak novel in which alienation and loneliness are major themes. In this work, a former President of the United States recalls his national program designed to eliminate loneliness and promote human decency by dividing the country's population into several thousand extended families, each with a unique middle name. In *Jailbird* (1979), a former advisor to President Richard Nixon contemplates his role in the Watergate conspiracy for which he was sent to prison. In this novel, Vonnegut examines several themes relating to contemporary America, including economics, violence, politics, and big business. *Deadeye Dick* (1982) concerns a boy who accidentally shot a pregnant woman and grows up under a burden of guilt as a town scapegoat and servant to his parents, who are bankrupt from lawsuits resulting from the woman's death. Like several of Vonnegut's works, this novel details an absurd catastrophe in which the townspeople are devastated by a neutron bomb and centers on an unfortunate protagonist who attempts to enjoy life through harmless pursuits, in this case gourmet cooking.

Galápagos (1985) was hailed as one of Vonnegut's finest works. This novel is typically concerned with human futility and Vonnegut's distrust of scientific ideologies. In this apocalyptic satire of Charles Darwin's theory of evolution, Vonnegut entertains the notion that humankind is doomed to evolutionary failure because its oversized brain has resulted in its destructive overdevelopment as a species. The novel centers on a group of tourists marooned on the Galápagos Islands by a nuclear war and a worldwide economic collapse. Descendants of the tourists eventually attain a more peaceful existence by developing fins, beaks, and smaller, less dangerous brains. Michael Bishop called this novel Vonnegut's "most controlled and inventive, and so his best, since 1969's *Slaughterhouse-Five*."

In addition to his novels and short stories, Vonnegut has written several plays. His best-known work for the stage is *Happy Birthday, Wanda June* (1971), a satirical play featuring an egocentric male whose inflated self-worth denies dignity to women, ethnic groups, and anyone else differing from himself. Although considered less successful than his novels, several critics found the play witty, plausible, and uncharacteristically optimistic. Vonnegut has also written a screenplay for television, *Between Time and Timbuktu* (1972), a space fantasy based on *Cat's Cradle* and *The Sirens of Titan*. *Wampeters, Foma & Granfalloons: Opinions* (1974) and *Palm Sunday: An Autobiographical Collage* (1981) are collections of reviews, essays, interviews, speeches, and personal reflections. *Slaughterhouse-Five* and *Happy Birthday, Wanda June* have been adapted for film.

(See also *CLC*, Vols. 1, 2, 3, 4, 5, 8, 12, 22; *Contemporary Authors*, Vols. 1-4, rev. ed.; *Contemporary Authors New Re-* *vision Series*, Vol. 1; *Dictionary of Literary Biography*, Vols. 2, 8; *Dictionary of Literary Biography Yearbook: 1980;* and *Dictionary of Literary Biography Documentary Series*, Vol. 3.)

BENJAMIN DeMOTT

Deadeye Dick is the life story, told by himself, of one Rudolph Waltz, born in Midland City, Ohio, in 1932 and now residing in Port-au-Prince, Haiti, where he's the chef and co-owner (with his older brother) of a well-known hotel. Like many other books from the pen that brought us *Jailbird, Slapstick* and *Welcome to the Monkey House,* it's a riot of randomness. At age 12 young Rudy, schoolboy, fires off an unaimed round from a rifle belonging to his father's gun collection and accidentally kills a pregnant woman named Eloise Metzger, who's vacuuming her living room several blocks away when hit. Jailed for the deed, both Rudy and his eccentric father are viciously beaten by the police. . . . Lawsuits from the bereaved Mr. Metzger ruin the Waltz family financially (Rudy's father is heir to a drugstore chain fortune), and Midland Cityites bestow a mocking nickname on Rudy—the nickname that gives this work its title.

Act Two: Released from prison into adolescence and early manhood, Rudy confronts unique problems of career choice. He himself likes to cook, but his high school English teacher believes Rudy is a literary genius and pushes him to become a professional writer. Rudy's far-out father, Otto, is opposed. Blaming his own parents for forcing him into a career in the arts he didn't want and heedless of the possibility that his son might want such a career, Otto insists that Rudy ignore his English teacher and take up business. . . . Rudy earns a degree in pharmacology at Ohio State and cooks for his parents at home (this book includes recipes). Then Rudy works at night at Schramm's Drugstore and completes a play in the daytime that wins a foundation prize and flops on Broadway. . . . (pp. 1, 32)

Comes midlife. Rudy relocates to Haiti, where he cooks and has a circle of intimates that includes his brother and a Haitian adept at raising the dead. More recipes are presented, but disasters keep looming. An Ohio blizzard kills Rudy's parents. An explosion, possibly accidental, of a neutron bomb destroys the population of his hometown. . . . Rudy observes, "We are still in the Dark Ages. The Dark Ages—they haven't ended yet."

Fini.

In my estimate *Deadeye Dick* is a cut above *Jailbird,* which I found overly dependent on stale Watergate material and perhaps a cut below this author's best performances, such as *Slaughterhouse-Five.* The account of Midland City after the neutron bomb explosion is strongly imagined (at the Holiday Inn all guests have expired, all applicances are Go—phones, television sets, ice-cube makers, the rest). So too is the portrait of the town's Police Headquarters in the grip of brutal moral outrage. . . . On the other hand, the satirical thrusts struck me as less telling than the splendid assault on altruistic bigots in *Mother Night,* and no moment of comic invention is as fully realized as the death of the computer in *Player Piano.*

What will chiefly matter to Vonnegut fans, though, is that the book's tone, content, arrangements and assumptions nowhere diverge far from this writer's norms. This means, first, that the hero is sweet and hapless and bears a silly-sounding name. It means that strange folk abound—among them . . . an Ohio farmer who, after reading James Hilton's *Lost Horizon,* takes off for keeps to Katmandu; an NBC president who, after making the ten-best-dressed-men's list, has his suits vandalized (hundreds of buttons sliced off) by one of his estranged wives, and an Oberlin graduate who dies at 77, victim of a radioactive mantelpiece.

It means, in addition, that respect for The Authorities is held to a minimum. The initial targets in *Deadeye Dick,* obviously, are opinionated parents . . . and violence-prone police. But other kinds of lawgiving self-inflaters also come in for review—drug corporation executives who create an age of "pharmaceutical buffoonery" in the name of progress, [and] Nuclear Regulatory honchos to whom catastrophe teaches only a single lesson ("the most important thing [is] that nobody panic"). . . . (pp. 32, 34)

The continuity with the author's past also means that the new Vonnegutisms introduced here harmonize well with those met in earlier books. In *Deadeye Dick* one isn't born, one has one's peephole opened; one doesn't die, one has one's peephole closed, after which one becomes what one was before—"a wisp of undifferentiated nothingness." (People who detest Vonnegut's stylistic special effects—"So it goes" in *Slaughterhouse-Five* is probably his best-known tag phrase—find them intolerably cute; people less finicky are charmed by the unique quality of resignation they hear in them, and that quality is present in the wisp and peephole routines.)

And, more important than any of this, the grand old Vonnegutian comedy of causelessness still holds center stage. Traditional novelists and traditional people inhabit a world wherein things happen for reasons; they're forever connecting threads, limning webs of influence and interdependency, shading and lighting, so that in the end the *why* of this or that momentous event or feeling will blaze across the mind's sky—AHHhhhh—marvellously incontestable and vivid. (Absurdist novelists abolish feelings altogether.) But Vonnegut lives in a world scrubbed clean of reasons. Why does the child of a gun safety specialist, using a rifle from his father's collection, emerge as a double murderer? A tough question. Why do human beings take satisfaction in creating a neutron bomb that destroys "only" human beings, not their accoutrements? Another toughie. Why should grief-struck Rudy Waltz, headed for a presumably moving moment at his parents' graveside, allow his train of thought to light on a certain cookie, whereupon—nod to Proust?—instead of grief we're provided with a recipe for almond macaroons?

Don't ask. And don't mutter, either, about paradox, irony or absurd, incongruous juxtaposition. Such mutterings aren't apposite. Irony presupposes the existence, somewhere, of a straight road out of irony, and that's not on Vonnegut's map. . . . Sentence on sentence, paragraph on paragraph, chapter on chapter, so it goes: a tissue of unanswerables.

But never mind: The good reader knows how to cope. (p. 34)

The secret of [Vonnegut's] following, according to the standard judgment, lies in the author's hostility to authority. I disagree. In my opinion the secret lies in a whole congeries of attitudes toward logical explanation—in Vonnegut's relaxed, conta-

gious, oddly untendentious presentation of doubt that any of us really can locate the causes of which we're the results. . . .

The voice of Vonnegut fans, in my experience (in the classroom as well as on the road), tends to be that of people whose life stories to this moment strike the tellers *themselves* as having no more gravity or resonance than a choice of complimentary beverage. (I'll have apple juice, thank you.) The young love Vonnegut because he's in closer touch than most of us with the thinness of the membrane, the insubstantiality of the fabric. He knows what it's like to search for and fail to find the connective tissue; he's capable of being simultaneously superior to Rudy Waltz yet tender and inward with the poor soul's puzzlement.

Vonnegut can also be, of course, something rather less interesting than this. Often the comic poet of weightlessness, the magician who freshens, for a time, in grown-ups, knowledge of the insides of unsettledness, dwindles into a mere fabricator of one-liners. . . . Often toward the end of his tales he forgets he's a mystery-multiplier and tries his hand at Explaining All (witness the Dark Ages business at the close of *Deadeye Dick*). I understand why some critics find Vonnegut vexingly soft on both the cartooning and preaching sides of his nature. . . .

But I know that on some days this very odd writer is good medicine, whatever one's age: on the day when, for instance, you hear that the shelling hasn't stopped, or that the liveliest young mind in your acquaintance can't find work, or that it's been decided, in the newspapers, that the operations mutilating a loved one are no longer regarded as correct procedures. One reason for this is that Vonnegut's inexplicables are admirably plain, homely, abundant, up front; there's no epistemological complication, few philosophical conundrums, just the improbable mess of any probable human week. And the other reason is that there's no cruelty in the man. He is, evidently, playing; take away the ever-present question (namely, How on earth can you explain this?) and his activities might not be easily distinguishable from those of a child setting up and batting down toy soldiers on a rug. But gloating and meanness are excluded from the game, and the observing eyes are sad, humorous, *kind.*

I predict that many Vonnegutians will grow up and away from their favorite author. I also predict that, a decade or two after they do so, many will grow back. The old rule applies: As soon as you put on weight on this earth, you discover it makes a kind of sense to lose it. (p. 35)

> Benjamin DeMott, "A Riot of Randomness," in The New York Times Book Review, *October 17, 1982, pp. 1, 32, 34-5.*

GARY GIDDINS

Like many of his novels, *Deadeye Dick* is a case history from the holocaust, though this time Vonnegut gives us his smallest and most painless holocaust to date. Having destroyed the world in *Cat's Cradle* and the United States in *Slapstick,* he now localizes his devastation in Midland City, Ohio—a provincial town not unlike the one in which Vonnegut was raised—which is accidentally depopulated by a neutron bomb. The narrator, Rudy Waltz, who shares Vonnegut's diction and several biographical details . . . , can easily identify with murderous accidents. At the age of 12, he celebrates Mother's Day by firing a rifle into the air; the bullet lands several blocks away, between the eyes of pregnant Eloise Metzger, who is vacuuming at the time. Nicknamed Deadeye Dick, Rudy becomes the town pariah and an affectless servant to his misfit parents, who have been rendered bankrupt by Mr. Metzger's lawsuits. . . .

[Yet] Rudy ends up in better shape than the witnesses to previous Vonnegut holocausts. . . .

[Vonnegut] gives Rudy, an accomplished cook, his own hotel in Haiti, where he lives with his much-divorced brother, Felix (formerly the president of NBC),and Hippolyte Paul De Mille, a Haitian who can raise the dead; there he whips up delicacies like banana soup and polka-dot brownies.

So here we have all the ingredients for a whimsically pessimistic meditation on the lunacies of contemporary life, with sharply focused assaults on parents who tyrannize their children, doctors who prescribe nerve-decaying drugs, expatriates who search for Shangri-La everywhere but home and a gun culture predicated on the assumption that life is cheap. Yet *Deadeye Dick* is stilted in comparison with Vonnegut's best work—*Cat's Cradle, Mother Night* and *Slaughterhouse-Five*. Vonnegut's voice, that dispassionate croon that pretends to misanthropy while somehow intimating affection for even the most pathetic of his characters, has soured. It's as though he's allowed his anger to bully his wit at the expense of his imagination. His final sentences have the ring of desperation and the inconsequence of a non sequitur: "You want to know something? We are still in the Dark Ages. The Dark Ages—they haven't ended yet." On one hand, Rudy Waltz's story lacks the momentum to justify so sweepingly brutal a generalization; on the other, the Dark Ages seem positively sunny compared with a world capable of imagining, let alone building, a neutron bomb. (p. 500)

Vonnegut appears stymied by this bomb that kills people but leaves their property undamaged. In his preface, he writes that a real neutron bomb—as opposed to his "fantasy borrowed from enthusiasts for a Third World War"—would cause far more "suffering and damage than I have described." Why mute that reality? For a joke? The joke is thin. In *Cat's Cradle*, Vonnegut invented Ice-Nine, which destroyed the world by freezing all its water and freed him to play God with the comic buoyancy of a writer who has out-imagined science. The neutron bomb, however, is beyond the imagination of most humans. Vonnegut can do little more than state its existence and wryly describe an episode in which Rudy and company . . . wander through lifeless Midland City, now under martial law. Rather than animating the novel, the bomb is merely inserted—a kind of howdy-do from the world of current events.

In any case, it's no wonder that Rudy thinks of people as "undifferentiated wisps of nothingness." They aren't born and they don't die; rather, their peepholes are opened and closed. This bit of information is found on page 1, and though it may sound like an awfully cute conceit, it's actually handled well. Page 1 ends with the phrase "Blah blah blah," and I suspect that Vonnegut enjoyed imagining how his readers would tremble with the apprehension that those words—like the catch phrases "So it goes" and "Hi ho" from earlier novels—would appear every page or so. They never appear again, but there are other catch phrases, judiciously inserted, like "Imagine that" or "Think of that"; in addition, Rudy passes time by scat singing, so there are occasional "skeedy wahs" and "foodly yahs." Vonnegut is a masterly stylist, much in the way Count Basie is a masterly stylist—economic, droll, rhythmic. Consequently, many people think they have no style; but try and

imitate them—it can't be done. *Deadeye Dick* has its share of well-turned phrases ("festive inhumanity") and jokes. . . . There are several amusing set pieces, notably a plane ride with the founder of the Mildred Barry Cultural Arts Center, and a few dramatically compelling playlets that make you wonder how Rudy's real play (or, for that matter, Vonnegut's real play, *Happy Birthday, Wanda June*) could have turned out so awful.

Still, some of the familiar mannerisms are intrusive and betray bad comic timing. There must be two dozen sentences that position a climactic phrase after a colon (i.e., "The words were these: Deadeye Dick"), and in almost every instance the colon strains the humor. Expected yowls fall flat, ironies fail to resonate. Rudy's father palled around with Hitler when they were both art students, but little is made of it. A couple of Italian immigrants, the Maritimo brothers, promise to be major characters, but they never come alive. Random observations—pro capital punishment, anti modern art—and unmodulated spleen, conspire to rob Vonnegut's voice of its usual disenchanted wisdom. He is frequently capricious: Celia Hoover's son is shown in her thrall on one page; on the next, he's grown into a "notorious homosexual" (whatever that is). So much for him. But then, nobody's children come to any good in *Deadeye Dick*.

Vonnegut is ambivalent about the Midwest of his youth. The little house (complete with white picket fence and all modern appliances) given to Rudy and his mother by the Maritimos is invariably described as a "shitbox," but it's the kind of shitbox many people would kill for. Reading *Deadeye Dick,* it's hard to understand what motivates Vonnegut's undying nostalgia for "the American Middle West of my youth." Yet he turns the horrific barn of a house in which Rudy grows up into the town's very own Mount Fuji. This happens when the Maritimos replace the structure's cupola, from which Rudy fired his fateful shot, with a large white cone. Thus Midland City itself aspires to Shangri-La; in fact, now that the original inhabitants have been vaporized, the government is thinking of turning it into a refugee center. But nostalgic or not, Vonnegut is unlikely to join those refugees. More probably, he'll turn up in Port-au-Prince, Haiti, eating Rudy Waltz's spuma di cioccolata. (pp. 500-02)

        Gary Giddins, "Vaporizing Midland City," *in* The
        Nation, *Vol. 235, No. 16, November 13, 1982, pp.
        500-02.*

JEFFREY BRODRICK

Better preheat the oven for this one—Vonnegut [in *Deadeye Dick*] has things for us to eat. Food, not ideas—recipes contributed by the various characters. Rudy, the neutered pharmacist who conducts this reminiscence, makes great chili. (p. 1558)

Rudy hangs out in the kitchen with the black servants and learns how to cook; Mr. Waltz parades around in a panther-skin uniform when Felix brings his prom date home; Mrs. Waltz gets zapped by a radioactive mantelpiece; and Midland City is wasted by a neutron bomb, courtesy of the U.S. Government. . . . Vonnegut—in his totally natural, most offhand conversational manner—is mixing in these crazy recipes like Haitian banana soup or Eggs à la Rudy Waltz. . . . Every novelist should serve food!

The story is wacko. It offends one's sense of dignity. If you disliked Vonnegut before, you'll loathe him after this one. But then, reading Vonnegut for plot has always been like going to Italy for Chinese food. This book should be either eaten or played, like a record. . . . (pp. 1558-59)

Deadeye Dick is to be celebrated for its language, its sound, its smell, its color, its nonliteralness. Vonnegut is like a jazz improviser: he has no idea where he's going, but he has an uncanny sense of timing. He snores great sentences, sneezes top-flight metaphors. Sometimes he's on, sometimes he's off, but always fluid, always melodic, sending weird birds of images flapping through his sentences. Call it *white funk:* the finest swing and rumble in American prose since Kerouac. Yet while Kerouac is amphetamine-mad, Vonnegut is languid, effortless, and slick.

He also whines a lot less than he used to. In the past Vonnegut would stop at nothing to get a good fight going in the comic ring of his imagination. He seemed to have a fetish for human suffering. Even as late as 1980, in *Jailbird*, he was administering a *post facto* to Nixon and the Watergate gang. . . . [In] *Deadeye Dick* he takes shots at the neutron bomb, the NRA, the pharmacology industry, and Hitler. But he's not ranting against fascism now; he's saying Gee, Father hooked up with the wrong guy, it could happen to anybody. Nor does he rant against technology. In fact, Rudy admits to deriving an "inordinate" amount of pleasure from driving his Mercedes. And the neutron bomb that does in the folks of Midland City (so we are told in the preface) in fact represents Vonnegut's anxiety at the loss of his childhood friends. Finally, Vonnegut has stripped *Deadeye Dick* of the annoying infrastructure that typified his earlier works, such as the fake planet Tralfamadore that Billy Pilgrim used to frequent in *Slaughterhouse Five* or the imaginary machine-world of Ilium in *Player Piano* (everything in *Deadeye Dick* transpires on planet Earth).

Indeed, the more seriously this novel is examined the richer it becomes. What on its face appears to be just another Vonnegut extravaganza conceals about nine hundred coruscating little stories, all manner of stylistic tricks, digressions on Roman history, etymology, how to sing scat, three endings, and finally a hushed ending, metric, breath-taking, best read aloud in a darkened theater. . . . [*Deadeye Dick* displays] the intensely imagistic, dissociative mind of a writer facing up publicly to the epilogue of his own life: resigned, compassionate, even patriotic, saddened by the incessant manifestation of human folly, yet still buckling to the floor in service to laughter.

I gave up on Vonnegut years ago. Now I eat meals cooked by him. (p. 1559)

Jeffrey Brodrick, "On and Off," in National Review, *Vol. XXXIV, No. 24, December 10, 1982, pp. 1558-59.*

KHACHIG TÖLÖLYAN

[*Deadeye Dick* is a] book that's carefully put together and eager to help the reader along. The narrator is Rudolph Waltz, who tells the story of his life vaguely chronologically, in the short installments that are a hallmark of Vonnegut's style; he may strain your tolerance or credulity, but never your attention span. Rudy's voice is mild and confiding, and rarely wavers from the tone established in the opening pages, no matter how grim the details he narrates. . . .

It helps to know something about Vonnegut's past as a survivor of the bombing of Dresden and a publicist for General Electric, where "progress is our most important product." Progress, Vonnegut intimates, is an ugly mid-American city left standing

and corpse-free, a technological improvement over the charnelhouse that was Dresden.

In its orientation toward disaster, *Deadeye Dick* looks back to *Slaughterhouse-Five* and *Cat's Cradle.* But the technical innovations that made Vonnegut an "experimental" writer in the '60s are gone: no Tralfamadorean narratives, no intercutting from the land of fact to the terrain of science fiction. What remains is a distilled sense of the doom always impending in a world dominated by technocrats and military men; it is palpable on every page, and permeates even events that have no direct relation to Midland City's bomb factories. Whether routine or catastrophic, events are narrated in the patented Vonnegut style: plain to the point of blandness, capable of large whimsy and small expressions of outrage that are almost immediately retracted with self-deprecating humor, punctuated with the little aphorisms that are his most recognizable trademark. It's a style that Vonnegut seems to think is both stoically moral and, with its jingle-like refrains, appropriate for a mass readership; he uses it to depict a world in which large mistakes, like neutron bombs, are the only thing apt to put an end to the small mistakes that form the grain and pattern of existence. His characters' lives are always shaped by what they neither expect nor plan for. "It is too easy, when alive, to make perfectly horrible mistakes," Rudy says, remembering that his father helped keep young Hitler alive by buying a painting from him when he was a starving artist in Vienna. Variations of this sentiment are everywhere: small decisions balloon into large disasters, and Rudy responds by saying, "this was quite a mistake"; then, because he is a cook, he gives us a recipe. The book is full of them, presumably on the theory that as formulas go, a recipe is less likely to result in something catastrophic than, say, Dr. Hoenikker's Ice-9 in *Cat's Cradle.*

Deadeye Dick is a much better book than *Slapstick* and *Jailbird;* in fact, it serves to reiterate Vonnegut's implied claim that he is a competitor (with Updike, Roth, and Mailer) for the right to dominate the large literary terrain between Sidney Sheldon and Thomas Pynchon. And yet it also demonstrates what's fatally constricting about his work. I don't see in it the squishy sentimentality attributed to him by most critics, maybe because I think the skillfully disguised coarseness of thought and loutishness of feeling in the work of someone like Bellow is more dangerous. Instead, what never stops being problematic in Vonnegut is the calculated naiveté and blandness of the style, coupled to the equally simplified view—what used to be called the "absurd vision"—of the wrongness of the world.

Vonnegut's sense that life is a series of inexplicable errors, made deadly by increasing technocratic power concentrated in a few hands, seems almost as right as it is simple. The understanding sadness and the small jokes that permeate his work are so appealing that I feel guilty even as I feel sad. It seems necessary, still, to say that a writer depicting the collapse of the traditional ways of making sense in a senseless world is busy committing a book, which is itself one of the most traditional ways of making sense. The notion that great evil is not necessarily complex, and that the injustices which preoccupy Vonnegut are simple in their enormity, is no reason to write books that resist complexity and evade difficulty.

Vonnegut's directness and simplicity are not malignant, the way, say, Reagan's are, because he has the imagination of disaster in him. He shares with some post-Holocaust Jewish writers and with Pynchon the feeling that World War II is not just our past but also quite possibly our future. Yet he writes nothing that matches the complexity of that present relationship between past and future; he remains smug in the conviction that a demure stoicism in the face of what can't be helped is all that's required. So he writes page after page of narrative vignettes as stylized as sonnets: 10 or 20 lines of story, then a sentence of the sort that once said "so it goes" and now says "no harm done, luckily," "waste not, want not," or "let sleeping dogs lie." Old wisdom follows new event, allegedly to distill its meaning, while undercutting the bankrupt saws by which such meaning was once understood. Vonnegut does a good enough job of demonstrating the inadequacy of cliché in the face of the sequential disasters that are his characters' lives, but this is no excuse at all, in the end, for providing nothing better than a new and slightly wiser set of clichés. Is it a tribute to Vonnegut's qualities as a human being and a writer, I wonder, or a measure of the Machiavellian nature of his calculated simplicity, that I feel like a clumsy socialist critic (even as I think I am right) in attacking his aesthetic of innocence, which writes off the social facts of life in order to forge a link between large universals and polished down-home truths? I think it's an indictment, a measure of the insidiousness of simple charms.

> *Khachig Tölölyan, "Kurt Vonnegut's New Improved Clichés," in* The Village Voice, *Vol. XXVIII, No. 8, February 22, 1983, p. 50.*

CHARLES BERRYMAN

Kurt Vonnegut has continued after *Slaughterhouse-Five* to explore the images of a haunted memory, but he has produced a very uneven series of novels. One scene near the end of *Deadeye Dick* is perfectly emblematic of Vonnegut's fiction of the past fifteen years. A minor character suddenly amazes the narrator of the novel by successfully raising a spirit from the grave. The scene is comic, the supernatural feat is inexplicable, but the ghostly reminder of crime and death is genuine Vonnegut.

Billy Pilgrim in *Slaughterhouse-Five* (1968) survives the bombing of Dresden, a plane crash in Vermont, and the accidental death of his wife. . . .

Vonnegut introduces himself in *Breakfast of Champions* (1973) as a comic figure who is injured by one of his own creations. The persona of the author is hurt during the mad and violent rampage of Dwayne Hoover. . . .

The setting of *Slapstick* (1976) is the island of Manhattan after it has been largely depopulated by a mysterious plague. (p. 96)

The story of *Jailbird* (1979) is told against a background of the Cuyahoga Massacre and the deaths of Sacco and Vanzetti. . . . The narrator of *Jailbird* is in prison for a time because of his connection with the crimes of the Nixon administration, but the guilt he feels goes back to his role during the McCarthy hearings. His mind is haunted by the victims of injustice.

The narrator of *Deadeye Dick* (1982) spends less time in jail despite the fact that his crime is more destructive. As a twelve-year-old boy, he is initiated into manhood with the single firing of his father's rifle. The bullet happens to kill a pregnant woman, and from that moment forward, his life is haunted by guilt and shame. . . .

Vonnegut himself admits to a version of the nightmare which appears in all five of his novels from *Slaughterhouse-Five* to *Deadeye Dick*. An autobiographical passage in *Palm Sunday* describes the "bad dream I have dreamed for as long as I can remember." The nightmare of crime and guilt—"I know that I have murdered an old woman a long time ago"—resembles

the plot of *Crime and Punishment*. Vonnegut even acknowledges that he and Dostoyevsky have the same birthday. Puzzled by the recurring dream, Vonnegut asked a psychiatrist if the dead woman could be his mother. The ambivalent response—"the woman might not even be a woman"—is typical of the uncertain truth Vonnegut expects from any oracle. (p. 97)

Vonnegut's fiction has always included a measure of autobiography, but in his recent work this trend has become more explicit. The first chapter of *Slaughterhouse-Five* depicts a persona of the author attempting to come to terms with the idea of writing about the bombing of Dresden. The autobiographical basis for the fiction is explored more fully in the introduction Vonnegut added in 1976 for a new edition of the novel.

Breakfast of Champions not only begins with an autobiographical preface, Vonnegut also introduces himself as a character in the narrative. The novelist pretends to offer freedom to the other characters, but his gift turns out to be an image of the forbidden fruit. The freedom his characters will be granted amounts to the crime and guilt of the fallen world. (pp. 97-8)

[The prologue to *Jailbird* is also] autobiographical. Vonnegut talks about his father as a failed architect and his mother as a probable suicide, but the family relationships are set against the background of the Cuyahoga Massacre and the references to Sacco and Vanzetti. In this way, Vonnegut uses history to support the personal narrative which in turn reinforces the fiction. In all three, the theme is unjustifiable violence and death. The narrator of *Jailbird* feels guilty for crimes which history and circumstance have forced him to inherit. His life has been a nightmare for longer than he can remember. (p. 98)

Vonnegut dreams repeatedly about the murder of a woman, and all of his recent novels have important female characters who come to tragic ends. Billy Pilgrim's wife is killed by carbon monoxide in *Slaughterhouse-Five*. Dwayne Hoover's wife swallows the detergent in *Breakfast of Champions*. Wilbur Swain's sister is killed by an avalanche in *Slapstick*. Walter Starbuck's former love and present benefactor dies after being hit by a car in *Jailbird*. And the women in *Deadeye Dick* are either shot to death, poisoned by radiation, or commit suicide. This record does not have its equal in American literature since Poe first advocated the subject of the death of a beautiful woman in his "Philosophy of Composition."

The single deaths in Vonnegut's recent fiction are often overshadowed by the vision of a massacre. The bombing of Dresden in *Slaughterhouse-Five* is the most famous example, but the vision is recreated for different novels. A tide of industrial waste is threatening to bury Midland City in *Breakfast of Champions*. The island of Manhattan has been devastated by changing gravity and a mysterious plague in *Slapstick*. The story of the Cuyahoga Massacre is retold in the prologue to *Jailbird*, and the familiar Midland City is recreated in *Deadeye Dick* so that Vonnegut can depopulate it with a neutron bomb. Is there another contemporary novelist more concerned with visions of destruction and mortality?

If the images of a massacre haunt the characters in Vonnegut's fiction, it is not surprising that so many of his narrators behave as passive victims of a hostile fate. One of the many ironies of *Slaugherhouse-Five* is that Billy Pilgrim, who merely wants to die at the beginning of the novel, should be the survivor of the bombing of Dresden, not to mention his wife's death and a plane crash. The price for his survival is a memory haunted by fear and death. He moves from one disaster to another unable to either banish or accept the experience of Dresden. The images of the massacre are so deeply repressed that the full memory does not surface until near the end of the novel.

No matter how comic and forlorn the character of Billy Pilgrim may appear as he enters Dresden in his Cinderella boots, the enormity of what is about to happen is enough to insure the sympathy of Vonnegut's audience. In the novels which follow, however, the weight of history is often lacking, and the narrators who suffer a private trauma are apt to appear more absurd than tragic. Wilbur Swain, for example, may suffer as long as he wants from his grotesque childhood or the loss of his sister, but he will always seem more or less ridiculous. There is no credible reference point in *Slapstick* for his state of mind. How can a reader possibly respond to an avalanche on Mars?

Vonnegut has a similar problem with the narrator of *Jailbird*. Walter Starbuck is more sympathetic than the absurd Wilbur Swain, but his connection with history is still rather tenuous and often unconvincing. . . . Who cares whether the narrator of *Jailbird* is sentenced to another term in prison or to be a vice president of the RAMJAC Corporation?

It is typical of the narrator of *Jailbird* to feel so inhibited by guilt and fear that he is incapable of any genuine passion. . . . The same is characteristic of all the Vonnegut narrators who are haunted by images of crime and death. The latest example is the narrator of *Deadeye Dick*. He describes himself as a "neutered pharmacist" who is "so sexless and shy that he might as well be made out of canned tuna fish." How does Vonnegut expect his audience to respond to a main character who has all of the passion and courage of tuna fish? The emotional growth of the narrator has been arrested at the age of twelve when the killing of a pregnant woman filled his life with guilt and shame. For decades thereafter, he denies himself almost all freedom in a vain attempt to make amends to his own parents. No peace of mind, not to mention love or happiness, is available to the repressed and tormented narrator. His only chance for self-expression comes in the form of writing a pathetic play about the search for Shangri-La. (pp. 99-100)

[The drama about the search for Shangri-La reflects one] of Vonnegut's favorite devices for coping with the ghosts of failure. The narrator of *Deadeye Dick* attempts to compensate for his impoverished life by imagining a promised land: "There's room for everybody in Shangri-La." . . . It is the old mistake of Eliot Rosewater [in *God Bless You, Mr. Rosewater*], who tried to banish his guilt by giving away his fortune. Vonnegut's characters know that the fallen world cannot suddenly be converted back into the lost paradise, but that does not stop them from trying.

All of the narrators who try to escape from the fear and guilt of a fallen world are attempting to regain an innocence which they feel was lost in childhood. The subtitle for *Slaughterhouse-Five* is "The Children's Crusade," and Vonnegut describes himself in the preface to *Breakfast of Champions* as "programmed at fifty to perform childishly." The style of the novel with its drawings of a light switch, a cow, and a hamburger is so apparently childish that perhaps Vonnegut should be taken at his word. (p. 101)

"The museums in children's minds," Vonnegut suggests [in *Slapstick*], "automatically empty themselves in times of utmost horror—to protect the children from eternal grief." But in novel after novel, he has dramatized just the opposite. The children are exposed to horror, and the experience is then repressed to a level of the mind where it continues to haunt

their conscious behavior. The mind is never empty, and the children cannot be protected.

The uneven quality of Vonnegut's recent fiction may be the difference between feeling "programmed at fifty to perform childishly" and the vital expression of "the museums of children's minds." Vonnegut is true to the latter when he allows the memory of the "children's crusade" to break through the limits of repression in *Slaughterhouse-Five*. The prevalence of this psychological drama may also contribute to the success of *Jailbird* and *Deadeye Dick*, while its absence may help to explain the weakness of *Breakfast of Champions* and *Slapstick*.

Vonnegut identifies his own fiction with the voice of a child, and in *Palm Sunday* he cites Henry David Thoreau as his literary ancestor: "Thoreau, I now feel, wrote in the voice of a child, as do I." In so far as Thoreau can be viewed as the "American Adam" attempting to live at Walden Pond as if it were paradise regained, he foreshadows the efforts made by Vonnegut's narrators to regain the innocence of their lost childhoods. (pp. 101-02)

When it comes to writing in the voice of a child, however, Vonnegut's most important literary ancestor is not Henry David Thoreau but Mark Twain. It was Twain who "wrote childishly" when he created a world seen through the eyes of Tom Sawyer. Such a world is often viewed with satire, but it is very limited in psychological depth. Tom Sawyer would be good at writing a fantasy play for Midland City, about a treasure hunt perhaps or a search for Shangri-La, but there is no convincing fear and guilt in his soul. It was also Twain, however, who at times could truly enter "the museums in children's minds," and then he created the haunted and wonderful imagination of Huckleberry Finn. Here is the prototype for many of Vonnegut's narrators: a child marked by the loss of parents, not ready yet for marriage, love, or responsibility, but lighting out for the territory with a mind haunted by images of death and destruction. The territory ahead, of course, is not Tralfamadore or Shangri-La—it is the great river of life with fugitives and charlatans. The territory ahead includes *Slaughterhouse-Five*, *Jailbird*, and *Deadeye Dick*. (p. 102)

Charles Berryman, "After the Fall: Kurt Vonnegut," in Critique: Studies in Modern Fiction, *Vol. XXVI, No. 2, Winter, 1985, pp. 96-102.*

MICHAEL BISHOP

Consider the human brain, urges Kurt Vonnegut in *Galápagos*, his first novel since *Deadeye Dick*. The size of that brain (next to the cognitive instruments of the "lower" animals, a disastrously *big* organ) has doomed us to evolutionary failure, suckering us down a primrose path of misconceptions, neuroses, and crackpot notions to our own inevitable extinction.

But suppose that we could sidestep extinction by jettisoning large pieces of our cerebral furniture, trading in our hands for flippers, and dieting exclusively on fish. In the long run, wouldn't these sacrifices turn out to be improvements, utterly happy evolutionary adaptations? In *Galápagos,* which often has the flavor of a jeremiad delivered more in sorrowful whimsy than in angry disgust, Vonnegut expertly stacks the deck to force us to conclude that forfeiting our big brains would be far better than either (1) continuing to inflict our vicious selves on this lovely planet or (2) going the way of the dodo as a viable species.

In fact, to structure this simultaneously funny and harrowing novel—his most controlled and inventive, and so his best, since 1969's *Slaughterhouse-Five*—Vonnegut has stood a hoary science fiction cliché on its head. Almost to a person, sf writers have bought the premise that only greater brainpower will ensure humanity's survival and of course its total triumph over the physical cosmos. . . . Vonnegut, who rigorously eschews genre classification not only to write whatever he deems important but also to keep from artificially limiting his audience, frog-marches the post-Darwinian concept of the superman right back to the sea. *Galápagos,* then, is both a harrowing litany of big-brain abuses against life and good order and a semi-hilarious paean to the joys of devolution.

The story resists easy summary. Seven people have gathered in the Ecuadoran seaport, Guayaquil, to take passage aboard the *Bahia de Darwin* for a trip to the historic Galápagos Islands. The trip's promoters have billed it as "the Nature Cruise of the Century," but a world monetary crisis and the outbreak of war between Peru and Ecuador—among other disasters, including the sudden appearance of a bacterium that renders human women permanently infertile—conspire to turn a couple of these would-be passengers, and six girls of the local Kanka-bono cannibal tribe who are hustled aboard under desperate circumstances, into the ancestors of the happily devolved sea-going human beings who people the Ecuadoran isles in the year 1,001,986 A.D.

Oh, yes. The novel's narrator is a ghost—specifically, the ghost of Leon Trotsky Trout, son of the not-so-famous sci-fi writer Kilgore Trout. Leon is also a Marine deserter who helps build the *Bahia de Darwin* in Malmo, Sweden, after fleeing Vietnam. Leon's ensuing spirituality—a crane at the dockyard decapitates him—permits him to get inside the other characters' heads and also to provide sardonic commentary on the action—the bulk of which takes place between 1986 and 2016—from a vantage one million years down our common timeline. Most of this gentle rant centers on the duplicity and the domineering arrogance of humanity's three-kilogram brains. (pp. 1, 10)

No more about the story or its characters. Vonnegut has nearly always resorted to *reductio ad absurdum* to score points against our species' most dismaying follies, and in *Galápagos* he does so again, as precisely as he has ever wielded this instrument. I can imagine hostile readers indicting him for easy pessimism or simplistic misanthropy, but Vonnegut—in keeping with his advocacy of smaller brains?—has never pretended to be a deep thinker along the lines of Sartre or Bellow. He prefers common sense to arcane intellectualism, grotesque exaggeration to austere despair, and humor to hysteria. Therefore, his best work may sometimes seem a rare combination of the unsubtle and the subtle—a sledgehammer blow to the forehead followed by a series of tenderly administered feather tickles. No one else writing in America today can duplicate this wily effect, and an eagerness to experience it anew has always typified the most avid Vonnegut freaks.

Galápagos is a book that makes me glad to declare my membership in that *granfalloon* ("a proud and meaningless association of human beings"). I am equally glad that my brain has sufficient size and weight to allow me a perplexed appreciation of this newest addition to the Vonnegut canon. (p. 10)

> Michael Bishop, "Kurt Vonnegut and the Next Million Years," in Book World—The Washington Post, September 22, 1985, pp. 1, 10.

MICHIKO KAKUTANI

[With *Galápagos* we are] back in familiar Vonnegut territory: the subject is the end of the world (or at least the end of the world as we know it); the objects of lamentation are man's cruelty to man, contemporary society, modern technology and, of course, the horrors of war—World War II and Vietnam, as well as the more generic variety. Although there are no sing-song refrains like "hippity hop," "hi ho" or "so it goes," the narrative voice still has the quality of a verbal shrug—flip, careless and willfully casual ("the people would eat up all the food, gobble, gobble, yum, yum, and it would become nothing but excrement and memories"), and the characters still bear more of a resemblance to cartoon figures than regular human beings. The narrator is a Vietnam veteran named Leon who happens to be the son of the erstwhile Kilgore Trout, the hero of *God Bless You, Mr. Rosewater* and *Breakfast of Champions.*

Leon also happens to be a ghost, who is telling this story from a vantage point in the future—one million years from now, to be exact. This gives him the same sort of historical perspective that Billy Pilgrim had from the planet Tralfamadore in *Slaughterhouse Five*—and it enables him and Kurt Vonnegut to jump back and forth in time, comment on a lot of 20th-century atrocities, make some sci-fi-like speculations about the future and, in general, ignore the day-to-day complexities of life in favor of the Big Picture. The result is a novel that has the satisfactions of a well-crafted comic strip: though it often settles for easy jokes instead of real humor, though it tries to amuse us rather than move our emotions, *Galápagos* does have plenty of whimsical charm. It's fun to read, often clever and almost always entertaining. . . . [As] Mr. Vonnegut notes, *Galápagos* might well be subtitled "A Second Noah's Ark," though as related by Leon Trout, it more often sounds like a surreal episode of "Gilligan's Island" or "Love Boat." It seems that Leon was killed while working on a luxury cruise liner named the Bahia de Darwin and his ghost now haunts the ship, which is scheduled to embark on "the Nature Cruise of the Century." While the likes of Jacqueline Onassis, Mick Jagger and Henry Kissinger had originally signed up for this trip to the Galápagos Islands, the sudden economic collapse of the Western world has left the Bahia de Darwin with a handful of anonymous passengers: Mary Hepburn, a schoolteacher widow given to suicidal despair; James Wait, a con man in search of a rich woman to make his 18th wife; Zenji Hiroguchi, a Japanese computer genius, and his disaffected wife, Hisako; Andrew MacIntosh, a boisterous American entrepreneur, and his blind daughter, Selena.

Along with the ship's captain, Adolf von Kleist, and several Kanka-bono Indian girls, these passengers—or rather, those passengers who actually survive assorted accidents and medical disorders—will form the gene pool from which all future generations of mankind will develop. Shipwrecked on Santa Rosalia, the outermost of the Galápagos Islands, these people will somehow survive the coming apocalypse, and their little colony will become the new "cradle of civilization."

Mr. Vonnegut spins out this fantastical story with admirable, if somewhat disorganized, inventiveness, decorating the main plot with touching meditations about the animals who live on the Galápagos Islands and lots of shaggy-dog digressions about individual characters. . . .

Unfortunately, many of Mr. Vonnegut's conceits—like having Mandarax [a computer invented by Zenji Hiroguchi] continually quote famous people at appropriately ironic moments, and putting asterisks by the names of people who have died—

grow tiresome as the novel progresses; we come to expect them, like the irritating nervous tics of an old friend. Even more disturbing is the author's tendency to repeatedly italicize the moral of his story: as in most of Mr. Vonnegut's fiction, deciphering the message is never the reader's problem, and *Galápagos* is obvious enough without our having to be told, point-blank, that Mandarax stands for "the Apple of Knowledge" or that Captain von Kleist represents the "new Adam."

> *Michiko Kakutani, in a review of "Galápagos," in* The New York Times, *September 25, 1985, p. C17.*

LORRIE MOORE

Yes, American culture is more smart than wise. But Kurt Vonnegut, that clown-poet of homesickness and Armageddon, might be the rare American writer who is both. He dances the witty and informed dances of the literary smart, but while he does, he casts a wide eye about, and he sees. He is a postmodern Mark Twain: grumpy and sentimental, antic and religious. He is that paradoxical guy who goes to church both to pray fervently and to blow loud, snappy gum bubbles at the choir.

None of this, of course, is news to Mr. Vonnegut's fans, and neither is this: His most recent novels have not been his strongest. . . . Despite its courage and farsightedness, much of Mr. Vonnegut's recent work has seemed fatigued, marred by sloppy writing. It is prose that makes a beeline for a punch line—like a man for a water fountain, only to find it dribbling, not working right at all.

Galápagos, however, seems to scrabble back toward the energies of earlier works. It is the story, sort of, of a second Noah's ark, a 1986 nature cruise booked with celebrities (Mick Jagger, Paloma Picasso, Jacqueline Onassis and others) that in the wake of planetary catastrophe—famine, financial crises, World War III and a virus that eats the eggs in human ovaries—is fated to land on the Galápagos Islands and perpetuate the human race. Humanity "was about to be diminished to a tiny point, by luck, and then, again by luck, to be permitted to expand again."

All this may sound like a glittery and Darwinian "Gilligan's Island"—not really what *Galápagos* is at all. Although certainly the novel has something to do with the giant crush America has on celebrity, the famous people never really do make it into the story, and what we end up with is a madcap genealogical adventure—a blend of the Old Testament, the Latin American novel and a lot of cut-up comic books. . . .

Leon Trout, Mr. Vonnegut's doppelgänger, speaks to us, moreover, from a million years hence, from the afterlife, whence he can best pronounce on what was wrong with us 20th-century folk—our brains were too big—and reveal what, through evolution and for purposes of survival, we became: creatures with smaller brains and flippers and beaks. Even if people of the future "found a grenade or a machine gun or a knife or whatever left over from olden times, how could they ever make use of it with just their flippers and their mouths" Leon Trout asks. . . .

Mr. Vonnegut has probably always been a better teller than maker of stories. One continually marvels at the spare, unmuddied jazz of a Vonnegut sentence and too often despairs of his ramshackle plots. *Galápagos* is, typically and perhaps aptly, structured spatially, like an archipelago, tiny islands of prose detached from that apparently dangerous continent of time—childhood reminiscences, parables, interviews, real and invented history, nature writing, sapient literary quotations, a

soldier's confession. (The novel, alas, has always lacked a natural form.) This is a narrative style engendered by emergency, the need to get directly to something. It is susceptible, however, to an unhelpful chaos and can defeat its own purpose by blithely wandering off and turning whole characters and events into charmless non sequiturs, whole chapters into scrapbooks of blather and dead end.

But Mr. Vonnegut seems eventually to get where he wants, shining his multicolored lights and science fiction "what ifs" on the huge spiritual mistake that is the Western world. He wants to tell us things: It is not the fittest who survive—it is merely those who happen to survive who survive. The earth is a "fragile habitat" that our big brains have failed to take care of. We must hope for flippers and beaks—or nothing at all. . . .

Although not as moving as, say, *Slaughterhouse-Five*, *Galápagos* does have moments (of father-son vis-à-vis) that bring a glug to the throat. And although more wobblingly cobbled and arrhythmic comically than *Breakfast of Champions*, *Galápagos* can be as darkly funny. Mr. Vonnegut asterisks the names of characters who are going to die and, after their inevitably gruesome deaths, kisses them off with the elegiac "Oh, well—he wasn't going to write Beethoven's Ninth Symphony anyway." Early in the novel, he even puts Captain von Kleist on "The Tonight Show," and what follow are the best laughs in the book.

Mr. Vonnegut's work long ago broke ground for such writers as Richard Brautigan, Thomas Pynchon, Donald Barthelme, Tom Robbins—all curators of the rhetorical and cultural non sequitur. But Mr. Vonnegut's grumbly and idiomatic voice has always been his own, unfakable and childlike, and his humanity, persisting as it does through his pessimism, is astonishing, seeming at times more science fiction than his science fiction. As for his suspended concern for the well-made, big-brained novel, Mr. Vonnegut has opted to zoom in directly for the catch, the idea, the oracular bit. His books are not only like canaries in coal mines (his own analogy) but like the cormorants of the Galápagos Islands, who, in their idiosyncratic evolution, have sacrificed flight for the getting of fish.

> *Lorrie Moore, "How Humans Got Flippers and Beaks," in* The New York Times Book Review, *October 6, 1985, p. 7.*

MARTIN AMIS

[*Galápagos*] is far and away Kurt Vonnegut's best novel since *Slaughterhouse 5*. However, that's not saying very much, in itself—especially if you look at Kurt Vonnegut's novels *before Slaughterhouse 5*. These include a beautifully intricate space-fantasy, *The Sirens of Titan,* a coruscating satire on human destructiveness, *Cat's Cradle* (usually referred to by fans as 'Ice Nine' or simply 'the ice-nine book'), and a work of moral and comic near-perfection, *Mother Night. Mother Night* remains, to my knowledge, the only funny book about the Holocaust ever written, or indeed ever attempted. . . .

Galápagos begins brilliantly with a description of a Vonnegut villain. Nobody writes about villains the way Vonnegut writes about villains (as *Mother Night* proves): he makes them look like lab rats, stupidly pursuing their projects and programmes, quite deaf to the disgusted laughter up there in Rat Control. James Wait, for example, first seen at the bar of the Hotel El Dorado in Guayaquil, Ecuador, presents himself as entirely unexceptional, 'drab and friendless,' tamed by deep sorrows: 'he was pudgy, and his colour was bad, like the crust on a pie in a cheap cafeteria.' In fact, Wait is a one-time homosexual prostitute who has made a million in the confidence-trickster business, marrying and ruining rich old widows. Vonnegut views human infamy as, in the end, a condition of chronic indifference. . . .

Wait has come to Ecuador to embark on 'the Nature Cruise of the Century,' a luxury excursion to the Galápagos Archipelago. Joining him on the trip are a familiar bunch of megalomaniacs and nobodies, each of them in thrall to laughable or mischievous non-value systems: big business, blind scientific advance, battered American innocence. . . .

Vonnegut is not embarrassed by the Darwinian perspective, since he has always gazed down on Earthling confusions as if from some cosmic vantage of space and time. A million years hence, according to Leon Trout (1946—1,001,986), human beings will be no more intelligent than the blue-footed booby. In evolutionary terms, man went wrong when his brain outgrew his soul. . . .

The first half of the book teems with the kind of odd connections and telling metaphors that I reverently associate with early, pre-*Slaughterhouse* Vonnegut. The organised exposure of various animals to the effects of nuclear blasts was, in the disturbed mind of a Bikini veteran, 'the exact reverse of Noah's ark.' Killing people is here called 'outsurviving' them (an armed madman rampages, hoping 'to find more enemies to outsurvive'). All evils, for the purposes of this satire, come from ideas, from big brains.

The second half of *Galápagos* I reluctantly associate with late, post-*Slaughterhouse* Vonnegut: it tends towards the formless, the random, the diffuse, the anecdotal. Always tempted by the delights of playful inconsequentiality, Vonnegut grows too attached to his pet grotesques and loses sight of their structural function. Perhaps this is a vestige of another weakness of the late phase, namely sentimentality. But it is only a vestige, and *Galápagos* is his most tough-minded book since *Mother Night*.

One of the purest delights of early Vonnegut was the phrasing. As with the very best chapters of Chandler (in some ways a comparable popular artist), you can read for hours without hearing a single false quantity. *Galápagos* kicks off with that relaxed musicality and swing. It makes the reader sweat with pleasure, but also with suspense. And if in the end the novel doesn't quite come good, it makes some marvellous noises along the way.

> Martin Amis, "Kurt's Cosmos," *in* The Observer,
> *November 3, 1985, p. 25.*

LOREE RACKSTRAW

The other day a friend who had just finished reading Kurt Vonnegut's new novel, *Galápagos,* remarked that it would be nice if at this stage in Vonnegut's career people overcame their fear of taking him seriously and gave him the accolades he really deserves. . . .

Surely an accomplished author more committed to the responsibility of his profession is rare, and it has puzzled those who think Vonnegut's work is important why he has been the brunt of more than his share of inept if not rancorous criticism in the past few years. The reason is probably the central theme in most of his fiction. The critics are offended because Von-

negut is so serious about the damage done by humanity's insistence on taking itself too seriously. In fact, he pushes this theme so far that he questions the singular "Truth" of any literature, including his own. And he obstinately uses an idiomatic vernacular to drive the point home. As every academic knows, those who defame both the Canon and the queen's English are trampling on sacred ground.

Never mind that Vonnegut holds up his own work, and even himself, as so much unpretentious bathos. If life is absurd, well then so is he and what he does. But like Samuel Beckett, he goes on anyway, and he puts forth considerable literary energy to see life as a joke rather than a tragedy. The kind of candor he has allowed publicly about his own life and work are seen by his admirers as the courageous humility of a droll savant. But for those who yearn for the nobility of the virtuous tragic hero, Vonnegut not only falls short; he becomes a literary scandal.

Vonnegut persists in *Galápagos,* his eleventh novel, in reiterating the ponderous themes he first raised in his 1959 novel, *The Sirens of Titan:* the universe is an accident from which has evolved the serendipity called life; chronological time is an idea that lures people into believing in linear causality and intelligent purpose; absolute Truths are illusions humanity tells itself to make life seem purposeful, and those Truths often become self-destructive paradoxes.

Galápagos is a remarkably well-crafted work that offers a million-year slice of the largely random interconnectedness of all life. It echoes Vonnegut's [*Slaughterhouse-Five*] in its development of the powerful role of chance, though from a somewhat different angle. . . . In *Galápagos,* World War III triggers the fortuitous devolution of the human race in a million-year biological process of Natural Selection that turns human beings into harmless and contented "fisherfolk."

As usual, wacko humor masks profoundly serious concerns about the fate of humanity. The "only real villain" of the novel is the oversize brain of human beings, an accident of Natural Selection that also failed to give people teeth that would last a lifetime. Nature corrects the brain mistake when a hapless crew of ten people flees a missile attack on Ecuador in 1986 and is shipwrecked on a little island in the Galápagos. These are the survivors who become the forebears of the human race over the next million years: a race of people with small-brained, sleek skulls and flippers, who learn to live compatibly with the mild, blue-footed boobies that supply them with eggs. (p. 78)

A major theme in this novel is the blatant exploitation of the poor by powerful corporate entrepreneurs who try to sustain the illusion that money has a real value. The entrepreneurs are afflicted, we are told, with a pathology that allows them to cause pain to those around them. They believe they are entitled to any behavior money allows because the Darwinian concept of "survival of the fittest" gives them scientific justification for their actions.

It is this wrong-headed use of Darwin's theory of evolution to justify cruelty to the weak that gives the novel one of its most powerful ironies: World War III begins over possession of the Galápagos Islands, that archipelago Darwin visited in the 19th century, whose curious inhabitants gave him his insight into the Law of Natural Selection.

In Vonnegut's *Galápagos,* the island called Santa Rosalia becomes the ironic refuge for the only humans who escape the war and an ovum-eating virus. A more hilariously unfit group of survivors is not to be found in any Vonnegut novel. It is mostly by dumb luck that they become the sole progenitors of "a perfectly cohesive family" of people who live on barren volcanic rock that evolves, over a million years, to a paradise of blue lagoons and white sand beaches.

One of their first lucky breaks is their escape from Peru's missile attack on Guayaquil which, like most of the rest of South America, is pregnant with violence brought on by starvation and bankruptcy. (pp. 78-9)

Vonnegut's analogy between the male "happy-go-lucky adventure" of missile launching and coitus is surely one of the most elegant satires of military mentality ever written. We see a young Peruvian pilot high in the stratosphere activate a computer capable of the flawless delivery of a missile rod slung underneath his plane. . . . The release of the rod is a transcendental experience for the pilot who realizes ". . . that the rod which became a dot and then a speck and then nothingness so quickly was somebody else's responsibility now. All the action from now on would be on the receiving end. He had done his part. He was sweetly sleepy now—and amused and proud."

Meanwhile, in the harbor below, the Captain of the "Bahia de Darwin," Adolph Von Kleist (whose physical description is a caricature of Vonnegut himself) thinks a shower of meteors is falling. His ship has been ransacked by desperately hungry people, and his "Nature Cruise of the Century" aborted because of the deteriorating political situation.

Readers interested in following the clue of Vonnegut's caricature will take a closer look at the Captain, knowing that Vonnegut often takes a role as a character in his own fiction. Surely in *Galápagos* the name Kleist must direct us to an important 19th century German writer, Heinrich Von Kleist, in whom one finds an uncanny parallel to Kurt Vonnegut. Not only are they remarkably similar in their life experiences; they both perceive the essentially paradoxical and fortuitous nature of life and create intricately crafted literary forms to contain and express the absurdly chaotic nature of reality. Both were influenced by experiences in Dresden in their early careers. Both were haunted by man's inhumanity to man and both were largely rejected by the traditional literary establishment. Kleist wrote tragedies, but he was also one of the few successful humorists of his time. Like Vonnegut, he perceived that the irony of tragedy taken to its extremes is stunningly close to comedy.

And when we realize that we know what's happening to Captain Kleist because of ghostly Leon Trout, the narrator who at that moment is inhabiting the Captain's head, and when we recall that the narrator's father, Kilgore Trout, in previous novels was clearly a persona of Vonnegut, we may find ourselves reeling with delight at the density of the linguistic brilliance he is treating us to. Vonnegut has created *doppelgangers* of himself in quadruplicate partly to provide clues for the careful reader to unravel the complex structure of the novel, partly to demonstrate the post-modernist vision of intertextuality, and partly to objectify his perceptions of the non-linearity of time, the human artifice of literary work, and the illusory nature of human identity.

Not everyone, to be sure, will be excited by the intellectual, psychological and philosophical density of *Galápagos*, but it's puzzling that so many critics seem to miss Vonnegut's artistry altogether. In fact, of course, that is his point. We view reality at its surface and skate along the rationally tolerable highs and lows, oblivious to the complex contradictions and ambiguities at the center. Such surface tripping has worked for the modern world, says *Galápagos*, until 1986 when the center finally erupts out of the miseries created by those whose power comes from money or social class or corrupt leadership.

What the novel is trying to tell us, with the most calm and controlled and simple voice of the author's literary career, is that humanity has been living illusions that are about to explode. . . . (pp. 79-80)

Ironic symmetries occur throughout the novel, along with an intricately woven time-space development that ranges back and forth and up and down from 1535, when the Galápagos Islands were first discovered, to a million years into the future, to eternity itself where we are addressed by the outraged voice of the deceased Kilgore Trout from the "blue tunnel leading to the Afterlife." Events that range wildly in time and space are knitted together by the web of ironic and accidental interdependencies. The novel is the literary equivalent of a complex ecosystem that includes everything from the bizarre to the sublime. It approaches a Lear-like structure with its symmetrical undergirding of paradox. The Chrysler Tower on the island of Manhattan, where the "Nature Cruise of the Century" is conceived, finds its symmetry with the island where humanity gets its new start. Both are Edens connected ironically by the planned and the actual cruise of the "Bahia de Darwin," the ship built by Leon Trout, Vonnegut's ghost writer.

As luck would have it, humanity gets its second chance only because an aging former biology teacher, Mary Hepburn, takes up with the aging Captain, the only male to make it to the island. She becomes a modern creator-Goddess when she inseminates six Kanka-bono girls (survivors of a primitive, cannibalistic tribe) by passing the Captain's semen from herself to them with her right index finger. Her parallel is Leon Trout who writes his story in the air with his left index finger. Both engage in the creative act because of their big brains, and without much regard for the consequences. Both produce for an indifferent universe and both create something that turns out to be harmless. . . .

Vonnegut's humbling message is one he has given before, but it appears in *Galápagos* with a more eloquent simplicity than in his previous novels. The message is that the human race has muddled its way to such splendid and horrific achievements because of the accidental evolution of a brain that does not seem to comprehend the danger of its own arrogance, and that how we perform the dance of life is largely a matter of luck and genes, whether the critics like it or not. (p. 80)

Loree Rackstraw, "Blue Tunnels to Survival," in The North American Review, *Vol. 270, No. 4, December, 1985, pp. 78-80.*

Diane Wakoski

1937-

American poet, essayist, and critic.

Wakoski's singular poetic vision has earned her a distinguished position in contemporary American literature. Her poems are personal narratives through which she weaves repeated images and themes, forming a rich texture of metaphor and critical reflection based in individual experience. In her essay "Creating a Personal Mythology," Wakoski describes her idea of the poet's mission: it involves "carving out a territory, creating the subject matter or content which helps the reader identify his voice or style as a poet." Wakoski's territory is inhabited by such characters as George Washington, The King of Spain, and The Man Who Shook Hands, all of whom attain mythical stature and embody the concepts Wakoski develops in her poetry. She usually centers on relations between men and women and chronicles a search for beauty and fulfillment in love that often ends in the ugliness of betrayal. Although she is sometimes accused of overwriting and of adopting a self-pitying stance, most critics detect in her work a determined, resilient persona who, while often emotionally wounded or angry, also possesses a wry sense of humor. Wakoski has published over fifty books, including collections of poetry, chapbooks, and volumes of prose. Her work is widely praised for its originality, intelligence, and imaginative power.

Wakoski's first two volumes, *Coins and Coffins* (1962) and *Discrepancies and Apparitions* (1966), established her, according to Sheila Weller, as "a poet of fierce imagination." In *The George Washington Poems* (1967), Wakoski uses the figure of George Washington to develop a number of themes, including that of an absent father who is romanticized by his daughter. In an interview, Wakoski called *Inside the Blood Factory* (1968) "the turning point in my career from being a young poet, perhaps talented and perhaps accomplished in certain ways, to someone who . . . had established a real and original voice, different from anyone else." In this book, Wakoski explores rejection and betrayal, themes further expanded upon in *The Motorcycle Betrayal Poems* (1971). Many of the poems in this volume center on a mythical motorcycle mechanic whose love the speaker has lost. *The Motorcycle Betrayal Poems* also contains the poem "I Have Had to Learn to Live with This Face," in which Wakoski develops another of her primary concerns—what she perceives as her lack of physical beauty.

In such volumes as *Smudging* (1972), *Dancing on the Grave of a Son of a Bitch* (1973), and *Waiting for the King of Spain* (1976), Wakoski continues her exploration of love and loss and her search for both physical and emotional beauty. With *Virtuoso Literature for Two and Four Hands* (1975) and *The Man Who Shook Hands* (1978), music becomes a dominant theme. In many of the poems in these volumes, Wakoski employs a digressive technique similar to that in musical works, allowing her naturally associative verse to wander away from its central concerns while maintaining a thread of continuity and eventually bringing the poem back to its main themes. In *Cap of Darkness* (1980), Wakoski again employs digression and also continues to delve into the past for the materials with

which to construct her "personal mythology," focusing particularly on the process of aging. *The Collected Greed, Parts 1-13* (1984) represents the culmination of an ongoing project. The "Greed" poems had previously been published in four separate volumes, at irregular intervals, beginning in 1968. This series documents Wakoski's struggles with self-definition and with her sometimes conflicting desires; she defines greed as "an unwillingness to give up one thing / for another." Kenneth Funsten claimed that although Wakoski is often termed a confessional poet, in *The Collected Greed, Parts 1-13* she produced "something immensely more promising than naive confession."

Wakoski's critical works have helped establish her as an intelligent, sometimes controversial commentator on the literary world. In particular, *Creating a Personal Mythology* (1975) and *Toward a New Poetry* (1979)—the latter a collection of essays, interviews, and columns written for *The American Poetry Review*—provide a theoretical basis for Wakoski's individualistic poetry. In characterizing Wakoski's accomplishment, Rochelle Owens observed: "With clarity, wit, and elegantly stunning imagery, [she] charters and restructures . . . a whole new subjective biography."

(See also *CLC*, Vols. 2, 4, 7, 9, 11; *Contemporary Authors*, Vols. 13-16, rev. ed.; *Contemporary Authors New Revision*

Series, Vol. 9; *Contemporary Authors Autobiography Series,* Vol. 1; and *Dictionary of Literary Biography,* Vol. 5.)

SARA PLATH

Diane Wakoski is extremely reluctant to see herself as a critic or theorist of any kind. She vowed when she was a young poet—she tells us in her preface [to *Toward a New Poetry*]—never to become a translator, editor, or critic. Over the years she has managed to publish a great deal of writing on contemporary poetry while still keeping that vow. Included in this volume are some of her columns from *American Poetry Review,* miscellaneous essays, and interviews. Wakoski has developed a unique and interesting way of talking about contemporary poetry. Personal and concrete in her approach rather than scholarly and general, the author relates her ideas about the medium in much the same context in which her own poems are found—an open, associative, metaphorical state of mind. Wakoski has interesting thoughts on almost every phase of contemporary poetry—writing, teaching, publishing, earning a living as a poet, the place of poetry in one's daily life.

> *Sara Plath, in a review of "Toward a New Poetry," in* Booklist, *Vol. 76, No. 19, June 1, 1980, pp. 1404-05.*

SARA PLATH

It's hard not to like Diane Wakoski's poems, so skillful and yet relaxed a writer is she. In this book [*Cap of Darkness*], as in her others, there is hardly a poem that fails to produce a stunning image or two. On the other hand, it is difficult to like her work unconditionally. It is part of Wakoski's personal aesthetic to present for public viewing much (maybe most) of what she writes, but in a poetry as personal, as emotional as this, readers may begin to feel worn down by the repetition of certain themes—love, loneliness, despair. Although the poems in this new volume evoke a calmer, if no less pessimistic, persona, one's affections for this talented writer may best be maintained by not reading everything she publishes.

> *Sara Plath, in a review of "Cap of Darkness," in* Booklist, *Vol. 77, No. 1, September 1, 1980, p. 26.*

D. EARNSHAW

The "new poetry" toward which Wakoski [as she explains in *Toward a New Poetry*] would have us move is based on the longer narrative poem, the "personal narrative" of the poet. This "new art" is not the traditional lyric with its forms of meter and strophe, but "a kind of cross between religion, philosophy, and story telling. It is a meditative art, and it's very personal, as opposed to the story teller who feels much more involved in telling the stories of other people." Epic has moved into fiction, she tells us, and poetry is the contemporary speech of our most sensitive people. Her gripe against critics is that they are historically minded and judge a modern poet with the sound of seventeenth-century diction in their heads. She teaches for a community of poets, those who understand. Defending herself against elitism, she claims that a self-selected group of poetry lovers is not anti-democratic. . . .

[In *Toward a New Poetry,* she] comments on many areas of life and poetry: dreams, oral readings (she is a very popular reader on the college circuit), academic critics (Helen Vendler comes in for heavy opprobrium) and specific opinions (she disputes Adrienne Rich's objections to Stevens's "The Dolphins"). Her critical judgment is professional; the **"Letter to the Finalists of the Walt Whitman First-Book Poetry Contest"** illustrates the application of her principles to a specific situation and is full of interest.

In spite of the sound doctrines put forth here, many readers will be exasperated by the aggressive narcissism; "I," "me," "mine" and "my poems" stud each paragraph with monotonous repetition.

> *D. Earnshaw, in a review of "Toward a New Poetry," in* World Literature Today, *Vol. 55, No. 2, Spring, 1981, p. 327.*

DONNA BROOK

Increasingly, publishing Diane Wakoski seems to be an activity with a logic and momentum all its own, for it is hard to establish a necessity for these two books [*Toward a New Poetry* and *Cap of Darkness*]. . . .

Toward a New Poetry . . . contains nothing even mildly revolutionary despite its title. Wakoski repeats and repeats "form is an extension of content" as a kind of talisman, announcing that, "It has become apparent to me that what is different about twentieth-century literature is the notion that 'form is an extension of content.'" This "notion" has been so generally "apparent" for several decades that writing about it should amount to more than chanting it, and Wakoski's other keynote, the creation of a "personal mythology," feels less inviting as one watches Wakoski's own superstructure turn into a cage. When she first brought in George Washington, I was as interested as everybody else; but, now that she has invented enough characters for a Diane Wakoski Muppet troupe, I'm less enthralled. By the time, "the Man from Receiving at Sears / the crippled brother of the King of Spain" shows up, it is not enough that even Wakoski seems to suspect the absurdity. Instead of mythology, it is machinery, and it creaks.

This apparently mechanical difficulty should be startling, for Wakoski has always possessed extraordinary talent. She's shown her readers a distinctive voice, vivid images, music, passion, all the goodies. She's written memorable, moving poems. Yet these essays mainly ramble rather than develop; the poems are not as lush. Form really being an extension of content, maybe ideas aren't developing in the prose; maybe myth is disintegrating into magic tricks? Wakoski's "myth" is, and always has been, one where woman is object, the action coming from men, the emphasis on them. Wakoski, in the poems at least, never does anything to drive lovers away; they abandon and cause pain. As this individual scenario of longing and betrayal becomes less and less reflective of, supported by the culture in which she lives, what happens to a poet like Wakoski? If she has become a well-known poet by showing her wounds, is her career jeopardized by changing times and fading scars?

Frankly, I find a whole range of things unnerving in [both *Toward a New Poetry* and *Cap of Darkness*]: Wakoski's continual insistence on her own "specialness;" . . . her homophobia, if that's a strong enough word, ("I want to slip a noose around the necks of those beautiful men / who make love / to other men / and mock woman's sacrificing body"); her accusation that "... we know that you will never win a Yale Younger Poets award if you do not know the judge" right after **"Letter to the Finalists of the Walt Whitman First-Book Poetry Contest,"** in which she describes her torment and indecision judging the manuscripts, and awarding the prize to "an author I know very well." But, of all that distresses or confuses here, nothing feels as Enough Already! as Wakoski's search for a rescuer. She not only insists on Prince Charming, she promotes the fellow....

> putting your arms around me when I am
> 　　　　　cold
> so that I smell the tobacco smoke in your
> 　　　　　clothes
> and feel assured that a man might take
> 　　　　　care of me,
> 　　　　　　　　someday.

Instead of moving toward "a new poetry" and a "personal mythology" this seems to head for an old social arrangement. "I have been asked," Wakoski writes in **"The Emerald Essay,"** "to talk about the subject of what women are up to, today, and have chosen to ignore the social implications of that question...." Well, OK. Every woman should be free to pick her issues, and Wakoski's continued insistence that to be called Woman Poet rather than just Poet is diminishing makes a certain sense, but, whatever else one may say about her, whatever the growth or decay of her language or technique may or may not be, a central question remains: as more and more women find the role of victim less and less inevitable and appealing, who reads Wakoski?

Of course, where this review is steering is just where Wakoski hates going. ("Poetry and politics really don't mix," she tells an interviewer. "I hate being read politically.") And yet, how can one avoid the social implications in an author who insists on, dwells on the role of woman and the relations between women and men? Whether any individual wishes it so or not, gender is currently political, and no one is so special as to escape this development. Wakoski constantly covers the same material that feminists discuss, and any modern woman must deal with.... Wakoski appears to be outside time, unable to give up the role of sufferer, the special one who is deserted while other women are successful. She seems to believe in themes propagated by *The Ladies Home Journal* in the 50s. "I have never been able to make myself into that wife and mother / that woman of the hearth," Wakoski reiterates, as if that were an individual inability, as if thousands of women had found happiness as Betty Crocker look-alikes. Rather than forming a personal mythology, Wakoski often seems to be buying into an outdated, damaging legend. And, as she chases herself in this circle, exploring the position of women and refusing to go beyond a certain point, Wakoski is pushed into the corners denial forces anybody into. She begins to take stances that range from silly to outrageous....

Furthermore, these difficulties in Wakoski's stance intimately connect with her attitudes toward violence, which seem to me the flip side of female passivity, the products of entrapment.... I find the popularity of women authors who seek out and simulate violence as Wakoski does (I think here of Joyce Carol Oates and Ai) as mystifying, at best, as the success of infamous "masculinists" like Dickey and Bukowski, ... and I find it important to distinguish between authors who record and/or discuss the violence of our times and those who romanticize it and/or confuse it with sex. Many people who have really lived through violence may not applaud writers who pretend it is a literary technique, for the latter type of author (whatever his or her personal experience) is, underneath it all, only fostering a heritage of sado-masochism. And who stands to gain? Well, those who feel they have something to lose if poets—or substitute "women" or "artists"—stop "being" tormented special souls, unable to find fulfillment, and become real messengers and members in the world, the political social world.

> Donna Brook, in a review of "Toward a New Poetry," in The American Book Review, Vol. 3, No. 6, September-October, 1981, p. 11.

TAFFY WYNNE MARTIN

It is perhaps inevitable that post-modern poetry, scorned by an earlier decade's most dogmatic critics, has become somewhat of a stepchild in the internecine disputes of contemporary critical theory. Rejecting the nearly canonized, well-made poem of balanced tensions, some of America's best contemporary poets have written and continue to write what might be called poems in search of a critical method. (p. 156)

[Critics] today seem not to have found a replacement for the formalist prejudice which, in Diane Wakoski's words, "likes to see the struggle in the language" and promotes "the notion that the things that are corporeal and physical and emotional move away from intellectual solidity." Supporting Sherman Paul's call for "an open-field criticism that can in some way deal with open-field poetry," Wakoski [in *Toward a New Poetry*] claims that "structuralist criticism has moved in the direction of the anti-personal." ... In fact, many critics remain, as Nietzsche predicted, "entangled in error, *necessitated* to error, to precisely the extent that our prejudice in favor of reason compels us to posit unity, identity, duration, substance, cause, materiality, being, however sure we may be, on the basis of strict reckoning, *that* error is to be found here." The problem is twofold: the majority of postmodern, long poems will not lend themselves to methods which were appropriate for short lyrics; but the critic familiar only with the formalist tradition cannot escape the compulsion "to posit unity" and proceeds as though all poets must necessarily engage themselves in what T. S. Eliot described as the essential task "of controlling, of ordering, of giving a shape and a significance to the immense panorama of futility and anarchy which is contemporary history."

Diane Wakoski's poetry, which strays about as far as possible from the detached irony of a well-made modernist poem, undertakes, nevertheless, precisely the task which Eliot outlined. Her work suggests that while the "prejudice in favor of reason" which Nietzsche distrusted might lead to a misguided and futile search for modernist order, there is in post-modern poetry both an order and a method. In her attempt to confront the "futility and anarchy which is contemporary history," Wakoski not only accepts but embraces the experience of loss which underlies so much of her poetry. She begins with traditional or inherited myths and develops out of them her own malleable, often contradictory mythology, one which responds to irreversible absence by elaborating and thereby continuing desire. George Washington becomes the father of our (her) country; The Man With the Mustache reappears as frequently and as much on cue as Yeats' Maude Gonne; and The Man Who Shook Hands exists solely as an enigma. As the moon goddess, "Diane" either enchants men or wonders why she doesn't. George Washington's deflated image hardly replaces a stable father figure, and the elusive King of Spain dissolves into his crippled brother. In spite of this, Wakoski's quest for a personal mythology succeeds just because she controls and orchestrates every experience. Personal but very deliberately not confessional, Wakoski's poetry acknowledges loss—of children, of love, of sustaining myths—and develops out of that a coherent body of work in which desire functions as an enabling drive.

As if in direct dismissal of New Critical methodology, Wakoski writes poems which cannot be read as individual artifacts. That practice leads at best to individual, limited readings which eventually combine to produce a misleading interpretation unaware of the pervasive self-irony of her work. Only by considering Wakoski's poetry as what Robert Creeley, referring to Charles Olson's work, called "a structure possessed of its own organization in turn derived from the circumstances of its making," can one discern the internal structure. Rather than attempting to escape, deny, or diminish past loss and pain, Wakoski uses it creatively. A poem begins with the most ordinary people and events and turns them into emblematic fantasy figures. She embellishes this by employing digression as a musical structure to present "the real world and then its mirror image which is the vision of the real world." . . . By combining these dramatic and structural devices she creates a personal mythology which turns her recognition of absence and lost love into an ongoing post-modern song.

Wakoski begins from a position similar to Nietzsche's belief that "every culture that has lost myth has lost by the same token, its natural, healthy creativity" and that additionally "a culture without any fixed and consecrated place of origin [must be] condemned to exhaust all possiblities and feed miserably and parasitically on every culture under the sun." Nevertheless, she escapes from that predicament by creating a poetry which, like Nietzsche's Dionysian music, "offers us a universal mirror of the world will: every particular incident refracted in that mirror is enlarged into the image of a permanent truth." . . . (pp. 157-58)

The key to Wakoski's "escape" from and creative use of the past, a method not explicable in terms of contemporary narrative theory, is her Dionysian mirror which transforms any detail or event by creating the larger-than-life figures of her mythology. (p. 158)

Wakoski's entire mythology exists in her head, taking its cue from the dramatic demands of her poetry. . . . Her own description of the undertaking appears throughout the poetry. She attempts not to deny loss but to affirm and to continue desire. . . . Thus, "the little girl who read fairy tales / . . . grown into the woman / in them" . . . realizes that a poet's work

> is not
> the measure
> of his love. It is
> the measure
> of all he's lost, or
> never seen,
> or what has no life,
> unless he gives it life
> with words.

In the mythology, Wakoski gives life to lost love and lost lovers in a variety of disguises. It begins in *Coins and Coffins,* Wakoski's first volume, with the bizarre tale of her apocryphal brother. She explains in **"Creating a Personal Mythology"** that the invention of a "twin brother, David, who committed suicide when we were still children after we had sex together"

grew out of two impulses. As a young adult she had been fascinated by Thomas Mann's *Holy Sinners,* by Yeats' "Leda and the Swan," and by Greek tragedy which "made me very interested in incest, rape, sex which causes guilty feelings, taboos, etc." At the same time, she had begun to desire a replacement for "my true history, part of which was boring and part of which I was ashamed of and felt I could never tell anyone." . . . Following this first emblematic invention, the ever-present missing lover enters her mythology in *Discrepancies and Apparitions;* but *The George Washington Poems,* dedicated ironically "To My Father and My Husband," are the first to develop an absent figure fully. That volume begins by presenting Washington as "the ultimate / in the un-Romantic: / false teeth" . . . and moves him through a variety of roles, including, by means of Wakoski's puns on "my country" and "inaugural ball," that of an imaginary lover. This wordplay makes **"The Father of My Country"** reverberate when it appears more than half-way though the volume. The poem poignantly creates—in the person of George Washington—a father figure who in Wakoski's childhood was a name but "not in the telephone book / in my city," who "was not sleeping with my mother," and who "did not care if I studied the piano." . . . Once created as a mythological figure, George Washington can reappear in a variety of dramatic contexts, always disturbingly, as an absent replacement for love.

In later poems, The King of Spain and The Man With the Mustache join George Washington as betrayers and, more importantly, as members of her personal mythology. George Washington's initials, along with her father's "military origins," establish sufficient evidence for her claim to Washington as father. Once established, the mythology is at once malleable and completely under Wakoski's control. Like "Yeats [who] was hung up with a girl's beautiful face," Wakoski keeps her betrayers ready to appear whenever a poem needs one. Refracted in her Dionysian mirror, they become both more and less than individual men. (pp. 160-61)

Both the merging of her betrayers and the blending of trivial events made emblematic distinguish even Wakoski's most personal work from confessional poetry. . . . Rather than as an expurgation of emotions, poetry functions for Wakoski "to complete an act that can't be completed in real life. In other words, it's a problem-solving act . . . an act of completion. If you get what you want you don't write about it. You write about what you don't get. . . ." . . . (pp. 161-62)

Wakoski's problem solving, her attempt to create and make present the object of her desire, emerges as an ongoing process in the form of musical repetition. Thus, although she has been called a poet of the deep image and although many of her chant-like poems suggest an affinity with Williams and Olson and perhaps Robert Bly in their use of breath as the measure of the line, her autographic use of digression as a musical structure proves to be essential in moving her personal mythology beyond confession. By employing Creeley's "structure possessed of its own organization in turn derived from the circumstances of its making," she transcends simple replication of loss. Instead, the digression and repetition embellish the absence, perpetuate her desire, and create out of it a numinous presence. In **"The Blue Swan, an Essay on Music in Poetry,"** Wakoski explains the process. "First comes the story. Then comes the reaction to the story. Then comes the telling and retelling of the story. And finally . . . comes boredom with the story so that . . . we invent music and the nature of music is that you must hear all the digressions." . . . In that essay-poem, six attempts at telling the story of The Man Who Shook Hands stop short, falling into digression, before Wakoski completes her tale. When the tale finally emerges, it is as ignominious and simple as the story of her brother, David, was fantastic. . . .

Woven into this tale are phrases from Wallace Stevens' "Peter Quince at the Clavier" since that poem captures for Wakoski the contradictory nature of her quest. From desire, desire for an absent person, presence can be created; but the presence she creates is not a person but desire. (p. 162)

[Two] forces—Dionysian fantasy with the flesh as muse, and simultaneous desire for a life of the spirit—conflict in virtually every Wakoski poem. Digression is the structure through which she controls them. It is for Wakoski a form of music, "that movement which we follow, that sound which we recognize not because it says anything but because it is motion which suspends motion." . . . Like an enabling, calming chant, Wakoski's repetitions and digressions in "The Blue Swan" pass gradually into music so that by the time she completes it, the story of The Man Who Shook Hands has become, because of her digressions, not a "sad, silly, not very important, yet overwhelmingly terrifying story," . . . and not proof "that all of my life is . . . some very long and complicated soap opera of pragmatism." . . . It is instead an emblematic tale, invented music, which replaces the absence caused by the story before its transformation into myth. Rather than a resolution, it becomes a deliberate, lasting recreation of absence. (pp. 163-64)

Mythmaking, digression, and musical repetition operate simultaneously as Wakoski ends [*The Man Who Shook Hands*] with the poem, **"The Blue Swan, an Essay on Music in Poetry."** This time the mythmaking starts with Charles Olson as archaeologist and leads to Wakoski's interpretation of her own unfulfilled desire. Patterned repetition enacts the process of embellishment through which Olson's discovery of "a large piece of shaped clay / with what appeared / to be a blue swan / painted on it" gains mythic status. That, in turn, sparks a digression which is a return to the story of The Man Who Shook Hands. The progression is incremental. . . . What began as a digression rapidly shifts to what have been Wakoski's twin obsessions all along—The Man Who Shook Hands and her inability to articulate and understand either the loss she experiences or the unfulfilled desire that she still feels. In the last stanza, where Olson's mythmaking and Wakoski's loss merge, her desire gains mythic status, albeit merely as a digression. . . . In Wakoski's terms, the poem works as a problem solving device. It completes the mystifying loss of her encounter by continuing to keep it present as a part of her personal mythology. . . . [She] weaves any number of mythologized events into her poems whenever they demand a loss made present. Like Susanna's music, they become ironic scrapings more than adequate to their task. (pp. 164-66)

Wakoski is a distinctive reader. . . . Her musical training is obvious in her range of tone and expression, particularly in her chanting poems which "make the spoken word, the poem, into its own music." . . . These poems—the largest group is the collection **"Dancing on the Grave of a Son of a Bitch"**—demand being read aloud, often suggesting more than one voice. As phrases, sometimes just syllables and sounds, repeat and develop, they evoke moods which vary from outrage (at the motorcycle betrayer) to enchantment (with a variety of textures and colors), to despair (on realizing that she cannot control love and capture it permanently). Wakoski claims that she has "tried to set the poems down on the page so that you could read them in the most rhythmical way possible." Nevertheless, she considers "the cognitive aspect to be the most important one to me in poetry and would not want this element of spoken music to take over, either in a majority of my poems or in a majority of the lines of any poem." . . . (pp. 166-67)

In fact, the repetition which she employs in the chanting is just as effective cognitively. In her longer, narrative poems it represents the second way through which digression becomes a musical structure. The process begins when Wakoski transforms an everyday event into a part of her mythology. Once made emblematic, an event stands ready like Yeats' Maude Gonne to perform on cue whenever a poem needs a betrayer or a reminder of continuing desire. Thus by the time she writes **"Spending the New Year with the Man from Receiving at Sears"** [in *Cap of Darkness*] her sea captain father "whose bedroom never contained Lafcadio Hearn's / *Glimpses of Unfamiliar Japan*," her "teenage accident: first childbirth," "the loss of Rilke's mustache," and "the sagging couch in our house / in the orange grove" . . . appear in the new episode as familiar refrains. As these shadows of past experience repeatedly appear within each poem, they form a musical structure which resembles the process of incremental repetition Andrew Porter described in his review of the 1976 Philip Glass opera, *Einstein on the Beach*—one of "rhythmic patterns and short melodic motifs endlessly repeated but slowly altering." Porter explains further that "Glass asked for 'another mode of listening—one in which neither memory nor anticipation . . . has a place in sustaining the texture, quality, or reality of the musical experience." . . . Wakoski asks for an equally new mode of listening (reading). . . . (p. 167)

Just as the listener to glass cannot anticipate and then derive pleasure from encountering traditional musical patterns, so Wakoski's reader faces neither traditional narrative, nor confessional poetry, nor pure chant. Both demand active listening in order to recognize the pattern that is there. In Wakoski the problem is particularly challenging because while developing her mythology, she refuses to move it toward a resolution or toward a fulfillment of the desire on which it is based. Contradiction and false leads are also involved. In **"Having Replaced Love with Food and Drink, a poem for those who've reached 40,"** she concludes

> Yes, I have gladly given up love
> for all the objects made with love:
>   a poem
>   an orchid
>   this pasta, green and garlicky
>   made with my own hands. . . .

But in **"Precision"** we learn that memory inevitably continues desire.

> I arrived yesterday at the Los Angeles airport
> And could not help some part of me wishing/
>   expecting to see you,
> M.,
> waiting for me to return.
> I suppose that is what it means
> to be haunted.
> In my real life
> I neither expect
> nor want you. Yet, some rehearsal of the past
> is always with me.

In fact, the rehearsal of the past is deliberate and serves a complex purpose. As a problem-solving device it neither denies nor "confesses" past anguish but rather adopts a Nietzschean solution. Contrary to the benighted, cadaverous, and ghostly souls Nietzsche attacks, Wakoski refuses "to feed miserably and parasitically on every culture under the sun" or on her own past. Instead she willingly and imaginatively embraces that past by employing a transforming, mythmaking mirror to create her own Dionysian music. *Cap of Darkness,* Wakoski's most recent volume, continues this affirmation and transformation. The long Preface, beginning with a letter "Dear Michael" weaves a tale "that makes the scars / . . . look exotic / rather than ugly." . . . Incidents from her mythology echo throughout this volume in poems often shorter and more lyrical than those of earlier collections. Old memories, "Scene: / though dismissed, / not quite dismissed," blend with new ones—stories of friends, references to Robert Creeley, Clayton Eshleman, Norman Hindley, Stanley Kunitz, and William Stafford. Wakoski's mother still offers only "clothes squashed into flat wrinkled shapes / . . . Sears (E) gingham dress, in sizes 2, 4, 6 and 6x / Colors: red and blue" . . . and spends a life waiting for love. . . . (pp. 168-69)

The rehearsals continue to aid Wakoski as mythmaker. In the midst of a set of digressions in **"Spending the New Year with the Man from Receiving at Sears"** she interjects, "I am telling myself all these things / in order to try to understand. . . ." That understanding occurs gradually as new themes emerge and develop. In **"A Letter [to J] from Unwritten *Greed, Part 10*"** and in **"The Moth,"** which is part of **"Letter,"** Wakoski introduces a memory not yet understood, which she soon reintroduces and transforms.

> When I was a child I used to stand for hours,
> abnormally still for a child of five, in front of
> a hedge of lantana and catch butterflies in my
> bare fingers, something no child should have
> been able to do.

This recollection follows without transition her account of waking, terrified, one night to unusual sounds, and of discovering "no figure or person or animal or anything big enough to be dangerous." She found at her window "an enormous dusky moth, about five inches wide, half of his wing torn from beating against the blind where he had been caught." . . . Relieved, Wakoski admits, "I think there is a certain madness in my marauder turning out to be a butterfly—for, if I had to choose two symbols for myself, one would be the moon and the other would be a butterfly." In **"The Moth,"** the butterfly/moth and other figures of entrapment dominate the poem. The moth, "trapped behind blinds," reminds Wakoski that "the poet is the blind man." The whole incident sparks another memory—of J—"so much in my mind, / who have never been trapped." . . . This addition to the personal mythology reappears two poems later in **"Lantana"** where Wakoski's already familiar "thick little girl hands" possess for the first time a "murdering stillness." . . . She is astonished that her "hands that have shaken since adolescence / with nervous energy and mercurial power . . . should have started with this stillness." Even more striking is Wakoski's ambivalence toward this new recollection. Not yet understood—"I am telling myself these things / in order to *try* to understand . . ." (italics mine)—the incident is only partly mythologized. Thus we are told that "It continues to be the most I have to offer / this stillness." . . . She is the child desiring love and the poet "trapped in her own words / . . . which explain / and in explaining / lose love." Wakoski simultaneously assigns the murdering stillness to the past and makes it present, both rejects and embraces it. This contra-

diction, which she very deliberately neglects to resolve, works in two ways. It rejects pessimistic confession and opts instead for a creative solution—the evolving musical pattern and the problem-solving work of her mythology. All of her poetry, like this new incident, is a process which demands to be read not as individual poems but as a coherent and continuous body of work.

Wakoski's poetry, like much post-modern American verse, remains—as it should—in search of a critical method; and post-modern poetry still eludes easy definition. But her work does offer at least one imaginative response to Olson's question, which serves here as an epigraph. For Wakoski the way out of threatened burial in shallow graves is her Dionysian music which makes the past sing. Her work is a contemporary love poem which acknowledges loss, pain, and confusion. (pp. 169-71)

Taffy Wynne Martin, "Diane Wakoski's Personal Mythology: Dionysian Music, Created Presence," in boundary 2, *Vol. X, No. 3, Spring, 1982, pp. 155-72.*

ROCHELLE RATNER

As in all Wakoski's work, the concern with love and loss dominates, but with [*The Magician's Feastletters*] she turns to food as a metaphor and focus for the domestic life she was deprived of and now wishes to obtain. In tune with this, the poems are concerned mainly with a world of women. Individual poems, such as **"Saturday Night," "Making a Sacher Torte," "Leaving Waterloo,"** or **"Eleanor on the Cliff"** are excellent, but this collection is for the most part prosaic, and the themes often seem superficial or tacked on. Similarly, I see no reason for having divided the book into sections according to the four seasons.

Rochelle Ratner, in a review of "The Magician's Feastletters," in Library Journal, *Vol. 107, No. 11, June 1, 1982, p. 1100.*

CLAYTON ESHLEMAN

I don't believe anyone has addressed the suddenness with which American poetry has gone abstract in the past decade. In fact the "new" has, overnight, become a kind of writing in which story has disappeared from narration, and narration itself has become so discontinuous that nonsense, in many instances, seems to have usurped imagination. . . .

Relative to this new abstract poetry (on one level no more than the return of the Surreal, or the revenge of Gertrude Stein's ghost), Diane Wakoski's poetry looks like Grant Wood's "American Gothic." It is about concrete realities and has a stubborn objectlike presence. . . . At the same time, her sensibility, especially in these ravenously still new poems [collected in *The Magician's Feastletters*], is profoundly feminine and sensual, offering the language a kind of creamy substantiality of Ingres' women.

Here is the opening stanza of **"Making a Sacher Torte"**:

> Her hands, like albino frogs,
> on the keys of a Bosendorfer,
> nails short and thin like sliced almonds, fleshy fingers,
> with the lightning bolt gold and diamond wedding

ring, zigzagging up to her fat knuckle,
looking out of place
on the heavy working hand.

While such lines might appear as merely descriptive, I find, rereading them, that they contain a lot of character, that they are packed with discontinuous sensations, and are a kind of amoebalike egg, turning on its own inward straining, out of which the snake of the poem will wind. All of the half-images in this stanza are picked up and worked in the course of the poem (the "albino frogs" of the "hands" become a "Frog Prince"), and are finally elaborated into a synthesis of memory and experience.

[*The Magician's Feastletters*] is a fascinating continuation and elaboration of her last book, *Cap of Darkness*, . . . where she began to take on the ramifications of aging in America, a real challenge given the American obsession, all across the board, with youth and novelty. In *Cap of Darkness*, Wakoski began to reverse a whole system of frozen values geared to affirm youth/sexuality/summer/product and to denigrate aging/impotence/winter/soul. Especially in the light of current fashions in American poetry (where empty description is as touted as pretentious nonsense), Wakoski's poetry is extremely valuable. It is not enough to just say it is "about something," as opposed to "about nothing." She is increasingly able to register the contours of a world at once solid and bottomless in meditations across which the meaningfulness/meaninglessness of her own lived life is worked.

The Magician's Feastletters focuses on one aspect of aging tied up with converting sexual desire into sensual reception, where the need to perform must give way to a painstaking survey of the shapes of place into which the performance has bled. It is as if one awoke one morning (as one actually awakens throughout the span of a lifetime) in the grip of the details of, say, one's plants, or the food one enjoys cooking and eating—in short, to *one's own* things, which had, in the turmoil of forging an identity, been left unattended.

Diane Wakoski's poetry is poised on an alchemical edge in which, I feel, the paths of her task will increasingly lead to a valuing of the temporal while its eternal hollows will demand to be mined.

> Clayton Eshleman, *"Wakoski Poetry Aging with Concrete Realities,"* in Los Angeles Times Book Review, *July 18, 1982, p. 11.*

KENNETH FUNSTEN

Since 1962, when Diane Wakoski's first book of poetry, *Coins and Coffins,* appeared, she has enchanted fans and offended critics. No one, it seems, straddles the line. One camp calls Wakoski entertaining, sincere, instructive; the other scoffs—and often with angry contempt—that she is prosy, crude, sentimental, moralizing. The only opinion that both seem to share is that Wakoski writes a form of "confessional poetry." But as her newest book, *The Collected Greed, Parts 1-13,* shows, Wakoski is writing something immensely more promising than naive confession. . . .

[Wakoski] defines *greed* as *failing to choose,* "an unwillingness to give up one thing / for another." Polygamy is one form. The American norm of consumption—to have enough but want just a bit more—is another. . . .

Part 5, **"The Shark—Parents & Children,"** begins confessionally: "I gave up my children when I was young / because I had no money, no husband. . . ." But after accepting her loss, the poem switches gears: "I want to talk about / the greed that makes a parent want a child. / That makes a woman want to use her body / as a stretched, swollen, lumpy pocket in an old worn coat, / that makes a man want to see some squalling / smelly inarticulate baby animal take his name / and imitate his actions / What is that greed? / That mirror. / That desire for repeating ourselves. / Stamping ourselves on the world?" Wakoski's metaphor grows like a child, until it means more than just parenting, but stands for any type of creation. . . .

Part 10 is a mystery. A portion of it appeared in a previous collection, *Cap of Darkness.* In *The Collected Greed,* there is only a small note between Parts 9 and 11, stating that 10 was conceived to be about the greed of "Love, Sex and Romance" but never completed. Wakoski doesn't believe she'll ever finish it; nevertheless, she writes, "I still retain the option. . . ." But isn't this greed on the poet's own part, claiming a territory but failing to choose between a set past and an open, uncertain future?

Part 12, **"The Greed to Be Fulfilled,"** is one of the two parts here previously unpublished, and it is a *tour de force,* a dream voyage in which the confessional "Diane" is transported by a Dalmatian to the desert, where inside a glass house is a beautiful garden in which sits George Washington, president of the Society for Western Flowers.

What follows is reminiscent of Chaucer's "Parliament of Fowls." Part 12 takes Wakoski's lyric "I" and moves it into the dramatic mode, where it becomes as much a representation of something as Washington is. George and Diane discuss what it is she has been searching for "all these years." "A feeling of completion, fulfillment," she responds. While Washington's guests don flower masks, the "main event" of the evening is a masque, "The Moon Loses Her Shoes," with actors playing the parts of Diane and George, as well as of the King of Spain, the Blue Moon Cowboy and others, all further distancing Wakoski from simple confession. Poet Charles Bukowski is even fictionalized as the event's emcee.

Finally, "Diane"—representing the poet at mid-life—confronts the unresolved problem of Part 10, choosing to stop fighting for her completion in "Love, Sex and Romance" in order to start fighting for her ideas. In effect, a character, the confessional voice of the self-centered ego, reaches a new plane of maturity when it decides that intellectual things, not emotional ones, are what matter.

As if to reinforce that choice, Part 13 is about an idea—poetry's analogy to music. Wakoski takes three Beethoven sonatas and uses verbal descriptions of their thematic structures as paradigms by which to create three poems. This uncovering of technique is the sign of a mature poet, unimpressed by obfuscation *or* autobiography for their own sakes, but intent upon illuminating substance. Listening to this poetry's thematic structure rather than its verbal one, *what* is said becomes more important than *how*. Reemphasizing content and idea, Wakoski strikes a most refreshing note amid a century and world overcome by form, technique and method.

> Kenneth Funsten, *"More Than Naive Confessions,"* in Los Angeles Times Book Review, *November 4, 1984, p. 4.*

ROBERT McDOWELL

[*Toward a New Poetry*] is in a class by itself. It tells you everything you will ever want to know about the author and might better have been called *Wakoski—Why Not?* This is a book of snap judgments, bad girl posing, breaking into a critic's wardrobe and playing dress-up.

Specifically, Wakoski sees herself as the avenging angel-promoter of "new poetry." According to her, the "new" poet begins with inwardness and turns it outward. Incredibly, Wakoski believes this to be a twentieth-century phenomenon. But this sort of oversight is precisely the point. In columns . . . , articles, pamphlets, essays, notes, and interviews, Wakoski misuses terms, expresses herself in adolescent, slanderous generalizations, and seems to be saying to readers "I don't care how you take me." Two opinions involving teaching and criticism provide examples. At one point, she confesses that she doesn't know how to teach poems of the past. After all, dead poets are *dead*. Surprisingly, she has nothing to say about all of the dead poets who are still living. Later, she acknowledges that "there are practically no critics of contemporary poetry left . . ." and then proceeds to prove it by doing.

Robert McDowell, "The Mum Generation Was Always Talking," *in* The Hudson Review, *Vol. XXXVIII, No. 3, Autumn, 1985, pp. 507-19.**

Appendix

The following is a listing of all sources used in Volume 40 of *Contemporary Literary Criticism*. Included in this list are all copyright and reprint rights and acknowledgments for those essays for which permission was obtained. Every effort has been made to trace copyright, but if omissions have been made, please let us know.

THE EXCERPTS IN CLC, VOLUME 40, WERE REPRINTED FROM THE FOLLOWING PERIODICALS:

America, v. 152, June 15, 1985 for "Thought Patterns" by Paul J. McCarren. © 1985. All rights reserved. Reprinted by permission of the author./ v. 108, January 12, 1963; v. 116, March 25, 1967. © 1963, 1967. All rights reserved. Both reprinted with permission of America Press, Inc., 106 West 56th Street, New York, NY 10019.

The American Book Review, v. 3, September-October, 1981; v. 5, January-February, 1983; v. 5, July-August, 1983; v. 6, March-April, 1984. © 1981, 1983, 1984 by *The American Book Review*. All reprinted by permission.

The American Poetry Review, v. 8, November-December, 1979 for "The Second Self: Some Recent American Poetry" by Dave Smith; v. 11, January-February, 1982 for "Some Recent American Poetry: Come All Ye Fair and Tender Ladies" by Dave Smith; v. 11, July-August, 1982 for "'Midquest'" by Robert Morgan; v. 14, January-February, 1985 for "'Night Feed': An Overview of Ireland's Women Poets" by James McElroy. Copyright © 1979, 1982, 1985 by World Poetry, Inc. All reprinted by permission of the respective authors.

The American Spectator, v. 16, February, 1983; v. 16, August, 1983. Copyright © *The American Spectator* 1983. Both reprinted by permission.

Analog Science Fiction/Science Fact, v. CIV, July, 1984 for "Helliconia Summer" by Tom Easton. © 1984 by Davis Publications, Inc. Reprinted by permission of the author.

The Antioch Review, v. 40, Spring, 1982; v. 41, Spring, 1983. Copyright © 1982, 1983 by the Antioch Review Inc. Both reprinted by permission of the Editors.

The Armchair Detective, v. 17, Spring, 1984. Copyright © 1984 by *The Armchair Detective*. Reprinted by permission.

The Atlantic Monthly, v. 256, October, 1985 for "Blue Over the Bomb" by John Romano. Copyright 1985 by The Atlantic Monthly Company, Boston, MA. Reprinted by permission of the author.

Australian Book Review, v. 9, December, 1969 & January, 1970. Reprinted by permission.

Australian Literary Studies, v. 10, May, 1982 for "John Tranter and Les Murray" by Thomas Shapcott. Reprinted by permission of the publisher and the author.

Best Sellers, v. 25, August 15, 1965. Copyright 1965, by the University of Scranton. Reprinted by permission.

THE EXCERPTS IN CLC, VOLUME 40, WERE REPRINTED FROM THE FOLLOWING BOOKS:

Aggeler, Geoffrey. From *Anthony Burgess: The Artist as Novelist*. University of Alabama Press, 1979. Copyright © 1979 by The University of Alabama Press. All rights reserved. Reprinted by permission.

Blanchot, Maurice. From *The Sirens' Song: Selected Essays*. Edited by Gabriel Josipovici, translated by Sacha Rabinovitch. Indiana University Press, 1982. Copyright © 1982 by The Harvester Press Limited. All rights reserved. Reprinted by permission.

Bosmajian, Hamida. From *Metaphors of Evil: Contemporary German Literature and the Shadow of Nazism*. University of Iowa Press, 1979. © 1979 by The University of Iowa. Reprinted by permission.

Brooks, Gwendolyn. From a preface to *Poems from Prison*. By Etheridge Knight. Broadside Press, 1968. Copyright © 1968 by Etheridge Knight. All rights reserved. Reprinted by permission.

Chiari, J. From *Landmarks of Contemporary Drama*. Herbert Jenkins, 1965. © J. Chiari 1965. All rights reserved. Reprinted by permission.

Coale, Samuel. From *Anthony Burgess*. Ungar, 1981. Copyright © 1981 by The Ungar Publishing Company Inc. Reprinted by permission.

Curtis, Anthony. From *New Developments in the French Theatre: A Critical Introduction to the Plays of Jean-Paul Sartre, Simone De Beauvoir, Albert Camus and Jean Anouilh*. The Curtain Press, 1948.

Dillard, Annie. From a foreword to *Moments of Light*. By Fred Chappell. New South Company, 1980. © 1980 by The New South Company. Reprinted by permission.

Ellison, Fred P. From *Brazil's New Novel, Four Northeastern Masters: José Lins do Rego, Jorge Amado, Graciliano Ramos, Rachel de Queiroz*. University of California Press, 1954. Copyright 1954 by The Regents of the University of California. Renewed 1982 by Fred Pittman Ellison. Reprinted by permission of the University of California Press.

Falb, Lewis W. From *Jean Anouilh*. Ungar, 1977. Copyright © 1977 by The Ungar Publishing Company Inc. Reprinted by permission.

Hellmann, John. From *Fables of Fact: The New Journalism as New Fiction*. University of Illinois Press, 1981. © 1981 by the Board of Trustees of the University of Illinois. Reprinted by permission of the publisher and the author.

Henry, Peter. From an introduction to *Selected Stories*. By Konstantin Paustovskii. Pergamon Press, 1967. Copyright 1967, Pergamon Press. Reprinted with permission from Pergamon Press and Peter Henry.

Hirsch, Marianne. From *Beyond the Single Vision: Henry James, Michel Butor, Uwe Johnson*. French Literature Publications Company, 1981. Copyright 1981 French Literature Publications Company. Reprinted by permission of Summa Publications, P.O. Box 20725, Birmingham, AL 35216.

Huse, Nancy L. From *The Survival Tales of John Hersey*. The Whitston Publishing Company, 1983. Copyright 1983 Nancy L. Huse. Reprinted by permission of the author.

Konuk, Mutlu. From an introduction to *The Epic of Sheik Bedreddin and Other Poems*. By Nazim Hikmet, translated by Randy Blasing and Mutlu Konuk. Persea Books, 1977. Copyright © 1977 by Randy Blasing and Mutlu Konuk. All rights reserved. Reprinted by permission of the publisher, Persea Books.

Konuk, Mutlu. From an introduction to *Things I Didn't Know I Loved: Selected Poems of Nazim Hikmet*. By Nazim Hikmet, translated by Randy Blasing and Mutlu Konuk. Persea Books, 1975. Copyright © 1975 by Randy Blasing and Mutlu Konuk. All rights reserved. Reprinted by permission of the publisher, Persea Books.

Lenski, B. A. From *Jean Anouilh: Stages in Rebellion*. Humanities Press, 1975. Copyright © 1975 by Humanities Press, Inc. Reprinted by permission of Humanities Press International, Inc., Atlantic Highlands, NJ 07716.

McIntyre, H. G. From *The Theatre of Jean Anouilh*. Barnes & Noble, 1981. © H. G. McIntyre 1981. All rights reserved. By permission of Barnes & Noble Books, a Division of Littlefield, Adams & Co., Inc.

Murphy, Carol J. From *Alienation and Absence in the Novels of Marguerite Duras*. French Forum, 1982. Copyright © 1982 by French Forum, Publishers, Incorporated, P.O. Box 5108, Lexington, KY 40505. All rights reserved. Reprinted by permission.

Oates, Joyce Carol. From an introduction to *Had I a Hundred Mouths: New & Selected Stories 1947-1983*. By William Goyen. Clarkson N. Potter, Inc./ Publishers, 1985. Introduction copyright © 1985 by Ontario Review, Inc. All rights reserved. Used by permission of Clarkson N. Potter, Inc.

Literature Criticism Series
Cumulative Author Index

Author Index

This index lists all author entries in the Gale Literary Criticism Series and includes cross-references to other Gale sources. For the convenience of the reader, references to the *Yearbook* in the *Contemporary Literary Criticism* series include the page number (in parentheses) after the volume number. References in the index are identified as follows:

AITN: *Authors in the News,* Volumes 1-2
CAAS: *Contemporary Authors Autobiography Series,* Volumes 1-3
CA: *Contemporary Authors* (original series), Volumes 1-118
CANR: *Contemporary Authors New Revision Series,* Volumes 1-18
CAP: *Contemporary Authors Permanent Series,* Volumes 1-2
CA-R: *Contemporary Authors* (revised editions), Volumes 1-44
CLC: *Contemporary Literary Criticism,* Volumes 1-40
CLR: *Children's Literature Review,* Volumes 1-10
DLB: *Dictionary of Literary Biography,* Volumes 1-48
DLB-DS: *Dictionary of Literary Biography Documentary Series,* Volumes 1-4
DLB-Y: *Dictionary of Literary Biography Yearbook,* Volumes 1980-1985
LC: *Literature Criticism from 1400 to 1800,* Volumes 1-4
NCLC: *Nineteenth-Century Literature Criticism,* Volumes 1-13
SAAS: *Something about the Author Autobiography Series,* Volumes 1-2
SATA: *Something about the Author,* Volumes 1-44
TCLC: *Twentieth-Century Literary Criticism,* Volumes 1-21
YABC: *Yesterday's Authors of Books for Children,* Volumes 1-2

Author Index

Author Index

Author Index

Author Index

Author Index

CLC Cumulative Title Index

Title Index

Title Index

Title Index

Title Index

Title Index

Title Index

Title Index

Title Index

Title Index

Title Index

Title Index

Title Index

Title Index

Title Index

Title Index

Title Index

Title Index

Title Index

Title Index

Title Index

Title Index

Title Index

Title Index

Title Index

Title Index

Title Index

Title Index

Title Index

Title Index

Title Index

Title Index

Title Index

Title Index

Title Index